The Law of Contempt

The Law of Contempt

Third edition

Nigel Lowe   LLB (Sheffield), of the Inner Temple, Barrister, Professor of Law, Cardiff Law School, University of Wales

Brenda Sufrin   LLB (Birmingham), Solicitor, Reader in Law, University of Bristol

Butterworths
London, Dublin and Edinburgh
1996

United Kingdom	Butterworths a Division of Reed Elsevier (UK) Ltd, Halsbury House, 35 Chancery Lane, LONDON WC2A 1EL and 4 Hill Street, EDINBURGH EH2 3JZ
Australia	Butterworths, SYDNEY, MELBOURNE, BRISBANE, ADELAIDE, PERTH, CANBERRA and HOBART
Canada	Butterworths Canada Ltd, TORONTO and VANCOUVER
Ireland	Butterworth (Ireland) Ltd, DUBLIN
Malaysia	Malayan Law Journal Sdn Bhd, KUALA LUMPUR
New Zealand	Butterworths of New Zealand Ltd, WELLINGTON and AUCKLAND
Puerto Rico	Butterworth of Puerto Rico, Inc, SAN JUAN
Singapore	Reed Elsevier (Singapore) Pte Ltd, SINGAPORE
South Africa	Butterworths Publishers (Pty) Ltd, DURBAN
USA	Michie, Charlottesville, VIRGINIA

A CIP Catalogue record for this book is available from the British Library.

ISBN 0 406 02677 7

Printed by Mackays of Chatham plc, Chatham, Kent

Preface

The twelve years which have passed since the second edition of this book have demonstrated the continuing contemporary importance of this wide-ranging subject. In that time there has been extensive case law and the issues raised in many of the cases have led to widespread public debate and controversy. In the UK the House of Lords alone has considered contempt on at least nine occasions, dealing with such diverse issues as ministerial liability for breaking court orders, *M v Home Office*; employers' liability for breaking court orders, *Re Supply of Ready Mixed Concrete (No 2); third parties' liability for frustrating court orders, A-G v Times Newspapers Ltd* ('Spycatcher'); determining whether a mental health tribunal is a 'court' for the purposes of contempt of court, *Pickering v Liverpool Daily Post & Echo Plc*, and determining the ambit of s 8 of the Contempt of Court Act 1981 concerning publication of jury deliberations, *A-G v Associated Newspapers Ltd* and of s 10 concerning journalists refusing to reveal their sources, *X Ltd v Morgan Grampian (Publishers) Ltd, Re An Inquiry under the Company Securities (Insider Dealing) Act* and *Secretary of State for Defence v Guardian Newspapers Ltd*. It also considered the production by the *Observer* newspaper of a midweek edition containing a DTI inspectors' report just days before the House of Lords were to hear the appeal in judicial review proceedings challenging the non-publication of the report, *Re Lonrho Plc*.

Other jurisdictions have been similarly active. There have , for example, been at least eight contempt cases decided by the Australian High Court, including the key decisions of *Hinch v A-G (Victoria)* on publications creating a risk of prejudice; *Gallagher v Durack* on scandalising the court; *AMIEU v Mudginberri Station Pty Ltd* on the court's power to punish civil contempt and *Doyle v The Commonwealth* on the procedural safeguards when committing contemnors. In Canada, courts now have to wrestle with the relationship between the common law based contempt and both the Canadian Criminal Code and the Canadian Charter of Republic Rights and Freedoms and the leading cases are *R v Kopyto* (scandalising the court) in the Ontario Court of Appeal and the Supreme Court decision of *United Nurses of Alberta v A-G for Alberta* (on a disobedience to a court order). Other important Supreme Court decisions include *R v Vermette* on the procedure and power to punish contempts ex facie, *BCGEU v A-G for British Columbia* on a judge's power to punish for contempt picketing outside the court, *Videotron Ltée v Industries Microlec Produits Electronique Inc* on the compellability of witnesses in contempt cases; *Chrysler Canada Ltd v Competition Tribunal* on the contempt power of inferior courts and *Dagenais v Canadian Broadcasting Corporation* on prohibiting a television programme because of the risk of prejudice to a forthcoming trial.

There have been full scale reviews of contempt of court by the Australian Law Reform Commission, the Irish Law Reform Commission and in Hong Kong. As yet, however, no legislative reform has followed these reviews. Indeed the common law contempt jurisdiction has proved remarkably enduring throughout the Commonwealth common law world. Even in Canada (including Quebec) it continues to operate (except in respect of scandalising the court) notwithstanding the Criminal Code (which expressly preserves the common law powers) and the Charter of Rights and Freedoms. Ironically, it is only in the UK, the jurisdiction in which the contempt power first originated, that there has been any significant attempt to place contempt on a statutory footing. But even here the common law continues to operate not just in areas not covered at all by the Contempt of Court Act 1981 such as civil contempt but also, as a series of cases now show, where a publisher intends to prejudice a particular case.

The 1981 Act had only just begun to operate when the second edition was published and in the Preface we referred to the disappointment expressed by some that the legislation was not liberal enough. Ironically, the current concern is the lack of prosecutions. This was highlighted in the case of the Taylor sisters in which, notwithstanding the castigation of the prejudicial publicity by the Court of Appeal, no contempt prosecution was brought. The sisters' application for review of the Attorney-General's decision not to bring proceedings was dismissed by the Divisional Court but it is understood that an appeal to the House of Lords is underway. It is submitted that whatever the eventual outcome of the Taylor case may be, s 7 of the 1981 Act by which the Attorney-General is given (apart from the court) the exclusive right to bring prosecutions under the strict liability rule is in need of urgent review. The evident reluctance of Sir Nicholas Lyell, the current Attorney-General, to prosecute contempt cases has, we would argue, led to the media's own relaxation of standards which in turn has contributed to what we regard as a disturbing trend of halting and abandoning trials because of prejudicial publicity, of which the trial of Geoffrey Knights is the latest example. But quite apart from the office's idiosyncratic practice (which of course will vary with the particular Attorney-General), given that contempt cases can be highly politically charged, as the *'Spycatcher'* and *Lonhro* cases well illustrate, there does seem to be a strong case for removing the office's exclusive role to bring contempt cases.

Another provision in need of review is s 8, under which there is a total ban on inquiry into juries' deliberations. As the courts have pointed out on more than one occasion the prohibition is too Draconian in preventing even bona fide research. Moreover, as *R v Young* (the 'ouija board' case) shows, s 8 could seriously inhibit the court's own powers to investigate a case.

The scope and application of the Contempt of Court Act 1981 is of course specific to the UK but a problem faced by all jurisdictions is the globalisation of information and new technology. The Canadian experience in the infamous Bernado/Homulka trial in which the Canadian court struggled to prevent the American media coverage of the case reaching Canada and the problem of news reports of the committal proceedings involving Rosemary West intended for an overseas readership leaking back into the UK when an account of the evidence appeared on the Internet, are examples of problems increasingly likely to be experienced. Whether these problems could or should be controlled by international agreement or by greater emphasis being placed on jury selection will need to be addressed.

Another issue raised by the Rosemary West trial is payment of witnesses by the media. Whether such payments made or agreed upon before the witness has given evidence could or should be punished and, if so, whether by contempt or a specific offence is something that clearly needs to be considered.

To take account of all these changes and developments the book has been substantially revised and a new chapter added so that separate consideration is now given to the general common law position governing publications interfering with the due course of justice to particular legal proceedings (Chapter 3) and the general position under the Contempt of Court Act 1981 (Chapter 4). Like the second edition, the book continues to contain throughout a full discussion of the common law position as well as detailed consideration of the 1981 Act. The book has been written on the assumption that the Criminal Justice and Public Order Act 1994 is fully in force. It should also be said that this is the first edition which Brenda Sufrin has co-authored.

A number of people have been helpful in the preparation of this third edition. We wish to thank Richard Dawson of Edwards Geldard, Solicitors, Cardiff, Joshua Rozenberg, BBC Legal Correspondent, James Stirk of Tarmac Quarry Products and Tom Welsh, co-author of Essential Law for Journalists for their assistance.

We should like to extend particular thanks to Laura Hoyano of Bristol University Law Department, with whom we discussed many issues and who gave us invaluable help in relation to Canada. Contempt is a subject which touches many areas of law and we should like to thank our colleagues at Bristol and Cardiff, especially Cathy Cobley, Steven Greer, Stephen Jones, John Parkinson, Paul Skidmore, Paul Robertshaw, Lynden Walters and Chris Willmore who were so generous with their time and knowledge.

We are grateful to both Bristol Law Department's and Cardiff Law School's funding of student research assistants at various times and we record our appreciation of Sean Chou, Kirsty Lewis, Louise Webb, James Clarke, Emmanuel Khoza and Tony Graham for all their hard work.

The library staff at both institutions were enormously helpful and in particular we would like to thank Peter Clinch and Duncan Montgomery at Cardiff for their willing and instant service.

A tremendous debt of thanks is owed to Jennifer Roberts and in particular Ann Bladen for their patient typing of the many drafts at the Cardiff end of the production.

We should also like to acknowledge the help and patience of the staff at Butterworths.

Finally, the third edition of this book is dedicated to our children, Alexandra and Oliver, with all our love.

Nigel Lowe, Cardiff Law School
University of Wales
Brenda Sufrin, Law Department
University of Bristol

All Saints' Day 1995

Contents

Table of statutes

References in this Table to *Statutes* are to Halsbury's Statutes of England (Fourth Edition) showing the volume and page at which the annotated text of the Act will be found.

Table of statutory instruments

Table of cases

B

C

D

H

I

J

K

L

N

T

U

X

Y

Z

CHAPTER 1

Introduction

The rules embodied in the law of contempt of court are intended to uphold and ensure the effective administration of justice. Lord Simon said in *A-G v Times Newspapers Ltd* [1] that they are the means by which the law vindicates the public interest in the due administration of justice. The law does not exist, as the phrase 'contempt of court' might misleadingly suggest,[2] to protect the personal dignity of the judiciary nor does it exist to protect the private rights of parties or litigants.[3] Lord President Clyde said in *Johnson v Grant*:[4]

> 'The phrase "contempt of court" does not in the least describe the true nature of the class of offence with which we are here concerned. . . . The offence consists in interfering with the administration of the law; in impeding and perverting the course of justice. . . . It is not the dignity of the Court which is offended—a petty and misleading view of the issues involved—it is the fundamental supremacy of the law which is challenged.'

It has been well said[5] that the law of contempt is of ancient origin yet of fundamental contemporary importance. Contempt of court certainly has a long history—*contemptus curiae* is said to have been a recognised phrase in English law since the twelfth century,[6] and, as will be evidenced by the rest of this book, the law continues to play a key role in protecting the administration of justice. Essentially a creature of common law, contempt has been and continues to be developed and adapted to meet changing challenges to the 'supremacy of the law'. One result of this continuing development and concern to protect the many facets of the administration of justice is that there are many forms of contempt.

---

1 [1974] AC 273 at 315.
2 The phrase 'contempt of court' has often been criticised as being inaccurate and misleading: see in England, eg Lord Cross in *A-G v Times Newspapers Ltd*, ibid, at 322, and Salmon LJ in *Jennison v Baker* [1972] 2 QB 52 at 61; in Australia, eg Mahoney JA in *A-G (NSW) v Willesee* [1980] 2 NSWLR 143 at 161 and the High Court of Australia (comprising Gibbs CJ, Mason, Murphy, Wilson and Brennan JJ) in *Lane v Registrar of the Supreme Court of New South Wales* (1981) 55 ALJR 529 at 534; in New Zealand, eg Richmond P in *Solicitor-General v Radio Avon Ltd* [1978] 1 NZLR 225 at 229. The Phillimore Committee's Report on Contempt (1974, Cmnd 5794) para 12 acknowledged these criticisms but could not offer any suitable alternative name.
3 Although it should be said that such individuals undoubtedly benefit from the protection that the law of contempt provides.
4 1923 SC 789 at 790, cited with approval inter alia by Lord Edmund-Davies in *A-G v Leveller Magazine Ltd* [1979] AC 440 at 459.
5 Miller: *Contempt of Court* (2nd edn, 1989, Clarendon Press) p 1.
6 Fox: *The History of Contempt of Court* (1927) p 1. For other reviews of the history of contempt see Arlidge and Eady: *The Law of Contempt* (1982, Sweet and Maxwell) and R Dhavan: 'Contempt of Court and the Phillimore Report' (1976) Anglo-American LR 186. For an account of contempt at the beginning of the century see the classic work by Oswald: *Contempt of Court* (3rd edn, 1910).

One commentator[7] has described contempt as 'the Proteus of the legal world assuming an almost infinite diversity of forms', but equally it can be said that contempt of court is as diverse as are the means of interfering with the due course of justice.[8]

I   THE SCOPE OF THE LAW OF CONTEMPT

Contempt can be divided into two broad categories, contempt by interference and contempt by disobedience.

The former category comprises a wide range of matters such as disrupting the court process itself (contempt in the face of the court), publications or other acts which risk prejudicing or interfering with particular legal proceedings, and publications or other acts which interfere with the course of justice as a continuing process (for example, publications which 'scandalise' the court and retaliation against witnesses for having given evidence in proceedings which are concluded).

The second category comprises disobeying court orders and breaking undertakings given to the court. It is essential that the law provides sanctions for the enforcement of the process and orders of a court. Dealing with the case of a party in civil litigation who refused to answer interrogatories, Chief Justice McKean of the United States said in 1778:[9]

> 'Since, however, the question seems to resolve itself into this, whether you shall bend to the law, or the law shall bend to you, it is our duty to determine that the former shall be the case.'

Although at first sight interference and disobedience contempts seem quite distinct, in fact this is not always so. The boundaries become blurred, for example when persons are accused of aiding or abetting breaches of court orders or of frustrating their purpose. The classic example of this is the *Spycatcher* litigation,[10] in which certain newspapers were held to be in contempt not for breaking an injunction to which they were not a party but for 'frustrating' the order and thus interfering with the course of justice in those proceedings.

So far as the interference category is concerned a crucial distinction is between acts thought to interfere with the course of justice in particular proceedings and those which are thought to interfere with the course of justice as a continuing process. Although it is true that, in one sense, the first type of act is but a special form of the latter, as inteference with the due administration of justice is a characteristic common to *all* contempts,[11] holding an act to be a contempt although it has no effect on *particular* proceedings, can have far-reaching consequences for freedom of speech. The classic case here is *A-G v Times*

---

7   Joseph Moskovitz: 'Contempt of Injunctions, Civil and Criminal' (1943) 43 Col LR 780.

8   This passage was cited by Sir John Donaldson MR in *A-G v Newspaper Publishing plc* [1988] Ch 333 at 361–362, [1987] 3 All ER 276 at 294 . Cf Hodgson J's remark in *A-G v Sport Newspapers Ltd* [1992] 1 All ER 503 at 536 that 'if contempt be the Proteus of the common law then for my part I would hope that his repertoire will not be increased'.

9   Cited by Fox: *The History of Contempt of Court* (1927) p 47.

10 *A-G v Newspaper Publishing plc* [1988] Ch 333, [1987] 3 All ER 276, *A-G v Newspaper Publishing plc* (1989) Times, 9 May; on appeal (1990) Times, 28 February, and *A-G v Times Newspapers Ltd* [1992] 1 AC 191, [1991] 2 All ER 398.

11 See Sir John Donaldson MR in *A-G v Newspaper Publishing plc* ibid at 362 and 294 and Lord Diplock in *A-G v Leveller Magazine Ltd* [1979] AC 440 at 449, [1979] 1 All ER 745 at 749.

Newspapers Ltd [12] in which the debate was whether a publication could be condemned not for interfering with the particular litigation but because, by amounting to 'trial by newspaper', it was inherently inimical to the due administration of justice.

Criminal and civil contempt

Traditionally contempts have been classified as being either criminal or civil.[13] Under this scheme it can broadly be said that interference contempt is seen as criminal contempt and disobedience contempt as civil, although the position has been confused by cases in which the courts have talked of civil contempt which 'savours of criminality'.[14]

Sir John Donaldson MR said in *A-G Newspaper Publishing Plc* [15] that whatever value classifying contempt as criminal or civil had in earlier times it now tended to mislead rather than assist. He preferred to use the categorisation discussed above and distinguish between (a) conduct which involves a breach, or assisting in a breach, of a court order, and (b) any other conduct which involves an interference with the due administration of justice. He pointed out that in all cases the standard of proof is the criminal one and that there are common rights of appeal. He considered that what distinguished the two categories was that where breach of a court order is involved the matter is raised by the parties whereas cases of interference are generally matters for the Attorney General.[16]

There remain, however, other practical consequences of classifying contempt as civil or criminal and these, and the procedures for dealing with each type of contempt, are dealt with in Chapters 12 and 14.

In so far as contempt constitutes a crime it is best to regard it as a crime that is *sui generis* since there are a number of peculiarities associated with the offence of which perhaps the outstanding example is the summary process by which such crimes are prosecuted. One of the causes of the confusion between criminal and civil contempt is that there has always been a punitive element in civil contempt as well.[17] The rules of civil contempt are equally concerned to uphold the effective administration of justice and although civil contempt is basically a wrong to the person who is entitled to the benefit of the court order, the court can punish disobedience to its order (an injunction, for example) by a committal to prison, just as in the case of a criminal contempt.[18] In a major constitutional

---

12 [1974] AC 273.
13 No such distinction, however, is made in Scotland, see the Phillimore Report (1974, Cmnd 5794) at para 4.
14 See *Wellesley v The Duke of Beaufort* (1831) 2 Russ & M 639 at 667, 39 ER 538 at 548, per Brougham LC; *Re Freston* (1883) 11 QBD 545 at 555, per Brett MR.
15 [1988] Ch 333 at 362, [1987] 3 All ER 276 at 294.
16 See also Lord Scarman in *Home Office v Harman* [1983] 1 AC 280 at 310, [1982] 1 All ER 532 at 542 and Chs 12 and 14 of this book. This distinction became confused in *A-G v Newspaper Publishing plc* itself, where the Attorney General, as a minister and on behalf of the Crown, was the plaintiff: see the discussion of the *Spycatcher* litigation in Ch 6.
17 See *Videotron Ltée et al v Industries Microlec Produits Electroniques Inc* (1993) 96 DLR (4th) 376 (Can Sup Ct).
18 The Australian Law Reform Commission (Report No 35, *Contempt*, para 22) pointed out that this court-centred, rather than plaintiff-centred approach, whereby disobedience of a court order made for the benefit of a party to civil proceedings is punishable as an affront to the court, is foreign to the approach to the enforcement of judgments found in civil law systems, where the broad-ranging concept of contempt which exists in the common law is unknown.

development the House of Lords decided in 1993 that even ministers of the Crown and their departments commit contempt if they act in disregard of an injunction made against them. They are not above the contempt jurisdiction by which the the courts protect the due administration of justice.[19]

The rationale of both criminal and civil contempt is therefore essentially the same: upholding the effective administration of justice. If a court lacked the means to enforce its orders, and its orders could be disobeyed with impunity, not only would individual litigants suffer, the whole administration of justice would be brought into disrepute.[20]

II SOURCES OF THE CONTEMPT POWER

The power to punish as contempt conduct that interferes with the course of justice has largely been developed at common law. Inasmuch as it is not confirmed by statute the contempt power is properly regarded as an inherent power, which vests in courts of record only.[1] As one would expect, superior courts of record have more extensive contempt powers than inferior courts, the position being broadly that superior courts can punish contempts whether committed in or outside the court whereas inferior courts can only punish contempts committed in the face of the court.

The courts' non-statutory contempt powers have proved remarkably enduring. In many Commonwealth jurisdictions contempt of court is specifically preserved as a common law crime. In Canada for example, criminal contempt is not a codified criminal offence but exists as a result of the Criminal Code, which preserves the common law power of the court to punish for contempt.[2] In New Zealand contempt is the only crime that can now be prosecuted at common law. Ironically, in the United Kingdom, where the contempt power first originated, there has been some attempt to put the offence on a statutory footing. Hence, parts of criminal contempt, for example that dealing with publications interfering with the course of justice in particular legal proceedings, are now controlled by the Contempt of Court Act 1981. As we shall see, however, the 1981 Act does not by any means apply to the whole law of contempt and even in those areas where it does operate, the common law is still relevant.

The exercise of the contempt power by courts in the United Kingdom is to some extent affected by the European Convention on Human Rights. Decisions of the European Court of Human Rights are not binding upon domestic courts though they can be influential in the courts and can of course be instrumental in causing legislative change. It was the *Sunday Times*' successful application[3] in the Strasbourg court that prompted the passing of the Contempt of Court Act 1981.

---

19 *M v Home Office* [1994] 1 AC 377, [1993] 3 All ER 537.
20 See the citation of this passage in *AMIEU v Mudginberri Station Pty Ltd* (1986) 161 CLR 98 at 107 (Aust HC).
1 For a discussion of this inherent power see Ch 12.
2 *R v Kopyto* (1988) 47 DLR (4th) 213.
3 *Sunday Times v UK* (1979) 2 EHRR 245.

III   CONTEMPT AND FREEDOM OF DISCUSSION

One aspect of contempt that deserves special mention is that which operates to protect the fairness of trials and to maintain the authority of the courts. In pursuit of this objective the contempt rules place severe restrictions[4] on what may be published about particular legal proceedings, so that they are not prejudiced by what jurors, witnesses and parties read or see in the media. Although there is a public interest in doing this, the rules thereby imposed impede and ultimately conflict with another public interest, namely, freedom of discussion. Freedom of discussion is an important public interest for as Lord Simon said in *A-G v Times Newspapers Ltd* :[5]

> 'People cannot adequately influence the decisions which affect their lives unless they can be adequately informed on facts and arguments relevant to the decisions.'

It is not easy to reconcile these two interests and to a certain extent the contempt rules are a compromise between them. It must be stressed, however, that the results of the compromise reflect the fact that the courts regard the due administration of justice as being the paramount interest so that where they cannot be reconciled the protection of the administration of justice trumps freedom of speech. This should be contrasted with the position in the United States, where the First Amendment to the Constitution guarantees freedom of expression. In the United States freedom of speech is the paramount value and extensive pre-trial publicity is off-set by procedures such as intensive jury vetting. The consequences of the American system and the contrast with legal systems with contempt of court rules were never so well demonstrated as in 1994 and 1995 before and during the trial in the United States of O J Simpson. It is notable that the Canadian Charter of Rights and Freedoms of 1982 guarantees freedom of expression in s 2(b) but the individual right of the accused to a fair trial is guaranteed by s 11(d) and the *societal* interest in a fair trial has been held to be preserved by s 26 which provides: 'The guarantee in this Charter of certain rights and freedoms shall not be construed as denying the existence of any other rights or freedoms that exist in Canada'. This means that in Canada the contempt rules still serve to limit freedom of expression in the interests of the due administration of justice. However, it has been said in the Supreme Court of Canada[6] in the context of pre-trial publication bans, that under the Charter the right to free expression has equal status with the right to a fair trial and that it is inappropriate for the courts any longer to automatically favour the latter over the former. If the United Kingdom was to have a Bill of Rights the relationship between these interests would have to be worked out here too.

In the United Kingdom, and other common law jurisdictions apart from the United States, there seems to be general agreement that there should be *some* restriction on what can be said about current proceedings, particularly criminal proceedings. The arguments coalesce around what exactly those restrictions should be. The criticisms which are made of the contempt rules are that they are too wide, too uncertain, unnecessarily limit the publication of matters of which the public should be informed, and serve to reinforce the culture of secrecy which is a feature of (British) public life.

---

4   Which generally last only until the case is concluded, so that publications are *postponed* rather than prohibited for ever.

5   [1974] AC 273 at 315.

6   *Dagenais v Canadian Broadcasting Corporation* 120 DLR (4th) 12 at 37 per Lamer CJC.

It is submitted that once proceedings have begun the law is right to insist that freedom of the media should give way to the public interest in fair trials. That is not to say that the media should have no role to play in the administration of justice. Lord Denning MR once said:[7]

'. . . the Press plays a vital part in the administration of justice. It is the watchdog to see that every trial is conducted fairly, openly and above board . . . [But] the watchdog may sometimes break loose and have to be punished for misbehaviour.'

The difficulty is that whether or not the watchdog has broken loose may be a matter of opinion. The courts need to be vigilant to ensure that the watchdog is not curbed more than is absolutely necessary or it will not be able to do its job.

There are particular problems when publications are restricted because of their alleged effect on the due administration of justice as a continuing process, rather than in relation to particular proceedings. Restricting discussion in order to protect a general process, or the legal system as a whole, smacks more of censorship and the abrogation of democratic freedoms than does the protection of individual litigants. In this area of contempt, for example, the offence of 'scandalising the court' by publishing certain types of comment about the courts and the judiciary still exists and has the potential to be used as a way of stifling criticism of the legal establishment.[8]

The contempt rules as they affect freedom of discussion must be looked at in their context. This includes looking at the media not as some idealised entity operating altruistically to uphold democratic values in a framework of accepted ethical standards, but as a disparate collection of interests driven partly by purely commercial considerations. The contempt rules govern, for instance, both the sensational end of the tabloid press[9] and serious investigative journalism and it is not surprising that the rules which attempt to rein in the one sometimes have damaging effects on the other. It must also be remembered that in the United Kingdom the contempt rules are a major brake on the media (along with defamation and breach of confidence) in a legal system which has no laws on privacy. Some of the material which cannot be published because of the contempt rules is prohibited from publication in other countries by stringent privacy rules. In the United Kingdom we rely upon the *public* interest in the administration of justice to restrict publications rather than on the *private* interest which would be protected by privacy laws.

The public interest aspect of the contempt rules as they affect publications is reflected in the role of the Attorney General in bringing proceedings. The fact that proceedings under the strict liability rule are brought at the Attorney General's discretion means that he sets the boundaries of what it is permissible to publish.[10] If the Attorney General repeatedly declines to act over publications which arguably offend the contempt rules then the parameters of the permissible shift. The question of how far the courts can review his discretion goes to the Attorney General's constitutional position but also raises the issue of how far contempt by interference with proceedings can be a private interest of the litigants as well as a public one.[11]

7 Denning, *Road to Justice* (1955) p 78.
8 In the UK at present this type of contempt prosecution has fallen into disuse, but is still very much alive in some jurisdictions: see Ch 9.
9 Eg, the reporting of the murder trial in *R v Taylor* (1993) 98 Cr App Rep 361.
10 Under s 7 of the Contempt of Court Act 1981 it is possible for a court to act on its own motion: see the discussion of this in Ch 12.
11 In *R v Solicitor-General, ex p Taylor* (1995) Times, 14 August, the Divisional Court held that the Attorney General's discretion was not subject to judicial review.

New Challenges

The contempt rules on publications interfering with the course of justice today face new challenges from the globalisation of information and new technology. Rules which were developed in days before even radio was dreamed of now have to deal with cable and satellite communications and the Internet and cyberspace. Even the Contempt of Court Act 1981 was, in this context, passed in another world. We are now faced with a situation where it is in fact impossible to ensure that a jurisdiction is insulated from information which is available outside it. The issue that arose in *Spycatcher*,[12] concerning the futility of trying to ban in the United Kingdom a book that was being sold in the United States, becomes more acute with every new development in communication technology and electronic publication. News networks such as CNN and Sky News serve the world and it can hardly be supposed that they will restrict what they broadcast worldwide in case the information leaks back into the United Kingdom in breach of the contempt rules.[13] The Internet is still in its infancy but it is a revolution in the way that people communicate and presents fundamental difficulties for contempt as it does for defamation, copyright, confidentiality and laws on pornography. All legal systems with rules which restrict publications, on whatever grounds, will have to grapple with the seemingly insuperable problems which the new age of communication presents. For example, news reports of the committal proceedings involving Rosemary West in 1995[14] intended for an overseas readership leaked back into the United Kingdom when an account of the evidence appeared on a commercial service carried on the Internet.

It may be that these developments mean that there will have to be a radical reappraisal of the way that trials are protected from prejudice and that a greater emphasis on jury selection, as it is practised in the United States, will have to be introduced in the common law countries which have hitherto relied on contempt rules.

IV THE SIGNIFICANCE OF THE LAW OF CONTEMPT

The sanctions of the law of contempt are powerful ones, particularly the sanction of imprisonment, but it is important to put the rules and the sanctions into perspective. The law of contempt is only one of the ways in which the due processes of the law are supported and furthered. It does, however, play a key role in protecting the administration of justice. It is an important adjunct to the criminal process and provides the final sanction in the civil process. Inevitably when its procedures and sanctions have come down to us over the centuries there are features which seem unsuited to a modern system of law. To some extent the ill effects of such features have been mitigated or eliminated by erosion and the good sense of the courts when called upon to consider to what extent the law of contempt should be applied. Some of the more obvious defects such as lack of

---

12 *A-G v Newspaper Publishing Plc* [1988] Ch 333, [1987] 3 All ER 276, *A-G v Newspaper Publishing plc* (1989) Times, 9 May and (1990) Times, 28 February, and *A-G v Times Newspapers Ltd* [1992] 1 AC 191, [1991] 2 All ER 398.
13 The problem was recently faced in an acute form in Canada over the American media's coverage of the *Bernardo/Homulka* trial: see pp 280–281 below.
14 To which strict reporting restrictions applied: see Ch 8.

the right of appeal have been remedied by statute. However, the resulting law is still imperfect. Even with its imperfections, however, there are those who believe that the law of contempt does a good job and one commentator said in 1979:[15]

> 'However uncertain its definition and scope may be in some respects, contempt of court is undoubtedly one of the great contributions the common law has made to the civilised behaviour of a large part of the world . . .'.

One recent source of disquiet over the law is the role that it played in the *Spycatcher* affair, where its impact on a matter which was really to do with government secrecy demonstrated how wide, draconian, and, in some people's eyes dangerous, this ancient law can be and how far its tentacles spread.

V   THE STRUCTURE OF THE BOOK

The United Kingdom law of contempt was significantly amended by the Contempt of Court Act 1981. However, the Act does not apply to all aspects of contempt and even where it does apply it is now apparent from judicial developments since it came into force that the common law remains relevant. Bearing this in mind and mindful of the fact that the common law remains operative in many Commonwealth jurisdictions, we have maintained a discussion of the common law position as well as dealing, where appropriate, with the 1981 Act and the interplay between common law and statute.

15   F A Mann (1979) 95 LQR 348.

CHAPTER 2

Contempt in the face of the court

I INTRODUCTION

A The basis and nature of the jurisdiction

The interruption or disruption of the trial process itself constitutes a serious and direct threat to the administration of justice and the power to punish as contempt such conduct has long been recognised as a necessary incident of courts of record. In his celebrated opinion in *R v Almon* [1] Wilmot J said:

> 'The power, which the Courts in Westminster Hall have of vindicating their own authority, is coeval with their first foundation and institution; it is a necessary incident to every Court of Justice. . . . to fine and imprison for a contempt of court acted in the face of it.'

More recently Lord Denning MR commented in *Morris v Crown Office*: [2]

> 'The phrase "contempt in the face of the court" has a quaint old-fashioned ring about it; but the importance of it is this: of all the places where law and order must be maintained, it is here in these courts. The course of justice must not be deflected or interfered with. Those who strike at it, strike at the very foundations of our society. To maintain law and order, the judges have, and must have, power at once to deal with those who offend against it. It is a great power—a power instantly to imprison a person without a trial—but it is a necessary power.'

It is settled law that the power to punish contempts committed in the face of the court is an inherent power vested in both superior and inferior courts of record.[3] Being an inherent power means that it cannot be lost by technicalities such as by repeated adjournments[4] nor should it be regarded as being taken away, restricted or controlled by statute save where it is clear that that must be the intention of the legislature.[5] Despite the latter point the tendency both in England

---

1 (1765) Wilm 243 at 254. For the circumstances in which the opinion was made and published, see pp 336 and 470–471. See further *R v Davison* (1821) 4 B & Ald 329 at 333, per Abbott CJ and *Re Rea (No 2)* (1879) 4 LR Ir 345, 347.

2 [1970] 2 QB 114 at 122, [1970] 1 All ER 1079 at 1081. See also the similar observations by Moffitt P in *Registrar, Court of Appeal v Collins* [1982] 1 NSWLR 682, 707 (NSW CA).

3 *Ex p Pater* (1864) 5 B & S 299, especially per Blackburn J at 312. See also *R v Lefroy* (1873) LR 8 QB 134 which supersedes older authority such as *Sparks v Martyn* (1668) 1 Vent 1. For Canada see eg *Re Regina and Monette* (1975) 64 DLR (3d) 470 at 474; *R v Dunning* (1979) 50 CC (2d) 296; *Canadian Broadcasting Corpn v Cordeau* (1979) 101 DLR (3d) 24 and *Vaillancourt v R* (1981) 120 DLR (3d) 740. For Australia see eg *R v Metal Trades Employers' Association, ex p Amalgamated Engineering Union Australian Section* (1950-51) 82 CLR 208 per Latham CJ at 241–3.

4 *R v Shumiatcher* (1967) 64 DLR (2d) 24.

5 See eg in New Zealand *A-G v Taylor* [1975] 2 NZLR 138, SC; on appeal [1975] 2 NZLR 675, CA; in Australia, *Douglas v Douglas* [1976] Qd R 75, 10 ALR 285 and *Skouvakis v Skouvakis* (1976) 11 ALR 204, and in Canada, *Chrysler Canada Ltd v Competition Tribunal* (1992) 92 DLR (4th) 609. See also I H Jacob: 'The Inherent Jurisdiction of the Court' (1970) 23 Current Legal Problems 23–24 and Mason: 'The Inherent Jurisdiction of the Court' (1983) 57 ALJ 449.

and Wales and other jurisdictions has been for Parliament to regulate the contempt powers of inferior courts whilst leaving those of the superior courts at large.

The contempt powers are the most extreme means of dealing with those who disrupt court proceedings and should only be exercised as a last resort when other less drastic remedies such as ejecting the offender from the court and adjourning proceedings are thought to be inappropriate and in any event only in exceptional circumstances where the contempt can be clearly proved and cannot wait to be punished.[6] As Stephenson LJ said in *Balogh v Crown Court at St Albans*,[7] the contempt power is both salutary and dangerous:

> 'salutary because it gives those who administer justice the protection necessary to secure justice for the public, dangerous because it deprives a citizen of the protection of safeguards considered generally necessary to secure justice for him.'

Judges should guard against the over use of their contempt powers lest, to use the words of Lord President Normand 'a process the purpose of which is to prevent interference with the administration of justice should degenerate into an oppressive or vindictive abuse of the court's powers'.[8] As Lord Goddard CJ said in *Parashuram Detaram Shamdasani v King-Emperor* [9] the contempt power is 'a power which a court must, of necessity, possess; its usefulness depends upon the wisdom and restraint with which it is used . . .'.

B   The significance of classifying contempt as being 'in the face of the court'

Criminal contempts are traditionally classified into those committed in the face of the court (in facie curiae) and those committed outside the court (ex facie curiae). The chief significance of this distinction lies in determining the extent of the inherent jurisdiction of different courts, it being established that, whereas superior courts of record have jurisdiction over both forms of contempt, inferior courts of record can only punish contempts in their face.[10] There have also been, and in some cases still are, procedural consequences that are dependent upon the classification.

In England and Wales there has been no recent litigation upon the classification problem with regard to determining the scope of the inherent[11] contempt powers of the inferior courts. In part this is because it is well established[12] that the contempt jurisdiction of the principal inferior court, the county court, is entirely

---

6 Per Stephenson LJ in *Balogh v Crown Court at St Albans* [1975] QB 73 at 87. See also the South African case *S v Nel* 1991 (1) SA 730.
7 [1975] QB 73 at 91.
8 *Re Milburn* 1946 SC 301 at 315, 1946 SLT 219 at 224 (Court of Session, 1st Division Scotland). See also *Re Prior, ex p Bellanto* [1963] SR (NSW) 190 at 192 (NSW SC).
9 [1945] AC 264 at 270 (PC).
10 See n 3, above.
11 Aliter to determine the scope of statutory powers. See eg, *Bokhari v Blessed* (1995) Independent, 16 January, CA and *Bodden v Metropolitan Police Commissioner* [1990] 2 QB 397, discussed at p 21 and p 515 respectively. Note also *R v Griffin* (1989) 88 Cr App Rep 63, 69 where the court acknowledged that the classification issue might have been important had the court in question been an inferior court.
12 *R v Lefroy* (1873) LR 8 QB 134.

controlled by statute.[13] A similar position obtains with regard to magistrates' courts.[14] Nonetheless classifying whether or not a contempt is 'in the face of the court' remains a potential issue in determining the extent of the powers of (a) coroners' courts which, as is now established,[15] retain an inherent as well as a statutory contempt jurisdiction; (b) certain bodies[16] that are statutorily designated courts of record; (c) mental health[17] and industrial tribunals[18] both of which are now held to be 'courts' for at least certain purposes of contempt; and (d) of a court-martial to certify to any court of law an alleged contempt by a civilian.[19]

In procedural terms the classification issue is important in determining the ambit of the Queen's Bench Divisional Court's jurisdiction to hear committal applications for contempts committed in respect of criminal proceedings before other courts since RSC Ord 52, r 1(2)(a)(ii) expressly excludes contempts committed in the face of the court.[20] The issue might have been important in relation to the superior courts' powers to punish contempts acting upon their own motion. The former RSC Ord 44, r 2(2) expressly confined such a power of the High Court and Court of Appeal to contempts committed in the face of the court. The current rule, Ord 52, r 5, contains no such restrictions which means, as the Court of Appeal in *Balogh v Crown Court at St Albans*[1] has said, that it is no longer necessary to give an exact geographical definition of contempt in the face of the court.

If *Balogh*'s case closed an area where classification might have been important the Legal Aid Act 1988 has opened another. Section 29(1) provides that in:

> 'any proceedings where a person is liable to be committed or fined . . . (c) by any superior court for contempt in the face of that or any other court, . . . (2) . . . the court may order that he be granted representation under this section for the purposes of the proceedings if it appears to the court to be desirable to do so in the interests of justice.'[2]

In other words it appears that the superior courts' power to order legal aid for the accused is confined to contempts committed in the face of a court. We shall consider shortly how this should be interpreted.[3]

Outside England and Wales, the classification issue has proved of varying importance. In Scotland and New Zealand, for example, the problem does not appear to have troubled the courts[4] whereas in Australia and Canada, the distinction between contempts in facie and ex facie has proved very important. In both these latter countries there has been considerable litigation over the

13 See the County Courts Act 1984, Part VII, discussed post, at pp 510 ff.
14 Under the Contempt of Court Act 1981, s 12, discussed post pp 513 ff.
15 *R v West Yorkshire Coroner, ex p Smith (No 2)* [1985] QB 1096, discussed at p 508.
16 Eg, an election court and the Transport Tribunal: see p 508.
17 *Pickering v Liverpool Daily Post and Echo Newspaper Plc* [1991] 2 AC 370, HL, discussed at p 489.
18 *Peach Grey & Co (a firm) v Sommers* [1995] 2 All ER 513, discussed at p 489.
19 Under s 101(g) of the Army Act 1955 or the Air Force Act 1955 or under s 65(1)(c) of the Naval Discipline Act 1957, discussed at p 517.
20 Discussed at pp 485 ff.
1 [1975] QB 73.
2 This provision, which replaced that formerly provided by s 13(1) of the Contempt of Court Act 1981, came into force on 1 May 1991, SI 1991/790.
3 See p 14.
4 For the position in Scotland see eg *The Laws of Scotland, Stair Memorial Encyclopadia*, Vol 6, paras 301 ff and G H Gordon, *Criminal Law* (2nd edn) Ch 51. In New Zealand see Adams; *Criminal Law and Practice in New Zealand* (2nd edn) particularly at para 3598 where he doubts whether inferior courts have any inherent contempt jurisdiction.

inherent contempt powers of inferior courts[5] and until 1972 the classification of the contempt was important in Canada because in respect of contempts in facie appeals could only be made against punishment and not conviction.[6]

C   The meaning of 'contempt in the face of the court'

In general 'contempt in the face of the court' may be said to comprise the unlawful interruption, disruption or obstruction of court proceedings. Such conduct can take a variety of forms: hurling insults or objects at the judge, refusing to answer questions in court, threatening or harassing advocates, defendants being unfit through drink to plead in criminal proceedings, litigants undressing in court, wolf whistling a juror and members of the public demonstrating inside the court room, are but a few examples.

As with all criminal contempts the offending act must constitute an interference with the administration of justice.[7] Beyond this, however, unless the contempt jurisdiction is statutorily defined[8] it is difficult to give a comprehensive definition of the type of conduct involved.[9]

The principal definitional difficulty is the relevance of the geographical location of the offending act. Clearly, misconduct inside the court room and in the sight or hearing of the judge must be included but doubts may be raised about the classification of the following: misconduct in the court room but not in the sight or hearing[10] of the judge, misconduct in chambers (either before a judge or a master),[11] misconduct in the court precincts or outside the court building; misconduct which takes place both inside and outside the court; misconduct by lawyers, witnesses or jurors failing to appear in court on an appointed day. The very phrase 'contempt in the face of the court' particularly when it is used in contradistinction to contempts committed outside the court would seem to imply that location is important. Accordingly, it could be argued that an offending act

---

5   For Australia see generally the *Australian Digest* (2nd edn) Vol 5, paras 32 ff. For Canada see eg *Vaillancourt v R* (1981) 120 DLR (3d) 740; *R v Pinx* (1979) 105 DLR (3d) 143; *Canadian Broadcasting Corpn v Cordeau* (1979) 101 DLR (3d) 24 and *Re McLachlan and Lockyer and The Queen* (1980) 117 DLR (3d) 137 (the classification issue was not pursued on appeal; see *R v McLachlan and Lockyer* (1981) 125 DLR (3d) 730). See also the Law Reform Commission of Canada, Working Paper No 20 (1974) pp 17, 18 and the Final Report No 17 (1982) pp 51–52. The distinction is crucial in other jurisdictions not least in the US where summary punishment for contempt is limited under 18 USC, s 401 inter alia to misbehaviour of any person in the presence of the court or so near thereto as to obstruct the administration of justice.

6   Which was when the Canadian Criminal Code, s 9(1) was changed (by the Criminal Law (Amendment) Act 1972, s 4) to allow appeals both against conviction and punishment.

7   See *Parashuram Detaram Shamdasani v King-Emperor* [1945] AC 264 at 268, per Lord Goddard CJ; *Weston v Central Criminal Court Courts' Administrator* [1977] QB 32, [1976] 2 All ER 875; *Re Prior, ex p Bellanto* [1963] SR (NSW) 190 at 199; *Re Nash, ex p Tuckerman* [1970] 3 NSWR 23 and *Tippett v Murphy* (1982) 16 NTR 13.

8   As with county courts under the County Courts Act 1984, s 118 and magistrates' courts under the Contempt of Court Act 1981, s 12.

9   Indeed Lord Tucker said in *Izuora v R* [1953] AC 327 at 336 that it was not possible 'to particularise the acts which can or cannot constitute contempt in the face of the court'.

10 In most jurisdictions in Australia (see *European Asian Bank AG v Wentworth* (1986) 5 NSWLR 445, 456) it is common for the Rules to refer to the face or hearing of the court.

11 In *Re Johnson* (1887) 20 QBD 68 Lord Esher MR left the question open; cf *Weedow v Phillips* (1891) 12 ALT 166 (Victoria, Australia). Cf *Bokhari v Blessed* (1995) Independent, 16 January, CA, in which it was held that s 118 of the County Courts Act 1984, discussed at p 510, applied to arbitration proceedings before a district judge.

could only be considered contempt in the face of the court provided all the circumstances were within the personal knowledge of the court. This, at any rate, was the view of the Canadian judge, Laskin J, who delivered a powerful dissenting judgment in *McKeown v R* [12] saying:

> 'Contempt in the face of the court is, in my view, distinguished from contempt not in its face on the footing that all the circumstances are in the personal knowledge of the court. The presiding Judge can then deal summarily with the matter without the embarrassment of having to be a witness to issues of fact which may be in dispute because of events occurring outside.'

In *Balogh v Crown Court at St Albans* [13] however, Lord Denning MR called the above definition into question. He equated contempt in the face of the court with contempt which the court can punish of its own motion and thought that it really meant 'contempt in the cognisance of the court'. There must be 'a gross interference with the course of justice in a case that was being tried, or about to be tried, or just over ... and it must be urgent and imperative to act at once'. Subject to these requirements, he thought that the power to punish contempts on the court's own motion applied to acts committed (1) within the sight of the court, (2) within the court room but not seen by the judge, and (3) at some distance from the court. In support of this last example, he cited *Moore v Clerk of Assize, Bristol* [14] where a witness having given evidence was threatened in a cafe outside the court building.

A similarly wide view was taken in the Australian decision *Registrar, Court of Appeal v Collins*,[15] in which it was held that a man who, whilst standing on the pavement outside the entrance to certain court buildings, distributed pamphlets warning jurors against accepting police evidence was rightly convicted for 'contempt in the face of the court'. In so holding Moffitt P observed that the power of any court of record to punish as contempt in the face of the court extends to conduct which takes place outside the actual court room. It extends to conduct which is sufficiently proximate in time and space to the trial of the proceedings then in progress or imminent so as to present a 'confrontation to the trial'. In Moffitt P's view neither the geographical precincts of the court nor the personal observation of court officials prescribe the limits of the power.

In *European Asian Bank AG v Wentworth*,[16] however, Kirby P took a much narrower view holding that contempt in the face of the court embraces 'conduct coming to the notice of the court directly by one of its senses'. Accordingly, he held that the party striking another in the court room but after the judge had left did not constitute contempt in the face of the court. A strikingly similar approach was suggested in the English decision *Bokhari v Blessed*,[17] where a judge overheard insults between the parties after he left the court room. Bingham MR suggested, obiter,[18] that as the insult was directly 'witnessed by the judge's own senses' it might well have been considered contempt in the face of the court.

---

12 (1971) 16 DLR (3d) 390 at 408. In Ireland see the similar comment by Henchy Chambers J in *The State (DPP) v Walsh* [1981] IR 412, 432.
13 [1975] QB 73 at 83, 84; cf *Rooney v Snaresbrook Crown Court* (1978) 68 Cr App Rep 78 at 81.
14 [1972] 1 All ER 58, [1971] 1 WLR 1669.
15 [1982] 1 NSWLR 682 (NSW CA).
16 [1986] 5 NSWLR 445, 457. See also *Fraser v The Queen* [1984] 3 NSWLR 212. See also *Re Cooper's Marriage* (1980) 48 FLR 264, 272, per Watson J approving the Laskin test.
17 (1995) Independent, 16 January, CA, (LEXIS).
18 The case was actually decided under the statutory jurisdiction, see s 118 of the County Courts Act 1984, discussed at p 510.

Although the corpus of the modern case law is that contempt in the face of the court is not necessarily confined to acts taking place within the court there is no uniformity as to precisely what the phrase means. What then *should* it be taken to mean? Confining it to circumstances within the personal knowledge of the court would seem to be one of the narrower definitions, whilst equating it with the courts' power to punish contempts upon its own motion seems very wide. Neither definition is totally satisfactory. The former ignores, for example, the acceptance in some jurisdictions that a lawyer's wrongful absence from court is a contempt in its face[19] whilst the latter seems to extend inferior courts' contempt jurisdiction beyond what is traditionally accepted.[20] It is tempting to suggest some compromise definition but the true position may be better reflected if it were accepted that its meaning may vary according to the context in which the issue is raised.

So far as superior courts are concerned the wider tests of both Lord Denning MR in *Balogh*'s case and Moffitt P in *Collins* may well be acceptable. In this context the critical issue is not so much where the acts complained of took place (since such courts have jurisdiction over contempts committed both in and outside court) but of their impact on the court proceedings and of the urgency to deal with them. If, to use Lord Denning's phrase, the acts are within the 'cognisance of the court' and, to use Moffitt P's phrase, they 'present a confrontation to the trial', then immediate action seems justifiable. A similarly wide approach seems right when interpreting the Legal Aid Act 1988, s 29 which, it will be recalled, confines superior courts' powers to order legal aid for the accused with respect to contempts in the face of the court. In other words it seems right to facilitate legal representation whenever a court, acting upon its own motion, can instantaneously punish the offenders.

In contrast a more cautious approach seems appropriate with respect to inferior courts' inherent jurisdiction. As Kirby P surely rightly pointed out in *European Asian Bank AG v Wentworth*,[1] the power to act summarily is extraordinary and one should be wary of vesting too wide an extraordinary power in inferior courts. In this context therefore, it seems sensible to confine contempt in the face of the court, though even so one might be hesitant to adopt either the Laskin or Kirby tests. Instead one might suggest that however it is phrased the contempt power should extend to all misconduct occurring within the court room, at any rate whilst the court is in session,[2] brought to the court's notice whether or not it is seen or heard by the judge.[3] In such cases all the evidence will be available to the court and it seems right that the judge *should* be able to control events in his own court room. The power should also cover misconduct in the court precincts or immediately outside the court provided that misbehaviour actually interrupts the proceedings.[4] Although a case could certainly be made for

---

19 In Canada according to *McKeown v R* (1971) 16 DLR (3d) 390. For the position in England see *Weston v Central Criminal Court Courts' Administrator* [1977] QB 32, [1976] 2 All ER 875.

20 Ie to contempts clearly committed outside court.

1 (1986) 5 NSWLR at 445 at 457–458.

2 Aliter, perhaps, if as in *European Asian Bank*, ibid, the judge has already left the court room when the offending act takes place.

3 This will cover a case like *Lecointe v Central Criminal Courts' Administrator* (1973) Bar Library Transcript, 57A where a man distributed leaflets in the public gallery at the Old Bailey, inviting people to picket the courts.

4 This would be in line with the Court of Appeal discussion in *Bodden v Metropolitan Police Commissioner* [1990] 2 QB 397 in which it was held that magistrates' powers under s 12 of the Contempt of Court Act 1981 extend to acts outside court that actually interrupt the court proceedings. See further p 515.

saying that even inferior courts should have the immediate power to punish the type of behaviour encountered in *Collins*, it is submitted that a sensible distinction can be drawn between behaviour outside court which actually interrupts proceedings and that which does not. Only the former, it is submitted, should be treated as contempt in the face of the court. At all events it is suggested that where the misconduct is not seen by the judge summary punishment should only be exercisable where there is immediately available cogent evidence and that short of an admission by the offender this would require all the witnesses to be before the court.

II WAYS IN WHICH CONTEMPT IN THE FACE OF THE COURT MAY BE COMMITTED

Any person attending the court can commit contempt in the face of the court, be they litigants, counsel, witnesses, jurors, court officers, members of the press or members of the general public.

A Assaulting or threatening persons in court

Assaulting or threatening any person in the court room during proceedings constitutes an obvious and grave threat to the due administration of justice and can therefore be punished as a contempt. As Lord Denning MR emphasised in *Morris v Crown Office*[5] 'of all the places where law and order must be maintained it is here in the courts'.

1 *Assaulting or threatening judges*

Happily, personal outrages upon judges are uncommon, being mainly restricted to persons (usually defendants having just been found guilty) throwing missiles at the judge. The classic example is the case of 1631[6] where a prisoner having been adjudged guilty of a felony was reported to have 'ject un Brickbat a le justice que narrowly mist'. For this, the prisoner's right hand was cut off and fixed to the gibbet, upon which he was immediately hanged in the presence of the court. Another well-known case is *Re Cosgrave*[7] where an: 'unprecedented assault was committed by a man in Court throwing an egg at the Judge'. Oswald recites that:

> 'The Vice-Chancellor [Malins V-C] had sufficient presence of mind and sense of humour, it is said, to remark that the present must have been intended for his brother Bacon V-C, who was sitting in an adjoining Court.'[8]

For this the culprit was immediately imprisoned and discharged only after five months.

---

5 [1970] 2 QB 114 at 122, [1970] 1 All ER 1079 at 1081.
6 *Anon* (1631) 2 Dyer 188b n. See also the case of James Williamson cited by Oswald: *Contempt of Court* (3rd edn, 1910) p 42.
7 (1877) Seton's *Judgments & Orders* (7th edn) 457, (1877) Times, 17 March.
8 *Contempt of Court* (3rd edn, 1910) p 42. This story has been doubted by Sir John Fox (1922) 38 LQR 185.

More recently a litigant was imprisoned for an extra nine months for leaping from the dock and attacking Brabin J whose wig and glasses were knocked off,[9] whilst in Scotland a petitioner in a divorce case was imprisoned for three years for his contempt when, at the end of the case, he lost his temper, shouted and bawled and uttered threats against everyone in court.[10]

Notwithstanding the seriousness of assaults or attempted assaults upon a judge, lenience is likely to be shown to a disappointed litigant and even where objects are thrown a judge will often be content to give a stern warning not to repeat the offence.[11] As Davies LJ said in *Morris v Crown Office:*[12]

> 'On occasions one has the misfortune to encounter someone who makes a disturbance in court. Usually, when that happens it is a case of a disappointed litigant who, from a sense of rage or disappointment at the result of his case, loses control of himself and gives vent to his feelings by an outburst either by word of mouth or physically. That is a situation which has to be dealt with according to its seriousness. He may be fined, or, in serious cases, he may be sent to prison.'

Where a serious assault has been committed, such as attempting to shoot a judge, the more likely and proper course is to invoke the ordinary criminal process, although contempt proceedings could be used.[13]

2 Assaulting or threatening other persons

Assaulting or threatening other persons in the court room are regarded no less seriously than outrages upon judges. It has been held to be a contempt to assault or threaten parties,[14] witnesses,[15] jurors[16] or advocates.[17] Until the early seventeenth century offenders were commonly punished by cutting off their right hands.[18] Today, imprisonment is the major sanction for serious contempts. In *R v Wigley*[19] a witness was imprisoned for three days for striking the defendant in the lobby of the court immediately after the trial, and in *R v Craddock*[20] a prisoner who, on

9 The litigant was David Alfred Crowley, see (1973) Times, 2 March.
10 *Cordiner, Petitioner* 1973 SLT 125. The maximum term of imprisonment that can now be imposed is two years, s 14 (England) and s 15 (Scotland) of the Contempt of Court Act 1981.
11 From time to time isolated instances of such acts are reported in the press. A collection of amusing examples can be found in *Punch* (18–24 February, 1970), pp 251–2. See also *R v Astor, ex p Isaacs* (1913) 30 TLR 10 where Scrutton J, *arguendo* referred to a case in Scotland where ladies threw apples at Lord Salvesen. See also the case reported in (1970) Times, 12 February where a litigant threw books at Lord Denning MR (reported in 'The Times Diary').
12 [1970] 2 QB 114 at 127, [1970] 1 All ER 1079 at 1085.
13 As was done in the case of Judge Parry being shot and seriously injured by a disappointed bailiff, see Oswald, *Contempt of Court* (3rd edn, 1910) p 42.
14 *R v Wigley* (1835) 7 C & P 4.
15 *Rowland v Samuel* (1847) 9 LT OS 280; *Kirby v Webb* (1887) 3 TLR 763.
16 See *R v Sparks and Kingsnorth* (1995) 16 Cr App Rep (S) 480 – two members of the public comitted to prison for making threatening gestures at members of the jury from the public gallery. See also *R v Smithers and Bowen* (1983) 5 Cr App Rep (S) 248 and *Carlion's Case* (1345) 2 Dyer 188b.
17 See eg *Re Johnson* (1887) 20 QBD 68 and *Re Goldman* [1968] 3 NSWLR 325.
18 See eg *Davis's Case* (1560) 2 Dyer 188b. See also *Jones' Case* (1575) 2 Dyer 188b n, also reported as *Ballingham's Case* (1605) 2 Dyer 188b n; *Savel and Lord Worthley's Case* (1626) 2 Dyer 188b n; *Oldfield's Case* (1610) 12 Co Rep 71; and *Waller's Case* (1634) Cro Car 373. The last case where this type of punishment was discussed was *R v Earl of Thanet* (1799) 27 State Tr 821, 970.
19 (1835) 7 C & P 4.
20 (1875) Times, 18 March. See also *Rowland v Samuel* (1847) 9 LT OS 280 where the defendant addressed a witness with the words 'You perjured villain I'll kill you' and was imprisoned for his contempt, and, in Canada, *Paul v R* (1980) 111 DLR (3d) 626.

being acquitted, threatened his fellow prisoner in the dock with the words 'I will give it you for this splitting on me', was imprisoned for a year.

Whether assaults or threats made in the court precincts or even beyond can be regarded as contempts in the face of the court is, as already indicated, a moot point. There is some support for saying that assaults or threats upon persons having a duty to discharge in court can be so regarded. In *Re Johnson*[1] for example, Bowen LJ, said: 'The principle is that those who have duties to discharge in a court of justice are protected by the law, and shielded on their way to the discharge of such duties, while discharging them, and on their return therefrom, in order that such persons may safely have resort to courts of justice.' In *Purdin v Roberts*[2] Neville J said:

> 'It is most important the public should know that persons who attend the courts to give evidence as witnesses in any matter before the courts will be protected from assault whilst in the precincts of the courts.'

In Australia, assaults upon advocates in the court precincts have been punished as contempts. In *Brown v Putnam*[3] the Supreme Court of New South Wales, Court of Appeal, affirmed Bowen LJ's comments and expressly held that a judge of the Family Law Division of the Supreme Court of New South Wales had jurisdiction himself to deal with an alleged contempt comprising threats made against a barrister in the court precincts.

However, whilst assaults or threats upon persons having a duty to perform in court are undoubtedly punishable as contempts, especially since the courts are rightly vigilant to protect such persons, the above cases may establish nothing more than that superior courts can punish such contempts upon their own motion. If that is so, and such misconduct is not contempt in the face of the court, then, in the absence of statutory authority, inferior courts have no such comparable powers, unless perhaps where the misconduct actually disturbs the court proceedings.[4] It might be added that assaulting or threatening a member of the public in the court precincts (and a fortiori outside the court) should not (unless it actually disturbs the court hearing) be punishable by any court as a contempt, since it would be difficult to argue that the course of justice was thereby jeopardised.

B   Insulting the court

Insulting behaviour in the court's presence is a classic example of contempt in the face of the court. An obvious way of insulting the court, is to insult the judge personally. In what was described as a classic example of contempt, a man was

---

1 (1887) 20 QBD 68 at 74, cf *Re Clements, Costa Rica Republic v Erlanger* (1877) 46 LJ Ch 375, CA. *Re Johnson* was cited with approval in *Bokhari v Blessed* (1995) Independent, 16 January, CA.
2 (1910) 74 JP Jo 88. See also 9 *Halsbury's Laws* (4th edn) para 6, n 2.
3 (1975) 6 ALR 307. See also *Re Goldman* [1968] 3 NSWLR 325. For an account of the facts see the first edition of this work at pp 12, 13. Cf *European Asian Bank AG v Wentworth* (1986) 5 NSWLR 445, in which it was held that the striking of one party by another after the judge had left the court room did not constitute contempt in the face of the court.
4 A pointer in favour of this narrow approach is the tendency in legislation to confer on inferior courts the power only to deal with assaults inside the court room.

found guilty of contempt for shouting from the public gallery that the judge was biased and racist.[5] However, as Holroyd J said in *R v Davison*:[6]

> 'In the case of an insult to [the judge], it is not on his own account that he commits, for that is a consideration which should never enter his head. But, though he may despise the insult, it is a duty which he owes to the station to which he belongs, not to suffer those things to pass which will make him despicable in the eyes of others. It is his duty to support the dignity of his station, and uphold the law, so that, in his presence, at least, it shall not be infringed.'

It is also a contempt to insult the jury[7] and even fellow solicitors.[8] Under the County Courts Act 1984, s 118(1)(a)[9] and the Contempt of Court Act 1981, s 12[10] it is expressly stated that wilful insults in a county court or magistrates' court to the judge or magistrate or to any juror, witness or officer of the court are punishable as contempts.

What amounts to insulting the court is necessarily a question of fact. While some words are obviously insulting others may be considered insulting because of the tone and manner in which they are said. As Lord Denman CJ, said in *Carus Wilson's Case*:[11]

> 'A court may be insulted by the most innocent words, uttered in a peculiar manner or tone. The words . . . might or might not be contemptuous, according to the manner in which they were spoken.'

A blatant example is *Harrison's Case*[12] where one Thomas Harrison rushed into the Bar of the Common Pleas while that court was sitting and said: 'I accuse Mr Justice Hutton of High Treason.' For this, he was fined £5,000 and imprisoned during the King's pleasure.[13] In *Carus Wilson's Case*[14] Wilson interrupted the court, when it was about to deliver judgment, by uttering 'in the most unbecoming tone':

> 'I solemnly protest against the reading of the judgment, which you, an incompetent court, composed of a bailiff, and two lieutenant bailiffs, who have been recused, and who have not purged themselves of that recusation and have not the power to do so, have rendered.'

The Court of Appeal held that these words were sufficient to justify the Royal Court of Jersey fining the offender for contempt.

The authority just cited is old but there is no doubt that the power continues to exist. In *R v Tamworth Justices, ex p Walsh*,[15] for instance, a solicitor remarked

---

5 *R v Hill* [1986] Crim LR 457.
6 (1821) 4 B & Ald 329.
7 *Ex p Pater* (1864) 5 B & S 299, and *R v Powell* (1993) 98 Cr App Rep 224.
8 *Re Johnson* (1887) 20 QBD 68.
9 Discussed at pp 510–511
10 Discussed at pp 513–515.
11 (1845) 7 QB 984 cited with approval by Cockburn CJ in *Ex p Pater* (1864) 5 B & S 299.
12 (1638) Cro Car 503.
13 Hutton J also recovered £10,000 damages in a civil action for slander, see *Hutton v Harrison* (1638) Hut 131.
14 (1845) 7 QB 984. For other cases see *Earl of Lincoln v Fysher* (1597) Moore KB 470; *R v Rogers* (1702) 7 Mod Rep 28; *R v Langley* (1703) 2 Salk 697; *Ex p Marlborough* (1844) 5 QB 955; and *R v Jordan* (1888) 36 WR 797 (sub nom *R v Staffordshire County Court Judge* (1888) 57 LJ QB 483). See also *R v Watson* (1878) 23 Sol Jo 86 where the prosecution was a criminal information for slander, and not contempt.
15 [1994] COD 277. The conviction, however, was quashed because the contemnor had not been given the opportunity to reflect and to obtain advice and legal representation.

in court that 'any delay is a result of the ridiculous listing of the Clerk of this Court.' It was held that it could not be said that no reasonable Bench could have considered the remarks were wilfully insulting and there are modern Australian cases[16] in which courts have committed litigants for rude and insolent behaviour. A judge, however, should be slow to use his contempt powers with respect to insults directed against himself. As Lord Denning MR said in *Balogh v Crown Court at St Albans* [17] 'Insults are best treated with disdain—save when they are gross and scandalous.' In *Balogh*'s case itself, no action was taken over the defendant's uncouth insult addressed to the judge: 'You are a humourless automaton. Why don't you self-destruct?'[18]

On the other hand insults to others such as jurors or, possibly witnesses, may be thought more worthy of punishment since such persons are not used to, nor trained to withstand court room pressures. In *Ex p Pater*,[19] a barrister, following some extraordinary outbursts by the foreman of the jury during the case, said in his address to the jury:

'I thank God that there are twelve jurymen, for if it rested with one, and that one the foreman, there could be no doubt of the result; he ought to be removed from the box and another juror put in his place.'

These words were spoken in a loud, threatening and insulting tone with violent gestures and when asked to withdraw the expressions, the barrister refused and in fact repeated them. For this conduct he was fined £20 for his contempt, and this decision was upheld on appeal. Cockburn CJ said:

'We are bound to protect jurymen in the discharge of their duties, and if looking to the whole of the circumstances, we see evidence from which it might fairly be concluded that there was an intention to insult, we cannot interpose to prevent the consequences from a desire to uphold the privileges of the Bar.'

In similar vein in upholding a conviction under s 12 of the Contempt of Court Act 1981 that a wolf whistle addressed to a female juror by a member of the public amounted to a wilful insult to the court, Staughton LJ commented in *R v Powell*: [20]

'Judges are not so conscious of their own dignity or so afraid of losing it that they have to take action in all such cases. But jurors do not come to these Courts, as they are under a duty to do when summoned, in order to have comments, even flattering comments,[1] publicly made on their personal appearance. The administration of justice is not to be interrupted at the tense moment when the jury return with their verdict.'

In contrast to insulting the court, insults directed, during the course of argument, against opposing counsel or the other party are less likely to be thought to be a contempt. As Lord Goddard CJ said in *Parashuram Detaram Shamdasani v King-Emperor*: [2]

16   *Dow v A-G* [1980] Qd R 58 and *Reece v McKenna, ex p Reece* [1953] QSR 258.
17   [1975] QB 73 at 86G. Cf in Canada *R v Barbacki* (1993) 97 DLR (4th) 479.
18   Similarly no action was taken by Ward J when a defendant pulled down her trousers and 'did a moonie' at the judge from the dock. Written across her buttocks were the words 'Happy Christmas': (1995) The Lawyer, 3 January.
19   (1864) 5 B & S 299 (Appeal from Middlesex Quarter Sessions); see also *R v Skinner* (1772) Lofft 54, where a JP insulted the jury.
20   (1993) 98 Cr App Rep 224, 228.
 1   Apparently the juror in question found the wolf whistle flattering, see ibid at 227–228.
 2   [1945] AC 264.

'It must be rare indeed for words used in the course of argument, however irrelevant, to amount to a contempt when they relate to an opponent, whether counsel or litigant.'

He added that:

'An insult to counsel or to the opposing litigant is very different from an insult to the court itself or to members of a jury who form part of the tribunal.'

C   Disrupting court proceedings generally

Conduct which disturbs or disrupts court proceedings constitutes an interference with the due administration of justice, and is a contempt. In *Morris v Crown Office*[3] a group of students protesting against a court order made against one of the leaders of their organisation, invaded a court during the hearing before Lawton J of a libel case, and shouted slogans, scattered pamphlets and sang songs. Their contempt in interrupting the proceedings was aggravated by the fact that the disruption was a deliberate conspiracy and because the proceedings which were interrupted had no relevance to their cause of protest. As Davies LJ said:[4]

'They banded together and made the journey from Aberystwyth to London with the deliberate intention of interfering with the conduct of a case or cases in the Royal Courts of Justice—a deliberate invasion. Their purpose was to invade and interrupt a court of justice here in the Strand by singing and other means. They interrupted with the greatest contumely and brought to a halt an important trial which had nothing whatsoever to do with Wales, the Welsh people or the Welsh language.'

Lawton J sentenced eleven of the demonstrators each to three months' imprisonment. A further eight who had apologised for their behaviour were each fined £50. Several of those who were imprisoned appealed. The Court of Appeal upheld Lawton J's decision but as a gesture of mercy freed those students who had appealed, making it clear that such a course of conduct would not be tolerated in the future.

Salmon LJ said:[5]

'I believe that the very proper sentences imposed by Lawton J have served to bring home to these young people and to anyone else who may be tempted to follow their example that even in our so-called "permissive" society, it is unsafe to assume that "anything goes". Everyone has now been warned. If this sort of conduct is repeated by anyone in the future, whatever their motives, no excuse will be accepted, and a sentence of three months' or even six months' imprisonment should not in my view be regarded as in any way excessive.'

Since *Morris v Crown Office* there have been further incidents involving Welsh Nationalists. In one case[6] no less than 50 such demonstrators were held in custody for three days, after having disrupted a trial by singing and cheering. In a later case[7] three women and a man were removed from the public gallery after

---

3 [1970] 2 QB 114, [1970] 1 All ER 1079.
4 Ibid 128, 1086 respectively.
5 Ibid 130, 1087 respectively
6 See (1971) Times, 24 April.
7 See (1971) Times, 4 May. See also (1971) Times, 28 April. For disturbance in a Northern Ireland court in Belfast see (1971) Times, 17 April. Note also *R v Newbury Justices, ex p Du Pont* (1983) 78 Cr App Rep 255, discussed further at p 526.

shouting demands for justice for the Welsh language. Two of the women, who refused to give an undertaking that they would cause no further disturbance, were sent to prison for three months for their contempt. In *Lecointe v Central Criminal Court Courts' Administrator*[8] a man was committed for seven days for distributing leaflets in the public gallery of the Old Bailey inviting others to picket the courts. There is also a growing line of instances where defendants have deliberately set out to disrupt their trial.[9]

The above cases are extreme examples of disrupting proceedings but less reprehensible conduct may also be punished as a contempt. In *R v Stone*[10] after a jury had returned a verdict of not guilty, there was a considerable noise in the court and one man, who was jumping up in the middle of the court waving his hat and hallooing, was taken into custody and fined £20. It has also been held to be a contempt to disturb the court by applauding and even by exaggerated coughing.[11] Whether such apparently trivial conduct should be punishable as contempt is surely questionable. A court should be slow to punish spontaneous outbursts as a contempt, and particularly where members of the public are concerned, if a warning is insufficient, ejection from the court would seem in most cases to be the appropriate remedy.

Contempt by disturbing a court is not restricted to conduct in the court. In *Re Dakin,*[12] it was held that the carrying on of a noisy trade in the vicinity of the court, so as to obstruct court proceedings, after service of an order to desist, amounted to contempt. More recently it has been held in *Bodden v Metropolitan Police Commissioner*[13] that magistrates' courts powers under s 12 to punish interruptions of proceedings extended to conduct outside court (in this case the holding of a demonstration) that actually disturbed the proceedings.

Interrupting the court can take different forms. It can be a contempt to persist in addressing the court in defiance of a judge's order. Such conduct is more frequently associated with advocates[14] but this is not invariably so. In *Re Surrey (Sheriff)*[15] a High Sheriff was found guilty of contempt for repeatedly interrupting Blackburn J in order to persuade him to thank all those who had attended the proceedings for the purpose of serving as jurors. In *Re MacMichael,*[16] a member of the public began to address the court during the hearing of a case concerning copyright, stating his views on cruelty to animals. He said that he was rising as amicus curiae and replying to Pennycuick J, who did not wish to hear him, said 'You may not want to but I insist.' Pennycuick J said 'Sit down please.' MacMichael replied 'No, I stand on my rights. I have already sat down once.' Pennycuick J then directed the usher to remove MacMichael from the court, but after further resistance he was eventually committed for contempt of court, and

8 (1973) Bar Library Transcript No 57A, CA.
9 Many examples are given by Zellick: 'The Criminal Trial and the Disruptive Defendant Part I' (1980) 43 MLR 121 at 121–6.
10 (1796) 6 Term Rep 527 at 530. See also *R v Colledge* (1681) 8 State Tr 549.
11 These two examples are cited in (1963) 107 Sol Jo 669. In the second example the offender was originally fined 2s 6d, but because the offender only had 2s on him, the fine was reduced to 2s.
12 (1887) 13 VLR 522 (Victorian Supreme Ct). See also (1949) 99 LJ 674, where Croom-Johnson J threatened to order the grounding of all aircraft at a local RAF station if they continued to interrupt proceedings by flying low over the town centre.
13 [1990] 2 QB 397, CA.
14 See pp 31 ff.
15 (1860) 2 F & F 234.
16 (1961) Times, 14 and 17 January.

this decision was upheld by the Court of Appeal. An unusual example of interrupting proceedings is *Gohoho v Lintas Export Advertising Services* [17] where Gohoho, having been ordered to pay £50 by way of security as to costs, or else have his appeal dismissed, proceeded, as a form of protest, to lay down on the bench, from where litigants personally address the court, and to strip himself naked except for his shirt. The Court of Appeal, before which this spectacle had taken place, committed Gohoho to prison for a week for his contempt.

An intention to interrupt proceedings is not per se a contempt at least while the act in question is merely preparatory and no interruption is occasioned. This seems to be the result of *Balogh v Crown Court at St Albans*.[18] Balogh intended to 'enliven' proceedings by releasing 'laughing gas' into the court. To this end he had reconnoitred the roof of the court room building to decide where to put the gas and the following morning he brought into court a briefcase with a cylinder of gas inside it. His intention was, at an appropriate moment, to take the case into the roof and release the gas into the ventilation system. However, before he could carry out his plan, officers of the court found the briefcase and apprehended Balogh. The accused frankly admitted what he had done and what he intended to do. The Court of Appeal unanimously held that no contempt had been committed since the acts in question were merely preparatory. They were also agreed that the acts fell short of what would be required to constitute an attempt.[19]

Whether there is such an offence as attempting to commit a contempt has still to be authoritatively resolved. Stephenson LJ doubted its existence[20] though both Lord Denning MR and Lawton LJ seemed to imply that there was such an offence.

It is submitted that it is possible, particularly in view of the current trend in favour of punishing attempts, to be guilty of attempting to commit contempt.[1] If Balogh had, for example, actually released the gas into the system then even though there was apparently insufficient quantity to have any effect, there seems no reason, under the current law, why he could not be considered guilty of an attempted contempt. Whether a court would think such conduct worthy of punishment is another matter.

D   Disrespectful or other misbehaviour in court

There is a thin dividing line between insulting and disrespectful behaviour; nevertheless case law and statute do seem to recognise a distinction.[2] The jurisdiction to punish misconduct falling short of insulting or disruptive behaviour

---

17   (1964) Times, 21 January.
18   [1975] QB 73. For a discussion of the requisite mens rea see pp 64–66.
19   This approach seems to be in accordance with that laid down by the Criminal Attempts Act 1981, s 1(1).
20   [1975] QB 73 at 87C.
 1   In Zimbabwe, it has been held that there is such an offence, see *S v Benatar* 1984 (3) SA 588. Note that prosecutions may now have to be brought under the Criminal Attempts Act 1981 though this may depend upon the interpretation of s 1(4). See further p 82.
 2   The County Courts Act 1984, s 118 and the Contempt of Court Act 1981, s 12 refer to wilful insults, wilful interruption and other misbehaviour. In South Australia the Justices Act 1921–69, s 46 refers to 'disrespectful behaviour'.

is a delicate one. Not every act of discourtesy amounts to contempt.[3] Indeed the only justification for punishing disrespectful behaviour which does not otherwise interrupt proceedings is where it is considered to impair the authority of the court and so interfere with the administration of justice. Judges should be wary about punishing allegedly disrespectful conduct and should remember that the object of contempt is to protect the administration of justice and not to satisfy their personal feelings. An excessive use of the power will itself detract from the court's authority.

An example of the legitimate use of the power is the Australian decision in *Re Nash, ex p Tuckerman*[4] where by prearrangement several defendants as they entered the court raised their left arm with a hand or fist clenched. As no noise, grimace, violence or offer of violence accompanied this gesture they argued no contempt had been committed since their conduct did not interfere with the conduct of the court's business. The court thought otherwise, holding that the gesture was one of defiance and as such was calculated to lessen the authority of the court. As was pointed out:[5]

> 'The expression "interfere with the course of justice" is not confined to physical disturbance of particular proceedings in the court . . . it comprehends as well an interference with the authority of the courts in the sense that there may be a detraction from the influence of judicial decisions and an impairment of confidence and respect in the courts and their judgments.'

In contrast to *Re Nash* is the South Australian decision of *O'Hair v Wright*[6] where it was held not to be a contempt for an accused to reply when asked how he pleaded: 'I refuse to recognise the authority of this Court'.

A blatant example of the misuse of the power is the Scottish case of *Royle v Gray*[7] where a witness sitting in the public gallery having given evidence, shook his head during the summing up. For this he was fined £10 but this was reversed on appeal and the decision that the conduct amounted to contempt was roundly condemned.

Perhaps the more difficult examples are the failure to observe various traditions or customs of court procedure such as standing when the judge is ushered into court. The refusal to stand is clearly a mark of disrespect but should apparently trivial misconduct be considered a contempt? Once an issue has been made of the conduct and the offender still refuses to observe the tradition, the act goes beyond mere discourtesy and becomes the deliberate flouting of the court's authority thereby hardening into contempt. This is perhaps the best explanation of the Canadian decision in *Re Hawkins*.[8] It also explains *R v Pateley Bridge Justices, ex p Percy*[9] in which a litigant in person was held to be in contempt for

---

3 See *Izuora v R* [1953] AC 327, [1953] 1 All ER 827 and *Weston v Central Criminal Court Courts Administrator* [1977] QB 32, [1976] 2 All ER 875: discussed at p 36.
4 [1970] 3 NSWR 23 (NSW, CA).
5 Ibid at 27.
6 [1971] SASR 436 (South Australia Supr Court).
7 1973 SLT 31. Note also *Aitken v Carmichael* 1993 SCCR 889 in which it was held that a sheriff had greatly overacted in respect of a spectator who had put on a set of personal stereo headphones on his way out of court and *McMillan v Carmichael* 1993 GWD 32-2033 where a spectator 'yawned in an open and unrestrained manner, raising his arms above his head', where a contempt finding was quashed because no inquiry had been made as to the spectator's intention. Both these examples were cited by Orr: 'Contempt of Court' 1993 SLT 361.
8 *Re Hawkins' Habeas Corpus Application* (1965) 53 WWR 406 where Branca J stressed the importance of obeying court traditions. See especially p 411.
9 [1994] COD 453.

insisting, contrary to the court's wishes, on sitting in the place reserved for legal representatives. It is submitted that courts should show caution in treating acts of disrespect (particularly isolated acts) as contempt. Rebuking a woman for wearing a trouser suit whilst attending court,[10] for instance, is surely unjustified, and indeed impossible rationally to describe as an act of disrespect.

Frequently it is court officials rather than judges who are responsible for the maintenance of alleged traditions. Some check should be made on these. For example, a common but, it is submitted, an unnecessary[11] 'ruling' is that members of the public should not make notes during the sitting of the court. It is difficult to challenge such 'rulings' without appearing disrespectful.

E   Taking photographs or making sketches in court

There appears to be no specific common law authority holding it to be a contempt to photograph court proceedings. The activity however, is bound to be distracting to the court. As Judge Ellison Ch said in *Re St Andrews, Heddington* [12] 'Justice could not be properly administered if justices or witnesses suffered the pressures, embarrassment and discomfort of being photographed whilst playing their role in court'. It would be prudent, therefore, to assume that courts of record have the power to punish those who photograph court proceedings and probably to ban the taking of photographic equipment into court.[13] Whether there is a similar common law power to prohibit or punish sketches made during court proceedings is more doubtful. In England and Wales,[14] however, such activities are controlled by the Criminal Justice Act 1925. Section 41 provides:

'(1)   No person shall—
   (a)   take or attempt to take in any court any photograph, or with a view to publication make or attempt to make in any court any portrait or sketch, of any person, being a judge of the court or a juror or a witness in or a party to any proceedings before the court, whether civil or criminal or,
   (b)   publish any photograph, portrait or sketch taken or made in contravention of the foregoing provisions of this section or any reproduction thereof;
   and if any person acts in contravention of this section he shall, on summary conviction, be liable in respect of each offence to a fine not exceeding level 3 on the standard scale.'[15]

10   As reported in (1970) The Guardian, 24 February. Similar questionable decisions are that of the borough councillor being fined £5 for failing to remove his hat upon entering the court precincts and a barrister being fined for smoking in the robing room, both reported in (1926) 62 LJ 131.
11   Conceivably, it could be justified upon the basis that there is a statutory embargo (discussed below) on making sketches in court, though it is doubtful whether much thought has been given to the 'ruling'. Perhaps the matter could be resolved by practice directions.
12   [1978] Fam 121 at 125.
13   Such a power would seem to be within the principle that every court has an inherent power to regulate its own proceedings. See *A-G v Leveller Magazines Ltd* [1979] AC 440, [1979] 1 All ER 745 discussed at pp 275 ff. Apparently, it was common practice prior to 1925 for judges to forbid and prevent photographs being taken in court. See 183 HL Official Report (5th series) col 837.
14   Ie the Act does not apply to Scotland nor Northern Ireland.
15   Currently £1,000.

There are two separate offences: the taking of a photograph or the making of a sketch or portrait within the court and the publication of such photographs, sketches or portraits. It is assumed that the prohibition on photographs applies equally to filming by television cameras[16] or camcorders.

Any person taking a photograph etc inside the court will be guilty of an offence as well as any subsequent publisher. It would appear that while there is an absolute bar on taking photographs, the making of sketches or portraits only amounts to an offence under this section if they are made 'with a view to publication'.

The justification for the distinction is debatable—sketching in court may be as distracting as photographing and perhaps more pertinently can be equally damaging from the point of view of identification, particularly of jurors and witnesses. In any event what 'publication' means in this context is unclear. At its widest it could mean the showing of the sketch to any third party and if the prevention of identification is thought to be a major purpose of the section, that might be an appropriate interpretation. On the other hand, for the sake of uniformity, it could be interpreted in line with the Contempt of Court Act 1981, s 2(1) to cover a communication 'addressed to the public at large or any section of the public'. There appears to be no time limit on the embargo against publishing sketches made in court provided that at the time they were made 'with a view to publication'.

The making of sketches from memory outside the court is not caught by the section and indeed it is common practice to publish such sketches, particularly as an accompaniment to reports of court proceedings on television news programmes. Even the publication of sketches made in court is not necessarily an offence under the Act since the sketches must originally be made 'with a view to publication'. It may be, however, that sketches which identify witnesses or jurors can be considered a contempt at common law because of their tendency to interfere with the course of justice more generally.[17]

Curiously, the embargo against sketching in court only applies to sketches of judges, jurors, witnesses and parties and not to the parties' representatives nor members of the public. Though perhaps a nice point of interpretation it would seem that the embargo against photography is similarly confined.[18] Nevertheless all photographs are likely to be distracting to proceedings and as such may be punishable as contempt in the face of the court either at common law or under statute.[19]

Section 41 prohibits 'attempts' to take photographs etc, in court but the precise ambit of the prohibition is unclear.[20] At its widest it may be thought to include the taking of a camera into court at least where it can be shown that the offender intended to photograph a judge, juror, witness or party. In practice cameras are not allowed to be taken into court.

Another provision causing difficulty is s 41(2)(c) which reads:

16 It was taken to apply to television filming in *Re St Andrews, Heddington* [1978] Fam 121.
17 Eg it may deter future witnesses. See Ch 11. The Press Council, however, (see (1982) Times, 12 December) rejected a complaint along similar lines.
18 Cf Miller, *Contempt of Court* (2nd edn, 1989) p 62 and (1970) 134 JP 839. In 1970 a Durham magistrates' court ordered the destruction of photographs taken by the police from the upper room of the court of people arriving at the hearing. See (1970) Times, 21 October.
19 It is submitted that the activity would be 'misbehaving' within the meaning of the County Court Acts 1984, s 118(1)(b) and the Contempt of Court Act 1981, s 12(1)(b).
20 It would clearly cover the 'clicking' of the camera regardless of whether the picture came out.

'a photograph, portrait or sketch shall be deemed to be a photograph, portrait or sketch taken or made in court if it is taken or made in the courtroom or in the building or in the precincts of the building in which the court is held, or if it is a photograph, portrait or sketch taken or made of the person while he is entering or leaving the courtroom or any such building or precincts as aforesaid.'

The section provides in effect, a twin definition of when photographs, sketches or portraits will amount to an offence, namely (1) when the person taking the photograph, etc, is in the court room, or the building or the precincts of the building, and (2) when the person of whom a photograph is being taken is in the court room, the building or the precincts of the building. With regard to the second part of the definition, the position of the photographer himself is irrelevant. It would be an offence, for instance, to take a photograph of a person entering the court with a telephoto lens even if the photographer is himself a considerable distance away from the court.

The problem of s 41(2)(c) about which complaints are most often made is the meaning of the 'precincts of the [court] building'. The term defies easy definition. The Phillimore Committee[1] considered it impracticable to attempt a complete definition and recommended that a map or plan be displayed in each court premises defining the extent of what will normally be treated as the court and its precincts. Whilst such a recommendation would, if implemented, be helpful, its usefulness is diminished if it cannot be relied upon and the Committee envisaged that such a plan would be for assistance only and would not limit the courts' powers to determine or even to extend the limits of the precincts. In the event no action has been taken and there is still a need to define 'precincts'. Although it could certainly be argued that a photograph of judge, juror, witness or party which includes part of the court building would be within the court precincts in view of the common practice to do so[2] it may be more realistic to regard 'precincts' as being inside the court building including those areas of open space, such as an internal courtyard, to which public access is controlled.[3] Even this definition may not solve all problems. For example, it is uncertain whether it is an offence to photograph a judge whilst visiting the scene of the litigation.[4]

It remains an untested point as to whether s 41 applies to sketches or photographs of 'courts' when not in session. There seems no reason to prohibit such activity and permission has certainly been granted to film simulated proceedings.[5]

The foregoing powers extend to all 'courts of justice'[6] including a coroner's court, and the term 'judge'[7] is defined as also including registrars,[8] magistrates,

1 1974, Cmnd 5794, para 41.
2 It should not be necessarily assumed that such pictures can always be published with impunity. Apparently serious consideration was given to prosecuting under s 41 the *Sun* newspaper for publishing a photograph of an accused giving a 'V' sign in front of a court. In the event the newspaper was prosecuted under the 'strict liability rule'. See *A-G v News Group Newspapers Ltd* (1984) 6 Cr App Rep (S) 418, discussed at p 150.
3 In *Re St Andrews, Heddington* [1978] Fam 121 at 123 Judge Ellison Ch considered 'precincts' covered the church and the small area of churchyard which physically adjoined the church.
4 Such pictures are not unknown. Megarry J was extensively photographed whilst visiting Ocean Island in the course of determining the validity of the compensation claim of the Banabians. See *Tito v Waddell* [1975] 3 All ER 997, [1975] 1 WLR 1303.
5 Query whether a judge has power to waive the restrictions under s 41? Visitors to courts are commonly forbidden to take photographs even when the court is not in session.
6 S 41(2)(a).
7 S 41(2)(b). The reference to 'recorders' has been deleted by the Courts Act 1971.
8 Presumably this will now be taken to include reference to district judges of the Family Division.

justices and coroners. The precise ambit of 'courts of justice' has yet to be fully explored but in *Re St Andrews, Heddington*[9] it was held that it applied to consistory courts and the BBC were banned from filming proceedings inside a church while it was being used as a court. While it is clear that the power extends to all superior and inferior courts of record and to magistrates' courts it is an open question whether other bodies are included. The statutory definition of 'courts of justice' is not dissimilar to the approach of the House of Lords in *A-G v BBC*[10] and it may be that the power vests in industrial tribunals and mental health tribunals both of which have been held[11] to be 'courts' for other purposes of contempt.

Section 41 was apparently introduced as an 'experiment' to combat what had become 'an added terror to the administration of justice', namely, the photographing and subsequent pillorying of (mainly) accused persons.[12] Although some restrictions seem justifiable it will be evident from the foregoing discussion that s 41 is not well defined. It is time that the provisions were reviewed. Assuming that the same restrictions are to be maintained then at the very least some definitive meaning should be given to 'precincts'. It should also be made clear that *all* photographs taken in court are prohibited and, for the sake of clarity, that 'photographs' include television broadcasts and filming and video recording. But should the present level of restrictions be maintained? On the one hand there is a case for extending the restrictions to cover sketches of court scenes made from memory. After all if the object of the restrictions is to prevent litigants from publicity such sketches should also be banned. If it is not thought right to extend the restrictions, why should sketches made in court be banned? On the other hand there is a case for relaxing the restrictions to allow for controlled broadcasts of proceedings. This has long been allowed in parts of the United States and cameras have recently been allowed to film certain trials in Scotland.[13] Although there will be conflicting views on the wisdom of broadcasting court proceedings the time does seem ripe for considering this issue in England and Wales.

F   The use of tape recorders in court

It would seem to be within a court's inherent power in regulating its own proceedings to prohibit the unofficial use of tape recorders in court but there is little common law authority for this proposition. In the Canadian case of *R v Barker*[14] it seemed to be assumed that prior permission to use a recorder ought

---

9 [1978] Fam 121 at 124–5.
10 [1981] AC 303, [1980] 3 All ER 161; discussed at pp 487 ff.
11 See respectively *Re Peach Grey & Co (a firm) v Sommers* [1995] 2 All ER 513 and *Pickering v Liverpool Daily Post and Echo Newspaper Plc* [1991] 2 AC 370, HL, discussed at p 489. For the view that the section should be construed widely see Lowe and Rawlings: 'Tribunals and the Laws Protecting the Administration of Justice' [1982] PL 418.
12 As described by Sir W Joynson-Hicks, the Secretary of State to the Home Office: 188 HL Official Report (5th series) inter alia at cols 839 and 849. The whole debate on the clause at col 831 ff is instructive since the many problems discussed in the text had largely been foreseen by the opposers of the provision.
13 BBC2 broadcast a series 'The Trial' from 18 November 1994.
14 (1980) 4 WWR 202 (Alberta CA). Lord Roskill stated during the Lords debate on the Contempt Bill (HL Official Report (5th series) 416 col 382) that he had refused a request at the Central Criminal Court to permit a tape recording of the evidence. Permission was also refused in the *ABC* case, see Christopher Price MP's, comments in 1980–81 HC Standing Committee A on Contempt of Court, cols 205–6.

to be obtained from the court though in that case it was held that ignorance of the requirement was a defence.

The Phillimore Committee recommended[15] that statutory controls should be introduced and their recommendations have essentially been enacted by the Contempt of Court Act 1981, s 9 which applies to England and Wales, Scotland and Northern Ireland.

Section 9, which does not apply to recordings made or used in connection with official transcripts of proceedings,[16] creates two offences, namely, the unauthorised use of recorders during court proceedings and the subsequent publication of recordings whether or not they were lawfully made.

Under s 9(1)(a) it is a contempt of court:

> 'to use in court, or bring into court for use, any tape-recorder or other instrument for recording sound except with the leave of the court.'

In addition to any sanction that may be imposed for the contempt,[17] breach of s 9(1)(a) will also empower the court, pursuant to s 9(3), to 'order the instrument, or any recording made with it, or both, to be forfeited' and to dispose of the forfeited goods as it sees fit.

Under s 9(1)(a) it is an offence to use or to bring into court for use a recorder without prior permission. In the latter case the prosecution will have to prove that the accused intended to use the recorder in court, but beyond this there would seem to be[18] no mens rea requirement under the section. This could be productive of apparent injustice as, for example, where a foreign tourist wanders innocently into a law court because he wants to know what British justice is like and turns on his tape recorder.[19] No doubt such innocent offenders would be treated leniently[20] but the possibility that their recorders and recordings could be confiscated seems draconian. Notices explaining that the unauthorised use of recorders is forbidden, should surely be prominently be displayed in all courts.

Anyone wishing to use a recorder in court must, under s 9(1)(a), seek the court's permission beforehand. Although the precise mechanics for doing so have not been laid down, there have been no reported difficulties in practice.

Section 9(2) gives courts a complete discretion both as to whether to permit the use of recorders in court, and if so, upon what conditions. It is a contempt to break any condition that is imposed.[1] A court can subsequently withdraw or amend permission.

Notwithstanding the wide discretion conferred by s 9(2), a *Practice Direction* [2] suggests that the following factors may be relevant to its exercise:

---

15 1974, Cmnd 5794, paras 42, 43.

16 S 9(4).

17 The power to punish an offender for contempt is discussed at pp 524 ff.

18 The mens rea requirement under s 9(1) was, however, left open in *Re Hooker (Patricia) and the Contempt of Court Act 1981* [1993] C O D 190.

19 This was the example given by Peter Archer MP in 1980–81 HC Standing Committee A, col 211.

20 No penalty was imposed in the case of a freelance court shorthand writer who inadvertently omitted to ask the court's permission to use her recorder: *Re Hooker* [1993] COD 190.

 1 S 9(1)(c). It could be argued that the forfeiture sanction is not applicable to the breaking of a condition, since s 9(3) applies to s 9(1)(a) offences. However, it is submitted that a recording in breach of a condition would be using a recorder without leave of the court and so rank as a s 9(1)(a) offence.

 2 *Practice Direction (Tape Recorders)* [1981] 3 All ER 848, [1981] 1 WLR 1526 applicable to the Supreme Court and to county courts.

'(a)   the existence of any reasonable need on the part of the applicant for leave,
        whether a litigant or a person connected with the press or broadcasting, for
        the recording to be made;

(b)   in a . . . case in which a direction has been given excluding one or more
        witnesses from the court, the risk that the recording could be used for the
        purpose of briefing witnesses out of court;

(c)   any possibility that the use of a recorder would disturb the proceedings or
        distract or worry any witnesses or other participants.'

The *Direction* adds that consideration should always be given as to whether to impose conditions upon granting leave and that 'the identity and role of the applicant for leave and the nature of the subject matter of the proceedings may be relevant to this'. It also states that successful applicants' attention should be drawn to the absolute ban on publishing any recording. A permitted recording is not intended to be used as, or to compete with, the official transcript.

A Home Office Circular[3] has been issued for the guidance of magistrates. This states that there is 'no objection in principle' to the use of recorders 'especially by those connected with proceedings'. Accordingly, sympathetic consideration should be given to applications by parties or their legal representatives ('especially when the applicant is unable himself to take note of the proceedings') and accredited representatives of the press or broadcasting organisations. Like the *Practice Direction* the Circular draws attention to the risk that recordings might be used for briefing witnesses, though presumably this could be dealt with by imposing a condition against such use. It further suggests that practical objections that might lead to a refusal to permit the use of recorders:

'include the sensitivity of the subject-matter of the proceedings, the nervous disposition of a witness or any disturbance which the machine might cause in court, and the court should not hesitate to revoke permission already granted if use of a machine appears to distract any participant in the proceedings or otherwise cause a disturbance?'

Although the guidelines leave plenty of scope for refusing permission—'sensitivity of the subject matter of the proceedings' seems vague—the possibility that the use of recorders would 'disturb or distract any witnesses or other participants' seems wide; the underlying spirit, particularly that of the Circular is that litigants and their advisers and accredited press reporters[4] should normally be granted permission. Provided this spirit is followed then much of the sting will be taken from the major criticism[5] of the section that the burden is the wrong way round and that at least litigants and their advisers and news reporters should be allowed to use recorders in court unless the court otherwise directs. The exercise of discretion, however, is virtually unchallengeable[6] so that if, for example, a

---

3   Home Office Circular No 79/1981, 26 August 1981.
4   The Phillimore Committee (1974, Cmnd 5794) at para 43(a) and the Lord Chancellor at 416
    HL Official Report (5th series) col 383 envisaged that press reporters might obtain standing
    permission to use recorders but it is not entirely clear whether this is possible under the Act.
5   Eg by Lords Renton and Gifford, 416 HL Official Report (5th series) cols 380.1 and by James
    Young in (1981) 8 British Journal of Law and Society at 245.
6   The press have no right of appeal (the power given to aggrieved persons to appeal against a
    'publicity order' under the Criminal Justice Act 1988, s 159, discussed at pp 298–299, only
    applies to orders made under ss 4 and 11 of the Contempt of Court Act 1981) though in the case
    of inferior court rulings they could apply to the Divisional Court for judicial review (see
    further pp 513 and 516). Even then it would still be difficult to persuade the court to overturn
    the exercise of discretion. For examples see Robertson and Nicol, *Media Law* (3rd edn) 352.

particular court repeatedly refused permission and ignored the guidelines the only practical recourse is, it is suggested, to complain to the Lord Chancellor.

To what 'court' does s 9(1)(a) apply? For this purpose 'court' is defined by s 19 as including 'any tribunal or body exercising the judicial power of the State'. Although this definition is slightly different to that applying to the restrictions on photographing court proceedings under s 41 of the Criminal Justice Act 1925,[7] policy surely dictates that they should be treated as being co-extensive.[8]

All 'courts' to which the section applies can impose the forfeiture sanctions but the position is different with regard to punishing the offence as a contempt. Section 9(1)(a) breaches must be contempts in the face of the court and as such may be punished by superior courts of record and inferior courts of record (such as a coroner's court)[9] whose contempt jurisdiction is not otherwise controlled by statute. With regard to county courts and magistrates' courts, since s 9(1)(a) does not itself confer jurisdiction one must look instead to the County Courts Act 1984, s 118 and the Contempt of Court Act 1981, s 12 respectively.[10] These sections only confer jurisdiction to punish a person who either *wilfully* insults the court or who *wilfully* interrupts the proceedings or who otherwise misbehaves. As *Re Hooker (Patricia) and the Contempt of Court Act 1981* [11] confirms, the unlawful use of recorders ranks as 'misbehaviour' for these purposes. It was also held that unless there was some element of defiance or at least conduct such that a court could not reasonably be expected to tolerate[12] then no offence under s 12 can be committed. Whether in such a case a prosecution could successfully be brought in the Queen's Bench Divisional Court remains an interesting question.

Following the Phillimore Committee recommendation,[13] s 9(1)(b) places an absolute ban on the subsequent publication of any recordings, it being a contempt:

> 'to publish a recording of legal proceedings made by means of any [tape recorder or other instrument for recording sound] or any recording derived directly or indirectly from it, by playing it in the hearing of the public or any section of the public, or to dispose of it or any recording so derived, with a view to such publication.'

Precisely what is meant by playing it 'in the hearing of the public or any section of the public'[14] is not clear but presumably it is not intended to penalise parties playing it to their family or parties' representatives playing it to their secretary or even their colleagues, at least where it is done in the course of conducting the case. Similarly, it seems unlikely that a press reporter playing the tape back in his office, even in his colleagues' hearing, would be guilty of an offence or that he commits an offence by compiling, with the aid of the tape, a report which is subsequently published or broadcast.

---

7 Discussed at pp 26–27.
8 For a full discussion of s 19 see p 488.
9 See p 508.
10 Discussed at pp 510–511 and 513–515.
11 [1993] COD 190.
12 Presumably, this would cover a 'noisy' tape recorder.
13 Para 43(b).
14 The definition of publication is slightly different under s 2(1) which refers to 'public at large or any section of the public'. The meaning of this is discussed at pp 110 ff.

Section 9(1)(b) breaches would seem to be contempts committed outside the court[15] (although the Phillimore Committee recommended[16] that they should be treated as contempts in the face of the court) and accordingly should normally be prosecuted in the Queen's Bench Divisional Court.[17]

Although it might be argued that if proceedings are heard in open court then there is no reason to prohibit the publication of tape recordings, it is submitted that it was right to impose the absolute ban,[18] at any rate ahead of any full scale review of the general issue of televising or broadcasting court proceedings. Nevertheless if televising court proceedings is thought permissible (as it is in Scotland)[19] it is difficult to see why radio broadcasts should not also be allowed.

III CONTEMPTS COMMITTED BY PARTICULAR PERSONS

A Advocates[20]

The term 'advocates' is used here to include any person arguing a case before the court, that is, barristers, solicitors and litigants who conduct their own cases.

The ensuing passages are concerned with contempt but it is to be borne in mind that the professional advocate is also subject to the discipline of his or her own particular profession. An act whilst not amounting to contempt might well render an advocate liable to disciplinary procedures.[1]

1 *Misbehaviour in court*

The importance of advocates being allowed to argue their cases fearlessly and resolutely is reflected by the general reluctance to find such persons guilty of contempt. As Lord Tucker said:[2]

> 'It is not every act of discourtesy to the court by counsel that amounts to contempt, nor is conduct which involves a breach of his duty to his client necessarily in this category.'

Lord Goddard CJ[3] has gone further, saying that to use the summary power of

---

15 Query whether using a tape contrary to a court's condition, eg by playing it to a witness, should be treated as contempt in facie or ex facie?
16 Para 43.
17 Pursuant to RSC Ord 52, r 1(2), discussed at pp 485 ff.
18 There was only muted opposition to s 9(1)(b). See eg Mr Peter Archer MP in 1980–81 HC Standing Committee A Contempt of Court, cols 209, 210.
19 See p 27.
20 For contempts involving advocates, see generally P Butt: 'Contempt of Court and the Legal Profession' [1978] Crim Law Rev 463 and 'Contempt of Court—Extent of liability of members of the legal profession' (1978) 52 ALJ 151. For the position in the US see: 'Conduct of Counsel as Contempt' 14 L Ed 2d 234; 'Attorneys' Insulting Remarks as Contempt' 68 ALR (3d) 273; 'Conduct in Making Objections as Contempt' 68 ALR (3d) 314; and 'Attorney's Delay of Discovery—Contempt' 8 ALR (4th) 1181. See also *Disruption of the Judicial Process* (1970, American College of Trial Lawyers).
 1 Perhaps a good example of this is *Hilborne v Law Society of Singapore* [1978] 2 All ER 757, [1978] I WLR 841, PC. See also *Re a Solicitor* (1978) Times, 31 January.
 2 In *Izuora v R* [1953] AC 327 at 336.
 3 In *Parashuram Detaram Shamdasani v King-Emperor* [1945] AC 264 at 270. See also Abbott CJ in *R v Davison* (1821) 4 B & Ald 329.

punishing for contempt 'to suppress methods of advocacy which are merely offensive is to use it for a purpose for which it was never intended.'

The dividing line between 'merely offensive conduct' and conduct amounting to contempt is not easy to draw. In practice, an advocate is allowed considerable freedom in the conduct of his case. He can, in the interests of his client, cast reflections upon the character, conduct or credit of parties or witnesses with impunity, provided such comments are relevant to the issue before the court. He probably has a wider latitude with regard to comments addressed to opposing counsel.[4]

In the course of conducting his case an advocate may clash with a judge but again he has considerable freedom to act (and rightly so) without being at risk for contempt. When addressing the court he is free (in the words of Oswald):[5]

> 'to combat and contest strongly any adverse views of the Judge or Judges expressed on the case during its argument, to object to and protest against any course which the Judge may take and which the advocate thinks irregular or detrimental to the interests of his client, and to caution juries against an interference by the Judge with their functions, or with the advocate addressing them, or against any strong view adverse to his client expressed by the presiding Judge upon the facts of a case before the verdict of the jury thereon.'

Despite the undoubted latitude, advocates can commit, and have been punished for, contempt. Although the court will be more lenient towards litigants conducting their own cases, in general all advocates will be expected to respect the dignity and authority of the court and to behave responsibly. As Bayley J said in *R v Davison*:[6]

> 'every man who comes into a Court of Justice either as a defendant or otherwise, must know that decency is to be observed there, that respect is to be paid to the Judge, and that, in endeavouring to defend himself from any particular charge, he must not commit a new offence.'

Whether a higher standard of behaviour is expected of a professionally trained advocate is a moot point though he would surely be expected to know and to conform to the usages of the court and the rulings of the judge.[7] In the United States it has been said[8] that a lawyer participating in a trial has a duty not only to refrain from disorderly conduct but also to aid the court in preserving order in the court room.

---

4 See Lord Goddard CJ's comments in *Shamdasani*'s case [1945] AC 264 at 268 cited on p 20. See also *Re Prior, ex p Bellanto* [1963] SR NSW 190.
5 *Contempt of Court* (3rd edn, 1910) p 56. Note also the *Dean of St Asaph R v Shipley* (1784); Campbell, *Lives of the Lord Chancellors* Vol 6, p 432. Cited *arguendo* in *Ex p Pater* (1864) 5 B & S 299 in which following a discussion about the wording of the verdict delivered by a jury, the famous advocate Erskine said: 'I stand here as an advocate for a brother citizen and I desire that the word "only" may be recorded.' Buller J replied: 'Sit down, Sir; remember your duty, or I shall be obliged to proceed in another manner.' Erskine said: 'Your Lordship may proceed in what manner you think fit. I know my duty as well as your Lordship knows yours. I shall not alter my conduct.' The judge took no notice of this reply but did not repeat the threat of committal. Lord Campbell commenting on this incident said:

> 'This noble stand for the independence of the Bar would of itself entitle Erskine to the statue which the profession affectionately erected to his memory in Lincoln's Inn hall.'

6 (1821) 4 B & Ald 329 at 336.
7 That seemed to be Bayley J's view in *R v Davison* (1821) 4 B & Ald 329.
8 See *US v Sacher*, 182 F 2d 416 (1950); affd 343 US 1 96 L Ed 2d 1341 and see 14 L Ed 2d 934.

Clearly, no advocate can be allowed to use violence in court. In *Bryans v Faber and Faber*[9] for instance, a litigant in person after losing his appeal, hit opposing counsel on the head with a carafe of water and for this serious contempt he was imprisoned for three months. Similarly, an advocate will be guilty of contempt if he threatens or attempts violence in court. He may also be guilty of contempt if he uses abusive, blasphemous or even provocative language.[10] In *R v Davison*[11] a litigant conducting his own case was found guilty of contempt, even after allowing for the fact he was a layman, for repeatedly using blasphemous language.

The relationship between the advocate and the judge is a delicate one. On the one hand it is important to allow an advocate to be firm and resolute in the pursuance of his case while on the other the judge must maintain his authority in court.[12] Of course an advocate should avoid rude, insolent or insulting behaviour but a judge should not be oversensitive to remarks made against him. As Lord Denning MR has said: 'Insults are best treated with disdain—save where they are gross and scandalous.'[13] The Privy Council has also warned against the over zealous use of contempt. In *Maharaj v A-G for Trinidad and Tobago*[14] a barrister was held to be in contempt when he accused a judge of 'injudicial conduct'. Maharaj J considered the remark to be a 'vicious attack on the court's integrity' but the Privy Council were not satisfied that the remark should have been so interpreted and, because the accused was given no opportunity to explain himself, reversed the decision. Lord Salmon repeated[15] Lord Goddard CJ's earlier warning[16] that the contempt power should be used sparingly and only in serious cases.

There are, however, limits to judicial tolerance and though judicial sensitivity will vary with the judge, time and place it is wise to heed any warnings from the Bench. The courts seem most sensitive to accusations of bias. As Philip J said in the Australian case, *Reece v McKenna, ex p Reece*:[17] 'To impute injustice to a justice is to insult him in respect of the very title he wears; it is like imputing blindness to a bishop.' Even so, as one commentator has said,[18] it is clearly established that it is proper for counsel to raise the matter of bias or lack of

---

9 [1979] CA Transcript 316. Cf also *Re Johnson* (1887) 20 QBD 68 where a solicitor assailed his opponent outside the court room with 'foul and offensive names'. See also *Westcott v Lord* [1911] VLR 452.

10 In *Parashuram Detaram Shamdasani v King-Emperor* [1945] AC 264 at 269 Lord Goddard CJ suggested that language 'so outrageous and provocative as to be likely to lead to a brawl' could amount to contempt.

11 (1821) 4 B & Ald 329.

12 As was said in *Re Prior, ex p Bellanto* [1963] SR NSW 190 at 204 'as well as protecting the rights of the Bar, equally every judge must be ready and fearless at all times to protect the courts in the important duties which they have to discharge against insult and unseemly behaviour which tends to obstruct the course of justice'. See also *Disruption of the Judicial Process* (1970, American College of Trial Lawyers).

13 In *Balogh v Crown Court at St Albans* [1975] QB 73 at 86. Even so, advocates have been found guilty of contempt for insulting the judge. See eg *R v Jordan* (1888) 36 WR 797; sub nom *R v Stafford County Court Judge* (1888) 57 LJ QB 483. See also *Carus Wilson's Case* (1845) 7 QB 984 and *Fuller's Case* (1607) 12 Co Rep 41 at 43.

14 [1977] 1 All ER 411. The committal was also held bad because of the procedure, see p 520.

15 Ibid at 415.

16 Given in *Parashuram Detaram Shamdasani v King-Emperor* [1945] AC 264 at 270.

17 [1953] QSR 258 at 264. See also *Re Duncan* (1957) 11 DLR (2d) 616 and other cases cited by Peter Butt in [1978] Crim Law Rev at 466–7.

18 Peter Butt in [1978] Crim Law Rev at 467 relying on *R v Essex Justices, ex p Perkins* [1927] 2 KB 475 at 488–9 and *Cottle v Cottle* [1939] 2 All ER 535 at 540–1.

impartiality where there are reasonable grounds for doing so even if the judge is not in fact biased.

It is also unwise to accuse a judge of incompetence or that he is mishandling the case. In the Canadian decision, *R v Shumiatcher*, Davis J said:[19]

> 'It is inconceivable that any counsel worthy of the name would have the indelicacy—and the effrontery—to accuse one of Her Majesty's Justices of the Court of Queen's Bench in open Court and before a jury and a considerable audience (among whom were a number of young people) of pushing about and badgering a witness.'

The *Shumiatcher* decision, however, was one of those happily rare[20] cases where it was thought that counsel had indulged in 'the regrettable practice of needling the court in the hope that something might be said or done which would ensure a new trial, if one became necessary.' Given this belief Shumiatcher was fortunate only to be fined, for the deliberate misconduct by counsel aimed at obtaining another trial is surely a most serious contempt which a court should unhesitatingly punish.

An advocate may also commit contempt by completely disregarding the judge's ruling. An example is a persistent line of questioning in defiance of the judge's wishes.[1] Another example is *Watt v Ligertwood*[2] where contrary to the express orders of the court, and despite a warning that such conduct would amount to contempt, an advocate removed a material document from the court and destroyed it by throwing it on a fire. For this 'gross and unjustifiable contempt' the advocate was immediately imprisoned.

An advocate will be expected to conduct his case honestly, and deliberate deception of the court can amount to contempt. In *Linwood v Andrews and Moore*[3] it was held to be a contempt to read out false affidavits, and, in *R v Weisz, ex p Hector Macdonald Ltd*[4] to conceal the true nature of an action so as to deceive the court. But as Lord Denning MR said in *Abraham v Jutsun*,[5] an advocate:

> 'is not guilty of misconduct simply because he takes a point which the tribunal holds to be bad. He only becomes guilty of misconduct if he is dishonest. That is, if he knowingly takes a bad point and thereby deceives the court.'

As Miller has observed:[6]

> 'It seems professional etiquette, coupled with a recognition by the judiciary of the importance of an independent Bar, have greatly worked together to minimise the possibility of confrontation . . .'.

It can only be hoped that this mutual tolerance will continue and the high standards of behaviour maintained and while there is no room for complacency[7]

---

19 (1967) 64 DLR (2d) 24 at 32.
20 See also *Re Prior, ex p Bellanto* [1963] SR NSW 190.
 1 See eg the Australian cases of *Lloyd v Biggin* [1962] VLR 593 and *Re Prior, ex p Bellanto* [1963] SR NSW 190. In Canada see *R v Swartz* (1977) 2 WWR 751, 34 CCC (2d) 477. See also *R v Webb, ex p Hawkers* (1899) Times, 24 January.
 2 (1874) LR 2 Sc & Div 361.
 3 (1888) 58 LT 612. See pp 459–460.
 4 [1951] 2 KB 611, [1951] 2 All ER 408. See p 460. See also *R v Kopyto* (1981) 122 DLR (3d) 260 (Ontario CA) barrister allegedly misleading the court in seeking an adjournment.
 5 [1963] 2 All ER 402 at 404.
 6 *Contempt of Court* (2nd edn, 1989) p 110.
 7 For a disturbing case of a solicitor's misbehaviour see *Re a Solicitor* (1978) Times, 31 January.

neither does it seem necessary to suggest reforms. In other jurisdictions where confrontations between judge and advocate have become more common, consideration might be given to producing a written code of conduct. In this respect the report and recommendation of the American College of Trial Lawyers[8] makes interesting reading. They recommend that a lawyer has these professional obligations:

'(a)   to represent every client courageously, vigorously, diligently and with all the skill and knowledge that he possesses;
(b)   to do so according to law and the standards of professional conduct as defined in codes and canons of the legal profession;
(c)   to conduct himself in such a way as to avoid disorder or disruption in the courtroom;
(d)   to advise any client appearing in a courtroom of the kind of behaviour expected or required of him there, and to prevent him, so far as lies within the lawyer's power, from creating disorder or disruption in the court room.'

A lawyer is not relieved of these obligations by any shortcomings on the part of the judge, nor is he relieved of them by the 'legal, moral, political, social or ideological merits of the cause of any client'. They also recommend that a judge has the following obligations:

'(a)   to consider objectively any challenge of his right to preside: to deny it courageously if the challenge is unfounded; to allow it if it is well founded; and to disqualify himself without challenge if he is biased or plausibly may be suspected of bias;
(b)   to recognise the obligation of every lawyer to represent his clients courageously and vigorously, and to treat every lawyer with courtesy and respect due on performing an essential role in the trial process.
(c)   to avoid becoming personally involved in any case before him, to preside firmly and impartially, and to conduct himself and the trial in such a way as to prevent, if possible, disorder or disruption in the court room.
He is not relieved of these obligations by any shortcomings on the part of any lawyer, or by the legal, moral, political, social or ideological deficiencies of the cause of any litigant.'

2   Absence from court [9]

It is important that those who represent others in legal proceedings should be present at the hearing to conduct the case. Prima facie, therefore, absence from the proceedings is a dereliction of the representor's duty towards his client. Whether such absence is also a contempt is more problematic. As *Izuora v R* [10] shows, mere discourtesy to the court or breach of duty towards a client is not in itself a contempt. In that case at the end of a hearing counsel applied to be excused from attending the following day's proceedings when judgment was to be given.

---

8   *Disruption of the Judicial Process* (1970).
9   Curiously, this has been classified as contempt in the face of the court in Canada: *McKeown v R* (1971) 16 DLR (3d) 390 (Canadian SC). Some support for a similar classification in England might be gleaned from Lord Denning MR's judgment in *Weston v Central Criminal Court Courts' Administrator* [1977] QB 32 at 44D, at least in certain circumstances, though his Lordship equated such classification with the court's power to punish contempts upon its own motion. For the position in the US see generally 97 ALR (2nd) 431.
10   [1953] AC 327.

Permission was granted but when opposing counsel also sought to be absent the court ruled that as judgment could not be given in both counsels' absence, both would be ordered to attend. The appellant did not appear and for this 'contempt' he was fined £10. This conviction was reversed by the Privy Council which held:[11]

> 'It is not every act of discourtesy to the court by counsel that amounts to contempt, nor is conduct which involves a breach by counsel of his duty to his client necessarily in this category. In the present case the appellant's conduct was clearly discourteous, ... and it may, perhaps, have been in dereliction of his duty to his client, but in their Lordships' opinion it cannot properly be placed over the line that divides mere discourtesy from contempt.'

It should be noted that the barrister's absence did not prejudice his client's case nor did it delay the proceedings nor was it suggested that he intended to delay or hinder proceedings.

A similar standpoint was taken by the Court of Appeal in *Weston v Central Criminal Court Courts' Administrator.* [12] A solicitor, angered by what he considered high handed conduct by a court official in arbitrarily setting down a case for trial contrary to an earlier understanding and before he was ready, did not attend the first nor a second adjourned hearing nor did he instruct counsel to appear but instead let the client attend by himself. On the second occasion he informed the prosecuting solicitor that his case would not be ready. After his second non-appearance the judge purportedly ordered the solicitor to appear the following day to explain his conduct day but as this was communicated to him only by his client, he again declined to appear. He was then arrested upon a bench warrant and subsequently adjudged guilty of contempt. On appeal his non-appearance on the third occasion was held not to be a contempt since no order had actually been drawn up nor had it been served on him.[13] His non-attendance on the first two occasions was also held not to be contempt both because the solicitor's conduct though 'seriously discourteous' was not intended to, nor did it in fact, hinder or delay his client's trial. Lord Denning MR[14] had no doubts that the deliberate failure by a solicitor to attend with an intent to hinder or delay the hearing and doing so, would be a contempt. Bridge LJ[15] was more circumspect, doubting whether it could ever be a contempt for a solicitor to fail to instruct counsel on behalf of his client but that at any rate the omission would have to be shown to have the effect or possibly the object of frustrating or obstructing the legal process in question.

This apparent reticence to hold an advocate's non-appearance as contempt is not necessarily shared in other jurisdictions. In Scotland, for example, the basic principle seems to be that an advocate's unexplained failure to attend a court hearing when under an obligation to do so is prima facie a contempt. In *Muirhead v Douglas* [16] a solicitor whose case was second on the list left the court room (to pursue other work elsewhere) after ascertaining from a lawyer in the first case that that trial was estimated to last two hours. The solicitor made informal arrangements to be contacted in the event of an early conclusion of the first trial. In fact the first case ended 'prematurely' and the arrangements to contact the

---

11 At 336.
12 [1977] QB 32.
13 Following *Churchman v Joint Shop Stewards' Committee* [1972] 3 All ER 603, [1972] 1 WLR 1094 and *Danchevsky v Danchevsky* [1975] Fam 17, [1974] 3 All ER 934.
14 [1977] QB 32 at 43.
15 Ibid at 47, 48.
16 1979 SLT (Notes) 17, [1981] Crim LR 781.

solicitor failed and he arrived 20 minutes late for his case. The High Court of Justiciary held that he was rightly convicted of contempt and that his plea that his lateness was due to mere inadvertence or carelessness was an inadequate defence. In the court's view 'deliberate intent to cause prejudice to the administration of justice is not an essential element in contempt', though the solicitor was held to have deliberately chosen to take a risk 'that he might for his own professional benefit bring about (as in fact he did) an avoidable and quite possibly serious delay in the due dispatch of the court's criminal business'.

In contrast to *Muirhead* is *Macara v Macfarlane* [17] where a solicitor, realising that he might be unable to be present if his case was called before he was released from another, made arrangements, with the accused's consent, that another solicitor would conduct the case if the need arose. The need did arise and a plea of not guilty was entered and a request was made for an adjournment. In these circumstances the High Court of Justiciary had no doubts that no contempt had been committed and accordingly, quashed the fine of £30 imposed on the solicitor by a sheriff.

In Canada, too, support can be found for saying that the unexplained failure of an advocate to attend a court hearing when under an obligation to do so is prima facie a contempt. In *R v Hill*,[18] the accused lawyer represented two persons but failed to appear on the day fixed for their trial even though he was responsible for fixing the date. In fact he was elsewhere setting a date for the trial of another matter. Hill had sent an employee to represent the two accused but neither wanted the employee and complained about Hill's absence. After an abortive attempt to get Hill's attendance in the afternoon the judge ordered his attendance on the two following days but on each occasion he did not appear allegedly because he was ill. No medical evidence was tendered and the court rejected his defence of illness holding that his failure to appear was 'without justifiable excuse'. The British Columbia Court of Appeal upheld the finding of contempt saying that Hill's conduct went beyond mere discourtesy[19] and amounted to an interference with the process of the court and the administration of justice. McIntyre JA distinguished *Weston* [20] because unlike that case there was no explanation or justification for the absence particularly as Hill himself had fixed the date. Moreover unlike *Weston*, Hill had not communicated with Crown Counsel or any court official his intention not to appear, nor had he made effective arrangements acceptable to his clients[1] for the conduct of the trial. The result of his conduct was that the course of justice was hampered, witnesses had to be called on another day, expense was incurred and the trial delayed. Even if *Weston* could not be distinguished, McIntyre JA was not prepared to hold, as Lord Denning MR seemed to, that an intent to hinder or delay the trial was necessary, it being in his view sufficient that the conduct was 'calculated' to delay or disrupt proceedings.

However, by no means all Canadian courts agree that there is no mens rea requirement and indeed that increasingly seems to be a minority view.[2] It has

17 1980 SLT (Notes) 26.
18 (1976) 73 DLR (3d) 621 (BCCA). See also *Barrette v R* (1976) 68 DLR (3d) 260 (Supreme Court of Canada) per Pigeon J at 263.
19 Expressly distinguishing *Izuora v R* [1953] AC 327, [1953] 1 All ER 827.
20 [1977] 1 QB 32, [1976] 2 All ER 875.
 1 This would distinguish it from *Macara v Macfarlane* 1980 SLT (Notes) 26.
 2 See eg *R v Barker* (1980) 4 WWR 202 and *R v Anders* (1982) 136 DLR (3d) 316 where the Alberta CA and Ontario CA reporting concluded after analysing a number of cases that there *is* a mens rea requirement. Cf *R v Perkins* (1980) 4 WWR 763 where the British Columbia CA reached the opposite conclusion.

been held, on more than one occasion, that failure of counsel to appear due to mere inadvertence, at least where it falls short of indifference, will not be punished as a contempt.[3] In the most recent decision, *R v Glasner*,[4] Laskin JA observed that criminal contempt is not an offence of absolute liability. It requires mens rea. In his view:

> 'the fault requirement for criminal contempt calls for deliberate or intentional conduct, or conduct which demonstrates indifference, which I take to be akin to recklessness. Nothing short of that will do.'

It is submitted that Laskin JA is right. An advocate's avoidable absence from proceedings is something to be deprecated since it is wasteful of court time and unfair to clients. On the other hand the courts should not be overzealous to exercise their contempt powers. An advocate's absence should be explained but provided the explanation is reasonable no offence should be committed. Further it is submitted that absence due to mere inadvertence should not be punishable as a contempt. Even if the mens rea element can be established, contempt may not always be committed for, as Laskin JA pointed out in *R v Glasner*,[5] consideration should be given to the consequences of failing to appear. 'Conduct that has little or no effect on the administration of justice cannot support a conviction for contempt.'

3   *Withdrawal from proceedings*[6]

If an advocate's wrongful absence from a trial can be a contempt can it also be an offence for him to withdraw or attempt to withdraw during the court proceedings? The dangers of premature withdrawal are obvious. As Holroyd Pearce LJ said in *Brassington v Brassington*:[7]

> 'If it be open for counsel . . . to break off a losing battle when the court appears to be very much against him, and then to ask [an appeal court] for a rehearing, it would create an opportunity for many applications . . . by undeserving litigants. They might, by an opportune manoeuvre, take advantage of a recourse to [the appeal court] which should only be available to those who have suffered a real denial of justice.'

In *Brassington* no question of contempt arose since counsel was acting under his client's instructions when he did not call evidence but in the Canadian case, *R v Swartz*,[8] after being unexpectedly and apparently unjustifiably denied an adjournment the lawyer attempted to withdraw from the case. The issue quickly

---

3 See eg *R v Fox* (1976) 70 DLR (3d) 577 (lawyer late because of weather and car trouble but would probably have been late anyway) and *R v Jones* (1978) 42 CCC (2d) 192 (absence due to the breakdown of a system that was ordinarily effective). In *R v Pinx* (1979) 105 DLR (3d) 143 where a barrister was double booked to his knowledge 24 days beforehand but only tried to do something about it on the very day, the CA quashed conviction because, per the majority, the procedure was bad but Husband JA thought there was no contempt because absence was due to inadvertence. Monnin JA dissented.
4 (1995) 119 DLR (4th) 113, 130-131. Labrosse JA, however, dissented.
5 Ibid at 131.
6 See generally Shetreet, *Judges on Trial* (1976 North-Holland, ed Borrie) p 247 ff.
7 [1962] P 276 at 282.
8 [1977] 2 WWR 751, 34 CCC (2d) 477. But note *Leask v Cronin Prov J* [1985] 3 WWR 152: judge held to have no right to order counsel to continue in the case after counsel has advised that he will no longer do so.

developed into a confrontation with the judge and the lawyer found himself charged and later convicted of contempt. The Manitoba Court of Appeal reversed the decision considering that both lawyer and judge had overreacted and that on the facts the attempted withdrawal was at the worst an 'error of judgment' made in the heat of the moment. The implication of *Swartz*, however, was that had the lawyer's withdrawal been a deliberate tactic to gain a retrial that could properly have been treated as a contempt.

4   *Impersonating a barrister*

It is likely to be a serious contempt to impersonate a barrister.[9]

B   Witnesses

1   *Refusing to attend a court hearing or to produce documents*

There are different methods of enforcing the attendance of a witness, according to which court the witness is required to attend. The penalties for non-attendance differ according to which court is involved.

(a) The position in the High Court and analogous proceedings

When proceedings are in the High Court attendance can be secured by a writ of subpoena either by a subpoena ad testificandum, which simply directs that the person upon whom the writ is served shall attend a specified court at a specified time or a subpoena duces tecum, which directs a specified person to produce a particular and specified document[10] before a named court at a specified time.[11]

Normally a subpoena can be issued at any stage in the proceedings and without leave,[12] but where the proceedings are heard in chambers the writ will issue only on a note by the judge or master or registrar, as the case may be.[13] In addition to the High Court, an official referee[14] and arbitrator[15] can also issue subpoenas to secure the attendance of witnesses. Witnesses can also be subpoenaed to attend

---

9 See *In the Marriage of Slender* (1977) 29 FLR 267 (Fam Ct of Australia). Offender imprisoned for 90 days but ordered to be released after 14 days upon his entering into a recognisance in the sum of A $1,000 to be of good behaviour.

10 'Document' has been held to include tape recordings (*Grant v South-Western and County Properties Ltd* [1975] Ch 185, [1974] 2 All ER 465), cinematograph film (*Senior v Holdsworth, ex p Independent Television News* [1976] QB 23, [1975] 2 All ER 1009) and a database (*Derby & Co Ltd v Weldon (No 9)* [1991] 2 All ER 901, [1991] 1 WLR 652). Although the summons duces tecum is inappropriate to exhibit the film (or to play the tape) there is nevertheless an inherent power in both High Court and county court to order the addressee to exhibit the film or, presumably, to play the tape.

11 As to the nature of subpoenas see generally *Phipson's Evidence* (14th edn, 1990) Ch 8 and the *Supreme Court Practice*, 38/14–19/3, 19/4.

12 *Macbryan v Brooke* [1946] 2 All ER 688.

13 RSC Ord 32, r 7. In the case of the Family Division the reference to 'registrar' must now be taken to mean 'District Judge'.

14 RSC Ord 36, r 4.

15 Arbitration Act 1950, s 12(4), (5) and Supreme Court Act 1981, s 36.

before an examiner.[16] Tribunals set up under the Tribunals of Inquiry (Evidence) Act 1921 have the same powers as the High Court to secure the attendance of witnesses. Under RSC Ord 38, r 19 the High Court may also issue a subpoena in aid of an inferior court, or tribunal[17] but it has been established that such a procedure may only be used where there is no statutory regulation applicable to that particular inferior court. If there is a statutory regulation in force, then that statutory procedure must be followed.[18]

Under RSC Ord 38, r 13(1) the High Court can at any stage:

> 'order any person to attend any proceedings in the cause or matter and produce any document, to be specified or described in the order, the production of which appears to the Court to be necessary for the purpose of that proceeding.'

This power is, in effect, the equivalent to a subpoena duces tecum, but, although the order is widely phrased, in practice it is restricted to ordering the production of documents in the hands of the parties, and it cannot be made upon persons who are not parties, agents of parties, or witnesses. The object of the rule is to enable an order to be made at any stage of the proceedings, but it can only be made for the purposes of a particular proceeding.[19]

Once a subpoena has been duly issued and properly served,[20] and provided full conduct money has been tendered with the subpoena,[1] (this proviso only applies in civil proceedings) then failure to attend the court hearing can amount to contempt.[2] In the normal case contempt will only be committed where the non-attendance is wilful, and it has been held that the court will not punish the offender unless a clear case of contempt is made out,[3] the burden of establishing such a clear case being on the prosecution.[4] In *R v Daye*[5] it was held that the court could still enforce obedience to a subpoena duces tecum even though such disobedience was not wilful, but in that case the court ordered that no action should be taken unless the offender persisted in the disobedience. The conclusion to be drawn from these cases is that disobedience to a subpoena without a reasonable excuse will amount to contempt, but in practice the contempt will only be punished where such disobedience can be shown to be wilful. What amounts to a reasonable excuse will depend upon the facts, but it has been held that illness affords a reasonable excuse.[6]

---

16 RSC Ord 39, r 4.
17 For the meaning of 'tribunal' in this context see *Currie v Chief Constable of Surrey* [1982] 1 All ER 89, [1982] 1 WLR 215 discussed by Lowe and Rawlings: 'Tribunals and the Laws Protecting the Administration of Justice' [1982] PL 418 at 443–4. See also *Re Sterritt* [1981] CLY 1961.
18 *R v Hurle-Hobbs, ex p Simmons* [1945] KB 165, [1945] 1 All ER 273. For the provisions governing county courts and magistrates' courts, see below pp 41 and 44 respectively.
19 For more detail see, eg *Phipson's Evidence* (14th edn, 1990) para 8-06.
20 For rules as to the contents of a subpoena and rules as to its issue see RSC Ord 38, rr 14–19.
 1 See *Fuller v Prentice* (1788) 1 Hy Bl 49; *Brocas v Lloyd* (1856) 23 Beav 129; *Re Working Men's Mutual Society* (1882) 21 Ch D 831; cf *Re General Financial Bank* [1888] WN 47.
 2 See *Jeames v Morgan* (1616) Cary 56; *Anon* (1580) Cary 91; *Wyat v Wingford* (1729) 2 Ld Raym 1528. In Australia see eg *Registrar of the Court of Appeal v Maniam* (1991) 25 NSWLR 459.
 3 See, eg *Horne v Smith* (1815) 6 Taunt 9 and *Garden v Creswell* (1837) 2 M & W 319, per Lord Abinger CB.
 4 *Scholes v Hilton* (1842) 10 M & W 15.
 5 [1908] 2 KB 333.
 6 See *More v Woreham* (1580) Cary 99; *Scholes v Hilton* (1842) 10 M & W 15. For the application of these cases in New South Wales, Australia see eg *Registrar of the Court of Appeal v Maniam* (1991) 25 NSWLR 459.

Once a contempt has been established, the High Court can punish the offender as it sees fit, either by fine or imprisonment. Failure to attend can also render the offender liable in other ways. In civil cases the aggrieved party can recover a penalty of £10, with further compensation as the court issuing the process may assess,[7] and has a common law right to claim damages occasioned by the witness's non-attendance, provided it can be proved that there is actual loss or detriment suffered as a result of the non-attendance.[8] The amount of the damages is limited to the costs thrown away.[9] In practice it is almost impossible to bring a successful action for damages.[10]

Where a person is subpoenaed before an examiner,[11] the correct procedure for non-attendance is for the court, upon the action of the aggrieved party, to order the witness to attend (or to produce the document) at his own expense, and, in default of this order, a motion to commit the person for contempt may be made.[12]

Under RSC Ord 32, r 7 (which authorises masters, registrars and judges sitting in chambers generally to issue a subpoena to secure the attendance of witnesses)[13] it is generally considered that the issue of the summons is the correct procedure.[14] If a witness refuses to attend in answer to the summons an order for his attendance must be made before he can be committed.[15]

(b) The position in the county court

The power of the county court to secure the attendance of a witness, or to require a person to produce a particular document, is to issue a county court summons in accordance with the County Court Rules 1981, Ord 20, r 12(1), and by virtue of Ord 20, r 12(2) conduct money for the witness's expenses must be tendered at the same time as the summons. By the County Courts Act 1984, s 55(1):

> 'Any person who
> (a)   having been summoned in pursuance of county court rules as a witness in a county court refuses or neglects, without sufficient cause, to appear or to produce any documents required by the summons to be produced; or
> (b)   having been so summoned or being present in court and being required to give evidence, refuses to be sworn or give evidence,
> shall forfeit such fine as the judge may direct.'

A witness summoned to appear before the county court can only be punished under this section if:

> 'there has been paid or tendered to him at the time of the service of the summons such sum in respect of his expenses . . . as may be prescribed for the purposes of this section'.[16]

---

7 5 Eliz 1, c 9, s 12 made perpetual by the Statute Law Revision Act 1863.
8 *Crewe v Field* (1896) 12 TLR 405.
9 *Roberts v J & F Stone Lighting and Radio Ltd* (1945) 172 LT 240.
10 See Asquith J in *Roberts v J & F Stone Lighting and Radio Ltd* ibid.
11 RSC Ord 39, r 5.
12 *Re Evans, Evans v Noton* [1893] 1 Ch 252, CA.
13 RSC Ord 36, r 4.
14 See the *Supreme Court Practice*, Vol 1, 32/15/2. A similar procedure should be used with regard to a witness summoned under the Companies Act 1985, s 561; *Re Westmoreland Green and Blue State Co Ltd* (1891) 66 LT 52.
15 *Powell v Nevitt* (1886) 55 LT 728 and see RSC Ord 39, r 15(3).
16 S 55 (3).

However, where a person is present in court and is required to give evidence, there being no question of expenses to consider, the court can punish him if he refuses to be sworn or to give evidence. Under s 55(2) the maximum fine that can be imposed is currently £1,000.[17] However, where a fine is imposed, s 55(4) provides that the judge:

> 'may at his discretion direct that the whole or any part of any such fine, after deducting the costs, shall be applicable towards indemnifying the party injured by the refusal or neglect'.

(c) Applying to have the summons set aside

Once due application is made a court cannot refuse to issue a witness summons (or subpoena) for the production of documents. Instead, an aggrieved party must apply to have the summons set aside.[18] Indeed, any person whose legal rights will be interfered with by the execution of a subpoena duces tecum has locus standi to apply to set it aside.[19] Upon such application the court is empowered to set the summons aside if what is sought is irrelevant, oppressive, an abuse of process of the court or recognised by the law as privileged from protection. Even if the document sought is relevant and not privileged the court retains a residual discretion in certain circumstances to set the summons aside. In *Senior v Holdsworth, ex p Independent Television News* [20] an order to produce all film negative taken at a pop festival was held 'oppressive' and set aside since only parts of the film were relevant to the plaintiff's action. Scarman LJ commented[1] that though the court's power to set summonses aside afforded the press and broadcasting authorities some protection against oppressive applications, more protection was arguably needed. He questioned why the party seeking production of documents should not be called upon to show cause and suggested that the law might formulate guidelines designed 'to hold the balance between the right of the litigant and the protection of the media'.

Whether the media are or should be specially treated will be considered later but the problem of being liable to produce untransmitted films and tapes does seem to produce special, if not unique, problems and might be thought to merit special treatment. In particular it does not seem unreasonable, at least in this context, to require the party seeking the film etc to make out his case. It is to be hoped that Scarman LJ's suggestions will be considered further.

(d) Crown Court

The procedure for securing the attendance of a witness before the Crown Court is governed by the Criminal Procedure (Attendance of Witnesses) Act 1965. The

---

17 As substituted by the Criminal Justice Act 1991, s 17(3)(a), Sch 4, Pt 1. This sum may be raised by order made under the Magistrates' Courts Act 1980, s 143(1).
18 An appeal can be made against the refusal to set an order aside. An alternative to applying to set an order aside is for the party to wait until the trial and object to the production of the 'documents' then, per Lord Denning MR in *Senior v Holdsworth, ex p Independent Television News* [1976] QB 23 at 31.
19 *Marcel v Metropolitan Police Comr* [1992] Ch 225.
20 [1976] QB 23.
 1 Ibid at 43.

principal method is by issuing a witness summons[2] pursuant to s 2 (1) which states:[3]

> 'For the purpose of any criminal proceedings before the Crown Court a witness summons, that is to say, a summons requiring the person to whom it is directed to attend before the court and give evidence or produce any document or thing specified in the summons, may be issued out of that Court or out of the High Court.'

Under s 2(2) the witness summons may be declared to have no effect if the person summoned can satisfy the court[4] that he cannot produce any material evidence or that he cannot produce any document or thing likely to be material evidence. The power to issue a witness summons supersedes any power to issue a subpoena and testification or subpoena duces tecum.[5]

Failure to obey a witness summons renders the offender liable for contempt.[6] This is provided for by s 3(1) which states that:

> 'Any person who without just excuse disobeys a witness order or witness summons requiring him to attend before any court shall be guilty of contempt of that court and may be punished summarily by that court as if his contempt had been committed in the face of the court.'

A committal will, however, only be justified upon the strict proof that a duly issued summons[7] has been brought to the notice of the alleged offender.[8] However, provided these requirements are satisfied, the offence is absolute subject only to the words 'without just excuse'. Accordingly, culpable forgetfulness cannot amount to such an excuse.[9] The maximum penalty for such disobedience is, by virtue of s 3(2), three months' imprisonment.

It should be noted that the contempt is of the court before which the witness is required to attend (ie the Crown Court). The reason why the contempt is expressed to be punishable as if it had been in the face of the court can now be explained only on historical grounds. The Act formerly applied both to quarter sessions and assizes and it was therefore necessary to state that the punishment was to be treated as if it were contempt in the face of the court because the power of quarter sessions was limited to punishing contempts committed in its face[10] and because the High Court had no power to punish disobedience to a subpoena

---

2 The former power to make a witness order under s 1 of the 1965 Act was repealed by the Criminal Justice and Public Order Act 1994, Sch 11.

3 As amended by the Courts Act 1971, Sch 8, para 45(2).

4 Either the High Court or the Crown Court: s 2(2).

5 Under s 8.

6 For the reasons why the offence should be treated as contempt see the Criminal Law Revision Committee 6th Report (1964, Cmnd 2465), especially paras 48–52.

7 The summons must be in proper form, see RSC Ord 79, r 10, ie Forms 101 or 103 in Appendix A.

8 See *Chance v Central Criminal Court* [1980] CA Transcript 351. The CA held that in the case of a *summons*, knowledge of that document was an essential requirement but left open whether the position might be different in the case of an *order*. It may be that the court had in mind substituted service as provided for by the Magistrates' Courts Rules 1981, r 8(5) (as amended) which defines 'notice' as including leaving it with someone at the witness's last known or usual place of abode or by sending it by post in a letter addressed to him at his last known or usual place of abode. Query, however, whether a person should be committed if he did not know of the existence of the order?

9 *R v Lennock* (1993) 97 Cr App Rep 228, CA. Duress, on the other hand, is likely to be thought 'just excuse'; cf *R v K* (1983) 78 Cr App Rep 82, CA.

10 See *R v Lefroy* (1873) LR 8 QB 134.

issued out of quarter sessions.[11] However, this provision is now otiose since the Crown Court is a superior court of record[12] and its contempt jurisdiction is at large.[13]

A second way of enforcing attendance of witnesses before the Crown Court is by s 4(1) of the 1965 Act which provides that the High Court can, if satisfied upon the evidence made on oath that the witness in respect of whom a witness order or summons is made is unlikely to comply with that order or summons, issue a warrant for that person's arrest.[14]

(e) Magistrates' courts

Magistrates' courts can secure the attendance of a witness or the production of documents by means of a witness summons issued pursuant to the Magistrates' Courts Act 1980, s 97(1).[15] It is provided by s 97(3) that:

> 'On failure of any person to attend before a magistrates' court in answer to a summons under this section, if—
> (a)   the court is satisfied by evidence on oath that he is likely to be able to give material evidence or produce any document or thing likely to be material evidence in the proceedings; and
> (b)   it is proved on oath, or in such other manner as may be prescribed, that he has been duly served with the summons, and that a reasonable sum has been paid or tendered to him for costs and expenses; and
> (c)   it appears to the court that there is no just excuse for the failure, the court may issue a warrant to arrest him and bring him before the court at a time and place to be specified by the warrant.'

Upon being brought to the court, if that person refuses without just excuse to be sworn, or give evidence or to produce any document or thing, he can be imprisoned for a maximum period of one month or fined a maximum of £2,500 or both.[16] Any fine so imposed is deemed to be a fine adjudged to be paid on conviction.[17]

(f) Coroner's courts

Coroners can also enforce the attendance of witnesses[18] and any person duly summoned to give evidence who does not appear after being openly called three times to such summons is liable to a maximum fine of £1,000.[19]

---

11 *R v Judge, ex p Isle of Ely Justices* [1931] 2 KB 442.
12 Supreme Court Act 1981, s 45(1).
13 See pp 10–12 and 504–505.
14 For an example of the use of s 4 see *R v Sokolovics* [1981] Crim LR 788.
15 The Criminal Procedure (Attendance of Witnesses) Act 1965, s 8 (as amended by the Magistrates' Courts Act 1980, Sch 7, para 56) abolished the use of subpoenas in cases covered by this section (ie s 97 of the 1980 Act).
16 Magistrates' Courts Act 1980, s 97(4) as amended by the Contempt of Court Act 1981, Sch 2, para 7 and the Criminal Justice Act 1991, Sch 4. This power extends to all recalcitrant witnesses whether compulsorily or voluntarily appearing before the court. It does not, however, compel production of documents to which legal professional privilege is attached: *R v Derby Magistrates' Court, ex p B* (1995) 145 NLJ 1575, HL.
17 Magistrates' Courts Act 1980, s 97(5), as substituted by the Criminal Justice Act 1993, Sch 3.
18 The attendance of witnesses is secured either by a message or a formal summons: see 9 *Halsbury's Laws* (4th edn); *Coroners*, para 1097. Note *McKerr v Armagh Coroner* [1990] 1 All ER 865, HL.
19 Coroners' Act 1988, s 10(1) as amended by the Criminal Justice Act 1991, Sch 4.

Where a fine is so imposed, for the purposes of its collection, enforcement and remission, it is treated as having been imposed by the magistrates' court for the area in which the coroner's court was held. The coroner must give the particulars to the clerk of that court as soon as is practicable.[20]

2 Refusing to be sworn or to answer questions

(a) The general position

Any person attending the court can be compelled to give evidence, whether or not he has been subpoenaed[1] (provided such a person's evidence is not privileged) and therefore attendance at the court in pursuance of a subpoena will be deemed to waive any irregularity of the subpoena itself.[2]

In general, compellable witnesses[3] who unjustifiably refuse to take the oath or affirm or who unjustifiably refuse to answer a question properly put by the court and which is relevant to the case[4] will be held guilty of contempt.[5] As Watkins LJ put it in *R v Phillips*:[6]

> 'It is of the utmost importance that everyone called upon to testify in our courts recognises that he or she is under a duty to do so and that a refusal or neglect to perform that duty may have dire consequences for the proper administration of justice and for that person.'

Such unjustifiable refusals are treated as serious contempts and are generally punished by committals to prison. In *R v Montgomery*[7] Potter J said:

> 'An immediate custodial sentence is the only appropriate sentence to impose upon a person who interferes with the administration of justice, unless the circumstances are wholly exceptional.'

Notwithstanding the foregoing comments not all English courts have the power to commit in such circumstances and those that have do not necessarily have the same power. So far as the High Court is concerned it can punish the contempt either by imprisonment (the maximum term being two years)[8] or by fine (there being no maximum limit) or both. Such powers also extend to punishing offenders before Tribunals of Inquiry set up under the 1921 Act[9] and

---

20 Criminal Justice Act 1988, s 67.
1   *R v Flavell* (1884) 14 QBD 364; *Cutler v Wright* [1890] WN 28.
2   See *Cutler v Wright* ibid.
3   Not all witnesses are required to swear or affirm, eg children, witnesses merely producing documents, counsel, judges and the Sovereign. See generally Phipson: *Evidence* (14th edn, 1990) para 9-35.
4   See p 49.
5   *Hennegal v Evance* (1860) 12 Ves 201. For examples in England see eg *Ex p Fernandez* (1861) 10 CBNS 3; *Re Davies* (1888) 21 QBD 236 at 238; *A-G v Mulholland and Foster* [1963] 2 QB 477, [1963] 1 All ER 767; cf Lord Denning MR in *Balogh v Crown Court at St Albans* [1975] QB 73 at 86: 'Refusal to answer should be treated with admonishment save where it is vital to know the answer'. In Scotland see *HM Advocate v Airs* 1975 SLT 177. In Australia see *Smith v The Queen* (1991) 25 NSWLR 1 and the cases there cited. In Canada see eg *Vaillancourt v R* (1981) 120 DLR (3d) 740; *Re Couture and Hewison* (1980) 105 DLR (3d) 556; cf *Re Abko Medical Laboratories Ltd and The Queen* (1977) 77 DLR (3d) 295.
6   (1983) 78 Cr App Rep 88, 94.
7   [1995] 2 All ER 28, 32.
8   Contempt of Court Act 1981, s 14; for a similar restriction in Scotland see s 15.
9   Discussed in more detail in Ch 13.

similar powers are vested in official referees,[10] examiners[11] and Crown Courts.[12] Magistrates have more limited powers, being empowered to commit offenders for a maximum of one month or fine them a maximum of £2,500 or both.[13] However, alone of the major domestic English courts,[14] county courts have no power of committal. Instead all they can do is fine the recalcitrant witness a maximum of £1,000.[15] It is difficult to justify this singularity and it is suggested that at the very least county court powers should be brought into line with those of magistrates.

Another curiosity of the above mentioned powers is that the Crown Court's powers of punishment are greater in the case of witnesses refusing to be sworn or to affirm or to answer questions than in respect of witnesses refusing to attend court at all.[16] However, in *R v Montgomery*[17] it was held that while that difference was a relevant consideration it did not mean that the Crown Court could never impose a sentence longer than three months for refusing to answer questions etc, nor was it accepted that such an offence should, as a matter of principle, be visited with shorter sentence than for threatening jurors. Instead to determine the appropriate sentence, the court should consider (a) the gravity of the principal offence being tried;[18] (b) the effect on that trial of the witness's refusal to give evidence;[19] (c) the reason for the failure to give evidence; (d) whether or not the contempt is aggravated by impertinent defiance of the judge rather than a simple and stubborn refusal to answer;[20] (e) the antecedents, personal circumstances and characteristics of the contempt;[1] and (f) whether or not a special deterrent is necessary.

Montgomery also emphasised the need for the judge not to act precipitously and in any event to give the witness time to consider his refusal and to take independent legal advice.

(b) Defences

Despite the gravity of the offence, in an important ruling by the Court of Appeal in *R v K*,[2] it has been recognised that duress is a defence to a charge of contempt.[3]

10 RSC Ord 36, r 4.
11 RSC Ord 39, r 5.
12 Supreme Court Act 1981, s 45(4). It seems arguable that coroners have wide powers following the ruling in *R v West Yorkshire Coroner, ex p Smith (No 2)* [1985] 1 QB 1096.
13 Magistrates' Courts Act 1980, s 97(4) as amended by the Contempt of Court Act 1981, Sch 2, para 7, and the Criminal Justice Act 1991, Sch 4.
14 The powers to punish witnesses who refuse to answer questions before coroner's courts has yet to be established, but it is arguable that their inherent powers are as extensive as that of the High Court.
15 County Courts Act 1984, s 55 (1) (a), (2), as amended by the Criminal Justice Act 1991, Sch 4.
16 Under the Criminal Procedure (Attendance of Witnesses) Act 1965, discussed at pp 42 ff.
17 [1995] 2 All ER 28.
18 Compare *R v Jardine* (1987) 9 Cr App Rep (S) 41 (a case of robbery) and *R v Samuda* (1989) 11 Cr App Rep (S) 471 (attempted murder) with *R v Leonard* (1984) 6 Cr App Rep (S) 279 (criminal damage).
19 See eg *R v Phillips* (1983) 78 Cr App Rep 88.
20 As in *R v Leonard* (1984) 6 Cr App Rep (S) 279.
 1 See *R v Palmer* [1992] 3 All ER 289—effect of sentence would have been to separate a mother from her baby.
 2 (1983) 78 Cr App Rep 82.
 3 Thereby bringing contempt law into line with that of perjury, see *R v Hudson* [1971] 2 QB 202, [1971] 2 All ER 244.

Nevertheless this defence is not easy to establish.[4] For example, the fact that a witness has been threatened[5] may not necessarily amount to duress though it will be a mitigating factor. Apart from duress, refusal to take the oath or affirm will rarely be justifiable.[6] Refusal to answer questions on the other hand may be justifiable upon a number of grounds. For example, a witness, has been held to be entitled to refuse to answer until the sum paid for his attendance was sufficient to cover his costs.[7] More commonly, refusal to answer may be justified upon the basis of self-incrimination or privilege.

The right of a witness not to answer an incriminating question[8] is governed by the Civil Evidence Act 1968, s 14(1), which states:

> 'The right of a person in any legal proceeding other than criminal proceedings to refuse to answer a question or produce any document or thing if to do so would tend to expose that person to proceedings for an offence or for the recovery of a penalty:
> (a)   shall apply only as regards criminal offences under the law of any part of the United Kingdom and penalties provided for by such law; and
> (b)   shall include a like right to refuse to answer any question or produce any document or thing if to do so would tend to expose the husband or wife of that person to proceedings for any such criminal offence or for the recovery of any such penalty.'

It is to be noted that s 14 only justifies refusing to answer a question and not refusing to be sworn[9] (which would still be punishable as a contempt) nor does it extend to refusing to answer questions which merely incriminate co-defendants or others.[10]

Although a witness must pledge his oath that he honestly believes that the answer will incriminate him, the court is still entitled to see, from the circumstances of the case and the nature of the evidence, whether or not there are reasonable grounds to apprehend danger.[11] However, once it is established that there are reasonable grounds, great latitude will be allowed to a witness to judge for himself the effect of any particular question.[12]

---

4   The test would seem to be whether the threat of physical harm was of such gravity that a person of reasonable firmness sharing the accused's characteristics and placed in the same position, would have similarly refused to take the oath or affirm or to refuse to answer questions. See Archbold: *Criminal Pleading. Evidence and Practice* (1994) para 17–158 following *R v Howe and Others* [1987] AC 417, HL. It was thought that the defence would have been established in *R v Lewis* (1992) 96 Cr App Rep 412 (accused savagely attacked by accomplice in prison). See also *R v K* (1983) 78 Cr App Rep 82.
5   See eg *R v Phillips* (1983) 78 Cr App Rep 88 and *R v Shorten and Purves* [1981] Crim LR 620 where the fact that two prisoners had been threatened whilst in prison did not prevent the court imprisoning them for three months. Threatening a witness is in itself a contempt and now a statutory offence under the Criminal Justice and Public Order Act 1994, s 51. See Ch 11.
6   See the extraordinary case of *The Commercial Bank of Scotland Ltd and Maceachran v Lloyd's General Italian Assurance Co* (1886) 2 TLR 780. What amounts to a reasonable excuse was left open by Griffiths CJ in *Clough v Leahy* (1904) 2 CLR 139 (High Court of Australia). In Canada see *Re Yanover and Kiroff and The Queen* (1974) 53 DLR (3d) 241 where it was held to be no contempt to refuse to take the oath, etc before a commission acting under the Public Inquiries Act 1971 (Ont) Vol 2, c 49 pending adjudication of a bona fide dispute by the Divisional Court to which body the commission had to state a case.
7   *Re Working Men's Mutual Society* (1882) 21 Ch D 831. See also the County Courts Act 1984, s 55(3).
8   See generally *Phipson's Evidence* (14th edn, 1990) para 20-44 ff. For a recent Australian case see *Registrar, Court of Appeal (NSW) v Craven* (1994) 126 ALR 668.
9   *Boyle v Wiseman* (1855) 10 Exch 647.
10   *Kelly v Colhoun* [1899] 2 IR 199.
11   *Re Reynolds, ex p Reynolds* (1882) 20 Ch D 294, CA.
12   *Re Reynolds, ex p Reynolds*, ibid; *R v Boyes* (1861) 1 B & S 311.

The privilege subsists only as long as the liability exists. Once the liability ceases, for example because the offence is pardoned or the penalty waived, the privilege ceases.[13]

There are a number of exceptions to this privilege. For example, s 1 (e) of the Criminal Evidence Act 1898 states:

> 'A person charged and being a witness in pursuance of this Act may be asked any question in cross-examination notwithstanding that it would tend to criminate him, as to the offence charged.'

Subject to a number of exceptions, by s 1(f) he need not answer questions tending to show that he has committed other offences. It is by no means unusual for statute to require a witness to answer a question even though the answer may incriminate him or his spouse. In such cases it is usual to give statutory protection against the use of the answer in subsequent proceedings.[14]

A witness may also be justified in refusing to answer a question on the grounds that the evidence is privileged,[15] for example, that the evidence is part of a professional confidence (which privilege is confined to legal advisers), or, secondly, that the evidence relates to title deeds or a lien, or, thirdly, that the evidence formed part of the matrimonial confidence, (although this privilege now exists only in criminal proceedings).[16]

(c)   The position of journalists protecting their sources of information

(i) The common law position   Common law recognises no general[17] privilege protecting journalists from disclosing their sources of information. This was established by *A-G v Clough*[18] and *A-G v Mulholland and Foster*.[19] Both cases arose because certain journalists refused to reveal to the Vassall Tribunal under the chairmanship of Viscount Radcliffe (which was set up under the Tribunals of Inquiry (Evidence) Act 1921)[20] the sources of certain publications which the tribunal held to be pertinent to the scope of their inquiry. As Lord Denning MR put it:[1]

> 'The journalist puts forward as his justification the pursuit of truth. It is in the public interest, he says, that he should obtain information in confidence and publish it to the world at large, for by so doing he brings to the public notice that

---

13   Eg *R v Boyes*, ibid.
14   See eg Children Act 1989, s 98, Companies Act 1985, s 434 and Representation of the People Act 1983, s 141. See further *Phipson's Evidence* (14th edn, 1990).
15   See generally *Phipson's Evidence*, para 20-11; cf *Halsbury's Laws* (4th edn) para 235 ff. Note that in children cases it is established that the court can overrule professional privilege, see *Oxfordshire County Council v M* [1994] Fam 151, [1994] 2 All ER 269, CA.
16   The privilege was abolished in civil proceedings by the Civil Evidence Act 1968, s 16(3).
17   Cf the so-called 'newspaper rule' that in libel actions against newspapers interrogatories directed to discovering the source of information are not permitted: see eg *Adam v Fisher* (1914) 110 LT 537 and the discussion eg by Viscount Dilhorne in *British Steel Corpn v Granada Television Ltd* [1981] AC 1096 at 1178–9. RSC Ord 82, r 6 now provides for a general application of the above rule. Cf, in New Zealand, *Broadcasting Corporation of New Zealand v Alex Harvey Industries Ltd* [1980] 1 NZLR 163 (NZ CA).
18   [1963] 1 QB 773, [1963] 1 All ER 420. A similar position obtains in Australia, see *McGuinness v A-G of Victoria* (1940) 63 CLR 73, and in Scotland, see *HM Advocate v Airs* 1975 SLT 177. The position in the US is considered at p 57.
19   [1963] 2 QB 477.
20   Cmnd 2009.
 1   In *A-G v Mulholland and Foster* [1963] 2 QB 477 at 489.

which they should know. He can expose wrongdoing and neglect of duty which would otherwise go unremedied. He cannot get this information, he says, unless he keeps the source secret. The mouths of his informants will be closed to him if it is known that their identity will be disclosed. So he claims to be entitled to publish all his information without ever being under any obligation, even when directed by the court or a judge, to disclose whence he got it.'

However, after reviewing the authorities,[2] the Court of Appeal emphatically denied the existence of such a privilege. Lord Denning MR concluded:[3]

'It seems to me, therefore, that the authorities are all one way. There is no privilege known to the law by which a journalist can refuse to answer a question which is relevant to the inquiry and is one which, in the opinion of the judge, it is proper for him to be asked.'

That journalists have no privilege was again affirmed by the Court of Appeal in *Senior v Holdsworth, ex p Independent Television News*,[4] where it was held that cameramen were in no different a position with regard to untransmitted film than any other journalist, and confirmed by the House of Lords in *British Steel Corpn v Granada Television Ltd*[5] in which British Steel sought from Granada disclosure of names of those who supplied them with confidential documents.

This lack of privilege is counterbalanced by a discretion vested in the courts not to insist on disclosure. As Lord Denning MR put it in *A-G v Mulholland and Foster*[6] professional confidences would be respected and a question would not be required to be answered: 'unless not only is it relevant but also it is a proper and, indeed, necessary question in the course of justice to be put and answered'. In the same case, however, Donovan LJ[7] rather than use the term 'necessary' preferred to say that the question 'ought to be one the answer to which will serve a useful purpose in relation to the proceedings in hand'. That rather less generous standpoint from journalists' point of view might be taken to have been supported by Scarman LJ in *Senior v Holdsworth, ex p Independent Television News*[8] when he said that Donovan LJ's 'gloss' on Lord Denning MR's test represented the limit of the court's discretion not to direct questions to be answered. At any rate, he was not prepared to go as far as some American cases[9] and hold that a question must be answered only if it goes 'to the heart of the party's case'. Subsequently, however, the majority of the Law Lords in *British Steel*[10] held that there was no immunity protecting journalists from disclosing sources of information provided such disclosure was 'necessary in the interests of justice'.

---

2   Particularly the Australian High Court decision *McGuinness v A-G of Victoria* (1940) 63 CLR 73.
3   In *A-G v Mulholland and Foster* [1963] 2 QB 477 at 491.
4   [1976] QB 23, [1975] 2 All ER 1009. See also the case of Bernard Faulk, a BBC employee refusing to reveal the identity of an IRA member (1971) Times, 28 April.
5   [1981] AC 1096 at 1170–1 (Lord Wilberforce), 1178–82 (Viscount Dilhorne), 1196 (Lord Fraser) but cf the powerful dissenting judgment of Lord Salmon. Despite winning their case British Steel did not in the end insist on disclosure but if they had and Granada had persisted in their refusal, their refusal would have constituted *civil* contempt.
6   [1963] 2 QB 477 at 489.
7   Ibid at 492.
8   [1976] QB 23 at 42.
9   Eg *Baker v F and F Investment* 470 F 2d 778 (1972). For further discussion see below.
10 [1981] AC 1096, ie Lords Wilberforce (at 1169), Dilhorne (at 1179) and Russell (at 1203). Cf Lord Fraser (at 1196) who expressly referred to the 'useful' test, as per Donovan LJ in *Mulholland*.

In the subsequent decision, *A-G v Lundin,* [11] applying the test that the respondent could be in contempt of court if the question put was relevant and necessary, the Court of Appeal held that a journalist who refused to reveal who had given him a copy of a particular document did not commit a contempt because as Watkins LJ said:

> 'although the question put to the defendant was a relevant one, in the end the revealing of his source could not possibly be regarded as serving a useful purpose for in the circumstances it would have been rendered useless by the absence of much other related and essential evidence. *That which was useless could not conceivably be said to be necessary'.* (Emphasis added)

In summary therefore the common law position is that journalists have no special privilege to protect their sources of information in the sense that they are obliged on pain of contempt to answer questions or to disclose documents properly asked or sought by the court. On the other hand judges have a discretion not to make such orders and should not do so unless, in broad terms,[12] the information sought is necessary in the interests of justice.

(ii) Section 10 of the Contempt of Court Act 1981[13]   Introduced on the initiative of Lord Scarman, s 10 of the Contempt of Court Act 1981 provides:

> 'No court may require a person to disclose, nor is any person guilty of contempt of court for refusing to disclose, the source of information contained in a publication for which he is responsible, unless it be established to the satisfaction of the court that disclosure is necessary in the interests of justice or national security or for the prevention of disorder or crime.'

Although Lord Scarman initially considered[14] that the provision did no more than put on an authoritative statutory footing the judicial practice of generally avoiding asking journalists to reveal their sources of information unless it was absolutely necessary, in fact the section has generated considerable case law. Insofar as it governs the issue of whether a journalist *ought* to be asked to reveal his source of information s 10 is to be regarded as having superseded the common law.[15] However, as Lord Oliver put it in *X Ltd v Morgan-Grampian Ltd,*[16] the common law position, that no witness has any absolute privilege against answering a relevant question solely on the ground that the answer may involve disclosure of confidential source, applies once the hurdle of s 10 has been overcome and the source of information is properly sought. Any journalist refusing to comply will be in contempt of court. Put in a different way as Lord

11 (1982) 75 Cr App Rep 90, [1982] Crim LR 296. This prosecution was brought before the Contempt of Court Act 1981 came into force but was heard afterwards. As Miller points out in *Contempt of Court* (2nd edn, 1989) at p 121, this decision lends some support for saying that it is no contempt to refuse to obey an order if improperly made. Cf, the discussion at pp 555–556.

12 Cf Lord Bridge in *X Ltd v Morgan-Grampian Ltd* [1991] 1 AC 1, 40 who commented 'How far and in what circumstances the maintenance of this public interest operated to confer on journalists any privilege from disclosure of their sources which the common law would recognise admitted of no short and simple answer on the authorities'.

13 See generally S Palmer: 'Protecting Journalists Sources: Section 10, Contempt of Court Act 1981' [1992] P L 61, Y Cripps: 'Judicial Proceedings and Refusals to Disclose the Identity of Sources of Information' (1984) 43 CLJ 266 and Robertson and Nicol: *Media Law* (3rd edn, 1992) p 198 ff.

14 417 HL Official Report (5th series) 157.

15 See Lord Bridge in *X Ltd v Morgan-Grampian Ltd* [1991] 1 AC 1, 40 who considered in this context that no assistance is to be gained from the authorities preceding s 10.

16 Ibid at 52.

Diplock observed in *Secretary of State for Defence v Guardian Newspapers Ltd,*[17] s 10:

> 'confers no powers upon a court additional to those powers, whether discretionary or not, which already existed at common law or under rules of court, to order disclosure of sources of information, its effect is restrictive only.'

The ambit of s 10

Section 10 operates to restrict courts' power to compel disclosure of sources of information. 'Court' for this purpose is defined by s 19 to include 'any tribunal body exercising the judicial power of the State'. As we discuss in Chapter 12[18] the scope of this definition is by no means easy to state. However, suffice to say here that the definition undoubtedly includes all superior and the long established inferior courts (county courts, magistrates' courts,[19] courts-martial, coroners' courts and consistory courts) and, as has recently been established, mental health[20] and industrial tribunals.[1]

On occasion, however, s 10 might be applicable even where the body concerned clearly falls outside the definition of 'court' under s 19. For example, in *Re An Inquiry Under the Company (Insider Dealing) Act 1985,*[2] it was accepted that s 10 applied to an investigation by inspectors appointed under the Financial Services Act 1986 on the basis that it was imported into the general defence of 'reasonable excuse' provided for by s 178(2) of the 1986 Act.

On its face s 10 only operates to restrict the court from seeking disclosure of sources of information 'contained in a publication'. However, after initial doubts,[3] it has now been settled by the House of Lords in *X Ltd v Morgan-Grampian Ltd*[4] that it applies even where the information has not been contained in a publication provided at any rate the information has been communicated and received for such purposes. As Lord Bridge said:[5]

> 'The information having been communicated and received for the purposes of publication it is clearly right to treat it as subject to the rule which the section lays down, since the purpose underlying the statutory protection of sources of information is as much applicable before as after publication.'

This purposive interpretation is welcome for, as others have pointed out,[6] it avoids anomalies that would otherwise arise. As Lord Lowry observed in the *Morgan-Grampian* case:[7]

> 'I agree that the provision extends to protect from disclosure the source of information contained in an intended publication. This seems to be a necessary interpretation: otherwise a defendant would be worse off than if he had already

---

17 [1985] AC 339, 347.
18 See pp 488.
19 At any rate when experiencing a judicial as opposed to an administrative function, see p 491.
20 *Pickering v Liverpool Daily Post and Echo Newspapers Plc* [1991] 2 AC 370, [1991] 1 All ER 622, HL.
1 *Peach Grey & Co (a firm) v Sommers* [1995] 2 All ER 513.
2 [1988] AC 660, [1988] 1 All ER 203, HL.
3 See eg *Francome v Mirror Group Newspapers Ltd* [1984] 2 All ER 408, CA. The House of Lords in *Secretary of State for Defence v Guardian Newspapers Ltd* [1985] AC 339, clearly assumed s 10 only applied to publications.
4 [1991] 1 AC 1, HL.
5 Ibid at 40.
6 Miller, All ER Review 1990 at 51.
7 [1991] 1 AC 1 at 54–55.

published, with only such limited protection as the common law and a judge's exercise of discretion might afford.'

Insofar as s 10 is concerned with information contained in 'publications', it is to be noted that it is not necessarily confined to journalists or the news media generally but to everyone responsible for 'any speech, writing, broadcast, cable programme or other communication in whatever form, which is addressed to the public at large or any section of the public'.[8]

Of course the raison d'etre of s 10 is to protect journalists from having to reveal their sources but how certain must it be that the information sought would reveal the identity of the source before the defence comes into play? The leading case is *Secretary of State for Defence v Guardian Newspapers Ltd.* In the Court of Appeal[9] Slade LJ considered that s 10 could only be brought into play provided the publisher could positively show that disclosure of information would reveal the source's identity. However, this view was decisively rejected in the House of Lords. Lords Fraser and Bridge[10] thought that it was sufficient to show that the identity *may* be revealed. Lord Diplock[11] thought there had to be a 'reasonable chance' of the source being identified, while Lord Scarman[12] thought that the publisher must show that on the balance of probabilities his source would be identified, though if identification were the plaintiff's purpose in coming to court there would be little difficulty in inferring the probable result of the order.

Provided s 10 is triggered in the sense mentioned above then it is established that it applies equally to orders for discovery as well as to orders to answer questions in court,[13] and to orders to produce photographs as well as written documents.[14] It is also established that s 10 applies equally to interlocutory proceedings as well as to final hearings.[15] In general terms it applies regardless of the nature of the action[16] including, as the *Guardian* case importantly established,[17] actions based on proprietary rights. As Lord Roskill said,[18] the section provides four specific exceptions to the prohibition against ordering a publisher to reveal his sources and he could therefore:

'see no reason for adding to those four specific exceptions by cutting down the natural and unqualified meaning of the section's opening words.'

---

8 See ss 19 and 2(1) of the 1981 Act discussed at pp 110 ff.
9 [1984] Ch 156 at 170.
10 [1985] AC 339 at 356 and 372 respectively.
11 Ibid at 349.
12 Ibid at 363.
13 See *Secretary of State for Defence v Guardian Newspapers Ltd* [1985] AC 339 at 347 per Lord Diplock.
14 See *Handmade Films (Productions) Ltd v Express Newspapers plc* [1986] FSR 463, per Browne-Wilkinson V-C.
15 See the *Guardian* case [1985] AC 339 at 345, per Lord Diplock.
16 Aliter if Parliament itself provides otherwise. See, eg the Prevention of Terrorism (Temporary Provisions) Act 1989, Sch 7, para 4(5)(b) which provides:

'An order under paragraph 3 above . . . shall have effect notwithstanding any obligation as to secrecy or other restriction on the disclosure of information imposed by statute or otherwise.'

According to Miller, All ER Review 1993 at 95, this provision was the reason why s 10 of the 1981 Act was not pleaded in *DPP v Channel 4 Television Co Ltd* [1993] 2 All ER 517.
17 [1985] AC 339, in which the House of Lords unanimously rejected the assertion to the contrary by Donaldson MR and Slade LJ in the Court of Appeal.
18 Ibid at 368.

It will be seen from the foregoing discussion that s 10 has been given a wide ambit. This is reflective of a deliberate policy of the courts. As Griffiths LJ said in the *Guardian* case:[19]

> 'It is in the interests of us all that we should have a truly effective press and it seems to me that Parliament by enacting section 10 has clearly recognised the importance that attaches to the ability of the press to protect their sources . . . I can see no harm in giving a wide construction to the opening words of the section because by the latter part of the section the court is given ample powers to order the source to be revealed where in the circumstances of a particular case the wider public interest makes it necessary to do so.'

However, it is one thing to say that s 10 is prima facie applicable but quite another to decline to insist on disclosure on the basis of the section. It is to the application of s 10 that we now turn.

Applying the s 10 criteria

Once s 10 is deemed to be relevant then, as Lord Griffiths said in *Re An Inquiry Under The Companies Securities (Insider Dealing) Act 1985*:[20]

> 'a journalist is prima facie entitled to refuse to reveal his source and a court may make no order that has the effect of compelling him to do so unless the party seeking disclosure has established that it is necessary under one of the . . . four heads of public interest identified in the section.'

Alternatively, as Lord Diplock put it in the *Guardian* case, the establishment by the person seeking the order of one of the four exceptions is a condition precedent to a judge having any jurisdiction to order disclosure of sources of information.[1] Lord Diplock also made the point that the exceptions make no reference to public interest generally but it can be equally said that public interest per se neither justifies nor condemns a particular publication. If an exception cannot be proved then the court has no power to order the disclosure of the source, but if an exception can be proved then disclosure can be ordered[2] regardless of whether the publication is thought to be in the public interest.

'Necessity' The common requirement to the establishment of any of the exceptions is that disclosure must be shown to be 'necessary'. It is settled that 'necessary' means more than merely relevant or desirable, useful or expedient.[3] As Lord Griffiths said in *Re An Inquiry*[4] perhaps the best synonym is 'really needed'. Although it is settled that what is necessary in any particular case is a question of fact, as Lord Griffiths pointed out in *Re An Inquiry*,[5] necessity will take colour from its context and inevitably involves the exercise of judgment.

How that judgment will be exercised will inevitably be influenced by which of the exceptions it is sought to invoke. Case law seems to demonstrate that it

---

19 [1984] Ch 156 at 167 cited with approval inter alia by the House of Lords in the *Guardian* case, ibid, and by Lord Bridge in *X Ltd v Morgan-Grampian Ltd* [1991] 1 AC 1 at 41. Note also *Handmade Films (Productions) Ltd v Express Newspapers plc* [1986] FSR 463 at 470 per Browne-Wilkinson V-C.
20 [1988] AC 660 at 702.
1 [1985] AC 339 at 350.
2 But note that the establishment of an exception does not compel a court to order disclosure. See p 57.
3 See eg *Maxwell v Pressdram Ltd* [1987] 1 All ER 656, CA and *X v Y* [1988] 2 All ER 648.
4 [1988] AC 660 at 704.
5 Ibid. See also *X Ltd v Morgan-Grampian Ltd* [1991] 1 AC 1 at 41 per Lord Bridge.

might be harder to establish necessity with regard to the interests of justice exception than in relation to national security or the prevention of crime. However, regardless of which exception is in issue it seems clear that to establish necessity requires more than mere assertion and should ideally be as specific as possible in relation to the reasons why disclosure is sought.[6] Clearly relevant to the question of 'necessity' is how far, if at all, the person seeking the order has made any inquiries or attempts to discover the source.[7] However, it seems clear from the *Guardian* case[8] that s 10 is not to be interpreted as demanding evidence that there is no other available means of identifying the source or that all other possible means of obtaining such identification have been exhausted provided, at any rate, the court can be satisfied that there is an urgent need to discover who the source is.

The four exceptions

The courts have so far had occasion to consider three of the four exceptions. The only one not yet considered is the prevention of disorder. So far as national security is concerned, the leading and indeed first case to consider s 10 was *Secretary of State for Defence v Guardian Newspapers Ltd.*[9] In that case the plaintiff sought the return of a photocopy of a memorandum (dealing with the timing of the arrival in the United Kingdom of cruise missiles) prepared by the Secretary of State, individually marked copies of which had been sent to the Prime Minister's Office and certain other Departments. The copy in question had been sent by an employee of the plaintiff (subsequently identified as Sarah Tisdall) to the *Guardian* who published it. The Crown claimed that the fact that such a document marked 'secret' with a very restricted circulation concerning a matter of great significance in relation to defence had come into possession of a national newspaper was of the greatest importance to the continued maintenance of national security. The majority were prepared to accept that this evidence was sufficient to establish that disclosure was necessary in the interests of national security. The minority, however, were not convinced. Lord Fraser in particular stressed the strictness of the 'necessity' requirement commenting that there may have been other means of identifying the source and 'unless special urgency is proved, the requirements of section 10 are not . . . met merely by showing the easiest way of identifying the person is by calling on the publisher of the information to disclose it.' Since 12 days had elapsed between publication and the demand for the document's return, Lord Fraser did not think there could have been 'special urgency'. Both he and Lord Scarman thought it essential to have information about the class of persons having access to the documents and whether such documents were processed in the same system as sensitive defence documents or were processed with parliamentary or other political material. In contrast the majority were prepared to infer necessity from the evidence, their attitude neatly being summarised by Lord Bridge when he said:[10]

'The role of the [court] . . . was not that of a school mistress to scold the Crown for the poor quality of its evidence as if it were a piece of homework required to

6 See the *Guardian* case [1985] AC 339 at 346 (Lord Diplock), 360 (Lord Fraser), 364 (Lord Scarman), 368 (Lord Roskill) and 372 (Lord Bridge).
7 See eg *Broadmoor Hospital v Hyde* (1994) Independent, 4 March.
8 [1985] AC 339. See in particular Lords Roskill at 370 and Bridge at 373.
9 Ibid, commented upon by Lowe and Willmore: (1985) 48 MLR 592. See also Robertson and Nicol, *Media Law* (3rd edn, 1992) p 202.
10 [1985] AC 339 at 374.

be done over again. A potential threat to national security was clearly revealed and, assuming that the gravity of the threat could be weighed at all, it was certainly not to be weighed by the scruple. Any threat to national security ought to be eliminated by the most effective and speediest means possible.'

Nevertheless even the majority clearly signalled that the Crown's evidence fell short of what was ideal and that in future applicants would be expected to offer convincing evidence to prove their case.

The 'prevention of crime' exception was explored in *Re An Inquiry Under the Company Securities (Insider Dealing) Act 1985*.[11] In that case, a financial journalist, Jeremy Warner, published two articles in national newspapers which seemed to be based on leaked information about insider dealing. The House of Lords held that the case fell within the prevention of crime exception. They rejected Hoffmann J's first instance view that to establish this exception it had to be shown that in the absence of disclosure further crimes are likely to be committed. Instead it was held that the section imported a wider construction, stress being laid on the fact that the provision refers to the 'prevention of crime' rather than of a crime or even crimes. It was accordingly held sufficient if disclosure would enable prosecution of an offence already committed or could assist in the prevention of crime in the future. In this case the court was satisfied that it was of real importance that the inspectors should know the source for the purpose of their inquiry the aim of which was the prevention of crime. Warner was subsequently fined £20,000 for his continued refusal to reveal his source.

In contrast is *X v Y*,[12] in which, based on information supplied by one or more health authority employees, newspaper articles were written suggesting that there were doctors in Britain who were continuing to practise despite having contracted AIDS and that the (then) Department of Health and Social Security wished to suppress that fact. It was held that the plaintiffs (a health authority) had failed to establish their case for disclosure under s 10. In Rose J's view the plaintiffs failed to prove that disclosure was necessary for the prevention of crime since such prevention was not the plaintiffs' task and a criminal investigation would not be the likely consequence if the source were disclosed.

The most open ended of the exceptions is that of the interests of justice which Lord Hailsham[13] dubbed a 'mish mash of muddled thinking'. At one time, however, it seemed as though that it had an extremely limited application, for in the *Guardian* case Lord Diplock commented,[14] obiter, that:

'the expression "justice", the interests of which are entitled to protection, is not used in a general sense as the antonym of "injustice" but in the technical sense of the administration of justice in a court of law . . .'

However, this interpretation, insofar as it confined the proviso's application to court proceedings was rejected in the subsequent House of Lords' decision, *X Ltd v Morgan-Grampian Ltd*.[15] In Lord Bridge's view the proviso should enable persons: 'to exercise important legal rights and to protect themselves from serious legal wrongs whether or not resort to legal proceedings in a court of law

---

11 [1988] AC 660, noted by Ferran [1988] CLJ 160.
12 [1988] 2 All ER 648.
13 417 HL Official Report (5th Series) col 162. This exception was not included in the provision originally proposed by Lord Scarman, see 416 HL Official Report (5th series) col 210.
14 [1985] AC 339 at 350.
15 [1991] 1 AC 1, noted by Cram, (1992) 55 MLR 400 and Miller, All ER Review 1990, 50. See also Robertson and Nicol, *Media Law* (3rd edn, 1992) p 201.

will be necessary to attain these objectives.'[16] He instanced, by way of an example, an employer who is suffering grave damage from the activities of an unidentified disloyal servant in which case 'it is undoubtedly in the interests of justice that he should be able to identify him in order to terminate his employment, notwithstanding that no legal proceedings may be necessary to achieve this end'.

In the *Morgan-Grampian* case, a confidential document concerning the financial affairs of two private companies was wrongfully removed from their premises and disclosed to a journalist, William Goodwin. The companies inter alia sought disclosure of Goodwin's notes. It was held that disclosure should be ordered under the interests of justice proviso. In reaching this decision the Law Lords, contrary to their earlier decision, laid some stress on the balancing exercise that must be undertaken.[17] As Lord Bridge said:[18]

> 'In estimating the weight to be attached to the importance of disclosure in the interests of justice on the one hand and that of protection from disclosure in pursuance of the policy which underlies section 10 on the other hand, many factors will be relevant on both sides of the scale.'

Lord Bridge offered limited guidance on what factors may be significant, in favour of ordering disclosure, namely: where it is shown that the livelihood of the party who seeks disclosure is dependent upon disclosure; and where the information was obtained illegally. Factors leaning against disclosure include the source obtaining the material legitimately and where there is great public interest in the information published. Inevitably, however, the various factors can counterbalance one another. Lord Bridge said:

> 'If it appears that the information was obtained legitimately this will enhance the importance of protecting the source. Conversely, if it appears that the information was obtained illegally, this will diminish the importance of protecting the source unless, of course, this factor is counterbalanced by a clear public interest in publication of the information, as is the classic case where the source has acted for the purpose of exposing iniquity.'

Applying these factors in this case, namely the importance to the plaintiffs of obtaining disclosure to counter the threat of severe damage to their business and consequently to their employees' livelihood coupled with the gross breach of confidentiality in obtaining the material, it was held that disclosure should be ordered. For his continued refusal to comply Goodwin was subsequently fined £5,000.[19] However, notwithstanding Lord Templeman's belief[20] that the decision complied with Article 10 of the European Convention on Human Rights, the European Commission of Human Rights[1] considered that the order contravened that provision. The decision of the European Court is therefore awaited with some interest. Notably, since *Morgan-Grampian* there has been no reported example of the interests of justice proviso being successfully argued.[2]

---

16 [1991] 1 AC 1 at 43. See also Lord Oliver at 54.
17 Cram at (1992) 55 MLR 400 at 402 maintains that this construction harps back to the common law and that no authority exists to support its application to s 10.
18 [1991] 1 AC 1 at 44. See also Lord Oliver at 53.
19 (1990) Times, 11 April.
20 [1991] 1 AC 1 at 49.
 1 See (1995) 145 NLJ 720.
 2 The application failed in *Handmade Films (Productions) Ltd v Express Newspapers plc* [1986] FSR 463, *Maxwell v Pressdram Ltd* [1987] 1 All ER 656, CA and *Broadmoor Hospital v Hyde* (1994) *Independent*, 4 March.

The position where an exception is established

Although disclosure will normally be ordered where a proviso can be established, there is nevertheless a residual discretion not to make the order. This was made clear by Lord Griffiths in *Re An Inquiry*[3] where he pointed out that s 10 does not make it mandatory to order disclosure in any event. As he said:

> 'I can conceive of extreme cases in which the judge might properly refuse to do so if, for instance, the crime was of a trivial nature or, at the other end of the scale, the journalist's life might be imperilled if he revealed his source.'

However, Lord Bridge said in *Morgan-Grampian*[4] that if non-disclosure would imperil national security or enable a crime to be committed which might otherwise be prevented, then it is difficult to imagine that any judge would hesitate to order disclosure.

Once an order is made then, as Lord Oliver said in *Morgan-Grampian*,[5] the journalist is in no different position to any other witness and is, on pain of contempt, bound to comply, save possibly where he can raise the defence of duress.[6]

A comparative view[7]

Interestingly, English law is not out of line with other common law jurisdictions. A similar standpoint is taken at common law both in Australia[8] and New Zealand[9] and even in America the 'freedom of the press' provision of the First Amendment to the Federal Constitution has been held not to give journalists an absolute immunity under common law from revealing sources of information at least in connection with grand jury proceedings.[10] In general[11] a court will need to be convinced that there is an overriding public or national interest requiring a journalist to reveal his confidential information, and even then the information may have to be 'necessary' in the sense of going to the heart of the case.[12] It may be that in civil cases, at least where the 'news gatherer' is a non-party, the first amendment will more likely be held to confer a privilege and in any event the court will consider various factors such as whether the information sought to be disclosed could be obtained from other sources which have not been exhausted or whether the information is relevant or material or necessary (in the sense of

---

3   [1988] AC 660 at 703.
4   [1991] 1 AC 1 at 43.
5   Ibid at 52.
6   As established by *R v K* (1983) 78 Cr App Rep 82, discussed at p 46.
7   See Palmer, 'Protecting Journalists' Sources' [1992] PL 61.
8   See *McGuinness v A-G of Victoria* (1940) 63 CLR 73, and *Independent Commission Against Corruption v Cornwall* (1993) 116 ALR 97.
9   See the discussion by Palmer, [1992] PL 61 at 63 and Burrows, *News Media Law in New Zealand* (1991) p 397.
10   *Branzburg v Hayes* 408 US 665 (1972).
11   The authorities are collected in 99 ALR (3d) 37 and 81 Am Jur (2d) S 297. See also Mark Neubauer, 'The Newsman's Privilege After Branzburg–The Case For A Federal Shield Law' (1976–7) 24 UCLA Review 160, and 'Developments: Privileged Communications' (1985) 98 Harv LR 1450, 1600–1609.
12   See eg *Garland v Torre* 1958 CA 2 NY 259 F (2d) 545, *Baker v Fand F Investment* 470 F (2d) 778 (1972) and *Democratic National Committee v McCord* 1973 356 F Supp 1394. For a short account of these and other cases see Altes: 'The Journalistic Privilege: A Dutch Proposal For Legislation' [1992] PL 73, 79–82 and Miller, *Contempt of Court* (2nd edn, 1989) at 126–128.

'going to the heart of the claim') before demanding disclosure.[13] In short, in civil cases disclosure is certainly not ordered as a matter of course, and indeed the general position is probably more generous than under English law. Moreover a number of states have enacted 'Shield Laws' under which it is sought to protect journalists from having to reveal their sources in any proceedings.[14]

How satisfactory is the position under s 10? At the time of its implementation it was not expected to make a significant impact on court practice[15] at any rate in England and Wales.[16] However, as Lord Scarman pointed out in the *Guardian* case,[17] before its enactment, whether or not to put a question or to seek a document that might threaten the confidentiality of the journalist's source, was a matter of judicial discretion, whereas under s 10 it is a rule of law subject only to specifically stated exceptions that must be established to the satisfaction of the court. Although Lord Scarman considered this change to be 'of profound significance', so far, at any rate, there is little evidence to suggest that cases are being decided differently under s 10 than they would have been under the common law. Nevertheless it may be observed that in favour of the media s 10 has been held to apply equally to information contained in or about to be contained in publications and, importantly, to applications based on proprietorial claims. On the other hand, so far as the individual exceptions are concerned, the House of Lords have rejected the narrow interpretation both of the prevention of crime proviso, namely, that it is confined to the prevention of a particular crime, and of the interests of justice proviso, that it is restricted to the interests of justice in particular legal proceedings.[18] However, it is submitted that neither of the wider interpretations, namely, that the prevention of crime refers to crime generally and that the interests of justice proviso can apply outside the context of legal proceedings, does violence to the intention of Parliament. The main concern, however, is the apparent readiness of the courts to infer necessity from the facts presented. It is noticeable that in two of three House of Lords decisions,[19] disclosure was ordered notwithstanding that the evidence was not thought to be as well presented as it might (and some would say, should) have been.

Does s 10 therefore strike the right balance? It is submitted that important though it is to respect journalists' confidential sources, it is nevertheless right not to accord a complete privilege. There is no evidence that the courts readily demand that journalists reveal their sources (indeed s 10 is a statutory reminder that judges should not) and it seems right that sources should be revealed where national security is at stake or the prevention of crime or disorder is involved, both of which exceptions are taken from Article 10 of the European Convention on Human Rights. There may be more room for argument about whether it is right to include the interests of justice proviso,[20] and if so, what its ambit should be.

One issue that *Morgan-Grampian* brings into sharp relief is the responsibility for a refusal to comply. In that case Goodwin was only a trainee journalist and

13 See Neubauer, (1976–77) 24 UCLA Review 160 at 179.
14 For an account of the legality of Shield Laws see 99 ALR (3d) 37, para 2(a).
15 This was the view expressed in the second edition of this work at pp 45–47.
16 Aliter in Scotland, see the discussion on the impact of s 10 on *HM Advocate v Airs* 1975 SLT 177 in the second edition of this work at p 46.
17 [1985] AC 339, 361.
18 In *Re An Inquiry Under the Companies Securities (Insider Trading) Act 1985* [1988] AC 660 and *X Ltd v Morgan-Grampian Ltd* [1991] 1 AC 1, respectively.
19 The *Guardian* case [1985] AC 339 and *Morgan-Grampian* [1991] 1 AC 1.
20 This exception was not included in the provision originally proposed by Lord Scarman, see 416 HL Official Report (5th series) col 210. For their scathing comments about this exception see Robertson and Nicol, *Media Law* (3rd edn, 1992) p 199.

is now working freelance and so had to bear the responsibility personally for his continued refusal. But given that a newspaper or broadcasting agency normally takes the 'benefit' of the publication, should not a more responsible person (eg the editor or producer) take the burden of any contempt proceedings? Section 10 admittedly refers to a person 'responsible' for the publication, which would clearly cover an editor etc, but if that person does not know of the identity of the source, it is difficult to see how, under current law, he could be held guilty of contempt.

(d) Prevaricating

The deliberate evasion of a question is no less contempt than an outright refusal to answer. In either case the course of justice is being obstructed. On the other hand, as the Australian High Court said in *Coward v Stapleton*,[1] a witness can only rarely be properly convicted of contempt for refusing to answer a question which he has purported to answer. The court continued:

'It is essential not to lose sight of the sharp distinction that exists between a false answer and no answer at all. Of course a purported answer may be so palpably false as to indicate that the witness is merely fobbing off the question. His attitude in the box may show that he is simply trifling with the court and is making no serious attempt to give an answer that is worth calling an answer. In such cases it may well be right to say that the witness refuses to answer the question, but it cannot be too clearly recognised that the remedy for giving answers which are false is normally a prosecution for perjury or false swearing, and not a summary committal for contempt. Such a committal can be justified only by a specific finding of an evinced intention to leave a question or questions unanswered, or by a finding of contempt in some other defined respect.'

In the subsequent Australian High Court decision, *Keeley v Brooking*,[2] it was argued that not only did a judge have to be satisfied beyond all reasonable doubt that a witness was deliberately evading answering the question (ie that he was lying when he said that he could not remember) but also that the witness's allegedly false answers were in their nature absurdly and palpably false and would appear so to any objective bystander. This assertion was rejected. As Barwick CJ[3] said, it is difficult to see how the additional criteria could be used, adding:

'Adherence to the well-understood standard of proof in the trial of criminal charges is quite adequate to protect individuals charged summarily with contempt. To be satisfied beyond all reasonable doubt is, for the purposes of the law, to be certain.'

In deciding whether a witness's answer is so false as to amount to no answer at all, a third Australian case, *Thelander v Woodward and A-G (NSW)*,[4] held that

1 (1953) 90 CLR 573 at 578. Cf *Cotroni v Quebec Police Commission and Brunet* (1978) 80 DLR (3d) 490 (Can Sup Ct) (witness's answers were deliberately obscure, often ambiguous or simply unintelligible and amounting to a barely concealed refusal to testify). Conviction quashed because charges were not specific enough. Cf *Childs v McLeod* 1981 SLT (Notes) 27 (no evidence that witness had feigned her lack of recollection).
2 (1979) 53 ALJR 526. Reliance was also placed on American cases eg *US v Appel* 1913 211 F, 495; *Richardson v US* 1919 249 US 378; *Re Meekly* 1943 50 F Supp 274; *Gaylon v Stutts* 1954 84 SE (2d) 822; and *Collins v US* 1959 269 F (2d) 785. *Keeley v Brooking* was subsequently applied in *McGoldrick v Citicorp Finance Pty Ltd* [1990] VR 494.
3 (1979) 53 ALJR 526 at 527.
4 [1981] 1 NSWLR 644 (NSW CA).

the court can only consider what it saw and heard whilst the witness was in the witness box. In so holding the court followed Learned Hand J's comment in *US v Appel*:[5]

> 'If a court is to have any power at all to compel an answer, it must surely have power to compel an answer which is not given to fob off inquiry. Nevertheless, this power must not be used to punish perjury, and the only proper test is whether on its mere face, and without inquiry collaterally, the testimony is not a bona fide effort to answer the questions at all.'

It will be noted that both Learned Hand J and the court in *Coward* state that mere perjury should not be prosecuted as contempt. There are good policy reasons for this position since a contempt prosecution deprives offenders of many of the safeguards accorded them in perjury proceedings. The difficulty lies in distinguishing false testimony only amounting to perjury from that amounting to contempt. It is clear that the mere falsity of evidence is not enough to justify a contempt charge and that some additional element is necessary. That additional element must be related to the interference with justice since all contempts are in some respect an obstruction of justice.[6] Although it could be argued that any false testimony involves to some extent an obstruction of justice and could therefore be treated as contempt, the law does not go that far.[7] Indeed, there is some authority for the view that it is only false testimony amounting to no answer at all that can be prosecuted as a contempt. This is possibly what the court had in mind in *Coward* and what Mason and Aickin JJ contemplated in *Keeley v Brooking*.[8] A possible justification for this position is the line taken in the American case, *Re Michael*,[9] that deliberate falsehoods do not obstruct the administration of justice to the same extent as refusals to answer questions. As Mason and Aickin JJ said:[10] 'Refusals to answer questions deny to the court evidence which is required for the purposes of the judicial process.' Presumably false answers provide testimony which the court can evaluate.

As a matter of policy the above distinction might serve to limit contempt prosecutions[11] though it is doubtful whether the argument could be sustained on a point of principle. The more logical distinction (though one which is difficult to apply) is that stated by Barwick CJ in *Keeley v Brooking*:[12]

> 'If it could be concluded beyond all reasonable doubt that the false swearing was with the actual or inevitable intent or consequence of frustrating or obstructing the proceedings, the party or witness could be dealt with for contempt of the tribunal. But that intent or inevitable consequence would differentiate what I might call mere perjury from contempt. The contempt would lie in the obstruction or frustration of the proceedings actually intended or necessarily consequential.'

---

5   1913 211 F 495 at 496.
6   For a similar comment on American law see 89 ALR (2d) 1258.
7   Hence the statement in *Coward v Stapleton* (1953) 90 CLR 573 at 578 that mere disbelief in the truth of answer is insufficient for a contempt prosecution.
8   (1979) 53 ALJR 526 at 531. In both *Coward* and *Keeley* the courts were specifically concerned with purported non-answers rather than when in general false testimony can be properly prosecuted as a contempt.
9   1945 326 US 223 cited with approval by Mason and Aickin JJ in *Keeley* (1979) 53 ALJR 526 at 531.
10 In *Keeley v Brooking* (1979) 53 ALJR 526 at 531.
11 This seems to be Miller's position (*Contempt of Court* (2nd edn, 1989) at 118, 119) and possibly that in America but cf 89 ALR (2d) 1258.
12 (1979) 53 ALJR 526 at 528. See also *McGoldrick v Citicorp Finance Pty Ltd* [1990] VR 494.

(e)   Repeated lateness

It can be a contempt for a witness to be repeatedly late in attending court.[13]

(f)   Remaining in court

Witnesses remaining in court after an order has been given that he or all the witnesses are to leave the court room can be punished for contempt though a party is still entitled to rely on the evidence.[14]

C   Jurors

A duly summoned juror's absence from the relevant proceedings or his unfitness for service is punishable at common law as contempt. As with advocates' absence it is a nice point whether a juror's absence is properly classifiable as a contempt in the face of the court. In many jurisdictions the above two offences are governed by statute. In England and Wales, the Juries Act 1974 provides both a uniform procedure for the summoning of jurors to the High Court, Crown Court and the county court and a common set of penalties for non-attendance or unfitness.

The Juries Act 1974, s 20[15] provides:

'(1)   Subject to the provisions of subsections (2) to (4)[16] below
    (a)   if a person duly summoned under this Part of this Act fails to attend (on the first or any subsequent day on which he is required to attend by the summons or by the appropriate officer) in compliance with the summons, or
    (b)   if a person, after attending in pursuance of a summons, is not available when called on to serve as a juror, or is unfit for service by reason of drink or drugs, he shall be liable to a fine not exceeding level 3 on the standard scale.[17]

(2)   An offence under subsection (1) above shall be punishable either on summary conviction or as if it were criminal contempt of court committed in the face of the court.'

It should be noted that s 20(2) provides alternative methods of punishing the offender, by either trying the case as a contempt in the face of the court, ie by immediate punishment, or by allowing the case to be tried by a magistrates' court. This latter course may well prove to be the more convenient procedure, since it would relieve the higher court of unnecessary delay in trying the principal case.

Coroners are empowered under the Coroners Act 1988, s 10,[18] to punish a

---

13   See *R v Carter and Nailor* (1994) 16 Cr App Rep (S) 434.
14   *Skelton v Castle* (1837) 6 JP 154 n; *Chandler v Horne* (1842) 2 Mood & R 423 sub nom *Roberts v Garratt* (1842) 6 JP 154.
15   As amended by the Criminal Justice Act 1988, s 170(1) and Sch 15.
16   S 20(3) states that a summons must (apart from when issued under s 6) be duly served not later than 14 days before the date of the proceedings. S 20(4) provides for a defence for reasonable cause for failure. In a case reported in the (1982) *Daily Mail*, 13 May a juror was fined £75 when on the day of the trial he telephoned the court to say that he could not attend as he was appearing as the accused at another trial!
17   Currently £1,000.
18   As amended by the Criminal Justice Act 1991, s 17(1) and Sch 4, Pt 1. For the collection and enforcement of the fine see the Criminal Justice Act 1988, s 67.

person who, having been duly summoned, refuses without reasonable excuse to serve as a juror, by fining him a sum not exceeding £1,000.

Presumably, jurors remain under a duty to attend proceedings until discharged by the judge but it is perhaps a moot point whether a judge is empowered to order a jury's attendance after their finding of not guilty to listen to the sentencing of a co-defendant who had pleaded guilty.[19]

Jurors can commit contempt in other ways. In *R v Rhoder* [20] a juryman was seized with sickness and rushed out of the court before he could be stopped. For this he was fined £20, since he had left the court without permission. Although this particular case may seem harsh, it is important to remember that the correct conduct of a jury is of paramount importance to the validity of a trial. It is an obvious contempt, for instance, for a juror to discuss a case with members of the public before the verdict is given,[1] and it is therefore important that a juror should not leave the court without permission. Indeed, as a general rule, jurors should not separate from their fellow jurors during the hearing.

Jurors should be careful in arriving at their verdict. It has been held to be a contempt for a jury to 'toss up' to arrive at a verdict (they 'hustled halfpence in a hat').[2]

Jurors can also commit contempt by misbehaving in court. A man was fined £50 for wearing a horror mask as he was about to be sworn in on a jury.[3] In another case a juror was fined for contempt for being rude when he exclaimed, as he was about to be sworn: 'I want to know what the devil I'm brought here for'.[4]

It is also a contempt to impersonate a juror.[5] Deliberate impersonation is a serious contempt likely to be punished by imprisonment but where a case arises from ignorance or genuine misunderstanding as in *R v Levy* the punishment will be less harsh, for example, paying costs.

D   Parties

Parties, like anyone else, may be held guilty of contempt for their misbehaviour in court. Such misconduct commonly occurs at the end of their case particularly in the face of an adverse decision. At this stage the potential interference with the administration of justice, at least in the particular case, is minimal and, especially where the outburst is spontaneous, judges should be, and usually are, tolerant and

---

19 Judge King-Hamilton QC made such an order in the so-called 'Bayswater Anarchist' trial, see (1979) Times, 20 December.

20 (1894) Times, 12 February.

 1 Cited with approval by the Quebec Supreme Court in *R v Papineau* (1980) 58 CCC (2d) 72. See also *R v Macrae* (1892) Times, 19 November, the juror being fined £50. For the disclosure or publication of a jury's deliberations see the Contempt of Court Act 1981, s 8 discussed at pp 366 ff, and at common law *A-G v New Statesman and Nation Publishing Co Ltd* [1981] QB 1, [1980] 1 All ER 644.

 2 *Langdell v Sutton* (1737) Barnes 32. Cf *R v Young* [1995] QB 324, [1995] 2 WLR 430 (the 'ouija board' case) discussed at p 370 and note also the impact of s 8 of the Contempt of Court Act 1981.

 3 Reported in the (1979) Daily Telegraph, 11 September (Croydon Crown Court). See also *Welcden v Elkington* (1578) 2 Plowd 516 at 518 A (juror fined 20s for having a box of preserved sweetmeats, sugar-candy and liquorice). Query whether that would be regarded as a contempt now? For other examples see Oswald, *Contempt of Court* (3rd edn, 1910) p 69 ff.

 4 *Anon* Law Gazette Vol 1 299. Cited by Oswald, op cit, p 70.

 5 *R v Levy* (1916) 32 TLR 238. See also *Norman v Beaumont* (1744) Barnes 453. Impersonation usually renders the trial void. See *R v Wakefield* [1918] 1 KB 216; cf *Anon* (1642) March NC 81 pl 132.

understanding. An amusing example is the case of Vera Bath Stone[6] who threw two volumes of *Butterworth's Workmen Compensation Cases* at Lord Denning MR after the dismissal of her application for leave to appeal against a tax decision. She was restrained as she reached for her third book and was escorted from the court (the woman offered her congratulations to Lord Denning for his 'coolness under fire') and no further action was taken. Even at this stage, however, there are limits to judicial tolerance and judges may properly punish a party for contempt on the grounds that the conduct is liable to lower the court's authority. Clearly, violence cannot be tolerated[7] and even verbal abuse may be punished.[8]

Defendants who deliberately set out at the beginning of their case to disrupt the trial (and there is depressing evidence of a growing number of these cases both in England and elsewhere[9]) pose a greater threat to the administration of justice both in their own case and more generally. Although such disruptive defendants can be removed from the courtroom and the trial proceed in their absence such behaviour can properly attract punishment for contempt. In *R v Aquarius*,[10] the Court of Appeal upheld a contempt conviction of an accused who set out to disrupt his trial by refusing to plead or exercise his right to challenge the jury, by challenging the right of the court to try him and by introducing irrelevancies and attacking witnesses. He had been removed from the court on eight occasions. The accused, who had been sentenced to six months' imprisonment for theft, was originally sentenced to nine months' consecutive for his contempt but on appeal this was reduced to three months' consecutive, it being held that bad and provocative though the conduct was it did not justify a greater sentence for contempt than for the substantive offence.

Defendants who refuse to plead will have a plea of not guilty entered on their behalf. The refusal to plead often arises from the defendant's unwillingness to recognise the authority of the court. However, in the South Australian case, *O'Hair v Wright*[11] it was held that an accused's bare reply, when asked how he pleaded, namely 'I refuse to recognise the authority of this court' did not amount to contempt since the words were not in themselves disrespectful[12] nor did they come into the category of scandalising the court.[13]

---

6 Reported in (1970) Times, 12 February.
7 See the case of *Crowley* (1973) Times, 2 March discussed at p 16; *Bryans v Faber and Faber* [1979] CA Transcript 316 discussed at p 33, and the case of Miss Rohrberg 1980, unreported, who was sentenced for three months for throwing a glass tumbler in the direction of the clerk to the judge in chambers.
8 See *R v Logan* [1974] Crim LR 609, CA, where a contempt conviction was upheld on an accused who on being sentenced for an assault made an outburst using expletives that his conviction had been a 'carve up'. Sentence was reduced to three months consecutive. Comments, made even when outside the court, may amount to contempt by 'scandalising the court', see pp 335 ff.
9 For a comprehensive catalogue of instances and an excellent analysis of the options open to the court when dealing with disruptive defendants see Zellick, 'The Criminal Trial and the Disruptive Defendant' (1980) 43 MLR 121 and 284.
10 (1974) 59 Cr App Rep 165, [1974] Crim LR 373. As Miller (*Contempt of Court* (2nd edn, 1989) at 107) states, the English cases are but a pale reflection of some of their American counterparts: see eg *Mayberry v Pennsylvania* 400 US 455 (1971); *US v Dellinger; US v Seale* 69 CR 180 (ND 111, February 14–15 1970) reversed on appeal 461 F (2d) 345 and 389. See also *Illinois v Allen* 90 S Ct 1057 (1970).
11 [1971] SASR 436 (SA Supreme Ct).
12 Ie within the wording of the relevant statute, namely, the Justices Acts 1921–69, s 46.
13 Discussed in Ch 9.

Parties have been found guilty of contempt for their rude and insolent behaviour[14] in attempting to leave the court without permission[15] and, in the Canadian case, *R v Perkins*,[16] for arriving at court being unfit to plead by reason of drink. A case not dissimilar to *Perkins* is *R v Harbax Singh* [17] where a defendant, whilst on bail, was so drunk as to be incapable of appearing on the opening day of his trial at the Central Criminal Court. The defendant conceded at a later hearing that by his conduct he was in breach of the Bail Act 1976, s 6 and the judge exercising his option under s 6(5) to punish the offence 'as if it were for criminal contempt', sentenced him to three months' imprisonment. The Court of Appeal upheld the conviction but reduced the sentence to one month.

E   Officers of the court

Officers of the court can commit contempt in the face of the court, for example by interrupting court proceedings,[18] or by being absent without leave.[19]

IV   MENS REA

Although it seems clear that to sustain at common law a prosecution for contempt in the face of the court it must be proved that the accused intended to do the act in question,[20] it is not yet settled whether it must also be proved that the accused intended to interfere with the course of justice.[1] In Canada, for example, where this issue has been extensively litigated, there are conflicting lines of cases.[2] In England there is some support[3] for the view that an intention to interfere with the

14 See eg *Dow v A-G* [1980] Qd R 58 and *Re Fellows, ex p Stewart* [1972] 2 NSWR 317.
15 *Boyle v Vivean* (1579) Cary 104 and *Re Fellows, ex p Stewart* [1972] 2 NSWR 317. See also what is believed to be the first case under the Contempt of Court Act 1981 where a man who had been fined for a motoring offence was kept in custody for three and a half hours for walking out of court before he was released (1981) Times, 17 September.
16 (1980) 4 WWR 763 (British Columbia CA).
17 [1979] QB 319, [1979] 1 All ER 524, CA. See also *R v Tyson* (1979) 68 Cr App Rep 314. For the procedure to be followed under s 6 of the Bail Act 1976 see *Schiavo v Anderton* [1987] QB 20, [1986] 3 All ER 10 and *Practice Direction (Bail: Failure to Surrender)* (1986) 84 Cr App Rep 37, discussed in Archbold: *Criminal Pleading, Evidence and Practice* (1995) para 3-30 ff. Note also *Murphy v Director of Public Prosecutions* [1990] 2 All ER 390, [1990] 1 WLR 601 (no time limit for laying information before magistrates).
18 *Re Sheriff of Surrey* (1860) 2 F & F 234.
19 *R v Tichborne* (1892) Times, 7 December.
20 It would be a defence, for example, that the accused acted under duress, see *R v K* (1983) 78 Cr App Rep 82, discussed at p 46.
1   As the Irish Law Reform Commission in their Consultation Paper on Contempt of Court (1991) p 11, neatly put it: the 'authorities dealing with the question of mens rea in respect of in facie contempt are relatively few in number and unconvincing in their analysis'. See also the Australian Law Reform Commission's *Improper Behaviour in Court* (Research Paper No 2) para 23.
2   See eg *R v Perkins* (1980) 4 WWR 763 and *R v Hill* (1976) 73 DLR (3d) 621 (no mens rea required). Cf *R v Glasner* (1995) 119 DLR (4th) 113 (per Brooke and Laskin JJA, Labrosse JA, dissenting); *R v Fox* (1976) 70 DLR (3d) 577; *R v Jones* (1978) 42 CCC (2d) 192; *R v Swartz* (1977) 34 CCC (2d) 477. See also *R v Barker* (1980) 4 WWR 202 (mens rea required on the facts) and *R v Anders* (1982) 136 DLR (3d) 316.
3   *Weston v Central Criminal Court Courts' Administrator* [1977] QB 32 at 43, [1976] 2 All ER 875 at 881, per Lord Denning MR. Note also *R v Giscombe* (1984) 79 Cr App Rep 79.

course of justice is required though this may be confined to advocates' absence from the court.

The doubt with regard to the mens rea requirement for contempts in the face of the court reflects a general doubt as to the application of the doctrine in cases of criminal contempt. In the leading case, *A-G v Butterworth*,[4] there were conflicting views as to the mens rea requirement. Lord Denning MR thought[5] that in general contempt required a guilty mind so that an intention to interfere with the course of justice is normally required. In contrast, Donovan LJ[6] thought that if an act is clearly and of itself calculated to interfere with the administration of justice no further evidence of intent or motive is required. We examine these views in more detail in Chapter 11[7] where it is submitted that Donovan LJ's approach is preferable to that of Lord Denning MR.[8] On this basis it is submitted that where conduct clearly interferes with the course of justice there is no need to prove an intent beyond showing that the accused intended to do the act. Conduct falling into this category would seem to include disruptive behaviour during court proceedings and the refusal to answer questions in court.[9] It is perhaps a moot point as to whether an advocate's absence from court can be considered ipso facto a clear interference with the course of justice but it is submitted that where such absence cannot be justified a contempt will be committed regardless of the accused's intent.

The position with regard to mens rea is further complicated by statute. In a number of jurisdictions for example, statutes vesting contempt powers in lower courts commonly state that the misbehaviour must be 'wilful'.[10] It is submitted that while 'wilfulness' imports a requirement that the conduct must be deliberate or possibly reckless it does not import the requirement that the accused must be shown to have intended to interfere with the course of justice. More problematic is the application of the Contempt of Court Act 1981. Section 1 refers to the 'strict liability rule' which is defined as conduct which 'may be treated as a contempt of court as tending to interfere with the course of justice in particular legal proceedings regardless of intent to do so'. Section 2 confines the rule to publications creating a substantial risk of serious prejudice to particular legal proceedings. Read literally ss 1 and 2 require proof of an intention to interfere with the course of justice to establish a contempt in respect of any conduct, including contempt in the face of the court, that interferes with the course of justice in particular legal proceedings other than publications creating a substantial risk of serious prejudice.[11] However, since Parliament clearly did not have contempts in the face of the court in mind when enacting ss 1 and 2 it is submitted that courts should be slow to infer from these provisions a general mens rea requirement.[12] Even if such an inference was made it might be observed that not all conduct amounting to contempt in the face of the court can be said to interfere

4　[1963] 1 QB 696.
5　Ibid at 722, 723.
6　Ibid at 726.
7　See pp 410 ff.
8　This is also the view of certain Australian courts, see p 411.
9　Though this issue was left open in *Hancock v Lynch* [1988] VR 173 at 177 and see further the cases there cited.
10　See eg the County Courts Act 1984, s 118 and the Contempt of Court Act 1981, s 12, discussed in Ch 12.
11　This seems to be the interpretation favoured by Arlidge and Eady, *The Law of Contempt*.
12　Cf Miller, *Contempt of Court* (2nd edn, 1989) at 134 who considers that the Act has no direct application and offers only a weak inference as to the mens rea requirement.

with the course of justice in a particular case. This would be true, for example, of misconduct at the end of a trial. Indeed it could be argued that contempt in the face of the court generally could properly be regarded as conduct interfering with the course of justice as a continuing process and therefore falling outside the ambit of s 1.[13]

How much difference a need to prove mens rea would make is debatable. For example, disruptive conduct or refusing to answer questions is usually only dealt with as a contempt after the accused has been warned about the consequences if such conduct is repeated. In such cases the accused is unlikely to be able to show that he did not have the requisite mens rea. In other cases the extent of liability may depend on the interpretation given by the courts and in particular whether an accused can be guilty of contempt if he is reckless as to the consequences of his conduct. It is suggested that the mens rea requirement should include the concept of recklessness so as to cover the type of situation that was faced by the British Columbia Court of Appeal in *R v Perkins*[14] where the accused, finding his case had been postponed from the morning until the afternoon, spent his time drinking and became too drunk to plead in the afternoon.

13 See p 106.
14 [1980] 4 WWR 763. Cf the position in respect of contempt by publication, discussed at pp
    106 ff.

CHAPTER 3

Publications interfering with the due course of justice in particular legal proceedings—the general position at common law

A major area of the law of contempt is that which places restrictions on what may legally be published because of the likely effect of the publication on the due administration of justice. This conflicts with freedom of speech and although 'publication' in this context has a wide meaning and is not limited to what appears in the media, the effect of the contempt laws on the freedom of the press make this a sensitive and controversial area of law. The law on what may be published about current legal proceedings is popularly known as the sub judice rule.

In reporting court proceedings and the functioning of the criminal and civil justice systems the media serve a necessary role in an open and democratic society by keeping the public informed of what is being done in its name and of matters which are its proper concern. However, in most common law jurisdictions the media is not a monolithic public service institution dedicated simply to upholding the principles of a democratic society. In the United Kingdom, for instance, it is now a disparate collection of interests most of which exist for commercial purposes and those purposes are best served by maximising the size of the circulation or audience. It is undeniable that the reporting of shocking, scandalous or exciting events, particularly in a way which appeals to the popular imagination or prurience, increases circulation or viewing figures and this is an important consideration when newspapers are engaged in circulation wars. As Hoffmann LJ said in *R v Central Independent Television Plc*:[1]

> 'Newspapers are sometimes irresponsible and their motives in a market economy cannot be expected to be unalloyed by considerations of commercial advantage.'

However, newspaper editors and media proprietors are not always or solely motivated by commercial concerns. They may wish to publicise certain matters because they believe issues of important public interest are concerned and they wish to stimulate public discussion, raise public awareness or influence the course of events.[2] Such journalism may be good for business but it is also an integral part of what the media sees as its role in a free society and of what the public expects of it. The status of the news media was described by Sir John Donaldson MR in *A-G v Guardian Newspapers Ltd (No 2)*:[3]

> 'I yield to no-one in my belief that the existence of a free press, in which term I include other media of mass communication, is an essential element in maintaining

---

1 [1994] Fam 192 at 202–203, [1994] 3 All ER 641 at 651–652.
2 The thalidomide litigation, *A-G v Times Newspapers Ltd* [1974] AC 273, the *Spycatcher* cases (see *A-G v Newspaper Publishing plc* [1988] Ch 333, [1987] 3 All ER 276, *A-G v Newspaper Publishing plc* (1989) Times, 9 May and (1990) Times, 28 February and *A-G v Times Newspapers Ltd* [1992] 1 AC 191, [1991] 2 All ER 398) and *Re Lonrho Plc* [1990] 2 AC 154 are all good examples of this.
3 [1990] 1 AC 109 at 183, [1988] 3 All ER 545 at 600.

parliamentary democracy and the British way of life as we know it. But it is important to remember why the press occupies this crucial position. It is not because of any special wisdom, interest or status enjoyed by proprietors, editors or journalists. It is because the media are the eyes and ears of the general public. They act on behalf of the general public. Their right to know and their right to publish is neither more nor less than that of the general public. Indeed it *is* that of the general public for whom they are trustees.'

Contempt of court as it applies to publications which interfere with the due course of justice in particular proceedings had its origins in an age when there was no photography, the concept of the tabloid press and of newspapers as a virtual branch of the entertainment industry was undreamed of and indeed before the word 'media' was invented. In some jurisdictions the courts alone have developed the law to deal with these new phenomena but in the United Kingdom there has been statutory intervention in the shape of the Contempt of Court Act 1981.

Domestic pressures to relax the law had culminated in the report of the Phillimore Committee in 1974[4] but the greatest stimulus to reform came from the decision of the European Court of Human Rights in *Sunday Times v United Kingdom.*[5] This case, in which the United Kingdom was held to have violated the European Convention on Human Rights because of the House of Lords decision in *A-G v Times Newspapers Ltd,*[6] finally prompted the Government to act.

The Contempt of Court Act 1981 does not provide a complete code. The interplay between the statute and the common law presents many problems and some contempts fall outside the ambit of the Act. As Watkins LJ said in *A-G v News Group Newspapers:*[7]

'The common law is not a worn-out jurisprudence rendered incapable of further development by the ever increasing incursion of parliamentary legislation. It is a lively body of law capable of adaptation and expansion to meet fresh needs calling for the exertion of the discipline of law.'

Additionally, in jurisdictions where there has been no statutory intervention the common law still applies. For these reasons we begin with a discussion of the application of the common law to publications which interfere with the due course of justice and then deal in Chapter 4 with the position in the United Kingdom after the 1981 Act. Chapters 5 and 6 consider the specific application of the law to criminal and to civil proceedings respectively. Chapter 8 deals with matter of reporting court proceedings.

I OBJECTIVES AND DILEMMAS

A Protecting fair trials

It is commonly asserted that the law of contempt operates to restrict what may be published about particular litigation but it would be more accurate to say that it operates to *postpone* what may be said,[8] for once legal proceedings are over the

---

4 *Report on Contempt* (1974, Cmnd 5794).
5 (1979) 2 EHRR 245.
6 [1974] AC 273.
7 [1989] QB 110 at 133D, [1988] 2 All ER 906 at 920.
8 As Lord Reid said in *A-G v Times Newspapers Ltd* [1974] AC 273 at 301, 'The purpose of the law [of contempt] is not to prevent publication of material but to postpone it'.

restrictions imposed under the contempt laws are, in general, lifted.[9] Furthermore, even during the currency of legal proceedings the law of contempt does not impose a total embargo on references to the particular trial. The immediate object of limiting what can be said during the currency of legal proceedings is, in broad terms, to protect the fairness of that trial. The underlying fear is that without such protection there would be 'trial' by the media and participants in the proceedings, such as witnesses and jurors, could be influenced. As Lord Reid said in *A-G v Times Newspapers Ltd* [10] (hereinafter referred to as the *Sunday Times* case):

> 'There has long been and there still is in this country [ie England] a strong and generally held feeling that trial by newspaper is wrong and should be prevented.'

The objection to such 'trials' is that they usurp the power of the court without any of the safeguards that are to be found in legal proceedings such as those provided by rules of procedure and evidence. As Wills J put it in *R v Parke* [11] they:

> '. . . deprive the court of the power of doing that which is the end for which it exists—namely, to administer justice duly, impartially, and with reference solely to the facts judicially brought before it. Their tendency is to reduce the court which has to try the case to impotence, so far as the effectual elimination of prejudice and prepossession is concerned.'

In short, the immediate objection to 'media trials' is that they put at risk the due administration of justice in the particular case. The long-term fear, however, is that such trials could undermine confidence in the judicial system generally. Lord Reid said in the *Sunday Times* case that trial by newspaper is intrinsically objectionable: [12]

> 'not only because of its possible effect on that particular case but also because of its side effects which may be far reaching. Responsible "mass media" will do their best to be fair but there will also be ill-informed, slap-dash or prejudiced attempts to influence the public. If people are led to think that it is easy to find the truth disrespect for the processes of the law could follow and, if mass media was allowed to judge, unpopular people and unpopular causes will fare very badly.'

This comment shows that even when the law is operating to restrict what may be said about particular current litigation there is an element of protecting the administration of justice as a continuing process. It is a matter of some dispute, however, whether such a long-term aim can justify restricting what can be said during the currency of particular litigation regardless of the risk of prejudice to that case.[13] The majority of the Law Lords in the *Sunday Times* case were committed to the view that it could, but there seems little support in other common law jurisdictions for this view.[14] However, there *is* general support for saying that in restricting what can be published during the currency of particular litigation the law intervenes not so much to protect individuals' interests but to

---

9 See Chs 5 and 6: the position is different in respect of publications 'scandalising' the court, see Ch 9.
10 [1974] AC 273 at 300.
11 [1903] 2 KB 432 at 437.
12 Ibid at 300.
13 See pp 226 ff.
14 For a review of the relevant case law see p 227.

protect litigants' rights as a whole by preserving the due administration of justice generally.[15] As Lord Reid said in the *Sunday Times* case:[16]

'the law of contempt even when operating to protect the fairness of a particular trial is properly regarded as seeking to uphold the public interest in the due administration of justice.'

The public nature of contempt helps to explain why the law is concerned to protect the 'fairness' of all hearings before courts of law whether criminal or civil and why it is equally concerned in criminal cases to protect the prosecution's case as well as the defence. It is easy to appreciate the public interest in having a fair criminal trial. As one New Zealand judge put it:[17]

'The people of a nation as represented by the Crown in criminal proceedings are interested to have both sides of criminal trials presented fairly, so that, on the one hand, proved malefactors are convicted, and, on the other hand, no one is convicted except on a proper and fair trial according to the law.'

The theory behind the public need for protection in civil cases was adverted to by their Lordships in the *Sunday Times* case. For example, Lord Morris commented:[18]

'In an ordered community courts are established for the settlement of disputes and for the maintenance of law and order. In the general interests of the community it is imperative that the authority of the courts should not be imperilled and that recourse to them should not be subject to unjustifiable interference. When such unjustifiable interference is suppressed it is not because those charged with the responsibilities of administering justice are concerned for their own dignity, it is because the very structure of ordered life is at risk if the recognised courts of the land are so flouted that their authority wanes and is supplanted.'

While some caution should be sounded with regard to observations made in the *Sunday Times* case,[19] they do comprise the broad context within which the common law has provided a justification for imposing restrictions to protect the fairness of a particular trial.

B   Preserving freedom of speech

The need to protect the fairness of a trial is not the only consideration that the courts have to bear in mind. Another important concern is freedom of speech. That, too, is a public interest. Lord Simon said in the *Sunday Times* case:[20]

'The public interest in freedom of discussion (of which the freedom of the press is one aspect) stems from the requirement that members of a democratic society should be sufficiently informed that they may influence intelligently the decisions which may affect themselves.'

---

15 See *Re A-G's Application; A-G v Butterworth* [1963] 1 QB 696 at 723, per Donovan LJ. See also in Australia *Victoria v BLF* (1982) 41 ALR 71 (Australia HC) and *A-G (NSW) v Willesee* [1980] 2 NSWLR 143 (NSW CA). In South Africa see *S v Van Niekerk* 1972 (3) SA 711.
16 [1974] AC 273 at 294.
17 Henry J in *A-G v Noonan* [1956] NZLR 1021 at 1027.
18 [1974] AC 273 at 302. For a similar view see Lord Simon, ibid at 315–316.
19 Because of the consequences of that case, which are discussed at pp 100 ff.
20 [1974] AC 273 at 320.

It is important to society that freedom of speech should not be lightly or inadvertently whittled away. As Rumpff JA put it in the South African decision of *Publications Control Board v William Heinemann Ltd:*[1]

> 'When a Court of Law is called upon to decide whether liberty should be repressed —in this case the freedom to publish a story—it should be anxious to steer a course as close to the preservation of liberty as possible. It should do so because freedom of speech is a hard-won and precious asset, yet easily lost.'

The nature of freedom of speech was emphasised by Hoffmann LJ in *R v Central Independent Television Plc:*[2]

> '. . . a freedom which is restricted to what judges think to be responsible or in the public interest is no freedom. Freedom means the right to publish things which government and judges, however well motivated, think should not be published. It means the right to say things which "right-thinking people" regard as dangerous or irresponsible. This freedom is subject only to clearly defined exceptions laid down by common law or statute . . .
>
> It cannot be too strongly emphasised that outside the established exceptions (or any new ones which Parliament may enact in accordance with its obligations under the [European] convention) there is no question of balancing freedom of speech against other interests. It is a trump card which always wins.'

Contempt of court, however, is one of those well-established exceptions to which Hoffmann LJ referred.

C Reconciling fair trial and freedom of speech

The courts are well aware of the dilemma in reconciling the two ultimately conflicting public interests of protecting fair trials and preserving freedom of speech. As Lord Simon said in the *Sunday Times* case:[3]

> 'Each is a genuine interest of society and neither can be held to be universally paramount over the other.'

That neither interest is paramount does not mean, however, that one interest is not favoured more than another. In general where the two interests are thought to conflict, the common law tends to favour the protection of a fair trial at the expense of freedom of speech. Australian judges have talked of *balancing* the competing public interests of freedom of expression and the proper administration of justice. In *The Prothonotary v Collins*[4] McHugh JA said:

> 'The law of contempt, or as I would prefer to call it, the law relating to interference with the administration of justice, seeks to strike a balance between the competing values of a fair trial and freedom of expression. Many informed persons think that the present law of contempt unduly restricts freedom of expression. Opinions in a democratic society will inevitably differ as to where should be drawn the line which makes the communication of information, ideas and opinions a criminal offence. But that a line exists is not open to doubt.'

---

1 [1965] (4) SA 137 at 160E.
2 [1994] Fam 192 at 203, [1994] 3 All ER 641 at 652.
3 [1974] AC 273 at 319.
4 (1985) 2 NSWLR 549 at 562 (NSW CA)

In broad terms the position that obtains in most common law jurisdictions (though not necessarily applied with the same rigour)[5] is that freedom of speech is permitted save where to do so would be calculated to create a real risk of prejudice either to a particular trial or possibly, and more controversially, to the administration of justice generally. As Lord Reid said in the *Sunday Times* case:[6]

> 'Freedom of speech should not be limited to any greater extent than is necessary but it cannot be allowed where there would be real prejudice to the administration of justice.'

There are limits to how far the common law will go in protecting a fair trial. Moffitt P said in *A-G (NSW) v Willesee*:[7]

> 'It is beyond question that the law of contempt in its operation accepts some compromise between that which arguably has a tendency to prejudice a fair trial of particular proceedings and that which will, at some time, tend to interfere with the public interest in some other respect.'

One important 'compromise' is permitting fair and accurate reports of open court proceedings regardless of the risk of prejudice.[8] Openness of decision-making has long been regarded as an important right in a democratic society and as a vital check on judicial activity. Other examples of when the law chooses to favour freedom of speech are permitting the continuation of public discussion of matters of public interest despite supervening litigation[9] and allowing temperate public pressure upon litigants to settle or withdraw from civil proceedings.[10] These last two examples have, under English law at least, been established comparatively recently and are evidence of a discernible trend (arguably more evident in relation to civil proceedings) in favour of freedom of speech. Despite this the common law still treats the protection of the due administration of justice as the superior value. This is evident from the general refusal to recognise a defence of public interest[11] for it has yet to be authoritatively accepted that the public interest in the due administration of justice can be outweighed by the public interest in being informed about a particular matter or issue.

II   THE REQUIREMENTS OF THE DUE ADMINISTRATION OF JUSTICE

The law of contempt is concerned to prohibit publications that create a real risk of prejudice to the administration of justice. What then are the requirements of the due administration of justice? According to Lord Diplock in the *Sunday Times* case[12] they are:

5 In Australia, for example, contempt cannot be committed until proceedings are 'pending'; see *James v Robinson* (1963) 109 CLR 593. Cf the common law position as it applies in England, discussed in Ch 7. In South Africa contempt can be more readily committed where there is no jury than in other jurisdictions; see eg *S v Van Niekerk* 1972 (3) SA 711.
6 [1974] AC 273 at 294, cited with approval in *Victoria v BLF* (1982) 41 ALR 71 (Australia HC).
7 [1980] 2 NSWLR 143 at 149, para 12.
8 See the judgment of Jordan CJ in *Ex parte Bread Manufacturers Ltd; Re Truth & Sportsman Ltd* (1937) 37 SR NSW 242: reporting proceedings is discussed in Ch 8.
9 Discussed in Chs 5 and 6 at pp 171 ff and 231 ff.
10 Discussed in Ch 6 at p 204 ff.
11 Discussed in Ch 5 at p 170.
12 [1974] AC 273 at 399B–C.

'*first* that all citizens should have unhindered access to the constitutionally established courts of criminal or civil jurisdiction for the determination of disputes as to their legal rights and liabilities, *secondly*, that they should be able to rely upon obtaining in the courts the arbitrament of a tribunal which is free from bias against any party and whose decision will be based upon those facts only that have been proved in evidence adduced before it in accordance with the procedure adopted in courts of law; and *thirdly* that, once the dispute has been submitted to a court of law, they should be able to rely on there being no usurpation by any other person of the function of that court to decide it according to law. Conduct which is calculated to prejudice any of these three requirements or to undermine the public confidence that they will be observed is contempt of court.'

We discuss the application of these requirements in subsequent chapters but here we make these general observations. It is for the impairment of the second of the above requirements that publications are commonly held to be a contempt. Publications may fall foul of this requirement either by creating a risk of prejudicing the tribunal hearing the case or by potentially jeopardising the validity of evidence that may be presented in court. In either case the central concern is the effect publicity may have on the laymen involved in the judicial process since it is assumed that they, unlike the professionally trained lawyer, are unable to put out of their minds evidence that has not been properly adduced in court. The principal concern is the effect of publicity upon jurors but there is also concern with its effect upon witnesses and (possibly) lay magistrates. Since, as Lord Diplock pointed out,[13] trial by jury has been and still is the mode of trial of all serious criminal offences and, until comparatively recently, was also the mode of trial of most civil cases at common law likely to attract the attention of the public, it is not surprising that most cases have been decided under this category. Indeed, publications relating to criminal proceedings are almost invariably dealt with under this category and are likely to continue to be so. With civil proceedings, however, the other requirements adverted to by Lord Diplock have become more relevant because such proceedings are now normally heard without a jury and because the judge trying the case is generally assumed to be immune to the deleterious effect of media comment.[14]

Publications falling foul of Lord Diplock's first requirement of the administration of justice are essentially those which unfairly pressurise parties and would include, for example, the public pillorying of a litigant for taking or defending a particular legal action. Although not frequently given as a reason for holding a publication to be a contempt this category is nevertheless well established. In 1742, for example, Lord Hardwicke in the *St James' Evening Post Case* [15] referred to it as 'abusing parties who are concerned in causes here' and in 1990 a publication was held to be a contempt for holding a litigant 'up to public obloquy in terms neither fair nor temperate but of abuse'.[16] The difficulty lies in drawing the borderline between fair and unfair pressure on parties.[17]

According to Lord Diplock, publications which impair his third requirement are those which discuss or comment on the merits of a dispute which has been submitted to a court of law. This consideration can apparently restrict a publication

---

13 Ibid at 309D.
14 See p 196.
15 (1742) 2 Atk 469.
16 *A-G v Hislop* [1991] 1 QB 514 at 535G, [1991] 1 All ER 911 at 927, per McCowan LJ.
17 See the discussion in the *Sunday Times* case [1974] AC 273, and also pp 204 ff.

which, though thought not to create a risk of prejudice to the particular case, is nevertheless thought to impair the due administration of justice generally.

III   TEST OF LIABILITY

A   The actus reus

1   *Actual prejudice not essential to the offence*

It has long been established that to maintain an action for contempt it is not necessary to show that a publication is actually prejudicial to a trial. If a trial is in fact prejudiced the accused can appeal to have his conviction quashed[18] but it is sufficient in contempt proceedings that the publication has a *tendency* (or, as it sometimes expressed, is 'calculated') to prejudice the case. As Cotton LJ said in *Hunt v Clarke*:[19]

> 'It is not necessary that a judge or jury will be prejudiced, but if it is calculated to prejudice the proper trial of a cause that is a contempt and would be met with the necessary punishment in order to restrain such conduct.'

The phrase 'calculated to prejudice' or 'tending to prejudice' is intended to refer to a publication which, when objectively viewed, can reasonably be said to present a *risk* of prejudice. In *Bell v Stewart*,[20] Isaacs and Rich JJ commented:

> 'The tendency of an article, therefore, means that the nature of it—as distinct from its actual or even probable force in the specific circumstances—is such that prejudice might result.'

As will be seen the risk of prejudice has to be a real one.[1] A good working definition is that stated by the New South Wales Court of Appeal in *A-G (NSW) v John Fairfax & Sons Ltd*,[2] namely:

> '[C]ontempt will be established if a publication has a tendency to interfere with the due administration of justice in the particular proceedings. This tendency is to be determined objectively by reference to the nature of the publication; and it is not relevant for this purpose to determine what the actual effect of the publication upon the proceedings has been, or what it probably will be. If the publication is of a character which might have an effect upon the proceedings, it will have the necessary tendency, unless the possibility of interference is so remote or theoretical that the de minimis principle should be applied.'

The fact that actual prejudice is not required is illustrative of two aspects of contempt. First it is evidence of the law's aim that justice should not only be done but seen to be done. As Lord Diplock said in the *Sunday Times* case:[3]

> 'Whether in the result the publication will have had any influence upon jurors or witnesses is not known when the proceedings for committal for contempt are heard. The mischief against which the summary remedy for contempt of court is directed is not merely that justice will not be done but it will not be manifestly seen

18   See *R v Taylor* (1993) 98 Cr App Rep 361.
19   (1889) 58 LJ QB 490 at 492.
20   (1920) 28 CLR 419 at 432 (Australia HC).
1   See pp 77 ff.
2   [1980] 1 NSWLR 362 at 368, para 21.
3   [1974] AC 273 at 309.

to be done. Contempt of court is punishable because it undermines the confidence not only of the parties to the particular litigation but also of the public as potential suitors in the due administration of justice by the established courts of law.'

Secondly, the test emphasises that the law of contempt is a deterrent, being essentially concerned with the *prevention* of prejudice rather than merely applying sanctions to comments which have prejudiced a case. So viewed it is perfectly logical to hold publications to be a contempt on the basis of possible prejudice yet at the same time to hold (when it is sought to have a conviction quashed), that a trial has not in fact been prejudiced.[4] It also helps to explain why contempt actions may still be successful in cases where the publication is alleged to be calculated to prejudice the accused even though he has already been acquitted. Finally, the essential deterrent role of contempt defends the law against the charge made by one American commentator:[5]

> 'The greatest failure of English contempt law is its disrelation with its most valuable object—protection of fair trials. It is of little service to an accused person who is written into jail by a prejudiced press that the publisher or editor is fined or imprisoned. This victory is a hollow one unless the conviction is reversed.'

However the law of contempt is not concerned with the private rights of the individual (whose remedy lies elsewhere). The object of punishing those that transgress is to deter others from doing so. In that way it is hoped to protect litigants' rights generally. As the commentator himself says:

> 'The contempt vehicle is only indirectly curative of unfair trials, if at all, though this is its most valuable purpose.'

The protection of public interest through the contempt rules has been described by the New South Wales Court of Appeal:[6]

> '. . . the principles of law in question do not exist merely to protect the private interests of a person... in securing a fair trial in respect of his alleged crimes. They protect the interest of the public in having persons who are accused of crime in our community dealt with by the system established for the administration of justice according to law. Trial by media has no place in that system.'

R v Dyson[7] is a previously rare example of a conviction being quashed because of prejudicial publicity. However English courts seem now more ready to accept that trials can *actually* be prejudiced. In *R v McCann and others*[8] the defendants' convictions for conspiracy to murder were quashed by the Court of Appeal, which said that in view of the impact on the trial of the media coverage of certain comments by the Secretary of State for Northern Ireland and Lord Denning, the judge should have discharged the jury and ordered a re-trial. Moreover, the courts are prepared to stay criminal proceedings where publicity

---

4 As illustrated by the case involving Michael Malik in which the *Sunday Times* was found guilty of contempt for creating a serious risk of prejudice against the accused (see *R v Thomson Newspapers Ltd, ex p A-G* [1968] 1 All ER 268, [1968] 1 WLR 1, discussed at p 138) yet Malik failed to have the conviction quashed on the grounds of prejudice: *R v Malik* [1968] 1 All ER 582n, [1968] 1 WLR 353.

5 Goldfarb, *The Contempt Power* (1963, Columbia University Press) p 88.

6 *A-G for New South Wales v TCN Channel Nine Pty Ltd* (1990) 20 NSWLR 368 at 384.

7 (1943) 29 Cr App Rep 104.

8 (1991) 92 Cr App Rep 239 discussed in Ch 5 pp 146 ff.

has made it impossible for the defendant to have a fair trial.[9] In *R v Taylor*[10] the prejudicial reporting of a murder trial of two sisters was one of the reasons why the convictions were quashed. The Attorney General declined to bring contempt actions against the newspapers concerned and an action by the sisters for judicial review of this decision failed in the Divisional Court on the grounds that the Attorney General's discretion was not reviewable.[11] This case serves to highlight the public right aspect of the contempt laws and the lack of redress by way of contempt proceedings of those affected by the publication.

2   What amounts to actionable contempt?

The determination of what is an actionable contempt has been influenced in part by the summary procedure that has been adopted to deal with the offence. As the New South Wales Court of Appeal said in *A-G (NSW) v John Fairfax & Sons Ltd* ,[12] the courts have been anxious that in the absence of statutory authority the trial otherwise than by jury of a criminal offence is an anomaly to be justified only by the special consequences flowing from the nature of contempt. The courts have long been aware of the arbitrary power that they possess in relation to contempt. As Jessel MR said in *Re Clements and Costa Rica Republic v Erlanger*:[13]

> 'It seems to me that this jurisdiction of committing for contempt being practically arbitrary and unlimited should be most jealously and carefully watched, and exercised . . . with the greatest reluctance and the greatest anxiety on the part of judges to see whether there is no other mode which is not open to the objection of arbitrariness and which can be brought to bear upon the subject.'

(a) Technical contempts

It is against the background of an anxiety not to overuse the contempt power that there developed the notion of 'technical contempts'. Such contempts were referred to in *Hunt v Clarke* where Cotton LJ said:[14]

> ' . . . it does technically become a contempt if pending a cause, or before a cause has even begun any observations are made or published to the world which tend in any way to prejudice the parties.'

But he added:

9 In *R v Reade, Morris and Woodwiss* (1993) Independent, 19 October, Garland J stayed criminal proceedings against three police officers charged with conspiracy to pervert the course of justice, holding that the volume, intensity and coverage of the circumstances surrounding the case made a fair trial impossible although no question of contempt arose; in July 1994 the *Sun* was fined a total of £100,000 for publishing a photograph of the defendant prior to an identity parade with the result that the trial was abandoned.
10 (1993) 98 Cr App Rep 361, discussed at p 150.
11 *R v Solicitor-General, ex p Taylor* (1995) Independent, 3 August.. The Divisional Court also held that even if the discretion was reviewable the decision not to bring contempt proceedings was not so unreasonable that it could be overturned. The case is being appealed to the House of Lords. See further p 481.
12 [1980] 1 NSWLR 362 at 367, para 14.
13 (1877) 46 LJ Ch 375 at 383. See also in Canada *Re Depoe and Lamport* (1968) 66 DLR (2d) 46 at 49.
14 (1889) 58 LJ QB 490 at 491.

'where the offence complained of is of a slight and trifling nature and not likely to cause any substantial prejudice to the party in the conduct of the action or the due administration of justice, the party ought not to apply'.

This notion of technical contempts is apt to cause confusion. It is properly understood as referring to a publication which, having been adjudged a contempt, is nevertheless thought for a variety of reasons not to warrant punishment. It is wrong, therefore, to think that there are two types of contempt, one being technical and the other being actual contempt. As the court said in *A-G (NSW) v John Fairfax & Sons Ltd*:[15] 'Technical contempt is contempt.' In all cases, as Lord Reid said in the *Sunday Times* case[16] in agreeing with Cotton LJ in *Hunt v Clarke*:

'there must be two questions: first, was there any contempt at all and, secondly, was it sufficiently serious to require, or justify the court in making, an order against the respondent?'

In the past these two questions have not been clearly separated, and as the New South Wales Court of Appeal pointed out,[17] some of the reasons for not punishing a publisher have tended to obscure whether the question being dealt with is what constitutes contempt, or what the court should do in the particular case. The court agreed with Lord Reid's observation in the *Sunday Times* case that it is confusing to import into the question whether there is any contempt at all, or into the definition of contempt, matters which are related to the course of action which might be taken against the offender, the contempt having already been established.

(b) The need for a real risk of prejudice

According to Lord Reid in the *Sunday Times* case[18] the test of what constitutes a contempt at common law is that expressed by Lord Parker CJ in *R v Duffy, ex p Nash*,[19] namely, that there 'must be a real risk [of prejudice] as opposed to a remote possibility'. In Lord Reid's view this test is no more than an application of the ordinary de minimis principle and there can be no contempt if the possibility of influence is remote. On the other hand, 'if there is some but only a small, likelihood, that may influence the court not to impose any punishment. If there is a serious risk some action may be necessary'. Inasmuch as Lord Reid's test demands that a real risk of prejudice be shown before *any* contempt can be established his judgment might be thought to represent some theoretical relaxation in the position represented by Cotton LJ's definition of technical contempts referred to earlier. It echoes Russell J's view in *Carl-Zeiss-Stiftung v Rayner & Keeler Ltd*[20] that 'a finding of contempt of court must be based on a solid view of the likelihood of such interference and not on fanciful notions'. Lord Reid's test, however, does seem to leave open a category of what might still be called 'technical' contempts, namely, publications which create a small rather than a remote risk of prejudice, where punishment may not be appropriate. Since the

15 [1980] 1 NSWLR 362 at 367, para 16 (NSW CA).
16 [1974] AC 273 at 298G.
17 In *A-G (NSW) v John Fairfax & Sons Ltd* [1980] 1 NSWLR 362 at 367, para 16; and see now *A-G (NSW) v John Fairfax & Sons & Bacon* (1985) 6 NSWLR 695 at 708, discussed at p 78.
18 [1974] AC 273 at 298–299.
19 [1960] 2 QB 188 at 200.
20 [1960] 3 All ER 289 at 293.

media are expected to refrain from creating such risks this concept is less than helpful and the test potentially difficult to operate.

The Australian courts have taken a more radical attitude to what amounts to an actionable contempt by not recognising as contempts publications which fall within Lord Reid's 'small risk not deserving punishment' category. In deciding liability for contempt they apply the test of whether there is 'a real risk, as opposed to to a remote possibility' of prejudice.[1] They have also formulated the test in terms of whether 'the matter published has, as a matter of practical reality, a tendency to interfere with the due course of justice in a particular case',[2] an issue which is to be established objectively, by reference to the nature and circumstances of the publication.[3] However, the courts appear to no longer recognise technical contempts. In *A-G (NSW) v John Fairfax & Sons & Bacon*[4] McHugh JA said that the distinction between technical and actual contempts—between contempts which will be punished and those which will not be punished—should be abolished and that a publication should no longer be regarded as a contempt unless it fell within the class of case which would previously have been held as a punishable contempt: therefore a publication will *only* be a contempt if it satisfies the test of interfering, as a matter of practical reality with the due course of justice. The Australian and English positions on the concept of technical contempts at common law seem therefore to be at variance.[5]

(c)   The prejudgment test[6]

Before the *Sunday Times* decision the orthodox view was that to constitute an actionable contempt the publication should have created a real risk of prejudice to the administration of justice in the *particular* case. The House of Lords in the *Sunday Times* case, however, established a broader test. They held that a publication relating to particular proceedings can constitute a contempt not only because of the risks of prejudice to the case in hand but because of the risks of prejudice to the administration of justice as a whole. To be consistent with Lord Reid's test stated earlier such a risk must be a real one but in judging this he made it clear[7] that the publication should not be considered in isolation but in the light of the replies that it might provoke. With these considerations in mind the *Sunday Times* case laid down what has become known as the 'prejudgment test' namely, that anything in the nature of a prejudgment of the specific issues already pending before the courts should not be published. The rationale behind this view is best explained by Lord Cross when he said:[8]

'It is easy enough to see that any publication which prejudges an issue in pending proceedings ought to be forbidden if there is any real risk that it may influence the

1   *Victoria v Australian Building Construction Employees' and Builders' Labourers' Federation* (1982) 152 CLR 25 at 56 (Australia HC).
2   Per Dixon CJ, Fullagar, Kitto and Taylor JJ in *John Fairfax & Sons Pty Ltd v McRae* (1955) 93 CLR 351 at 370 (Australia HC).
3   See *A-G (NSW) v John Fairfax & Sons Ltd* [1980] 1 NSWLR 362 at 368 (NSW CA); *A-G (NSW) v John Fairfax & Sons Ltd and Bacon* (1985) 6 NSWLR 695 at 708 (NSW CA); *DPP v Wran* (1986) 7 NSWLR 616 at 626 (NSW CA); *Hinch v A-G (Victoria)* (1987) 164 CLR 15 at 27–28 (Australia HC); *A-G for NSW v Dean* (1990) 20 NSWLR 650 at 655-656 (NSW CA).
4   (1986) 6 NSWLR 695 at 708 relying on *Victoria v BLF* (1982) 152 CLR 25.
5   For the position where there is intent to interfere with the administration of justice see p 79.
6   For a detailed discussion of this see pp 221 ff.
7   [1974] AC 273 at 299.
8   Ibid at 322–323.

tribunal. . . . But why, it may be said, should a publication be prohibited when there is no such risk? The reason is that one cannot deal with one particular publication in isolation. A publication prejudging an issue in pending litigation which is itself innocuous enough may provoke replies which are far from innocuous but which, as they are replies, it would seem unfair to restrain. So gradually the public would become habituated to, look forward to, and resent the absence of, preliminary discussions in the "media" of any case which aroused widespread interest. An absolute rule, though it may seem to be unreasonable if one looks only to the particular case, is necessary in order to prevent a gradual slide towards trial by newspaper or television.'

By holding that a publication relating to particular proceedings can be held a contempt not because of the risk of prejudice to those proceedings but because of the risk to the administration of justice generally, the decision broke new ground.[9] This approach, however, has been widely criticised and was found to be in breach of the European Convention on Human Rights.[10]

(d) Intending to prejudice proceedings

As will be seen,[11] liability at common law for a publication held to create a real risk of prejudice is strict so that intent to prejudice is not required. There is no doubt, however, that a publication which is *intended* to prejudice is a very serious contempt. Whether publications intended to prejudice proceedings amount to contempt regardless of any risk to the due administration of justice is more problematic.

(i) Authorities suggesting there can be contempt without risk of prejudice　In *Re Ludlow Charities, Lechmere Charlton's Case* (a case concerning a letter written to a judge rather than a publication) Lord Cottenham LC commented:[12]

'All these authorities tend to the same point; they shew that it is immaterial what measures are adopted, if the object is to taint the source of justice, and to obtain a result of legal proceedings different from that which would follow in the ordinary course. It is a contempt of the highest order; and although such a foolish attempt as this cannot be supposed to have any effect, it is obvious that if such cases were not punished, the most serious consequences might follow.'[13]

It appears from Lord Cottenham's judgment that this was intended to be representative of a general principle:[14]

'Every writing, letter, or publication which has for its object to divert the course of justice is a contempt of the court.'

9　The function of contempt as protecting the administration of justice generally has long been relevant, however, to other areas of contempt: see Chs 9 and 11.
10　*Sunday Times v UK* (1979) 2 EHRR 245, discussed at p 100.
11　See p 89.
12　(1837) 2 My & Cr 316 at 342.
13　See also *Martin's Case* (1747) 2 Russ & M 674, 39 ER 551, in which one Thomas Martin sent a private letter to the Lord Chancellor which discussed the subject matter of a threatened suit against Martin and enclosed a £20 note: it was held that this amounted to contempt although it could hardly be supposed that the Lord Chancellor was likely to be influenced by the letter or the money.
14　(1837) 2 My & Cr 316 at 339.

A similar standpoint was taken by Blackburn J in *R v Castro, Skipworth's Case* [15] when he held an "utterly ineffectual" attempt intended, inter alia, to deter by vituperation the Lord Chief Justice from taking part in a trial, to be a contempt.

More recently, in *R v Duffy, ex p Nash* [16] Lord Parker CJ, while accepting that appellate judges are normally immune from the deleterious effect of newspaper comment, nevertheless said that it might be a contempt if 'the article in question formed part of a deliberate campaign to influence the decision of the appellate tribunal'.

In some cases the Australian courts have also accepted in principle the proposition that publications intended to prejudice proceedings can amount to contempt regardless of the risk of prejudice. In *A-G (NSW) v John Fairfax & Sons Ltd* [17] the court said, relying on the *Re Ludlow Charities* case:

> 'There is, however, another class of case where a publication will constitute contempt, even though the possibility of interference is remote or theoretical. These are cases where matter is published with the intention of interfering with the due administration of justice in the particular case.'

In *Registrar, Court of Appeal v Collins* ,[18] the contemnor had stood on the footpath outside the criminal courts buildings and distributed pamphlets indiscriminately to members of the public who included jurors and those summoned for jury service. The pamphlets warned jurors against accepting police evidence and advised them to disregard the directions of the trial judges. Moffitt P, with whom Street CJ and Hope JA agreed, thought that the risk of prejudice was irrelevant if there was an intention to prejudice:[19]

> 'Likewise, if the giving of a pamphlet to a juror would constitute contempt, contempt would be established, if the pamphlet were handed to a class of persons in the vicinity of the court wide enough to constitute jurors or potential jurors. It would not be necessary to prove that a person who in fact acted as a juror received a pamphlet or that in fact it influenced his decision. If the person handing out the pamphlets, did so intending that some should be received by jurors and influence their decision, there would be contempt even although it appeared that the possibility of a juror receiving one was remote or even although it appeared that what was done failed in its purpose...'.

In Zimbabwe it has been held that it is possible to be guilty of an attempt to commit contempt, although that was not in the context of contempt by publication.[20]

(ii) The counter authorities The fullest discussion of the issue is in *The Prothonotary v Collins* [1] in which the New South Wales Court of Appeal held that a bare intention to interfere with the administration of justice *as a continuing process* could not be a contempt in the absence of an objective act which was likely to interfere with the course of justice. McHugh JA restricted the *ratio* of

---

15 (1873) LR 9 QB 230. See also *Birmingham Vinegar Brewery v Henry* (1894) 10 TLR 586; *Re Cornish, Staff v Gill* (1893) 9 TLR 196 and *Re Crown Bank, Re O'Malley* (1890) 44 Ch D 649.
16 [1960] 2 QB 188, [1960] 2 All ER 891.
17 [1980] 1 NSWLR 362 at 369, para 22 (NSW CA) followed in *Registrar of the Supreme Court, Equity Division v McPherson* [1980] 1 NSWLR 688 at 697, per Moffitt P and Hope JA.
18 [1982] 1 NSWLR 682 (NSW CA).
19 Ibid at 691.
20 *S v Benatar* 1984 (3) SA 588, which concerned a man's attempt to communicate with a minor contrary to a court order.
1   [1985] 2 NSWLR 549.

the earlier *Collins* case to the proposition that 'the distribution of extraneous material to persons who include jurors is a contempt when made in circumstances where there is a tendency to influence their verdicts'.[2] He was unhappy with Moffitt P's suggestion that an act done with the intention of interfering with *particular proceedings* would constitute contempt even if the act was unlikely to succeeed. He thought this incompatible with the finding of the Australian High Court in *Lane v Registrar of the Supreme Court of New South Wales (Equity Division)*.[3] He also considered that in *A-G (NSW) v John Fairfax & Sons*[4] the judges' remarks quoted above were open to the interpretation that, given an intention to interfere, a case would not fail because the tendency of the publication or conduct does not result in *actual* interference with the course of justice: read this way the *John Fairfax* case was not authority for saying that a bare intention to interfere was contempt and did not support the dicta of Moffitt P with which he disagreed.

The principal counter English decision is *R v Ingrams, ex p Goldsmith*,[5] in which it was contended that even though there was no real risk of prejudice contempt could be established if the article was intended to have that effect. In the Divisional Court, Lord Widgery CJ, apparently rejecting the contention, said: 'simple intention by itself could not amount to contempt'. In saying this he relied on *Balogh v Crown Court at St Albans*[6] in which it was held that a mere preparatory act, even if done with an intention of interfering with the course of justice, did not amount to contempt nor even (assuming the offence exists) an attempt to commit contempt. With respect to Lord Widgery CJ, *Balogh*'s case was clearly distinguishable since the case before him concerned a publication by *Private Eye* which could hardly be described as a 'mere preparatory act'. Bearing this in mind it is difficult to follow what Lord Widgery meant when he commented:

> 'If it could be proved that someone had attempted to commit contempt, then intent might be sufficient to support contempt.'

Neither Eveleigh nor Peter Pain JJ reached a similar conclusion and indeeed the former expressly concluded that *Private Eye* did not intend to prejudice any pending action. It is therefore submitted that *Ingrams* cannot be relied upon as authority for saying that an article published with an intention to prejudice proceedings cannot be a contempt unless there is a real risk of prejudice.[7] In *A-G v Newspaper Publishing plc*[8] however, Sir John Donaldson MR agreed with counsel's submission that if the conduct of the newspapers did not constitute an actus reus, it mattered not whether they had the necessary mens rea. He added:

> 'That is quite right and perhaps fortunate. If ordinary citizens could be convicted of offences which they intended to commit, but never got round to committing, the prisons would be even fuller than they are at the moment.'

2 Ibid at 571. Kirby P agreed.
3 (1981) 148 CLR 245, discussed at p 82: this was the appeal from *Registrar of the Supreme Court, Equity Division v McPherson* [1980] 1 NSWLR 688.
4 [1980] 1 NSWLR 362.
5 [1977] Crim LR 40.
6 [1975] 1QB 73, [1974] 3 All ER 283, discussed in Ch 2.
7 See also the commentary in [1977] Crim LR 40 at 41.
8 [1988] Ch 333 at 373G, [1987] All ER 276 at 303.

(iii) Commentary   There are differences of judicial opinion in both English and Australian law. A possible approach to this problem is to eschew a general rule about whether or not a bare intention can constitute contempt in the absence of a real risk of prejudice and to take a contextual approach instead. Where publications are concerned the question of the creation of the risk of prejudice normally depends on the likely effect of the publication on the mind of another person,[9] and cases such as *Lane* [10] and *Balogh,* [11] which have nothing to do with publications, are not helpful. *Lane* concerned a company officer who advised the company directors that certain documents were not within a class of documents which a subpoena required the company to produce. Not surprisingly it was held that if a person is not required to produce certain documents it cannot be contempt to advise him not to produce them, whatever the intentions of the person proffering the advice. In *Lane* no act had been committed which could interfere with the administration of justice. In *Balogh* the defendant stole a cylinder of nitrous oxide ('laughing gas') intending to release it, via the roof, into the ventilating system of a court hearing a case about pornography in order (in Lord Denning MR's words) to 'liven it up'. He got no further than taking the cylinder into the public gallery before being apprehended. His plans were therefore thwarted before he could do any act which interfered with the proceedings and the Court of Appeal, as explained above, held that mere intention did not suffice. Lord Denning MR's description of the defendant's acts as 'merely preparatory' presages the terminology used in distinguishing those acts which amount to an attempt to commit an offence from those which do not, under s 1 of the Criminal Attempts Act 1981.

Where publications are concerned the production and circulation of the material must be seen as acts which are more than 'merely preparatory'. In *The Prothonotary v Collins* the tendency to interfere with the administration of justice was absent because the publication, distributed to jurors and potential jurors waiting ouside the court building, told them not to believe any evidence about oral confessions by the accused as the police habitually fabricated such evidence: however, as none of the trials to be heard that day featured oral confessions no trial was likely to be affected. The publication missed its target completely and Kirby P and McHugh JA were unwilling to punish an expression of opinion which, despite the intention, was so completely ineffectual. Similarly, in *Ingrams, ex p Goldsmith* it appears that despite the intent, the content of the publication was insufficient to create the required degree of risk of prejudice. These cases are to be distinguished from those such as *Ludlow Charities, Skipworth's Case* and *Duffy, ex p Nash* in which it was not something inherent in the publication or in what the defendant did which prevented the risk of prejudice occurring but the principle that it is impossible improperly to influence professional judges because they are immune from influence or persuasion.[12] To hold that as a consequence of the robustness of the judiciary it is impossible to convict of contempt a person who deliberately tries improperly to influence a

---

9   *A-G v Newspaper Publishing plc,* ibid, which was part of the *Spycatcher* saga, was an unusual case in that respect as the issue was that the publication had caused irremediable damage to the subject matter of the litigation, which was information which was allegedly confidential: for a discussion of the case see Ch 6.

10   *Lane v Registrar of the Supreme Court of New South Wales (Equity Division)* [1981] 148 CLR 245.

11   *Balogh v Crown Court at St Albans* [1975] QB 73, [1974] 3 All ER 283.

12   For a discussion of this principle, see pp 124 ff.

judge is surely a nonsense.[13] One can therefore conclude that although a bare intention unaccompanied by any relevant act at all cannot be a contempt, an intention accompanied by acts which were intended to cause prejudice but which fail to do so for some reason, may be punishable as a contempt. It will depend on what the acts were and the reason for the failure.

The Phillimore Committee thought that ineffectual intentional acts should constitute contempt.[14] Section 6(c) of the Contempt of Court Act 1981 says that the legislation does not affect liability for intentional contempts.[15] Although it does not expressly deal with the issue under discussion, the wording of s 6(c) that nothing in the foregoing provisions of the Act 'restricts liability for contempt of court in respect of conduct intended to impede or prejudice the administration of justice', by being silent about the necessity for a risk of prejudice could suggest that the risk is not required.[16]

Is it possible to view an intentional act which fails to create a risk of prejudice to proceedings as an attempt to commit contempt? In *Balogh* Lord Denning MR considered whether the defendant's actions amounted to an attempted contempt but concluded that they did not, because of their 'merely preparatory' nature,[17] while Stephenson LJ doubted whether an attempt to commit contempt was punishable. One problem is that the terminology of attempts fits oddly with the test of whether there is a *tendency* or a *real risk* of (rather than *actual*) prejudice created by a publication. It is unrealistic to talk of attempts to create a risk: the intention of the alleged contemnor will invariably have been to create *actual* prejudice, not a tendency or a risk. As has been said,[18] the actus reus of contempt, defined in terms of creating a risk of prejudice, could in itself be described as an attempt. Certainly the language of Blackburn J in *Skipworth's Case* [19] is couched in terms of an attempt to interfere with proceedings. Criminal attempts are now governed in English law by the Criminal Attempts Act 1981 and by s 1(2) of that Act attempting the impossible can lead to criminal liability. This would circumvent the problem caused by the principle that no attempt improperly to influence a judge can possibly succeed.

It is interesting to note the position with regard to the indictable offence of perverting the course of justice. This offence overlaps to a considerable extent with contempt of court but is not normally relevant where publications are concerned.[20] In *R v Machin* [1] Eveleigh LJ said that the gist of the offence of

13 An attempt to bribe a judge might, of course, be chargeable as an attempt to pervert the course of justice.
14 1974, Cmnd 5794, para 66.
15 See pp 106 ff.
16 Ibid.
17 At the time of *Balogh* the leading case on attempts generally was *Haughton v Smith* [1975] AC 476, [1973] 2 All ER 896; the law is now governed by the Criminal Attempts Act 1981 the interpretation of which has been a matter of controversy: see *Anderton v Ryan* [1985] AC 560, [1985] 2 All ER 355; *R v Shivpuri* [1987] AC 1, [1986] 2 All ER 334; *R v Gullefer* (1990) 3 All ER 882, discussed in Smith and Hogan, *Criminal Law* (7th edn, 1992) pp 304–324 and Clarkson & Keating, *Criminal Law: Text and Materials* (3rd edn, 1994) pp 443–486.
18 Arlidge and Eady, *The Law of Contempt* p 45 at para 2-21.
19 (1873) LR 9 QB 230 at 235 and 238.
20 The last known prosecution upon indictment against a newspaper for contempt was in *R v Tibbits and Windust* [1902] 1 KB 77 where although the judgments constantly refer to contempt of court the charge was in fact one of an unlawful attempt to pervert the course of justice. In *Re Lonrho Plc* [1990] 2 AC 154 the House of Lords said, approving *R v D* [1984] 1 All ER 574, that the proper remedy in the case of contempt of court by the media is by way of committal proceedings in the High Court: see pp 469 ff.
1 [1980] 3 All ER 151.

perverting the course of justice is conduct which may lead and is intended to lead to a miscarriage of justice whether or not a miscarriage actually occurs. He thought that the use of the word 'attempt' in this context was misleading as:

'To do an act with the intention of perverting the course of justice is not of itself enough. The act must also have that tendency.'[2]

In *R v Kellett*,[3] where the defendant was charged with perverting the course of justice by threatening potential witnesses with defamation proceedings, his counsel conceded that he was guilty of contempt.

(e)   The time at which risk is assessed

It is well established that the risk to the administration of justice is assessed at the time of publication and not with hindsight. As Lowe J said in the Australian decision, *R v Pacini*: [4]

'The tendency of the publication must be judged as at the time of publication and is not determined by the fact that for some reason no harm has resulted from the publication.'

It is irrelevant that the accused was acquitted or that, although a publication could have potentially jeopardised a trial, it involved matters that do not prove relevant at the hearing. For instance, it was held in *R v Daily Mirror, ex p Smith*[5] that the publication of a photograph of the accused prior to his appearance in an identity parade constituted a contempt even though the issue of identity was not raised at the trial. In *A-G v Times Newspapers Ltd*[6] Lord Ackner stated that:

'The contempt must be judged as at the date of commission of the acts complained of.'

In that case the appellant was charged with contempt for having published material which was the subject of an interlocutory injunction addressed to other parties. Lord Ackner said that the appellants could not claim in their defence that somebody else was also going to commit contempt of court or otherwise render the court's order useless and that therefore the interference with the course of justice, flagrant as it was on the day when it was committed, was irrelevant.

It seems that the tendency of a publication to prejudice a fair trial is to be judged on the probabilities existing at the date of publication. This problem has been discussed in relation to photographs. According to Lord Hewart CJ:[7]

'. . . there is a duty to refrain from the publication of a photograph of an accused person where it is apparent to a reasonable man that a question of identity arises.'

But in *Re Consolidated Press, ex p Auld*,[8] an Australian decision, Jordan CJ, commenting on Lord Hewart CJ's judgment said:

2   Ibid at 154.
3   [1976] QB 372, [1975] 3 All ER 468; for interference with witnesses, see Ch 11.
4   [1956] VLR 544 at 547; See also in Australia *R v David Syme & Co Ltd* [1982] VR 173 at 177; *R v Australian Broadcasting Corporation* [1983] Tas R 161 at 168; *Registrar of the Court of Appeal v Willesee* (1985) 3 NSWLR 650 at 656, 657; *A-G (NSW) v John Fairfax & Sons Ltd and Bacon* (1985) 6 NSWLR 695 at 697; *DPP v Wran* (1986) 7 NSWLR 616 at 626.
5   [1927] 1 KB 845, discussed at p 160.
6   [1992] 1 AC 191 at 215, [1991] 2 All ER 398 at 413. This was one of the cases which arose in the *Spycatcher* litigation: see Ch 6 pp 211 ff.
7   *R v Daily Mirror, ex p Smith* [1927] 1 KB 845 and at 850.
8   (1936) 36 SR NSW 596 at 598.

'It seems to have been supposed that his Lordship was setting up the probable views of the average reasonable and prudent man as the standard for determining whether, in a particular case, the publication of a photograph would be proper. It is plain that this was not intended. The test to be applied . . . is to see whether at the time when the photograph was published, there was a likelihood that the identity of the accused would come into question in some aspect of the case, so that publication would be likely to prejudice a fair trial. If the court is satisfied beyond reasonable doubt that there was such a likelihood . . . a case for intervention is made out. The question is not whether, on the facts then known, a defence based on identity is likely to be successful or to be set up; it is whether it is reasonably probable that identity may come into question.'

The test whether the court rather than the hypothetical reasonable man thinks a question of identity is likely to come into issue has subsequently been followed both in Australia[9] and New Zealand.[10] It is submitted that it is the preferable view and should be adopted in England.[11]

3   The publication requirement

As we have seen, intention apart, the actus reus of contempt by publication is the creation of a real risk of prejudice either to the administration of justice in particular proceedings or possibly to the administration of justice generally. Clearly, no matter how 'prejudicial' material in itself might be it can only become creative of a real risk of prejudice if it is *published*. As Lord Goddard CJ said in *R v Griffiths, ex p A-G*: [12] 'The offence is not the mere preparation of the article but the publication of it . . .'

(a)   The meaning of 'publication'

There has been remarkably little discussion as to what constitutes a 'publication' for the purposes of contempt.[13] By analogy with the law of defamation it could be argued that matter is 'published' whenever it is communicated to someone other than the author[14] but as a general definition this seems too strict for contempt since the concept should be in some way related to the risk of prejudice. To establish a real risk of prejudice to a particular case it should surely have to be shown not only that the article is likely to influence the reader but also that it is likely to be read by persons connected with the trial: jurors or potential jurors, witnesses or litigants. To meet this latter requirement it is suggested that in general material should only be regarded as 'published' when it is made available to the general public or at any rate a section of the public which is likely to comprise those having a connection with the case. On this basis private communications would not normally be regarded as 'publications'. Showing

9 *A-G (NSW) v Mirror Newspapers Ltd* [1962] NSWR 856; *R v Pacini* [1956] VY 544 and *R v Regal Press Pty Ltd* [1972] VR 67 at 73.
10 *A-G v Noonan* [1956] NZLR 1021.
11 An analogy can be drawn with the issue of whether at the time of publication proceedings appear to be imminent, see the discussion in Ch 7.
12 [1957] 2 QB 192 at 202.
13 For the meaning of publication in respect of s 12 of the Administration of Justice Act 1960 see pp 327 ff.
14 For the definition in defamation see eg Gatley: *Libel and Slander* (8th edn, 1981) para 222.

material to another person unconnected with the case cannot be said to be creative of a risk of prejudice. This would therefore exclude the newspaper reporter who merely sends information to his editor, assuming the editor is unconnected with the trial and that the information is not subsequently used in the newspaper.[15] Not all private communications can be excluded, however. It would hardly be open to someone who sends a letter containing prejudicial comments upon a pending trial directly to a juror or witness to say that the material has not been 'published'.[16] In that case there is a real risk of prejudice even though the letter is published to one person only.

It is not suggested that merely because prejudicial material is made available to the public at large that a contempt is necessarily committed. The speech maker at Speaker's Corner might be regarded as 'publishing' his material to the public at large but it is doubtful whether he could be said to be creating a real risk of prejudice to a particular case. It is submitted that it is an important requirement that the material is made available to a section of the public likely to comprise those having a connection with the case. It is in this connection that the extent of the publication's circulation can be important. The national press or national television or radio network can hardly argue that their publication is unlikely to come to the notice of a juror or potential juror, witness, etc since their circulation is nationwide. As Lord Goddard CJ said in *R v Odham's Press Ltd, ex p A-G* [17] in the case of a contempt concerning the *People* newspaper:

> 'considering the proprietors claim a circulation of over four million copies a week, there is a strong probability that it would be read by at least some of those summoned as jurors'.

Nor would it be open to a local newspaper reporting a local case to argue that the article was unlikely to be read by potential jurors. In *Higgins v Richards*,[18] for instance, the *Neath News* published articles which were held to be prejudicial to a case pending at Swansea Assizes. Bray J said:

> 'It mattered not that the jury who would try the case might not come from Neath itself or from the neighbourhood. The editor boasted of the extended circulation of the paper, and it was almost certain that at least some of the jury would read some of the articles . . .'

It may be possible for a local newspaper with a strictly limited circulation, or a regional television network or a local radio station to argue in appropriate cases that, although the material was admittedly prejudicial, the publication was so limited as not to present a real risk of prejudice, there being only a remote chance of a person connected with the trial reading or hearing of the publication. For example, if a small local newspaper in Cornwall commented on a trial held in Durham, it might be argued that there is only a 'remote' chance of the article being read by persons connected with that trial and that therefore even though the comment may be prejudicial, provided of course there was no intention to prejudice the proceedings, no contempt would have been committed. The same argument might also apply to a highly specialised publication, which is unlikely to be read by the general public. The courts did not accept such an argument in

---

15 If the material is subsequently published the reporter is not necessarily immune from prosecution see eg *R v Evening Standard Co Ltd, ex p A-G* [1954] 1 QB 578, [1954] 1 All ER 1026, discussed in Ch 10.
16 Indeed, such a contempt might be thought to be intentional.
17 [1957] 1 QB 73 at 78.
18 (1912) 28 TLR 202 at 203.

the *North West Evening Mail* [19] or *Border Television* [20] cases, where the place of trial was outside the circulation or reception area, but in *A-G v Independent Television News Ltd* [21] there was held to be no contempt where the publication comprised an insignificant number of a northern newspaper sold in London, the place of trial.

The Australian Law Reform Commission has considered the publication requirement in relation to a jurisdiction in which centres of population are far apart and over a vast geographical area and where radio and television stations may only have a licence for a limited service area.[1] It concluded that a 'functional approach' to what constitutes 'publication' is preferable to a statutory definition and that both in determining what is a publication and in ascertaining the range of publication the policy objectives of the particular rule of contempt law involved should be considered. These conclusions are to be compared with the reform of UK law, where a statutory definition of publication was adopted.[2]

(b)   Where and when material is regarded as being 'published'

The issue of where material can be said to be published can be crucial to the question of jurisdiction. This problem has not been considered by the English courts but in the Canadian case of *Re Ouellet* [3] it was argued that remarks made in Ontario province by a Minister of the Crown to a newspaper reporter could not be prosecuted for contempt in Quebec province.[4] The plea failed because as Hugesson ACJ said:[5]

> 'Where as here, the essential element of the offence charged is in the publication of words and where these words are spoken by a person occupying the respondent's position to a newspaper reporter who is known to be a representative of a national news agency (the Canadian Press) it seems to me to be extremely doubtful that one can say that the offence was committed "entirely" at the place where the words were uttered and nowhere else. Publication in the rest of the country becomes a virtual certainty in the circumstances.'

Following *Re Ouellet* the place where the offence is committed is the place where the material is made available either to the general public or at any rate a section of the public likely to comprise those having a connection with the case. Accordingly in the case of radio or television broadcasts the place of the offence is that of the reception area and in the case of newspapers or periodicals it is the place of sale.

The issue of *when* material is published is relevant to the question of whether an offence is committed at all since (a) there is a point of time both before and after proceedings when contempt by interference with the administration of justice in a particular case cannot be committed,[6] and (b) the probability of risk

19   (1981) Times, 7 February.
20   (1978) 68 Cr App Rep 375, [1978] Crim LR 221, (1978) Times, 18 January. Cf *Blackburn v BBC* (1976) Times, 15 December.
21   [1995] 2 All ER 370, a case decided under the Contempt of Court Act 1981.
1   See the Australian Law Reform Commission's publications *Contempt and the Media* (Discussion Paper No 26) para 20 ff and *Contempt* (Report No 35) para 248 ff.
2   See Contempt of Court Act 1981, s 2(1), discussed at p 110.
3   (1976) 67 DLR (3d) 73. The case was appealed see (1976) 72 DLR (3d) 95 but not on this point.
4   Relying on s 434(1) of the Canadian Criminal Code.
5   (1976) 67 DLR (3d) 73 at 81, 82. Reliance was also placed upon *R v Gillespie* (1898) 8 Que QB 8; *Fournier v A-G* (1910) 19 Que KB 431; *Farmers' State Bank of Texhoma v State* (1917) 164 P 132; and *Myers v US* (1924) 44 S Ct 272.
6   See Ch 7.

is judged at the date of publication.[7] Despite the potential importance of the question there appears to be no case that has considered this point. It is submitted that in the case of the broadcasting media the operative time is when the material is broadcast and in the case of newspapers or other periodicals when they are on sale to the public.

New problems arise with forms of communication such as the Internet and it is submitted that material on the Internet must be considered published wherever it is available on the system. So material placed on the Internet anywhere in the world can be considered as published in whatever jurisdiction it can be read.[8]

(c)   The medium of publication

Contempt is not restricted to any particular medium of publication. It is commonly committed via the written word published in a newspaper or magazine but a risk of prejudice can be created by newspapers publishing photographs or even cartoons.[9] It does not matter where in a newspaper or magazine the offending material is published. It may be published as a front-page headline as in *R v Bolam, ex p Haigh* [10] or as an item in the 'Stop-Press' as in *R v West Australian Newspapers Ltd, ex p Minister for Justice.* [11] Contempt has also been held to have been committed by words on a poster used to promote newspaper sales.[12] Obviously, front-page headlines are more noticeable and it may be held indicative of the newspaper's intention to 'pander to sensationalism', which would be regarded as a serious contempt deserving of the severest punishment. It should also be said that publication of items on separate pages is no guarantee of immunity from a contempt prosecution if when read together they are thought to be creative of a risk of prejudice. Contempts are not restricted to newspapers. As Swift J said in *R v Hutchison, ex p MacMahon*: [13] 'The film is no more immune from the rules regarding contempt of court than the newspaper is.' Similarly, the broadcasting agencies, be they radio or television, are subject to the laws of contempt, though possibly because (until the advent of the video recorder) of their more fleeting nature less prosecutions have been brought in respect of broadcasts.[14] Contempt may also be committed by the spoken word such as a speech[15] or a theatrical performance[16] and in *R v Gilham* [17] wax models were the subject of proceedings. It has been held in Australia that the public proceedings

---

7   See p 84.
8   The question of responsibility for publication on the Internet is considered in Ch 10. The Government has attempted to deal with some of the problems of defamatory material on the Internet in its Defamation (Responsibility for Publication) Bill.
9   See eg *R v Evening News, ex p Campbell* (1925) Times, 27 October and *R v Edmonton Sun Publishing Ltd* (1981) 62 CCC (2d) 318.
10   (1949) 93 Sol Jo 220.
11   (1958) 60 WALR 108.
12   *R v Daily Herald, ex p Rouse* (1931) 75 Sol Jo 119: 'Another Blazing Car Murder'.
13   [1936] 2 All ER 1514.
14   See also Brabin J's comment in *A-G v London Weekend Television Ltd* [1972] 3 All ER 1146 at 1152: 'We reject the suggestion that merely because the spoken word is more ephemeral than a written publication that it is therefore less likely by its impact to amount to a contempt'.
15   See eg *R v Castro, Onslow's and Whalley's Case* (1873) LR 9 QB 219.
16   *R v Williams* (1823) 2 LJOS KB 30; *Keegstra v One Yellow Rabbit Theatre Association* (1992) 91 DLR (4th) 532: in February 1994 the Attorney General's ban on a production in London of a musical about Robert Maxwell caused the loss of the money already invested in the production.

of a Royal Commission were capable of giving rise to a contempt.[18] The statutory definition of 'publication' in the Contempt of Court Act 1981 has already been amended twice, in order to keep abreast of developments in the way in which television services are provided[19] and the courts can be expected to extend the meaning of publication at common law to cover new broadcasting phenomena as they arise and to consider words or images on a computer screen as a publication.

B   The mens rea

In criminal law the general rule is that the prosecution must prove, beyond all reasonable doubt, not only that the accused committed the actus reus, but also that he intended the consequences of his act or at least that he was reckless as to such consequences. In other words the prosecution must prove that the accused had the necessary 'mens rea'. In exceptional circumstances, however, the state of the accused's mind is irrelevant and all that is required to be proved is that the accused committed the requisite act. These latter offences are known as 'strict offences'.[20] As will be seen from the discussion elsewhere in this book, the application in general of the doctrine of mens rea to *criminal* contempt is not entirely clear. With regard to publications thought to create a real risk of prejudice, however, the common law position seems settled, it being established that provided it can be shown that the accused intended to publish the relevant material then he can be guilty of contempt even if he had no intention to prejudice the trial. To this extent contempt can be described as a 'strict offence'. This does not mean that the accused's intentions are irrelevant; for they are a crucial factor in deciding the appropriate punishment. Moreover, as we have seen, if it can be shown that the accused intended to interfere with the course of justice, he may be held guilty of contempt even though the material is not inherently prejudicial. That an intention to prejudice proceedings is not a necessary requirement was first established by the *St James's Evening Post* case.[1] As a defence to a charge of contempt it was said on behalf of the printer that she did not know the contents of the offending publication. Lord Hardwicke LC rejected this defence. He said it was urged:

> 'that she did not know the nature of the paper; and that printing papers and pamphlets is a trade and what she gets her livelihood by. But, though it is true this is a trade, yet they must take care to do it with prudence and caution; for if they print anything that is libellous, it is no excuse to say that the printer had no knowledge of its contents, and was entirely ignorant of its being libellous; and so is the rule at law, and I will always adhere to the strict rules of law in these cases.'

17 (1828) Mood & M 165.
18 *State of Victoria v Australian Building Construction Employees' and Builders' Labourers' Federation* (1982) 41 ALR 71 (Australia HC).
19 See p 110.
20 For a discussion of 'strict offences' see Smith & Hogan, *Criminal Law* (7th edn, 1992) Ch 6.
 1 (1742) 2 Atk 469, followed by Lord Erskine LC in *Ex p Jones* (1806) 13 Ves 237 at 239. Cf *Re Truth and Sportsman Ltd, ex p Bread Manufacturers Ltd* (1937) 37 SR (NSW) 242 at 250.

More recently Lord Goddard CJ said in *R v Odham's Press Ltd, ex p A-G*:[2]

> 'The test is whether the matter complained of is calculated to interfere with the course of justice, not whether the authors and printers intended that result, just as it is no defence for the person responsible for the publication of a libel to plead that he did not know that the matter was defamatory and had no intention to defame.'

Lord Goddard CJ's judgment was later approved by Donovan LJ in the Court of Appeal decision, *Re A-G's Application; A-G v Butterworth*,[3] who said:

> '*R v Odhams Press Ltd, ex p A-G* ... makes it clear that an intention to interfere with the proper administration of justice is not an essential ingredient of the offence of contempt of court. It is enough if the action complained of is inherently likely so to interfere. A newspaper article accusing a man of crime after proceedings have begun [against him] and before his trial plainly answers that description.'

A similar position obtains in other common law jurisdictions. In Australia, for example, the High Court has said[4] that actual intention or purpose lying behind a publication is not a decisive consideration but that the ultimate question is as to the inherent tendency of the matter published.

Donovan LJ's approval of Lord Goddard CJ's judgment in the *Odham's Press* case has been cited with approval in the New Zealand Court of Appeal.[5] A similar principle has been held to apply in Canada[6] but since the 1982 Charter there has been considerable debate about the issue of offences of strict and absolute liability. In *United Nurses of Alberta v A-G for Alberta*[7] McLachlin J, speaking for the majority in the Supreme Court of Canada, said that mens rea was needed for criminal contempt. This, however, was said in the context of disobedience to a court order[8] and other courts have proceeded on the assumption that contempt in respect of prejudicial publications does not need mens rea.[9] It is submitted that the general apparent lack of a need to show that the accused has a guilty mind is evidence not of a particularly strict application of the law in this area but of the general principle explained by Donovan LJ in *Butterworth*'s case,[10] namely, that

2 [1957] 1 QB 73 at 80. Lord Goddard CJ also relied on the dissenting judgment of Palles CB in *R v Dolan* [1907] 2 IR 260 at 284 where he said: 'As to the law applicable to the case there is no doubt. Actual intention to prejudice is immaterial. I wholly deny that the law of this court has been that absence of an actual intention to prejudice is to excuse the party from being adjudged guilty of contempt of court, if the court arrives at the conclusion which I have arrived at that there is a real danger that it will affect the trial: or that absence of intention is to excuse the party from punishment.'
3 [1963] 1 QB 696 at 726.
4 See *John Fairfax & Sons Pty Ltd v McRae* (1955) 93 CLR 351 at 371; *Lane v Registrar of the Supreme Court of NSW (Equity Division)* (1981) 148 CLR 245 at 258; *Victoria v Australian Building Construction Employees' & Builders' Labourers' Federation* (1982) 152 CLR 25 at 56 and 133; *Hinch v A-G for the State of Victoria* (1987) 164 CLR 15 at 85.
5 In *Solicitor-General v Radro Avon Ltd* [1978] 1 NZLR 225 at 232.
6 See eg *Re A-G for Manitoba and Radio Ob Ltd* (1976) 70 DLR (3d) 311 at 323.
7 (1992) 89 DLR (4th) 609 at 637.
8 See also *R v Edge* (1988) 24 BCLR (2d) 145, [1988] 4 WWR 163, which involved the breach of a publication ban on court proceedings, where mens rea was thought relevant.
9 See *A-G for Manitoba v Groupe Quebecor Inc* (1988) 45 DLR (4th) 80, where the Manitoba Court of Appeal convicted a publication of contempt for publishing an accused's previous convictions without requiring intent, but specifically said that the law of contempt was consistent with the Charter; in *R v Southam Inc* (1992) 6 Alta LR (3d) 115 (Alberta QB) it was specifically held that *UNA v A-G for Alberta* had no application to cases of prejudicial publicity. Cf South Africa where, according to Claassen J in *S v Van Niekerk* 1970 (3) SA 655T, an intention at least with regard to scandalising the court is required (for scandalising see further the discussion in Ch 9).
10 [1963] 1 QB 696 at 725–6.

if an act is clearly and of itself calculated to interfere with the administration of justice no further evidence of intent or motive is required.[11]

An obvious consequence of not requiring an intention to prejudice is that it is no defence for the accused to argue that he did not know or think the material published was prejudicial or that he had some other motive for publishing. In *Littler v Thomson* [12] the editor stated he had published the prejudicial article under the conviction: 'that he was advancing and promoting the cause of truth and justice'. But as Lord Langdale MR said:[13]

> 'Whatever might have been [the editor's] belief at the time he published these articles, that belief will not protect him from the consequences, if his publication has been of such a nature as to disturb the free course of justice.'

Similarly, it is no defence to plead that the prejudicial publication was due to a mistake. For instance, in *R v Evening Standard Co Ltd* [14] a reporter inadvertently included in his report of proceedings a report of inadmissible evidence which was held to be prejudicial; but, though the court held that the reporter had made an 'honest' mistake, he was nevertheless held guilty of contempt.[15] It has been held no defence to plead that the accused mistakenly believed either that no proceedings had been instituted or that they had been completed. In *R v Odhams Press Ltd, ex p A-G* [16] the *People* newspaper published a series of articles dealing with prostitution and brothel-keeping in London, and in their issue of 15 July 1956 published an attack on one Micallef alleging that he was 'up to his eyes in the foul business of purveying vice and managing street women', and urged that he should be prosecuted. However, Micallef had been arrested on 13 June. The respondents admitted that the article was prejudicial but argued that, because they did not know that proceedings had been instituted against Micallef and so could not be said to have intended to prejudice proceedings, they could not be held guilty of contempt.[17]

The Divisional Court held that such a lack of knowledge was no defence. Lord Goddard CJ said:[18]

> 'It is obvious that if a person does not know that proceedings have begun or are imminent he cannot by writing or speech be said to intend to influence the course

---

11 Cf Lord Denning MR's view, ibid at 722, that 'contempt of court is a criminal offence . . . and like all criminal offences it requires in general a guilty mind'. It is submitted that this view is wrong. See further, *Registrar, of the Supreme Court, Equity Division v McPherson* [1980] 1 NSWLR 688 at 700, para 28.

12 (1839) 2 Beav 129.

13 Ibid at 132.

14 [1954] 1 QB 578, [1954] 1 All ER 1026.

15 It was held, however, (ibid at 586) that the reporter should not be punished: 'he did not deliberately send up that which he knew to be untrue, but, perhaps owing to ill health or other reasons, he had a confused idea in his mind'.

16 [1957] 1 QB 73, [1956] 3 All ER 494.

17 Such an argument was to a certain extent supported by two old cases, *Metropolitan Music Hall Co v Lake* (1889) 58 LJ Ch 513 and *Re Marquis Townshend* (1906) 22 TLR 341. In the former, Chitty J thought that it would be 'an extension of the doctrine to say that the respondent is bound by his peril to take cognizance' of every action that might be pending, but in the case before him he thought that the article was not prejudicial in any event, so that his observation could be said to be obiter. In the latter, Lord Collins MR seemed to be of the opinion that being aware that proceedings were pending was a precondition of being found guilty of contempt although again it was not clear that the article was considered to be prejudicial. Another case which supported this argument, but which was not cited is *Ex p Foster* (1894) Times, 5 February.

18 [1957] 1 QB 73 at 80.

of justice or to prejudice a litigant or accused person, but that is no answer if he published that which is in fact calculated to prejudice a fair trial.'

As a corollary to *R v Odhams Press Ltd, ex p A-G*, it will be no defence to argue that it was thought all proceedings had been completed. Such a defence was raised in *Grimwade v Cheque Bank Ltd* [19] but Kekewich J held that the person responsible for the publication was under a duty to inquire whether or not in fact the proceedings had been completed.

A person who is held to be responsible for a publication will be considered guilty of a contempt even though he personally may be ignorant of the contents of the article. Examples of this are the *St James's Evening Post* case [20] and *Ex p Jones*, [1] where the printers were held liable despite their personal ignorance of the contents of the newspapers. This principle extends to any person held responsible for a publication, such as the editor and the proprietors. In *R v Griffiths, ex p A-G* [2] it was applied to distributors. In this case the American magazine, *Newsweek*, published an article which was held to be prejudicial to a pending trial. The article was written in America and the European edition was printed in Amsterdam. Contempt proceedings were brought against the secondary publishers, Rolls House Company, and against WH Smith & Son who, having imported the magazine into this country, distributed it for sale either to wholesalers or direct to the general public. Both respondents argued that they were not guilty of contempt as they did not know that the magazine contained the offending paragraphs and had no reason to suspect it would. In other words, they sought to invoke the defence of innocent dissemination as is applicable in the law of defamation. The Divisional Court denied that there was any valid analogy with the law of defamation. Lord Goddard CJ said:[3]

'Cases of contempt by publication of matter tending to prejudice a fair trial stand in a class of their own and are not truly analogous to cases of defamation.'

Applying *R v Odhams Press Ltd, ex p A-G* [4] it was held that the lack of knowledge of the contents of the publication and the consequential lack of intention to prejudice the proceedings was no defence. Lord Goddard CJ added that as the defence of innocent dissemination was not available it was unnecessary to consider the issue of negligence.

Although contempt by publication might properly be regarded as a strict offence that does not mean to say that no mens rea is required. The authorities support the view that the accused must have intended to publish the material in question. In *McLeod v St Aubyn*,[5] where a newspaper known as the *Federalist* printed certain letters containing abusive and derogatory comments on St Vincent's Chief Justice, the person charged with the contempt was neither the printer or publisher of the newspaper nor the author of the letters. All the accused had done was to lend a copy of the newspaper to a librarian, the library not having received their usual copy. As the Privy Council held:[6]

19 (1897) 13 TLR 305.
20 (1742) 2 Atk 469.
 1 (1806) 13 Ves 237.
 2 [1957] 2 QB 192.
 3 Ibid at 203.
 4 [1957] 1 QB 73, [1956] 3 All ER 494.
 5 [1899] AC 549.
 6 Ibid at 562.

'On the evidence it must be assumed that he innocently and without any knowledge of the contents, handed . . . the copy of the newspaper to [the librarian].'

It was held that the accused had not committed a contempt, for as Lord Morris (who delivered the judgment) said:[7]

'It would be extraordinary if every person who innocently handed over a newspaper or lent one to a friend with no knowledge of its containing anything objectionable, could thereby be constructively but necessarily guilty of a contempt of a court because the said newspaper happened to contain scandalous matter reflecting on the court. [The colonial court] arrived at the conclusion that the appellant was guilty of negligence in not making himself acquainted with the contents of the newspaper ... This assumes there was some duty on the appellant to have so made himself acquainted. That is a proposition which cannot be upheld. A printer and publisher intends to publish, and so intending cannot plead as a justification that he did not know the contents. *The appellant in this case never intended to publish.*' (emphasis added)

This decision was approved by Lord Goddard CJ in *R v Griffiths, ex p A-G* [8] who said that the Privy Council:

'clearly regarded the contention that in such circumstances the appellant could be said to be guilty of publishing a contempt as extravagant, and we should take the same view.'

Despite the foregoing authority, it can also be argued that a person who knowingly sells or lends or delivers a newspaper to another obviously intends to publish it. This view depends for its validity in the concept of 'publishing' bearing the same meaning as for defamation which we have previously argued, is too strict for the purposes of contempt.[9] Another possible explanation of *McLeod* is that the lending of the newspaper to another individual could not possibly be said to have been creative of a real risk of prejudice to the due administration of justice. In other words it might be arguable that the accused has to have an intention to publish to the world at large to be guilty of contempt.[10] The drawback of this explanation is that it might be difficult to defend paper-boys, street sellers, or the ordinary employee of a newspaper, television or radio yet, as Lord Goddard CJ said in *R v Griffiths, ex p A-G*: [11]

'It was argued that if these two respondents [Rolls House Co and WH Smith & Son] are liable so every small newsagent or street seller who sells the paper would equally be liable. Logically this may be so, but the court would not regard with favour applications against such persons to whom no real blame would attach. This jurisdiction is discretionary and the court can be trusted not to exercise it except against those who can fairly be said to bear some real responsibility for the publication.'

The reason for not regarding such people as guilty of contempt may simply be one of policy. However, that policy would surely be better served by saying that such persons are properly regarded as not having committed a contempt at all rather than saying that in the exercise of its discretion the court will not punish

---

7 Ibid at 562.
8 [1957] 2 QB 192 at 203.
9 See p 85.
10 Cf in Canada *Cotroni v Quebec Police Commission and Brunet* (1978) 80 DLR (3d) 490 at 494 (Can Sup Ct) where *McLeod* is dismissed as a prosecution failing for insufficient evidence.
11 [1957] 2 QB 192at 204.

them. It should be emphasised that it is only open to a person to say that he has no intention to publish if he is *both* ignorant of the contents of the publication *and* bears no responsibility for the publication. A person selling or even lending a newspaper, knowing that it contained prejudicial material could not argue that he had no intention to publish. Even so it is doubtful whether such persons will normally be charged, it being more likely that charges will be brought against those exercising original responsibility for the publication, ie the editor or proprietor. However, if a person, knowing that a newspaper contained prejudicial comments, deliberately pointed such comments out to a person whom he is aware is directly concerned with a trial, such a witness or juror, it might be thought proper to prosecute. On the other hand, a person such as an editor or proprietor, who bears real responsibility for the publication cannot say that because he was personally ignorant of the contents of the publication, he did not intend to publish. Such persons, as we shall see, must always be regarded as intending to publish on the grounds of their ultimate responsibility for a publication.[12]

C   Defences

Once the constituent elements of the contempt offence are established the common law admits of few defences. As can be seen from the discussion above, liability is strict so that provided the defendant can properly be said to have 'published' the offending material it is no defence to say that he did not intend to prejudice proceedings or that he was unaware that proceedings were pending or imminent as the case may be or even (in some cases) that he was unaware of the contents of the publication. There is no defence of innocent dissemination at common law.

Nor has the common law developed a general defence of 'public interest' whereby it is a defence to show that the publication of prejudicial material is in the public interest. It does, however, appear to recognise the validity of the 'discussion of public affairs' as being an answer to a charge of contempt. This concept is popularly known as the '*Bread Manufacturers* defence' after the Australian case, *Re Truth and Sportsman Ltd, ex p Bread Manufacturers Ltd* [13] in which it was explained.[14] These matters are discussed in Chapter 5.[15]

A defence of 'statutory authority' has been discussed in Australia in the context of Royal Commissions holding inquiries about matters which are also the subject of legal proceedings. In *Lockwood v Commonwealth* [16] Fullagar J said:

> 'No court could hold . . . that what is expressly authorised by the Crown under a statute is a contempt.'

In *State of Victoria v Australian Building Construction Employees' and Builders' Labourers' Federation* [17] the High Court of Australia considered that this would not apply where the statute did not authorise the *specific* inquiry. Since

---

12 See generally Ch 10.
13 (1937) 37 SR (NSW) 242.
14 It was cited with approval by Lords Reid and Simon in *A-G v Times Newspapers Ltd* [1974] AC 273 at 296 and 321 respectively.
15 See pp 169 ff.
16 (1954) 90 CLR 177 at 185.
17 (1982) 41 ALR 71.

there is no reported case in which the proceedings of a Royal Commission have been held to prejudice a trial the matter remains untested.

IV CRITICISMS OF THE COMMON LAW POSITION

There is rightly concern about any law that operates to restrict freedom of speech and though the law of contempt is not the only law that restricts such freedom, it causes particular anxiety especially to those involved with the news media.[18]

Reasons contributing to this anxiety include the alleged uncertainty in the application of the law of contempt, the potential severity of the penalties and the summary nature of the prosecution process. There has also been increasing questioning of the very rationale of the contempt laws and it is to this that we shall now turn.

A The rationale of contempt at common law

The alleged justification for the common law position is that, important though freedom of speech is, it must nevertheless be curbed so as not to interfere with the interest of society in the right to a fair trial. Preservation of freedom of speech and protection of the right to a fair trial (in the sense of having an impartial tribunal trying the case upon properly submitted evidence) are both hallmarks of a democratic and free society. Both interests are commonly regarded as fundamental rights and are enshrined as such under various international conventions on human rights notably the Universal Declaration of Human Rights 1948, the European Convention on Human Rights and the American Convention on Human Rights.[19] The problem, which is not unique to common law jurisdictions, is whether the two interests are properly adjudged to conflict and, if so, how they should be balanced. The common law (at least outside the United States) perceives these two interests as ultimately conflicting public interests. It assumes that uncontrolled publicity about a particular trial will constitute a threat to the due administration of justice either in the particular case by potentially jeopardising the fairness of that trial or more generally by lowering public esteem in the courts' ability to try a case free from outside interference and so deter litigants from using the judicial process to settle disputes. Acting upon these assumptions and working on the principle that prevention is better than cure, the law of contempt operates strictly in that it is concerned to curb comments creating a *risk* of interfering with the course of justice. Furthermore, those adjudged to have offended against the restrictions can be punished regardless of their intent so to interfere.

18 As Charles Wintour, a former editor of the London *Evening Standard*, said: 'I probably spend more time worrying about the possibility of contempt of court than I do about all the other legal restrictions put together' (*Pressures on the Press* (1972) p 129).
19 However, it is post-Enlightenment, Western societies which ascribe such importance to freedom of speech: the controversy over the *fatwa* imposed on Salman Rushdie demonstrated that for some societies and communities it does not have the same status as a master value.

B   Alternative views

Neither the common law perception of conflict nor its resolution of the alleged conflict represent inevitable choices in upholding both the right to freedom of speech and the right of a fair trial. Furthermore, not everyone would accept that the right to a fair trial is properly classifiable as a *public* interest. The assumption that those involved in the judicial process, even lay people acting as jurors or witnesses, are susceptible to the influence of out-of-court publicity is largely an untested one[20] and not all jurisdictions are so ready to make such an assumption. In the United States, for example, Burger Ch J said in the leading case of *Nebraska Press Association v Stuart* [1] that 'pre-trial publicity—even pervasive adverse publicity—does not inevitably lead to an unfair trial.' Hence, it is difficult in that country to justify a court order restraining pre-trial publicity,[2] let alone punishing allegedly prejudicial publications through the contempt process.[3]

Even if the existence of a conflict is accepted the common law solution is still not inevitable. The solution commonly adopted in the United States, for example, is not to resolve the conflict by limiting what can be said but rather to quash any conviction resulting from a prejudiced trial.[4] This position could perhaps be rationalised by saying that in effect the right to a fair trial is really a *private* interest of the parties or litigants which is normally outweighed by the public interest in freedom of speech. The American solution has of course been in part influenced by the provisions of its Constitution emphasising the right of free speech[5] but nevertheless it does provide an alternative model to that of the common law. The appropriateness of the American model to England and other common law jurisdictions is a matter of debate and ultimately a value judgment. Allowance might have to be made for the fact that the system has been developed against a different societal and institutional background. Nevertheless some will undoubtedly see attraction in a system which clearly recognises freedom of speech as the superior value. Under the American system whilst some restrictions can be specifically imposed on what can be said before a trial (ie court orders can be made, with constitutional validity, in circumstances where influence seems a near certainty)[6] there is now a steadfast refusal to impose a general and automatic restraint on what can be said about particular trials.[7] The trial process is thought to be adequately protected by greater scrutiny of the prejudices of potential jurors and a readiness to quash a conviction resulting from a prejudiced trial. The critics of the American system will doubt whether the right to a fair trial is adequately protected.[8] Quite apart from whether it is right to subject those involved in a trial (criminal or civil) to the uncontrolled glare of publicity perhaps for no other

20   See the comments of the Phillimore Committee (1974, Cmnd 5794) para 50.
 1   1976 427 US 539 at 555, 49 L Ed 2nd 683 695.
 2   See *Sheppard v Maxwell* 1966 384 US 333, 16 Led 2nd 600, commented on by, inter alia, Alan Grant, 'Pre-Trial Publicity and Fair Trial: A Tale of Three Doctors' (1976) 14 Osgoode Hall LJ 275; Van Niekerk, (1978) 95 South African LJ at 551 and note the references there cited.
 3   See *Nye v US* 1941 313 US 33 and the discussion in Miller, *Contempt of Court* (2nd edn, 1989) at pp 90–96.
 4   See eg *Sheppard v Maxwell* 1966 384 US 333, 16 Led 2nd 600 and the comments by Miller ibid, at pp 192–194.
 5   As provided for by the First Amendment to the Constitution.
 6   See eg *Chicago Council of Lawyers v Bauer* 522 F 2nd 242 (7th Circ, 1975).
 7   *Nebraska Press Association v Stuart* 1976 427 US 539 at 555, 49 L Ed 2nd 683 695.
 8   Note the recommendations of the Reardon Committee, 'The Fair Trial—Free Press Standards' 54 ABA J 343 (April 1968) and Purver, 'Contempt—By News Media' 33 ALR 3d 1116: there was widespread criticism in the UK of the publicity surrounding the trial of OJ Simpson in 1995.

reason than it is a good story, it might be questioned whether it is sensible to allow or even court the possibility that guilty people should be acquitted because of adverse publicity. Furthermore, the system depends upon lengthy screening of potential jurors which is not a process with which everyone will agree nor does it guarantee that all jurors will have been uninfluenced by out-of-court publicity. In short there will be those who believe that the American system has got its priorities wrong.

In Canada, which does have contempt rules, the accused may choose,[9] with the consent of the Attorney General to be tried by judge alone instead of by judge and jury,[10] and this can protect an accused who believes that pre-trial publicity may have prejudiced potential jurors against him.

C The extent to which the common law standpoint is justified

It is submitted that inasmuch as the common law seeks to prevent a risk of prejudice to a particular trial (especially criminal trials) it adopts the preferable position. It is true that the perception of conflict is based on the assumption that out-of-court publicity does influence those involved in the trial process but nevertheless, given the undoubted power of the media, it does seem reasonable to suppose that laymen such as jurors and witnesses are likely to be influenced. Once it is accepted that publicity *can* interfere with the fairness of the trial (and even in the United States there is a limited recognition of such an effect) then it seems sensible to seek to eliminate the risk of prejudice rather than to endeavour to live with the consequences. The appropriateness of this position at least with respect to the protection of criminal trials is further strengthened by the fact that in the United Kingdom, at any rate, there is apparent support even from within the media for the law's basic standpoint.[11] The position with regard to the protection of civil proceedings is harder to justify, particularly if, as is generally accepted, the professional judge will not be unduly influenced by out-of-court publicity. It may be that the common law has yet to come to terms with the fact that most trials are now heard without a jury. While there is a case for applying some restrictions, if only to protect litigants and to prevent undue influencing of witnesses, there must be a doubt as to how much further the law can properly go. The more general the danger to the due administration of justice is perceived to be the more speculative the alleged risk becomes and the more speculative the risk, the harder it becomes to justify restricting freedom of speech. It is one thing to restrict publications thought to present a real risk of prejudice to a particular case but quite another to impose restrictions because the publication might undermine public confidence in the judicial system generally. It was in this latter respect that the application of the common law rules[12] brought the English courts into conflict with the European Court of Human Rights.[13] Although acceptance of the common law standpoint inevitably means that there must be some limitation on freedom of speech, the law has never been so strict as to prohibit

9 In respect of an offence listed in s 469 of the Criminal Code.
10 Charter of Rights and Freedoms, s 11(f) and s 473 of the Criminal Code.
11 For the example in para 73 of the Phillimore Report the Committee commented that: '[a]mong the substantial volume of evidence we received from the press and others there was no suggestion that the law was wrong in principle . . .'.
12 *A-G v Times Newspapers Ltd* [1974] AC 273, [1973] 3 All ER 54.
13 *Sunday Times v UK* (1979) 2 EHRR 245 discussed at pp 100 ff.

all references to pending litigation and in any event the restrictions that are imposed are, for the most part, only temporary. There is and always has been a right to criticise particular decisions once they have been made and informed criticism is aided by the fact that open court proceedings are freely reportable. Moreover, criticism of the law is permitted even during the currency of legal proceedings provided comment upon the particular case is avoided.[14] It can thus be fairly said that justice is not a cloistered virtue.

V   REFORM IN THE UNITED KINGDOM

A   The background to reform

In the period leading up to the Contempt of Court Act 1981 there was no serious pressure within the United Kingdom for the *abolition* of the contempt restrictions[15] but there was considerable pressure to relax them. Earlier pleas for reform notably from *Justice* [16] had brought some relaxation in the law in that under what was then s 11 of the Administration of Justice Act 1960[17] it became a defence if the publisher could show that he was, in effect, justifiably ignorant of the pendency or imminence of the proceedings alleged to be potentially prejudiced. Similarly, distributors had a defence if they were justifiably ignorant that a publication which they distributed contained potentially prejudicial material. Following the 1960 Act the pleas for reform subsided[18] but in the 1970s they began to be heard again. Naturally, pressure for reform came from the media, in the vanguard of which was the *Sunday Times* under its then editor, Harold Evans. However, the greatest pressure and stimulus for reform came first from the report of the Phillimore Committee[19] and then from the decision of the European Court of Human Rights in the *Sunday Times v UK*.[20] The latter decision, in which the United Kingdom was held to have violated the European Convention on Human Rights, finally prompted the Government to act with the result that in 1981 the Contempt of Court Act was passed.

Subsequently there has been considerable discussion in other common law jurisdictions about reform of the law. In Canada, the Canadian Law Reform Commission investigated the law of contempt for a number of years and in 1982 published their final report.[1] Since then the Canadian courts have had to reconcile the law of contempt with the guarantee of freedom of expression under the 1982 Charter of Rights and Freedoms. The Australian Law Reform Commission published a report on contempt in 1986[2] and the Irish Law Reform Commission published a consultation paper in 1991.

14 See in particular Lord Morris's comments in the *Sunday Times* case, ibid at 306.
15 Note the Phillimore Committee's comments (1974, Cmnd 5794).
16 Via their report, *Contempt of Court* (1959).
17 This has been re-enacted by s 3 of the Contempt of Court Act 1981, discussed at pp 398 ff.
18 Though *Justice*, this time in their report, *The Law and the Press* (1965), did call for further reforms, see paras 13–54.
19 The Committee was appointed on 8 June 1971 under the chairmanship of Phillimore LJ but Lord Cameron acted as chairman in the later stages due to Phillimore LJ's serious and ultimately fatal illness.
20 (1979) 2 EHRR 245.
1 Report No 17 (1982). Its Working Paper No 20 was published in 1977.
2 Report No 35, *Contempt*. The recommendations of this report are mentioned in the book in the context in which they arise.

We shall now concentrate on the position in the United Kingdom and prior to discussing the Contempt of Court Act 1981 we shall examine the Phillimore proposals and the European Court's decision.

B The Phillimore Report

The Committee accepted[3] that there was a need to have some degree of protection for the due administration of justice and that it was right in principle to limit what can be published in order to protect the course of justice in particular legal proceedings. The Committee seemed to endorse the common law assumption of the vulnerability of jurors[4] and witnesses[5] to undue influence by out-of-court publicity but thought it right to regard professional judges as being capable of withstanding such pressures.[6] It was also thought to be right in principle that there should be strict liability for potentially prejudicial publications.[7] In view of the power of the printed or broadcast word the due administration of justice in particular legal proceedings could be adequately protected only if there was a rule which required great care to ensure that offending material was not published. The Committee commented:

> 'A liability which rested only on proof of intent or actual foresight would favour the reckless at the expense of the careful. Most publishing is a commercial enterprise undertaken for profit and the power of the printed or broadcast word is such that the administration of justice would not be adequately protected without a rule which requires great care to be taken to ensure that offending material is not published.'

It recommended,[8] however, that strict liability should be limited to public conduct because (a) private conduct could not give rise to such dangers as creating a prejudicial atmosphere or undermining public confidence in the administration of justice, and (b) it would be neither reasonable nor practicable to penalise an ordinary individual who does not realise that his conduct may affect pending proceedings. Accordingly, the Committee recommended[9] that strict liability should apply only to 'publications' which it defined as 'any speech, writing, broadcast or other communication, in whatever form, which is addressed to the public at large'. However, whilst basically accepting the correctness of the common law standpoint the Committee's concern was (a) to eliminate uncertainty in the application of the contempt laws wherever possible, and (b) to adjust the balance a little in favour of freedom of speech. To this end a number of recommendations were made[10] including the proposal that there should be a new statutory test for when publications should be considered a contempt.[11]

In recommending a new statutory test the Committee had in mind that a number of different tests had been developed by the courts, ie variants on the need

3 Ibid at paras 10 and 73.
4 Though note the reservations expressed at para 50.
5 Paras 53–56.
6 Para 49.
7 Para 74.
8 Para 77.
9 Para 80. For a critisism of this definition see Lowe, 'Report of the Committee on Contempt of Court 1974' (1975) 125 NLJ 513 at 514.
10 Other recommendations are discussed throughout this book. For a discussion of the report see eg Borrie, [1975] Crim LR 127 and Lowe, (1975) 125 NLJ 513 and 526.
11 See paras 103–114.

to establish a risk of prejudice to particular legal proceedings and finally the 'prejudgment test' as formulated by the House of Lords in the *Sunday Times* case.[12] Whilst recognising the force of the Law Lords' arguments with respect to the dangers of 'trial by newspaper or television' the Committee nevertheless rejected the 'prejudgment' test as being at once too wide and too narrow; the former because it could prevent an opinion being expressed in a learned legal journal or in a scientific journal, the latter because it might exclude opinions which though influential could be so framed as to disclaim any intention to offer a concluded judgment. The Committee, considering that the only satisfactory test was one referring to the risk of prejudice to the due administration of justice, recommended a test of 'whether the publication complained of creates a risk that the course of justice will be seriously impeded or prejudiced'. The advantages of the proposed test, as the Committee saw it, were that it eliminated reference to the slippery concept of 'calculated' to;[13] by defining the degree of prejudice it eliminated 'technical' contempts[14] and the use of the word 'will' further emphasised the need for a serious risk of prejudice. When considered together with proposals such as the legitimacy of continuing public discussion of matters of public interest despite intervening litigation and the propriety of bringing public influence or pressure to bear upon a party to proceedings, the effect of the recommendation would have been to relax substantially the operation of the law of contempt in respect of civil proceedings.

The Phillimore proposals were widely applauded, particularly by the news media, but successive governments seemed prepared to ignore them and when in 1978 a Green Paper[15] on Contempt was published in which some of the Phillimore recommendations were questioned it seemed that the report would never be implemented. In the event fresh impetus for reform was given by the European Court of Human Rights' decision in the *Sunday Times* case.

C   The European Court of Human Rights' Decision in *Sunday Times v UK*

The immediate pressure for reform of the UK domestic law of contempt came from the European Court of Human Rights' decision in *Sunday Times v UK*.[16] The *Sunday Times* applied to Strasbourg following the granting of an injunction by the House of Lords to restrain the newspaper's proposed publication of an article dealing with the thalidomide tragedy at a time when several actions on behalf of the child victims of the drug were being negotiated with Distillers Ltd (the UK marketers) with a view to an out-of-court settlement. The newspaper's main claim[17] was that the injunction violated Article 10 of the European

12 [1974] AC 273, [1973] 3 All ER 54. The prejudgment test is discussed at pp 221 ff.
13 Discussed at p 74.
14 Discussed at pp 76 ff.
15 1978, Cmnd 7145.
16 (1979) 2 EHRR 245. For an excellent account of the whole of the *Sunday Times'* litigation see Murray Rosen, *The Sunday Times thalidomide case: Contempt of Court and the Freedom of the Press* (1979, Writers and Scholars Educational Trust). For a more critical account of the European decision see Lowe, 'The English Law of Contempt of Court and Article 10 of the European Convention on Human Rights' in *The Effect on English Domestic Law of Membership of the European Communities and of Ratification of the European Convention on Human Rights* (1983, Nijhoff, eds Furmston, Kerridge and Sufrin) pp 318 ff.
17 It also claimed that it had been unfairly discriminated against contrary to Art 14 (when read in conjunction with Art 10) because although other publications dealt with the thalidomide

Convention on Human Rights because it restricted its freedom of expression. Article 10(1) provides, inter alia:

'Everyone has the right to freedom of expression. This right shall include the freedom to hold opinions and to receive and impart information and ideas without interference by public authority . . .'

The Government argued that the restriction was justified within the terms of Article 10(2) which states:

'The exercise of these freedoms since it carries with it duties and responsibilities, may be subject to such formalities, conditions, restrictions or penalties as are prescribed by law and are necessary in a democratic society, in the interests of national security, territorial integrity or public safety, for the prevention of disorder or crime, for the protection of health or morals, for the protection of the reputation or rights of others, for preventing the disclosure of information received in confidence or for maintaining the authority and impartiality of the judiciary.'

Its main argument was that the restriction had been imposed for the legitimate purpose of maintaining the authority and impartiality of the judiciary.[18] It also argued that it was justified under 'the rights of others' exception since it protected Distillers' right (guaranteed by Article 6) to a fair trial. Article 6 provides, inter alia:

'In the determination of his civil rights and obligations or of any criminal charge against him everyone is entitled to a fair and public hearing within a reasonable time by an independent and impartial tribunal established by law.'

In any event Article 10, it was argued, was subject to an *inherent* limitation imposed by Article 6 so that where the two articles conflicted the former had to give way. None of the Government's arguments was accepted either by the Commission[19] or the Court and in each case by a narrow majority it was ruled that the injunction violated Article 10.[20] The argument that Article 10 was subject to an inherent limitation imposed by Article 6 was specifically disposed of by the Commission[1] which ruled that the justification of the restriction upon freedom of expression cannot be implied by interpretation of other provisions of the Convention independently of Article 10. Neither the Commission nor the Court considered it necessary to pursue the argument that the restriction was justified under the 'rights of others' exception since that purpose was held to be included in the notion of protecting the judiciary's 'authority'. The Court unanimously agreed that at least one purpose of the contempt laws is to maintain the authority and impartiality of the judiciary and that the injunction was specifically aimed at maintaining the judiciary's 'authority'. Hence, the restriction had a legitimate aim within Article 10(2) but the majority ruled[2] that this in itself did not justify

tragedy it was only its article which was restrained. Both the Commission and the Court unanimously rejected this claim. A further claim that the injunction prevented the applicants from exercising their duties as journalists thereby violating Art 18 (when read in conjunction with Art 10) was rejected by the Commission and not pursued before the Court.
18 Indeed this exception was first drafted by the British Delegation specifically, it is said, (see the Joint Dissenting Opinion in *Sunday Times v UK* (1979) 2 EHRR 245 at 285, para 2) to cover contempt of court.
19 Reported as Application No 6538/74, adopted on 18 May 1977.
20 The majorities were 8 to 5 in the Commission and 11 to 9 in the Court.
1 Report on Application No 6538/74, para 191 applying *De Becker v Belgium* (1960) Report of 8 January, para 263.
2 (1979) 2 EHRR 245 at 275, para 59. Following *Handyside v UK* (1976) 1 EHRR 737.

the restriction since it still had to be shown to be 'necessary'. 'Necessity' was ruled to mean something between 'indispensable' on the one hand and 'reasonable', 'useful' or 'desirable' on the other, and implied the existence of a 'pressing social need'. The crucial question, therefore, was whether the 'interference' complained of corresponded to a 'pressing social need', whether it was 'proportionate' to the legitimate aim pursued and whether the reasons given by the national authority were 'relevant and sufficient' under Article 10(2). With regard to the latter inquiry the majority noted that the Law Lords had emphasised their concern that the processes of the law might be brought into disrespect and the functions of the court usurped inter alia if litigants had to undergo 'trial by newspaper'. Though certainly 'relevant' to the maintenance of the authority of the judiciary it was doubted whether the particular article would have had that effect. However, it was acknowledged that the fear that publication of the proposed article might have provoked replies was also a 'relevant' concern but the question then was whether in all the circumstances this was 'sufficient' reason so as to make the restriction 'necessary'. In the majority's view it was not. Working from the principle that the:[3]

> 'Court is faced not with a choice between two conflicting principles but with a principle of freedom of expression that is subject to a number of exceptions which must be narrowly interpreted',

the majority were concerned with the public interest in the case. In its view a court cannot operate in a vacuum so there cannot be a total embargo against prior discussion of disputes outside the courts, indeed, it was incumbent on the mass media to impart information and ideas concerning matters that come before the court just as in other areas of public interest. In this case the thalidomide disaster was a matter of 'undisputed' public concern and that concern extended to the question of where responsibility for the tragedy actually lay. This public concern was not outweighed by any demonstrative need on the facts to maintain 'the authority of the judiciary'. Accordingly, the majority ruled that Article 10 had been violated.

The immediate significance of the European Court's decision was that the United Kingdom became obliged, by reason of Article 53, to amend its laws to conform with the ruling. This, however, is not its only significance for although the Convention in not directly applicable to UK domestic law and the decisions of the European Court are not binding precedents, nevertheless as Lord Scarman has said in *A-G v BBC*:[4]

> 'there is a presumption, albeit rebuttable that our municipal law will be consistent with our international obligations ... we must bear in mind the impact of whatever decision we may be minded to make upon the international obligations assumed by the United Kingdom under the Convention.'

Even in other common law jurisdictions outside Europe the European Court's decision is not totally irrelevant although it may not be regarded as persuasive as the House of Lords' decision.[5] For a number of reasons, therefore, it is important

---

3 (1979) 2 EHRR 245 at 281, para 65.
4 [1981] AC 303 at 354.
5 In *Commercial Bank of Australia Ltd v Preston* [1981] 2 NSWLR 554 at 562 Hunt J held that 'the majority judgment of the European Court at Strasbourg is of no assistance in the task of what the law is here in Australia'. That comment should, however, be considered in its context. Earlier in his judgment at 561, Hunt J said that both the European decision and that of the House of Lords were of 'very substantial persuasive authority' but held that the latter is 'the more persuasive'.

to appreciate what the European Court decided. The European decision cannot be regarded as a wholesale condemnation of the contempt laws. On the contrary, it was accepted that such laws had a legitimate aim within Article 10(2). Further, the Court was only concerned with that aspect of contempt aimed at protecting the 'authority' of the judiciary. It did not pass comment, nor therefore criticise the application of contempt when concerned to protect the 'impartiality' of the judiciary.[6] All that the European Court specifically disapproved of was the imposition of a particular restraint in the particular circumstances. In reaching this conclusion it disapproved of the 'prejudgment test' as laid down by the majority in the House of Lords. The majority in the European Court expressly concluded[7] that they had to weigh the balance in *each* case between freedom of expression and the maintenance of the authority of the judiciary. The prejudgment test amounted to an absolute prohibition irrespective of the risks of prejudice to an individual case and as such was inconsistent with the European Court's decision. It also seems reasonable to conclude that the European Court disapproved of the application on the particular facts of the so-called 'pressure test' (ie the public imposition of undue pressure upon litigants) as conceived by the minority of the Law Lords.

Precisely what reforms of the contempt laws were required of the United Kingdom has generated heated controversy. Few disputed the obligation to reverse the 'prejudgment test' but beyond this there was disagreement. The narrow view (perhaps not surprisingly favoured by the then Government)[8] was all that was required was the replacement of the prejudgment test by a test approximating to the concept of 'necessity' as conceived by the European Court. The wider view was that not only should the prejudgment test be reversed but that it should be replaced by a test that specifically refers to the requirement of a 'pressing social need' and it should be enacted[9] that bringing influence or pressure to bear upon a party to proceedings should not be a contempt unless it amounts to intimidation or unlawful threats to his person, property or reputation. Although the wider view probably more accurately reflected the spirit of the European Court's decision there is justification for taking a narrow view.[10] The decision was reached only by the narrowest of margins and the majority's approach is not beyond criticism, particularly as it seems to leave Contracting States with little discretion to decide the 'necessity' of restriction for themselves.[11]

---

6 In fact the 'impartiality' ground was not pleaded before the Court and was left out of account, see (1979) 2 EHRR 245 at 274, para 57.
7 Ibid at 281, para 65.
8 In particular by Lord Hailsham who as Lord Chancellor had prime responsibility for steering the contempt legislation through Parliament.
9 Following the recommendation of the Phillimore Committee (1974, Cmnd 5794).
10 See Lowe, 'The English Law of Contempt of Court and Article 10 on the European Convention on Human Rights' in *The Effect on English Domestic Law of Membership of the European Communities and of Ratification of the European Convention on Human Rights* (1983, Nijhoff, eds Furmston, Kerridge and Sufrin) pp 335–339.
11 The so-called 'margin of appreciation' seems in this instance to have been reduced almost to vanishing point for quite unsupportable reasons. See the minority view, (1979) 2 EHRR 245 at pp 289, 290, para 9. See also Clovis C Morrison Jnr, *The Dynamics of Development in the European Human Rights Convention System* (1981, Nijhoff) pp 110, 111. For a trenchant criticism of this aspect of the decision see FA Mann, 'Contempt of Court in the House of Lords and the European Court of Human Rights' (1979) 95 LQR 348 at 351–352. For criticism of this and other points of the majority's judgment see Lowe, op cit at pp 333–335.

Further the decision did not represent a wholesale condemnation of the law of contempt and in any event was really only concerned with the application of the restriction in the context of *civil* proceedings. Lastly, it can be argued that the facts of the *Sunday Times* case were such that one might justifiably be wary of drawing too many conclusions from the European Court's decision as to the validity of the general application of the law of contempt.[12]

Nevertheless, the *Sunday Times* case served as the spur to the reform of the law in the United Kingdom by the Contempt of Court Act 1981 which is discussed in the next chapter.

---

12 For a later, unsuccessful challenge to the contempt laws under the European Convention see *Times Newspapers Ltd and others v UK* (App No 10243/83) [1983] 8 EHRR 45 at 54 which concerned comments by Lord Diplock in *A-G v English* [1983] 1 AC 116, [1982] 2 All ER 903. See p 118.

CHAPTER 4

Publications interfering with the due course of justice in particular legal proceedings—the general position under the Contempt of Court Act 1981

I INTRODUCTION

The Contempt of Court Act 1981 was the legislative response to the pressures for reform described in Chapter 3. Sections 1–7 of the Act deal with publications likely to interfere with the course of justice in particular legal proceedings and introduce what is labelled the 'strict liability rule'. This part of the Act defines the circumstances in which proof of intent is or is not required.

A The strict liability rule—the broad objectives

According to Lord Hailsham LC[1] the enactment of the strict lability rule had the threefold objective of (1) implementing with 'minor deviations' the main recommendations of the Phillimore Report; (2) harmonising the law of England and Wales with the majority judgment of the European Court in the *Sunday Times* case; and (3) harmonising the laws of England, Scotland and and Northern Ireland into a coherent set of rules.

Parliament did not intend a *radical* reform of the law of contempt. All that was really intended was to relax some of the restrictions imposed by the law and to make its application more certain. In other words the Act was intended to maintain the basic stance of the ultimate supremacy of the due administration of justice over freedom of speech but to shift the balance a little in favour of the latter.

B The strict liability rule—the strategy

The strategy of the Act is to impose strict liability for unintentional contempts in more limited circumstances than under the common law.[2] Section 2(1) and (2) of the Act confines the imposition of strict liability to 'publications' which create a substantial risk of serious prejudice to particular legal proceedings. The

1 415 HL Official Report (5th Series) col 660.
2 As recommended by the Phillimore Report (1974, Cmnd 5794), paras 73–77.

Government believed[3] that by these provisions it was amending the contempt laws so as to comply with the European Court's ruling in the *Sunday Times* case.[4]

The Act also makes important changes by:

(a) redefining the time within which a contempt within the strict liability rule may be committed;

(b) providing certain specific defences (but without prejudice to other common law defences); and

(c) providing that (save in Scotland) proceedings for contempt under the strict liability rule must be brought or must be sanctioned by the Attorney General or by the motion of a competent court.

C   The limited application of section 1

Section 1 provides:

> 'In this Act "the strict liability rule" means the rule of law whereby conduct may be treated as a contempt of court as tending to interfere with the course of justice in particular legal proceedings regardless of intent to do so.'

It will be noted that s 1 refers to conduct being treated as contempt because it tends to interfere with the course of justice in *particular legal proceedings*. This would seem to exclude from its ambit conduct that is held to be a contempt because of its tendency to interfere with the course of justice *as a continuing process*. Such conduct continues to be governed by common law principles. On this basis publications or other conduct said to 'scandalise the court'[5] are unaffected by the Act, as is conduct such as victimising witnesses for giving evidence in a trial that had previously been concluded.[6]

The extent to which the prejudgment by a publication of the outcome of proceedings—referred to by the House of Lords in the *Sunday Times* case as 'trial by newspaper'—may still amount to a contempt at common law, on the basis that it may amount to interference with the administration of justice as a continuing process, is unclear. This question is further discussed below.[7]

D   The inapplicability of the rule to intentional conduct

Section 6(c) specifically provides that nothing in ss 1–5:

> 'restricts liability for contempt of court in respect of conduct intended to impede or prejudice the administration of justice.'

This exclusion of intentional contempts from the strict liability rule adopts the

---

3   See Lord Hailsham LC in HL Official Report 415 (5th Series) col 600 and Sir Michael Havers (the Attorney General) HC Debs Vol 1000, col 30.
4   *Sunday Times v UK* (1979) 2 ECHRR 245 discussed at pp 100 ff.
5   Discussed in Ch 9.
6   Discussed in Ch 11.
7   See pp 117 ff.

strategy recommended by the Phillimore Committee.[8] Intentional conduct continues to be governed by the common law.

However, what is meant by 'intended' in this context is problematic. As liability for contempt was previously strict it was not necessary to establish 'intent' and so the common law offers no guidance. In English criminal law generally there is some uncertainty as to the meaning of 'intent' and 'intention'.[9] It clearly covers the situation where the consequences which result from an act are the aim or objective of the actor. Problems arise when this 'direct' intent is not present but the consequences could have been foreseen as a result of the act. Following the House of Lords decision in *DPP v Hyam* [10] a person was considered to have intended the consequences of his act if he foresaw them as a *highly probable or likely result* of his actions.[11] The position is now[12] that this foreseeability does not constitute intent. It appears instead that a person will only be held to have intention on the basis of foreseeability if a result is objectively a virtually certain consequence of his action *and* he foresees it as virtually certain: in that case the jury may *infer* that the result is intended, although the foresight does not actually constitute the intention. Even foresight of a virtual certainty, therefore, does not in itself connote intent.[13]

This position on intention has been formulated in cases on murder, but in *R v Moloney* [14] and *R v Hancock* [15] the House of Lords stressed (albeit obiter) that it was dealing with all crimes of intention,[16] although some authorities have argued that intent should vary in meaning according to its context.[17] The narrow view of intent which now holds sway means that even in cases in which consequences of an act are foreseen by a party as a virtual certainty there will not necessarily be 'intent'. Instead, it may be an instance of 'recklessness', for what constitutes recklessness depends upon the definition of intention: foresight which is insufficient for intention may well suffice for recklessness.

There is nothing in s 6(c) to suggest that intent bears a special meaning which is different from that of the general law and s 6(c) does not expressly impose liability for reckless conduct. However, contempt of court is generally considered an offence sui generis. Before the Act, cases on reporting proceedings, where liability was not strict, suggest that the mens rea required was recklessness.[18] However, the two leading cases *A-G v Leveller Magazines* [19] and *Re F (Otherwise*

---

8 See Recommendation 6 and paras 66 and 72. Their recommendation was, however, that 'such conduct should normally be dealt with as a criminal offence unless there are compelling reasons requiring it to be dealt with as a matter of urgency by means of summary contempt procedures'.

9 See Smith & Hogan, *Criminal Law* (7th edn, 1992) Ch 4, pp 53–91; Clarkson & Keating, *Criminal Law: Text and Materials* (3rd edn, 1994) Ch 2, pp 131–188.

10 [1975] AC 55.

11 Although the decision in *Hyam* is open to various interpretations; see Buzzard, 'Intent' [1978] Crim LR 5; Smith, 'Intent: A Reply' [1978] Crim LR 14.

12 See *R v Moloney* [1985] AC 905; *R v Hancock and Shankland* [1986] AC 455; *R v Nedrick* [1986] 3 All ER 1, [1986] 1 WLR 1025; *R v Walker and Hayles* (1990) 90 Cr App Rep 226.

13 Although it can be argued that so likely is a jury to convict on evidence of such foresight that they do amount to the same thing. See Smith, 'Intent: A Reply' [1978] Crim LR 14.

14 [1985] AC 905.

15 [1986] AC 455.

16 See also *R v Bryson* [1985] Crim LR 669 (CA).

17 See Glanville Williams, 'Oblique Intention' [1987] CLJ 417, 431; R A Duff, 'The Obscure Intentions of the House of Lords' [1986] Crim LR 771,779.

18 For reporting proceedings, see Ch 8.

19 [1979] AC 440.

A) (a minor) (Publication of Information) [20] both preceded the House of Lords'
decision in *Moloney*. Since *Moloney* the courts have had to deal with several
cases of publications alleged to interfere with particular legal proceedings where
the circumstances took the case outside the strict liabilty rule. In all of them the
courts have had little difficulty in concluding that the interference with particular
proceedings was intended in that it was the express aim of the publication. In *A-
G v Times Newspapers Ltd* [1] the situation did not fall within the strict liability rule
because the proceedings interfered with were not 'active' at the time of publication.[2]
The case was part of the *Spycatcher* saga[3] and concerned publication of extracts
from a book which, at the time of publication, two other newspapers were
restrained from publishing by an interlocutory injunction pending trial of an
action that such publication would be in breach of the author's duty of
confidentiality. In the Court of Appeal the question was canvassed as to whether
s 6(c) required a specific or basic intent.[4] The judges all agreed that what s 6(c)
requires is intent rather than recklessness. As Lloyd LJ said:

> 'Now whatever else recklessness may or may not mean (and the cases show that
> the concept is not without its difficulties) it is clear that it is independent of, and
> frequently contrasted with, intent. Liability based on recklessness is thus liability
> regardless of intent. If that is so, then liability based on recklessness is included
> within the statutory description of the strict liability rule, and is therefore subject
> to the restrictions imposed by s 2. . . . Putting the matter another way, s 6(c) of the
> 1981 Act saves from the operation of ss 1 and 2 conduct which is intended to
> impede or prejudice the administration of justice. If it was the object of Parliament
> to save also conduct which is reckless, then Parliament would surely have said.
> Sections 1, 2 and 6(c) cover the whole ground. In cases covered by the Act to which
> the strict liability rule does not apply, there is no room for a state of mind which
> falls short of intention. There is no middle way.'[5]

In the House of Lords the newspapers conceded the issue of intent. Lord
Ackner said that the conclusion reached below that the publication was done with
intent to interfere with the administration of justice was 'in the circumstances
irresistible'[6] and both Lord Brandon and Lord Jauncey used the word 'knowingly'.[7]

The term 'specific intent' is used in criminal law in more than one sense, but
the usual one now is that offences of specific intent such as murder, unlike those
of basic intent, cannot be committed recklessly.[8] The importance of *A-G v Times
Newspapers Ltd* therefore is that it is persuasive authority[9] for the proposition
that s 6(c) applies where the objective of the publication is to interfere with
proceedings, and not where there is mere recklessness about this consequence.
It is the distinction between intent and recklessness that is crucial to contempt.

20 [1977] Fam 58.
 1 [1988] Ch 333, [1987] 3 All ER 276.
 2 For a discussion of when proceedings are active, see Ch 7.
 3 See Ch 6.
 4 See the judgment of Sir John Donaldson MR [1988] Ch 333 at 374–375, [1987] 3 All ER 276
   at 304.
 5 Ibid at 383 and 310 respectively.
 6 *A-G v Times Newspapers Ltd* [1992] 1 AC 191 at 211.
 7 Ibid at 206 and 231 respectively.
 8 See *R v Caldwell* [1982] AC 341: so intoxication will reduce the offence to a lesser one, such
   as murder to manslaughter; see *DPP v Majewski* [1977] AC 443. For a general discussion see
   Smith & Hogan op cit and Clarkson & Keating op cit.
 9 See the judgment of Lloyd LJ in *A-G v News Group Newspapers Ltd* [1988] 2 All ER 906 at
   916–917.

In *A-G v News Group Newspapers Ltd* [10] the Divisional Court also took the view that to be guilty of contempt the respondents needed to have a specific intent to interfere. The case concerned a campaign run by the *Sun* newspaper against a doctor who it alleged had raped a child, although the police and the DPP had decided not to prosecute as there was no corroboration of the child's story. The newspaper offered to fund the mother's private prosecution against the doctor and in the meantime published articles about the matter under headlines such as 'Rape Case Doc', and 'Doc groped me, says girl'. Watkins LJ (with whom Mann LJ agreed) said that it was not a matter of inferring intent from the articles alone but of considering the whole circumstances of the case, including the newspaper's financial support of the mother's action and the affidavit submitted to the court by the editor. He was unable to accept that so experienced an editor could have failed to foresee that what he was doing would incur a real risk of prejudicing the doctor's trial, in particular by influencing the views of those who might become the jurors. From this Watkins LJ inferred that the editor intended to interfere with the proceedings, and in drawing that inference he said that he bore in mind Lord Bridge's views on inferring intention expressed in *Moloney*.

Watkins LJ further considered, however, whether the editor would have been guilty of a contempt had he been merely reckless, but concluded[11] that it would not have been sufficient. He agreed with Lloyd LJ in *A-G v Newspaper Publishing plc* [12] that recklessness is liability regardless of intent and that had it been Parliament's object to exclude reckless conduct from the strict liability rule in s 2 of the 1981 Act it would have said so. As was submitted in the second edition of this book,[13] and is now confirmed by these cases, it would be wrong to subvert the apparent policy of the Act, which was to replace the common law applicable to potentially prejudicial publications with a slightly more relaxed statutory control, by bringing the notion of recklessness into s 6(c).

The view was also expressed in the second edition of this book[14] that, if 'intent' were narrowly interpreted it would be rare for a publisher to be guilty of intent to prejudice legal proceedings. However, cases since the Act demonstrate that it will not be that unusual. This is particularly so since it appears that publishing with an intent to influence a litigant to settle proceedings or not to insist on his strict legal rights may amount to a contempt within s 6(c). In *A-G v Hislop* [15] the defendants were charged with both common law and statutory contempt in respect of two articles appearing in the satirical magazine *Private Eye*. The articles concerned the defamation action which was at the time being brought by Sonia Sutcliffe, the wife of the mass murderer known as the 'Yorkshire Ripper', against the magazine. The Court of Appeal held that the contempt, in putting improper pressure on Mrs Sutcliffe to abandon her action, was both statutory within the strict liability rule, because the publications created a substantial risk of a serious prejudice to the course of justice in the defamation action, and also a common law contempt because the editor had intended to deter Mrs Sutcliffe from continuing with her action. However, the Court of Appeal considered that insofar as there was a contempt by reason of the risk of prejudice arising from the

10 [1988] 2 All ER 906 at 912.
11 Citing with approval the views expressed in the second edition of this book, pp 87–88.
12 [1987] 3 All ER 276 at 309–310, [1987] 3 WLR 942 at 983–984.
13 At p 88.
14 Ibid.
15 [1991] 1 QB 514, [1991] 1 All ER 911.

effect of the articles on potential jurors in the defamation action, this was only a statutory contempt as the editor had not had any intention in this regard.

Hislop shows that contempts committed by putting improper pressure on litigants have survived the Act, and can be either statutory or common law. This form of contempt is discussed in Chapter 6.

II APPLYING THE STRICT LIABILITY RULE

A The meaning of 'publication'

The 'strict liability rule' applies only to 'publications'. According to s 2(1):

> '"publication" includes any speech, writing, programme included in a programme service[16] or other communication in whatever form, which is addressed to the public at large or any section of the public.'

The first part of the definition confirms the common law view that contempt can be committed by any medium of publication.[17] Although the section uses the word 'includes', which suggests that there might be other forms of publication within the rule which are not specified in the words which follow, the definition seems comprehensive, particularly since it refers to 'communication in whatever form'. 'Includes' may, therefore, be better read as 'comprises' or 'means'. That was certainly Lord Diplock's view in *Secretary of State for Defence v Guardian Newspapers* [18] where he thought that the context of s 2(1) 'makes it clear that it is intended as a complete and comprehensive definition of the term'.

The second part of the definition is intended to implement the Phillimore Committee's view [19] that strict liability should be restricted to public conduct. In fact the definition is wider than that proposed by the Committee by reason of the words 'or any section of the public'. The additional words were thought necessary[20] to cover the case where 'less than the whole public were invited' yet where the publication is in reality still in the realm of the public conduct which the Committee thought should be covered. One example is a highly specialised publication.[1]

During the debate on the Bill Lord Simon of Glaisdale expressed the view[2] that the definition is reasonably clear and that the words 'the public' or 'section of the public' are used in contradistinction to 'a group of people aggregated in their private capacities'. It may be that his Lordship was too sanguine as to the clarity of the definition. As he said, a 'house magazine' might fall on either side of the

16 The words 'programme included in a programme service' were substituted by the Broadcasting Act 1990, Sch 20, para 31(1) for the words 'broadcast cable programme' which had been added to the 1981 Act by the Cable and Broadcasting Act 1984. A new s 2(5) of the 1981 Act provides that 'programme service' has the same meaning as in the Broadcasting Act 1990.

17 See Ch 3, p 88. The waxwork representation of the accused as the murderer in *R v Gilham* (1828) Mood & M 165 would be covered by 'communication in any form' in that it depicts an idea which is thereby communicated to the audience. So too, it is submitted, are words or images on a computer screen, however generated.

18 [1985] AC 339 at 348, [1984] 3 All ER 601 at 606 (HL).

19 Expressed in para 80. For a criticism of the proposal see Lowe, (1975) 125 NLJ 514.

20 Eg by Lord Mackay of Clashfern (the Lord Advocate) 416 HL Official Report (5th Series) col 180 and Lord Simon of Glaisdale at cols 180, 181.

1 This was an example given by Lord Simon ibid at col 181. The wisdom of including the extra words was questioned by Lord Gardiner, ibid at cols 181, 182.

2 416 HL Official Report (5th Series) col 180.

line and there must be doubts too about a communication circulated to a private club.

In other areas of the law the distinction between a section of the public and a group of private individuals has proved difficult to apply and the precedents may not necessarily be helpful.[3] The Race Relations Acts of 1965, 1976 and 1986 make it unlawful for any person concerned with the provision of goods, facilities or services to the public or a section of the public to discriminate on any of the grounds covered by the legislation. Problems have arisen as to whether the Acts cover members' clubs. In both *Race Relations Board v Charter* [4] and *Dockers' Labour Club & Institute Ltd v Race Relations Board* [5] the House of Lords held that a club which had a genuine selection procedure for membership was not a section of the public. This would suggest that a communication circulated in a private club to which admission is through a real selection procedure would fall outside s 2 (1). However, it must be remembered that the Race Relations legislation serves quite different policy objectives to the contempt of court rules. It is by no means clear that a communication published in the Garrick Club, for example, pertaining to a matter of interest to the members as members of the community at large rather than merely as members of the Garrick, would not be caught by the strict liability rule. On the other hand, it seems likely that an organization open to anyone who pays their money, such as computer users joining a bulletin board network, is a section of the public for the purposes of s 2(1) as well as for the Race Relations Act.

In the law of charities the distinction between a section of the public and a group of private individuals is crucial as a trust cannot be charitable unless its benefits are available to a sufficient section of the public. The leading cases establish that numbers alone are not decisive but that what comprises a sufficient section of the public will vary according to the nature of the charity in issue. Trusts for the relief of poverty require less 'public benefit' than do those falling under one of the other heads of charity.[6] So, a trust for the education of the children of the employees of a particular company will not be charitable[7] whereas a trust for the relief of poverty amongst the employees will be.[8] The reason for the difference is partly due to historical anomaly but it also reflects a matter of policy in that the classification of those who benefit from a charity cannot be judged in a vacuum but must be looked at in relation to the charity's purposes.

---

3 As the Phillimore Committee warned (at para 80), statutory definitions framed for a different mischief should be treated with caution.

4 [1973] AC 868.

5 [1976] AC 285.

6 Charitable trusts are usually classified under four 'heads', using the classification formulated by Lord McNaughten in *Commissioners for Special Purposes of Income Tax v Pemsel* [1891] AC 531, where he summarised the purposes listed in the Preamble to the Charitable Uses Act of 1601 on which the case law is based: the four heads are the relief of poverty, the advancement of education, the advancement of religion and other purposes beneficial to the community. See generally *Tudor on Charities* (8th edn,1995); Sheridan & Keeton, *The Modern Law of Charities* (4th edn, 1992); Picarda, *The Law and Practice Relating to Charities* (3rd edn, 1995).

7 *Oppenheim v Tobacco Securities Trust Ltd* [1951] AC 297, where there was said to be a 'personal nexus' between the members of the group which prevented them being a section of the public.

8 *Dingle v Turner* [1972] AC 601; note that in this case Lord Cross of Chelsea doubted, obiter, the conclusion reached in the *Oppenheim* case (above, n 7). In *Dingle v Turner* Lord Cross said (at 623) 'The phrase a "section of the public" is in truth a vague phrase which may mean different things to different people.'

The Charity Commission advises that funds raised by 'disaster appeals' can only be charitable if they are for the relief of poverty and the benefits restricted to those in need by reason of poverty, for otherwise the victims and their relatives and dependants will be a specific and identifiable group of private individuals incapable of constituting a section of the public.[9] Would such people be a section of the public for the purposes of s 2 if, for example, they held a meeting to discuss litigation arising from that disaster? Surely not, for any relevant 'publication' at that meeting would be to persons connected to one another by the very subject matter of that publication.[10] However, if the disaster litigation was discussed at a meeting of persons not personally connected with the matter, but interested merely as concerned citizens, then the same 'publication' might well satisfy s 2. The difficulty arises if there are some outsiders present at the relatives' meeting. At what point does this dilution turn those present into a 'section of the public'? If the press is invited,[11] or even has its uninvited presence at the meeting tolerated, that would seem to destroy the private nature of the meeting, but otherwise, it is submitted, it would be a question of degree.

As far as the media is concerned it *can* be argued that it is a 'section of the public' within s 2 so that any communication to the media, or between branches of the media, such as Reuters or the Press Association to the media, constitutes a 'publication' to a section of the public. There are occasions, however, on which the press is told matters on a confidential basis, often to help the police with a particular enquiry and, while it would be a contempt if the press then published the information, it is difficult to categorise the initial communication to the press as falling within s 2. On the other hand, the holding by the police of press conferences when they are investigating serious or particularly newsworthy crimes has become increasingly common, and such a media events are, it is submitted, within s 2.[12] The instigation of the police does not, however, absolve the media of liability for any contempt which is committed.[13]

The answer to the above problems, it is submitted, is that what constitutes a 'section of the public' will vary according to the circumstances and must be related (a) to the nature of the persons comprising the audience, (b) their relationship inter se and with the publisher, and (c) the nature of the communication and the purpose for which it is made. It must be remembered that for a publication to amount to a contempt within the strict liability rule the other conditions of s 2[14] must be fulfilled and the fact that the rule applies only to publications which create a '*substantial risk* that the course of justice in the proceedings in question will be *seriously* impeded or prejudiced' (emphasis added) will often rule out real problems in borderline cases. With regard to the press, for example, the risk to

---

9 See the Annual Report of the Charity Commission for 1981, paras 4–8.
10 Compare the defence of 'common interest' in the law of defamation: see Carter-Ruck, *Libel and Slander* (4th edn, 1992) Ch 13.
11 The Phillimore Committee (at para 80) recommeded including as a publication words addressed to public meetings, functions or entertainments and, if the press were invited, to private ones. It could, however, make a difference if the press were invited on the condition that matters were not to be reported until after the trial or litigation.
12 A notorious press conference was called by the police after the arrest of the so-called 'Yorkshire Ripper', at which much ill-judged comment was made: matters were exacerbated by how the press reported it. See Press Council Report: *Press Conduct in the Sutcliffe Case* (1983) and below, p 152.
13 See p 151.
14 See below.

the proceedings will usually arise only when they disseminate the material and not when it is communicated *to* them.

Section 2(1) says nothing about where or when matter will be regarded as published. It is submitted that the same considerations will apply as are discussed with respect to the common law position.[15] As will be seen, the courts have considered the matter of the area of publication in relation to the question of whether or not the risk is 'substantial'.

B The statutory test under s 2(2)

Under s 2(2) publications can only constitute a contempt under the strict liability rule if they create:

> 'a substantial risk that the course of justice in the proceedings in question will be seriously impeded or prejudiced.'

Section 2(2) is modelled on the test recommended by the Phillimore Committee[16] except that the word 'substantial' is added as a qualification of 'risk'. The Phillimore Committee said that the law should aim at preventing serious prejudice, not serious risks,[17] and argued that by defining the degree of prejudice required and by using the word 'will' rather than 'may' or 'calculated' a new statutory test would be both more certain and less restrictive than the old law. However, Phillimore specifically said that a risk of serious prejudice should always be prohibited unless the risk was de minimis[18] and it can be argued that the use of the word 'substantial' is nothing more than the expression of this.[19]

The crucial question is whether the requirement of a substantial risk of serious prejudice is more generous towards the media than the old requirement of a 'real risk of prejudice'. It is certainly not *more* restrictive; as Sir John Donaldson MR said in *A-G v News Group Newspapers Ltd*,[20] a case concerning an application for an injunction restraining publication:

> 'If the proceedings to be protected are "active" within the meaning of the Act *and* both limbs of the test in s 2(2) are met, not only will the strict liability rule apply, but I find it hard to think of any circumstances in which the conduct complained of would not, prior to 1981, have been held to be a contempt or, if it was apprehended, in which prior restraint would not have been ordered.'

In one respect s 2(2) has relaxed the law since by requiring a substantial risk of serious prejudice the Act cannot encompass the concept of 'technical contempts'.[1] Beyond that the effect of the statutory test depends on the way in which the courts interpret it. Lord Diplock's judgment in *A-G v English*,[2] the first case in which the House of Lords considered the Act, suggested that the

---

15 See Ch 3, pp 87 ff.
16 At para 113.
17 Ibid.
18 Ibid.
19 During the report stage of the Bill in the House of Lords Lord Hailsham LC said that he doubted whether the word 'substantial' would make any difference: 417 HL Official Report (5th Series) col 142.
20 [1987] QB 1 at 15, [1986] 2 All ER 833 at 841.
 1 See p 76 ff.
 2 [1983] 1 AC 116 at 142, [1982] 2 All ER 903 at 919, [1982] 3 WLR 278 at 286.

difference in the tests is little more than semantic as the effect of the test was merely to exclude remote risks:

> '"Substantial"' is hardly the most apt word to apply to "risk" which is a noumenon. In combination I take the two words to be intended to exclude a risk that is only remote. With regard to the adverb "seriously" a perusal of the cases cited in *A-G v Times Newspapers Ltd* discloses that the adjective "serious" has from time to time been used as an alternative to "real" to describe the degree of risk of interfering with the course of justice, but not the degree of interference itself. It is, however, an ordinary English word that is not intrinsically inapt when used to describe the extent of an impediment or prejudice to the course of justice in particular legal proceedings, and I do not think that for the purposes of the instant appeal any attempt to paraphrase it is necessary or would be helpful. The subsection applies to all kinds of legal proceedings, not only criminal prosecutions before a jury. If, as in the instant case and probably in most other criminal trials on indictment, it is the outcome of the trial or the need to discharge the jury without proceedings to a verdict that is put at risk, there can be no question that that which in the course of justice is put at risk is as serious as anything could be.'

In *A-G v Times Newspapers Ltd* [3] Lord Lane CJ explained that the test meant that a slight or trivial risk of serious prejudice was not enough and nor was a substantial risk of slight prejudice. In *A-G v News Group Newspapers Ltd* [4] Sir John Donaldson MR accepted counsel's submission that 'substantial' does not mean 'weighty' but rather means 'not insubstantial' or 'not minimal'.[5] He said that the risk part of the test would usually be of importance in the context of the width of the publication, such as the geographical area in which the publication was disseminated, while the 'serious' issue went to the likely effect on the trial if the risk did materialise:

> 'To declare in a speech at a public meeting in Cornwall that a man about to be tried in Durham is guilty of the offence charged and has many previous convictions for the same offence may well carry no substantial risk of affecting his trial, but, if it occurred, the prejudice would be most serious. By contrast, a nationwide television broadcast at peak viewing time of some far more innocuous statement would certainly involve a substantial risk of having some effect on a trial anywhere in the country and the sole effective question would arise under the "seriousness" limb of the test. Proximity in time between the publication and the proceedings would probably have a greater bearing on the risk limb than on the seriousness limb, but could go to both.'[6]

Cases since the Act show that with regard to criminal proceedings a substantial risk of prejudicing the jury is invariably regarded as 'serious'. However, in deciding whether there is a substantial risk, in respect of that or any other matter, the judges will carefully weigh up the content of the publication, the area in which it was published and how near it was to the time of the trial.[7] It is not a question

---

3 (1983) Times, 12 February (the Fagan case).
4 [1987] QB 1 at 15, [1986] 2 All ER 833 at 841.
5 This was followed by Lindsay J in *MGN v Bank of America* [1995] 2 All ER 355 in considering the interpretation of s 4(2) of the Act which provides for the postponement of reports of legal proceedings where it appears to be necessary to avoid 'a substantial risk of prejudice' to particular proceedings. The section differs from s 2(2) in not requiring a substantial risk of *serious* prejudice. See further Ch 8.
6 Parker LJ, using a slightly different geographical example (Devon and Newcastle), expressed the same ideas at [1987] QB 1 at 17, [1986] 2 All ER 833 at 843.
7 For a case in which the ephemeral nature of the publication, the limited circulation area and the delay before the trial were all factors in finding that there had been no contempt, see *A-G v Independent Television News Ltd* [1995] 2 All ER 370.

of whether the material is of a type which is inherently likely to create the requisite risk but whether, in any particular case, it actually does so.[8] As at common law the risk is to be assessed at the time of publication.[9] This last point sits somewhat uneasily with taking into account the delay before the trial. The important point when assessing risk must be the *likely* delay before the trial for to look at the actual delay would be to judge the matter with hindsight rather than at the time of publication. This means that those reponsible for publications must rely on their knowledge of the legal system in general and on the situation pertaining to the particular proceedings when deciding whether or not to publish.

The application of the statutory test to criminal proceedings and to civil proceedings is considered in detail in Chapters 5 and 6 respectively. Suffice it to say here that in a civil action where the trial is before a judge alone the major issues will be the risk of prejudicing witnesses and the extent to which public pressure may legitimately be put upon litigants. Where libel actions are concerned the presence of the jury, as in criminal trials, brings other considerations into play.

C The mens rea requirement

Although liability for publications that fall foul of s 2 remains 'strict', as at common law, it does not mean that no mens rea is required. It will still have to be proved that the accused intended to publish the offending material and the problems discussed[10] in relation to the common law will remain problems under the Act. Once the accused is shown to have the necessary mens rea it will be no defence to argue that he did not know or think that the material published was prejudicial or that he had some other motive for publishing.

D Proceedings to which the strict liability rule applies

The strict liabilty rule is subject to statutory time provisions in that it applies only in respect of proceedings which are 'active'. Section 2(3) of the Act provides:

> 'The strict liability rule applies to a publication only if the proceedings in question are active within the meaning of this section at the time of the publication.'

'Active' proceedings are defined by Schedule I to the Act. Despite these detailed provisions there are some difficulties in applying the concept 'active' in all situations. Also, the provisions do not apply to cases of intentional contempt falling outside the strict liability rule, which arc still govcrncd by thc common law.[11] Since the strict liability rule applies only to contempts committed through

---

8 *A-G v Guardian Newspapers Ltd* [1992] 3 All ER 38 at 45, where Mann LJ said that the risk must be practical rather than theoretical.

9 Ibid; and see also *A-G v Times Newspapers Ltd* (1983) Times, 12 February where Oliver LJ said that the degree of risk had to be assessed in the light of the situation as it actually existed at the date of publication and not in the light of the situation as it was thought to exist by those responsible for the publication. Cf the comments made by Bingham LJ in respect of intentional contempt in *A-G v Sport Newspaper Ltd* [1992] 1 All ER 503 at 517–518.

10 See pp 89 ff.

11 See eg *A-G v News Group Newspapers Ltd* [1988] 2 All ER 906, discussed at pp 144 ff. If, despite the Act, a publication may still be a contempt at common law because it is a 'prejudgment' affecting the administration of justice generally rather than 'particular proceedings', the statutory timing provisions would not apply: see Ch 7.

the medium of a 'publication' other forms of contempt are likewise still governed by the common law rules on time.

The issue of the timing of publications is dealt with in Chapter 7.

E   Qualification of the strict liability rule under s 5: discussion of public affairs or matters of general public interest

Section 5 of the Act contains a qualification to the strict liability rule. It provides:

> 'A publication made as or as part of a discussion in good faith of public affairs or other matters of general public interest is not to be treated as a contempt of court under the strict liability rule if the risk of impediment or prejudice to particular legal proceedings is merely incidental to the discussion.'

The purpose of this section is to ensure that there can be discussion of a matter of public interest despite the fact that there are active proceedings to which the matter is relevant. It is an example of the way in which the Act tries to balance the requirements of free speech and the due administration of justice.

Section 5 does not in the name of public interest give *carte blanche* to discuss the facts of a particular case. That would be to confuse it with the defence of 'public interest' which has yet to be recognised at common law.[12] No such defence was recommended by the Phillimore Committee and no such defence is provided for in the Act. Instead, s 5 takes out of the strict liability rule publications which are not *about* the proceedings as such but which make reference to the proceedings in the context of a more general discussion. The line between these two things can be a fine one and much turns on how the terms 'discussion in good faith' and 'merely incidental' are interpreted.

The House of Lords decision in *A-G v English*[13] and the Divisional Court decisions in the Fagan cases[14] show a liberal interpretation of s 5 which is to be welcomed. In the former case Lord Diplock, referring to the allegation that a newspaper article supporting a 'pro-life' candidate in a parliamentary by-election was a contempt because it appeared in the same week that the trial began of a paediatrician who was accused of starving to death a handicapped baby, said:

> 'Such gagging of bona fide public discussion in the press of controversial matters of general public interest, merely because there are in existence contemporaneous legal proceedings in which some instance of those controversial matters may be in issue, is what s 5 of the Contempt of Court Act 1981 was in my view intended to prevent.'[15]

It must be noted that s 5 is not a *defence* to the application of the strict liability rule but a provision which states criteria by which a publication is not to be considered a contempt at all. As such it is for the prosecution to show that s 5 does not apply rather than for the defence to show that it does.[16]

---

12   See below.
13   [1983] 1 AC 116, [1982] 2 All ER 903; see p 175.
14   *A-G v Times Newspapers* (1983) Times, 12 February; see p 76.
15   *A-G v English* [1983] 1 AC 116 at 144, [1982] 2 All ER 903 at 920.
16   Ibid.

III   THE CONTINUING RELEVANCE OF THE COMMON LAW

A   General

The Act does not render the common law irrelevant. As we have seen, the common law may continue to apply to publications intended to prejudice the administration of justice. It is also provided by s 6(b) that nothing in ss 1–5:

> 'implies that any publication is punishable as a contempt of court under [the strict liability] rule which would not be so punishable apart from those provisions.'

Section 6(b) has been interpreted[17] to mean that nothing under the strict liability rule can be considered to impose fresh liability for contempt. In other words if a publication would not have been a contempt at common law it cannot become so as a result of the strict liability rule.

The protection afforded by s 6(b) is further bolstered by s 6(a) which provides that nothing in ss 1–5:

> 'prejudices any defence available at common law to a charge of contempt of court under the strict liability rule.'

Section 6(a) and (b), particularly the latter, are important provisions which should not be overlooked when interpreting or applying ss 1–5 of the Act. For this reason alone common law decisions, particularly those relating to publications concerning criminal proceedings, will continue to be relevant under the Act. However, unless it is established *as a matter of principle* that a publication cannot be a contempt (for example because judges are thought to be immune from the deleterious effect of media comment) the mere fact that a prosecution failed under the common law does not ipso facto mean that prosecution in a similar type of case will fail under the Act because of s 6(b). Decisions as to what amounts to a real or substantial risk of prejudice must necessarily be related to their particular facts.

B   Publications which prejudge the outcome of proceedings

It is possible that publications which prejudge the outcome of proceedings— referred to by the House of Lords in the *Sunday Times* case[18] as 'trial by newspaper'—may still amount to a contempt at common law on the basis that such a publication may interfere with the administration of justice *as a continuing process* rather than in particular proceedings.[19] If this is so it is a serious matter because of the condemnation of the prejudgment test by the European Court on Human Rights in the *Sunday Times* case.[20] However, it is incontrovertible that ss 1 and 2 of the Act apply only to publications interfering with 'particular legal proceedings' and that the Act does not expressly abolish the prejudgment test. As the majority of the Law Lords in the *Sunday Times* case conceived the prejudgment

---

17   Per Lord Denning MR and Ackner LJ in *R v Horsham Justices, ex p Farquharson* [1982] QB 762 at 790–791 and 804, [1982] 2 All ER 269 at 284, 285 and 294–295. As was pointed out the wording is not dissimilar from that of s 12(4) of the Administration of Justice Act 1960, discussed in Ch 8.

18   [1974] AC 273.

19   See p 78.

20   *Sunday Times v UK* (1979) 2 EHRR 245; see p 100.

test as protecting the administration of justice as a whole it is therefore arguable that the test has survived the Act.

Remarks made by Lord Diplock in *A-G v English* [1] could suggest that a common law prosecution for prejudgment remains possible. In that case he held that the article complained of was not a contempt, contrasting it with the *Sunday Times* article and describing it as the 'antithesis' of the latter.[2] There are, however, powerful arguments for saying that a prejudgment which does not come within the criteria of ss 1–6 of the Act can no longer constitute contempt unless there is intention which brings the matter within s 6(c). The Act was passed in the aftermath of the decision of the European Court of Human Rights and it was the intention of the Government to amend the contempt laws so as to comply with the Court's ruling. The Lord Chancellor, Lord Hailsham, said of the Bill in the House of Lords:

> 'It puts an end, of course, to the prejudgment criterion which was adopted by your Lordships' House in the *Sunday Times* case.'[3]

In *R v Secretary of State for Home Department, ex parte Brind*,[4] a case concerning the broadcasting ban on direct statements by representatives of terrorist organisations in Northern Ireland, Lord Templeman said à propos Article 10 of the European Convention, which guarantees freedom of expression:[5]

> 'The United Kingdom adheres to the Convention and Her Majesty's Government are satisfied that the laws of the United Kingdom are in conformity with their obligations under the Convention.'

If the Act is not interpreted as having abolished the prejudgment test then Parliament's intention would be thwarted and the United Kingdom would have failed to comply with its international obligations. It is submitted that if it is possible to interpret the Act so that the law is in accordance with the European Convention as interpreted by the European Court then this should be done. In *A-G v BBC* [6] Lord Scarman said that although the European Court's decision in the *Sunday Times* case is not part of English law yet 'there is a presumption, albeit rebuttable, that our municipal law will be consistent with our international obligations'. The House of Lords has had on several occasions to consider the interpretation of domestic law in the light of the United Kingdom's international obligations. The general rule was expressed by Lord Diplock in *Garland v British Rail Engineering Ltd* [7] when he said:

> 'it is a principle of construction of United Kingdom statutes . . . that the words of a statute passed after the treaty has been signed and dealing with the subject matter

---

1 [1983] 1 AC 116 at 143, [1982] 2 All ER 903 at 920.
2 Lord Diplock's remarks were the subject of a complaint by the *Times* and the *Sunday Times* to the European Commission on Human Rights (Application No 10243/83) although those two newspapers were not involved in the *English* case. The complaint alleged that the remarks showed that the UK had not implemented the European Court's judgment in the *Sunday Times* case. The Commission dismissed the application on the grounds that the complainants had not made out a prima facie case of being victims of a violation of Art 10 of the European Convention on Human Rights and that there was no evidence of a violation of Arts 13 or 14: (1986) 8 EHRR 45 at 52.
3 415 HL Official Report (5th Series) col 660; see also the Attorney General (Sir Michael Havers) HC Debs Vol 1000, col 30.
4 [1991] AC 696, [1991] 1 All ER 720.
5 Ibid at 750 and 725 respectively.
6 [1981] AC 303 at 354.
7 [1983] 2 AC 751 at 771.

of the international obligation of the United Kingdom, are to be construed, if they are reasonably capable of bearing such a meaning, as intended to carry out the obligation, and not to be inconsistent with it.'[8]

The House of Lords expressly referred to the matter of how far the prejudgment test propounded in the *Sunday Times* case is still good law in *Re Lonrho Plc*.[9] Having quoted from Lords Reid and Cross in that case, Lord Bridge said that how far the *Sunday Times* case could still be relied upon as an accurate expression of the law was 'extremely doubtful', particularly in relation to the kind of contempt which is the subject matter of the strict liability rule under ss 1 and 2 of the Act: although the European Court's decision could not be directly relied upon as direct authority:[10]

> '. . . the 1981 Act, on any point on which any doubt arises as to its construction, may be presumed to have been intended to avoid future conflicts between the law of contempt of court in the United Kingdom and the obligations of the United Kingdom under the European Convention . . .'

Lord Bridge concluded that 'the only safe course' was to apply the test imposed by the statutory language according to its ordinary meaning, without any preconception derived from the *Sunday Times* case. He then proceeded to discuss the publication in issue solely in terms of whether it created a risk of prejudice to the particular proceedings which were active and did not consider the wider question of a risk of prejudice to the administration of justice as a continuing process.

The reluctance of Lord Bridge to settle the matter of the prejudgment test has to be understood in the light of the peculiar circumstances of *Re Lonrho*. The Appellate Committee of three judges was sitting, not to exercise the appellate jurisdiction of the House but as a 'superior court' within s 19 of the 1981 Act, in contempt proceedings brought by the House of its own motion.[11] Lord Bridge therefore felt inhibited from attempting the exposition and clarification of the law which he said would have been called for had the case arisen in the usual way.[12] First, he was uncertain as to the binding authority of a report of the Appellate Committee when it was not exercising the appellate jurisdiction and secondly, he considered that it was inappropriate for an Appellate Committee of three, sitting in circumstances where the issues concerned had not been discussed in the courts below, 'to attempt any wider exposition of the law than is strictly necessary for the decision of the specific issues arising for determination in the contempt proceedings'.

It may be possible, however, to settle the matter by reference to parliamentary materials rather than to presumptions as to Parliament's intention. The long-

---

8 See also *R v Chief Immigration Officer, Heathrow Airport, ex p Salamat Bibi* [1976] 3 All ER 843, [1976] 1 WLR 976; *Fernandez v Secretary of State for the Home Department* [1981] Imm AR 1; *Chundawdra v Immigration Appeal Tribunal* [1988] Imm AR 161; *R v Secretary of State for Home Department, ex p Brind* [1991] AC 696, [1991] 1 All ER 720.

9 [1990] 2 AC 154, [1989] 2 All ER 1100.

10 Ibid at 208 and 1116.

11 The alleged contempt arose during a long battle by Lonrho plc to challenge the takeover of Harrods by the Al Fayed brothers in 1985. In the course of this Lonrho brought an action for judicial review, inter alia of a decision of the Secretary of State not to publish a report of inspectors appointed under the Companies Act 1985. Twelve days before the House heard the appeal in that litigation Lonrho published the report in question in a newspaper and copies of the newspaper were sent to four of the five of the Law Lords who were to hear the appeal: the case is fully discussed in Ch 6.

12 [1990] 2 AC 154 at 201, [1989] 2 All ER 1100 at 1111.

standing rule that when seeking to ascertain Parliament's intention the courts could not have recourse to parliamentary material as an aid to statutory construction[13] has been considerably relaxed by the decision of the House of Lords in *Pepper (Inspector of Taxes) v Hart*.[14] The House of Lords held that reference to parliamentary material may be made where (a) the legislation is ambiguous or obscure or leads to an absurdity; (b) the material relied on consists of statements by a minister or other promoter of the Bill and, if necessary, other parliamentary material required to understand those statements; and (c) the statements relied on are clear. There is no doubt as to the clarity of the statements made by the Lord Chancellor, Lord Hailsham, when introducing the Bill. As well as commenting[15] that the Bill puts an end to the prejudgment criteria in the *Sunday Times* case, he said that the first of the three main purposes of the Bill's first six clauses[16] was to implement the recommendations of the Phillimore Report and that the second was:

> 'to harmonise the law of England and Wales with the majority judgment of the Strasbourg court in the *Sunday Times* case.'[17]

As to the criteria of ambiguity, the survival of the prejudgment test is not a matter of the ambiguity of particular words or phrases, as it was in *Pepper v Hart* itself, but of how one part of the Act relates to the common law. The application of *Pepper v Hart* to the Contempt of Court Act was raised in the House of Lords in *A-G v Associated Newspapers Ltd*[18] in respect of the meaning of s 8.[19] Lord Lowry (with whom the other judges agreed) did refer to statements by the Attorney General in respect of amendments made to s 8, but said that he deliberately refrained from discussing the question whether it would be appropriate to apply *Pepper v Hart* to the facts of the case 'having regard to the the complicated and controversial parliamentary history of s 8'.[20] The parliamentary history of ss 1 to 6 was quite different to that of s 8 and it is submitted that the Lord Chancellor's clear and uncontroverted statements should be treated as evidence that it was indeed Parliament's intention to comply with the United Kingdom's obligations under the convention as interpreted by the European Court and also to follow the Phillimore recommendations.

Section 6(c) expressly preserves liability for contempt where there is an intention to impede or prejudice the administration of justice.[1] This is not limited to the administration of justice in particular proceedings. A publication amounting to a prejudgment which is intended to prejudice the administration of justice as a continuing process would therefore still be a contempt at common law. In reality, such a scenario is unlikely to arise. A 'prejudgment' can only be made in

---

13 See *Millar v Taylor* (1769) 4 Burr 2303; *Black-Clawson International Ltd v Papierwerke Waldhof-Aschaffenburg AG* [1975] AC 591; *Davis v Johnson* [1979] AC 264; *Hadmor Productions Ltd v Hamilton* [1983] 1 AC 191.
14 [1993] AC 593, [1993] 1 All ER 42; in *Pickstone v Freeman Plc* [1989] AC 66, [1988] 2 All ER 803 the House of Lords, dealing with the construction of subordinate legislation, allowed reference to ministerial statements made in Parliament when introducing subordinate legislation.
15 415 HL Official Report (5th series) col 660, see p 118.
16 Which became ss 1–6.
17 415 HL Official Report (5th series) col 660; the third purpose was to harmonise the laws of England, Scotland and Northern Ireland.
18 [1994] 2 AC 238, [1994] 1 All ER 556.
19 Discussed in Ch 10.
20 [1994] 2 AC 238 at 261, [1994] 1 All ER 556 at 566–567.
 1 See pp 106 ff.

respect of particular proceedings. If there is a substantial risk of serious prejudice and the proceedings are 'active' within Schedule 1 to the Act, the strict liability rule will apply. Where there is intent to prejudice proceedings and the risk is 'real' within the common law meaning of that term there will be common law liability, preserved by s 6(c), even if the proceedings are not 'active'.[2] It would be a rare circumstance in which a court could be envisaged as finding that a contemnor had published a prejudgment of particular proceedings, with the *intention* of prejudicing not those proceedings but the administration of justice as a continuing process.

C Publications which put pressure on parties to proceedings

In the *Sunday Times* case[3] there was much discussion as to when it is a contempt to put pressure upon a party to proceedings to persuade them to abandon the proceedings, settle upon certain terms or otherwise act in a particular way in relation to the proceedings. A minority of the Law Lords considered that public pressure[4] was a contempt, not only because of its effect on the particular proceedings, but because it prejudiced the administration of justice as a continuing process. Lord Diplock said that holding up suitors to 'public obloquy' for availing themselves of their constitutional right to have their legal rights and obligations ascertained and enforced in the courts would have an inhibiting effect on litigants generally.[5] This view is clearly contrary to the European Court's judgment.[6]

The other view in the House of Lords, which seems to be that of the majority[7] was that fair and temperate public criticism of a litigant was not a contempt. The Phillimore Committee recommended[8] a legislative provision to this effect but one was not put in the 1981 Act, and it is therefore unclear how the Act affects this matter. Section 2(2) covers publications which amount to a substantial risk of serious prejudice to particular proceedings, but does not say whether it is a defence to show that the publication was fair, temperate and non-abusive or indeed whether fair, temperate and non-abusive comment is to be considered capable of creating such a risk at all. A publication which *intends* to interfere with the administration of justice by pressurising parties (which will often be the case) is still covered by the common law by virtue of s 6(c). However, the difficulty remains of ascertaining in the light of the *Sunday Times* case what exactly the common law *is* on this point, and where fair and temperate criticism ends and improper pressure begins.

Some guidance on this matter can be derived from *A-G v Hislop*[9] which showed that liability for contempt by putting pressure on a litigant has certainly survived the Act. In that case the editor of the magazine *Private Eye* was held guilty of contempt for publishing an article intended to deter a plaintiff from

---

2 See eg *A-G v News Group Newspapers Ltd* [1989] QB 110, [1988] 2 All ER 906.
3 [1974] AC 273.
4 Lord Simon was also concerned about private pressure, [1974] AC 273, 318–319.
5 [1974] AC 273, 310.
6 *Sunday Times v UK* (1979) 2 ECHRR 245.
7 It was definitely the view of Lord Reid and Lord Cross, and it is submitted that Lord Morris should be read as concurring with them on this issue.
8 At para 62.
9 [1991] 1 QB 514, [1991] 1 All ER 911.

pursuing a libel action against the magazine itself. The editor was held liable both under the strict liability rule in the 1981 Act, because there was a substantial risk of serious prejudice, and under the common law because he intended it. The Court of Appeal referred to the speeches in the *Sunday Times* case and the distinction between 'fair and temperate criticism' and 'public obloquy' and concluded that the *Private Eye* article went beyond the former. Nicholls LJ recognised that the observations in the *Sunday Times* case had to be read in the light of the 1981 Act but said that the Act left untouched cases such as this where the conduct was intended to impede or interfere with the administration of justice.[10]

The facts of *A-G v Hislop* were exceptional because of the allegation that the plaintiff was being pressurised to drop her action against the magazine itself and it was not surprising that the Court of Appeal had no hesitation in holding that the publication complained of went far beyond any fair discussion of the issues involved. The present position is therefore that it can still be a contempt to put *improper* pressure on parties and in Chapter 6 we explore further the question of what amounts to improper pressure.

10   Ibid at 532 and 924 respectively.

CHAPTER 5

Publications interfering with the course of justice in particular criminal proceedings

I INTRODUCTION

In Chapters 3 and 4 we discussed the principles upon which the law of contempt operates to restrict what may be published about particular legal proceedings. In this chapter we are concerned with the specific application of that law to particular criminal proceedings. The position at common law and the position under the Contempt of Court Act 1981 are dealt with together and divergences between them are considered when they arise. As we saw in the previous chapters, publications thought to create a real risk of prejudice to particular proceedings are held to be a contempt at common law. Under the 1981 Act the test for the strict liability rule is whether the publication creates a substantial risk of serious prejudice.

The belief that those, particularly laymen, involved in the criminal process are vulnerable to out-of-court publicity has led to fears that undue publicity may cause the tribunal hearing the case to be biased or otherwise not to try the case on properly adduced evidence. In other words publications relating to criminal proceedings are at risk of being held as contempt for jeopardising that requirement of the due administration of justice referred to by Lord Diplock in the *Sunday Times* case, namely, that citizens:[1]

> 'should be able to rely upon obtaining in the courts the arbitrament of a tribunal which is free from bias against any party and whose decision will be based upon those facts only that have been proved in evidence adduced before it in accordance with the procedure adopted in courts of law.'

There is a special vigilance to shield criminal proceedings from risk partly because the liberty of an accused might be in issue and partly to protect society's interest that the guilty be convicted and the innocent acquitted. Deane J said in the High Court of Australia in *Hinch v A-G (Victoria)*:[2]

> 'The right to a fair and unprejudiced trial is an essential safeguard of the liberty of the individual under the law. The ability of a society to provide a fair and unprejudiced trial is an indispensable basis of any acceptable justification of the restraints and penalties of the criminal law. Indeed, it is a touchstone of the existence of the rule of law.'

The general position on publications prejudicing proceedings was explained by Lord Bridge in *Re Lonrho Plc*:[3]

---

1 [1974] AC 273 at 309.
2 (1987) 164 CLR 15 at 58.
3 [1990] 2 AC 154 at 209B, [1989] 2 All ER 1100 at 1116; this was a case involving civil proceedings but Lord Bridge's comments are equally applicable to criminal proceedings.

'Whether the course of justice in particular proceedings will be impeded or prejudiced by a publication must depend primarily on whether the publication will bring influence to bear which is likely to divert the proceedings in some way from the course which they would otherwise have followed. The influence may affect the conduct of witnesses, the parties or the court. Before proceedings have come to trial and before the facts have been found, it is easy to see how critical public discussion of the issues and criticism of the conduct of the parties, particularly if a party is held up to public obloquy, may impede or prejudice the course of the proceedings by influencing the conduct of witnesses or parties in relation to the proceedings. If the trial is to be by jury, the possibility of prejudice by advance publicity directed to an issue which the jury will have to decide is obvious. The possibility that a professional judge will be influenced by anything he has read about the issues in a case which he has to try is very much more remote. He will not consciously allow himself to take account of anything other than the evidence and argument presented to him in court.'

II   PUBLICATIONS BEFORE AND DURING THE TRIAL

A   Influencing those involved in proceedings

1   *Judges and magistrates*

Lord Bridge's words quoted above reflect the generally accepted principle that professional judges cannot be improperly influenced by any publication which they see or hear about proceedings. Some of the strongest statements about this invulnerability have been in relation to appellate judges, but this is to some extent only a reflection of the circumstances in which those statements have been made. Lord Salmon was particularly definite when he said in *A-G v BBC*:[4]

'I am and always have been satisfied that no judge would be influenced in his judgment by what may be said by the media. If he were, he would not be fit to be a judge.'

There have been some counter views. In *R v Davies, ex p Delbert-Evans* for example, Humphreys J drew a distinction between appellate and first instance judges, and commented obiter:[5]

'it is a fallacy to say or to assume that the presiding judge is a person who cannot be affected by outside information. He is a human being and while I am not saying for a moment that it is likely that any judge would give a decision which he would not have given but for information which had been improperly conveyed to him, it is embarrassing to the judge that he should be told matters which he would much rather not hear and which make it much more difficult for him to do what is his duty.'

This comment, however, was disapproved of in *R v Duffy, ex p Nash*, by Lord Parker CJ[6] who was unhappy about the use of the term 'embarrassed':[7]

---

4 [1981] AC 303 at 342.
5 [1945] KB 435 at 442–443, [1945] 2 All ER 167 at 172; Oliver J agreed, ibid at 445.
6 [1960] 2 QB 188 at 200, [1960] 2 All ER 891 at 896.
7 The term was also used in the Australian case *Ex p A-G: Re Truth and Sportsman Ltd* (1958) 61 SR (NSW) 484.

'It is by no means clear what the judges in [the *Delbert-Evans* case] intended to convey by the word "embarrassed". If, in its context, the word means no more than this, namely, that the article had put on the judge, quite unnecessarily, the task of dismissing the offending matter from his mind, then we think that the dicta ... went too far. Embarrassment which has no effect on impartiality is not necessarily contempt of court.'

He also said:[8]

'Even if a judge who eventually sat on the appeal had seen the article in question and had remembered its contents, it is inconceivable that he would be influenced consciously or unconsciously by it. A judge is in a very different position to a juryman. Though in no sense superhuman, he has by his training no difficulty in putting out of his mind matters which are not evidence in the case.'

More recently, however, Viscount Dilhorne commented in *A-G v BBC*:[9]

'It is sometimes asserted that no judge will be influenced in his judgment by anything said by the media and consequently that the need to prevent publication of matter prejudicial to the hearing of a case only exists where the decision rests with laymen. This claim to judicial superiority over human frailty is one that I find some difficulty in accepting. Every holder of a judicial office does his utmost not to let his mind be affected by what he has seen or heard or read outside the court and he will not knowingly let himself be influenced in any way by the media, nor in my view will any layman experienced in the discharge of judicial duties. Nevertheless, it should, I think, be recognised that a man may not be able to put that which he has seen, heard or read entirely out of his mind and that he may be subconsciously affected by it.'

The comment that judges do not possess superhuman qualities to overcome influence might strike some as a pertinent observation. As one American judge put it:[10]

'I do not know whether it is the view of the court that a judge must be thick-skinned or just thickheaded but nothing in my experience or observation confirms the idea that he is insensitive to publicity.'

Indeed, Lord Bridge's reference in *Re Lonrho Plc,*[11] to a judge not *consciously* allowing himself to take account of anything other than the evidence and argument in court, does leave hanging the question of whether, as Viscount Dilhorne suggested, he could be *subconsciously* affected. Notwithstanding these occasional expressions of doubt the overwhelming trend of the cases, in England and Wales and in other jurisdictions, is that professional judges are immune from prejudicial comment.[12] In reality this position is one of policy, upholding the aura of the judiciary and its incorruptibility. It should also be remembered that it is the judges themselves who are pronouncing on judicial susceptibility to prejudicial comment: it is hardly surprising therefore that they tend to discount it. There is

8 [1960] 2 QB 188 at 198, [1960] 2 All ER 891 at 895.
9 [1981] AC 303 at 335. See also the comment of the Phillimore Committee at para 49.
10 Jackson J (dissenting) in *Craig v Harney* 1947 67 Sup Ct 1249 at 1264.
11 [1990] 2 AC 154 at 209B.
12 See eg Buckley J in *Vine Products Ltd v Green* [1966] Ch 484 at 496; Maugham J in *Re The William Thomas Shipping Co Ltd* [1930] 2 Ch 368 at 373; and Lord Denning MR in *A-G v BBC* [1981] AC 303 at 312. In Australia see eg *A-G for New South Wales v Mundey* [1972] 2 NSWLR 887 at 901–2, per Hope JA and *Victoria v BLF* (1982) 41 ALR 71 particularly per Mason J at 123–4; cf, however, *Kerr v O'Sullivan* [1955] SASR 204. In Canada see *Re Depoe and Lamport* (1968) 66 DLR (2d) 46; *Bellitti v Canadian Broadcasting Corpn* (1974) 44 DLR (3d) 407, but cf *R v Carocchia* (1973) 43 DLR (3d) 427.

an inherent unlikelihood in members of the judiciary holding that there is a serious risk of their brethren being influenced by anything they read in the *Sun*, even supposing that they could be imagined reading it in the first place.

In practice the question of prejudicing trial judges in criminal proceedings rarely arises because of the importance of the risk of prejudicing the jury: whether or not a publication is a contempt will have to be considered in relation to the jury and so the matter of the judge is irrelevant. However, there is also the question of magistrates to consider. Lay magistrates may be thought susceptible to the deleterious effect of media comment and it may be, though this has yet to be unequivocally established, that the type of publication thought likely potentially to prejudice trials by jury may also be a contempt if published in connection with summary trials or committal hearings tried by lay magistrates. This seems to be the view of Lord Diplock who in *A-G v Times Newspapers Ltd* commented:[12a]

> 'Laymen, whether acting as jurymen or witnesses (or, for that matter as magistrates), were regarded by the judges as being vulnerable to influence or pressure which might impair their impartiality or cause them to form preconceived views as to the facts of the dispute . . .'.

Other cases, both from England and Australia, have tended not to distinguish clearly between the position as regards lay and stipendiary magistrates.[13] Stipendiary magistrates, being legally qualified and professional judges, arguably share the immunity from influence which is attributed to the rest of the judiciary.[14]

In magistrates' courts there may be a distinction to be drawn between committal (or transfer for trial) proceedings[15] and summary trials. The statement in the Australian case *A-G for NSW v John Fairfax & Sons and Bacon*,[16] that it would be fanciful to suppose that a magistrate could be influenced by the extraneous material in issue in the case, was made specifically in relation to committal proceedings. The distinction between the magistrates' role in the different types of proceedings was discussed by the Australian Law Reform Commission,[17] who said that at committal proceedings the magistrate is usually shielded by the restraints on publication designed to protect the possible future jury and is, anyway, not finally determining the guilt or innocence of the accused. When magistrates conduct a summary trial, however, they are, like a jury, weighing evidence and deciding questions of guilt and innocence and as such can be seen as analogous to the jury rather than to the judge. Like a jury, magistrates are not told of the defendant's previous convictions[18] and by s 42 of the Magistrates' Court Acts 1980 a magistrate may not sit in a summary trial if he has heard the defendant's application for bail and thereby learned of his previous

---

12a [1974] AC 273 at 309.
13 See *R v Tibbits & Windust* [1902] 1 KB 77 at 88; *R v Regal Press Pty Ltd* [1972] VR 67 (Victoria Sup Ct); *A-G for NSW v John Fairfax & Sons and Bacon* [1985] 6 NSWLR 695 at 709.
14 See the Australian case of *Ex p McRae: Re John Fairfax & Sons* (1954) SR (NSW) 165 at 177; in *R v Regal Press Pty Ltd* [1972] VR 67 the court did appear to distinguish between lay and stipendiary magistrates in that the discussion concerned whether there would be a risk of prejudice if a lay ('honorary') rather than a stipendiary magistrate heard the case.
15 In England and Wales committal proceedings were replaced by transfer for trial proceedings by the Criminal Justice and Public Order Act 1994, s 44.
16 [1985] 6 NSWLR 695 at 709.
17 Report No 35, paras 376–380.
18 The Justices' Clerk, like the judge in a trial on indictment, does have this information. Previous convictions can be disclosed during a trial if the conduct of the defence brings them into issue: see Criminal Evidence Act 1968, s 1(f).

convictions.[19] It is possible to argue from this[20] that if a magistrate can be influenced by hearing of the defendant's criminal record during the trial he can also be influenced by reading such matters in the media.[1] On the other hand, magistrates do rule on the admissibility of evidence and are trusted to put out of their minds allegations they have heard which are inadmissible.

2   *The jury*

Most cases on the risk of prejudice to criminal proceedings centre on the risk of prejudicing the jury. It is considered that first instance proceedings before a jury are especially vulnerable to influence by out-of-court publicity because jury members generally have no legal training or legal knowledge.[2] They cannot be expected to be able to appreciate the rules of evidence and whether or not a particular statement is admissible evidence. Nor can they be expected to be able easily to ignore comments which attack the accused's character or which assert his guilt. As Abbott J said in *R v Fleet*: [3]

> 'Every person who has attended to the operations of his own mind must have observed how difficult it is to overcome preconceived prejudices and opinions, and that more especially in matters of sentiment and passion.'

A jury cannot be expected readily to overcome such preconceptions and the law is vigilant to see that they are not subjected to such prejudicial publications. As Lord Ellenborough said:[4]

> 'If anything is more important than another in the administration of justice, it is that jurymen should come to the trial of those persons on whose guilt or innocence they are to decide, with minds pure and unprejudiced. Is it possible they should do so, after having read for weeks and months before ex parte statements of the evidence against the accused, which the latter had no opportunity to disprove or controvert?'[5]

And as Blair J put it in the New Zealand case of *A-G v Tonks*:[6]

> 'A person accused of a crime is entitled to have the charge against him heard and adjudicated upon by a jury of his fellows, and he is entitled also to have his case presented to such jury with their minds open and unprejudiced and untrammelled by anything which any newspaper . . . takes upon itself to publish before any part of the case has been heard. . . . An excess of zeal on the part of a newspaper may

---

19 There are no such restraints on judges or recorders in the Crown Court.
20 See Miller, *Contempt of Court* (2nd edn) p 218.
 1 In reality magistrates may well know of the defendant's previous convictions because they have tried him before and they may also be able to deduce from how the defendant arrives in court whether or not he was refused bail, the most likely cause of which is that he had previous convictions.
 2 Under the Juries Act 1974, Sch 1 barristers and solicitors, whether or not in actual practice, are not eligible for jury service, nor are trainee solicitors, legal executives, barristers' clerks or other categories of people 'concerned with the administration of justice'.
 3 (1818) 1 B & Ald 379.
 4 In *R v Fisher* (1811) 2 Camp 563 at 570. See also *R v Daily Herald, ex p Bishop of Norwich* [1932] 2 KB 402.
 5 That members of a jury ever come to a trial with minds which are in any real sense 'pure and unprejudiced' is an unattainable ideal; the law of contempt can only seek to ensure that they are not further prejudiced by particular kinds of publication.
 6 [1934] NZLR 141 at 149 (not to be confused with *A-G v Tonks* [1939] NZLR 533).

be fraught with the gravest consequences either to the accused person himself or to the administration of justice.'

It is also possible for publications to be in contempt because they create a risk of prejudicing the prosecution's case.[7]

As we shall see, the time between when the publication occurred and the holding of the trial will often be an important factor in deciding whether the publication amounted to a contempt, for time can dull the memory and the courts recognise that people often retain little of what they see or hear. As Mason CJ said in the High Court of Australia in a case concerning a radio programme:[8]

> '. . . a broadcast may have a transient impact only on the mind of the listener and . . . this effect is the more likely as the mind of the listener is continuously bombarded with a never-ending kaleidosope of sensational and scandalous items of news so that the individual's recollection of each and every item is ephemeral.'

The public's constant diet of shocking news items was, for example, taken into account by the Divisional Court in *A-G v Independent Television News Ltd,* [9] where Leggatt LJ considered that broadcasts about IRA activities were so frequent that an individual one, even when it concerned the murder of a policeman, would not be particularly memorable.[10]

Judges sometimes comment on the robustness of juries and express confidence on their ability, once the trial is underway, to put from their minds what they have heard outside the court room. Lawton J said in *R v Kray:*[11]

> '. . . the drama, if I may use that term, of a trial, almost always has the effect of excluding from recollection that which went before.'

---

7   See eg *R v Castro, Onslow's and Whalley's Case* (1873) LR 9 QB 219; *Davis v Baillie* [1946] VLR 486 (Victoria Sup Ct); *DPP v Wran* [1986] 7 NSWLR 616 (NSW CA). In July 1994 the Attorney General was asked by pensioners who had lost their pensions as a result of the alleged fraud of Robert Maxwell to ban the publication of a book, *A Mind Of My Own,* by Maxwell's widow, Betty, until after the trial of her sons for their part in the fraud: the claim was that the book's depiction of the sons as dominated by their father would affect the jury's view of their culpability and create sympathy for them (see *Independent on Sunday,* 31 July 1994). The Attorney General did not accede to the request.

8   *Hinch v A-G* (1987) 164 CLR 15 at 31, citing, inter alia, *BLF* (1982) 152 CLR 25 at 132, *Duff v The Queen* (1979) 39 FLR 315 at 333, 28 ALR 663 at 677

9   [1995] 2 All ER 370.

10   On the other hand, there may be some matters which receive such wide publicity and become so ingrained in the public consciousness, that they cannot be erased from the mind. In *R v Reade, Morris and Woodwiss* (1993) Independent, 19 October proceedings in the Central Criminal Court against three officers charged with conspiracy to pervert the course of justice were stayed on the grounds that it would have been impossible for them to receive a fair trial. The charges were in respect of the conduct of the police in the investigation into the IRA Birmingham bombings in 1974 in which 21 people died, and for which six men, the so-called 'Birmingham Six', were convicted of murder. In 1991, after years of television programmes, books and articles attacking the convictions and two abortive appeals to the Court of Appeal, the convictions were finally quashed (*R v McIlkenny* [1992] 2 All ER 417). In *R v Reade, Morris and Woodwiss* Garland J held that the 'Birmingham Six' had become synonymous with forced confessions and that the publicity after the 1991 hearing had given the impression that the release was tantamount to finding the police officers guilty of perjury and conspiracy. Cf the trials of the policemen involved in the 'Guildford Four' case, where again the release of those originally convicted was attended with great publicity about the alleged misconduct of the police: the trials went ahead and the policemen were acquitted. In October 1995 the trial of Geoffrey Knights, the boyfriend of a soap opera star was abandoned because of the publicity in the tabloid press.

11   (1969) 53 Cr App Rep 412 at 415.

Sir John Donaldson MR expressed similar sentiments in a case concerning a libel action which would apply equally to a criminal trial:[12]

'. . . whilst I have never been a great believer in the efficacy of a conscious effort to put something out of one's mind, an acceptance of the fact that it is likely to remain there, but a determination not to take it into account, is more effective and, whilst I fully accept that judges may have an exaggerated belief in the extent to which juries are prepared to be guided by them in such mental gymnastics, the fact is that for one reason or another a trial, by its very nature, seems to cause all concerned to become progressively more inward looking, studying the evidence given and submissions made to the exclusion of other sources of enlightenment. This is a well-known phenomenon.'[13]

The Australian courts have reached the same conclusion. The Federal Court of Australia said in *Duff v The Queen*:[14]

'We live in an age when television, motion pictures, radio and newspapers inform us of acts of violence and other notorious happenings within minutes of their occurrence in remote or proximate places. Some of the accounts are accurate and fair, others are not. It is wrong to assume that jurors do not have or will not exercise a critical judgment of what they see, read or hear in the media.'

Nevertheless, the protection of jurors from exposure to prejudicial comments remains a major factor in the law of contempt.

3   *Witnesses*

There is concern too about witnesses, particularly 'lay' witnesses who are to be called upon to give evidence relating to events as they saw them. Publications potentially jeopardising their evidence can also be a contempt.[15] This is particularly so in respect of the publication of photographs of the accused where identification is likely to be an issue at the trial.[16] In *Vine Products v Green*[17] Buckley J appeared to accept counsel's contention that expert witnesses such as doctors would not be influenced by publicity but was doubtful about witnesses who gave 'expert evidence' about matters such as the practices in a particular trade: the judge's distinction seeems to have been between those he recognised as members

---

12   *A-G v News Group Newspapers* [1987] QB 1 at 16C, [1986] 2 All ER 833 at 822B (the Botham libel case).
13   There is a substantial body of work by behavioural scientists and psychologists about the accuracy of particular forms of evidence and about the reactions of the pool of potential jurors to particular types of evidence. For example, E Loftus in *Eyewitness Testimony* (1979, Harvard University Press, Cambridge, Mass) (see pp 176–177) conducted a survey about the extent to which people believe that an eyewitness will change their evidence after reading a mistaken and erroneous account of what happened in a newspaper. 'Cognitive filter' theories suggest that early impressions have tremendous power for tribunals of fact because a juror will early on start forming a picture about what happened and will strive to fit later evidence into that picture: see S M Kassin and L S Wrightsman, *The American Jury on Trial: Psychological Perspectives* (1988, Hemisphere Publications, New York); A J Morre, 'Trial by Schema: Cognitive Filters in the Courtroom' (1989) 37 UCLA Law Review 273–341. This has obvious implications in respect of jurors who have received strong early impressions from media coverage before the trial.
14   (1979) 39 FLR 315 at 333, 28 ALR 663 at 677.
15   See Ch 11 for the issue of the payment of witnesses.
16   See p 159.
17   [1966] Ch 484 at 496, a case involving civil proceedings, but the point is universal.

of a profession and those of humbler status. In *Pickering v Liverpool Daily Post and Echo* [18] Lord Bridge said of medical witnesses testifying before a mental health review tribunal that 'one would not, of course expect [them] to allow their judgment to be consciously influenced by the media'.

4   Parties

It is possible that the accused himself might react to out-of-court publicity in a way which prejudices his case. In *A-G v Times Newspapers Ltd* [19] Oliver LJ thought that certain matters published in a newspaper, although unlikely to create a substantial risk of influencing jurors, *did* constitute a contempt because it caused the defendant, upon legal advice, to opt for a summary trial because he *feared* that jurors might be prejudiced by what they had read.

There is also the question of that small minority of criminal actions which are begun by private prosecution. It can be a contempt to put improper pressure on a litigant in a civil action[20] and there is no reason why the position should not be the same as regards a person bringing a criminal prosecution. The contempt committed by the *Sun* in *A-G v News Group Newspapers plc* [1] involved a case in which the *Sun* was *encouraging,* and indeed financing, a private prosecution but a campaign of that intensity mounted against such a prosecution instead in favour of it could be condemned as improper pressure.

B   General considerations

Before examining the cases in more detail three further introductory points should be made. First, the application of the law of contempt can only be illustrated by examples. The risk of prejudice must necessarily be related to the particular facts of each case[2] so that what is held to be a contempt in one case does not automatically mean that it will be a contempt in another nor vice versa. Furthermore, the absence of an exact precedent must not be taken to mean that there can be no contempt. The concept of the risk of prejudice is sufficiently flexible to include any potentially real interference with a fair trial no matter how novel the interference is. The second point is that what the law is concerned about is the risk of prejudice and in general those risks become greater the nearer the date of the trial. The media should be especially vigilant to avoid comment during the trial when jurors are already empanelled and immediately before the trial since publicity is likely to be fresh in the minds of those subsequently empanelled as jurors. This should not be taken to mean that until the immediacy of the trial comment can be published with impunity but merely that the dangers of being found in contempt are greatest at this later time.

---

18   [1991] 2 AC 370 at 425, [1991] 1 All ER 622 at 637.
19   (1983) Times, 12 February, one of the first cases to be decided under the Contempt of Court Act 1981.
20   See Ch 6 and in particular *A-G v Times Newspapers Ltd* [1974] AC 273 and *A-G v Hislop* [1991] 1 QB 514, [1991] 1 All ER 911.
 1   [1989] QB 110, [1988] 2 All ER 906.
 2   See eg *A-G v Independent Television News Ltd and others* [1995] 2 All ER 370.

The final point to be made is that although pre-trial publicity is risky[3] the law has never been so strict to prohibit all reference to crimes or arrests or the forthcoming trial. As Griffith CJ said in *Packer v Peacock*:[4]

'Publishers of newspapers have not, of course, any greater rights with respect to publication than those enjoyed by other persons. It has nevertheless become part of the ordinary course of life in civilised communities to publish through the medium of the press information as to matters of interest to the public, using that term to mean matters as to which the public entertain a natural and legitimate curiosity. It would be unfortunate for civilisation if satisfaction of such a curiosity by this means were prohibited. . . . In our opinion the public are entitled to entertain a legitimate curiosity as to such matters as the violent or sudden death or disappearance of a citizen, the breaking into a house, the theft of property, or any other crime, and it is, in our opinion, lawful for any person to publish information as to the bare facts relating to the matter. By bare facts we mean (but not as an exclusive definition) extrinsic ascertained facts to which any eye witness could bear testimony, such as the finding of a body and its condition, the place in which it is found, the person by whom it was found, the arrest of the person accused, and so on. But as to the alleged facts depending upon the testimony of such particular person which may or may not be true, and may, or may not be admissible in a Court of Justice, other conditions arise. The lawfulness of the publication in such cases is conditional, and depends, for present purposes, upon whether the publication is likely to interfere with the fair trial of the charge against the accused person.'

However, although Griffith CJ's statement gives some indication as to what is or is not permissible, as Fullagar J said in another Australian case, *Davis v Baillie*[5] the problem remains:

'to find where the line lies which separates a legitimate purveying of news to a public which is entitled to be informed, from a wrongful publication of matter prejudicial to a party to pending proceedings. The line is not altogether easy to draw.'

The ensuing passages mainly comprise examples of where publishers have been thought to have overstepped the dividing line, but in referring to these cases it is hoped that the line itself will become clearer.

C   Publications which tend to impair the court's impartiality

Fundamental to the concept of a 'fair' trial is that the court approaches each case with complete impartiality. Publications that are thought calculated to jeopardise the court's impartiality are regarded as serious contempts. As Lord Hardwicke said in the *St James's Evening Post case*,[6] nothing is of more:

'pernicious consequence than to prejudice the minds of the publick against persons concerned as parties in causes before the cause is finally heard.'

In *R v Tibbits and Windust*[7] Lord Alverstone LJ commented:

---

3 There is a point in time before which contempt cannot be committed on the grounds of prejudice. See Ch 7.
4 (1912) 13 CLR 577 at 588 (Australian HC). See also *A-G v Mathison* [1942] NZLR 302.
5 [1946] VLR 486 at 494 (Vict Sup Ct).
6 (1742) 2 Atk 469.
7 [1902] 1 KB 77 at 88.

'A person accused of a crime in this country can properly be convicted in a Court of Justice only upon evidence which is legally admissible and which is adduced at his trial in legal form and shape. Though the accused be really guilty of the offence charged against him; the due course of law and justice is nevertheless perverted and obstructed if those who have to try him are induced to approach the question of his guilt or innocence with minds into which prejudice has been instilled by published assertions of his guilt or imputations against his life and character to which the laws of the land refuse admissibility as evidence.'

Publications held liable to impair the court's impartiality fall essentially into one or more of the following categories, namely, those which:

(a) reflect upon the personal character of the accused,

(b) reveal an alleged confession by the accused, or

(c) comment or reflect upon the merits of the particular case.

These categories are by no means mutually exclusive but provide a convenient starting point for examining the types of publications which have been held to be a contempt.

1　*Publications concerning the character of the accused*

'Observations calculated to excite feelings of hostility towards any individual who is under a charge . . . amount to a contempt of court . . .'.[8]

Publications which tend to excite 'feelings of hostility' against the accused amount to contempt because they tend to induce the court to be biased. Such 'hostile feelings' can be most easily induced by commenting unfavourably upon the character of the accused. Juries are particularly vulnerable to such comments, because it is common for the layperson to adjudge a person's guilt from his personal character, and in criminal cases evidence as to the character of the accused is not usually admissible before the verdict is given. Such publications amount to a gross contempt because they potentially bring to the notice of the jury facts, very damaging to the accused, which they are not entitled to know, and which have a tendency to create bias against the accused.

(a)　Revealing the accused's past criminal record

Publications revealing an accused's past criminal record are normally regarded as particularly serious contempts and satisfy the 'substantial risk of serious prejudice' test of the strict liability rule under the 1981 Act as well as the common law test. Moffitt P said in the Australian case *A-G (NSW) v Willesee* [9] that there is a:

'popular and deeply rooted belief that it is more likely that an accused person committed the crime charged if he has a criminal record, and less likely if he has no record.'

In criminal law, however, it is firmly established that the existence of a prior record is irrelevant and it has been said[10] to be one of the most 'deeply rooted and

8　Per Pigot CB in *R v O'Dogherty* (1848) 5 Cox CC 348 at 354 (Ireland).
9　[1980] 2 NSWLR 143 at 150, para 14.
10　Per Viscount Sankey LC in *Maxwell v DPP* [1935] AC 309 at 317.

jealously guarded principles of (the) criminal law' that evidence of prior convictions or crimes shall not be admissible in the trial of a person's guilt.

There are numerous examples of publications being held to be a contempt on this score. Cases in England, for instance, include *R v Parke* [11] where, after an accused had been remanded on a charge of forgery, the *Star* published articles stating inter alia that he had admitted an earlier conviction for forgery and that he had been sentenced to 12 months' imprisonment with hard labour. Wills J, said of the articles:

> 'They were unquestionably calculated to produce the impression that, apart from the charges then under enquiry, he was a man of bad and dissolute character.'

In *R v Davies* [12] a woman was arrested on a charge of abandoning her child. Subsequently, the *South Wales Daily Post* published articles including one with the headline: 'Antecedents of the Accused'. The paper not only alleged her to be guilty of wholesale baby-farming, but asserted that her real identity was one Dora Johnstone who, it was alleged, had been convicted of fraud on more than one occasion. There was little doubt that such articles were highly prejudicial to the accused, and indeed the newspaper readily conceded the point.

The strict liability rule in s 2 of the 1981 Act was applied in *Solicitor General v Henry and News Group Newspapers Ltd.* [13] There the Divisional Court accepted that publishing the previous conviction for rape of a man arrested for attempted robbery, who was also being questioned about a woman's disappearance, under the front page banner headline 'Bride Quiz Man Is Rapist' appeared to be 'an honest, if unprofessional mistake'. The newspaper admitted contempt and was fined £15,000 and the arrested man was subsequently convicted, inter alia, of murder.

However, publication of previous convictions will not invariably constitute a contempt under s 2. The risk of prejudice may not be substantial if the circumstances of the case, and the delay between the publication and the trial, are such that the publication is unlikely to affect the jurors. This was the main reason why no contempt was held to have been committed in *A-G v Independent Television News Ltd.* [14] That case concerned an item on the early evening television news and statements appearing in several newspapers which revealed the terrorist convictions and escape from jail of an Irishman arrested in connection with the murder of a policeman in Yorkshire. The Divisional Court said that the fact that the lapse of time before trial was likely to be (and in the event was) nine months was of 'overriding importance'. Leggatt LJ said that 'however horrible the incident described' the medium of television was ephemeral in nature and broadcasts about the IRA were so frequent that an individual one was less memorable as a result. His Lordship did not consider, therefore, that a viewer of this unrepeated news item would have retained the information for nine months. In the case of the newspapers it was relevant that the item appeared only in the first editions of the three daily papers concerned, which had a limited circulation in London (where the trial was to be held), and that only about 146 copies of the offending regional newspaper, the *Northern Echo*, were distributed in London, and those mostly at King's Cross station. Leggatt LJ took the same view as with the television broadcast of the likelihood of a potential juror recalling the articles

11 [1903] 2 KB 432.
12 [1906] 1 KB 32, cf *R v Armstrong* (1894) Times, 9 May.
13 [1990] COD 307.
14 [1995] 2 All ER 370.

and held that when the odds of having read any of the articles were multiplied against the odds of remembering there was only a very remote risk and such a risk did not satisfy the test for contempt under s 2(2). In reaching this conclusion the court emphasised the fact that in contempt cases the standard of proof is the criminal one. Given the combination of circumstances in this case the court was not satisfied that a substantial risk had been proved.

A-G v Independent Television News did raise interesting points about the issue of the area of circulation of the publication in relation to the place of the trial. The *Northern Echo's* main area of circulation was Yorkshire, where the crime had taken place. Some hours after the defendants were arrested in Yorkshire they were taken to Paddington Green police station in London. The court accepted that by the time of the publication the reasonable assumption was that the trial would take place at the Central Criminal Court and that there was no evidence that the trial might, after all, take place in Yorkshire. This meant that London was the relevant area of circulation[15] and demonstrates the importance of the point that the risk has to be assessed at the time of publication, for had the trial later been moved back to Yorkshire for some reason there would still, presumably, have been no contempt.

The A-G argued that the possibility of 'leakage' might occur, in that potential jurors visiting the principal area of circulation might see the publication, but the court held that such a risk could only be remote. A more interesting argument was that if regional or local papers could with impunity publish any prejudicial material they liked so long as they did it outside the potential catchment area for jurors, the policy of deterrence underlying the Act, which was referred to by Lord Diplock in *A-G v English*,[16] would be undermined. Leggatt LJ's reply to this was that the court simply had to apply the test in s 2(2) which means, of course, deciding whether there was a substantial risk to the particular proceedings. Another answer would be that a regional newspaper which had a policy of publishing sensational prejudicial material about forthcoming cases might be guilty of common law contempt as having 'intention' and the risk of leakage might be found to be more real than it was in the case of the merely careless *Northern Echo*.

Neither of the judges in *A-G v Independent Television News* suggested that the failure to satisfy the test in s 2(2) was because the statute produced a stricter test than the common law. They contrasted the statute's test of 'substantial' with what they found on the facts to be a 'remote' or 'insubstantial' risk. Indeed, Buxton J said:[17]

> 'The crucial question for this court . . . is whether the publication created a more than insubstantial risk that the information contained in the publication as to Mr Magee's record would be in the mind of a juror at the trial.'

In *A-G v Sport Newspapers* [18] the *Sport* published a photograph of a man sought by the police in connection with the disappearance of a schoolgirl, describing him as a 'sex monster' and giving detailed information about his previous convictions under the headline 'Anna: man on the run is a vicious rapist'. The 1981 Act did not apply because proceedings were not 'active' within the meaning of s 2(3) and Sch 1.[19] However the newspaper could be liable at

15 For the question of circulation, see pp 85 ff.
16 [1983] 1 AC 116 at 141 F; see pp 147 ff.
17 [1995] 2 All ER 370 at 384g–h.
18 [1992] 1 All ER 503, [1991] 1 WLR 1194.
19 See Ch 7.

common law if there was specific intention to cause a real risk of prejudice[20] and if the common law applied to proceedings which were neither in existence nor imminent. In the event both judges in the Divisional Court held that there was no contempt committed, agreeing that there was no intention proved, although disagreeing about the timing requirements.[1] They also disagreed about the existence of a real risk. Hodgson J was not satisfied that the publication created a real risk because of the police-inspired publicity about the hunt for the man[2] and the length of time likely to elapse before the trial. Bingham LJ, however, while conceding that 'most readers of the *Sport* would very quickly forget most of what they read in it', believed that such notoriety had attended the girl's disappearance and the subsequent police hunt[3] that potential jurors *would* remember this particular information, particularly if the trial was held locally.[4] Despite the small circulation of the *Sport* in the local area, a juror who had read the paper was likely to tell others, and so despite the lapse of time which was likely to occur before the trial his Lordship was convinced that the risk of prejudice was real.

There have also been a number of contempt prosecutions[5] in respect of public revelations that an accused had in open court entered guilty pleas to some but not all charges, such pleas being taken before the jury was empanelled and subsequently concealed from the jury so as not to influence them in their decisions on the charges to which he had not pleaded guilty. However, revealing that a defendant is awaiting trial on other charges does not necessarily create a substantial risk of serious prejudice. In *A-G v Guardian Newspapers Ltd,* [6] in the course of an article criticising the courts for too readily imposing reporting restrictions under s 4(2) of the 1981 Act in major fraud trials,[7] the paper published the information that one (unidentified) defendant in a current trial featuring six defendants was also facing charges in the Isle of Man. Mann LJ considered that the practical risk of the publication engendering bias in a juror of ordinary good sense was insignificant. A different outcome was reached, however, in a 1981 case where the *Guardian* was fined £5,000 for revealing, during the middle of a long fraud trial, that the two accused had previously been involved in an escape from custody.[8]

The Australian courts have been similarly vigilant to punish as contempts publications revealing an accused's past criminal record. In *A-G of New South*

---

20 Because of the saving provisions of s 6(c) of the 1981 Act; see Ch 4 pp 106 ff.
1   See Ch 7.
2   At both a press conference and in a fax to the Press Association, however, the police warned the media against revealing the suspect's previous convictions.
3   The girl was found murdered and the suspect eventually apprehended in France and extradited so the matter continued to attract widespread publicity for some time after the publication of the relevant edition of the *Sport*.
4   As would normally be the case in the absence of an application to hold it elsewhere.
5   See eg *R v Border Television Ltd, ex p A-G* and *R v Newcastle Chronicle and Journal Ltd, ex p A-G* (1978) 68 Cr App R 375. There have also been prosecutions against the *North West Evening Mail* (1981) Times, 7 February and the *Northampton Chronicle and Echo* (1981) Times, 31 March.
6   [1992] 3 All ER 38, [1992] 1 WLR 874.
7   See Ch 8.
8   Reported in (1981) Times, 31 March. The publications actually concerned the arrest in New York of a Mr Torri who, it was stated, had, along with the two (named) defendants in the current fraud trial escaped from Lambeth Magistrates' Court. The article appeared on the 127th day of the fraud trial. The trial was then abandoned throwing away costs of thousands of pounds.

Wales v Truth and Sportsman Ltd [9] the accused appeared before magistrates on a charge of possessing a pistol without a licence. An article was published, purporting to be a report of the proceedings, under the headline: 'Victorian Criminal Found in Sydney'. The article referred to the accused as a 'notorious Melbourne Criminal' and mentioned that the police had said that he had a record of escaping custody in Victoria. The publication was held to be a contempt and Street CJ warned the press against the use of 'colourful and emotional adjectives to attract attention to their columns'. In *R v Regal Press Pty Ltd* [10] the defendant newspaper published not only that the accused had been arrested and charged with 'driving under the influence' but also that he had previously served a sentence for murder. In its defence it was argued that the accused's prior conviction was common knowledge so that its publication did not add to any risk of prejudice. The argument was rejected on the basis that it overlooked the fact that knowledge or memory is not always at the forefront of a person's mind and that instant recall is not a faculty enjoyed by all magistrates and justices or for that matter judges.

In *A-G (NSW) v Willesee* [11] a television programme was held to be a contempt for revealing, at a time when the accused was charged with the murder, that whilst in prison he had previously assaulted two others officers with weapons. This information was broadcast during a television interview with another prisoner who at the time and in common with other prisoners had been confined to his cell because the prison warders had gone on strike following the death of their colleague. The defendants attempted to argue that the prisoner's remarks, including the reference to the prior crimes of the man charged were relevant to the discussion of a matter of great public interest, namely the state of affairs in that particular prison leading to confinement of prisoners to their cells and the reason for the prisoners' dissatisfaction. The argument was rejected, Moffitt P holding:[12]

> 'There is no authority that to broadcast to the public by newspaper, radio or television that a man has prior convictions, or has committed past crimes after he has been charged ceases to be a contempt because it is published in the course of some legitimate discussion upon a matter of public interest.'

The defence that the publication was in the course of a discussion on a matter of public interest was also raised in *Hinch v A-G (Victoria)*.[13] A man who had been ordained as a Roman Catholic priest,[14] and who had formed a non-profit making foundation which controlled a number of youth organisations and ran camps for young people, was arrested and charged with numerous sexual offences against children. Hinch made three broadcasts on the local radio station in which he drew attention to the fact that the priest had previous convictions for similar sex offences, implied that he was guilty of other offences where the victims had been too scared to come forward and raised the issue as to how a man

---

9 (1957) 75 WN (NSW) 70. See also eg *Davis v Baillie* [1946] VLR 486: publication describing an accused who had absconded from bail as an armed bandit who had gone back to his old habits of robbing houses and included information as to his prior convictions.

10 [1972] VR 67 (Victoria Sup Ct).

11 [1980] 2 NSWLR 143.

12 Ibid at 151, para 16. Cf Mahoney JA who was more sympathetic to the argument but who still held there to be a contempt. The public interest defence is discussed in more detail at pp 169 ff.

13 (1987) 164 CLR 15.

14 Although because of his subsequent conduct he no longer held any position within the Church.

with such a record could have been allowed to run a foundation for young people. The High Court of Australia held that although the trial might not take place until some two years after the first broadcast the lower courts were entitled to reach the conclusion that there was 'a substantial risk of serious interference with the fairness of the trial'.[15] The court considered that with such a sensational case involving a priest potential jurors were likely to remember the matter of the criminal record despite the lapse of time. The court, in fact, reached the same conclusion as the Divisional Court *A-G v Sport Newspapers Ltd* [16] about the way in which jurors were likely to recollect details about the accused in a sex case involving children, where issues such as 'why was this man allowed free to offend again?' were raised in the public mind by publications prior to the trial. The High Court held that the broadcasts in *Hinch* were not saved by the 'public interest defence'.[17] Gaudron J said:

> 'Where the impugned conduct goes directly to the question of guilt, it touches at the very heart of the public interest in ensuring that no person is convicted of a criminal offence save by verdict given after a fair trial on the evidence given in that trial.'[18]

In Canada, too, there is concern that publications should not reveal an accused's past criminal record. As Anderson J said in *Re Murphy and Southam Press Ltd*:[19]

> 'Except in the most unusual circumstances, the press should refrain from publishing criminal records of any accused person, alleged co-conspirator or witness.'

In that case, however, it was held not to be a contempt to reveal a *witness's* criminal record since that would have been revealed at the trial. In *Re A-G of Alberta and Interwest Publications Ltd* [20] a newspaper published an article about a man accused of murdering his wife, reporting his previous conviction for a firearms offence following an incident when the police were called to the man's home because he was threatening his family and using a shotgun. The article portrayed the man as explosive, moody, unpredictable and intimidating while painting a picture of the deceased as attractive and sensitive. Berger J held this to be contempt. He said that the public had a vital interest in knowing the facts, which was protected by the freedom of expression including freedom of the press contained in s 2(b) of the Canadian Charter of Rights and Freedoms, but that there was a distinction between the situation where a dangerous suspect is at large and public assistance may be required to apprehend him and the situation where he is custody awaiting trial: publication of the criminal record of a person who is not at large and who is not a danger to the community is prima facie a contempt of court.[1]

---

15 (1987) 164 CLR 15 at 31 per Mason CJ.

16 [1992] 1 All ER 503, discussed above.

17 This aspect of the case is considered at p 174.

18 (1987) 164 CLR 15 at 88; see also *R v Thompson* [1989] WAR 219 (W Australia Sup Ct) where a television programme was held to have committed contempt by revealing that a defendant accused of attempted unlawful killing had previously been convicted of multiple rape.

19 (1972) 30 DLR (3d) 355 at 359 (BC Sup Ct). See also *R v Froese and British Columbia Television Broadcasting System Ltd (No 3)* DLR (1979) 50 CCC (2d) 119; *R v Bannerman and Radio NW Ltd* (1979) 50 CCC (2d) 119; affd 54 CCC (2d) 315 (BCCA).

20 (1991) 73 DLR (4th) 83.

1 See also *R v Bowes Publishers Ltd* [1995] Alberta Weekly Law Digest, Issue 24, 16 June, p 2.

A similar position seems to obtain in New Zealand,[2] Northern Ireland[3] and Scotland.[4]

(b)   Other imputations on the accused's character

An accused's character can be damned in ways other than publishing his past criminal record. Editors appreciate that revelations of previous criminal convictions are likely to be considered a serious contempt and it is a relatively easy matter to ensure that nothing is published which refers to them. In *A-G v Independent Television News Ltd,* [5] for example, it was accepted that the publication of the accused's criminal record by ITN arose through 'carelessness'. It is more difficult to say when the way in which the defendant is described or referred to, or the way in which the circumstances surrounding the crime are discussed, will amount to a contempt as constituting such a reflection on the character of the accused that the fairness of the trial is put at risk. Certain sections of the press maintain their circulations because of their populist approach to news stories and it is (perhaps regrettably) true that the sensationalist treatment of crime attracts a large readership. When major crime stories break some newspapers send out journalists to investigate the backgrounds of those involved, often offering considerable sums of money for 'exclusive' stories, with a view to giving extensive coverage of these matters immediately the trial has ended.[6] The chances of prejudicial information about the accused's character infiltrating what is written before the trial is considerable.

A clear example of prejudicial reporting of the defendant's character from before the 1981 Act is *R v Thomson Newspapers Ltd, ex p A-G* .[7] An article was published in the *Sunday Times* about Michael Abdul Malik who was awaiting a retrial for an offence contrary to the Race Relations Act 1965. The following comment appeared beneath a photograph of Malik:

> 'Michael Abdul Malik, 34, West Indian. Came to UK 1950, took to politics after unedifying career as brothel keeper, procurer and property racketeer. Muddled thinker but natural flair for self-advertisement.'

In finding the newspaper guilty of contempt, Lord Parker CJ said:

---

2   See eg Burrows, *News Media Law in New Zealand* (NZ NPA) Ch 7, pp 248–9.
3   See *R v Beaverbrook Newspapers Ltd* [1962] NI 15.
4   There appears to be no direct authority specially concerning publication of past criminal records though there seems no doubt that it would be a contempt. In *HM Advocate v George Outram & Co Ltd* 1980 SLT (Notes) 13 *The Glasgow Herald* was fined £20,000 for what was described as an abominable contempt which included revealing that some of those arrested in a big drugs case were believed to be escapees from a prison in Holland. Radio Forth Ltd were fined £10,000 for reporting on the same case, see (1979) Times, 22 December.
5   [1995] 2 All ER 370.
6   Book publishers sometimes commission books with a view to publication immediately after the trial. Television companies do the same: on the evening of the conviction of two ten year old boys in 1994 for killing two year old Jamie Bulger ITV showed a documentary on the background to the case, including a discussion of the character and family circumstances of the boys, complete with a home video of one at a party. Possibly the most notable example of modern press behaviour in crime reporting occurred in 1994 when over a period of time the police unearthed 12 bodies at Frederick West's house and various other locations in Gloucester: the descent on the area by journalists and authors was described in the *Guardian* (1994) 10 June under the heading 'Making a Killing'.
7   [1968] 1 All ER 268, [1968] 1 WLR 1.

'That it is a serious contempt of court must be obvious to anyone when one realises that, except in special circumstances, a jury is not entitled to know anything of the prisoner's bad character.'

Another example of a publication blackening the defendant's character was in the Australian case *R v Saxon, Hadfield and Western Mail Ltd* [8] where shortly before her trial on a charge of perjury the newspaper published an article about the defendant's unsuccessful commercial career, alleging that she owed money to creditors and noting that she had previously been acquitted of a charge of false pretences. The fact that the defendant was subsequently acquitted of the perjury charge did not prevent the majority in the Supreme Court of Western Australia from finding that the publication was a contempt.[9] It was of particular relevance in that case first, that as the defendant's husband was a public figure potential jurors would be more likely to remember what they read, and secondly, that as the charge she faced was perjury the imputations in the article about the defendant's credibility were particularly serious.

In contrast, the New South Wales Court of Appeal found no contempt to have been committed when the *National Times* published an article about a police officer charged with attempted bribery of another policeman.[10] The article did not assert the accused's guilt on the bribery charge but discussed his character and past behaviour, making allegations against him of murder, attempted murder, supplying drugs, suborning witnesses and perverting the course of justice. In particular the article dwelt on a previous incident in which the accused had shot dead a heroin dealer. The basic theme of the article was corruption in the police force and the difficulties attendant on investigating it, with the case of the accused being used as a illustration of these matters. The reasons the court gave for finding that the publication did not, as a matter of practical reality, have a tendency to interfere with the trial included the length of time likely to elapse before the trial took place[11] and the fact that many of the allegations contained in the article, particularly the affair of the heroin dealer's death, had already been canvassed in the media. Given the circulation of the paper it was statistically unlikely that the article would have been read by a potential juror and any juror who had done so would be unlikely to remember it amid the welter of other publicity about the accused. McHugh JA referred to an academic article which suggested that the effect on jurors of pre-trial publicity had been overrated by the common law[12] and also said that the fact that when the (expedited) trial took place the accused was acquitted confirmed his opinion that there was no real risk of prejudice. He admitted that the final outcome was irrelevant, since a finding of contempt depends on risk of prejudice and not *actual* prejudice[13] and it is submitted that it is perhaps dangerous, however tempting, to look at a publication with hindsight.[14]

---

8 [1984] WAR 283.
9 For the reasons why an acquittal does not mean no contempt was committed see pp 74 ff.
10 *A-G (NSW) v John Fairfax & Sons & Bacon* (1985) 6 NSWLR 695.
11 This was said to be nearly 20 months although in the end the case was expedited and the trial took place only seven months later: the risk to the trial however has to be assessed on the basis of how matters stand at the time of publication, see p 84.
12 Simon: 'Does the Court's Decision in the Nebraska Press Association Fit with the Research Evidence on the Impact on Jurors of News Coverage?' (1978) Stanford Law Rev 515.
13 See Ch 3.
14 A temptation which was resisted, for example, by the Divisional Court in *A-G v News Group Newspapers Ltd* [1989] QB 110, [1988] 2 All ER 906, discussed at p 144.

The risk of prejudice was also dismissed in the Canadian case *Re A-G of Alberta and Interwest Publications Ltd* [15]. Berger J considered that publication at the time of arrest of the opinions and anecdotal accounts of neighbours and acquaintances about the accused's character might be seen by the public as merely idle rumour or gossip and therefore might not taint the mind of potential jurors: he contrasted this with the publication of the accused's criminal record which being a 'judicial pronouncement' would be a more substantial threat, as the public was likely to give it considerable credence and weight. This sanguine view of the discriminating judgment of the public on what they read is not, however, one which it would be safe for the media to assume is shared by all judges in all jurisdictions, as is apparent from the cases. The more shocking or memorable the material the greater the chance of jurors being held likely to recollect it, whatever the original source of the information.

The most striking case in England concerning this type of publication since the 1981 Act was the Divisional Court decisions in *A-G v Times Newspapers Ltd* [16] in which five national newspapers were prosecuted in respect of articles they published concerning Michael Fagan, who had intruded into the Queen's bedroom in Buckingham Palace. Most of the alleged contempts were reflections on the merits of the charges, and the case is considered as a whole below. [17]

In the examples given above the publications concerned the risk of prejudice to the defence but it is possibe that comments *favourable* to the accused's character can amount to contempt if thought to create a real risk of prejudging the case for the prosecution. [18]

In *Davis v Baillie* [19] articles were published which in the main disparaged the character of the accused, but there was one article favourable to the accused. Fullagar J said:

> 'In criminal cases it is not to be forgotten that it is immaterial whether the tendency of the matter complained of is for or against the accused person. The jurisdiction now invoked is concerned alike with the risk of conviction of the innocent and the risk of the acquittal of the guilty . . . I regard publication, while a charge is pending, of matters calculated to arouse sympathy with an accused person as objectionable in itself.'

15 (1991) 73 DLR (4th) 83, the facts of which are given at p 137.
16 (1983) Times, 12 February; the Divisional Court was particularly strong, comprising Lord Lane CJ and Ackner and Oliver LJJ.
17 See p 149. A more recent case of an allegation bearing on the defendant's character although not directly affecting the merits of the case against him was a front-page article in the *Sun* about a Gloucester builder, Frederick West, who at the time of publication, 10 June 1994, was facing 12 murder charges in respect of bodies unearthed at various properties he had owned. The article alleged that 'his dead lover', one of his alleged victims, had been pregnant and that they had planned to sell the baby when it was born: the photograph of them together which the *Sun* published was claimed to have been posed for as part of a campaign to impress 'potential buyers'. Although no contempt action was taken in respect of this publication an allegation that the defendant was a man who would sell his own children was certainly a prejudicial comment on his character.
18 See the moves in 1994 to ask the Attorney General to ban the publication of a book alleged to arouse sympathy for the Maxwell brothers, written by their mother (*Independent on Sunday*, 31 July 1994).
19 [1946] VLR 486 (Victoria Sup Ct). See also eg *R v Castro, Onslow's and Whalley's Case* (1873) LR 9 QB 219 discussed at p 153.

In other Australian decisions there is a hint that it might be harder to establish a real risk of prejudice to the prosecution.[20] However, Australian courts have certainly taken the view that a publication which directly discusses the merits of the case in a way favourable to the defendant is a serious contempt.[1]

2 Publication of confessions

Contrary to popular belief a pre-trial confession is not conclusive proof of an accused's guilt. As one Australian judge, Lowe J, explained:[2]

> 'No one at that stage [before committal proceedings] could know what would be the attitude of the accused or what defence he would set up. A confession of guilt signed by the accused would not preclude him from repudiating it and, indeed, experience of trials in the Criminal Courts suggests that, where the crime charged is serious, not infrequently, a confession is either repudiated by the accused or is alleged to have been obtained under circumstances which make it inadmissible. Nor would such a confession preclude the accused from setting up an alibi.'

It is possible for a pre-trial confession, therefore, never to be heard in court because the accused may change his mind, or because it may be inadmissible, as for example a confession obtained by force. Unless the confession is ruled admissible the jury is not entitled to know about it.

The fact that the accused has made an alleged confession is likely to be highly prejudicial, and premature publications of such information are regarded as a real threat to the court's impartiality and amount to a serious contempt. The truth of the published allegation is no defence to a charge of contempt.[3] The classic English decision is *R v Clarke, ex p Crippen*.[4] After Crippen had been arrested[5] in Canada the *Daily Chronicle* published the following statements, which had been cabled to the newspaper by a correspondent:

> 'I have confidence in the authority on which I cabled you the information last night and I am assured today from the same source that Crippen admitted in the presence of witnesses that he had killed his wife but denied the act was murder.'

and

> 'It is generally considered here that formal official denials that Crippen has made a confession hinge upon a distinction between the words "admission" and "confession". It is quite possible that what Crippen said may not be regarded officially as a confession, especially as he declared that he was not a "murderer" but that the prisoner made a statement to Inspector Drew last Monday I have reason to feel certain.'

The *Daily Chronicle* was found guilty of contempt, Darling J commenting: 'Anything more calculated to prejudice the defence could not be imagined.'

---

20 See eg *Consolidated Press Ltd v McRae* (1955) 93 CLR 325 (Australian HC) where the suggestion that a publication amounted to contempt because it aroused sympathy for the accused was dismissed. For a similar case see also *John Fairfax & Sons Pty Ltd v McRae* (1955) 93 CLR 351.
1 See *DPP v Wran* (1986) 7 NSWLR 616, discussed at p 154.
2 In *R v Pacini* [1956] VLR 544 at 549 (Victoria Sup Ct).
3 See *R v Clarke, ex p Crippen* (1910) 103 LT 636. See also, but in a different context, *R v Carocchia* (1973) 43 DLR (3d) 427 (Quebec CA).
4 (1910) 103 LT 636.
5 But not formally charged.

Under the strict liability rule in s 2(2) of the 1981 Act the *Daily Star* was found guilty of contempt in *A-G v Times Newspapers Ltd,* [6] the case concerning the intruder in the Queen's bedroom, because the article included the assertion that Fagan admitted stealing the wine, which was held to create a 'very' substantial risk of serious prejudice.

In Australia, the *Sun* was fined A$10,000 in *A-G (NSW) v John Fairfax & Sons Pty Ltd* [7] for publishing, pending a trial for murder, inter alia:

> 'Father Accused: Sick Baby Murder, "I couldn't bear to see him suffer in the future". Alleged Statement to Police and "A young father, heartbroken at learning that his baby son was mentally handicapped, killed him because he couldn't bear to see him suffer in the future," police said today.'

A police officer was found guilty of contempt by the New South Wales Court of Appeal in *A-G (NSW) v Dean* [8] when, in the course of a police media conference following the arrest of a suspect in a murder enquiry, he answered a journalist's question with a statement which suggested that the man was guilty of the charges and had confessed to them. The court considered that the police officer was a 'sincere and conscientious detective more at home in the field of homicide investigation than in a media conference' who had replied to the questions honestly and in ignorance of the law of contempt. Because of these factors, and despite the seriousness of the contempt, the officer was not fined. The court did point out that as the conference was not 'live' the principal responsibility for publishing the contempt really belonged to the media who had chosen to broadcast the statements.[9] The dangers of prejudicing the trial which are, to a certain extent, inherent in press conferences called by the police during an investigation or after a person has been charged, are discussed below.[10]

In Canada, in *Re A-G for Manitoba and Radio Ob Ltd*,[11] a broadcasting company was fined $750 (and the interviewer $250) for broadcasting a radio interview with a mother who revealed that her son, a juvenile, who had been charged with delinquency based on the murder of a school teacher, had earlier been diagnosed as psychotic and had confessed to the police.

Even where statements are made in court, which apparently amount to a confession, great care should be taken in reporting this fact. In *R v West Australian Newspapers Ltd, ex p Minister of Justice* [12] an accused, charged with murder, said in court that he had killed the woman concerned, but at no time did he admit to 'murdering' her. The *Daily News* published a statement to the effect that the accused had confessed to murder. It was held that the misreporting amounted to a contempt since by imputing that he was guilty of murder, the very point in issue, the article prejudiced the accused's chances of a fair and unbiased trial.

---

6   (1983) Times, 12 February, see p 149.
7   [1980] 1 NSWLR 362 (NSW CA). See also *R v David Syme & Co Ltd* [1982] VR 173 (Vict Sup Ct) and *Ex p Senkovitch* (1910) 10 SR (NSW) 738 (NSW Sup Ct).
8   (1990) 20 NSWLR 650.
9   For responsibility for publications, see Ch 10. Counsel for the Attorney General told the court that the proceeedings against the officer were brought in order to establish, or rather confirm, the matter of principle concerning contempt by the police.
10   See p 152.
11   (1976) 70 DLR (3d) 311 (Manitoba QB). See also *R v Willis* (1913) 9 DLR 646 (Manitoba KB).
12   (1958) 60 WALR 108 (W Australian Sup Ct).

3   *Publications which comment or reflect upon the merits of the case*

We have already suggested that the evil of 'trial by newspaper' is that the function of the court is usurped without any of the safeguards of court procedure such as the right to reply and to cross-examine. It is of the essence of a 'fair trial' that the court should assess the merits of any particular case, and in particular should decide the guilt or innocence of the accused. Publications which directly or indirectly prejudge the merits of a trial and particularly those which impute the guilt or innocence of the accused are classic examples of 'trial by newspaper'. Such publications have a tendency to prejudice the fair trial of an accused, since they could clearly create bias in the minds of those who have to try the case. It is therefore a serious contempt to impute directly or indirectly the guilt or innocence of an accused before he has been tried. It should be added, however, that it is prima facie permissible to publish the fact of an arrest and the exact nature of the charge. In *R v Payne* [13] the sub-editor of the *Huntingdonshire Post* was charged with attempting to set fire to the newspaper's premises. Two days after the arrest, the *Post* published an article which stated that the sub-editor had been arrested and that a charge of arson was pending. The Divisional Court held that this did not amount to contempt.

(a)   Assertions of guilt or innocence

Direct assertions of guilt or innocence are the most serious contempts. Such blatant assertions are rare, but *R v Bolam, ex p Haigh* [14] provides an outstanding example, and is one of the most serious contempts ever committed in England, resulting in the editor being imprisoned and the proprietors heavily fined. The *Daily Mirror* in front-page headlines described Haigh as a 'Vampire', gave reasons for that description, and:

> 'after saying that he had been charged with one murder went on to say not merely that he was charged with other murders but that he had committed others, and gave the names of persons whom, it was said, he had murdered.'

Lord Goddard CJ considered the article 'a disgrace to English journalism' which violated 'every principle of justice and fair play which it had been the pride of this country to extend to the worst of criminals'. He thought that:

> 'anyone who had the misfortune to read the articles must be left wondering how it could be possible for the applicant to obtain a fair trial after what had been published.'

In *R v Odham's Press Ltd, ex p A-G* [15] the *People* had been running a campaign against prostitution and brothel-keeping in London. An attack was made on one

---

13   [1896] I QB 577.
14   (1949) 93 Sol Jo 220 (Div Ct).
15   [1957] 1 QB 73, [1956] 3 All ER 494 (Div Ct); see also *R v Fisher* (1811) 2 Camp 563 where the article referred to the accused as a 'monster'; *R v Balfour, Re Stead* (1895) 11 TLR 492 where pending the trial of one Balfour it was commented by one journal: 'Another rare rogue in the shape of Jabez Balfour was a good deal before the courts last month. He will reappear at the Old Bailey and then we may expect to hear no more of him for some time to come', and *Re Thomas* [1928] SASR 210 (S Australian Sup Ct) where it was stated that the accused's arrest was a 'clean up' of many recent burglaries (thereby asserting guilt). See also *Re Associated Newspapers Ltd, ex p Fisher* (1941) 41 SR (NSW) 272 and *R v Parnell* (1881) 14 Cox CC 474 (Ireland).

Micallef under the headline: 'Arrest this beast'. The article alleged inter alia 'that he was up to his eyes in the foul business of purveying vice and managing street women'. At the time of publication, but unknown to the newspaper,[16] Micallef had already been arrested and charged with brothel-keeping. Lord Goddard CJ held:[17]

> 'With the truth or falsity of the various allegations in the article this court is not concerned, for it is not and could not be disputed that anything more calculated to prejudice a fair trial could not well be imagined . . . '.

A more unusual example is *R v Williams* [18] where the imputation of guilt conveyed by means of a theatrical play was held to be a contempt, the court commenting:

> 'Any attempt whatever to prejudge a criminal case whether by a detail of evidence or by a comment, or by a theatrical exhibition, is an offence against public justice.'

A more recent case involving a blatant assertion of guilt was *A-G v News Group Newspapers Ltd.*[19] Following the DPP's decision not to prosecute a consultant anaesthetist who, it was alleged, had raped an eight year old, the girl's mother considered bringing a private prosecution. The costs of this were beyond the mother's means but the matter was taken up by the *Sun* newspaper which offered, through its editor, Kelvin MacKenzie, to fund a prosecution in return for exclusive interviews and photographs and the mother undertaking not to talk to any other media. The *Sun* then published articles under such headings as 'Rape Case Doc: Sun Acts', 'He's a real swine', 'Beast must be named, says MP', and 'Doc groped me, says girl' which made various detailed allegations concerning the offence itself, statements said to have been made by the doctor and stories of an indecent assault by the doctor on a woman during a Mediterranean cruise. The first article did not name the doctor but he was then identified in the House of Commons by an MP (under the cloak of Parliamentary privilege) and the subsequent articles did name him. The private prosecution was launched about seven weeks later. The publications could not be a contempt under the strict liability rule in s 2(2) of the 1981 Act because at the time of the publication no proceedings were active within the meaning of s 2(3) and Schedule 1, but there was held to be a contempt at common law[20] because the court found that the articles were published with the *intention* of prejudicing proceedings.[1] Watkins LJ said:[2]

> 'No one could possibly resist the conclusion that in the circumstances I have assumed for the present purpose that the content of the articles complained of here

16 Justifiable ignorance that proceedings are 'active' is now a defence under s 3 of the Contempt of Court Act 1981, discussed at pp 398 ff.
17 [1957] 1 QB 73 at 78.
18 (1823) 2 LJOSKB 30; see also *R v Gilham* (1828) Mood & M 165 (wax models). In February 1994 the Attorney General banned the opening of a show featuring tunes adapted from Gilbert and Sullivan called *Mawxell the Musical* about the deceased tycoon and newspaper proprietor Robert Maxwell on the grounds that it could prejudice the trial of his sons, who were charged with various fraud offences; the Canadian cases *Canadian Broadcasting Corporation v Keegstra* (1987) 35 DLR (4th) 76 and *Keegstra v One Yellow Rabbit Theatre Association* (1992) 91 DLR (4th) 532 also concerned a play.
19 [1989] QB 110, [1988] 2 All ER 906.
20 The Divisional Court held that the proceedings were 'imminent' but also that the common law could apply even before proceedings became 'imminent': for this aspect of the case see Ch 7.
 1 For the matter of intention, see pp 107 ff.
 2 [1989] QB 110 at 125, [1988] 2 All ER 906 at 914.

posed a real risk of prejudice to a fair trial of Dr B. Publication of them during pending proceedings could not, in my view, have failed to have had that effect, so grave are the allegations made against the doctor and so prominent, widespread and so savage, in headline at least, is the publicity given to them.'

He continued:[3]

'Mr MacKenzie became so convinced of Dr B's guilt and incensed by that and the failure to prosecute him that he endeavoured to persuade readers of the *Sun* to take a similar view. Some of those obviously could possibly have formed part of a jury to try the doctor. That is trial by newspaper and strikes directly at a jury's impartiality.

Furthermore, what conceivable reason could there be for publishing the article headed "Doc groped me, says girl" unless it was intended to prejudice a fair trial by bringing to the notice of readers of the *Sun*, including possible potential jurors, extremely damaging matter affecting Dr B which would be inadmissible as evidence in his trial?'

Given the extreme facts of this case it was hardly surprising that a real risk of prejudice was found to have been created. Ironically, however, at the conclusion of the doctor's trial nine months after the appearance of the articles, he was acquitted. Perhaps the jurors did not read the *Sun*, or else that paper has less influence over its readers than might be thought.

As has been pointed out[4] the *Sun* case does not mean that any agitation for a prosecution to be brought (or dropped) against a particular person would be a contempt. What marked out the *Sun's* conduct was that at the time that the grossly prejudicial articles appeared the editor had already concluded its deal with the child's mother. The paper intended that the proceedings should be commenced and its conduct was such as to present a very real risk that those proceedings could not involve a fair trial. A campaign by a newspaper to have a person prosecuted is not by itself a contempt, nor is funding a prosecution in return for exclusive access to a party to the proceedings.[5] The contempt in the *Sun* case came about because the accused's character was blackened and revelations were made about him which a jury were not entitled to know.

Less blatant assertions of guilt can also be a contempt. For example, in the Australian case, *Re Smith's Associated Newspapers Ltd, ex p Higgs* [6] pending the trial of three brothers for murder, the *Daily Guardian* published a series of articles in which possible motives for the crime were discussed. Street CJ held that these articles amounted to a 'discussion as to the guilt or innocence of those three men who have been arrested'. He thought:

'that jurymen reading these articles . . . would find it difficult, if not impossible to come to the trial of these three men with unprejudiced minds.'

A not dissimilar situation arose in the Scottish case, *Atkins v London Weekend Television Ltd* [7] where, in the course of a television programme entitled 'The Living Dead', specific reference was made to a case due to be heard on the following day in which a nurse was accused of assault endangering the life of one of her patients in that she tried to block the air supply to a brain damaged 13 year old. Although the programme stated she would plead 'not guilty' to the charge,

---

3 Ibid at 916.
4 Robertson and Nicol, *Media Law* (3rd edn) p 287.
5 However distasteful that may be.
6 (1927) 28 SRNSW 85; cf *Packer v Peacock* (1912) 13 CLR 577.
7 1978 SLT 76 (High Ct of Justiciary).

by juxtaposing with this case reference to another case in which a life support machine was deliberately switched off because the brain-damaged patient was adjudged to be clinically dead, the programme conveyed the impression that the nurse did the act complained of. For this serious contempt London Weekend Television Ltd was fined £50,000.[8]

(b)   Assertions of guilt by innuendo

Imputation of guilt by innuendo can also be a contempt and it was upon this basis that Auberon Waugh was restrained, pending the trial of Jeremy Thorpe and others on a conspiracy to murder charge, from publishing his election address on behalf of his so-called 'Dog Lovers' Party'. The address stated inter alia:[9]

> 'CITIZENS OF BARNSTAPLE AND VOTERS OF NORTH DEVON
>   Unaccustomed as I am to public speaking I offer myself as your Member of Parliament in the General Election on behalf of the nation's dog lovers to protest about the behaviour of the Liberal Party generally and the North Devon Constituency Liberal Association in particular. Their candidate is a man about whose attitude to dogs—not to mention his fellow human beings—little can be said with any certainty at the present time.
>
>   But while it is one thing to observe the polite convention that a man is innocent until proven guilty, it is quite another thing to take a man who has been publicly accused of crimes which would bring him to the cordial dislike of all right-minded citizens and dog lovers, and treat him as a hero.
>
>   Before Mr Thorpe has had time to establish his innocence of these extremely serious charges, he has been greeted with claps, cheers and yells of acclamation by his admirers in the Liberal Party, both at the National Conference in Southport and here in the constituency. I am sorry but I find this disgusting.'

The situation which arose in *R v McCann* [10] should also be considered here, although no charge of contempt was brought in that case. The three appellants, who were all Irish, were found in suspicious circumstances close to the home in Wiltshire of the then Secretary of State for Northern Ireland, Tom King, and were arrested under the Prevention of Terrorism (Temporary Provisions) Act 1984. After extensive police investigations they were charged with conspiracy to murder the Secretary of State and other persons unknown. At their trial, which began on 10 October 1988, each of them elected to exercise their right of silence and not to give evidence. On 20 October, when counsel for one of the defendants was giving his closing speech, the Home Secretary announced in the House of Commons the Government's intention to change the law on the right to silence. This announcement became the main item on the evening radio and television news bulletins and immediately excited a great deal of comment. Tom King was interviewed several times on the different channels and made a number of statements to the effect that the right of silence allowed too many terrorists to be

---

8 See also in Scotland *HM Advocate v News Group Newspapers Ltd; HM Advocate v Scottish Express Newspapers* 1989 SCCR 150 where the publication of articles giving the impression that the arrested person was guilty was held to be contempt—the special and dramatic nature of the crime and the 110 day rule meant that the time lag between publication and trial was not enough to avoid substantial prejudice.

9 *Thorpe v Waugh* [1979] CA Transcript No 282; the shooting of the alleged victim's dog was a major feature of the case.

10 (1990) 92 Cr App Rep 239.

acquitted and that the change in the law would 'help the conviction of guilty men'. Lord Denning, the former Master of the Rolls, was also interviewed and said, inter alia:

> 'Too many people have been acquitted when they were guilty and that's because our rules favoured the guilty person far too much. Our rules of evidence should be so brought about that proper convictions can be had of the guilty.'

The defendants were convicted and sentenced to 25 years' imprisonment. They appealed, one of the grounds being that comments made on 20 October when, as the Court of Appeal said, 'the Secretary of State for Northern Ireland and a senior and greatly revered figure who had held very high judicial office were expressing in strong terms the fact that in terrorist cases a failure to answer questions or to give evidence was tantamount to guilt', were so prejudicial to their trial that the judge should have granted their request to discharge the jury and order a retrial. The Court of Appeal agreed with this and said that the only way in which justice could have been done and been seen to be done was by a new trial. The convictions were therefore quashed.[11]

Reference was made by the Court of Appeal to s 5 of the Contempt of Court Act 1981 which provides for a defence to a contempt action for publications which arise incidentally from a discussion of public affairs[12] and this was clearly a case in which that section would have been relevant had any contempt aspect ever been pursued.[13] The case does, however, provide a perfect example of how the guilt of a defendant can be implied without any express mention of the particular proceedings.

The first two prosecutions brought for contempt after the 1981 Act came into force also concerned publications which commented on the merits of a current criminal trial and implied guilt. The cases arose in connection with the trial of Dr Arthur on a charge of murdering a three day old baby boy with Down's Syndrome by giving instructions that he should be treated with a drug that caused him to die from starvation. One prosecution was brought against Express Newspapers and the editor of the *Sunday Express*, Sir John Junor, in respect of the article written by the editor and published during the Arthur trial.[14] The article commented:

> 'In the three grim days of his short, sad life, mongol baby John Pearson was given no nourishment. His parents had rejected him. So instead of being fed he was drugged. Even then, we know he fought tenaciously for life. Without a chance of success.
>
> And so he died. Unloved, unwanted.
>
> I blame no one. I condemn no one.
>
> And I make no comment on the case in Leicester Crown Court against child specialist Dr Leonard Arthur.
>
> Save this. The case is expected to go on for at least five weeks.
>
> Five weeks?
>
> If John Pearson had been allowed to live that long, might he not have found someone, apart from God, to love him?'

11 The appellants' notices of leave to appeal were given before s 43 of the Criminal Justice Act 1988 came into force. Lord Denning defended his part in the affair in a letter to the *Times*, 30 April 1990.

12 See p 175.

13 Proceedings in Parliament are privileged and cannot be the subject of contempt proceedings as a result of Art 9 of the Bill of Rights. A House of Commons resolution, however, bans references to criminal proceedings from the time of charge until after sentence (HC Official Report (5th series) vol 681, col 1417).

14 Reported as a news item in the *Times*, 19 December 1981.

There could be little doubt that this comment, which clearly implied Dr Arthur's guilt, amounted to a serious contempt and this was the view taken by the Divisional Court. As the court said: 'The article could not be regarded as anything but a scathing reference to the trial and the person on trial . . . It was of the utmost importance that "extraneous" irrelevant and emotional influences should not enter the minds of the jurors.' The editor was fined £1,000 and Express Newspapers £10,000.[15]

The second prosecution, *A-G v English*[16] was brought against Associated Newspapers Group Ltd and the editor of the *Daily Mail*, in respect of an article written by Malcolm Muggeridge and published by the defendant newspaper after the trial of Dr Arthur had begun. The article made no direct reference to the Arthur trial and was written in support of a 'pro-life' candidate who was standing in a forthcoming Parliamentary by-election. The article referred to the fact that this candidate was herself armless and then added:

> 'To-day, the chances of such a baby surviving would be very small indeed. Someone would surely recommend letting her die of starvation, or otherwise disposing of her.'

To use Lord Diplock's words:[17]

> 'The article then continued with a skilful piece of polemical journalism which concluded with the following passages derisive of those whose views he was condemning:
>   "Are human beings to be culled like livestock? No more sick or misshapen bodies, no more disturbed or twisted minds, no more hereditary idiots or mongoloid children. Babies not up to scratch to be destroyed, before or after birth, as would also the old beyond repair. *With the developing skills of modern medicine, the human race could be pruned and carefully tended until only the perfect blooms— the beauty queens, the Mensa IQs, the athletes—remained.*" [Mr Muggeridge's emphasis.]'

Although, as we shall see, the prosecution failed because of the operation of s 5 it was nevertheless held that the article did create a substantial risk of serious prejudice. Although no mention was made of the Arthur trial it was held that all sensible people including the jurors would take the quoted comments to refer to the trial. The Divisional Court thought[18] the 'undisguised assertions or insinuations that babies who are born with certain kinds of handicaps are caused or allowed by those in charge of them to die within days of birth of starvation among other means' created a substantial risk of serious prejudice. In the House of Lords, Lord Diplock agreed,[19] laying some emphasis on the timing of the publication, ie after the commencement of trial but still at a time when the jury did not know what the defence would be.

The finding that the article was creative of the risk envisaged by s 2(2) has been criticised[20] as robbing the section of all meaning. While this seems an unduly harsh criticism nevertheless, even making allowance for the sensitive timing of the publication, the finding seems a particularly restrictive one and at

---

15 It should be noted that at his trial Dr Arthur was acquitted.
16 [1983] 1 AC 116, [1982] 2 All ER 903.
17 Ibid at 138 and 916 respectively.
18 [1983] 1 AC 116, [1982] 2 All ER 903, [1982] 2 WLR 959.
19 [1983] 1 AC 116 at 142, [1982] 2 All ER 903 at 919.
20 Zellick, 'Fair Trial and Free Press' [1982] PL 343 at 344.

the time raised fears that the new Act would curtail further the freedom of the press.

(c)   The Fagan cases

A-G v English should be contrasted with the Divisional Court decisions in *A-G v Times Newspapers Ltd* [1] in which five national newspapers were prosecuted in respect of articles which both reflected on the merits of the case and cast imputations on the accused's character generally. Michael Fagan had achieved notoriety as the intruder into the Queen's bedroom at Buckingham Palace, and faced charges of burglary (based on the allegation that he drank some wine whilst in the Palace), taking a car without the owner's consent and assaulting his stepson.

The case against the *Sun* was that they made Fagan out to have a long-standing drug problem (asserting that he was a 'junkie'), that he was a glib liar and that he had stolen cigars from the Palace. This was held not to be a contempt as it was thought that the risk of prejudice that the article created was too remote to qualify as 'substantial'. The article published by the *Sunday People* contained allegations similar to that in the *Sun* and the prosecution was also dismissed.

The *Mail on Sunday* article contained the clear suggestion of a possible homosexual liaison between Commander Trestrail (the then royal bodyguard) and Fagan. It also referred to Fagan as a 'rootless neurotic with no visible means of support'. This was held to create a substantial risk of serious prejudice (though, as will be seen,[2] the newspaper was held to have a defence under s 5) for, although no mention was made of the burglary charge, 'everybody in the country reading any newspaper would be well aware of the charge against Fagan', and as Lord Lane CJ said:

> 'A suggestion of the rootless penniless neurotic being a guest of the homosexual royal bodyguard at the Palace created a picture which tended to stay in the mind and was not easy to dismiss.'

The *Daily Star* was found guilty in respect of an article which included the assertion that Fagan admitted stealing the wine for that was held to create a 'very' substantial risk of serious prejudice.

The *Sunday Times* was prosecuted in respect of two articles which, unlike those in the other papers, were contended to create a substantial risk of serious prejudice to the trial of the *assault* charge. The first article, which was prominently published on the front page, alleged that Fagan was charged with stabbing his stepson in the neck. The publication was false in that the charge against Fagan was for assault not stabbing, and it was held by the majority that this gross misrepresentation did create a substantial risk of serious prejudice. Oliver LJ doubted whether the article created a substantial risk of influencing the jurors but nevertheless thought it a contempt since it caused Fagan, upon legal advice, to elect for a summary trial because it was feared that jurors might be prejudiced by the media publicity. The second article, which suggested inter alia that the driving charge had been dropped and that the stepson's injuries had been received in some earlier incident before Fagan arrived, was also held to be contempt on the grounds that it was prejudicial to the prosecution's case.

1   (1983) Times, 12 February.
2   See p 176.

The *Sunday Times* was fined £1,000 and no penalty was imposed on the *Daily Star*. Both newspapers might be considered fortunate in being so lightly dealt with.

If s 2(2) was thought to be restrictively interpreted in *A-G v English*, it must be considered to be generously interpreted in the Fagan cases. As the *Times* said of the decisions,[3] the judges took a fairly robust view of the mentality of jurors and from the point of view of the administration of justice there may be some surprise at the width of the licence to dilate on the character and background of an accused before a trial. However, the commentary added that there was a glaring contrast between the enormity of Fagan's conduct and the triviality of the offence with which he was tried and concluded: 'similar licence might not be given, and ought not to be taken, in cases of more serious as well as notorious crime'. The Fagan cases also illustrate the fine judgment that has to be exercised for while it might fairly be said that in a broad way all the articles were prejudicial nevertheless the different ways each was written made a crucial difference in the result of the prosecution.

(d)   Photographs

The publication of photographs is most likely to be a contempt when identification is, or may become, an issue,[4] but it is also possible for a photograph to imply guilt. In *A-G v News Group Newspapers Ltd* [5] the *Sun*, which admitted contempt, was fined £5,000 for publishing, on the second day of a trial, a photograph of a man who was charged with causing serious injuries to his baby. The baby's mother was also accused of the offences and on the opening day of the trial it was clear that the Crown could not specifically attribute to either of the accused the actions which led to any of the particular injuries. The photograph showed the man gesturing towards the camera with two fingers of his right hand raised in an unpleasant manner, with the caption 'A gesture yesterday from accused Dad . . . '. The banner headline above this and the accompanying article about the day's proceedings said 'Baby was blinded by Dad'. Not only was the headline a misrepresentation of the Crown's allegations but, as Stephen Brown LJ said, 'the juxtaposition of the photograph undoubtedly carried with it the risk that the accused, who had pleaded not guilty, might be regarded in a very unpleasant light by those who saw this particular photograph and headline'.

The publication of a photograph during the trial was an important element in *R v Taylor* [6] where the coverage of the trial by some newspapers was described as 'unremitting, extensive, sensational, inaccurate and misleading'. Two sisters were accused of the murder of the wife of the former lover of one of them. Some newspapers obtained a copy of the video made at the deceased's wedding and froze a frame from the sequence of the guests emerging from the church, kissing first the bride and then the groom, so that it appeared as though the 'peck on the cheek' given by the accused to the groom, her former lover, was a mouth-to-mouth kiss. This photograph was given great prominence and was accompanied by headlines such as 'Cheats Kiss', 'Judas Kiss' and 'Tender Embrace—the Lovers share a kiss just a few feet from Alison'. The prejudicial press coverage

---

3   (1983) Times, 12 February.
4   See pp 159 ff.
5   (1984) 6 Cr App Rep (S) 418.
6   (1994) 98 Cr App Rep 361.

was one reason why the Court of Appeal quashed the convictions[7] and did not order a retrial.[8]

(e) Police activities

Another area where guilt can be implied is the way in which police activity or statements are reported. It can be perfectly proper to publish references to police activity surrounding a crime, such as the various searches, questioning of suspects, and any arrest that may be made but it should not be thought that there is an automatic immunity in so doing.[9] In *A-G(NSW) v TCN Channel Nine Pty Ltd* [10] the police launched a widely publicised manhunt for a particular suspect after brutal killings of two women and a child at two locations hundreds of miles apart. The suspect surrendered to the police, was interviewed, confessed and was then taken to the scenes of the crimes by the police where he demonstrated various significant matters to them. On these visits the police and the suspect were accompanied by a posse of journalists, including television crews. At one point a television crew travelled in the aircraft with the suspect and the police to the scene of the crime. The police held a press conference at which it was announced that the suspect had confessed. These matters were all broadcast on the television news. The New South Wales Court of Appeal said that the tendency of this publication to create a risk of prejudice to the accused's trial[11] was not lessened because of the very strong evidence against the accused and that:

'A notion that the rules relating to contempt of court somehow apply with less rigour to the case of a person against whom there is a very strong case would reflect a fundamental misunderstanding of the nature and purpose of those rules.'[12]

Nor was the contempt lessened because of the role of the police in encouraging the publicity. As the court said:[13]

'... as a general rule we regard it grossly offensive to the principles embodied in this aspect of the law, and to the proper administration of justice, for police to display for the benefit of the media persons in the course of being questioned or led around the scene of a crime.'

In the Canadian case, *R v Carocchia*,[14] a police officer was held guilty of contempt for issuing a press release referring to charges that had been brought

---

7 The others concerned matters which came to light after the trial, including documents relating to statements by witnesses which had not been disclosed to the defence.
8 The case raises serious issues about the way in which court proceedings are reported (considered further in Ch 8) and about the discretion of the Attorney General in bringing contempt proceedings (see pp 481 ff).
9 In the Australian case *R v Pacini* [1956] VLR 544, for example, a radio station committed a contempt by broadcasting, at a time when the accused was awaiting trial, an interview with a detective who had been concerned with the arrest of the accused, in which it was intimated that the detective's investigations had been brought to a successful conclusion with the accused's arrest, the implication being that the accused was guilty.
10 (1990) 20 NSWLR 368.
11 Which had in fact never taken place because the accused committed suicide while in custody.
12 (1990) 20 NSWLR 368 at 382.
13 Ibid at 381.
14 (1973) 43 DLR (3d) 427 (Quebec CA); see also, in Australia, *A-G (NSW) v Dean* (1990) 20 NSWLR 650, discussed above; cf *Re Letourneau-Belanger and Société de Publication Merlin Ltd* (1969) 6 DLR (3d) 451.

against a particular company and stating that more charges were to come and generally linking the accused company with organised crime.

These cases are a salutary warning to police forces both with respect to their press releases and to the access they give to the media. In England there have been occasions in which the police have overstepped the mark of prudence (though no prosecution has ever been brought) the most notorious example being the 'euphoric' press conferences held by the police following the arrest (on other charges) of Peter Sutcliffe who was later charged with being the so-called 'Yorkshire Ripper'.[15] There was much concern over the treatment of Sutcliffe's arrest but it was the press, rather than the police themselves, who bore the brunt of the criticism, no doubt because of the subsequent behaviour of the press over the case. The Press Council issued a report on the matter which was critical of the way in which the press had produced a 'highly and inexcusably prejudicial' composite general impression that 'the man who had been detained, even though he had not then been charged, was beyond doubt the killer of the 13 women and girls and that a trial was no more than a formality'.[16] After Sutcliffe's trial the Attorney General announced in the House of Commons that he would not be bringing any actions for contempt, explaining in a letter to the Chairman of the Press Council:

> 'Because of the nature of the plea at the trial there was no risk that the pre-trial publicity had prejudiced the fairness of the trial. My understanding of what happened was that in the excitement produced by the apparent detection of the Yorkshire Ripper, the media (with honorable exceptions) lost their heads. . ... I formed the opinion that it was not in the public interest that a very large number of editors and others should be paraded in front of the Divisional Court.'[17]

With respect to the Attorney General, he seems to have looked at the matter with hindsight in assessing whether the publicity created a risk of prejudice.

Irrespective of the responsibility that lies on the police the media themselves have a responsibility so that reliance on a police press release will not be a defence to charges of contempt brought against them if their publication is held creative of a real risk of prejudice.[18]

The need for care in describing a police operation is perhaps best illustrated by the Scottish decision, *HM Advocate v George Outram & Co Ltd*.[19] The *Glasgow Herald* was fined £20,000 for publishing under the headline: 'Armed Raids Smash Big Drugs Ring in Scotland', a detailed account of the arrest and police operation. The article began:

> 'Armed police raids on two luxury bungalows near Dundee and Edinburgh yesterday smashed a huge illicit drugs operation. Four Dutch citizens—three of them believed to be escapees from a prison in Holland—were arrested and last night police were confident they have now broken an amphetamines manufacturing ring equivalent in size and organisation to "Operation Julie", the LSD operation

15   Ie at the West Yorkshire press conference following Sutcliffe's arrest the Chief Constable announced that the huge operation set up to capture the 'Yorkshire Ripper' was being called off. See also in Scotland, the warning given in *Hall v Associated Newspapers Ltd* 1978 SLT 241 at 250 in connection with the Scott-Elliott murders.
16   Press Council Booklet No 7: *Press Conduct in the Sutcliffe Case* p 75.
17   Ibid pp 48–49.
18   As was demonstrated in *A-G(NSW) v TCN Channel Nine News Pty Ltd* (1990) 20 NSWLR 368.
19   1980 SLT (Notes) 13 (High Ct of Justiciary). The article published was based on information supplied by a release of the Press Association which in turn was based on information supplied by the police; cf *Hall v Associated Newspapers Ltd* 1978 SLT 241.

in England and Wales in which a large quantity of amphetamines was seized, [though the] value on the drug market has not yet been estimated.'

In holding the article to be a contempt the newspaper was said to have published alleged evidence of a highly incriminating character tending to suggest that the guilt of the accused persons might be presumed.

There is no doubt, however, that there are occasions on which the media assumes that it can publish highly prejudicial material safely because of the unlikelihood of there ever being a trial in respect of which there would be any risk. In July 1994, for example, the press gave saturation coverage to the arrest of a woman in Nottingham charged with abducting a newborn baby from a maternity ward. The baby was found at her house in a night-time operation which was filmed by a television crew, with the full co-operation of the police, whom the film-makers had been following around during the investigation. The film was shown on television the next night and although it did not feature the accused it did show her house and, in a window, the baby being lifted from its cot. The tabloid press over the next few days filled their pages with photographs of the accused and statements from her boyfriend, family and neighbours about her alleged pregnancy, state of mind, and previous behaviour. Presumably the media believed that the accused was bound to plead guilty (as in fact she did) and that there was therefore no risk of prejudicing the jury.

Whether publications made at the request of the police, for example to assist in the apprehension of a wanted man, can be a contempt raises different issues and will be discussed later.[20]

(f)   Imputations of innocence

There is some authority to show that publicity *adverse* to the police, even if relating to a specific case, might not be so readily considered a contempt.[1] On the other hand, direct imputations of the accused's *innocence* can be considered a contempt as *R v Castro Onslow's and Whalley's Case*[2] shows. This case arose out of the famous nineteenth century Tichborne Succession Claims. While the claimant was awaiting trial on charges of perjury and forgery, a public meeting was held at which the claimant and his friends were present. Two Members of Parliament took charge of the meeting, and in a speech one alleged that the accused was not guilty but had been the victim of a great conspiracy. Both were held guilty of a gross contempt, Cockburn CJ pointing out:[3]

'If it is open to those who take the part of the accused to discuss in public meetings the merits of the prosecution in the interest of the accused, it is obvious that it must be equally open to those who believe in the guilt of the party accused and the propriety of the prosecution, and believe a conviction is necessary to the ends of justice, to collect meetings and to hold language of the opposite tendency; and thus the course of justice might be interfered with and disturbed by discussions taking

---

20 See p 170.
 1 See eg *John Fairfax & Sons Pty Ltd v McRae* (1955) 93 CLR 351 and *Consolidated Press Ltd v McRae* (1955) 93 CLR 325.
 2 (1873) LR 9 QB 219. See also *Skipworth's Case* (1873) LR 9 QB 230; *R v Mason, ex p DPP* (1932) Times, 7 December (references to a 'frame-up' of the accused) *R v Nield* (1909) Times, 27 January (for article see 20 January: prosecution a waste of money) and *R v Bottomley* (1908) Times, 19 December (for article see 16 December).
 3 (1873) LR 9 QB 219 at 226.

place outside of the walls of a court of justice, but which might in the end influence proceedings within it.'

In Australia in *DPP v Wran* [4] the Premier of New South Wales was held to be in contempt for saying, in a response to a question from a journalist, subsequently published, that he believed in the innocence of a High Court judge who had been convicted of charges concerned with perverting the course of justice and that he believed that the retrial would reach a different verdict. The court said that despite the lapse of time likely before the retrial there was a tendency as a matter of practical reality to interfere with those proceedings because of the public standing of the person making the statements and the likelihood that they would be republished. The newspaper which published the statement (in a sensational way) was also fined for contempt.

(g)   Creating an atmosphere of prejudice

It may be sufficient to show that the creation of an 'atmosphere of prejudice' can also be a contempt. In *R v Hutchison, ex p McMahon* [5] a man had been arrested and charged with unlawful possession of a firearm, the charge arising from an occasion where whilst the King was riding in a procession in London a revolver fell close to the King's horses. A news film (distributed to some 262 cinemas) showed the man's arrest with the caption: 'Attempt on King's life'. It was held that this news film was a contempt, because the caption implied a charge which was more serious than the actual charge, and the film thereby created an atmosphere of prejudice against the accused. Swift J warned the proprietors that:

> 'if they want to produce these sensational films, they must take care in describing them not to use any language likely to bring about any derangement in the carriage of justice.'

It may be that *R v Daily Herald, ex p Rouse* [6] can be viewed in the same light. There, while Rouse stood committed for trial on a charge of murdering an unknown man in a car which was found burnt out, the following headline was published on a poster: 'Another Blazing Car Murder'. The poster in fact related to another case in which it was alleged that a young woman was murdered in a burning car. Nevertheless it was felt that the poster might prejudice the fair trial of Rouse because the words 'another murder':

> 'might well seem to suggest that the case on which Rouse was to be tried was a case of murder. That was the very issue which the jury would have to try'.

How far the 'atmosphere of prejudice' reasoning is representative of current law is difficult to say but in view of its possible application it might be wise, once the 'contempt period'[7] has begun, to avoid emotive descriptions of the offence, such as describing a killing as a 'murder' or worse still a 'vicious murder' or describing an attacker as a 'sex fiend'. There are situations, however, in which an 'atmosphere of prejudice' is hard to avoid unless the media is unnaturally self-denying in what it publishes. For example, over a period of many weeks in the first part of 1994 a large-scale police operation in Gloucester uncovered a number

---

4   (1986) 7 NSWLR 616 (NSW CA).
5   [1936] 2 All ER 1514.
6   (1931) 75 Sol Jo 119.
7   Discussed in Ch 7.

of bodies at a house owned by Frederick West, at a previous home of West and in a nearby field. West was arrested after the first body was discovered. The operation involved partly demolishing one house and extensive excavations at the other sites—matters which were impossible to hide. There was extensive press coverage of the affair and the police were often filmed carrying from the sites boxes reported to contain human remains. Several of the victims were revealed to have had a close family relationship to West. It is not surprising that in the circumstances some newspapers took to referring to West as 'the alleged mass-murderer' and that comments began to be made as to whether he could ever have a fair trial. When West committed suicide while on remand concern about the press coverage centred on its effect on the trial of his wife, Rosemary. It is in circumstances like these that the media needs to exercise great care.[8]

D Publications calculated to prejudice the court's ability to determine the true facts

The due administration of justice requires that each case be tried on all the available evidence which has been properly submitted. Publications calculated to impair this requirement amount to a contempt.

1 *Preventing the court hearing all the evidence*

If a witness is deterred from coming to court or from giving all his evidence, the court is deprived of hearing all the evidence, and this deficiency can obviously impede the fair trial of the accused.

Witnesses may be deterred if they become the object of public criticism. In *R v Bottomley*[9] Horatio Bottomley, a Member of Parliament, was on trial for conspiracy to defraud. The newspaper *John Bull*, of which the accused was the editor, referred to a 'relentless cross-examination' and commenting about a prosecution witness being cross-examined said: 'All this time the unhappy man was writhing in the toils of this relentless cross-examiner'. It was held that the article interfered with a fair hearing because it held up the witnesses for the prosecution to 'public opprobrium'. Such comments tended not only to prejudice the prosecution's case but also to deter future witnesses. As a general rule adverse comment upon a witness should be avoided since such comment can only add to the general reluctance of witnesses to appear before the court.[10]

Akin to deterring a witness is the type of publication which induces the court to ignore or treat with scepticism the evidence of a particular witness. This could be brought about by a publication which discredits a witness. In *Re Labouchere, ex P Columbus Co Ltd*[11] an article was published in *Truth* which attacked a

---

8 The banner headline in the *Sun* on 2 January 1995, the day after West hanged himself, read 'Happy Noose Year'. Despite the sensational press coverage of the matter, complete with the publication of letters allegedly written by West to one of his sons, it is submitted that nothing which appeared in the press following his death had any bearing on the question of his wife's involvement in the murders.

9 (1908) Times, 19 December.

10 See *R v Castro, Onslow's and Whalley's Case* (1873) LR 9 QB 219; *R v Daily Herald, ex p Bishop of Norwich* [1932] 2 KB 402.

11 (1901) 17 TLR 578.

certain witness. The article referred to: 'this masterstroke of ingenious impudence' and altogether discredited the character of the witness. It was held by Bruce J that:

> 'Looking at the whole of the article in question, he could not doubt that it was calculated to imply that Cowen was not a witness to be relied upon, that it held him up as a person whose conduct was to be condemned and that it might prejudice the mind of any juryman against Cowen, who happened to read it.'

Another example, though one which was not prosecuted, was the revelation made public during the trial of Jeremy Thorpe and others, that the leading witness, Peter Bessell, was being paid by a national newspaper, the amount reputedly being contingent on the final outcome of the case. Many of the jurors in the case felt that in view of this, weight should not be placed upon the witness's uncorroborated evidence.[12] It could certainly have been argued both that the revelation itself thereby impeded the due course of justice and that the behaviour of the newspaper was improper.[13]

It can also be a contempt for a publication to induce the court to treat the evidence of a class of witnesses in a particular way. In *Registrar, Court of Appeal v Collins* [14] and *The Prothonotary v Collins* [15] Collins believed that the police habitually indulged in 'verballing', that is that they fabricated confessions to criminal charges. On two occasions he went, with associates, to the criminal court complex where prospective jurors were arriving and addressed the public through a loud-hailer about the alleged malpractices of the police in this regard and distributed pamphlets about it. The pamphlets claimed that 'verballing' was widespread and had become an institution and that jurors should treat police evidence with scepticism. Both courts were of the opinion that this conduct was *capable* of causing a real risk to particular proceedings but they differed over the position when, as here, no proceedings were to be heard in which the type of evidence castigated in the publications was in issue so that there were no particular proceedings which could be prejudiced. The differences in the cases arose over whether an intention to prejudice is enough although the risk of prejudice never materialises, and the question of the intention to prejudice the administration of justice generally rather than in particular proceedings.[16]

2   *Premature publication of evidence*

The publication of evidence before it has been given in court may be a contempt because it can put in jeopardy the requirement of the due administration of justice that each case be tried only upon properly adduced evidence.

(a)   The publication of systematic private investigation

A newspaper conducting its own private investigation and publishing the results before or during the trial is perhaps the most blatant example of 'trial by

---

12 For a contempt prosecution following the revelation of the jurors' views see *A-G v New Statesman and Nation Publishing Co Ltd* [1981] QB1, [1980] I All ER 644, discussed in Ch 9.
13 For interference with witnesses, see Ch 11.
14 [1982] 1 NSWLR 682.
15 [1985] 2 NSWLR 549.
16 These matters are discussed at pp 79 ff.

newspaper'. Such publications hinder the court's determination of the facts and might otherwise be 'prejudicial'. There is no guarantee that the facts published by the newspaper (and therefore brought to the notice of potential jurors) are true, there being no opportunity to cross-examine nor to have the evidence corroborated, and further there is no guarantee that the published facts will be admitted in the trial at all, since such evidence could amount to hearsay or be irrelevant. The leading case is *R v Evening Standard, ex p DPP* [17] where the court found that certain newspapers 'had entered deliberately and systematically on a course which was described as criminal investigation'. It was argued in defence of the newspapers that it was part of their duty to elucidate the facts, but this defence was emphatically rejected by Lord Hewart CJ:[18]

> 'If he understood that suggestion [that there was a duty] when clearly expressed it came to something like this; that while the police or the Criminal Investigation Department were to pursue their investigations in silence and with all reticence and reserve, being careful to say nothing to prejudice the trial of the case, whether from the point of view of the prosecution or . . . of the defence, it had come to be somehow for some reason the duty of newspapers to employ an independent staff of amateur detectives who would bring to an ignorance of the law of evidence a complete disregard of the interests whether of the prosecution or the defence. They were to conduct their investigation unfettered, to publish to the whole world from time to time the results of these investigations, whether they conceived them to be successful or unsuccessful results, and by so doing to perform what was represented as a duty. . . .'.

Moreover, he pointed out that it was difficult, if not impossible, to predict events in a forthcoming trial: 'any one fact, however trivial on the face of it . . . may become of paramount importance'. To publish any results of such investigations (it is the publication of the results which is the offence, not the investigation itself) could prejudice a fair trial and will therefore amount to a contempt.

The penalty in the *Evening Standard* case was severe, the proprietors of the *Evening Standard* being fined £1,000 and two other newspapers which had repeated the reports, £300 each. Lord Hewart CJ noted that the practice of private investigations had become common and he commented: 'It is hoped that this day's proceedings would show that in the opinion of the court that view was entirely wrong.' He added that if the offence were repeated the punishment would be imprisonment.

Lord Hewart did not believe that it was the duty of newspapers to 'employ an independent staff of amateur detectives' but it has to be said that serious investigative journalism has in many common law countries a long and honorable history and has been responsible for uncovering many matters which are of rightful concern to the public.[19] Various recent well-known miscarriages of

---

17 (1924) 40 TLR 833. The other newspapers involved were the *Manchester Guardian* and *Daily Express*. A team of newspaper detectives were sent to the scene of the crime where they made full investigations including a door-to-door search for witnesses. Having made contact with witnesses they proceeded to publish their stories. See also *R v Surrey Comet, ex p Baldwin* (1931) 75 Sol Jo 311.

18 (1924) 40 TLR 833 at 835.

19 In the United States the Watergate affair is an obvious example. The leading contempt case, *A-G v Times Newspapers Ltd* [1974] AC 273, which was concerned with civil proceedings, arose out of investigative journalism by the *Sunday Times*.

justice have been corrected, partly at least, because of the work done by
journalists and the authors of books.[20]

(b)   The publication of interviews with witnesses

In principle, it can amount to contempt to publish the evidence which a witness
may later give in court. That is not to say, however, that no statement of witnesses
can be published pending a trial.

Contemporaneous eye witness accounts of crimes are commonly published
and, if confined to the 'bare facts' seem no more than the legitimate satisfaction
of proper public curiosity,[1] and should not be a contempt even if charges are
pending. In-depth interviews with witnesses on the other hand pose more
problems. There are obvious dangers in the publication of such interviews. These
were adverted to by the Salmon Committee which commented:[2]

> 'A witness could be bullied or unfairly led into giving an account which was
> contrary to or put a slant upon the truth. He could commit himself, particularly
> under the strain and tension of a television interview, to a badly expressed or
> inaccurately recollected version of events. Witnesses might also be tempted to
> give a version of facts which they thought most newsworthy, particularly if a fee
> were paid for the interview. When such witnesses came to give evidence before
> the tribunal they would either have to stick to what had already been said, however
> inaccurate it might be, or reveal the true facts. In the latter event, the weight of their
> evidence might be considerably shaken by the discrepancy between what they
> were telling the tribunal and what they had said previously. This might greatly
> hinder the tribunal, and, in an extreme case, prevent it from arriving at the truth.'

The Phillimore Committee endorsed the above views being particularly
worried about television interviews:[3]

> 'Television interviews import the added dangers of dramatic impact. For example,
> the "grilling" on television of a person involved in a case can seem to take the form
> of a cross-examination in court. It could obviously create a serious risk of affecting
> or distorting the evidence he might give at the trial. Such an interview could be
> regarded as a "trial by television".'

Having acknowledged the dangers neither Committee thought that such
publications should ipso facto be considered a contempt. As the Phillimore
Committee said:

> 'Having pointed to the dangers of contempt in television and press interviews it
> is only right to say that, responsibly conducted, they make a useful contribution
> to public information.'

The general propriety of publication of interviews with witnesses seems
confirmed by the general absence of prosecutions. A reminder of the possible
dangers, however, is the Australian decision, *A-G (NSW) v Mirror Newspapers
Ltd*,[4] concerning a coroner's inquiry into the deaths of seven people during a fire

---

20 Such as in the case of the Birmingham Six, whose appeal was finally allowed in *R v McIlkenny*
    [1992] 2 All ER 417.
 1 Cf Giffiths CJ's judgment in *Packer v Peacock* (1912) 13 CLR 577 at 588 cited at p 131.
 2 Committee on the Law of Contempt as it Affects Tribunals of Inquiry under the chairmanship
    of Salmon LJ (1969, Cmnd 4078) para 31.
 3 1974, Cmnd 5794, para 55.
 4 [1980] 1 NSWLR 374 (NSW CA).

at an amusement centre. One witness, who had already given evidence, was widely reported as saying in effect that an attendant had allowed two children to go on a 'ghost train' into the fire. The *Daily Telegraph*, believing that the attendant would not be giving evidence, published a detailed account by him in which he sought to defend himself from the previous witness's allegation. Part of the article read:

> 'It makes it sound as if I sent two kids to their death ... it just isn't so. I even had to wrestle with one young lad who was determined to follow his mates into the fire. I had to tear him from the car.'

The publication was held to be a serious contempt and the proprietors fined A$10,000.

The *conducting* of interviews, with a view to publication of 'background' material *after* the trial is generally regarded as legitimate practice[5] but would amount to contempt if it could be shown to have been of a 'bullying' kind such as to deter witnesses from giving evidence.[6] Payments of witnesses in current legal proceedings for their stories is contrary to Clause 8 of the Press Complaints Commission Code of Practice. The problems which can arise from payments to witnesses was well illustrated in the Jeremy Thorpe trial.[7]

(c)   Photographs

The publication of a photograph of an accused will amount to a serious contempt if it is published at a time when identification is likely to become an issue at the trial. As the Scottish judge, Lord Clyde, said:[8]

> 'Identification may be a really substantial issue in the trial and publication of . . . a photograph may gravely prejudice that trial by affecting the evidence of identification at the trial by witnesses who have already seen the photograph.'

Such a photograph can prejudice both the defence and the prosecution. It can prejudice the defence because it could induce the witness to make an identification not on the strength of the person's recollection of the actual incident in question, but from the memory of the published photograph. As the New Zealand judge, Blair J[9] pointed out, a witness:

> 'unable to form a mental picture . . . might, quite honestly, derive such a picture of the person whose photographs he [has seen] in the paper.'

On the other hand, the photograph can prejudice the prosecution because it can jeopardise the validity of an identification by a witness. A particularly good example of this can be found in the New Zealand case of *A-G v Noonan* [10] where a police constable who had been stabbed had seen the photograph of the accused in the newspaper, and this fact immediately called into question the validity of his identification, thereby prejudicing the case for the prosecution.

---

5   The practice was specifically endorsed by the Salmon Committee (1969, Cmnd 4078) para 29.
6   See Ch 11.
7   See p 409.
8   In *Stirling v Associated Newspapers Ltd* 1960 SLT 5 which was overruled, but not on this point, by *Hall v Associated Newspapers Ltd* 1978 SLT 241.
9   In *A-G v Tonks* [1934] NZLR 141 at 154.
10 [1956] NZLR 1021.

In the leading English case, *R v Daily Mirror, ex p Smith* [11] a picture was published of a man who had been arrested a few days earlier. The photograph was published on the same morning as an identification parade was due to be held with the following caption:

> 'Shot PC Charge, Edgar William Smith of Hykeham (Lincs) remanded at Newark on a charge of attempting to murder police constable Dainty, who, it is alleged was shot by a motorist on a Notts Co Road.'

Lord Hewart CJ, in finding the publication to be a contempt, likened the publication to a police officer saying to a potential witness:[12]

> "'I have arrested a man and I am going to put him up for identification by you", and then [showing] those persons a photograph of the suspected person. The unfairness of that course is manifest, because the witness approaches the difficult and it may be the crucial task of identification with his mind prejudiced by the knowledge that this particular person has been arrested and is in the hands of the police.'

More recently, the *Evening Standard* [13] was fined £1,000 for its admitted contempt in publishing on its front page, a picture of Peter Hain on the day that he was due to take part in an identification parade. In 1994 the *Sun* was fined £80,000 and its editor £20,000 for publishing a photograph of a defendant who was about to take part in an identity parade where as a result of the publication criminal proceedings against him had to be dropped.[14]

Not all pre-trial photographs of the accused will amount to contempt since it is a fundamental prerequisite of the offence that *at the time of publication*, identity must either be or reasonably likely to be in issue at the trial. An example of where identity was held not to be in issue is *R v Lawson, ex p Nodder*.[15] In dismissing proceedings for contempt, Swift J said that there was:

> 'no ground whatever for the suggestion that the publication of the photograph in the *Empire News* was in the least degree calculated to interfere with the fair trial of the proceedings which were taking place against Nodder. It had been urged that some question of identification of Nodder might, at some future time arise. All that they knew now was that, up to the time of the publication of the photograph, there was no such question. A full description of Nodder had been issued by the police, and he (his Lordship) could see no difference between the description and the photograph.'

Another example might be to take pictures of the apparent perpetrators of a publicised siege where, for instance, the building is surrounded by police.

If identity is thought to be an issue (which is determined objectively by the courts in the light of the circumstances existing at the time of publication)[16] it is no defence that identity is not subsequently raised at the trial,[17] nor that the published picture was so bad[18] that no identification could possibly be made from it, nor that no witness in fact saw the photograph.[19] In other words, the rule is that

---

11 [1927] 1 KB 845.
12 Ibid at 849.
13 *R v Evening Standard Co Ltd, ex p A-G* (1976) Times, 3 November.
14 Reported in (1994) Independent, 6 July.
15 (1937) 81 Sol Jo 280.
16 See p 84.
17 See *R v Daily Mirror, ex p Smith* [1927] 1 KB 845.
18 This argument was rejected in *A-G v Tonks* [1934] NZLR 141.
19 As in the *Daily Mirror* case and the *Evening Standard* case.

publication of a photograph at a time when identity is likely to be an issue amounts to a contempt. Given that, as Blair J pointed out,[20] it is 'abundantly plain' that 'when a man has been arrested only, and formally charged, it is impossible to say what his line of defence will be', it is a particularly perilous enterprise to publish the accused's photograph at that time. In Australia a judgment in the Tasmanian Supreme Court[1] has gone so far as to hold that where a person is charged with a crime in the ordinary calendar of criminal offences it is *always* likely that the question of identity may arise and that therefore the general rule is that no photograph of the accused should be published: the burden is on the defendant in the contempt action to show that some special circumstances applied in the case clearly indicating otherwise.

III   PUBLICATIONS AFTER VERDICT BUT BEFORE SENTENCE

Once a case has gone on appeal the law of contempt becomes substantially relaxed. This is because professional judges are generally thought to be immune from the influence of media comment. Similar considerations might therefore be taken to be applicable after the verdict[2] but before the sentence. This was the view taken by Zuber J in the Ontario High Court decision *Bellitti v Canadian Broadcasting Corp* [3] when he dismissed a contempt application against the defendant for broadcasting, pending sentence, a purely factual account of the facts of the case. In England, however, in a drugs case widely referred to as the *Operation Julie* case[4] Park J took a different view, warning the press that to publish a 'background report' on the accused pending sentence might amount to contempt not on the basis that it would influence him in deciding sentence but because others might think it would.

Park J's comments were widely criticised[5] and with respect to the judge they do seem hard to justify *once it is acknowledged there is no risk of influencing the sentencing tribunal.*[6] Some support for his approach might, however, be derived from the New Zealand decision in *A-G v Tonks* [7] where an accused, having pleaded guilty to the charge of indecent assault, was sent to the Supreme Court for sentence. Before the case was heard, New Zealand *Truth* published an article demanding that the accused 'should meet with the utmost vigour of the law'. Myers CJ held that the article amounted to a contempt, not because it could influence the decision of the court, but because:

> 'The court must not only be free—but it must also appear to be free—from any extraneous influence. The appearance of freedom from any such influence is just

20 In *A-G v Tonks* [1934] NZLR 141 at 150.
 1 *R v The Australian Broadcasting Corporation* [1983] Tas R 161, a case concerning a murder investigation which began with a human finger being found in a sewer.
 2 The position while the jury is still deliberating is quite different.
 3 (1974) 44 DLR (3d) 407.
 4 Heard at Bristol Crown Court, the warning being made in 1978.
 5 Eg by the Joint Committee of the Law Society and the Guild of British Newspaper Editors: see (1978) 75 Law Soc Gaz 237 and by the *Times*, Leader 23 March 1978, p 19.
 6 There might be thought to be a risk of influence where a case has been sent to the Crown Court for sentence where the court will be constituted in part by lay magistrates: for the question of prejudicing lay magistrates, see p 126.
 7 [1939] NZLR 533; cf *Re Depoe and Lamport* (1968) 66 DLR (2d) 46 where urging a court to impose a certain penalty was held not to be a contempt: Ontario HC.

as important as the reality. Public confidence must necessarily be shaken if there is the least suspicion of outside interference with the administration of justice. . . . If the court imposed [the sentence demanded] it might well be assumed by the readers of the paper that the court had been influenced by the newspaper's demands. If, on the other hand, a lesser sentence were imposed, the article was calculated in anticipation to arouse resentment against the court.'

Although the rationale of maintaining public confidence and respect for the independence, authority and fairness of the judiciary lies at the heart of other branches of contempt law[8] such consideration has generally not been applied with respect to comments about decisions pending their appeal and it may seem unduly restrictive to apply them to comments pending sentence. It is worth adding that since Park J's ruling there have been no subsequent warnings nor prosecutions and it has become standard practice for the media to comment between verdict and sentence.[9]

It should be added that different considerations apply where the trial has ended in a jury disagreement for then there is a distinct possibility of a retrial when the normal rules will apply.[10]

IV   PUBLICATIONS AFTER THE TRIAL, PENDING AN APPEAL

Although publications remain at risk of being in contempt pending an appeal[11] restrictions upon comment are in practice considerably relaxed. This is because the appellate tribunal is thought unlikely to be influenced by out of court publicity since there will be no jury and rarely any witnesses to influence and because according to the authorities shortly to be considered appeal judges are not thought likely to be unduly influenced by media comment. The Contempt of Court Act 1981, Sch 1, para 15 contains provisions as to when appellate proceedings become 'active' for the purposes of the strict liability rule, from which it can be argued that contempt must have some relevance to appellate proceedings. However, s 6(b) provides that nothing under the strict liability rule should be construed as creating liability where none existed under the common law and it is submitted that the Act therefore does nothing to change whatever the position was at common law.

A   Effect on witnesses

Normally, no witnesses appear in appellate proceedings although under the Criminal Appeal Act 1968, s 23(1)[12] witnesses can be required to appear before the

8 Eg 'scandalising the court', see Ch 9. The reasoning in *Tonks* might also be considered analagous to the wider concern expressed in the *Sunday Times* case. See also *In re Channel 4 Television Company Ltd* (1987) Times, 18 December and (1988) Times, 2 February.
9 Over vigorous demands for severe sentences (or the reverse) might be classifiable as a 'deliberate campaign' to influence the court and so be a contempt upon the basis mentioned by Lord Parker CJ in *R v Duffy, ex p Nash* [1960] 2 QB 188, [1960] 2 All ER 891.
10 The *News of the World* was fined £500 in respect of a publication in such circumstances in *A-G v News Group Newspapers Ltd* (1982) 4 Cr App R (S) 182.
11 As Lord Parker CJ said in *R v Duffy, ex p Nash* [1960] 2 All ER 891 at 896 'newspapers publish articles at their peril' during the pending of an appeal.
12 Under s 23 (1)(b) this power is limited to calling only those who were compellable witnesses in the earlier proceedings.

Criminal Division of the Court of Appeal. Publications appearing after such witnesses have been called[13] might conceivably be considered in contempt if it is thought that there is the requisite degree of risk of affecting their evidence.[14]

B   Effect on a jury

Although juries are not involved in appeals, there may be the question of a retrial. The Court of Appeal has a power, independent of statute, which it inherited from the Court of Crown Cases Reserved, to quash a conviction and issue a writ of venire do novo. This writ only issues where the proceedings in the trial court contained a fundamental irregularity and the proceedings were therefore so defective as to amount to a nullity. A venire do novo is, in effect, an order for a retrial although the court may, in its discretion, simply quash the conviction and do nothing else. The power is rarely used and the Court of Appeal normally relies on its statutory powers to order retrials under the Criminal Appeal Act 1968[15] as amended by the Criminal Justice Act 1988.[16] The Criminal Appeal Act 1968, s 7 formerly provided that a new trial could be ordered where fresh evidence suggests that had it been given at the trial it would have created a reasonable doubt in the mind of the jury. Such cases are not common. However the Criminal Justice Act 1988 amendments to s 7 provide in effect that whenever the Court of Appeal allows an appeal it has the discretion to order a retrial should the interests of justice so require. This makes the possibility of a retrial much more likely.[17]

It seems clear that once a retrial has been ordered, under whichever power, the law of contempt must begin to operate again[18] because the new trial will, of course, involve a jury. A more difficult question is whether the possibility of a retrial should stifle comment until after the time-limit for an appeal has passed. It was suggested in *R v Davies, ex p Delbert-Evans* [19] that such was the position. Lord Parker CJ in *R v Duffy, ex p Nash* [20] doubted this, as venire de novo (then the only procedure for a retrial) was very rare and there would be no risk of prejudice at the time of publication if there did not then appear to be any reason why the original proceedings should be considered a mistrial. However he warned that 'newspapers publish articles at their peril' during the pendency of an appeal.[1]

---

13   The possibility that they *might* be called and their evidence influenced seems too remote a risk to constitute contempt.

14   There is also the possibility of witnesses appearing at retrials, which are discussed below where the position of the juries is considered.

15   Previously s 1 of the Criminal Appeal Act 1964.

16   The venire de novo presupposes that the original trial was a complete nullity whereas the Criminal Appeal Act 1968 does not. If the irregularity at the trial was so fundamental that venire de novo can issue it seems that the Criminal Appeal Act does not apply: see *R v Rose* [1982] AC 822 and *R v Newland* [1988] QB 402.

17   From August 1989 to March 1991 four retrials were ordered by the Court of Appeal. This compares with nine retrials from 1966 to 1968 and fourteen retrials from from 1981 to 1986. However in 1991 15 retrials were ordered. See Zander, *Cases and Materials on the English Legal System* (6th edn, 1993, Butterworths) p 608; O'Connor, 'The Court of Appeal: Re-Trials and Tribulations' [1990] Crim LR 615.

18   The contempt in *DPP v Wran* (1986) 7 NSWLR 616 was in respect of an interview given to a journalist the day before the retrial of a judge charged with corruption. See also in New Zealand, *Macassey v Bell, Re Macassey* (1874–75) 2 NZ Jur 158.

19   [1945] KB 435.

20   [1960] 2 QB 188, [1960] 2 All ER 891.

 1   [1960] 2 QB 188 at 200, [1960] 2 All ER 891 at 896.

Normally comment made before the appeal is heard is not likely to influence a jury in a retrial because the article would have been published some considerable time before the trial, and is likely to be forgotten and therefore to present only a 'remote' risk of prejudice. There are, nevertheless, some cases of such notoriety that the after-trial publicity, especially if it included extensive 'background' material of a sensational nature, would be lastingly memorable. Indeed, one of the reasons that the Court of Appeal did not order a retrial in *R v Taylor* [2] was because of previous prejudicial publicity, including the prejudicial reporting of the original trial. The application of contempt to the possiblity of a retrial was discussed, but left open, in *Re Channel Four Television Company Ltd* [3] which involved the re-enactment of the 'Birmingham Six' appeal hearings. The Court of Appeal expressed some misgivings about the possibility that the appellants might appeal to the House of Lords who could order a retrial. In such circumstances the court thought that the programme could cause great prejudice in relation to the eventual jury.[4] The Attorney General submitted that the court was unable to consider the possible effect on a new jury because of Sch 1, paras 15 and 16 to the 1981 Act. This provides that appellate proceedings are 'active' for the purposes of the strict liability rule from the time they are commenced and that any further or new proceedings which result from the appeal are 'active' from the conclusion of the appellate proceedings. This, said the Attorney General, meant that all the court could consider was the likely effect on the House of Lords because no possible new trial proceedings were yet 'active'. The Court of Appeal declared themselves unconvinced by this argument but expressly did not pronounce upon it. If there was *intention* to prejudice, the Act would not apply and the question would then be whether a retrial was 'pending' or 'imminent' within the common law criteria.[5]

In *In re Channel Four Television* the appeal was already underway when the injuncted programme was to be transmitted. As a general principle, however, given that the rule is that the risk must be assessed at the time of publication and that the law can hardly be heard to say that there are such failings in the criminal justice system that there is a substantial likelihood that any particular conviction will result in a retrial, publications ought not to be at risk of contempt unless the retrial has been ordered.[6]

2   [1994] Cr App Rep 361; and note *R v Reade, Morris and Woodwiss* (1993) Independent, 19 October in which proceedings were stayed because of the intense and prolonged publicity which had attended other proceedings (the *Birmingham Six* appeal, culminating in *R v McIlkenny* [1992] 2 All ER 417 two and a half years earlier).
3   (1988) Times, 2 February; see further p 166.
4   Given the nature of the campaign about the 'Birmingham Six' and publicity afforded to their appeal the programme would have been likely to create a risk of prejudice to the prosecution rather than to the defence.
5   For the timing provision see Ch 7.
6   This could be undesirable where, upon conviction, the defendant immediately announces his intention to appeal and ask for a retrial. When the trial in *R v Bernardo* ended in Canada on 1 September 1995 with the conviction of the defendant he immediately made such an announcement. Meanwhile, details of the material which had been excluded from his trial as inadmissible in a voir dire, began to be circulated. The material was highly prejudicial and of such a nature that it was unlikely to be forgotten by potential jurors in any retrial. There is an argument for saying that in jurisdictions where appeal courts are likely to order a retrial such an announcement by a convicted person should cause the sub judice period to continue running.

C Effect upon the accused

Once the accused has been convicted and sentenced the onus is upon him as to whether he should appeal or not. Adverse comment may induce an accused not to appeal and it may be argued that this constitutes an interference with the due administration of justice in the same way that improper pressure upon a litigant in a civil case may.[7] There is no direct authority on this point but in view of the lack of case law despite numerous examples of outspoken criticism of decisions, particularly of sentences, it may be that this possibility of influence is not considered relevant. The possibility of deterring the accused from appealing was acknowledged by the Phillimore Committee[8] but they were not keen to see comment restricted on this ground saying: 'We have had no evidence of any case in which a party was shown to have been deterred from appealing . . .' In England Lord Parker CJ said[9] that it was irrelevant that an article might lead a prisoner to think that he will be or has been prejudiced in his appeal and seems not to have thought that a publication would be a contempt on those grounds. In Australia, however, it has been said that if a convicted person was aware of a campaign of vilification against him and newspapers were declaring that his sentence was inadequate 'this would be calculated to cause him to hesitate before instituting an appeal'.[10] Whether or not such a tendency could be described as a 'substantial risk' for the purposes of the strict liability rule in the Contempt of Court Act 1981 is difficult to say.

The position under the strict liability rule is complicated by the timing provisions. The rule aplies only if proceedings are 'active' within the meaning of the Act.[11] According to Sch 1, para 15 appellate proceedings are active only from the time they are commenced and it would therefore appear that a publication which deters a convicted person from appealing at all would fall outside the strict liability rule and could only be dealt with, if at all, at common law.

D Effect upon appellate judges

Under English law it seems to be accepted that professionally trained appellate judges are not open to undue influence by media comment and that therefore publications which might have been contempt at first instance will not be contempt at the appellate stage on the basis of the risk of prejudicing the appellate tribunal hearing the case. Despite the occasional doubt which has been expressed, particularly in regard to trial judges,[12] the immunity of judges in the appellate courts to prejudicial publications seems to be well established. In *Re Lonrho Plc,*[13] in which the question of a possible risk of prejudice to the House of Lords arose, Lord Bridge pointed out that no case had been drawn to the House's attention in which public discussion of the issues arising in, or criticism of the parties to,

---

7 See Ch 6 and in particular *A-G v Times Newspapers Ltd* [1974] AC 273 and *A-G v Hislop* [1991] 1 QB 514, [1991] 1 All ER 911.
8 At para 132; see also Miller, *Contempt of Court* (2nd edn, 1989) pp 222–223.
9 In *R v Duffy, ex p Nash* [1960] 2 QB 188 at 200, [1960] 2 All ER 891 at 896.
10 *Ex p A-G; Re Truth and Sportsman Ltd* (1958) 61 SR (NSW) 484 at 496.
11 See Ch 7.
12 See pp 124 ff.
13 [1990] 2 AC 154 at 210, [1989] 2 All ER 1100.

litigation already decided at first instance had been held to be a contempt on the ground that it was likely to impede or prejudice the course of justice in proceedings on appeal from that decision. In the *Sunday Times* case[14] Lord Reid commented:

> '. . . it is scarcely possible to imagine a case where comment could influence judges in the Court of Appeal or noble and learned Lords in this House. And it would be wrong and contrary to existing practice to limit proper criticism of judgments already given but under appeal.'

In *Re Lonrho* [15] Lord Bridge was quite certain:

> 'So far as the appellate tribunal is concerned, it is difficult to visualise circumstances in which any court in the United Kingdom exercising appellate jurisdiction would be in the least likely to be influenced by public discussion of the merits of a decision appealed against or of the parties' conduct in the proceedings.'

The matter also arose in *In re Channel 4 Television Company Ltd* [16] where the Court of Appeal granted an injunction forbidding transmission of a television programme reconstructing the appeal it was currently hearing and refused to discharge it until after the reserved judgment had been given. Lord Lane CJ said that the reconstruction would not affect the judgment of the court[17] and that, if there was a further appeal, the effect on the House of Lords would be negligible.[18] This was an extraordinary case, in which the programme makers planned to have actors playing the witnesses as well as counsel and the court. Lord Lane CJ's concern was that the public and the appellants might *think* that the appellate judges had been affected by the broadcast. In that regard the case was to do with the protection of the public's perception of the administration of justice rather than the particular proceedings themselves. As far as the appellants were concerned, the programme was sympathetic to their cause and they might have welcomed the idea of the judges being affected by it! An enactment of witnesses' evidence, however, is a dangerous matter, as Professor JC Smith commented:[19]

> 'However incorruptible the judicial mind, it may be unconsciously influenced by seeing the portrayal by an actor of what a witness has said. It would be all too easy to confuse the actual performance in the witness box with the re-enactment of it on the television screen.'

In reality it was extremely unlikely that the appeal court judges hearing the case would have contemplated watching the reconstruction on the television but Lord Lane CJ clearly did not believe that the public understood the standards of behaviour of the higher judiciary.[20] The idea that publications should be banned because of some speculative view of the public's perception is dangerously wide.

The English position adopted is essentially one of policy. It is not really suggested that a judge is immune from *any* influence (or academic lawyers might feel that they labour in vain) but rather that he will not be *improperly* influenced by media comment and that in any event risk of undue influence is more than

---

14 *A-G v Times Newspapers Ltd* [1974] AC 273 at 301.
15 [1990] 2 AC 154 at 209.
16 The injunction in this case was considered by the Court of Appeal three times: see (1987) Independent, 9 December, (1987) Times, 18 December and (1988) Times, 2 February and noted in [1988] Crim LR 237.
17 (1987) Times, 18 December.
18 In the judgment of 29 January 1988, (1988) Times, 2 February.
19 [1988] Crim LR 237.
20 Robertson & Nicol, *Media Law* (3rd edn, 1992) p 207 say that 'the worrying aspect of this decision was that it was essentially a public relations management exercise.'

outweighed by the importance of promoting freedom to comment upon or criticise court judgments. As one Australian High Court judge explained:[1]

> 'It is only natural that judges should prefer to decide cases in an atmosphere which is clinically free from prejudice. No one enjoys making a decision to which government or public is hostile or antagonistic. But the natural desire to avoid embarrassment of this kind is not enough to justify a restraint which deprives the public of knowledge of important matters which it has a legitimate interest in knowing.'

The outcome of the above considerations is that pending an appeal there is considerable freedom to criticise or otherwise comment upon court decisions or even to comment (subject to the laws of libel) upon the accused. That is not to say, however, that contempt can never be committed. Scurrilous abuse of the judge may amount to contempt known as 'scandalising the court'[2] and it may be that a deliberate campaign to influence an appellate court can amount to contempt.[3] It should also be said that where an appeal lies to the Crown Court there might be thought to be a risk of influencing lay magistrates.

In Australia there was some suggestion in *Ex p A-G; Re Truth and Sportsman Ltd*[4] that an appellate court might be susceptible to influence. In its 1987 Report on Contempt[5] the Australian Law Commission drew a distinction between courts hearing appeals in civil cases and those hearing criminal appeals. The Commission concluded that 'in the light of the relatively legalistic character of most of the judicial decision-making in a criminal appeal and the arguments for treating judicial officers as comparatively unsusceptible, it is safe, except in the matter of sentencing, to accept the proposition that no publicity will ever give rise to a substantial risk of prejudice in criminal appeal proceedings by virtue of influence on the judges concerned'.[6] The Commission believed, however, that special considerations arose where appeals against sentences were concerned because of the discretionary elements in sentencing and it considered that there was a particular danger that media campaigns about particular sentences could exert a conscious or unconscious influence even on appeal court judges. Although it was legitimate for the views of the 'community at large' to be taken into account in sentencing there was no reason to suppose that the media's comments reflected society's opinions as a whole, even supposing that any consensus existed. The Commission concluded, therefore, that publications expressing opinions on the sentence to be passed on any specific accused person or convicted offender should be prohibited until after sentence had been passed and, if an appeal was lodged, comment should again be restricted until after the appeal was heard.[7]

---

1 Mason J in *Victoria v BLF* (1982) 41 ALR 71 at 124.
2 See Ch 9.
3 This possibility was envisaged by Lord Parker CJ in *Duffy's* case [1960] 2 QB 188 at 197, [1960] 2 All ER 891 at 894, and see *Re Lonrho Plc* [1990] 2 AC 154, [1989] 2 All ER 1100, discussed in Ch 6.
4 (1958) 61 SR (NSW) 484.
5 Australian Law Commission Report No 35.
6 Ibid para 383.
7 Ibid para 384: this means that there might be an 'interregnum' between the sentence and the lodging of the appeal when comment would be permitted; however the Commission thought that such comment would be far enough away from the determination of the appeal 'to dispel any effect, real or apparent' which it might have.

E   Effect on appeals by the prosecution against sentence

Under the Criminal Justice Act 1988, ss 35 and 36[8] the Attorney General may refer to the Court of Appeal a sentence imposed by the Crown Court which he considers may be unduly lenient. The Court of Appeal then reviews the sentence and may substitute for it a sentence which is *more severe* (which must be one which the Crown Court could lawfully have passed). This change in the law (first announced at the 1987 Conservative Party Conference) was prompted by a concern about supposedly 'lenient' sentences articulated in particular by some Conservative backbenchers and by certain sections of the press. There is no doubt that press comment about allegedly lenient sentences is now partly directed towards having the sentence reviewed. The Attorney General is not a judge. Indeed, he is a politician as well as the chief Government law officer and as a politician may feel a proper sensitivity towards what he perceives as public sentiment. It is questionable however whether media comment, even if it was *intended* to influence the Attorney General, would amount to contempt. It could not be contempt under the strict liability rule because the proceedings would not at that stage be 'active' for the purposes of Sch 1 to the 1981 Act. Once the sentence is referred to the Court of Appeal the considerations discussed above in respect of appellate judges apply.

V   PUBLICATIONS AFTER THE FINAL CONCLUSION OF PROCEEDINGS

Once proceedings are finally concluded and no further appeal is possible the law of contempt ceases to operate at least so far as 'prejudicing' the case is concerned, for as Wills J said:[9]

'It is possible to very effectually poison the fountain of justice before it begins to flow. It is not possible to do so once the stream has ceased.'

In the *Sunday Times* case Lord Simon of Glaisdale commented:[10]

'once the proceedings are concluded, the balance of public interest shifts. It is true that the pan holding the administration of justice is not entirely cleared. The judge must go on to try other cases, so the court must not be scandalised. Further juries must be empanelled, so the departing jurors must not be threatened. Witnesses in future cases must be able to give honest and fearless testimony so witnesses in past cases must not be victimised. But, these things conceded, the paramount interest of the public now is that it should be fully appraised of what has happened (even being informed, if appropriate, of relevant evidence that could not lawfully be adduced at the trial), and hear unhampered debate on whether the law, procedure and institutions which it had ordained have operated satisfactorily or call for modifications.'

As Lord Simon intimated, though there is considerable freedom to comment upon and criticise concluded proceedings, it might still be possible to commit contempt, as for example, by scandalising the court or by creating a risk of prejudice to other proceedings and discussion of a concluded case should not be

8   This applies to England, Wales and Northern Ireland but not to Scotland.
9   In *R v Parke* [1903] 2 KB 432 at 438.
10   [1974] AC 273 at 320.

used as a pretence for interfering with another pending case. Concluded cases are sometimes the subject of savage criticism in the press and the point at which criticism of the case becomes scurrilous abuse of the judge is discussed in Chapter 9.

Under s 17 of the Criminal Appeal Act 1968 it was possible for a concluded case in which a person had been convicted on indictment to be reopened by the Home Secretary referring the case to the Court of Appeal. This procedure was abolished by the Criminal Appeal Act 1995, s 8 of which establishes a new body, the Criminal Cases Review Commission, which can at any time refer a conviction to the Court of Appeal.[11] Section 17 references were often made after a prolonged campaign on behalf of the convicted persons in which criticism of the judge, counsel and police involved in the case were made in the media and this will doubtless remain so in respect of references by the Commission. Until the reference is made the proceedings are not active and the idea that the merits of a concluded case could not be commented upon because of the possibility of a reference by the Commission would be a totally unacceptable restriction on press freedom. Such a suggestion was never made in respect of s 17 references. Once the case is referred[12] the normal position about the unlikelihood of influencing appellate judges, discussed above, applies.[13]

VI DEFENCES

As we said in Chapter 3, the common law admits of few defences. Liability is strict so that provided the defendant can properly be said to have 'published' the offending material it is no defence to say that he did not intend to prejudice proceedings or that he was unaware that proceedings were pending or imminent as the case may be or even (in some cases) that he was unaware of the contents of the publication. What, if anything, can be argued against liability at common law? We shall look at two matters: first, the possibility of a defence of public interest and second, the argument that the publication involves the discussion of public affairs and that the likelihood of prejudice was an incidental but not intended by-product. Under the Contempt of Court Act 1981, s 5 statutory provision is made for the discussion of public affairs and we shall discuss when this applies and how far it has liberalised the law.

Section 3 of the 1981 Act provides a defence of innocent publication or distribution and this will be dealt with in Chapter 10.

A Is there a defence of public interest?

It can be argued[14] in respect of both criminal and civil proceedings that the courts could and should recognise a general defence of public interest on the basis that

---

11 Criminal Appeal Act 1995, ss 9 and 11. The new procedure applies to convictions on indictment and summarily. The creation of the Commission implements some of the key recommendations of the 1993 Royal Commission on Criminal Justice on making new provision for handling alleged miscarriages of justice.

12 Criminal Appeal Act 1995, s 9(2) provides that when a reference is made it shall be treated for all purposes as an appeal by the person concerned under s 1 of the Criminal Appeal Act 1968.

13 Note that *In re Channel Four Television Company Ltd* (1987) Independent, 9 December, (1987) Times, 18 December and (1988) Times, 2 February, [1988] Crim L R 237, discussed at p 166 concerned an appeal being heard on an Attorney General's reference.

14 See eg the first edition of this book at p 146.

if the doctrine of contempt exists for the public good (ie to protect the public interest in the due administration of justice) then it is conceivable that a greater *public* interest could outweigh it so as to justify a publication irrespective of any prejudice that might result. An example of this would be where information is published at the request of the police both with a view to securing a man's arrest and at the same time warning the public that the man may be dangerous. Perhaps the classic example is where, pending his trial, a man escapes custody. As the report of the Justice Committee said, in such a situation:

> 'it would be nothing short of folly to label as "contempt" publication of his name and photograph and the crimes which he is suspected of committing, with a view to securing his arrest and protecting the public meanwhile.'[15]

However, the possibility of the courts upholding the propriety of such a publication, at any rate upon the grounds that it is in the public interest, has receded. This is because of the attitude taken in the *Sunday Times* case. In the Court of Appeal, Lord Denning MR had held[16] that in that unique case the public interest in being informed about the thalidomide tragedy outweighed the private interest of Distillers Ltd in having a fair trial. This proposition was, however, expressly rejected by Lords Reid[17] and Cross.[18] Lord Reid[19] thought that the proposition rested upon the false premise that contempt exists to protect the *private* interests of litigants whereas in reality the law exists to protect the public interest in the due administration of justice. He further held[20] that though the courts had to balance the two ultimately competing public interests, conduct influencing the tribunal hearing the case had to be absolutely prohibited.

If this latter view is right then there seems to be no scope for the application of a defence of public interest though it has to be said that no prosecution has been brought in the type of example we have been discussing.[1]

An alternative view for holding there to be no contempt in the mooted circumstances is that far from interfering with the course of justice such a publication helps its administration. This suggestion was made by Sir Michael Havers (as Attorney General) during the committee stage of the Contempt of Court Bill.[2] It is an interesting idea but it must remain doubtful whether the argument would succeed.

The conclusion one must reluctantly draw is that though perhaps unlikely to be prosecuted, publications made even at the request of the police with a view to apprehending escaped prisoners and warning the public of possible dangers are at risk of being held in contempt. This seems an unsatisfactory situation and it is perhaps surprising that the Phillimore Committee[3] did not recommend some kind of public interest defence. Their view was that such a defence would be too

---

15 *Contempt of Court* (1959) p 11.
16 [1973] QB 710 at 739–740. Lord Denning MR repeated this line of argument subsequently, see p 231.
17 [1974] AC 273 at 301E–F.
18 Ibid at 323F–G.
19 [1974] AC 273 at 301E–F.
20 Ibid at 296–297.
1   The prosecution in *A-G v Sport Newspapers Ltd* [1992] 1 All ER 503 was in respect of a report which revealed the wanted man's previous convictions, see p 134. When briefing the press and asking for their co-operation in their search for the suspect in that case the police had expressly warned journalists against revealing his criminal record.
2   1980–81 HC Official Report, SCA Contempt of Court, col 65.
3   At paras 143–145.

uncertain to be helpful and that situations of escaped prisoners during the pendency of proceedings were too rare to warrant special consideration.

B   The discussion of public affairs at common law

It has been recognised for some time in Australia that the de facto creation of a real risk of prejudice does not invariably mean that a contempt will be established. In a nutshell it seems to be accepted that if through public discussion of matters of public interest, supervening litigation might incidentally but unintentionally be potentially prejudiced, no contempt will be committed. The leading case is *Re Truth and Sportsman Ltd, ex p Bread Manufacturers Ltd* [4] where the respondent newspaper published a series of articles dealing with a matter of public interest, namely, the organisation of the bread trade and the selling price of bread, which was critical of the applicant company's activities. Some of these articles were published after the company had issued a libel writ against the newspaper. It was held that no contempt had been committed. Jordan CJ commented inter alia:[5]

> 'It is of extreme public interest that no conduct should be permitted which is likely to prevent a litigant in a court of justice from having his case tried free from all matter of prejudice. But the administration of justice, important though it undoubtedly is, is not the only matter in which the public is vitally interested; and if in the course of the ventilation of a question of public concern matter is published which may prejudice a party in the conduct of a law suit, it does not follow that a contempt has been committed.
>
> The case may be one in which as between competing matters of public interest the possibility of prejudice to a litigant may be required to yield to other superior considerations. The discussion of public affairs and the denunciation of public abuses, actual or supposed, cannot be required to be suspended merely because the discussion or the denunciation may, as an incidental but not intended by-product, cause some likelihood of prejudice to a person who happens at the time to be a litigant.
>
> It is well settled that a person cannot be prevented by process of contempt from continuing to discuss publicly a matter which may fairly be regarded as one of public interest, by reason merely of the fact that the matter in question has become the subject of litigation, or that person whose conduct is being publicly criticised has become a party to litigation either as plaintiff or as defendant, and whether in relation to the matter which is under discussion or with respect to some other matter.'

In Australia, Jordan CJ's comments have been cited with approval by, for example, Owen J in *Re Australian Consolidated Press Ltd, ex p Dawson* [6] and by Fullagar J in *John Fairfax & Sons Pty Ltd v McRae* [7] whilst in Engand, in the *Sunday Times* case, Lords Reid[8] and Simon[9] cited with approval respectively *Ex p Bread Manufacturers Ltd* and *Ex p Dawson*. There is therefore substantial

---

4   (1937) 37 SR (NSW) 242.
5   Ibid at 249.
6   (1961) SR NSW 573 at 575.
7   (1955) 93 CLR 351 (Australian HC).
8   [1974] AC 273 at 296.
9   Ibid at 321.

authority for the existence at common law of what may be regarded as a concession in favour of freedom of speech. Lord Simon commented:[10]

> 'There is one particular situation where the law might strike the balance between the competing interests either way, but in fact strikes it in favour of freedom of discussion. This is where a matter is already under public debate when litigation supervenes which the continuance of the debate might interfere with. The situation of public debate involves that there is probably at stake some matter of which the public has a legitimate interest to be informed; and the law, in pragmatic judgment, says that conditionally the debate may continue.'

Although the concession has been developed primarily in the civil context it appears also to apply in the criminal context. Lord Simon's comments indicate its wide application at common law in England[11] and it has been accepted in Australia that it applies to criminal cases.[12] In *Hinch v A-G (Victoria)*[13] Mason CJ said:

> 'there is no acceptable basis in principle or theory for drawing a distinction between the rules of the law of contempt as they apply to civil and criminal proceedings.'

However Deane J while agreeing that it applied in criminal cases, did admit that it was possible to see a valid distinction:[14]

> , 'There is something to be said for the view that the fair administration of criminal justice is of such fundamental importance to the social compact underlying a democratic society that a publication which has a clear tendency to interfere with it adversely could never be justified by countervailing public interest considerations'.

The ambit of the freedom to publish, particularly in the criminal context, is not easy to state. The Phillimore Committee pointed out[15] that given that at any moment many thousands of legal proceedings are in progress, one cannot halt all general public debate on any issue arising in any case. The Committee gave as an example a debate about hotel fire regulations which should not be halted simply because one hotel is being prosecuted for breach of the regulations. It must also be remembered that for there to be a contempt there must be a real risk of prejudice and in many cases this risk will not be present. It can be argued that a publication on a matter of public interest is permissible despite supervening prosecutions where there is no reference to the particular case (or at any rate when there is no detailed reference) and where the matter is not of such notoriety that it is impossible to disentangle the particular case from the general debate. On the other hand, it seems clear that even in the midst of a general discussion, detailed references to particular cases can be a contempt. A good example of this is the Scottish case of *Atkins v London Weekend Television Ltd*[16] where the television

---

10 Ibid at 321.
11 Cf Lord Reid who seemed to approve the concession only in the context of pressurising litigants and perhaps not where there is a risk of prejudicing the tribunal trying the case.
12 In *John Fairfax & Sons Pty Ltd v McRae* (1955) 93 CLR 351; *Registrar of Criminal Appeals v Willesee* (1985) 3 NSWLR 650; *Hinch v A-G (Victoria)* (1987) 164 CLR 15; see also *Re Whitlam, ex p Garland* (1976) 8 ACTR 17. See also the position under the Contempt of Court Act 1981, and *A-G v English* [1983] 1 AC 116, [1982] 2 All ER 903.
13 (1987) 164 CLR 15 at 22.
14 Ibid at 48.
15 At para 142.
16 1978 SLT 76.

programme dealt generally with the issue of brain death but referred to a specific case in such a way as to suggest that the accused did attempt to block a patient's air supply which was the very issue to be determined in the prosecution. The High Court of Judiciary rejected the defence based on *Ex p Bread Manufacturers Ltd*, commenting that that case:[17]

> 'dealt with the issue of contempt in general terms and not precisely with a case in which specific references to an immediately pending trial are made part of the commentary.'

The dividing line between an acceptable reference to a pending case and that which is not is obviously a fine one. One uncertainty is whether the concession only applies to general discussion begun before a prosecution or whether it extends to discussion prompted by a particular prosecution. The words 'suspended' and 'continuing to discuss' in the crucial passage from Jordan CJ's judgment in *Ex p Bread Manufacturers Ltd* suggests a discussion which is already underway and Lord Simon in the *Sunday Times* spoke in similar terms. However, the distinction is not always an easy one to make. There are some matters which are the subject of continuing public discussion in the sense that they involve a long-standing and ongoing debate in society and some which become an issue discussed by the general public only as the result of a particular case. An example of the former would be the treatment of severely handicapped newborn babies.[18] Examples of the latter are more difficult to give, but one might be the widespread discussion of children who kill other children which was engendered in 1993 by two ten year olds who killed Jamie Bulger. In many cases, however, the matter is one which *has* been raised in public discussion prior to the proceedings but has excited no particular current interest until the proceedings in question bring it to the fore. In such situations the court may be thrown back on considering how specific the publication is about the proceedings, whether public discussion about the matter of public interest is tantamount to a discussion of the particular proceedings, and whether the matter of public interest is of such importance that it outweighs, in this instance, the interest in the administration of justice.

Some doubt has been expressed in Australia as to how the principle in *Bread Manufacturers* is to be interpreted.[19] One interpretation is that it says that there is no contempt whenever the risk of prejudice is an incidental but unintended by-product of a discussion on a matter of public concern. The other is that even if the prejudice is incidental and unintended a 'balancing' act is required, whereby the public interest in the unprejudiced administration of justice is weighed against the competing public interest in the matter under discussion when the alleged contempt occurred.

This difference of interpretation arose in *Registrar, Court of Appeal v Willesee*[20] where the *Bread Manufacturers* defence saved a broadcaster from contempt even though the broadcast had led to a trial being aborted. There a television programme about police corruption was transmitted the night before

---

17 Ibid at 79. See also *A-G v Willesee* [1980] 2 NSWLR 143 at 162–3 per Mahoney JA (NSW CA) and in Canada *Re A-G for Manitoba and Radio Ob Ltd* (1976) 70 DLR (3d) 311.

18 This was the subject matter in *A-G v English* [1983] 1 AC 116, [1982] 2 All ER 903, the first case decided under s 5 of the 1981 Act: see the discussion below.

19 See *Victoria v Australian Building Construction Employees and Builders' Labourers' Federation* (1982) 152 CLR 25; *A-G (NSW) v Willesee* [1980] 2 NSWLR 143; *Registrar, Court of Appeal v Willesee* [1985] 3 NSWLR 650; Australian Law Reform Commission Report No 35: *Contempt*.

20 [1985] 3 NSWLR 650.

the jury was to give its verdict in a theft trial. The accused was one of the main protagonists in an inquiry into police corruption, which had been instigated largely because of his allegations. The programme made no reference to the theft charge but there were references to allegations that the accused had shot a man and doubts were cast on his general credibility. The New South Wales Court of Appeal held that the serious risk of prejudice to the trial created by the broadcast was unintentional and was incidental to the discussion. If, as Hope JA and Priestly JA suspected, the court was required to go further than this and evaluate the competing matters of public interest it was held that there was no contempt committed here because of the public interest in continuing the debate about police corruption.

The issue was discussed at length by the High Court of Australia in *Hinch v A-G Victoria.* [1] Mason CJ said that the question was whether the fourth sentence of the passage quoted above from Jordan CJ's judgment in the *Bread Manufacturers* [2] expresses a 'principle of law that governs references to pending criminal proceedings when such references form part of any discussion of public affairs or any denunciation of public abuses'. He held that it does not, and that the fourth sentence is not so much a statement of principle as an example of a publication which has not crossed the borderline into contempt.[3] His conclusion therefore was that even where the risk of prejudice is unintentional and incidental the court is required to balance the competing public interests and he doubted whether the public interest in the administration of justice would often give way:[4]

> 'No doubt there will be other occasions, apart from reports of the proceedings of Parliament and the continuation of discussion of a matter of public interest commenced before the institution of proceedings, when the balancing approach requires that the public interest in the administration of justice should give way to the public interest in freedom of discussion. The discussion of a major constitutional crisis or of an imminent threat of nuclear disaster are illustrations with overriding claims which immediately spring to mind. But this concession is a fragile foundation for the conclusion that once any topic of public concern or interest is identified, the public interest in the administration of justice must give way to discussion of that topic, provided that the likelihood of prejudice to pending litigation is no more than unintended and incidental to the discussion of the topic of public concern or interest.'

In *Hinch* a unanimous court held that the public interest in knowing that a convicted child sex offender was continuing to run a youth organisation while facing new charges did not justify the publication of the accused's previous convictions and suggestions that he had committed other offences in the past which had not resulted in charges. One notable thing about *Hinch* was that the prejudicial material was not incidental to the discussion but was the central issue. It *was*, however, incidental *to the pending trial* as the whole thrust of the broadcasts was not directed to the trial but to the fact that the accused was still

1 (1987) 164 CLR 15.
2 Ie the sentence at (1937) 37 SR (NSW) 242 at 249–250 which says 'The discussion of public affairs and the denunciation of public abuses, actual or supposed, cannot be required to be suspended merely because the discussion or the denunciation may, as an incidental but not intended by-product, cause some likelihood of prejudice to a person who happens at the time to be a litigant'.
3 Note that Mason CJ did not think that the test under s 5 of the Contempt of Court Act 1981, as interpreted by Lord Diplock in *A-G v English* [1983] 1 AC 116, discussed at pp 175 ff, reflects the common law in Australia.
4 (1987) 164 CLR 15 at 26.

in his post at the organisation despite his previous record being known to the authorities. In the Supreme Court of Victoria Young CJ commented that the broadcaster could have made his point effectively without referring to the previous convictions. It is, with respect, difficult to see how. The High Court considered that what *Bread Manufacturers* required was a balancing act, and in this case the public interest concerned did not take precedence over the fundamental one of protecting the administration of justice from risk of interference. Ultimately, therefore, it came down to a value judgment and the public interest in an unprejudiced trial won. The result was that once the priest was facing new charges it was impossible to warn parents publicly against committing their children to the care of a convicted paedophile without committing contempt.

To conclude from a comparison between these cases that discussion of police corruption is a greater public interest than the prevention of the sexual abuse of children would be an over-simplification, although one can have doubts about the hierarchy of values held by the High Court of Australia. Perhaps the key distinction is that in *Willesee* it was simply unfortunate that a person featured in the programme happened to be on trial for a relatively trivial offence at the time whereas in *Hinch* it was the criminal charges which had occasioned the broadcast.

Finally, it seems a nice point (despite the frequent shorthand references to the '*Bread Manufacturers* defence') as to whether discussion of public affairs is properly regarded as a defence or simply as an exception to the normal rule. This may be important in determining the burden of proof. Although this still has to be resolved at common law it has been held,[5] that under the similar statutory provision in the Contempt of Court Act 1981, the burden of proof lies on the prosecution to show that the risk of prejudice is not incidental. It may be that the position is the same at common law.

C   The discussion of public affairs under the Contempt of Court Act 1981

Although, as we shall see, it does not actually operate as a *defence*, the Contempt of Court Act 1981 contains a specific provision to deal with the discussion of public affairs in the context of the strict liability rule. Section 5 provides:

> 'A publication made as or as part of a discussion in good faith of public affairs or other matters of general public interest is not to be treated as a contempt of court under the strict liability rule if the risk of impediment or prejudice to particular legal proceedings is merely incidental to the discussion.'

Great care should be taken in interpreting s 5. It *does not* in the name of public interest give a carte blanche to discuss the facts of a particular case. That would be to confuse it with the defence of 'public interest' which, as we have seen, has yet to be recognised at common law. No such defence was recommended by the Phillimore Committee and no such defence is provided for in the Act.

The leading case on the meaning of s 5 is *A-G v English*.[6] This case establishes that the section does not operate as a defence and that it is incumbent upon the prosecution to show not only that a publication creates the necessary degree of risk but also that such a risk is not incidental to a discussion of public affairs. In

---

5   *A-G v English* [1983] 1 AC 116, [1982] 2 All ER 903.
6   [1983] 1 AC 116, [1982] 2 All ER 903: for the facts see pp 147–148.

other words it is for the prosecution to show that s 5 does not apply rather than for the defence to show that it does.

It was held that on the facts s 5 did apply so that no contempt had been proved. It was accepted that the article was written in good faith, and being in support of a candidate in a forthcoming by-election, was a discussion of public affairs. Being a 'pro-life' candidate it was a necessary part of the supporting argument that assertions be made that paediatricians commonly let severely physically or mentally handicapped new-born babies die. As Lord Diplock put it:[7]

> 'an article supporting [the] candidature in the by-election as a pro-life candidate that contained no such assertion would depict her as tilting at imaginary windmills.'

Lord Diplock considered that the term 'discussion' was not, as the Divisional Court had ruled, confined to 'the airing of views and the propounding and debating of principles and arguments' but that it embraced accusations without which the article would have been emasculated. Nor did his Lordship accept that the test was whether the article could have been effectively written without the offending passages. The sole question in his view was whether the risk of prejudice was no more than the incidental consequence of expounding its main theme. In this case there being no express mention of the *Arthur* case, and given that the main plank of the article was to support the pro-life candidate, in his view, the risk was properly described as 'merely incidental'.

A-G v English is a liberal interpretation of s 5. It is to be noted, however, that no mention of the case in hand had been made in the publication in issue and Lord Diplock himself stressed[8] that the *English* case was the very 'antithesis' of the *Sunday Times* case where the raison d'etre of the article was the particular litigation. The *English* case, therefore, did not decide what latitude, if any, would be given to direct references to particular cases. In this respect the subsequent Divisional Court decisions in the Fagan cases[9] are important for they seem to make it clear that s 5 can apply to direct references to the accused. The *Mail on Sunday* was held to be protected by s 5 in respect of the article suggesting a possible homosexual liaison between Fagan and the Queen's bodyguard because the publication was part of the discussion about the Queen's safety which subject was par excellence a public affair or a matter of general public interest. On the other hand, as the prosecution against the *Sunday Times* shows, the discussion must be of a matter of *public* concern and hence s 5 was held not to apply to the discussion of the incident resulting in injuries to Fagan's stepson since that incident was thought to be irrelevant to the public discussion of the matter of general public interest. As has often been said in the context of alleged press intrusion into people's privacy, there is a difference between matters of public interest and matters which are of interest to the public.

In *English* it was accepted that the article was published in 'undisputed good faith'. This leaves open what is meant by good faith. If it means no more than the lack of an improper motive then the good faith condition will normally be covered by the requirement of lack of intention to prejudice. Where there is intention to prejudice the strict liability rule will not apply but the publication can be prosecuted at common law because of s 6(c).[10] A publication could perhaps be

---

7 Ibid at 919 and 286 respectively.
8 [1983] 1 AC 116 at 143 G, [1982] 2 All ER 903 at 920.
9 (1983) Times, 12 February, see pp 149–150.
10 See Ch 4, pp 106 ff.

said to be in bad faith where it was in pursuit of a campaign or vendetta against a particular person. An example of this could be the use of a newspaper by its proprietor to wage a campaign in connection with his other business interests, as happened in 1988–89 over Tiny Rowland's campaign over the Al-Fayed's takeover of Harrods.[11]

English and the Fagan cases suggested that s 5 has brought a measure of relaxation into the law.[12] However s 5 does not give a carte blanche to discuss the merits of the particular case. In *A-G v TVS Television Ltd; A-G v H W Southey & Sons Ltd* [13] a television programme was broadcast concerning alleged harassment, Rachman-like behaviour and fraud on the DHSS on the part of a small number of landlords in Reading. A free distribution Reading newspaper previewed the programme under the headline 'Reading's new wave of harassment . . . TV focus on bedsit barons'. The publications coincided with a trial at Reading Crown Court in which a number of persons were charged with conspiracy to defraud the DHSS. Two of the defendants were recognisable in a 'stills' photograph used in the programme (although their faces had been blacked out). The TV company's plea that s 5 applied, because the prejudicial matter was incidental to the main theme of the programme which was the shortage of rented accommodation in the south of England resulting from government policies, failed. The Divisional Court said that the test of whether it was incidental was to look at the subject matter of the discussion and see how closely it related to the particular legal proceedings. The more closely it related the easier it was for the Attorney General to show that the risk of prejudice was not merely incidental to the discussion. Lloyd LJ said: 'The application of the test is largely a matter of first impression.'

Mann LJ in *A-G v Guardian Newspapers Ltd* [14] agreed that the 'test is largely one of impression' but he did not say 'first impression'. It is difficult to understand why a court's *first* impression on such a difficult matter should be relied upon in place of its more considered assessment. The *Guardian* case itself concerned a newspaper article in which the paper's city editor castigated the increasing tendency of judges hearing major fraud trials to make orders under s 4(2) of the 1981 Act restricting reports of the court proceedings.[15] He gave as an example the order made in a current trial, revealing in the course of his argument that it was because an (unnamed) defendant in the trial was also facing charges in the Isle of Man. The Divisional Court held that no substantial risk of serious prejudice had been created but that, if it had, s 5 would have applied because this was a case in which the revelation about the defendant really was incidental to a discussion of public affairs. This was an interesting case where, although the subject matter of the discussion was closely related to something which had happened in the proceedings, the article did not deal with the substance of the trial as such.

---

11 This resulted in the contempt case of *Re Lonrho Plc* [1990] 2 AC 154 which concerned civil proceedings but where it was held that there was no intention to prejudice, see Ch 6, pp 220 ff.
12 The finding in favour of the *Mail on Sunday* in the Fagan affair was particularly generous to the media.
13 (1989) Times, 7 July.
14 [1992] 3 All ER 38 at 45.
15 For reporting court proceedings, see Ch 8.

D   The relationship between the common law and s 5

Is s 5 a statutory enactment of the common law as expressed in the *Bread Manufacturers* case? In *A-G v News Group Newspapers Ltd* [16] Sir John Donaldson MR quoted Jordan CJ in *Bread Manufacturers* and said:

> 'This is the defence of public interest,[17] now confirmed by s 5 of the Act of 1981 and nothing in the authorities suggests that the defence at common law was wider than that available under the Act.'

In *A-G v Guardian Newspapers Ltd* [18] Brooke J, also quoting Jordan CJ, expanded on this:

> 'The language of the common law that "freedom of speech cannot be allowed where there would be real prejudice to the administration of justice" and that "the discussion of public affairs cannot be required to be suspended merely because it may, as an incidental but not intended by-product, cause some likelihood of prejudice to a person who happens at the time to be a litigant" has now been converted into the statutory language of ss 2(2) and 5 of the Contempt of Court Act 1981 . . . The language is slightly different but the underlying philosophy is the same.'

However a different view of the congruence of the *Bread Manufacturers* defence and statute has been expressed in Australia. In the High Court of Australia in *Hinch v A-G (Victoria)* [19] Mason CJ said that the s 5 test, at least as interpreted by Lord Diplock in *A-G v English*,[20] did not accurately reflect the common law in Australia. Toohey J said that s 5 operates in the special framework of the statute which includes limiting the operation of the strict liability rule and that 'it is not to be assumed that s 5 is intended only to restate the common law'. The common law as interpreted in *Hinch* [1] requires a balancing of the different public interest issues involved. As is clear from Lord Diplock in *English*, however, s 5 concentrates on what Toohey J rather inelegantly termed 'incidentalness'. The test is whether or not the risk is incidental to the discussion and once that discussion is adjudged to be in good faith and on a matter of public affairs or other matters of general public interest the incidental nature of the risk is all that matters. A balancing act does not take place.

Far from there being any suggestion of 'the defence at common law being wider than that available under the Act' (in the words of the Master of the Rolls in *A-G v News Group Newspapers Ltd* [2]) s 5 appears to be wider than the common law at least as it is currently interpreted in Australia. As said above, Lord Diplock gave s 5 an interpretation in *English* which is generous to the media. Whether or not the difference in approach would lead to a different outcome in practice is

---

16 [1987] QB 1 at 13. This was a case in respect of civil proceedings but there is no reason to think that the position would be different in respect of a criminal trial.
17 The Master of the Rolls seems to be using the term 'public interest defence' here as shorthand for the freedom to discuss matters of public interest. There is no suggestion in the case that he thought that *Bread Manufacturers* established a general public interest defence of the type discussed at pp 169 ff.
18 [1992] 3 All ER 38 at 47.
19 (1987) 164 CLR 15 at 29.
20 [1983] 1 AC 116, [1982] 2 All ER 903.
1 See the discussion of the facts of this case at pp 174 ff.
2 [1987] QB 1 at 13.

another matter. It is difficult to see a UK court excusing the exposure of the accused's past which happened in *Hinch* on the grounds that it was 'incidental'. On the other hand the narrow application which Mason CJ accorded to the *Bread Manufacturers* defence in *Hinch* could have boded ill for the press had it been applied to their behaviour in the Fagan cases.

VII PRE-TRIAL PUBLICATION BANS IN CANADA AFTER THE CHARTER

In Canada the Supreme Court has had to consider the constitutionality of pre-trial publication bans in the light of the Charter of Rights and Freedoms of 1982. Section 11(d) of the Charter protects the right of the accused to a fair trial, but s 2(b) guarantees freedom of expression 'including freedom of the press and other media of communication'. In *Dagenais v Canadian Broadcasting Corpn* [3] the Supreme Court of Canada, by a majority, refused to uphold a ban on the broadcasting of a film drama about the abuse of boys in a home run by lay brothers which had been imposed in order to protect the trial of four Christian brothers charged with sexual offences against boys in a Catholic institution. Lamer CJC held that the common law preference for a fair trail over free expression had been altered by the Charter. He said:[4]

> 'The pre-Charter common-law rule governing publication bans emphasized the right to a fair trial over the free expression interests of those affected by the ban. In my view, the balance this rule strikes is inconsistent with the principles of the Charter, and in particular, the equal status given by the Charter ss 2(b) and 11(d). It would be inappropriate for the courts to continue to apply a common-law rule that automatically favoured the rights protected by s 11(d) over those protected by s 2(b). A hierarchical approach to rights, which places some over others, must be avoided, both when interpreting the Charter and when developing the common-law.'

He said that a ban should only be ordered when:

(a) the ban is necessary in order to prevent a real and substantial risk to the fairness of the trial, because reasonably available alternative measures will not prevent the risk; and

(b) the salutary effects of the publication ban outweigh the deleterious effects to the free expression of those affected by the ban.

The alternative measures Lamer CJC suggested included changing the trial venue, isolating jurors and jury selection.

Lamer CJC's formulation of the situation in which a ban should be ordered clearly contemplates a situation in which a ban is necessary to avoid a risk of prejudice, but the risk is outweighed by its impact on free expresion. Since in the present case the first instance judge had not considered the alternative solutions to the problem, however, the Supreme Court did not have to decide whether the salutary effects of the ban were outweighed here.

3 (1995) 120 DLR (4th) 12.
4 Ibid at 37.

CHAPTER 6

Publications interfering with the course of justice in particular civil proceedings

I INTRODUCTION

Most case law in respect of publications interfering with the course of justice in civil proceedings was developed at a time when trial by jury in civil actions was commonplace.[1] Such a mode of trial is now unusual except in defamation actions.[2] Where there *is* a jury there is the same concern to protect jurors from out-of-court publicity as with criminal proceedings. Where there is no jury it will be difficult to show that a publication creates a real risk of jeopardising the impartiality of the court for, as is explained in Chapter 5,[3] it is generally held that publications cannot influence professional judges. The law is concerned in civil cases, however, as much as in criminal cases, to see that nothing is published which could interfere with or pressurise witnesses.

Particular issues arise in regard to the application of the contempt laws to civil proceedings which do not concern the presence or absence of a jury. In civil proceedings the parties themselves can determine the course of proceedings to a far greater extent than can the defendants in criminal cases and the possibility of a publication influencing their conduct in respect of the proceedings is consequently greater. The extent to which a publication influencing the parties can be a contempt and the point at which influence becomes improper pressure are difficult issues which the courts have had to address. Furthermore, the very existence of contempt laws which restrict publications regarding particular proceedings has led to the problem of the so-called 'gagging writ' whereby a writ is issued for the specific purpose of stifling comment rather than with any real intention of bringing an action.

There is no limit to the ways in which publications can be held to prejudice proceedings. Recently, for example, contempt has been used in a novel and controversial way to protect the subject matter of litigation from destruction.[4] An older controversy concerns the objections voiced by the House of Lords in *A-G v Times Newspapers Ltd*,[5] the *Sunday Times* case, to publications which *prejudge* an issue pending before the court. This objection was based not just upon the risks to the due administration of justice in the particular case but also upon the wider risks to the due administration of justice generally. This idea attracted widespread criticism, led to a case against the United Kingdom in the European Court on

1 See the comments by Lord Diplock in *A-G v Times Newspapers Ltd* [1974] AC 273 at 309.
2 For the details on when civil actions are heard before a jury see p 182.
3 See pp 124 ff.
4 *A-G v Newspaper Publishing Plc* [1988] Ch 333, [1987] 3 All ER 276; cf *Re Lonrho Plc* [1990] 2 AC 154: these cases are considered at pp 211 ff.
5 [1974] AC 273.

Human Rights[6] and was a catalyst in the reform of the contempt laws by the Contempt of Court Act 1981.[7] There remains some uncertainty about how far the 'prejudgment test' has survived the 1981 Act and about the position of the test in other jurisdictions.[8] The 'prejudgment test' is more of an issue in civil than in criminal proceedings because the absence of a jury makes a risk to the *particular* proceedings less likely.

As explained in the previous chapters the test for contempt at common law is whether the publication creates a 'real risk' of prejudice and under the strict liability rule of the 1981 Act it is whether there is a 'substantial risk of serious prejudice'. Two things must be remembered, however. First, which of these tests is applied may not make any difference to the outcome of the case[9] and secondly, the common law will still apply, even in the United Kingdom, to cases which for some reason fall outside the strict liability rule.[10]

II   PUBLICATIONS CALCULATED TO IMPAIR THE COURT'S IMPARTIALITY IN PARTICULAR PROCEEDINGS

A   Civil cases where there is a jury

Trial by jury in civil actions is very much the exception. In England and Wales, under s 69(1) of the Supreme Court Act 1981, either party can demand a jury in cases of libel, slander, malicious prosecution or false imprisonment and a defendant to allegations of fraud can also demand a jury. These are the only cases in which there is a *right* to a jury and even then, if the trial requires prolonged examination of documents or accounts, or any scientific or local investigation which cannot conveniently be made with a jury, the proviso to s 69(1) allows trial by jury to be dispensed with. Otherwise, under s 69(3) of the Supreme Court Act 1981 trial will be without a jury unless the court 'in its discretion orders it to be tried with a jury'. In practice, the discretion of the court to order a jury trial will be exercised only in exceptional circumstances.[11] As a result of this the most common civil action to be tried with a jury is an action for libel. Libel actions, however, are often the most newsworthy of civil proceedings and the most likely to attract media attention.

1   *Disparaging the parties or prejudging the merits of an action*

In cases where there is or is likely to be a jury then, as Buckley J said in *Vine Products Ltd v Green,*[12] it is a contempt if the publication is 'of a kind which will be apt to make a juryman approach the case without a completely open mind'.

6   *Sunday Times v UK* (1979) 2 EHRR 245.
7   All of which is discussed in Ch 3. The *Sunday Times* case is discussed in context at pp 221 ff.
8   See pp 117 ff and p 227.
9   See p 113.
10   See pp 117 ff.
11   See *Ward v James* [1966] 1 QB 273, [1965] 1 All ER 563; *Hodges v Harland & Wolff Ltd* [1965] 1 All ER 1086, [1965] 1 WLR 523; *H v Ministry of Defence* [1991] 2 QB 103, [1991] 2 All ER 834, [1991] 2 WLR 1192.
12   [1966] Ch 484 at 496.

Publications thought to have a real risk of having such an effect are essentially those which disparage either of the parties to the action and those which prejudge the merits of the case.

An example of disparagement is *Wilson v Collison, Re Johnson and Mitchell.* [13] A writ of libel had been issued by the leader of the National Sailors' and Fireman's Union, in respect of a pamphlet entitled 'J Havelock Wilson MP. Daylight on his career. Exposure and Challenge. Astounding Revelations', which had been published by the defendants. Some time after the issue of the writ the *Seaman's Journal* published several articles attacking the defendants. It accused them of being 'the tools of British Shipowners' and described them as 'abandoned wretches'. The article ended by appealing to the members of the National Sailors' and Fireman's Union to 'supply the sinews of war to help Mr Wilson, their own champion, to scotch these vampires'. As Day J said 'the publication of these articles in question was undoubtedly calculated to interfere with the course of justice'.

Prejudgments affecting particular proceedings can take a variety of forms but the most objectionable is the public assertion that one of the parties is going to lose. A good example is the *Finance Union* case.[14] The article read:

'A fierce battle is to be fought in the courts between the Yorkshire Provident Life Assurance Company and the *Review*. We never hesitate to back the winner, and in this case we say 100 to 1 on the *Review*. The executive of the Yorkshire Provident must be abundantly lacking in foresight and wisdom. Whoever is to blame for advising this puny, weak, and mismanaged company to squander the hard-earned savings of the people in courts of law has much to answer for. The result, in our opinion, to the Provident will be disastrous, and we would urge on the officials to withdraw the action.'

Wills J branded the article as being 'a most reprehensible attempt to interfere with the course of justice'.

In *Re Robbins, ex p Green* [15] the offending article stated that a forthcoming libel action 'will be a very short affair'. The article continued:

'it is stated in well-informed circles that there will be no cross-examination and no attempt to prove the allegations; that an apology will be tendered; and the business of the jury will be to fix such damages as under the circumstances [the plaintiff] may think fit to accept as compensation for the injury to his character and reputation.'

The article was held to be a contempt since it asserted there was to be no issue before the jury, the implication being that the defendants had no case.

Commenting upon the issues can also be a contempt. In *Daw v Eley* [16] pending a suit to restrain the infringement of a patent in which one issue was to be the novelty of the plaintiff's invention, the *Volunteer Service Gazette* was held to have committed contempt by publishing certain letters which tended to disprove the novelty of the invention. In *Wilson v Collison, Re Johnson and Mitchell* [17] the

---

13 (1895) 11 TLR 376. See also *Russell v Russell* (1894) 11 TLR 38; *R v Gossip* (1909) Times, 18 February; *Greenwood v Leather Shod Wheel Co Ltd* (1898) 14 TLR 241; and *Howitt v Fagge* (1896) 12 TLR 426.
14 *Re Finance Union, Yorkshire Provident Assurance Co v Review Publishers* (1895) 11 TLR 167. See also *Peters v Bradlaugh* (1888) 4 TLR 414.
15 (1891) 7 TLR 411. See also *Ex p Foster* (1894) Times, 5 February, and *Ex p The Standard* (1907) Times, 28 January.
16 (1868) LR 7 Eq 49.
17 (1895) 11 TLR 376. Presenting one side of the case may be risky. Cf *R v Barry, ex p Grey* (1939) 83 Sol Jo 872.

Seaman's Journal referred to the pamphlet which was the subject of libel proceedings as a 'tissue of infamous lies and blackguardly libel from beginning to end'. Day J said that 'newspapers had no right to prejudge the merits of an action in that way'.

Influencing jurors was one of the grounds of the action in *A-G v Hislop* [18] against the satirical magazine *Private Eye*, which arose out of the magazine's battle with Sonia Sutcliffe, the wife of the convicted mass-murderer known as the 'Yorkshire Ripper'. *Private Eye* had published an article alleging that Mrs Sutcliffe had cashed in on her husband's notoriety by selling her story to the *Daily Mail*. Three months before the trial, when the action was already on the 'warned' list, *Private Eye* published two further articles. These said that if Mrs Sutcliffe continued with her libel action she would be exposed in cross-examination to questioning designed to establish that she had known of her husband's murderous activities and that she had defrauded the social security authorities. The main objection to these articles was that they put pressure on Mrs Sutcliffe to abandon her action[19] but the Court of Appeal also held that they constituted a contempt under the strict liability rule in s 2(2) of the 1981 Act. The articles did not deal at all with the subject matter of the libel action—the allegations about the transaction with the *Daily Mail*—but the court held that a substantial risk of serious prejudice was created because any juror who read the articles would remember them three months later and be prejudiced generally against Mrs Sutcliffe. Parker and McCowan LJJ thought that a juror who had read the articles would be likely to mention the content to other jurors in the case.[20] In deciding whether the statutory test was satisfied[1] the court took into consideration the circulation of the magazine, 209,000, almost half of which was in London where the trial was to be held. That meant that it was, in McCowan LJ's words, 'quite on the cards' that a potential juror would have read the articles and would remember them and be influenced by them. 'Quite on the cards' appears in this instance to have equated to 'substantial risk'.

2   Publication of the fact of payment of money into court

Publication of the fact that one party has paid money into court can be a contempt on the grounds that it might jeopardise the jury's impartiality.

Payment of money into court arises in two separate circumstances. The first is where a newspaper wishes to plead an apology under Lord Campbell's Libel Act 1843, s 2, as amended by the Libel Act 1845, s 2. According to these provisions, this defence is only available to a newspaper or other periodical which has published a libel without malice or gross negligence, and which has published a full apology before commencement of the action or at the earliest opportunity afterwards. An essential requisite of such a defence is the payment

---

18 [1991] 1 QB 514, [1991] 1 All ER 911.
19 See p 207.
20 Perhaps the jurors were not *Private Eye* readers or were not so easily influenced as the Court of Appeal supposed because in the libel action Mrs Sutcliffe was awarded the then record sum of £600,000 damages against *Private Eye*. The magazine appealed and the Court of Appeal set aside the award but it was later stated in court (see (1989) Times, 7 November) that she had accepted £60,000 in settlement.
1   The Court of Appeal accepted that there was no *intention* to prejudice the jury.

into court of money by way of amends; failure to pay in money is fatal to the plea. In *R v Wealdstone News and Harrow News* [2] it was held that the newspaper had committed contempt by publishing the *amount* of money paid in under these provisions. According to Lord Hewart CJ:

> 'it was wrong to name the amount. It was for the jury to name the appropriate amount of damages without reference to any payment into court, and it was then easy to see whether the amount paid in was adequate.'

Lord Hewart CJ suggested that it might be a contempt to publish the fact that the payment in has been made, even without disclosing the amount, but he left the point open. This contention seems doubtful, since not only does the fact that payment has been made appear on the pleadings, but also such a fact is in any event likely to come to the jury's notice since the apology will be the sole defence.

This defence,[3] in practice, has become obsolete because it is better for a newspaper which has no other defence to publish an apology in the newspaper where the libel was published, pay a sum of money into court under RSC Ord 22 and plead the apology in mitigation of damages. If the defence under Lord Campbell's Act fails, the defendant may have to pay all the costs of the action even though the jury awards a sum less or no greater than the amount paid in. Nevertheless, *R v Wealdstone News and Harrow News* remains good authority if and when the defence is used and moreover provides a useful precedent in discussing payments into court under RSC Ord 22. Order 22 facilitates the settlement of actions (whether libel actions or not) before they reach court.[4] Once payment into court has been made the plaintiff has the choice of either accepting the payment in full satisfaction or continuing with the action. If he chooses to ignore the payment and continue with the action, and fails to recover in damages more than the amount paid, then he will be penalised in costs, having to pay *all* the costs of the action as and from the date of the payment in. Where the plaintiff does continue, the fact that there has been payment in does not appear on the pleadings, and moreover under Ord 22, r 7 the court must not be told of the existence of the payment into court until all questions of liability and damages have been determined.

Although none of the decisions which have been concerned with the disclosure of payments have ever dealt with the problem from the point of view of contempt,[5] it is submitted that to publish the fact that money has been paid into court under RSC Ord 22 and especially the amount paid into court will be a contempt if it is a jury trial. Suppose, for example, during libel proceedings one party paid a substantial amount of money into court, which was not accepted, should this fact be disclosed it would surely be highly prejudicial to the case, because if a juror learnt of this fact the likely effect would be that he would regard the payment in as an admission of liability.

2 (1925) 41 TLR 508.
3 For further cases and a detailed discussion of this defence see Gatley, *Libel and Slander* (8th edn 1981) pp 865–876, 1188–1197.
4 See Gatley, ibid pp 1188–1197.
5 But see *Millenstead v Grosvenor House (Park Lane) Ltd* [1937] 1 KB 717, [1937] 1 All ER 736 where the case was before a judge only and no question of contempt was raised. See also *Monk v Redwing Aircraft Co* [1942] 1 KB 182, [1942] 1 All ER 133 and the *Supreme Court Practice*, 22/7/1.

3　*Mere reference to pending trial, without comment, is not a contempt*

It must not be thought that any reference to a pending trial will amount to contempt. Publications which merely refer to an action which is pending, but without making any comment, are permissible as there is no risk of prejudice at all. In *R v Parke, ex p John Bull Ltd*[6] the *Star* published the following advertisement:

> 'We are requested, by Messrs Beardall & Co, solicitors to the National Cash Register Co, to state that they are taking proceedings against Mr Horatio Bottomley MP, and the proprietors and printers of *John Bull* in respect of a very serious libel that has appeared in this week's issue of *John Bull*.'

The words 'very serious' were inserted in the advertisement by the newspaper, but nevertheless it was held that no contempt had been committed. As Lord Alverstone CJ said:

> 'It seemed to him . . . that for a paper to publish that they had been requested by people named to state that an action was being brought in respect of it, did not come within the class of case in which the interference of this court should be invoked.'

In *R v Fitzhugh, ex p Livingston,*[7] contempt proceedings were brought against the *Evening News*, in respect of a statement, published after a writ for fraud and damages for breach of contract had been issued, which indicated the nature of the writ and gave the names and addresses of the parties, but which made no reference to the facts or details of the action. Lord Hewart CJ dismissed the action with costs and commented that the application ought never to have been made.

4　*Publication of pleadings not necessarily a contempt*

Although there is some support in certain nineteenth century cases[8] for the proposition that publication of pleadings automatically amounts to contempt, the better view is that unless the pleadings can be regarded as confidential (for example where the case itself will be heard in private[9]) such publications will only be a contempt if they create the requisite degree of risk of prejudice. As Lord Hewart CJ commented in *R v Associated Newspapers Ltd, ex p Beyers:*[10]

> 'it . . . might be perilous for a newspaper to publish a pleading or a summary of the pleadings in an action which was pending . . . but every case must be judged on its own particular facts.'

In *Gaskell and Chambers Ltd v Hudson Dodsworth & Co* Du Parcq J rejected the contention that the publication of a statement of claim must always amount to contempt, saying:[11] 'Publication of pleadings in an action may in certain circumstances amount to a contempt of court, while in other circumstances it may not.' He added:

6　(1909) Times, 27 July.
7　(1937) 81 Sol Jo 258. If the cause of action is described, care should be taken to describe it accurately since a misstatement could be prejudicial.
8　*Re Cheltenham and Swansea Railway Carriage and Wagon Co* (1869) LR 8 Eq 580 and *Re O'Connor, Chesshire v Strauss* (1896) 12 TLR 291.
9　Eg in children cases, discussed in Ch 8. Juries will not be involved in such proceedings.
10　(1936) 80 Sol Jo 247.
11　[1936] 2 KB 595 at 601.

'The pleading which was published was the pleading of the opposite side. It would seem rather absurd in most cases, I will not say in all cases, to say that the fair trial of the action was likely to be prejudiced, because one party to it showed to members of the public what was being said against himself by the other party.'

Gaskell's case, however, involved a publication by one of the parties—the position may be different where a third party (for example a newspaper) publishes one side's pleadings. If a newspaper had published the plaintiff's statement of claim in *Gaskell*'s case it might have been open to the defendants to argue that the trial could have been prejudiced against him. Clearly, to publish both parties' pleadings is not so likely to prejudice the trial as to publish just one party's pleadings.

It may also be a contempt for one side to publish his own pleadings if, for example, it is the plaintiff's intention to libel the defendant in his statement of claim. As Goddard J, said in *Gaskell and Chambers Ltd*:[12]

'The court will not allow its process to be made the vehicle of libel upon other persons, and . . . if the litigant uses the process as a means of disseminating a libel, the court will not put the injured person to the expense and delay of bringing an action to remedy the injury, but will, if asked to do so, interfere in a summary way by treating it as a contempt of court to use its process as a means of disseminating libels.'

5 Publications less at risk if published long before the trial

As it must be shown that there is a real (at common law) or substantial (under the 1981 Act) risk of prejudicing proceedings, there may be no contempt if comment is published so far in advance of the trial that it is likely to be forgotten by the jury. In civil proceedings of course the time between the issue of the writ and any subsequent court hearing can be significant. It is certainly likely to be some months and can be some years.[13]

In *Ex p The Standard*[14] during the pendency of libel actions brought by London County Councillors against the proprietors of the *Standard* newspaper, a well known Member of Parliament commented in a speech, 'What is the charge against these 12 councillors? I know it to be, as well as we all know it to be, unfounded, unfair and untrue.' He continued:

'I demand a justification of what has been said because I have memories . . . of the old *Standard*, against us politically, but a fair, honourable, decent, upright newspaper that would not condescend to the mischievous slander that has been produced by that paper today, but which it cannot justify by the test of evidence.'

Clearly, these comments could impair the impartiality of a jury—they not only disparaged the *Standard* but assumed that its owners would lose the libel actions brought against them. However, it was held by Darling J that, reprehensible though the comments may have been, there was no contempt. He observed that:

12 Ibid at 603. See also *Bowden v Russell* (1877) 46 LJ Ch 414 and see the discussion at pp 111–112 of the first edition of this work.
13 For the likely time scale involved see *Judicial Statistics,* Annual Report (1994, Cmnd 2891): the average waiting time on actions in the Queen's Bench Division, other than personal injury actions, in 1994 (based on a sample in February and November) was 177 (137 between issue of writ and setting down) weeks between the issue of the writ and the start of the trial or disposal of the case.
14 (1907) Times, 28 January; see also *Re Ehrmann* (1909) Times, 18 February and *R v Fox, ex p Mosley* (1966) Times, 17 February.

'they must consider whether [the comments] would be likely to influence the jury, so that they might not come to the case inclined to do justice fairly. That must always depend upon the expressions used, and, he thought, partly upon the nearness of the trial.'

He pointed out that the speech was made very early on in the proceedings (in fact the day after the issue of the writ).

More modern cases continue to support the general standpoint. For example, in the Australian decision, *Brych v The Herald and Weekly Times Ltd*,[15] Anderson J commented:

'Remoteness of the date of the trial may thus render the damage which might be caused by the words complained of negligible or non-existent depending on a variety of different circumstances.'

He dismissed the committal application made in respect of two articles published a fortnight after the issue of a writ, commenting inter alia:[16]

'The fear expressed . . . that a person, later to be selected as a juror in the libel action, might have engraved on his memory to the prejudice of the plaintiff the two articles complained of is, to my mind, so remote as to fit comfortably, with room to spare, within the de minimis principle mentioned by Lord Reid [in the *Sunday Times* case].'

The time factor was also a reason for holding there not to be a contempt in *R v Bulgin, ex p BBC*.[17] In that case the contention was that the two assessors sitting with the county court judge might have been influenced by the newspaper article complained of but Lord Widgery CJ did not think they would carry forward an impression created by an article in a newspaper from several months before.

The period of time, at least 11 months, which would elapse before the hearing of the action was the reason why the Court of Appeal found that there was no substantial risk of serious prejudice by influencing jurors in *A-G v News Group Newspapers Ltd*.[18] An action for libel had been commenced by a famous cricketer in respect of articles in the *Mail on Sunday* alleging that he had taken drugs, supplied drugs to girls whom he encouraged to have sex with him and generally 'behaved in an unseemly manner'[19] during a test match in New Zealand. The case was set down for trial no earlier than March 1987 and in April 1986 another newspaper, the *News of the World* published an article under the headline 'He snorted drugs on pitch. Botham Cocaine and Sex Scandal'. A further article along the same lines was planned for the following Sunday and the Attorney General applied for a prior restraint order prohibiting the paper from publishing allegations substantially the same as those in the original *Mail on Sunday* features.[20] In the Court of Appeal Sir John Donaldson MR considered at length the meaning of the words 'substantial risk' and 'seriously impeded and prejudiced' in s 2 (2)[1] and concluded, as did the other members of the court, that in the time elapsing before the trial 'many wickets will have fallen, not to mention much water having flowed under many bridges', and the impact of the publication would be blunted.

---

15 [1978] VR 727 at 731 (Victoria Sup Ct).
16 Ibid at 734.
17 (1977) Times, 14 July.
18 [1987] QB 1, [1986] 2 All ER 833.
19 In the words of Sir John Donaldson MR, ibid at p 6 and 835.
20 For prior restraint orders see Ch 12.
 1 See Ch 4, p 114.

The Attorney General therefore failed to obtain an injunction as the court did not consider that the statutory test was satisfied. The case illustrates once again the somewhat arbitrary nature of decisions made on the basis of what 12 unknown persons might or might not be expected to recall about what they had read in the tabloid press 11 months earlier.

Despite the foregoing authority it cannot be said that comment made early in the proceedings can *never* be a contempt. Much must depend upon the nature and context of the publication and the interest in the particular litigation. Although it is more likely, for example, that trenchant comments about a libel action involving a national figure will be remembered than comment upon an action involving a relatively unknown figure, *A-G v News Group Newspapers* shows that mere repitition of material which has already attracted widespread publicity will not necessarily be a contempt however famous the persons concerned. Secondly, there is a danger that the repeating of comments might produce a cumulative effect and are therefore more likely to prejudice the case, even if repeated early in the proceedings. Darling J commented in *Ex p The Standard*:[2]

> '. . . no one else must suppose for a moment that this decision in this case or any other gave freedom of discussion of cases before the courts. Each case of this kind when it comes before them would be judged on its merits and to his mind the repeating of such arguments as these when they had been advanced by others would give strong reason for thinking that such repetition would be more likely to result in causing prejudice to a fair trial than the original utterance.'

Particular problems arise in respect of defamation actions where a publication may not be so much a comment or discussion of proceedings as a reiteration of the material which is alleged to be libellous. The questions which arise are whether the mere repetition of the alleged libel prejudices the jury and how far the issue of a writ can 'gag' the press.

Even in cases not involving a jury, comment made early in the proceedings may be considered a contempt either as unduly interfering with the parties' freedom in pre-trial negotiations or for otherwise infringing the 'prejudgment test'.[3]

6 *Defamation actions and the problem of 'gagging' writs*

The fact that publications which create a risk of prejudice to particular proceedings can be a contempt of court has led to the problem of so-called 'gagging writs'. A 'gagging writ' is one issued with the specific purpose of stifling comment rather than with any real intention of bringing any action.[4] Defamation actions, which involve juries, are the most likely subject of gagging writs. As Miller[5] has commented, 'gagging writs' have caused the media some of the most acute and practical problems within the whole law of contempt. A newspaper, for example, having spent many months investigating a particular scandal which is a matter of legitimate public concern (for example manipulation of an insurance company, football bribery or suspected corruption in the police force) may find early in

---

2 (1907) Times, 28 January.
3 According to the *Sunday Times* case [1974] AC 273 discussed at p 204 and pp 221 ff.
4 Normally the writ issued is one for libel. In Australia gagging writs are also known as 'Stop Writs': see *Francis v Herald and Weekly Times Ltd* (1978) 52 ALJ 336.
5 *Contempt of Court* (2nd edn, 1989) p 247.

their campaign that a writ has been issued against them so presenting them with the problem of not only having to face the laws of defamation but also those of contempt.

The 1981 Act ameliorated the problem by limiting the period during which proceedings are sub judice for the purpose of the strict liability rule to the time when the proceedings are 'active'. Proceedings in the High Court become active when the case has been set down for trial.[6] Where s 2(2) applies therefore there is no longer a possibility of stifling comment merely by issuing a writ. The Act also altered the position in favour of the media by introducing the stricter test for contempt where the strict liability rule applies and by giving the media the chance of arguing that the comment is part of a discussion of public affairs under s 5.

The problem at common law can, however, be overstated. There seems to be general agreement that a writ issued solely to stifle comment will not have such an effect. Lord Reid said in the *Sunday Times* case[7] that 'a gagging writ ought to have no effect' while in the same case Lord Diplock referred[8] to the 'abuse' of the so-called gagging writs issued for the purpose of preventing repetition of statements that are defamatory but true. It is, however, often very difficult for the media to judge whether or not the proceedings are genuine. For example, in the course of its *Reference on Defamation* the Australian Law Reform Commission obtained information as to the number of defamation actions commenced and disposed of in a period of three and a half years in a number of jurisdictions in Australia. It found that only 5.4% of the number commenced were set down for hearing and only 3.25% were actually heard. There are many things which deter plaintiffs from continuing with defamation actions[9] and many may have been settled out of court, but the Commission concluded that 'many actions are commenced purely to deter further publication of material critical of the plaintiff'.[10]

One explanation for upholding the propriety of comments in cases where a writ is issued only to stifle comment is that there are no genuine legal proceedings at risk of being interfered with. Such reasoning seems to have been the basis of the decision in *R v Daily Mail, ex p Factor* [11] in which contempt proceedings were brought against the *Daily Mail* for publishing the following article after a writ for libel had been issued against the newspaper:

> 'JACOB FACTOR AND THE *DAILY MAIL*
> A WRIT FOR LIBEL
>
> The British public will be surprised to learn that Jacob Factor, the notorious share-pusher, who found England too hot for him after the Daily Mail exposure, is once again back in London. . . .
>
> We thought we had succeeded in chasing this arch-swindler back to his haunts in America for good, but it appears that he has managed to get into this country again. . . . His fraudulent share dealings have been repeatedly exposed in this newspaper and in our courageous contemporary *Truth*.
>
> If Jacob Factor imagines that the issuing of the writ will muzzle us while he is engaged on some new deal he is labouring under a misapprehension.'

---

6 S 2(3) and Sch 1, paras 12–14; for a discussion of the timing provisions, see Ch 7.
7 [1974] AC 273 at 301.
8 Ibid at 312.
9 Not the least of which, in England and Wales, is the lack of legal aid for defamation proceedings.
10 See the Australian Law Reform Commission Report No 11, *Unfair Publication: Defamation and Privacy*, (1979, AGPS, Canberra) para 53 and Law Reform Commission of Australia Report No 35, *Contempt*, (1987, AGPS, Canberra) paras 335–336.
11 (1928) 44 TLR 303.

In dismissing the motion for contempt it was held that the issue of the writ by Factor was not genuine, since no proceedings had been brought in respect of other similar articles in the past, and in any case the writ itself was very carefully phrased so that it did not actually deny the contention that the plaintiff was defrauding people all over the country. Lord Hewart CJ concluded:[12]

> 'The court was not satisfied that the article . . . coming as it did, after a long series of similar articles, being but a repetition of charges already made against Factor and not complained of . . . was calculated to prejudice the trial of the only issues which Factor had chosen to raise.'

Significantly he said that the dismissal of the action was not to be taken as authorising the *Daily Mail* to publish further and different charges against Factor up to the trial of the action, if it should be proceeded with.

A similar view was taken in *R v Fox, ex p Mosley*.[13] In 1962 Sir Oswald Mosley brought libel proceedings against the BBC in respect of an item broadcast on the television programme *Panorama*. The statement of claim was delivered in December 1962 and the BBC delivered its defence in February 1963, but no further action was taken. In November 1965 the *Radio Times* published an article previewing a programme entitled *The Thirties in Britain*, and Mosley claimed that the article was prejudicial to the pending libel proceedings. The action for contempt which Mosley brought against the BBC was dismissed, inter alia because it was held that he had no intention of pursuing the libel proceedings any further, having taken no action for over two years after the defence had been delivered: Mosley's sole object in bringing the contempt proceedings was to allow him to voice his views and not to have to justify his reputation in court.

From the media's point of view the drawback of upholding the propriety of comment upon the basis that there are no genuine proceedings to protect is that it is difficult to determine whether there is a real intention to pursue the action. There are, however, other cases which put the immunity from contempt on a somewhat wider basis. One line of cases has considered the rule in *Bonnard v Perryman*.[14] This says that where a defendant to a defamation action intends to plead justification the courts will not grant an injunction to restrain the defendant from repeating the allegations. The question therefore arises whether the contempt rules prevent the repetition of the alleged libel in those circumstances. In *Thomson v Times Newspapers Ltd*[15] Salmon LJ emphatically stated:

> 'It is a widely held fallacy that the issue of a writ automatically stifles further comment. There is no authority that I know of to support the view that further comment would amount to contempt of court. Once a newspaper has justified, and there is some prima facie support for the justification, the plaintiff cannot obtain an interlocutory injunction to restrain the defendants from repeating the matters complained of. In these circumstances it is obviously wrong to suppose that they could be committing a contempt by doing so. It seems to me equally obvious that no other newspaper that repeats the same sort of criticism is committing a contempt of court. They may be publishing a libel, and if they do so, and they have no defence to it, they will have to pay whatever may be the appropriate damages; but the writ does not, in my view, preclude the publication of any further criticism;

12   (1928) 44 TLR 303 at 307.
13   (1966) Times, 17 February.
14   [1891] 2 Ch 269.
15   [1969] 3 All ER 648 at 651. See also *The Law of Contempt as it Affects Tribunals of Inquiry* (1969, Cmnd 4078, under the chairmanship of Salmon LJ).

it merely puts the person who makes the further criticism on risk of being sued for libel.'[16]

The relationship between contempt and *Bonnard v Perryman* was discussed in *A -G v News Group Newspapers Ltd*,[17] the Ian Botham libel case. The defence argued that an injunction should not to be granted to the Attorney General on the grounds inter alia:

(i) that a publisher who asserts credibly that the publication can be justified requires special consideration in the context of an application to commit for contempt or for an interlocutory injunction to restrain publication;

(ii) that this consideration involves weighing in the balance the desirability of ensuring freedom of expression against the right of litigants to have their litigation tried without outside interference;

(iii) where this special consideration arises the balance will come down in favour of publication where the publication takes place, or will take place, before the proceedings come into the jury list.

Despite these arguments the Court of Appeal held that the rule in *Bonnard v Perryman* did not mean that a repetition of the alleged libel could not be a contempt. Parker LJ said:[18]

'If the court is satisfied that the threatened publication would be a contempt, ie would, if made, create a substantial risk etc, and the defendant cannot make out a defence under the Act, the court will in my view necessarily grant relief because to refuse it would license the commission of a criminal offence. The fact, if it be a fact, that the plaintiff could not himself obtain the relief is neither here nor there.'

Sir John Donaldson MR looked at the relationship in the light of the provisions of the 1981 Act. He said that the relationship seemed to have been changed by the Act:[19]

'The strict liability rule is quite as important as the rule in *Bonnard v Perryman* and each depends on wholly distinct, if potentially conflicting, considerations. However, if and in so far as [the Attorney General's] submissions might suggest that the strict liability rule is paramount, I do not think that this was necessarily true prior to the passing of the 1981 Act and, in theory, some such balancing operation as is indicated by the first three submissions of counsel for the defendants could still be called for. In practice I think that the rule in *Bonnard v Perryman* will be decisive unless and until the strict liability rule is invoked. Once it is invoked it will prevail, because, in the form in which it survives in the 1981 Act, if strictly construed and applied, the balance must always come down on the side of protecting the right to justice.'

In explaining this the Master of the Rolls referred to s 5 of the Act and said that he knew of no reported authority which would have led the courts to refuse to order prior restraint on the ground of a general public interest in allowing *general* discussion of the topic in circumstances which would not be protected by s 5. He pointed out that the Act only applied the strict liability rule to 'active' proceedings. Furthermore, s 2(2) laid down a double test which had to be satisfied

---

16 See also *Re Labouchere, Kensit v Evening News Ltd* (1901) 18 TLR 208; *Phillips v Hess* (1902) 18 TLR 400; *Cronmire v The Daily Bourse* (1892) 9 TLR 101.
17 [1987] QB 1, [1986] 2 All ER 833.
18 Ibid at 18 and 843.
19 Ibid at 14 and 840–841.

before there could be prior restraint. Given that these conditions were fulfilled he said:[20]

> 'I find it hard to think of any circumstances in which the conduct complained of would not, prior to 1981, have been held to be a contempt or, if it was only apprehended, in which prior restraint would not have been ordered. Accordingly, for practical purposes, those who are asked to make orders for prior restraint can, save in extraordinary circumstances, decide the matter solely by reference to the 1981 Act.'

He concluded that the rule in *Bonnard v Perryman* should therefore be put on one side and the case decided purely by reference to s 2(2) of the Act.

While the decision in *A-G v News Group Newspapers* as regards *Bonnard v Perryman* deprives the defendant of one advantage of pleading justification[1] it is not a judgment which is necessarily inimical to the media because, instead of looking at one issue, it takes a considered view of what the words 'substantial risk' and 'serious prejudice' really mean and takes a robust attitude of the susceptibility of jurors. There were, moreover, always problems as to whom, and for how long, the rule in *Bonnard v Perryman* applied. It was doubtful, whether, as Salmon LJ intimated in *Thomson v Times Newspapers*, such a defence is available to publishers other than the defendant who repeated the comment.[2] Furthermore Salmon LJ put no apparent time limit on when repeated comment can be published with immunity although in one decision[3] it was suggested that comments made 'especially on the eve of the trial' can amount to contempt.

Where defamation actions are concerned it appears always to have been assumed that repeating the alleged libel can, depending on the facts of the case such as the length of time before the trial,[4] amount to contempt as a prejudgment of the merits which is likely to influence the jury. This begs the question of how and why the jury is at risk of being prejudiced even if the allegations are repeated close to the trial. Jurors may have read the original publication (although they may well be taken to have forgotten it) and during the trial they will certainly read it. It is not like the accused's previous convictions in a criminal trial which will not normally be disclosed to the jury before their verdict. Is the problem that reading the material before the trial, outside the courtroom, they will already have made up their minds about its truth or falsehood before counsel seek to persuade them to their client's view? Or is there thought to be a cumulative effect, so that jurors reading the same comments over and over again may become convinced one way or the other by a kind of process of attrition?[5] Mere repetition of the original libel is, it is submitted, of less risk to the proceedings than is a publication which comments on the merits of the parties' claims or which publishes material which makes *other* allegations about a party which would cause a juror to think ill of them. *A-G v Hislop* [6] is an outstanding example of this,

20 Ibid at 15 and 841.
 1 Pleading justification can be a dangerous strategy because if the defence fails it may be taken as aggravating the injury to the plaintiff and so result in a higher award of damages.
 2 Repeated comment might produce the cumulative effect of prejudice referred to in *Ex p The Standard* (1907) Times, 28 January and there may be no immunity if the writ has caused the repeated comment.
 3 *R v Blumenfeld, ex p Tupper* (1912) 28 TLR 308.
 4 As in *Ex p The Standard* (1907) Times, 28 January, and *A-G v News Group Newspapers Ltd* [1987] QB 1, [1986] 2 All ER 833.
 5 See *Ex p The Standard* (1907) Times, 28 January for comments on the culmulative effect of prejudice.
 6 [1991] 1 QB 514, [1991] 1 All ER 911, discussed at pp 207 ff.

for the magazine did something more damaging than repeating the alleged libel—it alleged that the plaintiff was guilty of perjury, fraud and was privy to serial murder.

However, whether or not a publication goes further than simply repeating the alleged libel may be a difficult judgment. *Higgins v Richards* [7] is a good example of where there was both repetition and comment and where contempt was found. In September the Chief Constable of Neath issued a writ for libel against the editor and the proprietor of the *Neath News* in respect of an article criticising in general the action of Neath Police and, in particular, the personal conduct of the Chief Constable during a riot. The following December, and prior to the hearing, the newspaper published further articles in respect of which contempt proceedings were brought. The first article commented:

> 'I informed the editor of my resolve to resign my position as the "Quill" of the *Neath News* unless I was given a free hand and was allowed to make public the recent disgraceful "carryings on" of certain members of the borough police force. The result is, I have been given considerably more freedom. I therefore take this opportunity of informing my readers that the editor no longer intends to be intimidated and indefinitely muzzled by a 10s 6d writ. I am in a position to lay bare the facts of an astounding borough police scandal. The story is revolting and utterly degrading.'

Bray J held that this showed:

> 'that the editor deliberately allowed these articles to be put in, and, knowing his duty, deliberately elected to run the risk of contravening the plaintiff's rights.'

A further article commented:

> 'A Great Sensation—The recent developments in the *Neath News v the Police* case or the *Neath News v the Watch Committee* case have created almost unprecedented local interest. Everybody is talking about the extraordinary attitude adopted by the Watch Committee, and public feeling is strongly in support of the editor and the stand he has made for that which is right.'

This latter article assumed that the newspaper was fully supported by the public and Bray J had no doubt that contempt had been committed holding moreover that it was the editor's intention to influence the jury. For this contempt the editor was imprisoned.

It is important to discern the distinctions between *Higgins v Richards* and those cases accepting the propriety of repeated criticisms following the issue of the writ. The significant factors in *Higgins v Richards* seem to be that the articles commented trenchantly on the proceedings as well as repeating the criticisms of the police and that it was found that the editor *intended* to prejudice the proceedings. It should also be noted that the defendants had not sworn that they would plead justification at the libel proceedings. Moreover there was no doubt that the matter was intended to go to trial and this was not, therefore, a gagging writ.

Before the 1981 Act reduced the period during which unintentional contempt can be committed[8] Lord Denning MR, in *Wallersteiner v Moir*,[9] attempted

---

7   (1912) 28 TLR 202.
8   See Ch 7.
9   [1974] 3 All ER 217 at 230, [1974] 1 WLR 991 at 1004, 1005. For a criticism of this decision see Farrar and Lowe, 'Fraud, Representative Actions and the Gagging Writ' (1975) 38 MLR 455 at 456–458. Lord Denning MR repeated his comments in *A-G v BBC* [1981] AC 303 at 315–316.

to justify the propriety of continued comment following the issue of a writ, saying:

> 'I know that it is commonly supposed that once a writ is issued, it puts a stop to discussion. If anyone wishes to canvass the matter in the press or in public, it cannot be permitted. It is said to be "sub judice". I venture to suggest that it is a complete misconception. The sooner it is corrected, the better. If it is a matter of public interest, it can be discussed at large without fear of thereby being in contempt of court. Criticisms can continue to be made and be repeated. Fair comment does not prejudice a fair trial.'

The need to balance the 'public interest' in the right of free speech against a fair trial is a reiteration of his judgment in the *Sunday Times* [10] case which was rejected by the House of Lords. Lord Reid stated[11] that although there could be a balance of such interests in the case of publications likely to affect the mind of a litigant there was an absolute prohibition on comments likely to affect the minds of witnesses and of the tribunal. Since a libel action is likely to involve a jury there is a risk of influencing the tribunal and Lord Reid said that in cases involving witnesses or a jury 'even fair and temperate criticism might be likely to affect the minds of some of them so as to involve contempt'. It will also be remembered that in *A-G v News Group Newspapers* [12] the Court of Appeal gave precedence to the protection of the trial, with Sir John Donaldson MR saying that 'where the strict liability rule under the 1981 Act applies' the balance must always come down on the side of protecting the right to justice'. In that case the Master of the Rolls referred to Lord Denning's words in *Wallersteiner v Moir* and said in particular that the remark 'Fair comment does not prejudice a fair trial' was far too general a statement. He warned against taking sentences from the judgment and treating them as a considered and comprehensive statement of the law and pointed out that *Wallersteiner v Moir* was a case in which the court was reacting strongly to an extreme example of a 'gagging writ'.

On the other hand, in *A-G v News Group Newspapers* the Master of the Rolls laid stress on the role of s 5 of the Act which protects the discussion of public affairs and, given its generous interpretation by the House of Lords in *A-G v English,* [13] s 5 can be seen as the final death knell of the 'gagging writ' so far as 'public affairs' and 'matters of general public interest' are concerned.[14]

One particular feature of defamation actions, which clouds the issues of contempt and 'gagging writs', is the relationship between the parties concerned. The person who may be committing contempt by commenting on the proceedings and creating a risk of prejudice may be the defendant to the defamation action. This is different from a situation where the press is discussing an action between two separate parties. It is natural that the courts will be concerned about cases such as *A-G v Hislop* and *Higgins v Richards* in which the defendants can be seen as using their own publications to create a risk of prejudice against the plaintiff.

As the foregoing discussion shows, even at common law a writ which is truly a 'gagging writ', in that its sole purpose is to stifle further comment, is unlikely to be effective. The time limits for contempt in the 1981 Act, the new test and the enactment of s 5 have further reduced the problem where the statutory rule

---

10   [1973] 1 All ER 815 at 822.
11   [1974] AC 273 at 296C–D.
12   [1987] QB 1, [1986] 2 All ER 833 discussed at p 192.
13   [1983] 1 AC 116; see pp 175 ff.
14   The difficulty, particularly in defamation actions, is to decide what those phrases cover.

applies. One problem which remains, however, is that *if* and insofar as the prejudgment test as laid down by the House of Lords in the *Sunday Times* case[15] has survived the Act,[16] then, as the Phillimore Committee pointed out,[17] the risk of comment once a writ has been issued being held in contempt has arguably become greater. Moreover, in jurisdictions where the common law continues to apply, it is likely that a 'gagging writ' will remain a potent weapon because of the problems in proving that the proceedings *were* issued only to stifle comment.

B   Civil cases where there is no jury

In cases without a jury it will be difficult to show that a publication creates a real risk of jeopardising the impartiality of the court. It is only in the rarest circumstance that a publication, even in theory, could be considered likely to influence the first instance or appellate judges in a civil action.

In *Re William Thomas Shipping Co Ltd, HW Dillon & Sons Ltd v The Co* [18] Maugham J commented in relation to Chancery judges (at a time when there was more likely to be a jury in Queen's Bench cases):

'There is an atmosphere in which a common law judge approaches the question of contempt somewhat differently from that in which a judge who sits in this Division [ie Chancery] has to approach it. The common law judge is mainly thinking of the alleged contempt on the mind of the jury and also, I think, he has to consider the effect or the possible effect of the alleged contempt in preventing witnesses from coming forward to give evidence. In these days, at any rate, a judge who sits in this Division is not the least likely to be prejudiced by statements published in the Press as to the result of cases which are coming before him. He has to determine the case on the evidence, of course, and with regard to principles of law as he understands them, and the view of a newspaper, however intelligently conducted it may be, cannot possibly affect his mind.'

With the general demise of trial by jury in civil actions similar considerations now apply in the Queen's Bench Division except that there may still be a greater concern in the Queen's Bench Division over witnesses. As Buckley J said in *Vine Products Ltd v Green*:[19]

'although I suppose there might be a case in which the publication was of such a kind that it might even be thought that it would influence the mind of a professional judge, it has been generally accepted that professional judges are sufficiently well equipped by their professional training to be on their guard against allowing any such matter as this to influence them in deciding the case.'

The accepted immunity to influence of professional judges does not necessarily apply, for example, to assessors appointed to sit with High Court or county court

15 [1974] AC 273.
16 See pp 117 ff.
17 (1974, Cmnd 5794) para 85.
18 [1930] 2 Ch 368 at 373. See also *Metropolitan Music Hall Co v Lake* (1889) 58 LJ Ch 513 and *Grimwade v Cheque Bank Ltd* (1897) 13 TLR 305.
19 [1966] Ch 484 at 496, approved by Lord Denning MR in *A-G v BBC* [1981] AC 303 at 312 and 315–316. See also Lord Denning MR in *Re F (Orse A) (Publication of Information)* [1977] Fam 58 at 88; Lord Reid in the *Sunday Times* case [1974] AC 273 at 298A; *Schering Chemicals Ltd v Falkman Ltd* [1982] QB 1 at 29, [1981] 2 All ER 321 at 335 (per Shaw LJ); Lord Bridge in *Re Lonrho Plc* [1990] 2 AC 154 at 209–210; in Australia see, eg *Watts v Hawke, and David Syme & Co Ltd* [1976] VR 707 at 719 per Kaye J; and see also the cases discussed in Ch 5, pp 124 ff.

judges.[20] Accordingly, where such assessors are appointed there is a greater risk of influencing the court and publishers should be wary of this possibility. Apart from this circumstance it is unlikely that a publication will be considered a contempt on the grounds of influencing a judge.[1]

Although the judiciary can generally be regarded as not being at risk of influence by media comment this should not be taken to mean there is a carte blanche for publishers to comment on pending civil proceedings. The matters discussed below must also be taken into account.

C Tribunal proceedings

Some tribunals are 'courts' for the purposes of the contempt of court rules.[2] In *Pickering v Liverpool Daily Post and Echo Newspapers Plc* [3] the House of Lords considered whether members of a mental health review tribunal could be influenced by the media. Lord Bridge, giving the judgment, said in respect of both the members and the medical witnesses appearing before them that he did not, of course, expect them to allow their judgment to be consciously influenced. He continued, however:

'But it by no means follows from this that a media campaign against the release of a patient who has applied for his discharge will not create a substantial risk of serious prejudice to the course of justice in proceedings before the tribunal.'

It is difficult to see how the prejudice could occur if the members of the tribunal and the witnesses were not affected. It may be that Lord Bridge was thinking of them being *subconsciously* affected.

III DETERRING OR INFLUENCING WITNESSES

One reason why there is not a carte blanche to comment upon pending civil actions even if they are heard by judge alone is that in principle, as Buckley J said in *Vine Products Ltd v Green*,[4] it is a contempt if a publication is:

'likely to interfere with the proper adducing of evidence in the case either by discouraging witnesses from coming forward or by influencing them in some way in the kind of evidence that they are prepared to give'.

---

20 The power to appoint assessors is provided by s 70(1) of the Supreme Court Act 1981 and by s 63(1) of the County Courts Act 1984. For a contempt prosecution against a publication upon proceedings involving assessors, see *R v Bulgin, ex p BBC* (1977) Times, 14 July, discussed at p 188.

1 Under RSC Ord 22, r 7 there must be no disclosure to the court that the defendant has paid money into court. This is discussed in respect of contempt and jury trials at p 184. It is possible that it could also be contempt in a case where proceedings are tried by judge alone. RSC Ord 59, r 12 forbids disclosure that there was payment into court where the case goes on appeal to the Court of Appeal.

2 *Pickering v Liverpool Daily Post and Echo Newspapers plc* [1991] 2 AC 370, [1991] 1 All ER 622; *Peach Grey & Co (a firm) v Sommers* [1995] 2 All ER 513; for a discussion of the definition of a court under s 19 of the Contempt of Court Act 1981, see pp 486 ff.

3 [1991] 2 AC 370 at 426, [1991] 1 All ER 622 at 637.

4 [1966] Ch 484 at 495. See also *Tichborne v Mostyn* (1867) LR 7 Eq 55n where Wood V-C commented that the court had a duty to punish a publication which: 'can affect the minds of persons who might be willing to give evidence in the case, and may prevent them from coming forward when they will find that they will expose themselves to criticisms'.

A   Criticising witnesses

Witnesses may be reluctant to give evidence and that reluctance will only be increased if, pending the giving of evidence, they are subjected to personal criticism. The leading case is *Re Doncaster and Retford Co-operative Societies Agreement*,[5] where, some two months before the hearing of an action concerning a boundary agreement between the members of the Doncaster and Retford Co-operative Societies, the *Co-operative News* published an article commenting inter alia:

> 'One of the most disturbing aspects of this case is the probability that the chief officials of a number of societies will give evidence for the State against boundary agreements which in practice means against the Co-operative Union, which is carrying out Congress policy on this matter. . . . The fact, however, that a number of societies are now prepared to hit back at Congress decisions in the courts and to make co-operative policy a matter of public rather than of domestic discussion, poses the very serious question whether internal dissension will not cause more harm to the movement than all the overt hostility throughout the last century.'

Diplock J considered the article to be a serious contempt of court, being an 'obviously serious attempt to influence the evidence given before the court', and amounting to an attempt to intimidate witnesses. He said that everyone:

> 'must understand that witnesses who are called to give evidence in the courts, including this court [the Restrictive Practices Court], are performing a public duty, and that they are entitled to give their evidence without any shadow of interference from anyone.'

B   Criticising parties

Public criticism of witnesses is the most obvious and direct way of deterring or influencing them but it is not the only way. Publications which criticise a party have been impugned because of their possible effect upon witnesses. Attacks upon a party to an action can be read as implied attacks upon anyone (ie witnesses) supporting that party. A good example is *Hutchinson v Amalgamated Engineering Union, Re Daily Worker*.[6] The plaintiff sought an injunction against the AEU restraining the union from removing him as President, after having exhausted his right of appeal to the Union 'courts'. While the action was pending the *Daily Worker* commented:

> 'Not only will the appeals [to the Final Court of Appeal of the Union] be discussed [in a court of law] but the action of people seeking a further Court of Appeal at the hands of capitalist judges will also be discussed. At some future day the members will have an opportunity to ratify the decision of the Final Appeal Court [ie of the Union]. They will no doubt have no mercy upon those who seek to upset working class decisions in the capitalist courts.'

---

5   [1960] LR 2 RPC 129 (*Practice Note*). See also *Littler v Thomson* (1839) 2 Beav 129; *Felkin v Herbert* (1864) 33 LJ Ch 294 and *Tichborne v Mostyn* (1867) LR 7 Eq 55n. Cf *Dallas v Ledger, Re Ledger* (1888) 4 TLR 432 where the comment was published *after* the trial. Query whether hostile criticism of witnesses could be a contempt on the wider basis of deterring witnesses generally from giving evidence upon the principle established by *Re A-G's Application, A-G v Butterworth* [1963] 1 QB 696, [1962] 3 All ER 326 discussed in Ch 11.
6   (1932) Times, 25 August.

Goddard J held that the tenor of the article was to disparage the plaintiff as a litigant in the eyes of its readers, and amounted to contempt because:

> 'nothing [was] more calculated to make persons the plaintiff might desire to call as witnesses hesitate or refuse to give him their assistance: if no mercy was shown to him [ie the plaintiff] what was the probable fate that awaited those who assisted him?'

Another example is *Re Hinde, Thornhill v Steel Morris*.[7] There, a landowner sought an injunction to restrain a vicar from trespassing upon a certain garden. While this action was pending the *Derbyshire Courier* published an article asserting that the real reason for bringing the action was to compel the vicar to resign. The article concluded that the landowner's action was:

> 'the best evidence that the Liberal party is doing the nation a service by freeing it from the despotic rule of landed tyrants. Such people as this landowner are the best helpers in the Liberal cause, and it is not surprising that Liberalism flourishes in the village in question.'

The article was held likely to prejudice the plaintiff since it impugned the plaintiff's motives with 'language of studied offensiveness' and the political issues adverted to in the concluding part of the article were held likely to deter witnesses from supporting the landowner's suit.

C   Prejudging the merits of the action

Prejudging the merits of a case may also create prejudice against one party and thereby deter witnesses from coming forward. As Kaye J put it in the Australian decision, *Watts v Hawke and David Syme & Co Ltd*:[8]

> 'Public aversion towards a litigant can reduce his claim at law to an unpopular one and thereby cause witnesses to be unwilling to testify on his behalf.'

Contempt was held to have been committed at least in part on this basis in *Spurrell v De Rechberg*.[9] While an action was pending to determine the validity of a will, the *Daily News* published an article which included the following comment:

> 'It is contended that a will made under such circumstances is not legal, that it is to be assumed that a woman of 81 three days before her death [at which time she signed the will] acted under undue influence.'

The statement that the will had been made 'under undue influence' was branded by Sir Francis Jeune P as a 'misstatement of some moment' since no such

---

7   (1911) 56 Sol Jo 34. See also *Re Pall Mall Gazette, Jones v Flower and Hopkinson* (1894) 11 TLR 122. For other cases in which a party was disparaged, see *Morgan v Carmarthen Corpn* (1956) Times, 3 March; *R v Daily Herald, ex p Bishop of Norwich* [1932] 2 KB 402; *R v Gossip* (1909) Times, 18 February; *Greenwood v Leather-Shod Wheel Co Ltd* (1898) 14 TLR 241; cf *Oppenheim v Mackenzie* (1898) 42 Sol Jo 748. See also *Michigan (Great Britain) Ltd v Mathew* [1966] RPC 47.

8   [1976] VR 707 at 719. But note the criticism of this case at (1977) 51 ALJ 319. Cf *Burton v Harris* [1979] Qd R 548. See also *Victoria v BLF* (1982) 41 ALR 71 especially at 90–91 per Gibbs CJ.

9   (1895) 11 TLR 313. See also, *Herring v British and Foreign Marine Insurance Co Ltd* (1895) 11 TLR 345; *Fielden v Sweeting* (1895) 11 TLR 534; *Brodribb v Brodribb* (1886) 11 PD 66; *R v Barnado* (1892) Times, 29 November; *Tichborne v Tichborne* (1870) 39 LJ Ch 398.

plea of undue influence had been made by the defendants. It was held moreover that if such an assertion came to the notice of witnesses it might discourage them from coming forward, and the article was therefore held to be a contempt.

How far the courts will be prepared to pursue this line of reasoning must be a matter of some doubt. In *Re Duncan* [10] the *Evening Standard* published an article in which it was stated that the deceased's lawyer described him in a diary as being 'but a shadow of his former self'. Latey J dismissed the argument that the article might have deterred witnesses as 'failing to carry conviction'. In *Vine Products Ltd v Green*,[11] pending an action in which the plaintiffs sought a declaration that they were entitled to sell wine under various descriptions such as 'British Sherry', 'South African Sherry' or 'Cypriot Sherry', the *Daily Telegraph* published an article which after referring to a previous case *Bollinger v Costa Brava Wine Co Ltd* [12] which had decided that the word 'Champagne' meant only a wine produced in the Champagne district of France, concluded:

> 'If the Sherry Shippers' Association intend, as is reported, to bring a test case in defence of their own name, their position must be fundamentally the same [ie as in the Champagne case]. Sherry, to be fully entitled to that name, should come from Jerez (or the closely adjoining winefield of San Lucar, which makes manzanilla). To speak of South African or Cypriot Sherry is as anomalous as to speak of Spanish Champagne.'

Although the article seemed to amount to a prejudgment of the merits of the case Buckley J commented:

> 'I cannot see myself that this article would be likely to deter any witness whom the plaintiffs might want to call from coming to give evidence in the action, or that it would be likely to colour his evidence if he were called.'

It is difficult to disagree with this conclusion. The risk of influencing or deterring witnesses by commenting upon the merits of the action is at best speculative and it can surely only be in more extreme cases (for example where the comment is particularly vituperative or when there has been a concerted public campaign in support of the one side) that a risk of interference with witnesses could be established. At any rate on the strength of *Vine Products Ltd v Green* it seems that the courts will not readily hold that a discussion of the merits of the case carries a significant risk of deterring or influencing witnesses. This view is perhaps strengthened by *Schering Chemicals Ltd v Falkman Ltd* [13] where a film dealing with some of the issues in a forthcoming case was held not to create a risk of influencing witnesses. Buckley J's conclusions in *Vine Products v Green* rendered it unnecessary in that case to rule on the argument that *expert* witnesses

---

10   (1969) Times, 20 May (the better report), (1969) 113 Sol Jo 526. See also *State of Spain v Chancery Lane Safe Deposit and Offices Co Ltd* (1939) 83 Sol Jo 477; *Shaw v India Rubber (Mexico) Ltd* (1900) 44 Sol Jo 295; *Re Gates and London Congregational Union and East London Publishing Co, R v Mead* (1895) 11 TLR 204 where Wills J observed that there was 'No pretence for such an action, and to accede to it in such a case woud be to bring the jurisdiction of the court in such matters into ridicule and contempt'; *Bowden v Russell* (1877) 46 LJ Ch 414; *Fairclough v Manchester Ship Canal Co* (1896) 13 TLR 56, CA; *Re Hooley, ex p Hooley* (1899) 79 LT 706.

11   [1966] Ch 484, [1965] 3 All ER 58. Although this decision was criticised (particularly by Lord Reid) in the *Sunday Times* case [1974] AC 273 no comment was made in relation to the effect of the article upon witnesses.

12   [1961] 1 All ER 561, [1961] 1 WLR 277.

13   [1982] QB 1, [1981] 2 All ER 321. See particularly the comments of Shaw LJ, ibid at 29, 30 and 339 respectively. See also *Pickering v Liverpool Daily Post and Echo Plc* [1991] 2 AC 370 at 425.

are in any event unlikely to be influenced by media comment. Such an argument does seem plausible and it may be that where witnesses at a trial are confined to experts then it will be especially difficult to establish a risk of interference.

D   Trade warnings and contempt

To what extent is a party to a forthcoming action aimed at stopping alleged infringements of patents or trade marks free to warn others (who are potential witnesses in the action) against infringing his rights, when the right itself is the subject of the pending litigation? The generally accepted view is that provided the publication is confined to a warning to other members of the trade then no contempt will be committed. As Chitty J said in *Coats v Chadwick:* [14]

'The plaintiffs are at liberty to warn the trade as much as they like, notwithstanding the pendency of this action; but they are bound to refrain during its pendency from public discussion on the merits or demerits of the case.'

The leading modern case is *Carl-Zeiss-Stiftung v Rayner and Keeler Ltd.*[15] The plaintiffs, an East German company, brought a passing-off action against a company bearing the same name but which was a West German company. A motion to expunge certain trade marks including 'Carl Zeiss Jena' and 'Tessar' which were registered in the name of the West German company, had been brought by CZ Scientific Instruments Ltd, as agents for the East German company. While these actions were pending, the solicitors to the West German company (the defendants) wrote a letter addressed to the editor of a trade journal called the *Optician*, stating:

'It has been brought to our notice that you have published in your issue of the 10th instant an advertisement for Zeiss Binoculars on behalf of CZ Scientific Instruments Ltd. . . . We must inform you that our clients [the West German company] are the registered proprietors of the trade mark No 335738 being the words "Carl Zeiss Jena" as depicted in the lenticular device shown in that advertisement, while CZ Scientific Instruments are the agents of an East German nationalised concern . . . which has no right to use the trade marks of which our clients are the proprietors. We think it right to warn you that our clients will take all legal steps available to them to protect their rights in their registered trade marks.'

A second letter addressed to Dixons Camera Centre in Bristol, read:

'you are advertising for sale cameras with what are stated to have "Tessar" lenses but which are manufactured by an East German nationalised concern. . . . We must inform you that our clients [the West German company] are the registered proprietors of trade mark No 249457, being the word "Tessar". The East German nationalised concern has no right to use any trade mark registered in the name of our clients, and we think it right to warn you that our clients will take all legal steps available to them to protect their rights in their marks . . .'.

It was held that no contempt had been committed. With regard to Chitty J's observation that there was liberty to warn the trade, Russell J observed:

'How can you warn the trade, the retailers, not to sell the products . . . [of the East German company] under these trade marks except in the course of a letter saying

14 [1894] 1 Ch 347 at 350.
15 [1960] 3 All ER 289, [1960] 1 WLR 1145.

"We are entitled to the trade marks" mentioning also expressly that the other side
are not entitled to the trade marks? To go beyond that might come into the field
of discussion of the merits of the case but I cannot bring myself to think that it is
a discussion of the merits of the case to assert that which one is bound to assert in
the course of a warning letter, viz that the writer is entitled to the trade marks and
the other people concerned are not.'

In any event Russell J pointed out that the only way in which proceedings
could have been prejudiced was that the letters in question were:

'intended or likely to deter or discourage witnesses from giving evidence in favour
of the plaintiff in the one proceedings or the applicant in the other proceedings.'

On the facts of the case before him he concluded that witnesses were not at all
likely to be deterred.

A similar conclusion was reached in *Easipower Appliances Ltd and Frederick
Williams (Appliances) Ltd v Gordon Moore (Electrical) Ltd.* [16] While a passing-
off action was pending, the following statement was published in trade journals:

'Disclaimer by blankets manufacturer. The Directors of Easipower Appliances
Ltd wish to make it clear to the trade that the only electric blankets they market
bear the name "DREAMLAND". At the present moment, no other manufacturer
in this country has been given production rights of the patent "Safety Seal" process
which was invented by this company. It has been noticed in the last few days that
a brand of electric blanket has been mentioned in the trade press which the
directors of Easipower Appliances Ltd and their advisers consider could be
mistaken by the public and trade for a "DREAMLAND" product because of the
similarity of name and name-style together with a superficial similarity in
description of the blanket. Easipower Applicances Ltd wish it to be known that
they cherish their trade name and reputation and are not prepared to tolerate an
attempt at "passing-off" another product as a "DREAMLAND" blanket. With this
in mind, the company concerned with a product bearing the name "DREAMTIME"
has been warned that unless there is an immediate change of name, prompt legal
action will be taken with a view to enforcing withdrawal.'

Cross J, held that no contempt had been committed as he was:

'quite unable to see that this statement has any tendency whatever to prejudice the
fair trial of the action or to deter witnesses from coming forward to support the
defendants' case. It seems to me to fall on the right side of the line and to be no
more than what Chitty J described as a warning to the retail trade.'

It will be noted that in both the above cases no attempt was made to *discuss*
the merits of the case and the warnings were published to a limited trade audience.
Both factors may be important limitations in the freedom to warn. With regard
to the former, *Coats (J and P) v Chadwick* [17] perhaps[18] illustrates the danger of
trespassing too far upon the merits of the case. In that case, pending an action for
infringing a trade mark, the plaintiffs sent out the following circular to various
retail dealers:

'We regret to draw your attention to the fact that Messrs James Chadwick and
Brothers Ltd, have recently attempted to injure our trade by adopting a blue label

16 [1963] RPC 8.
17 [1894] 1 Ch 347.
18 The decision was in fact disapproved of in *R v Payne and Cooper* [1896] 1 QB 577 though in
    the *Carl Zeiss* case Russell J was content to treat it as good law. *Chadwick* and other relevant
    cases were thoroughly reviewed in the *Carl Zeiss* case.

for 400 yards six cord which so closely resembles ours as to produce the result of their goods being passed off as ours, nor can there be any doubt that this is intended, as Messrs Chadwick have previously and for a number of years sold their 400 yards six cord with a label of their own which in no way resembles ours. Being apparently unsuccessful in selling this class of goods with their own label, they have now adopted the device of imitating ours in order more readily to find purchasers for their thread. We are determined to use every means in our power to put a stop to unfair competition of this sort, and have therefore commenced proceedings against retail dealers selling goods manufactured by Messrs Chadwick and bearing the blue label which is an imitation of ours. We think it right to warn the trade in general of the course we are pursuing . . .'.

The circular was held to be a contempt and an injunction to restrain its further publication was granted. Chitty J considered the circular to be:

'a strong one-sided statement by one of the parties to the action on the merits of the case which is pending before the courts. It unhesitatingly imputes fraud and dishonesty to the defendants. It charges them, not merely with imitating the plaintiffs' goods but with the deliberate intention of imitating.'

To be safe from the possibility of committing contempt parties should therefore refrain from any disparagement of the defendants and from imputations of dishonesty.

E Advertisements offerings rewards for evidence

It is now established that an advertisement for evidence even if a reward is offered is not per se a contempt. In *Plating Co v Farquharson* [19] two advertisements were published, one appealing for money to pursue an appeal and the other offering a reward for further evidence. The Court of Appeal held[20] that no contempt had been committed since the advertisement contained nothing which could interfere with the course of justice. In *Butler v Butler* [1] Butt J said:

'I doubt very much whether a bona fide attempt to procure evidence in a suit, even by an advertisement offering a reward, is a contempt of court.'

The current position seems to be that such advertisements will only amount to contempt if they are calculated to create the requisite degree of risk of prejudice on the particular facts of the case.[2] Temperately expressed advertisements genuinely published for the purpose of discovering evidence are unlikely to be considered to create a real risk of prejudice.[3]

---

19 (1881) 17 Ch D 49.
20 Rejecting the contention, supported by *Pool v Sacheverel* (1720) 1 P Wms 675, that such advertisements tend to the suborning of witnesses.
1 (1888) 13 PD 73.
2 For examples see *Brodribb v Brodribb* (1886) 11 PD 66 and *Re Cornish, Staff v Gill* (1893) 9 TLR 196.
3 The matter of offers made by the media to witnesses or potential witnesses for their 'stories' is discussed in Ch 11.

IV   PRESSURISING PARTIES

A publication may constitute a contempt because it puts public pressure on a litigant to pursue a certain course of action in relation to legal proceedings in which they are involved. This may be to not insist upon their strict legal rights, for example, or to settle upon certain terms, or generally not to pursue or defend the action. It is possible also to commit contempt by *privately* pressurising a party to proceeedings, and this is discussed in Chapter 11. Here, however, we are concerned with the extent to which influencing parties through the media is legitimate. Restrictions upon this type of publication raise in acute form the perpetual dilemma of reconciling the administration of justice with freedom of the press and reference is often made in this connection to the position of the Venetian press—would it have been contempt for it to have urged Shylock not to insist upon his strict legal rights?[4]

This matter was considered at length by the House of Lords in the *Sunday Times* case.[5] The article in question was the first of a series published by the *Sunday Times* in a campaign to urge Distillers Ltd, regardless of their legal rights, to be generous to the unfortunate children who had been born deformed as a result of the thalidomide drug (which Distillers had marketed in the United Kingdom) taken by their mothers during pregnancy. At the time of this campaign Distillers were involved in pre-trial negotiations to settle claims relating to a number of children and were minded (without admitting negligence) to set up a fund of £3.25 million for their benefit. Under the headlines: 'Our Thalidomide Children: A Cause for National Shame' the article discussed whether those who put drugs on the market ought to be absolutely liable for damage done by them and whether the currently accepted method of assessing damages was inadequate. The sting, however, lay in the following:

> '. . . the thalidomide children shame Distillers. . . . There are times when to insist on the letter of the law is as exposed to criticism as infringement of another's legal rights. The figure in the proposed settlement is to be £3.25 million spread over 10 years. This does not shine as a beacon against pre-tax profits last year of £64.8 million and company assets worth £421 million. Without in anyway surrendering on negligence, Distillers could and should think again.'

The Law Lords were not in agreement as to the propriety of this article. Lord Reid[6] drew a distinction between conduct likely to influence the tribunal hearing the case (such as comment likely to affect the minds of witnesses and jurors) which had to be absolutely prohibited, and conduct influencing litigants, where

---

4   See, eg Lords Reid, Diplock and Simon of Glaisdale in *A-G v Times Newspapers Ltd* [1974] AC 273 and Robertson & Nicol, *Media Law* (3rd edn) p 290.
5   [1974] AC 273. For a similar type of case see in Australia *Fry v Bray* (1959) 1 FLR 366 (Commonwealth Industrial Court). Ironically, in the *Sunday Times* case the deliberations of the Law Lords on this point centred upon the propriety of an article already published by the newspaper which was not the subject matter of the proceedings. It is possible, therefore, to argue that their statements on this point are obiter: cf (in Australia) *Commercial Bank of Australia Ltd v Preston* [1981] 2 NSWLR 554 at 559, 600 where Hunt J considered that the Law Lords were discussing the legitimacy of pressure in the context of the *projected* article. With respect to Hunt J it seems clear that this is not so. In fact the discussion of the earlier article arose because it concerned the propriety of the decision of the Attorney General (whose role in contempt prosecutions was also under review, see Ch 12) to refuse to institute contempt proceedings in respect of it.
6   [1974] AC 273 at 296C–D.

a balance with freedom of speech could and should be drawn so as to allow fair and temperate criticism of a litigant. He said:[7]

'I would hold that as a general rule where the only matter to be considered is pressure put on a litigant, fair and temperate criticism is legitimate, but anything which goes beyond that may well involve contempt of court.'

In Lord Reid's view the above-mentioned article amounted to no more than fair and temperate criticism. Lord Cross agreed, with regard both to the general principle and to the propriety of the published article. With regard to the principle he said:[8]

'To seek to dissuade a litigant from prosecuting or defending proceedings by threats of unlawful action, by abuse, by misrepresentation of the nature of the proceedings or the circumstances out of which they arose and such like is no doubt a contempt of court; but if the writer states the facts fairly and accurately, and expresses his view in temperate language the fact that the publication may bring pressure—possibly great pressure—to bear on the litigant should not make it a contempt of court.'

Though more ambivalent, Lord Morris also seemed to accept the propriety of the published article[9] and considered it unobjectionable to call attention to the financial needs of the children and to inspire an appeal for national financial help or public generosity.[10] He saw:

'no reason why a temperate and reasoned appeal might not have been expressed inviting Distillers to consider whether, quite regardless whether they were in law in any way liable, they should make generous payments on the basis that it was as the result of purchases of that which they had sold that such unfortunate consequences had resulted.'[11]

Lord Diplock, however, considered the article to be a contempt because it held up Distillers to public obloquy for relying in the pending actions on the defence that they were not negligent.[12] In agreeing with this conclusion, Lord Simon thought the published article a contempt because:[13]

'it was intended to interfere with the terms of the settlement by holding Distillers up to execration.'

The majority view of the House of Lords appears to be, therefore, that fair and temperate criticism of a litigant in respect of proceedings in which he is engaged is not a contempt. Lord Simon, however, was not even prepared to draw a simple distinction between public and private pressure upon litigants. In his view[14] even private pressure was acceptable only within narrow limits, namely where there was a common interest such that fair, reasonable and moderate personal

---

7 Ibid at 297H–298A.
8 Ibid at 326B–C.
9 Eg at 306D he said 'Speaking for myself, and having in mind the guidance given in decided cases, I consider that the Attorney General was right in deciding that there was no necessity for him to bring the published articles to the attention of the court by way of complaint.'
10 Ibid at 307A–B.
11 Admittedly his Lordship did not make it clear *in this passage* whether such appeal could be public but given his apparent approval of the published article it seems reasonable to suppose that he was thinking of a public appeal. For a similar conclusion see in Australia *Commercial Bank of Australia Ltd v Preston* [1981] 2 NSWLR 554 at 560 per Hunt J.
12 [1974] AC 273 at 313H–314A.
13 Ibid at 321E.
14 Ibid at 319.

representation would be appropriate. Lord Diplock condemned the article as a contempt because public abuse and public obloquy of a litigant is not to be tolerated, not only on account of the likely effect on that particular litigant but also because future litigants might be dissuaded from enforcing their legal rights if they believed that using the courts would make them a legitimate target of public abuse.[15] He did not, however, consider the position of a publication which did *not* amount to 'public abuse'. This is a significant omission for, as has been noted, he condemned the *Sunday Times* for holding Distillers up to 'public obloquy' although the article in question was written in a measured and restrained way in what was a respected quality newspaper. This suggests that Lord Diplock's attention was fixed, not on the form and content of the publication itself, but on its possible effect on the litigant and that as a consequence the calm tones of the *Sunday Times* were to be classified as 'abuse'. What then, if anything, would constitute 'fair and temperate criticism' in Lord Diplock's estimation?

There is in theory something to be said for this approach if contempt is to do with a risk of prejudice. If that risk, in the shape of influencing the litigant, is created, why should the form of the material which produced that influence matter? However, it is submitted that in this aspect of contempt, if a balance is to be struck between freedom of the press and the administration of justice, the emphasis has to be on the factor that the majority thought decisive, which is the nature of the publication. In the *Sunday Times* case Lord Reid quoted[16] the famous passage from the *Bread Manufacturers* case[17] on the principle that discussion of public affairs should not be stifled just because those matters are the subject of litigation and Lord Cross expressly addressed the point[18] and asked what a layman reflecting on the issue would say, concluding:

> '"Surely" he would say "it ought to depend on the way in which the influence is exerted". That is, I think, the legal position.'

Obviously, the nature of the publication cannot be divorced entirely from its effect on the litigant. However, a well-reasearched and argued article in an influential newspaper may have more effect on the proceedings than a burst of vituperation in the tabloid press. Indeed, the *Sunday Times* article was the start of a campaign 'waged in the press and in Parliament which led to Distillers being forced to offer in settlement ... five or six times as much as they had been offering previously'.[19] When the effect on the litigant is considered the question of whether a subjective or objective standard applies arises, in that litigants, ranging as they do from private individuals to multinational companies, may not be equally susceptible to the same amount of pressure. The point was discussed in *A-G v Hislop* [20] but, for reasons which are explained below, did not have to be decided.

The Phillimore Committee recommended[1] that the matter of pressure on litigants should be dealt with by a statutory provision to the effect that 'conduct directed against a litigant in connection with the legal proceedings in which he is concerned, which amounts to intimidation or unlawful threats to person,

---

15 Ibid at 313E–F.
16 Ibid at 296–297.
17 *Re Truth and Sportsman Ltd, ex p Bread Manufacturers Ltd* (1937) 37 SR NSW 242 at 249–250, discussed in Ch 5, p 171 and at p 232.
18 [1974] AC 273 at 326A–C.
19 Ibid at 325, per Lord Cross.
20 [1991] 1 QB 514, [1991] 1 All ER 911 discussed below.
 1 At para 62.

property or reputation should be capable of being treated as a contempt of court; but that conduct falling short of that should not be a contempt'. Despite this recommendation the Contempt of Court Act 1981 does *not* include any specific provision on the matter. It is submitted, therefore, that the majority view in the *Sunday Times* case that fair and temperate criticism is not contempt, is still the law. Certainly, it must follow from s 6(b) of the Act[2] that the law cannot now be more restrictive than it was before the Act.[3] It would also be in keeping with the spirit of the Act, bearing in mind that it was intended[4] to amend English law so as to comply with the European Court of Human Rights' ruling in the *Sunday Times* case,[5] that the courts should not readily regard public criticism of a litigant for pursuing his legal rights as interfering with the course of justice.[6]

A situation similar to that in the *Sunday Times* case arose in the course of the *Eli Lilley* litigation which concerned the alleged side-effects of the drug Opren and which excited much media comment urging Eli Lilley, the manufacturers, to pay generous compensation. The judge issued a contempt warning to the media over their campaigns saying that 'the advertisements and the press releases might be thought not to be far from the dividing line between legitimate comment and illegitimate pressure' but no contempt proceedings were ever brought.[7] The first case to discuss the issue since the 1981 Act was therefore *A-G v Hislop,*[8] where unfortunately the facts were so extreme that it was not necessary for the court to consider all the facets of the problem. It arose from a libel action brought by Sonia Sutcliffe, the wife of a convicted mass murderer known as the 'Yorkshire Ripper', against *Private Eye* in respect of allegations that Mrs Sutcliffe had sold her story to the *Daily Mail* for a large sum of money. Three months before the trial of this action *Private Eye* published two further articles which implied that Mrs Sutcliffe gave a false alibi for her husband to the police, knew about his activities and furthermore was defrauding the social security system. The articles said that at the libel hearing Mrs Sutcliffe would be able to be cross-examined as to these matters. At first instance the judge held that although the articles were published with the intention of dissuading Mrs Sutcliffe from pursuing her libel action it was not established that there was substantial risk of serious prejudice to the libel action.

The Court of Appeal accepted the judge's finding that there had been an intention to deter Mrs Sutcliffe but disagreed with the finding that there had been no contempt and held *Private Eye* guilty of contempt both at common law, because there was intention to prejudice, and under the strict liability rule. The court stressed that the articles subjected Mrs Sutcliffe to the most serious charges and threatened to confront her with them in the libel action. The articles did not advert directly to the issue at stake in the libel action at all and could not be described as 'fair and temperate criticism' of her in relation to that action. Parker

---

2 This provides that nothing in the Act 'implies that any publication is punishable as contempt of court under [the strict liability rule] which would not be so punishable apart from those provisions'.

3 At least where there is no *intention* to prejudice: see the discussion on this below .

4 See Lord Hailsham: 415 HL Official Report (5th series) col 660.

5 *Sunday Times v UK* [1979] 2 EHRR 245.

6 See also Lowe, 'The English Law of Contempt of Court and Article 10 of the European Convention on Human Rights' in *The Effect on English Domestic Law of Membership of the European Communities and of Ratification of the European Convention on Human Rights* (1983, Nijhoff) 318, 341-342.

7 *Davies v Eli Lilley & Co* (1987) Independent, 23 July, (1987) Times, 23 July.

8 [1991] 1 QB 514, [1991] 1 All ER 911.

LJ described the articles as 'plain abuse'. Whether or not the editor had at the time of publication believed the charges he made against Mrs Sutcliffe to be true was held to be irrelevant.

The *Hislop* case highlights the issue of intention in cases of pressurising litigants. Before the Act, when the *Sunday Times* case was decided, whether or not there was an intention to prejudice went only to matters such as sentencing and not to the actual offence. The Court of Appeal in *Hislop* dealt with the issue of intention because the charge of contempt was of contempt at common law as well as under the strict liability rule. Where there is intention, and therefore the possibility of contempt at common law, two important consequences follow. First, the time limits are different so that contempt can be committed from the time of the issue of the writ rather than from the proceedings becoming 'active' and secondly, the contempt may arise from the risk to the administration of justice generally and not merely from any risk to the particular proceedings.[9]

It can be argued, however, that where the whole point of the publication is to have some effect on what the party does in relation to the proceedings an intention in this regard is inevitable. But does this mean that there is inevitably an intention *to impede or prejudice the administration of justice* within the meaning of s 6(c) of the 1981 Act? This raises the question of exactly what 'impede or prejudice' means. Are proceedings prejudiced because the plaintiff discontinues them? Nicholls LJ thought so in *Hislop* when he said:[10]

> 'The articles were published with the intention of deterring Mrs Sutcliffe from continuing. I see no reason to doubt that there was a substantial risk that Mr Hislop might have succeeded in his aim. Had he done so, the course of justice in Mrs Sutcliffe's action would have been seriously prejudiced, because she would have been deterred from having her defamation claim decided by a judge and jury.'

Equally, proceedings could be said to be 'prejudiced' when the publication causes a litigant to take some action such as settling on particular terms[11] which they would not otherwise have taken.

The answer to this conundrum is that either the concept of 'prejudicing' must be applied in a special way in regard to this kind of contempt or else the question of intention goes not to the result of the publication alone but to its nature. It is submitted that in the light of the majority opinion in the *Sunday Times* and of the judgments in *Hislop* the crucial factor is the nature of the publication. The question is whether those responsible for the publication intend 'fair and temperate' criticism or whether they intend to apply improper pressure. This was recognised in *Hislop* by Parker LJ when he said:[12]

> ' . . . once it is found that the articles were intended by Mr Hislop to deter Mrs Sutcliffe from pursuing her claim the conclusion [that they created a real risk of prejudice] must, as I see it, follow inevitably unless it can be shown that these articles contained no more than fair temperate and *relevant* criticism.' (Parker LJ's emphasis).

The conclusion from this is that if the publication is intended to influence the litigant and amounts to improper pressure then there is a possibility that proceedings may be at risk of being 'prejudiced', whereas an intention to deter will not be contempt if it is done through proper means. Proper means involves

9 See Ch 4.
10 [1991] 1 QB 514, [1991] 1 All ER 911 at 923.
11 Such as in the case of Distillers.
12 [1991] 1 QB 514 at 528.

'fair and temperate' criticism but also criticism which is related to the subject of the proceedings.

The Court of Appeal in *Hislop* concluded, differing from the trial judge, that there was a substantial risk of Mr Hislop succeeding in his aim of deterring Mrs Sutcliffe. There was some discussion about whether the risk had to be judged objectively or subjectively, that is, in respect of Mrs Sutcliffe or of a hypothetical reasonable litigant. The evidence about Mrs Sutcliffe's disposition was conflicting and Parker and McCowan LJJ thought there was no choice but to take the objective approach: they then had no trouble in holding that the articles would have a deterrent effect. Nicholls LJ, however, considered the effect on Mrs Sutcliffe was not important for he followed the point made by Lord Reid and Lord Diplock in the *Sunday Times* case[13] that the mischief in this sort of contempt lies in the deterrent effect it has on *other* litigants. Such an effect could be considered here because the intention to prejudice took the case outside the strict liability rule by virtue of s 6(c) of the 1981 Act and it was therefore unnecessary to show a risk of prejudice to *particular* proceedings. However, if the objection to pressure on litigants is not the effect on *them* but the effect on future would-be litigants, it may be that this type of contempt is not to do with particular proceedings at all but should be looked at as an act which interferes with the course of justice generally.

Nicholls LJ declined to give a view on how the strict liability rule, requiring risk to particular proceedings, would be applied in a case 'where there was evidence that the litigant was so committed to the proceedings that no amount of vilification would deter him'. The disadvantage of a subjective test is that it increases the uncertainty of the law in an area where uncertainty has a restrictive effect on freedom of speech. It is submitted therefore that an objective test is to be preferred. There may indeed be no alternative to an essentially objective test where the litigant is a company and judgments as to its sensitivity or robustnesses cannot sensibly be made. This is not to advocate a blanket test to be applied indiscriminately to all litigants from Distillers to the Mrs Sutcliffes of this world, for the law should assume that companies, although they may well be concerned about their image and reputation, can expect, and are able to withstand, a degree of discussion and criticism of their affairs, whereas a private individual should be considered far more vulnerable. There may need, therefore, to be some difference in the application of an objective test to companies and to individuals. Obviously this is to some extent a crude distinction and some 'private' individuals may have wealth and situation which makes them immune to any pressure (although if they are, in fact, players in the corporate world their position could be treated as analogous to that of a company[14]). What seems to be clear, however, is that the contempt laws cannot and should not turn on assessments about the personalities of individual litigants and their supposed susceptibility to pressure.[15] The media needs clearer guidelines if press freedom is not to be inhibited.

Objections to an objective test based on the wording of s 2(2) of the Act in cases in which the strict liability rule is to be applied can be answered by remembering that the law is concerned with *risk*. Abusive criticism of a private

13 [1974] AC 274 at 295 and 310 respectively.
14 Perhaps James Goldsmith, Rupert Murdoch and Richard Branson could tentatively be offered as examples.
15 In *Re Duncan, Deceased* (1969) Times, 20 May, for example, Latey J decided that the litigant was too determined to succumb to pressure.

litigant must at least run the *risk* of deterrence. Ultimately it must come down to a question of the nature of the contents of the publication. If they amount to what the court deems to be improper pressure then, as can be seen from *Hislop*, the elements of contempt are likely to be found. The real problem remains the central question of what amounts to 'fair and temperate criticism' and what amounts to improper pressure. *Hislop* is of little use here because it was so clearly the latter. One must fall back on saying that the dividing line between what is thought to be fair and temperate and that which is not is a matter for judgment in each case. Looking at past cases there is the example of the comment in *Re William Thomas Shipping Co Ltd* [16] which the majority of the Law Lords in the *Sunday Times* case thought fell on the wrong side of the line. In that case the company had suffered severely from the prevailing depression and debenture holders sought liquidation. The governing director published a statement in a Liverpool newspaper, inter alia, that the appointment of the receiver had 'smashed the goodwill and organisation of the business in one day' and that 'No one in shipping circles can understand this line of conduct'. He did not say that the appointment had been made on the ground of jeopardy, nor did he mention, as was the case, that the company could not have continued its business unless money had immediately been found. Maugham J held that the statements were likely to interfere with the course of justice. They not only misrepresented what took place in court, but also amounted to the suggestion that the plaintiffs had acted with gross impropriety, and were held likely to dissuade the plaintiffs from continuing the action. Accordingly, the director was held to have committed contempt.

The publication in *William Thomas Shipping* could hardly be considered 'fair' as it involved misrepresentations. To fall on the right side of the line a publication should not contain material factual inaccuracies or amount to threats, invective, fraud or intimidation. Those who believe that the law tends to err on the side of caution, however, will not have been encouraged by Hirst J's warning issued over full-page advertisements in the press appealing to Eli Lilley's conscience in connection with the litigation over the damage allegedly caused by their drug, Opren.

Another factor to be taken into account is any role which the authors or publishers of the publication have in the litigation which is being discussed or criticised. In *Hislop*, *Private Eye* was the defendant in the litigation concerned. For the media to attempt to influence the course of proceedings to which it is itself a party by publicly seeking to influence the other side is clearly a different matter from a case such as the *Sunday Times* in which a disinterested third party expresses views on litigation. Even fair and temperate criticism in such a situation would run the risk of being a contempt. Care should also be exercised by the press over litigation involving parties which are part of the same corporate group or media empire.

V   PRE-EMPTION OF LITIGATION BY AFFECTING THE SUBJECT-MATTER OF PROCEEDINGS

Two extraordinary recent cases have raised the question of whether it is a contempt for material to be published which in effect destroys the subject-matter

---

16   [1930] 2 Ch 368. For another example see *Commercial Bank of Australia Ltd v Preston* [1981] 2 NSWLR 554.

of litigation or pre-empts the decision of the court by removing the point of the proceedings. Both cases arose in rather extraordinary circumstances.

A Publishing material which frustrates an order made in litigation between third parties

This was the issue which arose in the first case, which was really a series of actions: *A-G v Newspaper Publishing Plc,* [17] *A-G v Newspaper Publishing plc* [18] and *A-G v Times Newspapers Ltd,*[19] which were part of the notorious *Spycatcher* affair (and which are therefore collectively referred to here as the *Spycatcher* cases). It is necessary to understand the chronology of events to appreciate the role which contempt of court played in this highly controversial and complex saga.

A former British secret service agent, Peter Wright, wrote a book of memoirs, entitled *Spycatcher,* which he proposed to publish in Australia where he then lived. The UK government, believing that the memoirs contained highly classified and sensitive information and made serious allegations,[20] was concerned that they should not be published. It therefore sought an injunction in the Supreme Court of New South Wales to restrain publication on the grounds that it would be a breach of the duty of confidentiality owed by Wright to the Crown as his former employers.[1] Before the action was heard two UK newspapers, the *Guardian* and the *Observer*, published details of some of the allegations. The grant of an interlocutory injunction to the (UK) Attorney General restraining further publication in the United Kingdom was upheld in the Court of Appeal.[2] Before the appeal against that decision was heard by the House of Lords, although after the first instance judgment in the Australian case, the *Independent* newspaper also published details of allegations and included what was claimed to be verbatim extracts from the memoirs.[3] The story in the *Independent* was reported in the *London Evening Standard* and the *London Daily News* on the same day. The Attorney General immediately made an application in the Queen's Bench Division against all three newspapers for contempt of court (the first contempt action) on the basis that they had broken the terms of the injunction against the *Guardian* and the *Observer*.

---

17 [1988] Ch 333, [1987] 3 All ER 276
18 (1989) Times, 9 May (Morritt J) and (1990) Times, 28 February (CA).
19 [1992] 1 AC 191, [1991] 2 All ER 398.
20 Such as that a former director of M15 had been a Soviet double agent and that M15 had bugged foreign embassies, plotted to assassinate Colonel Nasser and plotted to destabilise Harold Wilson's Labour Government.
1 That action was ultimately lost, but not before one of the witnesses, the Secretary to the Cabinet, Sir Robert Armstrong, had famously confessed to being 'economical with the truth': *A-G v Heinemann Publishers Australia Pty Ltd* (1987) 8 NSWLR 341, affd New South Wales Court of Appeal (1987) 10 NSWLR 86, and High Court of Australia (1988) 165 CLR 30.
2 *A-G v Observer Ltd* (1986) 136 NLJ 799, [1986] CA Transcript 696: somewhat disastrously from the Government's point of view the Court of Appeal made the injunction subject to the proviso that it did not prohibit publication of material disclosed in open court in the Australian proceedings. The House of Lords, when upholding the grant of the injunction, removed the proviso.
3 The *Independent* said that it had received an unsolicited copy of the book, which it had destroyed after using.

Browne-Wilkinson V-C decided that the matter should come before him on a fresh notice of motion[4] and that a preliminary point of law should be determined:

> 'Whether a publication made in the knowledge of an outstanding injunction against another party and which if made by that other party would be in breach thereof, constitutes a criminal contempt of court upon the footing that it assaults or interferes with the process of justice in relation to the said injunction.'

In other words the question was whether, in the circumstances of the case, what the three newspapers had done *could* be a contempt of court.

The Vice-Chancellor's answer to his preliminary point of law was 'no'.[5] The Attorney General appealed. On 10 July 1987 Viking Penguin Inc, which had already announced its intention to publish *Spycatcher* in the United States, sent out thousands of copies of the book to bookshops throughout the United States. On 12 July the *Sunday Times* published the first instalment of what was intended to be a serialisation of *Spycatcher*, having negotiated a licence from Viking Peguin. The next day the Attorney General began proceedings against the *Sunday Times* and its editor for contempt of court (the second contempt action). Two days later the Court of Appeal announced that it was allowing the Attorney General's appeal in the first contempt proceedings. There were therefore two independent sets of proceedings: first there was the action involving the *Guardian* and the *Observer* on the issue of whether an injunction should be granted prohibiting publication of *Spycatcher*, or details of its contents, in the United Kingdom and secondly there were the contempt proceedings against the *Independent* [6] and the *Sunday Times* for having published material which was the subject of an interlocutory injunction. The main case against the *Independent* and that against the *Sunday Times* were heard together at first instance before Morritt J[7] who found that they *had* committed common law contempt and this decision was upheld by the Court of Appeal.[8] The *Sunday Times* alone appealed to the House of Lords,[9] but only on the ground that they had not committed the actus reus of contempt: the paper did not contend, as both they and the *Independent* had below, that they did not have the necessary intention.[10]

In considering the contempt actions two preliminary points should be made. First, the Attorney General accepted that there could be no question of the strict liability rule applying in the case because the proceedings against the *Guardian* and the *Observer* were not 'active' for the purposes of the 1981 Act at the time of the publication.[11] Therefore the newspapers could ultimately be found to be in

---

4   This was because the *Guardian* and the *Observer* were seeking in the Chancery Division to have the injunctions against them discharged on the ground, inter alia, that it was wrong that others could publish what they were prohibited from publishing. The Vice-Chancellor considered that the validity of this ground largely depended on whether the *Independent* etc had committed contempt in publishing as they did and therefore had the proceedings against the *Independent* begun anew in the Chancery Division. See further Ch 12 which considers matters of procedure.

5   *A-G v Newspaper Publishing Plc* [1988] Ch 333, [1987] 3 All ER 276.

6   This is used as shorthand for the action against the *Independent*, the *Evening Standard* and the *London Daily News*. Ultimately, the Attorney General did not press for substantive relief against the latter two papers. He also began a third contempt action, against the *Sunday Telegraph* and the *News on Sunday* but, again, ultimately did not press for substantive relief.

7   (1989) Times, 9 May.

8   (1990) Times, 28 February.

9   [1992] 1 AC 191, [1991] 2 All ER 398.

10   See below.

11   For when proceedings are 'active' see s 2(3) of, and Sch 1 to, the 1981 Act, discussed in Ch 7.

contempt only if they had an *intention* to prejudice the administration of justice pursuant to s 6(c) of the Act. This meant that the Attorney General had only to satisfy the court that there was a 'real risk' of prejudice and did not have to satisfy the statutory test. Secondly, Sir John Donaldson MR was at pains to point out in the Court of Appeal that although the Attorney General was bringing proceedings against the *Guardian* and the *Observer* as a government minister and on behalf of the Crown, in the case against the *Independent* he was acting, as he normally would in contempt cases, as 'guardian of the public interest in the due administration of justice'.[12]

As noted above, in the case against the *Independent* at first instance the Vice-Chancellor held as a preliminary point of law that there could be no contempt in such a situation. He saw the matter in terms of a breach of the interlocutory injunction and thought it would be an unwarranted extension of the law of contempt to apply it to a person who had only done an act which was a breach of a court order *against other persons* and who had not been a party or privy to a breach of the order by those to whom it was addressed.

On appeal the Court of Appeal saw things differently and held that the three newspapers *had* done something which could be a contempt. The Court of Appeal considered it not as a question of committing contempt by breaching a court order, a type of contempt which is traditionally classified as 'civil' contempt,[13] but as a question of conduct which interferes with the administration of justice. This meant that to whom the injunction was or was not addressed was irrelevant. Rather, the issue was whether by publishing the material from the memoirs the second three newspapers thereby nullified the point of the proceedings between the Crown and the first two newspapers. The Master of the Rolls likened the subject-matter of the first action, which he considered to be the alleged confidential material in the memoirs, to an ice-cube. Like an ice-cube, confidential information is inherently perishable and left exposed it will disappear. It is impossible to restore confidentiality to material which has been published to the world and for that reason the Master of the Rolls considered it an interference in the administration of justice for a third party to publish allegedly confidential material which was the subject of litigation where the court had acted to preserve the confidentiality pending the full hearing of the proceedings.

The Master of the Rolls did not equate the outcome of this with holding that the injunction was binding on third parties. Lloyd LJ, however, recognised that if the interference with the administration of justice depended not simply on whether there was current litigation over confidential information but on whether the court had granted an interlocutory injunction, then it is difficult to resist the conclusion that the injunction did have some effect contra mundum.[14] If the actus reus of contempt consisted of destroying the subject-matter of current litigation why was the injunction relevant?[15] Lloyd LJ answered the conundrum by saying that once the court has made such an order it has announced how it intends to conduct the case and the third party can therefore be in contempt, not because he

---

12 For procedure in contempt actions, see Ch 12. This episode in the *Spycatcher* affair does highlight the multiplicity and apparently contradictory roles of the Law Officers of the Crown.
13 The classification of contempt into civil contempt and criminal contempt is unsatisfactory and was criticised in the present case by both the Master of the Rolls and by Lloyd LJ. The matter is discussed in Ch 14 at pp 663 ff.
14 [1988] Ch 333 at 378, [1987] 3 All ER 276 at 307.
15 The Attorney General did not, in fact, go so far as to argue that there could have been contempt in the absence of an injunction.

breaks the order, but because his actions prevent the court proceeding in accordance with its intentions.

Although the *Independent* could not be liable under the strict liability rule because of the timing complications, Lloyd and Balcombe LJJ both considered that s 2(2) of the Act *would* apply to the facts of this case if all the normal requirements of the section were satisfied. As it was, the extra element of intention had to be proved in order to bring the case within s 6(c). The type of intention that had to be proved was considered both by Sir John Donaldson MR and by Lloyd LJ, who both concluded that specific intent was necessary and that recklessness was not enough.[16] Such intention was proved to the court's satisfaction when the main issue was tried some time later.[17] At first instance Morritt J refused to equate merely knowing of the injunction with an intent to interfere with the administration of justice. He held that all the circumstances had to be taken into account before intention could be inferred from knowledge of the injunction.[18] It is, however, difficult to see when intention would be absent in a breach of confidentiality context if it was present in the *Independent*'s case. A newspaper which publishes material knowing it to be the subject of a breach of confidence action in which an interlocutory order has been made prohibiting the defendant from publication, does so in the knowledge that in publishing, the confidentiality is breached and, according to the courts in the cases now under discussion, that the subject-matter is therefore wholly or partly destroyed. The newspaper may not be interested in the litigation, in the sense that its actions are not directed towards the proceedings, for it will have an agenda of its own: its motive will not be to facilitate the first newspaper's publication, let alone to aid the party alleging confidentiality, but simply to publish itself. It is intending to interfere with the administration of justice only in the sense that it must foresee the destruction of the subject-matter as the inevitable outcome of its actions. Such foresight of the inevitable does, however, seem to satisfy the specific intent test which applies in contempt cases.[19] The only defence would appear to be that the newspaper, or other publication concerned, believes that, for some reason to do with the nature of its circulation or readership, its exposure of the material will not result in the confidentiality being wholly or partly lost.[20]

It is unfortunate that because the *Independent* did not appeal,[1] and the *Sunday Times* did not appeal the finding of intention, the House of Lords did not properly

---

16   [1988] Ch 333 at 373–375, and 381–383, [1987] 3 All ER 276 at 303–304 and 309–310 respectively. The question of what constitutes 'intention' for the purposes of s 6(c) of the 1981 Act is discussed at pp 107 ff.

17   *A-G v Newspaper Publishing plc* (1989) Independent, 9 May.

18   The Court of Appeal (*A-G v Newspaper Publishing Ltd* (1990) Times, 28 February) merely agreed that the newspapers had intention without saying anything further.

19   See *A-G v News Group Newspapers* [1989] QB 110, [1988] 2 All ER 906, *Spycatcher* itself and the discussion at pp 107 ff.

20   In fact, the upholding of the interlocutory injunction against the *Guardian* and the *Observer* by the House of Lords (*A-G v Guardian Newspapers Ltd* [1987] 3 All ER 316) was on the grounds that despite the revelations in the newspapers there was still some confidentiality left to protect. It is doubtful, however, whether any newspaper would wish to belittle its own power and influence by claiming that its publication of information was without effect.

1   The Court of Appeal, although upholding the finding of contempt, quashed the fines imposed below of £50,000 on each newspaper on the grounds that the law had been unsettled at the time and that although the legal advice given to the editors transpired, in the end, to be erroneous, it had corresponded with the first instance decision of the Vice-Chancellor on the preliminary point.

consider the matter of intention.[2] The application of a different test of intention in this particular situation might lessen the sweeping effects which the judgments in the *Spycatcher* contempt actions have on the freedom of the press, for once intention is found the matter is outside the constraints which attend the strict liability rule. Consequently, the period during which contempt can be committed is much longer (the point which was fatal to the newspapers in *Spycatcher*).[3] Secondly, s 5 of the 1981 Act, which protects a discussion in good faith of public affairs,[4] does not apply. As has been seen,[5] the courts have liberally interpreted s 5. The possible misdeeds of the country's security service would appear to be a good candidate for the application of s 5, certainly on a par with the security arrangements at Buckingham Palace,[6] although whether the courts, which displayed such abhorrence of Wright writing his book rather than of the matters which he alleged,[7] would have applied the section in *Spycatcher* must be seriously doubted. However, in a situation of less extreme political sensitivity, the application of s 5 would be much more feasible. That escape route is not available so long as the court can find intention, although it is true that the common law *Bread Manufacturers* defence, recognised by the House of Lords in the *Sunday Times* [8] case, could apply.[9]

In *A-G v Times Newspapers Ltd* [10] the House of Lords upheld the line of reasoning followed by the Court of Appeal on the preliminary point in *A-G v Newspaper Publishing Ltd* [11] in saying that the newspaper was in contempt not for breaking an order addressed to another, but in interfering with the course of justice by destroying, wholly or in part, the subject-matter of a breach of confidence action whose preservation the court had sought to safeguard by an interlocutory injunction. The *effect* of this was as if the interlocutory injunction was binding against the whole world. This is contrary to the normal rule that 'the courts have no jurisdiction to make orders against persons not . . . before them merely because an order made, or to be made, may or will not be effectual without it'.[12] The Law Lords looked to the same previous cases to justify their conclusions as had the Court of Appeal. They agreed that this was not a case of a person aiding or abetting the breach of an order,[13] but relied on statements in *Seaward v*

---

2 Lord Ackner referred to Morritt J's finding of intention and said 'Such a conclusion was in the circumstances irresistible', having first rehearsed how the *Sunday Times* handled the publication of the *Spycatcher* extracts. This had involved great secrecy, including producing a first edition of that Sunday's paper which did not include the material, in order, Lord Ackner said, to avoid the risk of the Attorney General having time to obtain an interlocutory injunction against it. However, although this showed cunning and a deliberate attempt to evade legal action it did not, it is submitted, necessarily show an intention *to prejudice the administration of justice*.
3 Because the sub judice period is not limited to that laid down in Sch 1 to the 1981 Act; see Ch 7.
4 See the discussion at pp 175 ff.
5 Ibid.
6 As in the *Fagan* cases, *A-G v Times Newspapers Ltd* (1983) Times, 12 February.
7 See the terms in which Wright was spoken of throughout the litigation, for example *A-G v Guardian* [1987] 3 All ER 316, [1987] 1 WLR 1248 in which 'treachery' and 'disloyalty' appear passim.
8 [1974] AC 273 at 296 and 321 (Lords Reid and Simon respectively).
9 For a discussion of this, see pp 171 ff.
10 [1992] 1 AC 191, [1991] 2 All ER 398.
11 [1988] Ch 333, [1987] 3 All ER 276.
12 *Brydges v Brydges* [1909] P 187 at 191 per Farwell LJ.
13 As in *Lord Wellesley v Earl of Mornington* (1848) 11 Beav 180, 181 where trees were cut down by the agent of a landowner enjoined by injunction from doing so: it does not seem that the

Paterson, [14] where, although the parties were actually charged with aiding and abetting the breach of an order by the person to whom it was addressed, Lindley LJ placed the matter on a wider footing when he said that a person who is not bound by an order may nevertheless be committed for contempt if he is 'conducting himself so as to obstruct the course of justice' for 'the court will not allow its process to be set at naught and treated with contempt'.[15] Their Lordships also drew comfort from *Z Ltd v A-Z and AA-LL,*[16] in which the Court of Appeal considered that a bank which disposed of assets subject to a Mareva injunction after it had been served with notice of it could be liable for contempt, not just for aiding and abetting but for conduct which 'knowingly interferes with the administration of justice by causing the order of the court to be thwarted'.[17] In the Court of Appeal the Master of the Rolls and Balcombe LJ referred to the judgment of the latter in *X County Council v A* [18] where, in the exercise of the wardship jurisdiction, he made an order, prohibiting the publication of information about the ward, which he held was binding on the whole world. Balcombe LJ had said then that had he not been exercising the parental jurisdiction in wardship he would not have had power to do this but in the present case he considered that there could be other exceptions to the general rule, of which the present situation was one.[19]

There was considerable discussion both in the Court of Appeal[20] and in the House of Lords about how far the principle they were laying down was applicable to the subject-matter of *any* litigation where an interlocutory order for its preservation had been made. There was much talk of shooting racehorses and demolishing houses.[1] The application of the principle to situations where the interference is not through the medium of a publication is dealt with in Chapter 14. As far as publication is concerned in cases where the issue at stake is not confidentiality, the Master of the Rolls briefly adverted to the position as regards defamation. He referred to *A-G v News Group Newspapers Ltd,* [2] where the Court of Appeal had held that the rule in *Bonnard v Perryman* [3] gave way to the rules on contempt of court, and would not exclude the possibility that the publication by a third party of a defamatory statement which the defendant in a defamation action is enjoined from repeating could be a contempt: it would all depend on whether it would in fact interfere with the administration of justice.[4]

As far as the application of the principle which emerges from the *Spycatcher* cases to breach of confidentiality actions is concerned, it is necessary to ask of

landowner himself was involved in this action in any way but an application was made to commit the agent for contempt 'in being party and privy to, and in aiding and assisting the breach of the injunction'. See further p 574.

14 [1897] 1 Ch 545, a case concerning an injunction against permitting premises to be used other than for a private club which had been breached by holding boxing matches there: see pp 574 ff.

15 Ibid at 554, 555–556; see also the judgments of A L Smith and Rigby LJJ.

16 [1982] QB 558.

17 Ibid at 578 per Eveleigh J.

18 [1985] 1 All ER 53, [1984] 1 WLR 1422, subsequently doubted in *R v Central Independent Television Plc* [1994] Fam 192 at 205, per Hoffmann LJ.

19 [1988] Ch 333 at 388, [1987] 3 All ER 276 at 314.

20 In the first contempt action, [1988] Ch 333, [1987] 3 All ER 276.

 1 See particularly [1988] Ch 333 at 380 (Lloyd LJ), [1987] 3 All ER 276 at 307 (Lloyd LJ); [1992] 1 AC 191 at 206–207 (Lord Brandon), 218–219 (Lord Oliver) and 230–231 (Lord Jauncey).

 2 [1987] 1 QB 1, see above pp 192 ff.

 3 [1891] 2 Ch 269, [1891–94] All ER 965.

 4 [1988] Ch 333 at 373–374, [1987] 3 All ER 276 at 303.

what the actus reus of this kind of contempt consists. It is clear that the confidentiality need not be completely destroyed by the publication. It is enough that there is damage or partial destruction. The Master of the Rolls spoke of conduct which 'interfered with the administration of justice by rendering the government's claims against the *Guardian* and the *Observer* less effective'.[5] This meant that the *Independent* could be in contempt even though its publication was 'not extensive'[6] and that enough confidentiality remained for the *Sunday Times* to be in contempt for the damage which it caused with its later publication. Indeed, even after the *Sunday Times* exposure the House of Lords considered there was enough confidentiality left for it to be worth affirming the interlocutory injunction.[7] It can be concluded, therefore, that the courts are not interested in looking at exactly *what* has been published and assessing the *amount* of damage. This is consistent with the fact that the actus reus of contempt regarding publications usually involves the creation of some degree of *risk* of prejudice.[8] However, risk creation did not figure in the arguments in the *Spycatcher* cases. It was sufficient that what had been published contravened the terms of the injunction and since the court had considered the prohibition was necessary to preserve the confidentiality until trial such contravention is equated with damage which interferes with the course of justice.

The immediate result of the *Spycatcher* cases is that an interlocutory injunction granted in a breach of confidentiality action can operate as a blanket ban on anyone who knows, or ought to know, of the injunction publishing material within the scope of the injunction. It is therefore a serious restriction on the freedom of the press.[9] In the circumstances of *Spycatcher* it amounted to banning the British press from publishing controversial material which raised matters of public concern and which was being published amidst much publicity in other countries.[10] Moreover, it operated by using contempt to impose a prior restraint against parties who had had no chance of being heard before the injunction was granted. Indeed, during the *Spycatcher* litigation, when copies of the book became available in the United Kingdom, Derbyshire County Council asked permission to stock it in its public libraries.[11] Knox J held that for it to do so would involve an interference in the proceedings involving the *Guardian* and the *Observer* and would therefore constitute the actus reus of contempt.

In the Court of Appeal Sir John Donaldson MR stressed that he was not concerned with official secrecy but with an action for breach of confidence:[12]

'So much has been said about state secrets that I must stress that the basis of the Attorney General's claim to be entitled to restrain publication was not that Mr Wright might be in breach of the Official Secrets Acts 1911 to 1939. It was that by the terms of his employment with the security service he had a duty of

---

5 [1988] Ch 333 at 373.
6 [1992] 1 AC 191 at 215 per Lord Ackner.
7 *A-G v Guardian Newspapers* [1987] 1 WLR 1248, [1987] 3 All ER 316, described by Geoffrey Robertson in *Freedom, the Individual and the Law* (6th edn, 1989) at p 263 as 'this century's most publicly derided legal decision'.
8 See Ch 3.
9 But for its wider application see pp 576–578.
10 And information about which was therefore widely known inside the United Kingdom: for instance, copies of the book published in the United States on 12 July 1987 were not distributed in the United Kingdom but no attempt was made to prevent people bringing in individual copies.
11 *A-G v Observer Ltd, Re An Application by Derbyshire County Council* [1988] 1 All ER 385.
12 [1988] Ch 333 at 357F, [1987] 3 All ER 276 at 291.

confidentiality which would be breached if he published his memoirs. Confidentiality, *not* official secrecy was, and still is the central issue.'

With respect, that is somewhat disingenuous. The government's main weapon in controlling the publication of state secrets was the Official Secrets Acts 1911 to 1939.[13] There were notorious difficulties with this legislation, including the problem of restraining threatened disclosures of information. Although the Attorney General *can* commence an action for an injunction to prevent breaches of the criminal law such an order will normally be made only where strict conditions are satisfied.[14] However, in *A-G v Jonathan Cape Ltd*[15] in 1975 the Attorney General sought to restrain the publication of the diaries of a former Cabinet Minister[16] on the novel ground that they revealed details of Cabinet discussions which were protected by the duty of confidence owed by all Cabinet ministers. Lord Widgery CJ accepted that breach of confidence could apply but said that before breach of confidence could be successfully invoked by the government it had to be shown not only that the material in question was held in confidence but also that it was in the public interest for it to be restrained. Despite this major limitation, *Jonathan Cape* did mean that breach of confidence, an action developed in the private law sphere, could be used in the public law area as a weapon by which the government could seek to enforce secrecy.[17] It had the advantage of making prior restraint easier to obtain because it ostensibly made the matter into a civil law issue.[18] It was this route which the government took in order to try to ban *Spycatcher*. To say that official secrets were not the central issue in the litigation is hardly a true representation of what was really going on.

The whole idea of confidential information of the kind in issue in *Spycatcher* being the 'subject-matter' of litigation which can be likened to ice-cubes or race-horses has been criticised[19] on the grounds that the subject-matter of such an action is not the information itself but the confidential relationship in the course of which it was acquired. It is argued that the publication of the material by the *Independent* and the *Sunday Times* did not affect the issue of whether the *Guardian* and the *Observer* had become a party to Wright's breach of duty to the Crown and that therefore it did not damage or destroy the 'subject-matter' of that litigation. However, it is submitted that that argument takes too abstract a view of the proceedings. Parties do not litigate breach of confidence actions in order to establish interesting points about the nature of relationships: they do it to restrain information imparted during that relationship from entering the public domain. If that information enters the public domain by the fault of the confidee damages may provide compensation if there are measurable economic

13 There is now an Official Secrets Act 1989, s 1 of which makes it a criminal offence for members or former members of the security and intelligence services ever to reveal anything which came into their possession by virtue of their position. A person who receives and publishes such information may be guilty of a criminal offence even if no injunction would have issued to restrain publication as a civil wrong.

14 See *A-G v Harris* [1961] 1 QB 74; *A-G v Chaudry* [1971] 3 All ER 938; *Gouriet v Union of Post Office Workers* [1978] AC 435.

15 [1976] QB 752, [1975] 3 All ER 484.

16 Richard Crossman.

17 For a general discussion of this see Feldman, *Civil Liberties and Human Rights in England and Wales* (1993, Oxford) Ch 14.

18 Only ostensibly, inasmuch as criminal contempt was then brought into play in *Spycatcher* with all the sanctions which that implies.

19 See eg Robertson, *Freedom, the Individual and the Law* (6th edn, 1989) p 291.

consequences, but in some instances damages are not an adequate remedy.[20] It has been suggested that the proper action to have brought against the *Independent* would have been another breach of confidence action but a breach of confidence action is far less effective than the contempt of court remedy which provides, in effect, a universal prior restraint order.

Spycatcher brought contempt of court into disrepute. However, in the way the courts approached the issue contempt of court was not left as a way of making all injunctions binding on the whole world. By saying that it is the interference with proceedings which is the contempt, rather than the breach of an order made against another party, contempt is limited to those cases in which independent third party action interferes with the actual operation of the order unfortunately, cases on confidential information are the obvious example of this category.[21]

It needs also to be borne in mind that the impact of the *Spycatcher* principle depends on the readiness of the courts to make interlocutory orders. Lord Oliver addressed this issue in the *Spycatcher* case itself.[1] The guidelines governing the grant of interlocutory injunctions were laid down by the House of Lords in *American Cyanamid Co v Ethicon Ltd* and Lord Oliver described these as having come to be treated as 'carved in tablets of stone, so that a plaintiff seeking interlocutory relief has never to do more than show that he has a fairly arguable case'. He pointed out that the effect of this practice, in conjunction with the decision in the present case, meant that a person seeking to restrain the publication of allegedly confidential information could by presenting an arguable case in effect 'stifle what may, in the end, turn out to be perfectly legitimate comment until it no longer has any importance or commands any public interest'. He suggested that this state of affairs could be ameliorated by the courts returning to pre-*Cyanamid* principles and concentrating more on the prima facie merits of the case.

The European Court of Human Rights considered the issues raised in *Spycatcher* when the newspapers' publishers petitioned under the European Convention.[2] The main concern of the European Court was whether the issue, modification and extension of the injunctions was compatible with Article 10(2) of the Convention which guarantees freedom of expression. The majority of the judges held that up to the time that the book was published in the United States in July 1987 the injunctions were justified. However, the publication in the United States so destroyed the confidentiality that restrictions on publication in the United Kingdom after that time served no useful purpose and the interference with the freedom of the press was no longer 'necessary in a democratic society'. This meant that there was no justification for the House of Lords upholding the

---

20 This raises the issue of the grounds upon which interlocutory injunctions are given: whether compensation in damages is adequate if a party is refused an injunction but ultimately wins the case is according to *American Cyanamid Co v Ethicon Ltd* [1975] AC 396 a major consideration, but see below for the suggestion that in cases of prior restraint the merits of the case should play a larger part.

21 See *A-G v Times Newspapers Ltd* [1992] 1 AC 191 at 231 per Lord Jauncey; see further Ch 14 pp 576 ff. In the Scots case *Lord Advocate v The Scotsman Publications Ltd (Inside Intelligence)* 1988 SLT 490 the Outer House and the Second Division of the Court of Session both resisted attempts to esatblish the terms of an interdict *contra mundum*; in the appeal to the House of Lords (1989 SLT 705) the issue was not addressed; see Walker [1990] Public Law 354.

1 [1992] 1 AC 191 at 226.

2 *Sunday Times v UK (No 2)* (1991) 14 EHRR 229; *The Observer and The Guardian v UK* (1991) 14 EHRR 153. See Feldman, *Civil Liberties and Human Rights in England and Wales* (1993, Oxford) pp 658–660: Leigh, 'Spycatcher in Strasbourg' [1992] PL 200.

injunction on the *Guardian* and the *Observer* on 30 July 1987 in *A-G v Guardian Newspapers Ltd.*[3]

The European Court considered the principles in *American Cyanamid* meant that the criteria for granting interim injunctions were 'prescribed by law' as required for limitations to Article 10 despite not having previously been applied to prevent interim publication in a breach of confidence action. The majority's opinion can be criticised[4] for not having appreciated that the 'balance of convenience' test in *American Cyanamid* is not consistent with the court's own case law on Article 10 and it is submitted that Lord Oliver's strictures on that test as being an inappropriate basis for granting interlocutory injunctions in cases concerning the freedom of the press should be heeded.

B   Publishing material which pre-empts an action to which the publisher is a party

Since a plaintiff can normally discontinue an action which he is pursuing at any time it will not be a contempt if he himself publishes material which nullifies the point of the action.

This is the principle which can be derived from the House of Lords' decision in *Re Lonrho Plc.*[5] This case arose in the course of the long battle waged between Lonrho plc (and in particular its chief executive, 'Tiny' Rowland) and the Al-Fayed brothers over the latters' takeover in 1985 of the House of Fraser company which controlled Harrods.[6] After the Al-Fayeds acquired Harrods Mr Rowland mounted a campaign to establish that they had been guilty of fraud and deceit so that they would be obliged to sell the company and Lonrho would be given the chance of acquiring Harrods. In April 1987, as a result of this campaign, the Secretary of State appointed inspectors under the Companies Act 1985 to investigate the takeover. However, the Secretary of State subsequently declined to publish the inspectors' report immediately on the grounds that he had sent a copy of it to the Serious Fraud Office and did not wish to prejudice their inquiry. He also declined to refer the takeover to the Monopolies and Mergers Commission. Lonrho then sought in judicial review an order that the Secretary of State publish the report and refer the takeover to the MMC. After losing this action in the Court of Appeal Lonrho appealed to the House of Lords. Meanwhile, Mr Rowland came into possession of a copy of the inspectors' report and ten days before the Appellate Committee sat to hear the appeal he caused the *Observer* newspaper, which was owned by Lonrho, to publish a special midweek edition containing details of the report and comment upon it. The Secretary of State obtained an injunction against the *Observer* but not before 200,000 copies had been sold and 2,000–3,000 copies had been sent to people on a mailing list to whom Lonrho had regularly been sending propaganda throughout the campaign. Among the recipients were four of the five Law Lords who were due to hear the judicial review appeal.

3   [1987] 3 All ER 316, [1987] 1 WLR 1248; Lord Bridge, dissenting in that case, had predicted that the UK government would face 'inevitable condemnation and humiliation by the European Court of Human Rights' if the ban continued.
4   See Robertson and Nicol: *Media Law* (3rd edn) p 193.
5   [1990] 2 AC 154, [1989] 2 All ER 1100.
6   This affair reverberated for some years and surfaced again in 1994 over accusations about 'sleaze' and payments to MPs.

Lonrho, the *Observer*, and others involved in the publication[7] were charged with contempt of the House of Lords both at common law and under the 1981 Act. The case therefore came before the Appellate Committee not acting in its appellate capacity.[8] Lord Bridge, delivering what was described as the 'report' of the Committee on the question of contempt, said that there were two issues of contempt involved. One was whether the publication amounted to a 'prejudgment': this aspect of the matter is considered below.[9] The other was whether the publication amounted to a 'pre-emption' of the decision of the Appellate Committee as regards the Secretary of State's action over the report, given that the whole point of that part of the proceedings was to compel him to publish it. If the injunction had not been granted the report would have been put fully into the public domain and the question of whether the Secretary of State had acted unlawfully would have been rendered academic.

Lord Bridge emphasised that in this case, unlike the *Spycatcher* cases,[10] the court had issued no injunction prior to the publication of the midweek *Observer* and the subject-matter of the proceedings was not protected by a court order made for its preservation. He said that the issue amounted to asking:

> 'whether there is any support in principle or authority for the proposition that a litigant who seeks a judicial remedy compelling a certain course of action creates a risk that the course of justice in the proceedings in which the remedy is sought would be impeded or prejudiced if he takes direct action to secure for himself the substance of the remedy sought without the assistance of the court.'[11]

He decided that there was no such support for this proposition and declined to extend the law of contempt in a novel way. It can therefore be concluded from *Lonrho* that where a litigant resorts to self-help in respect of a matter which is the subject of judicial proceeedings he will not be in contempt of court,[12] at least so long as the court has made no order for the preservation of the subject-matter pending the hearing.

Even where there is an order, it is doubtful whether action by a litigant would necessarily constitute a contempt. In *Spycatcher*, for example, had the UK government itself published or caused to be published the details of Wright's allegations after the interlocutory order had been made, this would have been tantamount to dropping the attempt to keep the material secret and it is difficult to see why this should be held a contempt,[13] even if the Attorney General had continued with his action in order to have the matters of principle involved resolved. It is submitted, therefore, that action by a litigant resulting in total or partial destruction of the subject-matter of a case will not amount to contempt if the effect of that action is equivalent to discontinuing the proceedings and ceding victory to the other side.

---

7 Including Lonrho's solicitors, Stephenson Harwood.
8 For this aspect of the case see Ch 12, p 477.
9 At p 225. In the course of his speech Lord Bridge considered the question of whether appellate judges can ever be said to be open to improper influence, see p 166.
10 See pp 211 ff.
11 [1990] 2 AC 154 at 212F, [1989] 2 All ER 1100 at 1119.
12 He may of course be guilty of other criminal offences or have opened himself to civil liability for damages.
13 For the liability of government ministers and civil servants for contempt, see Ch 14, pp 557.

VI   THE APPLICATION OF THE PREJUDGMENT TEST

It was explained in Chapter 3[14] that the *Sunday Times* case[15] established that at common law it was possible for a publication to constitute a contempt not because it created a real risk of prejudice to particular proceedings but because it prejudged a specific issue pending before the courts. Such prejudgments were prohibited because they usurped the function of the courts and created a danger of trial by media but it is uncertain to what extent this form of contempt has survived the 1981 Act. We consider here, therefore, the substance of the rule against prejudgments as laid down by the House of Lords in the *Sunday Times* case and how it might be applied insofar as it is still extant. Because of the absence of a jury in most civil actions and the attitude of the courts to professional judges' immunity from improper influence,[16] the prejudgment test is more likely to become an issue in civil than in criminal cases.

A   The facts of the *Sunday Times* case

The direct concern of the *Sunday Times* case was an application by the Attorney General to restrain publication of an article in a forthcoming issue of the defendant newspaper. The projected article was intended to further the newspaper's campaign to urge Distillers to be generous to the child victims of the thalidomide drug which they had marketed. Unlike previous articles, however, it dealt with one of the major issues at stake between Distillers and the claimants, namely, whether the company had been negligent. Although written in temperate terms the article contained a detailed and well-researched analysis of the evidence against Distillers, marshalling forcibly the arguments for saying that Distillers did not measure up to their responsibilities. The article concluded inter alia that 'it could be argued' that:

> '1.   [Distillers] should have found all the scientific literature about drugs related to thalidomide. It did not.
> 2.   It should have done further tests when it discovered that the drug had anti-thyroid activity and unsuspected toxicity. It did not.
> 3.   It should have had proof before advertising the drug as safe for pregnant women that this was in fact so. It did not.'

However, the article stopped short of saying that Distillers were actually negligent and attempted to marshall the arguments on the company's side concluding that in the end 'there appears to be no neat set of answers'. Despite the concluding remarks the article created a powerful impression that Distillers had in fact been negligent.

B   The decision

It was unanimously held that publication should be restrained primarily on the basis that by dealing with the question of negligence the proposed article

14   See pp 69 ff.
15   [1974] AC 273.
16   See pp 124 ff.

amounted to a prejudgment of an issue pending before the court. Such prejudgment was objected to not so much because of the effect on the case in hand—it was accepted[17] that the proposed article would have added little to the pressure already put upon Distillers by previous publicity and that neither witnesses nor judge would be improperly influenced by the article—but because of the long-term effect that permitting this type of article could have upon the administration of justice generally. As Lord Reid said:[18]

> 'I think that anything in the nature of a prejudgment of a case or of specific issues in it is objectionable not only because of its possible effect on that particular case but also because of its side effects which may be far reaching. Responsible "mass media" will do their best to be fair, but there will also be ill-informed, slapdash or prejudiced attempts to influence the public. If people are led to think that it is easy to find the truth, disrespect for the processes of the law could follow and, if mass media are allowed to judge, unpopular people and unpopular causes will fare badly.'

Lord Cross took a similar view.[19] Lord Diplock[20] with whom Lord Simon agreed,[1] was also worried about the long-term effect of allowing prejudgments to be published. He said:

> 'If to have recourse to civil litigation were to expose a litigant to the risk of public obloquy or to public and prejudicial discussion of the facts or merits of the case before they have been determined by the court, potential suitors would be inhibited from availing themselves of courts of law for the purpose for which they are established.'

Lord Morris was similarly concerned about prejudgments. He questioned whether it was right that when parties have submitted a dispute and the issues raised therein to the arbitrament of the courts there should be elaborate public debate and explicit expression of opinions as to what the court's decision ought to be and as to where the merits and rights lie. He pointed out that:[2]

> 'Even if some expressions of opinion were the result of honestly attempted sound reasoning how easy it would be for later statements by others to amount simply to advocacy inspired by partisan motives for the cause of the party, and how difficult it would be then to stem the tide of public clamour for the victory of one side or the other.'

He added:[3]

> 'the courts, I think, owe it to the parties to protect them either from the prejudices of prejudgment or from the necessity of having themselves to participate in the flurries of pre-trial publicity.'

It seems to have been the collective judgment of their Lordships that there is an objection to and a rule against publications (no matter how well researched or temperately expressed) which prejudge, at any rate in any detail, issues in particular cases that are pending before the courts. Moreover, prejudgments are

---

17 At any rate by Lord Reid at [1974] AC 273 at 299B and 301G.
18 Ibid at 300F–G.
19 See his comment at [1974] AC 273 at pp 322H–323A.
20 Ibid at 310F–G.
1 Ibid at 314C. Lord Simon, however, does not himself mention prejudgments though at 345 he did refer to the article as being a detailed discussion of one of the crucial issues in the actions.
2 Ibid at 303G.
3 Ibid at 304A.

objectionable whether or not they are thought to create a real risk of prejudice to the particular case. Lord Diplock, for example, said:[4]

'contempt of court in relation to a civil action is not restricted to conduct which is calculated (whether intentionally or not) to prejudice the fair trial of that action by influencing, in favour of one party or against him, either the tribunal by which the action may be tried or witnesses who may give evidence in it; it extends also to conduct that is calculated to inhibit suitors generally from availing themselves of their constitutional right to have their legal rights and obligations ascertained and enforced in courts of law, by holding up any suitor to public obloquy for doing so or by exposing him to public and prejudicial discussion of the merits or the facts of his case before they have been determined by the court or the action has been otherwise disposed of in due course of law.'

Lord Reid commented:[5]

'Most cases of prejudging of issues fall within the existing authorities in contempt. I do not think that the freedom of the press would suffer, and I think that the law would be clearer and easier to apply in practice if it is made a general rule that it is not permissible to prejudge issues in pending cases.'

C   Some difficulties in applying the decision

1   *The meaning and scope of 'prejudgment'*

Despite Lord Reid's claims as to its clarity and certainty, the prejudgment test is beset with problems not least of which is determining the meaning of 'prejudgment' itself.[6] No doubt it refers in general to the public canvassing of the factual merits of the case and presumably refers to publications that suggest what the court ought to decide or predict what the court will in fact decide or which attempts to evaluate the evidence by the opposing parties. All these examples might be said to be cases where the publication is usurping, or at least anticipating, the function of the court. On the other hand, an article that merely sets out the issues to be determined cannot be considered a 'prejudgment'. However, as one commentator has said[7] where such setting out is done by someone whose views are well known then it might be difficult to avoid inviting the reader to draw inferences. Would such a publication then be a prejudgment?

Another doubt is whether there is objection to prejudging *legal* issues in cases pending before the court. Lord Cross thought[8] that the prejudgment test did so apply but, as has been pointed out,[9] that would mean that an opinion expressed on a legal issue in a learned journal would be caught. It is perhaps doubtful,[10] however, whether even Lord Cross would have gone that far but it is not easy to see where the line should be drawn. A similar problem relates to learned

4   Ibid at 310F–H.
5   Ibid at 300G.
6   See the comments of the Phillimore Committee (1974, Cmnd 5794) at para 111.
7   Miller, *Contempt of Court* (2nd edn) p 162. See also his articles in (1974) 37 MLR 96, 98 and [1975] Crim LR 132, 134–6.
8   [1974] AC 273 at 322G.
9   By the Phillimore Committee (1974, Cmnd 5794) para 111.
10 See the arguments by Miller, *Contempt of Court* (2nd edn) p 162. Query whether media discussion of legal issues can be distinguished from scholarly treatises on the grounds that unlike the former the public will hardly be influenced by the latter publication and so the risks of descending to trial by newspaper is remote?

discussion in medical journals, for example, as to the manner in which thalidomide operates to produce deformities, published during the pendency of the action against Distillers.

2   The extent of the embargo against 'prejudgments'

Both Lords Reid and Cross seemed committed to the view that *any* prejudgment was wrong and should be avoided. It is evident, however, from their attitude towards *Vine Products Ltd v Green* [11] that even they did not think that every prejudgment *once published* constitutes a punishable or even actionable contempt. Lord Reid considered the publication in that case to be a technical contempt:[12]

> 'but the fault was so venial and the possible consequences so trifling that it would have been quite wrong to impose punishment or I think even to require the newspaper to pay the costs of the applicant. But the newspaper ought to have withheld its judgment until the case had been decided'.

Lord Cross too thought the publication a technical contempt and that it had been right to dismiss the application with costs.[13]

Given this attitude it may be that what the Law Lords really had in mind when laying down the prejudgment test was the type of article that canvasses in *some detail* the very issues that have to be tried by the court.

3   The relationship of the 'prejudgment test' to the 'real risk of prejudice test'

As we have seen, Lord Reid thought that most cases of prejudgment fell within the existing authorities on contempt and that, therefore, freedom of the press would not suffer if there were to be a general rule against prejudgments. This could be taken to mean that the prejudgment test was intended to replace the old 'real risk of prejudice to the particular case test'. It is submitted, however, that this is not so. Publications that create a real risk of prejudice to the particular case will remain a contempt at common law on that ground alone even if they do not amount to a prejudgment but, according to the *Sunday Times* case, prejudgments could be a contempt even if there is no real risk of prejudice to the particular case. It would appear that all Lord Reid meant was that as a guide to the press, prejudgments should be avoided, but not that that was now the sole criterion for what amounts to contempt.

There is, in this respect, some difficulty with the speech of Lord Bridge in *Re Lonrho Plc*,[14] the facts of which are given above.[15] Lord Bridge said that as well as the 'pre-emption' category, the issues raised in that case could most conveniently be considered under the heading 'prejudgment'. He was extremely doubtful how far the speeches in the *Sunday Times* case still represented the law in the wake of the 1981 Act,[16] saying that the 'only safe course' was to apply the statutory test

11   [1966] Ch 484, [1965] 3 All ER 58. The facts are set out at p 200.
12   [1974] AC 273 at 301A.
13   [1974] AC 273 at 325C. See also Lord Simon at 321E.
14   [1990] 2 AC 154, [1989] 2 All ER 1100.
15   See p 220.
16   This aspect of his judgment is considered in Ch 4, pp 119.

according to its ordinary language, without preconceptions derived from the *Sunday Times*. He said:[17]

> 'The vice at which the strictures in the speeches in *A-G v Times Newspapers Ltd* against "trial by newspaper" and "prejudgment" were directed is exhibited, if at all, in the editorial comment, in particular the accusation that the Secretary of State acted in bad faith in deciding to defer publication of the inspectors' report.'

He concluded that, however intemperate the language was in which this comment was couched, there was no risk that either the Secretary of State would be deterred from pursuing the appeal or that the Appellate Committee would be influenced in deciding that appeal and that there was therefore no contempt committed on those grounds.

With respect, it is difficult to see why Lord Bridge was concerned with 'prejudgment' if the matter was to be resolved entirely on whether a risk to the proceedings had been created through possible influence on the one of the parties or on the Committee. That is not the concept of 'prejudgment' with which their Lordships were concerned in the *Sunday Times* case. Lord Bridge did not consider whether the editorial comment might have a prejudicial effect on the administration of justice generally, or whether it should be held a contempt simply for prejudging an issue of which the courts were seised. He applied not the prejudgment test but the statutory test in s 2(2).

D   The reaction to and criticisms of the prejudgment test

The House of Lords' decision with regard to prejudgments was widely criticised as being an over-reaction to an imagined threat of 'trial by newspaper'. As one commentator said[18] 'Thus far we have managed to avoid the spectre of trial by newspaper without the rule'. The alleged certainty of the rule has been doubted[19] and in any event it has been said[20] that the price of the alleged certainty, namely, the curb on freedom to comment on issues directly before the court, is too high.

As we have seen,[1] these criticisms were endorsed by the Phillimore Committee which recommended its replacement.[2] This recommendation was impliedly endorsed by the Government Green Paper published in 1978.[3] It will also have been noted that the *Sunday Times* decision was held by the European Court of Human Rights to have been a violation of Article 10 of the Convention.[4]

It is submitted that the general criticism is justified. It seems dangerously wide to prohibit comment on the basis that it would lead generally to trial by newspaper.[5] There may well be objection to the detailed canvassing of issues to be tried by a court but it seems sound to base this objection on the risks of interference in the particular case. In the *Sunday Times* case it could have been plausibly argued that Distillers were unduly pressurised—after all they did bow

17 [1990] 2 AC 154 at 210.
18 Miller, (1974) 37 MLR 96 at 98.
19. See eg the Phillimore Committee (1974, Cmnd 5794) para 111.
20 Lowe, (1977) 127 NLJ 676 at 678.
1   See pp 99–100.
2   See paras 106–114.
3   1978, Cmnd 7145.
4   *Sunday Times v UK* (1979) 2 EHRR 245, discussed in Ch 3.
5   See also Borrie who at [1975] Crim LR 127, 130 commented: 'For the great mass of cases that are brought or might be brought, the fears of their Lordships are surely exaggerated'.

to the pressure and offer substantially more—nor should it be forgotten that the *Sunday Times* intended this result which may also be a ground for objecting to the publication.[6]

E The subsequent application of the prejudgment test

The 'prejudgment test' has yet to be directly applied in a subsequent case. In England there were some opportunities to apply the test before the passing of the 1981 Act. Indeed in *Blackburn v BBC*[7] the court was expressly invited to apply the test but refused. That case, however, concerned a relatively innocuous publication akin to that published in *Vine Products Ltd v Green*.[8] More importantly perhaps is *Schering Chemicals Ltd v Falkman Ltd*[9] where the background facts were strikingly similar to those of the *Sunday Times* case. An application had been made to restrain the broadcast of a film concerning the drug 'Primodos' which, like thalidomide, was the alleged cause of deformities in unborn children. At the time of the planned broadcast, actions by parents of some deformed children against the plaintiff company had been set down for trial. It seems apparent that the proposed film did deal with some of the issues to be raised in the court action though it was held not to amount to a prejudgment.[10] Nevertheless, the attitude of the Court of Appeal judges was that unless some harm to the course of justice in the particular case could be shown no injunction should be granted. Templeman LJ commented:[11]

> '. . . the court should not be anxious to accept submissions that discussions of a pending action must necessarily be unseemly or harmful to the administration of justice. Each case must be judged on its own merits. . . '

In other words the wider dangers of trial by newspaper that so appalled the Law Lords in the *Sunday Times* case did not figure large in the reasoning of the Court of Appeal.

As is explained above, the prejudgment test was discussed in *Re Lonrho*[12] but the test actually applied was that of risk to the particular proceedings. In that case Lord Bridge was understandably reluctant to apply a test which has been condemned by the European Court of Human Rights and which, whatever the imperfections of the legislation, Parliament appears to have intended to abolish.[13] In other jurisdictions, where there has been no statutory intervention, the full authority of the *Sunday Times* decision has yet to be established, at any rate with regard to the prejudgment test.[14]

6 This was certainly a factor relied upon by Lord Morris; see his comments at [1974] AC 273 at 307.
7 (1976) Times, 15 December.
8 [1966] Ch 484, [1965] 3 All ER 58. For a similarly innocuous case where the Divisional Court did not apply the prejudgment test see *R v Bulgin ex p BBC* (1977) Times, 14 July.
9 [1982] QB 1, [1981] 2 All ER 321.
10 See Lord Denning MR's conclusions [1982] QB 1 at 21.
11 Ibid at 40.
12 [1990] 2 AC 154.
13 See Ch 4, pp 118.
14 In Australia the *Sunday Times* decision has been referred to on a number of occasions but the 'prejudgment test' has yet to be relied upon as the *sole* ground for holding there to be a contempt. The closest a judge has come to doing this was in *Watts v Hawke and David Syme & Co Ltd* [1976] VR 707 but there Kaye J also relied upon the risk of prejudice to the particular proceedings. For a criticism of the case see in particular (1977) 57 ALJ 319. See also

VII   PUBLICATIONS PENDING AN APPEAL

As explained in Chapter 5, where criminal proceedings are concerned there is a major difference between the freeedom of speech as regards first instance proceedings and as regards appeals, because of the presence of the jury at first instance.

This difference is not so stark with civil proceedings, except for defamation, because of the greater freedom in respect of civil actions at first instance. As with criminal cases, the freedom to comment upon civil proceedings pending an appeal appears to be considerable. Appellate judges, as we have seen,[15] are assumed to be immune from the effect of media comment and there is normally no problem with witnesses. In *Re Lonrho Plc*[16] Lord Bridge commented that no case had been drawn to the court's attention in which public discussion of the issues arising in, or criticism of the parties to, litigation already decided at first instance had been held to be a contempt on the ground that it was likely to impede or prejudice the course of justice in proceedings on appeal from that decision. A different aspect of the susceptibility of appellate judges arose in *Re Lonrho* however, because of the wholly exceptional circumstances of that case.[17] When most of the Appellate Committee of the House of Lords about to hear Lonrho's appeal were sent the special edition of the *Observer* the Committee initiated contempt proceedings against Lonrho. Lonrho submitted that the contempt proceedings be heard by a differently constituted Committee as, in Lord Keith's paraphrase, 'since the contempt proceeedings had been initiated by those who were proposing to hear and adjudicate upon them, an objective observer might think that their Lordships were predisposed to decide against Lonrho and that in fact Lonrho did think so'.[18] Although there was held to be no possible question of any bias, the Appellate Committee nonetheless decided that a differently constituted Committee should hear the contempt proceedings.[19]

The matter of deterring a party to litigation from pursuing their case does need to be considered in the context of appeals. It raises similar issues to that of appeals against conviction in criminal cases.[20]

There is no reason in principle why improper pressure upon a party to a civil action to deter them from appealing should not be a contempt in the same way that it is over first instance proceedings. The question will again be the distinction between fair and temperate criticism and improper pressure.[1] In *Re South Shields*

Commercial Bank of Australia Ltd v Preston [1981] 2 NSWLR 554 where the *Sunday Times* decision was fully analysed with apparent approval. Other cases have attempted to distinguish the *Sunday Times* case. See in particular *A-G (NSW) v Willesee* [1980] 2 NSWLR 143. In the Australian High Court case, *Victoria v BLF* (1982) 41 ALR 71, no comment was made upon the prejudgment test though the *Sunday Times* decision was adverted to in other contexts. In New Zealand, on the basis of *A-G v Tonks* [1939] NZLR 533 (referred to in detail in the first edition of this work at pp 72–73) the *Sunday Times* case might be predicted to be more readily followed.
15 See pp 165 ff.
16 [1990] 2 AC 154 at 210.
17 Described at p 220.
18 [1990] 2 AC 154 at 177.
19 Lonrho also claimed that the fact that the father of one of the Law Lords had once been Tiny Rowland's dentist made his Lordship unsuitable to hear the case: not surprisingly the Appellate Committee dismissed this notion. For a consideration of the procedural aspects of *Re Lonrho* see Ch 12, p 477.
20 See Ch 5, p 165.
1   See above pp 204 ff.

(*Thames Street*) *Clearance Order 1931* [2] a publication asserted that the appellant, by appealing to the High Court against a clearance order, was responsible for keeping tenants out of new homes. The contention that the article was in contempt because of its tendency to deter the appellant from appealing was rejected. The report is short and the grounds for dismissing the claim not stated but Lord Reid in subsequently approving the decision said[3] that as the article did not go beyond fair and temperate comment on the owner's action it could not properly be regarded as contempt. In *Re Lonrho* Lord Bridge thought that as regards appeals:[4]

> 'in general terms the possibility that the parties will be influenced is remote. When a case has proceeded so far it is unlikely, save in exceptional circumstances, that criticism would deter an appellant from pursuing his appeal or induce a respondent to forgo the judgment in his favour or to reach a compromise of the appeal.'

He considered that there was no risk that 'however intemperate the language' that the editorial in the *Observer* could in any way have deterred or deflected the Secretary of State in that case. It is submitted, however, that a more vulnerable litigant could be influenced in respect of appeal proceedings by intemperate and unfair comment and that the type of conduct indulged in by *Private Eye* towards Mrs Sutcliffe[5] would be a contempt at any stage of the proceedings.

The strict liability rule will only apply once appeal proceedings are launched by the lodging of a formal notice of appeal or application for leave[6] and will not apply merely because the losing party announces his intention to appeal. If, however, it is a case where an intention to prejudice is found[7] then the wider common law time limits apply.[8]

VIII PUBLICATIONS AFTER THE FINAL CONCLUSION OF THE CASE

In general a similar position obtains with respect to comment published after the conclusion of civil proceedings as it does with regard to concluded criminal proceedings. Hence, provided proceedings have been heard in open court, detailed criticism of the decision or detailed reference to the facts of the case is permissible subject only to the reservations that publications that are, for example, scurrilously abusive may amount to contempt by scandalising the court[9] and comment about the concluded case might conceivably be a contempt if it is thought to create a real risk of prejudice to a forthcoming case. It should be noted that the same freedom to comment may not apply to proceedings heard in private. This is because of restrictions imposed by the Administration of Justice Act 1960, s 12 which prohibits publication of information relating to certain proceedings heard in private. We shall discuss the operation of s 12 in Chapter 8 but it may be that restrictions over and above that imposed by the

---

2 (1932) 173 LT Jo 76.
3 In the *Sunday Times* case [1974] AC 273 at 297. See also Lord Cross at 326.
4 [1990] 2 AC 154 at 210.
5 *A-G v Hislop* [1991] 1 QB 514, [1991] 1 All ER 911; see p 207. Obviously the exact threats of cross-examination would not apply to an appeal.
6 Contempt of Court Act 1981, Sch 1, para 15.
7 See p 208 for a discussion of intention in relation to improper pressure.
8 See Ch 7.
9 See generally Ch 8.

section apply to wards of court. One peculiarity of wardship[10] is that legal control of a ward vests in the court and indeed this control remains so vested throughout the wardship. As wardship continues unless the court orders otherwise this overall control also continues even after the court hearing. It is because of this continued control that it may be that publications interfering with the ward's welfare could be held a contempt. It is possibly with this in mind that in *Re T (AJJ) (an infant)*[11] Russell LJ issued the following warning:

> 'We decided to hear this appeal in camera with a view to protecting the infant from harm, and we now give our judgment in open court taking every care that we can to avoid identification of the persons concerned. No doubt diligent investigation would enable anyone interested to tear aside the veil. But it must be borne in mind that the infant is a ward of court under the judge's order, and if anyone is minded to question or interview the infant they may well be at risk of being in contempt.'

Exactly what Russell LJ had in mind is unclear.[12] He may have considered that the contempt would be committed by revealing the ward's identity or that the information gained and subsequently published contravened s 12 of the 1960 Act. But he may have considered that an interview alone could have constituted the contempt. Being hounded by the press could certainly be held to interfere with the ward's welfare and on this basis could constitute contempt. A subsequent publication could also be held a contempt.

If this is the correct view it is evident that the courts will not readily restrict publications even to protect wards of court. In *Re C (an infant)*[13] contempt proceedings were brought by a ward's foster parents against the BBC in respect of a proposed television programme. The child involved had been the subject of lengthy legal proceedings which ended when the House of Lords granted care and control to the English foster parents as against his Spanish natural parents. The proposed programme, which formed part of a series known as *Cause for Concern*, was called 'The Case of a Spanish Boy'. The producer of the *Cause for Concern* series had said:

> 'The series will dispassionately examine cases where individuals have suffered from bureaucracy, from our legal and welfare system and perhaps also from their own mistakes and who are still fighting for a fair deal.'

The foster parents argued:

> 'that the boy's identity would inevitably be revealed, and it was said that that was a contempt of court per se. They also said that public comment on the case which had now died down might be revived.'

Goff J held on the facts that no contempt had been committed. He said:

> 'While the foster parents might be right in saying that some viewers would identify the boy, they would probably be those who already knew.'

He also dismissed the foster parents' second contention:

> 'the House of Lords' reasons for their decision had been published only on 19 February, and having regard to the publicity given to the case already—and in

10 For a detailed account of the wardship jurisdiction see Lowe and White, *Wards of Court* (2nd edn, 1986). See also pp 451 ff.
11 [1970] Ch 688 at 689. For an extra-judicial criticism of this see Lord Denning MR's address to the Law Society's 1970 Conference.
12 See Lowe and White, *Wards of Court* (2nd edn, 1986) p 93.
13 (1969) Times, 18 June.

particular the publishing of the name of the Spanish parents and therefore the name of the ward—his Lordship could not, or ought not, to restrain the publication of the programme as being something that would be a contempt of court.'

Goff J concluded:

'the court would not lightly override the right of freedom of discussion on matters of public concern and interest. The court's restrictive powers should be exercised only where the welfare of the infant plainly required the ordinary right of bona fide comment to be restricted. It was almost certain the boy would not see the programme and it was improbable he would hear about it. His Lordship was not satisfied that there was any risk of injury to the ward or interference with the position of the foster parents.'

IX DEFENCES

Once it has been shown that an article interferes with the due course of justice either on the real risk of prejudice approach or upon the prejudgment test, then there are few defences recognised by the common law provided the defendant is properly adjudged to have published the offending material. Where the Contempt of Court Act 1981 applies, however, s 5 will be available.

A The defence of public interest at common law

As we saw in Chapter 5 the possibilities at common law of invoking the defence of public interest look slender in the light of the *Sunday Times* decision. Not only did Lords Reid and Cross reject the contention favoured by Lord Denning MR that the public interest in being informed about the thalidomide tragedy outweighed the *private* interest of Distillers in having a fair trial on the basis that it was misconceived—the right to a fair trial being a public interest—but they went further and seemed to rule out the possibility that the public interest in being informed could in certain circumstances outweigh the *public* interest in having a fair trial. Despite this Lord Denning MR referred to such a defence subsequently. In *Wallersteiner v Moir,* [14] for example, his Lordship said 'If it is a matter of public interest, it can be discussed at large without fear of thereby being in contempt of court'. He continued a little later:

'Lord Reid said in the *Sunday Times* case: "there must be a balancing of relevant considerations". The most weighty consideration is the public interest. The share holders of a public company should be free to discuss the company affairs at the company meetings. If a shareholder feels that there have been, or may be, abuses by those in control of the company, he should be at liberty to give voice to them.'

With respect to Lord Denning MR, he quoted Lord Reid misleadingly. What the latter actually said was:[15]

'There must be absolute prohibition of interference with a fair trial but beyond that there must be a balancing of relevant considerations.'

In other words, there can be no balancing of interests if a publication is thought creative of a real risk of prejudice to the particular case or is thought to prejudge

14 [1974] 3 All ER 217 at 230, [1974] 1 WLR 991 at 1004–1005.
15 [1974] AC 273 at 296D.

the issue. In view of this it would be unwise to rely upon Lord Denning MR's opinion.

It may be fair comment to say that the European Court of Human Rights' decision in the *Sunday Times* case was based on the notion that the public interest in the case outweighed in that case the public interest in the due administration of justice. However, this does not represent the common law view nor is it a binding judgment in any common law jurisdiction.

B   The discussion of public affairs

The common law does recognise that the discussion of matters of public interest will not be a contempt if it incidentally and unintentionally creates a real risk of prejudice to pending civil proceedings.

As Lord Reid said in the *Sunday Times* case[16] this means that the discussion, for example, of the propriety of local authorities or other landlords ejecting squatters from empty premises due for demolition does not have to cease merely because some proceedings are begun against some squatters—even if it is brought by the same authority that has already been criticised in the press. However, as the *Sunday Times* case shows, this defence (if it is properly so regarded) does not permit detailed reference to the particular case especially when it is intended to influence that case. On the other hand, some reference to the particular case might be permissible. In the Australian decision, *Ex p Bread Manufacturers* [17] it was held permissible for a newspaper to repeat criticisms against a particular company in the context of a discussion of an issue at large, despite the fact that that company had issued a writ of libel against the newspaper.

In the *Sunday Times* case Lord Morris thought[18] that criticism of the law during the pendency of proceedings was permissible, as for example in the thalidomide case, on whether the law was right on insisting that liability be based on fault and whether the principles of assessing damages was fair.

C   The application of s 5 of the 1981 Act

Where the strict liability rule under the 1981 Act applies, s 5 provides that a publication made as or as part of a discussion in good faith of public affairs or other matters of general public interest is not a contempt if the risk of prejudice is merely incidental to the discussion.[19] Even if it can be proved that a publication creates a substantial risk of serious prejudice it is still incumbent upon the prosecution[20] to prove that such a risk is not incidental. Section 5 has mainly been discussed in relation to criminal proceedings where, as we saw in Chapter 5, the courts have interpreted it generously.[1] However, Lord Diplock clearly served notice in *A-G v English* [2] that the type of comment published in the *Sunday Times*

16   Ibid at 296B, C.
17   (1937) 37 SR NSW 242. See Ch 5 pp 171 ff.
18   [1974] AC 273 at 306.
19   See pp 175.
20   Following *A-G v English* [1983] 1 AC 116, [1982] 2 All ER 903.
1   See pp 176.
2   [1983] 1 AC 116 at 143C, [1982] 2 All ER 903 at 920.

case would not be covered by s 5 since the risk of prejudice could not be said to be *incidental* to the discussion.

As far as civil proceedings are concerned, s 5 was pleaded in *A-G v Hislop* [3] but rejected at first instance and briefly dismissed in the Court of Appeal.[4] The section was also raised in *A-G v News Group Newspapers Ltd* [5] but as the Court of Appeal decided there was no risk of prejudice it was not relevant, and the same occurred in *Re Lonrho Plc.* [6]

D   Other defences

The statutory defence of innocent publication under s 3 of the Contempt of Court Act 1981 which is discussed in Chapter 10 applies to civil proceedings as do the common law defences preserved by s 6(a) such as the lack of intent to publish.[7]

---

3   [1991] 1 QB 514.
4   Parker LJ commenting 'Mr Lightman sought before this court to reverse the judge's finding on this point. He did so however with a brevity and lack of enthusiasm which were entirely appropriate. I need say no more about it than that the judge was in my view plainly right': ibid at 529 and 921.
5   [1987] QB 1.
6   [1990] 2 AC 154.
7   See Ch 3.

CHAPTER 7

The timing of publications

I INTRODUCTION

Before a publication can be held to be in contempt on the basis that it creates a risk of prejudice to particular legal proceedings it must satisfy a 'time requirement' since there is a point in time both before and after the trial when the law of contempt does not operate at all. The problem of time does not arise in relation to other types of contempt. Contempts in the face of the court[1] are only possible when the court is in session whilst words or conduct amounting to 'scandalising the court'[2] may amount to contempt whenever they occur.

The timing issue, or the 'sub judice rule' as it is sometimes referred to, has long been a thorny topic in contempt law. Not least of the problems has been to discover precisely what the law is and, as will be seen, this uncertainty has not been entirely resolved by the Contempt of Court Act 1981. The underlying problem, which the timing issue throws into prominence, is how to reconcile the interests of freedom of speech with that of a fair trial and at the same time produce reasonable certainty.

Although publications prosecuted under the 'strict liability rule' of the Contempt of Court Act 1981 will be subject to the statutory time provisions, the common law time limits still apply to publications intended to prejudice proceedings.[3] Moreover, jurisdictions outside the United Kingdom will be subject to the common law rules. For these reasons discussion of the time at which publications can be a contempt still requires consideration of the common law position.

II COMMON LAW

A Criminal proceedings

1 *When does the law of contempt begin to operate?*

(a) The English position

The question of when proceedings begin for the purposes of contempt is the most controversial aspect of the timing issue. The common law position in England seems to be that the law of contempt definitely applies when proceedings are

---

1 See Ch 2.
2 See Ch 9.
3 Discussed at pp 106 ff.

'pending' and almost certainly to when they can be said to be 'imminent'. There is, however, uncertainty as to the application of the law to 'imminent' proceedings which is compounded by the uncertainty of the concepts of both 'imminence' and 'pending'. Modern authorities[4] even suggest that contempt may apply *before* proceedings are 'imminent'. The difficulty, as always, is to balance the protection of trials from prejudice with upholding freedom of speech. Too early a starting point unduly restricts freedom of speech but uncertainty too has an inhibiting effect.

(i) Application of contempt to 'pending' proceedings   Throughout the nineteenth century it was accepted that the law of contempt applied to comments on 'pending' proceedings.[5] Little attention, however, was paid either to the meaning of 'pending' or to whether proceedings *had* to be 'pending' for contempt to apply. In *R v Castro, Onslow's and Whalley's Case*,[6] however, it was held that contempt applied to comments made after committal proceedings and the fixing of the date for trial before assizes but before that trial had taken place. Cockburn CJ said[7] that it made no difference in principle whether comments were made with reference to a 'trial actually commenced or going on or with reference to a trial which is about to take place'.

The law was extended by three cases decided early this century. In *R v Parke* [8] it was held that the law of contempt applied to comments made *before* the accused had been committed for trial. In *Parke* an accused had been arrested, charged, brought before magistrates and remanded for eight days. The offending comments were published during the remand period. It was held that the High Court had jurisdiction to punish the comments as contempt because the charge in question had to be tried by an assize court and since assizes was a branch of the High Court an offence against that branch was an offence against the High Court itself.

In *R v Davies* [9] the court went further, holding that contempt applied to comments made prior to a committal even if they related to a charge which could only be tried in an inferior court. Wills J justified this position[10] upon the basis that, as the Court of King's Bench was the custos morum of all the subjects of the realm and was invested with a superintendent jurisdiction over inferior courts to see that they did impartial justice, it was incumbent upon it not only to correct the misfeasance of the inferior courts themselves but also to correct others whose conduct tended to prevent the due performance of their duties by such courts.

R v Davies has been followed both in England[11] and elsewhere[12] and has been relied upon as authority for saying that proceedings are 'pending' whenever a

4 *A-G v News Group Newspapers Plc* [1989] QB 110, [1988] 2 All ER 906.
5 For a more detailed historical analysis see the first edition of this work at pp 130–1.
6 (1873) LR 9 QB 219. In *Re Syme, ex p Worthington* (1902) 28 VLR 552, the Supreme Court of Victoria held that the contempt jurisdiction applied only after committals.
7 Ibid at 227.
8 [1903] 2 KB 432.
9 [1906] 1 KB 32.
10 Ibid at 39, 40.
11 The principle has been used to apply contempt protection to proceedings before coroners courts, see *R v Clarke, ex p Crippen* (1910) 103 LT 636 at 641 per Lord Coleridge J; courts martial, see *R v Daily Mail, ex p Farnsworth* [1921] 2 KB 733; county courts, see *R v Edwards, ex p Welsh Church Temporalities Comrs* (1933) 49 TLR 383 and consistory courts, see *R v Daily Herald, ex p Bishop of Norwich* [1932] 2 KB 402.
12 In Australia see *John Fairfax & Sons Pty Ltd v McRae* (1955) 93 CLR 351 (Australian High Court) and *A-G (NSW) v Mirror Newspapers Ltd* [1980] 1 NSWLR 374. In Canada see eg *Re British Columbia Ferry Corpn and British Columbia Ferry and Marine Workers' Union* (1979) 100 DLR (3d) 705 (BC CA). In New Zealand see *R v McKinnon* (1911) 30 NZLR 884.

case is before magistrates, regardless of where the charge may eventually be tried.[13] Interestingly, however, the principle that whenever a power to correct an inferior tribunal exists so too does a power to protect it, upon which so much of the law of contempt was developed, would no longer be acceptable as a test for determining whether proceedings before a tribunal are protected by contempt.[14]

The law was extended by *R v Clarke, ex p Crippen*.[15] Following the issue of a warrant for his arrest on a charge of wilful murder, Crippen was arrested on board a ship in Canadian waters and brought before a Quebec judge under the Fugitive Offenders Act 1881 'in order that proper proceedings might be taken to have him returned to England'. The offending article was published while Crippen was in the course of being brought to London for trial but before he had been formally charged. Did contempt apply to comments made after the arrest but before a formal charge? It was held that it did. Darling J commented:[16]

> '. . . to say that after a magistrate has performed a judicial act upon sworn information laid before him there are no proceedings against the accused person, and where the person has been arrested upon a warrant and is in custody that there are no proceedings against the accused person in the sense that anybody is at liberty to say whatever he pleases concerning the case . . . would be gravely to narrow the jurisdiction of this court. . .'

As the above comments show, the court's reasoning was that proceedings are 'pending' once the criminal process has been formally set in motion by a judicial act. Indeed it was upon this basis that the court, albeit obiter, was prepared to say that contempt applied from the time that a warrant has been issued. This was most clearly stated by Lord Coleridge J:[17]

> '. . . after an information has been laid before the magistrate and he has issued a warrant . . . all comments after that, tending to prejudice the administration of justice, are in the nature of contempt. The issue of the warrant is an act of a magistrate not merely ministerial but involving the exercise of a judicial discretion. It is therefore the first step in the criminal process.'

Lord Coleridge J hinted that contempt could be applicable even earlier when he expressly declined any opinion as to whether it would apply when 'the sole thing that has been done was the swearing of an information upon which no further steps had been taken'. It is doubtful, however, whether proceedings can properly be said to be 'pending' at this stage, at least under the principle that the criminal process must have been formally set in motion by a judicial act rather than by mere police activity. However, if it is correct to say that proceedings

---

13 Including cases that can only be tried by magistrates, see *John Fairfax & Sons Pty Ltd v McRae* (1955) 93 CLR 351.
14 See *A-G v BBC* [1981] AC 303, [1980] 3 All ER 161, HL; *New South Wales Bar Association v Muirhead* (1988) 14 NSWLR 173, 202 per Mahoney JA (NSW, CA). The problem of which bodies' proceedings are protected by contempt is discussed in Ch 12. See also Lowe and Rawlings, 'Tribunals and the Laws Protecting the Administration of Justice' [1982] PL 418.
15 (1910) 103 LT 636.
16 Ibid at 639.
17 Ibid at 641. At 640 Pickford J said 'There is ample authority for holding that the prosecution has begun, at any rate, where the warrant is issued.' Darling J was more cautious for while he said (at 639) 'no case has been called to our attention where it has ever been held that the issue of a warrant is not the commencement of proceedings'; he later said 'I do not mean to say that the laying of the information alone, coupled with the granting of the warrant, would not have been quite sufficient without any assent at all. I am not going to say a word to prejudge that case.'

cannot be 'pending' until curial procedures have been invoked[18] then it is difficult to see why a case should be regarded as 'pending' upon an arrest without a warrant. On the other hand, a contempt law which distinguishes between arrest with and without a warrant can hardly be described as sensible. In the Australian High Court decision *James v Robinson* [19] the impugned publication took place while a murder suspect was being pursued in a massive manhunt. He was arrested without a warrant shortly afterwards. En route to deciding that no contempt had been committed because at the time of publication the proceedings were not 'pending' the court said that:[20]

> '(t)he proposition that proceedings are pending in criminal cases after a person has been arrested and charged is firmly established.'

No distinction was drawn between arrest with or without a warrant but given that the case concerned the latter scenario it is submitted that the case is authority for saying that proceedings are 'pending' at this stage. Whether, therefore, proceedings are 'pending' only if criminal proceedings have been set in motion by some judicial act is perhaps best regarded as an open question. As far as English common law is concerned there seems little doubt that contempt would apply to comments made after an arrest without a warrant. However, as will be seen, the English authorities are in favour of saying that contempt can begin to apply even *before* proceedings are 'pending' and consequently any difference between the two modes of arrest is less likely to be crucial.

A second point discussed in *Crippen's* case was whether the High Court had contempt jurisdiction to punish comments upon proceedings before coroners' courts. Darling J was careful to say that he was not going to decide that question but Lord Coleridge J thought there was jurisdiction upon the '*Davies* principle'.[1]

(ii)   Application of contempt to 'imminent' proceedings

a The position before the Contempt of Court Act 1981   The cases just cited should not be regarded as authority for saying that proceedings *have* to be 'pending' before contempt can apply. At common law in England it appears that it can also apply in respect of proceedings which are merely 'imminent' and perhaps, in special circumstances, even prior to that.[2]

Wills J certainly contemplated a wide role for contempt when he said in *R v Parke*:[3]

> 'Great stress has been laid by (counsel) upon an expression which has been used in the judgments upon questions of this kind—that the remedy exists when there is a cause pending in the Court. We think undue importance has been attached to it. It is true that in very nearly all the cases which have arisen there has been a cause actually begun, so that the expression, quite natural in the circumstances, accentuates the fact, not that the case has begun but that it is not at an end. That is the cardinal consideration. It is possible very effectually to

18 Cf the reasoning in the Scottish decision, *Hall v Associated Newspapers Ltd* 1978 SLT 241 at 249, discussed at p 247.
19 (1963) 109 CLR 593.
20 Ibid at 606 per Kitto, Taylor, Menzies and Owen JJ.
1   (1910) 103 LT 636 at 641. For the '*Davies* principle' see p 236.
2   See *A-G v News Group Newspapers Ltd* [1989] QB 110, [1988] 2 All ER 906, discussed at pp 240 ff.
3   [1903] 2 KB 432 at 437. See also Pickford J in *R v Clarke, ex p Crippen* (1910) 103 LT 636 at 640 where he says that he had not decided that it was necessary that proceedings should be 'pending'.

poison the fountain of justice before it begins to flow. It is not possible to do so when the stream has ceased.'

The idea that contempt might apply before proceedings are 'pending' was adverted to by Lord Hewart CJ when he commented in *R v Daily Mirror, ex p Smith*:[4]

'We are not called upon to consider the question whether there may be a contempt of court when proceedings are imminent but have not yet been launched.'

It is probably because of this statement that there developed the notion that the contempt laws apply to 'imminent' proceedings. In *R v Odham's Press Ltd, ex p A-G*[5] Lord Goddard CJ seemed to contemplate that contempt could begin before an arrest.

Added impetus to the belief that contempt applied to 'imminent' proceedings was given by the wording of s 11 (1) of the Administration of Justice Act 1960, namely:

'A person shall not be guilty of contempt of court on the ground that he has published any matter calculated to interfere with the course of justice in connection with any proceedings *pending or imminent* at the time of publication if at that time (having taken all reasonable care) he did not know and had no reason to suspect that proceedings were *pending*, or that such proceedings were *imminent*, as the case may be' (emphasis added).

It was upon the basis of the wording of this now repealed section that *R v Beaverbrook Newspapers Ltd*[6] was decided. Until 1988 this decision of the Northern Ireland High Court was the only known contempt prosecution in respect of 'imminent' proceedings to have succeeded. It concerned a reporter who entered a suspect's house which was surrounded by police, and conducted an interview. The ensuing article was published, with a photograph, shortly before the suspect was arrested and charged. The reasoning of this decision may be doubted since reliance was placed exclusively on the statute in holding that contempt applied to 'imminent' proceedings. No inquiry was made, as it should have been, as to whether the statutory provision truly reflected the common law position for it is a principle of statutory interpretation that a statute is presumed not to alter the pre-existing rules of common law. The purpose of s 11(1) was to provide a defence and it was framed in the negative: it is difficult to construe it as amounting to an intentional positive amendment to the common law.[7]

R v Savundranayagan and Walker[8] is more persuasive authority for the application of contempt to 'imminent' proceedings. There Savundra contended that his conviction for fraud should be quashed because his trial had been prejudiced by a notorious television interview with him by David Frost before his arrest. In referring to that interview Salmon LJ said, albeit obiter:[9]

'It must not be supposed that proceedings to commit for contempt of court can be instituted only in respect of matters published after proceedings have actually

---

4 [1927] 1 KB 845 at 851. Cf Talbot J who, at 852, had clear reservations about extending contempt protection beyond proceedings that are 'pending'.
5 [1957] 1 QB 73, [1956] 3 All ER 494. See the comment in *Justice: Contempt of Court* (1959) p 11.
6 [1962] NI 15. For a commentary on this case see (1964) 15 NILQR 219.
7 See AL Goodhart, (1964) 80 LQR 166.
8 [1968] 3 All ER 439.
9 Ibid at 441.

begun. No-one should imagine that he is safe from committal for contempt of court if, knowing or having good reason to believe that criminal proceedings are imminent, he chooses to publish matters calculated to prejudice a fair trial.'

Certain statements in the House of Lords lend further support. For example, Lord Reid said in *A-G v Times Newspapers Ltd*:[10]

'There is no magic in the issue of a writ or in a charge being made against an accused person. Comment on a case which is imminent may be as objectionable as comment after it has begun.'

And Lord Diplock said in *A-G v Leveller Magazine*: [11]

'Of those contempts that can be committed outside the courtroom the most familiar consist of publishing, in connection with legal proceedings that are pending or imminent, comment or information that has a tendency to pervert the course of justice . . .'.

Apart from these judicial pronouncements there is a plethora of support from extra judicial comments that contempt applies to 'imminent' proceedings. Lord Parker CJ said so in an address to the Judicial Council of Massachusetts[12] and the Salmon Report on the Law of Contempt as it affects Tribunals of Inquiry concluded:[13]

'Although there have been differences of opinion expressed on this subject the better view seems to be that as far as criminal proceedings are concerned the law of contempt bites when such proceedings are imminent.'

A similar conclusion was, perhaps more hesitantly, reached by the Phillimore Committee[14] and the 1978 Government Discussion Paper on contempt said:[15]

'The effect of the decided cases makes it prudent for the media to assume that strict liability for contempt applies as soon as legal proceedings are "imminent".'

b The position after the Contempt of Court Act 1981   Any idea that the uncertainty over 'imminence' had been rendered obsolete by the timing provisions of the Contempt of Court Act 1981[16] has been dispelled by the decisions after the Act which show that, using the saving provision in s 6(c), the courts are prepared to apply the common law to cases in which an *intention* to prejudice can be found.[17] Faced with cases to which the strict liability rule would not apply because the proceedings were not 'active' within the meaning of Schedule 1 of the Act the courts have therefore looked for 'intention' and applied the wider timing provisions of the common law.

The most striking of these cases is *A-G v News Group Newspapers* [18] in which the *Sun* newspaper helped to finance a mother's private prosecution against a doctor whom she accused of raping her young daughter but whom the DPP

---

10   [1974] AC 273 at 301B. See also Lord Diplock at 308C.
11   [1979] AC 440 at 449G
12   39th Report of the Judicial Council of Massachusetts, 1963, referred to by Goodhart, (1964) 80 LQR 166. See also Viscount Kilmuir, 222 HL Official Report (5th series) col 252.
13   (1969, Cmnd 4078) p 9.
14   (1974 Cmnd 5794) para 84.
15   (1978 Cmnd 7145) para 12.
16   See pp 255 ff.
17   See pp 106 ff.
18   [1989] QB 110, [1988] 2 All ER 906.

declined to prosecute. The *Sun* announced its intervention in the matter and ran a series of sensational condemnatory articles about the doctor and his alleged conduct.[19] The proceedings were not 'active' within the meaning of the 1981 Act and were not launched until some seven weeks after the appearance of the articles. The Attorney General nevertheless brought a contempt prosecution and the Divisional Court, having decided that the editor intended to prejudice the doctor's trial, had to consider whether the common law sub judice rules were satisfied.

Watkins LJ (with whom Mann LJ agreed) looked at *R v Parke*,[20] the Australian case *James v Robinson*,[1] the words of Lord Diplock in *A-G v Times Newspapers Ltd*[2] and the previous edition of this book[3] in considering when the sub judice period began at common law and what was meant by 'imminent' proceedings. He agreed that 'imminent' was a vague and uncertain concept but held that, if it was necessary to prove that the proceedings in this case were imminent,[4] the Attorney General had done so.

The 'imminent' problem and the decision in *A-G v News Group Newspapers* were considered by a differently constituted Divisional Court in *A-G v Sport Newspapers Ltd*[5] in which the *Sport* was prosecuted for common law contempt for revealing, before the warrant for arrest was issued, the previous criminal convictions of a man whom the police were hunting in connection with the disappearance of a schoolgirl. The newspaper was acquitted because the requisite intention to prejudice was not proved[6] but the Divisional Court discussed the timing issue.

Bingham LJ took the view that the judicial observations made prior to the Administration of Justice Act 1960 pointed to a growing consensus that contempt could apply to proceedings which were imminent although not in existence and that the draftsman of s 11(1) intended to recognise that consensus. He also made the point that the only sensible purpose s 6(c) of the 1981 Act would seem to serve is to preserve liability for contempt in respect of imminent proceedings where there is an intention to prejudice, for liability in respect of active proceedings is covered by s 2(2) regardless of intention.[7] He therefore concluded:[8]

> 'I accordingly have no doubt that a publication made with the intention of prejudicing proceedings which, although not in existence, are imminent may be contemptuous and punishable as such if it gives rise to the required risk.'

Hodgson J disagreed. He made an exhaustive review of the authorities and emphasised the point made above[9] that prior to the 1981 Act there may have been judicial dicta to the effect that contempt applied to imminent proceedings but there was no decision on the point and nor had the courts ever actually considered what 'imminent' meant. The Administration of Justice Act 1960, s 11(1) could

19 In exchange for its assistance the mother promised the *Sun* exclusive interviews and photographs and undertook not to speak to any other media. See further p 245.
20 [1903] 2 KB 432; see p 236.
1 [1963] 109 CLR 593; see pp 247 ff.
2 [1974] AC 273 at 308.
3 (2nd edn, 1982) pp 167–168.
4 As is discussed below, Watkins LJ was prepared to extend the sub judice period to a time before the proceedings became 'imminent'.
5 [1992] 1 All ER 503 (DC), [1991] 1 WLR 1194.
6 For the meaning of intention, see pp 106 ff.
7 [1992] 1 All ER 503 at 514–516, [1991] 1 WLR 1194 at 1206–1207.
8 [1992] 1 All ER 503 at 515, [1991] 1 WLR 1194 at 1207.
9 At pp 239–240.

not itself have widened the common law time limits. He relied heavily on the Scottish, Irish and Australian cases[10] which have held that imminent proceedings are not covered by contempt and was particularly concerned that the position in England should not differ from that in Scotland.

Above all, Hodgson J saw the matter as a question of principle. He considered that the exceptional power of judges to punish persons by a summary procedure and without trial by jury was to enable them to protect the proceedings over which they have control and the right to a fair trial of those who have entered their jurisdiction: where the proceedings had not reached that point there is no justification for such a power and the power should not be widened. The ordinary criminal law could deal with offences of perverting the course of justice. He also said also that in laying down strict rules about 'active' proceedings in the 1981 Act Parliament was clearly accepting the Phillimore recommendations as to certainty over time limits and that it was 'highly desirable' that there should be the same certainty over deliberate contempt by publication.

(iii)   Application of contempt to proceedings before they are 'imminent'   In *A-G v News Group Newspapers* (the *Sun* case, discussed above), Watkins LJ did not confine himself to holding that contempt could apply to 'imminent proceedings'. He accepted the argument that there was no authority which states that proceedings *have* to be imminent before contempt can be committed at common law and said:

> 'the circumstances in which a criminal contempt at common law can be committed are not necessarily, in my judgment, confined to those in which proceedings are either imminent or pending. . .'[11]

He therefore concluded that contempt had been committed whether or not the proceedings could be classified as 'imminent'.

There is, with respect, a fallacy in the argument that proceedings do not have to be imminent because there is no authority at common law proceedings which says that they do, for previous cases proceeded on the assumption that 'imminent' was the minimum requirement for the application of contempt and the argument had hitherto been about the meaning of that imprecise notion. It is not clear whether Watkins LJ considered that he was extending the ambit of contempt. On the one hand he said:[12]

> 'The common law is not a worn out jurisprudence rendered incapable of further development by the ever increasing incursion of Parliamentary legislation. It is a lively body of law capable of adaptation and expansion to meet fresh needs calling for the exertion of the discipline of law.'

On the other hand he cited Sir John Donaldson MR in *A-G v Newspaper Publishing Plc* [13] who said that the law of contempt was based on the broad principle that the courts cannot and will not permit interference with the due administration of justice:

---

10 Discussed at pp 247 ff.
11 [1989] QB 110 at 133, [1988] 2 All ER 906 at 920.
12 [1989] QB 110 at 133.
13 [1988] Ch 333 at 368; he also relied upon *A-G v Butterworth* [1963] 1 QB 696, discussed at pp 412 ff.

'Its application is universal. The fact that it is applied in novel circumstances . . . is not a case of *widening* its application. It is merely a new example of its application.'

At first sight it is startling that after the passing of a statute which deliberately limited the sub judice period the common law could be held to cover proceedings which have not even reached the 'imminent' stage. However, *A-G v News Group Newspapers* involved an unedifying scenario which presented a particular challenge to the administration of justice and it is understandable that Watkins LJ wished, whatever uncertainty attends the concept of 'imminent', to make it plain that contempt applied to the situation. As he said:

'The common law surely does not tolerate conduct which involves the giving of encouragement and practical assistance to a person to bring about a private prosecution accompanied by an intention to interfere with the course of justice by publishing material about the person to be prosecuted which could only serve to and was so intended to prejudice the fair trial of that person. This is especially so when the publisher of them makes it plain that he believes the person referred to in the articles is guilty of serious crime, that he is deserving of punishment for that and that he has committed some other serious crime.'

The question is whether, in order to catch this behaviour, it is necessary to hold that contempt applies before proceedings are imminent. It will be recalled that Watkins LJ himself thought that the proceeedings in this case *were* imminent.

When the issue was considered in *A-G v Sport Newspapers Ltd* [14] Bingham LJ doubted whether common law contempt could apply even before proceeedings were imminent, saying:

'If the question was at large, I would be much more hesitant whether that proposition could hold if proceedings were not imminent.'

However, he concluded that *A-G v News Group Newspapers* was such a clear, recent decision on the point that he should hold that common law contempt *can* be committed in respect of proceedings which are neither in existence or imminent. He raised the point of whether the decision in that case would have been reached had the ratio of the Australian case *James v Robinson* [15] been relied upon or the Scottish case of *Hall v Associated Newspapers Ltd* [16] been cited but said it would be idle to speculate. Instead he went for what he saw as certainty and clarity:

'In a matter of this nature it is very highly desirable that that the law should be clear so that it may be understood and observed. I am quite satisfied that we should not be justified in departing from the rule so recently and unambiguously laid down in this court.' [17]

It goes without saying that in rejecting the application of contempt to imminent proceedings[18] Hodgson J also rejected Bingham LJ's application of it to proceedings not yet imminent. *A-G v News Group Newspapers* was, he admitted 'plain authority' for the application of contempt prior to proceedings being pending but, nevertheless, it was wrong and he declined to follow it.

14 [1992] 1 All ER 503, [1991] 1 WLR 1194.
15 (1963) 109 CLR 593, see below.
16 1978 SLT 241, discussed at p 247.
17 [1992] 1 All ER 503 at 515, [1991] 1 WLR 1194 at 1207.
18 See pp 241–242.

What then is the position? There is clear authority for the application of contempt beyond the 'imminent proceedings' point. Nevertheless it is notable that Watkins LJ related his remarks very closely to the actual facts at issue in the *Sun* case. The complication in the case stemmed from the fact that where a private prosecution is concerned the usual landmarks of arrest, warrant and charge are missing and the only significant moment is the laying of an information before a magistrate. Moreover, crucially, the *Sun* was not in the position, as the media often are, of not knowing how events will turn out or how situations will develop because it was in control of matters since at the time of the first article it had already made the agreement with the mother concerning financial support in return for exclusivity of access.

The conduct disapproved of in the *Sun* case could conceivably also arise in the context of an ordinary criminal prosecution, if the Crown Prosecution Service publicised prejudicial matters about a person against whom they had decided to bring proceedings. It must be remembered, however, that in the UK common law contempt is committed only if there is an *intention* to prejudice and it may be that the indictable offence of perverting the course of justice would be a more suitable charge to bring in such circumstances.[19]

The question of the application of contempt to proceedings before they are imminent is inextricably bound up with the determination of the moment at which proceeedings *become* imminent. As is shown by the judgments of Watkins LJ in the *Sun* case and Bingham LJ in the *Sport* case, the attraction of pre-imminent contempt is that it circumvents the notorious difficulties of pinpointing that moment. However, there is no need to apply contempt to proceedings which are not yet imminent if imminence is itself an elastic enough concept.

(iv)   The meaning of 'imminent'   What, then, *does* 'imminent' mean? The concept admits of no easy definition. It is not even clear precisely *what* has to be 'imminent'. Definitions commonly refer to the proximity of the arrest but it would be perhaps preferable to relate the timing to proximity of court proceedings. On the other hand it *is* reasonably likely, although not inevitable, that once a suspect has been arrested, court proceedings will follow fairly quickly.

'Imminent' would suggest that the relevant event will take place in the immediate future. Viscount Kilmuir (when Lord Chancellor) commented in the House of Lords' debate on the Administration of Justice Bill, clause 11:[20]

> 'Proceedings may be imminent, for example, when no one has yet been charged with a crime but an arrest is expected hourly.'

R v Beaverbrook Newspapers Ltd[1] is a good example within this definition. The police had surrounded a suspect's house, but nevertheless, a reporter was allowed to enter the house where an interview, which was later published, took place. The article and a photograph were published shortly before the suspect was arrested and charged with murder. Sheil J said:[2]

> 'how any reasonable person, knowing the contents of the report and having expert advice available, could have failed to form the opinion that proceedings were imminent, passes my comprehension.'

19   The last time this charge was used in the case of a prejudicial publication was in *R v Tibbits and Windust* [1902] 1 KB 77.
20   222 HL Official Report (5th series) col 252.
  1   [1962] NI 15.
  2   Ibid at 21.

He also suggested that 'imminent' meant 'impending' or 'threatening'.

A somewhat wider view of 'imminence' was taken by Salmon LJ. In the report under his chairmanship on Contempt of Court as it affects Tribunals of Inquiry it was said:[3]

'There are cases, however, in which it is obvious that a certain individual is on the point of being arrested on a serious criminal charge—perhaps in 24 hours, perhaps in seven or eight days, it is impossible to lay down a precise scale.'

This approach is reminiscent of his Lordship's comments in *R v Savundranayagan and Walker*[4] that at the time of the interview with Savundra 'it must surely have been obvious to everyone that he was about to be arrested and tried on charges of gross fraud'.

The criteria of 'obviousness' is a very uncertain test. What is 'obvious' after the event is by no means clear beforehand. In *Savundra*'s case itself, it is doubtful whether the imminence of proceedings was 'obvious'. As David Frost pointed out in a letter to *The Times*: [5]

'There had been no police action in the seven months following the initial newspaper coverage and there was no official indication that there would be. Nevertheless, we checked privately with the Board of Trade and elsewhere and were informed: "We have nothing on Dr Savundra. Go ahead".'

The Divisional Court in the *Sun* case was prepared to hold the proceedings to be imminent, if that was necessary. Those proceedings were in the contemplation of the editor at the time. Crucially, the editor had at the time of the articles entered into an agreement with the child's mother to support her private prosecution. The matter would have been more difficult had that step not been taken. It is hardly possible to classify as 'imminent', proceedings in which no action at all has been taken and where the future prosecutor is merely considering the matter. Note should be taken of in *Re Crown Bank, in Re O'Malley*,[6] a civil case which concerned a contempt by publication prejudicing the fair trial of a winding-up petition. The shareholder who presented the petition had, prior to the presentation, 'put in motion' a series of newspaper articles containing unfavourable comments about the company and its directors. North J rejected the idea that these articles could be a contempt.[7] The petition was plainly contemplated by the shareholder, but he had not done anything towards it at the time of publication. If contempt is to be judged at the time of publication it is difficult to quarrel with this conclusion. However, it is not clear whether this was a case where the proceedings were held not to be imminent, or whether the court was rejecting the application of contempt to imminent proceedings.[8]

'Imminence' is an elusive concept, and while it would seem clearly to cover cases where 'a man is helping police with their inquiries' or the situation in *Beaverbrook Newspapers* where the publication appeared while the police were surrounding a suspect's house, it appears to go beyond that. Are proceedings

3   (1969, Cmnd 4078) p 9.
4   [1968] 3 All ER 439 at 441.
5   (1968) Times, 18 July.
6   (1890) 44 ChD 649.
7   Ibid at 651.
8   The case focused on articles published after the petition was presented which North J held *were* a contempt. In the *Sport* case Hodgson J thought that North J's dictum concerning the earlier articles were not obiter and that had the case been cited in the *Sun* case the court would have had to have overruled it in order to come to the conclusion that it did.

'imminent' when there is a massive manhunt in operation for a named man?[9] The answer might well depend on how quickly the suspect is arrested after the publication. The *Sport* case did concern a manhunt, but as one judge thought that contempt could apply before proceedings were imminent and the other thought that only pending proceedings were covered[10] the point was not answered. Are proceedings 'imminent' when a suspect is arrested abroad and extradition proceedings are in progress or about to begin?[11] Again the answer might depend on how quickly the case comes before the English courts.

The problem with this approach, which amounts in effect to looking at the matter with hindsight, is that it does not produce a test for determining whether or not publication is a contempt at the moment of publication. As Hodgson J said in *A-G v Sport Newspapers Ltd*,[12] it suggests a form of 'contingent contempt' the quasi-criminality of which has to wait upon events. Bingham LJ was prepared to solve this conundrum by drawing a distinction between apparent and actual imminence. What mattered, he said, was what appeared to the contemnor at the time as being likely to happen, rather than what did happen:[13]

> 'But in considering a common law contempt based on intention, it would seem to me that what would matter (if imminence were relevant at all)[14] would not be the factual record of what actually happened but what appeared to the alleged contemnor as being likely to happen. Thus an event might appear to be imminent and turn out not to be, or appear not to be but turn out to be so. If, contrary to the opinion expressed above, imminence is any longer an appropriate test at all, the test must (I think) relate to what is apparently imminent and not to what turns out to be so.'

This is not easy to understand, but Bingham LJ seems to be suggesting that the publisher must *himself* believe that proceedings are imminent: if he does not there can be no contempt regardless of actual events. If he does believe it, however, there can be contempt whatever transpires. The problem with this is that common law contempt can only be committed where there is an *intention to prejudice*. If the publisher has an intention to prejudice proceedings which appear to him to be imminent but which in fact are not one is back with the question discussed in Chapter 4[15] of whether intention alone, regardless of actual risk, can constitute contempt. If the proceedings do not appear to the publisher to be imminent it would be difficult to prove that he had an intention to prejudice them. There is the added complication too, of the situation when what is apparently imminent in the eyes of the world at large is not so in the opinion of the publisher. Is the apparent imminence purely subjective?

In reality one scenario where contempt in respect of imminent proceedings is likely to arise is where there is a police manhunt in respect of a named individual (as happened in the *Sport* case) or a similar operation. If the police are successful

9 In the situation that arose in *James v Robinson* (1963) 109 CLR 593.
10 See pp 241 ff.
11 Apparently, the *Sunday Times* once withdrew a background article on Stephen Raymond (later convicted of theft) when it was discovered that he had been detained in Switzerland. Query whether, prior to extradition proceedings, proceedings in England could be said to be 'imminent'?
12 [1992] 1 All ER 503 at 529 quoting Windeyer J in *James v Robinson* (1963) 109 CLR 593 at 616, discussed at pp 247 ff.
13 [1992] 1 All ER 503 at 517–518.
14 This is a reference to the fact that Bingham LJ had just said that proceedings do not *have* to be imminent for contempt to apply.
15 See pp 79 ff.

and proceedings follow then publications before the arrest may cause a real risk of prejudice. To this extent it cannot easily be gainsaid that liability for contempt is contingent. In such situations it is not difficult for the media to restrain themselves for a time from discussing the previous convictions and character of the persons concerned or generally discussing the merits of the case. Warnings to the public in the *Sport* case were satisfactorily communicated by the rest of the media to the public without disclosing the wanted man's previous convictions. The problem arises when time passes without an arrest and the lack of police success makes the proceedings look less likely. The police in the United Kingdom may in theory still be looking for Lord Lucan but one would hardly describe proceedings as 'imminent'. Indeed, it can be argued that once police operations are scaled down proceedings are no longer to be regarded as imminent. In the United Kingdom these difficulties are more theoretical than real because of the requirement of intention to prejudice in respect of imminent proceedings.

The *Sun* scenario, where proceedings yet to be begun are deliberately prejudiced by the potential prosecutor, present a particular problem and it is submitted that the difficulty of trying to define imminence with reference to this exceptional type of case clouds the general issue.

(b)   The Scottish position

At one time the law in Scotland seemed particularly draconian, for according to Lord Clyde in *Stirling v Associated Newspapers Ltd,* [16] contempt could apply 'once a crime has been suspected and once the criminal authorities are investigating it'. This dictum has, however, now been ruled unsound. According to *Hall v Associated Newspapers Ltd* [17] the test to be applied is whether proceedings have reached the stage when it can be said 'that the court has become seised of a duty of care towards individuals who have been brought into a relationship with the court'. Applying that test[18] it was held that contempt applied from the moment of arrest or (obiter) from the moment when a warrant for an arrest has been granted. With regard to the former it was felt that at that time the person arrested is within the protection of the court since he is vested with rights (for example he must be informed of the charge and must be brought before a magistrate within 24 hours) which he can invoke and which the court is under a duty to enforce.

(c)   The Australian position

In *James v Robinson* [19] the Australian High Court firmly rejected the contention that contempt can be committed when proceedings are 'imminent', with Windeyer J saying[20] 'imminent is an imprecise word by which to mark out a period of time'. The offending publication appeared while a 'manhunt' was in progress following a double killing and the suspect was caught and arrested within 24 hours of the publication. The defence contended that as no warrant for the suspect's arrest had been issued at the time of publication, the proceedings could not be said to be

16   1960 SLT 5 at 8.
17   1978 SLT 241 at 248.
18   Ibid at 249.
19   (1963) 109 CLR 593, followed in *R v Crew and IPEC Australia Ltd* [1971] VR 878 (Vict Sup Ct).
20   Ibid at 618.

'pending' even within the widest meaning of the concept and hence there could be no contempt. The court agreed.

One reason for the decision was the court's conclusion that the common law authorities supported the view that for contempt to apply proceedings *have* to be 'pending'. A second reason was that a publication must be a contempt at the time of publication. The majority said:[1]

> 'If a publication is to constitute contempt at all it must be a contempt at the time it is made, and the person aggrieved must be aggrieved in his capacity of a party to proceedings; therefore he must be a party at that time. It would be an astonishing state of affairs if a person responsible for a publication were to be held guilty or not guilty according as proceedings should or should not be commenced thereafter.'

A third reason justifying a restricted approach was that the case was said to concern a 'narrow kind of contempt' (ie a publication tending to interfere with the fair trial of a particular case) as opposed to a 'general contempt' (ie the type of contempt, such as scandalising the court, that involves an interference with the administration of justice generally).

None of the reasons given for the decision is entirely convincing. As discussed above the common law decisions in England at the time of *James v Robinson* were not committed to the idea that proceedings had to be 'pending'.[2] Secondly, there is little justification for distinguishing different types of contempt. All contempts involve an interference with the administration of justice generally and indeed it could be argued that the chief aim in punishing 'prejudicial' publications is to uphold the *public* interest in the administration of justice rather than the *individual's* right to a fair trial. The idea that a person aggrieved must be aggrieved as a party for contempt to apply is open to the objection that it excludes the possibility of contempt beginning at the time a warrant is issued for arrest (or even at the point of arrest). Yet in *James v Robinson* the court seemed to accept that contempt could begin at such a point.

The timing issue also arose in *A-G for NSW v TCN Channel Nine Pty Ltd* [3] in which a film of an arrested man being led around the scene of the crime by the police was shown on television, with a commentary which clearly implied that he had confessed to a number of murders (which was indeed the case). At the time of the broadcast the man had been arrested and charged but not yet brought before the court. The New South Wales Court of Appeal thought there was nothing in *James v Robinson* to suggest that in order for proceedings to be pending a person had to have been brought before the court and cited with approval the statement in *Hall v Associated Newspapers* [4] that 'from the moment of arrest the person arrested is in a very real sense under the care and protection of the court'. The court concluded that the critical moment for contempt was the time of arrest for from that moment:

> 'The processes and procedures of the criminal justice system, with all the safeguards they carry with them, applied to him and for his benefit, and . . .

---

1 Ibid at 607 per Kitto, Taylor, Menzies and Owen JJ.
2 While it may be superficially attractive to say, of *Crippen*'s case ((1910) 103 LT 636), for example, that the court would not otherwise have analysed the meaning of 'pending' it overlooks Pickford J's express caveat that he was not deciding that proceedings *had* to be 'pending'.
3 (1990) 20 NSWLR 368.
4 1978 SLT 241 at 249.

publications with a tendency to reduce those processes, procedures and safeguards to impotence are liable to attract punishment as being in contempt of court.'[5]

In *TCN Channel Nine* the court referred to the English courts' recent application of contempt to imminent proceeedings[6] and to the similar decision in New Zealand[7] but showed no inclination to follow the same path. The Australian position seems therefore to be that contempt applies from the moment of arrest, that being the time at which proceedings become 'pending'.

(d) The position in other jurisdictions

In New Zealand there seemed to be an assumption that the Australian position— that the proceedings had to be pending—applied.[8] However, in *Television New Zealand Ltd v S-G* [9] the Court of Appeal considered the application of contempt to a situation where the police were conducting a manhunt for a named man but no charge had yet been laid. In that case the Solicitor General obtained an interim injunction to prevent a television news broadcast which included comments and opinions about the hunted man from friends and neighbours. The court rescinded the injunction on the grounds that the material was unlikely to prejudice a fair trial but would have been prepared to uphold it had that not been so. The court cited *A-G v News Group Newspapers Ltd* [10] for the proposition that the circumstances in which criminal contempt at common law can be committed by pre-trial media publications are not confined to circumstances in which proceedings are either pending or imminent and said:[11]

> 'In our opinion the law of New Zealand must recognise that in cases where the commencement of criminal proceedings is highly likely the court has inherent jurisdiction to prevent the risk of contempt of court by granting an injunction.'

The court gave no indication of the meaning of 'highly likely'. It did however insist that freedom of the press was not lightly to be interfered with and that a real likelihood of serious prejudice must be shown. This leaves New Zealand with a more far-reaching contempt law than either Australia, where proceedings must be pending,[12] or the UK, where the application to anything other than active proceedings depends on the intention of the contemnor.

As far as Canada is concerned one Canadian commentator has stated[13] that the 'sub judice rule' begins to apply when the court obtains jurisdiction over the matter 'and in criminal cases that is when information is sworn before a justice of the peace upon which either a summons or warrant is issued or where a person is arrested by a police officer'. For this assertion he largely relies on English authorities.

---

5 (1990) 20 NSWLR 368 at 378, applying the 'seminal principle' stated in *R v Parke* [1903] 2 KB 432 at 436.
6 *A-G v News Group Newspapers* [1989] QB 110, discussed at pp 240 ff.
7 *Television New Zealand v S-G* [1989] 1 NZLR 1, see below.
8 Professor JF Burrows, *News Media Law in New Zealand* (1st edn, NPA of NZ) p 233.
9 [1989] 1 NZLR 1.
10 [1988] 2 All ER 906, preferring this to the Australian case of *James v Robinson* (1963) 109 CLR 593.
11 [1989] 1 NZLR 1 at 3.
12 See above.
13 Stuart M Robertson, *Courts and the Media* (1981, Butterworths, Toronto) p 48.

2   *When does the law of contempt cease to operate?*

It has long been accepted that once criminal proceedings have ended so too has the risk of prejudice to those proceedings. As Wills J said in *R v Parke:* [14]

> 'It is possible very effectually to poison the fountain of justice before it begins to flow. It is not possible to do so when the stream has ceased.'

There is broad agreement in the various common law jurisdictions as to when criminal proceedings are regarded as being at an end for the purposes of contempt. The generally accepted view is that proceedings remain sub judice until an appeal hearing is completed or the time has expired within which notice of appeal may be given. In other words not only must the original hearing be completed but so must the possibility of appeal be at an end. Although in England it is possible to find authority for the view that a criminal case is over once proceedings in the Court of Appeal have been completed,[15] the better view supported, albeit obiter, by Lord Parker CJ in *R v Duffy, ex p Nash* [16] is that proceedings are not over until the House of Lords stage has been exhausted.

It is to be emphasised that cases remain sub judice, irrespective of whether an appeal is actually lodged, until the period for appealing has expired.[17]

There is less certainty as to whether the possibility of a retrial can keep proceedings alive for the purposes of contempt. Where a trial ends in a jury disagreement it is submitted that because a retrial is likely proceedings are better regarded as sub judice unless and until it is decided not to proceed with a second trial.[18] In the event of a retrial being ordered by the Court of Appeal[19] proceedings must surely remain sub judice until that hearing and any subsequent appeals have been disposed of.

A further problem relates to the position where charges are adjourned sine die. In *A-G v Times Newspapers Ltd* [20] the Court of Appeal were firmly of the opinion that contempt could only apply to proceedings that were actively being pursued and this view seems to have been accepted in the House of Lords in that case. Assuming this to be so and accepting that the same view applies to criminal proceedings it would seem that proceedings adjourned sine die fall outside the contempt umbrella.[1]

It is important to emphasise that the foregoing discussion has merely been concerned to outline the period during which publications are *at risk* of being in contempt. It is one thing to say that proceedings during this period are protected by contempt but quite another to say that the offence will be committed. In fact, as we have seen,[2] publishers run little risk of being found guilty of contempt for publishing articles during the appellate period, at least on the grounds of possible prejudice.

14   [1903] 2 KB 432 at 438.
15   Humphreys J in *Delbert-Evans v Davies and Watson* [1945] 2 All ER 167 at 174; sub nom *R v Davies, ex p Delbert-Evans* [1945] 1 KB 435 at 444.
16   [1960] 2 All ER 891 at 893.
17   See in Australia, *Re Truth and Sportsman Ltd, ex p A-G* (1958) 61 SR (NSW) 484. In New Zealand see *A-G v Crisp and 'Truth' (NZ) Ltd* [1952] NZLR 84.
18   Cf *Re Labouchere, ex p Columbus Co Ltd* (1901) 17 TLR 578.
19   See the discussion in Ch 5, p 163.
20   [1973] QB 710, [1973] 1 All ER 815, CA, [1974] AC 273, [1973] 3 All ER 54, HL.
 1   Cf the position with regard to coroners' proceedings: *Peacock v London Weekend Television* (1985) 150 JP 71, discussed at p 262.
 2   At pp 162 ff.

B Civil proceedings

1 *When does the law of contempt begin to operate?*

The timing issue has not often been adverted to in relation to civil proceedings. However, it seems commonly accepted that the law of contempt operates once proceedings are 'pending'. *Dunn v Bevan* [3] is usually cited as authority for saying that civil proceedings become 'pending' immediately the writ is issued. Although this point was made obiter it appears correct. [4] It is sensible to regard civil proceedings as 'pending' as soon as any formal step is taken to commence such proceedings. This would include, for example, not merely issuing a writ but also the issuing of an originating summons or the presentation of a petition. It is authoritatively established that the case does not have to be set down for trial before the law of contempt can operate. [5]

Even if proceedings are 'pending' contempt may not operate if those proceedings are not being actively pursued. This, at least, was the firm view of the Court of Appeal and accepted by the House of Lords in the *Sunday Times* case. [6] There is, however, difficulty in determining when proceedings are being actively pursued. The Court of Appeal considered the 'proceedings' in the *Sunday Times* case to be dormant principally because beyond issuing a writ no formal steps in the action had been taken in the subsequent three or four years. As Scarman LJ said [7] 'The reality of the situation, therefore, is that no-one expects a trial; the writs were issued as moves towards a settlement.' The House of Lords rejected this approach. It was unanimously agreed that the law of contempt was as much concerned to protect pre-trial negotiations as to protect the trial itself. The proceedings in question could not be said to be 'dormant' since negotiations for a settlement were being actively pursued. As Lord Reid said [8] 'If there is no undue procrastination in the negotiations for a settlement I do not see how in this context actions can be said to be dormant.'

Whatever may be the merits of protecting pre-trial negotiations the House of Lords' approach makes it difficult to know whether proceedings are being actively pursued or not.

Does the law of contempt operate before civil proceedings can be said to be 'pending'? Although two nineteenth century cases [9] support the view that it does not apply at this earlier stage (ie when proceedings are merely threatened) it would be unsafe to rely on them since they pre-date *R v Parke* [10] and *R v Davies*. [11] There are, moreover, two statements in the *Sunday Times* case supporting the view that contempt applies when proceedings are 'imminent'. Lord Reid said: [12]

> 'There is no magic in the issue of a writ or in a charge being made against an accused person. Comment on a case which is imminent may be as objectionable as comment after it has begun.'

3 [1922] 1 Ch 276.
4 The case was actually concerned with proceedings that had ended but at 284 Sargant J cited with approval Oswald's statement to the above effect: *Contempt of Court* (2nd edn) p 62.
5 See Lord Cross in *A-G v Times Newspapers Ltd* [1974] AC 273 at 323C–D.
6 [1973] 1 All ER 815, CA, [1974] AC 273, HL.
7 [1973] 1 All ER 815 at 827.
8 [1974] AC 273 at 301D.
9 *Re Cornish, Staff v Gill* (1893) 9 TLR 196 and *Re Crown Bank* (1890) 44 Ch D 649.
10 [1903] 2 KB 432.
11 [1906] 1 KB 32.
12 [1974] AC 273 at 301B.

Lord Diplock said:[13]

> 'To constitute a contempt of court that attracts the summary remedy, the conduct complained of must relate to some specific case in which litigation in a court of law is actually proceeding or is known to be imminent.'

Neither of the above statements can be regarded as conclusive authority upon the point. However, if contempt *does* operate when criminal proceedings are 'imminent' it is rational to have a similar approach to civil proceedings. Indeed, the following example may be thought to justify the operation of the law at this earlier time: a company, learning that a minority shareholder is wishing to bring an action against it and is canvassing other shareholders for support, publishes a circular intending to discredit the shareholder so as to deter him from bringing the action and to deter other shareholders from supporting him or appearing as witnesses for him.[14] If contempt in civil proceedings does have a similar starting point that does not mean it will necessarily be found to be so readily committed. The time lag even from the inception of proceedings to the actual hearing will normally be much longer than in a criminal context and hence the risk of prejudice much less. A fortiori this will be so where civil proceedings can only be said to be imminent.

In Australia and Scotland, where the law of contempt does not apply to 'imminent' criminal proceedings, there is no reason to suppose that the law will be extended to 'imminent' civil proceedings.[15] For those jurisdictions where the timing issue is an open point a practical argument against applying the law to 'imminent' civil proceedings is the difficulty in defining the term in this context. Further, there is the important policy issue of whether it is right to restrict comment so far in advance of any eventual trial.

2   When does the law of contempt cease to operate?

It is submitted that there should be no difference between civil and criminal proceedings for the purposes of the time within which contempt can be committed. Accordingly, proceedings should be regarded as remaining sub judice until *all* the appeals have been concluded (ie including an appeal to the House of Lords) or alternatively until the period within which an appeal can be made has expired without such appeal. There is some authority for the view that once judgment has been given civil proceedings must be regarded as ended, provided no appeal has been made, even though the time for appealing has not expired. For the most part the cases supporting this view[16] pre-date the modern case law[17] except for the

---

13 [1974] AC 273 at 308C. It is also worth pointing out that s 11(1) of the Administration of Justice Act 1960 (now repealed) made no distinction between criminal or civil proceedings.
14 See *Commercial Bank of Australia Ltd v Preston* [1981] 2 NSWLR 554.
15 Cf *Commercial Bank of Australia Ltd v Preston*, ibid, where it was held (per Hunt J) that for public conduct pressurising a party, contempt could be committed *before* proceedings are 'pending'.
16 *Re ERA Newspapers, Dallas v Ledger* (1888) 4 TLR 432 and *Metzler v Gounod* (1874) 30 LT 264. See also in Scotland, *Glasgow Corpn v James Hedderwick & Sons* 1918 SC 639 (Court of Session) per Lord Strathclyde the Lord President. Cf Lord Johnstone.
17 *Delbert-Evans v Davies and Watson* [1945] 2 All ER 167 (although admittedly Humphreys J did say (at 169) 'I say nothing about the law generally, or of the law proceedings for contempt as it applies to civil proceedings') and *R v Duffy, ex p Nash* [1960] 2 QB 188, [1960] 2 All ER 891.

1961 Australian decision of *Re Consolidated Press Ltd, ex p Dawson.* [18] It is difficult, however, to defend a distinction between civil and criminal proceedings (which is what *Dawson* expressly does) and it is not sensible to allow for a temporary suspension of the sub judice period between judgment at first instance and the lodging of an appeal. The difference of view may be academic since the likelihood of a publication being held to create a risk of prejudice to appellate proceedings is remote.

Where a civil case ends in a jury disagreement it is submitted that proceedings should be regarded as sub judice unless and until it is decided not to proceed with a second trial. Similarly, if an appeal court remits a case for a rehearing those proceedings will remain sub judice until the case has finally been disposed of.

Wardship proceedings are better regarded as ended only when the child in question ceases to be a ward and not necessarily at the end of court proceedings.[19]

III THE PROPOSALS FOR REFORM

A The starting point

The Phillimore Committee[20] could see no case for retaining the concept of 'imminence' since it defies definition and could apply arbitrarily depending on the chance outcome of events. As the Committee said, the vagueness of 'imminence' has 'an inhibiting effect on the freedom of the press which is out of all proportion to any value there may be in preserving it'.

Moving away from the concept of 'imminence' does not resolve the difficulty of deciding when contempt ought to begin to apply. There remains the problem of selecting a starting point that is both sufficiently certain and early enough to afford real protection to any ensuing trial. The Phillimore Committee[1] recommended that for criminal proceedings the starting point should be (a) in England and Wales, when the accused person is charged or a summons served, and (b) in Scotland, when the person is publicly charged on petition or otherwise or at the first calling in court of a summary complaint. Had this recommendation been implemented, it is suggested that it would have tipped the balance too far in favour of freedom of speech. Quite simply, the suggested starting point would have been too late to afford real and necessary protection to the accused. A subsequent Government Discussion Paper seemed to take a similar view. As it said:[2]

> 'Charges often follow shortly after a serious crime becomes known; and indeed, from the point of view of an accused person it may be as important to have protection from prejudicial comment during the period immediately before he is charged, when media and public interest in the crime is strong, as it is after a charge has been formally laid.'

---

18 [1961] SR (NSW) 573 (NSW Sup Ct). For a criticism of the case see (1964–6) 2 Tasmanian University Law Review 71–4.
19 For the precise details on when a wardship order ends see Lowe and White, *Wards of Court* (2nd edn, 1986) Chs 4 and 5. For the law of contempt as it affects wardship see pp 451 ff.
20 (1974, Cmnd 5794) para 117.
 1 Ibid at paras 123 and 216(10).
 2 (1978, Cmnd 7145) para 14.

The Paper concluded that on that footing 'there is ground for the view that the Phillimore recommendation goes too far in allowing prejudicial publication before a formal charge is made, so endangering the fair trial of accused persons'.

The Canadian Law Reform Commission[3] was also impressed by the need for certainty but it too rejected the Phillimore recommendations and proposed instead that the sub judice period should begin at the moment an information is laid. The Australian Law Reform Commission[4] recommended that contempt should apply from the time when a warrant for arrest has been issued, a person has been arrested without a warrant, or charges have been laid, whichever is the earliest. However, it also recommended that if a person 'implicated' in a publication at an earlier point acted with the *intention* of prejudicing the relevant trial, so as to amount to an attempt to pervert the course of justice, he should be able to be prosecuted for that offence under s 43 of the Crimes Act 1914 (Cth). This has echoes of the position reached in the United Kingdom after the Contempt of Court Act 1981.[5]

The Irish Law Reform Commission[6] also recommended two tests. The first, which would apply in 'normal' cases, would apply contempt only to 'active' proceedings as defined in the UK Contempt of Court Act 1981.[7] The second would apply contempt to 'the rare case where, in relation to proceedings which are not active but are imminent, a person publishes material when he is actually aware of facts which, to his knowledge, render it certain, or virtually certain, to cause serious prejudice to a person whose imminent involvement in criminal or civil legal proceedings is certain or virtually certain'.

As will be seen in the next section UK law was reformed with an earlier starting point than recommended by Phillimore.

For civil proceedings the Phillimore Committee argued[8] for a later starting point for contempt, there being less need to protect such proceedings since the risk of prejudice was less and the liberty of the subject not in issue. There was no case, they thought, for applying contempt to 'imminent' proceedings and there were objections to applying it to 'pending' proceedings since the restrictions operated too far in advance of the trial and facilitated the tactic of issuing a so-called 'gagging writ'. Accordingly, the Committee proposed that[9] the starting point should be (a) in England and Wales, when the case has been set down for trial, and (b) in Scotland, when proof or jury trial has been ordered. The undoubted advantages of this are to create certainty, bring the law into line with the House of Commons sub judice convention[10] and go some way to resolving the problem of the 'gagging writ'.[11] Moreover shifting the balance significantly in favour of freedom of speech would seem more in accord with our obligations under the European Convention on Human Rights.[12] Its only disadvantage is that it leaves unprotected pre-trial negotiations but this may be thought a small price

3 1977 Working Paper No 20 on Contempt of Court, p 44 and see the 1982 Report No 17: *Contempt of Court*, pp 44, 54–6 (Cl 4(3)(b)).
4 Report No 35: *Contempt*, para 296.
5 See pp 240 ff.
6 *Contempt of Court* (July 1991) p 321.
7 For the details, see pp 255 ff.
8 At para 124.
9 At paras 127, 129 and 216(11).
10 Described by the Phillimore Committee at paras 118–120.
11 Discussed at pp 189 ff.
12 Particularly in view of the decision of the European Court of Human Rights in the *Sunday Times* case (1979) 2 EHRR 245.

to pay in the interests of certainty and freedom of speech. The Canadian Law Reform Commission[13] proposed the same starting point and, as we shall see, this is the point adopted under the Contempt of Court Act 1981. The Australian Law Reform Commission[14] took the view that this still resulted in too long a sub judice period and thought that contempt should only apply when (a) it is known that the trial will take place before a jury, and (b) pre-trial proceedings have reached the stage when the case is genuinely ready to proceed. Generally they thought that the fixing of a date for hearing would be sufficient.

2 The ending point

The question of the point at which contempt should cease to apply has attracted less comment than the question of where it should begin. In fact the Phillimore Committee proposed[15] that the law be relaxed so that save where there is a jury disagreement, or where a retrial is actually ordered, contempt should normally cease to apply at the conclusion of the first instance hearing. In criminal cases, it was made clear that this meant, in the event of a verdict of 'guilty', after sentence. In other words, except in the case of an appeal against conviction from magistrates' courts to the Crown Court, which was thought to merit special protection because it is by way of a rehearing, it was proposed that appellate proceedings should not be protected by contempt.

In view of the minimal risk of prejudice at this stage it might be felt that this proposal was fully justified though it attracted little attention at the time. The Canadian Law Reform Commission originally thought[16] that in the interests of certainty and (more plausibly) in the interests of maintaining the public image of the administration of justice and a desire to avoid unduly embarrassing judges, it was better to retain what it conceived to be the existing rules, namely, that the sub judice period should end at the conclusion of the final appeal. In their final report, however, the Commission felt that at the appellate stage the risks of prejudice were minimal and accordingly recommended that the sub judice period end at the determination of the trial or hearing at first instance.[17]

IV   THE TIMING PROVISIONS UNDER THE CONTEMPT OF COURT ACT 1981[18]

A   The concept of 'active' proceedings under the 1981 Act

Where the 'strict liability rule' applies the Contempt of Court Act 1981 introduces the notion of 'active' proceedings. Section 2(3) provides:

---

13 At p 45 of the Working Paper and see also pp 44, 54–56 (Cl 4(3)(a)) the Final Report.
14 At para 339.
15 (1974, Cmnd 5794) paras 132 and 216(12).
16 At pp 44–45 of the Working Paper.
17 See pp 30–31, 54-6 (Cl 4(3)) of the Final Report.
18 For a variety of contemporary comments on the provisions see eg SH Bailey, (1982) 45 MLR 301, 306–8; Miller, [1982] Crim LR 71, 74–77; Lowe, (1981) 131 NLJ 1167, 1168–9 and [1982] PL 20, 22 and 26; and ML Pearl, 1981 SLT 141–3. See also the extensive notes to the Act in Sweet and Maxwell's *Annotated Statutes* series.

'The strict liability rule applies to a publication only if the proceedings in question are active within the meaning of this section at the time of the publication.'

'Active' proceedings are defined by Schedule 1 to the Act.

B   Criminal proceedings

'Criminal proceedings' are defined[19] as proceedings against a person in respect of an offence, excluding appellate proceedings and proceedings commenced by motion for committal or attachment[20] in England and Wales or Northern Ireland.

1   *The starting point*

By Schedule 1, para 4, criminal proceedings *become* 'active' upon:

(a) arrest without warrant;

(b) the issue, or in Scotland the grant, of a warrant for arrest;

(c) the issue of a summons to appear, or in Scotland the grant of a warrant to cite;

(d) the service of an indictment or other document specifying the charge;

(e) except in Scotland, oral charge.

Paragraph 4 is a virtual enactment of the starting point in Scotland as laid down by *Hall v Associated Newspapers Ltd* [1] and in any event closely corresponds to what the common law in England and elsewhere understands as 'pending' proceedings.

For the most part, in theory at least, the provisions in para 4 are self-explanatory. The one area of doubt may be to determine the exact point at which a person can be said to be arrested without a warrant. There is no statutory definition of 'arrest', despite the Police and Criminal Evidence Act 1984,[2] but Blackstone described it as the 'apprehending or restraining of one's person in order to be forthcoming to answer an alleged or suspected crime'.[3] A person may be said to be arrested as soon as he is detained against his will.[4] However, there

---

19 Sch 1, para 1.
20 The reference to commencement by motion for committal or attachment is to contempt proceedings. However, it is no longer possible to proceed by motion for attachment for contempt: see pp 475–476.
1   1978 SLT 241.
2   Referred to in this work as the PACE Act.
3   *Commentaries* (1830) p 289. In Bevan and Lidstone, *The Investigation of Crime* (1991) at p 215 the authors suggest that an amended version of Blackstone in the light of PACE might read 'Arrest is the apprehending or restraining of one's person in order to detain him at a police station while the alleged or suspected crime is investigated and in order that he be forthcoming to answer an alleged or suspected crime'.
4   For the powers of the police in relation to the detention and questioning of suspects, see the Code of Practice for the Detention, Treatment and Questioning of Persons by Police Officers (Code C) passed under the PACE Act, Bevan & Lidstone, op cit, Chs 5–8, De Smith and Brazier, *Constitutional and Administrative Law* (6th edn) pp 462–466, Zander, *The Police and Criminal Evidence Act 1984* (2nd edn) pp 57–149, Wade and Bradley, *Constitutional and Administrative Law* (11th edn) pp 482–492, Feldman, *Civil Liberties and Human Rights in England and Wales* (1993) pp 169–172 and 207–231.

is a major problem area in respect of people said to be 'helping the police with their inquiries'. In fact the police have no general power to detain a person against his will 'to help with their inquiries.'[5] On the other hand there is nothing to stop a person going to the police station voluntarily. In theory as soon as a person is involuntarily detained at the station he is under arrest and must then be charged within the statutory periods.[6] In practice it may be difficult to say at what point a person becomes involuntarily detained although s 29 of the PACE Act attempted to clarify matters by providing:

> 'Where for the purpose of assisting with an investigation a person attends voluntarily at a police station or at any other place where a constable is present or accompanies a constable to a police station or any such other place without having been arrested—
> (a) he shall be entitled to leave at will unless placed under arrest;
> (b) he shall be informed at once that he is under arrest if a decision is taken by a constable to prevent him from leaving at will.'

A suspect may, however, still wrongly believe that he is under arrest when he is not[7] and it is virtually impossible for an outsider, such as an editor, to determine the position. The situation in Scotland is even more difficult because under the Criminal Justice (Scotland) Act 1980, s 2,[8] the police now have a limited statutory right to detain without a warrant any person who is reasonably suspected of having committed or committing an offence punishable by imprisonment.

Although proceedings are not 'active' whilst a person is *voluntarily* 'helping the police with their inquiries' in view of the above difficulties it may be wise for the media to refrain from commenting on the case at that time. In any event sanctioning comment is a risky enterprise at this stage particularly for newspapers as an editor cannot be sure that the person will not have been arrested by the time the newspaper is published.

At first sight it may seem curious that proceedings are not 'active' at this stage; after all adverse publications can at this point present a very real risk of prejudice to the eventual trial. The problem for the legislators, however, was that 'helping the police with their inquiries'[9] is not a legally recognised concept, while in the literal sense plenty of people who are in no way under suspicion, for example witnesses, help the police. In other words it would have been difficult to have included this situation without creating general uncertainty as to the starting point for contempt.

A major difficulty with the starting point under para 4 is the practical one of discovering whether a warrant for arrest has been issued or an arrest made. It was these difficulties that led the Phillimore Committee to reject either event being designated the starting point for contempt. As it said:[10]

---

5 See *R v Lemsatef* [1977] 2 All ER 835, [1977] 1 WLR 812 (CA); McKenzie, Morgan and Reiner, 'Helping the Police with Their Inquiries: The Necessity Principle and Voluntary Attendance at The Police Station' [1990] Crim LR 22–33.

6 Laid down in the PACE Act 1984, ss 41–44. Under the Prevention of Terrorism (Temporary Provisions) Act 1989, s 14 the police are allowed to detain a suspect held under that Act for up to 48 hours prior to charge and may have this period extended for up to five days with the consent of the Secretary of State.

7 See Zander, *The Police and Criminal Evidence Act 1984* (2nd edn), pp 65–67.

8 As amended by the Criminal Justice (Scotland) Act 1987 s 70(1) and Sch 1.

9 Zander, *The Police and Criminal Evidence Act 1984* (2nd edn), p 65 rightly describes it as a 'polite euphemism' and it seems probable that the phrase was originally used to avoid possible defamation actions.

10 Para 123.

'a warrant for arrest is usually issued in private, and even an actual arrest may not, for good reasons, be immediately announced by the police. In these circumstances the press might well not know whether they were at risk.'

These difficulties should not be underestimated and they can best be minimised by the police co-operating with the media. However, even if, on occasion, that co-operation is not as forthcoming as it might be, a publisher may still escape the rigours of the Act under s 3[11] provided that he can show that at the time of publication, having taken all reasonable care he neither knew nor suspected that the relevant proceedings were active and (probably) that he published in good faith. While s 3 might not provide a complete answer it goes a long way to meet the fears of the Phillimore Committee.

The timing provisions under para 4 are not as generous to the news media as the Phillimore Committee recommendation, which was that the sub judice period should begin only when the person was charged or a summons served.[12] However, despite the difficulties adverted to above it is submitted that the Act gets the timing about right. Paragraph 4 strikes a reasonable compromise between the Phillimore Committee's proposals, which would not have protected a trial from the real risk of prejudice that publicity prior to the charge can cause, and the undesirable uncertainties of the common law position. Indeed, it was the extraordinary publicity which followed the arrest of Peter Sutcliffe in January 1981, which began even before he had been charged with the 'Yorkshire Ripper' murders, which doomed any attempt in the later stages of the Bill to ease the sub judice provisions and follow the Phillimore recommendation.[13] Paragraph 4 should have had the advantage of creating a uniform and reasonably certain starting point applicable to England and Wales, Scotland and Northern Ireland. However, as we have seen,[14] this statutory certainty has been undermined by the continuing application of the common law, with its concept of 'imminence', to intentional contempts.

2   The ending point

By Schedule 1, para 5 criminal proceedings are concluded:

'(a)   by acquittal, or as the case may be, by sentence;
(b)   by any other verdict, finding, order or decision which puts an end to the proceedings;
(c)   by discontinuance or by operation of law.'

It will be noted that under para 5(a) proceedings remain 'active' until sentence rather than verdict. This confirms both the common law position[15] and the

---

11   Discussed at pp 398 ff.
12   Phillimore Committee Report, para 123. The recommendation with regard to Scotland was that the period should run from when the person is first publicly charged on petition or otherwise, or at the first calling in court of a summary complaint, as the case may be.
13   Sutcliffe was arrested in connection with the offence of the theft of motor-car licence-plates. While in detention he began to be questioned about the 'Ripper' murders. Before he had been charged with any of the murders or related offences, the police held the first of their 'congratulatory' press conferences which led to massive publicity about him in the media: see Press Council Booklet No 7: *Press Conduct in the Sutcliffe Case, A Report by the Press Council* (1983).
14   At p 240 ff.
15   Park J's ruling in the Operation Julie trial; discussed at p 161.

Phillimore recommendation. However, whether publications can create a 'substantial risk of serious prejudice' between conviction and sentence seems doubtful.[16] Paragraph 8, confirming the common law view, provides that criminal proceedings before a court-martial or standing civilian court are not concluded until the completion of any review of finding or sentence.

An interesting contrast to para 5(a) is the provision in para 6 that proceedings cease to be active upon a deferment of sentence.[17] In view of the normal six-month delay between conviction and the passing of a deferred sentence[18] it is understandable why it is provided that proceedings should cease to be active upon deferment of sentence.

In general terms para 6 explains that para 5(a) refers to any order or decision which disposes of the case 'either absolutely or subject to future events'. This would seem to cover a probation order or conditional discharge but *not* it is thought, remanding offenders for a social inquiry or medical report.

Paragraph 5(b) is intended to refer to cases where there has been a successful plea in law on the basis of autrefois acquit or autrefois convict (or, in Scotland, tholed assize); where indictment has been quashed and where a case has been adjourned sine die. Adjournments sine die, which must be distinguished from adjournments to a definite but unspecified date, are not thought to be covered by para 9. That provides that proceedings cease to be active where an order is made for the charge to lie on the file, but become active again if leave is later given for the proceedings to continue. Paragraph 10[19] provides, without prejudice to para 5(b), that proceedings cease to be active '(a) if the accused is found to be under a disability such as to render him unfit to plead or, in Scotland, is found to be insane in bar of trial' or (b) if a hospital order is made, but in either case proceedings become active again if they are later resumed.

By para 7 proceedings are discontinued within the meaning of para 5(c):

'(a) in England and Wales or Northern Ireland, if the charge or summons is withdrawn or a nolle prosequi entered;

(aa) in England and Wales, if they are discontinued by virtue of s 23 of the Prosecution of Offences Act 1985;[20]

(b) in Scotland if the proceedings are expressly abandoned by the prosecutor or are deserted simpliciter;

(c) in the case of proceedings in England and Wales or Northern Ireland commenced by arrest without warrant if the person arrested is released, *otherwise than on bail*, without having been charged.' (emphasis added)

Paragraph 7(c) requires some explanation. Normally a person is only released on bail after being charged, in which case proceedings obviously continue to be active, but para 7(c) refers to the case of the police granting bail after arresting a person but before charging him.[1] In that case, too, proceedings continue to be 'active'.

---

16 See the discussion in Ch 5, at pp 161–162.
17 Under the Powers of Criminal Courts Act 1973, s 1; the Criminal Procedure (Scotland) Act 1975, s 219 or s 432 (as amended by the Criminal Justice (Scotland) Act 1980, ss 53 and 54) or the Treatment of Offenders (Northern Ireland) Order 1976, SI 1976/226 Art 14.
18 Under the Powers of Criminal Courts Act 1973, s 1(1) the six-month period is the maximum time allowed but the common practice is to defer sentence for this maximum period.
19 As amended by the Mental Health Act 1983 and the Mental Health (Scotland) Act 1984.
20 Inserted by the Prosecution of Offences Act 1985, s 31(5), Sch 1, Pt 1, paras 4 and 5.
1 See the PACE Act 1984, s 47.

The Act does not expressly provide for a case in which a jury fails to reach a verdict, a situation about which there is some uncertainty at common law[2] although there is specific provision to cover the case where the Court of Appeal orders a retrial.[3] It is submitted that proceedings should be considered active until a formal decision not to proceed with a retrial is made.

Paragraph 11 provides that proceedings which have become active on the issue or grant of a warrant for arrest cease to be active at the end of the period of 12 months beginning with the date of the warrant unless the person in question has been arrested within that period, but become active again if he is subsequently arrested.

This provision[4] is intended to cover what has become known as the 'Lucan situation', ie where the suspect remains undiscovered or flees the country and cannot be extradited. The situation is not apparently that unusual.[5] Paragraph 11 goes some way to meet the objection that the Phillimore Committee had to the issue of the warrant for arrest being a starting point for contempt, namely, that if the wanted man was never found publication would be restricted for as long as the warrant existed.[6] To the objection that 12 months is too long a period it may be said that, though risky, a publication during this period at a time when it is likely, as in Lord Lucan's case, that the suspect would not be found, can only be a contempt if the suspect is ever brought to trial and even then only if there is a 'substantial risk of serious prejudice'.

C   Other proceedings at first instance

The phrase 'other proceedings at first instance' in Schedule 1, para 12 to the 1981 Act is intended to refer to proceedings other than criminal proceedings and appellate proceedings. In this context it primarily means first instance civil proceedings and proceedings commenced by motion for committal or attachment in England and Wales and Northern Ireland, ie contempt proceedings. The phrase also covers coroners' proceedings.[7]

1   *The starting point*

It is with the starting point for civil proceedings that the Contempt of Court Act 1981 made the most important changes to the sub judice period at common law. By para 12 proceedings become active from the time when arrangements for the hearing are made or, if no such arrangements are previously made, from the time the hearing begins. So far as England and Wales are concerned the arrangements for the hearing of proceedings are, by para 13:

---

2 See *Re Labouchere, ex p Columbus Co Ltd* (1901) 17 TLR 578 and p 250.
3 Sch 1, para 16.
4 Introduced at the Bill's third reading in the House of Commons, see 6 HC Official Report (5th series) col 952. It was first mooted at the Committee Stage in the Commons see 1980–81 HC Standing Committee A, Contempt of Court, col 64.
5 See Miller, [1982] Crim LR 75 who refers to the cases of Lord Kagan and John Gaul.
6 Para 123.
7 *Peacock v London Weekend Television* (1985) 150 JP 71.

'(a) in the case of proceedings in the High Court for which provision is made by rules of court for setting down for trial, when the case is set down;

(b) in the case of any proceedings, when a date for the trial or hearing is fixed.'

Paragraph 14 provides the equivalent starting point in Scotland, namely:

'(a) in the case of an ordinary action in the Court of Session, or in the Sheriff court, when the Record is closed;

(b) in the case of a motion or application, when it is enrolled or made;

(c) in any other case, when the date for a hearing is fixed or a hearing is allowed.'

Under para 12 any motion or application made in or for the purpose of any proceedings, (which includes interlocutory proceedings[8] and matters such as an application for discovery) and pre-trial reviews in the county court are treated as distinct proceedings.

These provisions are broadly what the Phillimore Committee recommended and represent a substantial relaxation of the common law position. An important object of the Phillimore Committee was to solve the problem of the so called 'gagging writ'[9] (ie writs issued solely for the purpose of stifling comment). Providing that a case must be set down for trial before proceedings can be 'active' will go some way to achieving this object though even so there may still be opportunity to procrastinate at this later stage. It has also been pointed out[10] that because pre-trial reviews in the county court are designated distinct proceedings for the purposes of para 12, and since the date of the pre-trial review is inserted by the court into an ordinary summons before it is issued, the proceedings will become immediately active.[11]

Pre-trial negotiations will not, unless the case has been set down for trial, be protected under the Act. This represents a reversal (on the timing point) of the House of Lords' decision in *A-G v Times Newspapers Ltd* [12] unless 'prejudice' was thought to be intended.

As with the starting point for criminal proceedings there are practical problems in determining when civil proceedings become 'active'. It is difficult to discover whether a case has been set down for trial, unless the precise name of the case, date of the writ and the Division of the High Court is known.[13] It will be similarly hard to discover if arrangements have been made for an interlocutory hearing. The Phillimore Committee recommended[14] that some information ought to be available as of right to an inquirer but this was not implemented though the Government did promise[15] that court staff would be co-operative.

Given that Parliament has decided that civil proceedings should be protected by contempt, the statutory timing provisions strike a reasonable balance. It cannot be denied that the time between setting down and the actual hearing can

8   See p 262 for complications over interlocutory proceedings.
9   Discussed at pp 189 ff.
10 See the comments on the Act in Sweet and Maxwell's *Annotated Legislation* series.
11 The device may not be effective, at least where it is clear that it is only a gagging writ, see pp 189 ff.
12 [1974] AC 273, [1973] 3 All ER 54; aliter if prejudice is intended, in which case the common law would continue to apply.
13 See the article by a *Times* reporter (1981) Times, 19 May.
14 Para 133.
15 Standing Committee A col 100, 12 May 1981.

be substantial[16] and that this might inhibit a publication which is in the public interest. Nevertheless it must be said that even if proceedings are 'active' the scope for comment is wide and in any case, as we have seen, s 5[17] allows a continuation of discussion of public affairs where the risk of prejudice is incidental to particular proceedings. Selection of any later moment in time, for example, a 'sub judice list' suggested by Robin Day[18] would, it is submitted, operate too late to afford real protection for litigants.

A coroner's inquest becomes 'active' within para 12 at the moment the inquest is opened.[19] Coroners usually now sit without a jury[20] but a jury is necessary in certain circumstances, including where there is reason to suspect that the death occurred in prison or in police custody.[1] Publications may therefore be in contempt because they create a risk of prejudicing the jury. This principle was applied in *Peacock v London Weekend Television* to ban the reconstruction of a death in police custody although a jury had not yet been sworn in and the inquest had been adjourned sine die.[2]

2   The ending point

Paragraph 12 provides that proceedings are 'active' until the proceedings are 'disposed of or discontinued or withdrawn'.

Since interlocutory proceedings are treated as distinct proceedings it means that proceedings cease to be active when the interlocutory hearing is over but will become active again when the main hearing or a subsequent interlocutory hearing is set down for trial. As one commentary has put it,[3] the Act has created 'a confusing pattern of periods of "activity", when the strict liability rule applies, interspersed by intervals when press comment may be fully made' unless, of course, there is an intention to prejudice proceedings. The effects of this were seen in the *Spycatcher* cases[4] in which the newspapers could not be prosecuted under the strict liability rule as the interlocutory proceedings were over and the main action had not been set down for trial. They were therefore prosecuted under the common law, which meant that it was necessary for the Crown to prove intention to prejudice the proceedings.

It was held in *Peacock v London Weekend Television* [5] that the proceedings of a coroner's inquest remain active even when they have been adjourned sine die while police investigations are carried out, as once opened the proceedings must

---

16 See eg the Botham libel case, *A-G v News Group Newspapers Ltd* [1987] QB1, [1986] 2 All ER 833, discussed in Ch 6.
17 Discussed at pp 175 ff and 232.
18 Phillimore Committee Report (1974, Cmnd 5794) pp 98–100 which suggestion was later criticised as being impracticable because of the cost and time involved in having to prepare such lists; see the Government Discussion Paper on Contempt of Court (1978, Cmnd 4078) para 18.
19 *Peacock v London Weekend Television* (1985) 150 JP 71.
20 Pursuant to s 8(1) of the Coroners Act 1988.
 1 Ibid s 8(3).
 2 (1985) 150 JP 71.
 3 In the annotated notes on the Contempt of Court Act 1981 in Sweet and Maxwell's *Annotated Legislation* series.
 4 *A-G v Newspaper Publishing Plc* [1988] Ch 333, [1987] 3 All ER 276; *A-G v Newspaper Publishing plc* (1989) Times, 9 May and (1990) Times, 28 February; *A-G v Times Newspapers Ltd* [1992] 1 AC 191 [1991] 2 All ER 398: see Ch 6, pp 211 ff.
 5 (1985) 150 JP 71.

at some time be resumed. This means that in respect of an inquest the contempt period can last for an indefinite time, which is a highly undesirable state of affairs and one which runs counter to the philosophy of the Act.

C Appellate proceedings[6]

By para 15 appellate proceedings *become* active when they are commenced:

> '(a)   by application for leave to appeal or apply for review, or by notice of such an application;
>
> (b)   by notice of appeal or of application for review;
>
> (c)   by other originating powers.'

By s 9 of the Criminal Appeal Act 1995 a reference by the Criminal Cases Review Commission to the Court of Appeal is to be treated for all purposes as an appeal by the person concerned under the Criminal Appeal Act 1968 and this means that appellate proceedings become active when such a reference is made.[7]

Proceedings cease to be active when they are disposed of, or abandoned, discontinued or withdrawn.

The inclusion of appellate proceedings in the active period for contempt was controversial. Paragraph 15 was widely misunderstood as introducing new restrictions.[8] In fact the statutory provisions are *more* generous than the common law since the active period only begins *following* notice of appeal etc whereas at common law the proceedings remain sub judice throughout the period in which notice to appeal may be given. In any event s 6(b)[9] prevents the imposition of fresh restrictions under the strict liability rule. In short the risks of committing contempt even if proceedings are active are no greater than at common law.

The statutory provisions are less generous than the Phillimore Committee's proposal which was to leave most appellate proceedings unprotected.[10] Was the Government right to reject the proposal? It is not an easy question. During the debates on the Bill great play was made of the difficulties even appellate judges had to face in the event of public outcry against a particular decision.[11] As is seen from the discussion in Chapters 5 and 6[12] recent authority comes down firmly on the side of the immunity of appellate judges from improper influence and there will rarely be any question of prejudicing appellate proceedings. However, it is, it is submitted, preferable to retain the possibility of contempt to cover those exceptional cases in which prejudice might arise.[13]

---

6   For the question of contempt in relation to appellate proceedings generally see Ch 5, pp 162 ff and Ch 6, p 228.

7   This procedure replaces references by the Home Secretary under s 17(1)(a) of the Criminal Appeal Act 1968, which also caused appellate proceedings to become active within para 15.

8   Admittedly, Lord Hailsham's comments during the debates (see eg 415 HL Official Report (5th Series) col 694–5 and 416 HL Official Report (5th series) col 407–9 where he doubted even appellate judges' immunity) may well have contributed to this confusion.

9   Discussed at p 117.

10   Except for appeals from magistrates, courts to the Crown Court in England and Wales which take the form of a complete rehearing: Phillimore Committee Report, para 132.

11   Particular reference was made to the public outcry following the decision in the *Maws Sisters'* murder trial, see House of Commons Standing Committee A, 7 May 1981, col 113.

12   See pp 165 ff and 228.

13   See, eg *In re Channel Four Television Company Ltd* (1987) Times, December 18 and (1988) Times, 2 February, concerning the re-enactment of the Birmingham Six appeal, discussed in Ch 5, p 166.

Under para 16 if in appellate criminal proceedings the court either remits the case to the court below or orders a new trial or a venire de novo or, in Scotland, grants authority to bring a new prosecution, then 'any further or new proceedings which result shall be treated as active from the conclusion of the appellate proceedings'.

That these proceedings continue to be 'active' despite the ending of the appellate hearing confirms what was thought to be the position at common law.

It is to be noted that the equivalent problem in civil proceedings is not specifically dealt with by the Act and presumably, such proceedings become 'active' again when the rehearing is set down for trial.

CHAPTER 8

Reporting court proceedings

I INTRODUCTION

It is a cherished principle of common law jurisdictions that justice should be openly administered. Jeremy Bentham once said:[1]

> 'Where there is no publicity there is no justice. Publicity is the very soul of justice. It is the keenest spur to exertion and the surest of all guards against improbity. It keeps the judge himself while trying under trial. The security of securities is publicity.'

The prima facie rule is that courts of law sit in public. This means that anyone, including members of the media, can attend proceedings and report to the public at large what they see and hear. As Lord Diplock has said:[2]

> 'As a general rule the English system of administering justice does require that it be done in public: *Scott v Scott*. If the way that courts behave cannot be hidden from the public ear and eye this provides a safeguard against judicial arbitrariness or idiosyncrasy and maintains public confidence in the administration of justice. The application of this principle of open justice has two aspects: as respects proceedings in the court itself it requires that they should be held in open court to which the press and public are admitted and that, in criminal cases at any rate, all evidence communicated to the court is communicated publicly. As respects the publication to a wider public of fair and accurate aspects of proceedings that have taken place in court the principle requires that nothing should be done to discourage this.'

The importance of attendant publicity was emphasised by Lord Scarman:[3]

> 'When public policy in the administration of justice is considered, public knowledge of the evidence and arguments of the parties is certainly as important as expedition ... the common law by its recognition of the principle of open justice ensures that the public administration of justice will be subject to public scrutiny. Such scrutiny serves no purpose unless it is accompanied by rights of free speech, ie the right publicly to report, to discuss, to comment, to criticise, to impart and to receive ideas and information on matters subjected to scrutiny. Justice is done in public so that it may be discussed and criticised in public.'

---

1 Cited by Lord Shaw in *Scott v Scott* [1913] AC 417 at 477, in which Lord Halsbury said 'Every court in the land is open to every subject of the King.'
2 In *A-G v Leveller Magazine Ltd* [1979] AC 440 at 449–50. In *MacDougall v Knight* (1889) 14 App Cas 194 at 200, Lord Halsbury commented that freedom to report open court proceedings rests on the principle that such a publication 'is merely enlarging the area of the court and communicating to all that which all had the right to know.'
3 In *Harman v Secretary of State for the Home Department* [1983] 1 AC 280 at 316, [1982] 1 All ER 532 at 547.

In theory, the media have no greater or lesser rights than any other members of the public but in practice they are generally recognised as the means by which the public are informed of court decisions. As Lord Widgery CJ observed:[4]

> 'Today, as everybody knows, the great body of the British public get their news of how justice is administered through the press or other mass media.'

Special places have long been provided for them in the press benches[5] and some statutory recognition of their unique role is witnessed by the fact that some proceedings in England and Wales are open to the press but not to other members of the public.[6]

The general rule of open justice requires that the names of those who sit in judgment should be known. In *R v Felixstowe Justices, ex p Leigh* [7] the Divisional Court held that the inherent power of magistrates' courts to control their own proceedings did not include the power to sit anonymously and withhold their names from the press and public.[8]

The law of contempt is concerned with the need to protect litigants' rights to a fair trial. This means that the right to report even those proceedings heard in open court is not absolute. At the very least the report must be fair and accurate. There is no public interest in permitting inaccurate or misleading reports and those which create a risk of prejudice to current or even future proceedings are as liable to be adjudged contempt as any other publication. The common law also on occasions reserves the right of the trial judge to order the postponement of a report or the withholding of information and, provided the order is lawfully made, publications in breach of it may be deemed a contempt. In some jurisdictions there are also statutory provisions governing these matters. The *postponement* of reports of proceedings is ordered because of a fear of prejudice to current or future proceedings. Once this danger has passed the reporting restrictions are lifted. Other types of restrictions are imposed because of a wish to protect the administration of justice generally or because it is considered undesirable and unnecessary for certain matters to be made public as, for example, the identity of victims of sexual assault and the details of cases of matrimonial breakdown.

It is not always considered desirable that proceedings should be heard in open court. As Viscount Haldane LC said in *Scott v Scott*:[9]

> 'While the broad principle is that courts in this country must . . . administer justice in public this principle is subject to apparent exceptions which, however, are themselves the outcome of a yet more fundamental principle that the chief object of courts of justice must be to secure that justice is done.'

Under this principle, even at common law, courts have power on occasion to

---

4 *R v Denbigh Justices, ex p Williams* [1974] QB 759 at 765.
5 One commentator has complained that 'sitting snugly in their privileged "press bench" reporters may have come to regard themselves as part and parcel of the court process rather than as the eyes and ears of the public': see Robertson and Nicol, *Media Law* (3rd edn) p 307.
6 In magistrates' family proceedings courts and youth court proceedings for example, see pp 310 ff.
7 [1987] QB 582, [1987] 1 All ER 551.
8 The court said that there was no duty to disclose addresses or telephone numbers and that the clerk to the justices would be justified in refusing to give the names of the justices to a person who he reasonably believed wanted the information solely for a mischievous purpose (per Watkins LJ at 595D–E). See also the Resolution of the Magistrates' Association Council Relating to Publication of Names of Justices, July 1985.
9 [1913] AC 417, 437.

sit in private in which case neither the public nor the press have right of access and there is no automatic freedom to report the proceedings.

There are basically three ways, therefore, in which reports of court proceedings may be restricted: first by limiting what can be published about what is disclosed in open court; secondly by not disclosing certain information in open court; thirdly by holding the proceedings in private. The first of these is becoming increasingly problematic. Once matters have been mentioned in open court they can be reported in the foreign media. This may not be of concern insofar as overseas readers will not be sitting on a jury but with every development in communications and information technology it becomes easier for matters originally broadcast or published abroad to 'leak' back into the jurisdiction where the proceedings are taking place. This is the same issue as arises with the prohibition on prejudicial publications generally.[10] Both England and Canada have recently had problems over foreign reporting of sensational criminal trials coming back into the jurisdiction despite reporting restrictions.[11] The response of the courts to these threats may well be to sit in private more frequently and so further erode the principle of open justice.

As we shall see in this chapter, the common law position on reporting court proceedings is not straightforward but, in addition, statutory provisions operate to restrict reports of proceedings in open court or empower courts to sit in private. In the United Kingdom such statutes are legion and, often being an ad hoc response to a particular problem, are complex, inconsistent and diverse. There is an urgent need for consolidation and rationalisation.[12] It is not in the public interest that there should be confusion as to what the public is allowed to hear about the administration of justice.

This chapter deals first with reporting proceedings heard in open court and secondly with proceedings heard in private. In each case the common law is considered and then the statutory position in the United Kingdom.

II REPORTING PROCEEDINGS HEARD IN OPEN COURT

A The position at common law

The general principle is that there is immunity from contempt for fair and accurate reports, published contemporaneously and in good faith, of proceedings heard in open court.

That such reports do not amount to contempt even if they create a risk of prejudice to current or future proceedings is supported by a number of authorities. Perhaps the clearest and most striking of the English authorities is *R v Evening News ex p Hobbs*[13] where the newspaper was held not guilty of contempt for publishing a fair and substantially accurate report of what in effect was a

---

10 See Chs 3–6.
11 In England with the reporting of the committal proceedings involving Rosemary West, held in Dursley, Gloucestershire in 1994–95 when she was sent for trial charged with ten murders and four sex offences; in Canada over the reporting of the trial of Karla Homulka, in *R v Bernardo* (1995) 121 DLR (4th) 42 (see p 280).
12 As an example one might cite the statutory restrictions on reporting proceedings concerning children, discussed at pp 310 ff.
13 [1925] 2 KB 158. See also the cases cited therein. See also *Buenos Ayres Gas Co Ltd v Wilde* (1880) 29 WR 43 where Malins V-C said 'As I understand the law is it is this, that any fair representation of what takes place in a Court of Justice is justifiable provided it is accurate.'

premature assertion of guilt made by the Recorder of London in delivering a charge to the grand jury. As Lord Hewart CJ said 'It would not be right to punish a newspaper for reporting a charge to the jury when the real sting of the criticism is against the charge itself'. A number of cases established, in effect, that at common law 'a fair and substantially accurate report of committal proceedings was lawful notwithstanding any resultant prejudice to the accused'.[14] In *R v Kray*[15] Lawton J commented:

> 'I can see no reason why a newspaper should not report what happens in court, even though there may be other charges pending. The reporting of trials which take place in open court is an important part of the functions of a newspaper, and it would not be in the public interest, in my judgment, if newspapers desisted from reporting trials merely because there was some indictment still to be dealt with. What is more, the mere fact that a newspaper has reported a trial and a verdict which was adverse to a person subsequently accused ought not in the ordinary way to produce a case of probable bias against jurors in a later case. I have enough confidence in my fellow-countrymen to think that they have got newspapers sized up and they are capable in normal circumstances of looking at a matter fairly and without prejudice even though they have to disregard what they may have read in a newspaper.'

A similar position obtains in Commonwealth jurisdictions. In Australia, for example, Jordan CJ commented in *Re Consolidated Press Ltd, ex p Terrill*:[16]

> 'So long as any account so published is fair and accurate and is published in good faith and without malice, no one can complain that its publication is defamatory of him, notwithstanding that it may in fact have injured his reputation, and no one can in general be heard to say that it is a contempt of court notwithstanding that it may in fact be likely to create prejudice against a party to civil or criminal litigation.'

Some doubt was cast upon the common law position in England in *R v Poulson and Pottinger*.[17] Poulson was involved in a series of cases and Waller J was concerned that the reporting of evidence in one might be prejudicial to another. With respect to certain evidence he is reported to have said:[18]

> 'I do not see myself how the press can properly report this evidence without running the risk of being in contempt of this other trial. When we are dealing with someone who is subject to another trial things have been said which might be highly prejudicial to that trial, and therefore must not be published.'

The implication of this statement is that the media are at risk of committing contempt even in the absence of judicial warning or directions if, in the course of reporting the proceedings, (albeit accurately) they create a risk of prejudicing another proceeding.[19] It is doubtful, however, whether Waller J actually did

---

14   See Ackner LJ in *R v Horsham Justices, ex p Farquharson* [1982] QB 762, 802; [1982] 2 WLR 430, 459, citing with approval Miller, *Contempt of Court* (1st edn) p 113.
15   (1969) 53 Cr App R 412 at 414.
16   (1937) 37 SR (NSW) 255 at 257–8. See also *Cassidy v Mercury Newspaper Pty Ltd* [1968] Tas SR 198. For the position in Canada, see Robertson, *Courts and the Media*, pp 44–5 and *R v Solloway, ex p Chalmers* [1936] 4 DLR 321 (Ont). In New Zealand see Burrows, *News Media Law in New Zealand* (3rd edn, Oxford) Ch 7, pp 202 ff.
17   [1974] Crim LR 141.
18   See (1974) Times, 4 January.
19   Some support for this might be derived from *Re Marquis Townshend* (1906) 22 TLR 341 where Lord Collins MR left the point open.

suggest or imply such a possibility. All that he seemed to be saying is that a judge does have the power to direct the postponement of such reports.[20]

We shall discuss the legality of such directions later. If, however, Waller J meant to imply such an inherent limitation on the freedom to report proceedings then it is submitted he was wrong to do so. Quite apart from flying in the face of the authority cited above, as the Phillimore Committee pointed out,[1] it would impose an unacceptably heavy burden upon court reporters. As the Committee said, 'It is not uncommon for evidence to emerge during a trial which is or may be damaging to others whether witnesses or persons who are not before the court at all. To require the press to check in each instance whether such persons are themselves involved in criminal or civil proceedings would be unreasonable'.

It is submitted that there is no such limitation on the freedom to report so that in the absence of judicial warning fair and accurate reports cannot be a contempt because of prejudice thereby occasioned to other proceedings.

It remains now to examine the requirements that must be satisfied to gain immunity.

1   When are proceedings in open court?

The first requirement is that the proceedings are in open court. For this purpose the simple test is whether members of the public have the opportunity to attend the hearing.[2] In the case of civil proceedings, provided they are heard in open court, they are prima facie freely reportable. The same rule applies both to interlocutory and final hearings as was made clear by Malins V-C, in *Buenos Ayres Gas Co Ltd v Wilde*.[3]

In the criminal context, however, it may not be enough that proceedings are heard in open court in the sense just described. Another important consideration is the presence or absence of the jury. It is only evidence heard during the jury's presence that is prima facie freely reportable. Material heard in the jury's absence and which the jury is not entitled to know is not freely reportable. The clearest example of this is a 'trial within a trial' ie where arguments are heard in the jury's absence to determine the admissibility of evidence.[4] Obviously, if evidence is ruled inadmissible it should not be reported until the trial is over. Premature publication will constitute a contempt. A further example arose in *R v Border Television Ltd, ex p A-G, R v Newcastle Chronicle and Journal Ltd, ex p A-G*,[5] where it was established that it is contempt to report guilty pleas entered to some

---

20 This is more apparent from the extract of the judgment which Waller J kindly gave to the authors.

1 (1974, Cmnd 5794) para 137.

2 For a discussion of the meaning of 'open' court see eg Harris, *The Courts, The Press and the Public* (1976, Barry Rose) Ch 1 and *R v Denbigh Justices, ex p Williams* [1974] QB 759, [1974] 2 All ER 1052. For an unusual contempt prosecution in this connection see the Australian decision in *Re Lucas, ex p Tubman* [1970] 3 NSWR 41—held not to be a contempt for police to lock the doors of a court as a means of controlling entry.

3 (1880) 42 LT 657, 29 WR 43.

4 See *A-G v Leveller Magazine Ltd* [1979] AC 440 at 450 per Lord Diplock. See also Lord Denning MR in *R v Horsham Justices, ex p Farquharson* [1982] QB 762 at 791–2; [1982] 2 WLR 430 at 450.

5 (1978) 68 Cr App Rep 375 (Note), (1978) Times, 17 January. Two further prosecutions for similar offences were against the *North West Evening Mail* (1981) Times, 7 February (proprietors fined £500) and against the *Northampton Chronicle and Echo* (1981) Times, 31 March (publishers fined a 'moderate' £500).

but not all charges before the jury is empanelled, about which the eventual jurors will be told nothing (the indictment having been amended).

The House of Lords[6] has affirmed that at common law the embargo against publicising matters heard in the jury's absence in the above circumstances does *not* depend upon the court warning against publication. This is because the prohibition is so elementary and well understood by the media that it calls for no explicit statement from the Bench.

There was some consternation in press circles about the *Border TV* ruling on the basis that it constituted an incursion upon the right to report on matters heard in open court. It is submitted, however, that the decision was correct. Such publications are obviously prejudicial and as one commentator put it[7] 'The rules laid down by the court seem to be both fair and simple—there must be no reporting of other offences or of any other material which has been deliberately kept from the jury's ears'.

2   Reports must be 'fair and accurate'

To gain immunity from contempt, reports of proceedings must be 'fair and accurate'. This does not mean that the report must be word perfect, it is sufficient that it is a fair representation of what has taken place in court. In *Brook v Evans*[8] Stuart V-C observed:

> 'I find a report of what took place, and although, as is generally the case with such reports, it is not, and cannot be expected to be, in every particular, a perfectly accurate report, yet it contains no such inaccuracy and no such impropriety in any part of it, as to justify the defendants in coming here and taking up the time of the court . . .'.

In *R v Evening News, ex p Hobbs*[9] certain words said by the Recorder were omitted in the newspaper report. What the Recorder actually said in his summing up to the jury was:

> 'The evidence in the case is of an extraordinary character, and there can be no doubt, I should say—*it is for you to judge*—that Hobbs was a party to a gigantic fraud, as monumental and perhaps as impudent a fraud as has ever been perpetrated in the course of our law' (emphasis added).

The newspaper report omitted the words 'it is for you to judge', but the court held that since it was clear that the Recorder's opinion was that the prisoner ought to be convicted, the report was on the whole fair and accurate. The omitted words did not materially alter the meaning of what was (improperly) said by the Recorder.

In *R v Daily Worker, ex p Goulding*[10] it was reported that a chief constable said during committal proceedings that the four accused were wearing 'knuckle-dusters', whereas he in fact said that their knuckles were heavily bound in insulating tape. It was held no contempt had been committed for nothing had been published which was likely unfairly to prejudice the future trial on indictment.

6 In *A-G v Leveller Magazine Ltd* [1979] AC 440, discussed below.
7 Professor JC Smith, [1978] Crim LR 222.
8 (1860) 29 LJ Ch 616.
9 [1925] 2 KB 158.
10 (1934) 78 Sol Jo 860.

On the other hand, even the misreporting of one word can amount to contempt. In *R v West Australian Newspapers Ltd, ex p Minister of Justice*[11] the *Daily News* published that the prisoner had confessed in court to murder, whereas in fact the prisoner had admitted only to killing. The newspaper was found guilty of contempt because the misreport was held likely to interfere with the course of justice.

There is Australian authority supporting the view that not only must the report be accurate but it must also be 'fair'. Undue selectivity or emphasis might not be considered 'fair'. As Jackson CJ said in *Minister for Justice v West Australian Newspapers Ltd*:[12]

'A report may be accurate as far as it goes but unfair either in its mode of presentation or in stressing unfavourable aspects of the proceedings or in accurately reporting some parts but omitting other parts of the proceedings.'

Although this observation would seem to be of general application it is relevant to add that in the above case the imbalance was caused by reference to a matter not stated in the court proceedings. In the majority view the report could not therefore be said to be 'fair and colourless'. Although one judge[13] took issue with the alleged dual requirement that a report be both fair *and* colourless (in his view the requirements amounted to the same thing) the latter reference does underline the point that *comment*, whether express or implied, can destroy immunity from contempt. In the *West Australian Newspapers* case itself, an accused was remanded both on a charge of wilful murder and for breaking and entering offences. At the same court sitting he was sentenced to 15 months' imprisonment for offences relating to the unlawful use of motor vehicles. All this was reported but the *Daily News* gave details of only one of the charges of breaking and entering, which related to the alleged theft of a rifle and ammunition and added, in a footnote reference, that the murder victim had been found shot through the heart. Virtue SPJ said:[14]

'The purpose of the introduction of the subject-matter is obvious and the natural connection between this and the modus operandi of the killer which the ordinary reader would no doubt be likely to draw makes the article a gross contempt.'

Another example of what has been held to be a 'coloured' report is the New Zealand case, *A-G v Davidson*.[15] There, a newspaper referring to the giving of evidence by a crucial witness under the headlines 'Smiles For Mouat' stated:

'As she spoke of her knowledge of the Mouats her gaze alternated between the Crown Prosecutor and the dock; from under a brown hat she spared many quick smiles for Mouat' (Mouat was on trial for murder).

Although what was stated was true, nevertheless by a majority the Court of Appeal held the report a contempt since it amounted to an insinuation that the witness was openly displaying her partisanship with the accused, thereby calling into question the truth of her evidence. Some may feel that this decision takes matters too far. There seems strength in the minority's assertion that a newspaper reporter cannot be treated as a law reporter. As Ostler J said[16] 'The vice lay in the

11 (1958) 60 WALR 108.
12 [1970] WAR 202 at 207.
13 Virtue, SPJ at 209.
14 [1972] VR at 210.
15 [1925] NZLR 849.
16 Ibid at 863.

facts themselves, not in the report of them'. On the other hand, when newspapers report proceedings in the way that was at issue in *R v Taylor*,[17] a case which falls to be considered under the English statutory provisions, they clearly go too far.

Care should be taken that what is reported did actually take place in court. In *Duncan v Sparling*[18] a report in the *Times* included statements contained in an affidavit which were not read out in court, and although it was not suggested that the report would prejudice proceedings, the court refused to order the applicant in the contempt proceedings to pay the costs.

It is usual for newspapers to take the precaution of reporting words used by counsel in the course of a trial in inverted commas, thus making it clear that these are merely allegations. One issue that does not appear to have been addressed by the courts in considering whether a report is 'fair and accurate' is that the coverage of any but the most sensational trials tends to be uneven, concentrating on dramatic statements made by prosecuting counsel at the begining, and perhaps the prosecution witnesses, and then losing interest.[19] It is unclear whether the press is obliged to be fair and accurate about *that day's* proceedings or whether it is fairness and accuracy *overall* which matters. This may depend on the view that is taken of the meaning of 'contemporaneous'.[20] The Press Complaints Commission has taken the view that it is the overall impression which matters:[1]

> 'Meticulous accuracy in reporting the whole of the case, part of which has been reported, is a fundamental requirement of the proper administration of justice.'

However, one must not lose sight of the object of the contempt rules. In this context the main concern is the effect on the jury.[2] The jury will have sat through the parts of the trial which the press have not bothered to report in detail and that omission should not affect them. It is not the role of contempt to police the general behaviour of the press and the imbalance in reporting could often only affect the due administration of justice *as a continuing process*. There should, however, be more concern over the situation where the first trial is, or is likely to be, one of a series for then the effect of future juries needs to be considered. It is to protect juries in subsequent trials that postponement orders may be made[3] and it was because of subsequent trials that the uneven reporting in *R v Saunders*[4] could be seen as problematic.[5] This requirement is considered further in the context of the statutory position under the 1981 Contempt of Court Act.[6]

---

17 (1993) 98 Cr App Rep 361, discussed at p 284.
18 (1894) 10 TLR 353.
19 The issue is, however, addressed by Beloff, 'Fair Trial—Free Press? Reporting Restrictions in Law and Practice' [1992] PL 92.
20 See pp 273 and 283.
1 Report No 4 of the Press Complaints Commission, November 1991.
2 In the *Taylor* case, for example, it was alleged that members of the jury were seen during the trial with copies of the offending newspapers.
3 See pp 275 ff and 284 ff.
4 The first 'Guinness' trial, which was the subject of the postponement order appeal in *Re Saunders* (1990) Times, 8 February.
5 See Beloff, 'Fair Trial—Free Press? Reporting Restrictions in Law and Practice' [1992] PL 92 at p 95.
6 See pp 284 ff.

3 *Reports must be published in good faith*

'Good faith' is a term which occurs in diverse areas of the law[7] but its meaning in this context must be seen in the context of the contempt rules. The good faith requirement was mentioned by Jordan CJ in *Ex p Terrill* in the passage already cited[8] and in a later Australian case, *R v Scott and Downland Publications Ltd,*[9] it was said to be a separate requirement. In other words a fair and accurate report can be a contempt if it is not published in good faith. One such example might be where the report is not published contemporaneously with the proceedings. In the *Scott and Downland* case Menhennitt J considered that a publication of an article a week before the trial but a year after the committal proceedings (of which proceeding the publication purported to be a report) 'does show an absence of good faith'.[10] Lack of contemporaneity, it should be said, will not always be evidence of an absence of good faith and hence, it is submitted, is not *of itself* destructive of immunity from contempt.

It will be noted that absence of good faith does not mean that bad faith has to be proved at least in the sense of having to show an intent to prejudice proceedings. In the *Scott and Downland* case Menhennitt J commented:

> 'I do not come to the conclusion that this article was published with the express object of prejudicing the trial of the accused . . . I come to the conclusion that it was published for its news value and in a complete and serious disregard of its consequences, its inevitable consequences on the trial of the accused and in that sense I conclude that it was not published in good faith.'

A report that is not 'fair' because of imbalance may also be evidence of a lack of good faith. As Jordan CJ said in *Ex p Terrill*:[11]

> 'The court will always be vigilant to see that sensational use is not made of a partial or incomplete statement of court proceedings for the purpose of, or with the likelihood of, causing prejudice to a litigant.'

Again, this requirement is discussed below in the context of the 1981 Act.[12]

4 *Does immunity extend to reporting everything that occurs in court?*

There is Australian authority for saying that provided the foregoing requirements are met a report of anything that occurs in a court of justice while it is performing its judicial duties is exempt from being treated as a contempt as long as the incident arises out of and is substantially connected with the matter which the court is investigating whether it be technically part of it or not. Hence, in *Re Associated Newspapers Ltd, ex p Fisher*,[13] it was held not to be a contempt to publish comments such as 'Dirty Mongrel' and 'Hope he burns' made by a father whilst a spectator at court proceedings against another man accused of murdering his baby daughter.

---

7 As in the law of property, where the purchaser for value in good faith without notice is popularly known as 'equity's darling'.
8 See p 268.
9 [1972] VR 663.
10 Ibid at 675.
11 (1937) 37 SR (NSW) 255 at 260.
12 At pp 281 ff.
13 (1941) 41 SR (NSW) 272.

One commentator[14] has said that in the absence of English and New Zealand authorities on this point 'caution would seem the best policy'. It is submitted, however, that the Australian viewpoint is sound and even if it is not, in most cases such reports will not be considered to create a real risk of prejudice either to the proceedings in hand or to future proceedings that may result from incidents occurring in court.

5   *Misreports*

It was established in *Dunn v Bevan* [15] that misreports are not per se a contempt. In that case Sargant J rejected counsel's contention[16] that there was a form of contempt which consisted of misrepresenting the judgment and proceedings of the court for the purpose of injuring one of the parties, regardless of lack of prejudice to the proceedings.

The question of whether misrepresenting the court proceedings is of itself a contempt was squarely raised in the case because all proceedings were considered to have been at an end and therefore it could not have been argued that the misrepresentation created any risk of prejudice. Sargant J said:[17]

'It seems to me that if proceedings in a court are ended, then, unless there is an attack on the court itself, the mere making of statements as to proceedings must be dealt with by way of the ordinary law of libel, or slander if they are misrepresentations and go beyond what is legally permissible.'

It is submitted that Sargant J's conclusions are of wider application so that, even if proceedings are not at an end, a misreport will only be a contempt at common law if it creates a real risk of prejudice to current or possibly future proceedings or if it is thought to be 'scandalous' to the court. This means that a misreport of civil proceedings heard without a jury, even if published during the currency of proceedings, is unlikely to be a contempt since the risk of prejudice is small. In the criminal context, on the other hand, the media must be careful not to misreport a trial which is still continuing because the empanelled jury will be especially interested in the case and will not easily forget any report they might have read. The risk of prejudice, therefore, is very real.

A blatant example of misreporting occurred in *R v Evening Standard Co Ltd, ex p A-G.*[18] The *Evening Standard* published a purported report of court proceedings which included the following statement:

'He told me that he was not married. After I had seen him in the same public house again and he had asked me to marry him, I asked him to show me his Army pay book.'

There was also a headline 'Accused man "asked me to marry"'. In fact the statement 'and he asked me to marry him' was wholly inaccurate. That evidence, which another witness had given at another hearing (the committal hearing), had

14 Burrows, *Media Law in New Zealand* (1st edn) p 251.
15 [1922] 1 Ch 276.
16 Who relied on Lord Hardwicke's statement in the *St James's Evening Post Case* (1742) 2 Atk 469 where he said 'Nothing is more incumbent upon courts of justice than to preserve their proceedings from being misrepresented'; see also *Ilkley Local Board v Oswald Lister* (1895) 11 TLR 176 per Chitty J at 176.
17 [1922] 1 Ch 276 at 280.
18 [1954] 1 QB 578, [1954] 1 All ER 1026. See also *R v Tibbits and Windust* [1902] 1 KB 77.

been ruled inadmissible. Lord Goddard CJ, in holding the newspaper guilty of contempt, said:

> 'The evidence which Miss Biggs might have given if the learned judge had not ruled that it was not to be admitted as it was highly prejudicial to Kemp was published in the *Evening Standard* and attributed to another witness who had not said anything of the kind. Consequently, the public at Chelmsford, including members of the jury, who are no longer locked up when the court has arisen, could have bought the paper and read that "Kemp had made an offer of marriage to Mrs Darmody" although he had not done so.'

Care should be taken not to mix up reports. In *R v Astor, ex p Isaacs* [19] an article was published which consisted of reports of civil and criminal proceedings (which had not then been completed) relating to the same share transaction. It was said by Scrutton J that:

> 'If a paper took upon itself to mix up together the reports of criminal proceedings and of civil proceedings relating to the same share transaction, he could come to no other conclusion than that it might tend to prejudice the jury trying the case, who were not trained lawyers able to distinguish the exact relevance of a charge of that kind.'

6   The court's power to delay or restrict reports

(a)   The nature and basis of the power

The freedom at common law to report proceedings heard in open court is subject to the power of the judge to delay or restrict such reports. It was recognised as long ago as 1821[20] that a judge could in certain circumstances order the postponement of a report but, for the most part, the ambit and basis of the judicial control has been developed comparatively recently.

Although the control itself takes different forms it broadly comprises the power to delay publication of reports or to prevent the disclosure of the identity of certain witnesses. The juristic basis of the control is not entirely settled. The leading English authority is the House of Lords' decision in *A-G v Leveller Magazine Ltd.*[1] There, the majority[2] doubted whether a court has specific power to make an explicit order directed to and binding upon the public ipso jure as to what might lawfully be published outside the courtroom in relation to proceedings before it. On the other hand, it was accepted that if, in the course of regulating its own proceedings, a court clearly makes an order designed to protect the administration of justice, then it is incumbent upon anyone who knows of the ruling not to do anything even outside the court which will frustrate the object of that ruling.[3] Furthermore, it was accepted that provided the object of the ruling is 'apparent to anyone'[4] it is not incumbent (though it might be preferable) upon the court to warn of the consequences of ignoring the ruling. The application of

---

19   (1913) 30 TLR 10.
20   Ie in *R v Clement* (1821) 4 B & Ald 218, discussed at p 279.
1   [1979] AC 440.
2   Ie Lords Diplock (ibid at 451) Dilhorne (at 455) Edmund-Davies (at 464); cf Lord Russell of Killowen (at 467).
3   See particularly Lord Scarman at 470.
4   Per Lord Diplock at 452.

this principle means that the publication of even a fair and accurate report of proceedings heard in open court can be a contempt if it frustrates the object of a ruling known to the publisher even if no specific warning about the publication has been given.

In New Zealand the position would appear to be different inasmuch as the Court of Appeal ruled in *A-G Taylor* [5] that a binding order can be made on outsiders and in particular upon the news media. However, it remains unclear whether *Taylor* should be regarded as establishing an *additional* power to that accepted in *A-G v Leveller Magazine Ltd* or merely an *alternative* power. In other words it has yet to be established under New Zealand law whether the judicial power to control reports has to be *expressly* imposed or whether as at common law in England, control can also be *impliedly* imposed. It is submitted that as there is nothing in the *Taylor* decision which is otherwise inconsistent with *Leveller Magazine* it should be regarded as authority for establishing *additional* powers in the New Zealand courts.

At first sight there may not appear to be much difference between the English and New Zealand authorities. On either basis there must be knowledge of the ruling or order and a publication in defiance of it would appear to be a contempt. It is submitted, however, that there are important differences. First, it would appear that the breaking of a binding order is ipso facto a contempt in New Zealand whereas under the English authorities it may be that a publication in 'defiance' of a ruling will only be a contempt if it constitutes a real risk of interfering with the administration of justice.[6] Secondly, the power to regulate their own proceedings seems to be vested in all courts of justice. Hence, even magistrates and inferior courts can, on the *Leveller* basis, indirectly restrict what can be reported. The power to make binding orders on outsiders, however, can surely only be made, if at all, by superior courts of record since such courts are the only bodies vested with inherent jurisdiction to punish contempts committed outside the court.[7] Thirdly, under the English position it would appear doubtful whether publication of information gained entirely through independent sources can be a contempt even if it relates to matters that are subject to a ruling made in court.[8]

It remains now to examine the application of judicial control.

(b)   The exercise of the power

(i) Anonymity orders or rulings   *A-G v Leveller Magazine Ltd* was specifically concerned with the court's ability to maintain the anonymity of witnesses outside the court room. The practice of allowing certain witnesses to give evidence in open court under a pseudonym so as to preserve their identity is a long standing

---

5   [1975] 2 NZLR 675.
6   At least Lord Edmund-Davies thought so in *A-G v Leveller Magazine Ltd* [1979] AC 440 at 465.
7   See Ch 12.
8   In the *Leveller* case the identity of the army officer, 'Colonel B', was discoverable because during cross-examination the witness gave the official name and number of the army unit to which he belonged and revealed that his posting to it was recorded in a particular issue of the Royal Corps of Signals magazine 'Wire' which was available to the public. As Lord Russell put it, in this way the 'gaff was blown' though but for this he would have found the defendants guilty.

one at least with regard to blackmail proceedings.[9] The effect of such anonymity orders was not, however, challenged until 1974 when the *Socialist Worker* published the names of two witnesses who, under the direction of the trial judge had given evidence in a much publicised blackmail trial under the pseudonyms, Y and Z. The Divisional Court, in a decision[10] subsequently approved in *A-G v Leveller Magazine Ltd*, held the publication to be a contempt not for breaking the trial judge's order as such (it was accepted that the order was not expressed to go beyond the four walls of the court) but because it constituted a 'blatant affront to the authority of the court' (ie in the sense of apparently destroying the court's ability to protect certain blackmail witnesses) and was calculated to prejudice the due administration of justice in the wide sense by discouraging potential witnesses in blackmail cases from coming forward in future proceedings.[11] In reaching this decision the Divisional Court rejected the contention that a judge had no power to make such orders and that he either has to sit in camera (provided there is power to do so) or sit in open court with no reporting restrictions. Lord Widgery CJ said:[12]

> 'I do not believe that we are faced with those stark alternatives. I think that there is a third course suitable and proper for this kind of case of blackmail where the complainant has done something disreputable or discreditable and has something to hide and will not come forward unless thus protected.'

It will be noted that Lord Widgery CJ confined his remarks to blackmail trials but later in his judgment, he doubted whether there was power to make binding anonymity orders to protect complainants in rape cases.[13] It has become evident, however, that at common law binding anonymity orders can be made to protect witnesses in cases other than blackmail trials. For example, it is clear that orders can properly be made to protect witnesses from the security services when giving evidence in Official Secrets prosecutions[14] and it has been held that anonymity can properly be accorded to certain prosecution witnesses in pornography trials.[15]

In the United Kingdom the Contempt of Court Act, s 11, provides for the courts to made anonymity orders but does not widen the circumstances in which they may be made. This means that the position at common law is still relevant despite the provision in the Act. The post-1981 case law is, however, dealt with below where s 11 is considered as a whole.[16]

Anonymity orders cannot be made simply because it is convenient. The basis of the power lies in the need to protect *the due administration of justice*. Hence, before anonymity is permitted the court should consider whether the publicly revealed identity would be prejudicial to and render impracticable the due administration of justice. It is not sufficient, for example, that publicity would

---

9 Professor Goodhart mooted the effect of such 'orders' in his article: 'Newspapers and Contempt of Court in English Law' (1935) 48 HLR 885 at 905.
10 *R v Socialist Worker Printers and Publishers Ltd, ex p A-G* [1975] QB 637.
11 Relying on *A-G v Butterworth* [1963] 1 QB 696, [1962] 3 All ER 326, discussed in ch 11.
12 [1975] QB 637 at 652. Permanent publication bans on the names of blackmail witnesses have been imposed in Canada, see *Toronto Sun Publishing Corp v A-G for Alberta* (1985) 6 WWR 36 (Alberta CA).
13 [1975] QB 637 at 652–3, sed quaere? The position is now otherwise under the Sexual Offences (Amendment) Act 1976, discussed at pp 318 ff.
14 *A-G v Leveller Magazine Ltd* [1979] AC 440 at 471 per Lord Scarman.
15 *R v Hove Justices, ex p Gibbons* (1981) Times, 19 June. It is common practice to make anonymity orders in pornography cases.
16 See pp 299 ff.

endanger national security, but if the factor of national security appears to endanger the due administration of justice, for example, by deterring the Crown from bringing prosecutions in the future, anonymity can properly be ordered.[17] According to Lord Scarman[18] there must be material, not necessarily formally addressed evidence, made known to the court upon which it can reasonably reach its conclusion. Failure to meet any of these criteria will render the order of no effect.

Unless the court is empowered to make an anonymity order no one can be held guilty of contempt for subsequently revealing a witness's identity and it is established that the court must make an *order* and not a mere request[19] before an obligation not to flout it can arise. Secondly, the order itself must be clear. In most cases this will mean that the court should expressly explain the result that the ruling was designed to achieve and what kind of information about the proceedings would, if published, tend to frustrate the ruling and so be at risk of being held a contempt. However, while such express warnings might be preferable in all cases, in circumstances where it would be apparent to anyone aware of the ruling that the result which the ruling was designed to achieve would be frustrated by a particular act, no warning is necessary. Anonymity accorded to witnesses in the blackmail cases was thought to be one such example.[20] Finally, the publisher must know (or have had a proper opportunity of knowing[1]) of the ruling. In the *Socialist Worker* case it seems to have been held sufficient that the publisher knew of the ruling even though he thought that it was a mere request and in any event did not believe it to be 'binding' upon him.[2]

Anonymity orders have been upheld in Canada as being consistent with s 2(b) of the Charter where no public interest would be served by publication and other persons might be deterred from coming forward to reveal wrongdoing[3] or would be put in physical danger if their identity was known.[4]

(ii) Delaying orders   Apart from making anonymity orders courts have, in the course of regulating their own proceedings to protect the administration of justice, power to make orders the effect of which will, on pain of contempt, delay publication of reports of proceedings. Two such powers were referred to in *A-G v Leveller Magazine Ltd*, namely, the power in criminal cases to exclude the jury and hold a 'trial within the trial' and the power to withhold from the jury information given before they were empanelled, namely, that the accused had

---

17   Per Lord Scarman in *A-G v Leveller Magazine Ltd* [1979] AC 440 at 471. In prosecutions under the Official Secrets Acts the Crown can apply for the whole or part of the evidence to be heard in camera. In an incident reported in the Observer, 22 August 1993, Ealing magistrates' court withheld the address of the defendant to a drink driving charge on the grounds that her husband was a senior serving member of the armed forces: no order was made withholding her name or the identity of her husband, and their address was in the telephone directory.

18   In *A-G v Leveller Magazine Ltd*, ibid at 473.

19   Per Lord Scarman in *A-G v Leveller Magazine Ltd* at 473 and Lord Widgery CJ in *R v Socialist Worker Printers and Publishers, ex p A-G* [1975] QB 637 at 646.

20   *A-G v Leveller Magazine Ltd* [1979] AC 440 per Lords Diplock, Dilhorne. Lord Edmund-Davies (ibid at 462) seemed dubitante on this point.

1   Per Lord Scarman in *A-G v Leveller Magazine Ltd*, ibid at 473.

2   See the affidavit referred to by Lord Widgery CJ in the *Socialist Worker* case [1975] QB at 646. The decision has been criticised on this point in [1974] Crim LR 711 at 712.

3   *Re Hirt and College of Physicians and Surgeons of British Columbia* (1985) 17 DLR (4th) 472, [1985] 3 WWR 350, 60 BCLR 273 (British Columbia CA).

4   *R v McArthur* (1984) 13 CCC (3d) 152, 10 CRR 220 (Ont HC).

pleaded guilty to some but not all the charges.[5] Those were thought to be examples of a departure from the general principle of open justice which were so obviously designed to protect the administration of justice as to require no further explanation nor warning that premature publication of the evidence would constitute a contempt.

Their Lordships did not, however, advert to the power first established in 1821 in *R v Clement*[6] to make express postponement orders. In *Clement* several persons were indicted for high treason in connection with the Cato Street conspiracy. They pleaded not guilty and elected to be tried separately. The trial judge, Abbott CJ, knowing that the evidence in each trial would be very similar, and fearing that if each trial was contemporaneously reported, it would give witnesses an opportunity to alter their evidence in the next trial, ordered that there should be no report of any trial until all the charges had been heard. In breach of this direction the *Observer* published 'a fair, true and impartial' account of the proceedings and evidence heard by the court and was fined £500 for contempt for disregarding the judge's direction.

In upholding this fine the Court of King's Bench stressed that as the defendants had originally been charged together, the several trials were properly regarded as one entire proceeding. The extent and basis of the decision was made most clear by Holroyd J who said:[7]

> 'The object for which [the order] was made was clearly, as it appears to me, one within their jurisdiction, viz the furtherance of justice in proceedings then pending before the court; and it was made to remain in force so long, and so long only, as those proceedings should be pending before them. Now I take it to be clear, that a Court of Record has a right to make orders for regulating their proceedings, and for the furtherance of justice in the proceedings before them, which are to continue in force during the time that such proceedings, are pending. It appears to me, that the arguments as to a further power of continuing such orders in force for a longer period do not apply. It is sufficient for the present case, that the court have that power during the pendency of the proceedings.'

Clement received some support in *Scott v Scott*[8] and the reasoning of Holroyd J would seem consistent with that in *A-G v Leveller Magazine Ltd.*

Holroyd J left open the question whether there is power to postpone reports beyond the pendency of the proceedings in hand. That further step seems to have been taken by Waller J in *R v Poulson and Pottinger*[9] when he directed that certain evidence should not be published because of the risk of prejudice to *other* proceedings against Poulson and others which had already begun. Although superficially the two situations appear similar *Poulson* represents a significant extension of *Clement* since it appears to involve the court going beyond regulating and protecting its *own* proceedings. Although *Poulson* received judicial support[10] it is questionable whether a court does have such a power at common law.[11] In the United Kingdom the issue is now academic because of the provisions of s 4(2) of the 1981 Act.[12]

5 Discussed at pp 269–270.
6 (1821) 4 B & Ald 218.
7 Ibid at 233.
8 [1913] AC 417 at 438 per Lord Haldane and at 453 per Lord Atkinson.
9 [1974] Crim LR 141.
10 Per Lord Denning MR in *R v Horsham Justices, ex p Farquharson* [1982] QB 762 at 792, [1982] 2 All ER 269 at 285–6.
11 See the discussion of this point in the second edition of this book at p 197.
12 See pp 284 ff.

Postponement orders have been made in Canada to protect from prejudice the future trials of other persons charged in connection with the same offence. In *R v Bernardo* [13] a husband and wife were charged with various offences in connection with the abduction, assault, rape and murder of two girls. The woman was tried first and the Crown accepted a negotiated plea of guilty to manslaughter. The Crown asked for a temporary publication ban to cover those proceedings. This was opposed by the husband, on the grounds that prior to the trial there had been widespread and sensational media coverage which had depicted the woman as herself victimised and dominated by the man, and that his trial would be prejudiced if that impression of their relationship was not corrected by publication of the evidence which he submitted would emerge at her trial. The case therefore raised the issue of the accused's right to control his own defence. Kovacs J held that society had a right and interest in ensuring that an accused had a fair trial and that if the court thought that a ban was necessary for this purpose it should be imposed notwithstanding the individual's objections. [14]

(iii) Evidence sensitive on other grounds   The House of Lords ruled in *Scott v Scott* [15] that at common law there was no power to hold proceedings in camera for the sake of public decency or morality. Their Lordships also said that even assuming an order for a hearing in camera was validly made it would not be effective to enjoin perpetual silence on pain of contempt. In English law there is now statutory provision on this in the shape of the Judicial Proceedings (Regulations of Reports) Act 1926 [16] and that statute and various others specifically deal with the reporting of family cases in which evidence of a sexual nature may arise. [17] The media cannot report, however, what they cannot see, and it is usual not to show photographs of dead bodies, autopsies etc to the press. In Canada this has been challenged as being contrary to the guarantee of right of access to the courts as an aspect of the guarantee to freedom of expression provided by s 2(b) of the Charter, but it has been held that these guarantees do not include a constitutional right of the press and public to examine physical evidence or documentary exhibits. [18]

Modern technology has presented the courts with new problems over the type of evidence which is available to be placed before the jury. In the Moors Murder trial in 1966 part of the evidence against the accused consisted of an audio tape made as one of the victims was tortured to death. The trial judge considered whether that evidence should be heard in camera but concluded that there had been so much talk about it that he had no right to exclude the public and it was played without anyone being asked to leave the court, although those who did not

---

13   5 July 1993 (Ont HC); the appeal to the Ontario Court of Appeal (1995) 121 DLR (4th) 42 was dismissed on the grounds that there is no appeal from a postponement of publication to the Court of Appeal and that the appropriate remedy was an application for leave to appeal to the Supreme Court of Canada. The *Bernardo* ban was so extensive that it prevented the proper reporting of the decision until after the second trial.

14   In *Re Church of Scientology of Toronto v The Queen (No 6)* (1986) 27 CCC (3d) 193 (Ont HCJ) it was suggested that the common law power to impose a temporary publication ban pending the future trial of a co-accused might only exist where the co-accused applied for it.

15   [1913] AC 417, which concerned a nullity petition on the grounds of the respondent's impotence.

16   See p 317.

17   See pp 314 ff for the English legislation; there are similar provisions in other jurisdictions.

18   See *R v Thomson Newspapers Ltd* (1983) 11 WCB 436 (Ont HCJ).

wish to listen were invited to leave.[19] The sounds on the tape were reported in the *Times* [20] but most of the rest of the press chose not to recount it in full.

A similar issue arose in Canada in 1995 during *R v Bernardo*.[1] The prosecution evidence included video tapes allegedly showing the rape, torture and murder of the victims. The trial judge ordered that only the judge, jury, prosecuting counsel, certain court officials and the accused and his lawyers should see the tapes, which would be shown on close circuit monitors turned away from the public and the press. The judge is reported as saying:[2]

> 'The public pictorial display of these videos has virtually no redeeming societal value. Public display of this evidence will seriously affect the families and perhaps others. Open justice is a concept, a principle, that can be more than adequately achieved without pictorially displaying the indignities suffered by these young victims.'

He did, however, order that there would be no restriction on the audio track of the tapes. The families of the victims appealed against this order to the Supreme Court of Canada, arguing that the judge erred in finding a distinction between the harms of the visual component of the videotapes and their audio component but the Supreme Court refused leave to appeal.[3] The judge in this case made his order in the exercise of his inherent common law powers but interpreted in the light of s 2(b) of the Canadian Charter guaranteeing free expression and the freedom of the media.

In this case the judge was trying to balance the freedom of the press with the emotional well-being of the victims' survivors. Publication bans are imposed to protect the administration of justice and it is submitted that in these extreme circumstances the administration of justice would not be well-served by the public display of appalling material the essential contents of which would be more than adequately communicated to the media through the testimony of a witness. It is to be noted that the media did not appeal against the viewing ban. The denial of access to the visual element of the tapes can be seen as analogous to the practice of not showing photographs of dead bodies, autopsies and similar to the press and this point was made by the judge in explaining his ruling.

B   The statutory position under English law

1   *General position*

The Contempt of Court Act 1981 contains specific provisions on protecting fair and accurate reports of legal proceedings from contempt. Section 4(1) provides:

---

19 See Times, 27 April 1966, and Emlyn Williams, *Beyond Belief* (1968, Pan Books) p 344.
20 Ibid.
 1 Not yet reported on this point; for the issue of postponement orders on publication of the first of the accused to be tried, see p 280.
 2 Edmonton Journal, 31 May 1995.
 3 On 15 June 1995. Three Canadian newspapers contested the appeal saying that turning off the soundtrack would 'greatly limit the ability of the media to understand and report on the evidence that is being presented to the jury'. The Supreme Court does not give reasons for refusal of leave. One of the points taken by the press was that the families had no locus standi to bring an appeal.

'Subject to this section a person is not guilty of contempt of court under the strict liability rule in respect of a fair and accurate report of legal proceedings held in public, published contemporaneously and in good faith.'

Section 4(1) was intended,[4] following the Phillimore Committee's recommendations,[5] to clarify the law so that in the absence of *specific* statutory or judicial directions, publications complying with the requirements of the section cannot be considered a contempt. This removes the possibility thought to be established by *R v Poulson and Pottinger*[6] that even a fair and accurate report could be held a contempt if it is prejudicial to another proceeding. From this point of view, s 4 is to be welcomed.

Failure to meet any of the requirements of s 4(1) does not ipso facto mean that a contempt is committed.[7] Under the 'strict liability rule' a publisher can only be found guilty of contempt where it is shown that the publication creates a substantial risk of serious prejudice.[8]

The requirement that proceedings should be held in public is to be noted. It would seem[9] to apply to all proceedings which members of the public are entitled to attend. Furthermore to attract the s 4(1) protection, proceedings must be before a 'court'. We discuss in detail in Chapter 12 the courts to which contempt applies, but in general it is submitted that it applies to 'courts of law'. It has been held that proceedings before licensing justices fall outside this definition[10] and the Attorney General has warned the press that s 4(1) does not apply to the reporting of such proceedings.[11]

The requirements that the report be fair and accurate and published in good faith mirror the common law requirements and the considerations discussed in that context continue to be relevant under the Act.[12] During the passage of the Bill[13] some anxiety was expressed about the good faith requirement as being open to the objection that it might depend upon the whim and capriciousness of the individual judge and that certain publications might fare better than others. However the burden of proof will lie on the prosecution and it is a burden which will be particularly difficult to discharge if the report is fair and accurate and published contemporaneously. In any event it must be remembered that lack of good faith is not in itself sufficient to justify a finding of contempt as there must be shown to be a substantial risk of serious prejudice to the course of justice. These considerations should act as a safeguard against capriciousness.

Section 4(1) has been considered in the context of the making of postponement orders under s 4(2),[14] where judges have sometimes refused to make such orders on the basis that any reporting of the trial will comply with s 4(1). In one such case, *Re Saunders*[15] the Court of Appeal upheld Henry J's refusal to make an order. Henry J said that 'in good faith':

---

4   See eg Lord Hailsham, *Hansard* HL Debs Vol 415 col 660–1 and the Attorney General, Sir Michael Havers QC, HC Debs Vol 1000 cols 36–7.
5   Paras 134–141.
6   [1974] Crim LR 141 discussed, at p 268.
7   Aliter, if a publication falls outside the strict liability rule because prejudice is intended. Cf liability for breach of s 4(2), discussed at pp 291–293.
8   S 2(2), discussed in Chs 3, 4, 5 and 6.
9   There is no definition of this requirement in the Act.
10 *Lewis v BBC* (unreported, 23 March 1979) [1979] CA Transcript No 193.
11 See the Daily Telegraph, 8 November 1981.
12 See pp 270 ff.
13 Eg Mr Jeffrey Thomas QC MP 1980–81 HC Debs SC A (Contempt of Court) col 154.
14 See pp 284 ff.
15 (1990) Times, 8 February; the trial concerned was *R v Saunders*, the first 'Guinness' trial. See Beloff, 'Fair Trial—Free Press? Reporting Restrictions in Law and Practice' [1992] PL 92.

'requires all those who compile and publish reports of the first trial to have regard both to the fact that there is to be a second trial, and to the need to preserve the fairness of that trial when compiling their reports on the first trial',

and that:

'To this end the media must ensure that they have proper internal disciplines to secure that standard of reporting, and to preserve the fairness of the second trial.'

This latter passage was specifically endorsed by the Court of Appeal, but as has been pointed out, it may be difficult for the media to ascertain the issues in the second trial if the preparatory hearings, as with a serious fraud trial, are in private.[16]

The requirement of contemporaneity poses further problems. It appears to mean that a report be published 'as soon as practicable' after the proceedings in question. This would seem to follow from the provisions of s 4(3)(a) and (b) which state that 'a report of proceedings shall be treated as published contemporaneously' if it is published 'as soon as practicable' after the expiry of a s 4(2) postponing order or after it becomes permissible pursuant to the Magistrates' Courts Act 1980 to report transfer for trial (formerly committal proceedings) respectively. This would seem to allow daily, weekly and monthly publications to publish in their next issue. It is unclear as to how the provision might apply to books. 'Publication' has not been defined for the purposes of contempt[17] but if an analogy is drawn with defamation it would mean that each fresh sale is a publication.[18] If this definition is applicable to contempt it would pose a particular problem for books which obviously have a longer sale life than newspapers. Could publication of a book which was unexceptionable when first published subsequently become a contempt because, for example, the man about whom the book is written is charged again? Could it be said that publication occurs 'as soon as practicable' after the proceedings. If not, does that mean that publishers and distributors have to withdraw the book if they become aware of subsequent proceedings?

However, it may be questioned whether lack of contemporaneity can destroy immunity. It was by no means clear that it was a separate common law requirement though lack of contemporaneity has been held to be evidence of lack of good faith.[19] If it was not a common law requirement then s 6(b)[20] would seem to prevent it from being a contempt under the Act. The issue of contemporaneity is not unique to contempt law. Contemporaneous publication of a fair and accurate report of proceedings also arises in connection with defamation. At common law such reports were afforded qualified privilege. The Law of Libel Amendment Act 1888, s 3[1] provides that such reports are privileged but in that section there is no reference to a requirement of good faith and it appears that the result of this is to confer absolute privilege upon the reports.[2] It has been

---

16 Beloff op cit at p 97.
17 For a discussion of this requirement see pp 85 ff.
18 See eg Gatley on *Libel and Slander* (8th edn, 1981) Ch 6, para 222; *Clerk and Lindsell on Torts* (16th edn) Ch 21, para 46.
19 In the Australian decision in *R v Scott & Downland Publications Ltd* [1972] VR 663, discussed at p 273.
20 S 6(b) prevents anything from being a contempt under the 'strict liability rule' that would not have been a contempt under the previous law. See p 117.
 1 Extended by the Defamation Act 1952, s 9(2).
 2 *McCarey v Associated Newspapers Ltd* [1964] 1 WLR 855 and see *Clerk and Lindsell on Torts* (16th edn) Ch 21, para 135, Winfield and Jolowicz: *Tort* (14th edn, 1994) p 357.

suggested that s 3 of the 1888 Act could be construed to cover contempt as well as libel[3] but the headnote to the Act, as well as the express mention of good faith in s 4(1), seems to militate against this.

It is submitted that the Act should be so construed that lack of contemporaneity alone cannot be a contempt. Hence, a book initially published in good faith as soon as practicable after the proceedings should not subsequently be treated as a contempt because it has become prejudicial to further proceedings.

There has been little discussion of the 'fair and accurate' requirement under the Act but the events occurring in *R v Taylor*[4] did raise this issue. In that case during a murder trial reports of the proceedings appeared in some newspapers under front-page banner headlines such as 'Butchered Bride' and 'Love Crazy Mistress Butchered Rival Wife Court Told'. In respect of the latter McCowan LJ remarked in the Court of Appeal[5] 'The Court had been told no such thing'. In respect of the misleading frozen frame from the wedding video accompanied by headlines variously saying 'Cheats Kiss', 'Judas Kiss', and 'Tender Embrace - the Lovers share a kiss just a few feet from Alison', McCowan LJ pointed out that the video had no relevance to the trial and was not played at it. Of the press coverage generally he said:[6]

> 'What, in fact they did was not reporting at all; it was comment, and comment which assumed guilt on the part of the girls in the dock.'

If one analyses this scenario in terms of contempt law[7] the photograph and accompanying text could not be construed as a report of proceedings at all. It would fall under the strict liability rule in s 2(2) of the Act. It is submitted that despite McCowan LJ's castigation the rest of the press coverage probably *was* an attempt to report the proceedings, but one which was so lacking in fairness and accuracy that it lost the protection of s 4(1) and so became subject to the strict liability rule.

2   Orders postponing publication: the Contempt of Court Act 1981, s 4(2)

(a)   General

The freedom to report open court proceedings under s 4(1) is qualified by s 4(2) which gives the courts a statutory power to make postponement orders. The section provides that in respect of legal proceedings held in public:

> 'the court may, where it appears to be necessary for avoiding a substantial risk of prejudice to the administration of justice in those proceedings, or in any other proceedings pending or imminent, order that the publication of any report of the proceedings, or any part of the proceedings, be postponed for such period as the court thinks necessary for that purpose.'

3   See Miller, *Contempt of Court* (2nd edn, 1989) p 330.
4   (1993) Cr App Rep 361.
5   Ibid at 369.
6   Ibid.
7   *Taylor* was not a contempt prosecution but an appeal against the murder conviction: the Attorney General declined to bring contempt proceedings despite the invitation to do so by the Court of Appeal. A subsequent attempt to challenge the Attorney General's decision by judicial review failed. See *R v S-G, ex p Taylor* (1995) Times, 14 August, discussed at p 481.

By providing that postponements of what can be reported can only be effected via an express court order, s 4(2) is intended both to clarify the law and to place the onus of safeguarding proceedings upon the judiciary. Accordingly, it is no longer possible to impose delaying restrictions by implication (as, for example, by hearing a 'trial within a trial') nor by mere judicial request.[8] Whether contempt can be committed even though no order under s 4(2) was made may depend upon the meaning given to the 'good faith' requirement under s 4(1). Suppose a judge forgets to make an order postponing publication of evidence heard in the jury's absence and ruled inadmissible, could it be said that an experienced journalist was acting in 'good faith' if he reported the evidence?[9] Neither the journalist nor editor may actually intend to prejudice the proceedings but they could be taken to appreciate that the publication is prejudicial to the proceedings. If the common law view as expressed by the Australian decision in *R v Scott & Downland Publications Ltd*,[10] that absence of good faith does not require proof of bad faith in the sense of having to show an intent to prejudice proceedings, is adopted under the Act, then it may be that a prosecution could be successful even in the absence of a court ruling. It is submitted, however, that such an interpretation would be contrary to the spirit of the legislation.

It will be noted that s 4(2) is concerned only with the power to order the *postponement* of publication of reports though such orders can apply to the whole[11] or part of the proceedings.

(b) When a postponement order under s 4(2) may be made

Courts do not have unlimited powers to make postponement orders. The requirement set out under s 4(2) is that the postponement must be necessary to avoid a substantial risk of prejudice to the administration of justice either in the proceedings before the court or in other proceedings pending or imminent. This means that the perceived danger must relate to the *administration of justice*. An order should not be made, for example, simply to protect the interests of national security or even the safety of the parties.

The making of postponement orders in order to protect other proceedings has arisen particularly in the context of serious fraud cases, where a preparatory hearing is often conducted in the Crown Court instead of going through transfer for trial (formerly committal proceedings) and then the judge decides to split up the indictment and hold several sequential trials.[12]

In deciding whether there is a substantial risk of prejudice to the administration of justice courts are obliged to consider the risk both to the proceedings before

8 *R v Horsham Justices, ex p Farquharson* [1982] QB 762, [1982] 2 All ER 269 (CA). That this was the intention of Parliament can be seen from the statements of Lord Hailsham, HL Official Report (5th series) cols 660–661 and Sir Michael Havers QC HC Debs Vol 1000 cols 36–7. Decisions like *R v Border Television Ltd, ex p A-G* and *R v Newcastle Chronicle and Journal Ltd, ex p A-G* (1978) 68 Cr App Rep 375 (Note); (1978) Times, 17 January, discussed at p 269. cannot therefore be made under the Act.
9 See also the discussion by Lowe, 'The Contempt of Court Act 1981: The Strict Liability Rule' (1981) 131 NLJ 1167, 1169.
10 [1972] VR 663, discussed at p 273.
11 Cf Ackner LJ in *R v Horsham Justices, ex p Farquharson* [1982] QB 762 at 806, [1982] 2 All ER 269 at 296, who said that 'the power can be exercised in relation to only a *part* of the proceedings'.
12 See eg *Re Saunders* (1990) Times, 8 February; *R v Nat West Investment Bank Ltd* (unreported, 11 January 1991, MacKinnon J, Central Criminal Court). For this, and other issues relating to postponement orders see Nicol, (1991) LSG 6 November p 17.

them and to other proceedings pending or imminent. The *Poulson* warning[13] is therefore statutorily embodied. In the *Horsham Justices* case[14] it was held that 'pending' and 'imminent' are terms of art reflecting the position established at common law. Hence, proceedings are to be considered 'pending' from the time a person is charged and 'imminent' even before that event.[15] As can be seen from the discussion in Chapter 7 of the sub judice rule[16] the question of when proceedings are 'imminent' is one of great difficulty and it is unfortunate that the uncertainty surrounding that concept is perpetuated in s 4(2). However, it must be remembered that the more distant actual proceedings are, the less likely a publication will create a *substantial* risk of prejudice and accordingly, postponement orders to protect 'imminent' proceedings will require special justification.

It is clear that s 4(2) cannot be used to postpone reports of events which are not 'legal proceedings held in public'. In *R v Rhuddlan Justices, ex p HTV Ltd* [17] a television company filmed the arrest of a man on drugs charges and wished to show it as part of a programme on drug trafficking. In the meantime the man had pleaded not guilty in the magistrates' court and the justices made an order under s 4(2) postponing the showing of the arrest. The Divisional Court held that the justices had no jurisdiction to do this and, if there was a substantial risk of serious prejudice to the trial, publication would have to be restrained under the strict liability rule.

In *Horsham Justices* the Court of Appeal accepted in principle that in committal proceedings magistrates were entitled and indeed obliged to take into account possible prejudice to the Crown Court proceedings, the latter proceedings being considered to be 'pending' even before a committal for trial is made.[18]

(c)   The application of the test in s 4(2)[19]

Before an order under s 4(2) can be made the danger to the administration of justice must be a substantial one. A remote or even a small risk of prejudice is therefore insufficient justification for ordering a postponement. It will be noted, however, that the requirement does not go as far as s 2(2), and provide that there must be a substantial risk of *serious* prejudice. According to Ackner LJ in the *Horsham Justices* case it is a less stringent test.[20] Lord Denning MR, on the other hand, thought that such orders should not often be made. He said:[1]

> 'In considering whether to make an order under s 4(2), the sole consideration is the risk to the administration of justice. Whoever has to consider it should remember

13   See p 279.
14   *R v Horsham Justices, ex p Farquharson* [1982] QB 762, [1982] 2 All ER 269.
15   See eg Ackner LJ at 807 and 297 respectively.
16   See pp 244 ff.
17   (1985) Times, 21 December.
18   Per Lord Denning MR [1982] QB 762 at 789, [1982] 2 All ER 269 at 283, Shaw LJ at 798 and 290 and Ackner LJ at 807 and 297 all adopting Glidewell J's position explained at 775–776 and 279, 280. Committal proceedings were replaced by the procedure of transfer for trial by s 44 of the Criminal Justice and Public Order Act 1994, which amended ss 4 to 8 of the Magistrates' Courts Act 1980, see p 290.
19   For a study of the use of s 4(2) (and s 11) orders from 1982 to 1989 see Walker, Cram and Brogarth, 'The Reporting of Crown Court Proceedings and the Contempt of Court Act 1981' (1992) 55 MLR 647.
20   [1982] QB 762 at 807, [1982] 2 All ER 269 at 296.
1   [1982] QB 762 at 794, [1982] 2 All ER 269 at 287.

that at a trial judges are not influenced by what they may have read in the newspapers. Nor are the ordinary folk who sit on juries. They are good, sensible people. They go by the evidence that is addressed before them and not by what they may have read in the newspapers. The risk of their being influenced is so slight that it can usually be disregarded as insubstantial and therefore not the subject of an order under s 4(2).'

The readiness of courts to make orders under s 4(2), therefore, partly depends on the judge's views on the robustness of juries. As with the application of s 2(2)[2] judges' attitudes vary but the Lord Chancellor's Department has issued guidance on the promulgation of s 4(2) orders.[3] In *Re Central Independent Television plc*[4] Lord Lane CJ said that even if there was some slight risk, judges would be well advised to bear in mind Lord Denning's words. In *Barlow Clowes Gilt Managers v Barlow Clowes,*[5] *Re Saunders*[6] and *R v Nat West Investment Bank Ltd,*[7] for example, postponement orders were refused but an order *was* made during the trial of Clive Ponting on Official Secrets Act charges[8] and in *R v HM Coroner for East Kent, ex p Spooner*[9] reports of a ruling that the owners of the ferry Herald of Free Enterprise could be liable for corporate manslaughter were postponed until after the coroner's court verdict on the disaster.

The question of what is meant by the word 'substantial' was considered by Lindsay J in *MGN Pension Trustees Ltd v Bank of America National Trust and Savings Association,*[10] considering it in the light of the interpretation of s 2(2)[11] but conscious of the fact that s 4(2) lacks the extra safeguard of requiring the possible prejudice to be 'serious'. He was concerned[12] that to take 'substantial' to mean 'not insubstantial' would, given 'the fine shades which language offers', result in a lower threshold for the operation of s 4(2) than the legislature intended. However, he assumed in favour of the Serious Fraud Office, which was applying for the order, that substantial meant 'not insubstantial' or 'not minimal'.

However, a risk of prejudice alone is not sufficient. Section 4(2) provides that 'the court may, where it appears to be necessary for avoiding' the risk, make an order. The word 'may' gives the court a discretion. There is some uncertainty about whether the discretion indicated by the use of the word 'may' is catered for by the requirement that the court may only make an order where it appears to be necessary for avoiding the risk, or whether it is a separate third element. If it is, then the court must decide first whether there is a substantial risk, secondly whether the making of an order is necessary to avoid the risk and thirdly whether

2   See Chs 4, 5 and 6.
3   See the circulars Court Business items B948 No 8/81 and 5/86 discussed in Walker, Cram and Brogarth, 'The Reporting of Crown Court Proceedings and the Contempt of Court Act 1981' (1992) 55 MLR 647.
4   [1991] 1 All ER 347 at 349, [1991] 1 WLR 4 at 8; see also Lord Taylor of Gosforth CJ in *Ex p Telegraph plc* [1993] 2 All ER 971 at 978.
5   (1990) Times, 2 February.
6   (1990) Times, 8 February.
7   Unreported, 11 January 1991, MacKinnon J, Central Criminal Court.
8   *R v Ponting* (1985) Times, 29 January, which involved re-enactments of the trial on television.
9   (1987) Times, 10 October.
10 [1995] 2 All ER 355 (the action was heard together with *Bishopsgate Investment Management Ltd v Credit Suisse,* with the Serious Fraud Office intervening). In *Ex p Telegraph plc* [1993] 2 All ER 971 at 975, [1993] 1 WLR 980 at 984 Lord Taylor of Gosforth CJ merely 'noted' that the risk of prejudice had to be substantial.
11 In cases such as *A-G v English* [1983] 1 AC 116, [1982] 2 All ER 903 and *A-G v News Group Newspapers Ltd* [1987] QB 1, [1986] 2 All ER 833, discussed in Chs 3, 4, 5 and 6.
12 [1995] 2 All ER 355 at 361.

in all the circumstances an order should be made. In *Ex p Telegraph plc* [13] Lord Taylor of Gosforth CJ pointed out that the courts had as a matter of practice tended to merge the requirement of necessity and the exercise of discretion together,[14] thus making it a two rather than a three-stage test. He said that in deciding whether it was necessary to make an order the courts would inevitably have regard to the competing public considerations of ensuring a fair trial and open justice and that the necessity for an order was statutory recognition of the principle of open justice.

In *MGN Pension Trustees Ltd v Bank of America* [15] Lindsay J preferred to consider s 4(2) as providing a three-stage test, in which the 'necessity' part is directed only at the practicalities of avoiding the risk with an additional stage at which the court exercises its discretion and considers the competing public interests. It is submitted that Lindsay J's approach has much to recommend it for it accords more naturally with the wording of the section and also emphasises the importance attached to the principle of open justice by making it clear that even if an order is the only way of avoiding a substantial risk it will not always be made.[16] In *MGN* the proceedings in issue were civil actions in connection with the Maxwell pension fund debacle. The Serious Fraud Office was concerned that reports of these proceedings could prejudice the future criminal trials of Maxwell's sons and others. Lindsay J concluded that there was no substantial risk of prejudice, but if there had been there would have been no way of avoiding it other than by a postponement order: he would not, however, have exercised his discretion and made the order because the risk would have been outweighed by the requirement of open justice and legitimate public interest and concern.[17]

As to whether it is necessary as a matter of practicality to make an order to avoid a risk of prejudice, the Court of Appeal made it clear in *Re Central Independent Television plc* [18] that the court must consider all reasonable alternatives and not lightly interfere with the freedom of the press. In that case the judge had considered the welfare of the jury in a fraud trial, who were confined overnight in a hotel, and he made a postponement order rather than deny the jury access to radio and television.[19] Lord Lane CJ thought that this showed

---

13 [1993] 2 All ER 971 at 975.
14 Citing *Re Saunders* (1990) Times, 8 February, *Re Central Independent Television plc* [1991] 1 All ER 347, *R v Beck, ex p Daily Telegraph plc* [1993] 2 All ER 177 and *R v Brooks* (unreported, 23 July 1992).
15 [1995] 1 All ER 355 at 363.
16 As is also clear from *R v Beck, ex p Daily Telegraph plc* [1993] 2 All ER 177 and *R v Clerkenwell Magistrates' Court, ex p Telegraph Plc* [1993] QB 462, [1993] 2 All ER 183.
17 The SFO's worry was that the civil actions involved claims of 'knowing receipt' and 'knowing assistance' by financial institutions in connection with the fraudulent designs of the defendants in the criminal trials (inter alia) and that the talk of 'fraud' in relation to the defendants might impress itself on the minds of future members of the criminal jury, unversed in the mysteries and terminology of constructive trusts. Lindsay J's attitude is to be contrasted with the more cautious stance of Millett J in a previous 'Maxwell' civil case, *Macmillan Inc v Bishopsgate Investment Trust plc* [1995] 1 WLR 978 where a s 4(2) order was made. As Lindsay J pointed out, moreover, the *MGN* trial had already been going on for 45 days when the SFO applied for the order and so far the press had not shown any interest in reporting the case.
18 [1991] 1 All ER 347.
19 One interesting point about the judge's order was it covered only reporting by radio and television and not newspapers. The Lord Chief Justice was prepared to concede that there might be occasions when legitimate distinctions could be made between broadcasting and other media but did not believe this to be one of them.

a wrong order of priorities.[20] In *R v Beck, ex p Daily Telegraph plc* [1] Farquharson LJ suggested that in a case where the risk of prejudice was to a further trial of the accused consideration should be given to measures such as extending the period between the trials, or transferring the second trial to another location, rather than making a s 4(2) order.

In both *Beck* and *Ex p Telegraph plc* [2] the Court of Appeal, as explained above, ran the issues of the necessity of the order and the exercise of the court's discretion together. *Beck* concerned the trial of three social workers charged with serious sexual and other offences against children in their care over a long period of time. There were a large number of counts in the indictment and there were to be three trials. The Court of Appeal thought that there was a substantial risk of prejudice but in deciding whether a postponement order was necessary alluded not only to the practical alternatives mentioned in the preceding paragraph, but stressed the grave matters of public concern which the trials raised and the importance of the public having the opportunity to know what was going on. Farquharson LJ saw it as a matter of 'balancing' these matters with the risk to the administration of justice and concluded that the order made by the trial judge should be reversed. In the *Telegraph* case, where a vital Crown witness was to give evidence in a number of drug-running trials the Court of Appeal accepted the media's contention that if they had to postpone reporting any matters pertaining to this witness they would be unable properly to report the first trial at all. The court 'on the second question of necessity'[3] therefore said that even if there was a substantial risk of prejudice (which they rejected):

'it is a case in which the public interest in open trial would, in any event, outweigh any possible risk, substantial or not, of prejudice that might result from publication of Vukmirovic's role.'[4]

In a study of s 4(2) orders between 1982 and 1989 at nine Crown Courts the authors found a considerable variation in the propensity of these courts to make postponement orders.[5] Recent cases suggest, however, that when these orders are appealed[6] the higher courts are either taking the view that the jury will not be influenced or else favouring the principle of open justice over a possible risk of prejudice. As Lindsay J in *MGN* said, having examined the recent Court of Appeal decisions:[7]

'By framing the section as it did, the legislature contemplated . . . that, as to prejudice, a risk which cannot be described as substantial has to be tolerated as the price of an open press and that even if the risk is properly to be described as substantial a postponement order does not automatically follow. An argument that wherever there is *some* risk of the described prejudice in *some* degree the balance should invariably favour the right of the individual to a fair trial is inconsistent with the framework of the section . . . '

---

20 Cf *R v Ponting* (1985) Times, 29 January, in which television re-enactments were banned in order to keep them from the jury.
1   [1993] 2 All ER 177.
2   [1993] 2 All ER 971.
3   Ibid at 978 per Lord Taylor CJ.
4   Ibid at 979.
5   Walker, Cram and Brogarth, 'The Reporting of Crown Court Proceedings and the Contempt of Court Act 1981' (1992) 55 MLR 647.
6   For the appeal procedure see p 298.
7   [1995] 2 All ER 355 at 368.

(d)   The application of s 4(2) to transfer for trial proceedings

Until 1996, magistrates' courts had a function as examining justices in committing for trial at the Crown Court persons accused of an indictable offence. By s 44 of the Criminal Justice and Public Order Act 1994 committal proceedings were abolished and replaced by a procedure called transfer for trial.[8]

The Criminal Justice Act 1967 (later s 8 of the Magistrates' Courts Act 1980) provided for reporting restrictions on committal proceedings.[9] These restrictions could be lifted upon the application of the accused.[10] The *Horsham Justices* case[11] raised the issue of the relationship between reporting restrictions on committal proceedings and postponement orders under s 4(2). It was argued that justices had no power to make a s 4(2) order in respect of committal proceedings in which reporting restrictions have been lifted. The Court of Appeal held that there was such a power and rejected the submission that what was later s 8 of the Magistrates' Courts Act 1980 provided a complete code on what may or may not be reported in committal proceedings. It was pointed out[12] that the functions of the two statutory provisions were different. The restrictions under s 8 were designed to protect the defendant, they were applied or lifted at the outset of proceedings and, if not lifted, operated to *prohibit* the reporting of most of the proceedings. Section 4(2), on the other hand, is concerned to protect the wider interests of the administration of justice and can be used to protect persons other than the defendant, the power is only a postponing one and can only be sensibly exercised after proceedings have commenced.

The Court of Appeal could see nothing necessarily inconsistent with lifting reporting restrictions under s 8(4) of the 1980 Act and subsequently making a postponement order under s 4(2) of the 1981 Act. However, as Forbes J pointed out at first instance,[13] in the case of a single defendant, if he has asked for reporting restrictions to be lifted that seems a fairly good indication that as far as he is concerned, there could be no prejudice to his fair trial by allowing reports to be published. To that extent it may be more difficult for *him* to convince justices of such prejudice if he makes a subsequent application under s 4(2).

The *Horsham Justices* case specifically concerned committal proceedings involving more than one defendant, but after s 8 of the 1980 Act was amended[14] it was no longer automatic that reporting restrictions would be lifted simply upon the request of one co-defendant. Magistrates had to be satisfied that it is 'in the interests of justice' that restrictions should be lifted. Forbes J commented that if justices have already been through the process of deciding whether the interests of justice require the lifting of restrictions something new might well be required before they could feel that the possibility of prejudice required the reimposition of any particular ban under s 4(2). However, as Shaw LJ said in the Court of Appeal,[15] under the amended s 8 the court could only consider the interests of

8   By Pt 1 of Sch 4 to the 1994 Act which replaces ss 4 to 8 of the Magistrates' Courts Act 1980. See further pp 304 ff.
9   See p 304.
10   Magistrates' Courts Act 1980, s 8(2).
11   *R v Horsham Justices, ex p Farquharson* [1982] QB 762, [1982] 2 All ER 269.
12   Per Lord Denning MR, ibid at 788–9 and 282–3, Shaw LJ at 795–6 and 288–9 and Ackner LJ at 802–804 and 293–4.
13   Ibid at 772 and 277.
14   By the Criminal Justice (Amendment) Act 1981 which inserted a new s 8(2A) into the 1980 Act.
15   [1982] QB 762 at 797, [1982] 2 All ER 269 at 289.

justice as affecting the defendants before the court and Ackner LJ pointed out[16] that there are no *postponing* powers under those provisions. It is submitted, therefore, that there is nothing inconsistent in lifting reporting restrictions but exercising powers under s 4(2) to postpone reports of certain aspects of the case.

The *Horsham Justices* case concerned committal proceedings. However, the making of s 4(2) orders by magistrates has been rendered a more urgent issue by the reporting restrictions provisions which accompany the new transfer for trial procedures.[17] What is now s 8A of the Magistrates' Courts Act 1980 (as substituted by the 1994 Act) provides for not dissimilar reporting restrictions to those which applied to committal proceedings. There are, however, significant differences. One is that the reporting restrictions apply only to an 'application for dismissal' that is, to the proceedings whereby the accused applies for the charges against him to be dismissed under s 6 of the Act. There are no longer reporting restrictions on remand proceedings.[18] They may, however, be the subject of s 4(2) orders. This situation produces the possibility that magistrates may routinely have to consider the imposition of s 4(2) orders. It has been suggested that given the nature of the delicate balancing exercise called for by s 4(2) and the way it has been interpreted and applied in the higher courts (discussed above) magistrates may find this a difficult task, particularly considering the time constraints under which they operate.[19] The 1994 reforms certainly open up a new area of application for s 4(2).

(e)   The relationship between s 4(2), the strict liability rule and the common law

The submissions made in the *Horsham Justices* case on behalf of the press raised the interesting issue of how s 4(2) relates to the common law. The question was whether a breach of an order made under s 4(2) is *in itself* a contempt of court or whether it will only be a contempt if the conduct complained of is also a breach of the strict liability rule and would have amounted to contempt prior to the 1981 Act.

Lord Denning MR was adamant that a breach of a s 4(2) order was not in itself a contempt. He did not believe that Parliament intended to cut down or abridge the freedom of the press as hitherto established. In his view the proper approach was to consider whether apart from s 4(2) a publication would have been punishable as a contempt and if it would have been an order could properly be made to postpone publication under s 4(2). In other words the sole function of s 4(2) is to create the need for a court order before liability for contempt can arise. He explained his view quite simply:[20]

> 'Section 4 (2) retains the common law about the occasions when a report (otherwise fair and accurate) may be a contempt of court, but with this improvement: Nothing is to be left to implication. It is for the court to make an order telling the newspapers what things they are not to publish. Thus, giving the newspaper that warning which the Lords felt was desirable in *A-G v Leveller Magazine Ltd.* . . .

16   Ibid at 803–804 and 294F.
17   For a full account of these, see p 305.
18   Remand proceedings are dealt with by what is now s 6 of the 1980 Act. One commentator has remarked a propos of the 1994 Act coming into force: 'Prosecutors will not suddenly stop making prejudicial remarks when applying for defendants to be remanded in custody. Defendants will not stop volunteering incautious confessions', see Welsh, (1995) 145 NLJ 1007.
19   See the discussion by Welsh, ibid.
20   [1982] QB 762 at 793, [1982] 2 All ER 269 at 286.

In short, s 4(2) only applies to cases where the courts themselves would at common law have jurisdiction to make an order postponing publication: but now it needs an order, not an implication. . . .

Such an order operates now so as to bind not only persons within the courtroom but also those outside, thus clearing up the doubts expressed by some of the Lords in the *Leveller* case.'

Lord Denning MR said that were s 4(2) to be construed differently, then 'every court in the land', including tribunals,[1] would be given a new power to postpone reports on proceedings and he could not accept that suggestion.

Ackner and Shaw LJJ accepted with equanimity, however, the idea that s 4(2) created a new head of contempt and that any court could make an order postponing reports of proceedings, breach of which would automatically be contempt.

The difficulty over s 4(2) arose partly because of doubts about the application of s 6(b) of the Act which reads:

'Nothing in the foregoing provisions of this Act . . .implies that any publication is punishable as contempt of court under that rule which would not be so punishable apart from those provisions.'

The reference in the subsection to 'that rule' means the strict liability rule.

Both Lord Denning MR and Ackner LJ were prepared to accept that s 6(b) was properly construed as providing that no one can in the future be found guilty of contempt who would not have been so found guilty under the pre-existing law. However, they disagreed as to whether s 6(b) applies to s 4(2). Lord Denning was convinced that it does,[2] seeing the provision as an important check on the court's powers. There is support for this view in that ss 1–7 of the Act are headed 'Strict Liability'. Ackner LJ on the other hand, ruled that s 6(b) has no application to s 4(2). He pointed out[3] that s 6(b) is confined to contempts falling under the 'strict liability rule' and in his view there are sufficient pointers in the language of s 4(2) (that orders can be made to protect pending and imminent proceedings from a substantial risk of prejudice as opposed to protecting *active* proceedings from a substantial risk of *serious* prejudice) to show that Parliament intended to create a new and separate head of contempt liability.

Though not beyond doubt it would seem that Shaw LJ sided with Ackner LJ on this point.[4] The majority view seems therefore to be that s 4(2) is properly regarded as the *sole* source of authority for making postponement orders. The effect of the decision is that the powers of the courts have been *extended* by s 4(2).[5] Whether or not this was the intention of Parliament it is a more sensible outcome to a situation caused by provisions which do not properly fit together, than that which would result from Lord Denning's approach. That would involve a 'double-take', in that if the press breached an order a court would still have to

---

1 Because of the definition of 'court' in s 19 of the 1981 Act as 'any tribunal or body exercising the judicial power of the State', discussed further pp 293 and 486 ff. Lord Denning MR had an alarming view of the propensities of tribunals to misuse their powers but his worries in that regard have proved unfounded: it would, anyway, be very rarely that the requirements of s 4 (2) will be fulfilled in respect of tribunal proceedings.
2 See especially ibid at 794 and 784 and at 284B–F and 287F–G.
3 Ibid at 806–7 and 296.
4 At any rate he found himself at variance with Lord Denning MR, see ibid at 798 and 290C.
5 It was doubtful for example whether, at common law, magistrates could delay the reporting of committal proceedings. See p 279.

decide whether there was a substantial risk of serious prejudice before finding them in contempt.

Some of the objections to the majority's view of the effect of s 4(2) were that the courts' new power would largely go unchecked since the media, not being party to the proceedings, had no right of appeal. Ackner LJ was dismissive of some of these fears saying[6] that the power was only to postpone, that it could be exercised in relation to only a part of proceedings, and only to avoid a substantial risk of prejudice. None of these points is a complete answer but subsequent developments over rights of appeal and the media being heard prior to making the order have greatly improved the situation.[7]

(f)   The bodies empowered to make a s 4(2) order

When s 4(2) refers to a 'court' making an order to which bodies does it refer? 'Court' is defined under s 19 as including 'any tribunal or body exercising the judicial power of the State'. We consider the ambit and general application of this definition in Chapter 12. As mentioned above[8] in the *Horsham Justices* case it seemed to be contemplated that the definition could apply to 'tribunals' as opposed to 'courts of law'.[9] Ackner LJ, however, did not believe that a tribunal properly directing itself in the terms of s 4(2) could find it necessary to order the postponement of the report of its proceedings. In policy terms it is suggested that his judgment in this regard should be followed if s 19 is thought properly construed to apply to tribunals at large.[10]

(g)   Evidence and procedure when making an order

In the *Horsham Justices* case it was argued that the bench should have embarked on some kind of inquisitorial examination of the material placed before them. Forbes J considered that this went too far. He thought[11] that all a reasonable bench had to do is satisfy itself that such material justifies a particular restriction. This seemed to be the Court of Appeal view.[12]

Since the enactment of s 4(2) the courts[13] have gradually become more willing to accommodate the legitimate concerns of the media over the making of postponement orders. A 1983 *Practice Direction*[14] states that it is necessary to keep a permanent record of s 4(2)[15] orders and for that purpose all orders have to be formulated in precise terms and committed to writing, either by the judge personally or by the clerk of the court under the judge's directions. An order must state:

(1)   its precise scope,

---

6   Ibid at 806 and 296.
7   See pp 298 ff.
8   See p 292.
9   See Lord Denning MR, ibid at 790E–F and 284E–F and Ackner LJ at 805-6 and 295-6.
10   For a discussion of the ambit of s 19 see pp 486 ff.
11   Ibid at 774 and 279.
12   See eg Ackner LJ, ibid at 807–8 and 297.
13   And the legislature, see below on challenging orders.
14   *Practice Direction (Contempt of Court Act: Reports of Proceedings: Postponement Orders)* [1983] 1 All ER 64.
15   The *Practice Direction* also applies to s 11 orders, see p 300.

(2) the time at which it will cease to have effect, if appropriate, and

(3) the specific purpose of making the order.

Courts will normally give notice to the press in some form that an order has been made and court staff should be prepared to answer any inquiry about a specific case. In *Re Central Independent Television plc* [16] the Court of Appeal stressed the importance of courts observing the provisions of the *Practice Direction*. In that case the judge made an oral order which was not reduced to writing until the next day. The written order then differed in material respects from the oral order. One publication complied with the oral pronouncement but contravened the written order. Lord Lane CJ was critical of the judge's procedure. He said[17] that the oral order should have been reduced to writing in precise form as soon as possible after it was made so that those affected by it knew exactly what they could and could not do.[18]

The *Practice Direction* stated that ensuring no breach of an order occurs is the responsibility of those reporting cases and their editors and that the onus rests with them to make inquiries in any case of doubt. In *A-G v Guardian Newspapers Ltd*,[19] however, the Divisional Court said that courts should be diligent in accommodating the legitimate interests of the press[20] and approved the practice of the Central Criminal Court in faxing all s 4(2) orders to the Press Association where they could be kept on file and inquiries from journalists dealt with at times, such as in the late afternoon and evenings, when court officials might not be available to answer queries. Mann LJ thought that other courts might usefully adopt this practice.

It was formerly a matter of criticism[1] that s 4(2) orders were made without the press being heard, while the parties to the case either supported the ban or took no view on it. The problem stems from the lack of statutory provision in regard to who can make representations about such orders. However, the courts have recently made it clear that the press should be heard and their views taken seriously.[2] This sympathetic attitude to the press is apparent in the *Guardian* case, discussed above. The practice of Crown Court judges in hearing representations from the press was recognised by the Court of Appeal in *R v Beck, ex p Daily Telegraph plc*.[3] Farquharson LJ said[4] that it is preferable for s 4(2) orders not to be made suddenly, because the press may not then have the opportunity to make representations. He suggested that the best course was for the matter to be dealt with at the preliminary hearing or summons for directions, or, if not, for a limited order to be made for a short time (such as two days) so that the press could be heard.

---

16 [1991] 1 All ER 347.
17 Ibid at 350.
18 This was reiterated by Mann LJ and Brooke J in *A-G v Guardian Newspapers Ltd* [1992] 3 All ER 38 at 46 and 50 where Brooke J said the orders should be drafted and made public in a way which made it 'crystal clear'.
19 Ibid.
20 Ibid at 50 per Brooke J.
 1 See eg, the second edition of this book, p 211, and Robertson and Nicol, *Media Law* (3rd edn, 1992) pp 345–346.
 2 This is in at least part due to the press now having some rights of appeal against s 4(2) orders and the courts having more cause, therefore, to consider how these orders are made: for appeals, see p 300 post.
 3 [1993] 2 All ER 177.
 4 Ibid at 182.

The question of whether magistrates' courts have power to hear representations from the press when making postponement orders was directly at issue in *R v Clerkenwell Metropolitan Stipendiary Magistrate, ex p Telegraph Plc.*[5] One of those involved in the Maxwell affair was charged with a summary offence under s 2(13) of the Criminal Justice Act 1987.[6] The metropolitan stipendiary magistrate, on the application of the accused, and with the support of the prosecution, made a s 4(2) order on the grounds that if these proceedings were made known to the public the trial of other serious fraud offences, with which the accused had already been charged, might be prejudiced. The magistrate held that he had no powers to hear the protestations of the press about the order because they were not parties to the proceedings. The Divisional Court rejected the submission that magistrates' courts, being creatures of statute, have only those powers expressly or by implication given to them by statute, which do not include the power to hear the press. Mann LJ said that the matter could not be decided with reference only to the rules about locus standi in proceedings contained in the Magistrates' Courts Act 1980 because the press were not asking to be heard *on the issue in the proceedings*. He said that any court exercising s 4(2) powers could hear the press representations on the matter:[7]

> 'I regard it as implicit in the enactment of s 4(2) that a court contemplating its use should be enabled to receive assistance from those who will, if there is no order, enjoy the right of making reports of proceedings before the court. They are in particular the best qualified to represent that public interest in publicity which the court has to take into account when performing any balancing exercise which has to be undertaken.'

The weakness in the position of the media is that, even after these cases, there is no *right* to be heard. It all depends on the discretion of the court. This was admitted by Mann LJ in the *Clerkenwell* case but he said that although the power to hear the media was discretionary he expected it to be exercised when the media asked 'because the court can expect to find assistance from the news media'.[8] It is submitted, however, that what is needed is a statutory *right* for the media to be heard. This would also have the virtue of putting the emphasis where it belongs—on the rights of the media—rather than on the discretionary powers of the courts.

In *Clerkenwell* it was said that it would be convenient if the media were able to present a single view.[9]

Another problem concerning s 4(2) orders is that the decision to make them may be made in camera,[10] but it is to be noted that in *A-G v Guardian Newspapers Ltd*[11] the Divisional Court held that publishing the fact that a postponement order has been made or the terms of the order may itself be prohibited, so that publication thereof would be a contempt.

---

5   [1993] QB 462, [1993] 2 All ER 183.
6   Which involves failing, without reasonable cause, to answer questions relevant to a serious fraud investigation by the Serious Fraud Office.
7   [1993] QB 462 at 471E–F.
8   Ibid at 471H.
9   Ibid at 471H and 472D.
10   *Re Crook* [1992] 2 All ER 687.
11   [1992] 3 All ER 38 at 46 per Mann LJ.

(h)   What information can be postponed?

Even if there is thought to be justification for ordering a postponement, care and restraint must still be exercised as to the width of the order. Given the requirement that there must be a substantial risk of prejudice, it should be a rare case where a blanket postponement on what can be reported can be justified. It is difficult to see why in all but exceptional cases it should be regarded as prejudicial to publish, for example, the names of the accused and the nature of the charge against him. The Court of Appeal in the *Horsham Justices* case thought the blanket order made in that case too wide. It was pointed out[12] that the order was more restrictive than that applying to committal proceedings (as they then were) where reporting restrictions are not lifted.

Despite this, following the 1981 Act the courts frequently made blanket bans.[13] This seemed to be evidence of a misuse of the power. The 1983 *Practice Direction*[14] stated that an order under s 4(2) must state its precise scope and specific purpose. These requirements were partly a response to the disquiet over the trials of some Rampton Hospital nurses, where blanket bans on reporting the trials prevented the press reporting the industrial action taken by other nurses in protest. When the *Observer* breached the order, the Court of Appeal would not grant an injunction on future breaches on the grounds that the order was too wide. The order was later rescinded by the trial judge.[15]

(i)   The duration of the order

The Act is silent as to how long an order may last but the reference in s 4(2) to 'other proceedings pending or imminent' means that an order can be expressed to stay in force beyond the conclusion of the proceedings in which the order was made. The duration of the order was one of the issues raised in the *Horsham Justices* case. There, during committal proceedings (the reporting restrictions upon which had been lifted), magistrates made an order 'prohibiting the reporting of any part of the proceedings until the commencement of any trial hearing'. Although the case was sent back to the magistrates for consideration as to whether the order was necessary to protect the administration of justice there seemed to be no objection in principle to the duration of the order. It was accepted, however, that magistrates have no power to make an order under s 4(2) covering not only the hearing before them but also a later trial in the Crown Court.[16] It is understandable that it should be held that a lower court should have no power to bind a superior one. It might be thought, however, that courts generally should be reluctant to make orders that purport to bind courts in other cases.

---

12 By Lord Denning MR [1982] QB 762 at 787 and [1982] 2 All ER 269 at 281.
13 It was reported in the *Daily Telegraph*, 12 July 1982 for example that in the Old Bailey alone, 16 of the 22 postponing orders made up until July 1982 were blanket prohibitions.
14 [1983] 1 All ER 64, discussed at p 293.
15 See Observer, 11 July 1982 and Robertson and Nicol, *Media Law* (3rd edn, 1992) p 344.
16 See per Lord Denning MR [1982] QB 762 at 789 and [1982] 2 All ER 269 at 283, Shaw LJ at 798 and 290 and Ackner LJ at 807 and 279, 280 and all adopting Glidewell J's position explained at 775 and 279–280.

(j)   Effect of an order

It is submitted that the law may be properly summarised by saying that provided a s 4(2) order is clear and certain and made intra vires it is incumbent upon all those who know of the order to obey it. Failure to do so will render the offender liable to be punished for contempt. The 1983 *Practice Direction* [17] states that the onus is on the press to inquire in cases of doubt and it is submitted that where an order is reduced to writing, given to representatives of the media and measures such as those suggested in *Guardian Newspapers* [18] taken, it would be not be tenable for the media to claim that they had no notice of the order.

The juristic basis of liability does not seem to have been made clearer by the legislation. It may be, therefore, that the explanation given in *A-G v Leveller Magazine Ltd* [19] will continue to apply, namely, that it is not for breaking the order as such that a contempt is committed but for deliberately frustrating a court ruling aimed at protecting the administration of justice. Lord Denning MR's suggestion in the *Horsham Justices* case[20] that an order is binding on those outside the court room by reason of s 11 seems out of place since that section applies to prohibitions rather than postponements. Even if it does apply it would seem a prerequisite of liability that the publisher knows of the order.

In the *Horsham Justices* case it was argued that it was not enough to show that the terms of the order had been broken but that it had to be shown that the publication creates a substantial risk of serious prejudice to the administration of justice in particular proceedings. The contention was that breach of an order merely removes a possible defence to a charge of contempt under the strict liability rule. This contention was rejected both by Ackner and Shaw LJJ. In their view, breach of an order is a contempt per se and no further inquiry is necessary. It is not clear whether Lord Denning MR acceded to the argument or not.

Shaw LJ considered[1] that a premature publication in contravention of an order of which the publisher is aware could not be said to be made in good faith. Ackner LJ thought[2] that it could not have been Parliament's intention that it would be necessary to look behind every order made under s 4(2).

It is suggested that the majority opinion is right. As Ackner LJ said,[3] it would be an odd situation if contravention of an order made because the court thought postponement necessary for avoiding a substantial risk of prejudice to the administration of justice could carry with it no sanction other than the removal of a defence to a charge of contempt under the strict liability rule.

Although both Shaw and Ackner LJJ considered breach of a s 4(2) order a contempt per se, it is submitted that this was based upon the assumption that the order was intra vires in the first place. It surely cannot have been contemplated that it is a contempt to ignore an order made ultra vires (for example, because it was not based on the need to protect the administration of justice).[4]

---

17   [1983] 1 All ER 64.
18   *A-G v Guardian Newspapers Ltd* [1992] 3 All ER 38, see p 294.
19   [1979] AC 440, [1979] 1 All ER 745 discussed at pp 275 ff.
20   [1982] QB 762 at 793, [1982] 2 All ER 269 at 286.
 1   Ibid at 798 and 290.
 2   Ibid at 806 and 296.
 3   Ibid at 805 and 295.
 4   Though it can be in other contexts, see *Isaacs v Robertson* [1985] AC 97, [1984] 3 All ER 140, PC and *Johnson v Walton* [1990] 1 FLR 350, CA discussed at pp 555–556.

(k)   Challenging the order

The point has already been made that the media have no *right* to be heard before a s 4(2) order is made. Until s 159(1) of the Criminal Justice Act 1988 came into force the media, not being parties to the proceedings, could not appeal against an order either. Judicial review was available to challenge orders made in magistrates' courts but was thought not to be available against orders made in the Crown Court because there they related to a trial on indictment which is excluded from the ambit of judicial review.[5] In *R v Leicester Crown Court, ex p S (a minor)*,[6] however, the Divisional Court held that it could review reporting restrictions under s 39 of the Children and Young Persons Act 1933 as it was not 'a matter relating to trial on indictment'. This was on the application of the party to the proceedings but it does suggest that the Divisional Court could likewise review s 4(2) orders at the behest of the press.

This apparent lacuna became an issue in 1984 over an attempted challenge to a s 11 anonymity order imposed by a Crown Court, where the same inability to challenge applied.[7] Faced with a challenge to this by the journalist concerned under the European Convention on Human Rights, s 159(1) was enacted. This gives a 'person aggrieved' a right to appeal (with leave) against a s 4(2) order[8] to the Court of Appeal. The press can be a 'person aggrieved' for this purpose.[9]

Section 159(1) has several drawbacks. First, it does not give the press an untrammelled right of appeal, but requires leave. Secondly, the decision of the Court of Appeal is final and there is no further appeal to the House of Lords. Thirdly, it applies only to trials on indictment and not to orders made by magistrates' courts or by civil courts. There is no equivalent provision made for orders in summary trials and therefore the press still has to rely on judicial review proceedings or on obtaining a statement of case on law or jurisdiction.[10]

An advantage of s 159(1), however, is that the Court of Appeal will actually look into the merits of the decision to impose the order and replace the judge's decision with their own if necessary. As Farquharson LJ said in *R v Beck, ex p Daily Telegraph plc*:[11]

> 'It has been correctly submitted to us . . . that in applying the subsection we, as the Court of Appeal, can exercise our own discretion. It is not a case of reviewing the exercise of the learned judge's discretion with the limitations imposed on the Court of Appeal in such circumstances. So we approach the case first of all by deciding whether there was such a substantial risk of prejudice and secondly whether, if we find that there is such a risk, in our discretion we should make the order.'

This contrasts with the position on judicial review from a magistrates' court order, where the Divisional Court can only decide whether the order was lawfully made and whether it was a decision which a reasonable tribunal could have come to. Yet a magistrates' court is at least as likely to come to a wrong decision about

5   See the Supreme Court Act 1981, s 29(3).
6   [1992] 2 All ER 659.
7   *R v Central Criminal Court, ex p Crook* (1984) Times, 8 November.
8   Or s 11 order, see p 304.
9   See eg *R v Beck, ex p Daily Telegraph plc* [1993] 2 All ER 177; *R v Clerkenwell Stipendiary Magistrate, ex p Telegraph Plc* [1993] QB 462, [1993] 2 All ER 183.
10 As a person 'aggrieved' within the meaning of s 111(1) of the Magistrates' Courts Act 1980, see *R v Clerkenwell Stipendiary Magistrate, ex p Telegraph Plc*, ibid.
11 [1993] 2 All ER 177 at 180.

a postponement order as is a Crown Court judge and it is submitted that this is an anomaly which should be corrected by statute.

An appeal can be heard against a s 4(2) order even though it is long spent and can no longer affect the actual events concerned. In *Re Central Independent Television plc* [12] the Court of Appeal reversed an order banning the reporting of a trial on television and radio while the jury were in a hotel overnight, some nine months after the event. The Court of Appeal held that they had jurisdiction to hear the appeal because otherwise s 159(1) would not be an effective remedy in that it would not be possible to correct the misleading impression that orders could be made in circumstances in which the Court of Appeal thought they should not be.

An application for leave to appeal under s 159(1) has to be made within 14 days (although this period can be extended). [13]

3   Prohibiting the publication of particular information: The Contempt of Court Act 1981, s 11

Section 11 of the Contempt of Court Act 1981 deals with prohibiting the publishing of information which has been withheld from being mentioned in open court. The section provides:

> 'In any case where a court (having power to do so) allows a name or other matter to be withheld from the public in proceedings before the court, the court may give such directions prohibiting the publication of that name or matter in connection with the proceedings as appear to the court to be necessary for the purpose for which it was so withheld.'

Unlike s 4(2), s 11 is concerned with the power to *prohibit* publication of certain information. As we have seen, there was such a power at common law but there was uncertainty both as to when a court had power to withhold information and as to the effect such withholding had outside the courtroom. Section 11 was apparently meant[14] to clarify the position but in this it lamentably fails. The section does not *confer* any power to withhold information. This is made clear by the words 'having power to do so'. Accordingly, one must continue to look to various other statutes and to an uncertain common law.

Provided there is power to order the withholding of information, s 11 allows the court to give 'such directions prohibiting the publication . . . as appear . . . to be necessary for the purpose for which it was so withheld'. Again this seems to do little more than confirm the pre-existing position. The section does not spell out the consequences of a breach nor does it make it clear whether an express order is necessary to bind the press. With regard to the latter, and to make sense of s 4, it is suggested that an express order *is* necessary. In any event it was established at common law that a mere request to withhold information is insufficient to impose liability.[15] Once an order is made it is incumbent upon all those who know of the order to obey it.[16] Those who do not obey are liable to be committed for contempt.

12   [1991] 1 All ER 347.
13   Criminal Appeal Rules 1968, 16(A) as amended by the Criminal Appeal (Amendment) Rules 1989, SI 1989/1102.
14   See eg Lord Hailsham comments in HL Official Report (5th series) col 664.
15   See p 278.
16   This appears to follow from *A-G v Leveller Magazine Ltd* [1979] AC 440. See the discussion at pp 275 ff about the *Leveller* case in the context of the common law.

Section 11 does not appear to settle the issue of whether an order made in court can be directly binding on outsiders, though in the *Horsham Justices* case[17] Lord Denning MR seemed to think it does so. Even if it does not, liability will accrue upon the indirect basis laid down by *A-G v Leveller Magazine Ltd*. [18] For the most part the exact juristic basis of an order will not matter since on either approach those who know of the order must obey it. One possible difference, however, relates to whether a court can make a binding order forbidding publication of a witness's identity gained from an independent source. If orders are directly binding, then it may be that they can, but not otherwise. Given its object of clarification the failure to spell out the juristic basis of a court order is a serious defect in s 11.

The *Practice Direction* [19] referred to earlier with regard to s 4(2) orders also applies to s 11. Hence an order should be committed to writing and should define the precise scope, the time at which it ceases to have effect if appropriate and include the specific purpose of making the order.

An order cannot be made in respect of information that was not withheld from the public during the court proceedings. This was demonstrated in *R v Arundel Justices, ex p Westminster Press Ltd* [20] where the Divisional Court quashed an order made by magistrates that an offender's name and address should not be published on the grounds that it had already been disclosed in open court.[1]

Courts, particularly magistrates' courts, may sometimes be tempted to withhold information by making s 11 orders to spare defendants from publicity. However, as Watkins LJ said in *R v Evesham Justices, ex p McDonagh*: [2]

> '... s 11 was not enacted for the benefit of the comfort and feelings of defendants.'

In that case the justices were trying to shield an ex-MP who was on a charge of driving his Land Rover without an MOT certificate, by prohibiting the publication of his home address. He was afraid of harassment from his ex-wife. This did not impress Watkins LJ, who said that the justices' action had nothing to do with the administration of justice:

> 'It seems to me that the concern shown by the justices for not giving publicity to Mr Hocking's home address was solely motivated by their sympathy for his well being if his former wife should learn of his home address and harass him yet again. That kind of predicament is not, unfortunately, unique. There are undoubtedly many people who find themselves defending criminal charges who for all manner of reasons would like to keep unrevealed their identity, their home address in particular. Indeed, I go so far as to say that in the vast majority of cases, in magistrates' courts anyway, defendants would like their identity to be unrevealed and would be capable of advancing seemingly plausible reasons why that should be so.'

A similar position applies in respect of making s 11 orders where publicity might cause the defendant to suffer economic damage and in *R v Dover Justices, ex p Dover District Council* [3] the court refused to sanction a ban on reporting the name of a restauranteur being prosecuted for public health offences.[4] The

17 [1982] QB 762 at 793, [1982] 2 All ER 269 at 286.
18 [1979] AC 440, [1979] 1 All ER 745 discussed at pp 276 ff.
19 [1983] 1 All ER 64, [1982] 1 WLR 1475, see pp 293 ff.
20 [1985] 2 All ER 390.
1   See also *R v Central Criminal Court, ex p Crook* (1984) Times, 8 November.
2   [1988] 1 QB 553 at 562, [1988] 1 All ER 371 at 384.
3   (1991) 156 JP 433.
4   And see also the Australian case *Raybos Australia Pty Ltd v Jones* [1985] 2 NSWLR 47, which concerned a solicitor involved in a civil action where there were accusations of fraud against him.

decisions are consistent with the effect of s 11 being confined to enabling the court to make an order where it has power to withhold information at common law for, as we have seen, anonymity orders at common law could not be made simply on the basis of convenience, but only to protect the due administration of justice.[5]

However, there are two cases in which the court *has* granted anonymity to parties to civil proceedings to spare them embarrassment and distress, but in neither case was there any argument put forward by the press or the Attorney General on the matter. The first case, *H v Ministry of Defence,* [6] concerned a claim for damages by a serviceman alleging that the medical negligence of the defendant's medical services had led to the amputation of his penis. Liability was admitted and the only issue was to damages, but the case went to the Court of Appeal because the plaintiff wanted the action to be tried by judge and jury and the defendant was resisting this. The Court of Appeal, taking into account the plaintiff's psychological trauma and suicide attempts, prohibited the naming or other identification of the plaintiff in any report of the case, saying that his personal identity was irrelevant to the matters of general public importance raised.[7] The second case, *R v Criminal Injuries Compensation Board, ex p A* [8] was an action for judicial review of a decision of the Criminal Injuries Compensation Board about a claim relating to the sexual abuse of the applicant by her stepfather. The court thought it right to withhold the applicant's name in view of her 'psychiatric and psychological interests' and made a s 11 order.

The limits to the courts' willingness to grant s 11 orders to protect privacy and avoid embarrassment was demonstrated in *R v Westminster City Council, ex p Castelli and Tristan-Garcia,*[9] where, unlike the two cases above, there was full argument of the s 11 point and the press and the Attorney General were represented. The applicants were bringing an action against the local authority claiming that they were unintentionally homeless and in priority need and that the authority had a duty to house them under the Housing Act 1985. The basis of their priority need claim was that they were both HIV positive which they said was a condition to which social stigma attached and therefore a s 11 order was justified.

Latham J refused to make an order. He accepted that anonymity had been granted in *H v Ministry of Defence* and *R v CICB, ex p A* and that the court had recognised in both cases that it had power to do so in the exercise of its inherent jurisdiction, but said that the applicant always had to establish that the failure to grant anonymity would render the attainment of justice really doubtful or in effect impracticable. He was concerned that the strict guidelines laid down in *A-G v Leveller Magazine Ltd*[10] should be applied and said that they were not satisfied here. He was not convinced by the general assertion that if the order was not made other persons who were HIV positive would be deterred from pursuing their rights.[11]

In is difficult to draw real distinctions between *Castelli and Tristan-Garcia* and the other two cases because in the latter there was, in fact, no discussion as

5   See pp 276 ff.
6   [1991] 2 QB 103.
7   Ibid at 107 per Lord Donaldson MR.
8   [1992] COD 379.
9   (1995) Times, 14 August.
10 [1979] AC 440, see pp 275 ff.
11 Latham J also considered the implications of the fact that the names of the applicants had already been revealed in the leave proceedings; this aspect is dealt with below.

to whether the attainment of justice would be rendered doubtful or impracticable without the order. The orders were made out of sympathy for the sufferings of the parties involved. However, *R v CICB, ex p A* can be seen as analagous to the grant of anonymity in sexual offences cases[12] where it is believed necessary to prohibit identification inter alia to encourage victims to come forward. One detects, on the other hand, a distinct lack of sympathy with the applicants in *Castelli* but it is also possible to argue that their identity *was* relevant in a way which did not arise in the other cases. Latham J pointed out that the reason that the case had attracted publicity was 'not so much the medical condition, but the fact that the applicants came from Italy and Spain and were seeking to obtain benefits in the United Kingdom' and saw that as a reason why they wanted to remain anonymous.

An over-enthusiastic approach to granting s 11 orders is a dangerous erosion of the principle of open justice, but it is difficult to quarrel with the decision in *H v Ministry of Defence*. Judicial indulgence is not, however, readily extended to those who are perceived as having brought their troubles on themselves, as was shown by *R v Evesham Justices, ex p McDonagh*.[13] In *R v CICB, ex p A* there was some discussion of the position of the stepfather, who had never been convicted, charged or (apparently) even interviewed by the police about the alleged abuse. A s 11 order was not thought appropriate to protect *him* but in fact the incidental effect of that covering the step-daughter was that he was not indentified.

Castelli and Garcia raised the issue of when s 11 orders should be made. The names had already been given in open court when applications for leave to move for judicial review were made and Latham J said that a s 11 order made at the substantive hearing could not relate back to the application for leave as it appeared to him that they were separate proceedings, and so an order made in respect of the substantive hearings would be ineffectual.[14] Asked how future applicants could protect themselves, he considered that in some cases it might be necessary to have an ex parte hearing (perhaps in camera) and possibly grant a s 11 order for a short time until the matter could be fully argued. He also thought that in cases where the appearance of the applicant's name in the cause list would attract publicity the applicant should not lodge the papers until he had the assurances of the Crown Office that his s 11 application could be dealt with immediately.[15]

Witnesses may be subject to different considerations. The common law was prepared to countenance bans on revealing the identity of witnesses in blackmail trials, for example,[16] where anonymity is required to encourage witnesses to come forward and thus to protect the due administration of justice. In *R v Central Criminal Court, ex p Crook*,[17] however, the Divisional Court suggested that it would, if it could, have quashed a s 11 order made by a Crown Court judge[18] prohibiting the publication of the name of a woman from a prominent family,

---

12 See pp 318 ff.
13 [1988] 1 QB 553, [1988] 1 All ER 371, see p 300.
14 And even if they were not separate, the publicity which had already taken place meant that an order would be inappropriate.
15 Otherwise there is a risk that a person can exercise their right under RSC Ord 63, r 4 to inspect the office documents.
16 See p 277.
17 (1984) Times, 8 November.
18 Since this was in a trial on indictment, it ran into the problem about the lack of an appeal from the making of s 11 and s 4(2) orders: this was the case which provoked the change in the law embodied in s 159 of the Criminal Justice Act 1988, see p 298.

recovering from drug addiction, who was the chief prosecution witness in the trial of persons charged with abducting her for the purpose of unlawful sexual intercourse. The court said that the principle of open justice should outweigh the interests of particular persons and that it was common for witnesses to be faced with the revelation of embarrassing facts during proceedings. It is submitted, however, that while it is undesirable that courts should seek to protect people simply because of the wealth or influence of their families there is a far greater argument for shielding witnesses than for shielding defendants, who usually have no choice but to appear in court. Witnesses innocently caught up in events which become the subject of proceedings may be deterred from coming forward if there is no way of protecting them from unwelcome publicity. This is yet another point where the principle of open justice conflicts with other urgent considerations. Once witnesses *have* come forward, of course, a refusal to cooperate can be met with subpoenas and ultimately with the sanction of contempt for failure to testify. Courts may, however, be more sympathetic to witnesses who fear for their physical safety. In *R v Watford Magistrates' Court, ex p Lenman* [19] the witnesses to a rampage by a group of youths through a shopping centre, in which bystanders were seriously injured, were allowed not only to remain anonymous but also to give evidence from behind screens with their voices disguised. The Divisional Court said that if the magistrates were satisfied of a real risk to the administration of justice it was entirely within their powers to take these steps so that the witnesses were not deterred. This approach was followed by the Court of Appeal in *R v Taylor (Gary)* [20] in which the appellant had been convicted of murder after one witness gave evidence from behind a screen and her name and address were not revealed.[1] The Court of Appeal said that the rare and exceptional circumstances in which the defendant should not see and know the identity of his accusers were a matter for the discretion of the trial judge, but they did lay down six guidelines. These were that (a) there should be real grounds for fear if the evidence was given in the normal way; (b) the evidence was sufficiently relevant and important to make it unfair for the Crown to have to proceed without it; (c) the Crown must satisfy the court that the creditworthiness of the witness had been investigated; (d) there would be no *undue* prejudice to the accused; and (e) the court could balance the need for protection of the witness against unfairness or the appearance of unfairness.

One way in which courts can prevent the publication of information is to sit in camera. In *R v Malvern Justices, ex p Evans* [2] the justices decided to sit in camera in order to prevent publication of the 'embarrassing and intimate details' of her private life which a woman on a drink driving charge wanted to put forward as reasons for not disqualifying her. This aspect of the matter is discussed below.[3] The court may sit in camera to decide whether to make a s 11 order. Indeed, in *R v Tower Bridge Magistrates' Court, ex p Osborne* [4] the Divisional Court said that when hearing applications for such orders the justices *should* accede to requests to hear them in private, so as to judge whether there is any substance in the application without prejudicing the applicant.

---

19 [1993] Crim L R 388.
20 [1994] TLR 484.
 1 Counsel and the jury could see her, and the defendants could see her on a video screen.
 2 [1988] 1 QB 540, [1988] 1 All ER 371.
 3 See pp 320 ff. The Divisional Court thought this a case where proceedings should not have been heard in camera.
 4 (1987) 88 Cr App Rep 28.

The position over actions for judicial review and appeals in respect of s 11 orders is the same as in respect of s 4(2) orders.[5]

4   Reporting transfer for trial proceedings (formerly committal proceedings)

(a)   The replacement of committal proceedings by transfer for trial proceedings

Until the coming into force of s 44 of the Criminal Justice and Public Order Act 1994 someone accused of an indictable offence would first be dealt with by committal proceedings in a magistrates' court. The object of these proceedings was to determine whether there was a prima facie case to be answered and therefore whether he should be sent for trial by jury in the Crown Court. At committal proceedings the *prosecution's* evidence would be presented but in practice the accused usually reserved his defence. In what became termed 'old style' committal proceedings, evidence used to be invariably tendered in open court in the usual way but under the Magistrates' Courts Act 1980[6] it was possible to hear committal proceedings by taking written depositions from witnesses.[7]

For many years it was felt that reports of the committal proceedings were prejudicial to the accused, particularly as potential jurors reading such reports would read one side of the case only. Impetus for reform was created by a prosecution for murder against Dr Bodkin Adams in 1957 where the prosecution, having led evidence of earlier deaths which they alleged were attributable to the accused in the committal proceedings, did not offer the evidence at the trial itself. In the wake of that case,[8] the Tucker Committee[9] was set up and it recommended the introduction of reporting restrictions. This recommendation was belatedly implemented by the Criminal Justice Act 1967 and consolidated under s 8 of the Magistrates' Courts Act 1980.[10] These provisions severely limited the information which could be published about committal proceedings to the barest facts.[11]

Committal proceedings were abolished by s 44 of the 1994 Act. The transfer of trial procedure which replaces them[12] involves no oral advocacy where the accused is represented, except in limited cases, and is essentially an administrative procedure. The court will consider written representations, generally in the absence of the accused.

---

5   See p 298.
6   See ss 6 and 102.
7   So-called 'paper committals'. By the time evidence was presented to the Royal Commission on Criminal Justice it was estimated that full committal hearings represented only 7% of all committals (Report, 1993, Cmnd 2263).
8   Albeit that the doctor was acquitted.
9   Report of the *Departmental Committee on Proceedings before Examining Justices* (1958, Cmnd 479).
10 As subsequently amended by the Criminal Justice Act 1982, the Courts and Legal Services Act 1990 and the Broadcasting Act 1990.
11 See the second edition of this book, p 213.
12 By Sch 4, Pt I to the Act, whose provisions become ss 4 to 8C of the Magistrates' Courts Act 1980 in substitution for the previous provisions.

(b)   What may be reported about transfer for trial proceedings

The transfer for trial procedure is subject, like the committal proceedings it replaces, to severe reporting restrictions. These are set out in what is now s 8A of the Magistrates' Courts Act 1980.[13] Unless reporting restrictions are lifted (see below) the only permissible reports are, by reason of s 8A(9), those which confine themselves to the following information:

'(a)   the identity of the magistrates' court and the names of the justices composing it;

(b)   the names, age, home address and occupation of the accused;

(c)   the offence, or offences, or a summary of them, with which the accused is or are charged;

(d)   the names of legal representatives engaged in the proceedings;

(e)   where the proceedings are adjourned, the date and place to which they are adjourned;

(f)   the arrangements as to bail;

(g)   whether legal aid was granted to the accused or any of the accused.'

Failure to observe these restrictions renders the offender liable to a fine not exceeding level 5 on the standard scale.[14] Under s 8A(11) liability rests on (a) in the case of a newspaper or periodical, any proprietor, editor or publisher, (b) in the case of any other written report, the publisher, and (c) in the case of a 'relevant programme':[15]

'any body corporate which is engaged in providing the service in which the programme is included and any person having functions in relation to the programme corresponding to those of the editor of a newspaper.'[16]

Under s 8A(12) proceedings can only be brought by or with the consent of the Attorney General.

These restrictions, with certain exceptions, are similar to those which applied to committal proceedings. The major difference is that the restrictions apply, according to s 8A(1)(a), only to an 'application for dismissal' under s 6 of the 1980 Act. The application for dismissal is initiated by the defence[17] and the court will grant the application 'if it appears to the court that there is not sufficient evidence against the accused to put him on trial by jury for the offence charged'.[18] As discussed above,[19] unlike the previous provisions[20] these restrictions appear not to cover the reporting of remand applications. The magistrates will have to

---

13 As added by Sch 4, Pt I to the Criminal Justice and Public Order Act 1994.
14 S 8A(11). Currently £5,000.
15 'Relevant programme' means a programme included in a programme service (within the meaning of the Broadcasting Act 1990).
16 For the question of liability generally see Ch 10.
17 S 6(1).
18 S 6(10). This is similar to the test in the old s 6(1) and it has been suggested that the criteria laid down in the *Practice Direction (Submission of No Case)* [1962] 1 WLR 227 will apply (see *Blackstone's Criminal Practice* (1995) at D 7.21).
19 At p 291.
20 See the old s 8(8).

consider the making of a postponement order under s 4(2) if there is a risk of prejudice to the future Crown Court proceedings.[1]

It is to be expected that the courts will take the same attitude to the breach of reporting restrictions in respect of dismissal applications under the transfer for trial proceedings as they did in respect of committal proceedings. This means that they are strict in the sense that as Lord Denning MR has said:[2]

> 'nobody has to consider whether the reporting of the proceedings will cause any risk of prejudice to anyone. No one has to consider what parts should be allowed to be reported and what parts not. No one has to consider whether the administration of justice will be prejudiced or not.'

Prosecutions, however, are not common but the precedents, such as there are, emphasise the strictness of the restrictions.[3] The best example of this is the first defended case against a prosecution under the restrictions. There, the *Eastbourne Herald*[4] was fined a total of £250 for reporting under the headlines 'Organist for trial on Sex Charges' (to which no objection was taken) the following: (i) the further headline 'New Year's Day Bridegroom Bailed', (ii) the description that the offence was 'serious', (iii) the description that the accused was 'bespectacled and dressed in a dark suit', (iv) the fact that he had been married in a particular church on New Year's day, and (v) a reference to the way the solicitor handled the case.

It may be thought that none of the infringements amounted to serious breaches though the fact that there were a number of infringements may have accounted for the prosecution being brought. Whether a prosecution would have been brought for any *one* of the above infringements may be doubted though the infringements listed at (ii) and (v) above may be thought more serious than the others. Item (ii) was an infringement because what is now s 8(A)(9)(c) does not permit the offence to be described by qualifying adjectives. The description 'bespectacled and dressed in a dark suit' seems particularly innocuous and indeed it has now become common practice to include such descriptions in reports of such proceedings. It may, indeed be arguable that such a description is not a report of part of the proceedings.[5] Certainly it is not clear that any reference to the time and place of the accused's marriage was made in court and this suggests that a report of committal proceedings cannot, technically, include any information other than that permitted, whether it emerged from the proceedings, was gleaned elsewhere, or was merely general knowledge.[6]

The fact that apparently innocuous details, impossible to envisage as prejudicing the trial, can infringe the reporting restrictions has been condemned elsewhere.[7] The restrictions are wide but on the other hand they are clear and certain which seems a distinct advantage over the provisions, say, under s 4 of the Contempt of

1 For a discussion of this issue see Welsh, (1995) 145 NLJ 1007.
2 In *R v Horsham Justices, ex p Farquharson* [1982] QB 762 at 789, [1982] 2 All ER 269 at 283.
3 Basic details of the first three prosecutions were given by Sir Peter Rawlinson: Hansard HC Deb Vol 859 col 4378. In the first (see (1968) Times, 13 September) the BBC was fined £500 on two summons for broadcasting that a police officer, on applying for a remand in custody on a charge of taking away a child, had said that 'sticking plaster had been stuck over the mouth of a girl and that she had been assaulted'. A second prosecution was made against the *Bicester Journal Ltd* also in 1968 and a third against *Kosmos* in 1972. A fourth prosecution against the *Eastbourne Herald* is discussed in the text below.
4 See (1973) Times, 12 June.
5 See Robertson and Nicol, *Media Law* (3rd edn) p 325.
6 See the criticisms in Miller, *Contempt of Court* (2nd edn) p 325.
7 Miller, op cit at pp 324–325, Robertson and Nicol, op cit at pp 324–325.

Court Act. Moreover, the need to have a prosecution brought by or with the Attorney General's consent should act as a safeguard against prosecutions against what may be called de minimis breaches. However, as the *Eastbourne* case shows this is not a total answer. The re-enactment of the restrictions in the 1994 Act, however, shows the Government's imperviousness to the criticisms of them.

What undoubtedly should be restricted is the publication of anything that might be considered to create a real risk of prejudice. In this regard mention should be made of bail decisions. Section 8A(9)(f) merely permits mention of 'arrangements as to bail'. This, it is submitted, should properly be interpreted as permitting a bare statement as to whether or not bail has been granted. It should not be taken as permitting the publication of the reasons either for opposing or refusing bail. Such evidence can obviously be most prejudicial particularly if it involves revealing the accused's past criminal convictions.

A further difference between the new restrictions and the old is that the former allowed the publication of the names, addresses, occupations and ages of witnesses.[8] The new provisions make no reference to witnesses. Normally there will be no witnesses in a transfer for trial procedure although statements from witnesses will be among the documents on which the prosecution relies, but the lack of mention of witness particulars in s 8A(9) means that should the media learn these details they will not be able to publish them unless reporting restrictions are lifted.

The above reporting restrictions do not apply if the application for dismissal is successful[9] for then there will be no trial on indictment which can be prejudiced. If the magistrates proceed to try the case summarily those proceedings may be reported even if there are other accused whose application for dismissal is dismissed.[10] Restrictions cease to apply once the Crown Court trial is over[11] though of course by this time the news value of the report will probably have been lost.

(c)   Lifting the reporting restrictions

Before the 1994 Act came into force the accused could, under s 8(2), apply for the restrictions on reporting committal proceedings to be lifted.[12] Where a single accused made such an application the restrictions had to be lifted.[13] Where, however, there was more than one accused it was provided under the Criminal Justice (Amendment) Act 1981[14] that if one of the accused objected to the lifting of reporting restrictions the court should make a lifting order:

> 'if, and only if, it is satisfied, after hearing the representations of the accused, that it is in the interests of justice to do so.'

---

8 S 8(4)(b) as it formerly was: why it was thought necessary to report the ages of adults who just happened to be appearing as witnesses is not clear.
9 S 8A(5).
10 The report may contain a report of so much of the application for dismissal as took place before the determination to proceed summarily, even if it contains matters other than those permitted by s 8A(9): s 8A(8), the equivalent to the previous s 8(3).
11 S 8(7).
12 It was incumbent upon the court to explain to the accused his right to apply for the lifting of reporting restrictions; see the Magistrates' Courts Rules 1981, r 5.
13 Magistrates' Courts Act 1980, s 8(2). Once lifted they could not be reimposed.
14 Inserting what was then s 8(2A) into the 1980 Act.

If none of the accused objected to the lifting of restrictions then justices were bound to make the order. The decision whether or not to lift reporting restrictions could be reported but not apparently other details of the application.[15]

The 1981 Amendment Act ended the anomaly highlighted by the trial of Jeremy Thorpe and others that reporting restrictions had to be lifted simply upon the request of one defendant regardless of the wishes of others.[16] In *R v Leeds Justices, ex p Sykes* [17] the Divisional Court stressed that only if a very powerful case had been made out for the restrictions to be lifted should that be done against the wishes of the co-accused. In that case one of the accused wanted the restrictions lifted to give publicity to his grievance against the police and the justices' order sanctioning this was quashed on the grounds that the interests of justice, which meant ensuring a fair trial, would not be advanced by publicity.[18]

Under the transfer for trial proceedings there continue to be provisions on lifting reporting restrictions but they differ in certain material respects from the previous rules. Previously they could be lifted on the application of the accused only.[19] The new s 8A(2), provides:

> 'A magistrates' court may, on an application for the purpose made with reference to proceedings on an application for dismissal, order that subsection (1) above shall not apply to reports of those proceedings.'

It appears, therefore, that someone other than the accused may make an application to lift restrictions and that the court is no longer *bound* to make an order. It does not say what the position is where there is only one accused and he objects to the lifting of restrictions. As s 8A(3) reiterates the wording of the old s 8(2A), however, it is still provided that *where there are two or more accused* and one of them objects to lifting restrictions it may only be done if it is in the interests of justice.[20] This seems anomalous but it resembles that which pertains in the notice of transfer procedure, discussed below.[1] It is submitted that normally the court should only lift the restrictions against the will of a single accused person if it was convinced that the 'interests of justice' demand it. Be that as it may, the effect is to take the power of decision from the accused person and give it to the court.

It will be noted that under both the old and new provisions the restrictions either operate in toto or are entirely lifted. This decision is taken at the outset of the proceedings. However, as we have seen,[2] it is established that there is nothing necessarily inconsistent with lifting reporting restrictions and subsequently imposing a postponement order under s 4(2) of the Contempt of Court Act. Even where there are no statutory restrictions care should be taken to see that reports are fair and accurate etc.[3]

15 Under s 8(2B) as added by the 1981 Act.
16 That the restriction had to be lifted was first established by *R v Russell, ex p Beaverbrook Newspapers Ltd* [1969] 1 QB 342, [1968] 3 All ER 695.
17 [1983] 1 All ER 460.
18 It was also important that all the co-accused be given the opportunity to make representations about the lifting of restrictions since failure to do so was is a breach of natural justice, rendering the lifting of the restrictions procedurally invalid and ultra vires: see *R v Wirral District Magistrates' Court, ex p Meikle* (1990) 154 JP 1035.
19 Magistrates' Courts Act 1980, s 8(2).
20 It may be assumed that the previous case law on the meaning and operation on this criterion will apply to s 8A(3).
 1 Except that with the latter the court appears to be able to act on its own initiative, without an application from anyone.
 2 See at pp 290 ff.
 3 Ie the normal requirements discussed at pp 282 ffapply.

The decision whether or not to lift reporting restrictions may be reported but not other details of the application where the co-accused object pursuant to s 8A(3).[4]

5 Reporting restrictions on alternatives to transfer for trial procedure

(a) Notice of transfer

(i) Cases of serious fraud The Criminal Justice Act 1987 introduced a new procedure[5] whereby in serious or complex fraud cases the necessity of going through transfer for trial (formerly committal proceedings) can be avoided.[6] The prosecuting authorities give a 'notice of transfer' and thereupon the magistrates' court which would otherwise be seised of the case ceases to have jurisdiction and the prosecution can, by virtue of the notice, prefer a bill of indictment. The matter therefore goes straight to the Crown Court. The accused can apply to the Crown Court for the charges to be dismissed.[7] If the charges are not dismissed the judge can order a preparatory hearing,[8] which he will conduct before the jury is sworn,[9] which the public and the press can attend.

The application for dismissal and the preparatory hearing are subject to reporting restrictions[10] similar to those which applied to committal proceedings, except that 'relevant business information' may also be published.[11] In line with comparable restrictions, prosecutions can be brought only by the Attorney General[12] and the penalty is a maximum of a level 5 fine.[13]

By s 11(2) reporting restrictions can be lifted by the judge (or by the Court of Appeal on an interlocutory appeal under s 9(11)). This leaves the lifting of restrictions to the court's discretion and it would seem that it can act on its own initiative without waiting for a party to make an application. However, s 11(3) makes the same provision as does s 8A(3) of the Magistrates' Courts Act 1980[14] in the case where there is more than one accused and the same considerations would seem to apply.[15]

(ii) Notice of transfer in child witness cases By s 53 of the Criminal Justice Act 1991 cases concerning offences of a violent or sexual nature where there is a child witness[16] may be transferred straight to the Crown Court under a similar system as described in (i) above, likewise avoiding the necessity for transfer for trial (formerly committal) proceedings. There are similar reporting restrictions,[17]

---

4 Magistrates' Courts Act 1980, s 8A(4).
5 Following the Fraud Trials Committee Report, 1986, chaired by Lord Roskill.
6 Criminal Justice Act 1987, s 4.
7 S 6(1).
8 S 7.
9 S 7.
10 S 11.
11 S 11(4). This means the name and address of a business carried on by the accused on his own account or in partnership, or a business of which he was a director.
12 S 11(13).
13 S 11(12), currently £5,000.
14 As substituted by the Criminal Justice and Public Order Act 1994, Sch 4.
15 See the discussion at pp 307 ff.
16 See s 32(2) of the Criminal Justice Act 1988.
17 Criminal Justice Act 1991, Sch 6, para 6.

which apply to the application for dismissal of the charges which the accused can make to the Crown Court.[18] Reporting restrictions can be lifted by the judge but, as with s 11(2) of the 1987 Act, it does not stipulate that he may only do so upon an application. The usual provisions about the situation where there is more than one accused apply.[19]

(b)   Voluntary bill of indictment

The voluntary bill of indictment procedure is another way by which a person may stand trial on indictment at the Crown Court without having first gone through the transfer for trial (formerly committal) proceedings. The procedure is provided for by the Administration of Justice (Miscellaneous Provisions) Act 1933, s 2(2)(b). The procedure does not take place in open court[20] and is therefore subject to the rules about reporting proceedings heard in private.[1]

6   *Reporting restrictions on proceedings concerning children*

(a)   Youth court proceedings

It is perhaps a moot point whether such proceedings can properly be regarded as taking place in open court. Members of the public have no right to attend the proceedings though somewhat unusually bona fide reporters of newspapers or news agencies[2] have.[3] If they are properly regarded as open court proceedings, then apart from the following restrictions, fair and accurate reports of the proceedings are permissible.[4]

Under the Children and Young Persons Act 1933, s 49(1):[5]

'(a)   no report shall be published which reveals the name, address or school of any child or young person concerned in the proceedings or includes any particulars likely to lead to the identification of any child or young person concerned in the proceedings; and

(b)   no picture shall be published or included in a programme service as being or including a picture of any child or young person concerned in the proceedings.'

This provision makes it clear that not only must the report avoid naming any child or young person concerned in the proceedings (ie whether a party or witness) but it must also avoid publishing any information which may lead to identification of the child.

---

18   S 5.
19   Sch 6, para 6(3).
20   See Indictments (Procedure) Rules 1971 (SI 1971/2084) r 10.
 1   See p 320.
 2   Presumably this includes television and radio reporters.
 3   S 47(2) of the Children and Young Persons Act 1933. For a discussion of this provision see Lowe, 'Publicity in Court Proceedings Concerning Children' (1981) 145 JPN 256 at 258.
 4   If they are properly classified as 'private' proceedings they may be caught by the Administration of Justice Act 1960, s 12 discussed below.
 5   As substituted by the Criminal Justice and Public Order Act 1994, s 49.

The penalty for infringing this provision is a fine not exceeding level 5 on the standard scale.[6] These restrictions can be lifted by the court if satisfied that it is appropriate to do so for the purpose of avoiding injustice to a child or young person.[7]

The Darlington based *Northern Echo* was fined £200 for publishing a photograph and the names and addresses of children who were being supervised by a local authority under a court order.[8] The publication appeared the day after magistrates had granted a two year supervision order and stated inter alia that the magistrates had decided that the children need not be kept in care. This was clearly in breach of s 49 and it was held to be no defence that information came from the mother. Indeed, the reporter had not even attended the court hearing.

Section 49 primarily applies to youth court proceedings but by s 10(1)(b) of the Children and Young Persons Act 1969 the restrictions also apply to appeals from such proceedings. In such cases, however, there is a duty upon the court to announce that s 49 applies and failure to do so will mean that the restrictions do not apply.[9]

There may be occasions when these provisions and other provisions apply simultaneously to the same set of proceedings. This happened in *Re L*[10] where a 17 year old was the subject of proceedings for returning him to the Republic of Ireland to face criminal charges. The Backing of Warrants (Republic of Ireland) Act 1965 requires the magistrates to consider the application in open court but because of his age the suspect had to be dealt with by the juvenile court. The Divisional Court heard that the restrictions in the Children and Young Persons Act prevailed over the open court requirement in the 1965 Act.

(b)   Adult court proceedings

Section 49 only applies to youth courts. Where a youth appears as a defendant or witness before an adult court, s 39 of the 1933 Act applies. Under s 39 *any court* in relation to *any* proceedings *may* expressly direct that:

'(a)   no newspaper report[11] of the proceedings shall reveal the name, address, or school, or include any particulars calculated to lead to the identification, of any child or young person concerned in the proceedings, either as being the person by or against or in respect of whom the proceedings are taken, or as being a witness therein;

(b)   no picture shall be published in any newspaper as being or including a picture of any child or young person so concerned in the proceedings as aforesaid.'

The penalty for infringing this provision is a fine not exceeding level 5 on the standard scale.[12] It should, however, be emphasised that the court must expressly prohibit the publication. It must also be emphasised that the section does not empower the court to forbid the publication of any specific matters other than the

---

6   S 49(9), currently £5,000.
7   S 49(5). The former power of the Secretary of State to lift the restrictions was removed by the 1994 amendments.
8   (1980) Times, 16 December.
9   S 10(2) of the Children and Young Persons Act 1969.
10 (1990) Independent, 11 December.
11 Or sound or television broadcast: Children and Young Persons Act 1969, s 57(4).
12 Under the Criminal Justice Act 1982, ss 37, 39(2), 46 and Sch 3, currently £5,000.

name, address and school of the child. Beyond that the court can only prohibit, in general terms, the publication of matters likely to lead to his or her identification. This was demonstrated in *R v Crown Court at Southwark, ex p Godwin* [13] when the court, at the urging of defence counsel, ordered that the names of the defendants on trial for indecent assault on young children should not be published, on the grounds that, since the defendants and the children were all members of a very close-knit orthodox Jewish community, naming them would readily identify the children. The Court of Appeal [14] held that the order was not validly made. The judge could only prohibit matters calculated to lead to identification and should phrase the order in the terms of s 39(1) or in words to like effect. The press then had to use its judgment as to what it could publish and if it went too far it could be prosecuted. In fact, in cases of this type Crown Court judges often indicate to the press what matters, including the identity of the defendants, would be likely to lead to the child's identification, but this is different from making the order in those terms. Where it will be apparent from any report of the case that the defendants and the child are related, for example, it is normally impossible to name the defendant and comply with a s 39(1) order.

That was, indeed, the situation in *Ex parte Crook* [15] in which the defendants were charged with the manslaughter of one of their children and cruelty to the three surviving children. An order was made under s 39 forbidding any publication of particulars calculated to lead to the identification of the surviving children. The judge made it clear that he considered that identifying the defendant parents (or the deceased child) would inevitably lead to the identification of the children. Journalists (who had made representations against the making of the order) appealed under s 159 of the Criminal Justice and Public Order Act 1988. The Court of Appeal upheld the order, saying that the judge was quite correct in deciding that in this instance the likely harm to the children outweighed the freedom to publish. The court distinguished the situation from *R v Central Independent Television plc* [16] in which the freedom to publish was held to outweigh the harm to a child because there the child had not been involved in proceedings and the harm would be caused by identifying her father, who was already in prison for offences against *other* children. [17]

It was made clear in *Re Crook* that when making a s 39 order the judge has a complete discretion about who can make representations about it. In the instant case the judge listened to the local authority who had the children in care and to their guardian ad litem, who both said that the children were disturbed and that further publicity would cause more damage. The Court of Appeal approved such a procedure and it does seem sensible that s 39 orders should be made on the basis of proper information about the children and not on judicial assumptions.

It must be emphasised that under s 39 the court has a *discretion* as to whether to impose reporting restrictions. In *R v Leicester Crown Court, ex p S (a minor)* Watkins LJ said: [18]

> 'The mere fact that the person before the court is a child or young person will normally be a good reason for restricting reports of the proceedings in the ways

13   [1992] QB 190, [1991] 3 All ER 818.
14   On an appeal by journalists under s 159(1) of the Criminal Justice Act 1988.
15   [1995] 1 WLR 139.
16   [1994] Fam 192.
17   Whose identity had been the subject of a s 39 order at the trial.
18   [1992] 2 All ER 659 at 662.

permitted by s 39 and it will, in our opinion, only be in rare and exceptional cases that directions under s 39 will not be given or having been given will be discharged.'

In that case the Divisional Court quashed the decision of a Crown Court judge[19] removing the s 39 restrictions previously imposed at an earlier hearing. The juvenile concerned had been convicted of arson causing damage of £2.5 million. The judge said that in the exceptional circumstances of the case he concluded that the reporting restrictions should be removed, but gave no further indication of his reasons[20] and the Divisional Court considered that this was inadequate. However, Watkins LJ's approach to the issue, quoted above, was held by the Court of Appeal in *R v Lee* [1]to be unduly rigid, because there was nothing in s 39 to indicate that reporting restrictions would not be imposed only in rare and exceptional cases. The Court of Appeal was unwilling to fetter the discretion of the court in this way and was concerned that the distinction between youth and Crown Court proceedings would become blurred. The court therefore refused, on an application for judicial review, to hold that the judge's refusal to forbid identification of a 14 year old rapist was incorrect.[2] The Divisional Court has said that young offenders should not be named simply to ensure publicity for some general rule or principle that the court wants to emphasise. It considered the matter in *R v Inner London Crown Court, ex p Barnes (Anthony)* [3] where the judge had said 'grave crimes attract grave sentences' but concluded that he had been concerned with the disgrace, and thus the deterrence, directed at the offender himself as well as the general deterrent effect of the disgrace. The court thought that where the judge does take into account the age of the offender and the potential damage to him of identification and balances those factors against the competing value of open justice, the Divisional Court would be very slow to interfere with the exercise of his discretion.

It is tempting for judges to refuse to impose restrictions where the crime appears particularly heinous or has caused exceptional public disquiet. After the trial in 1994 of two ten year olds convicted of murdering a two year old called James Bulger, a matter which had been the subject of enormous nationwide publicity, the judge allowed them to be identified and the result was saturation coverage dissecting every detail of their lives, families and backgrounds. It was questionable what public interest was served by this.

The Court of Appeal clarified the procedure to be followed in making a s 39 order in *Ex parte Crook*.[4] This is that a written order should be drawn as soon as possible after the judge or magistrate has orally made the order and it should be available in the court office for the press to inspect. The fact that the order has been made should be made clear to those not present when it was made (it was suggested that this be done by a notice in the daily list). Finally, it should be stated

19 Holding in doing so that the Divisional Court *did* have the power of judicial review in respect of reporting restrictions imposed at a trial on indictment: see p 298.
20 It was assumed it was because of the amount of damage caused.
1 [1993] 2 All ER 170.
2 This case demonstrated that an appeal under s 159 of the Criminal Justice Act 1988 can only be brought by a person aggrieved by the *making* of an order restricting reporting, not by a person aggrieved at it being withheld. Nor does the Court of Appeal have jurisdiction to impose an order restricting publication of proceedings in the Crown Court. It does, however, have jurisdiction to hear an application for judicial review.
3 (1995) Times, 7 August.
4 [1995] 1 WLR 139. It is also clear that the court, upon application, can later revoke an order, for example where it believes publicity would be in the child's interests: see *R v Cambridge and Huntingdon Area Health Authority, ex p B (No 2)* (1995) Times, 27 October, CA.

what the exact terms of the order are. The journalists suggested in *Crook* that, had the judge made it clearer that the dead child could be identified, they could have published a full account of the manslaughter trial and left the cruelty charges out.

(c)   Family proceedings

Proceedings specifically concerning children are, like most proceedings before the magistrates' family proceedings court, automatically designated 'family proceedings'. This is provided for by the Magistrates' Courts Act 1980, s 65(1),[5] and applies in particular to proceedings under the Children Act 1989, the Adoption Act 1976, the Child Support Act 1991, Part I of the Domestic Proceedings and Magistrates' Courts Act 1978 and s 3 of the Marriage Act 1949. The significance of the designation is that access to and the reporting of such proceedings is restricted. In these two important respects, however, adoption proceedings are singled out for special treatment. The position is further complicated by additional reporting restrictions applicable to (1) proceedings under the Children Act 1989, and (2) any family proceedings heard in private.

(i) Who can attend 'family proceedings'   In the case of 'family proceedings' (as defined above) other than adoption proceedings, no person is entitled to be present other than officers of the court, the parties and their legal representatives, witnesses and any other persons directly involved in the case, representatives of newspapers or news agencies and any other person whom the court permits to be present.[6]

As with youth court proceedings, therefore, members of the public have no right to attend family proceedings but, surprisingly, representatives of newspapers or news agencies do have a right of attendance. However, this latter right is subject to the magistrates' court's power to exclude the press during the taking of any indecent evidence 'if it thinks it necessary in the interests of the administration of justice or of public decency'[7] and to their power to sit in private.[8]

In the case of adoption proceedings before magistrates the press have no right of attendance nor does the court appear to have any power to permit anyone other than officers of the court, the parties and their legal representatives, witnesses and other persons directly involved, to attend the hearing.[9] Notwithstanding the press's inability to attend proceedings, as will be seen, they can publish limited reports.

(ii) What can be reported   As intimated earlier, the law on what may be reported is complex in that different restrictions apply to different types of 'family proceedings'. For convenience consideration will first be given to the general restrictions provided for under s 71 of the Magistrates' Courts Act 1980,

---

5   As amended, inter alia, by the Children Act 1989, ss 92, 108(6), (7), Sch 11, para 8 and the Maintenance Orders (Backdating) Order 1993 (S1 1993/623), art 3, Sch 2.
6   Magistrates' Courts Act 1980, s 69(2).
7   Ibid s 69(4).
8   See s 69(5) and, in the case of Children Act proceedings, the Family Proceedings Courts (Children Act 1989) Rules 1991 (S1 1991/1395), r 16(7).
9   S 69(3). This apparent limitation on magistrates' ability to allow anyone else to attend seems hard to justify and is clearly out of line with other proceedings. See Lowe, 'Publicity in Court Proceedings Concerning Children' (1981) 145 JPN 256 at 2.

then to the position in Children Act 1989 proceedings and finally to adoption proceedings. In each case the following discussion assumes that the court has *not* opted to sit in private. Where the court does so opt *additional* restrictions apply by reason of s 12 of the Administration of Justice Act 1960 which is discussed later.[10]

(iii) 'Family proceedings' affecting children other than Children Act 1989 or adoption proceedings In 'family proceedings' involving children other than those under the Children Act 1989 or adoption proceedings it is an offence to print or publish or procure to be printed or published in a newspaper or periodical or to include or cause to include or procure to be included in a programme service[11] for reception in Great Britain, particulars of the proceedings *other* than those set out by s 71(1A) of the 1980 Act, namely:

'(a)   the names, addresses and occupations of the parties and witnesses;

(b)   the grounds of the application, and a concise statement of the charges, defences and counter-charges in support of which evidence has been given;

(c)   submissions on any point of law arising in the course of the proceedings and the decision of the court on the submissions;

(d)   the decision of the court, and any observations made by the court in giving it.'

Those found guilty under this section are liable, on summary conviction, to a fine not exceeding level 4 on the standard scale.[12] No prosecution for this offence may be started without the consent of the Attorney General.[13] Although there are now few proceedings involving children to which s 71(1A) applies in full it seems extraordinary, not to say bizarre, to restrict reporting yet expressly allow the names and addresses of the parties and witnesses to be published.

Preventing the media from revealing children's identities must surely rank as the highest priority in any rational system of restricting reports.[14] Indeed, it is evident that little thought has been given to the situations contained in s 71(1A) as they apply to children. For example, the reference in s 71(1A)(b) to a 'concise statement of the charges' etc fits unhappily in the family context.

(iv) Proceedings under the Children Act 1989 Under the Children Act 1989, s 97(2) it is an offence to publish any material intended or likely to identify any child involved in Children Act proceedings or that child's address or school. 'Publishing' is defined[15] as including a programme service within the meaning of the Broadcasting Act 1990 or causing to be published and 'material' includes any picture or representation. As under the 1980 Act those contravening s 97 are liable on summary conviction to a fine not exceeding level 4 on the standard scale. However, unlike the 1980 Act it is a defence if the accused can prove that

10 At pp 320 ff.
11 Within the meaning of the Broadcasting Act 1990, as set out in s 201. Those restrictions were extended to broadcasts by the 1990 Act, s 203(1), Sch 20, para 29(2), as from 1 January 1991.
12 Currently £2,500: s 71(3).
13 S 71(4).
14 See eg the recommendation to this effect by the Report of the Inquiry into Child Abuse in Cleveland 1987 (the 'Butler-Sloss Report') (1988, Cm 412) at p 253.
15 Children Act 1989, s 97(5).

he did not know and had no reason to suspect that the published material was intended, or likely, to identify the child.[16] On the other hand a prosecution under the 1980 Act does not require the Attorney General's consent. The court or Secretary of State may, if satisfied that the child's welfare requires it, lift the restriction.[17] This power, which is modelled on that which formerly existed under the Children and Young Persons Act 1933, s 49,[18] is to allow for the rare case where it is in the child's best interests for the facts to be fully published rather than to have rumours and speculation flourish.

In addition to the above-mentioned restrictions, s 71 of the Magistrates' Court Act 1980[19] limits publication in a newspaper or periodical or broadcasts included in a programme service for reception in Great Britain[20] to reports of the grounds of the application, submissions on points of law and the court decision including any observations made by the court in giving it.[1] It is an offence to publish any other details of the proceedings.[2]

(v) Adoption proceedings   The law governing the reporting of adoption proceedings before magistrates' courts solely derives from s 71 of the Magistrates' Courts Act 1980. Under this provision, as it applies to adoption proceedings,[3] it is an offence[4] to publish any particulars other than submissions on any point of law and the decision of the court including any observations made by the court in giving it. It specifically states that in relation to the child it is an offence to publish his name, address or school, any picture as being, or including, a picture of the child, and any other particulars calculated to lead the child's identification.[5]

Although reports of adoption proceedings are understandably restricted it seems odd not to admit the press yet allow albeit limited reports of the proceedings. It means that the press are permitted to publish information gained from the parties or their advisers. At best, however, this can only be second-hand information and does not seem to provide the most satisfactory basis for allowing reports.

(vi) Commentary   Although the law on reporting children proceedings before magistrates' courts has undoubtedly been improved both by the new restriction under s 97 of the Children Act 1989 and by the long overdue extension of the restrictions under s 71 of the Magistrates' Courts Act 1980, to radio and television broadcasts, it is still in need of a substantial overhaul. The current law is far too complex and remains inconsistent. Why should prosecutions under the 1980 Act be only brought by the Attorney General and yet not under the 1989 Act? Why should there be a defence of no knowledge under the 1989 Act and yet not under the 1980 Act? Why should children not involved in Children Act and adoption proceedings be treated differently?

---

16 Ibid s 97(3).
17 Ibid s 97 (4).
18 Now amended by the Criminal Justice and Public Order Act 1994, s 49 which removes the Secretary of State's, but not the court's, power to lift restrictions. See p 311 n7.
19 Expressly preserved by s 97(8) of the Children Act 1989.
20 These restrictions were extended to broadcasts from 1 January 1991.
 1 Ie those particulars set out by s 71 (1A) of the 1980 Act (see p 315), not otherwise implicitly excluded by s 97(2) of the Children Act 1989.
 2 For the amount of the fine etc see the Magistrates' Courts Act 1980, s 71(3), and p 315 above.
 3 See s 71(2).
 4 For the amount of the fine etc see s 71(3) and p 315 above.
 5 By s 71(2) (a)-(c).

(d)   Family proceedings only involving adults

Family proceedings are not exclusively those concerned with children. Matrimonial disputes purely between spouses are also designated 'family proceedings' and the restriction on who can attend and what may be reported are those respectively provided by ss 69(2) and 71(1A) of the Magistrates' Courts Act 1980.

(e)   Judicial Proceedings (Regulation of Reports) Act 1926

The 1926 Act does what the House of Lords ruled in *Scott v Scott* [6] could not be done at common law, namely, restrict the publication of indecent material or matter. According to s 1(1)(a):

> 'It shall not be lawful to print or publish, or cause or procure to be printed or published—(a) in relation to any judicial proceedings any indecent matter or indecent medical, surgical or physiological details being matter or details the publication of which would be calculated to injure public morals.'

This Act was designed to prevent the publication of the unsavoury details of matrimonial cases and s (1)(1)(b) deals specifically with reports of such cases. Section 1(1)(a) could, on the face of it, have a wider application. There have been, however, no modern prosecutions under this provision. In cases (such as sex murders for example) where the details might fall within the description in this subsection it is more likely that the judge would hold the proceedings in camera (as the judge is reported as having considered doing in the Moors Murders trial[7]) or refuse the media physical access to the material (as has recently become an issue in Canada[8]). It is unlikely that the Attorney General[9] would prosecute the media for a report of proceedings held in open court which complied with s 4(1) of the 1981 Act and which the judge had taken no steps to withhold from the media.

Under s 1(1)(b) where proceedings are brought for the dissolution of marriage, nullity of marriage or judicial separation, the report of proceedings must be restricted to the following details:

> '(i)   the names, addresses and occupations of the parties and witnesses;
>
> (ii)   a concise statement of the charges, defences and countercharges in support of which evidence has been given;
>
> (iii)   submissions on any point of law arising in the course of proceedings and the decision of the court thereon;
>
> (iv)   the summing-up of the judge and the finding of the jury (if any) and the judgment of the court and the observations made by the judge in giving judgment.
>
> Provided that nothing in this part of this subsection shall be held to permit the publication of anything contrary to the provisions of paragraph (a) of this subsection.'

6   [1913] AC 417 discussed at pp 280 and 322 ff.
7   See p 280.
8   See p 281.
9   See s 1(3) and below.

The Domestic and Appellate Proceedings (Restriction of Publicity) Act 1968 (as amended) has extended the provisions of s 1(1)(b) of the 1926 Act so as to cover petitions for a declaration of status[10] and paternity[11] (in which case particulars of the declaration may be published[12]) and maintenance proceedings under s 27 of the Matrimonial Causes Act 1973.[13]

The maximum penalty for infringing these provisions is four months' imprisonment or a fine not exceeding level 5 on the standard scale[14] or both. These restrictions, however, do not apply to bona fide law reports[15] nor to 'any publication of a technical character bona fide intended for circulation among members of the legal or medical profession'.

According to s 1(3), proceedings can only be brought with the sanction of the Attorney General. However, it was held by Ungoed-Thomas J, in *Duchess of Argyll v Duke of Argyll* [16] that the Act also gives the courts jurisdiction to grant an injunction restraining publications which would breach the 1926 Act, on the application of one of the parties named in the proceedings, since s 1(1)(b) is designed to protect the parties themselves and not just to protect public morals.

(f)   Anonymity of complainants in cases of rape and other sexual offences

The law on the anonymity of complainants in cases involving sexual offences has been the subject of somewhat tortuous development since it was first introduced in 1976.

The Sexual Offences (Amendment) Act 1976 Act originally provided for the general anonymity of both complainant and accused in rape trials. The parties in cases of sexual offences other than rape, however serious, were not granted anonymity. In respect of complainants the Act implemented, but in respect of the accused went against, the recommendations of the Heilbron Committee.[17] The Committee recommended anonymity for complainants 'not only to protect victims from hurtful publicity for their sake alone, but in order to encourage them to report crimes of rape so as to ensure that rapists do not escape prosecution'.[18] In other words, the justification for anonymity lies in the protection of the administration of justice in much the same way as the common law recognised when according anonymity to victims in blackmail cases.[19] As the Committee pointed out,[20] however, there is no such justification for the anonymity of the accused and in truth it is illogical to single out the accused in rape cases for this treatment. The Criminal Justice Act 1988 amended the 1976 Act[1] and removed the cloak of anonymity from the accused.[2]

10   Under Pt III of the Family Law Act 1986.
11   Under s 56(1) of the 1986 Act.
12   See s 2(3) of the 1968 Act.
13   The 1968 Act has been amended in this respect by Sch 2, para 7(1) of the 1973 Act.
14   As substituted by the Criminal Justice Act 1982, ss 38, 46, currently £5,000.
15   S 1(4). To be a bona fide series of law reports they must not form part of any other publication and consist solely of reports of proceedings in courts of law.
16   [1967] Ch 302, [1965] 1 All ER 611.
17   Report of the Advisory Group on the Law of Rape (1975, Cmnd 6352).
18   See para 177 in particular and paras 150–162 in general.
19   See para 152. For the position in blackmail cases see p 277.
20   At para 177.
 1   S 158 of the Criminal Justice Act 1988 repealed s 6 of the 1976 Act, which dealt with those accused of rape.
 2   This remains, however, a contentious issue and men acquitted of rape after widely and sensationally reported trials have complained bitterly that their lives and reputations are ruined while the complainant shelters behind the anonymity rules.

The Sexual Offences (Amendment) Act 1992 made a long overdue amendment to the 1976 Act and extended anonymity to complainants in sexual offences other than rape. These offences, listed in s 2, include unlawful sexual intercourse, incest, indecent conduct with a young child, buggery, indecent assault and conspiracy or incitement to commit any of these offences. Section 142 of the Criminal Justice and Public Order Act 1994 redefined 'rape' to include non-consensual anal intercourse with a woman *or a man*. Accordingly, complainants in cases of what is known as 'male rape' are granted anonymity[3] by the provisions of the 1976 Act rather than the provisions of the 1992 Act, as are women victims of non-consensual anal intercourse.[4]

The anonymity of complainants in rape cases is provided for by s 4(1) of the 1976 Act, as amended by the Criminal Justice Act 1988, s 158 and the 1992 Act. The 1988 amendments were a legislative response to the weaknesses in the legislation which became apparent from the behaviour of some newspapers, particularly in regard to the 'Ealing Vicarage' case in 1983. The 1976 Act protected the complainant only from the time a person is charged. The protection now applies from the moment that an allegation of rape is made, and what is prohibited[5] at that time is the publication[6] of the complainant's name, address, or a still or moving picture[7] of that person during their lifetime if:

> 'that is likely to lead members of the public to identify that person as an alleged victim of [rape].'

Once a person is accused of rape the prohibition covers:

> 'any matter likely to lead members of the public to identify that person as the complainant.'

The embargo on identifying the complainant is couched in similar terms under s 1(1) and (2) of the 1992 Act in respect of other sexual offences.

Breach of either s 4(1) of the 1976 Act or s 1(1) or (2) of the 1992 Act renders the offender liable on summary conviction to a fine not exceeding level 5 on the standard scale.[8] Liability will rest[9] on (a) in the case of a newspaper, or periodical, the proprietor, any editor and any publisher, (b) in the case of any other publication, the publisher, and (c) in the case of a broadcast, any body corporate which transmits or provides the programme and any person having functions in relation to the programme corresponding to those of an editor of a newspaper.

It should be noted that the embargo applies to *publications* and *broadcasts* in England and Wales[10] and read literally this could mean that the restrictions still apply even if the trial itself is outside England and Wales. It may be doubted,

3 Sch 10, para 36 to the 1994 Act makes the necessary amendments to s 4 of the 1976 Act.
4 This offence in respect of a woman was previously charged as buggery.
5 The words which follow have been amended by the 1994 Act, Sch 10, para 36, to include male as well as female victims.
6 Or inclusion in a 'relevant programme' within the meaning of the Broadcasting Act 1990.
7 Defined as a 'likeness however produced'.
8 Currently £5,000.
9 According to s 4(5) of the 1976 Act and s 5 of the 1992 Act.
10 Save for offences before courts martial, the Act does not apply to Scotland. Hence it appears that if a Scottish celebrity was accused of a rape offence in England and the restrictions were not lifted and he was acquitted the English press would be unable to reveal his identity but the Scottish press could.

however, whether the Acts have this effect. The whole structure of the Acts and of ss 4 and 1 in particular,[11] assumes the trial to be in England or Wales.[12]

The restrictions under both the 1976 and 1992 Acts are subject to a proviso,[13] that they do not apply to prohibit the publication of matter which consists only of 'a report of legal proceedings other than proceedings at, or intended to lead to, or an appeal arising out of, a trial at which the accused is charged with' the rape or other sexual offence.

The restrictions may be lifted by order of the court on the application of the accused where publicity is necessary to induce witnesses to come forward and the conduct of the defence is likely to be substantially prejudiced otherwise.[14] They may be lifted by an appellate court if the court is satisfied that it is required in order to obtain evidence for an appeal and the applicant may otherwise suffer injustice. The trial judge can order the lifting of restrictions either partially or in toto if he is satisfied that the anonymity imposes a substantial and unreasonable restriction on reporting the trial *and* that it is in the public interest to remove or relax the restriction. The possibility of the ban being lifted means that a victim of sexual assault, when deciding whether to report the matter to the police, can *never* be certain that their identity will not be revealed in the press. As has been pointed out,[15] although the press has no right to apply for the lifting of the restrictions they may be able to suggest it through the court clerk or the lawyers in the case. Some sections of the press will invariably want the ban lifted.

Section 4(3)[16] provides that a removal of restrictions will not be justified by reason only of the outcome of the trial which means that the mere fact that the accused is acquitted does not necessarily expose the complainant to publicity. The complainant may also consent to the removal.[17] Consent must be given in writing[18] and must not have been obtained as a result of interference with the complainant's peace or comfort.[19] This is to guard against consent being obtained through harassment or intimidation.

III   REPORTING PROCEEDINGS HELD IN PRIVATE

A   The position at common law

1   *The nature and basis of the restrictions on reporting at common law*

Sitting in private is a manifestation of the court's right to regulate its own proceedings. A court may sit in private either by sitting in camera or in chambers.[20] It sits in camera when the judge orders the court to be closed during

---

11   Eg applications to lift restrictions have to be made to the Crown Court or magistrates' court.
12   Widespread coverage is sometimes given in the English press to rape cases going on abroad and it has never seriously been suggested that an offence has been committed.
13   In s 4(7) and s 1(4) respectively.
14   Ss 4(2) and 3(1) respectively.
15   Robertson and Nicol, *Media Law* (3rd edn) p 337.
16   See also s 3(3).
17   See *R v Gilligan* [1987] Crim LR 501, where the mother of a victim of rape and murder consented to the anonymity being lifted.
18   S 4(5)A of the 1976 Act as amended by s 3 of the 1988 Act, and s 5(2) of the 1992 Act.
19   Ss 4(5B) and 5(2) ibid.
20   See the Law Commission No 8, Report on the Powers of Appeal Courts to sit in Private and the Restrictions upon Publicity in Domestic Proceedings (1966, Cmnd 3149) para 3.

the whole or part of the trial. The judge is still sitting in court in every sense, however, and judge and counsel remain in wigs and gowns. When a judge sits in chambers he is technically not sitting in court at all. The proceedings may, in fact, take place in the normal court room but wigs and gowns are not worn and the rules of audience do not apply so strictly.

The effect of sitting in private is to deprive members of the public and therefore, the press, of the right to attend the hearing. However, a reporter, though excluded from the hearing, may of course obtain information relating to the proceedings from those (such as a party, a witness or a lawyer) who are lawfully present. One might have expected that since the whole object of sitting in private is to deprive the public of the right of access to the hearing, the publication of a purported report of or information relating to such proceedings would ipso facto be a contempt. However, while the common law position is not entirely free from doubt it seems that such publications are not automatically contempts.[1]

In any event contempt liability will depend upon whether the decision to hear the case in private was lawfully made[2] and whether the publisher is aware that his publication relates to private proceedings.[3] Provided, however, these two requirements are satisfied, then, where the court sits in camera in the exceptional cases recognised by the Law Lords in *Scott v Scott*,[4] it is a prima facie contempt at common law, regardless of intent, to publish (at any rate without judicial permission), an account (whether accurate or otherwise) of the private proceedings.[5] Although there is authority[6] supporting the view that the law applies at least as strictly with regard to proceedings heard in chambers in relation to interlocutory or administrative matters, the position is far from settled and it may be doubted whether it does so apply.[7] Even in the exceptional areas it seems that the decision to hear a case in private does not impose a perpetual obligation to remain silent so that in some cases publication might be permissible after the passage of time or change of circumstances, even without judicial consent.[8] A distinction might also be drawn between reporting proceedings and reporting the order. It seems to be established, at any rate, with respect to wardship proceedings that unless the judge (who has a complete discretion in the matter) orders otherwise it is not a contempt to publish the order or a fair and accurate summary of the order.[9]

The juristic basis of holding reports of proceedings heard in private to be a contempt has still to be established but it is arguable that the courts are reaching towards the same position as that previously discussed in relation to other

1 For the statutory position see pp 327 ff.
2 *Scott v Scott* [1913] AC 417.
3 *Re F (Orse A) (a minor) (Publication of Information)* [1977] Fam 58, [1977] 1 All ER 114. Discussed at pp 326–327.
4 [1913] AC 417.
5 Per Scarman LJ in *Re F*, ibid at 95 and 127.
6 See eg *Alliance Perpetual Building Society v Belrum Investments Ltd* [1957] 1 All ER 635, [1957] 1 WLR 720 and *New Procedure Summons in Chambers* [1932] WN Misc 185.
7 This seems to be indicated by Lord Denning MR in *Re F* [1977] Fam 58 at 87, [1977] 1 All ER 114 at 121.
8 See Lord Shaw in *Scott v Scott* [1913] AC 417 at 483 who suggested that publicity may be resumed when eg a ward attains his majority or when confidentiality has been abandoned or the secrets become public property. See also Wynn-Parry J in *Re De Beaujeu* [1949] Ch 230 at 435. See also Geoffrey Lane LJ in *Re F* [1977] Fam 58 at 107, [1977] 1 All ER 114 at 137.
9 *Re De Beaujeu's Application for Writ of Attachment Against Cudlipp* [1949] Ch 230, [1949] 1 All ER 439 cited with approval in *Re F*, ibid. The position in Victoria, Australia was left open in *Critchley v Australian Urban Investments Ltd* [1979] VR 374 at 376.

directions made in the course of regulating proceedings[10] ie it is not for breaking the judge's ruling as such that a publication amounts to contempt but for what amounts to a deliberate frustration of the court's effort to protect justice from interference. Implicit in this statement, however, is the requirement that the publication does interfere with the course of justice.[11] Where the court sits in private specifically to protect the administration of justice then a publication of those proceedings will prima facie frustrate the court's object and accordingly the publisher with the requisite mens rea will be guilty of contempt. Where, however, a court sits in private to hear interlocutory or administrative matters, for example, it does not automatically follow that a publication of those proceedings will interfere with the course of justice and it is submitted that unless it is calculated to create a real risk of doing so, it should not be regarded as a contempt.

It should be emphasised, however, that even if the foregoing proposition is accepted, no automatic immunity from contempt attaches to fair and accurate reports of proceedings heard in private. Such reports, if thought prejudicial to the due administration of justice, can be held a contempt. Furthermore, it seems that no privilege from defamation attaches to such reports. This was made clear by Lord Atkinson in *Scott v Scott* when he said:[12]

> 'if anything which took place in camera were published it must be published without the privilege which protects the publication of a full and fair report of proceedings in public open courts of justice, and would subject the publishers to all the risks attending the publication of anything which takes place in a private house or at a private meeting. If the matter published amounted to a libel or to a slander, the person defamed could sue for damages, or possibly in the former case, prosecute for criminal libel. If the printed matter published were, in addition, indecent, the public authority might prosecute for the publication of an obscene libel, etc.'

2   When can a court sit in private?

The power to sit in private derives from a number of sources. The Law Commission[13] identified the following, namely:

> '(a)   when this is permitted under the exceptions to the rule in *Scott v Scott*;
>
> (b)   in interlocutory and administrative matters;
>
> (c)   when the jurisdiction has been validly delegated to a single judge in chambers;[14]
>
> (d)   where there is express statutory provision.'

If the power to sit in private is neither authorised by statute nor by the Rules of Court then it must be justified upon common law principles. The leading case in this respect is *Scott v Scott*. There, the House of Lords affirmed the general principle that justice must be administered in public. It was recognised, however,

---

10   See particularly Lord Scarman's judgment in *A-G v Leveller Magazine Ltd* [1979] AC 440 at 469.
11   In the wide sense. It is not necessary to show that the particular proceedings are at risk of being prejudiced. See Geoffrey Lane LJ in *Re F* [1977] Fam 58 at 104, [1977] 1 All ER 114 at 134.
12   [1913] AC 417 at 452.
13   (1966, Cmnd 3149) para 6.
14   See eg RSC Ord 32.

that in exceptional circumstances courts of law had an inherent jurisdiction to sit in private. The exceptional circumstances were where the proceedings concerned wards of court, lunatics or a secret process (such as trade secrets or confidential documents where the whole point of the proceedings would be lost by holding them in public). There was a division of opinion as to whether a court could also hear a case in camera as a means of protecting the administration of justice. The majority seemed to think that there was a power though, as Lord Scarman has subsequently observed,[15] their Lordships did so in markedly different ways. Earl Loreburn considered it permissible where:[16]

> 'the administration of justice would be rendered impracticable by [the public's] presence, whether because the case would not effectively be tried, or the parties entitled to justice would be reasonably deterred from seeking it at the hands of the court.'

Viscount Haldane LC said:[17]

> 'I think that to justify an order for hearing in camera it must be shown that the paramount object of securing that justice is done would really be rendered doubtful of attainment if the order were not made.'

Lord Halsbury[18] was more doubtful though apparently not against the principle while Lord Shaw[19] considered Lord Halsbury's suggestion 'very dangerous'. Lord Atkinson did not express a view. All their Lordships were agreed, however, that there was no justification for hearing a case in camera merely because the evidence was of an unsavoury or delicate nature. Hence, it was held that there was no general power to hear a nullity suit in camera and that the first instance judge was wrong to have done so.

Subsequently the propriety of Earl Loreburn's apparent readiness to allow cases to be heard in camera was doubted[20] so that it was held insufficient justification to allow a legitimacy suit to be heard in camera that the parties would not otherwise proceed with their petitions. On the other hand, Lord Scarman in *A-G v Leveller Magazine Ltd,*[1] relying on Viscount Haldane LC, considered that there was power to sit in private in cases involving national safety provided such a factor 'appears to endanger the due administration of justice, for example by deterring the Crown from prosecuting in cases where it should do so . . .' More recently, the principle in *Scott v Scott* seems to be generally stated as being that a court has power to sit in private where the ends of justice would otherwise be liable to be defeated.[2] Sir John Donaldson MR considered *Scott v Scott* in *R v Chief Registrar of Friendly Societies, ex p New Cross Building Society* and said:[3]

---

15 In *A-G v Leveller Magazine Ltd* [1979] AC 440 at 471.
16 [1913] AC 417 at 446.
17 Ibid at 439.
18 Ibid at 442. His Lordship was concerned that the acceptance of the principle could vest too wide a power in individual judges.
19 Ibid at 485.
20 See *Greenway v A-G* (1927) 44 TLR 124 and *B (Otherwise P) v A-G* [1967] P 119, [1965] 3 All ER 253. The latter decision prompted an investigation into the subject by the Law Commission.
1 [1979] AC 440 at 471 and *Re F (Otherwise A) (Publication of Information)* [1977] Fam 58, [1977] 1 All ER 114. See the note on this case by Munro (1977) 40 MLR 343; cf Lowe, (1977) 93 LQR 180.
2 See eg the Law Commission Report No 8 (1966, Cmnd 3149) and the commentary in the *Supreme Court Practice*, at 33/4/3 and Ord 59/10/1.
3 [1984] QB 227 at 235, [1984] 2 All ER 27 at 31.

'The guidance which I get from their Lordships' speeches can be summarised as follows. The general rule that the courts shall conduct their proceedings in public is but an aid, albeit a very important aid, to the achievement of the paramount object of the courts, which is to do justice in accordance with the law. It is only if, in wholly exceptional circumstances, the presence of the public or public knowledge of the proceedings is likely to defeat that paramount object that the courts are justified in proceeding in camera. These circumstances are incapable of definition. Each application for privacy must be considered on its merits, but the applicant must satisfy the court that nothing short of total privacy will enable justice to be done. It is not sufficient that a public hearing will create embarrassment for some or all of those concerned. It must be shown that a public hearing is likely to lead, directly or indirectly, to a denial of justice.'

New Cross Building Society is a good example of a case where a public hearing would have nullified the point of the proceedings. The Chief Registrar of Building Societies made orders[4] whose effect was to revoke the society's designation as a trustee investment and to prevent it accepting money from the public. The society applied for judicial review and the orders were quashed, whereupon the Chief Registrar appealed to the Court of Appeal. All these proceedings were held in camera,[5] it being held that public knowledge that the orders had ever been made, even if they were ultimately quashed, would result in such a loss of public confidence and consequent withdrawal of funds that the society could not survive. The Master of the Rolls thought that if the Court of Appeal upheld the quashing of the orders there would be a problem about reporting the judgment which the interests of justice required to be published, since it turned on important issues of statutory construction. The Court of Appeal therefore provisionally decided that either the judgment should not identify the society concerned or else only an edited version of it should be published. In the event the Court of Appeal reversed the quashing of the Registrar's orders and their judgment was delivered in camera and made available three weeks later.[6]

When the court sits in private and excludes the public it will normally, but not always, mean that the press is excluded as well.[7] In exceptional cases there may be good reasons for only excluding the public.[8] The Court of Appeal has said that members of the public, such as the families of the defendant and victim, have as much right to be present as the press and it would not be right to favour the latter over the former.[9]

4 Under the House Purchase and Housing Act 1959 and the Building Societies Act 1962.
5 The power of the Court of Appeal to sit in private was reviewed by the Law Commission (1966, Cmnd 3149) and see *Re Agricultural Industries Ltd* [1952] 1 All ER 1188 and *Re Green (a bankrupt)* [1958] 2 All ER 57. The Court of Appeal has a common law right to sit in camera but cannot sit in chambers. Under the Domestic and Appellate Proceedings (Restriction of Publicity) Act 1968, s 1(1) an appeal court may sit in private if the trial court could.
6 After 5.00 pm when the society's branches had closed and the arrangements for transferring the society's engagements to the Woolwich were in place. See also *Polly Peck International plc v Nadir* (1991) Times, 11 November.
7 *Re Crook* [1992] 2 All ER 687.
8 See *R v Waterfield* [1975] 2 All ER 40, where the press was allowed to remain during the showing of allegedly indecent films so that they could report what type of 'censorship' was being imposed while the ordinary public was excluded to prevent the atmosphere which would be created by 'persons with a taste for the nasty' (per Lawton LJ at 44) just coming in to watch. Cf the Canadian case *R v Bernardo*, discussed above, p 281 at which the visual, but not the audio element of pornographic videos of the terminal sufferings of the victims was denied to both press and public.
9 *Re Crook* [1992] 2 All ER 687 at 694. There is no reason, however, why selected members of the public, such as those having some direct interest in the case cannot be admitted while the rest of the public is excluded.

Despite s 121(4) of the Magistrates' Courts Act 1980, which provides that a magistrates' court 'shall sit in open court' justices have an inherent power to sit in camera.[10] This power should, however, only be exercised in exceptional circumstances and should be avoided if there is any other way of serving the interests of justice.[11]

Appeals against orders to hold trials on indictment in camera may be made to the Court of Appeal by 'a person aggrieved'[12] pursuant to s 159(1)(b) of the Criminal Justice Act 1988. The application for leave to appeal and the appeal itself may be determined without a hearing.[13] Where magistrates make such orders the only remedy is to apply for judicial review.[14]

The principle of open court proceedings applies only to the trial itself and not to the preliminary interlocutory matters or matters of an administrative character. The disposal of these matters in private is, in most cases, now expressly authorised by statute or by the rules of court.[15] Judges and Masters in the Queen's Bench Division and county court district judges hear pre-trial applications in chambers but in the Chancery Division pre-trial applications are heard in open court. Appeals to the Crown Court against the refusal by magistrates to grant bail are also heard in chambers, as are 'pre-trial reviews' in criminal cases. A Crown Court judge may exercise in chambers the jurisdiction to hear any application relating to procedural matters preliminary or incidental to proceedings in the Crown Court[16] and this includes matters to do with the jury, such as an application that the jury should sit where they could not be seen from the public gallery.[17]

As can be seen elsewhere in this chapter statutory provisions have made considerable inroads upon the priniciple of open justice, both in providing for courts to sit in private and in providing for reporting restrictions. Statutory provisions particularly affect family proceedings and other proceedings concerning children. The Official Secrets Acts 1920 and 1989 should also be noted. These provide for all or part of the evidence in an Official Secrets Acts prosecution to be heard in the absence of the public.[18]

---

10 *R v Ealing Justices, ex p Weafer* (1982) 74 Cr App Rep 204; *R v Reigate Justices, ex p Argus Newspapers and Larcombe* (1983) 5 Cr App R (S) 181; *R v Malvern Justices, ex p Evans* [1988] QB 540, [1988] 1 All ER 371; this is in addition to the statutory powers conferred upon them in respect of particular types of proceedings. In *R v Governor of Lewes Prison, ex p Doyle* [1917] 2 KB 254 it was held that courts martial have an inherent power to sit in camera despite provisions made under what was then the Army Act 1881 that they should be held in open court.

11 See Watkins LJ in *R v Malvern Justices* [1988] QB 540, [1988] 1 All ER 371 at 378.

12 Which includes the press, see *R v Clerkenwell Stipendiary Magistrate, ex p Telegraph* [1993] QB 462, [1993] 2 All ER 183; *Re Crook* [1992] 2 All ER 687.

13 This is the combined effect of Criminal Justice Act 1988, s 159(6) and rules 16B(6) and (7) of the Criminal Appeal Rules 1968 as amended: these rules were held to be intra vires s 159 by the Court of Appeal in *R v Guardian Newspapers* [1994] Crim LR 912. S 159(9) gives the Court of Appeal power to stay the trial while the appeal is determined (and see Crown Court Rules 1982, r 24A).

14 See the discussion in respect of postponement orders under s 4(2) of the Contempt of Court Act 1981, at pp 298–299.

15 See *Re Bellman* [1963] P 239 at 242, citing *Smeeton v Collier* (1847) 1 Ex 457 and *Re Davidson* [1899] 2 QB 103 where it was said 'where Parliament has conferred a jurisdiction upon the High Court or any of its predecessors, the court has power to delegate that jurisdiction to a single judge sitting in chambers unless Parliament has also provided that the court itself, and not a single judge, is to exercise the jurisdiction'.

16 Crown Court Rules 1982, r 27(2)(c).

17 *R v Crook* [1992] 2 All ER 687.

18 Ss 8(4) and 11(4) respectively (the sentence has to be passed in public). If such an order is to be applied for (which has to be after the defendant has pleaded but before the jury is

3   *The publisher must be aware that proceedings have been heard in private*

That the publisher must be aware that the material published relates to proceedings heard in private was established by the Court of Appeal in *Re F (Orse A) (a minor) (Publication of Information* [19]*). Re F* specifically concerned wardship proceedings but the decision seems of more general application.

In deciding that knowledge was a common law requirement, reliance was placed on *Re Martindale* [20] where North J dismissed with costs, but with little discussion, contempt motions against three newspapers for publishing references to certain wardship proceedings in ignorance of the fact that those proceedings had been heard in private and upon an obiter statement of Wynn-Parry J in *Re De Beaujeu's Application for Writ of Attachment against Cudlipp* [1] reserving his opinion on whether a publisher could be guilty of contempt if he was unaware that the proceedings were heard in private. In addition to this somewhat slender authority it was thought appropriate to draw an analogy with contempt committed by disobeying court orders where it is clearly established that the defendant must have notice of the order. The analogy was thought appropriate because in each case it is a specific act of the court which imposes liability (ie the decision to sit in private or the decision to make an order) rather than a general rule such as that the courts are not to be scandalised or a fair trial prejudiced.

Although the analogy is not beyond criticism [2] there seems force in the argument. Moreover, the reasoning is consistent with the approach later laid down by the Lords in *A-G v Leveller Magazine Ltd* [3] in relation to other directions made by the court in the course of regulating its own proceedings.

The exact requirement of a mens rea is not beyond doubt. Scarman and Geoffrey Lane LJJ [4] described the defence in terms of 'no notice' so that no offence can be committed unless the publisher is aware that he is publishing information relating to private proceedings. Lord Denning MR, however, commented: [5]

> 'a person is only to be found guilty . . . if he has published information relating to wardship proceedings in circumstances in which he knows that publication is prohibited by law, or recklessly in circumstances in which he knows that the publication may be prohibited by law, but nevertheless goes on and publishes it, not caring whether it is prohibited or not.'

In other words, the publisher must not only know of the existence of the wardship proceedings but also that publication of those proceedings is prohibited by law. This latter requirement would, it was thought, give adequate protection

empanelled) seven days' advance warning has to be given and once the court has decided to sit in camera it adjourns for 24 hours to allow an appeal against it to the Court of Appeal: see Crown Court Rules 1982, r 24A. Note also that under the Defence Contracts Act 1958, s 4(3) evidence about defence contracts in civil proceedings can be given in camera. It was under these provisions that the 116-day 'Cyprus Secrets Trial' was heard in camera in 1985.

19   [1977] Fam 58, [1977] 1 All ER 114. See the note on this case by Munro, (1977) 40 MLR 343; cf Lowe, (1977) 93 LQR 180.
20   [1894] 3 Ch 193 at 203.
1   [1949] Ch 230 at 236.
2   See Lowe, (1977) 93 LQR at 183.
3   [1979] AC 440, [1979] 1 All ER 745 discussed above.
4   [1977] Fam 58 at 96 and 107 respectively.
5   This quotation is taken from [1977] 1 All ER at 123 as there appears to be a series of misprints at [1977] Fam 90.

to 'ordinary folk' while not giving too much freedom to newspapers since they would be taken to know that such publications are prohibited.

Whilst sympathising with Lord Denning MR's desire to cut down the scope of the offence as far as the parties to the case are concerned, his views are not without difficulties. It could mean, for example, that unless warned against publishing details of the proceedings, parties (provided they are ignorant of the law) would be free to talk not only to their friends about the case but also to give details to the press with the consequent possibility of these details being subsequently published by the press in ignorance of the fact that they relate to private proceedings. Indeed this is more or less what happened in *Re F* itself. To avoid this possibility it seems incumbent upon the judge to make a specific warning to those concerned not to reveal details of the case outside the court.[6]

A second difficulty of the definition given to the mens rea required concerns the obligation, if any, of the press to check whether their information related to proceedings heard in private. It seems clear that once it is known that the information relates to wardship proceedings newspapers must be taken to know such proceedings are normally heard in private but it remains unclear how far a newspaper is obliged to discover whether there are wardship proceedings. None of their Lordships expressly refer to this point though Lord Denning MR, in mentioning the concept of recklessness, might be taken as saying that there is some obligation to check the existence of such proceedings. The extent of such obligations, however, remains unclear.[7]

B The statutory position under English law

The reporting of proceedings properly heard in private is prima facie governed by s 12 of the Administration of Justice Act 1960, which states:[8]

'(1) The publication of information relating to proceedings before any court[9] sitting in private shall not of itself be contempt of court except in the following cases, that is to say:
(a) where the proceedings:
(i) relate to the exercise of the inherent jurisdiction of the High Court with respect to minors;
(ii) are brought under the Children Act 1989; or
(iii) otherwise relate wholly or mainly to the maintenance or upbringing of a minor;
(b) where the proceedings are brought under Part VIII of the Mental Health Act 1959[10] or under any provision of the Act authorising an

---

6 In wardship proceedings a specific warning against publication is now attached to the Official Solicitor's report—see Lowe and White, *Wards of Court* (2nd edn, 1986) para 8.16. For the position in family proceedings concerning children see Family Proceedings Rules 1991, r 4.23(1) and Family Proceedings Courts (Children Act 1989) Rules 1991, r 23(1).
7 On the facts of *Re F* the obligation to make checks does not seem to be that great, see Lowe and White, ibid.
8 As amended by the Children Act 1989, Sch 13, para 14.
9 It is submitted that the court must be in England or in Wales. It would not, for instance, apply to proceedings in the European Court of Human Rights. Query whether s 12 would apply to the reporting of proceedings in the European Court even if it contained information relating to English court proceedings?
10 Pt VIII of the Mental Health Act 1959 has been replaced by Pt VII of the Mental Health Act 1983.

application or reference to be made to a Mental Health Review Tribunal or to a county court;

(c)   where the court sits in private for reasons of national security during that part of the proceedings about which the information in question is published;

(d)   where the information relates to a secret process, discovery or invention which is in issue in the proceedings;

(e)   where the court (having power to do so) expressly prohibits the publication of all information relating to the proceedings or of information of the description which is published.

(2)   Without prejudice to the foregoing sub-section, the publication of the text or a summary of the whole or part of an *order* made by a court sitting in private shall not of itself be contempt of court except where the court (having power to do so) expressly prohibits the publication' (emphasis added).

'Sitting in private' is defined in s 12(3) to include a court sitting in camera or in chambers, while 'court' is defined to include 'references to a judge and to a tribunal and to any person exercising the functions of a court, a judge or a tribunal'.

1   *Publishing information relating to proceedings*

(a)   The prima facie rule

Save in the exceptional cases mentioned in s 12(1) the reporting of proceedings heard in private is *not* of itself a contempt of court. This prima facie rule, which applies principally to interlocutory or administrative matters heard in chambers, brings much needed clarity to a hitherto uncertain area of the law.[11] According to Lord Denning MR,[12] the prima facie rule applies not just to the reporting of proceedings but also to the reporting of or the publishing of information relating to the pleadings, affidavits and reports etc that are filed in the court preparatory to the hearing.

It is to be noted that s 12(1) states that a report of private proceedings is not of *itself* a contempt. As Lord Denning MR has said[13] such reports can, however, be a contempt if calculated to create what must now[14] be a substantial risk of serious prejudice to the administration of justice in particular legal proceedings or possibly a real risk of prejudice to the administration of justice generally. In this respect there would appear to be no automatic immunity for even fair and accurate reports of the proceedings (s 4(1) of the Contempt of Court Act 1981 only applies to proceedings heard in open court). On the other hand, since reports will be made in the context of civil proceedings, as we have seen,[15] the risk of prejudicing the case in hand will be small. Hence, as Lord Denning MR has said, speaking generally:[16]

---

11   Discussed at pp 320–322.
12   In *Re F (Orse A) (a minor) (Publication of Information)* [1977] Fam 58 at 87.
13   *Re F,* ibid at p 88.
14   Under s 2(2) of the Contempt of Court Act 1981.
15   In Ch 6.
16   *Re F* [1977] Fam 58 at p 88.

'the effect of s 12(1) of the Act of 1960 is that a newspaper may publish information about proceedings in chambers in a civil action, and about the pleadings, affidavits and reports therein, without any fear of being thereby in contempt of court.'

It should be added, however, that even fair and accurate reports of private proceedings attract no privilege from defamation actions,[17] so publishers must be careful not to offend against the law of libel. Care should also be exercised not to reveal details prohibited by the Judicial Proceedings (Regulation of Reports) Act 1926.[18]

(b)   The specified instances under s 12

For s 12 to operate at all, in relation to the specific instances mentioned in s 12(1) the offending material must be (a) published, and (b) contain information relating to proceedings heard in private.

(i) Publishing   Given that the prohibition under s 12 is against publishing material, the mere receipt of information cannot constitute a contempt. In the previous edition we suggested[19] 'publication' meant the communication of information in any form, be it printed, broadcast or simply passed on by word of mouth. If that is the case, the embargo is very strict so that even communication within a litigant's family would be caught. There are, however, cases (all in the context of wardship or other children proceedings) which support the view that the embargo extends to making information available to any person who is not a party. It has been held, for example, that it is a serious breach of confidentiality and therefore presumably a potential contempt to show the wardship papers to an independent social worker.[20] It is also clear that it is a contempt to show the papers to medical officers,[1] and to prospective adopters and their legal advisers[2] without prior court leave.

Whether similar constraints apply to proceedings other than those concerning children has yet to be established but even in the child context, the wide meaning given to publishing surely casts the contempt net too wide. It means, for example, that showing papers to International Social Services is a contempt unless leave of the court has first been obtained. This surely cannot be right. It is therefore suggested that 'publishing' under s 12 ought to have the same meaning as it does under the Contempt of Court Act 1981,[3] namely 'any speech, writing, programme included in a service[4] or other communication in whatever form, which is addressed to the public at large or any section of the public'.

This definition would presumably exclude communications within the family and, it is suggested, communicating information to experts instructed in the case.

---

17   See Lord Atkinson in *Scott v Scott* [1913] AC 417 at 452. Scrutton J in *R v Madge, ex p Isaacs* (1913) 30 TLR 10 at 12, 13 and Lord Denning MR in *Re F*, [1977] Fam 58 at 88.
18   Discussed at p 317.
19   At 223.
20   *Re C (Wardship: Independent Social Worker)* [1985] FLR 56, and *Practice Direction* [1983] 1 All ER 1097.
1   *Practice Direction* [1987] 3 All ER 640.
2   *Practice Direction* [1989] 1 All ER 169.
3   S 2(1), discussed at p 110.
4   As defined by the Broadcasting Act 1990, see s 2(5) of the 1981 Act.

On the other hand, on any definition, it is clearly 'publishing' for a parent to give an interview to the press about the case.[5]

(ii) Information relating to proceedings   What s 12 prohibits in the specified instances is publishing information about the proceedings. It does not:

(a) prevent references to the fact that proceedings have been instituted;

(b) prevent references being made to the parties;

(c) prohibit publication of information about the court *order*.

With regard to (a) the leading case is *Pickering v Liverpool Daily Post and Echo Newspapers Plc*,[6] in which the House of Lords held that it was not contrary to s 12(1)(b) to publish the fact that a named patient had made an application to a Mental Health Tribunal for his discharge nor to publish information as to the date, time or place at which the proceedings had been or were to be heard. As Lord Bridge observed:[7]

> 'The essential privacy which is protected by each of the exemptions in paragraphs (a) to (d) of s 12(1) attaches to the substance of the matters which the court has closed its doors to consider, not to the fact that the court will sit, is sitting or has sat at a certain date, time or place behind closed doors to consider those matters.'

With regard to (b) there is a substantial body of case law in relation to wards of court[8] which establish that unless the court has expressly ordered otherwise, the mere reference to the fact that the child is a ward of court is not caught by s 12. As Scarman LJ said in *Re F (Otherwise A) (a minor) (Publication of Information)*:[9]

> 'What is protected from publication is the proceedings of the court; in all other respects the ward enjoys no greater protection against unwelcome publicity than other children. If the information published relates to the ward, but not to the proceedings, there is no contempt.'

On this basis it has been held[10] that in the absence of an express court order it is not a breach of the automatic restrictions imposed by s 12 in wardship proceedings to publish the name and address or to identify the ward.

With regard to (c), s 12(2) expressly provides that 'publication of the text or a summary of the whole or part of an order made by the court sitting in private shall not of itself be contempt of court except where the court (having power to do so) expressly prohibits the publication'.

It is to be noted that s 12(2) does not itself confer a power to prevent publication of the order. Regard must therefore be had to the previous law. Although is seems to be accepted that the court has such a power in wardship proceedings beyond this the position is unclear.[11]

---

5 See the warning given by Dunn LJ in *Re B and G (minors) (Custody)* [1985] FLR 493, at 503.

6 [1991] 2 AC 370, [1991] 1 All ER 622.

7 Ibid at 423 and 635.

8 The nature of the wardship jurisdiction is discussed at p 451.

9 [1977] Fam 58 at 99, [1977] 1 All ER 114 at 130.

10 In *Re L (A Minor) (Wardship: Freedom of Publication)* [1988] 1 All ER 418. See also *Re W and Others (Wards) (Publication of Information)* [1989] 1 FLR 246. A fortiori s 12 has no application to publications that are not concerned with the care or upbringing of the child: *R v Central Independent Television Plc* [1994] Fam 192, [1994] 3 All ER 641, CA.

11 See p 321.

Although s 12 refers to publication of information relating to proceedings it is well established that the restriction encompasses the publication of information relating both to the actual hearing and the evidence filed for the hearing such as affidavits and pleadings, statements of witnesses, reports and account of interviews.[12] In cases involving children the embargo extends to publishing the Official Solicitor's, court welfare officer's or guardian ad litem's report.[13]

Warning has also been given that the embargo extends to *speculation* as to the evidence being heard. In Lord Widgery CJ's view:[14]

> 'It is just as damaging for information of that kind to leak out as it is to have the representatives of the press present and taking their notes at the time. It is even more serious if people can let themselves speculate as to what may or may not be going on in the courts during periods when they are in camera. . . . There is in each of these articles a measure of speculation as to what was going on in closed court . . . and I wish to bring to the notice of the press that that is irregular and a potential contempt of court.'

(iii) Is the publication of information relating to the specific proceedings heard in private necessarily a contempt?

Even if a publication does comprise information relating to the specified proceedings heard in private, it may still not be a contempt despite the apparent absolute prohibition under s 12(1).[15] Whether it was intended to be absolute has been obscured by s 12(4), which states:

> 'Nothing in this section shall be construed as implying that any publication is punishable as contempt of court which would not be so punishable apart from this section.'

Although the subsection might have been interpreted as meaning that *apart* from the express provisions of s 12(1) a publication will not amount to a contempt unless it was a contempt according to the common law,[16] the Court of Appeal ruled in *Re F (Otherwise A) (a minor) (Publication of Information)*[17] that s 12(4) has the effect of preserving any defence which would have been available at common law. In other words s 12 read as a whole does not create any new instances of contempt and therefore even the express instances provided for by s 12(1) are subject to the common law. This interpretation has since been approved by the House of Lords in *Pickering v Liverpool Daily Post and Echo*[18] though as Lord Bridge pointed out[19] in relation to a court, such as a mental health

---

12 As summarised by Lord Donaldson MR in *Pickering v Liverpool Daily Post and Echo Newspapers Plc* [1991] 2 AC 370 at 384, [1990] 1 All ER 335, at 344 following *Re F* [1977] Fam 58, *Re L (a minor) (Wardship: Freedom of Publication)* [1988] 1 All ER 418, *Re W and others (Wards) (Publication of Information)* [1989] 1 FLR 246 and *Re M and N (Minors) (Wardship: Publication of Information)* [1990] Fam 211.

13 Specific warnings against publishing the contents of welfare reports are now attached to court welfare officers' and the Official Solicitor's Reports see *Practice Direction* [1984] 1 All ER 827, Family Proceedings Rules 1991, r 4.23(1) and Family Proceedings Courts (Children Act 1989) Rules 1991, r 23(1).

14 Expressed during the trial of Nicholas Prager (1971) Times, 17 June, (1971) 121 NLJ 548.

15 Ie read literally the words 'a publication shall not of itself be a contempt except in the following circumstances' certainly seemed to mean that in those instances publications would automatically be a contempt.

16 This was the view favoured in the first edition of this work, see pp 119 ff.

17 [1977] Fam 58, [1977] 1 All ER 114.

18 [1991] 2 AC 370, [1991] 1 All ER 622. It also seems in line with Viscount Kilmuir's view who said when introducing the Bill (at HL Debs Vol 222 col 254): 'Nothing in Clause 12 will have the effect of making something punishable as contempt of court which would not have been so punishable as contempt under the existing law'.

19 [1991] 2 AC at 421, [1991] 1 All ER 622 at 633.

review tribunal, exercising a novel and purely statutory jurisdiction the common law principle can only be applied by analogy.

Following *Re F*, s 12 is now interpreted as meaning that publication of information relating to the specific instances referred to in s 12(1) in which proceedings are heard in private *may* be a contempt, it being left to the court's discretion to determine when, 'remembering', as Lord Denning MR said,[20] 'that the courts are not to make punishable anything which would not previously be punishable'. Following this interpretation it was held that a publisher is not guilty of contempt if he did not know or could not be taken to know that the publication related to proceedings heard in private.[1] Further, s 12 does not prejudice the common law defence whereby the passage of time or change of circumstance can allow 'the rule of publicity' to resume.[2]

It is perhaps a moot point whether it is a defence that the information published is already in the public domain. Such a defence was held to exonerate the *Daily Mirror* in *Re W and Others (Wards)(Publication of Information)*[3] but that was in respect of a publication allegedly in defiance of a specific court ban, rather than in respect of an alleged breach of s 12.

In reaching its decision on the interpretation of s 12 in *Re F* the Court of Appeal confirmed an earlier decision by Rees J in *Re R (MJ) (a minor) (Publication of Transcript)*[4] that a judge has a discretion to allow publication of information relating to proceedings (referred to in s 12(1)) heard by him in private. In fact in wardship proceedings publicity is not infrequently sought to enable a missing ward to be traced.[5] *Re F* also confirms the ruling in *Re R (MJ)* that the *Practice Direction,*[6] whereby in wardship and other proceedings relating to children heard in private, parties can without leave and non-parties with special leave obtain transcripts, is intra vitres.

(iv) Summary The position with regard to the instances contained in s 12(1)(a)–(d) can be summarised as follows: (1) the court does not have to sit in private, and (2) if it does, the judge still has a discretion to allow publication of information, but (3) in absence of express authorisation, publication of information relating to such proceedings is a prima facie contempt, unless (4) the publisher can show that he did not know nor could be taken to have known that his publication related to proceedings in private or that the passage of time or change of circumstances has removed the embargo on publicity, or, possibly, the information published is already in the public domain.

(v) Express prohibitions under s 12(1)(e) Unlike the cases referred to in s 12(1)(a)–(d), in the instances governed by s 12(1)(e), prohibition against

---

20   In *Re F* [1977] Fam 58 at 87, [1977] 1 All ER 114 at 120.
1   For a discussion of the mens rea see pp 326–327.
2   Per Scarman LJ in *Re F*, ibid at 99 and 131.
3   [1989] 1 FLR 246.
4   [1975] Fam 89, [1975] 2 All ER 749. There is now a considerable body of case law on how to exercise the discretion to allow the use of documents relating to court proceedings concerning children for other purposes. See eg *Re S (minors) (Wardship Police Investigation)* [1987] Fam 199, [1987] 3 All ER 1076, *Re Manda* [1993] Fam 183, [1993] 1 All ER 733, *Re X (minors) (Wardship: Disclosure of Documents)* [1992] Fam 124, [1992] 2 All ER 595, *Brown v Matthews* [1990] Ch 662, [1990] 2 All ER 155 and *Re K (minors) (Disclosure)* [1994] 1 FLR 377.
5   See *Practice Note* [1980] 2 All ER 806 and *Clarke Hall and Morrison on Children,* 2 [22].
6   [1972] 1 All ER 1056, [1972] 1 WLR 401.

publication of information is dependent upon an express court order to that effect. The problem, however, is to determine in what circumstances such an order may be made, it being clear from the words 'having power to do so' that s 12(1)(e) does not itself *confer* the power.

As Viscount Kilmuir explained during the Parliamentary debate on the provision,[7] the residual power to prohibit publication derives from three sources namely, statute, as for example under the Defence Contracts Act 1958, s 4(3); rules of procedure such as those under the Mental Health Act 1983, s 78(2)(e)[8] or finally from a court's own inherent powers as, for example, where publicity would defeat the object of the proceedings.[9]

Although Viscount Kilmuir's explanation is helpful it was only intended as a guide as to when orders may be made and his Lordship was perhaps unduly sanguine when he said that the provision was 'perfectly clear'. The precise scope of the section remains in doubt. In the past, for example, there has been some dispute as to whether anonymity orders can be thought of as being made under s 12(1)(e)[10] though this inquiry now seems academic in view of the Contempt of Court Act 1981, s 11. It has also been mooted whether orders prohibiting information relating to children can be made under s 12(1)(e) rather than s 39(1) of the Children and Young Persons Act 1933[11] and whether details relating to persons other than debtors who have been examined in private in bankruptcy hearings can properly be prohibited under s 12(1)(e).[12] The failure to clarify this residual power is another example of the regrettable uncertainties that s 12 has generated. In this instance the uncertainty is serious since if a court does prohibit publication, unless it clearly specifies the powers under which it is acting, a newspaper may well be justifiably unclear whether the express prohibition must be obeyed.

(c) The effect of publication in breach of s 12

It is clear that a publication made in breach of s 12 amounts to contempt of court but the section fails to clarify whether it is a civil or criminal contempt. It is sometimes said[13] that such contempts are properly thought of as civil contempts reliance being placed on *Scott v Scott*.[14] It is submitted, however, that if it is right that the publication is a contempt because it frustrates a court ruling designed to protect the administration of justice,[15] rather than being a breach of court order, then the contempt is properly regarded as *criminal*.

---

7 HL Debs Vol 222 col 253.
8 Under the Mental Health Review Tribunal Rules 1983.
9 For further discussion see p 322–325.
10 See Lord Scarman's judgment in *A-G v Leveller Magazine Ltd* [1979] AC 440 at 473, [1979] 1 All ER 745 at 768.
11 Miller, (1st edn) at p 214.
12 Miller, (1st edn) at p 215, n 20.
13 See the first edition of this work at p 121 and Miller, (2nd edn) at p 347, n 24.
14 [1913] AC 417.
15 Following *A-G v Leveller Magazine Ltd* [1979] AC 440, [1979] 1 All ER 745 discussed on this point at p 322.

CHAPTER 9

Publications interfering with the due course of justice as a continuing process

Lord Diplock said in *A-G v Leveller Magazine Ltd:* [1]

> 'although criminal contempts may take a variety of forms they all share a common characteristic: they involve an interference with the administration of justice either in a particular case or more generally as a continuing process.'

In previous chapters we discussed publications thought to interfere with the course of justice in the particular case, though as we saw, in protecting the individual case the underlying concern is to protect the administration of justice as a whole. In this chapter we deal with publications that can be impugned *solely* upon the basis that they interfere with the due course of justice as a continuing process.[2] In this connection we shall discuss two types of publication, namely, those which are said to 'scandalise' the court and those which reveal the deliberations of jurors in arriving at their verdict.

I   SCANDALISING THE COURT

A   Introduction

The phrase 'scandalising the court' has its origins in Lord Hardwicke's classic judgment in the *St James's Evening Post* case[3] but the standard definition of the type of publication it refers to is that of Lord Russell of Killowen CJ in *R* v *Gray*.[4] He said:

> 'Any act done or writing published calculated to bring a court or a judge of the court into contempt or to lower his authority, is a contempt of court.'

The rationale for this branch of contempt lies in the idea that without well-regulated laws a civilised community cannot survive. It is therefore thought important to maintain the respect and dignity of the court and its officers, whose task it is to uphold and enforce the law, because without such respect, public faith in the administration of justice would be undermined and the law itself would fall into disrepute. Wilmot J expressed this basic premise in *R* v *Almon* [5] when he said:

1   [1979] AC 440 at 449.
2   For conduct other than publications that constitute contempt on this wider basis see Ch 11.
3   (1742) 2 Atk 469, where he stated baldly 'One kind of contempt is scandalising the court itself'.
4   [1900] 2 QB 36 at 40.
5   (1765) Wilm 243 at 255. See also *Re The Evening News Newspaper* [1880] 1 NSWLR 211 at 237 where Sir James Martin CJ said:

> 'What are such courts but the embodied force of the community whose rights they are appointed to protect? They are not associations of a few individuals claiming on their

'The arraignment of the justice of the judges, is arraigning the Kings justice; it is an impeachment of his wisdom and goodness in his choice of his Judges, and excites in the minds of his people a general dissatisfaction with all judicial determinations, and indisposes their minds to obey them; and whenever men's allegiance to the law is so fundamentally shaken, it is the most fatal and most dangerous obstruction of justice, and, in my opinion, calls out for a more rapid and immediate redress than any other obstruction whatsoever. . . . To be impartial and to be universally thought so are both absolutely necessary for . . . justice . . .'.

Richmond P put the matter more succinctly when he said in the New Zealand case, *Solicitor-General v Radio Avon Ltd:* [6]

'The justification for this branch of the law of contempt is that it is contrary to the public interest that public confidence in the administration of justice should be undermined.'

The origins of this type of contempt are both dubious and controversial.[7] Wilmot J's opinion in *Almon*, which was never actually delivered,[8] was a product of the great constitutional battles of the eighteenth century featuring John Wilkes, the *North Briton* and Lord Mansfield, Chief Justice of King's Bench. It arose from the actions taken against Wilkes for the 'Candor' pamphlets which attacked Mansfield and the King's Bench.[9] It was crucial to these events that proceedings by way of summary attachment for contempt, unlike proceedings for seditious libel, avoided the awkward necessity of trial by jury. Wilmot J's opinion, with its ringing phrases and picturesque language, has often been described as rhetoric rather than a judgment and indeed it contains little in the way of precedent or authority. The doctrine it propounded was used later in the 1760s, particularly against William Bingley, who published attacks on Lord Mansfield while Wilkes was in exile, but despite some judicial flirting with it during the early nineteenth century[10] it fell into disuse for nearly a hundred years.

Its continued existence, at least in England, was called into doubt in 1899 when Lord Morris commented in *McLeod v St Aubyn:* [11]

'Committals for contempt of court by scandalising the court itself have become obsolete in this country.'

However, the comment proved premature. The very next year, in *R v Gray* [12] the Divisional Court held an article in the *Birmingham Daily Argus* to be a contempt of this kind for heaping 'scurrilous abuse' on Mr Justice Darling. In

personal account special privileges and peculiar dignity by reason of their position. A Supreme Court like this, whatever may be thought of the separate members composing it, is the accepted and recognised tribunal for the maintenance of the collective authority of the entire community . . . it derives its force from the knowledge that it has the whole power of the community at its back. This is a power unseen but it is efficacious and irresistible and on its maintenance depends the security of the public.'

6 [1978] 1 NZLR 225 at 230 (NZ CA).
7 See Fox, *The History of Contempt of Court: the Form of Trial and the Mode of Punishment* (1927, Clarendon Press, Oxford; reprinted 1972, Professional Books, London); Hay, 'Contempt by Scandalizing the Court: A Political History of the First Hundred Years' (1987) Osgoode Hall Law Journal 431; Hughes: 'Contempt of Court and the Press' (1900) 16 LQR 292.
8 For the history of the opinion see pp 470–471.
9 Almon was the publisher of the pamphlets. Lord Mansfield was in conflict, inter alia, with Charles Pratt, Chief Justice of Common Pleas (and later, as Lord Camden, Lord Chancellor) who is generally supposed to have had some part in writing the 'Candor' pamphlets.
10 See *R v Clement* (1821) 4 B & Ald 218 at 233, per Holroyd J.
11 [1899] AC 549 at 561.
12 [1900] 2 QB 36 discussed further at p 341.

England there were a number of subsequent prosecutions in the next two decades but they have now once again become a rarity. The last time a publication was held to be in contempt for scandalising the court in England was in 1931.[13] This does not mean that this branch of contempt law can be considered extinct. In 1982 Lord Hailsham LC[14] commented in the Privy Council in *Badry* v *DPP of Mauritius*:[15]

> 'whilst nothing really encourages courts or Attorneys General to prosecute cases of this kind in all but the most serious examples, or courts to take notice of any but the most intolerable instances, nothing has happened in the intervening eighty years to invalidate the analysis by the first Lord Russell of Killowen CJ in *R v Gray*.'

This type of contempt continues to exist in other jurisdictions. Although the frequency with which prosecutions are brought varies from jurisdiction to jurisdiction they have generally been more common than in England. Scandalising the court still has life in New Zealand[16] and has recently been applied in Australia[17] where, over the years, prosecutions have been relatively common. In Singapore there have been recent prosecutions against publications alleging that the judiciary favour the government.[18]

The most interesting recent discussion has taken place in Canada. Contempt by scandalising the court has been alive and well in Canada throughout this century and there seem to have been markedly more prosecutions than in other Commonwealth countries.[19] Inevitably, however, the courts have had to face the question of the compatibility of this concept with s 2(b) of the Charter of Rights and Freedoms which guarantees 'freedom of thought, belief, opinion and expression, including freedom of the press and other media of communication'. In *R v Kopyto*[20] the judges of the Ontario Court of Appeal differed on the matter. One (Houlden JA) held that contempt by scandalising was completely inconsistent with the Charter and that there was no scope left for it at all. Two (Cory and Goodman JJA) thought that it could only be compatible with the Charter if very strictly limited and the other two (Dubin and Brooke JJA) held that contempt of

---

13 *R v Colsey* (1931) Times, 9 May. In a private prosecution, *R v Meteropolitan Police Comr, ex p Blackburn (No 2)* [1968] 2 QB 150, [1968] 2 All ER 319, the publication was held not to be a contempt.
14 Ironically, as the then Quintin Hogg MP, Lord Hailsham was the alleged contemnor in *R v Metropolitan Police Comr, ex p Blackburn,* ibid.
15 [1982] 3 All ER 973 at 979, [1983] 2 WLR 161 at 168, PC.
16 The reservations expressed by some judges in *A-G v Blomfield* (1914) 33 NZLR 545 now seem to have been dispelled, see particularly Richmond P in *S-G v Radio Avon Ltd* [1978] 1 NZLR 225 at 237–8 and see also *Re Wiseman* [1969] NZLR 55.
17 *Gallagher v Durack* (1983) 45 ALR 53; *Fitzgibbon v Barker* (1992) 111 FLR 191; previous prosecutions included eg *R v Dunbabin, ex p Williams* (1935) 53 CLR 434 and *A-G for New South Wales* v *Mundey* [1972] 2 NSWLR 887. For discussion and criticism of the law in Australia see Burmester, 'Scandalizing the Judges' (1985) 15 Melbourne Univ LR 313 and Walker, 'Freedom of Speech and Contempt of Court: The English and Australian Approaches Compared' (1991) 40 ICLQ 583 (which also deals with contempt by publication generally).
18 See *A-G v Wain* [1991] 2 MLJ 525 and the judgment against the *International Herald Tribune* of 17 January 1995. In South Africa, the case of *S v Van Niekerk* 1970 (3) SA 655(T), discussed at p 359 was a reflection of the political preoccupations of the time.
19 For a discussion of the Canadian cases in the context of a highly critical article about the Canadian judiciary see Martin, 'Criticising the Judges' (1982) 28 McGill Law Journal 1, and also Watson, 'Badmouthing the Bench: Is there a Clear and Present Danger? To What?' (1992) 56 Saskatchewan Law Review 113.
20 (1987) 47 DLR (4th) 213.

court was not an abridgement of freedom of speech at all and that it was therefore unnecessary to decide the issue of its compatibility with the Charter.

We shall now consider what kinds of publication are capable of being impugned for scandalising the court. It must always be remembered, however, that the cases have to be looked at in their historical and cultural context because this branch of contempt, above all others, is subject to changes in judicial and political sensibilities and to shifts in perceptions of what constitutes legitimate comment on the institutions of the state.

It should be said at the outset that in England scandalising the court remains a common law offence since it falls outside the strict liability rule under the Contempt of Court Act 1981[1] as it comprises the interference with the course of justice as a continuing process.

B   The actus reus

1   *The need for a real risk of undermining public confidence in the administration of justice*

In general the actus reus of scandalising the court is the publication of material that is calculated to lower the repute of the court or judge and so undermine public confidence in the due administration of justice. An important qualification, however, is that established by the Privy Council in *Badry* v *DPP of Mauritius* [2] namely, that it is only 'courts of justice properly so-called' and the judges of such courts of justice that can be scandalised at common law. As we shall see,[3] the law of contempt is similarly limited when protecting the course of justice in particular legal proceedings. In general this means that in this context the common law is not concerned to protect tribunals or even courts of law when sitting in an administrative capacity.

A further qualification, at least according to the New Zealand decision *Solicitor-General* v *Radio Avon Ltd,*[4] is that to establish an actionable contempt it must be proved beyond reasonable doubt that there is a real risk as opposed to a remote possibility that public confidence in the administration of justice will be undermined. This seems a reasonable stand-point in principle and probably underlines what in practice the courts in the various jurisdictions had already acted upon. Assuming the need for a real risk it would seem a minimum requirement that the publication has a wide circulation at any rate in the area where it is claimed that public confidence is impaired. For example, a specialist journal read by a few can hardly be said to be likely to create a real risk of undermining *public* confidence in the administration of justice.

Perhaps the risks are greater where well-publicised attacks are made on courts or judges serving small communities[5] and especially where the publisher is an influential and respected member of society.[6] That is not to say, however, that in

---

1 See p 360 for a discussion of the relevance of the Act in determining the requisite mens rea.
2 [1982] 3 All ER 973, [1983] 2 WLR 161.
3 See ch 12. See also Lowe and Rawlings, 'Tribunals and the Laws Protecting the Administration of Justice' [1982] PL 418.
4 [1978] 1 NZLR 225 at 233–4 (NZ CA).
5 See for example *Re A-G of Canada and Alexander* (1976) 65 DLR (3d) 608 (NWT Sup Ct).
6 See eg *Re Ouellet* (1976) 67 DLR (3d) 73 at 93 where Hugessen ACJ commented: 'the position of the contemnor can sometimes be a critical factor. A scandalous comment by a private citizen might well pass unnoticed . . . the same comment by a person occupying a position of power

England, for example, the mass media can publish attacks with impunity on the basis that national confidence in the judiciary cannot be undermined. In the past prosecutions have succeeded against such publications and in principle can still do so.

In Canada two of the judges in *R v Kopyto* who believed that contempt by scandalising *could* survive the Charter[7] considered nevertheless that the common law test was not strict enough to satisfy it. Cory JA[8] said that to meet the constitutional requirements of the Charter the Crown would have to prove, for example:

> 'that an act was done or words were spoken with the intent to cause disrepute to its administration of justice or with reckless disregard as to whether disrepute would follow in spite of the reasonable foreseeability that such a result would follow from the act done or the words used;
>
> and that the evil consequences flowing from the act or words were extremely serious;
>
> and as well demonstrated the extreme imminence of those evil consequences, so that the apprehended danger to the administration of justice was shown to be real, substantial and immediate',

for then punishing the act or words would be in order to ensure the functioning of the judicial process. Goodman JA formulated the required test in terms strongly reminiscent of the 'clear and present danger' test which is applied in the United States[9] when he said:[10]

> '. . . the offence of contempt is constitutionally valid, however, only where the utterance or statement is found to result in a clear, significant and imminent or present danger to the fair and effective administration of justice. In that case it meets the test of proportionality and becomes a reasonable limitation prescribed by law which can be demonstrably justified in a free and democratic society.'

The adoption of such a test would render the position of the actus reus of scandalising significantly different from that pertaining in the other jurisdictions.

2 The mode and timing of the publication

Scandalising the court is not confined to a particular medium. Commonly, it is committed through the publication of written comment in a newspaper or

---

and authority may create a serious and dangerous impediment to the independence and integrity of the judicial process'. In that case comment was made by a minister of the Federal Cabinet. His conviction was upheld by the Quebec CA in *Re Ouellet* (1976) 32 CCC (2d) 149, 72 DLR (3d) 95. The prominence of the trade union official concerned in *Gallagher v Durack* (1983) 45 ALR 53 was a major factor in finding his comment to be a contempt.

7 Cory and Goodman JAA.

8 (1988) 47 DLR (4th) 213 at 241.

9 Contempt by scandalising is not known in the United States but in contempt charges in relation to pending cases (where the law operates quite differently from how it does in other common law jurisdictions, as is explained in Ch 3) the position was summed up by Black J in *Bridges v State of California*, 314 US 252 (1941) who said (at 263): 'What finally emerges from the clear and present danger cases is a working principle that the substantive evil must be extremely serious and the degree of imminence extremely high before utterances can be punished'.

10 (1988) 47 DLR (4th) 213 at 265.

broadcast on television or radio but it has been held to have been committed via a speech,[11] by words displayed on a poster[12] and even by means of a carton.[13]

This is not to say, however, that the medium of publication is never relevant. For example, it may be relevant that comment is published in satirical or humorous magazines or television or radio programmes. It could be argued that since the magazine or programme is meant to be humorous, most information can be taken with a pinch of salt and so could hardly be said to undermine public confidence in the administration of justice.

Since a court's or judge's repute can be impugned at any time, the offence of scandalising can be committed regardless of whether the words said or acts done occur before, during, or after a trial or indeed without reference to a particular trial at all.[14] Of course where the publication occurs before or during proceedings there is the additional risk of committing contempt by interfering with the course of justice in the particular case.

3   The types of contempt that 'scandalise' the court

The classic examples of publications held to scandalise the court are those that are said to be 'scurrilously abusive' and those which impugn the impartiality of the court or its officers. In either of these cases comment can be directed against a particular judge or against a court or judges in general. The seriousness of the offence does not differ according to the direction of the criticism. There are, however, comparatively fewer cases where a court has been held to be scandalised than where a single judge has been scandalised and it may be that comment has to be more outrageous when directed against a court or judges in general.

In addition to the classic examples, publications that are thought to lower the repute of a judge or court may also amount to contempt.

Some cases do not fall neatly into one or other of these categories and the lines between the categories are blurred. Nevertheless, they constitute a convenient starting point. As we will see, modern cases show that prosecutions for scandalising the court are most likely to be brought against allegations of partiality or bias.

(a)   Scurrilous abuse

(i) Scurrilous abuse of a judge   It is a well-established principle that publications that are considered to be scurrilously abusive of a judge amount to contempt by scandalising the court. As a number of decisions emphasise the rules of contempt do not exist to protect a judge personally but operate to protect the public interest in the administration of justice. Bowen LJ, said in *Helmore v Smith (No 2):* [15]

> 'The object of discipline enforced by the court is not to vindicate the dignity or the person of the judge, but to prevent undue interference with the administration of justice.'

11   *R v Ogilvie* (1928) 23 Tas LR 69 (Tasmanian Sup Ct).
12   *R v Vidal* (1922) Times, 14 October.
13   *A-G v Blomfield* (1914) 33 NZLR 545.
14   Contra, Hughes, 'Contempt of Court and the Press' (1900) 16 LQR 292, who argues that proceedings must be 'pending'. However, in *R v Gray* [1900] 2 QB 36 it was held that contempt by scandalising had been committed even though no proceedings were 'pending' and this position seems well established by the subsequent twentieth century cases.
15   (1886) 35 Ch D 449 at 455.

Similarly, Lord Morris said in *McLeod v St Aubyn* [16] that the power to commit for contempt 'is not to be used for the vindication of the judge as a person. He must resort to an action for libel . . .'. The principle is perhaps best explained by Dodds CJ, in the Tasmanian case of *R v Fowler* [17] when he said:

> 'These powers [ie powers to commit for contempt] are given to judges in order to keep the course of justice free. These powers are of great importance to society, for by their exercise of them law and order prevail. They have nothing to do with the personal feelings of the judge, and no judge would allow his personal feelings to have any part in the matter; the powers are exercised simply for the good of the people and whenever judges have exercised these powers they have done so from a sense of duty and under pressure of some grave public necessity.'

Whenever there are proceedings for contempt concerning comments on a judge, the first question is whether such comments reflect on the judge in his public capacity as a judge. It is clear from *Re Johnson* [18] that a judge sitting in chambers is acting judicially just the same as if he is sitting in court but the law of contempt has no application where reference is made to the behaviour of a judge when acting in his personal capacity or in an extra-judicial capacity. In *Badry v DPP of Mauritius* [19] it was held that comments upon a judge in his capacity as a commissioner on a Commission of Inquiry also fell outside the scope of the offence. [20]

The leading case on scurrilous abuse of a judge is *R v Gray*, [1] the case which marked the reawakening in England of scandalising the court after nearly a century of sleep. At the commencement of a trial concerning the publication of an obscene libel, Darling J warned the press that no protection would be afforded to them if they published a full account of the proceedings in court (which report would, of course, have included the details of the obscene matter), adding that:

> 'although he hoped and believed that his advice would be taken, if it was disregarded he should make it his business to see that the law was in that respect enforced.'

After the trial had finished (and no appeal was pending) the *Birmingham Daily Argus* published an article entitled 'A Defender of Decency'. The article described the judge as an: 'impudent little man in horse-hair', a 'microcosm of conceit and empty headedness', adding:

> 'No newspaper can exist except upon its merits, a condition from which the Bench, happily for Mr Justice Darling, is exempt. Mr Justice Darling would do well to master the duties of his own profession before undertaking the regulation of another.'

---

16 [1899] AC 549 at 561. See also *Debi Prasad Sharma v King Emperor* (1943) Times, 27 July.
17 (1905) 1 Tas LR 53.
18 (1887) 20 QBD 68.
19 [1982] 3 All ER 973, [1983] 2 WLR 161 (PC).
20 Judges frequently, at least in the United Kingdom, chair committees or public inquiries set up by government or Parliament to investigate particular matters of public concern. Lord Denning famously chaired the Profumo inquiry, Tayor LJ (later Lord Taylor of Gosforth CJ) chaired the inquiry into the Hillsborough football disaster; Scott LJ conducted the 'arms to Iraq' enquiry in 1994 and Lord Nolan chaired the 'sleaze' committee on standards in public life in 1995. These last three examples all gave the judges concerned a high profile and earned them much *complimentary* coverage in the media.
1 [1900] 2 QB 36. The article is published in full in (1900) 81 LT 534.

This article was held by the Divisional Court to be a grave contempt, for as Lord Russell of Killowen CJ said:[2] 'It is not criticism: I repeat that it is personal, scurrilous abuse of a judge as a judge'.

Another example is *Re Sarbadhicary*[3] where a barrister, having been interrupted by a judge during the course of his argument in court and been told to hold his tongue, published an article in his own paper, part of which read:

> '. . . then our honourable Chief Justice, who might not be qualified enough for the due discharge of the routine of work but . . . is . . . most competent, in hurling his unerring javelin at the counsel will too readily do so, inflicting a deep wound which will not cure in the process of time, which will fester and bleed afresh, and the wound only heals up when the aggrieved party courts death. So our readers can easily see that we have a wonderful Chief Justice who punishes an assailed and not an assailant with miraculous readiness and activity. He punishes not the wrongdoers, but the wronged and thus he upholds justice.'

The Privy Council held the article to be a contempt.

Further examples can be found in a trilogy of English decisions decided between 1922 and 1930. In the first, *R v Vidal*,[4] the accused, being dissatisfied with a court decision, displayed the following on a poster:

> 'Is Judge Sir Henry Duke afraid to prosecute me? I accuse him to be a traitor to his duty and defrauding the course of justice for the benefit of the kissing doctor.'

Vidal was sentenced by the Divisional Court to four months' imprisonment for his contempt (notice was also taken of his unrepentant attitude in court). In *R v Freeman*[5] another dissatisfied litigant sent letters to the presiding judge 'containing the grossest calumny and vituperation'. In one letter he wrote 'You are a liar, a coward, a perjurer. You aided Lord Sheffield in a felony'. Avory J, one of the judges hearing the case in the Divisional Court, thought that it 'constituted as gross a contempt as had lately been brought to the knowledge of the court'.

The third case was *R v Wilkinson*[6] in which an article in the *Daily Worker* said:

> 'Rigby Swift, the judge who sentenced Comrade Thomas, was the bewigged puppet and former Tory Member of Parliament chosen to put the Communist leaders away in 1926. The defending counsel, able as he was, could not do much in the face of the strong class bias of judge and jury.'

Lord Hewart CJ, said that the newspaper had committed contempt by scandalising the court because the comments had the effect of bringing the judge into contempt and lowering his authority.

A more recent example is the Canadian decision, *Re Ouellet*,[7] where a federal Cabinet Minister was held to have committed contempt for making the following disparaging remarks regarding a judge who dismissed a prosecution brought by his ministry:

> 'I find this judgment completely unacceptable. I think it is a silly decision. I just cannot understand how a judge who is sane could give such a verdict. It is a complete shock and I find it a complete disgrace.'

2 Ibid at 40.
3 (1906) 95 LT 894 see also *Mcleod v St Aubyn* [1899] AC 549.
4 (1922) Times, 14 October.
5 (1925) Times, 18 November.
6 (1930) Times, 16 July.
7 (1976) 72 DLR (3d) 95 (Quebec CA).

The above cases are cited as examples of what has been held in the past to amount to 'scurrilous abuse'. It is, however, a question which will be judged by different standards according to the time and place of the publication—very much a matter of *autres temps, autres moeurs*. Moreover, as we shall see, scurrilous abuse must be distinguished from criticism, even trenchant criticism, the propriety of which is equally well established. The foregoing English authorities are all over 60 years old and it cannot be assumed that what was held to amount to 'scurrilous abuse' in 1900 or 1930 would be held to amount to scurrilous abuse in the 1990s. For example, the May 1992 issue of the magazine *Legal Business* published a ranking order of High Court judges called *The Most Respected and the Least Respected*, which it claimed was the results of a survey it had conducted amongst members of the legal profession. Of the judge who came bottom of the poll, whom we will call X, the editor wrote:

> 'The judge should be seen to be even-handed, fair and reasonable. . . . It is my submission that, on this test [X] fails abysmally—and his conduct should therefore disqualify him from being a High Court judge . . . sheer bloodymindedness and rudeness . . . his behaviour in court . . . undermines the very credibility of English law and he does a disservice to all involved in the legal process . . .the behaviour of [X] is unacceptable. He is not suited for the bench . . . he holds a public office and his behaviour reflects upon the integrity of that office . . . [X] is an embarrassment to the bench.'

All this was gleefully recounted by Bernard Levin in *The Times*,[8] thereby giving it a much wider currency. In its terms the passage quoted above is not so different from the scandalising article in *R v Gray*, but although the whole episode raised many eyebrows no contempt action was taken against it.[9] Another incident in respect of which no action was taken was the *Daily Mirror*'s response to the *Spycatcher* injunction in 1987—upside-down photographs of the Law Lords below the headline 'You Fools!'

Society is more tolerant today of strong language and has lost the habit of respect. Judges, like other figures of the establishment, have had to become used to being addressed and criticised in terms which can be described as neither gentlemanly nor ladylike. The Law Officers may well prefer to ignore isolated abusive comments on the judiciary rather than give them greater prominence by a prosecution and provoke a cause célèbre. However, the *principle* remains the same, namely, that *abuse* of a judge amounts to contempt if it reflects upon his capacity as a judge. On the other hand, *criticism* of a judge's conduct, so long as no aspersions are cast on a judge's personal character, do not amount to scurrilous abuse.

(ii) Other examples of scurrilous abuse　Our examples so far have been solely concerned with abuse of a judge but the offence is not so confined. Abusive comments directed against a jury may also amount to contempt. In the Canadian case *Re Nicol*,[10] for instance, an article was published in the form of an elaborate allegory in which there was an imaginary trial of a judge after his death. This judge had in reality just conducted a case in which the accused had been sentenced to death. The article began as follows:

8　15 June 1992.
9　For a similar episode in Canada see 'Canadian Lawyer's Survey on the Provincial Court Bench: The Worst of the Provincial Court' (1991) 15:2 Canadian Lawyer 18 at 20.
10　[1954] 3 DLR 690. See also *R v White* (1808) 1 Camp 359n.

'Although I did not myself spring the trap that caused my victim to be strangled in cold blood, I admit that the man who put the rope around his neck was in my employ. Also serving me were the 12 people who planned the murder, and the judge who chose the time and place and caused the victim to suffer this exquisite torture of anticipation.'

One of the reasons that it was held that contempt had been committed was that a possible effect of the article was to deter future juries from 'observing their duty' when sitting on a capital murder charge.

Publications may also be a contempt for being scurrilously abusive of a court rather than an individual judge. For example, in *R v Dunbabin, ex p Williams* [11] (an Australian High Court decision) the Sydney *Sun* published an article entitled 'Courts and Cabinets', the general theme of which was 'the manner in which the High Court knocked holes in the Federal Laws'. The article included the following comment on a decision by the High Court to allow a certain Czech immigrant to remain in the country despite the fact that he had entered illegally:

'Jumping ashore, and spraining his ankle in the process, he was promptly put in gaol under the Act which gave the Government the right to keep undesirables out. Friends of the humbled and oppressed tested the law, and to the horror of everybody except the Little Brothers of the Soviet and kindred intelligentsia, the High Court declared that Mr Kisch must be given his freedom. We all, of course, ought to thank this distinguished litterateur for his discovery of a flaw in one of our most important Acts, a flaw which is to be mended sometime or other, when Parliament deigns to sit again. When the amendments are made we should invite him to jump ashore again to see whether the new Act pleases the High Court any better than the old, or whether the ingenuity of five bewigged heads cannot discover another flaw.'

The article ended with these words:

'Well may the Caseys and Kelleys cry, like the historic British monarch, for some gallant champion to rid them of this pestilent court. Perhaps there is a better way. If the High Court were given some real work to do the Bench would not have the time to argue for days on the exact length of the split in the hair, and the precise difference between Tweedledum and Tweedledee.'

Rich J, in holding the article a contempt, said that its effect and purpose was 'to represent that the court exercises its ingenuity in order to defeat legislation to which great public importance attaches.' This, together with the suggestion that only the 'Little Brothers of the Soviet' were pleased by the decision, was held to have the tendency to weaken the confidence of the public in court decisions.

In *R v Murphy* [12] a Canadian decision, an article published in a university newspaper contained the author's account of his personal experience of a particular case. The general tone of the account was one of disdain:

'That court was a mockery of justice. I, along with any of the other defence witnesses, might as well have testified to the bottle-throwing mob that on several occasions gathered outside. . . .

---

11   (1935) 53 CLR 434.
12   (1969) 4 DLR (3d) 289. See also *R v Ivens* (1920) 51 DLR 38 where the article commented that the accused was tried 'by a poisoned jury, by a poisoned judge and was in gaol because of a poisoned sentence', and *Chokolingo v A-G of Trinidad and Tobago* [1981] 1 All ER 244, [1981] 1 WLR 106, publication of a story entitled 'The Judge's Wife' held to be 'under a thin disguise of fiction' an 'attack upon the probity of the judiciary of Trinidad and Tobago as a whole'.

The courts in New Brunswick are simply the instruments of the corporate elite. Their duty is not so much to make just decisions as to make right decisions (ie decisions which will further perpetuate the elite which controls and rewards them). Court appointments are political appointments. Only the naive would reject the notion that an individual becomes a justice or judge after he proves his worth to the establishment.'

Bridges CJNB said:

'There is a limit to what a person may say or write of a judge or court. In my opinion, the defendant exceeded that limit in his malignment of Mr Justice Barry. He was not even satisfied with that but proceeded to make a most uncalled for attack on the integrity of the Courts of New Brunswick. I have no hesitation in holding the article was calculated to bring Mr Justice Barry and the Courts of New Brunswick into contempt. The defendant must be found guilty.'

As with cases on scurrilous abuse of a judge, allowance has to be made for the prevailing attitudes at the time of publication. The comment in *Dunbabin*, for example, is unlikely to attract the sanction of contempt today[13] and the decision is perhaps explicable only on the basis that fear of communism (the unfortunate Czech was seen as a potential spy) was endemic at the time. The more insecure the judicial system the more sensitive it is to sarcastic comments.

To put the examples into perspective one should refer to the 1968 English Court of Appeal decision in *R v Metropolitan Police Comr, ex p Blackburn (No 2)*.[14] A private prosecution was brought against Mr Quintin Hogg QC, MP (later Lord Chancellor) for an article published in *Punch* in which he criticised the courts' handling of the gaming legislation. The article contained the following comments:

'The recent judgment of the Court of Appeal is a strange example of the blindness which sometimes descends on the best of judges. The legislation of 1960 and thereafter has been rendered virtually unworkable by the unrealistic, contradictory and, in the leading case erroneous decisions of the courts including the Court of Appeal. So what do they do? Apologise for the expense and trouble they have put the police to? Not a bit of it . . . [they] blame Parliament for passing Acts which they have interpreted so strangely. Everyone, it seems, is out of step, except the courts. . . . The House of Lords overruled the Court of Appeal . . . it is hoped that the courts will remember the golden rule for judges in the matter of obiter dicta. Silence is always an option.'

The Court of Appeal had no hesitation in deciding that no contempt had been committed, and the witticism one associated with *Punch* was echoed by the opening words of Salmon LJ's judgment:[15]

'The authority and reputation of our courts are not so frail that their judgments need to be shielded from criticism, even from the criticism of Mr Quintin Hogg.'

The article was outspoken but bona fide and not abusive and the Court of Appeal's decision demonstrates that in recent times, when the courts are confident of their stability and strength, scope for comment on the actions of the courts and the conduct of the judges is quite considerable. As Cory JA said in *R v Kopyto*:[16]

13   Especially in view of Hope JA's comments in *A-G for New South Wales v Mundey* [1972] 2 NSWLR 887 at 909–10.
14   [1968] 2 QB 150, [1968] 2 All ER 319.
15   Ibid at 155.
16   (1988) 47 DLR (4th) 213 at 227.

'. . . the courts are not fragile flowers that will wither in the hot heat of controversy.'

(iii) Criticism is not abuse   A simple recital of the decided cases may give a distorted impression that the right to criticise the judiciary is severely restricted whereas in practice, as McKenna J said extra-judicially,[17] 'As to scandalising the court there is almost perfect freedom to criticise the decision of any court or the conduct of any judge.' Scurrilous abuse is to be distinguished from criticism. It has long been held that mere *criticism* is permissible. As Lord Russell CJ said in *R v Gray:* [18]

> 'Judges and courts are alike open to criticism and if reasonable argument or expostulation is offered against any judicial act as contrary to law or the public good, no court could or would treat that as contempt of court.'

The classic exposition of the right to criticise is that of Lord Atkin when he said in *Ambard v A-G for Trinidad and Tobago:* [19]

> 'The path of criticism is a public way: the wrong headed are permitted to err therein: provided that members of the public abstain from imputing improper motives to those taking part in the administration of justice, and are genuinely exercising a right of criticism, and are not acting in malice or attempting to impair the administration of justice, they are immune. Justice is not a cloistered virtue: she must be allowed to suffer the scrutiny and respectful, even though outspoken, comments of ordinary men.'

The last time a scandalising prosecution was brought in England the right to criticise the work of the courts was strongly upheld by the Court of Appeal, Lord Denning MR commenting:[20]

> 'It is the right of every man, in Parliament or out of it, in the press or over the broadcast, to make fair comment, even outspoken comment, on matters of public interest. Those who comment can deal faithfully with all that is done in a court of justice. They can say we are mistaken, and our decisions erroneous, whether they are subject to appeal or not. All we would ask is that those who criticise us will remember that, from the nature of our office, we cannot reply to their criticisms.'

In the same case Salmon LJ said:[1]

> 'It follows that no criticism, however vigorous, can amount to contempt of court, providing it keeps within the limits of reasonable courtesy and good faith.'

It is prima facie therefore legitimate to criticise a judge's conduct in a particular case or the decision that is given by the courts. There can be no objection, for example, to criticism of a judgment or series of judgments on points of law, provided at any rate that aspersions are not cast on the motives of a judge or court. Were this not so then most legal writers would have committed contempt![2] The freedom to criticise is not, however, confined to comments on points of law nor is it restricted to academic journals. It is equally permissible for

---

17 'The Judge and the Common Man' (1969) 32 MLR 601 at 603.
18 [1900] 2 QB 36 at 40.
19 [1936] AC 322 at 335.
20 In *R v Comr of Police, ex p Blackburn (No 2)* [1968] 2 QB 150 at 155.
 1 Ibid at 155.
 2 For an article (dealing with contempt of court, inter alia) containing scathing criticism of the quality of a country's judges as a whole see Martin, 'Criticising the Judges' (1982) 28 McGill Law Journal 1.

a mass circulation daily newspaper to criticise, for example, a decision as being against the overall policy of the law or contrary to the spirit of the legislation or being out of tune with present-day needs. There are countless examples of such criticism that the media regularly publish.

Comments on sentences or judgments or on the law in general are generally regarded as legitimate. In *Ambard v A-G for Trinidad and Tobago* [3] the Port of Spain *Gazette* published a long article under the title 'The Human Element'. The article was concerned about the discrepancy between the sentences given in two apparently similar cases. The article concluded that the difference must have been attributable to the personal attitude of the judge concerned. The language used was temperate, and the criticism related only to the sentences; moreover, the article expressly disclaimed the suggestion that the judge was habitually lenient or harsh. Lord Atkin held that:[4]

> 'The writer is ... perfectly justified in pointing out, what is obvious, that sentences do vary in apparently similar circumstances with the habit of mind of the particular judge.'

Again there are numerous modern examples of such criticism and indeed the media have become noticeably more outspoken.[5] There are regular outcries over alleged light sentences and over insensitive comments made by male judges about female rape and sexual assault victims which are often expressed, especially in the tabloid press, in the most intemperate language and are inevitably accompanied by cries for the judge's resignation or dismissal. Other notable examples are the vilification suffered by Sir John Donaldson when he was President of the National Industrial Relations Courts in the 1970s[6] and the sustained and sometimes quite vitriolic criticism directed at the members of the judiciary involved in the major miscarriages of justice which were corrected in the early 1990s.[7]

(iv) Limits of the right of criticism   The right to criticise is subject to certain provisos. For example, as we have seen, the right to criticise does not mean that there is a licence to be scurrilously abusive. Unfortunately it is not always easy to predict how the courts, particularly in some jurisdictions, will react to critical comment, although after 60 years it is understandable if the English media become quite blasé. As Lord Taylor CJ remarked at a *Times* symposium in 1994:[8]

3   [1936] AC 322, [1936] 1 All ER 704.
4   Ibid at 336.
5   Certainly in England and Wales as compared with earlier in the twentieth century. One must not forget, however, that the Victorian press could be vitriolic and in the second half of the eighteenth century the events surrounding John Wilkes and the *Almon* case (see p 336, and Hay, 'Contempt by Scandalizing the Court: A Political History of the First Hundred Years' (1987) Osgoode Hall Law Journal 431) well demonstrate the outspoken language in which the criticism of the courts was couched.
6   The Phillimore Committee (1974, Cmnd 5794) para 160, thought that things were said and published in this regard which *could* have been prosecuted for contempt.
7   Most of which involved terrorist offences, such as the 'Guildford Four'(whose convictions were finally quashed in *R v Richardson, R v Conlon* etc (1989) Times, 20 October) and the 'Birmingham Six' cases (the appeals were finally allowed in *R v Mclkenny* [1992] 2 All ER 417). Particularly trenchant criticism was directed at Lord Lane CJ in this connection. A notable player in this was Bernard Levin in the *Times* whose column on 18 March 1991, entitled 'Hoist by their own arrogance' called in very colourful language for Lord Lane to go. When the LCJ did retire Levin wrote (15 June 1992) 'the odious nature of Lord Lane's retirement bunfight suggests that many of them [the judiciary] still don't know why they are distrusted and even despised'.
8   See Times, 22 July 1994.

'There was a time when judicial decisions were reported with a reasonable degree of restraint. Nowadays, if a judge passes a sentence the tabloid press regards as lenient, they use the most extreme language—it is quite new, and, I think, regrettable.'

In *R v Kopyto* Goodman JA considered that it was the *content* of the criticism which mattered, saying:[9]

'In my view, the expression of an opinion which may be lawfully expressed in mild, polite, temperate or scholarly language does not become unlawful simply because it is expressed in crude, vulgar, impolite or acerbic words.'

Past cases show that opinions as to whether comment passes into contempt can differ and differ quite strongly, even in the same court. An excellent example is the Australian case, *A-G (NSW)* v *Bailey*.[10] An article entitled: 'The Case of Grant' purported to be a criticism of the harshness of the sentence imposed: 'He got 15 years for saying 15 words'. The concluding paragraph, however, went much further than just a criticism. It read:

'If this is Judge Pring's idea of mercifulness, heaven keep me out of his clutches. If that is a sample of what is known as "British Justice", God help us all. It is one of the most ghastly atrocities that the law has ever been guilty of, and that is saying something.'

One judge (Cullen CJ) thought that the article did not warrant the use of the summary procedure to punish it as a contempt while a second judge (Sly J) did, and a third judge (Gordon J) expressed no opinion on the matter.

An interesting contrast to *Bailey's* case is another New South Wales decision, *Re Truth and Sportsman Ltd, ex p A-G*,[11] where the *Daily Mirror* was held to be in contempt for publishing two articles in the following circumstances: a man driving too fast and who had been drinking ran over and killed two girls on a zebra crossing. After the accident the driver did not stop and later took steps to remove evidence of the accident and tried to frame an alibi. He was sentenced to two years' imprisonment. The first article read:

'Judge Brennan Shocks the Community. The fantastically light sentence that Judge Brennan yesterday imposed on a man whose car knocked down and killed two young sisters is a shocking thing. In the opinion of this newspaper there is no possible justification for treating a monster of this kind with such leniency.'

Some days later another case concerning death by driving came before the same judge. In this case the accused had stolen the vehicle and had a long record of driving offences. He was sentenced to four years' imprisonment. An article appeared the next day:

'Judge Brennan Shocks Again. For the second time in a week Judge Brennan has shocked the Community with the leniency of a sentence he imposed upon a driver killer.'

The court took the view that the article amounted to a contempt since it constituted an unjustified attack and the object was 'to intimidate the court and to prevent it from deciding matters brought before it in a calm and judicial

---

9 (1988) 47 DLR (4th) 213 at 259.
10 (1917) 17 SR (NSW) 170. See the comments on this by Hope JA in *A-G for New South Wales v Mundey* [1972] 2 NSWLR 887 at 909.
11 [1958] SR (NSW) 484. See also *R v Fletcher ex p Kisch* (1935) 52 CLR 248 and *A-G v Butler* [1953] NZLR 944.

atmosphere'. It is extremely doubtful whether in England, at any rate, that such comment would be considered a contempt.

A second proviso to the right of criticism relates to the bona fides of the publisher. One requisite common to all the judgments we cite[12] in support of the right to criticise is that the comment must not be made with malice. Although it is unclear whether it can properly be said that immunity only attaches to comments made bona fide (which issue, as we shall see, is inextricably bound with whether there is a mens rea requirement about which there is also doubt) it is clear that comments made mala fide fall outside the protective umbrella of the right to criticise.

How can mala fides be proved? One way is to look at the language in the publication. It is easy for example to infer an intention to vilify the courts where outrageous and abusive language is used especially where the article is one-sided containing little or no reasoning. In *R v White,* [13] an early English decision of 1808, Grose J decided that a censure of judge and jury in abusive terms constituted a contempt because the article:

> 'contained no reasoning or discussion but only declamation and invective . . . written not with a view to elucidate the truth but to injure the character of individuals, and to bring into hatred and contempt the administration of justice in this country.'

Cases of 'scurrilous abuse' of a judge, particularly *R v Gray,* [14] where Lord Russell CJ said that the comment went beyond criticism, clearly by their language show an intention to vilify rather than to correct; if an article is written in abusive language, the bona fides of the writer will immediately be brought into question.

The actual language used in an article is not of course conclusive proof of intention. Such factors as the party's attitude in court can also be important.[15] In *R v Glanzer* [16] an intention to vilify was inferred not only from the language of the article in question, but from the fact that the article was one of many. In fact, it was said that over 30 such articles had been contemplated as the subject of the proceedings. McRuer CJHC concluded that the writer had no intention to engage in bona fide criticism:

> 'Why have these attacks been carried on for many months? Obviously it is because the perpetrator of the attacks is engaged in a commercial enterprise and he thinks it is popular to attack the county court judges.'

In judging intention regard should be had to the meaning of the article taken as a whole. Where there is any doubt as to the real intention of the writer, since the offence of contempt is of a criminal character, the accused must be given the benefit of the doubt.[17] In *R v Brett* [18] O'Bryan J found it difficult to be sure of the writer's intention and the charge of contempt failed. Such doubts will only arise

---

12 See p 346–347.
13 (1808) 1 Camp 359n.
14 [1900] 2 QB 36 at 40.
15 Eg a refusal to apologise in court can be taken as an indication of bad faith—see *R v Vidal* (1922) Times, 14 October.
16 (1963) 38 DLR (2d) 402.
17 Cf *Re Ouellet* (1976) 67 DLR (3d) 73 where the defendant's claim that his choice of words was affected by his imperfect command of English and that his words had been misinterpreted, failed on the facts.
18 [1950] VLR 226.

where the language is ambiguous. Outright abusive comments are not likely to provide such room for doubt.

How far does mistake vitiate the bona fides of a comment? In *Re The Evening News* [19] it was pointed out that though mistakes of themselves do not necessarily mean that contempt will be committed, there is a point when 'mistakes become pernicious'. O'Bryan J said in *R v Brett:* [20]

> 'It is clear that an untruthful statement of facts upon which the comment is based may vitiate that which otherwise might be considered "fair" and justifiable. . . . Malice, and an intention or tendency to impair the administration of justice are elements in contempt of the kind which scandalises the court or the judge.'

Where, therefore, comment is based on a mistake, the major question in deciding whether contempt has been committed is in deciding whether the writer honestly believed the statement.

Evidence of bona fides is therefore a key factor. In *Perera v R* [1] the appellant, a member of the Ceylon legislature, during an annual inspection of prisons, wrote in the prison's visiting book the following comment:

> 'The present practice of appeals of remand prisoners being heard in their absence is not healthy. When represented by counsel or otherwise the prisoner should be present at the proceedings.'

Mr Perera mistakenly thought he was criticising prison practice whereas in fact his criticism was directed at court procedure. The Ceylon Court held Mr Perera's action to be a contempt but the Privy Council decided that:[2]

> 'Mr Perera was acting in good faith and in discharge of what he believed to be his duty as a member of the legislature. His information was inaccurate, but he made no public use of it, contenting himself with entering his comment in the appropriate instrument, the visitor's book, and writing to the responsible minister. . . . Finally, his criticism was honest criticism on a matter of public importance. When these and no other are the circumstances that attend the action complained of there cannot be a contempt of court.'

In *R v Metropolitan Police Comr, ex p Blackburn (No 2)* [3] where Mr Quintin Hogg's article published in *Punch* criticised the courts' handling of the gaming legislation, he wrongly alleged that a decision of the Court of Appeal had been overruled by the House of Lords but this mistake was held not to vitiate the bona fides of the article.

A third proviso to the right to criticise relates to impugning the impartiality of a judge or court.

(b)   Allegations of partiality or impropriety

Allegations of partiality or impropriety are probably the most common way in which the court has been held to be 'scandalised'. The courts are particularly sensitive to allegations of partiality, it being a basic function of a judge to make an impartial judgment. The law goes to some lengths to ensure that a judge has

19   [1880] 1 NSWLR 211.
20   [1950] VLR 226 at 229.
 1   [1951] AC 482 at 488, PC.
 2   Ibid at 488.
 3   [1968] 2 QB 150, [1968] 2 All ER 319. Cf *S-G v Radio Avon Ltd* [1978] 1 NZLR 225 at 231.

no personal interest in the case, his decision being considered void and of no effect if bias is proved: nemo judex in sua causa. Allegations of partiality are treated seriously because they tend to undermine confidence in the basic function of a judge.[4] Most of the more recent convictions for contempt by scandalising have involved allegations of bias or partiality.

The leading English case, *R v Editor of New Statesman, ex p DPP*,[5] illustrates that even a serious and seemingly respectful article which alleges bias on the part of the judge, may be adjudged to amount to a contempt. The article in this case was a comment on a court's decision involving a well-known pioneer of birth control, Dr Marie Stopes:

> 'We cannot help regarding the verdict given this week in the libel action brought by the editor of the Morning Post against Dr Marie Stopes as a substantial miscarriage of justice.[6] We are not at all in sympathy with Dr Stopes' work or aims, but prejudice against those aims ought not to be allowed to influence a court of justice in the manner in which they appeared to influence Mr Justice Avory in his summing up. . . . The serious point in this case, however, is that an individual owning to such views as those of Dr Stopes cannot apparently hope for a fair hearing in a court presided over by Mr Justice Avory and there are too many Avorys.'

Lord Hewart CJ said that:[7]

> 'the court had no doubt that the article complained of did constitute a contempt. It imputed unfairness and lack of impartiality to a judge in the discharge of his judicial duties. The gravamen of the offence was that by lowering his authority it interfered with the performance of his judicial duties.'

An extreme example is that of *R v Colsey*[8] where the editor of the magazine *Truth* was fined for contempt for publishing the following article:

> 'Lord Justice Slesser, who can hardly be altogether unbiased about legislation of this type, maintained that really it was a very nice provisional order or as good a one as can be expected in this vale of tears.'

It should be said that as Solicitor General in the 1924 Labour Government, Lord Justice Slesser had steered the relevant legislation through Parliament. This case,[9] again decided before Lord Hewart CJ, has been much criticised. Professor Goodhart thought that the decision seemed:

> 'To carry the doctrine of constructive contempt to its extreme limits for the administration of justice can hardly have been seriously endangered by the editor's mild but expensive humour.'[10]

Colsey does seem an example of overreaction by the court and it is perhaps ironic that it should be the last time that a successful prosecution for contempt by scandalising has been brought in England and Wales.

In other jurisdictions prosecutions are still brought and are illustrative of continued sensitivity to allegations of partiality or impropriety. In Australia, for

---

4   This paragraph has been cited with approval by Disbery J in *Re A-G of Canada and Alexander* (1976) 65 DLR (3d) 608 at 622.
5   (1928) 44 TLR 301.
6   *Gwynne v Stopes.*
7   (1928) 44 TLR 301 at 303.
8   (1931) Times, 9 May.
9   Slesser LJ did not in fact want any proceedings brought. See Slesser, *Judgment Reserved*, p 256.
10 'Newspapers and Contempt of Court' (1935–6) 48 HLR 883 at 904.

example, in *A-G for New South Wales v Mundey* [11] the secretary of a trade union was held to have committed contempt for commenting upon a decision to fine his president and another man following the infliction of damage upon goal posts during the course of a protest against the visit to Australia of the South African rugby team:

> 'Well I think it's a miscarriage of justice . . . it showed that the judge himself was a racist judge. It shows you the extent to which racism exists within our society and it shows you what a tremendous problem we have, all Australians, to overcome this deeply ingrained racism . . . I think the main purpose, the industrial action by the workers here this morning, the spontaneous action of workers walking off jobs, stopped the racist judge from sending these two men to jail; that's the real position.'

An edited version of the statement was shown by at least one television station on its evening news. Hope JA held that a contempt by scandalising the court had been committed not because of the imputation of racial bias as such, but because of the suggestion that the judge had been overawed by the action of workers congregating in the vicinity of the court and that it was this alone which had caused him to refrain from imposing a prison sentence.

Gallagher v Durack [12] concerned allegations that a court had been influenced by industrial action. A trade union secretary had been imprisoned for contempt of court in connection with a labour dispute. His appeal was successful and on being released he said 'I'm very happy to the rank and file of the union who has shown such fine support for the officials of the union and I believe that by their actions in demonstrating in walking off jobs. . . . I believe that that has been the main reason for the court changing its mind.' He was promptly imprisoned for contempt again, and the High Court of Australia refused to release him, saying that in insinuating that the Federal Court had bowed its head to outside pressure in reaching its decision he had imputed to the court a grave breach of duty and that:[13]

> 'There can be no doubt that the offending statement amounted to a contempt of court, and if repeated was calculated to undermine public confidence in the Federal Court'.[14]

It might be thought that the High Court was demonstrating undue sensitivity but the court stressed that this statement was made by someone very well known to the Australian public, holding an important office in a large national trade union and 'some members of the public might have been the more ready to accept the assertions of the applicant as true because of their awareness that on some occasions employers and even governments are influenced by the pressure which trade unions are able to bring to bear'.[15]

Recent Australian cases have shown that it is possible for contempt by scandalising to be committed by what is said or done in court, although courts will be slow to hold counsel to be in contempt for the way they conduct their case. In *Lewis v Judge Ogden* [16] counsel suggested in his address to the jury that

---

11 [1972] 2 NSWLR 887.
12 (1983) 152 CLR 238.
13 (1983) 152 CLR 238 at 245 per Gibbs CJ, Mason, Wilson and Brennan JJ.
14 This suggests, rather strangely, that the *initial* statement did not in itself have an undermining effect and that the contemnor was being imprisoned as a precaution.
15 Ibid at 244.
16 (1984) 153 CLR 682. The charge was brought under s 45A of the County Courts Act 1958 (Victoria) which confers on a county court judge a power to punish for contempt any person

remarks made by the judge showed him to be biased against his client. The High Court of Australia declined to hold this to be contempt:[17]

'... mere discourtesy falls well short of insulting conduct, let alone wilfully insulting conduct which is the hallmark of contempt. The freedom and the responsibility which counsel has to present his client's case are so important to the administration of justice, that a court should be slow to hold that remarks made during the course of counsel's address to the jury amount to a wilful insult to the judge, when the remarks may be seen to be relevant to the case which counsel is presenting to the jury on behalf of his client.'

The High Court reiterated the point[18] that the contempt power is exercised to vindicate the integrity of the court and of its proceedings and rarely, if ever, to vindicate the personal dignity of the judge and that the summary power should be used sparingly and only in serious cases. In an earlier case, however,[19] the comments of a disappointed litigant on the character of a District Court judge who had found against him were condemned as scandalous and outrageous and would have resulted in a 'substantial term of imprisonment' had the contemnor not apologised.[20]

The possibility that liability for contempt can arise during court proceedings can lead to some difficult situations. In *Bainton v Rajski* [1] the New South Wales Court of Appeal was careful in the procedure it adopted for dealing with a request from a litigant that certain of the judges should disqualify themselves from hearing his appeal on grounds of bias[2] for fear that the litigant, who was appearing in person, might otherwise be put in jeopardy of committing contempt.

In Canada, before the Charter, there were a number of prosecutions. In *R v Western Printing and Publishing Ltd* [3] the *Western Star* published the following:

'The stern warning intoned earlier in the week by the Chief Justice and his colleagues taking the St John's press and radio to task for publicising the *Valdmanin* case, has a faint tinge of the iron-curtain to it. It is intimidation of the most blatant variety (the shut-up-or-else type, that is). After reading the articles to which the eminent jurists objected and finding them in my opinion quite innocent of anything that might tend to prejudice a fair trial, I can only assume the admonition was another move in the "jump-on-the-press" campaign. The next step will be the seizure and shut down of all the Island's papers (except one) à la Juan Peron.'

In holding this article to be contempt, Walsh CJ said that the article exceeded 'the bounds of temperate and fair criticism' because it 'imputed improper motives to those taking part in the administration of justice' and apart from its insulting words 'it accuses them of the assumption of dictatorial powers.' In *Re*

---

who, inter alia, 'wilfully insults any judge ... in or in the vicinty of the court'. See also *MacGroarty v Clauson* (1989) 167 CLR 251, a case brought under the corresponding legislation in Queensland, the District Courts Act 1967, s 105(1), in which the High Court of Australia dismissed a charge of contempt against counsel who reacted impolitely to a suggestion from the judge that he terminate his cross-examination, on the grounds that the charge did not sufficiently identify the alleged insults.

17 Ibid at 689.
18 See pp 340–341.
19 *Ex p A-G; Re Goodwin* (1969) 70 SR (NSW) 413 (NSW CA).
20 As he did apologise, he was fined $2,000.
 1 (1992) 29 NSWLR 539.
 2 On the grounds of having previously turned down a legal aid application.
 3 (1954) 111 CCC 122 (Newfoundland Sup Ct).

A-G of Canada and Alexander[4] a newspaper was held to have committed contempt for publishing allegations (made without foundation) of a 'cover-up' by court officials and participated in by the Supreme Court judge, Morrow J, in shielding a public figure from adverse publicity by hearing a case against him at a specially constituted court.

The leading case since the Charter is *R v Kopyto*.[5] The alleged contemnor was a lawyer whose client had brought an action against the police. After the action was dismissed the lawyer gave a statement to the press, part of which said:

> 'This decision is a mockery of justice. It stinks to high hell. It says it is okay to break the law and you are immune so long as someone above you said to do it . . .
>
> We're wondering what is the point of appealing and continuing this charade of the courts in this country which are warped in favour of protecting the police. The courts and the police are sticking so close together you'd think they were put together with Krazy Glue.'

Goodman JA[6] thought that this would have constituted contempt at common law, because it was intended or was likely to bring the administration of justice into disrepute, but that it did not meet the much stricter requirements of the Charter. Dubin JA,[7] however, who did not believe that scandalising the court was affected by the Charter, thought that the publication did not amount to common law contempt. He called it 'disgraceful' but did not believe it could have any effect on public confidence in the administration of justice:

> 'The suggestion that there was some overall conspiracy between all the judiciary in this province and the police to deny a fair trial to the appellant's client, and, indeed, to all those engaged in litigation where the police were involved, is so preposterous that no right-thinking member of society would take it seriously.'[8]

There have also been a number of prosecutions in New Zealand. In *A-G v Blundell* [9] for example, a newspaper reported a speech made by the President of the New Zealand Labour Party as saying that 'he had never known the Supreme Court to give a decision in favour of the workers where it could possibly avoid it', and:

> 'While he agreed that they would not get fair play from the Court of Arbitration he was of the opinion that they had to have the court to do the job.'

Myers CJ, in holding the article to be contempt said:

> 'In this case we can entertain no doubt that the passages complained of are calculated to depreciate the authority of both the Supreme Court and the Court of Arbitration. The implication of the statements is that the workers have been and are unable to obtain justice in those courts. Such statements are calculated to diminish the confidence of the public in the courts and they are clearly contempts of court.'

In *Re Wiseman* [10] a solicitor was held to have committed contempt for alleging that during a previous case certain judges had been guilty of forgery, of

---

4   (1976) 65 DLR (3d) 608. See also *Re Borowski* (1971) 19 DLR (3d) 537.
5   (1988) 47 DLR (4th) 213 (Ont CA). Because of the defendant's acquittal the case did not reach the Canadian Supreme Court.
6   At 260
7   At 291; Brooke JA agreeing.
8   Ibid at 290.
9   [1942] NZLR 287. See also *Vidyasagara v R* [1963] AC 589 (PC) and the Irish High Court cases, *A-G v O'Kelly* [1928] 1R 308 and *A-G v Connolly* [1947] 1R 213.
10 [1969] NZLR 55.

fabricating evidence and of deliberately showing partiality to Wiseman's opponents. North P, said:

'It is quite impossible to regard these statements as being within the widest limits of legitimate criticism and, in our opinion, clearly have the tendency to lower the authority of the courts . . . We have no doubt whatever that the respondent must be convicted of contempt of court.'

In *S-G v Radio Avon Ltd* [11] the defendant radio station was held guilty of contempt for broadcasting inter alia:

'Supreme Court Judge, Mr Justice Roper, is at the centre of another closed court controversy. This one is the Moby Dick's arson case. It's just been revealed that he has dismissed the arson charge against night-spot manager, Ernest Hunter in a hearing behind closed doors 10 days ago. . . . A few months ago, Mr Justice Roper's son was given what's claimed to be a light sentence in a drinking driving hearing out of normal hours before a city magistrate.'

The Court of Appeal accepted the Supreme Court's judgment that the clear and unambiguous inference which listeners would take from the broadcast was that the judge had permitted a hearing before him to take place in private when it should have been heard in public and that there had been some preferential treatment.

The courts in Singapore are currently treating with utmost seriousness publications alleging partiality towards the government. In *A-G v Wain* [12] the Prime Minister, Lee Kuan Yew, had sued the publisher of the *Far Eastern Economic Review* for libel. He won and the next day the *Asian Wall Street Journal* published an article about the case which said, inter alia, that the original article was essentially accurate, that the court had given judgment based on an article that the Prime Minister had found personally offensive and that 'solely because it was read to be critical of Mr Lee, however, it has resulted in this unwarranted determination against the *Review*. We can only hope the *Review's* punishment will not, as doubtless intended, still honest and independent voices in Singapore'. The editor, publishers, proprietors and printers were all held to have committed contempt for this publication. Thean J took the view that it is settled law in Singapore since *A-G v Pang Cheng Lian* [13] that any publication which alleges bias, lack of impartiality, impropriety or any wrongdoing concerning a judge in the exercise of his judicial function which has terminated is a contempt.

In January 1994 an American academic and the editor, publishers, printers and distributors of the *International Herald Tribune* were fined for contempt by the High Court in Singapore because of an article written by the former and published in the *International Herald Tribune* on 7 October 1994.[14] The offending passage did not mention Singapore but referred only to 'intolerant regimes in the region' some of which relied 'upon a compliant judiciary to bankrupt opposition politicians'. The Attorney General said that this was not, as the defendants claimed, meant to refer only to military and communist regimes but would be understood as referring to Singapore because government politicians there were known for suing opposition figures for defamation. This is an interesting, and it

11 [1978] 1 NZLR 225.
12 [1991] 2 MLJ 525.
13 [1975] 1 MLJ 69.
14 (1995) Independent, 17 and 18 January. The combined fines, over $20,000 were the highest ever in Singapore.The writer of the article had already had to resign from his job in Singapore and had returned to the United States.

is submitted, dangerous case where the scandalising nature of the publication is not apparent on its face and has to be implied in the light of other facts which it is assumed the public would know.

It should also be noted that in England and Wales an allegation of more generalised bias is frequently made against the judiciary as a whole—that of class, sex and race. The judiciary is often charged with being drawn from too narrow a section of society and therefore subconsciously biased towards the upholding of certain interests. The response to these criticisms has not been contempt actions but, on the contrary, the declared intention of the Lord Chancellor to 'recruit' judges more widely, and the training of the judiciary on sensitive matters such as race. As Murphy J said (dissenting) in *Gallagher v Durack:*[15]

> 'If all those who advocate that the courts are involved in the class struggle were to be imprisoned for criminal contempt there would not be enough gaols.'

(i) The defence of fair comment   *R v Colsey* [16] tends to suggest that even the slightest suggestion of bias will be a contempt and, despite criticisms of the decision, it has not yet been judicially disapproved. Lord Atkin's classic statement (cited earlier) as to what is permissible criticism expressly excluded imputations of improper motives. Does this mean that allegations of partiality, corruption or other improper motives are always contempts? There is a body of authority which suggests that such allegations are not necessarily a contempt if what is published can be properly classifiable as 'fair comment'.[17] The leading judgment is that of Griffith CJ in the Australian High Court decision, *R v Nicholls:* [18]

> 'I am not prepared to accede to the proposition that an imputation of want of impartiality to a judge is necessarily a contempt of court. On the contrary, I think that, if any judge of this court or of any other court were to make a public utterance of such a character as to be likely to impair the confidence of the public, or of suitors or any class of suitors in the impartiality of the court in any matter likely to be before it, any public comment on such an utterance, if it were fair comment, would, so far from being a contempt of court, be for the public benefit, and would be entitled to similar protection to that which comment upon matters of public interest is entitled under the law of libel.'

Although obiter[19] Griffith CJ's statement has been subsequently followed in Australia[20] and has been accepted as good law by the New Zealand Court of Appeal.[1] Hope JA went further in *A-G for New South Wales v Mundey* [2] saying that in addition to the defence of fair comment:

> 'it does not necessarily amount to a contempt of court to claim that a court or judge had been influenced, or too much influenced whether consciously or unconsciously,

---

15 (1983) 152 CLR 238 at 251.
16 (1931) Times, 9 May.
17 Ie, as in libel, a fair and honest opinion on a matter of public interest.
18 (1911) 12 CLR 280 at 286.
19 Because it was decided on the facts that there had been no imputation of partiality.
20 *R v Fletcher, ex p Kisch* (1935) 52 CLR 248 at 257–8; *R v Brett* [1950] VLR 226 at 229; *R v Foster, ex p Gillies* [1937] QSR 368 at 378 and *A-G for New South Wales v Mundey* [1972] 2 NSWLR 887 at 910. As the Australian Law Reform Commission (*Contempt*, Report No 35, para 416) pointed out, however, the case does not conclusively establish a formal defence of fair comment.
1 In *S-G v Radio Avon Ltd* [1978] 1 NZLR 225 at 231.
2 [1972] 2 NSWLR 887 at 910.

by some particular consideration in respect of a matter which has been determined. Such criticism is frequently made in academic journals and books, and the right cannot be limited to academics . . .'.

Whether the defence of fair comment will be recognised in England and Wales, has yet to be established[3] though Hope JA's comment might be thought to represent the de facto if not the de jure (in view of *Colsey*) position.

The defence of fair comment was assumed to be part of English law by Salmon LJ and his colleagues in their report: *The Law of Contempt as it affects Tribunals of Inquiry.*[4] It is submitted that provided the allegation of partiality is free from the taint of scurrilous abuse and can be properly considered as fair comment it ought not to amount to contempt.

Assuming there to be a defence of fair comment it would seem right to say that it is not available to publications made mala fide.[5]

(ii) Justification   To what extent is the truth of the allegation a defence? In defamation, of course, justification and fair comment are both regarded as defences. In contempt, however, it seems doubtful whether justification is a defence. In the New Zealand decision *A-G v Blomfield,*[6] for example, Williams J said that as regards admitting justification as a defence:

> 'That has never been done, and cannot be done in summary proceedings, for contempt. The court does not sit to try the conduct of the judge.'

The New Zealand Court of Appeal in *S-G v Radio Avon Ltd*[7] also seemed to doubt the existence of such a defence. In England and Wales the truth of a publication is not a defence to a charge of contempt based on the risk of prejudice to the administration of justice in the particular case and it might be thought that a similar position would be taken in respect of scandalising the court. The Australian Law Commission[8] thought that the weight of authority was against justification being a defence.

Whether justification *should* be a defence has given rise to different views. The problem, of course, is that in considering such a defence the judge would have to decide whether the courts *were* biased, corrupt or whatever. *Justice* commented in their 1959 report, *Contempt of Court:*[9]

> 'Clearly if someone wishes, in good faith, to make a charge of partiality or corruption against a judge he ought to have the opportunity of making it; but we do not consider the press to be the appropriate organ for this purpose. We consider that he should be able to do so by letter to the Lord Chancellor or his Member of Parliament without fear of punishment, and would deplore the use of the law of contempt to prevent him from doing so. The charges could then be considered either administratively in the House of Commons or the House of Lords.'

This view is not without its difficulties because the procedure for raising such a matter on the floor of Parliament means that such a question will rarely be

---

3 In *R v Griffiths, ex p A-G* [1957] 2 QB 192 at 203 Lord Goddard CJ said 'Cases of contempt by publication of matter tending to prejudice a fair trial stand in a class of their own *and are not truly analogous to cases of defamation*' (emphasis added).
4 (1969, Cmnd 4078) para 36.
5 See *S-G v Radio Avon Ltd* [1978] 1 NZLR 225 at 231.
6 (1914) 33 NZLR 545. See also *Re The Evening News* [1880] 1 NSWLR 211.
7 [1978] 1 NZLR 225 at 231.
8 Report No 35, para 421.
9 At p 15.

discussed there. Parliamentary procedure only permits debate on the conduct of judges on a substantive motion which admits of a distinct vote, and, apart from such debate, it is not permissible to cast reflections on a particular judge or on judges in general.

The Phillimore Committee, on the other hand, though aware of its ensuing difficulties recommended[10] that it should be a defence to show that the allegations are true provided the publication was for the public benefit. The Committee added, however, that in their view the public benefit requirement would be unlikely to be met unless the defendant had previously taken steps to report the matter to the proper authority. As we shall see shortly, however, the Law Commission[11] recommended that only false allegations should be subject to sanctions at all.

The Australian Law Reform Commission's view was that there *should* be a defence to the effect that the allegedly scandalising remarks, so far as they related to questions of fact, were true, or that the person making them honestly believed them to be true and was not recklessly indifferent as to truth or falsity. Evidence that the accused knew the remarks to be false, or was recklessly indifferent as to truth or falsity, would nullify the defence.[12]

(c) Lowering the repute of the court or judge

Although scandalising the court is more immediately associated with scurrilous abuse and imputations of bias etc there seems a wider ambit to the offence. In the Canadian case, *R v United Fisherman and Allied Workers Union*,[13] the British Columbia Court of Appeal upheld a contempt conviction against a trade union for publicly initiating a vote on whether the union should obey a court order. The court emphasised that the contempt involved was not for breaking the injunction but for bringing the court and its process into contempt by suggesting that it was a matter of choice as to whether its orders should be obeyed.

The recent Australian case *Fitzgibbon v Barker*[14] can also be categorised under this head although in its judgment the court relied on cases such as *R v Dunbabin, ex p Williams, Gallagher v Durack* and *A-G (NSW) v Mundey* which have been dealt with above under different headings. A contempt was held to have been committed by a newspaper which published a report of demonstrators protesting that a man had been imprisoned for wanting to see his children. In fact he had a long history of breaching orders prohibiting him from molesting, intimidating or harassing his wife. The newspaper was, however, merely reporting the demonstration and the idea that a newspaper may be in contempt for faithfully reporting factual events without pointing out the mistaken ideas of those involved is an alarming one. The Family Court of Australia held that the publication scandalised the court because it was a gross distortion of the case and would give the public the erroneous impression that the courts jailed fathers for no good reason at all, which was quite different from a publication criticising

---

10 Paras 165–167.
11 Offences Relating to Interference with the Courts of Justice (1979) Law Com No 96, paras 3.64–3.70
12 Report No 35, para 458. See also the Irish Law Reform Commission proposals on Contempt, July 1991, pp 281–286.
13 (1968) 65 DLR (2d) 579. See also Chaudhary 'Contempt of the Trinidad and Tobago Industrial Court' (1981) 30 ICLQ 260.
14 (1992) 111 FLR 191.

what is seen to be a bad or unworkable law. It scandalised the court, therefore, because it impaired the public's confidence in the court's judgments.

Whether the English courts will be similarly disposed to find a contempt on such broad grounds as *United Fishermen and Allied Workers Union* remains to be seen though in one instance a judge is said to have warned the BBC not to televise a demonstration outside a court on the basis that it would be calculated to lower the court's repute. In the event the BBC did televise the event but no action was taken. This is *Fitzgibbon v Barker* country and does, it is submitted, raise serious concern about censorship of the news.

C The mens rea

1 The common law position

There is disagreement among common law jurisdictions as to whether the offence of scandalising the court requires mens rea in the sense of intending to lower the repute of a judge or court. The orthodox view, it is suggested, is that there is no such requirement there being no distinction between publications scandalising the court and those interfering with the course of justice in the particular case, where it seems well established that no intention to interfere is required.

That no such intent is required under English common law was made clear by Lord Hewart CJ in *R v Editor of New Statesman, ex p DPP*.[15] The article was held to have 'imputed unfairness and lack of impartiality to a judge in the discharge of his judicial duties and Lord Hewart CJ commented:[16]

> 'If they had come to the conclusion that that was intended by the writer who was also the editor, the only proper course would have been to commit him to prison for contempt. But it was right to look at the circumstances . . . the court accepted the explanation and the apology, and abstained from committing the respondent.'

The respondent was held guilty of contempt although there was no intent to 'scandalise'. The lack of such intention merely disposed the court to impose no penalty other than the payment of costs.

A similar position obtains in Australia as laid down by *A-G New South Wales v Mundey*[17] where Hope JA thought that whether publications constituted contempt must be determined by reference to their inherent tendency to interfere with the course of justice; and in New Zealand as confirmed by the Court of Appeal decision in *S-G v Radio Avon Ltd*.[18]

A different view, however is taken in South Africa. *S v Van Niekerk*[19] concerned a prosecution against a legal academic for an article he wrote for the *South African Law Journal* in which he imputed, albeit in sober and responsible language, racial bias to South African judges. The prosecution failed because in Claasen J's view:[20]

---

15 (1928) 44 TLR 301.
16 Ibid at 303.
17 [1972] 2 NSWLR 887 at 911–2
18 [1978] 1 NZLR 225 at 232–4.
19 1970 (3) SA 655 (T).
20 *Ibid* at 657. See also *S v Kaakunga* 1978 (1) SA 1190 and *S v Gibson* 1979 (4) SA 115.

'I think that before a conviction can result the act complained of must not only be wilful and calculated to bring into contempt but must also be made with the intention of bringing the judges in their judicial capacity into contempt or of casting suspicion on the administration of justice. For this type of intention it is sufficient if the accused subjectively foresaw the possibility of his act being in contempt of court and he was reckless as to the result. . . . Subjective foresight, like any other factual issue, may be proved by inference.'

In Canada, Hugessen ACJ said in *Re Ouellet* [1] that 'mens rea' is clearly an important element in the offence. Some support for this view might also be derived from Macfarlane J's comments in *R v Fotheringham and Sun Publishing Co Ltd* [2] that the essential elements of the offence are that the article:

'(a) was calculated or tended to impute proper motives to those taking part in the administration of justice; (b) *was written in malice, and not in good faith*; and (c) constituted an attempt to impair the administration of justice' (emphasis added).

2   The position after the Contempt of Court Act 1981

It has been argued[3] that since the passing of the Contempt of Court Act 1981 mens rea is required in this form of contempt. The basis of the argument is that s 1 in defining the 'strict liability rule' is by implication providing that those kinds of contempt that involve interfering with the due course of justice as a continuing process require a mens rea.[4]

However, the better view is that the 'strict liability rule' under the 1981 Act leaves untouched the common law relating to publications interfering with the due course of justice as a continuing process.

D   Criticisms of the law and proposals for reform

1   Two schools of thought [5]

Perhaps more than any other branch of contempt law scandalising the court is most open to question. The rationale of the offence, namely, the undermining of

---

1 (1976) 67 DLR (3d) 73 at 92, not referred to on appeal (1976) 72 DLR (3d) 95.
2 (1970) 11 DLR (3d) 353 at 360.
3 See Aldridge and Eady, *The Law of Contempt* (1982, Sweet and Maxwell) paras 2-01 to 2-01d, 2.07 and 2.72. Some support for this unconvincing argument might be drawn from Eveleigh LJ's comment in *Z Ltd v A-Z and AA-LL* [1982] QB 558, [1982] 1 All ER 556 at 567: 'It does not seem to me to be in the public interest that a person with no wrongful intent should be brought before the court, let alone be punished, unless there is some overriding public interest to the contrary. Recognition for this argument is to be found in the Contempt of Court Act 1981 which limits the scope of strict liability in relation to contempt of court as tending to interfere with the course of justice in particular legal proceedings.' Walker, 'Scandalising in the Eighties' (1985) 101 LQR 359, 369–370 takes the view of the present authors.
4 Ie the Act in general and s 1 in particular confines strict liability in *all* cases of contempt to the instances caught by s 2.
5 The ensuing text is based in part on the excellent exposition of the schools of thought by the Canadian Law Reform Commission in their 1977 Working Paper No 20 on Contempt of Court, pp 31–35. See also the Phillimore Report at para 162 and the Australian Law Commission Report No 35, paras 409–461. There is a large body of (mainly highly critical) literature about scandalising, see in particular Walker, 'Scandalising in the Eighties' (1985) 101 LQR 359.

public confidence in the administration of justice seems highly speculative and some say that it is too vague a principle to justify imposing restrictions upon freedom of speech. In any event it could be argued that it is hardly likely that the public of today is so naive that it will lose confidence in the administration of justice as a result of insults or abuses heaped upon a judge. It might also be wondered why the system of justice is apparently so unsure of itself that it has to suppress attacks even if they are unfounded or malicious. Ought not the public be the final judge of such criticism without resorting to a seemingly self-serving process that seems to turn the judicial system into both judge and plaintiff? As one Australian judge put it:[6]

> 'There is no more reason why the acts of courts should not be trenchantly criticised than the acts of public institutions, including parliaments. The truth is of course that public institutions in a free society must stand upon their own merits: they cannot be propped up if their conduct does not command respect and confidence of a community; if their conduct justifies the respect and confidence of a community they do not need the protection of special rules to shield them from criticism.'

Another criticism of the offence of scandalising the court is that it apparently vests arbitrary powers in the judiciary to suppress criticisms of themselves. As the Canadian Law Reform Commission said, it is the form of contempt that has the greatest potential for arbitrary use by the courts. In any event it might be asked why special protection should be given to members of the judiciary when it is not given to important members of society such as politicians, administrators and public servants. If laws such as that of defamation are thought adequate protection for everyone else why not for the judiciary?

The foregoing criticisms can be met by the arguments that (a) publications, particularly those which impute improper or corrupt judicial conduct, can realistically be said to create a real risk of impairing public confidence in the administration of justice; (b) defamation is an inadequate way of protecting such a public interest because it is concerned with *personal* reputations and anyway would not apply to attacks made upon an unspecified group of judges. In any event such actions might unduly prolong the debate and so prejudice the administration of justice since until the matter is resolved the judge will be in an awkward position; (c) unlike other public figures, judges have no other proper forum in which to reply to criticisms because they cannnot debate the issue in public without destroying their appearance of impartiality. In fact this last point has lost much of its force, in England at least, where judges have become more willing to engage in public debate. For example three present or recently retired judges wrote to *The Times* in 1991 in answer to a characteristic blast of criticism from its columnist Bernard Levin[7] and in 1993 Lord Taylor CJ appeared on the BBC programme *Question Time*.[8] The judiciary seems to be far more willing than previously to indulge in public relations. It is only the Queen who can never answer back.

---

6 Hope JA, in *A-G for New South Wales* v *Mundey* [1972] 2 NSWLR 887 at 908.
7 See Times, 7 February 1991, p 10 and 18 February 1991, p 13; the correspondents were Rougier J, Sir John Stephenson and Sir Michael Davies.
8 28 October 1993.

2   Reform proposals

It was because of these latter considerations that bodies such as the Phillimore Committee,[9] the English Law Commission,[10] the Australian Law Reform Commission,[11] and the Canadian Law Reform Commission[12] all recommended that the offence be retained in some form. The latter body's proposals[13] would most nearly preserve the law as it currently exists in jurisdictions other, ironically, than Canada.[14] The Canadian proposal[15] was that there should be a new offence known as an 'affront to judicial authority[16] which would be committed through conduct calculated to insult the court or attacks upon the independence, impartiality or integrity of a court or of the judiciary. The offence would still be triable summarily,[17] though not by the judge subject to attack.[18] In arriving at these recommendations there was much debate as to whether to allow a defendant to plead and prove the truth of the facts of a defence. The Commission finally decided[19] against this partly because such a defence would leave the way open to 'judicial guerilla warfare' since it would allow people to make charges simply to discredit the judicial system and thereby gain 'an ideal platform for waging their campaigns—all at minimal risk.'

The English bodies have proposed a much more limited role for scandalising the court. Both the Phillimore Committee[20] and the Law Commission[1] consider that a new separate criminal offence to cover this area is more appropriate than leaving it to be dealt with by the law of contempt, ie the summary procedure cannot be justified since there is usually no particular urgency to prosecute. The Phillimore Committee thought[2] that the new offence should be confined to imputations of improper or corrupt judicial conduct published with the intention of impairing confidence in the administration of justice and that it should be a defence to show that the allegations are true and the public action is for the public benefit. The Law Commission, however, thought the scope of the proposed offence too wide with the inclusion of 'improper' conduct and also that the proposed mens rea was difficult to apply.[3] They propose[4] that the offence be confined to publications or distribution of false statements alleging that a court or judge is corrupt in the performance of its or his functions and 'at the time when he [the accused] publishes or distributes it he intends it to be taken as true but knows it to be false or is reckless whether it is false . . .'. Such prosecutions which

---

9 1974, Cmnd 5794.
10 Law Com No 96 (1979): *Offences Relating to Interference With The Course of Justice*. See also the Working Paper No 62 (1975).
11 Report No 35 (1987).
12 Report No 17: *Contempt of Court* (1982). See also the Working Paper No 20 (1977).
13 Contained in the final report on Contempt of Court No 17 (1982) pp 24–27 and 52–54.
14 Where the effect of the Ontario Court of Appeal decision in *R v Kopyto* (1987) 47 DLR (4th) 213 (discussed at p 339) is that in that jurisdiction at least the common law offence no longer applies.
15 See cl 3 of the proposed draft insertion in Part III of the Criminal Code.
16 The new label was thought to be more accurate than the traditional one.
17 Under cl 6, see p 57 of the Final Report.
18 As explained at p 27 of the Final Report.
19 See pp 25–26 of the Final Report.
20 See para 163.
 1 See para 3.64.
 2 See paras 163, 164.
 3 See paras 3.67 and 3.66 respectively.
 4 See cl 13 of their draft Administration of Justice (Offences) Bill and para 3.70.

could only be instituted by or with the Attorney General's consent[5] would be triable either summarily or upon indictment and subject to a maximum punishment of two years.[6] These proposals would virtually remove the threat of prosecution. The Law Commission perhaps underestimates the difficulties of allowing truthful allegations of corruption and perhaps ignores the beneficial preventative function of the current law.

The Australian Law Reform Commission too, advocated a more limited version of scandalising. It concluded[7] that it should be an offence to publish an allegation imputing misconduct to a judge or magistrate in circumstances where the publication is likely to cause serious harm to the reputation of the judge or magistrate in his or her official capacity. The offence should be indictable and only triable summarily with the consent of all concerned. The Commission suggested three defences—fair, accurate and reasonably contemporaneous reporting of legal proceedings or of parliamentary proceedings, and truth or honest and reasonable belief in the truth of the allegations.

The Irish Law Reform Commission[8] recommended that abuse of the judiciary, even if scurrilous, should not be a contempt. It recommended that it should still be contempt to impute corrupt conduct to a judge or court, although the truth of the communication should render it lawful, and that it should also constitute contempt by scandalising to publish to the public a false or misleading account of legal proceedings.

3　*Commentary*

There is a natural tendency to look with suspicion upon a law which arose from the efforts of the political establishment to silence its critics and which can punish those who transgress it by speaking out freely with summary trial and imprisonment. In England and Wales there has been little pressure in recent times to reform this branch of contempt law because of the lack of prosecutions. Such a view, however, overlooks the 'chilling' effect that the *potential* application of the law has. In the past this effect has been considerable[9] although in 1974 the Phillimore Committee commented:[10]

> 'There is not much evidence that the press is unduly inhibited by this aspect of the law.'

Certainly, the amount of scathing comment on the judiciary, and individual members of it, that has been allowed to pass unchallenged since the Phillimore Committee made that remark does suggest that at present the law does not chill very coldly. Nevertheless the fact that English judges, albeit sitting in the Privy

5　See Sch I, Part II, para 6 of the draft Bill.
6　See Sch I, Part I, para 5 of the draft Bill. It seems wrong to allow the offence to be tried summarily by magistrates.
7　Para 460, and see the Discussion Paper DP 26: *Contempt and the Media* (1986) para 479.
8　Consultation Paper of Contempt of Court, July 1991, p 280.
9　Mr Cecil King, the proprietor of the *Daily Mirror*, is once reported as saying 'The actual operation of the rules against contempt . . . has meant that in recent years no serious criticism of judicial proceedings above the level of magistrates' courts has been thought possible. In fact there has been little or no such criticism, though a great deal from time to time would have been in the public interest' (quoted in Street, *Freedom, the Individual and the Law* (1963) p 171).
10　At para 160, citing in particular the comments made with respect to the former National Industrial Relations Court.

Council,[11] are prepared still to countenance the existence of the offence means that, in theory at least, the threat of prosecution still hangs over publishers. An action could be brought at any time, although it would itself no doubt attract enormous criticism. It can also be argued that the lack of prosecutions is at least suggestive of a need to reform the law to bring it into line with the de facto practice rather than justifying leaving the law as it is.

It is in Canada, where the offence had shown more signs of life in modern times, that the compatibility of scandalising with democratic freedoms has been most fully analysed. When the Ontario Court of Appeal held the offence up to the light of the Charter the majority concluded that, at least as it is known to the common law, it is no longer supportable.[12]

It is ironic that while this has gone on in Canada, the Australian courts, in a society superficially not so different from that of Canada, but without the disciplining effect of the Charter, have prosecuted scandalising actions which do not seem, on their face, to present the threat of rocking society to its foundations.[13]

The dangers of the common law scandalising offence are still present in any jurisdiction which still recognises it and it can be seen that a government with authoritarian tendencies can turn it on its critics far too readily for comfort. The whole idea that criticism of the judiciary or the courts can be silenced in such a peremptory manner is disturbing. On the other hand, opposition to the retention of the offence is based on the assumption that the press and the other media are on the side of the angels. We are no longer living in a world of the pamphleteer, of the *North Briton* and the *Letters of Junius* but in a world of powerful multinational media empires where media ownership is concentrated into the hands of interests which have their own agendas. In such a world it may, perhaps, be tempting to retain the old powers against the day when there are attacks on the courts which even libertarians might wish to repel.

One of the specific problems with the present law is its uncertainty and arbitrariness and what should certainly be done is to draw the parameters of the offence more tightly. It should certainly only be used in the gravest of situations. Charging disgruntled litigants[14] with contempt because of wild allegations of bias made while they are trying to come to terms with their defeat is totally unacceptable, as is punishing newspapers for reporting factual events such as demonstrations.

II PUBLICATION OF A JURY'S DELIBERATIONS

A The common law position

Although jurors are commonly entreated not to disclose what has happened in the jury room even after the conclusion of proceedings the precise extent of the obligation at common law, if any, to respect the confidentiality of jurors' deliberations is a matter of some doubt. In England it was suggested in *Ellis v Deheer* [15] that publication of an account of what took place in the jury room might

---

11 *Badry v DPP of Mauritius* [1982] 3 All ER 973, [1983] 2 WLR 161 and *Chokolingo v A-G of Trinidad and Tobago* [1981] 1 All ER 244, [1981] 1 WLR 106.
12 *R v Kopyto* (1987) 47 DLR (4th) 213.
13 *Gallagher v Durack* (1983) 152 CLR 238 and *Fitzgibbon v Barker* (1992) 111 FLR 191.
14 Or their equally disgruntled lawyers, as in *R v Kopyto* (1987) 47 DLR (4th) 213.
15 [1922] 2 KB 113 at 118 per Bankes LJ cited in *A-G v New Statesman and Nation Publishing Co Ltd* [1981] QB 1 at 9, [1980] 1 All ER 644 at 648.

be treated as a contempt but in the Australian case *Re Matthews and Ford* [16] the Full Court of Victoria thought it significant that the point was not actually decided.[17] In *Re Matthews and Ford*, however, the court did deplore the publication of disclosures by jurors, saying that it would 'set in train a process whereby the institution of trial by jury may be eroded and ultimately destroyed'.[18] There is also unreported authority[19] for saying that it could be a contempt to approach jurors to discover what had influenced them when reaching their verdict. On the other hand, in *Re Donovan's Application* Barry J said in the Victoria Supreme Court:

> 'No constraint can be placed upon a juror who wishes to discuss experiences at the trial and views he formed in the deliberations which took place in the jury room.'[20]

In Canada it has been said[1] that a juror may be guilty of contempt for revealing confidences as could any person pressing a juror to make such disclosures. A member of a firm of lawyers was held to be in contempt for attempting to obtain from a juror who had been discharged what the other jurors thought about the case.[2]

The leading English decision in this area is *A-G v New Statesman and Nation Publishing Co Ltd*.[3] The defendant magazine was prosecuted for publishing an unpaid for and unsolicited account by an unnamed juror of significant parts of the jury's deliberations in the course of arriving at their not guilty verdicts in the trial of Jeremy Thorpe and others on a conspiracy to murder charge. In the words of the Divisional Court the article recorded the juror as saying inter alia:

> 'that all the jury were agreed that the accused were guilty of a conspiracy of some kind, that 11 of them, after little more than an hour's deliberation on the first day, agreed that it was not proved that there had been a conspiracy to murder and that, on a charge of incitement to murder, the jury could not accept the uncorroborated word of a prosecution witness who had agreed to accept money from a newspaper, the amount to be increased in the event of a conviction.'

The prosecution argued that the publication amounted to contempt by constituting an interference with the due administration of justice as a continuing process in that disclosure of what happened in the jury room tended (a) to imperil the finality of jury verdicts and so diminish public confidence in the general correctness and propriety of such verdicts, and (b) to affect adversely the attitude of future jurors and the quality of their deliberations.

Although the Divisional Court seemed disposed to accept the prosecution's arguments of principle it did not agree that the mere publication of jurors'

---

16 [1973] VR 199 at 213.
17 Bankes LJ said at 118 that he had seen with outrage and disgust the publication in a newspaper of a statement by a juror as to what had taken place in the jury room but 'I do not think it necessary to express any opinion as to whether such a publication amounts to contempt of court.'
18 Ibid at 213. See the similar remarks by the English Court of Appeal in *R v Armstrong* [1922] 2 KB 555 at 568.
19 *Re A Solicitor, ex p Hartstein* (unreported, 4 June 1971) see (1972) 46 ALJ 367.
20 [1957] VR 333 at 337, although he added that that was 'vastly different from the state of affairs which arises when legal representatives of the prisoner take it upon themselves to question jurors'.
1 Haines J in *R v Dyson* [1972] 1 OR 744 at 751 and 753 (Ont HC).
2 *R v Papineau* (1981) 58 CCC (2d) 72 (Quebec Sup Ct). Under the Canadian Criminal Code, RSC 1985, s 649 it is an offence, punishable on summary conviction, for a juror to disclose information about the proceedings of the jury when it was absent from the courtroom.
3 [1981] QB 1, [1980] 1 All ER 644.

deliberations necessarily had such an effect.[4] In the court's view[5] each case had to be judged in the light of the circumstances in which the publication took place, and, on the facts of the case before it, held that no contempt had been committed. The court refused to lay down any further guidelines as to what might or might not amount to contempt, and from this point of view the decision is not helpful. Nevertheless, bearing in mind the facts of the case and remarks of the court the following propositions seem to flow from the decision:[6] (a) it is not a contempt per se to publish an account of a jury's deliberations in an identified case (a fortiori if the case is not identified), and (b) the finality of the verdict is not imperilled merely by saying that the jury thought the accused guilty of something else but not of the offence charged. The position might be otherwise if particular jurors are identified and if the juror's account is solicited and/or paid for. As we shall see, the position in England has now been changed by statute. Whether other jurisdictions will be disposed to follow the *New Statesman* case remains to be seen. As a matter of policy it is difficult to find the right decision, for while a blanket prohibition against disclosures might seem too draconian, banning, for example, bona fide research, the permissibility of some disclosures does potentially open the door to possible harassment of jurors and by not preserving the absolute confidence of the deliberation might inhibit jurors expressing their views in the jury room. It is submitted, however, that the *New Statesman* decision leaned too far in favour of publication. It seems wrong to permit publications identifying the particular proceedings and it might also be thought that on the facts doubt was cast in broad terms on the 'innocence' of the accused.

B   The position under the Contempt of Court Act 1981

1   *The background to and provisions of s 8*

The decision in the *New Statesman* case prompted the Government to include provisions dealing with the point in the Contempt Bill. It was originally intended to prohibit publication of jury deliberations save where the particular proceedings and individual jurors could not be identified. However, this was thought by some to be unsatisfactory because it still left the door open to jurors being harassed or pressurised into giving information, which in turn could undermine public confidence in juries and could even put at risk the finality of verdicts. In a well-orchestrated campaign led by Lords Hutchinson and Wigoder a last minute amendment was passed by the Lords banning in effect all communications by or with jurors. Although neither the Lord Chancellor or Attorney General supported the 'draconian' amendment the government decided not to oppose it when the Bill returned to the Commons.

By s 8(1) it is a contempt:

> 'to obtain, disclose, or solicit any particulars of statements made, opinions expressed, arguments advanced or votes cast by members of a jury in the course of their deliberations in any legal proceedings.'

By s 8(2), however, the section does not apply to any disclosure of any particulars:

4 Ibid at 10E; 649C–D.
5 Ibid at 10F; 649F–G.
6 See also [1980] Crim LR 236–8.

'(a)   in the proceedings in question for the purpose of enabling the jury to arrive at their verdict or in connection with the delivery of that verdict, or

(b)   in evidence in any subsequent proceedings for an offence alleged to have been committed in relation to the jury in the first mentioned proceedings, or to the publication of any particulars so disclosed.'

By s 8(3), save in Scotland, prosecutions for s 8 offences can only be instituted by or with the Attorney General's consent or on the motion of a court having jurisdiction to deal with it.

2   The interpretation and application of s 8

(a)   Obtain, disclose or solicit

The three things forbidden by s 8 in respect of the jury's deliberations are obtaining, disclosing and soliciting. Of these the first and third relate to the actions of third parties who seek information about the deliberations while the second (disclosing) covers both the actions of the jurors themselves and of third parties who pass on what they have learned from the jurors.[7]

The ordinary meaning of 'solicit' would seem wide enough to cover *attempts* to obtain information about jury deliberations. However, it is submitted that s 8(1) only applies to *actively* obtaining information and does not cover a person who is the passive recipient of the unsolicited confidences of a juror. The necessity of the Attorney General's involvement in proceedings pursuant to s 8(3) would, anyway, be a safeguard against prosecution in such a situation.

Section 8 does not say from whom the information about the deliberations has to be obtained but it seems that it is equally an offence under s 8 to obtain it from a third party rather than directly from the juror. The point was not considered in *A-G v Associated Newspapers Ltd* [8] where the newspaper obtained the information from a third party for there the argument concerned the question of whether the newspaper was guilty of disclosure.

Obtaining or soliciting information from jurors may also involve the common law contempt of interfering with jurors. In *A-G v Judd* [9] the defendant, who had been convicted of unlawful harassment, asked a juror whom he recognised at a car boot sale how the jury had voted and made various comments about hoping her conscience would go with her to the grave, looking out for her at car boot sales and suggesting she wrote to the judge to say she had made a mistake. The defendant's behaviour in general was held to constitute a common law contempt of interfering with jurors[10] but the specific question about the jury votes was a breach of s 8.

The meaning of 'disclose' was considered by the House of Lords in *A-G v Associated Newspapers Ltd* [11] which involved the publication of revelations by jurors about their deliberations in the 'Blue Arrow' serious fraud trial.[12] That trial

---

7   *A-G v Associated Newspapers Ltd* [1994] 2 AC 238, [1994] 1 All ER 556.
8   [1994] 2 AC 238, [1994] 1 All ER 556.
9   [1995] COD 15. For interfering with jurors, see Ch 11, p 423. There is now also a stautory offence of intimidating jurors in concluded proceedings—s 51(2) of the Criminal Justice and Public Order Act 1994. See Ch 11.
10   See Ch 11.
11   [1994] 2 AC 238, [1994] 1 All ER 556.
12   *R v NatWest Bank* (unreported).

lasted a year[13] but five months later the Court of Appeal allowed the appeals of the convicted defendants on the grounds that there was a material irregularity in the summing up.[14] Two weeks after the original trial an advertisement in the London *Evening Standard* offered a reward to the jurors in the Blue Arrow trial if they contacted a box number because an American researcher was seeking data for a comparative study. As a result various of the jurors came forward or were contacted. Ten days before the Court of Appeal decision the *Mail on Sunday* published an article about the trial which purported to reveal how the jury had reached their verdicts.[15]

When charged with contempt for this publication the *Mail on Sunday* contended that it was not guilty of an offence because s 8 covers only the initial disclosure of information *by a juror* to another person and not further revelations by that person to another person in his turn. The paper argued that there was a distinction between disclosure and publication and that once the juror had disclosed the information the newspaper's dissemination of it amounted to a publication but not to a disclosure within s 8.

Rejecting this argument, the House of Lords upheld the Divisional Court's finding[16] that the newspaper was guilty of contempt in that their actions did amount to 'disclosure' within s 8. Their Lordships thought that to confine 'disclosure' to the initial revelation by the juror only would be to restrict the natural meaning and effect of the word in a way which was not justified by anything in either s 8 or the other provisions of the Act. Lord Lowry said:[17]

> 'There is no conflict or contrast between publication and disclosure. The latter activity has many manifestations and publication is one of them. To disclose is to expose to view, make known or reveal and in its ordinary meaning the word aptly describes *both* the revelation by jurors of their deliberations *and* further disclosure by publication in a newspaper of the same deliberations, provided always—and this will raise a question of fact—that the publication amounts to *disclosure* and is not a mere republication of known facts.'

The distinction made by Lord Lowry between publication which is to be equated with disclosure, and republication which is not, may be a difficult one to apply in practice. It depends what is meant by known facts. Known to whom? It can be argued that disclosure in a specialist research paper, for example, would not prevent repetition in a mass circulation newspaper from being publication. However, the position once the latter has published the material is more problematic. If the *Mail on Sunday* publishes the material can the daily papers on the following Monday morning repeat it with impunity? Lord Lowry's 'question of fact' surely cannot relate to how the readerships of different newspapers overlap. Saying that the readers of the *Financial Times* would not be familiar with the contents of the *Mail on Sunday* whereas those of the *Daily Mail* would be, and that therefore only the *Financial Times* can be guilty of contempt under s 8, would reduce the law to an absurdity. If there is a distinction between disclosure and republication it must relate to some concept of whether the information has

13   From 11 February 1991 to 14 February 1992.
14   Because the trial judge had summed up on only one issue.
15   This included the thoughts of some of the jurors on the evidence, one juror's opinion that another had understood nothing of the case but agreed with the verdict because he wanted to go home, and accounts of how some jurors had been persuaded to change their minds or had their reluctance to convict overcome.
16   [1993] 2 All ER 535.
17   [1994] 2 AC 238 at 255.

entered the public domain. Since information about jury deliberations can only be revealed through the commission of a criminal contempt the courts should be slow to hold that it is in the public domain. Otherwise the one media outlet which is the first to publish will be the scapegoat for the others which follow. Of course, if later publishers obtain the information otherwise than by reading the first publication they may infringe s 8 by 'obtaining' or 'soliciting' rather than by 'disclosing'.

Lord Lowry's view was that if an item has been published in a newspaper it has become a matter of public knowledge.[18] This comment was made, however, in answer to the argument that a wide interpretation of 'disclose' would mean that a person who read the information in the paper and communicated what he had read to his neighbour would be guilty of contempt. Lord Lowry said that this was to confuse disclosure with republication. There is a sensible distinction to be made, however, between the conversations of private individuals about what they have read in the press and the publication of that material by the media to the world at large.

These problems with s 8 arise from the fact that the word 'publication' does not appear in the section: 'disclosure', with its meaning of making known or revealing, is an inadequate substitute. *If* it is desirable to prohibit the publication of matters to do with jury deliberations (and there are persuasive arguments for saying that it is not[19]) then *any* publication should be prohibited. The safeguard against the prosecution of individuals for private conversations concerning matters of which they have read elsewhere is the need for the involvement of the Attorney General in prosecutions which is provided in s 8(3). There is, for example, no record of prosecutions under s 8 of jurors who have told their spouses about the deliberations although technically such communications would appear to be covered by 'disclose'.

As is seen from the above, quite apart from the objections which can be made against the principle of s 8, the section is unhappily worded. A further peculiarity is that since 'disclose' can only relate what *actually* happened, people who publish lies about what happened during the deliberations do not appear to commit an offence under s 8.[20]

Section 8 is not temporally limited. It is an offence to make the prohibited disclosures however long ago the events occurred. The publication of a centenarian's reminiscences about the deliberations of the jury he served on in his 20s would be an offence, although one would not expect the Attorney General to prosecute. More relevant, however, would be the recollections of jurors of trials decades ago when there is a move to reopen the case.[1]

(b)   In the course of their deliberations

It is a popular misconception that s 8 prohibits the disclosure etc of *any* comment by a juror about the trial. In fact, the prohibition in s 8 is quite narrow in scope and covers only details about the jury deliberations themselves. Jurors may

18   Ibid at 259.
19   See p 000.
20   It could possibly constitute contempt by scandalising. The Irish Law Reform Commission, pp 278–279 recommended that publishing a false or misleading account of legal proceedings should be capable of constituting contempt by scandalising, see p 363.
1   As in the case of Timothy Evans, who was hanged in 1952.

express opinions, which the media can publish freely, about what they thought about the conduct of the trial, the judge, counsel, the sentence—anything, in fact except what was said or done in the course of their deliberations. It appears that a juror can even say what they themself thought of a particular piece of evidence so long as this does not relate to what they said in the jury-room or the way in which they voted.[2]

What is meant by 'in the course of their deliberations' was considered by the Court of Appeal in *R v Young*.[3] The defendant appealed against his conviction for murder on the grounds that there had been a material irregularity in the course of the trial. The jury had retired to consider their verdict and when they were unable to reach a decision that day they were accommodated overnight in a Brighton hotel. Back in court the following day they returned a unanimous guilty verdict. Some days later one of the jurors went to a solicitor and said that during the night in the hotel four (other) jurors had met in the room of one of them and conducted a seance with an ouija board. They apparently succeeding in contacting one of the victims and asked him, inter alia, 'Who killed you?' The glass spelt out the name of the defendant and went on to make various other statements adverse to the defendant in reply to questions about matters such as motive, concluding with 'Vote guilty tomorrow'. Other jurors were told about this by those present at the seance when they met at breakfast the next morning.

The Court of Appeal held that it was not precluded from enquiring into these events by s 8(1) because once the jury had been sent to the hotel it was no longer 'deliberating' within the meaning of the section. The Court relied on the Oxford English Dictionary definition of 'deliberation' as including 'consideration with a view to a decision', 'weighing . . . in the mind', 'careful consideration' etc and concluded that the jury was sent to the hotel precisely so that they could have a break from their deliberations. It was absurd to suggest that jurors were in the course of their deliberations while they were in separate hotel rooms. The court also took into account that the trial judge had given the usual instruction to the jury that they should not deliberate at the hotel.[4] As a result the court held that it was entitled to enquire about what happened in the hotel but not what happened the following day in the jury room. It could not enquire, therefore, about whether the seance influenced the deliberations but had to conclude that there was a real danger that some of the jurors may have been influenced by it. A retrial was ordered.[5]

---

2   The foreman of the jury which in 1978 convicted four men of the murder of Carl Bridgewater has supported the campaign for their release. In June 1992 he wrote to the Home Secretary saying that the confession of one of the defendants decisively influenced his judgment in respect of the others. He has also said this in the press and on television. No contempt action has been brought against him.

3   [1995] QB 324.

4   See Appendix 5B to the *Crown Court Manual* which deals with guidelines for overnight stays by juries in hotels.

5   Lord Taylor CJ said at [1995] QB 324 at 333 'Although many, perhaps most, people would regard attempts to communicate with the dead as futile, there can be no doubt that the four jurors were going through the motions of asking questions to that end and apparently receiving answers. It seems to us that what matters is not whether the answers were truly from the deceased, but whether the jurors believed them to be so or whether they may have been influenced. . .'. Wisely, perhaps, he did not address the issue that, if the answers were *not* from the deceased or some other supernatural agency, one of the jurors may have been manipulating the seance in a way highly prejudicial to the defendant.

(c)   Particulars of statements made, opinions expressed, arguments advanced or votes cast by members of a jury

As noted above, s 8 applies only to revelations about the jury's deliberations. There are, however, some matters arising during the period of deliberation about which enquiries may properly be made. In *R v McCluskey* [6] the Court of Appeal said that enquiries about whether a juror had used a mobile phone in the jury room did not offend s 8. It did, however, recommend that in view of the threats to the secrecy of the jury room that *any* enquiry about what happens there poses, investigations about any alleged irregularities should be embarked upon only with the consent of the Court of Appeal. In *R v Mickleburgh* [7] allegations were made by the foreman of the jury to the defendant, 18 months after the guilty verdict, about prejudicial comments made by an usher to the jury. The defendant appealed against his conviction on the grounds of a material irregularity. The Court of Appeal said that while statements obtained from the foreman about the alleged remarks were not a breach of s 8, statements which purported to give information about the reactions of the members of the jury did breach it. The court reiterated what was said in *McCluskey* about the extreme danger of taking statements from jurors and emphasised that the consent of the Court of Appeal should always be obtained. The Court of Appeal is not, however, able to authorise the taking of a statement which would entail disclosure of any of the matters mentioned in s 8.

The reference in s 8(1) to 'votes cast by members of a jury' needs some examination. The final collective 'vote' of a jury in a guilty verdict is known in that it is declared either to be unanimous or to be by a majority, with the number agreeing on a conviction and those dissenting being made known.[8] Where there is an acquittal, however, s 8(1) forbids disclosure of whether the decision was in fact a majority one. The words also cover any interim vote taken by the jurors in the course of their deliberations.[9]

(d)   Who can commit an offence under s 8

Anybody who obtains, discloses or solicits the secrets of the jury's deliberations breaches s 8. As is apparent from *Young*, *McCluskey*, and *Mickleburgh* this includes the courts themselves. In *Young* the Court of Appeal rejected the argument that it was not bound by s 8(1) and should, as a matter of public policy, be able to look into any irregularities alleged to have occurred in the jury room. The court said that s 8(1) is expressed in the widest terms and contains no exceptions. It also pointed out that if the courts themselves were not bound by s 8(1), s 8(2)(a) would be unnecessary. That paragraph allows the court to receive notes from the jury, to ask them if they require help on any point and to ask how many agreed and dissented when a majority verdict is returned. Section 8(2)(b) allows a court to receive evidence in subsequent proceedings over possible offences relating to the jury (such as bribery or intimidation).

---

6   (1993) 98 Cr App Rep 216.
7   [1995] 1 Cr App Rep 297.
8   See *R v Pigg* [1983] 1 All ER 56.
9   For a further discussion of this point see Joseph Jaconelli, 'Some thoughts on jury secrecy' (1990) Legal Studies 91.

These cases demonstrate that s 8 reinforces the long-standing principle that the court cannot enquire into the deliberations of the jury. The courts have resolutely refused to consider after the verdict what took place between the jurors during their deliberations or how they reached their verdict or to entertain appeals based on these matters.[10] This reinforcement is, however, an incidental side-effect of s 8. The section was primarily intended, as explained above, to prevent revelations of jury deliberations being made to the media. It is submitted that issues of how alleged irregularities in proceedings are dealt with and on what grounds appeals can be brought should be dealt with by rules of criminal procedure[11] specifically addressed to those important issues. Faced, for example, with the allegations of the extraordinary goings-on in *Young* it does not seem sensible that the court had to be concerned about committing contempt of court. Whether or not the Court of Appeal could consider information, for example, that a jury had conducted a seance to commune with the victim *in the jury room* should not be decided by reference to the side-wind of s 8.

3   *Should the law be reformed?*

Section 8 was disavowed by the Lord Chancellor and it is submitted that it goes too far. Although there are powerful arguments for preserving complete secrecy of jurors' deliberations there is also force in the assertion that an institution which represents the very cornerstone of the legal system ought to be open to reasonable scrutiny and public accountability. The conflicting arguments have been well rehearsed in law reform publications from different common law juridictions[12] and by many commentators.[13]

The arguments in favour of jury secrecy can be subsumed under two heads: the need to safeguard the integrity of the criminal[14] justice system and the need to protect the individual juror.[15]

There is general agreement that individual jurors should be protected from reprisal, harassment and intimidation but less agreement about whether jury verdicts in specific cases should be shielded from scrutiny in order to safeguard the system. It is often said that *interest reipublicae ut sit finis litium* and it is argued that without jury secrecy verdicts would never be 'final' but would be open to endless dissection, with the result inter alia that public confidence would be undermined both in individual verdicts and in the system as a whole and that jurors would be inhibited in their discussions. On the other hand, it is argued that

10 See eg *R v Thompson* [1962] 1 All ER 65; *R v Bean* [1991] Crim LR 843; *R v Less* (1993) Times, 30 March.
11 And civil procedure, where there is a jury.
12 Canadian Law Reform Commission Report No 16: *The Jury* (1982); Australian Law Reform Commission Report No 35: *Contempt*, Ch 7; Irish Law Reform Commission Consultation Paper on Contempt, July 1991, pp 364–375.
13 See eg McConville and Baldwin, 'The Effect of the Contempt of Court Act on Research on Juries' (1981) 145 JPN 575; Blackshield, 'After the Trial: the Free Speech Verdict' (1985) 59 Law Institute Journal 1187; The Hon Michael McHugh, 'Jurors' Deliberations, Jury Secrecy, Public Policy and the Law of Contempt' in *The Jury Under Attack* (1985, eds Findlay and Duff); Jaconelli, 'Some Thought on Jury Secrecy' (1990) Legal Studies 91; Robertson and Nicol, *Media Law* (3rd edn, 1992) pp 299–301.
14 And in some situations, the civil.
15 See Jaconelli: 'Some Thought on Jury Secrecy' (1990) Legal Studies 91 at 97; this classification is, as he says, not watertight. For example, people will be less willing to serve as jurors, thus hindering the workings of the legal system if they are not protected from reprisals afterwards.

greater openness about the way a verdict was reached would help in the correction of miscarriages of justice.

Whatever controversies abound about the wisdom of allowing disclosure of individual cases there is a general consensus that in its present form s 8 is unjustifiably restrictive and inimical to the proper development of the legal system. It prevents all research into how juries operate and how they reach decisions. In 1986 the Roskill Fraud Trials Committee admitted[16] that it was hampered in its consideration of whether juries should be wholly or partly abolished in serious fraud trials by its inability to investigate how juries *do* reach decisions:

> 'Ideally one would investigate systematically the way that juries undertake their task and interview them during and after the trial . . .
>
> We have not been able to obtain accurate evidence whether there have been many doubtful acquittals or convictions in fraud cases or whether many retrials have been caused by failure to secure jury agreement.'

In 1993 the report of the Royal Commission on Criminal Justice[17] pointed out that although 'we are conscious that the jury system is widely and firmly believed to be one of the cornerstones of our system of justice':

> '. . . we were barred by s 8 of the Contempt of Court Act 1981 from conducting research into juries' reasons for their verdicts. We recommend, however, that such research should be made possible for the future by an amendment to the Act so that informed debate can take place rather than argument based only on surmise and anecdote. Such research might throw light on a variety of issues on which we have not felt able to make any recommendations—such as whether there is a case for raising the age limit for jury service, whether there is a case for a literacy requirement for jurors, whether the arrangements for majority verdicts should be changed or whether the disqualification rules require amendment.'

This is in line with the report on the jury by the Canadian Law Reform Commission which recommended an exception to the offence of a juror disclosing information relating to the proceedings of the jury room if it assists the 'furtherance of scientific research about juries which is approved by the Chief Justice of the Province'.[18] The proposals of the Australian Law Reform Commission[19] were more complex. They recommended the creation of a number of statutory offences which would distinguish between the *disclosure* of jury deliberations (the prohibition of which would last only until the discharge of the jury or the passing of the sentence) and their *publication* (which would, with certain exceptions, be prohibited indefinitely). The Irish Law Reform Commission recommended[20] that there should be no absolute rule of jury secrecy because miscarriages of justice[1] must be capable of being brought to light and they agreed with the Canadian Law Reform Commission that properly authorised research should be permitted.

It is submitted that s 8 should be amended along similar lines so as to permit research being undertaken upon the prior approval of, say, the Lord Chancellor's

16 Fraud Trials Committee Report (1986, Chairman Lord Roskill) paras 8.10 and 8.12.
17 Cm 2263 at Ch 1, para 8.
18 In their final Report No 16: *The Jury* (1982). The present offence is contained in s 649 of the Criminal Code but the recommended exception has not been enacted.
19 Paras 53–58.
20 Pp 370–374.
 1 They gave as an example the jury deciding on the toss of a coin–presumably the holding of a seance would be another.

Department or the Home Office.[2] This could be limited to research which did not identify any particular trial or juror. This is allowed in Victoria, Australia.[3] Such a reform would be in the public interest and ensure that at least when the next Royal Commission is set up to enquire into the workings of the criminal justice system it is not precluded from investigating the revered institution which lies at its very heart. It would mean that alterations to the jury system are not made on the basis of guesswork, instinct or general received wisdom but on proper methodologically sound research. The question of whether jury disclosure about deliberations in particular trials should be allowed in cases of miscarriages of justice raises more difficult issues about the circumstances in which a miscarriage of justice is held to arise from events in the jury room, which must be a matter for the law of criminal procedure.

It has also been suggested[4] that by imposing a blanket ban on publication of jurors' deliberations regardless of the risk of prejudice to particular proceedings or even to the administration of justice as a whole, s 8 could be regarded as a potential violation of Article 10 of the European Convention on Human Rights. It was argued for the defendant in *A-G v Associated Newspapers Ltd*[5] that 'disclosure' should be given a narrow interpretation because of otherwise offending Article 10. The House of Lords, however, took the view[6] that the reasons for ensuring the secrecy of jury deliberations fell within the proviso in Article 10(2).[7]

---

2 Putting the approval into those hands is open to the objection of quis custodet ipsos custodes but it is unlikely that any reform of s 8 would provide for anything less. The approval of an independent body such as the ESRC might be a possibility, however.

3 Juries Act, s 69A as amended by the Juries (Amendment) Act 1985.

4 See Lowe, 'The English Law of Contempt of Court and Article 10 of the European Convention on Human Rights' in *The Effect on English Domestic Law of Membership of the European Communities and of Ratification of the European Convention on Human Rights* (1983, Nijhoff, eds Furmston, Kerridge and Sufrin) pp 318, 344–5.

5 [1994] 2 AC 238.

6 Ibid at 262.

7 Which provides for the circumscribing of freedom of expression as far as is necessary, in a democratic society, inter alia for maintaining the authority and impartiality of the judiciary.

CHAPTER 10

Responsibility for contempt by publication

We have seen that the actus reus of contempt by publication is the publication of material which is likely or, possibly, which is intended to interfere with the course of justice and the necessary mens rea is simply the intention to publish. The question now to be examined is, who can be said to have committed the actus reus with the necessary mens rea. In other words who will be held responsible for the publication?

The problem of responsibility is made more difficult by the fact that contempt is not restricted to any particular medium of publication. In the simple case of a speech delivered from a public platform, such speech being in contempt of court, responsibility will fall solely on the speaker. Where, however, contempt has been published by a newspaper or broadcast by television or radio, the question of who can be held responsible is more difficult. In these cases a considerable number of people are involved in the publication of the newspaper or in the broadcasting of a television or radio programme. Developments in information technology pose new problems about responsibility for material appearing on computer screens. The question is, are all those involved in the publication guilty of contempt or does responsibility devolve upon selected persons only, such as those exercising overall control?

In general, the answer to this question is that only those who can be said to bear some real responsibility for the final publication will be held liable.

I RESPONSIBILITY FOR A NEWSPAPER OR MAGAZINE PUBLICATION

The principal persons who can be said to bear a real responsibility for a newspaper or magazine publication and who can, therefore, be regarded as 'intending to publish' are: the editor, the proprietors, the printers, the persons responsible for supplying the information to the newspaper such as a reporter or news agency and, lastly, the persons responsible for the distribution of the newspaper.[1] The relative responsibility of these persons will be considered in turn.

A   The editor

1   *De facto responsibility*

The editor is the most obvious person to hold responsible for a newspaper publication since he has ultimate control over the contents of his newspaper.[2] In

---

1   Cited with approval by the New South Wales Court of Appeal in *A-G for NSW v TCN Channel Nine Pty Ltd* (1990) 20 NSWLR 368 at 379.
2   Cited with approval by Marks J in *R v David Syme & Co Ltd* [1982] VR 173 at 178.

practice, English courts always hold the editor responsible, although he may not necessarily be punished or even prosecuted. As Lord Goddard CJ said in *R v Odhams Press Ltd, ex p A-G:* [3]

> 'It has always been a tradition of English journalism that the editor takes responsibility for what is published in his paper and this was held to be a rule of law in *R v Evening Standard Co Ltd, ex p A-G.*'[4]

A person held responsible for publication may be held guilty of contempt, although he has no personal knowledge of the contents of the article in question. In *Re O'Connor, Chesshire v Strauss* [5] the editor of the *Sun* was shown a very short version of a proposed article, and since he was about to go on a journey he hardly had time to read it, though he did warn his sub-editor to be very careful. Despite the warning and without the editor's personal knowledge, the complete article was published and held to amount to contempt. The editor was held liable, even though he was not personally guilty of 'any very serious misbehaviour'.

In *R v Evening Standard Co Ltd,*[6] the editor was held to have committed a contempt by publishing a misreport of a case based on inaccurate information as supplied by a reporter even though it was expressly acknowledged that the editor had every reason to believe and did in fact believe the information to be accurate. In *R v Thomson Newspapers, ex p A-G* [7] the editor of the *Times* was held responsible for a prejudicial publication even though 'he had devised, so far as it is humanly possible, a system which would prevent this sort of thing'. Although the courts have recognised the undoubted difficulties involved in producing a newspaper and, in particular, the difficult position of the editor, the strict doctrine of holding the editor guilty has nevertheless been thought to be justifiable. Lord Hewart CJ said in *R v Evening Standard, ex p DPP:*[8]

> 'nobody who knew anything of the organisation and management of a newspaper could be ignorant of the fact that the work of newspapers was very often done in circumstances of great hurry by many different minds not always fully aware of what others might be doing. The result was a composite thing, but *there must be central responsibility*. It was impossible to say that men occupying responsible positions should be excused because they themselves were not personally aware of what was being done' (emphasis added).

This principle of editorial responsibility is accepted in Scotland,[9] Australia[10] and Canada[11] but in New Zealand, the Court of Appeal preferred to leave the question open.[12] Although the editor will always be held responsible (when he is

---

3 [1957] 1 QB 73 at 80.
4 [1954] 1 QB 578, [1954] 1 All ER 1026.
5 (1896) 12 TLR 291.
6 [1954] 1 QB 578, [1954] 1 All ER 1026.
7 [1968] 1 All ER 268, [1968] 1 WLR 1.
8 (1924) 40 TLR 833 at 836.
9 *HM Advocate v George Outram & Co Ltd* 1980 SLT (Notes) 13.
10 *R v David Syme & Co Ltd* [1982] VR 173 at 183 per Marks J relying on inter alia *A-G New South Wales v Willesee* [1980] 2 NSWLR 143 and *Brambles Holdings Ltd v Trade Practices Commission* (1980) 32 ALR 328 at 341 (though both these cases were on different points); *R v Day and Thompson* [1985] VR 261; *R v Australian Broadcasting Corporation* [1983] Tas R 161; *Fitzgibbon v Barker* (1992) 111 FLR 191.
11 *R v Western Printing and Publishing Ltd* (1954) 111 CCC 122 and *Steiner v Toronto Star Ltd* (1956) 1 DLR (2d) 297.
12 In *Solicitor-General v Radio Avon Ltd* [1978] 1 NZLR 225 at 241. In fact the case was concerned with the responsibility for a broadcast. Cf *Macassey v Bell* (1875) 2 NZ Jur 59 and *R v McKinnon* (1911) 30 NZLR 884.

made a party) for the contents of his newspaper he may not always be punished. Provided he has taken all reasonable precautions and has not been negligent, the tenor of recent decisions suggests that the editor is unlikely to be punished. Most newspapers have lawyers on hand to give advice—morning newspapers are usually 'night-lawyered'—and mistakes when they happen will not be visited upon the editor, especially if an apology is tendered. No punishment was imposed upon the editor in *R v Evening Standard Co Ltd, R v Thomson Newspapers, ex p A-G*, or *Solicitor-General v Henry and News Group Newspapers Ltd* [13] although fines were imposed on the proprietors of £1,000, £5,000 and £15,000 respectively.[14] In *R v Thomson Newspapers, ex p A-G* Lord Parker CJ said:[15]

> 'So far as Mr Harold Evans is concerned, he, of course, as editor takes full responsibility; on the other hand, when one is considering the question of penalty one must consider his personal culpability. It is quite clear that he knew nothing about this. It is also quite clear that an editor in his position could not possibly be expected to know everything that was happening. It cannot be said that he acted recklessly or turned a blind eye. Indeed in the opinion of the court, he had devised, so far as it is humanly possible, a system which would prevent this sort of thing. In those circumstances this court has come to the conclusion that it is quite unnecessary to impose a sentence of imprisonment or, in the circumstances of this case, any penalty whatever on him.'

In England and Wales the Attorney General sometimes does not bring an action against the editor at all, but only against the proprietors although the practice on this seems inconsistent, even in cases in which the editor took a more active role in the decision to publish. For example, the editor was not made a defendant in the leading common law decision on disclosing the secrets of the jury room, *A-G v New Statesman and Nation Publishing Co Ltd*,[16] but was in the prosecution under s 8 of the Contempt of Court Act 1981 in *A-G v Associated Newspapers Ltd*. [17] In Australia the trend is to bring the action against the editor (and others involved in the publication) as well as against the proprietor. In *DPP v John Fairfax & Sons Ltd* [18] the action was brought against both the editor and the sports editor who had sub-edited the item,[19] although neither was punished, partly because they had relied on in-house legal advice. Had contempt been found in *Re Lonrho Plc,* [20] a case in which the publication was instigated by the proprietor, it would have been interesting to see whether the court would have imposed any punishment on the editor, who was made a party to the action but appears merely to have been obeying orders.

In some cases the editor clearly plays the central role in the decision to publish. This was true, for example, in *A-G v Times Newspapers Ltd* [1] of Harold Evans'

---

13 (1990) COD 307.
14 The differences in the sums is a more a reflection of inflation than of a change in the level of fines.
15 [1968] 1 All ER 268 at 271. Cf in Scotland, *HM Advocate v George Outram & Co Ltd* 1980 SLT (Notes) 13—editor held liable and fined £750 though he was not on the spot when the critical decisions had to be made and when he went off duty he understood that legal advice would be sought and that it would be worth seeking. See also *R v Beaverbrook Newspapers Ltd, Associated Newspapers Ltd* [1962] NI 15.
16 [1981] QB 1, [1980] 1 All ER 644, discussed in Ch 9, p 365.
17 [1994] 2 AC 238, [1994] 1 All ER 556.
18 (1987) 8 NSWLR 732 (NSW CA).
19 As well as against the publisher and the journalist who had written the story.
20 [1990] 2 AC 154, [1989] 2 All ER 1100.
1 The *Sunday Times* case [1974] AC 273.

involvement with the thalidomide articles and that of the editors in the publication of Peter Wright's memoirs in the *Spycatcher* affair.[2] While absence of moral responsibility may, as we have seen, relieve the editor of punishment, the editor who intends to interfere with the course of justice or who completely disregards the interests of the due administration of justice or is reckless about the consequences of a publication, may be punished severely. As Lord Parker CJ, said in *R v Thomson Newspapers, ex p A-G*:[3]

> 'the seriousness of a contempt of court can be looked at from two angles: first, the seriousness of the contempt judged by the likely prejudice to the fair trial of an accused and, secondly, the seriousness of the contempt from the point of view of what I may call the culpability of those concerned.'

The classic illustration of an article published in complete disregard for the due administration of justice is *R v Bolam, ex p Haigh*,[4] where the *Daily Mirror*, while a murder trial was pending, published a front-page article describing the accused as a 'vampire' and asserting not only that he was guilty of the murder with which he was charged, but also that he had murdered five other named persons. The court held that the article was deliberately published for the purpose of increasing the circulation of the newspaper, at the expense of paying regard to the due administration of justice. In these circumstances it was held that it:

> 'was of the utmost importance that the court should vindicate the common principles of justice and in the public interest see that condign punishment was meted out to persons guilty of such conduct. What had been done was not the result of an error of judgment but had been done as a matter of policy in pandering to sensationalism for the purpose of increasing the circulation of the newspaper.'

For this aggravated contempt the editor was imprisoned for three months. Imprisonment was also threatened in *A-G v Hislop*[5] where the Attorney General applied for Ian Hislop, the editor of *Private Eye*, to be committed because of the degree of personal responsibility he bore for the offending article, but the Court of Appeal decided on a fine of £10,000 instead.[6] In taking all the responsibility for the article Mr Hislop said in evidence that he had taken legal advice about whether to publish but he declined to reveal what the advice was and merely said 'I took advice, as I always do, and then I come to my own decisions'.[7]

The role of the editor has become more crucial in England and Wales since the Contempt of Court Act 1981 because of the fact that prosecutions outside the strict liability rule can still be brought at common law if there is an intention to prejudice proceedings.[8] The 'intention' looked at in the cases on this so far has been that of the editor. This was so in *Hislop* and there was also a detailed discussion of the intentions of the then editor of the *Sun*, Kelvin MacKenzie, in *A-G v News Group Newspapers Ltd*.[9] In that case, surprisingly, the Attorney General did not bring the action against Mr MacKenzie but only against the

2 *A-G v Newspaper Publishing Plc* [1988] Ch 333, and *A-G v Times Newspapers Ltd* [1992] 1 AC 191, discussed in Ch 6, pp 211 ff.
3 Ibid at 269.
4 (1949) 93 Sol Jo 220.
5 [1991] 1 QB 514, [1991] 1 All ER 911.
6 Despite McCowan LJ's remarking that he was not filled with great confidence that Mr Hislop's promises as to his future conduct would be kept.
7 [1991] QB 514 at 536, [1991] 1 All ER 911 at 928.
8 See p 106.
9 [1989] QB 110, [1988] 2 All ER 906.

proprietors and publishers, who were therefore found liable for contempt on the basis of the intentions of their editor.[10]

2   The legal basis for the responsibility the editor

(a)   Vicarious responsibility

The precise basis upon which an editor's responsibility rests, in cases in which the contempt is not intentional, is not clearly established. According to Lord Goddard CJ, in *R v Evening Standard Co Ltd*,[11] it rests upon the principle of vicarious responsibility. In that case the editor was held vicariously liable for the mistake of a reporter. Lord Goddard CJ said:[12]

> 'Sir Hartley Shawcross said that, while his clients desired to abide by the well understood rule of journalism that the editor and proprietors of papers must in a case such as this take responsibility, he would suggest to the court that vicarious liability, as it is called, ought not in law to be visited upon them and that they ought not to be made vicariously liable for the mistake or misconduct of the reporter. I do not think we can possibly agree with that submission . . . the principle of vicarious liability is well established in these cases and must be adhered to.'

An editor has also been held liable for contempt on the basis of vicarious liability in the Ontario High Court case, *Steiner v Toronto Star Ltd*[13] where McRuer CJHC relying on Lord Goddard's above cited judgment seemed to regard the matter as entirely settled.

Despite the foregoing judgment there must be some doubt as to whether the principle of vicarious liability can properly be involved in this context.[14] The term 'vicarious liability' is usually taken to refer to the principle that an employer is responsible for the wrongful acts of an employee performed in the course of his employment. Three objections have been raised against the application of this principle to an editor's responsibility in the law of contempt for the contents of a newspaper:

(i)   It has been argued[15] that Lord Goddard CJ was wrong to say that the editor was vicariously liable for the acts of the reporter, as the reporter cannot be said to have committed a contempt at all. The reason, it is said, that the reporter has not committed a contempt is that the essence of the offence is the publication of the material and publication is the act of the proprietors and the editor, not of the reporter, who has merely supplied the information to the newspaper. This argument is said to be supported by Lord Goddard CJ's statement in *R v Griffiths, ex p A-G*[16] that the offence 'is not the mere

10   See further p 385. Mr MacKenzie was not always so lucky: in 1994 he was fined £20,000 for publishing the photograph of a suspect who was about to take part in an identity parade, see (1994) Independent, 6 July.
11   [1954] 1 QB 578, [1954] 1 All ER 1026.
12   Ibid at 585.
13   (1956) 1 DLR (2d) 297. See also *Re A-G for Manitoba and Radio OB Ltd* (1977) 70 DLR (3d) 311 at 324 per Solomon J.
14   See, eg the doubts expressed by the New Zealand Court of Appeal in *Solicitor-General v Radio Avon Ltd* [1978] 1 NZLR 225.
15   See eg Smith & Hogan, *Criminal Law* (5th edn, 1983) pp 723–724, (the 7th edn, 1992 does not cover contempt of court) and Miller, 'Contempt of Court—Sub Judice Rule' [1968] Crim Law Rev 63 at 195.
16   [1957] 2 QB 192 at 202.

preparation of the article, but the publication of it during the proceedings'. However, although it is true that the essence of the contempt is the publication of the offending material (so as to present a real risk of prejudice), it is surely a narrow view to regard the reporter as bearing no responsibility at all, under any circumstances, for the final production. We shall deal with this problem more fully when we consider the responsibility of the reporter,[17] but it is sufficient to say at this stage that a reporter who supplied information, knowing that it is likely to be published, can be said to be guilty of a contempt if it is in fact published. He has committed the actus reus by causing the information to be published and must be said to have the necessary mens rea of intending to publish. Accordingly, this objection cannot be supported.

(ii) Contempt by publication is a common law crime and, while the principle of vicarious liability is readily applicable in respect of a *tort* [18] committed by an employee, the principle is not generally applicable in respect of common law crimes. As Raymond CJ said in *R v Huggins*:[19]

> 'in criminal cases the principal is not answerable for the act of the deputy as he is in civil cases: they must each answer for their own acts, and stand or fall by their own behaviour ... to affect the superior by the act of his deputy, there must be the command of the superior ...'

The application of vicarious liability in respect of a common law crime[20] is not, however, entirely unprecedented as it has been said to apply both to a common law public nuisance[1] and to a criminal libel.[2] According to Glanville Williams,[3] it could be said that contempt of court provides a third exception, albeit of recent origin. The application of the principle of vicarious liability may be justified on the grounds that contempt of court is closely analogous to a criminal libel although the criminal libel cases are themselves of doubtful authority.[4] The most recent development in vicarious liability in respect of common law crimes has been the concept of corporate criminal liability.[5] The idea of corporate liability, however, is to fix a corporate body with liability for the acts of a natural person and is not, it is submitted, relevant to the question of whether one natural person (the editor) should be liable for the acts of another (the reporter or journalist).

---

17 See p 389.
18 For vicarious liability in tort see generally Atiyah, *Vicarious Liability in the Law of Torts* (1967); *Clerk & Lindsell on Torts* (16th edn, 1989 and supplements), Ch 3.
19 (1730) 2 Stra 882 at 885. For a discussion generally of vicarious liability in criminal law see Glanville Williams, *Criminal Law—The General Part* (2nd edn, 1961) p 266; Smith & Hogan: *Criminal Law* (7th edn, 1992) Ch 9; Clarkson & Keating, *Criminal Law: Text and Materials* (3rd edn, 1994) pp 231–232.
20 Some statutory crimes impose vicarious liability, see Smith & Hogan, *Criminal Law* (7th edn, 1992) and the 'delegation principle', for example, has been held to impose vicarious liability on licensees for the acts of their managers (see *Allen v Whitehead* [1930] 1 KB 211 and Smith & Hogan, ibid pp 172–175). See further the discussion at pp 383 ff in the context of the responsibility of the proprietor.
1 *R v Stephens* (1866) LR 1 QB 702.
2 *R v Gutch* (1829) Mood & M 433, 173 ER 1214; *R v Walter* (1799) 3 Esp 21, 170 ER 524. For a discussion of the common law exceptions, see generally Glanville Williams, *Criminal Law—The General Part* (2nd edn, 1961) p 267 ff.
3 Ibid p 269.
4 See pp 383–384.
5 See generally C Wells, *Corporations and Criminal Liability* (1993).

These matters are discussed further below in relation to the proprietors' liability.[6]

(iii) A more cogent reason for not applying the principle in respect of the liability of the editor is that, as it operates in the law of tort, vicarious liability is generally applicable only where there is a relationship of master and servant. In the case of an editor and a reporter the relationship is that of superior servant and inferior servant, not master and servant.

(b) Primary responsibility

There is an alternative ground on which to base the editor's responsibility in contempt, namely, that he is *primarily* liable. This avoids the necessity of having recourse to the principle of vicarious liability and therefore is not open to any of the objections already discussed. It is thought that this may provide a sounder basis for the editor's liability.[7] An essential element of the actus reus is the 'publication' of offending material, while the only mens rea necessary is the intention to publish. It is submitted that an editor of a newspaper commits the actus reus and has the necessary mens rea (in that he intends to publish) and his liability may therefore be considered personal or original rather than vicarious. With regard to the actus reus, it is submitted that an editor can properly be regarded as 'publishing' the contents of his newspaper, since he is the person who exercises ultimate and overall control and, as Lord Hewart CJ said,[8] there must be a 'central responsibility'. The editor can properly be regarded as 'publishing' an article, since he is the person who ultimately decides whether an article should be published. For example, in the *Evening Standard* case, it was the editor's decision to publish the reporter's account of the trial that led to the contempt— if he had decided to reject the account no contempt would have been committed. With regard to the necessary mens rea there is little difficulty, since a person occupying such a key position in a newspaper enterprise could hardly argue that he has no intention to publish. On this basis, therefore, it is submitted that the editor may be regarded as having himself committed the contempt, his liability being personal or original rather than vicarious.

It should be added that statutes such as the Judicial Proceedings (Regulation of Reports) Act 1926, s 1(2), and the Magistrates' Courts Act 1980, s 8A(11),[9] and the Sexual Offences (Amendment) Act, 1976, s 4(5),[10] expressly state that the editor can be held responsible for a publication which contravenes the relevant provisions of these statutes.

3   Commentary

It might plausibly be argued that editorial responsibility is too strict a doctrine to be applied in the context of contempt which after all is a criminal offence. It is

---

6 Se pp 382–384.
7 See also Peter Butt, 'Contempt of Court and the Legal Profession' [1975] Crim LR 463 at 465.
8 In *R v Evening Standard* (1924) 40 TLR 833.
9 Replacing the previous s 8(5): see the Criminal Justice and Public Order Act 1994, s 44 and Sch 4.
10 See Ch 8, p 318.

true that an editor who is not morally culpable can expect to be treated leniently but there is no guarantee of exoneration. Despite the strictness of the position it seems in accord with English newspaper tradition and it was noticeable that despite editorial responsibility being a specific question raised in a questionnaire circulated by the Phillimore Committee[11] there was no pressure to reform the law. The Phillimore Committee itself recommended no change.[12]

B   The proprietors

1   *Proprietors*

Most newspaper and magazine proprietors are limited companies, ie corporate bodies, though it is possible that ownership may be vested in an individual or a partnership. Newspaper proprietors are clearly responsible for the contents of their newspaper and will always (subject to the defence in s 3 of the 1981 Act, discussed below) be held responsible for a contempt by publication. However, whereas absence of moral culpability may relieve the editor from punishment, the proprietors can expect no such leniency. In *R v Thomson Newspapers, ex p A-G*[13] a fine of £5,000 was imposed on Times Newspapers Ltd, even though the court was satisfied:

> 'that this newspaper, with a clean record of some 150 years had devised, and the editor . . . had ensured was operated, an elaborate and reasonable system to avoid contempts of this sort, or indeed any contempt of court. They were fully alive to their obligations as a responsible newspaper and devised this system.'

It may, however, reduce the fine if the proprietors have taken care to set up a system to guard against committing contempt. In *A-G v News Group Newspapers Ltd*,[14] for example, a nominal fine of only £500 was imposed on the *News of the World*, the judge remarking that this was the paper's first contempt offence for 40 years, despite it concentrating on an area of life which rendered it more at risk.

2   *The legal basis for responsibility*

It will only be in very rare cases that the proprietor interferes in the running of the newspaper sufficiently to be *in fact* responsible for the contempt. Where the proprietor is a body corporate that interference can only come through the human agency of the directors or executives, and in such cases they may be held personally liable. Such a situation occurred in *Re Lonrho Plc*[15] where the chief executive and three directors of the company which owned the *Observer* were made parties to the action.[16]

In most cases, however, the proprietor will be held responsible for the contempt simply on the basis of the ownership of the newspaper, but as in the case of editors the exact legal basis of proprietors' responsibility remains unsettled.

11 1974, Cmnd 5794.
12 Ibid paras 147–148.
13 [1968] 1 All ER 268, [1968] 1 WLR 1.
14 (1982) 4 Cr App R (s) 182.
15 [1990] 2 AC 154, [1989] 2 All ER 1100.
16 See p 387.

(a)   Vicarious liability

In *R v Evening Standard Co Ltd*[17] Lord Goddard CJ, again invoking the principle of vicarious responsibility, held the proprietors liable, fining them £1,000. Although his Lordship seemed to hold the proprietors liable for the reporter's contempt, if it is accepted that the editor by deciding to publish has himself committed the contempt, it would be possible to base the proprietors' vicarious liability on the editor's contempt.

The question remains, does the principle of vicarious liability apply to contempt of court? There are certainly stronger grounds for applying the principle with respect to the proprietors since their relationship with the editor and reporters is that of master and servant. However, there is still the objection that vicarious liability is generally inapplicable in respect of common law crimes. Should contempt of court be regarded as one of the exceptions?[18] Perhaps the best reason for saying that it should is that contempt is closely analogous to criminal libel which is said to be one of the two accepted exceptions. There are two possible objections to this analogy. First, it is not altogether certain that the principle of vicarious liability was ever truly applicable to a criminal libel. The reasoning of the cases which are said to establish the principle are not altogether conclusive of the matter; for, while they certainly held the innocent proprietor liable, the precise grounds for this liability were not unequivocally stated. For instance, in *R v Gutch, Fisher and Alexander*,[19] Lord Tenterden CJ, in holding the proprietor liable said:

> 'surely a person who derives profit from, and who furnishes means for carrying on the concern, and entrusts the conduct of the publication to one whom he selects, and in whom he confides, may be said to cause to be published what actually appears, and ought to be answerable, although you cannot shew that he was individually concerned in the particular publication.'

While it is certainly possible to explain the decision by saying the proprietor was held vicariously liable, it cannot be said that Lord Tenterden CJ's decision unequivocally established this, indeed, it is at least arguable that this decision supports the view that the proprietor was originally liable. But even supposing that the cases definitely established that the proprietors were vicariously liable, as Glanville Williams has said, the cases:[20]

> 'were of doubtful authority, for not only did they introduce an almost unprecedented principle of liability into the criminal law, but they were contrary to other judicial pronouncements.'

It may therefore be at least a tenable proposition to say that vicarious liability was never truly applicable with regard to criminal libel.

The second objection is that even supposing that there is no doubt as to the application of the principle of vicarious liability to a criminal libel, it does not

17 [1954] 1 QB 578, [1954] 1 All ER 1026. See also the Phillimore Committee's comments, at
   para 153, that proprietors' contempt liability is an example of ordinary vicarious liability, and
   we believe it to be right in principle.
18 Some support for its application might be drawn from the House of Lords' decision in *Heatons
   Transport (St Helens) Ltd v Transport and General Workers' Union* [1973] AC 15, [1972] 3
   All ER 101 (discussed at p 569), although this was a case of civil contempt.
19 (1829) Mood & M 433. A similar argument can be used with regard to Lord Kenyon's
   judgment in *R v Walter* (1799) 3 Esp 21.
20 *Criminal Law—The General Part* (2nd edn, 1961) p 68.

follow that contempt is necessarily analogous. It is significant that both the alleged exceptions to the principle that vicarious liability has no application to common law crimes, ie, criminal libel and public nuisance, have direct counterparts in tort, whereas, of course, contempt does not.

The conclusion to be drawn is that while there is some authority for the view that vicarious liability is applicable to contempt of court it might, because of the general proposition that such a principle is inapplicable to a common law crime, be thought preferable to find an alternative basis for liability.

Corporate criminal liability [1]   In the case of incorporated proprietors it might be possible to consider them liable on one of the other bases developed by the courts to deal with the problem of how far companies can be held criminally responsible. Liability is well established in respect of strict liability offences where a statute imposes a duty on the entity itself as the occupier of premises or the operator of an industrial process.[2] In two exceptional cases the criminal law has long recognised vicarious liability: one is the 'delegation' situation, in which a statutory duty is cast upon the owner, licensee or keeper of premises, who will then be liable for the acts of a person to whom he delegates the management of the premises, and the other is where the courts interpret the words of a statute such as 'sell' or 'supply' as applying to the employer where it is the employee who has actually performed the relevant act.[3]

Matters become more difficult, however, where offences requiring mens rea are concerned. A company cannot have a guilty mind in the normal sense. The courts have therefore developed the idea that the minds of certain senior company officers can be deemed to be that of the company itself. This is known as the direct, 'alter ego' or identification doctrine. In *HL Bolton (Engineering) Co Ltd v TJ Graham & Sons Ltd,*[4] Denning LJ commented:

> 'A company may in many ways be likened to a human body. It has a brain and a nerve centre which controls what it does. It also has hands which hold the tools and act in accordance with directions from the centre. Some of the people in the company are mere servants and agents who are nothing more than hands to do the work and cannot be said to represent the mind or will. Others are directors and managers who represent the directing mind and will of the company and control what it does. The state of mind of these managers is the state of mind of the company and is treated by the law as such.'

As is shown by the leading case of *Tesco Supermarkets Ltd v Nattrass*[5] the key point in applying such a principle is to show that the person concerned represents the 'brain' and not merely the 'hand'; but once this is shown, that person's acts are treated as if they were the company's. Attempts to use this principle to affix companies with criminal liability for disasters have demonstrated

---

1   See Ashworth, *Principles of Criminal Law* (2nd edn, 1995) pp 111-118; Parkinson, *Corporate Power and Responsibility* (1993) pp 349-364; Wells, *Corporations and Criminal Responsibility* (1993).
2   See eg *R v Birmingham and Gloucester Rly Co Ltd* (1842) 3 QB 223; *Alphacell Ltd v Woodward* [1972] AC 824.
3   See *Coppen v Moore (No 2)* [1898] 2 QB 306. These exceptions are necessary if the purpose of certain statutes is not to be defeated.
4   [1957] 1 QB 159 at 172.
5   [1972] AC 153, [1971] 2 All ER 127. See also *Canadian Dredge & Dock Co Ltd v The Queen* (1985) 19 DLR (4th) 314 and the Law Commission No 177: *Draft Criminal Code for England and Wales* (1989) at 215.

its limitations[6] and the courts now seem to be slowly developing notions of corporate liability which do not depend on the notion of the directing mind and which might be more useful in that type of case.[7]

The alter ego or identification principle might, however, be thought to be applicable to contempt of court. The principle has been held to be applicable to the common law crime of conspiracy where there was no problem of imputing the mens rea of the managing director of a two-director family firm to the company.[8] An editor could be regarded as the 'brain' of the newspaper being a superior officer in day-to-day control of what the newspaper publishes. Alternatively, it could be argued that even if he is not a superior officer the proprietors (who are clearly the company's 'brain') might be regarded as having delegated sufficient powers to the editor as to identify the latter with the company. On either basis by regarding the editor as the 'alter ego' of the newspaper company, the company may be held originally liable for the publication.

The problem has been given a new twist by the issue of mens rea in respect of contempts outside the strict liability rule. As noted above in the context of the editor's responsibility[9] it is the intention of the editor to prejudice proceedings which will normally be relevant in common law contempt prosecutions. In the cases on intentional contempt since the 1981 Act, such as *A-G v Hislop,* [10] *A-G v News Group Newspapers* [11] and *Spycatcher* [12] the proprietors have been held to have committed contempt on the basis of the mens rea of the editor. In *Spycatcher* the Court of Appeal discussed whether the requisite mens rea was recklessness or specific intent but did not suggest that there was any difficulty about holding the proprietors liable for intentional contempt. The alter ego principle, would, in fact, provide a basis for imputing the editor's intention to the proprietor.

(b)   Primary liability

The alter ego principle is not, however, a totally satisfactory way of dealing with the proprietors' liability. A major difficulty of applying the 'alter ego' principle to contempt of court is that it can only apply to the incorporated proprietor and not to the proprietor who is a natural person. Since, however, the functions of the two types of proprietor are in reality the same, it seems illogical to apply different bases for liability, especially when there is a further ground on which to base liability. That ground is primary liability: it is suggested that it is possible to regard the proprietors as having *themselves* committed the offence and, therefore, as being originally liable.

6   Where the issue has been liability for manslaughter: see the cases which have resulted from the *Herald of Free Enterprise* disaster: *P & O European Ferries (Dover) Ltd* (1990) 93 Cr App R 72 and *R v HM Coroner for East Kent, ex p Spooner* (1989) 88 Cr App Rep 10.

7   See *Seaboard Offshore Ltd v Secretary of State for Transport* [1994] 1 WLR 541: a prosecution for manslaughter did succeed against the managing director of an outdoor adventure centre in *R v OLL Ltd* (1994) Times, 9 December, after the deaths of a numbers of teenagers in a canoeing accident, but that was a small business in which the directors were (or should have been) involved in the day-to-day management at ground level. A change of approach can also be detected in *Tesco Stores Ltd v Brent LBC* [1993] 2 All ER 718 and *Meridian Global Funds Management Asia Ltd v Securities Commission* (1995) Times, 29 June.

8   *R v ICR Haulage Co Ltd* [1944] KB 551, [1944] 1 All ER 691.

9   And see Ch 4, pp 106.

10   [1991] 1 QB 514.

11   [1989] 1 QB 110.

12   *A-G v Newspaper Publishing Plc* [1988] Ch 333.

It is also suggested that the reasoning of Lord Tenterden CJ[13] can be used to support this, namely, that a person who furnishes the means to carry on the concern and who entrusts the publication to a person whom he selects, can himself be said to have caused to be published what actually appears. In other words the proprietors can be regarded as having committed the actus reus because, although they have no personal knowledge of the contents of the newspaper, by setting up and running the newspaper concern, they have caused the article to be published. With regard to the mens rea, as with the editor, it can hardly be argued that the proprietors have no intent to publish, as that is the purpose of their enterprise. It should be added that, as in the case of editors, certain statutes, notably, the Judicial Proceedings (Regulation of Reports) Act 1926, s 1(2), the Magistrates' Courts Act 1980, s 8(A)(11)[14] and the Sexual Offences (Amendment) Act 1976, s 4(5), expressly provide that proprietors may be held responsible for a publication which contravenes the relevant provisions of these statutes.

It seems right to impose liability upon newspaper proprietors since they provide the means whereby publication is effected. The law of contempt as a deterrent instrument would be weakened if the proprietors did not have a strong incentive not only to choose a responsible editor but to take appropriate action if the editor or another member of staff began to make or allow comment which might subject the proprietors to liability. Subject to the reservation as to the proper legal basis of proprietors' liability, which it is submitted should be a primary responsibility, the current law seems satisfactory. This was the view taken of liability by the Family Court of Australia in *Fitzgibbon v Barker*.[15]

C The directors

Closely allied to the question of proprietors' liability is the question of whether a director of a newspaper company could be held personally responsible. Although it is a very unusual step[16] to prosecute a director personally, it *is* possible. In *R v Bolam, ex p Haigh* [17] Lord Goddard CJ warned that under certain circumstances such a step could be taken. He said:

'Let the directors beware; they know now the conduct of which their employees were capable, and the view which the court took of the matter. If for the purpose of increasing the circulation of their paper they should again venture to publish such a matter as this, the directors themselves might find the arm of that court was long enough to reach them and to deal with them individually.'

In other words, as a result of the conduct of the employees, the directors themselves were put on inquiry as to the future conduct of their employees and they could be held responsible for any further misconduct.

13 In *R v Gutch, Fisher and Alexander* (1829) Mood & M 433. Some support for supposing liability to be primary may be drawn by way of analogy from *Whitehouse v Lemon* [1979] AC 617, sub nom *R v Lemon* [1979] 1 All ER 898 (HL) (blasphemous libel).
14 Formerly s 8(5); see the Criminal Justice and Public Order Act 1994, s 44 and Sch 4.
15 (1992) 111 FLR 191 at 202–203, citing with approval this paragraph in the last edition of this work.
16 But see *R v Mason, ex p Director of Public Prosecutions* (1932) Times, 17 December, where the directors of a printing company were personally fined.
17 (1949) 93 Sol Jo 220; see also *Beard v WR Rolph & Sons Pty Ltd* [1955] Tas SR 19.

Re Lonrho Plc [18] is an exceptional case in which the publication alleged to constitute a contempt was instigated by the chief executive of the proprietor company. The facts of this case are recounted in Chapter 6 but, briefly, involved the *Observer* (normally a Sunday newspaper) coming out in a special midweek edition solely devoted to a DTI inspectors' report about persons with whom the proprietors of the *Observer*, Lonrho plc, and in particular its chief executive Mr Tiny Rowland, were engaged in a long-running feud over the ownership of Harrods. The newspaper was therefore being used purely as a weapon in a battle of Lonrho's which had nothing directly to do with the paper. Unsurprisingly the contempt proceedings were brought against Mr Rowland and two Lonrho directors as well as Lonrho itself, The Observer Ltd (which was a subsidiary company of Lonrho) and the hapless editor of the *Observer*, Donald Trelford. The liability of Mr Rowland and the directors was undoubtedly primary liability.[19]

D The importance of classifying the editor's and proprietors' liability

Since it is clear that the courts will hold both the proprietors and the editor responsible for the contents of their newspaper, it may be thought that classification of their liability is merely academic. But this is not so; for it could be important in relation to the operation of the Contempt of Court Act 1981. Section 3(1)[20] gives the publisher a defence if, having taken all reasonable care, he did not know and had no reason to suspect that proceedings were active. So far as the editor is concerned, if Lord Goddard CJ's view in *R v Evening Standard Co* is adopted, namely, that he is vicariously liable for the act of the reporter, it would be sufficient if the reporter has taken all reasonable care. On the other hand, if the editor is held personally liable, as, it is submitted, is the preferable view, the editor would have to show that he himself had taken all reasonable care. As Miller has said:[1]

> 'where an editor has relied entirely upon the investigations of a reporter the relevant question should not simply be that of whether the reporter has exercised reasonable care. It should rather be whether the editor's reliance upon the reporter was reasonable in all the circumstances of the case, having regard to, inter alia, the latter's experience and competence, the adequacy of the editor's communications with him and the reasonableness of the conclusions drawn from such circumstances.'

Similarly, in the case of the proprietors, if Lord Goddard CJ[2] was right in his view that their liability is a vicarious liability for the reporter's wrong, they too would have a defence if the reporter had taken all reasonable care. If they were considered to be vicariously liable for the editor, the defence would succeed only if it could be shown that the editor had taken all reasonable care. If, however, the proprietors were held to be primarily liable they would have to show not only that the editor had taken all reasonable care, but also that they had taken reasonable

---

18 [1990] 2 AC 514, [1989] 2 All ER 1100.
19 Mr Michael Foot made Rupert Murdoch, the owner of News International, a defendant to the libel action he brought in 1995 in respect of articles appearing in the *Sunday Times* alleging that he had been a KGB agent. The action was settled out of court.
20 Formerly s 11 (1) of the Administration of Justice Act 1960. Section 3 is further considered at p 398.
1 [1968] Crim Law Rev 63, 198. See also Miller, *Contempt of Court* (2nd edn, 1989) p 299.
2 In *R v Evening Standard Co Ltd* [1954] 1 QB 578, [1954] 1 All ER 1026.

care in appointing, and retaining the services of, the editor.[3] However, in neither event would it be necessary for the proprietors to show that they had personally inquired into the question of whether the proceedings were active.

Complications arise also from the question of publications outside the strict liability rule. If the responsibility is affixed to the proprietors under the alter ego principle the mens rea of a reporter might not be sufficient to make the proprietors liable for contempt because he is in too junior a position to be a 'brain' within the *Tesco v Nattrass* formulation. The outcome would therefore depend on whether the *editor* had taken all reasonable care. If he had, it is difficult to see how the proprietors could be liable. These difficulties are avoided if the proprietors and editor are primarily liable.

E   Printers

The liability of the printers is based on the fact that they are the persons who actually print the articles. Such persons can be regarded, therefore, as 'publishing' the contents of the newspaper and guilty of the actus reus and as having the necessary intent. Personal ignorance of the contents of the publication will be no defence at common law; for as Lord Morris said in *McLeod v St Aubyn*[4] 'A printer or publisher intends to publish, and so intending cannot plead as justification that he did not know the contents.'[5]

In *R v Mason, ex p Director of Public Prosecutions*[6] the managing director and another director of the printers of the *Daily Worker,* Utopia Press Ltd, were held liable for publishing an edition of that paper which included a prejudicial article. In *American Exchange in Europe Ltd v Gillig*,[7] the foreman printer of the London edition of the *New York Herald*, who was held out to the public as being the publisher, was held to be guilty of contempt. In both these cases the court rejected the defence of personal ignorance of the contents, citing the *St James's Evening Post* case,[8] which, as we have seen, is the basic authority for holding that personal ignorance of the contents is no defence. In practice, the printers are rarely charged with contempt,[9] for as the printing is usually done by the newspaper concerned itself, the proprietors and the editor will be held responsible. However, where the printing is not done by the newspaper the printers can be charged as well. Printers who were ignorant of the contents of the article[10] were held liable by the Singapore High Court, again relying on the *St James's* case, in *A-G v Wain & Ors (No 1)*[11] (although no fine was imposed).

As we shall see below, where the strict liability rule applies, the Contempt of Court Act 1981 provides printers (as 'publishers'of the material) with a defence

3   But where the proprietors are a body corporate and the editor is deemed to be the alter ego thereof, they would then have to show that the editor had taken all reasonable care.
4   [1899] AC 549 at 562.
5   This paragraph was cited with approval in *Fitzgibbon v Barker* (1992) 111 FLR 191 at 202 (Family Court of Australia).
6   (1932) Times, 17 December.
7   (1889) 58 LJ Ch 706.
8   (1742) 2 Atk 469, see also *Ex p Jones* (1806) 13 Ves 237.
9   In *R v Thomson Newspapers Ltd* [1968] 1 All ER 268, [1968] 1 WLR 1, the printers were charged but a separate fine was not thought appropriate.
10   See below.
11   [1991] 2 MLJ 525; and see *R v Scott and Downland Publications Ltd* [1972] VR 663 and *R v David Syme & Co Ltd* [1982] VR 173 (Australia);

of 'innocent publication' if they did not know that the prejudiced proceedings were 'active'. That defence is very limited and, even if it was ever justifiable to fix innocent printers with liability for publications the contents of which they were entirely ignorant, it is submitted that the law needs amendment in view of modern advances in printing methods. The virtual impossibility of the printers intervening in modern printing processes to check for objectionable material is well illustrated in *A-G v Wain* where the film negatives of the pages of the *Asian Wall Street Journal* were transmitted to the printers by facsimile via satellite and then processed and printed onto printing plates which were installed on the printing presses. This happened extremely quickly: the last negative was received by the printers at 6.59 am, the last printing plate was ready by 7.02 am, and the print run of 12,650 copies was completed by 7.32 am.

Indeed, information technology means that printers can now produce a printed work without seeing the material in written form at all. The revolution in printing techniques has led to government proposals[12] that the defence of 'innocent dissemination' in the law of *libel* should be modernised to match the modern world. Clause 1 of the draft Bill published in July 1995 provides that in proceedings for defamation it is a defence for a person to show that he was not primarily responsible for the publication and did not know, and having taken all reasonable care had no reason to suspect, that the publication was defamatory. Printers are specifically mentioned as persons who are not to be regarded as primarily liable. This is, in effect, the extension of the innocent dissemination defence to printers. It is difficult to avoid the conclusion that this defence should also be available to printers in respect of contempt.

Under the Judicial Proceedings (Regulation of Reports) Act 1926, s 1(2), it is expressly stated that the master printer or publisher can be held liable for a publication contravening the provisions of that Act.

F Persons responsible for supplying information

It can be argued[13] that a reporter who supplies prejudicial information to a newspaper cannot himself be said to have committed a contempt, since he has not committed the actus reus of 'publishing' the information to the general public. All the reporter has done is to publish the information to the newspaper editor which, as we have said, cannot be sufficient 'publication' for the purposes of contempt, since it cannot be said to occasion a 'real risk' of prejudice. Such an argument, it is said, is supported by Lord Goddard CJ in *R v Griffiths, ex p A-G* [14] where he stated:

> 'The offence is not the mere preparation of the article, but the publication of it during the proceedings. . . . It has never yet been held that a reporter who supplied objectionable matter to his editor or employer, which the latter published, is himself guilty of contempt.'

Lord Goddard must have overlooked the *Evening Standard* case of three years previously; and, in any case, it is submitted that such a view does not satisfactorily explain the position of reporters. It is true that an essential part of the actus reus

12 Lord Chancellor's Department, *Reforming Defamation Law and Procedure, Consultation on Draft Bill* (July 1995).
13 See eg Miller, *Contempt of Court* (2nd edn, 1989) pp 290–291.
14 [1957] 2 QB 192 at 202.

is the publication of the article. However, it is submitted that persons who cause an article to be published to the general public must also be considered to have committed the actus reus.[15] Whether or not a person can be said to have 'caused an article to be published' will depend upon that person's responsibility towards the final publication.

There are basically three types of reporter: first, there is the reporter whose sole responsibility is to gather and collect all the available information on a particular topic, but who will neither be expected to appreciate the significance of such information nor bear any responsibility for the final publication. Second is the type of reporter who, being experienced, will not only be expected to appreciate the significance of the information, but whose reports will be published more or less as they stand. Third is the reporter who is not only responsible for collecting information, but who will also write the whole article himself.

The first reporter can arguably be considered to be not guilty of a contempt because (a) he lacks the necessary mens rea—he only intends to give the information to the editor, and (b) he does not commit the actus reus, since he cannot be said to have published the information or to have caused it to be published because he bears no responsibility for the final publication. This argument, however, does not altogether sit easily with cases which have imposed liability for contempt on persons who have made contemptuous statements *to* reporters. In *DPP v Wran* [16] the Premier of New South Wales was held to have committed contempt in the remarks he made about a forthcoming trial to a journalist in an interview. The New South Wales Court of Appeal took the view that the Premier knew that his statements would be published by the organisations to whose journalists he was speaking and that he therefore intended to make a *public* statement. The same court has held a policeman liable for contempt for statements made to a press conference after a suspect's arrest.[17] The policeman argued that he did not intend his words to go beyond the media representatives and that he relied on them to purge the material of anything which might amount to contempt. This argument was rejected on the grounds that he made the statements with the intention that they should be included in material on the basis of which the media would later compose their programmes.

This principle could also be applied to the purely news gathering reporter—that his communication to the editor is not a private conversation because he knows (or hopes) that the editor will use his material as the basis for an item in the paper and that the intentional communication of material to a person whose job it is to publish to the world makes the source of the material liable for the publication himself. On the other hand, it is equally possible to argue that the reporter is not the source of the material and is not *making* the news himself, but merely acting as a conduit for the transmission of information. It is the editor who decides what to do with it. It is submitted that this argument is the most persuasive and that reporters of the first type should not be liable for contempt. As will be seen below, authority supports this view.

The second and third type of reporter may be held responsible for contempt. In both cases the reporters must be said to have the necessary mens rea (ie the

---

15 Support for this argument may be drawn from Solomon J's judgment in *Re A-G for Manitoba and Radio OB Ltd* (1977) 70 DLR (3d) 311 at 323 (radio interviewer held guilty of contempt 'for causing information to be published').

16 (1986) 7 NSWLR 616.

17 *A-G for NSW v Dean* (1990) 20 NSWLR 650; see similarly *R v Carocchia* (1973) 43 DLR (3d) 427.

intent to publish) because they know that what they have written may be published. It is also submitted that both reporters have committed the actus reus, because they have caused the information to be published to the general public. In such cases it would surely be a narrow view to say that a reporter, on whom the newspaper has relied and who knows that he will be relied on, should bear no responsibility for the article once it is published.

The three leading cases of the 1950s demonstrate the validity of this view of the liability of different types of reporter. The first is *R v Evening Standard Co Ltd*.[18] Here the reporter had telephoned an account of the trial, but by mistake had included in his account inadmissible evidence which was held to be prejudicial. The reporter was held to be guilty of a contempt. This decision can be explained on the ground that the reporter's information was entirely relied upon; as Lord Goddard CJ said,[19] the editor 'had no reason to suppose that the report telephoned to him by the reporter was otherwise than accurate'. This reporter was within our second category, namely, a reporter on whom the newspaper would rely and who would know that his information would be relied upon. As Sir Hartley Shawcross QC said in his argument in defence of the editor:[20]

> 'In the present case the newspaper published a story received from a *reliable and experienced reporter*; the editor thought that the message received from the reporter was perfectly correct and genuine and he published it in good faith, as did the proprietors' (emphasis added).

The second case, *R v Odhams Press Ltd, ex p A-G*[1] illustrates the liability of a reporter who falls into our third class, namely, a person who not only gathers information but who also writes the article. In this case, the printer and publishers of the *People*, its editor and a reporter called Webb had been found guilty of contempt for publishing a prejudicial article. Webb, who was described as an 'experienced crime reporter and investigator' was not only responsible for gathering the information (in some instances other reporters were paid to relay certain information) but he also wrote the offending article. Webb thus played a most important part in the publication of the article and the Divisional Court fined him £500.[2]

The third case is *R v Griffiths, ex p A-G*,[3] in which an article published in *Newsweek* was held to be a contempt, as it was prejudicial to a pending trial. *Newsweek* was American owned, but its 'European' edition was printed in Amsterdam, and the circulation manager resided in Paris. Griffiths, who was one of the persons charged with the contempt, was head of the company's English office in London and the paper's chief European correspondent. The copies of *Newsweek* which were distributed in England were despatched direct from Amsterdam by air 'to and distributed by or under the direction of the Rolls House Company, without the intervention of the London office'. Such a finding

18 [1954] 1 QB 578, [1954] 1 All ER 1026.
19 Ibid at 586.
20 Ibid at 580.
1 [1957] 1 QB 73, [1956] 3 All ER 494.
2 A modern Australian example of the same type of scenario is *R v Saxon, Hadfield and Western Mail Ltd* [1984] WAR 283 in which a reporter wrote an article based on a four-week investigation into the financial affairs of a politician's wife who was facing trial for perjury. Although the article was substantially amended before it appeared (as a two-page spread in the newspaper) he was held liable for contempt.
3 [1957] 2 QB 192, [1957] 2 All ER 379.

excluded Griffiths' responsibility for the actual distribution of the magazine. Griffiths' role in relation to the particular publication was as follows. He swore:[4]

> 'that he takes no part in the preparation of the magazine; his duties are, so he says, merely those of a reporter. He collects items of news in this country and sends them by cable to New York and there it is decided what, if any, use is to be made of them; the stories are written there and apparently the European edition is made up in New York and then sent for printing to Amsterdam.'

Although Griffiths admitted that he sometimes wrote articles he swore that he did not write the article in question. The Divisional Court essentially accepted Griffiths' explanation of his role and held that:[5]

> 'it does not seem to the court that responsibility for this article or for its publication can be imposed on . . . Griffiths. The offence is not the mere preparation of the article, but the publication of it during the proceedings. It seems that the article was written in America, printed in Amsterdam and distributed by commercial houses in this country. It has never yet been held that a reporter who supplied objectionable matter to his editor or employer which the latter published is himself guilty of contempt.'

Griffiths was accordingly found not guilty of contempt. His role was simply to supply information to the head office and nothing more. In other words, he fell into our first category of reporter, who cannot be considered to have intended to publish nor be said to have caused to be published the information, since it was up to the New York office to decide what, if any, use was to be made of it. Seen in this context, Lord Goddard CJ's statements are unexceptionable but should not be thought to be applicable to reporters generally.

Journalists (and others) who write articles or columns of comment and opinion must be considered in the same category as the third class of reporter. The same argument applies to a person who writes a prejudicial letter or article to the newspaper[6] and in *Daw v Eley*,[7] a solicitor was found to have committed a contempt for writing, under a pseudonym, a prejudicial letter upon a pending suit in which he was involved.

Although it is submitted that those individuals, who can be said to be responsible for a particular newspaper article, may be properly held guilty of contempt, such individuals are in practice rarely charged. It is notable that Malcolm Muggeridge was not charged over the article he wrote which was the subject of the proceedings in *A-G v English* [8] and it is perhaps right as a matter of policy to confine prosecutions to those such as the editor and proprietors who bear an overall responsibility for the newspaper. However, recent prosecutions have been brought against journalists designated as City editors where they have actually written the offending articles themselves. One of these cases, *A-G v Associated Newspapers Ltd,* [9] concerned the major issue of revealing the deliberations of the jury[10] while another, *A-G v Guardian Newspapers Ltd,* [11] involved the breach of an order under s 4(2) of the Contempt of Court Act 1981

4 Ibid at 200.
5 [1957] 2 QB 192 at 202.
6 On this basis liability may devolve upon a newsagency. See *Re Robbins, ex p Green* (1891) 7 TLR 411.
7 (1868) LR 7 Eq 49.
8 [1983] 1 AC 116, [1982] 2 All ER 903.
9 [1994] 2 AC 238, [1994] 1 All ER 556.
10 See Ch 9, p 364.
11 [1992] 3 All ER 38.

on reporting court proceedings in which the Attorney General applied to commit the city editor to prison.

G   Distributors

The distributors of newspapers, etc, may be held liable for contempt on the ground that they are responsible for the widespread publication of the newspaper's contents. However, a paper boy, a street seller, or even the small retail shop, ought not to be held guilty of contempt because, following the principle of *McLeod v St Aubyn*,[12] they cannot be said in any real sense to have intended to publish, since they will be ignorant of the contents and under no duty to be acquainted with them.

The leading case on the liability of distributors is *R v Griffiths, ex p A-G* [13] where it was held that Rolls House Company and WH Smith & Son Ltd were guilty of contempt for distributing the American magazine, *Newsweek*, which contained comments prejudicial to a pending trial. In imposing liability Lord Goddard CJ said:[14]

> 'We shall impose a fine ... to emphasise the risk which is run by dealing in foreign publications imported here but which have no responsible editor or manager in this country. The distributors are the only persons who can in these circumstances be made amenable in the courts of this country.'

It should be noted that *R v Griffiths, ex p A-G* was solely concerned with a foreign publication and liability was imposed upon the distributors because, as Lord Goddard CJ said, they were the only persons who could be held responsible. In such cases the distributors' liability can be explained in these terms. They have obviously committed the actus reus of publishing the magazine and have the necessary intent to publish; for, although they may be personally ignorant of the contents, they were expected, at least at common law, to be acquainted with them. Whether or not the same can be said for an English publication is more doubtful. It may well be that with regard to an English publication, as the editor and proprietors will be amenable to the jurisdiction of the English courts, there is no duty upon the distributors, large or small, to be acquainted with the publication's contents.

In any event, in the United Kingdom in these circumstances the distributors are not likely to be charged with the contempt. Section 3(2) of the Contempt of Court Act 1981[15] now gives the distributors a defence if, having taken all reasonable care, they had no reason to suspect that the publication contained material which was calculated to interfere with the course of justice. This defence operates only in respect of contempt under the strict liability rule but applies irrespective of whether the publication is foreign or English.[16] Section 3 as a whole is discussed further below.[17]

---

12   [1899] AC 549.
13   [1957] 2 QB 192, [1957] 2 All ER 379.
14   Ibid at 204.
15   Formerly s 11(2) of the Administration of Justice Act 1960. The defence now applies to Scotland.
16   No change in the law relating to distributors' liability was recommended by the Phillimore Committee (1974, Cmnd 5794) para 154.
17   See pp 398–400.

II   RESPONSIBILITY OF PERSONS ENGAGED IN BROADCASTING, FILM AND TELEVISION MEDIA

Although the same principles are applicable to a television or radio broadcast as to a newspaper publication, the difficulty is to delineate the relative functions of the various persons concerned in the broadcast.

It is submitted that, as in the case of newspapers, liability at common law will devolve only on those really responsible for the broadcast, and so a technician or cameraman cannot be considered guilty of contempt, as he will be unaware of the contents of the broadcast and, being under no duty to be acquainted with them, cannot be said to have intended to publish. This principle will also exclude sound engineers; for, although they are persons who actually broadcast the programme, they have no control over what they broadcast and they will not know the subject matter of the broadcast until after it has been published.[18] Such persons cannot, therefore, be said to have the mens rea of intending to publish; and, bearing in mind that it is the producer who selects which 'camerashot' to use, it might also be said that the cameraman at least does not commit the actus reus of publishing the broadcast.

Who then can be considered to be responsible for a broadcast? There can be little doubt that liability must devolve upon the corporation or company running the broadcasting station. Such bodies are the equivalent to newspaper proprietors. In the United Kingdom this means ascribing responsibility to the BBC[19] or to the programme contractors in independent television or radio. In *R v Border Television Ltd, ex p A-G*,[20] action was brought and liability established against the television company, while in two Scottish cases, namely, *Atkins v London Weekend Television Ltd*,[1] and a case against *Radio Forth Ltd*,[2] not only was there held to be corporate liability but also the companies' managing director and chief executive respectively were held liable.

In the *Atkins* case the prosecution was also brought against Scottish Television Ltd, and its managing director but neither were held liable because neither could be said to be responsible for the programme—they had been obliged by direction of the Independent Broadcasting Authority (the IBA) acting under statutory power to provide facilities for the transmission of the programme in Scotland.[3] *Atkins* is to be contrasted with the Australian decision in *A-G New South Wales v Willesee*[4] where a licensee of a television channel was held liable for contempt for broadcasting a programme that it helped to produce albeit under contract with another company. It may be that the true distinction between the decisions lies in the respective statutory conditions under which the companies operated. In *Atkins* Scottish Television Ltd were obliged to show the programme;[5] in *Willesee* the company had a statutory obligation to exercise some control over the

18   Like printers using modern electronic techniques, but cf the position of printers using older printing methods, see p 388.
19   The Phillimore Committee at para 151 thought that the BBC Director General could be held responsible for programmes broadcast by the Corporation.
20   (1978) 68 Cr App Rep 375.
1   1978 SLT 76.
2   (1979) Times, 22 December.
3   The IBA was abolished by the Broadcasting Act 1990 and replaced by the Independent Television Commission, whose statutory functions are significantly different (ss 1–7).
4   [1980] 2 NSWLR 143.
5   Ie pursuant to the direction of the IBA acting under statutory power (ie what is now the Broadcasting Act 1981) to make such direction.

particular type of broadcast made.[6] However, there is another distinction, namely, that while Scottish Television Ltd were but a passive agent, in *Willesee* the company did provide facilities for the making of the programme.[7]

Where programmes are provided by one company to another with little chance for the second company to vet the programme's contents difficulties will inevitably arise. In *R v The Australian Broadcasting Corporation and others* [8] the two television channels concerned were both subsidiaries of the same company. The first, the Tasmanian channel TVT 6, sent the offending film[9] to the second, TNT 9 in Sydney, under an arrangement whereby TNT 9 compiled a news programme and retransmitted it to TVT 6. TVT 6 duly received and telecast a transmission from Sydney of a programme which included the piece of film it had sent to Sydney ten minutes previously. It was broadcast again on the evening news seven hours later. Nobody at TNT 9 saw the material before it was broadcast the first time, and only an acting news editor saw it before the second. Nobody at TNT 6 had any control over what was received back from Sydney or knew what the programme contained before it was broadcast. Holding both channels guilty of contempt the court said that no thought had been given to instituting a system to ensure that contempt was not committed and advised that some means be devised to control the transmission of sensitive material. In another Australian case, *A-G for NSW v TCN Channel Nine Pty Ltd* [10] the prejudicial material was supplied by one company to another who broadcast it immediately. In that case the company supplying the material alone was charged with contempt and held liable, the court saying that it was known that the second company would transmit it in the form it was supplied. Unlike the Tasmanian case the receiving channel was not the source of the prejudicial material in the first place.

A similar approach to this has been taken in the United Kingdom. Only Independent Television News was charged with contempt in *A-G v Independent Television News Ltd* [11] in which its early evening news bulletin, which was shown across the independent television network, revealed the previous IRA convictions of a person arrested for murder. The television companies which carried the bulletin were not charged. This is a realistic approach to liability, for the ITN news goes out live and there is no way in which the companies can intervene short of blacking out the bulletin in the middle of the offending sentence. Unlike *Australian Broadcasting Corporation* there was no repitition in a later broadcast. In *ITN* the strictures by the Divisional Court, about tightening up procedures and ensuring there was no recurrence of the broadcasting of this type of material, were directed solely towards ITN and not to the other companies.[12]

As far as the liability of individuals is concerned there seems little doubt that the producer of the programme can be held responsible. He is the person who has de facto control over the contents of the programme and even in a 'live' production he can 'cut' the broadcast. A programme producer was held liable for contempt in *Atkins v London Weekend Television Ltd* and fined £1,000. There is an increasing tendency, even within the BBC, for programmes to be made by independent production companies and it is submitted that such a producer

6 Under the Broadcasting and Television Act 1942.
7 See also *R v Thompson* [1989] WAR 219.
8 [1983] Tas R 161.
9 Which included pictures of a man arrested for murder.
10 (1990) 20 NSWLR 368.
11 [1995] 2 All ER 370.
12 In fact the Divisional Court held that on the facts no contempt had been committed because there was not sufficient likelihood of a risk of prejudice: see Ch 5, p 133.

would be liable for contempt even though it is the television company which buys the programme which takes the decision to broadcast it.

Difficult questions arise with regard to persons occupying positions of authority in the hierarchy other than the producer, such as the head of a particular network or station, for example the head of BBC 1 or of Radio 1, 2, 3 or 4 or of a regional or local television or radio station, or the regional head, or the person in charge of a particular type of programme, for example the head of current affairs.[13] In these cases, it could be argued that they are the persons equivalent to the editor since they exercise overall control, and are responsible for deciding which programmes are to be broadcast. In the second edition of this work we suggested [14] that where such persons are aware of the contents of the programme or are ultimately responsible for the contents, then liability can be established on the same grounds as the editor of a newspaper. Support for this proposition might be drawn from the *Atkins* decision where the editor of the feature who was said to have 'immediate and direct responsibility and control' was fined £5,000. In New Zealand, however, the Court of Appeal in *Solicitor-Generalv Radio Avon Ltd*,[15] declined to find a news editor guilty on the proposition we advanced. However, in jurisdictions where the principle of editorial responsibility is accepted there is no reason for not applying it in the broadcasting context. In Australia there appears to be a greater tendency than in the United Kingdom to charge responsible individuals with contempt and editors of news programmes and programme managers have been held liable in several cases.[16]

The position of a reporter will closely correspond with that of a newspaper reporter, and liability will therefore depend upon whether his report is edited and whether the reporter is experienced and likely to be relied upon. Closely allied with the reporter is the interviewer. An interviewer can in principle be held personally liable though the liability may depend upon his experience and responsibility for the questions asked and replies provoked. In the Canadian case, *Re A-G for Manitoba and Radio OB Ltd*,[17] an experienced radio reporter was held guilty of contempt and fined $250. Where radio and television journalists have their 'own' programme over whose content they exercise editorial control they are likely to be held personally liable. Such was the position in *Hinch v A-G for the State of Victoria* [18] where the High Court of Australia upheld a term of imprisonment imposed on an experienced journalist with his own daily programme who discussed an accused's past convictions and present circumstances on a number of occasions.

The newscaster could also be held responsible for a contempt, if he is the person who actually edits the news, since responsibility for the publication could then be attributed to him personally.

Any person, including a member of the public, who makes an unscripted remark must be regarded as being personally liable for that remark.[19] The extent

13 As the Phillimore Committee (1974, Cmnd 5794) at para 151 pointed out Independent Television News has an editor who is in charge and whose responsibility is clearly the same as that of a newspaper editor. However, no individuals were charged with contempt in *A-G v Independent Television News Ltd*.
14 At pp 264–265.
15 [1978] 1 NZLR 225.
16 See eg *R v Australian Broadcasting Corporation, A-G (NSW) v TCN Channel Nine Pty Ltd* and *R v Thompson*, discussed above.
17 (1976) 70 DLR (3d) 311 at 323. See also *Taylor v A-G* [1975] 2 NZLR 675 (NZ CA).
18 (1987) 164 CLR 15.
19 See eg, *Gallagher v Durack* (1983) 152 CLR 238, (1983) 45 ALR 53 (Aust HC), discussed in Ch 9, at p 352.

to which others should bear responsibility for unscripted remarks is more problematic. In general it seems sensible to distinguish 'live' broadcasts from recordings. In the case of the latter, given that there is opportunity to vet the contents of the programme, there is no reason to think that those bearing general responsibility for the programme should escape liability. However, in the case of a 'live' broadcast it could plausibly be argued that as the unscripted reply is completely outside the control and knowledge of those running the programme liability should be confined to the person making the remark, at least if they are a member of the public. The British Columbia Supreme Court in *R v Bannerman* [20] has held that a body running a broadcasting station cannot hope to escape liability for a contempt committed by a regular broadcaster who is given a carte blanche to select his material.[1] It was acknowledged, however, that the company might escape liability for a contempt uttered spontaneously by a person being interviewed. Even in this situation, however, it is suggested that it can only be where the remark is entirely unexpected that no other person should be held liable. If the remark is provoked then those persons responsible for the programme, such as the programme contractor, may also be held responsible. For example, if a person was interviewed in connection with a pending trial, then those responsible for the programme must surely be legally liable for any prejudicial answers, even if they are unexpected, since the interviewer is the direct cause of the answers.[2]

The Phillimore Committee thought that editorial responsibility should remain strict in all cases though absence of real responsibility could be reflected in mitigating the penalty.[3]

Liability for broadcasts in contravention of the Magistrates' Courts Act 1980, or the Sexual Offences (Amendment) Act 1976 [4] seems more limited, being said to rest upon:[5]

> 'in the case of the inclusion of a report in a relevant programme, any body corporate which is engaged in providing the service in which the programme is included and any person having functions in relation to the programme corresponding to those of the editor of a newspaper.'

This provision seems to exclude interviewers and individuals from liability.

Although contempt is very rarely committed by means of a film shown in a cinema, such a case did arise in *R v Hutchison, ex p McMahon*,[6] where a news-film was held to be prejudicial. The contempt proceedings were brought against the distributors of the film, and against the owners and the manager of the cinema which showed the film. Swift J said that it was not necessary:

> 'to say anything about this case except to call to the attention of the proprietors of film houses and of the exhibitors of films, the fact that they are in no different position than anybody else. . . . The film is no more immune from the rules regarding contempt of court than the newspaper is. *Proprietors of cinemas and*

---

20 (1980) 17 BCLR 238.
1 The proprietor radio station was liable for the contempt, and fined, in *Hinch v A-G (Victoria)* (1987) 164 CLR 15.
2 It could hardly be supposed, for example, that had contempt proceedings been brought in respect of David Frost's interview with Dr Savundra (see *R v Savundranayagen and Walker* [1968] 3 All ER 439, discussed at p 239) that the company or indeed the interviewer could have hoped to have escaped responsibility for the programme.
3 (1974, Cmnd 5794) para 152.
4 These provisions are discussed in Ch 8.
5 S 8A(11)(c) of the 1980 Act and 4(5)(c) of the 1976 Act (as amended) respectively.
6 [1936] 2 All ER 1514.

distributors of films must realise that, if they want to produce these sensational films, they must take care in describing them not to use any language likely to bring about any derangement in the carriage of justice' (emphasis added).

III   RESPONSIBILITY FOR PUBLICATIONS BY ELECTRONIC MEDIA

Modern developments in information technology raise the issue of responsibility for material on computer systems.[7] Although the person who originates the material may be said to have 'published' it for the purposes of contempt by placing it onto a bulletin board or the Internet, what is the position of operators of online computer host services, Internet Usenet newsgroups or World Wide Web pages? Some online service providers and Usenet newsgroups do exercise some editorial control but others control access rather than content. It is merely a matter of time before the problem of liability for material which is in contempt of court arises.

The draft Bill on Defamation published in July 1995 has grappled with the problem of new technology as it affects defamatory material.[8] The Bill provides that those not 'primarily responsible' for the publication of the defamatory statement will not be liable.[9] Those who are to be considered *not* primarily liable include:

'in the case of a defamatory statement published by electronic means, a person involved only—
(i)   in processing, making copies of, distributing or selling any electronic medium in or on which the statement is recorded, or
(ii)   in operating any equipment by means of which the statement is retrieved, copied or distributed.'

As with the liability of printers, discussed above, it is submitted that it would be desirable for the law of contempt to take a similar attitude.

It should be added that the defences provided by the Contempt of Court Act 1981, s 3, discussed in the next section, will apply to television or radio broadcasts, or films; for, although the section uses the word 'publishes', by analogy with the law of defamation it is clear that a broadcast constitutes a publication.[10]

IV   THE DEFENCE OF INNOCENT PUBLICATION OR DISTRIBUTION UNDER SECTION 3 OF THE CONTEMPT OF COURT ACT 1981

Following a widespread outcry against the decisions in *R v Odhams Press Ltd, ex p A-G* [11] and *R v Griffiths, ex p A-G* [12] in which it was respectively held to be no defence at common law to a charge of contempt that the publisher was

7   See the discussion of this problem in relation to defamation in Braithwaite, 'The Internet and Bulletin Board Defamation' (1995) 145 NLJ 1216.
8   See p 389 for the proposals regarding the liability of printers.
9   So long as they do not know, and having taken all reasonable care had no reason to suspect that their acts were contributing to the publication of the libel.
10   See, eg *Youssoupoff v Metro-Goldwyn-Meyer Pictures Ltd* (1934) 50 TLR 581.
11   [1957] 1 QB 73, [1956] 3 All ER 494, see p 90.
12   [1957] 2 QB 192, [1957] 2 All ER 379, see p 92 and 393.

unaware that proceedings had begun against the accused and that the distributor was unaware that a magazine they imported to and sold in this country contained potentially prejudicial material, the law was amended by s 11 of the Administration of Justice Act 1960. That section was repealed[13] and replaced by s 3 of the Contempt of Court Act 1981. Section 3 states:

'(1)   A person is not guilty of contempt of court under the strict liability rule as the publisher of any matter to which that rule applies if at the time of publication (having taken all reasonable care) he does not know and has no reason to suspect that relevant proceedings are active.

(2)   A person is not guilty of contempt of court under the strict liability rule as the distributor of a publication containing any such matter if at the time of distribution (having taken all reasonable care) he does not know that it contains such matter and has no reason to suspect that it is likely to do so.

(3)   The burden of proof of any fact tending to establish a defence afforded by this section to any person lies upon that person.'

The statutory defence applies both to Scotland and Northern Ireland as well as England and Wales.

The limited application of s 3 should be noted. First it can only be pleaded as a defence to a prosecution under the 'strict liability rule'. The defence will not therefore be available to prosecutions outside the rule, for example, where it is claimed that a publication is in breach of s 12 of the Administration of Justice Act,[14] that it scandalises the court or where it is prosecuted under the common law on the grounds that it was intended to prejudice proceedings.

Even if the defence is prima facie available, s 3 has done nothing to amend the *general* position with regard to intention. Hence, as under the common law it is still no defence for an editor or proprietor, for example, to plead that they had no personal knowledge of the contents of the offending article or that the publication was made in good faith, reliance for its accuracy being made upon an experienced reporter.[15]

It is to be noted that under s 3(3) the burden of proof lies on the defendant.[16] Following the principle laid down in *R v Carr-Briant*[17] it will be sufficient if the defence is proved on the balance of probabilities and not, as the prosecution must prove, beyond all reasonable doubt. A further point is that the section would seem to offer no protection to a person who *in fact* suspects that either proceedings are active,[18] and it would be in accord with general principles that the defence will not be afforded to an accused who 'wilfully' shuts his eyes to such facts.[19]

There is a remarkable dearth of case law on s 3(1). It seems clear that some inquiries have to be made by the publisher prior to publication but the difficulty for the media is that, pending a definitive ruling, it remains unclear how far they should be expected to go. Will it be sufficient, for example, that they had made

---

13   By s 3(4) of the Contempt of Court Act 1981.

14   It had previously been held that s 11 of the 1960 Act did not apply to s 12, see *Re F (Orse A)(a minor) (Publication of Information)* [1977] Fam 58, [1977] 1 All ER 114.

15   Ie *R v Evening Standard Co Ltd* [1954] 1 QB 578, [1954] 1 All ER 1026 is not affected.

16   Attempts were made during the passage of the Bill to reverse the burden of proof but the pleas fell on deaf ears.

17   [1943] 1 KB 607, [1943] 2 All ER 156 and followed in *R v Dunbar* [1958] 1 QB 1, [1957] 2 All ER 737.

18   Cf such cases as *R v Banks* [1916] 2 KB 621 and *R v Harrison* [1938] 3 All ER 134.

19   Following such cases as *Knox v Boyd* 1941 JC 82 at 86 per Lord Normand; *Taylor's Central Garages (Exeter) Ltd v Roper* (1951) 115 JP 445 at 449 per Devlin J; *Westminster City Council v Croyalgrange Ltd* [1986] 2 All ER 353 at 359 per Lord Bridge.

enquiries of the police and what happens if the police prove unco-operative?[20] Their difficulty in this respect is that, as we shall see, proceedings become 'active'[1] from the moment a warrant for arrest has been issued so that from this point the media are at risk of committing contempt. However, warrants for arrest are frequently issued in private, and without police co-operation it may not be possible to discover that proceedings have been started. In these cases, at any rate, it is surely sufficient if enquiries have been made of the police[2] although once a person is being questioned at a police station it would be difficult to say that a journalist had 'no reason to suspect' that proceedings were active. It may also be difficult for the media to ascertain whether civil proceedings are 'active' (ie set down for trial)[3] and, as with criminal proceedings, journalists should protect themselves by keeping a record of the inquiries they make in trying to ascertain the stage proceedings have reached.

The defence provided by s 3(2) to distributors is a more generous one. Again, there is a dearth of case law on this subsection. It *would* be open to the courts to adopt the view expressed earlier in the 1959 *Justice* report that:[4]

> 'distributors should be regarded as having reason to suspect contemptuous matter in well-known disreputable types of publication, and even in reputable foreign publications whenever a trial in England or Wales is of so sensational a nature as to excite the interest of the world.'

20 By analogy with *Re F* [1977] Fam 58, [1977] 1 All ER 114 such enquiries may be deemed sufficient: for the details of that case see p 327.
1 For the concept of 'active' proceedings, see Ch 7.
2 The Phillimore Committee did not recommend that proceedings should become 'active' at such an early point but (at para 133) they did recommend that information as to whether a criminal charge has been laid might be made available as of right to an inquirer. This recommendation might be extended to include whether a warrant for an arrest has been issued.
3 This is further discussed in Ch 7, p 261.
4 *Contempt of Court* (1959) p 10.

CHAPTER 11

Acts which interfere with the course of justice

In this chapter we examine conduct other than publications that can amount to contempt on the grounds that they interfere with the course of justice. As with publications, acts can amount to contempt either because they interfere with the due course of justice in a particular case or because they interfere with the course of justice as a continuing process.

By s 1 of the Contempt of Court Act 1981 'the strict liability rule' means the rule of law whereby 'conduct' may be treated as a contempt by tending to interfere with the course of justice in particular legal proceedings regardless of intent to do so. Section 2, however, limits the rule to 'publications'[1] and it seems, therefore, that in the United Kingdom conduct other than publications can amount to contempt in relation to particular legal proceedings only if there is mens rea. However, whether conduct can amount to a contempt on the basis that it interferes with the administration of justice as a continuing process only if there is mens rea is more uncertain both in the United Kingdom,[2] and in other common law jurisdictions.

The conduct discussed in this chapter covers interference with persons having duties to discharge in a court of justice, interference with parties to an action, breach of duty by persons officially connected with the court or its process, interfering with the court's jurisdiction over certain persons, abuse of the court's process, and other miscellaneous examples of interference with the administration of justice.

I INTERFERENCE WITH PERSONS HAVING DUTIES TO DISCHARGE IN A COURT OF JUSTICE

The general principle by which interference with persons having duties to discharge in a court of justice amounts to contempt was explained by Bowen LJ in *Re Johnson*: [3]

> 'The law has armed the High Court of Justice with the power and imposed on it the duty of preventing brevi manu and by summary proceedings any attempt to interfere with the administration of justice. It is on that ground, and not on any exaggerated notions of the dignity of individuals that insults to judges are not allowed. It is on the same ground that insults to witnesses or to jurymen are not allowed. The principle is that those who have duties to discharge in a court of justice are protected by the law, and shielded on their way to the discharge of such duties, while discharging them, and on their return therefrom, in order that such persons may safely have resort to courts of justice.'

1 For the definition of 'publications' see p 85.
2 This depends upon what is thought to be the ambit of s 1 of the 1981 Act, see pp 105–106 and 412.
3 (1887) 20 QBD 68 at 74.

The phrase 'persons having duties to discharge in a court of justice' is interpreted widely—it includes judges, jurors, witnesses and court officers such as process servers, sheriffs, bailiffs, admiralty officers, liquidators, receivers, solicitors etc.

A Interference with witnesses[4]

The protection of witnesses is vital to the due administration of justice. Lord Langdale MR said in *Littler v Thomson*: [5]

> 'if witnesses are . . . deterred from coming forward in the aid of legal proceedings it will be impossible that justice can be administered. It would be better that the doors of the courts of justice were at once closed.'

We have already seen[6] that publications even though not personally addressed to witnesses can nevertheless amount to contempt if they are likely to deter or influence witnesses; a fortiori direct attempts to deter or influence witnesses personally are regarded as serious contempts of court.

In the past there has been some suggestion that a distinction can be drawn between interfering with witnesses in civil proceedings and those involved in criminal proceedings. In *Schlesinger v Flersheim* Williams J commented:[7]

> 'interfering with witnesses in criminal prosecutions [is] essentially different from the present (civil suit) for there the public is directly interested in the punishment of the supposed delinquent, while in civil suits the public is at least only remotely interested in the due course of justice being upheld.'

It is submitted that no such distinction can validly be drawn. The law of contempt is concerned to uphold the due course of justice in all proceedings, whether criminal or civil. In any event it is wrong to emphasise the harm done to an individual since contempt law does not primarily exist to protect individuals' interests but to protect the public interest in the due administration of justice as a whole.[8]

---

4 The following discussion is concerned with contempt of court but it should be noted that interference with the witnesses at common law was a misdemeanour punishable on indictment or information. See eg *R v Lady Lawley* (1731) 2 Stra 904 and *R v Steventon* (1802) 2 East 362. Interference with witnesses can also be indicted for the crime of perverting the course of justice (see eg *R v Kellett* [1976] QB 372, [1975] 3 All ER 468 and *Archbold* (1994 edn) paras 28–10 ff) and can be covered by the statutory offence of intimidating, threatening or harming witnesses which was introduced by s 51 of the Criminal Justice and Public Order Act 1994 (discussed below). See also Law Com No 96: *Offences Relating to the Administration of Justice* (1979) paras 3.3–3.6.
5 (1839) 2 Beav 129 at 131.
6 See Chs 5 and 6.
7 (1845) 14 LJ QB 97.
8 As emphasised particularly by Lord Reid in the *A-G v Times Newspapers Ltd* (the *Sunday Times* case) [1974] AC 273 at 301. See also Wills J in *R v Davies* [1906] 1 KB 32 at 40, Bowen LJ in *Re Johnson* (1887) 20 QBD 68 at 74 and Swinton Thomas J in *R v Bashir and Azam* (1988) 10 Cr App Rep (S) 76 at 77.

1   *Interference with witnesses before or during the trial*

(a)   The actus reus

Witnesses can be interfered with in different ways but the particular form of interference is of no consequence for liability in contempt. Kay J said in *Rowden v Universities Co-operative Association Ltd* [9] all that has to be considered is 'did the act complained of interfere with the course of justice; or . . . did it interfere with the freedom of a witness's evidence?' Expressing the principle in a more modern way it is submitted that the actus reus of the offence is the commission of an act which creates a real risk of interfering either with the due course of justice in the particular case or with the administration of justice as a continuing process.[10]

Interfering with a witness before or during the trial with the design or (possibly[11]) effect of either actually preventing or deterring witnesses from giving evidence altogether or influencing them in the evidence that they are to give is obviously prejudicial to the due course of justice in the particular case and can therefore amount to contempt. It is established, however, that whether or not an approach amounts to contempt does not depend upon whether the witness is actually deterred or influenced. Cross J said in *Re B (JA) (An Infant)*: [12]

> 'the mere fact that no harm has been done in this particular case is neither here nor there. It would be unfortunate if the idea got abroad that if people threaten witnesses in this way, the worst that is likely to happen to them will be that they will have to pay some costs and make an apology.'

Cross J's statement may be justified either by saying that it is sufficient for an offence to be committed that the act creates a real risk of interfering with the due course of justice in the particular case or by saying that it is illustrative of the general principle that by protecting individual witnesses the law is safeguarding the due administration of justice as a continuing process.[13] It is suggested that where the interference occurs before the witness has given evidence the law operates to protect both interests.[14] However, where the interference occurs after the evidence has been given the law intervenes to protect the general interest in upholding the due administration of justice as a continuing process.

(i)   The time of the interference

The time at which the interference with a witness occurs can be important for although, as we shall see, the law continues to exercise its protective function even after the witness has given evidence and the legal proceedings are completed, there may be a point of time *before* which contempt cannot operate. As we saw in Chapter 7 there is some uncertainty about the time from which publications can be considered to be a contempt at common law. The way in which publications may prejudice the course of justice is quite different from the way in which interference with witnesses may, and the time

---

9   (1881) 71 LT Jo 373.
10   This would be in line with Lord Reid's judgment in the *Sunday Times* case [1974] AC 273 at 298–299.
11   Subject to the mens rea requirement, see pp 410 ff.
12   [1965] Ch 1112 at 1123; see also *Welby v Still* (1892) 8 TLR 202.
13   Under the principle expounded by *A-G v Butterworth* [1963] 1 QB 696, [1962] 3 All ER 326 discussed below.
14   This would be consistent with the reasoning in the *Sunday Times* case [1974] AC 273, [1973] 3 All ER 54. See Ch 3.

limits for these different modes of contempt need not necessarily be the same. However, it is suggested that if an improper approach is made to a potential witness when proceedings are, at the most, only imminent, a charge of perverting the course of justice is more suitable than dealing with the matter as contempt. The time limits on perverting the course of justice are wide: in *R v Rafique* [15] the Court of Appeal held that persons who threw away the evidence of a crime before anyone else knew it had been committed and therefore before any investigations had begun, were rightly charged with perverting the course of justice because they knew that an act had occurred which was likely to lead to criminal proceedings. Provided intention is proved, therefore, perverting the course of justice will lie whether the acts are done before or after the alleged offence was investigated or even discovered.[16]

(ii)   Examples of actionable contempts   Acts which prevent a witness reaching the court obviously amount to serious interference with the due administration of justice, and it is for this reason that arresting a witness while on his way to give evidence can amount to contempt.[17] A police officer was held guilty of contempt in *Connolly v Dale* [18] when he sought to prevent an agent of the defendant's solicitors from interviewing potential witnesses and showing them the defendant's photograph. His motive was to safeguard a possible identity parade but the Divisional Court said that it was a contempt to interfere with proper and reasonable attempts by a party's legal adviser to identify and interview potential witnesses.

It is a contempt to *assault* a witness, whether or not the witness is actually prevented from giving evidence.[19] Witnesses are not only protected from assaults while on their way to the court, but also while they are at court, and while they are returning from court.[20] County court judges have a statutory power to punish assaults on witnesses *in* court by committal for contempt because such conduct would amount to 'otherwise misbehaving' in court under the County Courts Act 1984, s 118(1)(b).[1] Magistrates have a statutory power to punish those who misbehave in court under s 12 of the Contempt of Court Act 1981. Strangely, there is no statutory power allowing these courts to punish assaults on witnesses going to or returning from court[2] and recourse must be had to the supervisory jurisdiction of the High Court or to the ordinary criminal law.

15   [1993] QB 843, [1993] 4 All ER 1.
16   See also *R v Kiffin* [1994] Crim LR 449; *Rafique*, supra, returns to the position established in *R v Vreones* [1891] 1 QB 360 which was always difficult to reconcile with *R v Selvage* [1982] QB 372. See also *R v Panayiotou* [1973] 3 All ER 112, [1973] 1 WLR 1032 (interfering with a woman who had made a complaint of rape); *R v Andrews* [1973] QB 422, [1973] 1 All ER 857 and *R v Sharpe* [1938] 1 All ER 48. For a discussion of this offence see eg *Archbold* (1994 edn) paras 28–1 ff; The Phillimore Report (1974, Cmnd 5794), Appendix 11 pp 104–106; The Law Commission Working Paper No 62: *Offences Relating to the Administration of Justice* (1975) pp 5–10 and Law Com No 96: (1979) paras 3.3–3.5.
17   Eg *R v Hall* (1776) 2 WBI 1110. For a general discussion on privilege from arrest see Ch 14.
18   (1995) Times, 13 July. Cf *R v MacDonald* [1994] VLR 414 (Vic Sup Ct), discussed at p 462, n 19.
19   Cf *Anon* (1356) YB 30 Edw 3, Fo 2, B, pl 14, cited in Oswald, *Contempt* (3rd edn, 1910) p 43. In *Purdin v Roberts* (1910) 74 JP Jo 88 it was held to be a contempt to assault a witness in the precincts of the court.
20   Per Bowen LJ in *Re Johnson* (1887) 20 QBD 68 at 74 quoted above at p 401.
 1   For further discussion of the statutory powers of county court judges see pp 433 and 509.
 2   Cf the case of *insulting* witnesses or officers of the court (see below) and the case of *assaults* on officers of the county court, which is dealt with by s 14 of the County Courts Act 1984, discussed at p 433.

It can be contempt to *insult* a witness during attendance in court or in going to or returning from court. As far as county court and magistrates' courts are concerned there is a statutory power to punish for this type of contempt.[3] Superior courts have a comparable common law power.[4]

It is undoubtedly a contempt to intimidate or threaten a witness and indeed the line between insults and intimidation can be a very fine one. Threats and intimidation take many forms. In the old case of *Shaw v Shaw* [5] Mrs Shaw brought a suit against her husband for judicial separation on the grounds of cruelty. One of the witnesses, a servant of Mrs Shaw, had witnessed many of the instances of the alleged cruelty. Pending the suit, the husband summoned the servant, and during a 'bullying' conversation threatened her with an action for perjury if she gave evidence against him. It was also found that the husband had written an offensive letter to another key witness. It was held that Mr Shaw, in intimidating the witnesses for the purpose of preventing them from giving evidence as witnesses, had committed a gross contempt. Similarly in *Bromilow v Phillips*,[6] a plaintiff in a pending action was held to have committed contempt when, accompanied by a police sergeant in uniform, he demanded of a witness, 'in a threatening tone of voice', what he meant by certain statements contained in his affidavit, and further accused him of having sworn a false oath. There was also evidence that both the witness and the defendant had received threatening letters, which were probably written by the plaintiff. In *Re B (JA) (An Infant)* [7] a man threatened a girl, who was to be a witness in a wardship case, that if she gave evidence he would contact the college authorities where she was studying as a trainee teacher, tell them that she had given birth to an illegitimate child, and have her 'thrown out'. Cross J held that this threat amounted to a very serious contempt and committed Woodhall to prison for four weeks. Public criticism of witnesses in a forthcoming case may be serious enough to constitute intimidation.[8]

It is established by *R v Kellett* [9] that for the purposes of the crime of perverting the course of justice it is no defence per se[10] to argue that the threat used to persuade a witness to alter or withhold his evidence was the exercise of a legal right. In *Kellett* it was held that the appellant was rightly convicted for threatening to bring an action for slander against his next door neighbours unless they withdrew statements made to an enquiry agent which were going to be used by the appellant's wife in divorce proceedings against him. It is submitted that the position is the same in contempt cases.[11]

3 County Courts Act 1984, s 118(1)(a); Contempt of Court Act 1981, s 12(1)(a) (magistrates).
4 See eg *R v Smithers and Bowen* (1983) 5 Cr App Rep (S) 248. The tone of insults seems to have deteriorated over the years, cf the 'd - d perjured scoundrel' of *Re Johnson* (1887) 20 QBD 68 with *Smithers and Bowen's* 'f***ing bastard'.
5 (1861) 2 Sw & Tr 517, 31 LJ PM & A 35. See also *Partridge v Partridge* (1639) Toth 40.
6 (1891) 40 WR 220, 8 TLR 168.
7 [1965] Ch 1112, [1965] 2 All ER 168.
8 See *Hutchinson v Amalgamated Engineering Union, Re Daily Worker* (1932) Times, 25 August, discussed in Ch 6, p 198.
9 [1976] QB 372, [1975] 3 All ER 468; For an excellent note on this decision see [1975] Crim LR 578. Cf *Webster v Bakewell RDC* [1916] 1 Ch 300 where a threat made against a party to exercise a legal right was held permissible. See p 445.
10 Stephenson LJ emphasised (ibid at 386–7) that not all interferences with witnesses are contempts. It is relevant for example whether the witness is telling the truth—it would be no offence if a person 'went privately to a witness who had made a false statement and by reasoned argument tried to dissuade him from committing perjury ...'.
11 See eg *Chapman v Honig* [1963] 2 QB 502, [1963] 2 All ER 513 discussed at pp 418–422.

Most modern cases of interfering with witnesses concern intimidation or threats of violence.[12] As Swinton Thomas J said in *R v Bashir and Azam*:[13]

'Threats of violence made to witnesses are things which were virtually unknown in years gone by, but are now, as has been pointed out, on the increase. It is comparatively rare that threats of this nature come to light and perpetrators can be brought to justice.'

His Lordship may have been unduly sanguine about the past but it is certainly thought that the cases which are discovered now are but the tip of a very large iceberg. The concern of the Government about such allegations resulted in a new statutory offence of intimidating, threatening or harming witnesses being created in 1994 which will exist alongside contempt and the offence of perverting the course of justice.[14]

It may also be a contempt to bribe or attempt to bribe a witness. In *Lewis v James*,[15] an attempt was made to bribe a witness to conceal herself, so that the defendant could not find her. Kay J said:

'To tamper with a witness in an action and induce her to go away by an offer of money was a gross contempt of court and an interference with the fair trial of the action.'

In *Re Hooley, Rucker*'s case,[16] during bankruptcy proceedings at which Hooley was being publicly examined, directors of a certain company agreed to pay his wife[17] £1,500 if Hooley would keep silent as to the part of the evidence which was adverse to the directors. Wright J held that, in endeavouring by bribery to induce a witness to suppress evidence which it was his duty to give, the directors had committed a contempt and they were fined £200.

An attempt to influence a witness can amount to contempt, even without evidence of intimidation or bribery. In *Welby v Still*,[18] it was held to be a contempt for the plaintiff's solicitor and his son to write letters to persons who would probably be called as witnesses. The contents of the letters were not threatening in any way, but they did disparage the defendants. One letter concluded with the following statement:

'I am obliged to adopt this course, especially having regard to the systematically dishonest and dishonourable course of conduct which the defendants have pursued towards the ... plaintiff.'

Other letters tended to prejudge the case by asserting that the defendants had 'robbed the estate', when the subject of the action was a charge against a firm of solicitors that they had failed to account for certain mortgage moneys advanced

---

12 See eg *R v Mulvaney* (1982) 4 Cr App Rep (S) 106; *R v Pittendrigh* (1985) 7 Cr App Rep (S) 221; *R v Maloney* (1986) 8 Cr App Rep (S) 123; *R v James* (1988) 10 Cr App Rep (S) 392; *R v Smith* (1989) 11 Cr App Rep (S) 353. It is doubtful whether the statement 'If he goes down I will kill the f***ing lot of you' directed in *R v Palmer* [1992] 3 All ER 289 by the girlfriend of the accused at the assembled prosecution witnesses as she physically assaulted them in the court foyer when she returned drunk from lunch, was a serious threat to their lives; at any rate the Court of Appeal commuted her three months custodial sentence, having regard to the circumstances which included the fact that she had young children: see further p 526.
13 (1988) 10 Cr App R (S) 76 at 77.
14 Criminal Justice and Public Order Act 1994, s 51, discussed at pp 426–429.
15 (1887) 3 TLR 527. See also *Clement v Williams* (1836) 1 Hodg 382, 2 Scott 814.
16 (1898) 79 LT 306, not to be confused with *Re Hooley, ex p Hooley* (1899) 79 LT 306.
17 The court held that the arrangement to pay the money to Mrs Hooley was a mere sham.
18 (1892) 66 LT 523, 8 TLR 202.

to a deceased. Obviously such assertions were prejudicial, and if they had been publicly published they would have been adjudged to have been contempt—the fact that they had been sent to potential witnesses personally could only increase the risk of prejudice. Kekewich J had not 'the slightest doubt or hesitation' that such letters amounted to contempt. He said:

> 'The stream of justice was, unfortunately, in the present day slow in its course, but he hoped it was still possible to keep it pure and unpolluted . . . It was true . . . there had been no intimidation here; but there had been an endeavour to warp the minds of possible witnesses. That could not be allowed . . .'.

It can also be a contempt to attempt to persuade a witness to alter his evidence. An approach might be made, for example, after the witness has given evidence at transfer for trial (formerly committal) proceedings, but before the actual trial has begun.[19]

It is a contempt during proceedings, to victimise or threaten a witness for having given evidence either because of the potential effect upon other witnesses in that case or because of the danger of affecting witnesses generally. An example of the former is *Rowden v Universities Co-operative Association Ltd*[20] where an employee of the Association had given evidence in support of a motion against the Association. Before the trial of the action came to be heard, the general manager wrote the following letter:

> 'It having come to my knowledge that you have sworn an affidavit against the association (your employers) I am compelled to at once suspend you from your duties pending the decision of the directors.'

The employee's son was also suspended and as a result of this action other employees were afraid to give evidence. Kay J had no doubts that this action amounted to contempt:

> 'he could not conceive a grosser offence against a court of justice than to endeavour to exercise a power, legal or illegal, in order to punish a witness for giving evidence, or to induce him to pervert evidence. A gross and flagrant contempt had been perpetrated.'

An example of the latter is *Moore v Clerk of Assize, Bristol*[1] where a schoolgirl having been released by the judge at the end of her evidence (the hearing still continuing) went to lunch near the court. Moore called the girl over and asked her what she meant by 'splitting on his brother' and then said 'You had better get out of here quick' and clenched his fist. The girl was frightened and told a policeman what had happened. The Court of Appeal held that Moore's action amounted to a contempt, as:

> 'The court would always preserve the freedom and integrity of witnesses and not allow them to be intimidated in any way, either before the trial, pending it, or after it.'

(iii) Not every approach to a witness amounts to an actionable contempt Not every approach to a witness will amount to an actionable contempt. In some

19 See *R v Greenberg* (1919) 83 JP 167.
20 (1881) 71 LT Jo 373.
 1 [1972] 1 All ER 58, [1971] 1 WLR 1669 following *A-G v Butterworth* [1963] 1 QB 696, [1962] 3 All ER 326 discussed below. Bowen LJ's statement in *Re Johnson* (1887) 20 QBD 68 at 74 (cited at p 401) is also supportive of the wide principle that interference with witnesses affects the administration of justice generally. See also *Purdin v Roberts* (1910) 74 JP Jo 88.

cases, although there may be a risk of influence the court may hold that the risk is not serious enough to warrant its intervention. In the Scots case, *Forkes v Weir*,[2] Lord Kyllachy said that it was:

> 'not unlawful to approach witnesses and ascertain what they have got to say. In the course of such communications an altercation may arise and foolish things may be said. But the question is whether there is . . . such a serious case of intimidation as to make it necessary for me to have a trial of the matter within this case.'

The dividing line between lawful and unlawful approaches is not always easy to draw and there is difficulty in stating the extent to which it is permissible to seek to influence witnesses. The Court of Appeal in *R v Toney*[3] was far less tolerant than Lord Kyllachy when it held that a conversation between the accused's brother and a witness in which the former tried to dissuade the latter from giving evidence amounted to perverting the course of justice, despite the fact that there was no bribery, threats, force or intimidation used, but just persuasion.[4] On the other hand, discussions between an expert witness and his colleagues about the evidence the former will give cannot, it is submitted, be considered a contempt even though the discussions result in the witness changing his mind, unless the colleagues had set out to warp his judgment. On the other hand, acts such as assaults, intimidation and bribery speak for themselves and the only issue in any contempt action will be with regard to the mens rea.

One difficult issue concerns media interviews with witnesses with a view to obtaining background material for stories to be published after the trial. Such conduct is generally regarded as being legitimate practice.[5] However, such interviews normally involve payment and that raises the problems discussed below.

(iv)   The position with regard to the payment of witnesses[6]   As we have seen it is a contempt to bribe or attempt to bribe a witness but not all payments to witnesses will amount to bribery and neither will they all amount to contempt. A litigant offering to pay a witness money to pay his expenses in return for his agreeing to give evidence clearly does not commit a contempt so long as the amount does not go beyond expenses. Expert witnesses may be paid, and may even be paid for discussing their evidence in a television programme.[7]

It is common practice for newspapers to 'buy' witnesses' stories for publication after the trial. Perhaps surprisingly this has not hitherto been the subject of contempt proceedings, although it is a practice which arouses considerable disquiet. It can be argued that it offers a general inducement to witnesses to embellish and sensationalise their evidence with a view to increasing the market rate for their story. It may be disclosed in court that they have sold their stories and the spectacle of a procession of people already signed up to the press giving evidence in a serious criminal trial is an unedifying and worrying one.[8] A practice

2   1897 5 SLT 194; see also *Re Cornish, Staff v Gill* (1893) 9 TLR 196.
3   (1993) 97 Cr App Rep 176.
4   On the lines that the accused and the witness had been at school together etc.
5   See the discussion on interviews with witnesses in Ch 5 at pp 159.
6   See Lanham, 'Payment to Witnesses and Contempt of Court' [1975] Crim LR 144.
7   *Schering Chemicals Ltd v Falkman Ltd* [1982] QB, [1981] 2 All ER 321.
8   The muddying of the waters that such deals can cause was demonstrated in the Rosemary West trial in October 1995. Several of the prosecution witnesses had already 'sold' their stories to the Press and in one case defence counsel suggested to the witness in cross-examination that she was exaggerating what had happened to her because of this. Counsel later accepted that she had not changed her story from the allegations she had originally made 20 years before.

that gives rise to particular concern is the agreement to pay a witness for his story, the amount being contingent upon the verdict. The lawfulness of such agreements has yet to be directly tested in the courts. It is submitted, however, that such an arrangement could amount to contempt since it seems to provide an inducement to the witness to 'tailor' his evidence so as to secure the more financially lucrative result.

From time to time this alleged practice comes into public prominence. There was, for example, widespread disquiet following allegations in the 'Moors Murder' trial[9] that the leading witness was being paid £15 a week during the trial by a newspaper which also promised to pay him a large lump sum for his 'exclusive story' the amount being reputedly contingent upon the verdict. The trial judge observed that the alleged payment 'seems to be a gross interference with the course of justice'. As a result of these allegations an investigation was ordered to be undertaken by the Attorney General, but no further proceedings were brought. The Attorney General said in the House of Commons:[10]

> 'There is no evidence that the testimony of any witness in the murder trial referred to was affected by the payments in question. I have decided not to take proceedings in respect of the newspaper concerned. However, the practice of paying witnesses for information about the subject matter of a trial and interviewing them about the information before they give evidence does give rise to serious problems in relation to the administration of justice. Accordingly, the Government proposes to examine these problems with a view to making such changes in the law as may prove necessary.'

With regard to the allegation that the amount of money was contingent upon the result, the Attorney General said that this had not been proved but:

> 'the most important factor which decided me not to take proceedings was the knowledge that, in any event, the evidence of the two witnesses . . . was not affected by any of these payments at all.'

He concluded:

> 'I am aware of the public feeling on this matter and I am grateful that these questions and the opinions that have been expressed in this House have underlined the importance of this matter. I hope that, even before any Government action is taken, Fleet Street will now put its house in order.'

No changes in the law were made and the Phillimore Committee urged[11] that an inquiry into this practice should be carried out but again no action was taken. The issue again came into prominence in connection with the trial of Jeremy Thorpe[12] and others with allegations that the leading witness, Peter Bessell, had agreed to sell his story to the *Sunday Telegraph*, the amount of the fee being reputedly contingent on a verdict of guilty. Again no legal action was taken though the Press Council did condemn the *Sunday Telegraph*'s dealings with Bessell. It was decided not to legislate on the issue in the Contempt of Court Bill, the Attorney General being apparently satisfied with the Press Council's action.[13]

It is submitted that the practice of paying witnesses' fees, the amount of which is contingent upon a particular verdict, is undesirable as it is likely to create a risk

9 *R v Brady and Hindley* (unreported).
10 728 HC Official Report (5th series) cols 400-403. See also (1966) Times, 12 May.
11 At para 79.
12 *R v Holmes* (22 June 1979, unreported).
13 1000 HC Official Report (5th series) col 30.

of prejudice. As we know from the revelations published by the *New Statesman*,[14] the jurors in the Thorpe trial were greatly influenced by the agreed payments to Bessell and in any event such agreements seem obvious inducements to witnesses to embellish and tailor their evidence.

The Code of Practice enforced by the Press Complaints Commission (PCC) since January 1991 states, in Clause 8, that payments, or offers of payment, should not be made, inter alia, to 'witnesses or potential witnesses' in current criminal proceedings unless 'the material concerned ought to be published in the public interest and the payment is necessary for this to be done'. However, it is clear that 'enforcement' by the PCC[15] is no substitute for contempt laws. It seems a pity that no action was taken during the passage of the Contempt of Court Bill and in view of legislative inaction since then it is suggested that the next time the issue arises the Attorney General should prosecute and have the matter directly tested in the courts. Indeed, even where the payment is not contingent on the outcome, media payment to witnesses is, it is suggested, a matter which should be addressed urgently because of the suspicion of taint on the evidence such payment produces.

(b)   The mens rea

(i)   At common law   In *Re A-G's Application, A-G v Butterworth* [16] it was argued that the correct test to apply in considering whether a person is guilty of contempt, is a purely objective one, so that, provided that the act tended to interfere with the course of justice, the state of the alleged contemnor's mind was irrelevant. Although the Court of Appeal rejected this contention, the reasoning of their Lordships differed. According to Lord Denning MR:[17]

> 'the law requires a guilty mind in these cases of intimidation or victimisation of witnesses . . . It seems to me that the intimidation of a witness is only a contempt of court if it is done with the purpose of deterring him from giving evidence or influencing him to give it in a sense different from that which he would otherwise have given it, and the victimisation of a witness is only a contempt of court if it is done with the purpose of punishing him for having given evidence in the sense he did.'

Donovan LJ, however, said:[18]

> 'I conceive the position . . . to be this. *R v Odhams Press Ltd, ex p A-G* [19] makes it clear that an intention to interfere with the proper administration of justice is not an essential ingredient of the offence of contempt of court. It is enough if the action complained of is inherently likely so to interfere. A newspaper article accusing a man of crime after proceedings have begun [against him] and before his trial plainly answers that description. But there may be other actions where the likely effect is not self-evident, and further inquiry will have to be made.'

14   For which publication they were prosecuted: see *A-G v New Statesman and Nation Publishing Co Ltd* [1981] QB 1, [1980] 1 All ER 644, discussed in Ch 9. It is ironic that the only contempt proceedings which arose from this sorry affair were brought against the *New Statesman* for airing the problem rather than against the *Sunday Telegraph*.

15   For an account of the Press Complaints Commission, its predecessor the Press Council, and the Code of Practice and its origins, see Robertson and Nicol, *Media Law* (3rd edn) pp 521–540.

16   [1963] 1 QB 696, [1962] 3 All ER 326.

17   Ibid at 722,723.

18   Ibid at 726.

19   [1957] 1 QB 73, [1956] 3 All ER 494.

Donovan LJ went on to explain that victimisation of a witness for having given evidence was an example of a case where further inquiries would have to be made.

The tests laid down by Lord Denning MR and Donovan LJ differ in one important respect, namely, that whereas according to Lord Denning MR, in order to establish that an approach to a witness amounts to contempt, it must be shown that the alleged contemnor intended to influence the witness, according to Donovan LJ it could be sufficient to show that the approach was itself inherently likely to interfere with the witness's evidence. Whichever test one applies, it seems clear that before an approach made to a witness can amount to a contempt, it must be shown that the alleged contemnor knew that the person he approached was a witness or a potential witness. Cross J said in *Re B (JA) (An Infant):*[20]

> 'it is not, as I understand the law, necessary in these days that the alleged contemnor should know that the person to whom he is uttering a threat has made a statement or made up his mind to give evidence. It is quite sufficient that he should know that he is a potential witness—a person who, unless prevented, will very likely give evidence.'

To the extent that there must be knowledge that the person approached is a witness or a potential witness, the test is subjective. However, once it is shown that the alleged contemnor knew he was approaching a witness or potential witness, then it is submitted the correct test to apply is that of Donovan LJ, rather than that of Lord Denning MR, namely, that it is enough that the action complained of is inherently likely to interfere with the course of justice. This was the approach taken by the Divisional Court in *Connolly v Dale* [1] where there was a threat to *particular* proceedings. Balcombe LJ, giving the judgment of the court, said that an intention to interfere with the course of justice connoted an intention to bring about a state of affairs which, objectively construed, amounted to such interference. He relied, inter alia, on Lloyd LJ's words in *A-G v Newspaper Publishing Plc* [2] that 'As in other branches of the criminal law, that intent may exist even though there is no desire to interfere with the course of justice'. Donovan LJ's approach has also been preferred to that of Lord Denning MR's in Australian cases.[3]

Most impugned acts will be accompanied by an intention to influence witnesses[4] but one example where the matter could be significant is if an action is brought against a newspaper for paying witnesses for their story, as discussed above. In such a case it is doubtful that an editor would have intended to influence the witness but the effect of payment could be thought to interfere with the due course of justice.

---

20 [1965] Ch 1112 at 1122.
1 (1995) Times, 13 July, for the facts see p 404.
2 [1988] Ch 333 at 383.
3 *Brambles Holdings Ltd v Trade Practices Commission* (1980) 32 ALR 328 at 340, 44 FLR 182 at 194, 5 (Aust FC) and *Supreme Court Registrar, Equity Division v McPherson* [1980] 1 NSWLR 688 at 700 per Hope JA (NSW CA). In *Gregory v Philip Morris Ltd* (1987) 74 ALR 300 Gray J said that it must be proved that the contemnor had some appreciation that the person threatened was a potential witness and some intention to dissuade him from giving (truthful) evidence and that the requirement of intention could be satisfied by reckless disregard of the likely effect of the threat.
4 *Connolly v Dale* was an unusual situation in that the contemnor was trying to *shield* witnesses from what he perceived as interference from others.

(ii)   The effect of the Contempt of Court Act 1981   As we have seen in Chapters 3 and 4, the Contempt of Court Act 1981, s 1, introduced a 'strict liability rule' by which conduct tending to interfere with the course of justice in particular proceedings is treated as contempt regardless of intent to do so. Section 2, however, confines the strict liability rule to publications.[5] It follows from this that insofar as interference with witnesses affecting *particular* legal proceedings does not involve a publication, it requires mens rea—which presumably means an intention to interfere with the course of justice in particular legal proceedings. However, as we have argued above, interference with witnesses can also be seen as interfering with the course of justice as a *continuing process.*

Interference with witnesses *after* the trial however, as we shall see,[6] can only affect the course of justice generally. It is submitted that it is quite illogical to make the mens rea requirements for contempt by interfering with witnesses differ depending on the time at which the interference takes place. They should be the same. Insofar as *all* interference with witnesses is an interference with the course of justice generally it is submitted that the mens rea requirements are not affected by the Act and that the common law alone applies. This view is in line with *Connolly v Dale,* which was decided without any reference to the Act, and with the comments by Sir John Donaldson in *A-G v Newspaper Publishing Plc.*[7] A further argument in support of this view is that the purpose of the Act was to deal with contempt by publication[8] and not with interference with witnesses (and jurors). Conduct interfering with the course of justice as a continuing process lies outside the Act and conduct so impugned will therefore continue to be governed by the common law as exemplified by *A-G v Butterworth.*

2   Interference with witnesses after the trial

(a)   The principle

That it can be a contempt to take reprisals against witnesses in respect of the evidence that they have given even though the case itself has been concluded was first established by *Re A-G's Application, A-G v Butterworth.*[9] In that case Greenlees, who was the honourary treasurer and London delegate of the Romford Branch of the National Federation of Retail Newsagents, Booksellers and Stationers, had given evidence before the Restrictive Practices Court against a restrictive agreement known as RENA to which the Federation was a party. After the case was over the Romford Branch passed a resolution strongly deprecating Greenlees for having given evidence and removing him from his office. In fact these resolutions were invalid as they did not follow the Federation's own rules, but the amended contempt motion brought by the Attorney General against ten

---

5   As the Attorney General commented in a debate on the Bill (1000 HC Official Report (5th series) col 30), the practice of promising payments to witnesses in a pending case:

'is not, of course, itself a publication, and therefore, in so far as it could now be held to be a contempt under the strict liability rule, it will cease to be such by virtue of clause 2(1).'

As we have seen above, however, the payment of witnesses has *not* hitherto been prosecuted as a contempt at all.

6   See below.
7   [1988] Ch 333 at 374, quoted at p 415.
8   For the background to the Act, see Ch 3.
9   [1963] 1 QB 696, [1962] 3 All ER 326.

members who had attended the meeting was that the respondents should be committed for contempt for purporting or attempting to relieve Greenlees of his appointment.

The Court of Appeal held that in principle such acts could amount to contempt even though the legal proceedings had been concluded. Lord Denning MR said:[10]

'there can be no greater contempt than to intimidate a witness before he gives evidence or to victimise him afterwards for having given it. How can we expect a witness to give his evidence freely and frankly, as he ought to do, if he is liable as soon as the case is over, to be punished for it by those who dislike the evidence he has given? . . . If this sort of thing could be done in a single case with impunity, the news of it would soon get round. Witnesses in other cases could be unwilling to come forward to give evidence, or, if they did come forward, they would hesitate to speak the truth, for fear of the consequences.'

Donovan LJ commented[11] that the question to be decided:

'as in all cases of alleged contempt of court, is whether the action complained of is calculated to interfere with the proper administration of justice. There is more than one way of so interfering. The authority of a court may be lowered by scurrilous abuse. Its effectiveness to do justice may be diminished or destroyed in a pending case by frightening intending witnesses from the witness box. After giving evidence a witness may be punished for having done so, thereby deterring potential witnesses in future cases from risking a like vengeance. I see no such difference between any of these three methods as makes the first two contempt of court, and the third not. Each is calculated to do the same thing, namely, to interfere with the proper administration of the law in courts of justice.'

It was thus held that attempting to injure or harm a witness for having given evidence amounts to contempt on the broad ground that such conduct was likely to deter potential witnesses from giving evidence in future cases. Two cases in particular[12] were said to support this broad principle. The first concerned contempt of Parliament.[13] A stationmaster who had given evidence against the interests of his employers before a House of Commons' Select Committee was later dismissed from his employment. The House resolved that the employers' action amounted to a breach of privilege. The Speaker told them:[14]

'The breach of privilege which you have committed is, that you have by your conduct intimidated a witness before this House; that your conduct towards him is calculated to deter witnesses in giving evidence before the House or its committees . . . A great principle has been infringed, the principle that evidence given before this House shall be free and unrestrained.'

As a result of this case the Witnesses (Public Inquiries) Protection Act 1892 was enacted to provide a more convenient machinery for punishing such contempt. According to s 2:

'Every person who commits any of the following acts, that is to say, who threatens, or in any way punishes, damnifies, or injures, or attempts to punish, damnify, or injure, any person for having given evidence upon any inquiry ... shall, unless such

10 Ibid at 719.
11 Ibid at 723.
12 Other cases referred to included: *Littler v Thomson* (1839) 2 Beav 129; *Rowden v Universities Co-operative Association Ltd* (1881) 71 LT Jo 373; *Re Taylor, Industrial Registrar v Smith* (1949) 65 Comm AR Vol 4 1137 (Aust).
13 The case of *John Hood*.
14 147 HC Journals (1892) 167.

evidence was given in bad faith, be guilty of a misdemeanour, and be liable on conviction thereof to a maximum penalty of level three on the standard scale, or to a maximum imprisonment of three months.'

Under s 1, the Act does not apply to 'any inquiry by a court of justice,' but both Lord Denning MR and Donovan LJ[15] considered that the only sensible inference from the limitation was that Parliament must have considered that the courts already had their own powers to commit for such contempt.

The second case was an Irish decision, *R v Martin.* [16] The foreman of a jury had returned home after the conclusion of a case in which one John Martin had been convicted. The brother of the convicted man called at the house and challenged the foreman to mortal combat for allegedly having bullied the jury into returning a verdict of 'Guilty'. In holding this to be a contempt, Pigot CB made no reference to the timing of the challenge (which was after the trial) but instead based his decision on the broad ground [17] 'that juries should be protected from every interference with them in reference to the discharge of their important and sacred duties'. Donovan LJ commented:[18]

'I can see no essential difference between an attempt to punish a juror for having done his duty in court and an attempt to punish a witness for having done the same thing.'

(b) The mens rea requirement

As we have seen, Lord Denning MR and Donovan LJ had different views about the general need for mens rea in contempt cases. However, both agreed that in the *Butterworth* case it was not enough to show that Greenlees had been removed from his offices and that it could only be a contempt, if the action was taken to punish him for having given evidence. Donovan LJ explained the relevance of intention in this regard in the following way:[19]

'*R v Odhams Press Ltd, ex p A-G* [20] makes it clear that an intention to interfere with the proper administration of justice is not an essential ingredient of the offence of contempt of court. It is enough if the action complained of is inherently likely so to interfere. A newspaper article accusing a man of crime after proceedings have been begun and before his trial plainly answers that description. But there may be other actions where the likely effect is not self-evident, and further inquiry will have to be made. The present case is an instance. The respondents were within their legal rights in seeking to relieve Greenlees from his honorary posts. But if the object of doing so was not merely to exercise that right for the good of the branch but to punish him for the evidence which he gave before the Restrictive Practices Court, and if the taking of such revenge was calculated to interfere with the administration of justice, then it will be no answer for the respondents to say that, while intending to punish Mr Greenlees, still they had no intention of interfering with the administration of justice. Thus far the case is no different from *R v Odhams Press Ltd, ex p A-G*. But where it differs is that in order to determine the

15 [1963] 1 QB 696 at 721 and 724 respectively.
16 (1848) 5 Cox CC 356. The court might have also relied upon Bowen LJ's statement in *Re Johnson* (1887) 20 QBD 68 at 74 that the law protects those having duties to discharge in a court of justice inter alia on their return from the court.
17 Ibid at 359.
18 [1963] 1 QB 696 at 725.
19 Ibid at 726.
20 [1957] 1 QB 73, [1956] 3 All ER 494.

likely effect of what the respondents did one has to inquire into their motives. The mere fact that the court has to do this cannot, in my view, involve the consequence that contempt of court has not been committed. No doubt there are cases where such an inquiry will present difficulties, but they are not so overwhelming as to justify the conclusion that the jurisdiction does not exist, and the burden of proof will always be on those who allege contempt.'

Lord Denning MR said:[1]

'It is easy to imagine cases where dismissal of a witness from his employment or his suspension or expulsion from a trade union might well be done and justified for reasons quite apart from the evidence he has given, and that clearly would not be a contempt of court. It seems to me that ... the victimisation of a witness is only a contempt of court if it is done with the purpose of punishing him for having given evidence in the sense he did.'

The question therefore, in the *Butterworth* case was, what was the motive of the various members present at the meetings in voting to remove Greenlees from his offices? If the sole motive was to punish him for having given evidence against the Federation, that clearly amounted to contempt, but if on the other hand the sole motive was to remove him for the benefit of the Federation, no contempt would have been committed. The question of motives must necessarily be a question of fact and the Court of Appeal relied upon the findings of the Restrictive Practices Court in this respect.[2] As will most often be the case, the court found that most of the members had mixed motives. It was found that in the case of three members it was their predominant motive to punish Greenlees for giving evidence. In the case of three others it was found that though they intended to punish Greenlees, this was not the predominant motive. In the case of the four remaining members there was not enough evidence to show what their intention was. The position as regards mixed motives was clearly explained by Lord Denning MR:[3]

'If it is done with the predominant motive of punishing witnesses, there can be no doubt that it is a contempt of court. But even though it is not the predominant motive, yet nevertheless if it is an actuating motive influencing the step taken, it is, in my judgment, a contempt of court. I do not think the court is able to, or should, enter into a nice assessment of the weight of the various motives which, mixed together, result in a victimisation of a witness. If one of the purposes actuating the step is the purpose of punishment, then it is a contempt of court in everyone so actuated.'

Accordingly, six members were found to have committed contempt.

Sir John Donaldson MR commented in *A-G v Newspaper Publishing Plc,*[4] in referring to the definition of the strict liability rule in s 1 of the 1981 Contempt of Court Act, that:

'there may well be instances of conduct which would be treated as contempt of court regardless of intent to do so but which do not fall within this defined term. One example may be *A-G v Butterworth* because the act complained of . . . was calculated to interfere with future proceedings in general.'

1 [1963] 1 QB 696 at 722.
2 Sub nom, *Re A-G's Application* (1962) LR 3 RP 1 at 24–28.
3 [1963] 1 QB 696 at 723. For a discussion of the decision particularly with regard to the motive requirement see Goodhart, (1963) 79 LQR 5 at 8–9.
4 [1988] Ch 333 at 374.

The Master of the Rolls was not, it is submitted, saying that *Butterworth* suggests that *no* mens rea is required in this type of contempt but rather that the mens rea requirement does not entail an intention to interfere with the course of justice in future proceedings. All that is needed is an act which disadvantages the former witness which is motivated by a wish to punish him for having given evidence. There is no need for the contemnor to contemplate the effect on the administration of justice generally.

As is argued above,[5] the strict liability rule in s 2 of the Contempt of Court Act 1981 leaves untouched acts which interfere with the course of justice as a continuing process and the common law rules continue to apply. As is seen from the comment of the Master of the Rolls in *A-G v Newspaper Publishing Plc* quoted above, he considered that interference with witnesses after the trial was outside the strict liability rule as defined in the Act.

(c)   Does the victimisation have to be public?

In *Chapman v Honig*,[6] Pearson LJ suggested[7] that victimisation of a witness is not per se a contempt and that an additional element had to be proved, namely, that the victimisation has to be public. This is because the determining factor in deciding whether a contempt is committed is not the 'harm done to the individual but [the] harm done to the administration of justice' and in Pearson LJ's view witnesses in general will only be deterred from giving evidence if they know of the victimisation. The majority,[8] however, disagreed. Lord Denning MR was particularly critical, commenting:[9]

> 'If that is right, it would mean this, that if the tenant proclaims his grievance upon the housetops, telling everyone about it, the landlord is guilty of contempt. But if the tenant should keep his suffering to himself, without telling his neighbours why he is evicted, the landlord does no wrong. That cannot be right ... In my judgment the victimisation of a witness is a contempt of court and unlawful, irrespective of whether other people get to know it or not. It is a gross affront to the dignity and authority of the court ...'.

In the subsequent case of *Moore v Clerk of Assize, Bristol* [10] Edmund-Davies LJ expressly adopted Lord Denning MR's view so that it would seem that the weight of authority is that victimisation of a witness amounts to a contempt irrespective of whether other people get to know of the action.

Despite the apparent logic of Pearson LJ's views it is submitted that it ought still to be a contempt even if no-one other than the alleged contemnor and witness is aware of what has happened. At the very least in such cases the witness himself is likely to be deterred from giving evidence in other cases and that is itself damaging to the administration of justice. In any event if it is known that the law does not regard private victimisation as a contempt that in itself is likely to operate as a general deterrence against giving evidence.

5   See p 412.
6   [1963] 2 QB 502, [1963] 2 All ER 513.
7   Ibid at 518–519.
8   Ie Lord Denning MR and Edmund-Davies LJ.
9   Ibid at 511–12.
10   [1972] 1 All ER 58 at 59.

(d)   The subsequent application of the '*Butterworth* principle'

Although the principle established in the *Butterworth* case arguably[11] significantly extended the law of contempt it has now become firmly established.[12] With regard to its particular application to the victimisation of witnesses it has been followed in England,[13] Australia[14] and New Zealand.[15] One English case was *Roebuck v National Union of Miners (Yorkshire Area)*[16] where it was held to be a contempt to punish a witness for statements made to a party's solicitors and to be no defence to argue that the witness was punished not for giving evidence but for giving misleading evidence to the party's solicitor. Judge Rubin said if that argument had been right:[17]

> 'every other witness who has given a statement to a union's solicitor will be under pressure when he goes into the witness box to give evidence in accordance with that statement whether it be the truth or not. In my judgment, that is truly muddying the course of justice. A witness should be free to go into the witness box and give evidence according to his view of the truth, without any fear of the consequences or of being punished by any body thereafter.'

An interesting case in New Zealand is *Adams v Walsh*.[18] The following resolution was adopted at the Federation of Labour's Annual Conference of 1960:

> 'That as the undesirable publicity given to disputes between Unions and Union officials is bringing the Labour Movement into disrepute we support a Policy of resolving such differences within the Movement itself.'

In adopting this resolution it was added:

> 'that any Union or individual member of an affiliated Union failing to act in conformity with this recommendation be suspended from membership of the Federation of Labour and the individual concerned be denied delegateship.'

This resolution was reaffirmed both in 1961 and in 1962 and clearly showed that it was the policy of the Federation 'to discourage if not to prevent outright the resolving of disputes between members, unions and union officials in the courts'. It was also clearly stated that anyone who contravened the rule would be suspended from membership.

---

11   Though it was evident from contempt by scandalising the court that the law has long been prepared to protect the administration of justice as a continuing process.

12   For the application of the '*Butterworth* principle' in other contexts see eg *R v Socialist Worker Printers and Publishers, ex p A-G* [1975] QB 637, [1975] 1 All ER 142 which was approved by the House of Lords in *A-G v Leveller Magazine Ltd* [1979] AC 440, [1979] 1 All ER 745 (see p 276). See also *Supreme Court Registrar, Equity Division v McPherson* [1980] 1 NSWLR 688 discussed at pp 463–464.

13   See eg *A-G v Royal Society for the Prevention of Cruelty to Animals* (1985) Times, 22 June, where a charity brought disciplinary proceedings against one of its officers for not appearing to be a reluctant witness when he gave evidence for the defence at the hearing of a private prosecution brought by the charity. The RSPCA was fined £10,000

14   See *R v Wright* [1968] VR 164, *Re Samuel Goldman* [1968] 3 NSWR 325. Also cited in *James v Robinson* (1963) 109 CLR 593.

15   *Morris v Wellington City* [1969] NZLR 1038.

16   [1977] 1CR 573, (1976) Times, 27 July. See also *Roebuck v National Union of Miners (Yorkshire Area) No 2* [1978] ICR 676.

17   Ibid at 591. Judge Rubin also rejected the argument that a distinction should be made between witnesses voluntarily giving evidence and those doing so under subpoena.

18   [1963] NZLR 158.

In the event, an action against the Federation was brought before the courts by someone who was not a Federation member. Two Federation members were, however, called as witnesses, and as a result of this both were deprived of delegateship. It was held, relying on *A-G v Butterworth*, that the punishment of the two witnesses amounted to contempt. Barrowclough CJ added, however:[19]

> 'The court has not been asked to pronounce upon the resolution of the Annual Conference of May 1960 and the conforming resolutions of May 1961 and 1962 but it may be advisable to say that in so far as they impose a penalty of loss of membership or delegateship for those who venture to give evidence in court they are probably not only void, as being contrary to public policy . . . but may themselves be a form of contempt if they are allowed to continue as the policy of the Federation of Labour and binding on all its members.'

Whether such a resolution would be regarded as a contempt in other jurisdictions remains a moot point, but the fact that it might be is evidence of the potential width of the *Butterworth* principle. The problem for the courts is where the line should sensibly be drawn. In this particular instance it could be said that until some proceedings are pending (or possibly imminent) the resolution cannot be a contempt though it might still be possible to argue that it amounts to perverting the course of justice.

The issue of the victimisation of witnesses could arise more often following the decision of the Divisional Court in *Peach Grey & Co v Sommers*[20] that industrial tribunals are courts within the definition in s 19 of the Contempt of Court Act 1981. The question as to whether the victimisation of complainants in sex discrimination cases constitutes contempt is discussed below,[1] and it is submitted that the same issues arise in respect of witnesses in such cases. Employees who are witnesses to incidents of sexual harassment, for example, are easily vulnerable to victimisation by an employer and, unlike witnesses in criminal cases, are not protected by the new statutory offence created by s 51 of the Criminal Justice and Public Order Act 1994.[2]

(e)   Are damages available in respect of victimising witnesses?

(i)   The common law position   The question of whether the victimisation of witnesses is also a tort such that the victim can recover damages was the point at issue in *Chapman v Honig*.[3] A landlord, Honig, gave one of his tenants notice to quit his flat but before the expiry of the notice, Honig's father (who was in close communication with his son) entered the flat, moved the furniture, padlocked the doors and installed a new tenant. The evicted tenant brought an action for trespass and wanted Chapman, who occupied the flat below, to testify on his behalf. Chapman was reluctant to give evidence against his landlord, and only did so in obedience to a subpoena. The following day the landlord served notice to quit on Chapman and it was established that the landlord's sole reason was to punish Chapman for having given evidence against him. Although Chapman obtained an injunction restraining Honig from trespassing on his flat or placing padlocks on the doors or cutting off the electricity, he found it necessary to leave the flat

19 Ibid at 164.
20 [1995] 2 All ER 513.
 1 And see Ellis and Miller, 'The Victimisation of Anti-Discrimination Complainants—Is it Contempt of Court' [1993] PL 80.
 2 Discussed at p 489.
 3 [1963] 2 QB 502, [1963] 2 All ER 513.

because his wife had found the events so disturbing as to endanger her health. Chapman brought an action against Honig contending that he was entitled to damages in respect of the contempt (it was conceded that if it was shown—which it was—that the service of the notice to quit was prompted by a vindictive motive it was a contempt of court) reliance being placed on a statement made by Lord Denning MR in *Butterworth's* case, namely:[4]

> 'I would add that if the witness had been damnified by [the contempt] he may well have redress in a civil court for damages.'

Chapman succeeded in the county court and was awarded £50 damages but this decision was reversed by the Court of Appeal.

The key issue in the Court of Appeal was whether as between the parties the notice to quit was valid. If it was, then it was agreed that there could be no action for damages, for as Pearson LJ said:[5]

> 'the same act cannot be as between the same parties both a lawful exercise of a contractual right and at the same time unlawful as being tortious and giving rise to an action for damages. No such complication has yet existed in the law and it is not necessary or desirable to introduce it.'

In the majority's view (ie Pearson, and Davies LJJ) the notice to quit was valid since it was given in the lawful exercise of a contractual right duly implemented in accordance with the provisions of the tenancy agreement and that being so motive was regarded as irrelevant. This finding would have in itself been sufficient to dismiss the case but Pearson LJ had further objections to allowing the action. First, he pointed out that the object of the contempt jurisdiction is the protection of justice and not the individual.[6] Secondly, he thought a landlord could easily avoid the supposed liability by waiting for a suitable time and by putting forward some plausible excuse for evicting the tenant. Thirdly, he thought that whenever there was a continuing contractual right, damages could never be much more than nominal, because the tenant could only retain his tenancy subject to the landlord's right to terminate it lawfully, and as he said[7] 'The tenant could not reasonably be allowed to gain security of tenure by giving evidence against his landlord.' Davies LJ substantially agreed with Pearson LJ, emphasising the practical difficulties that would result from allowing an action for damages both with regard to the length of time for which a notice to quit would be tainted and to the problem of assessing damages. With regard to the former he commented:[8]

> 'one wonders . . . for how long the exercise of a legal right can, by reason of its amounting to a contempt, remain, as between the parties, one which gives rise to a claim for damages.'

With regard to the latter he asked:

> '. . . suppose a valet gives evidence against his master in a divorce suit. On the next day the master, in order to punish his valet, terminates his service by proper notice,

---

4 [1963] 1 QB 696 at 719.
5 [1963] 2 QB 502 at 521.
6 However, note that in *Midland Marts Ltd v Hobday* [1989] 3 All ER 246 Vinelott J held that where the contempt consists of a breach of an undertaking given to the court which necessarily involves a breach of a contract between the parties, the court dealing with the contempt may order an inquiry into damages and not make the plaintiff bring a separate action.
7 [1963] 2 QB 502 at 522.
8 Ibid at 524.

say, one month. What damage has the valet suffered? And if the notice were bad, for what period of time will any subsequent notice given by the master to the valet entitle the latter to claim damages?'

Lord Denning MR dissented. In his view the notice to quit was invalid because it was not lawful in itself:[9]

'For the landlord here was exercising his contractual right in contempt of court: and that is to my mind unlawful: and being unlawful, he can acquire no rights under it.'

In his Lordship's view:[10]

'The principle upon which this case falls to be decided is simply this. No system of law can justly compel a witness to give evidence and then, on finding him victimised for doing it, refuse to give him redress. It is the duty of the court to protect the witness by every means at its command. Else the whole process of the law will be set at naught. If a landlord intimidates a tenant by threatening him with notice to quit, the court must be able to protect the tenant by granting an injunction to restrain the landlord from carrying out his threat. If the landlord victimises a tenant by actually giving him notice to quit, the court must be able to protect the tenant by holding the notice to quit to be invalid. Nothing else will serve to vindicate the authority of the law. Nothing else will empower the judge to say to him: "Do not fear. The arm of the law is strong enough to protect you".'

He was unimpressed with the practical difficulties raised by the majority. With regard to the time factor he thought that:

'If the landlord has been guilty of such a gross contempt as to victimise a tenant, I should have thought that any court would hold that a subsequent notice to quit was invalid unless he could show that it was free from the taint.'

As regards damages, with respect to the example about the valet, he thought the assessment of damages would be based on the loss of the chance of being kept on longer. Moreover, he pointed out that the courts would have to assess damages in relation to victimised witnesses in public inquiries since, under the Witness (Public Inquiries) Protection Act 1892, it is provided that the court has power to award to the complainant:

'any sum of money which it may think reasonable, having regard to all the circumstances of the case, by way of satisfaction or compensation for any loss of situation, wages, status, or other damnification or injury suffered by the complainant through or by means of the offence of which such person shall be so convicted.'

Lord Denning MR saw no reason to distinguish witnesses in public inquiries and those in courts of law.

It is submitted that the majority decision in *Chapman v Honig* is unduly restrictive and that Lord Denning MR's approach is to be preferred. Inasmuch as the decision turned on the validity of the notice to quit (and it is to be emphasised that Pearson LJ left open[11] the question as to whether damages are recoverable where the act is unlawful in itself) the case has been said[12] to be an extreme example of the *Allen v Flood*[13] principle, namely, that the exercise of right (here

9 Ibid at 511.
10 Ibid at 513.
11 Ibid at 522.
12 *Clerk and Lindsell on Torts* (16th edn, 1989) para 15-19 at p 854.
13 [1898] AC 1.

the contractual right to give the tenant notice) will not be rendered unlawful only because of the evil motive of the person exercising it. The extent to which motive can render unlawful an otherwise lawful act is a conundrum that arises from time to time in the field of torts.[14] It is difficult to predict what solution the courts will arrive at in a particular case since the outcome seems to depend upon the premise from which the court starts, ie is the lawfulness of the act to be determined without reference to the motive or must motive be taken into account at the outset? It is this difference of approach that characterises the majority and minority approach, in *Chapman v Honig*. The most convincing reply to the majority's approach, it is submitted, is that suggested by Miller,[15] namely, that the notice to quit was not lawful in itself, since being intended to victimise the tenant, it was given in breach of an implied term of the contract.

It may be that in any event the majority approach will not be followed in the light of the subsequent Court of Appeal decision in *Acrow (Automation) Ltd v Rex Chainbelt Inc.*[16] Acrow had been granted a licence by S to manufacture certain equipment in England. S were later restrained from impeding Acrow inter alia in the manufacture of the products and, in breach of the injunction and therefore in contempt, S ordered Rex Chainbelt to refuse to accept orders from Acrow for the supply of chains which were essential to the manufacture of the equipment by Acrow. As Rex Chainbelt knew all the facts it was held that they were guilty of aiding and abetting S's contempt and were therefore themselves in contempt. Accordingly, an injunction was granted against Rex Chainbelt to stop them obeying S's orders and to use all reasonable endeavours to supply the chains. The basis of the injunction rested on the fact that Rex Chainbelt were said to be acting 'unlawfully'. Lord Denning MR commented:[17]

> 'if one person, without just cause or excuse, deliberately interferes with the trade or business of another, and does so by unlawful means, that is, by an act which he is not at liberty to commit, then he is acting unlawfully. He is liable in damages; and in a proper case, an injunction can be granted against him.'

As Miller has commented:[18]

> 'If therefore, contempt by assisting another to act in breach of an injunction is an unlawful act for the purposes of this newly recognised tort (and this of itself may be thought to provide support for the view that *Chapman v Honig* was wrongly decided), it is not a big step thereafter to say that contempt by victimisation is itself a tort and that a person may recover damages if he suffers loss as a result of the victimisation.'

Whether or not *Chapman v Honig* remains good law it is submitted that policy dictates that it should not be followed. There seems little doubt that the administration of justice would be better protected if the law did provide damages for contempt irrespective of whether the defendant's act was unlawful in itself. Deterrence against victimisation is likely to be more fully effective if the law provides a personal remedy to the victim as well as a criminal penalty against the

14 See *Clerk and Lindsell on Torts* (16th edn, 1989) paras 1-66–1-70.
15 *Contempt of Court* (2nd edn) at p 363.
16 [1971] 3 All ER 1175, [1971] 1 WLR 1676. It is generally said that this case is difficult to reconcile with *Chapman v Honig* and that the *Acrow* decision is to be preferred. See eg Wedderburn, (1972) 35 MLR 184 and Raynor, (1972) 88 LQR 177. The latter's assertion that *Acrow* involved civil contempt is probably wrong. See Ch 14 at p 657.
17 Ibid at 1181.
18 *Contempt of Court* (2nd edn) at p 364.

contemnor. It is a hollow protection for a tenant that while the landlord may be fined or imprisoned for contempt, the eviction (if lawful in itself) is nevertheless valid, and the tenant is left with no other remedy. Moreover the practical difficulties in allowing the remedy are perhaps not as great as the majority in *Chapman v Honig* envisaged. According to *Butterworth's* case[19] the applicant has the burden of establishing an improper motive and in any personal action would have to show that the defendant intended to punish him for having given evidence. Hence, the problem with regard to the timing of the action should not present insuperable difficulties, it merely means that the longer the time between the plaintiff giving evidence and the defendant's act, the more difficult it will be for the plaintiff to establish an improper motive.

The difficulty that damages might be considered to be purely nominal since at any time subsequent to the landlord giving the offending notice to quit he could lawfully give another notice seems well answered by Lord Denning MR when he said [20] that such subsequent notice would be invalid unless the landlord could show that it was 'free from taint'. The question of assessing damages is more problematic but although the amount may be difficult to assess this should not be a fundamental objection to existence of the action particularly as Lord Denning MR pointed out,[1] the courts are already bound to assess damages in similar circumstances in relation to witnesses in a public inquiry.[2]

(ii)   The position under the Powers of Criminal Courts Act 1973

The common law position in England and Wales seems tempered by the Powers of Criminal Courts Act 1973, s 35(1) which provides that:

> 'a court by or before which a person is convicted of an offence . . . may, on application or otherwise, make an order . . . requiring him to pay compensation for any personal injury, loss or damage resulting from that offence . . .'

It should be noted that s 35 only vests a discretion to award damages, ie the victim has no *right* to compensation.

This provision would, it is submitted, have given the court in *Chapman v Honig* the statutory power to make a compensation order. Miller[3] has doubted whether s 35 applies to contempt upon the basis that a committal for contempt might not amount to a 'conviction'. However, in another context the Privy Council in *Izuora v R*[4] rejected such an argument holding that 'conviction' must be given its plain meaning. It is true that other statutory provisions apparently having general application have in the past[5] been ruled inapplicable to contempt but there seems no reason to do so in this context.

Under s 51(2) of the Criminal Justice and Public Order Act 1994 it is an offence (triable summarily or on indictment) to harm or threaten to harm, inter alia, a witness who has given evidence. 'Harm' is defined in s 51(4) to include financial harm and harm to property. If the victimisation of a witness is dealt with as a statutory offence under this provision[6] it would appear, therefore, that damages can be awarded.

---

19   [1963] 1 QB 696 at 726.
20   [1963] 2 QB 502 at 513.
 1   Ibid at 514.
 2   Ie under the Witnesses (Public Inquiries) Protection Act 1892, s 4.
 3   *Contempt of Court* (2nd edn) at p 365.
 4   [1953] AC 327 at 334–5.
 5   See eg *Morris v Crown Office* [1970] 2 QB 114, [1970] 1 All ER 1079, discussed in Ch 12.
 6   See the discussion below.

3   *Intimidating, etc witnesses as a statutory offence*

Section 51 of the Criminal Proceedings and Public Order Act 1994 creates a new statutory offence of intimidating, threatening or harming persons who are taking part, or have taken part, in criminal proceedings. Since this offence covers jurors and others as well as witnesses this section is considered in toto below.[7]

B   Interference with jurors

The principle upon which interfering with jurors amounts to contempt is perhaps best explained by Pigot CB in *R v Martin*.[8] He said:

'It is important that there should be no improper interference with the administration of justice; and above all, that juries should be protected from every interference with them in reference to the discharge of their important and sacred duties; they form a portion of the tribunals by which the law of the land is administered.'

As Bowen LJ said in *Re Johnson*[9] jurors are not only protected while they are discharging their duties[10] but also while they are travelling to or from the court. It may also be a contempt to threaten or intimidate a juror even after he has returned home. In *R v Martin* a foreman of a jury was accused of bullying a jury and was then challenged to mortal combat by the brother of a person whom the jury had found guilty. This approach was made after the case had been completed, and after the juror had arrived home. Pigot CB, in holding that a contempt had been committed, said that it was:

'necessary for the court, when such a case as this is brought before it, to exercise the powers which the law has vested in it for the protection of those engaged in the administration of justice, and above all to protect jurors from intimidation and outrage.'

Contempt may be committed by approaches to jurors some time after the end of the trial. In *A-G v Judd*[11] a defendant, two days after the end of the trial at which he had been convicted, approached a juror when he recognised her at a car boot sale. He asked her to write to the judge saying that she had been mistaken as to his guilt, hoped that her conscience would go with her to the grave, and told her that he attended a lot of car boot sales and would look out for her. He was sentenced to 42 days' imprisonment.[12] There is, logically, no period after which interfering with a juror should cease to be a contempt. Since the object of the law is to ensure the protection of the course of justice as a continuing process, jurors should be assured that the sanctions of the law protect them from interference forever.[13]

Usually interference with jurors cannot occur before the trial because of the way in which juries are empanelled. However, it can amount to a contempt for

7   See pp 426–429.
8   (1848) 5 Cox CC 356 (Ireland).
9   (1887) 20 QBD 68 at 74 cited at p 401.
10   For examples see *R v Goult* [1983] Crim LR 103; *Nash v Nash, Re Cobb* [1924] NZLR 495. For abuse of jurors in the face of the court see eg *Ex p Pater* (1864) 10 LT 376 discussed in Ch 2.
11   [1995] COD 15.
12   He was also held to have committed a contempt for soliciting details of the jury's deliberations, contrary to s 8 of the Contempt of Court Act 1981, but was not imprisoned in respect of that.
13   See also the statutory offence in s 51(2) of the Criminal Justice and Public Order Act 1994 which shifts the burden of proof after a certain time: this is discussed at p 429.

an employer to dismiss or threaten to dismiss a person before serving as a juror. An example of this type of case occurred in 1966 before Sussex Assizes held in Lewes.[14] There, an employer who threatened to dismiss one of his workmen if he obeyed a summons to serve as a juror was brought before Melford Stevenson J. The learned judge is reported as saying:

> 'Fortunately for you the police have on my direction investigated the serious contempt of court which you have committed. Uttering a threat of dismissal was an inexplicable thing to do. I am satisfied that what you said was said in a moment of bad temper and rather childish petulance.
>   If I had thought you had seriously threatened to sack an employee if he obeyed a jury summons, nothing would have saved you from going to prison for a substantial period. You have expressed sincere regret on two occasions for what you have said. I propose to accept the apology and say no more about it.'

But he added 'Any future conduct of this kind will be followed by very grave consequences'.

An unusual example of interference with jurors before a trial arose in the Australian cases concerning Mr Collins, *Registrar, Court of Appeal v Collins*[15] and *The Prothonotary v Collins*,[16] in which Collins distributed pamphlets, accusing the police of falsifying confessions, to prospective jurors waiting at the courts. Since there were no cases involving confessions to be heard on those days, the cases revolved around questions of intending to do the impossible, particularly in relation to contempt by publication,[17] but there was no doubt that such activities were capable of constituting contempt.

The actus reus of interfering with jurors after the trial can comprise any behaviour which reasonably threatens or intimidates the jurors concerned. In *R v Goult*[18] it involved staring at the jurors while in court, driving a car slowly in front of one while leaving a car park and rushing up and jumping behind two of them in the street. In *R v Giscombe*[19] it was argued that acts which were not serious enough in themselves to amount to contempt could not be rendered so by the actor's mens rea. The Court of Appeal did not have to decide the point, having taken the view that the acts were sufficiently serious, when looked at in context, for although he had only said to a juror en route to the car park 'Don't I recognise you?', 'Aren't you on the jury?', 'Were/are you a screw?', 'Is your brother a screw?' he had demonstrated his attitude to authority throughout the trial. This included being brought to court in handcuffs as a hostile witness, attending every afternoon in the public gallery after his evidence, and calling out during a police officer's evidence that the latter was a liar. The court said that he was 'of striking appearance'[20] and that both that fact and his behaviour had caused the jury to note his continued presence in the public gallery and be concerned when he approached

---

14 (1966) 130 JP 622 (*R v Lydeard*) cited with apparent, though not express, approval by Lord Denning MR, in *Balogh v Crown Court at St Albans* [1975] QB 73 at 84-5. See also *R v Lovelady, ex p A-G* [1982] WAR 65 (W Aust Sup Ct) where the principle was accepted but the prosecution failed on the facts.
15 [1982] 1 NSWLR 682 (NSW CA).
16 [1985] 2 NSWLR 549 (NSW CA).
17 See the discussion of these cases at pp 80 ff.
18 (1983) 76 Cr App Rep 140.
19 (1985) 79 Cr App Rep 79.
20 It would be unfortunate if possessing a 'striking appearance' makes one more vulnerable to charges of contempt, and it is to be regretted that the court did not elaborate on this—presumably they were trying to be tactful.

them. Clearly, the identity of the person approaching the juror is relevant—the question 'Are you a juror?' coming from a hostile, handcuffed witness in an armed robbery trial is likely to be treated differently by both the juror and the court from the same words said as a pleasantry by an interested passer-by.

The mens rea of interference with jurors raises the same issues as are discussed above in relation to interference with witnesses.[1] So far as interference during (and as far as is relevant, before) the trial is concerned, it can be considered as interfering with both the particular proceedings and with the course of justice as a continuing process. Interference after the trial can be impugned only as interference with the course of justice as a continuing process. It is submitted that there is no reason to apply different mens rea requirements to interference with witnesses and to interference with jurors and that the provisions of the Contempt of Court Act affect (or do not affect) them equally.

The result of this would be that mens rea is required only to the extent that the alleged contemnor must be proved to have intended to do an act which, objectively construed, is calculated to interfere with the course of justice. This would be in line with *Connolly v Dale*,[2] with Sir John Donaldson MR in *A-G v Newspaper Publishing Plc*,[3] and, as is argued above, with Donovan LJ's views in *A-G v Butterworth*.[4] It is submitted that the Court of Appeal's reference in *A-G v Judd* to the fact that 'the court had of course . . . to be satisfied that the necessary intention had been proved'[5] is confused by the reliance, for the test to be applied, on *A-G v Sport Newspapers Ltd*,[6] which is a case concerning publications interfering with particular legal proceedings. When Lord Lane CJ said in *R v Giscombe*[7] that 'we are content to take the view that it is contempt of court if the defendant knowingly does an act which he intends, and is calculated, to interfere with the course of justice and is capable of having that effect' he qualified his remarks by saying that this was not 'the occasion upon which to decide the precise meaning of this sort of contempt', that the passages from Donovan LJ and Lord Denning MR in *A-G v Butterworth*[8] were not wholly in accord with one another, and that his own remarks about intention were 'for the purpose of this case only'. It is submitted, therefore, that one is justified in not according too much weight to his views on intention in that case.

Persons interfering with jurors can in theory be indicted for the common law offence of embracery but in England, at any rate, that offence might properly be regarded as obsolescent. In *R v Owen*[9] Lawton LJ said that where only one person was involved the better course was to proceed for contempt.[10] Where the interference occurs during the trial, as happened in *Owen*, then even though the interference may take place outside the courtroom the offender can be brought forthwith before the judge and tried on the spot. In such cases the court acts upon its own motion and is said to be ruling ex mero motu. The immediacy of the

1 See pp 410 and 414.
2 (1995) Times, 13 July, discussed at p 411.
3 [1988] Ch 333 at 374, discussed at p 415.
4 [1963] 1 QB 696.
5 [1995] COD 15 at 17.
6 [1992] 1 All ER 503.
7 (1985) 79 Cr App Rep 79.
8 Discussed at pp 414 ff.
9 [1976] 3 All ER 239, [1976] 1 WLR 840. Cf on procedure *R v Lovelady* [1982] WAR 65.
10 Lawton LJ (ibid at 240) thought that the more likely charge, where more than one person is involved, is conspiracy to pervert the course of justice, but if the summary method is appropriate for one why not more than one offender?

prosecution provides an effective and on occasion necessary means of protecting the administration of justice by preventing the offender approaching other jurors and at the same time reassuring jurors awaiting their call to duty in court. On the other hand, the very swiftness of the prosecution demands that it should be sparingly used. We shall discuss in Chapter 12[11] precisely when a court should punish an offender upon its own motion; suffice to say here that the power should be exercised only where it is imperative and urgent to act immediately and where the facts are incontrovertibly proved.[12] It has been held [13] that judges should state their findings of fact and where appropriate the process of reasoning by which those findings were arrived at.

When interference with jurors after the trial is concerned and the matter is therefore less urgent as there are no current proceedings to protect it is submitted that it may be preferable to proceed by way of a prosecution under s 51 of the Criminal Justice and Public Order Act 1994, discussed below.

C   The statutory offence of intimidating, threatening and harming witnesses and jurors in UK law under the Criminal Justice and Public Order Act 1994

In 1994 the UK Government dealt with widespread concern about what was believed to be an increasing and serious incidence of witness intimidation and jury 'nobbling' by introducing new statutory offences of intimidating a juror or witness and of harming, or threatening to harm, a juror or witness. These offences were created by s 51 of the Criminal Justice and Public Order Act 1994. Insofar as the section creates new statutory offences it is strictly outside the purview of this book. However, as it is an offence which deals with the same matters as this area of contempt it is relevant to examine the ambit of the offences and to consider when a prosecution under the section might be more or less suitable than dealing with the issue as a contempt. The new statutory offences are specifically stated to be in addition to, and not in derogation of, the common law offences.

1   Intimidation of witnesses, jurors and others

(a)   The provisions of s 51(1)

Section 51(1) provides that a person commits an offence if he does to another person:

(a)   an act which intimidates, and is intended to intimidate, that other person;

(b)   knowing or believing that the other person is assisting in the investigation of an offence or is a witness or potential witness or a juror or potential juror in proceedings for an offence; and

(c)   intending thereby to cause the investigation or the course of justice to be obstructed, perverted or interfered with.

11   See pp 502–503.
12   Cf *Rooney v Crown Court at Snaresbrook* (1979) 68 Cr App Rep 78, [1979] Crim LR 109.
13   *R v Goult* [1983] Crim LR 103.

The use of the present tense in s 51(1)(b) (as well as its juxtaposition to s 51(2)) shows that this subsection is limited to acts done before or during proceedings. Intimidation is not defined in the Act,[14] although s 51(4) provides that the harm threatened by an intimidatory act which consists of threats may be physical harm to the witness or juror or to his property, or financial harm. It may, by s 51(3), consist of threats not only to the juror or witness himself but also to third parties (which would cover, for example, threats to his family). The maximum penalty for the offence on indictment is five year's imprisonment, a fine or both; and summarily, six months' imprisonment or a fine not exceeding the statutory maximum, or both.

(b) Comparison between s 51(1) and contempt

Although there are many similarities between the statutory offence in s 51(1) and contempt, the former appears to be narrower in significant respects. The following points should be noted in particular:

(i) Section 51(1) is limited (s 51(1)(b)) to investigations of, and proceedings for, an offence (and is, of course, contained in an act concerned with criminal justice). It applies, therefore, only to criminal, and not to civil proceedings.

(ii) Section 51(1)(a) requires an act which intimidates, and is intended to intimidate. If 'intimidation' connotes causing fear or anxiety, an act which is intended to do so might fail because, for example, of the robustness of the other party. If so, it would appear to fall outside the wording of the section, although it would be covered by the Criminal Attempts Act 1981.[15] The second level of mens rea is that the act must be intended to obstruct, pervert or interfere with the investigation or the course of justice. This may be a stricter test of mens rea than the common law test for contempt which, as we discussed above, may involve only the intentional committal of an act which is inherently calculated to interfere etc with the course of justice.[16] However, s 51(7) provides that once the intimidation and intent to intimidate are proved, along with the knowledge or belief that the peron intimidated is a witness or juror etc, the intention to interfere etc with the course of justice is presumed, so that the burden will be on the defence to disprove it. Section 51(5) provides that the intention to interfere etc need not be the only or predominating intention, thus following the position explained with regard to motive in *A-G v Butterworth*. [17]

(iii) Since the subsection deals only with intimidation it does not cover those who seek to persuade witnesses to give or withhold certain evidence, or jurors to take a particular view of the case without, however, indulging in what could be classified as 'intimidation'. The conversation at the garden

---

14 Intimidation is defined in the Shorter Oxford English Dictionary as making timid or fearful, but especially forcing a person to act, or deterring them from acting by fear, which is the sense in which it appears to be used in s 51(1).
15 In which case it would be subject to the criteria which apply in the application of that Act, see Smith and Hogan, *Criminal Law* (7th edn, 1992) pp 304–317.
16 See pp 410 ff.
17 [1963] 1 QB 696 at 723 per Lord Denning MR, discussed at pp 414 ff.

gate in *R v Toney* [18] which was held to be perverting the course of justice would not appear to fall within the subsection, for example. The subsection also does not include bribery or payments unaccompanied by threats.

(iv) The types of harm, threat of which may amount to intimidation, set out in s 51(1), (4) are unduly restricted. It would, it is submitted, have been preferable to use the word 'economic' rather than 'financial'. The loss of the tenancy in *Chapman v Honig*,[19] for example, would not necessarily involve *financial* harm and is not happily described as harm to a person's property. The type of threat which occurred in *Hillfinch Properties Ltd v Newark Investments Ltd* [20]—excommunicating an orthodox Jew—is not dealt with at all.

2   Threatening or harming witnesses and jurors etc

(a)   The provisions of s 51(2)

This sub-section deals with the victimisation *after the trial* of witnesses, jurors and others who have assisted in the investigation.

Section 51(2) provides that a person commits an offence if he does or threatens to do to another person—

'(a) an act which harms or would harm, and is intended to harm, that other person;

(b) knowing or believing that the other person, or some other person, has assisted in an investigation into an offence or has given evidence or particular evidence in proceedings for an offence, or has acted as a juror or concurred in a particular verdict in proceedings for an offence; and

(c) does or threatens to do the act because of what (within paragraph (b)) he knows or believes.'

(b)   Comparison between s 51(2) and contempt

Some of the points made above in relation to s 51(1) apply equally to this subsection. Like s 51(1) it covers only criminal proceedings, and the restricted nature of 'harm' as set out in s 51(4) is the same. Looking at the contempt cases on victimising witnesses, it must be doubtful whether any of *A-G v Butterworth*,[1] *Chapman v Honig*,[2] *Hillfinch Properties v Newark Investments Ltd* [3] or *A-G v RSPCA* [4] would fall within the subsection, unless a very liberal interpretation is given to the definition of harm. Additional points to be noted however are:

(i) Section 51(2) does not require any mens rea as far as intending to interfere with the course of justice is concerned. The only mens rea required is in

18 (1993) 97 Cr App Rep 176, discussed at p 408.
19 [1963] 2 QB 502, [1963] 2 All ER 513, see pp 418 ff.
20 (1981) Times, 1 July, discussed further at p 444.
 1 [1963] 1 QB 696.
 2 [1963] 2 QB 502.
 3 (1981) Times, 1 July.
 4 (1985) Times, 22 June.

respect of an intention to harm. What s 52(2)(c) requires is the *motive* (and it is described by that term in s 51(5)) of doing or threatening to do the act because of what the person concerned knows or believes the witness or juror has done.

(ii) Where the threat or harm occurs within the 'relevant period' set out in s 51(7), which is generally 12 months after the trial,[5] the motive required by s 51(2)(c) is presumed once the requisite elements of s 51(2)(a) and (b) are proved. After the 'relevant' period, victimisation is still an offence but the burden of proof as regards the motive reverts to the prosecution.

3   The use of s 51 rather than contempt

As is shown by the above discussion, there will be some situations in which it will not be possible to use the statutory offence. Where both are available, it may depend on the urgency of the case. Where interference with witnesses and jurors before or during the trial is concerned it may be advantageous for the court to deal with the matter as speedily as possible by using the summary contempt procedure.[6] When victimisation after the trial is concerned the element of urgency will not normally be present and it will, it is submitted, usually be preferable to proceed by using the statutory offence. Using the latter within twelve months will also have the advantage to the Crown of the presumption as to motive.

One significant difference between the offences is that of penalties. Section 51 provides, on indictment, for a maximum of five years imprisonment to be imposed whereas the maximum under the Contempt of Court Act, s 14(1) is two years.[7] The higher penalty may well be more suitable in cases of very serious intimidation or interference.

D   Interference with judges

It is important to the due administration of justice that a judge should be able to conduct a trial entirely free from outside interference, and any act that jeopardises this freedom will therefore amount to contempt. It seems clear from cases such as *A-G v BBC*[8] and *Badry v DPP of Mauritius*[9] that the law of contempt is confined to protecting the administration of justice in courts of law. Hence the type of conduct we have in mind is that which interferes with judges of a court of law (which term includes magistrates, coroners, masters,[10] district judges[11] and, probably, members of those tribunals which are considered as 'courts'

---

5   The date the 12 months runs from depends on whether the person concerned is a witness, a juror, or a person who assisted the investigation without being a witness.

6   Although see *R v Griffin* (1989) 88 Cr App Rep 63 for a case in which dealing with an alleged interference with witnesses summarily was not, as events turned out, a good idea.

7   Or one year in the case of an inferior court.

8   [1981] AC 303, [1980] 3 All ER 161, discussed in detail in Ch 12.

9   [1982] 3 All ER 973, [1983] 2 WLR 161, discussed in Ch 9.

10   See *Re Ludlow Charities Lechmere Charlton's Case* (1837) 2 My & Cr 316. Cf *R v Faulkner* (1835) 2 Cr M & R 525.

11   Formerly registrars.

within the definition in s 19 of the Contempt of Court Act 1981[12]) while they are
acting in the judicial capacity.

Happily, physical attacks upon a judge outside the court are rare[13] but it seems
consistent with principle that it can be a contempt to assault a judge not only while
he is sitting in court but also while he is travelling to or from the court. However,
according to Oswald[14] the proper course to adopt is to try them on indictment and
in support of this contention is cited Wilmot J's statement in *R v Almon* [15]
'Striking a judge walking along the street is not contempt.' It is submitted,
however, that what Wilmot J meant was not that striking a judge outside the court
can never amount to contempt but that striking a person who happens to be a
judge, without any knowledge of his status, will not amount to contempt. Could
it not be a contempt, for example, deliberately to prevent a judge from attending
the court, either by physical assault or by blocking the road so as to stop the
judge's car from passing?[16]

While an intention to 'divert the course of justice' may be inferred from a
private communication with a judge in respect of a case pending before him, such
an intention is not necessarily inferred.[17] The proper course to adopt if a
complaint is thought necessary is to bring any matter to the judge's notice in open
court.

The majority of cases of interference with a judge are concerned with private
communications. The general principle involved was expressed by Lord
Cottenham LC in *Re Dyce Sombre*:[18]

> 'Every private communication to a judge, for the purpose of influencing his
> decision upon a matter publicly before him, always is, and ought to be reprobated;
> it is a course calculated, if tolerated, to divert the course of justice, and is
> considered, and ought more frequently than it is, to be treated as what it really is,
> a high contempt of court.'

Examples of private communications that have been held to be a contempt
include *Martin's Case* [19] where Martin sent a private letter to the Lord Chancellor
which not only discussed the subject-matter of a threatened suit against him, but
also included a banknote for £20. In *Re Ludlow Charities, Lechmere Charlton's*

---

12 Such as industrial tribunals, held to be 'courts' within s 19 in *Peach Grey & Co v Sommers*
   [1995] 2 All ER 513.
13 Oswald, *Contempt* (3rd edn, 1910) p 43 cites two cases of physical violence: *R v Dodwell*
   (1875) Times, 16 March and *R v Arnemann* (1890) Times, 10 March. Dissatisfaction with the
   Family Court of Australia, however, led to a number of violent incidents in the 1980s which
   included the murder of a judge and of the wife of another judge. Obviously, such incidents
   result in murder trials rather than contempt proceedings. Cf publications which verbally attack
   the judge, see Ch 9.
14 *Contempt* (3rd edn, 1910) p 43. In serious cases, the action is, however, likely to be tried on
   indictment.
15 (1765) Wilm 243 at 255.
16 Cf *Skipworth's Case* (1873) LR 9 QB 230 where according to Blackburn J, the parties
   attempted by vituperation to prevent the judge from taking part. The mens rea requirement is
   discussed more fully at pp 410 ff and 414 ff. In cases where judges travel to the court, fully
   robed, it will be more obvious that such persons are judges and the necessary mens rea could
   be inferred: the defendant could, however, have understandably mistaken the judge for the
   Lord Mayor.
17 Eg a trade union writing to the Industrial Relations Court, stating that it does not accept the
   court's jurisdiction. See *Heaton's Transport (St Helens) Ltd v Transport and General
   Workers' Union* [1972] 2 All ER 1214 at 1229. See also *Re Milburn* 1946 SLT 219.
18 (1849) 1 Mac & G 116 at 122, 41 ER 1207 at 1209.
19 (1747) 2 Russ & M 674.

Case [20] a barrister wrote a threatening letter to a Master during the pendency of a case in which the barrister was himself a party. According to Lord Cottenham LC, the tendency of the letter 'was to induce the Master to alter the opinion he was supposed to have formed upon the case', and accordingly the barrister was held to have committed a contempt. A novelist who sent a hand-written fax to a judge hearing an appeal against a destruction order on a dog was described by him as having committed a blatant contempt of court, although no action was taken against her.[1] It is also a contempt to write abusive letters to a judge, as Lord Cottenham LC said[2] 'Every insult offered to a judge, in the exercise of the duties of his office is a contempt'.

It is not necessary that a private communication should be threatening or abusive before it can amount to contempt. In *Re Dyce Sombre*, for example, Lord Cottenham LC accepted that the letter was not intended to be in any way disrespectful, but he nevertheless held that the communication amounted to contempt. In *Chester Corpn v Rothwell* [3] a litigant wrote a letter during the course of proceedings being heard in a county court. The letter was headed 'Justice' and began:

> 'I am enclosing herewith a copy of a letter I have forwarded to [a Cabinet Minister] mainly concerning the gross Travesty of Justice as exemplified in your Court on Tuesday last.'

The letter also contained eight pages detailing what had happened in court. Judge Whitmore Richards said:

> 'for a litigant to approach the judge, or a juror, during the hearing of a part-heard case behind the back of his opponent is an interference or attempted interference, with the course of justice. What the defendant has done prima facie constitutes, in my judgment, a serious contempt of court.'

Various communications were received by senior members of the judiciary from Lonrho plc during that company's long campaign in the 1980s about the takeover of Harrods by the Al Fayed brothers. The company regularly despatched propaganda literature to a mailing list which included members of both Houses of Parliament, and being members of the House of Lords the Lords of Appeal in Ordinary were among the recipients. One one occasion in 1987 Lord Keith received some of this literature a few days before presiding over an Appellate Committee hearing of an appeal directly or indirectly involving Lonrho and the Al Fayeds.[4] Although he described this as improper, no contempt proceedings were brought.

---

20 (1837) 2 My & Cr 316. See also *Macgill's Case* (1748) 2 Fowler's; Exch Practice (2nd edn) 404—a letter containing a scandalous offer to his Lordship relating to a judgment to be given in a pending case.

1 The novelist was Jilly Cooper, and the fax was handed to the judge as he was about to give his ruling. According to the *Guardian*, 24 August 1994, the offending message read 'Your Honour, please, please reprieve Buster. He's a lovely dog. He is certainly not a pit bull, the RSPCA inspector should have his eyes tested. I would be with you, but I've been away. Please help us, love Jilly Cooper'.

2 In *Lechmere Charlton's Case* (1837) 2 My & Cr 316, at 339, 370, cf *R v Freeman* (1925) Times, 18 November (see p 342) where the grounds for the decision were that the letter amounted to contempt by 'scandalising the court'. See also *Re Wallace* (1866) LR 1 PC 283.

3 (1940) 7 LJ CCR 58. See also *Taylor v Asmedh Konwar* (1865) 4 WR 86 (India); *Thomas v Nield* (1911) 30 NZLR 1208 (New Zealand).

4 This was the case of *House of Fraser Plc v ACGE Investments Ltd* [1987] AC 387.

Two years later in 1989, on the eve of an Appellate Committe hearing of another case in the saga[5] the *Observer* newspaper published a special midweek edition consisting of the DTI inspectors' report, the non-publication of which was the subject of the case. Some members of the Appellate Committee received copies of the newspaper through the post. Lord Keith also received another document.[6] Lonrho was prosecuted for contempt for the publication of the newspaper under the strict liability rule in s 2 of the Contempt of Court Act 1981, on the grounds that it created a risk of prejudice to the proceedings.[7] The matter of the document sent to Lord Keith was not pursued. These events raised interesting issues about interfering with judges which were not dealt with in the proceedings because their Lordships chose to concentrate on the publication aspect and not to pursue the question of whether Lonrho had deliberately attempted to influence the minds of the Appellate Committee.[8] However, if the communications were received by their Lordships as members of the Upper House and Lonrho did not intend to influence them in their judicial capacity it seems that no contempt by way of interference could have been committed. Lord Bridge clearly considered that Lonrho was not liable unless the attempt to influence was deliberate, and the sworn evidence from staff at Lonrho was that they had been instructed by a director to remove the Law Lords' names from the mailing list.[9] However, as contempt by interference requires mens rea there is, as with contempt by publication, the issue of who can supply the mental element when a company is involved. It is submitted that in such a situation the intentions of the directors who are responsible for the communication being sent can affix the company with liability but it would also be possible for them to be individually liable.[10]

According to *Oswald on Contempt* [11] once the case is over, private communications with a judge, unless amounting to 'scandalising the court', will not amount to contempt. He cites the amusing case of the defeated litigant, who having been warned during the case not to behave like a monkey, telegraphed the judge every morning for some time after the trial, 'Why did you call me a monkey? Reply paid'. It should be emphasised that abusive letters written to a judge after the case is over can amount to contempt by 'scandalising the court'.[12] However, it is submitted that other types of communications could also amount to contempt even though proceedings have been completed. To write a letter to a judge threatening physical harm by way of punishment for a decision he has given, could, it is submitted, be considered a contempt upon the principle laid down by *A-G v Butterworth.*[13]

---

5   The appeal from *Lonrho plc v Secretary of State for Trade and Industry* [1989] 2 All ER 609.
6   A document called *Birds of a Feather* which made serious allegations about the good faith of the Secretary of State and implied that the Prime Minister's husband was involved with sinister characters said to be associates of the Al Fayeds.
7   This was the case of *Re Lonrho Plc* [1990] 2 AC 154, [1989] 2 All ER 1100, discussed at pp 220 ff.
8   Partly because of the cross-examination problem, see [1990] 2 AC 154 at 204 and see p 220.
9   His secretary explained in an affidavit how an administrative error resulted in this not being done.
10 See Ch 10 for a discussion of responsibility for contempt by publication and Ch 14, p 569 for the question of the liability of companies for the actions of their employees in breaching court orders.
11 (3rd edn, 1910) pp 48, 49.
12 See eg *R v Freeman* (1925) Times, 18 November.
13 [1963] 1 QB 696 discussed at p 412.

E   Interference with officers of the court

Acts which prevent or which are intended to prevent officers of the court from carrying out their duties constitute a contempt of court, provided at any rate, they are committed in the knowledge that the person obstructed is an officer of the court.[14]

By 'officers of the court' is meant those persons having official duties to perform in connection with court proceedings. There is no definitive list of those who may rank as 'officers' for this purpose but as will be seen it has been held to be a contempt to obstruct or interfere with solicitors, sheriffs and their deputies (for example bailiffs), receivers, liquidators, sequestrators, admiralty marshalls and their substitutes and process servers.[15] It seems, however, that not all court officials are necessarily protected by contempt. In *Weston v Central Criminal Court Administrator*,[16] a solicitor, annoyed that his case had suddenly been put in the list, wrote what the court described as a scurrilous letter to the court administrator. In holding that no contempt had been committed, Bridge LJ said:[17]

'No doubt solicitors should not write discourteous and abusive letters to anybody; but a discourteous and abusive letter written to a court official in respect of his conduct of the purely administrative business of the court could no more be a contempt of court than an abusive and discourteous letter written by a solicitor to any other citizen.'

Whether this means that it can never be a contempt to obstruct a court administrator remains to be seen, but it is submitted that it would be dangerous to assume that it cannot be.[18] It might, for example, be considered a contempt to bribe or attempt to bribe an administrator to put a case in or take a case out of the list. At any rate such an act could be thought to interfere with the due course of justice.

1   Abuse of officers of the court

Abuse of officers of the court, especially where physical violence is involved, can obviously impede the due administration of justice and may therefore amount to contempt. County court judges have statutory powers under ss 14 and 118(1)(a) of the County Courts Act 1984 respectively to punish persons assaulting officers in the execution of their duties or wilfully insulting an officer not only while attending court but also while he is 'going to or returning from the court'.[19] Magistrates, too, have power under the Contempt of Court Act 1981[20] to punish

---

14   Cf *Blackburn v Bowering* [1994] 3 All ER 380, CA, discussed in Ch 12 at pp 511–512.
15   The tipstaff must also rank as an officer of the High Court for these purposes, cf Lowe and White, *Wards of Court* (2nd edn, 1986, Barry Rose) para 6-65. NB 'officer in relation to the court' is defined in the County Courts Act 1984, s 147 as 'any registrar [district judge], deputy registrar [district judge] or assistant registrar [district judge] of that court, and any clerk, bailiff, usher or messenger in the service of that court'.
16   [1977] QB 32, [1976] 2 All ER 875, CA.
17   Ibid at 47.
18   Particularly in the light of Stephenson LJ's judgment, since he upheld the appeal upon the basis (ibid at 46) that the solicitor's conduct did not go 'beyond the limits of non co-operation or discourtesy as to harden into contempt of court'.
19   Query why the two sections differ on when the act can be a contempt? For the powers of punishment under these sections see Ch 12 at pp 510–513.
20   S 12, discussed in Ch 12, at pp 513–516.

those wilfully insulting an officer of the court during his sitting in attendance in court or in going to or returning from the court. We discuss these statutory powers in Chapter 12.

Although the two above Acts give only limited powers in limited circumstances the High Court has a supervisory jurisdiction over all inferior courts and has a residual jurisdiction to punish contempts both of the county court and magistrates court.[1] If, therefore, the contempt is thought serious enough to warrant greater punishment than that prescribed by statute, or if the act falls outside the scope of the statute, it is always possible to take the contempt proceedings before the High Court. Such a procedure may be appropriate, for example, where an officer is assaulted rather than 'insulted' on his way to or from the court.

The question remains as to what is meant by 'abusing' an officer of the court. Physical abuse can clearly be a contempt. An old example is *Williams v Johns*,[2] in which the defendant, having been served with a subpoena, made the person serving it eat the parchment and wax of the process, beat and kicked the server and, considering him to be dead, directed his servants to throw his body into a river. In *Price v Hutchison*,[3] a clerk to a firm of solicitors served a copy of a bill upon Hutchison who refused to take the papers and insisted the clerk should take them back. When the clerk refused to do this, Hutchison locked the door and refused to let the clerk out, unless he took the papers with him. The clerk tried to leave the room but Hutchison and another forcibly detained him and threatened to throw him out of the window. The clerk was fortunately saved by two policemen who entered the room having heard cries for help. Malins V-C, considered the case to be one of the most extraordinary cases to be brought before the courts and he had no hesitation in committing the defendants to prison. In *Lewis v Owen*[4] a bailiff was prevented from levying distress for a certain tithe rent charge because the owner had locked the gate to the field and when the bailiff tried to get over a hedge, the defendant thrust him back. It was held that this conduct amounted to contempt.

A modern example is *Benerecetti v Gilbert Perkin*[5] where a director was committed for 14 days for assaulting a bailiff.

Whether or not mere verbal abuse will amount to contempt is perhaps less settled. Under an old Chancery Order[6] it was expressly stated that violent or abusive language to a process server was punishable by committal, but the Order was later annulled with no corresponding rule being substituted. There are, however, old cases at common law which held that verbal abuse amounted to contempt. Some of these cases involved picturesque language such as where the

---

1 The High Court's supervisory jurisdiction is discussed in Ch 12 at pp 467–468 and 486 ff.
2 (1773) 2 Dick 477. See also *Osborne v Tuthell* (1583) Ch Cas in Ch 168; *Dastoines v Apprice* (1580) Cary 91 and *Giles v Lackington* (1584) Ch Cas in Ch 177. For details of these cases see p 234 of the first edition of this work. See also *Rove v West* (1558) Cary 38; *Buffin v Heyward* (1584) Ch Cas in Ch 175; *Barker v Shepheard* (1633) Toth 102, *Morgan v Jones* (1745) cited in 1 Dick 91.
3 (1870) LR 9 Eq 534; see also *Emery v Bowen* (1836) 5 LJ Ch 349.
4 [1894] 1 QB 102. This case was decided under the County Courts Act 1888 but the principle extends to all bailiffs. See also *Southam v Smout* [1964] 1 QB 308, [1963] 3 All ER 104 and *Caress v Deal* [1976] CA Transcript 144A.
5 [1981] CA Transcript 032. See also *Gibbons v Registrar of Stroud* (1990) Independent, 8 October, CA in which it was stressed that the contemnor should be given the opportunity to explain his conduct. In Australia see eg *Re Barnes* [1968] 1 NSWR 697 (NSW Sup Ct).
6 Ord 42, r 2 Consolidated Chancery Orders 1860, See Oswald: *Contempt* (3rd edn, 1910) pp 84–85.

defendant, on being served with a rule, said[7] 'He did not care a fart for the rule of court' and in another where the defendant said[8] 'Take the rule back again to those from whom it came and bid them wipe their backsides with it.' Other cases have held verbal abuse not to amount to contempt. In *Giles v Venson* [9] the court refused to find a person guilty of contempt who threatened to make a server eat the writ, and in *Adams v Hughes* [10] no order was made even though it was asserted that the defendant:

> 'collared him, shook him violently, and ordered him to quit his presence. . . . The court said they would lay down no rule, whether every collaring and shaking of an officer, however improper such conduct were, should or should not be deemed a contempt of the court, it sufficed to say that no case was here shown to the court.'

The tenor of these decisions[11] is that trivial conduct which does not actually prevent service will probably not amount to contempt. In view of the current attitude of the courts to discourage trivial applications for contempt[12] these latter cases are likely to be adopted. Thus mere verbal abuse is unlikely to be considered a contempt and even trivial assaults may be overlooked.

An assault upon an officer of the court may not be considered to be a contempt if it takes place at a time when the officer is acting in excess of his powers. Assaults are only punishable under the County Courts Act 1984 when they are made upon an officer of the county court in the execution of his duties, and it seems reasonable to suppose that at common law no protection is afforded to an officer who is acting outside his duties. A case which considered, for the purposes of what is now s 14 of the County Courts Act 1984, the meaning of 'while in execution of his duty' is *Southam v Smout* .[13] A warrant had been issued to commit a widow to prison for non-payment of a debt and two bailiffs went to arrest her. Having discovered where she was the bailiffs went to her daughter and son-in-law's home, where one of them opened the door and entered the house (letting the other in by the back door). The son-in-law ordered them out and, following the bailiffs' refusal, assaulted one of them. The success of the action depended upon whether the bailiffs were trespassers. The Court of Appeal held that they were not. Although the bailiffs were executing a civil process (ie to enforce a debt) and as such could not break into property,[14] entry can nevertheless be lawful even though a door is closed provided no force is used.[15] The fact that the bailiffs had entered a stranger's property was held to be lawful in this case because the person sought was actually there, but it was made clear that such entries can only be justified if the person sought is actually found on the property—reasonable suspicion is not enough.[16] In a later case, *Vaughan v McKenzie* [17] it was held not to be lawful for a bailiff, executing a civil process, to enter the dwelling house of a debtor, if the debtor physically resists entry, even

7 *Anon* (1711) 1 Salk 84.
8 *R v Jermy* (1752) Say 47. See also *R v Kendrick* (1754) Say 114; *R v Jones* (1719) 1 Stra 185.
9 (1728) 1 Barn KB 56.
10 (1819) 1 Brod & Bing 24.
11 See also *Myers v Wills* (1820) 4 Moore CP 147 (tearing up a writ after being served not contempt) and *Weeks v Whitely* (1835) 3 Dowl 536 (mere rude behaviour on being served not contempt).
12 As expounded in *R v Payne and Cooper* [1896] 1 QB 577 per Lord Russell of Killowen CJ.
13 [1964] 1 QB 308, [1963] 3 All ER 104, CA.
14 Cf criminal process where there is power to break in.
15 In this case the bailiff knocked at the door and it fell open.
16 See especially Lord Denning MR [1964] 1 QB 308 at 323–4.
17 [1969] 1 QB 557, [1968] 1 All ER 1154.

though the door is unfastened. In such a case the bailiff would again be acting outside his powers in trying to enter and it is submitted that no contempt would be committed in assaulting him[18] in these circumstances.

It follows from *Southam v Smout* that had the bailiffs entered a stranger's property and not found the person sought, assaults on them would not have been actionable under the statute, nor, it is submitted, would it be actionable as contempt at common law. This latter contention is illustrated in a wider context by *Re Clements and Costa Rica Republic v Erlanger* [19] where a solicitor returned to another solicitor's office to fetch back a document 'which had ceased to be a document material to the case'. During the meeting the visiting solicitor was more or less forcibly ejected from the other solicitor's room, and was also verbally abused. The Court of Appeal held that no contempt had been committed for, as Jessel MR said, it was difficult to see how the ordinary course of justice had been interfered with, since under the circumstances such conduct could have no influence upon the case. Mellish LJ said:

> 'If we were to hold this to be contempt it would really amount to this, that whenever solicitors in an action, or clerks to the solicitors in an action, happen to meet each other with reference to some matter respecting the action, and one or other loses his temper and uses words which he ought not to use, that is to be considered as a contempt of court. It appears to me most undesirable that such a rule should be laid down. [The solicitor] has not disobeyed any order of the court; on the contrary, he has done nothing which obstructs the proper administration of justice in court.'

2   Other acts which interfere with or obstruct officers of the court

Acts which obstruct or interfere with the execution of an officer of the court's duties need not of course be acts involving physical attack upon such officers. It should be made clear, however, that as s 14 of the County Courts Act 1984 refers only to assaults, the county court has no jurisdiction of its own to punish such acts, but in these cases the High Court will be able to exercise its supervisory jurisdiction.

In certain cases it has been held that refusal to allow persons to be served with process will amount to contempt. In *Danson v Le Capelain and Steele* [20] the governor of a prison (complying with an order of visiting justices) refused to allow a writ to be served upon a prisoner serving a criminal sentence. Pollock CB held that the order of visiting justices was an interference with justice and that if the governor persisted in his refusal he would be imprisoned for contempt.[1] However, in *Wylam v Wylam and Roller* [2] an action failed for an alleged interference with the court's process. There an enquiry agent had four material witnesses in his employment, on whom the plaintiff's solicitor wished to serve subpoenas. A solicitor's clerk who went to the agent's offices to serve the

18 The proper course for the bailiff to adopt would be to report the matter to the court. It would then issue a committal order for the contempt which, consisting of a wilful refusal to obey an order, would justify a forcible entry being made. See, eg *Harvey v Harvey* (1884) 26 Ch D 644.
19 (1877) 46 LJ Ch 375.
20 (1852) 21 LJ Ex 219.
 1 See also *Denison v Harding* (1867) 15 WR 346, where a keeper of an asylum refused to allow a writ of service on a lunatic.
 2 (1893) 69 LT 500.

subpoenas was told that he could not serve the employees in question, but that if he left the subpoenas, the agent would see that they were served. The court held that it was the duty of the solicitors to serve the witnesses personally, but although the agent had failed in his duty 'to afford every reasonable facility for the service of subpoenas on his employees', it could not be said that the agent had prevented the witnesses from being served since there had been no force or obstruction involved. *Wylam's* case should not, however, be taken as authority for saying that preventing service can only amount to contempt if force is involved. If, for instance, the agent had said the persons sought to be served had left his employment, or that they were abroad, when in fact that was not the case, such an act would probably be regarded as a contempt.

The court has the power to commit for contempt any person who frustrates or attempts to frustrate a writ of possession. In *Alliance Building Society v Austen*,[3] a sheriff's officer in executing a writ of possession evicted the defendant from a flat and gave vacant possession to the plaintiffs. When it was discovered that the defendant had reoccupied the flat, the plaintiffs sought to have the defendant committed for contempt but the proceedings were adjourned for one week since the defendant had stated that he had vacated the premises and promised not to return. At the resumed hearing it was found that the defendant had remained in possession and the court had no hesitation in committing the defendant for contempt. Although it was held that the court did have power to commit for contempt, Roxburgh J made it clear that such a remedy would only be exercised in extreme cases,[4] and that the normal remedy to recover possession was to apply ex parte for a writ of restitution.

In *R v Edwards, ex p Welsh Church Temporalities Comrs* [5] it was held to be a contempt to obstruct the due process of Denbighshire County Court and its officers, by preventing the levying of distraint. After Edwards had refused to pay a tithe rent charge, an order was made under the Tithe Act 1891 to levy a certain sum of money. In order to raise this money a sale of cattle distrained was arranged to take place at Edwards' farm. However, on the day of the sale a large crowd of farmers attended and rendered the holding of the sale impossible. It was held that Edwards, by words, acts and conduct interfered with and incited others to obstruct the due process of the county court and its officers.

Once an officer of the court has been appointed to manage and control property it is a contempt to disturb or interfere with that officer's possession. It has thus been held to be a contempt to disturb or interfere with the possession of receivers, liquidators, sequestrators and admiralty officers or their substitutes. Most of the cases have been concerned with disturbing the possession of receivers in connection with bankruptcy proceedings.[6] The general principle involved was expressed by Lord Romilly MR in *Ames v Birkenhead Docks Trustees*:[7]

---

3   [1951] 2 All ER 1068. See also *Re Hogg and Christie* (1901) 19 NZLR 856.
4   For another case where the remedy of contempt was granted see *Lacon v De Groat* (1893) 10 TLR 24 (defendant regained possession by intrigue).
5   (1933) 49 TLR 383.
6   Receivers can also be appointed under the Mental Health Act 1983, by the Court of Protection, s 99(1).
7   (1855) 20 Beav 332 at 353. See also Lord Truro LC in *Russell v East Anglian Rly Co* (1850) 3 Mac & G 104. For a recent Australian case see *McIntyre v Perkes* (1987) 15 NSWLR 417 (NSW CA) in which it was held that the contemnor could properly be ordered to make good to the receiver the loss or expense occasioned by the contempt. See also *Re Penning, ex p State Bank of Australia* (1989) 89 ALR 417.

'There is no question but that this court will not permit a receiver appointed by its authority, and who is therefore its officer, to be interfered with or dispossessed of the property he is directed to receive, by anyone, although the order appointing him may be perfectly erroneous; this court requires and insists that application should be made to the court, for permission to take possession of any property of which the receiver either has taken or is directed to take possession.'

Once a receiver has been appointed the proper course to adopt is to apply to the court in respect of any dispute with regard to the property. Interfering with a receiver's possession (even if his appointment is invalid) without the court's permission is a contempt. While it is obviously a contempt for a person to take forcible possession of property over which a receiver has been appointed,[8] it has also been held to be a contempt to oust the receiver from possession of goods over which the defendant holds a valid bill of sale;[9] to bring an action against a receiver without permission of the court, even though it was held that the receiver had acted outside his authority and to the prejudice of the plaintiff;[10] and for a subsequent encumbrancer, with notice of the appointment of a receiver, to issue a sequestration against the receiver.[11] As Kindersley V-C said in *Hawkins v Gathercole*:[12]

'it is quite clear that when this court has appointed a receiver, it will not allow the possession of that receiver to be disturbed by anybody, however good his right may be, but the party thinking he has a right paramount to that of the receiver . . . must, before he can presume to take any steps of his own motion, apply to this court for leave to assert his right against the receiver.'

In *Re Plant, ex p Hayward*,[13] a receiver sent out the usual notices to the creditors informing them of his appointment, and asking for particulars of claims, and he sent out applications to some debtors for the debts due. The debtor's solicitor informed the receiver not to collect or apply for further debts as it would ruin the business and goodwill. He also told the receiver that it was unnecessary for him to interfere with the management beyond holding possession no further than the solicitor would direct from time to time as the business was being attended to under his superintendence. After a disagreement about this arrangement the solicitor told the receiver that he (the solicitor) would see to the management and he offered a written indemnity to the receiver. In holding this action to be a contempt Cotton LJ said:

'It is not for giving bad advice that the [solicitor] is to be held liable but for his interference. It has been clearly shown that the order of the court was stopped to some extent from having effect by what was done. The proper method, if the order was not considered to be right, was to apply to have such order altered. The solicitor however, did not take that view of the case. He in fact said to the receiver "Do not act under that order, but do as I tell you to do, and I will indemnify you from the consequences of your disobedience." That appears to me to have been a contempt of court.'

8   As in *Broad v Wickham* (1831) 4 Sim 511.
9   *Re Mead, ex p Cochrane* (1875) LR 20 Eq 282.
10   *Searle v Choat* (1884) 25 Ch D 723.
11   *Hawkins v Gathercole* (1852) 1 Drew 12.
12   Ibid at 17.
13   (1881) 45 LT 326. Cf *Re Mayhew, ex p Till* (1873) LR 16 Eq 97, which established as the one exception to the rule that an application must be made to the court in respect of property over which a receiver has been appointed, that a landlord may levy distraint for rent without leave of the court. For the relevant statutory provision see now the Insolvency Act 1986, s 347(1).

Contempt may be committed by less direct means of interfering with receivers. In *Helmore v Smith (No 2)* [14] pending an appeal against the dissolution of a partnership, a receiver was appointed in order to keep the business as a going concern. Helmore, a former employee of the partnership who after his dismissal had set up his own firm, wrote a letter to the customers of the firm, the effect of which, according to Kay J, was to say: [15] 'The business is at an end, subject to the chance of an appeal from the Vice-Chancellor's judgment; send your orders to me'. The Court of Appeal held that Helmore had committed a gross contempt. As Bowen LJ said: [16]

> 'I will not discuss the cases as to what interference with a receiver and manager will justify the court in interfering, or lay down any rule upon the subject. All I say is that this was a wrongful act calculated to destroy property under the management of this court, and that it was done deliberately. Are the hands of the court so tied that it cannot protect its officers, and must relegate them to the ordinary legal remedy, and the consequent delay of execution? Where it is necessary for the protection of its officers or of the property itself the court must show that it has a long arm.'

Upon the same principle it has been held to be a contempt to set up a rival business after the appointment of a receiver. [17] In *Dixon v Dixon* [18] the defendant, having been dismissed by the receiver, took an active part in establishing a rival business. He told employees of the firm managed by the receiver, that the business was to be sold and induced them to end their employment and join him. In this way three key employees left to join him, but as Swinfen Eady J said:

> 'The defendant contends that as the employees gave proper notice to terminate employment . . . so that no breach of contract was instigated or committed, there was no interference with the receiver and manager. I am unable to take that view. In my opinion, any deliberate act calculated to destroy property under the management of the court by means of a receiver and manager is an interference with that receiver and manager, although it may not induce the breaking of any contract. The object of the court is to prevent any undue interference with the administration of justice, and when anyone, whether a party in a business, a party to the litigation, or a stranger, interferes with an officer of the court, it is essential for the court to protect that officer.'

Although the above cases were concerned with interference with a receiver [19] there can be little doubt that the same rules apply with respect to sequestrators [20] and to liquidators appointed by the court, [1] but liquidators and receivers not appointed by the court are unlikely to be protected as they are not officers of the court. [2]

It is also a contempt to interfere with the possession of property of Admiralty Marshalls or their substitutes. In *The Jarlinn*, [3] the Admiralty Marshall had

14   (1886) 35 Ch D 449, CA.
15   At 451.
16   At 457.
17   *King v Dopson* (1911) 56 Sol Jo 51.
18   [1904] 1 Ch 161 but cf *Re Gent, Gent-Davis v Harris* (1892) 40 WR 267.
19   The same principles apply to all types of receivers appointed by the court.
20   See *Lord Pelham v Duchess of Newcastle* (1713) 3 Swan 289n; *Angel v Smith* (1804) 9 Ves 335.
 1   *Re Henry Pound Son & Hutchins* (1889) 42 Ch D 402.
 2   *Re Hill's Waterfall Estate and Gold Mining Co* (1896) 1 Ch 947 at 954.
 3   [1965] 3 All ER 36. See also *Re The Jarvis Brake* [1976] 2 All ER 886 (owner tried to remove arrest papers and sell ship).

ordered the arrest of 'The Jarlinn'. The telegram[4] ordering the arrest was nailed to the superstructure of the wheelhouse and a copy served on the master by the Admiralty Marshall's substitute who expressly told the ship's master and agent that the ship could not be moved without his permission. The next day the warrant of the arrest and a copy of the writ having arrived by post, the warrant was duly served on the master. Later however, and contrary to the express orders of the substitute, the master, fearing that his ship would be 'neaped' for over a week if he did not move, decided to move the ship outside the jurisdiction and delivered its cargo in the Republic of Ireland. The master was arrested on his return and found guilty of contempt. Hewson J, though conceding that there were mitigating circumstances, held that the master had sailed in defiance of the substitute's orders and that although he was an Icelandic citizen he had understood enough to know that what he was doing was wrong. He was accordingly fined £300 and it was pointed out that in appropriate cases the court would not hesitate to imprison the offender. Hewson J concluded his judgment with the following warning:

> 'In times past not only has the master of a ship, but also a pilot, an agent and a dockmaster have been brought before this Court in contempt for breaking, or being privy to the breaking of arrest of a ship.[5] I mention these facts because there has been no case of this kind for so many years and this present case may serve to bring to the notice of all those whose business is with ships within this jurisdiction that they defy an order of this Court at their peril.'[6]

F   Reform

The application of the law of contempt with regard to the interference with those having duties to discharge in a court of law was touched upon in the wide-ranging report of the Phillimore Committee.[7] Overall the Committee recommended that the ambit of the contempt offence should be reduced because it did not think that the summary procedure by which contempts are triable is always justifiable and that recourse should be had instead to the normal criminal process. It was their basic recommendation [8] that the contempt jurisdiction should be invoked only where an offending act does not fall within the definition of any other offence or where urgency or practical necessity requires the matter to be dealt with summarily. Consistent with this basic standpoint the Committee recommended[9] that conduct intended to pervert or obstruct the course of justice should only be capable of being dealt with as a contempt if proceedings to which the conduct relates have started and have not yet been finished. Following this recommendation the Committee proposed[10] that to take or threaten reprisals against a witness after the proceedings have been concluded should no longer be a contempt but that instead it should be made an indictable offence. In fact the new offence that they

---

4   It was held in *The Seraglio* (1885) 10 PD 120 that notice of arrest by telegraph was sufficient service, and was not to be disregarded even if the telegram's authenticity was in doubt.
5   See, eg *The Petrel* (1863) 3 Hag Adm 299.
6   For other cases see *The Abodi Mendi* [1939] P 178; *The Selina Stanford* (1908) Times, 17 November; The Seraglio (1885) 10 PD 120; *The Harmonie* (1841) 1 Wm Rob 179.
7   1974, Cmnd 5794.
8   At para 21.
9   At para 72.
10   See Ch 6.

recommended included reprisals or threatened reprisals against jurors as well as witnesses.[11]

The recommendation that there should be a new offence for taking reprisals against witnesses and jurors was included by the Law Commission[12] in their draft Administration of Justice (Offences) Bill. In fact, the Commission proposed two offences, namely, taking or threatening to take reprisals against persons for attending or having attended proceedings as jurors or witnesses[13] and taking or threatening to take reprisals inter alia against witnesses for the evidence that they have given.[14] In the latter instance it would be a defence if the alleged offender can establish that the reprisals were to punish a person for giving false evidence and that the witness knew that the evidence was false at the time when he gave it or was reckless whether it was false.[15]

The above two proposed offences would have a wider ambit than the current contempt law because they would extend to judicial proceedings[16] defined inter alia as proceedings 'before any person or body having by law power to hear, receive and examine evidence on oath'.

The above proposals were two of a number made by the Law Commission as a result of their inquiry into the operation of the laws protecting the Administration of Justice. The Commission's basic overall objective[17] in making their proposals was to provide a series of specific and relatively tightly defined offences which would replace a number of common law offences that now exist, and thereby provide a simpler and more rational law to protect the administration of justice. To this end they propose that there should be inter alia specific offences relating to threats or bribery to induce others to suppress or not to give evidence[18] and that the common law offences relating to the perversion of the course of justice, embracery and personating a juror etc should be abolished.[19]

The Law Commission made no specific recommendation with regard to contempt partly in the hope and expectation that the Phillimore proposals would be implemented[20] and partly because they felt that the codification of contempt merited separate consideration.[1]

It seems right when considering reform of contempt in this area that regard should also be had to the existence of other offences.[2] However, when the Government legislated in the Criminal Justice and Public Order Act 1994[3] on the intimidation etc of witnesses and jurors it produced offences which are in

11 See Part V, recommendation 20.
12 No 96: *Offences Relating to the Interference with the Course of Justice*. (1979). See also the Working Paper No 62: (1975). For an assessment of the report, see generally Roger Leng, [1981] Crim LR 151.
13 Cl 19.
14 Cl 18. The clause also refers to reprisals taken against judges and magistrates, members and officers of courts and tribunals, members of juries etc. See cl 18(1)(b) and 11(2).
15 Cl 18(2).
16 For the definition see cl 1. For a discussion of the definition see Lowe and Rawlings, 'Tribunals and the Laws Protecting the Administration of Justice' [1982] PL 418, 440ff.
17 See para 3.19.
18 Under cls 8 and 9 of the Draft Bill. Other proposed offences are referred to elsewhere in this chapter.
19 Under cl 35.
20 See para 1.7. For a criticism of this see Leng, [1981] Crim LR 151.
1 See para 14 of Working Paper No 62.
2 For a similar conclusion see the Canadian Law Reform Commission Working Paper No 20: (1977) pp 34–37.
3 Section 51, discussed at pp 426–429.

addition to the common law offences. The same conduct may now amount to contempt, perverting the course of justice, and the statutory offence. Confusion has been increased rather than lessened and, as has been explained above, there are considerable anomalies in the new offences, not the least of which is that they apply only to criminal proceedings. Section 51 looks more like a political response to a particular scenario than a properly thought out measure of law reform, and it offers little except higher sentences. In October 1995[4] the Home Secretary was reported as planning new measures to counteract the increasingly serious problem of jury 'nobbling' and it is hoped that any future provisions produce more coherence.

II   INTERFERENCE WITH PARTIES TO AN ACTION

A   The general principle

According to Lord Diplock in the *Sunday Times* case[5] it is a requirement of the due administration of justice that:

> 'all citizens should have unhindered access to the constitutionally established courts of criminal or civil jurisdiction for the determination of disputes as to their legal rights and liabilities . . .'.

Conduct calculated to impair this requirement is punishable as a contempt of court.

The first question to consider is whether the same principles apply to interference with litigants as they do to interference with witnesses. As both courts[6] and commentators[7] have pointed out there is a key difference between the witness and the litigant (at any rate in civil proceedings), namely, that the former can be compelled to give evidence whereas the latter has a choice whether or not to bring or defend proceedings. It has become apparent that whereas the courts will brook no real interference with a witness, a litigant can and should expect to suffer some pressure. As we have seen[8] the majority of the Law Lords in the *Sunday Times* case held that *public* pressure in the form of publication of fair and temperately expressed criticism does not constitute a contempt.[9] Here we have to consider *private* pressure. It is suggested that as a general principle it can be said that *improper* pressure aimed at deterring or preventing a party from bringing an action or inducing a party to suppress certain evidence or to give false evidence constitutes an unacceptable interference with the due administration of justice and amounts to contempt.

---

4   See the *Independent*, 24 October, 1995.
5   [1974] AC 273 at 309.
6   See eg the *Sunday Times* case per Lord Simon at 319 and *R v Kellett* [1976] QB 372 at 390 per Stephenson LJ.
7   See eg the Law Commission, Working Paper No 62: *Offences relating to the Administration of Justice* (1975) para 75 and in their full report (No 96) at para 3.41. See also the commentary on *Kellett* at [1975] Crim LR 576 at p 579.
8   In Ch 6.
9   See also *A-G v Hislop* [1991] 1 QB 514, discussed in Ch 6.

B   The actus reus

1   *Actionable interference does not require actual deterrence*

If improper pressure has been brought to bear upon a litigant, such conduct constitutes a contempt whether or not the party is actually deterred from bringing an action. As Stuart V-C said in *Smith v Lakeman*,[10] the letter sent to a defendant pending the suit:

> 'was a threat for the purpose of intimidating him as a suitor, and, therefore, *whether it had had that effect or not*, it was unquestionably a contempt of court' (emphasis added).

It would be consistent with the general principle applicable in contempt cases, however, that to constitute an actionable contempt even improper pressure must present a real risk of interference. For example, it may not be thought to be an actionable contempt for an individual to threaten a powerful corporation that unless they withdraw an action against him or someone else, he will take some action which will make little impact against them. It is dangerous, however, to take this de minimis principle too far and it may be that it has no place where a litigant's access to the courts has been denied. In *Raymond v Honey*[11] a prisoner successfully brought a contempt action against the governor of Albany Prison on the basis that he had prevented the prisoner from applying to the High Court for leave to commit the Governor for contempt on another matter by refusing to forward the necessary documents and accompanying letter which the prisoner had given him. It was argued for the defence[12] that no contempt had been committed as there had been no substantial interference with the course of justice since the prisoner had not been denied access to his solicitor and so at the worst his contempt application had been delayed. Evidently, however, this argument fell on deaf ears, and it is submitted rightly so, for a person's very access to the courts should be jealously safeguarded.

2   *What constitutes actionable interference through improper pressure*

As we have seen, *Raymond v Honey* establishes the point that denying a potential litigant access to the courts even for a short time constitutes an actionable contempt. Other examples of actionable contempts are physically harming or threatening a party with physical harm.[13] In *Ex p Halsam*[14] it was held that a husband had committed contempt when he induced his wife by 'menaces' to give untrue evidence.

Actionable contempts are not confined to threats of violence and once more subtle forms of pressure are involved the issue becomes more difficult. As said above, the majority of the Law Lords in the *Sunday Times* case held that fair and temperately expressed criticism in a publication was not a contempt. A fortiori

---

10 (1856) 26 LJ Ch 305.
11 [1983] 1 AC 1, [1982] 1 All ER 756; cf in Canada *Re Pereira and Minister of Manpower and Immigration* (1979) 91 DLR (3d) 706.
12 See Jones, 'Prisoners' Rights and Contempt of Court' (1982) 45 MLR 707 at 709.
13 See, eg *Re Bentley Macleod* (1842) 6 Jur 461; Anon (1356) YB 30 Edw 3, Fo 2B, pl 14, cited in Oswald, *Contempt* (3rd edn, 1910) p 43; *R v Craddock* (1875) Times, 18 March.
14 (1740) 2 Atk 50. See also *R v Carrol* (1744) 1 Wils 75.

on this view such *private* pressure is legitimate and in this respect one of the minority in the *Sunday Times* case, Lord Diplock, agreed. Lord Simon on the other hand took the strict line that even private pressure to deter a litigant amounts to a contempt unless there is a common interest between the person exerting pressure and the party such that 'fair, reasonable and moderate personal representations would be appropriate'.[15]

The distinction between proper and improper pressure is a difficult one to draw, and the cases give examples on what falls on either side of the line.

It was held in *Hillfinch Properties Ltd v Newark Investments Ltd*[16] that to threaten practising orthodox Jews with excommunication for the alleged sin of prosecuting litigation in the courts would constitute a contempt and it may be a contempt for a person to threaten to seek to invoke such action.

In *Smith v Lakeman*[17] the following letter sent to a defendant pending a suit was held to be a contempt:

'Sir, I learn from good authority that you have a suit pending in Chancery and should it go up for judgment, you will at once be indicted for swindling, perjury, and forgery, and thus bring disgrace on your family and ruin for ever the prospects of your gallant son.'

Stewart V-C held that the letter:

'was a threat for the purpose of intimidating him as a suitor, and therefore whether it had had that effect or not, it was unquestionably a contempt of court.'

In a similar case, *Re Mulock*,[18] Mulock wrote a letter to a plaintiff involved in a pending divorce suit threatening that if she did not withdraw her suit by a certain date he would:

'publish the full truth of the case, founded upon my own various communications with your own friends, and accompanied with a statement of facts concerning yourself from before your marriage up to the present time, borne out by irrefragable documents.'

It was held that the letter amounted to an attempt by a third person to prevent the suit being brought before the court by threats of bringing her into disgrace and disrepute:

'From the pressure of their threat Mrs Chetwynd seeks protection, and she claims the right to approach this court, free from all restraint or intimidation. It is a right that belong to all suitors.'

Mulock was accordingly found guilty of contempt and was fined £300.[19]

However, on the strength of the *Sunday Times* case it seems that exhortations to a party to settle or not to stand upon their strict legal rights will not be a contempt even if publicly expressed by a disinterested third party, provided the comment is fair and temperately expressed. A fortiori, private exhortations are permissible.

Parties are, of course, entitled to settle out of court and an approach by an opposing party, his agent or his solicitor with an offer of money by way of

---

15   [1974] AC 273 at 319.
16   (1981) Times, 1 July.
17   (1856) 26 LJ Ch 305.
18   (1864) 3 Sw & Tr 599, 33 LJ P M & A 205.
19   For other cases see *Kitcat v Sharpe* (1882) 52 LJ Ch 134; *Sharland v Sharland* (1885) 1 TLR 492; *Pavlova v Harvey* (1914) Times, 27 November.

settlement will not amount to a contempt. Such an offer could, however, be considered a contempt if it was accompanied by an unlawful or improper threat. However, on the strength of *Webster v Bakewell RDC* [20] it may be permissible for a person to say to a party:

> 'I will assert my legal rights against you if you choose to go on with your action which to my mind is detrimental to my interest in the property.'

In this case the plaintiff had brought an action against the council for trespass to property of which he was a yearly tenant. The owner of the tenancy, through her solicitor, heard about the damage and wrote to the council complaining about damage, not just to the plaintiff's tenement but to several tenements. The council agreed to rectify matters provided the plaintiff's writ was withdrawn. The owner's solicitor thereupon wrote a letter to the plaintiff which included the following:

> 'Mrs Thornhill [the owner] is determined that this action shall not go forward, and she is anxious to stop it with as little inconvenience to anybody as possible. She does not wish to take the extreme course of turning you out of the cottage, so as to place you in such a position that you would have no locus standi in the matter, but she will not hesitate to do so if her wishes are not carried out. I hope however that you will not drive her to take this course'.

The plaintiff contended that the letter was a contempt since it contained threats calculated to deter him from prosecuting the action, but Neville J rejected the contention. He considered the effect of the letter to say:

> '"I do not intend to interfere with the way you carry on the action at all, but it is injurious to me and, if you do carry it on and assert what you allege to be your legal rights in that way, I, on my part, shall give effect to the legal rights I possess and resume possession of my cottage." I must say I cannot think that can be considered a contempt of court'.

The extent to which it is permissible to threaten to exercise a legal right unless a litigant desists from his legal action remains in doubt. It is generally agreed[1] that the *Webster* case was perhaps special in the sense that the landlord genuinely thought it was in her interest to put a stop to the litigation which affected the property held by her tenant as well as other nearby property which she owned. Motive in pressing a threat might well be relevant and it is unclear whether a third party has a similar latitude to threaten to exercise a legal right. In *R v Kellett* [2] a threat to deter a *witness* by bringing a slander action was held to be an attempt to pervert the course of justice, but there is, as we have already said, a difference in the courts' attitudes to deterring witnesses and deterring parties.

3 *Victimisation in employment cases*

The effect of much of the modern statutory protection given to employees may be severely weakened unless the victimisation of those who try to invoke it is punished. There is considerable evidence of the prevalence of the victimisation

---

20 [1916] 1 Ch 300 at 304; see also *A-G v Hislop* [1991] 1 QB 514.
1   See eg the Law Commission in their Working Paper No 62 at para 74.
2   [1976] QB 372.

of employees who complain of discrimination,[3] and it has been argued that the 'somewhat limited protection accorded to anti-discrimination complainants by the Sex Discrimination and Race Relations Act is capable of being supplemented by invoking the deterrent powers of the law of contempt'.[4] Now that industrial tribunals have been held to be courts within s 19 of the Contempt of Court Act[5] the way is open to hold such victimisation before and during proceedings to be a contempt, on the grounds that it interferes with a litigant. The nature of the relationship between the parties in employment cases is such as to lend itself to pressure being put on the complainant which goes far beyond the 'private exhortation' category and it is submitted that in the contempt powers there is a weapon available to combat this which the courts could use, should they be so minded. However, it has to be recognised that there could be special problems with mens rea in such cases.[6] The hope would have to be that the threat of liability for contempt might deter employers from victimising conduct, because a finding of contempt would appear not to give the victim damages[7] or a right to reinstatement where the victimisation had resulted in the loss of the job or a particular position.

4 *Other types of improper interference*

It is also a contempt to bribe or attempt to bribe a party, either to induce him not to bring an action at all, or to suppress certain parts of his evidence, which it is his duty to disclose to the court.[8] It is a contempt to prevent a party from obeying a court order. In *Thomas v Gwynne* [9] a minor was ordered by the court to execute a conveyance and having not done so, a further order was made, namely, that the infant should execute the conveyance within 14 days after the order had been personally served on the minor. The minor's mother thereupon hid the infant so that he could not be personally served. It was held that the mother's action amounted to a contempt.

5 *Service of process on a party in the court precincts*

More doubtfully, it may be a contempt to serve process upon a party in the court precincts. According to *Cole v Hawkins* [10] decided in 1738 'the service of process

---

3 See Leonard, *Pyrrhic Victories* (1987, HMSO); Graham and Lewis, *The Role of ACAS Conciliation in Equal Pay and Sex Discrimination Cases* (1985, EOC). Sex discrimination includes sexual harassment.
4 Ellis and Miller: 'The Victimisation of Anti-Discrimination Complainants—Is it Contempt of Court?' (1993) PL 80 at 92.
5 *Peach Grey & Co v Sommers* [1995] 2 All ER 513.
6 See pp 414 ff.
7 See pp 418–422.
8 *Re Hooley' Rucker's case* (1898) 79 LT 306. For the facts of this case see p 406. Cf *Cox v Cox* (1893) Times, 18 July, p 14. In this case a possible witness threatened that if the defendant did not pay her £2,000 she would give evidence on the other side. The court, however, refused to commit since it found that the party had begun the communications. Sed quaere? Surely both the party and the potential witness had committed contempt?
9 (1845) 8 Beav 312.
10 (1738) 2 Stra 1094. See also *Newton v London Brighton and South Coast Rly Co* (1849) 19 LJ QB 12; cf, the position in Parliament. As Miller (in *Contempt of Court*, 2nd edn, p 406, n 43) points out, the Committee for Privileges of the House of Commons has held it to be a contempt

in the sight of the court is a great contempt', but this decision has yet to be followed. In *R v Jones, ex p McVittie*,[11] Lord Hewart CJ said:

> 'Speaking for myself I do not say that there may not be circumstances in which the service of process within the precincts of the court may amount to contempt, but on the particular facts of this case I think it is not possible to say that there was any contempt committed here.'

Lord Hewart CJ was careful to confine his decision to the particular facts of the case, which admittedly were rather extreme: a judgment had been obtained against McVittie but he paid nothing. Later he was served with a bankruptcy notice and he still paid nothing. An order for the payment of the judgment order by instalments was then obtained and McVittie disobeyed this order. Finally, a series of judgment summonses was issued, but all efforts to serve him with the summonses had failed because he kept out of the way. MacKinnon J thought that in these circumstances to argue that the service of process amounted to a contempt was 'farcical'. MacKinnon J, was more ready to say that the decision in *Cole v Hawkins* was obsolete. He said:[12]

> 'It is possible, as has been pointed out by the Lord Chief Justice, that there might be circumstances in which service of a writ within the precincts of court might amount to a contempt of court. Personally, I cannot conceive what those circumstances could be.'

It is hard not to sympathise with MacKinnon J's view and it is a pity that *Coles v Hawkins* has not been overruled. However, the possibility that service within the precincts could be a contempt was again left open in a more recent case, *Ex p Brantschen*.[13] What circumstances would justify a finding of contempt has yet to be established though it seems that service of process in the court precincts as a last resort does not constitute a contempt. Indeed it seems unlikely that any action for contempt would now succeed on the sole ground that service of process was made in the precincts of a court since it is difficult to see how the administration of justice is thereby jeopardised. In any case it seems illogical to hold that while such service is valid,[14] it is nevertheless a contempt.

The modern position seems well summarised by Lindgren J who said in the Australian case *Re O'Sullivan*:[15]

> 'In my view it is not the law that service of any process within the precincts of a court constitutes a contempt of court, and even if it were, it could not follow that service would be set aside ... No doubt the physical proximity of conduct to a court may be a factor sometimes to be taken into account when a contempt of court of a relevant kind is alleged. It cannot be said that service of process within the precincts of a court can never with other circumstances constitute a contempt. But this is hardly a useful statement: analysis shows that it signifies only that service within the precincts of a court is not precluded from being part of contemptuous conduct.'

of the House to serve a copy of a writ on a Member within the precincts of the House where Parliament is sitting: see (1973) Times, 23 February.

11   [1931] 1 KB 664 at 669. See also *Poole v Gould* (1856) 1 H & N 99.
12   Ibid at 671.
13   (1970) Times, 7 December. For the position in Australia see *Re O'Sullivan* (1995) 129 ALR 295; *Baldry v Jackson* [1976] 1 NSWLR 19 and *Re Tole, ex p Tole* (1933) 50 WN (NSW) 216.
14   The validity of the service was definitely established by *Ex p Brantschen* (1970) Times, 7 December, and in Australia by *Re O'Sullivan* (1995) 129 ALR 295, but see also *Newton v London, Brighton and South Coast Rly Co* (1849) 19 LJ QB 12.
15   (1995) 129 ALR 295 at 305–306.

One example of an additional element that could make service of process a contempt is where the requirement of attendance was a sham or subterfuge to lure the other party to the courts.

6   *The timing of the interference*

Wrongful interference with a party during the pendency of proceedings clearly constitutes an actionable contempt. *Raymond v Honey* [16] stands as authority for saying that contempt can apply to the interference with a potential party, ie before any proceedings have been brought, though the extent to which this decision can be relied upon is perhaps doubtful. It may be that in this respect *Raymond v Honey* should be regarded as turning on its special facts. At any rate, unless some legal proceedings are eventually brought, it is suggested that unlawful approaches to potential parties are better indicted for perverting the course of justice.

To what extent can contempt apply to interference with parties after the conclusion of proceedings? There is some authority that it can apply. In *William v Lyons* [17] after the jury had given a verdict in favour of the plaintiff, and damages of £200 had been awarded, the defendant sought to induce the plaintiff to take a small sum of money and release the damages. To this end, he obtained a warrant from a Justice of the Peace to arrest the plaintiff for a pretended murder and while in custody he was arrested in an action for £500 at the suit of the defendant. It was held that the defendant had committed contempt 'for endeavouring to intimidate a plaintiff for the purpose of inducing him to take less damages than the jury gave'.

Whether the *Butterworth* principle extends to the victimising or punishing of parties after the trial has been concluded remains to be decided. It could certainly be argued that, for example, a company that dismisses an employee for bringing a legal action against it could deter future employees from bringing an action. However, Lord Simon seemed to hint in the *Sunday Times* case that such reprisals were not contempt [18] and it may be that this is another example of where the difference between the litigant who has a choice whether or not to bring an action and a witness who can be compelled to give evidence, is crucial. On the other hand, we have considered above [19] the argument that the problem of the victimisation of complainants in discrimination complainants could be partly dealt with by applying the contempt rules, [20] and it is submitted that there should be no difference between victimisation before or after the conclusion of the tribunal hearing. The probability or possibility of victimisation by the employer after the case is a real deterrent to complainants and there is surely no problem about fulfilling the 'interference with the course of justice as a continuing process' criteria. There may, however, be a difficulty with mens rea.

---

16 [1983] AC 1, [1982] 1 All ER 756.
17 (1723) 8 Mod Rep 189. See also *Re Higg's Mortgage, Goddard v Higgs* [1894] WN 73.
18 [1974] AC 273 at 320.
19 At pp 445–446.
20 See Ellis and Miller, 'The Victimisation of Anti-Discrimination Complainants—Is it Contempt of Court?' (1993) PL 80 at 92.

C   The mens rea

The question of what is the mens rea required has not really been considered in relation to interfering with parties, because in the cases that have arisen, it has been obvious that there has been an intention to interfere with the course of justice. It is submitted that the requirement of mens rea should be the same with regard to interfering with parties as it is with regard to interfering with witnesses. It is therefore essential that the alleged contemnor should know that the person with whom he is interfering is a party to the action. In most cases such knowledge will be apparent, but in other cases knowledge must be proved before a contempt could be said to have been committed. For instance, there is no doubt that assaulting a party on his way to court, or preventing a party from reaching the court by physical force, can amount to contempt. However, in order to establish a case for contempt it would have to be shown that it was known that the person assaulted was a party to an action.

Once it has been shown that the act in question was committed in the knowledge that the 'victim' is a party the courts will readily infer an intention to interfere with the course of justice. In *Smith v Lakeman*, Stuart V-C said:[1]

> 'In *Re Ludlow Charities, Lechmere Charlton's Case*, Lord Cottenham had said, "The power of committal is given to courts of justice for the purpose of securing the better and more secure administration of justice. Every writing, letter or publication, which has for its object to divert the course of justice is a contempt." A threatening letter must be considered as having equally that object, whether addressed to a suitor seeking justice or to a judge or an officer of the court.'

There could, however, be problems if contempt were held to apply, as is discussed above[2] to the victimisation of discrimination complainants. Employers might plausibly argue that the case had had the effect of rendering it impossible for the employee comfortably to carry on working for them. The question of mens rea where victimisation *after* the case is concerned are discussed above in relation to witnesses[3] and what is really is at issue here is *motive*. There is no reason why motive cannot be examined by the court in the normal way, and it should be noted that in the statutory provisions on threatening witnesses and jurors after a criminal trial, introduced by the Criminal Justice and Public Order Act 1994, the motive of punishing the person concerned is presumed for a certain period thereafter.

D   Reform proposals

It seems right that a litigant should be given some protection though whether this should be under the law of contempt and how much protection should be given is more debatable. The Law Commission[4] proposed two offences dealing with this area, namely, making an unwarranted demand with menaces that another shall not institute or shall withdraw or settle judicial proceedings[5] and taking reprisals against a party for instituting or not withdrawing or settling disputes.[6]

1   (1856) 26 LJ Ch 305.
2   At pp 445–446.
3   See pp 414 ff.
4   Law Com No 96: (1979).
5   See cl 15.
6   See cl 16.

III   BREACH OF DUTY BY PERSONS OFFICIALLY CONNECTED WITH THE COURT OR ITS PROCESS

Contempt may not only be committed by interfering with persons having duties towards the court, but also by those persons themselves in the execution of their duties. It is a contempt for a receiver not to perform his duties as, for example, by not paying money due from him as a receiver.[7] Similarly, a sequestrator may also be held guilty of contempt if he abuses his powers.[8]

A sheriff, under-sheriff, bailiff or officer of a sheriff can be punished by a superior court of record in a 'like manner as for any contempt of court', if he has committed certain offences under the Sheriffs Act 1887[9] as, for example, by granting a warrant for the execution of a writ before actually receiving the writ[10] or where such a person:

'is guilty of any offence against or breach of the provisions of this Act, or of any wrongful act or neglect or default in the execution of his office or of any contempt of any superior court.'[11]

Any person purporting to act as an under-sheriff, bailiff or officer of a sheriff when not entitled to do so will also be guilty of contempt of the High Court and liable to punishment as if he were an under-sheriff guilty of such a contempt.[12] The maximum penalty prescribed under the Act is a fine of £200 which is in addition to payment of all the damages suffered by any person or persons aggrieved.[13] If the summary mode of proceeding against the offender is adopted, proceedings must be taken before the end of the next sitting of the court, after the offence has been committed.[14]

A sheriff may also be ordered by the High Court or Court of Appeal under RSC Ord 46, r 9(2) to comply with a notice served on him,[15] to indorse on a writ of execution a statement of the manner in which he has executed it and to send to the party at whose instance the writ was issued, a copy of the statement.

The court also exercises a special disciplinary jurisdiction over solicitors, since solicitors are officers of the Supreme Court.[16] Solicitors can be held guilty of contempt for not carrying out their undertakings, even if they were not given directly to the court. They can also be held guilty of contempt for not obeying court orders or for wrongfully disposing of funds belonging to clients. In addition to this special jurisdiction, under s 20(2) of the Solicitors Act 1974, any person

---

7   See *Re Gent, Gent-Davies v Harris* (1888) 40 ChD 190; *Re Bell's Estate, Foster v Bell* (1870) LR 9 Eq 172. A liquidator may also commit contempt if he disobeys a court order requiring him to comply with his statutory duties under the Insolvency Act 1985, s 192(1), see *Re Grantham Wholesale Fruit, Vegetable and Potato Merchants Ltd* [1972] 1 WLR 559 and *Re Diane (Stockport) Ltd* (1982) Times, 15 and 16 July and 4 August.

8   *Lord Pelham v Lord Harley* (1713) 3 Swan 291n. See also *Roe v Davies* (1878) WN 147. It may be noted the sequestrators owe a duty of care to the owner of the sequestered property, see *IRC v Hoogstraten* [1984] 3 All ER 25, CA, discussed further at p 606.

9   S 29(5). This summary mode of procedure is an alternative to other forms of prosecution.

10 S 29(2)(c). S 29(2) (a) also provides that it is an offence to withhold 'a prisoner bailable after he has offered sufficient security'. S 29(2) (b) was repealed by the Theft Act 1968, Sch 3.

10 S 29(2) (d).

12 S 29(6) as amended by the Theft Act 1968, Sch 3.

13 S 29(2).

14 S 29(7). S 29(8) provides that a person is not liable to be punished twice for the same offence.

15 Under the provisions of RSC Ord 46, r 9(1).

16 Under s 50 of the Solicitors Act 1974, see also Ch 14; Cf the position in Australia see eg *Barristers' Board of Western Australia v Tranter Corpn Pty Ltd* [1976] WAR 65.

who purports to act in any action or matter as a duly qualified solicitor without actually being so qualified shall be guilty of contempt of the court[17] in which the action cause or matter arose, and may be punished accordingly.[18] The offender will also be incapable of maintaining any action for any costs in respect of anything done by him in the course of so acting.[19]

Under s 40 no solicitor whilst in prison shall as a solicitor in his own name or in the name of any other solicitor issue a writ or process or commence, prosecute or defend any action or any matter in bankruptcy. Breach of s 40 renders the offender guilty of contempt.[20]

The rationale of these provisions was explained by Bargrave Deane J in *Re Watts, Davies and Davies*,[1] when he said that it was:

> 'essential that the work of the court should be done by duly authorised persons, and that no outsiders should come in and take advantage of the public by posing as solicitors or solicitors' clerks.'

IV INTERFERING WITH THE COURT'S SPECIAL JURISDICTION OVER CERTAIN PERSONS

A Wards of court[2]

The court has long exercised a special jurisdiction over wards of court,[3] indeed a unique feature of wardship is that as soon as the child becomes a ward of court, legal control of that child vests in the court. Furthermore, that control only ends when the child ceases to be a ward.[4] In other words the court's special control always precedes any court hearing and will often continue to exist after the hearing and in any event does not depend upon a specific court order.

It is sometimes said[5] that it is a contempt to interfere with the welfare of a ward but while this may be a convenient shorthand statement of the position, it is apt to be misleading.[6] Though rooted in the need to protect the ward's welfare the essence of the contempt with which we are now concerned[7] lies in interfering

---

17 The offender can, however, be indicted instead, s 20(2) (a).
18 Presumably by imprisonment up to a maximum of two years, see the Contempt of Court Act 1981, s 14, discussed at pp 626–627and/or an unlimited fine.
19 S 25(1).
20 Under s 40(2).
1 (1913) 29 TLR 513.
2 See generally *Clarke Hall & Morrison on Children,* 1 [1051] ff. Lowe and White, *Wards of Court* (2nd edn, 1986, Barry Rose). For the modern operation of the wardship jurisdiction in the light of the Children Act 1989, see White, Carr and Lowe, *The Children Act in Practice* (1995, Butterworths) Ch 12.
3 As Lowe and White, op cit at para 1-1 put it 'The law knows no greater form of protection for a child than wardship'. For the history of wardship see Lowe and White, op cit, Ch 1 and Seymour, 'Parens Patriae and Wardship Powers: Their Nature and Origins' (1994) 14 Ox Jo of Legal Studies 159, and the authorities there cited.
4 For when a child ceases to be a ward see the Supreme Court Act 1981, s 41(2), (3) and FPR 1991, r 5.3.
5 Arlidge and Eady, *The Law of Contempt* (1982, Sweet & Maxwell) at 4-24 and 9 *Halsbury's Laws* (4th edn), para 36. See also the *Supreme Court Practice* at 52/1/10 which refers to 'Interference with wards of court'.
6 Particularly when considering whether the contempt power extends to protecting children who are not wards of court see p 456.
7 Cf disobeying a court order or interfering with evidence. On this latter point see *Re B (JA) (An Infant)* [1965] Ch 1112, [1965] 2 All ER 168 discussed at p 405.

with the special protective jurisdiction which the court has over its wards. As Cross J said:[8]

> 'Any action which tends to hamper the court in carrying out its duty [to protect its wards] is an interference with the administration of justice and a criminal contempt.'

It is to be noted that Cross J classified such interference as *criminal* contempt. That view which reflected the much earlier decision in *Wellesley v Duke of Beaufort*,[9] has since been supported by Watkins LJ in *R v D* [10] who said:

> 'There seems to be no doubt that to take a ward of court out of the jurisdiction without consent is a criminal contempt.'

Since it is only those which interfere with the court's protective jurisdiction, not all acts which may be harmful to a ward are necessarily contempts. As Lowe and White say:[11]

> 'assaulting a ward may no doubt be harmful to him, yet even if the offender knows that the child is a ward such an act will not, unless intended to influence court proceedings[12] . . . normally constitute a contempt. As Lord Denning MR said, in *Re F (Otherwise A)* [1977] Fam 58 at 86 "The existence of wardship does not give the ward privilege over and above other young people who are not wards."[13] His Lordship was specifically referring to publications concerning children who happen to be wards, but his statement applies equally to other acts. Were the position otherwise the protection afforded a ward would be too wide to be practicable.'

What then constitutes a contempt in this area?

To answer this question in general terms one might have regard to the notice of wardship accompanying an originating summons, namely that:

> 'without leave of the court a ward of court may not marry or go outside England and Wales nor should there be any material change in arrangements for his or her welfare, care and control or education without such leave.'

Taking any of the above mentioned steps without court leave is prima facie a contempt. It remains now to examine some of the steps in more detail.

1   Marrying or removing a ward from the jurisdiction

The two classic and long-established interferences with the court's protective jurisdiction are respectively, the marriage of the ward and the removal of the ward from the jurisdiction, in each case without the court's consent. Both

---

8   *Re B (JA) (an infant)* ibid at 1117 and 171. See also *Z Ltd v A-Z and AA-LL* [1982] QB 558 at 579, [1982] 1 All ER 556 at 567 in which Eveleigh LJ referred to contempts committed by interfering 'with the protective power of the court dealing with a ward of court'.
9   (1831) 2 Russ & M 639.
10   [1984] AC 778 at 791, [1984] 1 All ER 574 at 583, not commented upon on appeal by the House of Lords.
11   *Wards of Court* (2nd edn, 1986) at 8-1.
12   As in *Re B (JA)*, [1965] Ch 1112, [1965] 2 All ER 168, where it was not to prevent the ward from giving evidence.
13   See also *R v Central Independent Television Plc* [1994] Fam 192, 204, [1994] 3 All ER 641, 653 in which Hoffmann LJ commented that it was not for the courts to create via their inherent powers what in effect was a right of privacy for children.

instances of contempt have been regarded as strict offences in that it is no defence that the defendant did not know that the child was a ward.[14] However, in *Re F (Orse A) (a minor) (Publication of Information)*[15] Lord Denning MR said that neither should be a strict offence and it is difficult not to agree. As Miller has said:[16]

> 'There is no sense in holding an offence to have been committed by a person who lacks knowledge of the status of the person with whom he is dealing and whose interference with the protective jurisdiction of the court was no more than a matter of bad luck.'

Arlidge and Eady argue[17] that in any event the common law position has been reversed by the Contempt of Court Act 1981. It is their contention that s 2(1) confines the application of the 'strict liability rule'_defined in s 1 as 'the rule of law whereby conduct may be treated as a contempt of court as tending to interfere with the course of justice in particular legal proceedings regardless of intent to do so'—to publications 'addressed to the public at large or any section of the public'. Accordingly, they argue that since marrying or removing a ward are not 'publications' the Act has introduced a mens rea requirement. At first sight the argument seems right as a matter of interpretation and desirable in terms of policy. However, as Lowe and White comment:[18]

> 'It must be doubted, however, whether s 1 was intended to refer to wardship. What Parliament had in mind , it is submitted, is conduct which potentially jeopardises the fair hearing of a case. It is by no means certain that the courts will treat conduct which interferes with their special jurisdiction as falling within the ambit of s 1.'

It may also be noted that in *Z Ltd v A-Z and AA-LL*[19] Eveleigh LJ assumed (admittedly obiter) that even after the 1981 Act, there continues to be strict liability in these instances.

Accordingly, it is submitted that the common law continues to govern those instances of contempt. Nevertheless it remains to be seen whether even at common law the court will continue to apply the strict liability approach either to marriage or removal from the jurisdiction. It may be hoped that the courts will be disposed to follow Lord Denning MR's views, but even if they do not, ignorance that the child is a ward is likely to be regarded as an important mitigating factor.[20] At all events it seems unlikely that the courts will apply strict liability to other types of interference.

Reflecting the historical importance of controlling a ward's marriage[1] there is a well-developed jurisprudence of what constitutes a contempt. *Warter v Yorke*[2] establishes that it is the attempt to marry the ward which is the contempt and that

---

14 *Herbert's Case* (1731) 3 P Wms 116. *Richardson v Merrifield* (1850) 4 De G & Sm 161 and *Re H's Settlement, H v H* [1909] 2 Ch 260 (marriage) and *Re Witten (an infant)* (1887) 4 TLR 36 and *Re J (an infant)* (1913) 108 LT 554 (removal from jurisdiction).
15 [1977] Fam 58 at 88, [1977] 1 All ER 114 at 112.
16 *Contempt of Court* (1st edn) at p 224. See also Munro (1977) 40 MLR 343.
17 *The Law of Contempt*, 1-32.
18 *Wards of Court* (2nd edn) 8-5.
19 [1982] QB 558 at 599, [1982] 1 All ER 556 at 567.
20 See Warrington J in *Re H's Settlement* [1909] 2 Ch 260 at 264 where he said 'the court is entitled to and ought to take into consideration her ignorance of the fact that he was a ward of court in determining whether it ought to resort to the punishment of imprisonment for contempt'.
1 See Lowe and White, *Wards of Court*, Chs 1 and 5.
2 (1815) 19 Ves 451; see also *Salles v Savignon* (1801) 6 Ves 572.

therefore the validity of the marriage is of no consequence in a contempt issue. All parties involved in the marriage of the ward of court may be regarded as having committed a contempt[3] including, as was established in *Re Leigh, Leigh v Leigh*,[4] the ward. Nevertheless it is within the court's discretion whether or not to punish any or all the parties.[5] In *Re Crump (an infant)*[6] where the ward and her husband had married contrary to the known, express orders of the court both parties were committed to prison for 28 days, Faulks J said that:

'Once it had become publicly known that an order of the court had been deliberately flouted the court must make it plain that such disobedience would not be disregarded.'

The embargo against marrying a ward has further declined in importance since the age of majority was reduced to 18.[7] Once the child has attained his majority he ceases to be a ward and it cannot then be a contempt to marry him.[8]

Removing the ward from the jurisdiction without the court's consent is another long-standing instance of contempt,[9] the original underlying reason being that removal effectively deprived the court of its power to supervise the child's upbringing. At one time the court was so jealous of its jurisdiction that it would never allow a ward to be taken outside the jurisdiction[10] but today consent is readily given.[11]

According to the notice of wardship issued with the originating summons the child's removal from England and Wales without court leave is prohibited. In fact, however, if divorce, nullity or judicial separation proceedings are continuing in Scotland, Northern Ireland or the Isle of Man or if the ward is habitually resident there then he or she may be freely removed to that jurisdiction without court leave.[12]

The embargo lies against anyone be they the parents or strangers[13] and on the cases as they stand it is no defence to plead ignorance of the fact that the child is a ward nor that the act was done on the solicitation of the ward.[14] By analogy

---

3   See *Long v Elways* (1729) Mos 249; *Edes v Brereton* (1738) West temp Hard 348.
4   (1888) 40 Ch D 290, followed in *Re H's Settlement, H v H* [1909] 2 Ch 260.
5   In *More v More* (1741) 2 Atk 157 it was held that the clergyman did not commit contempt but in *Nicholson v Squire* (1809) 16 Ves 259, it was said that the parson was liable to censure, at least where he makes no enquiries. For other cases involving a marriage of a ward see: *Hannes v Wough* (1713) 2 Eq Cas Abr 754 (and see generally Cap CXVII 'Wards' 2 Eq Cas Abr 754); *Brandon v Knight* (1752) 1 Dick 160; *Butler v Freeman* (1756) Amb 301; *Priestley v Lamb* (1801) 6 Ves 421; *Millet v Rowse* (1802) 7 Ves 419; *Cox v Bennett* (1874) 31 LT 83; *Brown v Barrow* (1883) 48 LT 357; *Ball v Coutts* (1812) 1 Ves & B 292.
6   (1963) 107 Sol Jo 682. For a critical comment on the case see (1963) 113 LJ 585; see also *Re Elwes* (1958) Times, 30 July and comment in (1958) 108 LJ 562.
7   By s 1 of the Family Law Reform Act 1969.
8   *Bolton v Bolton* [1891] 3 Ch 270.
9   See eg *Harrison v Goodhall* (1852) Kay 310; *Re O (infants)* [1962] 2 All ER 10, [1962] 1 WLR 724; *Symonds v Symonds and Harrison* (1872) LR 2 P & D 447.
10 See eg *Mountstuart v Mountstuart* (1801) 6 Ves 363; *De Manneville v De Manneville* (1804) 10 Ves 52.
11 Particularly if the removal is temporary, see *Practice Directions* [1984] 2 All ER 407 and [1973] 2 All ER 512.
12 Family Law Act 1986, s 38. Even so the embargo in wardship is stricter than under s 13 of the Children Act 1989 by which those with residence orders are forbidden to take the child outside the *United Kingdom* for periods of a month or over without court leave or the written consent of every person having parental responsibility.
13 *Re Harris (an infant)* (1960) Times, 21 May.
14 *Re J (an infant)* (1913) 108 LT 554; *Re Witten (an infant)* (1887) 4 TLR 36.

with marrying a ward it is probably a contempt to attempt to remove the ward from the jurisdiction.[15]

2 Concealing the ward's whereabouts

Another well-established instance of contempt is the concealing of the ward's whereabouts.[16] All parties who either know or are supposed to know the whereabouts of the ward's residence can be summarily ordered to attend the court and give such information as is within their knowledge.[17] Refusal to answer such questions constitutes a contempt. Even a solicitor is obliged to give the court any information which may lead to the discovery of the ward's whereabouts, nor can he withhold such information on the basis that it has been imparted to him during the course of his employment.[18]

3 Other important steps

Conduct liable to be treated as contempt is not confined to the instances already cited. *In Re S (an infant)* [19] Cross J commented:

> 'When a child is made a ward of court no important step in the child's life can be taken without the court's consent.'

The implication of this statement is that if such steps are taken without consent the offender could be guilty of contempt. The context in which Cross J issued his warning was where one party sought to have a ward examined by a psychiatrist with a view to putting a report in evidence. There have been several subsequent warnings against this practice[20] and in *Barnes (formerly Tyrell) v Tyrell* [1] Dunn LJ specifically said that such conduct 'might well amount to contempt'.

Although precisely what constitutes an 'important step' has still to be settled, as the notice of wardship suggests it would seem to include changing the child's education and making material changes to the arrangements for the child's welfare and care and control.[2] Specifically it is established that the following

---

15 *Warter v Yorke* (1815) 19 Ves 451. It is not yet established whether there is an offence known as attempting to commit contempt but on the basis of *Balogh v Crown Court at St Albans* [1975] QB 73, [1974] 3 All ER 283, discussed at p 81, mere preparation to take the child out of the jurisdiction may not be enough to constitute contempt. Query whether buying an airline ticket in the ward's name would be a contempt?

16 See *Mustafa v Mustafa* (1967) Times, 11 and 13 September. It is also a contempt to refuse to deliver a ward to the guardian appointed by the court: see *Burton v Earl of Darnley* (1869) LR 8 Eq 576n. See also *Hockly v Lukin* (1762) 1 Dick 353.

17 See eg *Rosenberg v Lindo* (1883) 48 LT 478 where a Roman Catholic bishop and a lady superior were ordered to attend.

18 *Ramsbotham v Senior* (1869) LR 8 Eq 575. It may be noted, however, that the court can now override professional privilege in other proceedings involving children following *Oxfordshire County Council v M* [1994] Fam 151, [1994] 2 All ER 269, CA.

19 [1967] 1 All ER 202 at 209.

20 See eg *B(M) v B(R)* [1968] 3 All ER 170 at 174 per Willmer LJ; *Re R(PM) (an infant)* [1968] 1 All ER 691n, [1968] 1 WLR 385 and *Re A-W (minors)* (1975) 5 Fam Law 95.

1 (1981) Times, 8 October. The embargo, which does not appear to apply to *physical* examinations, see *Practice Direction* [1985] 3 All ER 832, now applies by reason of FPR 1991, r 4.18.

2 See *Re CB (a minor)(wardship: local authority)* [1981] 1 All ER 16.

need court leave: instituting adoption proceedings,[3] or freeing for adoption proceedings,[4] placing a child for adoption,[5] major non-therapeutic treatment,[6] police interviews of wards,[7] the administration of a caution by the Crown Prosecution Service,[8] application to the criminal injuries compensation board on the ward's behalf[9] and interviewing a ward on behalf of a defendant in a criminal trial.[10] In each case failure to obtain prior consent from the court might render the offender guilty of contempt.

B   Other persons over whom the court exercises a special jurisdiction

As we have said, the jurisdiction over wards of court is special in that legal control of the child is vested in the court. It is this unique factor that distinguishes wardship from all other jurisdictions[11] concerned with children and given that it is the interference with this special protection that constitutes the contempt, it is suggested that save for wardship, outside the context of the court hearing there is no special protection for children enforceable by contempt.[12] This is not to say that children are without protection *within* other proceedings. For example, leave is generally required for medical experts to examine the child,[13] the proceedings are private so that leave to disclose the papers for other purposes is required,[14] and children involved in Children Act proceedings should only be interviewed for the purpose of obtaining evidence in related criminal proceedings with court leave.[15] In each case failure to obtain leave could be treated as a contempt. Finally, there seems growing acceptance that a child can be sterilised only with High

---

3   *F v S (Adoption: Ward)* [1973] Fam 203, [1973] 1 All ER 722 and *Re F (Wardship: Adoption)* [1984] FLR 60, CA.
4   *Practice Direction* [1985] 2 All ER 832. Note also *Practice Direction* [1989] 2 All ER 169, which states that leave is required before the wardship papers can be shown to prospective adopters and their legal advisers.
5   *Re CB (a minor) (Wardship: Local Authority)* [1981] 1 All ER 16.
6   *Re D (a minor) (Wardship: Sterilisation)* [1976] Fam 185, [1976] 1 All ER 326; *Re G-U (a minor)(Wardship)* [1984] FLR 811 and *Havering London Borough Council v S* [1986] 1 FLR 489.
7   *Re K (minors)(Wardship: Criminal Proceedings)* [1988] Fam 1, [1988] 1 All ER 214; *Practice Direction* [1988] 2 All ER 1015. Aliter if the ward is aged 17 see *Re B (a minor)* [1990] FCR 469 or if he has been arrested, see *Re R, Re G (minors)* [1990] 2 All ER 633.
8   *Re A (a minor)(Wardship: Police Caution)* [1989] Fam 103, sub nom *Re A (a minor)(Wardship: Criminal Proceedings)* [1989] 3 All ER 610.
9   *Re G (a minor)(Ward: Criminal Injuries Compensation)* [1990] 3 All ER 102, CA.
10 *Re R (minors)(Wardship: Criminal Proceedings)* [1991] Fam 56, [1991] 2 All ER 913. Query whether interviewing a ward per se can be considered a contempt? Cf *Re T (AJJ)(an infant)* [1970] Ch 688, [1970] 2 All ER 865, discussed at p 230.
11 Including the High Court's so-called inherent jurisdiction, discussed in Clarke Hall & Morrison at 1 [1123] ff and by White, Carr and Lowe, *The Children Act in Practice* Ch 12. See *Re W (a minor)(Medical Treatment: Court's Jurisdiction)* [1993] Fam 64, [1992] 4 All ER 627 in which Lord Donaldson MR expressly said that the exercise of the inherent jurisdiction does *not* place the child under the ultimate responsibility of the court.
12 Cf in Australia *P v P* [1985] 2 NSWLR 401 in which it is suggested (wrongly it is submitted) that the court's special protective jurisdiction over children goes beyond wardship.
13 FPR 1991, r 4.18.
14 See eg the Administration of Justice Act 1960, s 12, discussed at pp 327 ff, FPR 1991, r 4.23 and *Brown v Matthews* [1990] Ch 662, [1990] 2 All ER 155, CA.
15 See *Re F (Specific Issue: Child Interview)* [1995] 1 FLR 819, CA and *Re M (Care: Leave to Interview Child)* [1995] 1 FLR 825.

Court leave[16] so that again failure to obtain leave could lead to contempt proceedings.

Until the passing of the Mental Health Act 1959 lunatics were in a similar position to wards of court in that the High Court exercised an inherent paternal jurisdiction over them and punished as contempt any undue interference with their welfare.[17] The Mental Health Act 1959, however, substantially altered the position in that it finally ended the High Court's inherent parens patriae jurisdiction over persons of unsound mind.[18] Accordingly, it must now be accepted that jurisdiction to protect person of unsound mind solely derives from statute, currently the Mental Health Act 1983.[19] Under that statute the patient's property is protected and administered by the Court of Protection[20] and it is specifically enacted[1] that any act or omission which would have amounted to contempt in the High Court will also be regarded as a contempt with regard to the Court of Protection. Thus, for instance, interference with a receiver appointed by the Court of Protection will amount to contempt.[2] The Act also contains provisions relating to offences with regard to patients.[3] On the other hand, acts interfering with the welfare of the patient, such as marrying that person without the court's permission, and which fall outside the statutory provisions can no longer be considered a contempt.[4]

V   ABUSE OF THE COURT'S PROCESS

The term 'abusing the court's process' can be applied to many different types of conduct but generally the term connotes some misuse of the court's process.

The most serious example of abuse of process is conduct which is intended to deceive the court, for example, by the deliberate suppression of facts or by the presentation of falsehood, but the term also includes the bringing of frivolous or vexatious proceedings.

Not all acts which may be termed 'abuse of process' will be punished as contempt. Courts are generally reluctant to commit for contempt and will

---

16   See eg *Re B (a minor) (Wardship: Sterilisation)* [1988] AC 199 at 205, [1987] 2 All ER 206 at 214, per Lord Templeman and *Re W (a minor)(Medical Treatment: Court's Jurisdiction)* [1993] Fam 64 at 79, [1992] 4 All ER 627 at 635h, per Lord Donaldson MR, but cf *Re E (a minor) (Medical Treatment)* [1991] 2 FLR 585 (consent not required to perform an operation for therapeutic reasons even though a side-effect, but not main purpose, is sterilisation). In Australia see *Secretary, Department of Health and Community Services v JWB and SMB* (1992) 175 CLR 218 (Australian High Court). In Canada see *Re Eve* (1987) 31 DLR (4th) 1 (Can Sup Court).

17   See eg *Ash's case* (1702) Prec Ch 203; *Lord Wenman's case* (1721) 1 P Wms 701; *Re B (an alleged Lunatic)* [1892] 1 Ch 459.

18   See the analysis in *Re F (Mental Patient: Sterilisation)* [1990] 2 AC 1, [1989] 2 All ER 545.

19   Although, it may be noted, that the court can still make declarations as to the lawfulness of operations such as sterilisation, see eg *Re F* ibid, *Re C (Sterilisation: Mental Patient: Procedure)* [1990] 2 FLR 527 and *Re W (Mental Patient) (Sterilisation)* [1993] 1 FLR 381.

20   See Part VII of the Mental Health Act 1983.

 1   By s 104(2). Under s 104(1) the judge has the same powers as those of the High Court to secure the attendance of witnesses and the presentation of documents. Under s 104(3) the actual power of committal is limited to the Lord Chancellor or a nominated judge.

 2   For interference with receivers generally see at pp 437–439.

 3   Ss 125-131.

 4   Cf *Ash's case* (1702) Prec Ch 203, in which it was held under parens patriae jurisdiction that marrying a lunatic without the court's permission was a contempt.

exercise the jurisdiction only in extreme cases.[5] In any event they have adequate alternative powers to deal with abuse of process. For example, under RSC Ord 18, r 19 the court can strike out or amend:

> 'any pleading or the indorsement of any writ in the action, or anything in any pleading or in the indorsement, on the ground that:
> (a)　it discloses no reasonable cause of action or defence, as the case may be; or
> (b)　it is scandalous, frivolous or vexatious; or
> (c)　it may prejudice, embarrass or delay the fair trial of the action; or
> (d)　it is otherwise an abuse of the process of the court,'

and may (though even this power should be used with circumspection)[6] order the action to be stayed or dismissed or judgment entered accordingly, as the case may be. Courts can also strike out the pleadings or stay the action under their inherent jurisdiction.[7] A litigant who persistently and without any reasonable ground institutes vexatious legal proceedings may be declared, upon an application by the Attorney General to the High Court, a vexatious litigant with the result that the person may then bring legal proceedings only if the High Court gives leave.[8]

The court can also set aside subpoenas where the issue of such subpoenas has been misused, as, for example, where a witness was subpoenaed not for the purpose of giving evidence but for the sole purpose of being asked to stand up in the court in order to confront a person in the witness box.[9]

In the normal case these powers vested in the High Court will be sufficient and no further action will be taken. Some of the older cases must now be regarded as obsolete in view of the powers already outlined. It is unlikely, for instance, that *Milward v Welden*[10] will be followed, where a litigant who filed a long replication of some six score sheets was fined £10 and ordered to be brought by the Warden of the Fleet:

> 'into Westminster Hall on Saturday next about ten of the clock in the forenoon and then and there shall cut a hole in the myddest of the same engrossed replication, which is delivered unto him for that purpose, and put the said Richard's head through the same hole, and so let the same replication hang about his shoulders with the written side outward, and then, the same so hanging, shall lead the same Richard, bareheaded and barefaced, round Westminster Hall whilst the courts are sitting, and shall show him at the bar of three courts within the Hall.'

On the other hand, it must not be thought that the courts will never use their contempt jurisdiction. As Lord Merrivale P said in *Apted v Apted and Bliss*:[11]

> 'There is a general presumption that the sole penalty for suppression of fact or presentment of falsehood in cases such as this [ie a divorce suit] is the allowance of the King's Proctor's intervention, rescission of the decree nisi and the dismissal

---

5　Especially after *R v Payne and Cooper* [1896] 1 QB 577.
6　See eg *Halliday v Shoesmith* [1993] 1 WLR 1, CA.
7　See eg *Reichel v Magrath* (1889) 14 App Cas 665. For other cases see the *Supreme Court Practice* 18/19/1 and Oswald, *Contempt* (3rd edn, 1910) p 82. In Australia see eg *Turner v Bulletin Newspaper Co Pty Ltd* (1974) 131 CLR 69, (1974) 3 ALR 491 (Aust HC).
8　Under the Supreme Court Act 1981, s 42.
9　*Farulli v Farulli and Pederroli* [1917] P 28. See also *Raymond v Tapson* (1882) 22 Ch D 430; *Re Mundell, Fenton v Cumberlege* (1883) 52 LJ Ch 756; *Steele v Savory* (1891) 8 TLR 94; *London and Globe Finance Corpn v Kaufman* (1899) 69 LJ Ch 196; *R v Baines* [1909] 1 KB 258.
10　(1565) Toth 101. See also Oswald, *Contempt* (3rd edn, 1910) p 61. See also *Whitlock v Marriot* (1686) Dick 16; *Bishop v Willis* (1749) 5 Beav 83; cf *R v Gregory* (1843) 2 LT OS 193.
11　[1930] P 246 at 262.

of the suit, with an order for the payment of costs—an order not infrequently found incapable of enforcement. This is not an adequate view of the matter. One of the safeguards of legal procedure in this country is the presumptive authority of courts of record to visit with summary punishment persons who purposely obstruct or divert the course of justice.'

Acts amounting to 'abuse of process' which have been punished as contempt can be classified as follows:[12]

(1) Acts which involve the forging or altering of the process itself.

(2) Acts which involve falsehoods intended to deceive the court.

(3) Acts which misuse the process thereby prejudicing other persons.

Forging or altering any official court documents is an obvious example of contempt. It has been held to be a contempt to forge the signature of counsel,[13] to fill in a writ after it has been sealed[14] and in *Re Jacobs* [15] it was held to be a 'gross and most outrageous contempt of court' to erase from the back of a summons the words 'nor order' thus concealing from the master the fact that the judge had already adjudicated upon the summons and for which Jacobs was imprisoned for six months. Altering or adding a name on a warrant[16] or altering the date of the jurat on the affidavit[17] are practices which have been condemned but in the absence of an intention to defraud have not been considered punishable contempts. In *Re Taylor* [18] a barrister wishing to secure the attendance of two witnesses applied for subpoenas, which were duly granted. Upon discovering that they knew nothing about the case the barrister wanted to subpoena two further persons, but instead of applying for two new subpoenas as he should have done, he substituted the two names upon the subpoenas already issued. Although the Master knew of these alterations, he had made no objection and so the altered subpoenas were duly served. The Privy Council, although disapproving of the practice, found that there was no intention to defraud and held that 'At the most he [ie the barrister] committed an irregularity for which some pecuniary penalty on his part was an adequate penalty'.

Acts which deceive the court whether by falsehood or by the suppression of facts can amount to contempt. In *Lord v Thornton* [19] a litigant pleaded infancy in defence to an action when in reality he was 63(!) and was held to have committed a contempt. *In Linwood v Andrews and Moore*,[20] a barrister was held guilty of contempt by being party to the reading to the court of a false affidavit and for this

---

12 See also 2 Hawk PC (2nd edn), c22, ss 38-43.
13 *Bull v Griffin* (1795) 2 Anst 563; see also *Fawcett v Garford* (1789), cited in Oswald, *Contempt* (3rd edn, 1930) p 62.
14 *Anon* (1704) 6 Mod Rep 310.
15 (1874) Times, 13 June. See also the comment in (1874) 18 Sol Jo (Part II) 642 – see now Theft Act 1968, s 20, where the penalty for altering or destroying a public document may be seven years' imprisonment. See also *Stout v Towler* (1700) 12 Mod Rep 372.
16 See *Doydige v Penkvell* (1605) Nov 101, sub nom *Dag v Penkevell Moore* KB 770; *Hale v Castleman* (1746) 1 Wm B1 2.
17 *Finnerty v Smith* (1835) 1 Bing NC 649.
18 [1912] AC 347.
19 (1614) 2 Bulst 67. See also *Royson's case* (1628) Cro Car 146, 79 ER 729; cf *R v Pepper* (1724) 8 Mod Rep 227. In Australia see eg *In the Marriage of Bugg* (1978) 30 FLR 155 (falsely swearing an affidavit of service of court process) and *Malsen v The Official Receiver* (1947) 74 CLR 602 (non-party producing false receipts to the court).
20 (1888) 58 LT 612.

deceit was imprisoned. In *R v Weisz, ex p Hector MacDonald* [1] it was held to be a contempt for a solicitor to disguise the true nature of an action by means of a fictitious indorsement. In this case the solicitor was instructed by a client to bring an action to recover a gambling debt, which is of course not enforceable in a court of law.[2] The indorsement stated that the debts were due on accounts stated, this being a device to disguise the true nature of the action, since there had been no accounts stated. Lord Goddard CJ said:

> 'It is, in our opinion, beyond question that to disguise a cause of action so as to conceal its true nature when in truth it is one prohibited by statute is a contempt . . .'.

In both *Linwood* and *Weisz* the lawyers either perpetrated or were party to the deceits in question but in the Australian case, *Ditford v Brown*,[3] a solicitor was charged with contempt for failing to intervene in court proceedings by pointing out to the court that another party had given false evidence. In that case the defendant solicitor had been in court when another solicitor, appearing in answer to a subpoena to produce certain documents, informed the court that no documents were produced. The defendant was aware of the existence of certain documents falling within the terms of the subpoena but there was no evidence that the defendant either knew that the answer to the court was false or had no honest belief in its truth. In dismissing the charges Samuels AP observed:[4]

> 'we were not referred to any case, and I have not been able to discover one, in which an officer of the court has been found guilty for failing to intervene in proceedings in which he was engaged by pointing out to the court that a party for whom he does not act, has, without instigation or prior concurrence on his part, given a false answer. Contempt of the kind which the claimant seeks to establish here . . . requires positive conduct by some person directly involved in the relevant process of the court . . .'.

It has been held that merely to bring an action which is unenforceable, even if brought for the purpose of bringing the pressure of publicity upon the person not paying, will not normally be punished as contempt, unless such an action is, for example, repeatedly brought before the courts.

It may be a contempt to suppress, or give false, facts. In *Re Elsam* [5] an executor who caused a special case to be stated comprising an elaborate but wholly fictitious story solely for the purpose of obtaining a decision upon an obscure point of law, was held to have committed a contempt. In *Coxe v Phillips* [6] the defendant's marriage to one Muilman was declared void on the grounds that the defendant was already married. The defendant later (and after Muilman had married someone else) began a suit to repeal the determination of nullity by pretending that the man she was already married to was himself at the time married to another. Consequently, her first marriage was void and her marriage to Muilman was therefore valid. The court held that this deliberate pretence amounted to a contempt.

1   [1951] 2 KB 611, [1951] 2 All ER 408.
2   Following the Gaming Act 1845, s 18.
3   (1988) 19 NSWLR 49 (NSW CA).
4   Ibid at 53.
5   (1824) 3 LJOSKB 75.
6   (1736) Lee temp Hard 237.

The deliberate[7] suppression of facts was also held to be a contempt in *Apted v Apted and Bliss*.[8] That case concerned a divorce petition in which the petitioner represented that he had been deserted by his wife while he was on active service abroad during the First World War and that when so deserted he was guilty of one isolated act of adultery and that under the erroneous belief that his wife had procured a divorce he cohabited with another woman. In fact, the husband had committed adultery on numerous occasions before the date of the alleged desertion and far from the wife deserting the husband, in answer to a letter from the wife asking why he had refused to live with her again, he wrote 'You can do as you please . . . I have been unfaithful to you not once but many times since we parted . . .'. The petitioner, in suppressing the true facts and presenting a wholly false petition, was held to have committed a contempt.[9]

Misusing the court's process, at least where other parties are thereby prejudiced, may also amount to a punishable contempt. It is a contempt to issue double process as, for example, in *Anon* [10] where an attorney caused a person to be arrested twice for the same debt. It has been held to be a contempt to sue a person in a civil action, without leave of the court, while that person is a prisoner executing a fine,[11] to issue a summons without the court's authority,[12] and even to serve an imitation of a writ by way of a joke,[13] although in this case the person served had been put to the expense of seeking legal advice. In *R v Newton* [14] a solicitor who represented a client on a charge of forgery was held to have abused the court's process by using the threat of an action for contempt in order to extort money from a newspaper. The action arose as a result of several newspapers publishing articles which the solicitor claimed to be prejudicial to his client and accordingly he obtained two rules nisi against two newspapers. One of the newspapers offered 50 guineas as settlement and this offer was accepted; the solicitor then wrote to the other newspaper a letter which the court held to be an unlawful demand for money. Lord Alverstone CJ said:

> 'it must be plainly understood that applications for contempt of court ought not to be regarded in the nature of actions for damages. Such proceedings were analogous to, and in the nature of, criminal informations, which were incapable of settlement.'

In *Pitcher v Nokes* [15] it was held to be a contempt for the plaintiff to issue execution and seize the defendant's goods on the same day as a rule nisi had been obtained to deprive the plaintiff of his costs and in *Anon* [16] it was held to be a contempt to apply for a search warrant on false grounds merely to make it easier

---

7 Cf *R v B* (1972) 20 FLR 368 where the innocent omission to disclose adultery was held not to be a contempt (Fam Ct of Australia).
8 [1930] P 246. See also *Hopkins v Hopkins* [1933] NZLR 1486.
9 Note the suggestion (by Jennifer Levin, (1970) MLR 632, 639) that in cases where a wholly false petition for divorce is presented rather than deny the decree in cases of deception the better course would be to punish offenders either for contempt or perjury.
10 (1586) Gouldsb 30; see also *Higgins v Sommerland* (1614) 2 Bulst 68.
11 *Anon* (1703) 6 Mod Rep 88.
12 *Re Christie* (1856) 27 LTOS 67.
13 *Re Banks* (1845) 4 LTOS 375.
14 (1903) 19 TLR 627; the solicitor was only fined the costs since the practice of settlements in such cases had been common. This case clearly warned against the continuance of such a practice. See also *Re Cooper's Marriage* (1980) 48 FLR 264 (Fam Ct Aust), contempt by filing an affidavit of the child in a contested custody dispute.
15 (1848) 12 JP Jo 473.
16 *Anon* (1758) 2 Kenny 372. See also *M'Gregor v Barrett* (1848) 6 CB 262, a case involving collusion to avoid the payment of a debt. See also *Smith v Bond* (1845) 13 M & W 594.

to arrest a person for some other cause. In *Re Taylor*,[17] however, it was held that where a plaintiff, who had been refused a warrant for the detention of a defendant by a civil court, immediately began a criminal process on the same subject matter and by means of allegations to which the civil court attached no credit, thereby obtaining a warrant from a different court, had not committed a contempt, since the law did not restrict a person to a single remedy. The Privy Council, however, observed that the taking of such a course was prone to serious risks.

It may also be a contempt unlawfully to deprive the court of jurisdiction over an action. In *Re Septimus Parsonage & Co*[18] a petition had been lodged by a creditor of the company for a compulsory winding-up. On the same day a circular was drawn up in which it was stated that a certain Grace, purporting to be a large independent shareholder who was hostile to the directors, was determined upon a thorough investigation of the management of the business at his own expense and accordingly he asked for proxies to be used against the directors. In fact the circular was false and Grace was a man of straw put up by the two directors who had drawn up the circular. In this way 60,000 proxies were collected and these proxies were used to support a motion for a voluntary liquidation, thereby depriving the court of jurisdiction in the case. Wright J, in holding that a contempt had been committed, said:

> 'It seems to me an obvious inference that all that was done by the respondents was done for the purpose of defeating the creditor's petition, and that what they wanted to avoid was a compulsory winding-up . . .
>
> Where there is a real interference with the jurisdiction of the court, which is perhaps a better phrase than contempt of court, the court has no option but to act, however unwilling it is to deal with matters affecting the liberty of the subject and inasmuch as a case of the kind I have stated is made out, it is my duty to commit Parsonage to prison for six weeks [and the other director for four weeks].'

VI   MISCELLANEOUS EXAMPLES

The principle that conduct can constitute contempt because it is thought likely to interfere with the course of justice in a particular case or with the course of justice as a continuing process is a wide one. Not all cases fall within the foregoing instances discussed so far in this chapter. An interesting example is *Dobson v Hastings*.[19] In that case in the course of investigating the collapse of a public company and in particular the activities of Sir Edward Du Cann, a journalist visited the court offices to inspect the originating summons in certain proceedings relating to the disqualification of company directors. Having been told that she needed leave of the registrar to inspect the court file, she was given the file and sent to see the registrar. Contrary to a warning, whilst waiting to see the registrar she examined the file and in particular the official receiver's report and quite openly made notes. She admitted to the registrar that she had done so because she thought that obtaining permission was a formality (in fact a formal application in writing with supporting evidence was required). The registrar telephoned the

---

17   [1912] AC 347.
18   [1901] 2 Ch 424.
19   [1992] Ch 394, [1992] 2 All ER 94 and noted by Miller, *1992 All ER Review* 81–83. See also *R v Macdonald* [1994] VLR 414 (Vic Sup Ct) in which two police officers were held to be in contempt for searching and seizing part of a counsel's brief during the progress of a case, believing that the documents in question were stolen.

newspaper explaining the situation but the city news editor gained the impression that publication of extracts of the report would be embarrassing rather than unlawful. Accordingly, the newspaper published two articles containing information from the report, whereupon two directors of the company under investigation brought contempt proceedings against the journalist, editor and the managing director of the publishers.

The first question that had to be decided was whether there could have been a contempt of court at all in these circumstances. The problem was that although the relevant rules, RSC Ord 63, rr 4 and 4A,[20] clearly provide for restricted access, they do not expressly prohibit the inspection and taking copies of documents otherwise than in accordance with the rules. In the absence of any direct authority on the point Sir Donald Nicholls V-C commented that he was 'very conscious of the need for the court to take great care and exercise much caution, when confronted with an apparently novel application of the established principles relating to contempt of court'.

Nevertheless having referred to Lord Reid's observations in the *Sunday Times* case:[1]

> 'The law on this subject is and must be founded entirely on public policy. It is not there to protect the private rights of parties to a litigation or prosecution. It is there to prevent interference with the administration of justice and *it should in my judgment be limited to what is reasonably necessary for that purpose.* Public policy generally requires a balancing of interests which may conflict. Freedom of speech should not be limited to any greater extent than is necessary but it cannot be allowed where there would be real prejudice to the administration of justice' (Sir Donald's emphasis),

his Lordship concluded that knowingly interfering with the court's documents was a contempt of court. As he said the contrary conclusion:[2]

> 'would lead to results which are self-evidently unacceptable. So to decide would mean, for instance, that there could be publication to the world of documents containing trade secrets, a course which might wholly nullify a pending trial. Thus it would countenance conduct which would indeed be severely prejudicial to the administration of justice. That cannot be right. In my view it is reasonably necessary to proscribe such conduct as contempt of court.'

On the facts none of the defendants were held guilty of contempt since they all lacked the necessary mens rea. In the journalist's case she had neither indulged in trickery nor dishonesty. In short the 'court system was at fault far more than she was'.[3] In the city editor's case he had not realised that there was a legal impediment to publishing so that consequently neither the editor or newspaper could be fixed with liability. It was made clear, however, that in the light of this ruling if the newspaper were to publish further extracts from the official receiver's report they would commit contempt.[4]

---

20 The court rejected the contention that the Insolvency Rules 1986 (which permit wider inspection) applied.
1 [1974] AC 273 at 294. Sir Donald Nicholls V-C also referred to *A-G v Times Newspapers Ltd* (*Spycatcher*) [1992] 2 AC 191, [1991] 2 All ER 398, HL and to *A-G v Leveller Magazine Ltd* [1979] AC 440, [1979] 1 All ER 745, HL.
2 [1992] Ch 394 at 404, [1992] 2 All ER 94 at 102.
3 Ibid at 408 and 105. NB the practice has now been tightened.
4 On this basis the court was confident that the newspaper would not publish further extracts and therefore declined to grant an injunction to that effect.

Another example is the New South Wales case, *Supreme Court Registrar, Equity Division v McPherson*,[5] where the Court of Appeal was called upon to decide whether it was a contempt to destroy documents that were likely to be subpoenaed in proceedings that had already started. It was held that provided the intention in destroying the documents was to prevent their being used by the court then a contempt would be committed. In reaching this conclusion the court rejected the charge that they were extending the boundaries of contempt.

How far the general principle will continue to spawn new applications of the law remains to be seen. It has been argued,[6] for example, that industrial action by justice's clerks would constitute a contempt though whether it would be wise to invoke the jurisdiction is another matter. No doubt other examples may be thought of but a note of caution might be entered in the field of speculation. The principle that contempt can be committed generally by interfering with the administration of justice is a dangerously wide one. It would be all too easy to brand many acts as contempt upon this basis, and the courts should be cautious in so doing. Two factors might help to limit the expansion. The first is the mens rea requirement. It is a noticeable feature both of *Dobson v Hastings* and *McPherson* that the contempt was dependent upon there being proof of an intention to interfere with the course of justice. Secondly, is the key limitation mentioned by Lord Reid in the *Sunday Times* case and adverted to in *Dobson* that contempts should be limited to what is reasonably necessary to prevent interference with the administration of justice.

---

5 [1980] 1 NSWLR 688, not overruled on this point by *Lane v Registrar of Supreme Court of NSW* (1981) 148 CLR 245. Destroying evidence can be indicted for perverting the course of justice cf *R v Rafique* [1993] QB 843, [1993] 4 All ER 1, discussed at p 414.
6 By White, 'Courting Disaster' 1979 SLT (News) 197 and Lowe, 'Striking Clerks and Contempt of Court' (1980) 144 JP Jo 261.

CHAPTER 12

Jurisdiction, procedure and powers of the courts in respect of criminal contempts

I GENERAL CONSIDERATIONS

A Jurisdiction and powers

1 The contempt jurisdiction of courts of record forms part of their inherent jurisdiction

The power that courts of record enjoy to punish contempts is part of their *inherent* jurisdiction.[1] The juridical basis of the inherent jurisdiction has been well described by Master Jacob[2] as being:

'the authority of the judiciary to uphold, to protect and to fulfil the judicial function of administering justice according to law in a regular, orderly and effective manner.'

Such a power is not derived from statute nor truly from the common law but instead flows from the very concept of a court of law.[3] Accordingly, courts should be slow to hold that the power has been abrogated or restricted by Parliament. It has been repeatedly held that Parliament can only restrict or abrogate the contempt power if it does so in the clearest terms.[4] A further consequence is that

---

1 In England see Oswald, *Contempt* (3rd edn, 1910) p 11 and the cases there cited. See also I H Jacob, 'The Inherent Jurisdiction of the Court' (1970) 23 Current Legal Problems 23 (a scholarly treatise on the whole topic of inherent jurisdiction). In Australia, see Mason: 'The Inherent Jurisdiction of the Court' (1983) 57 ALJ 449, and *R v Forbes, ex p Bevan* (1972) 127 CLR 1 at 7 per Menzies J and *A-G (NSW) v Mirror Newspapers Ltd* [1980] 1 NSWLR 374. In Canada see eg *Re Gerson; Re Nightingale* (1946) 87 CCC 143 and *Canadian Broadcasting Corpn v Cordeau* (1980) 101 DLR (3d) 24 and the cases there cited. In New Zealand, see *Taylor v A-G* [1975] 2 NZLR 675. In Scotland see Gordon: *Criminal Law* (2nd edn) para 51.01.
2 (1970) 23 Current Legal Problems 23 at 28.
3 See generally Jacob, ibid, *Connelly v DPP* [1964] AC 1254, [1964] 2 All ER 401 and *R v Forbes, ex p Bevan* (1972) 127 CLR 1.
4 Thus in Australia it has been held that s 108 (1) of the Family Law Act 1975 does not displace the inherent contempt jurisdiction, see eg *Re Cooper's Marriage* (1980) 48 FLR 264; *Taylor v Taylor* (1979) 53 ALJR 629; *Skouvakis v Skouvakis* (1976) 11 ALR 204, at 208. See also *Douglas v Douglas* (1976) 10 ALR 285 in connection with s 107 of the 1975 Act. In Canada, it has been held in *Vaillancourt v R* (1981) 120 DLR (3d) 740, that notwithstanding the provisions of the Juvenile Delinquents Act RSC 1970, CJS a juvenile can be dealt with by the trial judge for a contempt. For the relationship of the Canadian Criminal Code and the inherent powers in contempt see eg *R v Vermette* (1987) 38 DLR (4th) 419, *R v Clement* [1981] 6 WWR 735; *Re Regina and Monette* (1975) 64 DLR (3d) 470; *Foothill's Provincial General Hospital Board v Broad* (1976) 57 DLR (3d) 758; *Re A-G of Nova Scotia and Miles* (1970) 15 DLR (3d) 189 and the cases there referred to. For the relationship between the Canadian Charter of Rights and Freedoms and contempt see eg *Dagenais v Canadian Broadcasting Corpn* (1995) 120 DLR (4th) 12 (Can Sup Ct) and *A-G for Manitoba v Groupe Quebecor Inc* (1987) 45 DLR (4th) 80. In New Zealand see *Taylor v A-G* [1975] 2 NZLR 675 where the relevant statutes,

rules of court should not be regarded as restricting or abrogating the contempt power.[5] It has also been said that because it is inherent the power cannot be lost by technicalities such as repeated adjournments.[6]

Whether *all* courts of record are vested with an inherent contempt jurisdiction has still to be directly tested. Although the general presumption of the case law is that they are,[7] it might be possible to argue either that the jurisdiction is confined to the 'common law courts'[8] or that, precedent apart, the inherent contempt jurisdiction vests only in superior courts.[9] In other words doubts may be raised as to whether the simple statutory designation that a body is a court of record[10] automatically means that a contempt jurisdiction is thereby vested. It is submitted that in the absence of any other explanation[11] statutory courts of record should be regarded as having an inherent contempt jurisdiction unless the statute expressly declares to the contrary.

2 The inherent contempt jurisdiction is confined to court of record

Although the proposition that the inherent jurisdiction resides exclusively in courts of record has not gone unchallenged,[12] it is now accepted to be the case.[13] The corollary, that non-courts of record have no contempt jurisdiction save that expressly vested by statute, has been affirmed both by the Privy Council in *Badry v DPP of Mauritius*[14] and by the Canadian Supreme Court in *Canadian*

the Official Secrets Act 1951, s 15, the Criminal Justice Act 1954, s 46 and the Crimes Act 1961, s 375 were held not to have abrogated the inherent jurisdiction to order witnesses' names to be suppressed nor the power to punish for contempt the subsequent breaking of the order. Cf in England where it was held in *R v Lefroy* (1873) LR 8 QB 134 that statute did confine the county court's jurisdiction. See also *R v Daily Mail, ex p Farnsworth* [1921] 2 KB 733.

5 See eg *Balogh v Crown Court at St Albans* [1975] QB 73 at 89 per Stephenson LJ. The absence of a rule of procedure is not necessarily fatal to a contempt action, see eg *Con-Mech Ltd v Amalgamated Union of Engineering Workers* [1973] 1 CR 620 at 626. In Australia see eg *Registrar, Court of Appeal v Ritter* (1994) 34 NSWLR 638 (decided in 1985) and see the Canadian decisions of *Re Regina and Monette* (1975) 64 DLR (3d) 470 and *R v Scherbank* [1967] 1 OR 412 at 416. For the relationship generally between the inherent jurisdiction and Rules of Court see Jacob (1970) 23 Current Legal Problems 23 at 25 and 50–51.

6 *R v Shumiatcher* (1967) 64 DLR (2d) 24.

7 This seems implicit in decisions such as *Ex p Pater* (1864) 5 B & S 299, and *R v Lefroy* (1873) LR 8 QB 134. The point was expressly conceded in *Fournier v A-G* (1910) 19 Que KB 431 and 436 and cited with apparent approval in *Re Gerson, Re Nightingale* (1946) 87 CCC 143 (Can Sup Ct).

8 Some support for this may be derived from Menzies J's comment in *R v Forbes, ex p Bevan* (1972) 127 CLR 1 that 'Inherent jurisdiction is the power which a court has simply because it is a court of a particular description. Thus *the courts of common law* without the aid of any authorising provision had inherent jurisdiction to prevent abuse of their process and to punish for contempt' (emphasis added).

9 This would seem to be the basis of the comment in Adams, *Criminal Law and Practice in New Zealand* (2nd edn) at para 3598, that inferior courts of record in New Zealand have no inherent contempt powers.

10 For the relevant courts in England and Wales see p 508.

11 It may be that the intention, in the case of the Transport Tribunal (and of the former Iron and Steel Arbitration Tribunal), is to do nothing more than to give the bodies an official seal which is to be judicially noticed.

12 See *Sparks v Martyn* (1668) 1 Vent 1, cited with approval in *R v Almon* (1765) Wilm 243 at 254. See also 10 *Halsbury's Laws* (4th edn), para 709 notes 4 and 7.

13 See Oswald, *Contempt* (3rd edn, 1910) p 12. See also *McDermott v British Guiana Justices* (1868) LR 2 PC 341.

14 [1983] 2 AC 297.

Broadcasting Corpn v Cordeau.[15] Where statute is the sole source of the contempt jurisdiction it should be construed strictly against the prosecution like any other criminal legislation, but where an Act purports to confer a contempt jurisdiction upon a court of record then, in accordance with the principles set out above, a court should only hold that the inherent jurisdiction is restricted if that is the clear intention of the legislature.[16]

3 All courts of record have an inherent jurisdiction to punish contempts committed in their face but the inherent power to punish contempts committed outside the court resides exclusively in superior courts of record

The above proposition was firmly established by *R v Lefroy* [17] and has not been seriously judicially challenged since.[18] It is of course open to a legislature to extend an inferior court's contempt jurisdiction,[19] but as the Canadian Supreme Court has observed in *Chrysler Canada v Competition Tribunal:*[20] 'there is a presumption, in construing statutes conferring powers on inferior tribunals, that they will not be considered to possess the power of contempt outside the presence of the court, unless the language of Parliament is clear and unequivocal'.

4 Superior courts of record have an inherent superintendent jurisdiction to punish contempts committed in connection with proceedings before inferior courts

The above proposition was first established by *R v Davies* [1] and was based upon the principle that the superintendent jurisdiction vested in the court of King's Bench as the *custos morum* of the people of the realm extended not merely to correcting inferior tribunals but to protecting them from those whose conduct tends to prevent the due performance of their duties. Wills J commented[2] that the mischief to be stopped in the case of inferior courts was identical with that which exists when the due administration of justice in the superior courts is improperly interfered with. The only difference is that whereas superior courts

15 (1980) 101 DLR (3d) 24 and the authorities (English and Canadian) there cited. In Australia see eg *Re Dunn, Re Aspinal* [1906] VLR 493 and *Reece v McKenna, ex p Reece* [1953] QSR 258.
16 Cf in New Zealand, *Taylor v A-G* [1975] 2 NZLR 675.
17 (1873) LR 8 QB 134. See also *Ex p Pater* (1864) 5 B & S 299, *ex p Fernandez* (1861) 10 CBNS 3.
18 In Australia see eg *R v Metal Trades Employers' Association, ex p Amalgamated Engineering Union, Australian Section* (1951) 82 CLR 208 (Australian High Court) and *Re Dunn; Re Aspinal* [1906] VLR 493. In Canada, see *Canadian Broadcasting Corpn v Cordeau* (1980) 101 DLR (3d) 24 and the authorities there cited (Can Sup Ct). In New Zealand, however, the position might be different inasmuch as inferior courts of record might not have any inherent contempt powers, see Adams, *Criminal Law and Practice in New Zealand* (2nd edn) para 3598. If this is true it is in marked contrast to the rest of the Commonwealth.
19 But it must do so in clear terms, cf *Re Hawkins and Halifax County Residential Tenancies Board* (1974) 47 DLR (3d) 117.
20 (1992) 92 DLR (4th) 609, 628 (per McLachlin J). See also *Canadian Broadcasting Corpn v Cordeau* (1980) 101 DLR (3d) 24; cf *Braaten v Sargent and A-G for British Columbia* (1967) 61 DLR (2d) 678.
1 [1906] 1 KB 32, discussed also in Ch 7.
2 Ibid at 47.

have ample powers to deal with the mischief themselves, inferior courts have no such powers.

Although it is now well established both in England and Wales[3] and elsewhere[4] that superior courts are vested with an inherent superintendent contempt jurisdiction, the precise ambit of that jurisdiction has been called into question. In *R v Daily Mail, ex p Farnsworth,* Avory J[5] took *R v Davies* to establish that:

> 'Wherever and whenever this court [ie the High Court, King's Bench Division] has power to correct an inferior court, it also has power to protect that court by punishing those who interfere with the due administration of justice in that court.'

For some time this became the established view of the principle.[6] However, given that in many jurisdictions the power to correct by prerogative order became greatly extended, had the '*Davies* principle' been similarly extended it would have meant that contempt would have applied to a whole host of tribunals, which would have had disturbing implications for freedom of speech.[7] It is now recognised, however, that the power to supervise by prerogative writs and the power to protect against contempt are not co-extensive. Instead, following the House of Lords decision in *A-G v BBC*,[8] the superintendent contempt jurisdiction only extends to protect 'courts of law'.

B   Practice and procedure

1   *Introductory observations*

Although criminal contempt has some of the characteristics of any criminal offence,[9] particularly since the offender can be punished by imprisonment, or fine, it is best to regard it as an offence *sui generis*. As Davies LJ said in *Morris v Crown Office* [10] 'the procedure, if that is the apt expression, is entirely different in cases of criminal contempt from that which applies in ordinary criminal cases.' Like any other offence a criminal contempt must be proved beyond all reasonable

3 See pp 486–487.
4 In Australia see eg *John Fairfax & Sons Pty Ltd v McRae* (1955) 93 CLR 351 (Aust HC) removing the earlier doubts expressed in *Packer v Peacock* (1912) 13 CLR 577. In Canada see eg *Re R v Solloway, ex p Chalmers* [1936] 4 DLR 321 at 328 and *Canadian Broadcasting Corpn v Cordeau* (1980) 101 DLR (3d) 24 (Can SC). In New Zealand see *R v McKinnon* (1909) 30 NZLR 884, *A-G v Blundell* [1942] NZLR 287 and *Quality Pizzas Ltd v Canterbury Hotel Employers' Industrial Union* [1983] NZLR 612.
5 [1921] 2 KB 733 at 752.
6 See *R v Daily Herald, ex p Bishop of Norwich* [1932] 2 KB 402. In Australia, see eg *A-G (NSW) v Mirror Newspapers Ltd* [1980] 1 NSWLR 374 and in Canada, see *Re British Columbia Ferry Corpn and British Columbia Ferry and Marine Workers' Union* (1980) 100 DLR (3d) 705.
7 For a critical consideration of the issues involved, see Lowe and Rawlings, 'Tribunals and the Laws Protecting the Administration of Justice' [1982] PL 418.
8 [1981] AC 303, [1980] 3 All ER 161, discussed at p 487. See also in Australia *NSW Bar Association v Muirhead* (1988) 14 NSWLR 173 at 201ff (per Mahoney JA).
9 See Lord Denning MR, in *Morris v Crown Office* [1970] 2 QB 114 at 123–4; cf in Scotland where in *HM Advocate v Airs* 1975 SLT 177 at 179 it was said that contempt was an offence *sui generis* and not a crime within the meaning of Scottish criminal law. In Canada it is established that the 'offence' of criminal contempt is of a different character to a Criminal Code offence, see *R v Vermette* (1987) 38 DLR (4th) 419, (Can SC) and falls outside s 11 of the Canadian Charter of Rights and Freedoms, see *A-G for Manitoba v Groupe Quebecor Inc* (1987) 45 DLR (4th) 80 (Man CA).
10 [1970] 2 QB 114 at 127.

doubt, but, unlike other offences, there is no prosecution, no summons or warrant for arrest, nor is there a right to trial by jury. At common law there is no theoretical limit either to the length of the term of imprisonment or the amount of the fine which may be imposed. Furthermore, general statutory restrictions on imposition of penalties are not necessarily applicable to contempt.[11] For contempts committed in the face of the court, the punishment can be immediate and is imposed by the judge sitting in the court at the time even if the contempt is directed against the judge himself.

Other peculiarities of contempt as it applies in England and Wales are that the offence can be tried at first instance by a Divisional Court or even by the Court of Appeal and appeals that lie to the latter court lie to the Civil rather than the Criminal Division. On rare occasions contempts are tried at first instance by the House of Lords.[12] Contemnors who have been committed to prison are treated under special prison rules and are kept out of contact with convicted prisoners as far as possible and are not compelled to wear prison dress.

Many of the above peculiarities have arisen either through inadvertence or historical accident but perhaps the most remarkable and fascinating development relates to the general use of the summary process. It is to this development that we will now turn.

2   The summary process by which criminal contempts are tried

(a)   Historical basis

A unique distinction of the law of criminal contempt is that it is triable summarily without a jury. As Lindley LJ said in *O'Shea v O'Shea and Parnell*[13] it is 'the only offence that I know of, which is punishable at common law by summary process'. In fact it is generally accepted that at common law all contempts are indictable[14] but in England and Wales, where the last known prosecution upon indictment against a newspaper for contempt was in *R v Tibbits and Windust* in 1901,[15] the practice has been to proceed summarily and in *Re Lonrho Plc*[16] Lord Keith said that procedure by indictment 'ought not to be revived'. This practice to proceed summarily is common to other jurisdictions.[17]

11   See eg in England and Wales *Morris v Crown Office* [1970] 2 QB 114, and *R v Selby Justices, ex parte Frame* [1992] 1 QB 72, [1991] 2 All ER 344, discussed at p 526 and in Canada *Vaillancourt v R* (1981) 120 DLR (3d) 740.

12   See *Re Lonrho Plc* [1990] 2 AC 154, [1989] 2 All ER 1100, discussed at pp 220–221.

13   (1890) 15 PD 59 at 64.

14   See eg *R v Parke* [1903] 2 KB 432 at 442; *John Fairfax & Sons Pty Ltd v McRae* (1955) 93 CLR 351 at 364; JC McRuer, 'Criminal Contempt of Court: A Protection to the Rights of the Individual' (1951) 30 Can Bar Rev 225 at 236–7 cited with approval in *Re Tilco Plastics Ltd v Skurjat* (1966) 57 DLR (2d) 596 at 610.

15   [1902] 1 KB 77. In fact the charge was the unlawful attempt to pervert the course of justice though the judgments constantly refer to contempt of court.

16   [1990] 2 AC 154, 177 [1989] 3 All ER 1100 at 1106.

17   In Australia, see eg *Registrar, Court of Appeal v Willesse* [1984] 2 NSWLR 378, 379 in which Hutley AP commented that trial upon indictment for contempt 'is for all practical purposes obsolete'. See also *A-G (NSW) v John Fairfax & Sons Ltd and Bacon* (1985) 6 NSWLR 695, 707 per McHugh JA and *DPP v Australia Broadcasting Corporation* (1987) 7 NSWLR 588, 595. In Canada see *R v Vermette* (1987) 38 DLR (4th) 419 in which the Canadian Supreme Court held that although the common practice is to proceed summarily it remains possible to proceed on indictment. NB in New Zealand it is not possible to proceed on indictment nor by way of criminal information. See *Solicitor-General v Radio Avon Ltd* [1978] 1 NZLR 225 at 235.

The power to proceed summarily in respect of contempts committed in the face of the court seems to have been vested in superior courts from the moment of their creation and has long been accepted as an appropriate procedure for any other court vested with powers to punish such contempts.[18] Such a power may properly be considered part of a court of record's inherent jurisdiction.

The power to proceed summarily against contempts committed outside the court is of more recent and questionable origin. The basic authority for the exercise of the jurisdiction is founded not upon an authoritative decision but upon an Opinion. This celebrated Opinion[19] was written over 200 years ago by Wilmot J (as he then was) in the following circumstances. In 1765, in *R v Almon*, a rule nisi was obtained to attach Almon for publishing a libel on Lord Mansfield, Chief Justice of the Court of King's Bench. Judgment was reserved, but when it was ready to be delivered, it was discovered that the rule nisi was incorrectly entitled 'The King against Wilkes'. The defendant's counsel was pressed to consent to an amendment, but without success: 'Wilmot J asked the defendant's counsel Serjeant Glynn, "as a gentleman" to consent, to which the Serjeant replied that "as a man of honour" he could not'.[20] The case therefore had to be abandoned, but a new rule nisi was obtained, the arguments on which stood over until the next term. In the meantime the Government resigned and the new Ministry decided to proceed no further in the matter. Wilmot J's judgment was therefore never delivered, but it was later published (in 1802) when his son edited his papers. Although the judgment was prepared after the argument on the rule to 'shew cause' had been heard, since the matter never came to a final decision, it can only be considered an Opinion and not a judgment. It says much for the reputation of Wilmot J (who later became Chief Justice) that his Opinion should have been considered at all let alone to have acquired 'the singular distinction of becoming a leading authority by citation and approved in subsequent cases'.[1]

Rejecting the argument that the procedure by attachment, being a 'summary' mode of proceeding, was inapplicable to contempts committed out of the court and that the proper procedure was, as in the case of ordinary crimes, to try the case on indictment, Wilmot J said:[2]

> 'The power which the courts in Westminster Hall have of vindicating their own authority, is coeval with their first foundation and institution; it is a necessary incident to every court of justice, whether of record or not, to fine and imprison for contempt to the court, acted in the face of it.... And the issuing of attachments by the Supreme Courts of Justice in Westminster Hall, for contempts out of court, stands upon the same immemorial usage as supports the whole fabric of the common law; it is as much the "lex terrae," and within the exception of Magna Carta, as the issuing of any other legal process whatsoever.
>
> I have examined very carefully to see if I could find out any vestiges or traces of its introduction, but can find none. It is as ancient as any other part of the common law; there is no priority or posteriority to be discovered about it, and therefore cannot be said to invade the common law, but to act in an alliance and friendly conjunction with every other provision which the wisdom of our ancestors has established for the general good of society. And though I do not mean to compare and contrast attachments with trials by jury, yet truth compels me to say,

18 In this respect Wilmot J's opinion in *R v Almon* (1765) Wilm 243, may be regarded as correct. See Fox, '*R v Almon II*' (1908) 24 LQR 266 and the authorities there cited.
19 *R v Almon* (1765) Wilm 243. See further the discussion in Ch 9 at p 336.
20 See Fox, '*R v Almon II*' (1908) 24 LQR 184.
 1 Fox, *The History of Contempt of Court* (1927) p 8.
 2 (1765) Wilm 243 at 254.

that the mode of proceeding by attachment stands upon the very same foundation and basis as trials by jury do—immemorial usage and practice; it is a constitutional remedy in particular cases, and the judges in those cases are as much bound to give an activity to this part of the law as to any other part of it. Indeed it is admitted that attachments are very properly granted for resistance of process, or a contumelious treatment of it, or any violence, or abuse of the ministers, or others, employed to execute it. But it is said that the course of justice in those cases is obstructed, and the obstruction must be instantly removed; that there is no such necessity in the case of libels upon courts or judges, which may wait for the ordinary method of prosecution without any inconvenience whatsoever. But when the nature of the offence of libelling judges for what they do in their judicial capacities, either in court or out of court, comes to be considered, it does, in my opinion, become more proper for an attachment than any other case whatsoever.'

In concluding that the summary process was applicable in cases of constructive contempt, Wilmot J relied not upon specific authority but upon 'immemorial usage and practice'. Although this historical assessment has never been challenged in subsequent English decisions, a fine piece of scholarly research by Sir John Fox seriously undermined the historical validity of the opinion.[3] Nevertheless, masterly though the research may have been, it can now only be a matter of academic interest. *R v Almon* has been relied on as authority and the practice to proceed summarily has been followed in England and elsewhere ever since. As Frankfurter J has commented:[4]

'The fact that scholarship has shown that historical assumptions regarding the procedure for punishment of contempt were ill-founded hardly wipes out a century and a half of the legislative and judicial history of federal law based on such assumptions.'

This comment has equal force in England and Wales and other common law jurisdictions.

(b)   The meaning of a 'summary' exercise of the power to punish for contempt

Although it has become established that all criminal contempts are triable summarily there are several degrees of summary process.[5] The most extreme form (sometimes referred to[6] as the 'classic summary' procedure) is where the

3 His research was first published in a series of articles in the *Law Quarterly Review*: (1908) 24 LQR 184 at 266; (1909) 25 LQR 238 at 354; (1920) 36 LQR 394; (1921) 37 LQR 191; (1922) 38 LQR 185 and (1924) 40 LQR 43. For the most part these articles are embodied in Fox, *The History of Contempt of Court* (1927). After exhaustive research, Fox found that the earliest recorded case in which the summary process had been used was *R v Wilkins* decided in 1720 and indeed he found that following the abolition of the Star Chamber, 'scandalising' the court had almost invariably been punished on indictment or information. These conclusions of course, are directly contrary to Wilmot J's statement that recourse to summary procedure had been exercised since 'time immemorial'. See also Hay, 'Contempt by Scandalising the Court: A Political History of the First Hundred Years' (1987) Osgoode Hall Law Journal 431; Frankfurter and Landis, 'Power of Congress Over Procedure in Criminal Contempts in "Inferior" Federal Courts etc—A Study in Separation of Powers' (1923-4) 37 HLR 1010 at 1046 ff and Goodhart: 'Newspapers and Contempt of Court in English Law' (1935) 48 HLR 885 at 899.
4 *Green v US* 356 US 165 (1958) cited by Windeyer J in *James v Robinson* (1963) 109 CLR 593 at 614.
5 See eg per Gale CJHC in *Re Tilco Plastics Ltd v Skurjat* (1966) 57 DLR (2d) 596 at 610 and *Re Bengert et al (No 2)* (1981) 23 BCLR 181 per Nemetz CJBC.
6 Eg by the Canadian Law Reform Commission Working Paper No 20 (1977) p 53. See also their Final Report No 17 (1982).

accused is charged on the spot, the judge formulating the charge and then asking the accused to show cause why he ought not to be immediately convicted. In these cases the judge is said to be acting *brevi manu*, ie without the intervention of any further court proceedings.[7] Slightly less immediate but no less drastic is the procedure used where the contempt is committed outside the court though usually at a time when proceedings are continuing, namely, for the court to proceed *ex mero motu* to bring the offending party immediately before the bar of justice and to impose punishment in a summary manner.

In England and Wales both these procedures are thought of as being where the judge acts upon his own motion,[8] which, as will be seen, is a power expressly preserved by the Contempt of Court Act 1981, s 7 and by the Rules of the Supreme Court.[9] Although it is theoretically possible for a judge to proceed upon his own motion in all cases of criminal contempt, in practice the procedure is now adopted only in cases of contempts committed in the face of the court and those committed outside the court which pose an immediate threat to the proceedings such as the intimidation or harassment of witnesses.[10] It would be a rare and questionable prosecution for a judge to proceed upon his own motion against a newspaper editor for publishing an allegedly prejudicial article.[11]

For most criminal contempts committed outside the court, notably those allegedly committed by the news media, the prosecution process has become markedly less summary. The practice adopted in England and Wales[12] and elsewhere[13] is for an application to be made to the court for a committal order. Under this process the accused has notice of the charge and time to prepare a defence. In fact this procedure lacks few of the safeguards accorded to defendants in a normal trial.[14] It is true that in England and Wales, as the Phillimore Committee pointed out,[15] evidence is usually given on affidavit so that there is no cross-examination of the applicant but the person sought to be committed does apparently have a right to require the applicant and his witnesses to be present for cross-examination.[16] The accused also has a right to give oral evidence on his own behalf.[17] The major difference between this form of summary process and a normal trial is the denial in the former case of a right to a trial by jury. The significance of this denial is discussed below.

(c)   Justifying the continued use of the summary process

Although the practice of trying contempts summarily has been criticised from time to time it remains the method most commonly resorted to in the United

7   See *Mathieson v Mathieson* (1974) 48 DLR (3d) 94 at 104 per Allen JA. See also *Re Johnson* (1887) 20 QBD 68 at 74 per Bowen LJ.
8   See eg *Balogh v Crown Court at St Albans* [1975] QB 73, [1974] 3 All ER 283.
9   Ie RSC Ord 52, r 5.
10 See *Balogh v Crown Court at St Albans* ibid.
11 See p 502. A similar position obtains in Canada. See Canadian Law Reform Commission Working Paper No 20 (1977) p 53.
12 Discussed at pp 476 ff.
13 Eg in Canada see McRuer, 'Criminal Contempt of Court Procedure: A Protection of the Right of the Individual' (1951) 30 Can Bar Rev 225 at 236–237 cited with approval in *Tilco Plastics Ltd v Skurjat* (1966) 57 DLR (2d) 596 at 610.
14 See Gale CJHC in *Re Tilco Plastics* ibid at p 610.
15 (1974, Cmnd 5794) para 16.
16 According to the Phillimore Committee ibid at para 16.
17 RSC Ord 52, r 6(4).

Kingdom and the major Commonwealth jurisdictions. Repeated use, however, does not in itself justify the process and there does seem a need to justify any recourse to the summary process no matter what form it may take. The more extreme the summary process the greater is the need to justify it.

The justification commonly advanced is that the summary process provides a speedy and efficient means of trying the contempt which is necessary for the protection of the due administration of justice. As Wills J said in *R v Davies*:[18]

'the undoubted possible recourse to indictment and criminal information is too dilatory and too inconvenient to afford any satisfactory remedy. It is true that the summary remedy, with its consequent withdrawal of the offence from the cognisance of a jury, is not to be resorted to if the ordinary methods of prosecution can satisfactorily accomplish the desired result, namely, to put an efficient and timely check upon such malpractices. But they do not.'

The Phillimore Committee similarly concluded[19] that the 'principal merit of the summary procedure is that it can be set in motion rapidly in order to deal with a threat to the administration'. Indeed one of their main underlying guiding principles was that the contempt jurisdiction should be invoked only where urgency or practical necessity require that the matter be tried summarily.[20]

According to Hope JA, in the Australian decision, *A-G (NSW) v Mundey*:[1]

'The reported decisions show that such a charge [ie of contempt] should be dealt with summarily only where it is established clearly and beyond reasonable doubt, and where the case can be described as exceptional. The justification for the summary disposition of contempt charges has been said to be the need to remove at once the immediate obstruction to the administration of justice.'

The need for speed seems a plausible justification for the most extreme summary process, namely, where the judge acts upon his own motion to deal with disorder in the face of the court or the intimidation and harassment of a witness during a trial. Such acts pose an immediate and direct threat to the due administration of justice and have to be dealt with quickly. Moreover, there seems little need for a jury since the facts should not be in dispute and sentence is quite properly a function of the judge. Judges are well aware that their apparently arbitrary powers need to be exercised with the greatest restraint. There is no evidence that the power is abused and with the added safeguard of a right of appeal contemnors' rights are reasonably protected. The process is by no means perfect but it does seem a necessary one.

The need for the speedy removal of an obstruction to the due administration of justice might also justify the less extreme summary process used to prosecute other types of criminal contempt committed outside the court, notably, allegedly prejudicial publications. As the Phillimore Committee said[2] 'A prejudicial publication shortly before a trial may need to be brought before the court without

18 [1906] 1 KB 32 at 41. See also *R v Castro, Skipworth's Case* (1873) LR 9 QB 230 at 233 per Blackburn J.
19 At para 17.
20 See para 21.
1 [1972] 2 NSWLR 887 at 912. But note also Glass JA's subsequent comment in *Registrar of Court of Appeal v Willesee* [1984] 2 NSWLR 378, 381: 'I believe that the time has come to recognise that the summary trial is now the ordinary and normal procedure. Although it should be sparingly employed and only in clear cases there are no preconditions such as the need for urgent action requiring fulfilment before it is available for exercise'.
2 At para 17.

delay in order to prevent a recurrence'. However, in the case of publications allegedly prejudicial to criminal proceedings, the modern practice in England and Wales and elsewhere is to delay the hearing of the contempt application until after the relevant trial has been completed.[3] Given this delay it might be questioned whether the summary process can be considered 'necessary' since, if the relevant trial has been concluded, there is arguably no pressing need for the prompt disposal of the contempt application. The lack of urgency has sometimes been said to be the reason against proceeding summarily in cases where it is alleged that the court is 'scandalised'.[4] In England and Wales, where such prosecutions are a rarity, there has been no suggestion made judicially that the summary procedure should not be used in such cases. In another context, however, namely, the punishment of witnesses after the trial has been completed, Pearson LJ commented in *Re A-G's Application, A-G v Butterworth:*[5]

> 'In this case it has not been contended on either side that there is an alternative procedure by indictment (which, though said to be disused, could be revived) and that it would be a more suitable procedure in a case such as the present since after the conclusion of proceedings there is prima facie no pressing need for prompt disposal of the matter and trial by jury would be appropriate for determining the intention or purpose of each of the defendants in voting for or otherwise helping to procure the removal of Greenlees from his offices. The decision in this appeal does not preclude any submission on those lines which might be made in any future case.'

It may be, however, that the possible dispute of fact, namely, the motive for taking action against the witness which could sensibly be left to a jury to decide, might justify distinguishing reprisals against witnesses from other types of contempt. Be that as it may, the Phillimore Committee recommended[6] that both scandalising the court and taking reprisals against witnesses after the trial is concluded should cease to be triable summarily and instead be statutory offences triable upon indictment. Their recommendation was endorsed by the Law Commission[7] and both offences were included in their draft Bill on offences against the administration of justice. Although no immediate legislative action has been taken, s 51 of the Criminal Justice and Public Order Act 1994[8] now makes it an offence to intimidate a witness or juror involved in criminal trials.

Unless there is a dispute of fact it seems sensible to treat all media contempts alike, ie whether the publication is alleged to be contempt because of the risk of prejudice or because it scandalises the court. With regard to prejudicial publications the Phillimore Committee recommended[9] no change to the procedure, noting that there was not much concern in press circles about 'this peculiarity of contempt'. It is submitted that they were right to recommend no change. Although speed

---

3   Discussed at p 498.
4   Eg in Australia see *A-G (NSW) v Mundey* [1972] 2 NSWLR 887, but cf *Gallagher v Durack* (1983) 152 CLR 238 (Aust HC) and *Fitzgibbon v Barker* (1992) 111 FLR 191 and in Canada see eg *R v Sommer* (1963) 46 DLR (2d) 49, but cf *R v Kopyto* (1987) 47 DLR (4th) 213 and *Re Ouellet* (1976) 32 CCC (2d) 149, (1976) 72 DLR (3d) 95. Scandalising the court is discussed in Ch 9.
5   [1963] 1 QB 696 at 728.
6   At Chs 6 and 7.
7   Law Com No 96: Offences Relating to Interfering with the Course of Justice (1979) paras 3.58–3.75.
8   Discussed at pp 426–429.
9   At para 17.

might not always justify the procedure (the Phillimore Committee overlooked the practice to delay hearing contempt applications in the cases mentioned above) there are other advantages. The very peculiarity of the procedure helps to emphasise the gravity of the offence, an impression further enforced by the fact that the contempt is dealt with by an authoritative court. In England and Wales, most media contempts come before the Queen's Bench Divisional Court which is often presided over by the Lord Chief Justice and often comprises three judges. This in itself might help deter the otherwise powerful media from jeopardising the due administration of justice. It is doubtful whether a trial by jury before the Crown Court would have a similar impact. As Professor Goodhart said 'if it were necessary to try before a jury every case of constructive contempt, such as prejudicing the jury or threatening the parties, the present control of the press would lose much of its efficacy'.[10] Another virtue of the present procedure is that it interferes as little as possible with the normal business of the criminal courts.

The above arguments, however, may not be thought to justify proceeding summarily if defendants' rights are seriously prejudiced. It is submitted that they are not, for as we have said, the current summary procedure as it is used in connection with media contempts does not deprive a defendant of most of the safeguards found in a normal trial. The major difference, of course, is the denial of a right to trial by jury. But what role could a jury have and would it benefit the particular defendant or the media in general? There will normally be no dispute as to the facts and sentence is not part of a jury's function but jurors could plausibly be asked to decide whether a particular publication created a substantial risk of serious prejudice. At first sight this might seem a valuable role since for the most part the contempt laws are designed to shield jurors from the possibility of influence and it might seem sensible to ask a jury whether a particular article carried such risks. However, there is surely a risk of greater inconsistency between one decision and another and this in turn will lead to greater uncertainty in the law.

C   Attachment and committal

Formerly, courts of common law and Chancery proceeded summarily in cases of criminal contempt either by attachment or by committal.[11] The main difference between the processes lay in the means of execution: in the case of an attachment the person is seized by the sheriff's officer acting under a writ of attachment issued by leave of the court, but in the case of a committal the process was less formal and more direct, the offender being seized by the tipstaff acting under the orders of the judge.[12] In *R v Lambeth County Court Judge and Jonas*,[13] Wills J commented that there was no other practical difference between a committal and

10 'Newspapers and Contempt of Court in English Law' (1935) 48 HLR 885 at 899.
11 The following passage was cited with approval by Allen JA in *Mathieson v Mathieson* (1974) 48 DLR (3d) 94 at 109 (Alberta SC).
12 For the difference between committal and attachment see Oswald, *Contempt* (3rd edn, 1910) pp 23–32 and for a short account see *The Annual Practice 1966*, pp 1071–73. See also in Australia *La Trobe University v Robinson* [1972] VR 883, at 900–901 (not commented on in appeal at [1973] VR 682).
13 (1887) 36 WR 475.

an attachment: 'One was enforced by the tipstaff of the court, and the other by the sheriff. That is all the distinction, and it comes to little if anything'.

However, it must be remembered that while either remedy was available in cases of criminal contempt, this was not true in cases of civil contempt where there were a number of technical rules determining which remedy was available in which circumstances. In these cases the applicant chose his remedy at his peril and a wrong choice was fatal to the action.[14]

Happily, so far as England and Wales[15] is concerned all such technicalities have been rendered academic since under RSC Ord 52, r 1 the remedy of committal is available in all cases of contempt.[16] The current rules do not refer to attachment and accordingly that remedy must be considered obsolete, for although theoretically it may still be possible to proceed by way of attachment since the remedy has not been expressly abolished, the procedure is unlikely to be adopted.[17]

II   THE CURRENT PROSECUTION PROCESS IN ENGLAND AND WALES

A   Contempts committed outside the court

1   *General observations*

As we have seen, only superior courts of record have inherent jurisdiction to punish contempts committed outside the court. In England and Wales, the following are superior courts of record: the House of Lords, Court of Appeal,[18] High Court of Justice,[19] Crown Court,[20] the Restrictive Practices Court,[1] the Employment Appeal Tribunal[2] and the Courts-Martial Appeal Court.[3] Although on the face of it their status would seem to invest such courts with wide contempt powers in practice their jurisdiction is more circumscribed.

The contempt jurisdiction can be invoked either by formal application to commit or by the court acting upon its own motion. Certain courts are also empowered to grant injunctions restraining contempts or threatened contempts.

Outside the House of Lords[4] the procedure by which formal applications for committal can be made is provided by RSC Ord 52. Under that Order the major original jurisdiction is vested in the Queen's Bench Divisional Court, in particular under Ord 52, r 1 (2)(a) (ii) it has sole jurisdiction to make committal orders in

---

14 See *Kemp v Kemp* (1957) Times, 26 November. See also *The Annual Practice 1966*, p 1072.
15 Aliter in Queensland, Australia, see eg *Re Intex Consultants Pty Ltd* (1986) 2 Qd R 99, 109.
16 As from March 1979 the procedure in the county court has been brought into line with the High Court. See Booth J in *Whitter v Peters* [1982] 2 All ER 369 at 374, [1982] 1 WLR 389 at 395. See now County Court Rules 1981, Ord 29 discussed at p 643.
17 See Stephenson LJ in *Balogh v Crown Court at St Albans* [1975] QB 73 at 88 F.
18 Supreme Court Act 1981, s 5(1).
19 Supreme Court Act 1981, s 19(1).
20 Supreme Court Act 1981, s 45(1).
 1 Restrictive Practices Court Act 1976, ss 1(1), (4).
 2 Employment Protection (Consolidation) Act 1978, s 135(6), Sch 11, para 12.
 3 Courts-Martial (Appeals) Act 1968, s 1(2).
 4 Discussed at p 477.

respect of criminal contempts committed in connection with criminal proceedings other than those committed in the face of the court.[5]

Notwithstanding the terms of Ord 52, r 1, all superior courts have the power to act upon their own motion. Indeed, properly understood such a power is not in itself circumscribed by the Rules of the Supreme Court nor by Ord 52 in particular.[6] However, as will be seen, a court's power to act upon its own motion is a restricted one which should not be invoked in all cases of contempts committed outside the court. In particular, it should not normally be invoked in respect of 'media contempts'.

The restricted ambit of Ord 52, r 1 and the restricted use of the power to act upon the court's own motion combine, as we shall see, to limit the Crown Court's jurisdiction in respect of contempts committed outside the court.

Applications to restrain conduct on the basis that it does or would amount to contempt should be treated like any other application for an injunction and should be made to the High Court. It may be, however, that all superior courts of record have jurisdiction to grant injunctions and might properly be invited to do so, at least in emergencies.

2   Committals under RSC Order 52

(a)   When applicable

(i) Not applicable to the House of Lords   Order 52 has no application to contempts of the House of Lords. This has become clear following *Re Lonrho Plc*[7] in which, pending the hearing of an action for judicial review of the Secretary of State for the Department and Trade's refusal inter alia to publish an inspector's report on the takeover of Harrods, copies of a special edition of the *Observer* containing extracts from the report were sent to four of the five Law Lords about to hear the case. After considering various suggestions on to how best to proceed with the alleged contempt, it was held that there was no authority vesting jurisdiction in the Divisional Court of the Queen's Bench Division or any other court, to deal with an alleged contempt relating to proceedings before the House and not involving any other crime. Accordingly, it was resolved that the House should hear the contempt itself before a differently constituted committee.

(ii) Not applicable to application for injunctions   Order 52 is concerned with applications for committal and not applications for injunctions. In an unreported decision (the *Novac Case*[8]) an application was made in the Queen's Bench Divisional Court under Ord 52 to restrain the BBC from screening a film entitled 'Johnny go home' because it related to proceedings then before the Old Bailey. The application was refused on the basis that the Divisional Court had no jurisdiction under Ord 52 to issue an injunction.

---

5   And those before the Court of Appeal. See further at pp 485–486.
6   See Stephenson LJ in *Balogh v Crown Court at St Albans* [1975] QB 73 at 89E–F, [1974] 3 All ER 283 at 292b–d. This is a consequence of the contempt power being inherent see pp 465–466.
7   [1990] 2 AC 154, [1989] 2 All ER 1100, discussed at pp 220–221.
8   1975. We are grateful to the late Lord Justice James for the details about this case.

In *A-G v Times Newspapers Ltd*[9] and *A-G v BBC*,[10] however, applications to restrain a planned publication made because of possible prejudice to legal proceedings, came first before a judge in chambers and then before the Queen's Bench Divisional Court. In the *Times Newspaper* case, by consent of the parties, the judge in chambers ordered the matter to be transferred to the Divisional Court. In the *BBC* case the judge, at the request of the Attorney General, adjourned the matter so that it could be heard by the Divisional Court. In neither case was this point of jurisdiction taken[11] at any level and both must be regarded as dubious precedents.[12] The procedure in the *Times Newspaper* case might possibly have been justified upon the basis that at the time of the application there was already pending in the Divisional Court an application for a committal against London Weekend Television[13] for a broadcast about the same subject-matter. It was therefore convenient for the Divisional Court to hear both cases. Even so there is no other authority for a judge in chambers to transfer an application to a Divisional Court in a matter not within the jurisdiction of that court. There seems even less justification for the procedure adopted in the *BBC* case.

It is submitted that on the rules as they stand the Divisional Court was wrong to accept jurisdiction in either of the cases just referred to. On the other hand, it may well be thought that because of the urgency and convenience it was nevertheless sensible that the Divisional Court heard the applications. Moreover, since the law of contempt lies at the heart of an application whether it be for a committal or an injunction there seems no sensible reason for distinguishing the procedure by which they are tried. Accordingly, it is suggested that consideration should be given to amending Order 52 so as to allow application to be made to restrain publication on the basis of their possible contempt of current proceedings.

(b)   Who can apply for committals?

(i) The position before the Contempt of Court Act 1981   Before the Contempt of Court Act 1981 it was open to any interested person[14] to apply to the relevant court for an order for committal under RSC Ord 52. However, the practice had evolved 'for persons complaining of a publication to make an informal approach to the Attorney General and, if it appears desirable in the public interest that a case should be brought before this court, an application is made by the Attorney General for leave to move'.[15] Nevertheless, if the Attorney General did not feel

---

9 [1973] QB 710, DC and CA; [1974] AC 273, HL.
10 [1978] 2 All ER 731, [1978] 1 WLR 477 DC; [1981] AC 303, CA and HL.
11 In fact this jurisdiction point was argued by the BBC in *A-G v BBC* but the Divisional Court did not think it important. Ironically, however, the central point in the *BBC* case was whether there was jurisdiction under Ord 52 to hear the application since it referred to proceedings before a local valuation court. See p 487.
12 Particularly as both were appealed from the Divisional Court to the Court of Appeal on the basis that they were applications for injunctions rather than contempt cases. For the route of appeal in 'contempt' cases see p 534.
13 *A-G v London Weekend Television Ltd* [1972] 3 All ER 1146, [1973] 1 WLR 202.
14 The applicant would normally be the 'aggrieved' party in the particular proceedings which it is claimed are prejudiced by the publication. Applicants, however, were not restricted to this class. See eg *R v Metropolitan Police Comr, ex p Blackburn (No 2)* [1968] 2 QB 150, [1968] 2 All ER 319, where a member of the public, albeit an MP, brought the prosecution; cf the position with injunctions, see p 500.
15 Per Sir Reginald Manningham-Buller QC arguendo in *R v Duffy, ex p Nash* [1960] 2 QB 188 at 192.

disposed to bring the action an individual was entitled to institute proceedings himself. In fact private prosecutions had become unusual and tended to be confined to 'aggrieved' parties in civil proceedings.[16]

It was established that the decision of whether or not to apply for a committal lay entirely within the Attorney General's discretion. As Lord Reid said in *A-G v Times Newspapers Ltd*,[17] 'It is entirely for him to judge whether it is in the public interest that he should act.' The decision to seek a committal, however, does not, as Lord Denning MR had asserted,[18] put 'the authority of the Crown behind the complaint'. As Lord Cross put it in *A-G v Times Newspapers Ltd* [19] in taking up a complaint the Attorney General 'does not do so as a minister of the Crown . . . but as "amicus curiae" bringing to the notice of the court some matter of which he considers that the court shall be informed in the interests of the administration of justice'. Hence, his role in bringing committal applications is equally valid whether the complaint is in respect of criminal or civil proceedings.[20]

The practice of referring complaints to the Attorney General probably dates from 1953 when Lord Goddard CJ commented in *R v Hargreaves, ex p Dill (No 2)*:[1]

'In this class of case I have always taken the view that it would be a good change if these actions were moved only by a Law Officer or on the instructions of the Attorney General, because the object is to punish an editor who has committed contempt, not to assist the defence.'

The view that such contempt prosecutions should only be brought by the Attorney General was subsequently repeated by such bodies as *Justice*.[2] On the other hand the then practice was eloquently defended by Sir Elwyn Jones when, as Attorney General, he said:[3]

'Ought the Attorney General of the day to have the last word? Suppose, for example, the complaint is made about some comment on proceedings in which a Ministerial colleague of the Attorney General as representing the Crown is a party. Is the complainant going to be satisfied with the Attorney General's decision in those circumstances not to act, or is he going away saying, "Dog don't eat dog?". I suggest it is much better if the Attorney General can say, "I do not think your complaint justifies me in instituting proceedings for contempt, but you are welcome to test my opinion by taking it to court yourself and persuading the court that my view is wrong . . .". I fear that I do not think it would be in the interests of the ordinary citizen or leave him with a full sense of satisfaction if the power was wholly taken from him.'

---

16 See eg *Vine Products Ltd v Green* [1966] Ch 484, [1965] 3 All ER 58 and *Re Duncan* (1969) 113 Sol Jo 526.
17 [1974] AC 273 at 294.
18 In *A-G v Times Newspapers Ltd* [1973] QB 710 at 738. See also Phillimore LJ at 742.
19 [1974] AC 273 at 326.
20 Both Lord Denning MR and Phillimore LJ thought it questionable that the Attorney General should act in relation to complaints about civil proceedings.
1   [1954] Crim LR 54. See also *R v Associated Newspapers Ltd, ex p Beyers* (1936) 80 Sol Jo 247.
2   In their reports *Contempt of Court* (1959), pp 34 and 42 and The *Law and The Press* (1965) p 17. See also the proposed Freedom of Publication (Protection Bill) discussed in [1969] Crim LR 124.
3   776 HC Official Report (5th series) col 1726. However, he subsequently appears to have changed his mind, see 415 HL Official Report (5th series) col 666 and indeed unsuccessfully attempted to amend the Contempt of Court Bill so as to provide for the need for the Attorney General's consent. See 416 HL Official Report (5th series) col 205 ff.

The Phillimore Committee recommended no change to the practice.[4] They considered it essential that the Attorney General should retain his right to act in the public interest where he thinks fit to do so but nevertheless thought it important that the individual should have the right to test the matter in the courts himself.

Despite these and other reservations[5] an amendment to the Contempt of Court Bill was successfully introduced at the Committee stage in the House of Commons[6] for the Attorney General's fiat in certain cases.

(ii) Committal applications under the 'strict liability rule'   The Contempt of Court Act 1981, s 7 provides:

> 'Proceedings for a contempt of court under the strict liability rule (other than Scottish proceedings)[7] shall not be instituted except by or with the consent of the Attorney General or on the motion of a court having jurisdiction to deal with it.'

The precise application of s 7 is not beyond question. Prima facie it appears to be confined to prosecutions under the 'strict liability rule'. Accordingly, it would appear to apply only to publications caught by s 2, ie those thought to create a substantial risk of serious prejudice to particular legal proceedings. On this basis s 7 does not apply to publications said to 'scandalise' the court[8] since that constitutes an interference with the administration of justice as a continuing process rather than interfering with a particular case. Similarly, s 7 might have been thought to have no application to publications intended to impede or prejudice a particular case since s 6(c) excludes such publications from the strict liability rule.[9] However, as Falconer J pointed out in *Roger Bullivant and Others v Ellis and Others*,[10] s 6 is carefully phrased to apply to foregoing provisions and not therefore to s 7. In his Lordship's view s 7 applies to any matter falling within s 1 (ie conduct tending to interfere with the course of justice in particular legal proceedings regardless of an intent to do so) and that therefore the Attorney General's consent is required in the case of an 'intentional contempt'. Even on this view s 7 has no application to conduct alleged to interfere with the course of justice as a continuing process. On the other hand it would apply to any conduct,[11] not just 'publications', thought to interfere with the course of justice in particular legal proceedings. Whether the appellate courts will accept this wider application remains to be seen.

It has been held that s 7 does not apply to applications to restrain future publications. As Watkins LJ said in *Peacock v London Weekend Television Ltd*,[12]

4   Ibid at para 187.
5   Eg whether an individual would have a remedy under Article 13 of the European Convention on Human Rights in the event of a refusal of consent by the Attorney General (a problem adverted to by Sir Michael Havers, HC Official Report, 1980-81 SCA, Contempt of Court, col 126 ff). See further below.
6   SCA col 121.
7   In Scotland the Lord Advocate commonly initiates contempt proceedings but, as *Robb v Caledonian Newspapers* 1995 SLT 631 confirms, an individual may still petition directly, see Bonnington, 'Press and Prejudice' (1995) 145 NLJ 1623. The provision does apply to Northern Ireland. By s 18(1): 'referred to the Attorney General shall be construed as referred to the Attorney General for Northern Ireland'.
8   Discussed in Ch 9.
9   Discussed at p 106 ff.
10 (1986) Financial Times, 16 April. Full transcript on Lexis.
11 Including, eg threatening witnesses on their way to court. But for whether individuals can nevertheless initiate court proceedings see pp 500–501.
12 (1985) 150 JP 71, full transcript on Lexis, CA. See also *A-G v News Group Newspapers Ltd* [1987] QB 1, 8, [1986] 2 All ER 833, 836, per Sir John Donaldson MR.

s 7 'comes into play when and only when a contempt of court has been committed and it is thought that the Attorney General ought to invite the court so to find and to consider what penalty, if that finding is made, should be inflicted on the contemnor'. On this reasoning it is open to any interested party (including the Attorney General) to apply for an interlocutory injunction to prevent an anticipated contempt.[13]

Where s 7 applies an individual must bring his complaint either before the Attorney General or a judge.[14] So far as the Attorney General is concerned there is no formal procedure for seeking his fiat. Applications are normally made simply by writing to him.

What is the position where the Attorney General refuses to give his consent? There is no right of appeal and, as *R v Solicitor-General, ex p Taylor* [15] recently confirmed the Attorney General's decision is not subject to judicial review. In the *Taylor* case the convictions of two sisters for murder were set aside partly because of the prejudicial media coverage[16] and the Court of Appeal ordered the papers to be sent to the Attorney General to consider whether it was appropriate to take any further action. Although leave to seek judicial review of the A-G's decision was granted to the sisters, the Divisional Court ruled that his decision not to prosecute for contempt was not reviewable. As Stuart-Smith LJ said, s 7 took away the right of citizens to move for committal for contempt and if the Attorney General's decision was reviewable Parliament would have said so.

An alternative possible remedy in the event of the Attorney General's refusal to consent is for an aggrieved individual to bring an action in the European Court of Human Rights on the basis of Articles 6 and 13. Such an action was discussed during the passage of the Contempt of Court Bill.[17]

Article 13 states:

> 'Everyone whose rights and freedoms as set forth in this Convention are violated shall have an effective remedy before a national authority notwithstanding that the violation has been committed by persons acting in an official capacity.'

Article 13 has to be read with Article 6 which is concerned with a right to a fair trial. A publication falling foul of the 'strict liability rule' would certainly interfere with the accused's right to a fair trial which is guaranteed by Article 6 and it was argued that the blocking of a remedy that formerly existed (ie the individual's right to bring an action for contempt on his own behalf) could be a breach of Article 6 when read together with Article 13.[18]

---

13 Under s 37 of the Supreme Court Act 1981, but cf *Pickering v Liverpool Daily Post and Echo Newspapers Plc* [1991] 2 AC 370, discussed at p 500.
14 Failure to do so is fatal to the action, see *Roger Bullivant and Others v Ellis and Others* (1986) Financial Times, 16 April, and *Taylor v Topping and Others* (1990) Times, 15 February.
15 (1995) Times, 14 August. This was also the view expressed in the second edition of the work (at p 328) relying on inter alia *Gouriet v Union of Post Office Workers* [1978] AC 435, [1977] 3 All ER 70, HL (on which see Feldman, 'Injunctions and the Criminal Law' (1979) 42 MLR 369, especially at 372 ff), *Raymond v A-G* [1982] QB 839, [1982] 2 All ER 487, CA and *Turner v DPP* (1978) 68 Cr App R 70. There is no right to review his decision to prosecute, see *London County Council v A-G* [1902] AC 165, HL.
16 Discussed at pp 75–76 and pp 150–151.
17 HC Official Report, 1980–81, SCA col 126 ff and 6 HC Official Report (5th series) cols 915–16.
18 The denial of an individual's right to bring an action for contempt cannot constitute a breach of Article 6 in the sense that the article upholds an individual's right of access to the courts (as interpreted by *Golder v UK* [1975] 1 EHRR 524) since the article is confined to the right to bring a *civil* action.

The Government's considered view was that the risk of being held in breach was in any event small but as Sir Michael Havers, the Attorney General, said:[19]

> 'The accused person's right to a fair trial is to be vindicated not in contempt proceedings but in the proceedings in the trial court. It is there that Article 6 rights are protected. It is there, not in separate contempt proceedings that the accused person has the remedy required by Article 13.'

It is submitted that the whole argument is misconceived. A contempt action cannot be considered a 'remedy' for the individual.[20] Holding a publisher guilty of contempt does not invalidate the verdict. The individual's 'remedy' is, as Sir Michael Havers said, to appeal against conviction on the grounds that the trial has been prejudiced and this right has not been affected by s 7. The fact that there is little chance of an appeal being successful on these grounds[1] does not convert a contempt action into a 'remedy' though a dismissal of an appeal in a particular case might itself be subject to a claim that Article 6 has been broken.[2]

Where the Attorney General consents to the institution of contempt proceedings he generally takes the case himself and bears its costs. However, it is to be noted that under s 7 he can give an individual leave to bring proceedings in which case the individual will have to bear the burden of costs.[3] Although it seems possible for this secondary route to be adopted where the Attorney General sees no *pressing* public need to bring the action but where nevertheless there is some merit in the application, there is no evidence that this option has been exercised.

It will be noted that s 7 does not prevent the Attorney General from acting upon his own initiative.

The main thrust of s 7 is to channel contempt applications via the Attorney General but the section also preserves the superior courts'[4] inherent power to institute proceedings upon their own motion. In practice, however, this power is not normally exercised in respect of publications which are now subject to the 'strict liability rule'.[5] Nevertheless the reservation of the power does provide at least certain individuals with a choice how to proceed. A party to proceedings before the Crown Court or the High Court could, for example, bring to the judge's notice a publication which is alleged to be potentially prejudicial rather than referring the matter to the Attorney General. The advantage of this course of action is that the litigant can have his complaint presented by counsel which might be more persuasive than a letter to the Attorney General. No doubt the proper practice would then be for the judge (if he thinks further action should be taken) to refer the matter to the Attorney General,[6] though, as we have seen,[7]

---

19   6 HC Official Report (5th series) col 916.
20   The argument might be well founded had s 7 applied to applications to restraining publications on the basis of their *potential* prejudice to active proceedings since these actions are properly considered 'remedies'.
1   But see *R v Taylor and Taylor* (1993) 98 Cr App Rep 361 and *R v McCann, Cullen and Shanahan* (1990) 92 Cr App Rep 239, discussed at pp 75–76.
2   See the notes to s 7 in the Annotated Notes on the 1981 Act published in Sweet and Maxwell's *Annotated Legislation Series*.
3   In relator actions the individual bears the costs. See *A-G, ex rel McWhirter v Independent Broadcasting Authority* [1973] QB 629, [1973] 1 All ER 689.
4   Inferior courts have no power to punish contempts committed outside the court, see p 467.
5   See the discussion at pp 502 ff. Cf, however, *Re Lonrho Plc* [1990] 2 AC 154, [1989] 2 All ER 1100.
6   Such a referral was made in *A-G v English* [1983] AC 116, [1982] 2 All ER 903. NB the referring judge's observations are not binding upon the Divisional Court per Watkins LJ ibid at 965.
7   See *R v Taylor and Taylor* (1994) 98 Cr App Rep 361, discussed above.

such a referral does not necessarily mean that a contempt action will be brought.

(iii) Critique   Although it may be right that the Attorney General should have the major role in bringing contempt applications,[8] (for as Lord Diplock said in *A-G v Times Newspapers Ltd*:[9] 'He is the appropriate public officer to represent the public interest in the administration of justice'), it is submitted that it was a mistake to enact s 7.[10] One of objects of the law of contempt is to maintain public confidence in the administration of justice. An aspect of this confidence is being able to see that justice is being done, and it is from this point of view that it is important that the individual, particularly in politically charged cases, should be able to test the law for himself.

A good example of the type of dilemma that can arise is *Re Lonhro Plc*[11] in which one of the reasons the House of Lords rejected the matter being referred to the Attorney General was that he and the Secretary of State, who was the respondent to the appeal by Lonrho (against the Secretary of State's refusal to publish an inspector's report and refer the Harrods take over to the Monopolies and Mergers Commission) 'were members of the same governmental administration which was or could have been affected by the contempt'.

As Professor Wade said[12] the Attorney General has a remarkable ability 'to detach himself from his political and personal ties when he has to act in his capacity of guardian of the law and of the public interest' but added 'Creditable though this ability is, it is not easily understood by the public'.

(iv) Other roles of the Attorney General   Apart from bringing, consenting or refusing to consent to prosecutions for contempt, the Attorney General may also apply for an injunction to restrain a planned publication on the grounds that it would amount to contempt. As will be seen[13] this step was first taken in *A-G v Times Newspapers Ltd*.[14] The procedure there was unusual in that during the course of investigating a complaint made by Distillers Ltd against the *Sunday Times* in respect of a previous article, the newspaper showed the Attorney General a copy of a further article which they intended to publish and it was agreed that that matter should go to court.[15] The Attorney General was also apparently shown, prior to its broadcast on BBC, a film about Lord Lucan, though no action was deemed necessary.[16]

The fact that proposed publications have been shown to the Attorney General may suggest that he provides an informal vetting service, but there are obvious limitations to when such a course of action can be undertaken. As Sir

---

8 But see further the discussion below.
9 [1974] AC 273 at 311.
10 The motivation behind the enactment was to give added protection to the media by providing a screening process for contempt applications, but this seems unnecessary given that under RSC Ord 52, r (2)1 (discussed at p 493) court leave must be obtained before committal proceedings can be brought.
11 [1990] 2 AC 154 at 176 per Lord Keith.
12 Wade and Forsyth: *Administrative Law* (7th edn) p 1010.
13 See p 500 for a discussion of injunctions to restrain possible contempts.
14 [1974] AC 273.
15 See the comments made by Sir Michael Havers as Attorney General during the committee stage of the Contempt of Court Bill in HC Official Report, SCA, 1980–81, col 133 (1981).
16 See the comments made by Sir Michael Havers as Attorney General during the committee stage of the Contempt of Court Bill in HC Official Report, SCA, 1980–81, col 133 (1981).

Michael Havers, the Attorney General, said during debate on the Contempt of Court Bill:[17]

> 'I should not like it to be thought that the Royal Courts of Justice will be a free legal aid bureau, that anyone can just pop along and say "I want to publish this next week. You won't mind will you?" Certainly we could not allow that to happen.'

The Attorney General has also been known to issue warnings against prejudicial coverage of certain notorious cases. One such warning was given in the Frederick and Rosemary West cases; another in the Peter Sutcliffe (the 'Yorkshire Ripper') case.[18]

(v) Assessment of the Attorney General's role The Attorney General plays a key role in the contempt prosecution process. It is a sensitive role and the decision whether or not to prosecute is an important one not just for its own sake in the particular case but because inaction (particularly if it is repeated) could well be taken as a yardstick by which publishers should be guided. It was noticeable, under the pre-1981 Act for example, that successive Attorneys did not prosecute, despite some clear cases, alleged contempts committed while proceedings were 'imminent' and so it might have been doubted (despite dicta suggesting it did) whether in fact the law applied so early.[19] The problem of relying on the Attorney General, however, is that there is no guarantee of consistency—some Attorneys have been more active than others.[1] Another possible criticism is the failure to prosecute in notorious cases particularly where the alleged offence has been committed by several of the media on the same matter.[2] There is a feeling in some quarters that the national media can 'get away' with more than the local press perhaps because of their collective strength and influence. Whether this is a fair criticism of the Attorney's General's office may be doubted. At any rate suggestions that the national media are always collectively immune from prosecution were dispelled by the prosecution in 1994 of ITN, the *Daily Mail*, *Today*, the *Daily Express* and the *Northern Echo* [3] and the earlier prosecution against five national newspapers in connection with the Michael Fagan (the intruder of the Queen's bedroom) case.[4] Another serious criticism is the Attorney General's role in politically sensitive cases. Mention has already been made of *Re Lonrho Plc* [5] in which the House of Lords were reluctant to leave the contempt prosecution to the Attorney General because Lonrho were already involved in an action against the Government. But perhaps more striking still was the 'Spycatcher' litigation in which the Government were seeking to use contempt to protect its own interests of confidentiality. In cases such as these the

17 HC Official Report 1980–81, SCA col 133.
18 In the Sutcliffe case a letter was in fact sent to newspapers by the Solicitor General (see eg *UK Press Gazette* 1981, p 775) and this was followed by a warning statement made by the Attorney General in Parliament.
19 For a discussion of when contempt applies see Ch 7.
1   The current Attorney General, Sir Nicholas Lyell, seems to have been particularly reluctant to bring contempt prosecutions, as his failure to do so in *R v Taylor and Taylor* (1994) 98 Cr App R 361 (discussed at p 150) and his refusal to seek an injunction to restrain publication of Betty Maxwell's book *A Mind of My Own* (see fn 18, p 140) well illustrates.
2   A particularly blatant example was the failure to prosecute in the *Sutcliffe* case despite the publicity surrounding his arrest.
3   *A-G v Independent Television News Ltd* [1995] 2 All ER 370, discussed at p 133.
4   *A-G v Times Newspapers Ltd* (1983) Times, 12 February, discussed at pp 149–150.
5   [1990] 2 AC 154, [1989] 2 All ER 1100.

Attorney's role, though as a matter of law quite distant from the Government, does smack of partisanship. In these cases there seems the need for another official to have the pivotal role.

Despite these criticisms, political cases apart, it is not sought to cast doubt upon the competence of the Attorney General and his staff to handle contempt cases. On the contrary, the office seems well suited to the task. On the other hand, handling contempt cases is but one of the many tasks falling upon the Attorney General. His office does not and could not undertake any systematic scrutiny of publications. Apart from notorious cases, impetus for action will come mainly from the litigants allegedly prejudiced by publicity. Whether this relatively haphazard scrutiny is thought to be satisfactory can be debated but it is difficult to see how the process can be improved without a massive injection of resources.

(vi) Committal applications not covered by s 7 Even in cases of criminal contempt not caught by s 7 it was nevertheless argued in *Dobson v Hastings* [6] that it is the exclusive right of the Attorney General to represent the public interest and that therefore individuals do not have *locus standi* to initiate contempt actions. In the event, however, the issue was left open. If this argument were to be accepted it would not only be contrary to the accepted practice before the 1981 Act of allowing individuals to apply for committals in respect of publication alleged to create a risk of prejudice to the proceedings in which they were involved, but it would also render pointless the enactment of s 7.

(c) Jurisdiction

(i) The Divisional Court of the Queen's Bench Division RSC Ord 52, r 1(2) provides that save in respect of contempts of the Court of Appeal the Divisional Court of the Queen's Bench Division has *sole* jurisdiction to make an order for committal in the following circumstances, namely, where contempt of court:

> '(a) is committed in connection with:
>> (i) any proceedings before a Divisional Court of the Queen's Bench Division, or
>> (ii) criminal proceedings, except where the contempt is committed in the face of the court or consists of disobedience to an order of the court or a breach of an undertaking to the court, or
>> (iii) proceedings in an inferior court, or
> (b) is committed otherwise than in connection with any proceedings.'

The effect of para 2 is that with regard to criminal contempts committed outside the court and in particular 'media' contempts the Queen's Bench Divisional Court has the major *original* jurisdiction.

(a) Paras 2 (a) (i) and 2 (b) In practice, the two important sub-paragraphs are 2(a)(ii) and (iii). Para 2(a)(i) covers the comparatively rare cases of disobedience to prerogative orders issued by the Divisional Court[7] and publications allegedly

---

6 [1992] Ch 394, 411, per Nicholls V-C. Cf *Pickering v Liverpool Daily Post and Echo Newspapers Plc* [1991] 2 AC 370, where the not dissimilar arguments over the *locus standi* of individuals to seek injunctions to restrain threatened contempts, was also left open. See p 500.
7 This would amount to civil contempt, see Ch 14.

prejudicial to proceedings before that court. Para 2 (b) refers to publications or acts said to 'scandalise' the court, prosecutions for which are unusual in this country.[8] Though not beyond doubt, para 2(b) also seems to refer to cases of victimising jurors and witnesses[9] at least where the proceedings in question have ended.[10]

It is to be noted that where the contempt is of the Court of Appeal, for example, that it is allegedly 'scandalised', that court has jurisdiction to hear the contempt application.[11] Whether the Divisional Court also has jurisdiction is unclear. The concluding words of r 1(2) are:

> 'This paragraph shall not apply in relation to contempt of the Court of Appeal.'

This could be read either as a denial of jurisdiction to the Divisional Court or simply a denial of *exclusive* jurisdiction in such cases. In the interests of flexibility the latter interpretation might seem preferable,[12] though a possible pointer against this is *Re Lonrho Plc* [13] in which it was held that Ord 52 had no application to the House of Lords and that the Divisional Court had no jurisdiction to hear committal applications respect of alleged contempts of the House.

(b) Para 2(a)(ii) Para 2(a)(ii) in practice covers most 'media contempts'. Criminal proceedings are not defined but seem to cover criminal proceedings before magistrates' courts, the Crown Court[14] and, depending upon the interpretation of the reservation under r 1(2) of the Court of Appeal's powers, the Court of Appeal (Criminal Division). In its commentary to the sub-paragraph the *Supreme Court Practice* [15] also includes proceedings before courts-martial. The Divisional Court has no jurisdiction in respect of contempts of the House of Lords.

(c) Para 2(a)(iii) The scope of para 2(a)(iii) is important since the corollary of holding that the Divisional Court has jurisdiction to hear a case is that the law of contempt applies to that tribunal. Denial of jurisdiction means a denial of the application of contempt to the tribunal.

Para 2(a)(iii) was originally drafted to reflect[16] the '*Davies* principle'[17] namely, that the High Court's contempt jurisdiction (now exercised by the Queen's Bench Divisional Court) was coextensive with its jurisdiction to correct

---

8   See Ch 9. Ironically, the last contempt prosecution for allegedly 'scandalising' the court was dealt with by the Court of Appeal at first instance. See note 11 below.
9   Miller, *Contempt of Court* (2nd edn) p 65 believes this to be the case.
10 The need for this qualification would seem to follow from the requirement under para 2(b) that the contempt is committed 'otherwise than in connection with any proceedings'.
11 See *R v Metropolitan Police Comr, ex p Blackburn (No 2)* [1968] 2 QB 150, [1968] 2 All ER 319.
12 Miller, *Contempt of Court* (2nd edn) p 65 assumes the latter interpretation applies.
13 [1990] 2 AC 154, [1989] 2 All ER 1100. Cf *DPP v Channel Four Television Co Ltd* [1993] 2 All ER 517, in which it was held in relation to breaches of orders made in criminal proceedings before the Crown Court , either that court or the Divisional Court could hear the application for committal.
14 Though as Miller (2nd edn) p 65, points out, this is despite the fact the Crown Court is a *superior* court of record. See further at pp 504–505. It does not cover breaches of orders made in criminal proceedings since they are clearly caught by the proviso. See *DPP v Channel Four Television Co Ltd.* [1993] 2 All ER 517, discussed at p 505.
15 52/1/13.
16 As noted earlier, the rules of court cannot properly be thought of as confining the inherent contempt power, see pp 465–466.
17 *R v Davies* [1906] 1 KB 32, discussed at pp 467–468.

tribunals by prerogative order. It was upon this principle that it became established that the Divisional Court had, in its supervisory capacity, jurisdiction to punish contempts committed in connection with proceedings before consistory courts,[18] courts-martial,[19] county courts[20] and probably, coroners' courts.[1]

In *A-G v BBC*,[2] however, the House of Lords ruled that para 2 (a) (iii) and therefore the law of contempt had a restricted ambit and in effect qualified the application of the *Davies* principle.

(d) The BBC Decision   The issue in the *BBC* case was whether a local valuation court constituted an 'inferior court' within para 2(a)(iii). It was unanimously held that it did not. Lord Salmon was content to dismiss the case upon the basis that:[3]

> 'public policy requires that most of the principles relating to contempt of court which have for ages necessarily applied to the long-established inferior courts such as county courts, magistrates' courts, courts-martial, coroners' courts and consistory courts shall not apply to valuation courts and the host of other modern tribunals which may be regarded as inferior courts; otherwise the scope of contempt of court would be unnecessarily extended and accordingly freedom of speech and freedom of the press would be unnecessarily contracted.'

Lord Edmund-Davies, similarly minded to confine contempts, attempted to do so by means of a conceptual definition of 'inferior court' but concluded[4] that there was 'no unmistakable hallmark by which a "court" or "inferior court" may unerringly be identified. It is largely a matter of impression.' His own 'firm' view was that a local valuation court was not such a body.

The majority (Viscount Dilhorne and Lords Fraser and Scarman) held that the contempt laws only protected courts discharging judicial rather than administrative functions, that is[5] 'courts of law which form part of the judicial system of the country' rather than 'courts which are constituted to resolve problems which arise in the course of administration of the government of this country'. They held that valuation courts fell on the administrative side of the line.

(e) The court of law test   The overall test that emerges from the case is that contempt only protects 'courts of law'. Identifying a 'court of law' is not easy and again their Lordships' approach differed. Viscount Dilhorne envisaged a two-fold test, namely, (1) is the body a 'court' and (2) is it a 'court of law'? With regard to the first question he thought that the parliamentary description of the body was important.[6] In his view, apart from the Lands Tribunal, any tribunal not otherwise labelled a 'court' by the relevant statute fails the first hurdle and is not protected by contempt. On this approach all bodies mentioned in what is now Schedule 1 to the Tribunal and Inquiries Act 1992 would be excluded save the Lands Tribunal, the Transport Tribunal (a statutory court of record[7]) and local valuation

18   *R v Daily Mail, ex p Farnsworth* [1921] 2 KB 733.
19   *R v Daily Herald, ex p Bishop of Norwich* [1932] 2 KB 402.
20   *R v Edwards, ex p Welsh Church Temporalities Comrs* (1933) 49 TLR 383.
 1   *R v Clarke, ex p Crippen* (1910) 103 LT 636 per Lord Coleridge J obiter at 641.
 2   [1981] AC 303, [1980] 3 All ER 161. For a detailed and critical analysis of this case see Lowe and Rawlings, 'Tribunals and the Laws Protecting the Administration of Justice' [1982] PL 418.
 3   [1981] AC 303 at 342E–F.
 4   Ibid at 351F.
 5   Per Viscount Dilhorne at 339H.
 6   Ibid at 338D–E.
 7   By the Transport Act 1985, Sch 4, para 1.

courts (which of course are held not to be 'courts of law'). In contrast, Lord Scarman, while adopting the same two-stage approach, thought that the parliamentary label was not conclusive one way or another.[8] According to him a 'court of law' can be identified:[9]

> 'as a body established by law to exercise either generally or subject to defined laws the judicial power of the state.'

All their Lordships had in mind the need to limit the application of contempt. It may be that they would all agree with Lord Salmon's policy orientated but less conceptual judgment that contempt only protects 'long established inferior courts', ie county courts, magistrates' courts, courts-martial,[10] coroners' courts and consistory courts. The 'court of law' test and in particular Lord Scarman's 'judicial power of the state' approach, however, permits a wider application for contempt. An added complication to determining the ambit of contempt is s 19 of the Contempt of Court Act 1981 which apparently following Lord Scarman's approach, defines 'court' for the purposes of the Act as including:

> 'any tribunal or body exercising the judicial power of the state.'

The ambit of this definition is a matter of some controversy being reminiscent of a clause[11] purporting to define the High Court's jurisdiction to protect inferior courts which was dropped from the Bill because of the difficulty in interpreting it and its potential wide ambit. However, it seems sensible that s 19 should be interpreted in line with the *BBC* decision[12] and perhaps in particular with Lord Scarman's judgment because (1) in the case of the 'strict liability rule' s 6(b)[13] provides that the Act cannot extend common law contempt liability and it seems sensible to give the same meaning to the definition for all purposes of the Act, and (2) the definition is so like Lord Scarman's approach, Parliament must have intended that approach to be followed.

An important limiting factor of their Lordships' approach is their insistence that merely because a body has to act judicially it does not follow that it is a court of law and according to Lord Scarman[14] a body's functions can remain administrative even though it has to perform duties which are judicial in character.

8   At least for the purposes of contempt: see [1981] AC 303 at 358D–E; cf his earlier statement at 358A, 'It ill behoves a judge to say that what Parliament says is a court is not a court.' Perhaps an added reason for not following Viscount Dilhorne's view is that s 19 of the Contempt of Court Act 1981 (see below) refers to a 'court' as including 'any tribunal or body exercising the judicial power of the state.'

9   [1981] AC 303 at 359G.

10 There may be some doubt as to whether courts-martial are courts of law. See the statutory provisions referred to at p 517.

11 Cl 7 in the original Bill provided inter alia: 'The jurisdiction of the High Court . . . to prohibit and punish contempt of court in or in respect of the proceedings of inferior courts extends to the proceedings of all inferior courts, tribunals and bodies (however described and whenever established) which are constituted by law and exercise any part of the judicial power of the state'.

12 Cf Geoffrey Robertson who in (1981) 106 The Listener 35, 171 asserted that because of s 19 the contempt laws protect 'industrial tribunals, sex discrimination tribunals and a host of inferior bodies that exercise in some form or other "judicial power" .' Cf Robertson and Nicol, *Media Law* (3rd edn) pp 382–86.

13 Discussed at p 117.

14 [1981] AC 303 at 359. It is submitted that this observation eliminates a number of tribunals that might otherwise have been categorised as 'courts of law'.

(f) The post BBC decisions In *Badry v DPP of Mauritius* [15] the Privy Council took the *BBC* case to have:

> 'plainly established—that, in the absence of statutory provision to the contrary, the law of contempt of court applies by definition only to courts of justice properly so called and to the judges of such courts of justice.'

In *Peach Grey & Co v Sommers* [16] Rose LJ said that it was 'clear from *A-G v BBC* that nomenclature as such is not decisive'. It has also become clear that s 19 of the 1981 Act cannot be interpreted as applying to tribunals at large. As Lord Donaldson MR (whose reasoning was approved by the House of Lords) said in *Pickering v Liverpool Daily Post and Echo Newspapers Plc*:[17]

> 'this definition must be intended to reflect the common law concept of what is a "court" for the purposes of the common law jurisdiction of the courts in relation to contempt of court.'

The two key decisions since the *BBC* case are *Pickering* and *Peach Grey*. The former established that mental health tribunals are 'courts' for the purpose of contempt. As Lord Donaldson MR pointed out,[18] following the ruling of the European Court of Human Rights in *X v United Kingdom*,[19] the function of mental health tribunals were changed under the Mental Health Act 1983 so as to include the power and the duty of applying statutory criteria and on the basis of their findings ordering or refusing to order the release of restricted patients from detention. They also have the power to subpoena witnesses.[20] In his Lordship's view if these tribunals are not 'courts' for all purposes then the United Kingdom would continue to be in breach of the European Convention on Human Rights since there is no indication that 'court' in that Convention has any different meaning from that which it bears in English Law. These considerations led Lord Donaldson MR to conclude that mental health tribunals were 'courts' for the purposes of contempt.[1] Lord Donaldson's reasoning was expressly upheld by the House of Lords but Lord Bridge added[2] that in his view the inclusion of proceedings before a mental health tribunal in s 12(1)(b) of the Administration of Justice Act 1960[3] was in itself an unequivocal indication that Parliament always intended that the tribunal should be a court to which the law of contempt applied.'

Peach Grey established that an industrial tribunal is an inferior court within the meaning of Ord 52, r 1 because, in the words of Rose LJ:[4]

15 [1983] 2 AC 297 at 307 per Lord Hailsham LC.
16 [1995] 2 All ER 513 at 520.
17 [1991] 2 AC 370 at 380. Cf however *R v Horsham Justices, ex p Farquharson* [1982] QB 762, [1982] 2 All ER 269, where it was assumed that s 4(2) applied, by reason of s 19, to tribunals at large.
18 [1991] 2 AC 370 at 380–81.
19 (1981) 4 EHRR 188.
20 Under the Mental Health Review Tribunal Rules 1983, r 14(1).
 1 In so concluding he overruled a previous decision to the contrary, namely, *A-G v Associated Newspaper Group Plc* [1989] 1 All ER 604.
 2 [1991] 2 AC 370 at 417.
 3 This provision, discussed in Ch 8, prohibits publications of information relating to certain proceedings heard in private.
 4 [1985] 2 All ER 513 at 519–520. This decision vindicates the view of Ellis and Miller, 'The Victimisation of Anti-Discrimination Complainants—Is it Contempt of Court?' [1993] PL 80, 88–89 and Lowe and Rawlings, 'Tribunals and the Laws Protecting the Administration of Justice' [1982] PL at 424. It is of interest to note that such tribunals were included in the list of tribunals proposed by the Opposition in connection with the then cl 7 of the Contempt of Court Bill (which clause was subsequently dropped), HC Official Report, 1980–81 SCA,

'It sits in public to decide cases which affect the rights of subjects and it has power to compel the attendance of witnesses, administer oaths, control the parties' pleadings by striking out and amendment and order discovery; it has rules of procedure relating to the calling and questioning of witnesses and addresses on behalf of the parties; it can award costs, it must give reasons for its decision which, on a point of law, can be appealed to the Employment Appeal Tribunal and Court of Appeal. In all it appears to me to exercise judicial functions.'

In the light of the above mentioned case law the Divisional Court has jurisdiction over the following bodies:

(1) the 'long established inferior courts' referred to by Lord Salmon in the *BBC* case[5]. It will be noted that this includes coroners' courts[6] although it has to be admitted that the distinction between the discharge of judicial and administrative functions is not particularly appropriate in this context;

(2) the Lands Tribunal;[7]

(3) mental health tribunals; and

(4) industrial tribunals.

Whether any other tribunal listed in Schedule 1 to the Tribunal and Inquiries Act 1992 can be considered a 'court of law' can be debated. However, in the light of the *Peach Grey* decision there is an argument that the Child Support Appeal Tribunals are 'courts'.[8] Like industrial tribunals their decisions affect the rights of subjects, they can compel the attendance of witnesses; parties can be legally represented; they have to give reasons for their decision, which on a point of law can be appealed to a Child Support Commissioner and these to the Court of Appeal.[9] Not dissimilar arguments can be made in favour of Social Security Appeal Tribunals.[10] There must also be a strong case for considering Immigration Appeal Tribunals.[11] Of the bodies outside the 1971 Act a strong case can be made for considering Election Courts.[12] Some have argued that the Prison Board of

---

Contempt of Court, col 182 and Lord Hailsham expressed the view, 416 HL Official Report (5th series) col 230, that they ought to be protected since they directly affect the liberty of the subject.

5   Ie county courts, magistrates' courts, courts-martial, coroners' courts and consistory courts. The judicial power of the *state* might be thought to exclude courts-martial and consistory courts but Lord Scarman (ibid at 360) expressly included them saying that 'the judicial system is not limited to the courts of the civil power.'

6   Apart from Lord Salmon both Viscount Dilhorne, [1981] AC 303 at 338E and Lord Edmund-Davies ibid at 349D, thought them 'courts' and implied that they were protected by contempt. See also *R v R v West Yorkshire Coroner, ex p Smith (No 2)* [1985] 1 QB 1096, [1985] 1 All ER 100, discussed at p 508 and *R v Surrey Coroner, ex p Campbell* [1982] 2 All ER 545 at 553, per Watkins LJ. In Australia see *A-G (NSW) v Mirror Newspapers Ltd* [1980] NSWLR 374.

7   This was expressly singled out by Viscount Dilhorne, [1981] AC 303 at 338H as having a different status from the rest of the tribunals listed under what was then the Tribunal and Inquiries Act 1971, Sch 1.

8   Such tribunals were set up by the Child Support Act 1991, s 21 and the procedure is controlled by the Child Support Appeal Tribunals (Procedure) Regulations 1992 (S1 1992/2641).

9   Child Support Act 1991, ss 24 and 25.

10 Set up originally by the Social Security Act 1975 and now controlled by the Social Security Administration Act 1992, ss 40, 41 and Sch 2.

11 Set up originally under the Immigration Appeals Act 1969, and now controlled by the Immigration Act 1971, s 12 and Sch 5.

12 Not least because they are statutorily designated courts of record under the Representation of the People Act 1983, s 110(2). See further p 508.

Visitors when exercising their disciplinary actions constitute 'courts of law' but it is submitted that this is not so.[13] On the other hand a stronger case can be made for Parole Boards since not unlike mental health tribunals they have the final say on whether to release (and to recall) long-term prisoners.[14]

(g) Courts of law exercising administrative decisions A further complication is that a body generally designated a 'court of law' can exercise both judicial and administrative functions. It seems that when exercising the latter function the proceedings are not protected by contempt. Magistrates, for example, when acting as licensing justices, discharge an administrative function and, as such, have been held not to be protected by contempt.[15] The Crown Court also has dual functions[16] and will only be protected in respect of its judicial function.

(h) The application of the 'court of law' test to other types of contempt As Rose LJ said in *Peach Grey* [17] the emphasis on the importance of freedom of speech underpinned the obvious concern of their Lordship's in the *BBC* case 'not to extend to multifarious fringe bodies the protection conferred on courts and judges by the inhibitions of free speech inherent in this form of contempt'. It could be argued therefore that different policy considerations in other types of contempt, for example, contempt in the face of the court and interfering with the witness, could lead to a different definition of 'court'.[18] In fact it has been hinted that in relation to interfering with witnesses the Divisional Court may have wider inherent powers than those contained 'in what may be the purely procedural provisions of Ord 52'.[19]

(i) The position in other jurisdictions Not surprisingly the problem of which bodies the law of contempt protects has been discussed in other jurisdictions. In South Africa, for example, a similar if less detailed conclusion than that given by the House of Lords in the *BBC* case was reached by the Supreme Court of South Africa (Transvaal Provincial Division) when it ruled that contempt did not apply to the Erasmus Commission.[20] In Australia it has been ruled, following the *BBC* case, that the Investigating Committee set up under the Medical Practitioners Act 1938, s 27, was not a body within the protection of the Supreme Court's powers in relation to contempt of court.[1] On the other hand it has been held that a Commissioner appointed under the Workers' Compensation Act 1987 was a 'court' for contempt purposes.[2]

---

13 They do have functions which are 'judicial' in character. See *R v Hull Prison Board of Visitors, ex p Germain* [1979] QB 425,[1979] 1 All ER 701 though as eg Lord Scarman said in the *BBC* case ([1981] AC 303 at 359H) that in itself would not make them 'courts of law'. On the other hand they have been held to fall outside Article 6 of the European Convention on Human Rights, see *Kiss v UK* (1976) 7 D & R 55 and *Campbell v UK* (1978) 14 D & R 186. See also Lowe and Rawlings, 'Tribunals and the Laws Protecting the Administration of Justice' [1982] PL at pp 424–5.

14 Criminal Justice Act 1991, s 50 and the Parole Board Rules 1992 (SI 1992/1829).

15 *Lewis v BBC* [1979] CA Transcript 193 approved by Lord Edmund-Davies in the *BBC* case [1981] AC 303 at 348F.

16 See *Kavanagh v Chief Constable of Devon and Cornwall* [1974] QB 624, [1974] 2 All ER 697.

17 [1995] 2 All ER at 520.

18 See Lowe and Rawlings, [1982] PL at 425–428.

19 Per Rose LJ in *Peach Grey* [1995] 2 All ER 513 at 520, relying in turn on Lord Salmon in *A-G v BBC* [1981] AC 303 at 344.

20 *S v Sparks* 1980 (3) SA 952 at 960–961 and *S v Gibson* 1979 (4) SA 115.

1 *X v Amalgamated Television Services Pty Ltd* (1987) 9 NSWLR 575.

2 *New South Wales Bar Association v Muirhead* (1988) 14 NSWLR 173.

(ii) Single judges of the High Court and Court of Appeal   RSC Ord 52, r 1(3) provides inter alia:

'Where contempt of court is committed in connection with any proceedings in the High Court, then, subject to paragraph (2), an order of committal *may* be made by a single judge of the Queen's Bench Division except where the proceedings were assigned or subsequently transferred to some other Division, in which case the order *may* be made *only* by a single judge of that other Division' (emphasis added).

The effect of this paragraph is that where contempt is alleged to have been committed in connection with civil proceedings (for example by means of publications likely to prejudice such proceedings or threatening witnesses connected with the proceedings) before any judge of any Division of the High Court, then a single judge of that Division has jurisdiction to hear the case.

It will be noted that whereas r 1(3) provides in effect that a judge of the Chancery or Family Division has *sole* jurisdiction to hear contempt applications in connection with proceedings before the respective Divisions,³ the position is less certain where the application relates to proceedings before the Queen's Bench Division. One commentator⁴ considers that in such cases either a single judge or the Divisional Court has jurisdiction. However, although that course has been adopted,⁵ it is not the invariable practice.⁶ Moreover, it is worth pointing out that Ord 52 does not confer contempt jurisdiction on the Divisional Court in respect of *civil* proceedings in the Superior Courts.

Ord 52, r 1 (4) provides:

'Where by virtue of any enactment the High Court has power to punish or take steps for the punishment of any person charged with having done anything in relation to a court, tribunal or person which would, if it had been in relation to the High Court, have been a contempt of that Court, an order of committal may be made by a single judge of the Queen's Bench Division.'

The effect of this paragraph is to give a single judge of the Queen's Bench Division jurisdiction to hear cases of contempt concerning, for example, tribunals of inquiry established under the Tribunals of Inquiry (Evidence) Act 1921, which provides that where a person does anything which, if the tribunal were a court of law having power to commit for contempt would have been a contempt of court, his offence may be certified to the High Court, which may punish the offender as if it were a contempt of the High Court.⁷

Order 52, r 1 also expressly reserves the power of the Court of Appeal to hear cases of alleged contempt of that court, as for example, where it is alleged that a publication is prejudicial to civil proceedings before that court. It also seems that where a publication is allegedly scandalous of the Court of Appeal (irrespective of the Division), the Court of Appeal (Civil Division) will hear the case.⁸

---

3   For examples, see in the Chancery Division: *Vine Products Ltd v Green* [1966] Ch 484, [1965] 3 All ER 58 and *Re Duncan* (1969) Times, 20 May and in the Family Division, *Re F (a minor) (Publication of Information)* [1977] Fam 58, [1976] 3 All ER 274 and *Re B (JA) (an infant)* [1965] Ch 1112, [1965] 2 All ER 168.

4   Miller, *Contempt of Court* (2nd edn) p 67.

5   *A-G v London Weekend Television Ltd* [1972] 3 All ER 1146, [1973] 1 WLR 202 was heard in the Queen's Bench Divisional Court.

6   See eg *A-G v Hislop* [1991] 1 QB 514, [1991] 1 All ER 911.

7   See also the Army Act 1955, s 101; Air Force Act 1955, s 101; Naval Discipline Act 1957, s 65; Nuclear Installations (Licensing and Insurance) Act 1959 Sch 1, para 7, the Pipe Lines Act 1962 Sch 5, para 7 and the Parliamentary Commissioner Act 1967, s 9 (1).

8   As in *R v Metropolitan Police Comr, ex p Blackburn (No 2)* [1968] 2 QB 150, [1968] 2 All ER 319.

(iii) House of Lords and Privy Council   As we have discussed, *Re Lonrho Plc*[9] establishes that RSC Ord 52 has no application to contempts of the House of Lords but, as that case shows, the House has power to prosecute contempts both outside and, a fortiori, in the face of the court, on its own motion.

The full ambit of contempt power of the Judicial Committee of the Privy Council has yet to be explored but it is to be noted that s 7 of the Judicial Committee Act 1843 provides that for 'better punishing contempts, compelling appearances and enforcing judgements' the Judicial Committee has the same power as a judge of the High Court of Admiralty.

(d)   Procedure

(i) Applications to a Divisional Court   No application can be made to a Divisional Court for an order of committal unless leave to make such an application has first been granted.[10] To obtain such leave, an application must be made, ex parte, to a Divisional Court, except in vacation when the application may be made to a judge in chambers. The application must be supported by a statement setting out the name and description of the applicant, the name, description and the address of the person sought to be committed, and the grounds on which the committal is sought. The facts relied upon must be verified by affidavit, and filed before the application is made.[11] It should be noted that an applicant must normally rely on the grounds set out in this statement, since unless the court gives leave no new grounds can be relied upon at the hearing.[12]

Notice of the application for leave must be given by the applicant not later than one day before the application is made, such notice being given to the Crown Office, and at the same time, copies of the statement and affidavit must also be lodged in that office.[13]

If a judge in chambers refuses to grant leave, a fresh application may be made to a Divisional Court,[14] in which case the application must be made within eight days of the judge's refusal, but if the Divisional Court does not sit within that period, the application must be made on the first day on which the Divisional Court sits.[15]

Once leave has been given, the applicant may proceed to apply for an order of committal. The application for such an order must be made by motion to a Divisional Court, and unless the court or judge granting leave has directed otherwise there must be at least eight clear days between the service of the notice of the motion and the day named therein for the hearing.[16] If no motion is entered for hearing within 14 days of leave being granted, then the leave will lapse.[17]

Notice of motion accompanied by a copy of the statement and affidavit in support of the application for leave must be served personally upon the person sought to be committed,[18] but the court or judge can dispense with service if the

 9   [1990] 2 AC 154, [1989] 2 All ER 1100, discussed at p 477.
10   RSC Ord 52, r 2(1).
11   Ord 52, r 2 (2).
12   Ord 52, r 6(3), see p 498.
13   Ord 52, r 2(3).
14   Ord 52, r 2(4).
15   Ord 52, r 2(5).
16   Ord 52, r 3(1).
17   Ord 52, r 3(2).
18   Ord 52, r 3(3), for the meaning of 'personal' service, see Ch 14.

court or judge thinks it just to do so.[19] In practice, however, personal service will rarely be dispensed with in cases of criminal contempt but one situation where it would be theoretically possible for service to be dispensed with is where the offender is deliberately evading service.[20]

It is now established that a litigant in person may move both the application for leave and the motion for committal in the Divisional Court.[1]

(ii) Applications to a single judge of the High Court (other than the Family Division) and to the Court of Appeal   Where an application may be made to a single judge of the High Court (ie where the contempt is committed in connection with civil proceedings before one of the various Divisions other than the Family Division of the High Court) or to the Court of Appeal, the application must be made by motion and be supported by an affidavit.[2] Unlike committal applications in a Divisional Court, therefore, there is *no* requirement to apply for leave to apply. Notice of motion stating the grounds of the application and accompanied by a copy of the affidavit in support of the application, must be served personally on the person sought to be committed,[3] although the court can dispense with service of the notice of motion if it thinks it just to do so,[4] but again this will rarely, if at all, occur in cases of criminal contempts.

The notice of motion[5] should be entitled in the cause in connection with which the contempt has arisen, and it is also convenient and proper to so entitle it where the application is directed against a stranger to the cause, in which case it should also be entitled in the matter of the particular application.[6] Though not beyond doubt it seems that where the application is directed against a stranger it ought then to be filed and dealt with as an originating application.[7]

It now seems that litigants can apply in person for a committal order.[8]

(iii) Applications to a single judge of the High Court (Family Division)   Rule 7.2(1) of the Family Proceedings Rules 1991 provides that committal applications in matrimonial proceedings in the High Court are to be made by *summons* rather than motion which means that applications are heard in chambers rather than in

---

19   Ord 52, r 3(4).
20   The dispensing with service is more usually associated with cases of civil contempt, and even then only in exceptional circumstances, see *O'Donovan v O'Donovan* [1955] 3 All ER 278, [1955] 1 WLR 1086, discussed at p 620.
1   See the *Supreme Court Practice* 52/2/1 citing *Practice Note, Divisional Court* [1947] WN 218 and *Ex p Collet* (unreported, 10 October 1952, QBD). See also 9 *Halsbury's Laws* (4th edn) para 91 n 2.
2   Ord 52, r 4(1).
3   Ord 52, r 4(2). At the hearing the applicant will only be allowed to rely on the grounds set out in this statement: Ord 52, r 6(3). See p 498.
4   Ord 52, r 4(3).
5   The notice in the Chancery Division is of a motion before a judge of the appropriate group. In the Queen's Bench Division the notice of motion is set down in the Crown Office to be heard before a judge sitting in court, and a judge will be assigned. The motion is a two-day motion.
6   See *O'Shea v O'Shea and Parnell* [1890] 15 PD 59, and *Alliance Perpetual Building Society v Belrum Investments Ltd* [1957] 1 WLR 720 at 722.
7   Such at any rate was the view of Oswald, *Contempt* (3rd edn) p 208 and seems to be implicit in the commentary in the *Supreme Court Practice*, 52/4/1. Cf *Re B (JA) (an infant)* [1965] Ch 1112, [1965] 2 All ER 168, dealt with below.
8   See *Bevan v Hasting Jones* [1978] 1 All ER 479, [1978] 1 WLR 294, where Goulding J reluctantly held that the former embargo no longer applied in the Chancery Division, and *De Vries v Kay* (1978) Times, 7 October in which it was held that the embargo no longer applied in the Queen's Bench Division.

court.[9] It is not yet established whether applications can be made by litigants in person but the trend in other Divisions would suggest that they can.[10] Apart from these points the position at least with regard to matrimonial proceedings is the same as in the other Divisions.[11]

The position with committal applications in wardship proceedings and other child proceedings under the High Court's inherent jurisdiction[12] is perhaps less certain. Prima facie r 7.2(1) of the Family Proceedings Rules 1991 applies equally to these proceedings as it does to any other 'family proceedings'.[13] However, the *Supreme Court Practice* continues to state[14] that in wardship (and, presumably, in proceedings under the High Court's general inherent jurisdiction with respect to minors) applications may be made by motion. This comment is no doubt based on *Re C (a minor) (Contempt)*[15] in which the Court of Appeal indicated that a motion was the proper procedure. That decision, however, pre-dates the new Rules and it is perhaps a moot point whether it remains good law. Certainly both before and after the decision the Family Division has accepted committal applications by summons.[16]

The essential difference between procedure on motion and procedure by summons is that a motion is heard in court and a summons in chambers, though its distinction is blurred because under Ord 52, r 6 motions can be heard in private while in practice summonses are listed for hearing in open court, though again they can be heard in private. However, because of this technical difference, it used to be thought[17] that procedure by motion was more appropriate in case of contempt by strangers (as in the case of unlawful publications of proceedings)[18] since as such matters are essentially outside the domestic context it was difficult to justify proceeding in chambers. Whether this thinking remains valid is debatable though no doubt provided the defendant has properly been served with notice the court would override any objection to the precise procedure adopted.

Where application is by motion it is established[19] that, even if the contempt does not directly concern the ward, the proper practice is (1) to bring a motion within the wardship proceedings rather than to proceed by originating motion, and (2) for evidence to be by formal affidavit exhibiting a statement of the facts relied on by the person making the affidavit. The reason for this is that unlike a normal affidavit, a formal affidavit exhibiting a statement prevents the public having access to the evidence. Such a rationale would seem to justify extending

9   This distinction is blurred by the fact that by Ord 52, r 6 (to which FPR 1991, r 7.2(1) is expressly subject) motions for committal can be heard in private. See below.
10 See the cases cited in n 8 above.
11 Ie RSC Ord 52, r 4 applies save for its reference to a motion.
12 For a discussion of the scope of this inherent jurisdiction and its relationship to the wardship jurisdiction see White, Carr and Lowe, *The Children Act in Practice* (1995) Ch 12.
13 Rule 1.2 defines 'family proceedings' for these purposes by reference to s 32 of the Matrimonial and Family Proceedings Act 1984, which in turn defines such proceedings as those assigned to the High Court, Family Division which, by Sch 1, para 3(b)(ii) to the Supreme Court Act 1981, includes the inherent jurisdiction with respect to minors.
14 See the 1985 edition at 52/4/1.
15 [1986] 1 FLR 578 (CA).
16 For the pre-1986 practice see Lowe and White, *Wards of Court* (2nd edn) pp 8–31 and the second edition of this work at 339. For a post-1991 example see eg *Official Solicitor v News Group Newspapers* [1994] 2 FLR 174.
17 See Lowe and White at pp 8–31 and the second edition of this work at pp 339–340.
18 Application was by motion in *Re F (Orse A)* [1977] Fam 58, [1977] 1 All ER 114, CA. See also *Re R (MJ)* [1975] Fam 89, [1975] 2 All ER 749.
19 *Re B (JA) (an infant)* [1965] Ch 1112, [1965] 2 All ER 168 per Cross J and see the *Supreme Court Practice* 52/4/1.

the practice to other cases concerning children where the proceedings are heard in private.

(iv) The need for strict compliance with the rules of procedure   The rules concerning an application for committal will normally be strictly construed particularly those designed to protect the alleged contemnor. As Cross J (as he then was) said in *Re B (JA) (an infant)*:[20]

> 'Committal is a very serious matter. The courts must proceed very carefully before they make an order to commit to prison; and rules have been laid down to secure that the alleged contemnor knows clearly what is being alleged against him and has every opportunity to meet the allegations. For example, it is provided that there must be personal service of the motion on him even though he appears by solicitors, and that the notice of motion must set out the grounds on which he is said to be in contempt; further, he must be served as well as with the motion, with the affidavits which constitute the evidence in support of it.
>
> It is clear that if safeguards such as these have not been observed in any particular case, then the process is defective even though in the particular case no harm may have been done. For example, if the notice has not been personally served the fact that the respondent knows all about it, and indeed attends the hearing of the motion, makes no difference. In the same way, as is shown by *Taylor v Roe*,[1] if the notice of motion does not give the grounds of the alleged contempt or the affidavits are not served at the same time as the notice of the motion, that is a fatal defect, even though the defendant gets to know everything before the motion comes on, and indeed answers the affidavits.'

On the other hand not every defect in the notice of motion will be fatal to the action, for provided that the alleged contemnor can in no way be prejudiced by the defects:[2]

> 'then it seems . . . that there is no reason why the courts should be any slower to waive such technical irregularities in a committal proceeding than they would be in any other proceeding.'

In *Taylor v Roe* it was held that a notice of motion marked before 'Mr Justice Kekewich' instead of before 'Mr Justice Stirling' was a defect which could be remedied by giving leave to amend the notice of motion. In *Re B (JA) (an infant)* it was held that the omission on the notice of the words 'Solicitors for the Plaintiffs' was a mere technical irregularity which could be waived. Further objections were taken in the same case, for example, that certain affidavits were defective for containing the following statement:

> 'I of [giving the description] make oath and say as follows: There is now produced and shown to me marked . . . a statement of facts signed by me . . . I depose to the matters set out in my said statement of fact of my own knowledge.'

Cross J, did not think that the form of the affidavit was very satisfactory, it being better to say that: 'the statements in the exhibited statements are to my knowledge true', but it was not so defective as to render the affidavit bad. It was also argued that the affidavits were defective because the commissioner of oaths had not stated his address but it was held that while there may have been force in that argument had the affidavits been sworn in London, since the object of the requirement was to ensure identification of the commissioner in case of difficulty,

20 [1965] Ch 1112 at 1117–18.
1 [1893] WN 14.
2 *Re B (JA) (an infant)* [1965] Ch 1112 at 1118, per Cross J. For numerous other cases see Ch 14 at pp 619–621 and 631–632.

this was not the case here since in a small town there would be no more than one or two commissioners altogether. As Cross J said:[3]

> 'The absence of the address seems to me to be a matter of little importance, although I think strictly it should be given. But assuming that it is a defect it is an irregularity which is certainly not in any way fatal.'

It was further argued that the affidavits were defective because one party did not give her address or occupation but again it was held that this omission amounted to an irregularity that could be waived.

(v) Legal aid   Although, as will be seen,[4] the position with regard to obtaining legal aid in respect of contempts committed in the face of the court is clear, the position is far less certain with regard to contempts committed outside court. Assuming contempt proceedings are classified as 'criminal proceedings' for the purposes of s 19 of the Legal Aid Act 1988 then criminal legal aid is prima facie available in any contempt proceedings before magistrates' courts,[5] the Crown Court, the criminal division of the Court of Appeal or the Courts-Martial Appeal Court and the House of Lords when hearing appeals from either of those courts. It is not available for proceedings before the High Court or the civil division of the Court of Appeal. It is, however, by no means certain that contempts committed outside court are classifiable as 'criminal proceedings' for these purposes. The fact that special provision is made under s 29 of the Legal Aid Act 1988[6] for contempts in the face of the court could be taken to indicate that s 19 does not apply to contempts at all. If that interpretation is right (and in any event in the case of prosecution for contempts not committed in the face of the court before the High Court or *civil* division of the Court of Appeal) application must be made for civil legal aid.[7]

(e)   The hearing of the application

(i) Hearing normally in open court   Under RSC Ord 52, r 6(1) an application for a committal order must normally be heard in open court but the hearing may take place in private in the following circumstances:

'(a)   where the application arises out of proceedings relating to the wardship or adoption of an infant or wholly or mainly to the guardianship, custody, maintenance or upbringing of an infant, or rights of access to an infant;

(b)   where the application arises out of proceedings relating to a person suffering or appearing to be suffering from mental disorder within the meaning of the Mental Health Act 1983;

(c)   where the application arises out of proceedings in which a secret process, discovery or invention was in issue;

(d)   where it appears to the court that in the interests of the administration of justice or for reasons of national security the application should be heard in private . . .'

---

3   Ibid at 1120.
4   See p 521.
5   In fact any contempt punishable by magistrates is covered by s 29 of the Legal Aid Act 1988, see p 521.
6   Discussed at p 521.
7   Ie the anomaly first adverted to in the first edition of this work (see pp 275–277) still applies.

If the court hears the proceedings in private and makes an order of committal Ord 52, r 6(2) provides that the name of that person, the general nature of the contempt committed and the length of the period of committal should be stated in open court.[8] It has been held, however, that the failure to comply with these requirements can be remedied by the court under Ord 2, r 1 by a subsequent statement in open court.[9]

(ii) The timing of the hearing   In *R v Hargreaves, ex p Dill* [10] and *R v Editor of the Sunday Express* [11] Lord Goddard CJ commented that where a publication is alleged to constitute contempt because of possible prejudice to particular proceedings, the application to commit should not be heard until after the relevant proceedings have been completed. As he said: 'if the publication has in fact done any harm, the hearing of the application only emphasises that harm.' This comment seems well made in relation to criminal proceedings and has since been adopted as regular practice.[12] However, it is less apposite to civil proceedings since they may not be heard for some time after the publication in question. Accordingly, contempt hearings are sometimes heard before the civil proceedings are completed.[13]

(f)   Evidence

Unless the court hearing the application gives leave, the applicant at the hearing of the application for a committal order can only rely on the grounds set out in the statement accompanying either (a) the application for leave to apply for a committal order before the Divisional Court, or (b) the notice of motion[14] before the other courts.[15] This statement will have been personally served upon the person sought to be committed thereby giving the offender an opportunity of preparing a defence.[16]

---

8   This provision followed the recommendation of Justice in their report: *Contempt of Court* (1959) pp 21–22.
9   *Re C (Contempt: Committal Order)* [1989] 1 FLR 288, CA. As is commented at [1989] Fam Law at 189 'the oversight in no way prejudiced the contemnor, nor was it in the public interest that the contemnor be let free upon such a technicality'.
10   [1954] Crim LR 54, (1953) Times, 4 November.
11   (1953) Times, 25 November.
12   Lord Goddard CJ's recommendation had been supported by *Justice: Contempt of Court* (1959) p 34 and has been commended as a wise practice by an Australian judge ie Connor J in *Re Whitlam, ex p Garland* (1976) 8 ACTR 17 at 19–21. See now *A-G for NSW v John Fairfax & Sons* [1980] 1 NSWLR 362 and *Hinch v A-G* [1987] VR 721. One consequence of this procedure is that the decision whether to prosecute for contempt is delayed. There is some evidence to suggest that an accused's plea at the relevant trial can influence the decision whether to prosecute for contempt. Query whether this is desirable?
13   See eg *Vine Products Ltd v Green* [1966] Ch 484, [1965] 3 All ER 58 where the contempt proceedings were heard six months before the action was due to be heard, and *A-G v News Group Newspapers Ltd* [1987] QB 1, [1986] 2 All ER 833 (the 'Botham libel case') where the contempt proceedings were heard ten months before the estimated time when the libel action could have been heard. (In fact the main proceedings were never heard.) Cf *A-G v Hislop* [1991] 1 QB 514 where the contempt was delayed until after the main libel action had been completed.
14   And, presumably, summons.
15   Ord 52, r 6(3). A committal based on contempts proved by the judge which are not set out in the committal notice is invalid: *Javadi-Babreh v Javadi-Babreh* (1992) Independent, 16 November. This is without prejudice to Ord 20, r 8 which allows inter alia correcting any defects or errors in the proceedings.
16   Ord 52, r 2(2) and r 4(2).

Evidence is by way of affidavit[17] but if the person sought to be committed expresses the wish to give oral evidence on his own behalf he is entitled to do so.[18] As evidence is normally given on affidavit there is usually no cross-examination of the applicant.[19] However, according to the Phillimore Committee[20] the person sought to be committed has the right to require the applicant and his witnesses to be present for cross-examination. It would seem though that the court has a discretion whether or not to allow cross-examination on the affidavit.[1]

The defendant is not a compellable witness but if he voluntarily chooses to give evidence he cannot as of right refuse to be cross-examined.[2]

It has been held in Canada that statements contained in affidavits based solely on information and belief cannot be used or relied upon to support a conviction for criminal contempt but the court has a discretion to accept those parts of any affidavit based on the affiant's personal knowledge.[3]

In *Re Bramblevale Ltd*[4] Lord Denning MR, said that:

> 'contempt of court is an offence of a criminal character. A man may be sent to prison for it. It must be satisfactorily proved. To use the time honoured phrase, it must be proved beyond all reasonable doubt.'

That case was a case of civil contempt, and although there is no English case directly in point, if the requisite standard of proof in a civil contempt is the same as in a crime, a fortiori this must be true in a case of criminal contempt. Accordingly, before a person will be committed for a criminal contempt the offence must be proved beyond all reasonable doubt. In practice there will rarely be a dispute about the facts, especially in 'newspaper contempts', but occasionally there may be a doubt as to the true meaning of the words in a published article and in these cases the person sought to be committed should be given the benefit of the doubt.

3 Injunctions

(a) Jurisdiction and procedure

It is well established that an injunction can properly be granted to restrain an obstruction to justice and in particular to certain publications or planned publications that are calculated to prejudice proceedings actually in progress or those about to be heard.[5]

---

17 See 9 *Halsbury's Laws* (4th edn) para 96 and see the authorities cited in note 3.
18 Ord 52, r 6(4).
19 See the Phillimore Committee's Report (1974, Cmnd 5794) para 16.
20 Ibid at para 16.
1 See 9 *Halsbury's Laws* (4th edn) para 96.
2 *Comet Products UK Ltd v Hawkex Plastics Ltd* [1971] 2 QB 67 at 76, [1971] 1 All ER 1141 at 1145–6 per Megaw LJ.
3 See *Re New Brunswick Electric Power Commission and Electrical Workers' Union* (1976) 73 DLR (3d) 94 at 98 relying on *Gilbert v Endean* (1878) 9 Ch D 259.
4 [1970] Ch 128 at 137.
5 See eg *Brook v Evans* (1860) 29 LJ Ch 616 (injunction refused); *Coleman v West Hartlepool Harbour and Rly Co* (1860) 2 LT 766; *Kitcat v Sharpe* (1882) 52 LJ Ch 134; *A-G v Times Newspapers Ltd* [1974] AC 273, [1973] 3 All ER 54; *Thorpe v Waugh* [1979] CA Transcript No 282 (Civil Division); *A-G v BBC* [1981] AC 303, [1980] 3 All ER 161; *Peacock v London Weekend Television* (1985) 150 JP 71; *A-G v News Group Newspapers Plc* [1987] QB 1, [1986] 2 All ER 833 and *Pickering v Liverpool Daily Post and Echo Newspapers Plc* [1991] 2 AC 370 (though in the latter two cases the application failed). See also 24 *Halsbury Laws* (4th edn) para 1032.

Application for such injunctions are treated like any other such application, that is, they are subject to RSC Ord 29.[6] Although originally associated with the Court of Chancery, under the Supreme Court Act 1981, s 37(1) every branch of the High Court has jurisdiction in appropriate cases. Nevertheless it is not unknown for an application to restrain a publication of potentially prejudicial material to be dealt with by the Divisional Court of the Queen's Bench Division.[7] In the Queen's Bench and Family Division application is made to a judge in chambers on summons[8] but in the Chancery Division it should be made on motion.[9]

(b)　Who can apply?

The Attorney General undoubtedly has locus standi to apply for an injunction to restrain possible contempts. The first such application was in *A-G v Times Newspapers Ltd*[10] and he has since sought an injunction in *A-G v BBC* [11] and *A-G v News Group Newspapers Ltd.*[12]

Whether the Attorney General has the exclusive right to seek such injunctions is more problematic. In this respect there are two issues, namely, the relevance of s 7 of the Contempt of Court Act 1981[13] and the effect of the decision in *Gouriet v Union of Post Office Workers.*[14]

So as far as s 7 is concerned it was settled by the Court of Appeal in *Peacock v London Weekend Television Ltd* [15] that it has no relevance to an application to restrain publication. In that case the Police Federation successfully sought an injunction to restrain the broadcast of a television programme on the grounds that it would cause a substantial risk of serious prejudice to a pending coroner's inquest into the death of a youth whilst questioned by the police.

Despite *Peacock* it was subsequently argued in *Pickering v Liverpool Daily Post and Echo Newspapers Plc* [16] that only the Attorney General can seek an injunction to restrain a threatened contempt. On the facts the plaintiff was held not to have locus standi to seek an injunction because as a mental patient he had no cause of action for breach of statutory duty in respect of an unauthorised publication about the proceedings on his application to a mental health tribunal for discharge.[17] In reaching this decision Lord Bridge (giving judgment for the House) expressly disapproved[18] of the majority of the Court of Appeal approval

6　Ie not Ord 52, see p 477.
7　As in *A-G v Times Newspapers Ltd* [1974] AC 273, [1973] 3 All ER 54; *A-G v BBC* [1981] AC 303, [1980] 3 All ER 161. Cf *A-G v News Group Newspapers Ltd* [1987] QB 1, [1986] 2 All ER 833 and *Pickering v Liverpool Daily Post and Echo Newspapers Plc* [1991] 2 AC 370, in which the application was dealt with by a single judge.
8　Save where it is ex parte in which case application can be made on affidavit, see the *Supreme Court Practice* 29/1/7.
9　Though in a very urgent case application may be made ex parte on affidavit, see the *Supreme Court Practice* 29/1/7.
10　[1974] AC 273, [1973] 3 All ER 54.
11　[1981] AC 303, [1980] 3 All ER 161.
12　[1987] QB 1, [1986] 2 All ER 833.
13　Discussed at pp 480 ff.
14　[1978] AC 435, [1977] 3 All ER 70.
15　(1985) 150 JP 171, full transcript available on Lexis.
16　[1991] 2 AC 370.
17　Ie no right of action accrues to a patient for breach of r 21(5) of the Mental Health Review Tribunal Rules 1983.
18　[1991] 2 AC 370 at 425.

of Lord Denning MR's earlier minority view in *Chief Constable of Kent v V* [19] that s 37 of the Supreme Court Act 1981 overrode previous case law and that the only limitation upon the court's power to grant injunctions is that the plaintiff must have a 'sufficient interest'. On the other hand Lord Bridge declined to decide the general locus standi point and indeed expressly left open the question of whether a party to the proceedings could properly seek to restrain someone else from publishing part of the evidence.[20] Lord Bridge gave no further explanation for this particular reservation. However, it is certainly arguable that in the light of *Gouriet*, which establishes[1] that in general private individuals cannot sue in their own name on behalf of the public to restrain a threatened breach of the criminal law they can if they would suffer some special damage from the crime, that litigants or parties (but not any other member of the public) to a criminal prosecution who claim that a threatened publication is potentially prejudicial to their case do have locus standi.[2]

(c) Evidence

In *A-G v BBC*[3] both Lord Denning MR and Lord Scarman stressed that the prior restraint of publication is a drastic interference with freedom of speech and an injunction should be granted only in a clear case where it would manifestly be a contempt for the publication to take place. Further evidence that a strong case is needed is the decision in *Schering Chemicals Ltd v Falkman Ltd*[4] where, in circumstances strikingly similar to that of the *Sunday Times* case,[5] an injunction to restrain the broadcasting of a film about the drug 'Primodos' was refused even though it was evident that the proposed film dealt with some of the issues raised in a pending action against the plaintiff company.

An injunction was also refused in *A-G v News Group Newspapers Ltd*[6] (the Botham libel case) but in that case it was held that the appropriate test was the same as that for establishing a contempt under the strict liability rule, namely, did the proposed publication create a substantial risk of serious prejudice to the proceedings in question. If the answer is yes then the Court of Appeal held an injunction would be granted notwithstanding the rule in *Bonnard v Perryman*[7] that repetition of libel cannot be restrained where the publisher intends to plead justification. In the Botham case itself no substantial risk was thought to be occasioned by a publication so far in advance of the projected date of the hearing (at least ten months).[8]

19 [1983] QB 34, [1982] 3 All ER 36.
20 [1991] 2 AC 370 at 425.
1 See Feldman, 'Injunctions and the Criminal Law' (1979) 42 MLR 369.
2 The locus standi point was not raised in *Thorpe v Waugh* [1979] CA Transcript 282 (Civil Division).
3 [1981] AC 303 at 311 and 362. For a similar approach in Australia see *Victoria v BLF* (1982) 152 CLR 25 in which Mason J said (at 96–97) that the view of Lord Scarman as expressed in *A-G v BBC* 'more nearly reflects the existing common law position in Australia than does the approach taken in *Times Newspapers*'. See also Wilson J at 135. In Canada see *Dagenais v Canadian Broadcasting Corpn* (1995) 120 DLR (4th) 12, (Can Sup Ct).
4 [1982] QB 1, [1981] 2 All ER 321.
5 NB Lord Denning MR's distinction that whereas the Attorney General brought the prosecution in the *Sunday Times* case and so involving the *public* interest, in this case the action was brought by the individual in their own interest, ibid at 20–21. This, with respect, seems an unconvincing argument.
6 [1987] QB 1, [1986] 2 All ER 833.
7 [1891] 2 Ch 269.
8 For a detailed discussion of this case, see Ch 6, pp 188 ff.

It is submitted that the approach in the *Botham* case has the dual merit of being logical and at the same striking the right balance between freedom of speech and fair trial.

4   Courts acting upon their own motion

All superior courts of record have inherent jurisdiction to punish upon their own motion contempts committed in or out of the court in connection with proceedings before that court.[9] The Contempt of Court Act 1981, s 7 specifically reserves this power[10] as does RSC Ord 52, r 5 with regard to the High Court[11] and Court of Appeal. It is also established that the Crown Court has such powers[12] and it is submitted that such powers are also vested in the Courts-Martial Appeal Court.[13]

(a)   When applicable

The circumstances when a court should act upon its own motion were considered in detail by the Court of Appeal in *Balogh v Crown Court at St Albans*.[14] That case established that the power should only be used where it is imperative and urgent to act immediately so that the contempt in question must therefore constitute a clear threat to the administration of justice either in a case being heard, about to be heard or possibly, just over,[15] and the contempt must be clearly proved beyond any reasonable doubt. If *any* of these requirements cannot be satisfied then a judge should not as a matter of practice[16] proceed upon his own motion but instead refer the matter to the Attorney General who can then proceed by a motion to commit under RSC, Ord 52. In *Balogh* itself, it was thought that there was no urgency to justify immediate action since the defendant had been apprehended before his plan to disrupt court proceedings could be put into action.[17] Subsequently, in *Rooney v Snaresbrook Crown Court*,[18] it was thought improper for the court to proceed upon its own motion because the alleged contempt (dismissal of a man from his employment allegedly as punishment for serving as a juror) could not be proved with sufficient certainty.

Although it was accepted that the criteria justifying immediate action are more likely to be satisfied with regard to contempts committed in the face of the court,

---

9 See p 467.
10 Cf *A-G v English* [1983] 1 AC 116, [1982] 2 All ER 903, where the trial judge, Farquharson J is reported (at 121 and 907) as saying that 'under the new Act I am only really concerned with contempts in the face of the court in dealing with them myself.' See also Lord Diplock's comment at 138A and 916a that the Attorney General's consent is now a requisite under the 1981 Act. Both seem to have overlooked s 7 which specifically preserves the court's right to act upon its own motion.
11 Including the Restrictive Practices Court, see p 506.
12 See *Balogh v Crown Court at St Albans* [1975] QB 73, [1974] 3 All ER 283, the Supreme Court Act 1981, s 45(4) and see p 504.
13 See p 505.
14 [1975] QB 73, [1974] 3 All ER 283.
15 Per Lord Denning MR ibid at 84. Query the 'urgency' in such cases?
16 As a matter of law there is jurisdiction notwithstanding the absence of urgency. See *R v Griffin* (1989) 88 Cr App Rep 63, at 69, per Mustill LJ.
17 See also *Weston v Central Criminal Court, Courts Administrator* [1977] QB 32, [1976] 2 All ER 875, CA.
18 (1978) 68 Cr App Rep 78, CA. See also *R v Griffin* (1989) 88 Cr App Rep 63, a case involving interfering with witnesses where the judge was held to have acted too precipitously.

it was acknowledged that they could be satisfied in respect of contempts committed outside the court. There was general agreement that the power could properly be exercised in respect of threats made against witnesses[19] or jurors.[20] Lawton LJ went further suggesting[1] that, depending upon the circumstances, it could well be proper for a judge to proceed upon his own motion against 'persons out of court who publish comments about a trial going on by revealing a defendant's criminal record when the rules of evidence exclude it'.

Lawton LJ was the only judge to contemplate a prosecution, upon the court's own motion, of a newspaper for alleged contempt by publication though it is to be noted that his example was confined to publications of the accused's past criminal record. Such prosecutions are not unknown. In the case involving the *North West Evening Mail*,[2] the editor was fined by the trial judge at Preston Crown Court for publishing during the trial that an accused had entered certain guilty pleas (this was done before the jury had been empanelled). Now that it seems incumbent upon judges to make a specific order forbidding such publications[3] it might be expected that they will be more ready to deal with any subsequent contempt themselves.[4]

It is submitted that judges should be extremely slow to act upon their own motion against the media in respect of alleged contempt by publication.[5] Such a procedure deprives defendants of many of the safeguards of a normal trial and it would be better to deal with the matter by a motion for committal. In any event once the offending article has been published or broadcast the damage is done and in that sense it might be thought that there is no 'urgency' to try the case immediately. However, speed might be thought justifiable where a damaging publication is threatened or where some damage has already been done but repetition is threatened. It may then be proper for the trial judge to make an interim injunction restraining publication.[6]

(b) Procedure

The procedure to be followed when the court acts upon its own motion will be considered when dealing with prosecutions of contempts in the face of the court.

(c) Private judicial warnings

Akin to acting upon their own motion is the practice resorted to by some judges of privately warning alleged offenders against repeating particular acts. Although not officially reported journalists and editors in particular are apparently not infrequently asked to go before a judge to explain their conduct. This is done usually quite informally (ie before the judge privately) and the journalists so appearing are not normally legally represented. Private warnings are to be distinguished from public warnings that are sometimes issued by a judge in open

19 See *Moore v Clerk of Assize, Bristol* [1972] 1 All ER 58, [1971] 1 WLR 1669.
20 See (1966) 130 JP 622 and *R v Gough* (1982) Times, 15 November.
 1 [1975] QB 73 at 93C–D.
 2 (1981) Times, 7 February.
 3 Under s 4(2) of the Contempt of Court Act 1981, discussed in Ch 8.
 4 Ie the contempt will then be the disobedience of a specific order.
 5 Though s 7 of the Contempt of Court Act 1981 preserves this possibility.
 6 For the power to grant injunctions see pp 499–502.

court warning the press against committing contempt in a particular or even general respect. These in turn are to be distinguished from formal orders.[7]

The propriety of private warnings seems questionable especially as there is no check on whether the judge is applying the law correctly. On the other hand, given that journalists are not actually punished a warning is likely to be as effective a deterrent as a formal prosecution and might be justified in so protecting the administration of justice. It should be said, however, that it would seem quite in order for those thus informally called to appear before a judge, to take a legal adviser with them.

5   Jurisdiction and power of specific courts

(a)   Crown Court

The Crown Court which replaced both quarter sessions and assizes was created by the Courts Act 1971. Its contempt jurisdiction is now[8] set out by the Supreme Court Act 1981, s 45(4) which states:

> 'Subject to s 8 of the Criminal Procedure (Attendance of Witnesses) Act 1965 (substitution in criminal cases of procedure in that Act for procedure by way of subpoena) and to any provision in or having effect under this Act, the Crown Court shall, in relation to the attendance and examination of witnesses, any contempt of court, the enforcement of its orders and all other matters incidental to its jurisdiction, have the like powers, rights, privileges and authority as the High Court.'

Prima facie the Crown Court has, both by its status as a superior court of record and by s 45(4), the same contempt powers and jurisdiction in relation to contempts committed in connection with proceedings before it, as the High Court. In practice, however, its jurisdiction is more circumscribed.

A particular problem is the relationship between the Crown Court's contempt powers and RSC Ord 52. As we have seen,[9] according to Ord 52, r 1(2)(a)(ii) the Queen's Bench Divisional Court has sole jurisdiction to make committal orders in respect of criminal contempts committed in connection with *criminal* proceedings[10] other than those committed in the face of the court. Insofar as this purports to restrict the Crown Court's power to punish contempts committed outside the court, Ord 52, r 1 seems incompatible with the court's inherent powers and s 45(4). The resolution of this apparent conflict is provided by the Court of Appeal's decision in *Balogh v Crown Court at St Albans*.[11] There it was held, in effect, that although it is not open to the Rules to confine the inherent contempt jurisdiction yet they can and do provide the procedure.

Hence, properly construed, all that Ord 52, r 1 does is to provide a procedure by which applications for committal may be made. However, this does not prevent a superior court, including therefore the Crown Court, acting upon its own motion. The result of *Balogh* is that applications for committal in relation

---

7   Eg under s 4(2) of the Contempt of Court Act 1981.
8   Formerly the Courts Act 1971, s 4(8).
9   See p 486.
10   Cf contempts comprising the breaking of a court order or undertaking: *DPP v Channel Four Television Co Ltd* [1993] 2 All ER 517, discussed below.
11   [1975] QB 73, [1974] 3 All ER 283.

to criminal proceedings before the Crown Court can only be made to the Queen's Bench Divisional Court. On the other hand, the Crown Court retains its power to act upon its own motion. However, as we have seen,[12] *Balogh* also established that such a power should not be readily resorted to particularly with regard to contempts committed outside the court. Hence, in practice the Crown Court's powers to deal with contempts committed outside the court are restricted to those which can be clearly established[13] and which require immediate action, the least controversial examples[14] being the intimidation or harassment of witnesses or jurors during the trial.

Special mention needs to made of *DPP v Channel Four News Co Ltd*,[15] which concerned the breach of an order made in criminal proceedings in which the television company was asked to produce documents relating to a programme that they had broadcast. It was held that as this type of contempt fell into the proviso under Ord 52, r 1 (2)(a)(ii),[16] prima facie both the Crown Court and the Divisional Court had jurisdiction. Woolf LJ added, however, that in the case of breach of orders made under Schedule 7(3) to the Prevention of Terrorism (Temporary Provisions) Act 1989, committal applications should invariably be heard by the Divisional Court.[17]

It is submitted that the Crown Court can grant injunctions to prevent repeated contempts since it has a like power to that of the High Court. It would seem proper to invite the judge to grant an (interim) injunction to prevent a threatened contempt.[18]

(b)   The Courts-Martial Appeal Court

The Courts-Martial Appeal Court was established by the Courts-Martial (Appeals) Act 1951. There is no direct statutory reference to the court's contempt jurisdiction but some jurisdiction would seem to be vested by virtue of the fact that it is a superior court of record. Such an inference is not negatived by the general jurisdiction provisions under the Courts-Martial (Appeals) Act 1968.[19] Section 1 provides inter alia:

'(2)   The Appeal Court shall be a superior court of record and shall for the purposes of this Act and subject to its provisions have full power to determine, in accordance with this Act, any question necessary to be determined for the purpose of doing justice in any case before the Court.

(3)   The powers of the Appeal Court shall be exercisable by them so far as they think it necessary or expedient in the interests of justice that they should be exercised, and the Court may issue any warrants necessary for enforcing their orders or sentences.'

12   See pp 502–503.
13   Cf *Rooney v Snaresbrook Crown Court* (1978) 68 Cr App R 78 and *R v Harbax Singh* [1979] QB 319, [1979] 1 All ER 524, CA.
14   Though Lawton LJ ([1975] QB at 93) contemplated the procedure being used against persons 'who publish comments about a trial going on by revealing a defendant's criminal record when the rules of evidence exclude it'.
15   [1993] 2 All ER 517, CA.
16   A contempt that 'consists of disobedience to an order of the court or a breach of an undertaking given to the court'.
17   [1993] 2 All ER 517 at 520 h–j.
18   For a detailed discussion on the power to grant injunctions see pp 499–502.
19   Which Act replaced the 1951 Act.

Being a superior court of record would seem to vest the court with power to act upon its own motion[20] with respect to contempts committed both in and out of the court.

(c)   Restrictive Practices Court

The Restrictive Practices Court is a superior court of record.[1] Its contempt jurisdiction is set out by s 9(3) of the Restrictive Practices Court Act 1976, namely:

'In relation to the attendance and examination of witnesses, the production and inspection of documents, the enforcement of its orders, and all other matters incidental to its jurisdiction, the Court shall have the like powers, rights, privileges and authority—
(a)   in England and Wales, as the High Court;
(b)   in Scotland, as the Court of Session; and
(c)   in Northern Ireland, as the High Court of Northern Ireland.'

It is established that these provisions confer upon the Restrictive Practices Court a wide contempt jurisdiction. The court can therefore not only, as it is expressly empowered to do, enforce the attendance and examination of witnesses, the production and inspection of documents and enforce its orders, but can also punish both contempts committed in its face and those committed outside the court (eg publications creating a risk of prejudice to proceedings before the court). As Diplock J said in *Re Cement Makers' Federation's Agreement*:[2]

'it is desirable to state publicly that this court [ie the Restrictive Practices Court] is by statute a superior court of record, and possesses in relation to all matters incidental to its jurisdiction the like powers, rights, privileges and authority in England and Wales as the High Court. Proceedings before it are sub judice, and the publication of any matter tending to interfere with the due course of justice in proceedings before this court is subject to the ordinary sanctions as respects contempt of court'.

Diplock J continued by saying that this does not mean that no comment may be made about the proceedings since the:

'jurisdiction of the court is peculiar and relates to matters which are properly of public interest, and controversy. But the publication of any matter calculated to deter or influence witnesses who may appear before the court,[3] or to substitute trial by newspapers for trial by this court while a hearing is proceeding amounts to contempt of court and will be dealt with accordingly.'

The court can also punish contempts committed after the proceedings have been completed, as for example, where witnesses have been punished for having given evidence.[4]
Section 9(4) of the 1976 Act provides:

'No person shall be punished for contempt of the Court except by or with the consent of a judge who is a member of the Court.'

---

20 See pp 502–503 for when it is proper so to proceed.
1   By s 1(1) of the Restrictive Practices Court Act 1976.
2   [1961] 2 All ER 75 at 96.
3   See eg *Re Doncaster and Retford Co-operative Societies' Agreement (Practice Note)* (1960) LR 2 RP 129 discussed at p 198, *Practice Note* (1961) LR 2 RP 168 (questionnaire sent to customers).
4   *Re A-G's Application, A-G v Butterworth* [1963] 1 QB 696, [1962] 1 All ER 321, see Ch 11.

Although s 9(4) does not state that the contempt must always be *tried* by a judge of the Restrictive Practices Court, it seems doubtful whether any other court and in particular the Queen's Bench Divisional Court has jurisdiction save possibly where the alleged contempt comprises a publication or other act said to 'scandalise' the court. Even then it seems unlikely that a party would wish to take the case to the Divisional Court, after having first obtained the necessary consent from the Restrictive Practices Court, especially since the powers of the courts are synonymous. Whether it was intended that the Restrictive Practices Court should have sole jurisdiction in this way may be questioned since it would seem that the court can only proceed upon its own motion, which as we have seen is not normally an approved procedure for prosecuting media contempts. Any committal order that is made by the Restrictive Practices Court may be executed on the authority of a warrant signed by the presiding judge, or one of the judges sitting as a member of the court making the order.[5] Presumably, before a publisher can be found guilty of contempt for *unintentionally* creating a risk of prejudice to proceedings before the Restrictive Practices Court, the requirements of the 'strict liability rule' under the Contempt of Court Act 1981 must be satisfied. Hence proceedings must be 'active', which in this context will be when the case has been set down for trial,[6] and the publication must create a 'substantial risk of serious prejudice' to those proceedings.[7] The publisher will also have the defences under ss 3 and 5 of the 1981 Act.[8]

B Contempts committed in the face of the court

1 Jurisdiction and powers

(a) Courts vested with an inherent contempt jurisdiction

As we have seen, the authorities favour the view that *all* courts of record whether superior or inferior have an inherent jurisdiction to punish contempts committed in their face. Such inherent jurisdiction can, however, be fettered, extended or replaced by statute provided that is the legislature's clear intention. Parliament can also confer a contempt jurisdiction upon non-courts of record. So far as England and Wales is concerned, all courts of record previously referred to have inherent jurisdiction to deal with contempts committed in their face. As we have dealt with the scope of the inherent jurisdiction in Chapter 2 no further explanation is required.

An *inherent* jurisdiction to punish contempts in the face of the court seems to vest in coroners' courts and might also vests in other bodies that are statutorily designated courts of record. The major inferior courts, the county court and magistrates' courts have a statutory contempt jurisdiction as do courts-martial. We shall consider these statutory jurisdictions shortly but first we shall examine the claims of other courts to an inherent contempt jurisdiction.

---

5 *Practice Direction* [1961] 2 All ER 11.
6 Ie because they will be proceedings other than criminal or appellate proceedings and will be governed by Sch 1, paras 12–14 of the 1981 Act. On timing generally see Ch 7.
7 Under s 2(2) of the 1981 Act, discussed at pp 113 ff.
8 Discussed at pp 175 ff and 398 ff respectively.

(i) Coroners' courts   *R v West Yorkshire Coroner, ex p Smith (No 2)*[9] seems finally to have settled the question of whether coroners' courts are courts of record and as such have an inherent power to punish contempts committed in their face. The Divisional Court ruled on the basis of 'an overwhelming body of judicial opinion[10] and learned academic opinion'[11] that such courts were inferior courts of record which have the power to commit for contempt in the face of the court. In Stephen Brown LJ's view this conclusion was further supported by Lords Salmon and Scarman's assumption in *A-G v BBC*[12] that a coroner's court was a court of law and by the fact that the terms of what is now the Coroners Act 1988 makes a similar assumption. In this latter respect s 10 (3) states:

> 'The power conferred upon a coroner by this section [to enforce attendance of jurors and witnesses[13]] shall be in addition to and not in derogation of any other power which the coroner may possess:
>
> (a)   for compelling any person to appear and give evidence before him in any inquest or other proceedings; or
>
> (b)   for punishing any person for contempt of court in not so appearing and giving evidence but a person shall not be fined by the coroner under this section and also be punished under any such other power.'

Accordingly, the Divisional Court upheld the coroner's decision to fine Smith £50 for his serious contempt in accusing one of the witnesses during the inquest of murdering his daughter.

(ii) Statutorily designated courts of record   A number of courts in England are statutorily designated courts of record which status, prima facie at least, seems to vest them with power to punish contempts in their face.[14] Whether it was Parliament's intention so to vest such courts is far from clear and remains so far an untested point. Although the statutory designation seems haphazard it is nevertheless suggested that in the absence of any other explanation[15] it should be taken that the status, court of record, does in fact vest such bodies with a contempt jurisdiction. Accordingly, on this basis the following have such a jurisdiction: the Transport Tribunal under the Transport Act 1985, Sch 4, para 1, the Election Court under the Representation of the People Act 1983, s 123(2) and the Court of Appeal against the refusal to institute an incumbent under the Benefices Act 1898, s 3(1).

Perhaps the strongest claim of the above courts to a contempt jurisdiction, at least on the wording of the statute, is the Election Court for s 110(2) of the above mentioned Act states:

9 [1985] 1 QB 1096, [1985] 1 All ER 100.
10 *Garnett v Ferrand* (1827) 6 B & C 611 at 625, per Tenterden CJ; *Thomas v Churton* (1862) 2 B & S 475 at 478, per Crompton J, arguendo; and *R v Clarke ex p Crippen* (1910) 103 LT 636 at 641, per Lord Coleridge J. Contra *Jewison v Dyson* (1842) 9 M & W 540 at 586, *Garnett v Ferrand* was cited with approval by Watkins LJ in *R v Surrey Coroner, ex p Campbell* [1982] QB 661, [1982] 2 All ER 545. The coroners' court has been held to be a court of record in Canada by *Davidson v Garrett* (1899) 30 OR 653 at 656 and in Australia by *Chippett v Thompson* (1868) 7 NSW SR 349, and *A-G (NSW) v Mirror Newspapers Ltd* [1980] 1 NSWLR 374.
11 Coke's *Institutes* (1797 edn, 4 Co Inst 271), 9 *Halsbury's Laws* (4th Edn) paras 1002 and 1103, *Jervis on the Office and Duties of Coroners* (9th edn, 1957) p 23 and the second edition of this work at p 351. See also *Blackstone* 4 BL 271 repeated in Stephen's *Commentaries*, Bk 4, p 341.
12 [1981] AC 303 at 342 and 355–56; [1980] 3 All ER 161 at 169 and 179.
13 Ie as provided by s 10(1) and (2).
14 See pp 466–467.
15 See p 466, n 11.

'The Election Court shall, subject to the provisions of this Act, have the same powers, jurisdiction and authority as a judge of the High Court (or, in Scotland, a judge of the Court of Session providing at the trial of a civil cause without a jury) and shall be a court of record.'

(b) Courts vested with a statutory contempt jurisdiction

(i) County courts *(a) Jurisdiction exclusively statutory* It is well established that county courts have no inherent contempt jurisdiction but that instead their powers solely derive from statute, namely now, the County Courts Act 1984. This issue was first authoritatively determined in *R v Lefroy* [16] in which Cockburn CJ commented that the:[17]

'statute itself under which the county courts are constituted points out what was the extent of the power of punishing for contempt intended to be conferred upon them. . . . We therefore must understand the legislature to have confined the power to the instances given and to the extent limited.'

It was thus held that a county court judge had no power to punish the author of a letter (published in a local newspaper) which strongly condemned the conduct of a county court judge in a certain case. This decision was followed in *R v Brompton County Court Judge* [18] where it was held that a county court had no jurisdiction to punish as for contempt a person who acted as a solicitor in an action in the county court without being qualified. Cave J said:[19]

'The legislature decided . . . that it could not entrust such a general and unlimited power to the county court judges, but gave them, instead, a special jurisdiction to punish by a limited fine or by imprisonment of limited duration certain specified offences, all of which were of the nature of contempts of court.'

More recently, *Lefroy* was applied in *Bush v Green* [20] in which it was held that a county court judge had no jurisdiction to punish a litigant for contempt for giving information about proceedings in which she was involved to the local press. In so holding the Court of Appeal also rejected the argument based on s 38 of the County Courts Act 1984 that, in this instance, the county courts' powers were as extensive as those of the High Court. The court held that an application for committal was a proceeding on its own and did not arise out of a 'cause of action for the time being within [the court's] jurisdiction'. Section 38 therefore could not be considered to confer jurisdiction to hold the defendant in contempt. In other words although s 38 confers equal powers with the High Court when enforcing orders (ie when dealing with civil contempt)[1] it does not confer jurisdiction to punish criminal contempts.

In those cases where the alleged contempt falls outside the statutory jurisdiction application to commit should be made to the Queen's Bench Divisional Court

---

16 (1983) LR 8 QB 134.
17 Ibid at 138.
18 [1893] 2 QB 195.
19 Ibid at 200.
20 [1983] 3 All ER 721, [1985] 1 WLR 1143, CA. See also *R v Bloomsbury County Court, ex p Brady* (1987) Times, 16 December (full transcript on Lexis) and *Bokhari v Blessed* (1995) Independent, 16 January, CA (full transcript on Lexis).
 1 Hence on this basis county courts have been held to be able to enforce their orders by way of sequestration, see *Rose v Laskington* [1990] 1 QB 562, [1989] 3 All ER 306.

which has a supervisory jurisdiction to protect county courts.[2] It remains now to examine the statutory jurisdiction.

(b) The statutory powers   The main provision dealing with contempt is s 118(1) of the 1984 Act under which any person who:

> '(a)   wilfully insults the judge of a county court, or any juror or witness, or any officer of the court during his sitting or attendance in court, or in going to or returning from the court; or
> (b)   wilfully interrupts the proceedings of a county court or otherwise misbehaves in court'

can, by order of the judge (including for these purposes, a district judge, assistant district judge or deputy district judge),[3] be taken into custody and detained until the rising of the court. Additionally, an offender can be imprisoned for a maximum period of one month or fined an amount not exceeding level 4 on the standard scale,[4] or both.

The leading case on the application of s 118 is *Bokhari v Blessed*[5] which establishes that the section applies equally to proceedings in chambers[6] as well as to proceedings in open court and to arbitration proceedings as well as to full court proceedings. In that case, the Court of Appeal upheld a £500 fine imposed on Bokhari for wilfully insulting[7] a witness after leaving the court room but still in the hearing of the district judge. In reaching this conclusion the court rejected the argument that s 118 had no application since this was not a contempt in the face of the court. It was held that s 118 could not be confined to contempts in the face of the court for, as Bingham MR pointed out, s 118(1)(a) expressly applies to wilful insults to a judge, juror, witness or officer of the court 'during his sitting or attendance in court, or in going or returning from the court'. In his Lordship's view the conduct in question was certainly caught by s 118, though he added that in any event, given that the insults were 'directly witnessed by the judge's own senses, in as much as he himself directly heard what was said and the tone of the voice in which it was said', was in the face of the court.

The ruling in *Bokhari* that s 118(1)(a) is not confined to contempts in the court's presence is in line with that of the Court of Appeal in *Bodden v Metropolitan Police Commissioner*,[8] that 'wilful interruptions' under the equivalent provision protecting magistrates' proceedings under s 12 of the Contempt of Court Act 1981[9] applies to conduct in or outside the court provided it actually disrupts the proceedings. No doubt a similar interpretation should be placed on s 118(1)(b).

In contrast to *Bokhari* and *Bodden* is *R v Bloomsbury County Court, ex p Brady*.[10] In that case a husband, who was involved in proceedings against his

---

2   Ie under RSC Ord 52, r 1(2)(a)(iii) discussed at p 486. See *Bush v Green*, supra and *R v Bloomsbury County Court, ex p Brady*, supra. Query whether the supervisory jurisdiction can be used in cases *within* s 118? If so, contemnors could be subject to larger penalties but this would seem to be contrary to *Gouriet v Union of Post Office Workers* [1978] AC 435, [1977] 3 All ER 70.
3   S 118 (3).
4   Currently £2,500.
5   (1995) Independent, 16 January, full transcript on Lexis.
6   Relying inter alia on *Friend v Wallman* [1946] KB 493 and *Re Johnson* (1887) 20 QBD 68.
7   By saying 'If you come near me I'll break your f . . . neck' and thereafter abusing him with foul language.
8   [1990] 2 QB 397, [1989] 3 All ER 833.
9   Discussed at p 513.
10 (1987) Times, 16 December, full transcript on Lexis.

estranged wife, alleged that he had been threatened by her and another man in connection with his defence in the proceedings and the evidence which he might have given. It was held that as the contempt in question was not in the face of the court, it fell outside s 118. In reaching this conclusion Lloyd LJ expressly said that the section 'is clearly dealing with contempt in the face of the court'.

Although the approach in *Bloomsbury* is inconsistent with that of the Court of Appeal in *Bokhari* both decisions seem clearly right. It is submitted that they are best reconciled upon the basis of whether or not the conduct in question fell within the terms of s 118 rather than on whether or not the contempt was in the face of the court. Although the legislation undoubtedly reflects the former common law position[11] by limiting county courts' jurisdiction essentially to dealing with contempt in the face of the court, the statutory position is not an exact replica since it includes the power to punish those who insult judges, jurors, witnesses or officers of the court on their way to or return from court. Hence while it might be right to say that conduct falling outside the terms of s 118 cannot be regarded as contempt in the face of the court, it does not necessarily follow that conduct within s 118 must necessarily be contempt in facie curiae. The proper approach, it is submitted, when determining county courts' jurisdiction to punish a contempt, is to have regard to the wording of s 118 bearing in mind that since it deals with criminal offences the section should be construed strictly against the prosecution. In this latter regard it may well be right in cases of difficulty, to bear in mind the common law distinction between contempts committed in the face of the court and those committed outside the court. On this basis it is submitted that in *Chester Corpn v Rothwell* [12] a county court judge was wrong to have committed a litigant to prison for his contempt during an adjournment in sending a letter to the judge 'mainly concerning the gross Travesty of Justice as exemplified in your Court'.

For further discussion of how s 118 should be applied, regard should be had to the growing body of case law on the application of the almost identically worded s 12 of the Contempt of Court Act 1981 which we discuss in relation to magistrates' powers.[13]

In addition to s 118, s 14(1) of the 1984 Act provides:

'If any person assaults an officer of a court while in the execution of his duty, he shall be liable—(a) on summary conviction, to imprisonment for a term not exceeding three months or to a fine of an amount not exceeding level 5 on the standard scale,[14] or both; or (b) on an order made by the judge in that behalf, to be committed for a specified period not exceeding three months to prison or to such a fine as aforesaid, or to be so committed and to such a fine, and a bailiff of the court may take the offender into custody, with or without warrant, and bring him before the judge.'

As the Court of Appeal observed in *Blackburn v Bowering*,[15] s 14(1)(b) enables the county court to exercise what is in effect a contempt jurisdiction.[16] However, notwithstanding that s 14 provides two procedures, one by way of summary prosecution, the other on application to the county court judge, the

11 See *R v Lefroy* (1873) LR 8 QB 134 at 138 per Cockburn CJ.
12 (1940) 7 LJCCR 58. Writing letters to judges are not normally classified as contempts in the face of the court; cf in Canada *R v Vallieres* (1973) 47 DLR (3d) 378.
13 See pp 513–515.
14 Currently £5,000.
15 [1994] 3 All ER 380, [1994] 1 WLR 1324.
16 Hence appeals lie to the Civil Division of the Court of Appeal under s 13 of the Administration of Justice Act 1960, see p 535.

choice of procedure cannot affect the nature of the conduct which must be proved to establish liability.[17]

The 1984 Act does not define 'assault' for these purposes but the Court of Appeal in *Blackburn v Bowering* held that it must have the same meaning as in other areas of criminal law and that accordingly to be guilty it must be proved that the defendant 'knew that his use of force was unlawful, or, put another way, that he did not believe his use of force to be lawful'.[18] In *Blackburn* the Court of Appeal accepted the following propositions, namely, (1) before an offence under s 14 can be established it must be shown that the other person was an officer of the court who was at the material time acting in the execution of his duty;[19] (2) it does not have to be proved that the defendant knew the person to whom he applied force was a court officer or that he knew that the officer was acting in the execution of his duty;[20] but (3) the section does require proof of an assault. To satisfy this third requirement a court must judge the defendant on the basis of what (reasonably or unreasonably) he believed to be the facts of the case. If as in *Blackburn*, a plea of self-defence is raised on the basis that the defendant did not know the plaintiffs' capacity but had acted on the mistaken but honest belief they were victims of an unlawful attack, then an offence can only be established, if in the light of the facts as they were assumed to be, the force used was excessive.

It will be noted that only 'officers of the court' are protected. For these purposes such officers are defined[1] as any county court registrar (district judge), deputy registrar (district judge) or assistant registrar (district judge) and 'any clerk, bailiff, usher or messenger in the service of that court'.

Surprisingly, therefore, assaults upon barristers or solicitors cannot be protected under s 14, though where such conduct takes place in the court room they could be punished under s 118.[2]

In addition to s 14, the court has power under s 92 to punish any person who 'rescues or attempts to rescue any goods seized in execution under process of a county court'. Like s 14, s 92 provides two procedures either by way of summary prosecution or upon application to the judge. The maximum penalty is imprisonment for one month or a fine of an amount not exceeding level 4 on the standard scale,[3] or both.

(c) Warrant of committal   Normally a warrant of committal for contempt is bad unless it specifies the exact nature of the contempt,[4] but it has been established by *Levy v Moylan* [5] that where the contempt committed consists in insulting the court, the nature of the insult need not be specified in the warrant.

It has also been established that a warrant of committal which has been regularly made out at the rising of the court is not void on account of a previous irregular oral sentence having been pronounced by the judge, and entered in the

17 Per Bingham MR in *Blackburn v Bowering* [1994] 3 All ER 380 at 382–383, [1994] 1 WLR 1324 at 1327.
18 Per Roche LJ ibid at 1333.
19 For discussion of the meaning of 'in the execution of his duty' see p 435.
20 Following *R v Forbes and Webb* (1865) 10 Cox CC 362, *R v Prince* (1875) LR 2 CCR 154 and *Mc Bride v Turnock* [1964] Crim LR 456. In Australia see *R v Reynhoudt* (1962) 107 CLR 381.
 1 See County Courts Act 1984, s 147.
 2 Note, however, that a committal application could be made to the Queen's Bench Divisional Court. See n 2, p 509.
 3 Currently £2,500.
 4 See *R v Lambeth County Court Judge and Jonas* (1887) 36 WR 475; *McIllraith v Grady* [1968] 1 QB 468, [1967] 3 All ER 625, CA.
 5 (1850) 10 CB 189, per Wilde CJ.

registrar's book. In *R v Jordan*[6] the judge said, during the hearing of a case, that he would impose a fine of £5, or a committal for six days, upon an offender guilty of contempt by insulting the judge. At the end of the hearing the judge, having had no apology, ordered the warrant of committal to be made out, in which the only punishment specified was the committal for six days. It was held by the Court of Appeal that this order was perfectly valid, as Lindley LJ said:

> 'This warrant only recites a committal for six days. And such a committal he was authorised to make under the section. In point of law no fine was imposed.'

(d) Appeals Appeals from order made under ss 14, 92 and 118 lie to the Court of Appeal (Civil Division).[7] However, where it is sought to challenge an order for want of jurisdiction then it may be appropriate to seek judicial review.[8]

(ii) Magistrates' courts *(a) Jurisdiction* Prior to the Contempt of Court Act 1981 it was generally accepted that magistrates in England and Wales had no general jurisdiction to deal with contempts committed in their face.[9] Based on the Phillimore Committee's recommendations s 12(1) of the 1981 Act provides:

> 'A magistrates' court has jurisdiction under this section to deal with any person who:
> (a) wilfully insults the justice or justices, any witness before or officer of the court or any solicitor or counsel having business in the court, during his or their sitting or attendance in court or in going to or returning from the court; or
> (b) wilfully interrupts the proceedings of the court or otherwise misbehaves in court.'

Section 12(1) is modelled on, what is now, the County Courts Act 1984, s 118 but it will be noted that unlike s 118(1) wilful insults of solicitors and barristers are included in s 12(1). On the other hand, s 12(1)(a) does not include assaults and there is no comparable section to s 14 of the 1984 Act. Furthermore it was held in *R v Havant Justices, ex p Palmer*[10] that a 'threat' is not an 'insult' for the purposes of s 12. Consequently, magistrates[11] had no power to punish a witness who threatened to 'get' the defender and solicitor who were waiting outside the court room while the magistrates were considering their decision.

The general issues and problems already noted[12] with respect to county court powers under s 118 of the County Courts Act 1984 also apply to s 12 of the 1981 Act.

Another general problem of interpreting s 12 is whether 'wilfully' qualifies 'otherwise misbehaves' and what 'wilfully' means anyway.[13] It has been held that[14] 'wilfully' does qualify 'otherwise misbehaves' which is in line with the

---

6 (1888) 36 WR 797, sub nom *R v Staffordshire County Court Judge* (1888) 57 LJQB 483.
7 Under s 13 of the Administration of Justice Act 1960, discussed at p 533.
8 Judicial review was successfully sought in *R v Bloomsbury County Court, ex p Brady* (1987) Times, 16 December (full transcript on Lexis).
9 For the previous law see the first edition of this work at p 273.
10 [1985] Crim LR 658, (1985) 149 JP 609, full report on Lexis.
11 Application for committal could, however, have been made to the Queen's Bench Divisional Court. See pp 486–487.
12 See pp 510–511.
13 Its use was condemned by Ashworth: [1981] Crim LR 73. In its defence see the Attorney General HC Official Report, 1980-81 SC A Contempt of Court, 14 May 1981, col 222.
14 See *Re Hooker (Patricia) and the Contempt of Court Act 1981* [1993] COD 190.

view that the section read as a whole imports a general 'mens rea' requirement. The meaning of 'wilfully' is more problematic, but in *Bodden v Commissioner of Police of the Metropolis* [15] the Court of Appeal held that in relation to interrupting proceedings:

> 'it is necessary for there to be established, in addition to the deliberate commission of the acts causing the interruption, the mental element of intending this should interrupt the proceedings of the court.' [16]

It was further held, relying on *R v Sheppard*, [17] that in addition to an intention to interrupt court proceedings 'wilfully' also includes:

> 'the state of mind of an interruptor who knew that there was a risk that his acts would interrupt the proceedings of the court but nevertheless went on deliberately to do those acts. In that sense recklessness would be a sufficient state of mind to make the interruptor guilty of an offence under s 12(1)(b).'

It is submitted that a similar approach is applicable to interpreting 'wilfully insulting the court' under s 12(1)(a). In this respect regard can usefully be had to the approach of the Australian High Court in *Lewis v Judge Ogden* [18] in interpreting a similarly worded provision. In that case it was held that:

> 'wilfully means intentionally and deliberately in the sense that what is said or done is intended as an insult . . . The mere voluntary utterance of words is not enough. "Wilfully" imports the notion of purpose.'

The fact that 'wilful' imports an element of recklessness is likely to prove of importance in determining whether alleged offences committed by persons who are drunk fall within the section. [19]

As we have said, it was held in *R v Havant Justices, ex p Palmer* [20] that 'threats' fall outside the scope of s 12(1)(a) since 'insult' must be given its ordinary English meaning. According to the *Shorter Oxford English Dictionary* 'insult' means 'to assail with scornful abuse or offensive disrespect' and, presumably, threats accompanied by scornful abuse etc (as they commonly will be) will be caught by s 12(1)(a).

It may be noted that in *R v Tamworth Magistrates' Court, ex p Walsh* [1] where a solicitor, having been made to wait until the end of the court sitting, remarked 'any delay is as a result of the ridiculous listing of the Clerk of this Court,' it was

---

15   [1990] 2 QB 397, [1989] 3 All ER 833.
16   Per Beldam LJ at 405 and 837.
17   [1981] AC 394, [1980] 3 All ER 899, HL.
18   (1984) 153 CLR 682, (1984) 58 ALJR 342. See also *G v Moss* [1985] 37 SASR 9: mother of child who had just been fined held not to be in contempt for standing up and saying 'That's just ridiculous'. See also *R v The Coroner at Melbourne, ex p Erikson* [1981] VR 205 in which the Victorian Supreme Court commented when interpreting 'wilfully misbehaves':

> 'The expression "wilful misbehaviour" is not defined . . . but the words "wilful" and "misbehaviour" are words well known to the law and in the context which the phrase appears they connote misbehaviour which is deliberate and intentional and it may include the spoken word.'

19   Eg a litigant arriving so drunk that proceedings have to be adjourned; cf the Canadian decision of *R v Perkins* [1980] 4 WWR 763. For another example of the type of difficulty that could arise see *R v Barker* [1980] 4 WWR 202. Both these cases are discussed in Ch 2.
20   [1985] Crim LR 658.
1   [1994] COD 277.

held that it could not be said that no reasonable Bench of Justices would have concluded that the remark was wilfully insulting.[2]

Palmer left open the question whether a solicitor and client awaiting the court's decision were 'attending in court' or 'going to or returning from' court for the purposes of s 12(1)(a) but it is submitted that it would be an unjustifiably narrow interpretation to hold that they were not.

So far as s 12(1)(a) is concerned, in an important ruling, the Court of Appeal in *Bodden v Commissioner of Police of the Metropolis*[3] rejected the contention that 'or otherwise misbehaves in court' qualifies 'wilful interruption'. Accordingly, it was held that provided the court hearing was actually disrupted it does not matter for these purposes that the source of interruption (in this case a demonstration immediately outside the court building) is outside the court. However, interruption alone is not enough to constitute the offence since to be 'wilful' the defendant must either have intended to disrupt the proceedings or, knowing that such interruption was a risk, deliberately continued with his behaviour.[4]

The corollary of *Bodden* is that 'or otherwise misbehaves in court' is a separate offence. Clearly this must take place in the court. Examples of misbehaving are disputing with the court as to where to sit[5] and wrongfully using a tape-recorder in court.[6]

(b) Powers of punishment By s 12(2) of the 1981 Act:

> 'the court may order any officer of the court, or any constable, to take the offender into custody and detain him until the rising of the court; and the court may, if it thinks fit, commit the offender to custody for a specified period not exceeding one month or impose on him a fine not exceeding £2,500,[7] or both.'

A magistrates' court may revoke a committal and if the offender is in custody, order his discharge.[8] Justices must observe a number of restrictions particularly relating to the sentencing of young offenders before imposing any sentence.[9]

Any fine imposed is deemed, for the purposes of any enactment, to be a sum adjudged to be paid by a conviction.[10] The court has no power to make a probation order.[11] Like any other court magistrates should not be precipitous in punishing offenders and should allow defendants time for reflection and to obtain legal advice and representation.[12]

---

2 Nevertheless it was held that the magistrates had been wrong to have punished the solicitor without first giving him the opportunity to reflect and to obtain advice and representation.
3 [1990] 2 QB 397, [1989] 3 All ER 833.
4 On this basis it must be highly questionable whether causing a commotion in the cells below the court could, without any warning, be regarded as a 'wilful interruption'; cf *R v Selby Justices, ex p Frame* [1992] 1 QB 72, [1992] 2 All ER 344.
5 See *R v Pateley Bridge Justices, ex p Percy* [1994] COD 453 (litigant in person insisting, contrary to the courts' wishes, to sit in the place reserved for legal representatives).
6 Cf *Re Hooker (Patricia) and the Contempt of Court Act 1981* [1993] COD 190.
7 As amended by the Criminal Justice Act 1991, s 17(3)(a), Sch 4, Pt 1.
8 S 12(4).
9 See s 12 (5) and *R v Selby Justices, ex p Frame* [1992] 1 QB 72, [1992] 2 All ER 344, discussed at p 526.
10 S 12(2A) added by the Criminal Justice Act 1993, s 65(3), Sch 3, para 6(4).
11 *R v Palmer* [1992] 3 All ER 289, CA.
12 *R v Tamworth Magistrates' Court, ex p Walsh* [1994] COD 277, following eg *R v Moran* (1985) 81 Cr App Rep 51, CA and *R v Newbury Justices, ex p Du Pont* (1983) 78 Cr App Rep 255.

(c) Appeals   Section 12(5) of the 1981 Act provides:

> 'The following provisions of the Magistrates' Courts Act 1980 apply in relation to an order under this section as they apply to a sentence on conviction or finding of guilty of an offence, namely . . . s 108[13] (appeal to the Crown Court).'

Although prima facie this provision seems intended to provide a general right of appeal to the Crown Court, it has been held in *R v Havant Justices, ex p Palmer*[14] that because s 12(5) only refers to an 'order' the Crown Court's jurisdiction is limited to hearing appeals against the penalty imposed. It has no jurisdiction to hear an appeal against a finding of contempt. Furthermore s 13 of the Administration of Justice Act 1960[15] was not to be regarded as applying to contempts covered by s 12 of the 1981 Act. Accordingly, where it is sought to challenge a finding of contempt the proper remedy is judicial review.

Whether the Divisional Court's analysis in *Havant Justices* is right has yet to be authoritatively tested. There have certainly been other cases in which judicial review was successfully sought,[16] but there has also been at least one case in which an appeal under s 13 of the 1960 Act has been allowed.[17] It is submitted that while s 12(5) might not be ideally worded it is unduly narrow to confine it to providing for appeals against sentence. It is still more questionable, having so confined its application, to holding that s 13 of the 1960 Act has no application to s 12 contempts. If *Havant Justices* is right about the ambit of s 12(5) then, as a matter of principle, it could be argued that s 13 of the 1960 Act should certainly be applicable to appeals against findings of contempt, since this will give the appellate court[18] marginally more discretion than under judicial review and, most importantly, will provide a speedier method of dealing with the matter.

(iii) Courts martial   If a person who is subject to military[19] or air-force law[20] or is a person subject to the Naval Discipline Act 1957:[1]

> '(a)   having been duly summoned or ordered to attend as a witness before a court-martial, fails to comply with a summons or order, or
>
> (b)   refuses to swear an oath when duly required[2] by a court-martial to do so, or
>
> (c)   refuses to produce any document in his custody or under his control which a court-martial has lawfully required him to produce, or
>
> (d)   when a witness, refuses to answer any question which a court-martial has lawfully required him to answer, or
>
> (e)   wilfully insults any person, being a member of a court-martial or a witness or any other person whose duty it is to attend on or before the court, while that person is acting as a member thereof or is so attending, or wilfully

13   Not s 198 as originally printed in the Act.
14   [1985] Crim LR 658, full report on Lexis.
15   Discussed at pp 532 ff.
16   See eg *R v Pateley Bridge Justices, ex p Percy* [1994] COD 453 and *R v Tamworth Magistrates' Court, ex p Walsh* [1994] COD 277.
17   *Re Hooker (Patricia) and the Contempt of Court Act 1981* [1993] COD 190.
18   Ironically the same court, the Queen's Bench Divisional Court, has jurisdiction to hear a s 13 appeal or an application for judicial review.
19   In the case of the Army, persons subject to military law are defined by the Army Act 1955, ss 205–208 as amended by the Armed Forces Acts 1971 and 1976.
20   In the case of the Air Force, persons subject to Air-Force law are defined by the Air Force Act 1955, ss 205–208, as amended by the Armed Forces Acts 1971 and 1976.
 1   As defined by the Naval Discipline Act 1957, ss 111–118, as amended by the Armed Forces Acts 1971 and 1976.
 2   The Naval Discipline Act 1957, s 38(1) (b) reads: 'refuses to take an oath or make an affirmation when duly required by a court-martial to do so.'

insults any such person as aforesaid while the person is going to or returning from the proceedings of the court, or

(f)   wilfully interrupts the proceedings of a court-martial or otherwise misbehaves before the court',[3]

he is liable, on conviction by a court-martial, other than the court[4] in relation to which the offence was committed, to a maximum punishment[5] of a term of imprisonment not exceeding two years. It is further provided[6] that the court before which the offence is committed, has itself the power, where it is thought expedient to do so, to punish the offender summarily. In this case the offender if an officer, can be imprisoned for a period not exceeding 21 days or a fine imposed not exceeding his pay for a period of 28 days and in any other case to imprisonment or detention for a like period or to a similar fine. Such an order should be made under the hand of the president of the court.

These provisions also apply to civilians who are employees of the regular forces or are dependants who accompany those forces if they are on active service[7] and to such civilians in peacetime who are outside the United Kingdom.[8]

If any other civilian commits any of the offences already outlined[9] or:

'does any other thing which would, if the court-martial had been a court of law having power to commit for contempt, have been contempt of that court . . .'[10]

then the court has no power of its own to punish the offender but must instead certify the offence:

'to any court of law in the part of the United Kingdom or in the colony, as the case may be, where the offence is alleged to have been committed, being a court having power to commit for contempt.'[11]

The court of law to which the offence has been referred must then enquire into the alleged offence and after hearing all the evidence including any statement offered in defence it can:

'punish or take steps for the punishment of that person in like manner as if he had been guilty of contempt of the court to which the offence is certified.'[12]

---

3 The Army Act 1955, s 57 (1), the Air Force Act 1955, s 57(1) and the Naval Discipline Act 1957, s 38(1).
4 The provision that the offender must be punished by another court is not enacted in the Naval Discipline Act 1957, see s 38(1). See further the difference in the wording of s 38(3) of the 1957 Act and s 57(2) of the Army Act 1955, and of the Air Force Act 1955.
5 The sanction need not be imprisonment since the offence can be punished by 'any less punishment provided by this Act'. See the Army Act 1955, s 57(1), the Air Force Act 1955, s 57(1) and the Naval Discipline Act 1957, s 38(1). Special provision is made for offenders aged between 17 and 21 see the Army Act 1955, ss 57 (12A) and 71AA, the Air Force Act 1955 ss 57(2A) and the Naval Discipline Act 1957, ss 38(3A) and 43AA.
6 The Army Act 1957 s 57(2), the Air Force Act 1955, s 57(2); the Naval Discipline Act 1957, s 38(3) as amended by the Armed Forces Act 1971, s 23.
7 S 209(1).
8 S 209(2).
9 Such offences are restated by the Army Act 1955, s 101 and the Air Force Act 1955, s 101 and by the Naval Discipline Act 1957, s 65(1).
10 The Army Act 1955, s 101(g), the Air Force Act 1955, s 101(g) and the Naval Discipline Act 1957, s 65(1)(c). Interestingly the words of the provisions suggest that such courts might not be courts of law yet they are assumed to be for the purpose of the supervisory jurisdiction of the Queen's Bench Divisional Court. See p 487.
11 The offence must be certified by the President of the court.
12 The Army Act 1957, s 101 and the Air Force Act 1955, s 101; the Naval Discipline Act 1957, s 65(2).

2   Procedure

Although it is technically possible to proceed upon indictment, contempts committed in the face of the court are generally prosecuted summarily.[13] Commonly, the judge, in whose court the misconduct took place, will institute the contempt proceedings upon his own motion and try the case himself. It is possible, however, for another judge of the Crown Court or High Court[14] to act upon his own motion and hear the case. In *Balogh v Crown Court at St Albans*,[15] for instance, the offender was brought before the presiding judge who was present in the same building, rather than before the judge, the proceedings before whom the offender intended to disrupt. Stephenson LJ[16] could see no reason why one judge of the Crown Court or High Court should not commit for contempt of another, and though everything depends upon the circumstances he thought it 'may be better for a presiding judge available in the same building to commit for a contempt of a circuit judge's court'.

Apart from proceeding upon his own motion it is open[17] to the judge to report the incident to the Attorney General with a view to the matter being dealt with by a motion to commit under RSC Ord 52. This course of action might be considered appropriate for contempts which are not likely to disturb the trial or affect the verdict or judgment.

The power to proceed upon the court's own motion is, in the case of the High Court and Court of Appeal, expressly preserved by RSC Ord 52, r 5, and by reason of s 45(4) of the Supreme Court 1981, the Crown Court is vested with similar powers.[18] Ord 52, r 5 may, however, be considered as being no more than declaratory of the common law,[19] and unless Parliament prescribes otherwise, all courts vested with powers to punish contempts committed in their face can proceed summarily upon their own motion. Accordingly, county courts, magistrates' courts and coroners' courts can so prosecute contempts committed in their face.

As Stephenson LJ said in *Balogh's* case,[20] where a court does proceed of its motion the proceedings are even more summary than for motions for committal

13   Per Lord Denning MR in *Morris v Crown Office* [1970] 2 QB 114 at 123–124 and see Lawton LJ in *Balogh v Crown Court at St Albans* [1975] QB 73 at 93. But note the suggestion referred to by Woolf LJ in *DPP v Channel Four Television Co Ltd* [1993] 2 All ER 517 at 521 that the Director, through the Crown Prosecution Service, could on being informed of the alleged contempt, make an application to the court and conduct the proceedings 'in the same way as it would if there were to be a trial on indictment'. For the position under Scottish Law see *HM Advocate v Airs* 1975 SLT 177.
14   It is submitted that a county court judge or a magistrate would not be so empowered since it would be outside their statutory powers.
15   [1975] QB 73, [1974] 3 All ER 283.
16   Ibid at 90 and 292. See also *DPP v Channel Four Television Co Ltd* [1993] 2 All ER 517 at 521 per Woolf LJ. For a similar standpoint in Canada see *R v Barker* [1980] 4 WWR 202 (Alberta CA) per Morrow JA, but cf in Australia *Brown v Putnam* (1975) 6 ALR 307 (NSW CA) where the consequential delay in referring the matter to another judge was one reason why the proceedings were dismissed.
17   Per Lawton LJ in *Balogh* [1975] QB 73 at 93. Cf Archbold, *Criminal Pleading, Evidence and Practice* (1994) para 28-27 where it is said that in non-urgent cases 'the judge should leave it to the Attorney General or to the party aggrieved to make a motion in accordance with the rules in RSC Ord 52'. A similar option is available in Scotland, see *HM Advocate v Airs* 1975 SLT 177. Cf *DPP v Channel Four Television Co Ltd* [1993] 2 All ER 517 in which it was suggested that a referral could be made to the Director of the Crown Prosecution Service.
18   See *Balogh v Crown Court at St Albans* [1975] QB 73.
19   See Lawton LJ in *Balogh* ibid at 92.
20   Ibid at 90.

under RSC Ord 52.[1] The process was well described by Mustill LJ in *R v Griffin*[2] when he said:

'there is no summons or indictment, nor is it mandatory for any written account of the accusation made against him to be furnished to the contemnor. There is no preliminary enquiry or filtering procedure, such as committal. Depositions are not taken. There is no jury. Nor is the system adversarial in character. The judge himself enquires into the circumstances, so far as they are not within his personal knowledge. He identifies the grounds of complaint, selects the witnesses and investigates what they have to say (subject to a right of cross-examination), decides on guilt and pronounces sentence.'

Provided the offender is before the court, he may be punished instantly and no notice or formal institution of proceedings is necessary.[3] Where the offender is not before the court he must be notified that his presence is required. Although it is desirable in such cases to serve on the accused a formal notice ordering attendance to answer a charge of contempt, it may not always be necessary.[4] It may be that, if the accused (particularly a lawyer) knows that his presence is required to answer a charge of contempt, and actually attends the hearing, he could still be properly convicted without formal notice. It is clear, however, that without formal notice to attend, an accused cannot be found guilty of contempt for failing to attend at the appointed time.[5]

The fact that the process is so summary does not mean that there are no procedural requirements. On the contrary, as the Privy Council was at pains to point out, in *Re Pollard*:[6]

'no person should be punished for contempt of court, which is a criminal offence, unless the specific charge against him be distinctly stated, and an opportunity of answering it given to him.'

It seems that the accused must at least be made aware that he is being charged with contempt.[7] However, the degree of precision with which the charge must be stated will depend upon the circumstances. Provided the gist of the allegation is made clear to the accused it is not always necessary to formulate the charge in a series of specific allegations.[8] However, as the Canadian Supreme Court has observed, the 'fundamental rule is beyond question: a vague charge is a fatal defect.'[9] The general rule may therefore be better stated by saying that the charge

---

1 The procedure for committals under Ord 52 is discussed at pp 493 ff.
2 (1988) 88 Cr App Rep 63 at 67.
3 *Watt v Ligertwood* (1874) LR 2 Sc & Div 361, HL. See also in Australia, *Dow v A-G* [1980] Qd R 58 at 63.
4 At least according to the Canadian decision of *R v Pinx* (1979) 105 DLR (3d) 143 at 148 per Freedman CJM (Manitoba CA). Cf *Weston v Central Criminal Court, Courts Administrator* [1977] QB 32 which might be taken to suggest the contrary. In that case, however, the defendant's solicitor did not attend the hearing until a bench warrant was issued.
5 See Lord Denning MR in *Weston* ibid at p 44.
6 (1868) LR 2 PC 106 at 120. Approved inter alia by *Chiang Hang Kiu v Piggott* [1909] AC 312, PC; *Appuhamy v R* [1963] AC 474, PC; *Maharaj v A-G for Trinidad and Tobago* [1977] 1 All ER 411. In Australia see *R v Foster ex p Isaacs* [1941] VLR 77 at 81, *Coward v Stapleton* (1953) 90 CLR 573 at 579–80 (Aust HC) and *G v Moss* (1985) 37 SASR 9 at 14 and in Canada see *Cotroni v Quebec Police Commission and Brunet* (1977) 80 DLR (3d) 490 (Can SC).
7 See the Canadian decision in *R v Pinx* (1980) 105 DLR (3d) 143.
8 *Chang Hang Kiu v Piggott* [1909] AC 312 (a case on perjury) approved by *Coward v Stapleton* (1953) 90 CLR 573 at 580 (Aust HC) and by *Cotroni v Quebec Police Commission and Brunet* (1977) 80 DLR (3d) 490 (Can SC). As Mustill LJ said in *R v Griffin* (1988) 88 Cr App Rep 63, it is not mandatory for any written account of the accusation to be made.
9 *Cotroni v Quebec Police Commission and Brunet* (1977) 80 DLR (3d) 490.

must always be specific enough to leave the accused in no doubt as to what conduct is being complained of. For example, if it is alleged that the whole of a witness's testimony is false then a charge of contempt is specific enough if it simply says that.[10] But if objection is only taken to part of the testimony, the charge must specify which part of the testimony is complained of.[11] In *Maharaj v A-G for Trinidad and Tobago*,[12] after a barrister accused a judge of 'unjudicial conduct', the judge simply told the barrister that he was being 'formally charged with contempt of court'. In his written reasons for his decision, however, Maharaj J made it clear that he regarded the barrister's conduct as a 'vicious attack on the integrity of the court', and it was held by the Privy Council that the failure to make this specific in the charge vitiated the committal for contempt.

The failure to make the charge specific enough jeopardises the second requirement that the accused be given an opportunity to answer the charge. This, however, is no more than a general requirement for although it would seem at the very minimum that an accused must be given an opportunity to answer the charge before a finding of guilt is pronounced,[13] there is no specific requirement allowing adequate time for the accused to prepare a defence. On the other hand, as the court said in *R v Pateley Bridge Justices, ex p Percy*:[14] 'It is clear in contempt cases that the court should never act in haste but always give the alleged contemnor an opportunity to have legal advice where appropriate and to consider apologising'.

It is not yet established whether an accused has a right to call witnesses, though the Canadian Supreme Court has said with apparent justification that before the question can arise there must be facts in issue which are contestable.[15] It is well established that the accused contemnor has no *right* to legal advice and representation[16] but save in cases of extreme urgency[17] courts should offer such representation. This standpoint was well explained by Lawton LJ in *R v Moran*[18] when he said:

> 'Sometimes situations arise in court when the judge has to act quickly and to pass such sentence as he thinks appropriate at once; so there cannot be any right to legal advice. Justice does not require a contemnor in the face of the court to have a right

---

10 This was the case in *Chang Hang Kiu v Piggott* [1909] AC 312 and in *Coward v Stapleton* (1953) 90 CLR 573. See also *Re Prior, ex p Bellanto* [1963] SR (NSW) 190.

11 See *Appuhamy v R* [1963] AC 474 at 483 and *Cotroni v Quebec Police Commission and Brunet* (1977) 80 DLR (3d) 490 at 497.

12 [1977] 1 All ER 411.

13 See *Re Fellows, ex p Stewart* [1972] 2 NSWLR 317 (accused charged with contempt was asked to apologise rather than explain her conduct) and *R v The Coroner at Melbourne, ex p Ericksen* [1981] VR 205 (a coroner held a witness guilty of contempt and before giving an opportunity to answer the charge, proceeded to discuss the question of penalty and possible mitigation).

14 [1994] COD 453. Quite frequently though a judge will order the offender to be detained in custody, until the end of the day before dealing with the contempt issue: cf *Morris v Crown Office* [1970] 2 QB 114, [1970] 1 All ER 1079.

15 *Cotroni v Quebec Police Commission and Brunet* (1977) 80 DLR (3d) 490.

16 See *R v Newbury Justices, ex p Du Pont* (1983) 78 Cr App Rep 255 (in which it was expressly held that s 21(1) of the Powers of Criminal Courts Act 1973, discussed at p 526 did not apply to contempt), *R v Moran* (1985) 81 Cr App Rep, 51, *Maharaj v A-G for Trinidad and Tobago* [1977] 1 All ER 411 at 416 per Lord Salmon and *Balogh v Crown Court at St Albans* [1975] QB 73 at 90 per Stephenson LJ.

17 See eg *R v Newbury Justices, ex p Du Pont* (1983) 78 Cr App Rep 255. In *Balogh*'s case Stephenson LJ at 90 thought that *Morris v Crown Office* [1970] 2 QB 114, [1970] 1 All ER 1079 was an example of such an urgent case.

18 (1985) 81 Cr App Rep at 53. See also *R v Bromwell* (1995) Times, 9 February, CA.

to legal advice. But, if the circumstances are such that it is possible for the contemnor to have advice, he should be given an opportunity of having it. In practice what usually happens is that somebody gives the contemnor advice. He takes it, apologizes to the court and that is the end of the matter. Giving a contemnor an opportunity to apologise is one of the most important aspects of this summary procedure, which in many ways is Draconian. If there is a member of the Bar in court who could give advice, a wise judge would ask that member . . . if he would be willing to do so. The member of the Bar is entitled to say no, but in practice never does.'

An added incentive to ensure that a contemnor is legally represented is provided for by the Legal Aid Act 1988, s 29.[19] By s 29(1) and (2), magistrates, when acting under s 12 of the 1981 Act, county courts when acting under the County Courts Act 1984, ss 14, 92 or 118 and superior courts[20] when dealing with contempts in their face or in the face of any other court 'may order that he be granted representation under this section for the purposes of the proceedings if it appears to the court to be desirable to do so in the interests of justice'.[1]

Where a court grants representation to a person for the purpose of contempt proceedings it may also assign for this purpose, any legal representative who is within the court precincts at the time of the order.[2] Where representation is granted the costs are paid for out of the legal aid fund.[3] There is no provision for a test for financial eligibility for representation nor are there any contribution or enforcement regulations.[4] This provision ends at least in this respect the anomaly that contemnors only qualify for civil legal aid.[5]

Although there is no English authority on the point, it is doubtful whether there would be dissent from the view that an accused should be allowed, if he so desired, to make a plea in mitigation pending sentence. At any rate there is Scottish authority for this point.[6] It is more doubtful whether a judge should always specifically give the accused the opportunity to make a plea in mitigation, but it would seem good practice to do so.

(i) Justifying the summary procedure It seems right that the disruption or interruption of the trial process should be punishable. However, the process for dealing with contempts in facie curiae is summary in the extreme. The judiciary

---

19 Which came into force on 1 May 1991, see SI 1991/790. This provision replaced s 13 of the Contempt of Court Act 1981.
20 Defined by s 29(3) as 'the Court of Appeal, the High Court, the Crown Court, the Courts-Martial Appeal Court, the Restrictive Practices Court, the Employment Appeal Tribunal and any other court exercising in relation to its proceedings powers equivalent to those of the High Court, and includes the House of Lords in the exercise of its jurisdiction in relation to appeals from courts in England and Wales'.
1 S 29(2).
2 S 32(5) as amended by the Courts and Legal Services Act 1990, s 125(3), Sch 18, paras 59, 63(3)(b). S 32(1), which entitles a person receiving representation to choose his legal representative, does not extend to contemnors, s 32(4). A single standard fee payable for each day of appearance (currently £71–£75) but exceptional circumstances may justify a higher sum being paid: Legal Aid in Contempt Proceedings (Remuneration) Regulations 1995 (SI 1995/948), regs 6 and 7.
3 Legal Aid Act 1988, s 25, which applies by reason of s 30(3).
4 See 27(2) *Halsbury's Laws* (4th edn), *Legal Aid*, para 2008.
5 The anomaly was serious in respect of contempts committed in the face of the court since the provisions for emergency legal aid under the civil scheme were quite inappropriate to summary prosecutions. For the position with respect to other criminal contempts see p 497.
6 *Macara v Macfarlane* 1980 SLT (Notes) 26.

are aware of this and have repeatedly urged caution in its use. As Stephenson LJ said in *Balogh v Crown Court at St Albans*,[7] the procedure:

> 'must never be invoked unless the ends of justice really require such drastic means; it appears to be rough justice; it is contrary to natural justice; and it can only be justified if nothing else will do. . .'

These sentiments echo the Phillimore Committee's recommendation that the summary procedure should only be invoked when considerations of immediate urgency dictate.[8] However, even the infrequent use of the contempt power is only acceptable if the summary procedure can be justified.

The consensus of opinion among the judiciary and commentators alike is that despite the objections that the judge deals with the contempt himself and that the contemnor has little opportunity to defend himself, there is a residue of cases where not only is it justifiable to punish on the spot but that it is the only realistic way of dealing with certain offenders.

The fact that the judge tries and punishes the case himself is open to the obvious criticism that he is simultaneously judge, witness, prosecutor and plaintiff. The criticism is most pertinent where the alleged contempt comprises conduct directed against the judge personally. However, strictly speaking this procedure does not offend against the principle of natural justice, namely, *nemo judex in sua causa*, since the prosecution is not aimed at protecting the judge personally but protecting the administration of justice. Nevertheless some would argue that in such cases justice is not being seen to be done.

The Phillimore Committee justified[9] the judge's role on the following grounds: (1) The judge will be in the best position to deal with the case since he will usually have witnessed the incident. (2) In the event of misconduct being directed against the judge personally he may treat it more leniently than another judge might feel able to do. (3) The threat of immediate punishment is the most effective deterrent against misconduct. Not all their arguments are convincing. With regard to the first, for example, Miller[10] has rightly said that convenience does not normally provide a sufficient reason for dispensing with the ordinary criminal process, and personal knowledge of the circumstances would generally be a reason for a judge to step down, rather than a reason for him to hear the case. Miller is also critical of the second, on the basis that it is important for justice to be seen to be done. However, as the Canadian Law Reform Commission has said[11] there are more persuasive arguments, namely, that the judge must remain in full control of the hearing and that he must be able to take steps to restore order as quickly and effectively as possible. As they say:[12]

> 'The time factor is crucial: dragging out the contempt proceedings would mean a lengthy interruption to the main proceedings, thereby paralysing the court for a time, and indirectly impeding the speed and efficiency with which justice is administered.'

7   [1975] QB 73 at 90.
8   (1974, Cmnd 5794) para 34.
9   Ibid at para 30.
10 *Contempt of Court* (2nd edn) 136. As he said 'No one would seriously contend that an ordinary trial should be denied to the assassin who stabs his victim in front of a large audience which immediately overpowers him. Still less would it be suggested that a judge forming part of that audience or, even worse, being the victim, should preside at the hearing'.
11 Working Paper No 20: *Contempt of Court* (1977).
12 Ibid at 23.

Moreover, the alternative of having another judge hear the case is not a practical solution since, as the Commission and others[13] point out, there is no guarantee that the offender will not interrupt the second proceedings so that the matter would have to be referred to a third judge and so on. There is strength too in the deterrence factor especially as it empowers a judge to increase gradually the pressure upon the offender to behave himself, by warning him and later perhaps imposing a suspended sentence and so on.

It is submitted that the above arguments do support the use of the summary process. However, Miller argues,[14] with some justification, that the procedure can only be *fully* justified when dealing with persons such as an accused, juror, witness and, one might add, an advocate, whose continued presence serves to promote the due administration of justice and even then only to punish misconduct occurring during rather than at the end of the proceedings. Miller questions the deterrent value of the threat of immediate punishment but it is submitted that it does play an important part in the judge's ability to maintain order and as such justifies the punishment of those such as members of the public whose presence is not essential to the trial, who, for example, deliberately set out to disrupt the trial. *Morris v Crown Office* [15] provides a good example of the legitimate use of the power in this respect.

(ii) Improving the summary procedure   Given that the summary procedure can be justified can or should it be improved? It is a serious criticism of it that it affords the contemnor little opportunity to defend himself. Indeed there must be concern as to whether the procedure complies with Article 6(3) of the European Convention on Human Rights which provides inter alia:

'Everyone charged with a criminal offence has the following minimum rights:
(b)   to have adequate time and facilities for the preparation of his defence;
(c)   to defend himself in person or through legal assistance of his own choosing or, if he has not sufficient means to pay for legal assistance, to be given it free when the interests of justice so require;
(d)   to examine or have examined witnesses against him and to obtain the attendance and examination of witnesses on his behalf under the same conditions as witnesses against him.'

There seems to be a good case for saying that at least in some cases, the procedure as applied in the English courts is in danger of being in breach of Article 6(3) (b), (c)[16] and possibly (d).

The Phillimore Committee were concerned about these possible breaches and recommended:[17] (1) that an accused be entitled to legal representation (2) that in all cases where more than a small fine (undefined) is considered a period of delay should be interposed between determination of the issue of contempt and the imposition of the penalty (this already apparently reflects the practice in Scotland)[18]

---

13 See eg the Phillimore Report (1974, Cmnd 5794) at p 31 and the American College of Trial Lawyers' report and recommendations on Disruption of the Judicial Process.
14 *Contempt of Court* (2nd edn) at p 136. This also seemed to be view of the Irish Law Reform Commission: *Contempt of Court* (1991) 242.
15 [1970] 2 QB 114, [1970] 1 All ER 1079. As does *R v Newbury Justices, ex p Du Pont* (1983) 78 Cr App Rep 255.
16 See DJ Harris, 'The European Convention on Human Rights and English Criminal Law' [1966] Crim LR 266 at 269.
17 Ibid at paras 32, 33.
18 See eg *Royle v Gray* 1973 SLT 31 and *Re Cordiner, Petitioner* 1973 SLT 125.

and (3) that before sentence an accused should be entitled both to be heard in mitigation and legal representation for this purpose with legal aid, if necessary.

As we have seen, since these recommendations were made provision for legal representation under s 29 of the Legal Aid Act 1988 has been implemented. Although this provision stops short of giving an accused contemnor the right to such representation, once an order has been made he is entitled to the costs being paid for out of the legal aid fund. It is submitted that this provision, coupled with the practice of only denying the opportunity of representation in truly urgent cases,[19] goes a long way to accommodating the Phillimore Committee's recommendations.

It is not suggested, even with the above reforms, that the procedure is a perfect one. Instant justice can never be completely satisfactory yet it does provide the simplest, most effective and least unsatisfactory method of dealing with disruptive conduct in court. With the suggested reforms and the final safeguard of an appeal it is submitted that the contemnor's interests are as adequately safeguarded as the peculiar nature of the offence allows.

III PUNISHMENT OF THE OFFENDER

A Imprisonment

1 *Powers*

One sanction that can be imposed upon those found guilty of contempt either in committal proceedings or where the judge is acting upon his own motion, is imprisonment. Formerly, there was no theoretical limit on the length of the term of imprisonment which could be imposed but following the Phillimore Committee's recommendation[20] s 14(1) of the Contempt of Court Act 1981 now provides that in England and Wales[1] the maximum term of imprisonment on any one occasion is two years in the case of superior courts and one month in the case of inferior courts.[2]

It has been held by the Court of Appeal in *Villiers v Villiers*[3] that s 14 applies to the occasion when the order was made and applies regardless of whether it related to one or more applications. Accordingly, a court cannot on the same occasion activate a suspended sentence and impose a new sentence which together exceeds the maximum limit allowed by the section.

The Court of Appeal, High Court and Crown Court (by reason of the Supreme Court Act 1981, s 45(4)) have the discretionary power to suspend a committal order.[3a] This power is provided for by RSC Ord 52, r 7(1) which states:

19 In fact committals have been quashed in a number of cases for failing to allow a contemnor to have legal representation, see eg *R v Selby Justices, ex p Frame* [1992] 1 QB 72; *R v Pateley Justices, ex p Percy* [1994] COD 453 and *R v Tamworth Magistrates' Court, ex p Walsh* [1994] COD 277.
20 Paras 201 (England) and 206 (Scotland).
1 The maximum penalties that can be imposed by Scottish courts are provided by s 15. The maximum term is two years (s 15(2)) but sheriffs' powers are limited to three months (s 15(2)(a)) and district courts to 60 days (s 15(2)(b)).
2 Ie those courts that have inherent jurisdiction to punish contempts, eg coroners and possibly the various statutorily designated courts of record referred to above at p 508.
3 [1994] 2 All ER 149.
3a There is, however, no power to defer a contempt sentence, ie to detain a contemnor in custody pending consideration of the appropriate sentence to be imposed on him: *Delaney v Delaney* (1995) Times, 2 November, CA.

'The court by whom an order of committal is made may by order direct that the execution of the order of committal shall be suspended for such period or on such terms or conditions as it may specify.'

Where the court does so suspend the order, Ord 52, r 7(2) provides that unless the court directs otherwise, the applicant must serve on the person against whom the order was made, a notice informing him of the making and terms of the order. In exercising this power it is not constrained by limitations as to the imprisonment of young offenders and first offenders.[4] If a suspended committal order for a fixed period is made it is established that in the event of non-compliance with a condition the court retains a discretion to do what is just in the circumstances.[5]

2 *Impact of statutory restrictions*

One problem with respect to imposing terms of imprisonment is the relevance of general statutory restrictions on imposing custodial sentences. In *Morris v Crown Office*[6] the Court of Appeal held that despite their apparently general application statutory restrictions then relating to *mandatory* suspension of certain sentences and to the imprisonment of young offenders did not apply to contempt.[7] Indeed, Davies LJ considered[8] that not only were such restrictions inapplicable but so were the statutory alternatives to imprisonment such as probation and the sending of young offenders to detention centres. Since *Morris*, however, the legislature has been more aware of contempt and certain statutory restrictions are now expressly applicable. For example, following the Phillimore recommendation,[9] s 14(4) of the Contempt of Court Act 1981 (as amended) provides:

'Each of the superior courts shall have the like power to make a hospital order or guardianship order under s 37 of the Mental Health Act 1983 or an interim order under s 38 of that Act in the case of a person suffering from mental illness or severe mental impairment who could otherwise be committed to prison for contempt of court as the Crown Court has under that section in case of a person convicted of an offence.'[10]

Under s 14 (4A)[11] each superior court has the power to make an order for remand for reports on the accused's mental condition whenever there is reason to suspect that a person who could be committed to prison for contempt is suffering from mental illness or severe mental impairment. For the purposes of ss 14(4) and (4A) a county court ranks as a 'superior court'.[12]

---

4 Per Sir Thomas MR in *Villiers v Villiers* [1994] 2 All ER 149, 153 relying on *Morris v Crown Office* [1970] 2 QB 114, [1970] 1 All ER 1079, discussed below.

5 *Re W(B) (an infant)* [1969] 2 Ch 50, [1969] 1 All ER 594. See also *Banton v Banton* [1990] 2 FLR 465, CA.

6 [1970] 2 QB 114, [1970] 1 All ER 1079.

7 Ie the Criminal Justice Act 1967, s 39 and the Criminal Justice Act 1948, s 17(2), respectively.

8 At para 127.

9 At para 203.

10 As amended by the Mental Health (Amendment) Act 1982, s 65(1), Sch 3, para 59 and the Mental Health Act 1983, s 148, Sch 4, para 57. For Scotland see s 15(5).

11 Added by Mental Health (Amendment) Act 1982, s 65(1), Sch 3, para 60 and amended by the Mental Health Act 1983, s 148, Sch 4, para 57(b).

12 S 14 (4A), inserted by the County Courts (Penalties for Contempt) Act 1983, s 1. It should presumably have been numbered s 14 (4B).

Replacing what was originally s 14(3) of the 1981 Act, the Criminal Justice Act 1982, s 1(1) provides that no court can imprison any offender under the age of 21 for 'any reason'.[13] However, s 9(1) provides that, subject to believing that no other method of dealing with the offender is appropriate,[14] a court can commit a young person, aged 18–20,[15] to be detained at a young offenders' institution, if guilty of contempt of court.[16] In determining whether there is no other appropriate method of dealing with the offender the court is enjoined[17] to 'take into account such information about the circumstances of the default or contempt (including any aggravating or mitigating factors) as is available to it'. It may also take into account any information before the court about the accused.

This limited obligation to obtain information about the accused is in marked contrast to other offences and indeed in *R v Selby Justices, ex p Frame* [18] it was held that the requirement under s 2 to obtain a social inquiry report before committing a person under 21 to be detained did not apply to contempts. Although at first sight this may seem harsh the need to act quickly precludes lengthy inquiry into an offender's background. On the other hand some inquiries ought to be undertaken. At the very minimum it would seem incumbent upon the court to ascertain the age of an offender if anything more than a fine is being considered.

Another express restriction on the court's powers to deal with young offending contemnors is that provided by s 14(2A)[19] which forbids a court from making an attendance centre order if it appears that the offender is under 17.

Aside from these aforementioned provisions which expressly apply to contempt it seems to remain the case that general statutory provisions are not usually held to be directly applicable to criminal contempts. For example, in *R v Newbury Justices, ex p Du Pont*,[20] it was held that s 21 of the Powers of Criminal Courts Act 1973, under which magistrates' courts and Crown Courts are barred from imprisoning a person who is not legally represented and who has not previously been imprisoned, does not apply to contempt. The Divisional Court's reasoning was that persons committed for contempt had not been 'summarily convicted' for the purposes of s 21.

A similar line of reasoning led the Court of Appeal reluctantly to conclude in *R v Palmer*,[1] that s 2(1) of the 1973 Act does not apply to contempt and hence the court had no power to place a contemnor on probation. On that basis it seems that there is no power to order a contemnor to do community service.[2]

---

13   Any such order is unlawful but not necessarily uncorrectable. See *Mason v Lawton* [1991] 2 All ER 784, CA.
14   See s 1(5).
15   This age range was amended by the Criminal Justice Act 1991, s 63(1), (5).
16   Where a magistrates' court does commit a person to be detained under s 9 it must state in open court the reason for its opinion that no other method was appropriate and to enter that reason on the warrant for committal: s 1 (5A)(a) and (b).
17   By s 1(5)(a) and (b) of the 1982 Act.
18   [1992] 1 QB 72, [1991] 2 All ER 344. The end result is very much the same as obtained following *Morris v Crown Office* [1970] 2 QB 114, [1970] 1 All ER 1079, discussed at p 364 of the second edition of this work.
19   Inserted by the Criminal Justice Act 1982, s 77, Sch 14, para 60.
20   (1983) 78 Cr App Rep 255.
 1   [1992] 3 All ER 289.
 2   Under s 14 of the Powers of Criminal Courts Act 1973 community service can only be imposed of those 'convicted' of an offence. Cf in Australia where such an order was imposed in *Registrar of the Court of Appeal v Maniam (No 2)* (1991) 25 NSWLR 459, discussed further at p 641.

3 Execution

The practice of issuing to the tipstaff an order of the Lord Chancellor has been discontinued and instead the committal order is now executed on the authority of a warrant signed by the judge, or one of the judges of the court making the order.[3]

If the contemnor is present in court (as will be usual in cases of criminal contempt) the tipstaff takes him to prison. If the contemnor is elsewhere and has a settled address the tipstaff will travel there with the order and arrest him, but if the contemnor does not have a settled address or is likely to move, the tipstaff will communicate with the local police who will hold him in the cells of the police station until the tipstaff arrives and takes him to London and lodge him in gaol.[4]

A person guilty of a criminal contempt has no privilege from arrest.[5] Indeed it is probably the duty of the officer charged with the execution of such an order, if necessary and after due notice has been given, to break open the outer door of the house of the person to be arrested.[6] An arrest for a criminal contempt may possibly be made on a Sunday.[7]

4 When imposed

The court's power to imprison is the major sanction[8] which can be imposed for contempt and accordingly should be exercised only in the most serious cases. The seriousness will be judged by reference to the likely interference with the due administration of justice and the culpability of the offender[9] with the latter perhaps being the key factor. Terms of imprisonment are commonly imposed upon witnesses who have refused to be sworn or to answer questions, upon persons who have intimidated parties, jurors, or witnesses and upon those who have interrupted court proceedings.

Imprisonment is rarely imposed in cases of 'media' contempts. This is usually because the potential interference with the due administration of justice is unintentional. Were it to be concluded, however, that such interference was intended or that the editor was indifferent or reckless as to the consequences of the publication then the court would have no hesitation in imprisoning the offender. In *R v Bolam, ex p Haigh* [10] the editor of the *Daily Mirror* was imprisoned for three months for publishing an article which was described as: 'violating every principle of justice and fair play which it had been the pride of this country to extend to the worst of criminals'.

It was held that the publication:

3 (1961) 111 L Jo 109 (Practice Note). County court practice is referred to at p 510.
4 See *Supreme Court Practice* 52/7/2.
5 See eg *Wellesley v Duke of Beaufort* (1831) 2 Russ & M 639; *Re Freston* (1883) 11 QBD 545; *Stourton v Stourton* [1963] P 302, [1963] 1 All ER 606. See also Ch 14 and Feldman, *Entry, Search and Seizure* (1983, Butterworths) Ch 8.
6 *Burdett v Abbot* (1811) 14 East 1; *Harvey v Harvey* (1884) 26 Ch D 644.
7 *Ex p Whitchurch* (1749) 1 Atk 55; *Burdett v Abbot* (1811) 14 East 1 at 162, see also Ch 11.
8 Formerly, the court could order mutilation, eg the cutting off of an offender's right hand, see Oswald, *Contempt* (3rd edn) p 43 ff. An offender could also be ordered to forfeit all his property.
9 See Lord Parker CJ in *R v Thomson Newspapers Ltd, ex p A-G* [1968] 1 All ER 268 at 270.
10 (1949) 93 Sol Jo 220, see also *Higgins v Richards* (1912) 28 TLR 202. A similar reticence is shown in other jurisdictions. In Canada for example the only case where a member of the media has been imprisoned for publishing comment is *R v Bryan* [1954] 3 DLR 631.

'was not the result of an error of judgment but had been done as a matter of policy in pandering to sensationalism for the purpose of increasing the circulation of the newspaper.'

The *Daily Mirror* case is the last known instance of imprisonment being imposed in respect of a 'prejudicial' publication.

5   *Treatment of the offender in prison*

A person who is committed to prison for contempt of court is treated under special prison rules.[11] For certain purposes the contemnor has the same privileges as an unconvicted prisoner,[12] so that he is allowed to wear his own clothing and 'to arrange for the supply to him from outside prison of sufficient clean clothing'.[13] He is also allowed to send and receive as many letters and receive as many visits as he wishes 'within such limits and subject to such conditions as the Secretary of State may direct'.[14] Such prisoners are treated as a separate class of prisoner[15] so that, like unconvicted prisoners, they are kept out of contact with convicted prisoners, so far as this can reasonably be done,[16] but if they are willing to do so, persons committed for contempt are permitted to associate with other classes of prisoners.[17]

Under s 45 of the Criminal Justice Act 1991 contemnors committed for a term of less than 12 months must be released after serving half the sentence, while those committed for 12 months or more must be released after serving two-thirds of their sentence.[18] This provision is without prejudice to the Secretary of State's power in exceptional circumstances to sanction the release of a prisoner on compassionate grounds,[19] nor conversely is without prejudice to the power to add extra days for disciplinary offences.[20] More importantly this power is without prejudice to the court's power, expressly preserved by s 14(1) of the Contempt of Court Act 1981, to order an earlier discharge. Accordingly it is always open to a prisoner[1] to apply to the court for a discharge. RSC Ord 52, r 8(1) provides that: 'The court may, on the application of any person committed to prison for any contempt of court, discharge him'. Rule 8(1) supersedes the decision in *A-G v James*[2] that once a court had made a fixed-term committal it had no further jurisdiction to interfere with the sentence. Rule 8, however, only applies to the Court of Appeal, High Court and Crown Court[3] and it is a moot point whether in spite of s 14 the *James* ruling continues to apply to other courts. However, it is suggested that the rule is wide enough to allow an application for discharge to be made to say the High Court even though a lower court made the original

11 Prison Rules 1964 (SI 1964/388) r 63.
12 R 63 (1).
13 R 20 (1).
14 R 34 (1).
15 By r 63 (2), such prisoners are treated as a separate class for the purposes of r 3.
16 R 3 (2).
17 R 63 (2).
18 See respectively s 33(1)(a) and (b) as amended by s 45(3) and note the discussion in *Re R (a minor) (contempt sentence)* [1994] 2 All ER 144.
19 Under s 36.
20 Under s 42.
 1 For the role of the Official Solicitor in seeking discharge on behalf of contemnors, see Ch 14.
 2 [1962] 2 QB 637.
 3 By reason of the Supreme Court Act 1981, s 45(4).

committal. Alternatively, application for a discharge can be made to the Home Secretary.[4] An application for discharge before the expiration of the term should, if possible, be made to the particular court which made the committal order[5] and the practice is for such application to be made by motion.[6] It is the practice in the Family Division of the High Court to require the contemnor to attend the court where an application for his release is being heard.[7] A motion to discharge a prisoner has priority over all other motions.[8]

Once the term of imprisonment prescribed by the committal order has expired the gaoler is bound to discharge the prisoner.[9] If a release has been made by mistake there is no jurisdiction to make a second order for committal for the same offence for as Vaughan Williams LJ said 'You cannot punish twice in respect of the same offence'.[10]

B Other forms of punishment

As RSC Ord 52, r 9 makes clear, in an application for committal a judge is not bound to commit to prison an offender found guilty of contempt. Rule 9 provides:

> 'Nothing in the foregoing provisions of this Order shall be taken as affecting the power of the court to make an order requiring a person guilty of contempt of court, or a person punishable by virtue of any enactment in like manner as if he had been guilty of contempt of the High Court, to pay a fine or to give security for his good behaviour, and those provisions so far as applicable, and with the necessary modifications, shall apply in relation to an application for such an order as they apply in relation to an application for an order of committal.'

Similarly, judges acting upon their own motion have wide powers to punish offenders.

An important power is that of fining contemnors. Formerly, there were no statutory limits to the amount which could be imposed by courts acting under their inherent jurisdiction. This remains the case for superior courts but in so far as inferior courts so act, s 14(2) of the Contempt of Court Act 1981 now provides a maximum limit of £2,500.[11]

In deciding the amount of the fine the courts will consider the seriousness of the interference or potential interference with the due administration of justice, the culpability of the offender and the offender's means. So far as culpability is concerned, as Lord Parker LJ said in *R v Thomson Newspapers Ltd, ex p A-G*[12]

4 [1962] 2 QB 637 at 640 per Lord Parker CJ. Such applications are rare.
5 See *Supreme Court Practice* 52/8/83.
6 At any rate this is the practice in the Chancery Division, see *Practice Direction (Chancery Division)* [1952] WN 121.
7 *Practice Direction (Family Division: Contempt of Court)* [1983] 2 All ER 1066 1 WLR 998.
8 *Supreme Court Practice* 52/8/3, relying on *Ashton v Shorrock* (1880) 29 WR 117.
9 *Re Edwards, Brooke v Edwards* (1882) 21 Ch D 230.
10 *Church's Trustee v Hibbard* [1902] 2 Ch 784 at 791. Where the offence is a continuing offence, it may be possible to re-arrest the offender under the original order, see *Church's Trustee v Hibbard*, per Mathew LJ at 792. This case was concerned with civil contempt but the same argument may be possible in cases of criminal contempt, eg where the offender refuses to answer a question. See also the *Supreme Court Practice* 52/8/3.
11 As amended by the Criminal Justice Act 1991, s 17 (3)(a), Sch 4, Pt 1. For the restrictions on sheriffs' and district courts in Scotland see s 15(2) (a) and (b) respectively as amended by the Criminal Justice Act 1982, s 56(4), Sch 7—maximum limits are level 4 on the standard scale (currently £2,500).
12 [1968] 1 All ER 268, at 270, [1968] 1 WLR 1 at 4, cited with approval by Parker LJ in *A-G v Hislop* [1991] 1 QB 514, 529, [1991] 1 All ER 911 at 921.

the most serious contempts are 'publication of matter done intentionally, with the very object of prejudicing a fair trial'. So far as media contempts are concerned in England and Wales the heaviest fine in real terms probably remains that imposed in *R v Bolam, ex p Haigh* [13] where the proprietors of the *Daily Mirror* were fined £10,000 in 1949. However, the highest reported fine is £80,000 imposed on the publishers of the *Sun* newspaper and £20,000 on its then editor, Kelvin Mackenzie, for publishing a photograph of man charged with murder shortly before he was picked out of an identity parade.[14] The proprietors of the *Sun* were also fined £75,000 for their contempt in publishing articles 'Rape case Doc' and 'Doc groped me, says girl' just after agreeing to finance a private prosecution against the doctor concerned.[15] These, however, are outstandingly severe penalties for what were regarded as particularly serious contempts.[16] In fact it is relatively unusual to impose fines in excess of £10,000, though in *A-G v Hislop* both the editor and the publisher of *Private Eye* were fined £10,000.[17] Generally, however, publications with small circulations and the local press can expect to be fined less than the national media. For example, in *A-G v TVS Television Ltd*,[18] whereas the television company was fined £25,000, the publishers of the *Reading Standard* were fined £5,000 for similar contempts.

Of course, in addition to the pecuniary penalties, those found guilty will also be liable for costs which themselves may exceed the fine. Indeed in some cases the imposition of costs alone will be deemed sufficient penalty. In *R v Border Television Ltd, R v Newcastle Chronicle and Journal Ltd, ex p A-G*,[19] for example, the *Chronicle* and *Journal* were ordered to pay two-thirds and Border Television one-third of the Attorney General's costs.

The propriety of ordering payment of costs as a penalty has been questioned in two Canadian cases[20] (though costs were commonly awarded in Canada[1]) and it may be that if a particular limit is had in mind that amount is better expressed as a fine. What according to the Court of Appeal in *Weston v Central Criminal Court, Courts' Administrator*[2] cannot be done in contempt proceedings is to order the contemnor to pay the costs thrown away by wasted proceedings resulting from the contempt.

13 (1949) 93 Sol Jo 220.
14 Reported in (1994) Independent, 6 July.
15 *A-G v News Group Newspapers Ltd* [1989] QB 110, [1988] 2 All ER 906, discussed in Ch 5 at pp 144–145.
16 Other high fines include £25,000 on TVS in *A-G v TVS Television Ltd* (1989) Times, 7 July, and £15,000 in *Solicitor-General v Henry and News Group Newspaper Ltd* [1990] COD 307. Cf in Scotland where in a series of contempt cases before the 1981 Act high fines were imposed. For example, in *Atkins v London Weekend Television Ltd* 1978 SLT 76 the television company was fined £50,000, the editor and managing director each £5,000 and the producer, £1,000; in *HM Advocate v George Outram & Co Ltd* 1980 SLT (Notes) 13 the publishers of the *Glasgow Herald* were fined £20,000 and the editor £750, while (as reported in the *Times*, 22 December, 1979) *Radio Forth Ltd* was fined £10,000 and its chief-executive £1,000 for a publication about the same case.
17 [1991] 1 QB 514, [1991] 1 All ER 911, discussed at pp 207 ff.
18 (1989) Times, 7 July, full transcript on Lexis. For earlier examples note that the proprietors of the *North West Evening Mail* (1981) 131 NLJ 1270, (1981) Times, 7 February and the publishers of the *Northampton Chronicle and Echo* (1981) Times, 31 March were each fined £500 for their offending publications; while in *R v Socialist Worker Printers and Publishers Ltd, ex p A-G* [1975] QB 637, [1975] 1 All ER 142, Paul Foot, as editor, and the magazine's publisher were each fined £250.
19 (1979) 68 Cr App R 375, [1978] Crim LR 221.
20 *Re Letourneau—Belanger and La Société de Publication Merlin Ltd* (1969) 6 DLR (3d) 451 and *Re Ouellet* (1976) 72 DLR (3d) 95.
 1 See Robertson, *Courts and the Media* (1981).
 2 [1977] QB 32, [1976] 2 All ER 875.

Costs that are awarded may be taxed 'on the common fund basis'[3] or, as in *R v Daily Herald, ex p Bishop of Norwich*[4] as between 'solicitor and client'.

The court is not bound to award costs against the offender even if found guilty of contempt.[5] Indeed it has power to dismiss the motion and order the prosecution to pay costs, if it is thought that the contempt in question is 'too venial to justify its being brought to the attention of the court at all'.[6]

The court can also take security for good behaviour. This was done in *R v Castro, Skipworth's Case*[7] where the offender was ordered to give his own security of £500 and find one or more sureties to the amount of £500:

> 'that he be of good behaviour and not guilty of any contempt of this court for the space of three months from the present time, and to be imprisoned until such security is given.'

The court also has the further option[8] both in committal applications and, it is submitted, upon its own motion to grant an injunction either to restrain further repetition of the act of contempt[9] or to prevent a contempt from being committed.[10] The former has been ordered by way of leniency but there is no reason why such injunctions cannot be accompanied by a fine etc.

IV APPEALS

A The right of appeal

Formerly, under English law the right of appeal could only be exercised against a decision concerning *civil* contempt. The reason that there was no right of appeal against a decision concerning a *criminal* contempt lay not in any conscious intention of the legislature but a result of a quirk in parliamentary drafting. The Criminal Appeal Act 1907 gave for the first time a general right of appeal in criminal cases to the Court of Criminal Appeal but as it applied only to those 'convicted on indictment'[11] it did not cover contempt prosecutions since they were tried summarily. At the same time no appeal could lie to the Court of Appeal since it was expressly provided[12] that no appeal lay to that court 'in any criminal cause or matter' and a criminal contempt was held to be such a 'criminal cause or matter'.[13] As Lord Shaw of Dunfermline commented in *Scott v Scott*:[14]

3 As in *Michigan (Great Britain) Ltd v Mathew* [1966] RPC 47.
4 [1932] 2 KB 402.
5 Eg in *Cronmire v Daily Bourse Ltd* (1892) 9 TLR 101 no order was made.
6 In *A-G v Times Newspapers Ltd* [1974] AC 273 at 312. See also *Plating Co v Farquharson* (1881) 17 Ch D 49 at 57 per James LJ.
7 (1873) LR 9 QB 230 at 241.
8 Ordering an offender to apologise publicly was held in *Re Ouellet* (1976) 72 DLR (3d) 95 not to be an appropriate or worthwhile penalty.
9 See *Lewis v James* (1887) 3 TLR 527 and *Coleman v West Hartlepool Harbour and Rly Co* (1860) 2 LT 766. See also *Critchley v Australian Urban Investments Ltd* [1979] VR 374.
10 *Kitcat v Sharp* (1882) 52 LJ Ch 134; *A-G v Times Newspapers Ltd* [1974] AC 273, [1973] 3 All ER 54.
11 Ss 3, 20.
12 Formerly by the Judicature Act 1873, s 47(1), replaced by the Judicature Act 1925, s 31(1)(a). See now the Supreme Court Act 1981, s 18(1)(a).
13 See eg *O'Shea v O'Shea and Parnell* (1890) 15 PD 59, CA.
14 [1913] AC 417 at 486. A similar problem was created in Scotland by the wording of the Criminal Appeal (Scotland) Act 1926, s 1 (which only applied to convictions on indictment) and the inappropriateness of the Summary Jurisdiction (Scotland) Act 1954 to appeals before the High Court. However, it was held in *Wylie v HM Advocate* 1966 SLT 149 that this lacuna

'In the year 1908 Parliament interposed to give a right of appeal in criminal causes. The Court of Appeal in the present case has held that no appeal lies from the judgment of Bargrave Deane J, because the decision of the learned judge is in a criminal cause or matter. Grant, accordingly, that this is so; yet, nevertheless, the Criminal Appeal Act 1907 affords no remedy to the unfortunate appellants. Under the argument against them they have been denied a civil appeal because their conduct was indictable, and under the Act of 1907 they can obtain no remedy by way of criminal appeal because they have not been convicted on indictment. In juggles of that kind the rights of the citizen are lost.'

This historical anomaly was finally remedied[15] by the Administration of Justice Act 1960, s 13 which now provides, at least in England and Wales,[16] but not in Scotland,[17] a *uniform* procedure for appeal in respect of *both* criminal and civil contempt. During the Parliamentary debates on the provision there was some opposition to providing appeals in respect of contempt in the face of the court[18] but, fortunately,[19] the opposition did not prevail and s 13 applies to all types of contempt tried summarily.[20] In cases of criminal contempts appeals can be made both against conviction and sentence.

Section 13(1) expressly states that the provisions for appeal in contempt cases replace any former channels of appeal. Accordingly, it was held in *Re Rudkin-Jones (a bankrupt), ex p The Bankrupt v Trustee of the Property of the Bankrupt (Practice Note)*[1] that whereas appeals from a county court in insolvency matters normally lie to the Divisional Court, in contempt they lie to the Court of Appeal. However, not all litigation over contempt issues is classifiable as an 'order or decision of a court in the exercise of jurisdiction to punish for contempt of court' to which the section refers. For example, applications to restrain publications because of possible prejudice to active legal proceedings are not thought to be contempt cases for these purposes.[2]

could be overcome by invoking the nobile officium of the High Court. See also *Green v Smith* 1988 SLT 175 in which a sentence of nine months' imprisonment was successfully challenged by bill of suspension.

15 This anomaly had been heavily criticised, see especially the 1959 *Justice* report: *Contempt of Court*, pp 35–38.

16 The provision formerly applied to Northern Ireland but s 13 in so far as it applied to Northern Ireland was repealed by the Judicature (Northern Ireland) Act 1978, s 122(2) and Sch 7. For the current routes of appeal see s 44 of the 1978 Act.

17 S 20(2) save where it is an appeal from the Courts-Martial Appeal Court. For the routes of appeal see *The Law of Scotland, Stair's Memorial Encyclopaedia*, Vol 6, *Contempt of Court* paras 325-400.

18 Notably by Lord Goddard in the second reading of the Bill. See generally 222 HL Official Report (5th Series) col 253 ff. See also Barwick CJ's reservations as to the value of such appeals, *Keeley v Brooking* (1979) 53 ALJR 526 at 528, 9 (High Court of Australia). Until 1972 the Canadian Criminal Code limited appeals in cases of contempt in the face of the court, to appeals against punishment and not sentence. Section 9 now gives a right of appeal in all cases. Similarly in New Zealand there is now a statutory right of appeal in all cases of contempt, see the Crimes Act 1961, s 384 and Summary Proceedings Act 1957, s 115B.

19 In view of such cases as *Balogh v Crown Court at St Albans* [1975] QB 73, [1974] 3 All ER 283 and *Weston v Central Criminal Court, Courts Administrator* [1977] QB 32, [1976] 2 All ER 875 where the first instance decisions were overturned on appeal and *Morris v Crown Office* [1970] 2 QB 114, [1970] 1 All ER 1079 where the first instance decision was tempered.

20 Appeals against decisions in contempt cases tried on indictment are controlled by Part I of the Criminal Appeal Act 1968: s 13(6) of the Administration of Justice Act 1960 as amended by the Criminal Appeal Act 1968, Sch 5. Note also the exclusion under s 13(5) as amended, see below.

1 [1964] 3 All ER 750, [1964] 1 WLR 1470.

2 Ie they are treated as injunctions and though in some cases, eg *A-G v Times Newspapers Ltd* [1973] QB 710, [1973] 1 All ER 815; [1974] AC 273, [1973] 3 All ER 54, HL and *A-G v BBC* [1981] AC 303, [1980] 3 All ER 161 they have been heard at first instance by the Queen's

Section 13(1) refers to appeals from any order or decision of a *court*, etc and under s 13(5) 'court' is widely defined as including 'any tribunal or person having power to punish for contempt' and such a definition therefore includes any court having inherent jurisdiction to punish for contempt. The section also states that any references to 'an order or decision of a court in the exercise of jurisdiction to punish for contempt of court *includes* [3] references' (a) to an order or decision of the High Court, Crown Court[4] or county court under any enactment enabling that court to deal with an offence as if it were contempt of court; (b) to an order or decision of a county court, or of any court having the powers of a county court, under the County Courts Act 1984, ss 14, 92, 118;[5] (c) to an order or decision of a magistrates' court, under the Magistrates' Courts Act 1980, s 63 (3).[6] The section expressly excludes orders made under the Debtors Act 1869, s 5, and any provision not already mentioned of the Magistrates' Courts Act 1980 and of the County Courts Act 1984 except for ss 38 and 142 of the latter Act insofar as they confer jurisdiction for contempt of court.[7]

The Act clearly intends to provide for appeals against the decisions of the various courts whether they are exercising their inherent or statutory jurisdiction. However, with regard to the exercise of their statutory jurisdiction it is not altogether clear whether the phrase 'order or decision of a court' extends to other courts not expressly mentioned in the section. Would for instance a coroner's court acting under its statutory jurisdiction be included?[8] The answer will depend upon the construction of the word 'includes', and while it could be argued that only the courts expressly mentioned should be included (ie applying the maxim *expressio unius exclusio alterius*) it is submitted that the better view is that appeals lie from all courts exercising a statutory jurisdiction in punishing a contempt.

According to s 13(2):

> 'An appeal under this section shall lie in any case at the instance of the defendant and, in the case of an application for committal or attachment, at the instance of the applicant . . .'

Although s 13(2) makes it clear that either party may appeal it seemed to be intended that an applicant should have a more limited right of appeal, for whereas a defendant may appeal 'in any case' an applicant can appeal only in respect of an application for committal or attachment. Read literally this would mean that the applicant could not appeal where only a fine was being sought, which in turn would mean that, since no committal lies against a company, no appeal would

Bench Divisional Court in fact they were appealed to the Court of Appeal before going to the House of Lords. For the effect of such classification upon (a) applications under RSC Ord 52 see p 477 and (b) the application of the Contempt of Court Act 1981, s 7 see pp 480–481. See also *R v Horsham Justices, ex p Farquharson* [1982] QB 762, [1982] 2 All ER 269 where an application to challenge a ruling made under s 4(2) of the Contempt of Court Act 1981 (see pp 284 ff) was not thought to be a contempt case for the purposes of s 13 ie the case was properly treated as an application for judicial review. Cf *A-G v Leveller Magazine Ltd* [1979] AC 440, [1979] 1 All ER 745 where an application was made to commit the defendants for publishing information contrary to a court order.

3 Emphasis added.
4 Amended by the Courts Act 1971, Sch 8, para 40(2).
5 S 13(5)(b).
6 S 13(5)(c) as amended by the Magistrates' Courts Act 1980, Sch 7, para 37. S 63(3) is discussed in Ch 14.
7 S 38 gives the county court the same general ancillary jurisdiction as the High Court, see pp 641–643; while s 142 gives the county court the same powers as the High Court to enforce undertakings given by solicitors, see p 642.
8 Eg under the Coroners' Act 1988, s 10, see p 508.

ever lie against a refusal to find a company[9] guilty of contempt. These contentions were expressly rejected by the Court of Appeal in *A-G v Hislop*.[10] In that case the court accepted the Attorney General's submission that the words 'and, in the case of an application for committal or attachment, at the instance of the applicant':[11]

> 'are intended to do no more than distinguish those cases in which the decision or order sought to be appealed resulted from an application to punish for contempt from those cases in which there was no application and the order or decision was made by the court of its own motion.'

As Nicholls LJ pointed out:[12]

> 'the phrase is applicable in all cases where an alleged contempt is brought before the court on an application regardless of the particular form of punishment which, either in the application or otherwise, the applicant says he is seeking. Punishment is a matter for the court, not for the applicant. As other construction of the phrase . . . would produce bizarre results which Parliament plainly could not have intended.'

On this basis appeals will also lie against a refusal to issue a writ of sequestration.[13]

Although s 13(2) refers to appeals lying at the instance of the defendant it has been held[14] that where a committal order has been made the Official Solicitor can appeal on behalf of the person committed if that person does not move the court on his own behalf.

B   Where appeals lie

1   *To a Divisional Court of the High Court*

Under s 13(2) of the 1960 Act appeals lie to the Divisional Court 'from an order or decision of any, inferior court not referred to in the next following paragraph'. Precisely what is meant by 'inferior court' in this context is still not entirely clear although apparently, the real intention of this paragraph was to provide a channel of appeal from quarter sessions,[15] which courts have now been abolished.[16] Nevertheless the words 'inferior court' have a wider meaning[17] and could plausibly refer to any inferior court[18] purportedly exercising a contempt jurisdiction.[19] On this basis it would include magistrates' courts, coroners' courts, consistory courts and any other statutory court of record.[20] In the case of

---

9   Attachments, which did lie against a company, have now disappeared; see pp 475–476.
10   [1991] 1 QB 514, [1991] 1 All ER 911.
11   Ibid at 523 and 917.
12   Ibid at 533 and 925.
13   See eg *Hoffman–La Roche (F) & Co, A-G v Sieczko* [1968] RPC 460 in which such an appeal was heard but no reference was made to the wording of s 13(2). See also *Lenton v Tregoning* [1960] 1 All ER 717, [1960] 1 WLR 333, CA.
14   *Churchman v Joint Shop Stewards' Committee of the Workers of the Port of London* [1972] 1 WLR 1094 at 1101.
15   Viscount Kilmuir, 222 HL Official Report (5th series) col 297.
16   By the Courts Act 1971, s 3.
17   This was the view of one contemporary commentator, see DGT Williams, 'The Administration of Justice Act 1960' [1961] Crim LR 87, 98.
18   Excluding county courts from where appeals lie to the Court of Appeal, see below.
19   Cf the discussion on the ambit of RSC Ord 52, r 1(2)(a)(ii), see p 486.
20   See above p 508.

magistrates' courts, however, s 12(5) of the Contempt of Court Act 1981 provides that appeals against orders made under s 12 of that Act lie to the Crown Court and, as we discussed earlier, May LJ in *R v Havant Justices, ex p Palmer*,[1] said that that provision precluded the operation of s 13 of the 1960 Act. Whether the appellate courts will be disposed to agree with their suggestion remains to be seen,[2] though there does seem some merit in saying that s 13 operates only insofar as Parliament has not subsequently provided a statutory route of appeal. Bearing this caveat in mind it is suggested that s 13(2) of the 1960 Act is to be regarded as providing a route of appeal to the Divisional Court against contempt decisions of any inferior court in any case where no other statutory route of appeal has since been provided.[3]

Where appeals do lie to the Divisional court under the 1960 Act they lie to the Queen's Bench Divisional Court.[4]

2 To the Court of Appeal

By s 13 (2), as amended,[5] appeals lie to the Court of Appeal:

'(b) . . . from an order or decision of a county court or any other inferior court from which appeals generally lie to the Court of Appeal, and from an order or decision . . . of a single judge of the High Court, or of any court having the powers of the High Court or of a judge of that court, . . . (bb) from an order or decision of the Crown Court . . .'

In general appeals lie to the Civil Division of the Court of Appeal, irrespective of whether the contempt itself is civil or criminal.[6] The exception, pursuant to the Supreme Court Act 1981, s 53(2)(b), is that appeals from Crown Court contempt decisions lie to the Court of Appeal (Criminal Division).[7] The phrase 'any other inferior court from which appeals generally lie to the Court of Appeal' formerly referred to certain local inferior courts of record, for example the Salford Hundred Court and the Liverpool Court of Passage, which have since been abolished.[8] The phrase also referred to the Mayor's and City of London Court, but although this court was abolished it was re-established under the same name but with county court status,[9] and accordingly an appeal concerning contempt will still lie to the Court of Appeal.

1 [1985] Crim LR 658, full report on Lexis, discussed at p 516.
2 As pointed out at p 516, there is at least one reported case where one such appeal was allowed under s 13, see *Re Hooker (Patricia) and the Contempt of Court Act 1981* [1993] COD 190.
3 On this basis *R v Havant Justices, ex p Palmer* was wrong to have allowed judicial review since there was a right of appeal under s 13 against a finding of contempt. See the discussion at p 516.
4 RSC Ord 109, r 2(1).
5 By the Courts Act 1971, Sch 8, para 40(1) and Sch 11, Pt 11. NB the Attachment of Earnings Act 1971, s 23(9) which provides that s 13 of the 1960 Act also applies to appeals against orders made under s 23 of the 1971 Act.
6 As emphasised by Lord Widgery CJ in *R v Tibbitts* (1978) 122 Sol Jo 761.
7 Similarly, the Court of Appeal (Criminal Division) is the correct appellate court for hearing appeals against an order or decision of the Crown Court dealing with an offence under the Bail Act 1976, s 6 as if it were a contempt, see *R v Harbax Singh* [1979] QB 319, [1979] 1 All ER 524.
8 By the Courts Act 1971, s 43(1).
9 Courts Act 1971, s 42(1)(2).

The phrase 'of any court having the powers of the High Court or of a judge of that court' refers to the Restrictive Practices Court and to the Lord Chancellor and 'nominated judges' acting under Part VII of the Mental Health Act 1983.

3   To the House of Lords

By s 13(2)(c) appeals lie to the House of Lords from a decision of a Divisional Court, Court of Appeal (Civil and Criminal Division[10]) and the Courts-Martial Appeal Court. Since in practice most cases of criminal contempt (particularly those concerning the news media) are tried at first instance by the Divisional Court, the appellate jurisdiction of the House of Lords assumes more than usual importance. Furthermore, as will be seen shortly, the rules for requiring leave are relaxed where the appeal to the House of Lords is the first appeal. In fact it took some time before advantage was taken of this right of appeal[11] but they have now become a little more common.[12]

C   Procedure for appeal

1   To a Divisional Court of the High Court

An appeal must be brought by originating motion,[13] every notice of the motion must state the grounds of appeal, and:

> 'if the appeal is against a judgment, order or other decision of a court, must state whether the appeal is against the whole or part of that decision and, if against a part only, must specify the part.'[14]

Unless the court gives leave to the contrary, there shall not be more than four clear days between the date on which the order or decision appealed against was made and the day named in the notice of the originating motion for the hearing of the appeal.[15] The notice must be served and the appeal entered not less than one

10 See DGT Williams: [1961] Crim LR 87 at 981; Criminal Appeal Act 1968, s 33(3) as substituted by Supreme Court Act 1981, Sch 5.
11 The first case of a direct appeal from the Divisional Court under s 13(2)(c) was *A-G v Leveller Magazine Ltd* [1979] AC 440, [1979] 1 All ER 745. Cf *Heaton's Transport (St Helens) Ltd v Transport and General Workers Union* [1973] AC 15 and *Home Office v Harman* [1983] 1 AC 280, [1982] 1 All ER 532 which were first appealed to the Court of Appeal under s 13(2)(b) and then to the House of Lords under s 13(2)(c).
12 Eg *A-G v Associated Newspapers Ltd* [1994] 2 AC 238, [1994] 1 All ER 556; *Raymond v Honey* [1983] 1 AC 1, [1982] 1 All ER 756; *A-G v English* [1983] 1 AC 116, [1982] 2 All ER 903. Other contempt cases heard by the House of Lords came via different routes eg *A-G v Times Newspapers Ltd* [1974] AC 273 [1973] 3 All ER 54 and *A-G v BBC* [1981] AC 303, [1980] 3 All ER 161 which were both applications to restrain publications. In neither case was a certificate required since they were appeals from the Court of Appeal in a civil matter. Note also *A-G v Times Newspapers Ltd* [1992] 1 AC 191, [1991] 2 All ER 398 (*Spycatcher*) in which the litigation as a whole was complex but in which the contempt action against the *Sunday Times* came before the House of Lords on appeal from the Court of Appeal; and *X Ltd v Morgan-Grampian (Publishers) Ltd* [1991] 1 AC 1, [1990] 2 All ER 1, *Re An Inquiry under the Company Securities (Insider Dealing) Act* [1988] AC 660, [1988] 1 All ER 203, *Secretary of State for Defence v Guardian Newspapers Ltd* [1985] AC 339, [1984] 3 All ER 601—cases involving a refusal by journalists to reveal sources of information which were all appeals from the Court of Appeal.
13 RSC Ord 55, r 3(1).
14 Ord 55, r 3(2).
15 Ord 109, r 2(4) ie Ord 55, r 4(2) does not apply; Ord 109 r 2(3).

clear day before the day named in the notice for the hearing of the appeal[16] and the notice must be served on the clerk or registrar or district judge of the court from whose order or decision the appeal is brought and on any party to the proceedings in which the decision was given who is directly affected by the appeal.[17]

2 To the Court of Appeal

Notice of the appeal must be served both on the proper officer of the court, from whose order or decision the appeal is brought, and on the party or parties who are directly affected by the appeal.[18] By means of *Practice Directions* it has been established that the proper officer of the Chancery Division is the Chief Registrar[19] and in the case of the Restrictive Practices Court, it is the Clerk of that Court.[20] It had also been established that the proper officer of the Probate Divorce and Admiralty Division was the senior registrar[1] and presumably the proper officer of the Family Court Division is the senior district judge of that division.

A separate order[2] governs appeals from county courts and notice of appeal must be served on the district judge[3] of the county court and on the party or parties who are directly affected by the appeal. In *Brown v Crowley*[4] it was held though 'with considerable doubt', by Pearson LJ, that it was not strictly necessary to serve notice of appeal upon a bailiff, who had been assaulted (thereby giving rise to the contempt action)[5] since he was not 'directly affected' by the appeal.

Affidavit evidence is receivable in both criminal and civil contempt cases,[6] and in all cases the admission of fresh evidence is governed by the practice of the Court of Appeal (Criminal Division), namely, that it should be admitted where justice so requires.[6a]

3 To the House of Lords

By the Administration of Justice Act 1960, s 13(4), many of the rules regarding appeals to the House of Lords in criminal cases generally are also applicable to such appeals in contempt cases.

An appeal can only be made with leave,[7] and such leave can either be obtained from the court below, or if that court refuses, from the House of Lords. Normally, leave cannot be given unless the court below certifies that a point of law or a point of general importance is involved, and where it appears either to the court below or the House of Lords that the point ought to be considered by that House.[8] However, s 13(4) provides that where the appeal is from a court of first instance

16 Ord 109, r 2(5).
17 Ord 55, r 4(1)(a).
18 Ord 59, r 20(1).
19 [1961] 2 All ER 494.
20 [1961] 2 All ER 11.
1 Ibid.
2 RSC Ord 59, r 19.
3 Although the rules still refer to 'registrar'.
4 [1963] 3 All ER 655, [1963] 1 WLR 1102, CA.
5 Ie under what is now the County Courts Act 1984, s 14.
6 *Brown v Crowley (No 2)* [1964] 1 All ER 72n, [1964] 1 WLR 147, CA.
6a *Irtelli v Squatriti* [1993] QB 83, [1992] 3 All ER 294, CA. This means that appeals in civil contempt cases are not governed by *Ladd v Marshall* [1954] 3 All ER 745, CA.
7 The Administration of Justice Act 1960, ss 1(2) and 13(4).
8 The Administration of Justice Act 1960, s 1(2).

such as the Divisional Court (which in practice tries at first instance most cases of 'newspaper' contempt) and both Divisions of the Court of Appeal (eg which try at first instance contempts committed in its face), then although leave of either the House of Lords or of the lower court is still required, leave may be given without a certificate.[9]

An application for leave to the court below should be made within 14 days of the decision of that court and an application to the House of Lords for leave should be made within 14 days of the refusal to grant leave by the court below,[10] although these times can be extended by the House of Lords upon an application by the defendant.[11]

Section 13 is apparently intended to allow one appeal *as of right* [12] but if that is the case why is it necessary to obtain leave, albeit without a certificate, to appeal from a Divisional Court at first instance to the House of Lords? Alternatively, when a Divisional Court hears a contempt case at first instance, why should not an appeal lie as of right to the Civil Division of the Court of Appeal which does have appellate jurisdiction over criminal contempt cases heard by a High Court judge, Crown Court or a county court?

D   Powers of the Appeal Courts

The Administration of Justice Act 1960, s 13(3) states that:

> 'The court to which an appeal is brought under this section may reverse or vary the order or decision of the court below, and make such other order as may be just . . .'.

It was established by *Linnett v Coles* [13] that s 13(3) gives the Court of Appeal wide powers including not merely reversing or varying the order under appeal but also to make such other order as may be just. Accordingly, it was held that under this provision the appellate court has jurisdiction to remedy an irregularity in the original committal order. In that case the committal order was defective since it had been made for an indefinite period,[14] but it was held that under s 13(3) the court could substitute a just sentence for the original one.

Clearly, given that the liberty of the subject is concerned, such a power should not be readily used[14a] and indeed it seems to be a rule of practice not to exercise the discretion to remedy a defective committal order if it has already been exercised with the contemnor taken to prison.[14b] Nevertheless, as the Court of

9   See also *Practice Direction* (1989) 88 Cr App Rep 105.
10   The Administration of Justice Act 1960, s 2(1).
11   S 2(3). Presumably, the Official Solicitor acting on the contemnor's behalf can apply for an extension of time, if the contemnor does not apply on his own behalf. See by way of analogy *Churchman v Joint Shop Stewards' Committee of Workers of the Post of London* [1972] 1 WLR 1094 at 1101. As regards the form of appeal, which is by petition, and for other rules of procedure see generally the *Supreme Court Practice* (1995) Vol 2, paras 16–001 ff.
12   Per Viscount Kilmuir, 222 HL Official Report (5th series) col 586–7.
13   [1987] QB 555, [1986] 3 All ER 652.
14   Under s 16 of the Contempt of Court Act 1981 committals must be for a fixed period not exceeding two years.
14a   See eg *Loseby v Newman* [1995] 2 FLR 754 in which Balcombe LJ commented that a court would not normally rectify a defective committtal order unless there were exceptional circumstances.
14b   See *Smith v Smith (Contempt: Committal)* [1992] FLR 40, CA, applying *Hegarty v O'Sullivan* (1985) 135 NLJ 557, CA and *Linkleter v Linkleter* [1988] 1 FLR 360, CA, and relied upon in *C v Hackney London Borough Council* [1995] 2 FCR 306 at 308 per Leggatt LJ.

Appeal subsequently observed in *M v P and Others (Contempt of court: Committal Order), Butler v Butler,* [15] in deciding whether to exercise its corrective powers the court has to take into account not only the interests of the contemnor but also of those affected by the contempt and the need to maintain the court's authority. If the irregularity has caused the contemnor no injustice it should not be set aside. However, whether a distinction should be made between a defect in the committal application and one in the order is not entirely clear. In *Harmsworth v Harmsworth* [16] the Court of Appeal thought such a distinction ought to be drawn and considered, for example, that defective notice could be so prejudicial as not to be curable. However, although it may be right to say[17] that the appellate court is more likely to make a substitute order in cases, other than where the contemnor has already been imprisoned (see above), where there is a defect in the committal order, particularly where it triggers an otherwise valid suspended order,[17a] rather than in the application, nevertheless it may be doubted whether there is a binding principle to this effect. In any event it may simply be another way of saying that a substituted order should not be made where the contemnor's interests have been prejudiced. In the latter respect the Court of Appeal decision in *Duo v Osborne (Formerly Duo)* [18] that s 13(3) also empowers the court to order a rehearing is important since some alleged injustices (in this case that insufficient fine had been given to the contemnor's legal representative to obtain instructions and to call witnesses) can be cured at the subsequent hearing.

Apart from the difficulty of being able to predict when the court will use its corrective powers under s 13(3)[19] another problem is determining the relationship between s 13(3) and RSC Ord 59, r 10(3). Under the latter provision the Court of Appeal is empowered to replace an order of a court below with 'such other order as the case may require'. Some cases, for example, *Linkleter v Linkleter,*[20] only considered this provision. However, as *Linkleter* itself shows the corrective powers under Ord 59, r 10(3) are much more limited and it is submitted that in the light of *Linnett v Coles* and *Duo v Osborne (Formerly Duo)*, s 13(3) should now always be used in preference to Ord 52.

Despite the apparent generality of s 13(3) not all appellate courts have such wide powers. Divisional Courts' powers are circumscribed by RSC Ord 55, r 7(5) which provides:

> 'The court may give any judgment or decision or make any order which ought to have been given or made by the court, tribunal or person and make such further or other order as the case may require or may remit the matter with the opinion of the court for rehearing and determination by it or him.'

15 [1993] Fam 167, [1992] 4 All ER 833.
16 [1987] 3 All ER 816.
17 Cf Miller, *Contempt of Court* (2nd edn) at p 426.
17a See *C v Hackney London Borough Council,* supra.
18 [1992] 3 All ER 121. Note that according to Lord Donaldson MR a possible reason why the power to order a rehearing had never previously been exercised was that it was only after the passing of s 43 of the Criminal Justice Act 1988 that the Court of Appeal (Criminal Division) had an unfettered power to order a retrial. Previously, such a power was contingent upon there being further evidence subsequent to the original trial.
19 See eg apart from *Linnett v Coles* [1987] QB 555, [1986] 3 All ER 652 and *Harmsworth, Mason v Lawton* [1991] 2 All ER 784, where new orders were made. Cf *B v B (Contempt: Committal)* [1991] 2 FLR 588, *Clarke v Clarke* [1990] 2 FLR 115 and *Smith v Smith (Contempt: Committal)* [1992] 2 FLR 40 where the court refused to cure the defect and ordered the contemnor's release.
20 [1988] 1 FLR 360. See also *Re C (a minor) (Contempt)* [1986] 1 FLR 578 and *Hill Samuel & Co v Littaur* (1985) NLJ Rep 556.

In other words a Divisional Court can only make an order which was within the powers of the court below. In *B (BPM) v B (MM)*[1] an appeal was made from a magistrates' court which, purporting to exercise its jurisdiction under what was then the Magistrates' Courts Act 1952, s 54(3),[2] sentenced the offender to imprisonment for two months but suspended the sentence for one year. It was held by the Divisional Court that the magistrates had acted in excess of their powers in imposing a suspended sentence and in imposing a sentence of imprisonment which would continue to apply even if the offender remedied his default. The Divisional Court did have the power to impose such sentence as the magistrates could properly have made, but on the facts it was held that it was unnecessary to impose any term of imprisonment pending the remedying of the default.

Where the Divisional Court's decision is further appealed to the House of Lords, it would appear that the latter court's powers are then similarly fettered because by s 1 (4) of the Administration of Justice Act 1960 for the purpose of disposing of an appeal the House of Lords may exercise any of the powers of the court below or may remit the case to that court.

While the Court of Appeal's powers do not appear to be fettered it is doubtful whether a greater sentence would in practice be imposed in the case of an appeal from a county court than that lower court could itself impose.

The appeal is by way of a re-hearing[3] which of course enables the appeal court to re-examine the facts and although the court would naturally be reluctant to disagree with the trial court's findings of fact, it nevertheless does have the power to do so, and will do so in appropriate cases.[4]

E Bail pending appeal

Provision has been made for an applicant who is in custody at the time of appeal to apply for bail. Where an appeal is made to the Court of Appeal or to the House of Lords from the Court of Appeal, RSC Ord 59, r 20(2)[5] provides that:

> 'the Court of Appeal may order his release on his giving security (whether by recognisance,[6] with or without sureties, or otherwise and for such reasonable sum as that Court may fix) for his appearance within 10 days after the judgment of the Court of Appeal or, as the case may be, of the House of Lords, on the appeal shall have been given, before the court from whose order or decision the appeal is brought unless the order or decision is reversed by that judgment.'

Application for such release on bail is made by motion, and a 24-hour notice must be served on the proper officer of the court below and on all parties affected.[7]

---

1 [1969] P 103, [1969] 1 All ER 891.
2 Now s 63(3) of the Magistrates' Courts Act 1980.
3 See, eg RSC Ord 55, r 3.
4 See *Hoffman-La Roche (F) & Co, A-G v Siezko* [1968] RPC 460. See also *Lenton v Tregoning* [1960] 1 All ER 717, [1960] 1 WLR 333 and *Mouser v Clark* (1962) Times, 20 March.
5 RSC Ord 59, r 20(4) provides that Ord 79, r 9(4) (6A), (6B) and (8) shall apply. NB by RSC Ord 59, r 20(8) the powers under rr 20(2) and (4) may be exercised by a *single* judge.
6 For rules relating to recognisances see RSC Ord 59, r 20(5) (as amended) and r 20(6). NB by RSC Ord 59, r 20 (8) these rules may be exercised by a *single* judge.
7 RSC Ord 59, r 20(3).

In the case of an appeal to the Divisional Court or to the House of Lords from a Divisional Court, the High Court may, according to RSC Ord 109, r 3(1):[8]

> 'order his release on his giving security (whether by recognisance, with or without sureties, or otherwise and for such reasonable sum as the court may fix) for his appearance, within 10 days after the judgment of the Divisional Court or, as the case may be, of the House of Lords, or the appeal shall have been given, before the court from whose order or decision the appeal is brought unless the order or decision is reversed by that judgment.'

F Privy Council

Resolving earlier doubts *Ambard v A-G for Trinidad and Tobago*[9] established that the Privy Council is competent to entertain appeals against orders even of courts of record overseas imposing penalties for contempt of court.[10] Lord Atkin added, however:[11]

> 'In such cases the discretionary power of the Board will, no doubt, be exercised with great care. Everyone will recognise the importance of maintaining the authority of the courts in restraining and punishing interferences in particular civil or criminal cases, or take the form of attempts to depreciate the authority of the courts themselves. It is sufficient to say that such interferences, when they amount to contempt of court, are quasi-criminal acts, and orders punishing them should, generally speaking, be treated as orders in criminal cases, and leave to appeal against them should only be granted on the well-known principles on which leave to appeal in criminal cases is given.'

V PARDONS

The prerogative of the Crown to pardon or remit sentences extends to criminal contempts,[12] and it is therefore still open to a person found guilty of such an offence to apply for a pardon or remission. The Crown's power to pardon does not in practice extend to cases of civil contempt, for 'though the Crown could interfere, it would be unconstitutional to do so'.[13]

Although the Crown enjoys the exclusive right of granting pardons, in England a pardon is usually granted on the advice of the Home Secretary[14] and accordingly an application should be made to that office.[15] In the Commonwealth,

---

8 RSC Ord 109, r 3(2) provides that Ord 79, r 9(1) to (6) and (8) shall apply. For a comment on the effect of granting bail pending appeal, see *Re W (B) (an infant)* [1969] 1 All ER 594 at 597, per Winn LJ.

9 [1936] AC 322. The early case law is reviewed at 326–329.

10 The Privy Council's competence in such matters was regarded as beyond argument in *Maharaj v A-G for Trinidad and Tobago* [1977] 1 All ER 411 at 412.

11 [1936] AC 322 at 329.

12 *Re Special Reference from Bahama Islands* [1893] AC 138, PC; *Seaward v Paterson* [1897] 1 Ch 545 at 559, CA; *Phipps v Earl of Anglesea* (1721) 1 P Wms 696 which held the Crown's prerogative to pardon extended to contriving the marriage of a ward of court without authority. See also Oswald, *Contempt* (3rd edn, 1910), pp 3, 4 and ATH Smith, 'The Prerogative of Mercy. The Power of Pardon and Criminal Justice' (1983) 42 CLJ 398, 411-412.

13 *Re Special Reference from Bahama Islands* [1893] AC 138 at 145, per Lord Hannen.

14 See 8 *Halsbury's Laws* (4th edn) p 951.

15 See eg *A-G v James* [1962] 2 QB 637 at 640 per Lord Parker CJ; *Sutherland v Sutherland* (1893) Times, 6 May.

where applicable, the power to pardon is usually delegated to colonial governors and to governors-general.[16]

In practice, however, applications for pardon have never been very common,[17] even though until 1960 there was no right of appeal in cases of criminal contempt.[18] Such applications are now even less likely to be made: in the first place there is a right of appeal in cases of a criminal contempt[19] and secondly, the Court of Appeal and High Court now have a general power to discharge a prisoner at any time upon the prisoner's application.[20]

16 8 *Halsbury's Laws* (4th edn), 985. See also *Re Special Reference from Bahama Islands* [1893] AC 138.
17 It was recommended to be exercised in *Rainy v Sierra Leone Justices* (1853) 8 Moo PCC 47 and *Re Ramsay* (1870) LR 3 PC 427 both cases involving contempt of colonial courts. For earlier examples see *Carlions* case (1345) 2 Dyer 188b and see Oswald: *Contempt* (3rd edn, 1910) p 4.
18 See p 531.
19 Administration of Justice Act 1960, s 13, discussed at pp 532 ff.
20 See p 528.

CHAPTER 13

The application of criminal contempt to tribunals of inquiry

I INTRODUCTION

From the seventeenth century until 1921, the usual method of inquiring into alleged misconduct of ministers or other public servants was by a Select Parliamentary Committee or Commission of Inquiry. A characteristic defect of parliamentary inquiries was that they were activated by party political motives and, after the Marconi Scandal of 1912 followed by a politically divided parliamentary Committee of Inquiry, the need was felt for a non-parliamentary method of inquiry into alleged public misconduct. By the Tribunals of Inquiry (Evidence) Act 1921, if both Houses of Parliament resolve that a tribunal should be established for inquiring into a definite matter described in the resolution as of 'urgent public importance', and in pursuance of such resolution a tribunal is appointed by the Crown or by a Secretary of State, the instrument by which the tribunal is appointed may provide that the tribunal should have all the rights, powers and privileges vested in the High Court.[1] It can enforce the attendance and examination of witnesses[2] and can compel the production of documents.[3] A tribunal of inquiry will normally be presided over by the holder of high judicial office and have two other members who will probably be Queen's Counsel.

The Royal Commission on Tribunals of Inquiry (the Salmon Commission)[4] considered that there were from time to time alleged instances of lapses in accepted standards of public administration and other matters causing public concern which could not be dealt with by ordinary civil or criminal processes and required inquisitorial investigation to allay public anxiety. The report cited the Lynskey Tribunal into alleged bribery of ministers and other public servants in 1948, the Bank Rate Tribunal in 1957, and the Vassall Tribunal in 1962. Nevertheless despite these conclusions inquiries under the 1921 Act have never been common and in recent times seem not to be resorted to.[5] Modern inquires such as the Bingham Report into the collapse of BCCI, the Scott Inquiry into the Sale of Arms to Iraq, and the Nolan Inquiry into Standards in Public Life have notably not been set up under the 1921 Act.

---

1 S 1(1).
2 S 1(1)(a).
3 S 1(1)(b).
4 1966, Cmnd 3121, under the chairmanship of Lord Justice Salmon.
5 In all there have been only 19 inquiries set up under the 1921 Act. Among the last ones was that set up in 1974 to investigate the circumstances which led to the Crown agents requesting financial assistance from the Government, that in 1972 into the so called 'Bloody Sunday' deaths in Northern Ireland and that in 1971 into the collapse of the Vehicle and General Insurance Company. For a criticism of this reluctance to use the 1921 Act see Segal, 'Tribunals of Inquiry: A British Invention Ignored in Britain' [1984] PL 207.

II HOW THE LAW OF CONTEMPT AFFECTS TRIBUNALS OF INQUIRY

A   The Tribunals of Inquiry (Evidence) Act 1921

The Tribunals of Inquiry (Evidence) Act 1921, s 1(2) provides:

'If any person
(a)   on being duly summoned as a witness before a tribunal makes default in attending; or
(b)   being in attendance as a witness refuses to take an oath legally required by the tribunal to be taken, or to produce any document in his power or control legally required by the tribunal to be produced by him, or to answer any question to which the tribunal may legally require an answer; or
(c)   does any other thing which would, if the tribunal had been a court of law having power to commit for contempt, have been contempt of that court; the chairman of the tribunal may certify the offence of that person under his hand to the High Court, or in Scotland the Court of Session, and the court may thereupon inquire into the alleged offence and, after hearing any statement that may be offered in defence, punish or take steps for the punishment of that person in like manner as if he had been guilty of contempt of the court.'

Sections 1(2)(a) and (b)[6] are self-explanatory though it is worth pointing out that as there is no provision in the 1921 Act for the payment of witnesses' costs,[7] no witness will be justified in refusing to answer questions until his costs have been paid.[8] It is also clear that s 10 of the Contempt of Court Act 1981 applies to tribunals of inquiry so that before a witness is under a duty to disclose a source of information contained in a publication, the tribunal must be satisfied that 'disclosure is necessary in the interests of justice or natural security or for the prevention of disorder or crime'.[9]

Sections 1(2)(c) is not so clear, though it is generally accepted that whatever else it may mean it includes other types of contempt committed in the face of the tribunal. Hence hurling abuse or missiles at the tribunal's chairman or members or interrupting its proceedings would be prosecutable as a contempt under this provision. The more difficult point, first brought into prominence in connection with the Aberfan Inquiry,[10] is whether s 1(2)(c) also includes contempts committed outside the tribunal and in particular publications creating a risk of prejudice to the inquiry. There are two possible views. The narrow one is that as s 1(2)(a) and (b) both refer to specific instances of contempts committed in the face of the tribunal so s 1(2)(c) is intended to refer (though more generally) to contempts committed in the tribunal's face. The counter view is that the language of the

---

6   For prosecutions under this provision see *A-G v Clough* [1963] 1 QB 773, [1963] 1 All ER 420 and *A-G v Mulholland and Foster* [1963] 2 QB 477, [1963] 1 All ER 767 (journalists refusing to reveal sources of information to the Vassall Tribunal, referred to at p 48).
7   Payments are however made ex gratia: see the Salmon Commission at p 25, para 60: the Commission recommended that express provision should be made for the payment of witnesses' costs.
8   Cf courts of law: see *Re Working Men's Mutual Society* (1882) 21 Ch D 831.
9   The provisions of s 10 are discussed in detail in Ch 2.
10   Particularly by a wide sweeping statement made in the House of Commons by Sir Elwyn Jones (then Attorney General) 734 HC Official Report (5th series) col 1315. See also Lord Gardiner 227 HC Official Report (5th series) col 529. For details of these speeches and press reaction see the first edition of this work at pp 298–299.

subsection is so wide that Parliament must have intended it to encompass all types of contempt.

Although there has been no judicial consideration of s 1(2)(c) the generally accepted view is that the wider interpretation applies. Perhaps the most weighty conclusion is that of the Salmon Commission which was specifically set up to consider the law of contempt as it affects tribunals of inquiry. The report concluded:[11]

> 'In our view the language of paragraph (c) of section 1(2) is in such wide terms that it would be impossible to hold that its application is restricted to contempt in the face of the tribunal. No doubt, the powers it confers upon tribunals of inquiry makes them unique. But they undoubtedly are unique because they possess many other powers not enjoyed by any other type of tribunal.'

Lord Hailsham also had no doubts about the application of the law of contempt to tribunals of inquiry[12] and the provision in the Contempt of Court Act 1981[13] is clearly based on this assumption.

On the strength of the above admittedly extra-judicial opinion, the better and certainly prudent view is that by s 1(2)(c) the law of constructive contempt does apply to tribunals of inquiry.[14]

B The current relevance of s 1(2)(c)

It has been argued[15] that it is unnecessary to determine the exact scope of s 1(2)(c) since in any event the High Court has a supervisory jurisdiction to punish contempts of a tribunal of inquiry.[16] Inasmuch as this view was based on the then accepted test that the Divisional Court's contempt jurisdiction was coextensive with that to correct tribunals by prerogative order there was some merit in the argument.[17] However, as we have seen[18] such a test has been qualified by the 'Court of Law' test laid down by the House of Lords in *A-G v BBC*.[19] It is extremely doubtful whether tribunals of inquiry could satisfy such a test[20] and accordingly it is submitted that the Divisional Court has no direct jurisdiction under RSC Ord 52, r 1(2)(a)(iii).

Section 1 (2)(c) of the 1921 Act must also be considered in the light of the Contempt of Court Act 1981. Section 20(1) states:

11 At para 12. This conclusion was unreservedly accepted in a Government White Paper published subsequently: (1973, Cmnd 5313) para 43. See also Miller, *Contempt of Court* (2nd edn) p 74.
12 See 416 HL Official Report (5th series) cols 389–390.
13 Ie s 20, see below.
14 And in the light of the Contempt of Court Act 1981, s 20 it certainly seems to be Parliament's intention that it should apply.
15 By Miller, 'Contempt of Court—Sub-Judice Rule' [1968] Crim LR 63 at 70 n 54.
16 Following *R v Davies* [1906] 1 KB 32 and more particularly *R v Daily Mail, ex p Farnsworth* [1921] 2 KB 733. Therefore applications for committal can be made direct to the Divisional Court under RSC Ord 52, r 2.
17 Though as we suggested in the first edition at p 298, the principle probably did not apply to tribunals of inquiry since they make no decisions which the High Court can correct.
18 See pp 487 ff.
19 [1981] AC 303, [1980] 3 All ER 161.
20 As Lord Hailsham said in one of the debates on the Contempt of Court Bill (HL Debs 416 HL Official Report (5th series) col 389): 'A tribunal of inquiry is not a court and proceedings before it are not judicial proceedings between parties at all . . .' At col 390 he said 'They do not exercise any part of the judicial power of the state.'

'In relation to any tribunal to which the Tribunals of Inquiry (Evidence) Act 1921 applies, and the proceedings of such a tribunal, the provisions of this Act (except subsection (3) of section 9) apply as they apply in relation to courts and legal proceedings; and references to the course of justice or the administration of justice in legal proceedings shall be construed accordingly.'

Although s 20(1) seems clearly intended to apply the general provisions of the 1981 Act to tribunals of inquiry, s 1(2)(c) of the 1921 Act continues to be relevant in two ways. First, the 1981 Act does not deal with all types of contempt. Thus if contempts such as 'scandalising' the tribunal or punishing witnesses apply to tribunals of inquiry they must do so by virtue of s 1(2)(c). Secondly, although on the face of it s 20(1) of the 1981 Act clearly applies the 'strict liability rule' to tribunals of inquiry, in fact because s 6(b) prevents the imposition of fresh contempt liability,[1] it can only do so provided publications creating a risk of prejudice could formerly be prosecuted for contempt. Again the only reason they could be so prosecuted was because of s 1(2)(c) of the 1921 Act.

It can be seen, therefore, that the generally held view that s 1(2)(c) should be widely interpreted continues to be important. It now remains to consider how the law of constructive contempt applies to tribunals of inquiry.

III   THE APPLICATION OF THE LAW OF CONSTRUCTIVE CONTEMPT TO TRIBUNALS OF INQUIRY

The most important consequence of the law of constructive contempt being applicable to tribunals of inquiry is that it restricts freedom of comment upon the subject-matter of the inquiry. Precisely how the restriction operates in this context is difficult to say though in principle it can be said that not all comment can or would be treated as contempt.[2] In broad terms what must be avoided is comment which is either thought to create a substantial risk of serious prejudice to the proceedings or which is thought to be scurrilously abusive of the tribunal's chairman or other members. The former restriction is consequential upon the operation of the 'strict liability rule', the latter upon the operation of the common law on 'scandalising the court'.

A   Applying the 'strict liability rule'

1   *Timing—proceedings must be 'active'*

Before any comment can amount to contempt under the 'strict liability rule', proceedings must first be 'active'. Section 20(2) of the Contempt of Court Act 1981 makes special provision for when proceedings before tribunals of inquiry are 'active', namely:

'The proceedings of a tribunal [of inquiry] shall be treated as active within the meaning of section 2 from the time when the tribunal is appointed until its report is presented to Parliament.'

---

1   Under the 'strict liability rule', see p 117.
2   Cf Sir Elwyn Jones' statement made in connection with the Aberfan Disaster Inquiry. See 734 HC Official Report (5th series) col 1315 where he said any comments were undesirable.

Section 20(2) noticeably refers to the 'time' of appointment rather than the 'date'. This was apparently[3] deliberately chosen so that in the event of a tribunal being appointed in the afternoon there would be no risk of liability for publications appearing that morning. As the appointment of a tribunal requires a resolution passed by both Houses of Parliament, there is no appointment until both Houses have concurred.

The statutory starting point implements the recommendation of the Salmon Commission[4] in this regard and is intended to replace the possibility under the common law (which nevertheless can still apply to publications *intended* to prejudice proceedings[5]) that contempt could begin when the appointment of the tribunal was 'imminent'.

The virtue of s 20(2) is that the starting point and indeed the whole of the 'contempt period' is certain. As the Salmon Commission acknowledged[6] this certainty is bought at a price, namely, the risk of undesirable and potentially prejudicial publicity prior to the tribunal's appointment.[7]

2   A publication must create a 'substantial risk of serious prejudice'

A publisher can only be liable under the 'strict liability rule', if the publication creates 'a substantial risk that the course of justice in the proceedings in question will be seriously impeded or prejudiced'.[8]

There is of course no jury to influence and since the chairman is usually a High Court judge and the other members Queen's Counsel, the risk of influencing the tribunal itself is small. The Salmon Commission was certainly dismissive of such a risk.[9] The real area of concern is the effect publications may have upon witnesses. Since it is the sole function of a tribunal of inquiry to investigate and find the facts it is of the utmost public importance that the tribunal should not be impeded in that function. Hence, as with courts of law, publications which have the effect of influencing or deterring witnesses can be considered contempt on the basis that they interfere with the course of justice by impeding the tribunal's ability to determine the truth.

The publication most at risk of being in contempt of a tribunal of inquiry and about which the Salmon Commission was most concerned is the publication of an interview with a witness or a potential witness. The danger of such interviews, as the Salmon Commission said, is that:[10]

> 'Witnesses whose evidence is vital to the matters under investigation are questioned without any of the safeguards which obtain in our courts of law or before tribunals of inquiry. . . . A witness could be bullied or unfairly led into giving an account which was contrary to or put a slant upon the truth. He could commit himself,

3   See Lord Hailsham's comments to this effect: 416 HC Official Report (5th series) col 390.
4   Para 24, which recommendation had been accepted in the Government White Paper (1973, Cmnd 5313) para 44.
5   See p 106 ff.
6   See para 24 and the Government White Paper, para 44.
7   Eg the broadcast of a television interview with a potential witness after the Government has announced its intention to set up a tribunal but before the appointment.
8   Contempt of Court Act 1981, s 2(2).
9   At para 26 they said 'No doubt comment may to some extent be embarrassing to a judge or to members of a tribunal. The risk, however, of their being improperly influenced by such comment certainly ought to be—and we are satisfied is—minimal.'
10   At paras 30 and 31.

particularly under the strain and tension of a television interview, to a badly expressed or inaccurately recollected version of facts which they thought most newsworthy, particularly if a fee were being paid for the interview. When such witnesses came to give evidence before the tribunal they would either have to stick to what they had already said, however inaccurate it might be, or reveal the true facts. In the latter event, the weight of their evidence might be considerably shaken by the discrepancy between what they were telling the tribunal and what they had said previously. This might greatly hinder the tribunal, and, in an extreme case, prevent it from arriving at the truth.'

The above comments were concerned with television interviews but similar dangers attach to interviews broadcast on the radio or published in the press.

The Commission considered[11] that it is the publication which amounts to a contempt and not the mere conducting of the interview which may have 'the entirely legitimate object of obtaining background material for stories to be published after the appearance of the tribunal's report'. However, although the conducting of the interview will not usually by itself deter or influence the witness, and so will not amount to contempt, on rare occasions it could have such an effect, if, for example, a witness has been 'bullied'.

The Commission did not think[12] that all published interviews with witnesses should amount to contempt but only those that present a real risk of deterring or influencing the witness. In practice, however, it will be difficult to draw the line between an acceptable interview and one which presents a substantial risk of deterring or influencing witnesses. It is therefore a perilous enterprise to publish any interview with a potential witness while proceedings before the tribunal are 'active'.

It must also be risky to publish personal comments about witnesses (particularly outright criticism or vilification) since that might have a general deterrent effect against witnesses giving evidence.[13] It is to be emphasised that publications remain at risk even if the particular witness has completed his evidence since the concern will be the effect that might be had on those still to give evidence.[14]

It might also be risky to publish comments upon the subject-matter of the inquiry since such publications could be contempt on the basis of their impact upon witnesses.[15] Of course to succeed under the 'strict liability rule' the prosecution must under the 1981 Act show that a particular publication created a substantial risk of serious prejudice in this regard and that might be difficult to prove. The Salmon Commission were rather dismissive of the risks for while recognising that complete freedom of comment upon the subject-matter of a tribunal would allow views or theories to be 'plugged' by the news media, and therefore did involve the risk that witnesses might be deterred from coming forward with evidence to support contrary views or theories, it nevertheless considered[16] 'that the risk is worth taking in order to preserve complete freedom of discussion and comment about the subject-matter of the inquiry'. No doubt the Salmon Commission's views would militate against a prosecution being brought in respect of published comments but the principle remains that if such comment

---

11 At para 29.
12 At para 32.
13 See the general discussion at p 158.
14 Following the principle established by *Re A-G's Application, A-G v Butterworth* [1963] 1 QB 696, [1962] 3 All ER 326, discussed at pp 412 ff.
15 Cf *Vine Products Ltd v Green* [1966] Ch 484, [1965] 3 All ER 58.
16 At para 27.

is clearly likely to deter or influence witnesses and thereby jeopardise the tribunal's ability to determine all the facts a contempt will be committed. However, there may be a defence to the charge under the Contempt of Court Act 1981, for by s 5 it is provided:

> 'A publication made as or as part of a discussion in good faith of public affairs or other matters of general public interest is not to be treated as a contempt of court under the strict liability rule if the risk of impediment or prejudice to particular legal proceedings is merely incidental to the discussion.'

It unclear how s 5[17] will operate in relation to tribunals of inquiry but the subject-matter of proceedings will be a 'public affair' and of 'general public interest' and it is at least arguable that any effect on witnesses is 'merely incidental' to a bona fide discussion.

B Scandalising the tribunal

The law of contempt also operates to restrict comments which 'scandalise' a court[18] and bearing in mind that the basic rationale of this type of contempt is not to uphold the personal dignity of the judges but to maintain public confidence in the courts, it seems apt to apply this branch of contempt to tribunals of inquiry.

As we discussed in Chapter 9 'scandalising' essentially comprises comments that amount to scurrilous abuse and those which attack the good faith or impartiality of the court. However, the courts have not readily held that comments amount to 'scandalising' and in practice only the most outrageous comments are even likely to be at risk of being considered 'scurrilous abuse'. Furthermore, the Salmon Commission suggested[19] that it would be permissible to publish a justifiable attack on the integrity of a member of the tribunal. However, the authority cited for this statement is an Australian case, namely, *R v Nicholls*,[20] which at best can only be regarded as of persuasive authority in England. The English authorities are to the effect that the truth of the allegation is of no consequence[1] and it may therefore be unwise to rely on this view of the Salmon Commission.

C Other types of conduct amounting to contempt

Apart from publications other types of conduct can amount to contempt. An obvious example is to threaten or intimidate, bribe or harm witnesses[2] and, as with proceedings before courts of law, such conduct will amount to contempt whether it occurs before, during or after the witness has given evidence.[3]

It will also be a contempt to bribe or to attempt to bribe members of the tribunal, or to attempt to influence them by means of private communications.[4]

---

17 For a discussion of this defence see pp 175 ff.
18 See Ch 9.
19 At para 36.
20 (1911) 12 CLR 280 at 286.
 1 See eg *R v Castro, Skipworth's Case* (1873) LR 9 QB 230 and in New Zealand see *A-G v Blomfield* (1914) 33 NZLR 545, discussed at p 357.
 2 See Ch 11 for details of this type of contempt.
 3 See eg *Re A-G's Application, A-G v Butterworth* [1963] 1 QB 696, [1962] 3 All ER 326.
 4 Cases on private communication with a judge are discussed at pp 429 ff.

D   Further consequences of the application of the Contempt of Court Act 1981

1   *Reporting proceedings*

Normally proceedings before tribunals of inquiry are held in public though power is given by s 2 of the 1921 Act to exclude the public when 'it is in the public interest expedient so to do for reasons connected with the subject-matter of the inquiry or the nature of the evidence to be given'. The provision has been interpreted[5] as requiring hearings to be held in public except when this would constitute a security risk.

Where proceedings are heard in public then s 4(1) of the Contempt of Court Act 1981 will operate so that bona fide fair and accurate reports cannot constitute contempt. However, s 4(2) will also operate and this will allow the inquiry to make specific orders postponing the reporting of part or even the whole of the proceedings on the basis of avoiding 'a substantial risk of prejudice to the administration of justice in these proceedings or in any other proceedings pending or imminent'.[6]

One can certainly envisage the possibility of both criminal and civil proceedings following the inquiry's report. However, it is to be hoped that an inquiry will not be too disposed to exercise their powers under s 4(2) since the publicity given to the proceedings is an important means of allaying public fears at times of national crisis.

Whether s 11 will also apply to tribunals is more problematic. That section[7] provides that where a court allows a name or other matter to be withheld from the public it may prohibit publication but s 11 only applies where the court already had power to allow a name or other matter to be withheld. Whether a tribunal of inquiry had such a power has not been established though it would seem a sensible adjunct to its powers since it might otherwise sit in private.

2   *The use of tape recorders*

The provisions controlling the use of tape recorders under the Contempt of Court Act 1981, s 9[8] apply to proceedings before tribunals of inquiry as they do to courts of law save that it is expressly stated[9] that a tribunal has no power under s 9(3) to order the forfeiture of the recorder or recording.

It is perhaps interesting to note that the provisions relating to photographs under the Criminal Justice Act 1925, s 41 do not appear to apply to tribunals of inquiry.[10]

---

5   See the Government White Paper (1973, Cmnd 5313) para 38.
6   For a full discussion of s 4(2) see Ch 8.
7   Discussed in detail in Ch 8.
8   Discussed in detail in Ch 2.
9   Contempt of Court Act 1981, s 20(1).
10   The powers are confined to 'courts of justice'. For details see p 30.

IV PROCEDURE

Section 1(2) of the 1921 Act does not give the tribunal itself the power to punish for contempt, but instead provides that the chairman of the tribunal must certify the offence to the High Court.[51] The High Court must then itself investigate the evidence before it can punish. As Lord Denning MR, said in *A-G v Mulholland and Foster*:[12]

> 'The certificate of the tribunal is not binding on the courts. The judge before whom it comes must inquire into the matters afresh to see if an offence has been committed.'

Lord Parker CJ said in *A-G v Clough* [13] that it was not for the High Court to 'rubber stamp' the opinion of the tribunal but added that where the tribunal was fully versed with all the details of the case (as the Vassall Tribunal under the chairmanship of Lord Ratcliffe was in *A-G v Clough* where a witness refused to answer a question) he would 'certainly hesitate in a case of inquiry which has gone on for a number of days, to refuse to follow a tribunal'.

Lord Parker CJ's statement seems appropriate to all cases of contempt committed in the face of the tribunal, and not just where a witness refuses to answer a question.

This 'double' investigation of an alleged contempt might be thought a clumsy procedure, especially where the alleged contempt is committed in the face of the tribunal. The problem of whether the tribunal itself should have the power to commit for a contempt was considered by the Salmon Commission in relation to compelling witnesses to give evidence. The Commission thought that the:[14]

> 'process of certification to the court and the procedural steps which have to be taken give opportunity for reflection by the tribunal and the offender. The offender has the advantage of being dealt with by a court approaching the matter with a fresh mind.'

The Commission envisaged two difficulties if the power to commit for contempt were to be vested in the tribunal. First, provision would have to be made for an appeal to the High Court and the Commission thought that it might be an undesirable precedent to make a decision of the tribunal directly subject to an appeal to the High Court. Secondly, the sentence of imprisonment might exceed the time during which the tribunal would be in office and:

> 'it is clearly preferable that the authority which commits should be in existence and approachable by the offender at any time during which he is serving his sentence.'

It was also stated that it might be considered inappropriate that the tribunal should have the power to commit as this:

> 'would reflect adversely upon the impression that the tribunal makes upon the public. It is inappropriate that an inquisitorial tribunal should have power to commit.'

11 For a similar procedure in Ontario, Canada see the Public Inquiries Act 1971 (Ont) and *Re Yanover and Kiroff and R* (1974) 53 DLR (3d) 241. Cf in British Columbia, Canada, the procedure under the Combines Investigation Act, RSC 1970, c C-23, s 17(3) and *Re Couture and Hewison* (1980) 105 DLR (3d) 556.
12 [1963] 2 QB 477 at 487; cf in Canada, *Re Yanover and Kiroff and R* (1974) 53 DLR (3d) 241.
13 [1963] 1 QB 773 at 785.
14 At para 127.

The arguments in favour of the tribunal having the power to commit for contempt were thought to be as follows:[15]

> 'The tribunal will always be presided over by a holder of high judicial office and is in no sense to be compared with the usual ad hoc tribunal to which it might be thought inadvisable to grant the exceptional power of depriving a person of his liberty. It may be thought to be derogatory of such a tribunal that it is not entrusted with the power to commit. The Restrictive Practices Court has such a power. Under the present practice, members of the Tribunal might find themselves liable to be called as witnesses and cross-examined in the High Court proceedings.'

Furthermore the tribunal would be in the best position to assess the seriousness of the contempt and the effect it has upon the inquiry. It would also have the advantage of seeing the witness concerned and judging his behaviour at the inquiry. Moreover, the Commission thought that if:

> 'the matter is dealt with by the tribunal, the delay which would be incurred in referring the matter to the court would be avoided.'

The Commission concluded that the question of whether the tribunal should have the power to commit was 'an intransigent problem to solve. On the whole, however, we incline to the view that the existing procedure might well be retained'.

Not all the above arguments against the tribunal having the power to commit are entirely convincing. For instance, would it be an undesirable precedent to have the tribunal's decision on the contempt question subject to an appeal in the High Court? Under the present procedure, since the High Court may not act as a 'rubber stamp' but must consider the evidence afresh, there is already, in effect, an appeal to the High Court on the decision of the tribunal to certify the offence. A stronger argument against the tribunal having the power to commit is the fact that the term of imprisonment might exceed the 'life' of the tribunal with the consequence that a person will be in prison at a time when the tribunal is functus officio. One answer to this might be to vest in the tribunal limited powers of punishment, but the objection to this suggestion is that a limited power of punishment might be insufficient in the face of a serious contempt. In view of the public importance of a tribunal of inquiry arriving at the truth, a refusal to answer a question must be considered a serious contempt and indeed this was the view taken by the courts in *A-G v Clough* [16] and *A-G v Mulholland and Foster* [17] where the offenders Clough and Foster were imprisoned for three months, and Mulholland for six months. In such cases a limited power of punishment would be inadequate, and from this point of view the present procedure of certifying the offence to the High Court, which has extensive powers of punishment, is more satisfactory.

The most serious argument against the present procedure is the delay involved in having the case tried before the High Court, and more especially where an appeal is made to the Court of Appeal. However, such proceedings before the High Court (and Court of Appeal) would no doubt be expedited, as indeed they were, for instance, in *A-G v Clough* where the judgment of the High Court was delivered nine days after the offence was certified.[18] The Commission considered

---

15 See para 128.
16 [1963] 1 QB 773, [1963] 1 All ER 420.
17 [1963] 2 QB 477, [1963] 1 All ER 767.
18 In *A-G v Mulholland and Foster* the decision of the Court of Appeal was delivered three weeks after the offence was certified.

that the cases concerning the Vassall Tribunal[19] 'proved to be procedurally satisfactory'. The Commission's overall conclusion,[20] therefore, that the present procedure ought to be retained, does seem to be a sound one. The court is able to approach the matter with a fresh mind and it should be remembered that although in practice the tribunal is presided over by a person holding high judicial office, this may not always be the case, and it would be highly undesirable to give the power of committal to a person not holding judicial office.

The Commission was specifically concerned with compelling witnesses to give evidence, but of course contempt may be committed in other ways, and the question must be asked whether the procedure is also appropriate to these other cases. With regard to contempt by interrupting the proceedings of the tribunal, as for instance by hurling insults or missiles at the members of the tribunal or by means of a demonstration, it might be thought reasonable to give the tribunal a limited power to fine such offenders, and to avoid the present procedure of having the High Court try the case after the tribunal has certified the offence. As the Salmon Commission commented[1] the present procedure: 'is perhaps not the most practical method that could be devised for dealing effectively with such interruptions'. However, a limited power might be inadequate to deal with a serious contempt. As *Morris v Crown Office* [2] shows, interrupting proceedings by means of a planned demonstration can amount to a serious contempt, and such cases would be better dealt with by the High Court. Again, therefore, on balance, probably the best solution is to retain the present procedure for these types of contempt.

Whether the procedure is satisfactory for contempts committed outside the tribunal is more questionable. It seems unnecessary and a waste of tribunal's time to notify such offences. As we have seen, the certificate is not binding upon the High Court. Moreover, the High Court will equally be able to judge whether a contempt has been committed since the facts of the case will not be within the exclusive knowledge of the tribunal. Allowing the High Court direct jurisdiction to try a case of alleged contempt of a tribunal would bring the superior court's jurisdiction into line with the existing power to deal with alleged contempts of inferior courts.[3] A former counter argument might have been that the certificate provides a useful check on the number of contempt applications but this can be equally[4] provided for by the requirement under the strict liability rule,[4] that proceedings for contempt cannot be instituted except by or with the consent of the Attorney General.

It is suggested that the above considerations militate against having, in cases of constructive contempt, a mandatory[5] requirement of a certificate and that applications for committal direct to the Divisional Court ought to be permissible, under RSC Ord 52.

19 Cmnd 2009.
20 This conclusion was endorsed by the Government White Paper (1973, Cmnd 5313) para 48.
1 (1969, Cmnd 4078) at para 37.
2 [1970] 2 QB 114, [1970] 1 All ER 1079. See also *R v Newbury Justices, ex p Du Pont* (1984) 78 Cr App Rep 255.
3 Discussed at pp 467–468.
4 Under s 7 of the Contempt of Court Act 1981.
5 The retention of the certificate seems a useful way of preserving the tribunal's own powers to initiate proceedings.

V   SHOULD CRIMINAL CONTEMPT APPLY TO TRIBUNALS OF INQUIRY?

The Salmon Commission had no doubts that proceedings before tribunals of inquiry ought to be protected by contempt. They could see[6] no 'profound difference between a trial before a judge alone and proceedings before a tribunal of inquiry as would justify affording the protection of the law of contempt to persons involved in the one but not in the other'.

They rejected the argument[7] that as the tribunal's sole function is to investigate and to find facts and to make a report to Parliament, the worst that can happen if the tribunal makes wrong findings of fact, is that Parliament will be misinformed. As the Commission pointed out, the whole future of a number of persons depends upon the tribunal's findings since their 'political, commercial, and social reputations may be (and sometimes have been) utterly ruined and their careers brought to an abrupt end', and as the Committee stated:

> 'It is certainly of no less public importance that justice should be done to individuals by tribunals of inquiry than that it should be done by the courts.'

A second important reason for a broad application of the law of contempt to tribunals of inquiry is to enhance its ability to arrive at the truth:

> '. . . on the very rare occasions when crises of public confidence occur, it is essential in the public interest that the evil, if it exists, shall be exposed so that it may be rooted out, or if it does not exist the public shall be satisfied that in reality there is no substance in the prevalent rumours or suspicions by which the public has been disturbed. It is only thus that the purity and integrity of our public life can be preserved; and without it a successful democracy is impossible.'[8]

It is submitted that the Salmon Commission were right. There seems a particularly strong case for affording protection to the conduct of the proceedings. It seems vital that there should be some speedy means of trying to ensure that witnesses answer questions. The contempt process, at least if speedily implemented, seems apt.[9] Though no doubt some could argue that there is no need to involve a summary process in such cases, the dangers of the procedure can be exaggerated and it is submitted that the Salmon Commission were right in saying that offenders are reasonably protected.[10]

More contentious perhaps is the application of contempt to publications about the subject-matter of the proceedings. The Salmon Commission were conscious of the importance of preserving, so far as possible, freedom of speech, especially about the matters of public concern. Equally, however, they were concerned about the possible 'contamination of evidence' by such publications. Both are proper concerns and would justify at least a limited application of contempt. In fact this is how the Committee saw contempt operating[11] but it may be that they were sanguine in thinking that commenting on the subject-matter of the inquiry carries no risks of contempt.

6   At para 16.
7   Put forward by the Press Council. See the Press Council Booklet No 1 (1965) p 12.
8   At para 19.
9   The Salmon Commission thought 'speed' to be the major justification of the contempt process.
10   See para 39.
11   Their recommendation in this regard (see paras 32 and 41) was that s 1(2) of the 1921 Act should be amended so as to relate specifically to anything said or done which is 'intended or obviously likely to alter this fact, or withhold some evidence from the tribunal'. The Government White Paper at para 46 did not think this amendment would clarify the law.

CHAPTER 14

Civil contempt

I INTRODUCTION

In this chapter we discuss that aspect of contempt known as civil contempt which is essentially concerned with the enforcement of judgments or orders of the court.

The administration of justice can obviously only be effective if it has the means to enforce court judgments or orders and it is in part upon the law of contempt that such enforcement depends. It is a contempt to disobey a judgment or order either to do a specified act within a specified time or to abstain from doing a specified act. It is also a contempt to break an undertaking given to the court, on the faith of which the court sanctions a particular course of action, or inaction. Further, it is a contempt not to comply with an order for interrogatories, or discovery, or inspection of documents. Solicitors, as officers of the court, are subject to a special jurisdiction of the court, and undertakings given in their professional capacity can be summarily enforced even if such undertakings are not given directly to the court. The court also has the power to punish as for contempt other acts of misconduct committed by solicitors in their official capacity.

Before discussing in detail the various ways in which civil contempt may be committed and the powers that the various courts have in consequence, certain introductory points ought to be made.[1]

(1) Coercive orders made by the courts should be obeyed and undertakings formally given to the court should be honoured unless and until they are set aside. Furthermore it is generally[2] no answer to an action for contempt that the order disobeyed or the undertaking broken should not have been made or accepted in the first place. The proper course, if it is sought to challenge the order or undertaking is to apply to have it set aside. As Romer LJ put it in *Hadkinson v Hadkinson*:[3]

'It is the plain and unqualified obligation of every person against or in respect of whom an order is made by a court of competent jurisdiction to obey it unless and until that order is discharged. The uncompromising nature of this obligation is shown by the fact that it extends even to cases where the person affected by an order believes it to be irregular or even void.'

Again as Lord Donaldson MR said in *Johnson v Walton*:[4]

'It cannot be too clearly stated that, when an injunctive order is made or when an undertaking is given, it operates until it is revoked on appeal or by the court itself,

1 See also *Re Marriage of Sahari* (1976) 11 ALR 679 at 681–693.
2 But see further below.
3 [1952] P 285 at 288.
4 [1990] 1 FLR 350 at 352.

and it has to be obeyed whether or not it should have been granted or accepted in the first place.'

This general point was confirmed in *Isaacs v Robertson* [5] in which the Privy Council upheld a finding that the appellant was in contempt for disobeying an injunction of the High Court of St Vincent notwithstanding that the order ought not to have been made in the first place. In so ruling, the court rejected the contention that there was a distinction between 'void' orders in the sense that they can be ignored with impunity and 'voidable' orders which may be enforced until they are set aside. Lord Diplock said that such contrasting concepts:[6]

'are inapplicable to orders made by a court of unlimited jurisdiction in the course of contentious litigation. Such an order is either regular or irregular. If it is irregular it can be set aside by the court that made it upon application to the court; if it is regular it can only be set aside by an appellate court upon appeal if there is one to which an appeal lies.'

Whether this general proposition is *invariably* true can be questioned. It has been pointed out[7] that even at common law there was some authority for the view that a journalist was not guilty of contempt for refusing to reveal his source if it was subsequently ruled that such a question was unnecessary,[8] while under s 10 of the Contempt of Court Act 1981 it is now established that before a finding of contempt can be made it is for the prosecution to show that the question falls into one' of the four exceptions provided by the Act.[9] Similarly, it seems to be a defence to alleged breaches of anonymity orders made under s 11 of the 1981 Act[10] and to orders made under s 12(2) the Administration of Justice Act 1960 directing that there be no publication of an order made by a court sitting in private, that the orders were properly made in the first place.[11]

(2)   Given that orders and undertakings are meant to be obeyed the motive for disobedience is irrelevent for the purposes of establishing a case of contempt. As Lord Sterndale MR said in *R v Poplar Borough Council (No 2)*:[12]

'Unless and until the time comes when the law of this country is that a person may disobey an order of the court or the laws as much as he likes if he does it conscientiously the question of motive is immaterial.'

Furthermore it is no defence to a finding of contempt that it is the defendant's first breach of the order in question. As Leggatt LJ said in *A v D (Contempt: Committal)* [13] it is a heresy to think that in cases of injunctions to restrain domestic violence, for example, there is a concept of 'one free breach'.

---

5   [1985] AC 97, [1984] 3 All ER 140. See also *M v Home Office* [1994] 1 AC 377 at 423, [1993] 3 All ER 537 at 565, per Lord Woolf.
6   Ibid at 103 and 143.
7   See Miller, [1984] All ER Annual Review at 66 and *Contempt of Court* (2nd edn) pp 438–440. There may, however, be less scope for questioning the general proposition with regard to undertakings, cf the comment on *Johnson v Walton* at [1990] Fam Law 260.
8   As pointed out by Miller, op cit, relying on *A-G v Lundin* (1982) 75 Cr App Rep 90.
9   See Ch 2 at pp 54 ff.
10   Discussed in Ch 8 at pp 299 ff.
11   Discussed in Ch 8 at p 330.
12   [1922] 1 KB 95 at 103, CA; see also *R v Leicester Union* [1899] 2 QB 632; *Re Thompson, R v Woodward* (1889) 5 TLR 565 and 601.
13   [1993] Fam Law 519, in which it was pointed out that such a heresy was firmly scotched in *Jordan v Jordan* [1993] 1 FLR 169, CA.

(3)   The Crown apart, court orders bind (and may be enforced by sanctions for contempt) everyone against whom they are made[14] including a government department or a minister of the Crown in his official capacity. This point, which of course is of huge constitutional significance, was established by the House of Lords in *M v Home Office*.[15] In that case Garland J issued a mandatory order requiring the Home Secretary to return M, a citizen of Zaire who had unsuccessfully claimed political asylum, to the jurisdiction of the court. Kenneth Baker, the then Secretary of State for the Home Office, received legal advice that Garland J had no power to issue the order against the Crown and that the appropriate course was to apply to set it aside. It was also decided not to return M to England because of the difficulties in removing him thereafter if, as was confidently expected, it was found that asylum had been properly denied. It was held, rejecting the contention that a contempt finding cannot be made against a government department or a minister of the Crown in his official capacity, that it was incumbent on the Secretary of State to obey the order and that by not doing so he had committed contempt. However, unlike the Court of Appeal, the House of Lords ruled that the contempt had been committed by the Secretary of State in his official capacity rather than his personal one.[16]

(4)   Notwithstanding the general obligation to obey court orders, unless they are coercive or injunctive in form they cannot be enforced by committal or sequestration. This was first established by *Webster v Southwark London Borough Council* [17] in which it was held that because a declaration is declaratory rather than coercive it was not a contempt for the party affected by it to refuse to comply with the order. A similar line of reasoning has since been applied to certain child related orders such as access to children and directions against removing children from the jurisdiction.[18]

(5)   The contempt remedy is a drastic one (those adjudged to have committed civil contempt can be imprisoned, fined or have their property sequestered) and it should not be readily resorted to as a means of enforcing court orders. It is worth remembering that while, for example, the threat of being committed to prison for failure to comply with court orders is often the only effective sanction that can be brought to bear, nevertheless every instance of a committal for civil contempt represents a failure of the sanction. At best contempt is a blunt weapon by which to enforce obedience and those wishing or having to maintain a relationship after the court hearing, for example members of a family or those in an industrial relationship should think hard before invoking the contempt process. Particular

14   Even non-parties can commit contempt if they aid and abet a breach, or if they knowingly do an act that frustrates the very purpose of the order, see pp 573 ff.
15   [1994] 1 AC 377, [1993] 3 All ER 537, on which see in general Harlow, 'Accidental Loss of an Asylum Seeker' (1994) 57 MLR 620, and on the contempt aspects; Miller, [1994] All ER Annual Review 105–106. Cf in Australia *R v Watt, ex p Slade* [1912] VLR 125 in which Madden CJ considered that the court had power to attach a Minister of the Crown for a failure to comply with a writ of mandamus requiring him to discharge duties cast him by statute. In Canada see *Minister of Employment & Immigration v Bhatnager* (1990) 71 DLR (4th) 84 (Can SC).
16   For a criticism of this part of the decision see Harlow: (1994) 57 MLR at 623, and see further p 572.
17   [1983] QB 698, [1983] 2 WLR 217, per Forbes J.
18   *D v D (Access: Contempt: Committal)* [1991] 2 FLR 34, CA, and *Re P (minors) (Custody Order: Penal Notice)* [1990] 1 WLR 613, CA, discussed at pp 590–592.

caution should be exercised when seeking to invoke contempt powers in family matters. Ormrod LJ commented in *Ansah v Ansah*:[19]

> 'Breach of . . . an injunction is, perhaps unfortunately, called contempt of court, the conventional remedy for which is a summons for committal. But the real purpose of bringing the matter back to the court, in most cases, is not so much to punish the disobedience as to secure compliance with the injunction in the future. It will often be wiser to bring the matter before the court again for further directions before applying for a committal order. *Committal orders are remedies of last resort; in family cases they should be the very last*' (emphasis added).

(6) Even if the contempt powers are sought to be invoked the courts will be reluctant to exercise their powers and will do so only in the clearest cases, namely, where an offender, having had proper notice of the order, has been shown beyond all reasonable doubt to have committed the contempt.[20] In most cases this will mean that the offender will have been shown to have deliberately or wilfully disobeyed the court order.[1]

(7) Although this aspect of contempt is designated civil,[2] because of the penal sanctions, it has been said to[3] 'partake of a criminal nature' and many of the rules that normally apply when seeking to prove an accused guilty of a crime, apply when seeking to show that the defendant has committed civil contempt. It also means that the rules safeguarding contemnors' rights must be strictly complied with.[4]

(8) Civil contempt provides the means by which an individual can, in his own interests and if he chooses to, seek to enforce a court order made in his favour. In many ways, therefore, this branch of contempt law exists to protect the private interests of litigants, and its prime function is coercive rather than punitive. However, the underlying object of this aspect of contempt law, even where invoked in the normal context of a private dispute between two litigants who hope and intend never to cross each other's path again, is to protect the public interest, namely, that every court must have the means of enforcing its own orders. As one Canadian judge put it:[5]

> 'To allow court orders to be disobeyed would be to tread the road toward anarchy. If orders of the court can be treated with disrespect, the whole administration of justice is brought into scorn . . . If the remedies that the courts grant to correct . . . . wrongs can be ignored, then there will be nothing left for each person but to take the law into his own hands. Loss of respect for the courts will quickly result in the destruction of our society.'

---

19 [1977] Fam 138 at 144. See also *Danchevsky v Danchevsky* [1975] Fam 17 at 22 per Lord Denning MR and *Marshall v Marshall* (1966) 110 Sol Jo 112 where it was held that committal was a serious matter and should not be treated as a weapon in domestic affairs. But note *Jones v Jones* [1993] 2 FLR 373 in which Russell LJ said that Ormrod LJ's comment should not be treated as laying down a general principle that 'irrespective of circumstance, an immediate custodial sanction should not be imposed'.
20 See pp 565 ff.
1 See p 568.
2 But for a discussion of the continued validity and use of this designation, see pp 663–664.
3 Per Lord Denning MR in *Re Bramblevale Ltd* [1970] Ch 128 at 137, discussed at p 565.
4 Discussed at pp 620–621, 624–626, 631–632.
5 O'Leary J in *Canadian Metal Co Ltd v Canadian Broadcasting Corpn (No 2)* (1975) 48 DLR (3d) 641 at 669 (Ont).

This public interest in the enforceability of court orders and therefore in civil contempt becomes more obvious where the disobedience is public, particularly if the offender is deliberately pursuing a policy of challenging a court's authority. In England and Wales such challenges were experienced in connection with trade union opposition to the Industrial Relations Act 1971 in general and the National Industrial Relations Court in particular.[6] In such cases the issue[7] is not simply one of enforcing a court order but also involves the need to maintain the authority of and respect for the court. The sanctions imposed are not therefore simply coercive but are also punitive and the individual in whose favour an order has been made may no longer be able to choose whether to bring to the notice of the court any breach of its orders, it being imperative for the maintenance of respect for the court to act upon its own initiative to have the offenders brought to account.[8]

II THE WAYS IN WHICH CIVIL CONTEMPT MAY BE COMMITTED

A Breach of injunction

An injunction is a most solemn and authoritative form of order made by the court expressly enjoining a party either to do a particular act, in which case the injunction is known as a mandatory injunction, or to refrain from doing a particular act, in which case the injunction is known as a prohibitory injunction. The general rule is that it is the duty of those so enjoined strictly to observe the terms of the injunction. As Kindersley V-C said, it is of the:

> 'greatest importance that either an order for an injunction or an interim order should be implicitly observed, and every diligence exercised to observe it.'[9]

In *Spokes v Banbury Board of Health*,[10] Wood V-C said:

> 'the simple and only view is that an order must be obeyed, that those who wish to get rid of that order must do so by the proper course, an appeal. So long as it exists, the order must be obeyed, and obeyed to the letter . . .'

More recently Sachs LJ commented in *Knight v Clifton* [11] that:

> 'when an injunction prohibits an act, that prohibition is absolute, and is not to be related to intent unless otherwise stated on the face of the order . . .'

---

6 See eg *Heatons Transport (St Helens) Ltd v Transport and General Workers' Union* [1973] AC 15; *Goad v Amalgamated Union of Engineering Workers (Engineering Section) (No 2)* [1973] ICR 42; *Goad v Amalgamated Union of Engineering Workers (Engineering Section) (No 3)* [1973] ICR 108 and *Con-Mech (Engineers) Ltd v Amalgamated Union of Engineering Workers (Engineering Section)* [1973] ICR 620. Similar problems have been encountered in Canada, see eg *Skeena Kraft Ltd v Pulp and Paper Workers of Canada Local (No 4)* (1970) 17 DLR (3d) 17; *R v United Fishermen and Allied Workers' Union* (1968) 65 DLR (2d) 579; *Tony Poje v A-G of British Columbia* [1953] 2 DLR 785 and *United Nurses of Alberta v A-G for Alberta* (1992) 89 DLR (4th) 609 (Can SC).
7 See Sir John Donaldson in *Con-Mech (Engineers) Ltd v Amalgamated Union of Engineering Workers (Engineering Section)* [1973] ICR 620 at 625.
8 Indeed in Canada these contempts are classified as criminal, see the Canadian cases cited at n 6 above and see further pp 657–658.
9 *Harding v Tingey* (1864) 12 WR 684.
10 (1865) LR 1 Eq 42 at 48. As was emphasised by the Manitoba Court of Appeal in *Re Swan River—The Pas Transfer Ltd* (1975) 51 DLR (3d) 292 at 308, orders must be obeyed even pending appeal.
11 [1971] Ch 700 at 721, [1971] 2 All ER 378 at 393, CA.

While in *Howitt Transport v Transport and General Workers' Union*[12] Sir John Donaldson explained:

> 'orders of any court must be complied with strictly in accordance with their terms. It is not sufficient by way of answer to an allegation that a court order has not been complied with for the person concerned to say that he "did his best". But if a court order requires a certain state of affairs to be achieved the only way in which the order can be complied with is by achieving that state of affairs.'

No distinction is made for these purposes between prohibitory and mandatory orders, though in the latter case it has been held that it is the duty of the party bound by the injunction to find out the proper means of obeying the order.[13] Interim and interlocutory injunctions have the same force as a final order, so that the same principles of obedience apply.[14] Because strict observation of an injunction is expected, courts should and usually are wary of the orders that they make. No court, for example, should order action to be taken that is impossible.[15] They should also be wary of making vague orders which will in any event be difficult to enforce for it is an equally well-established principle that 'no man's liberty is to be taken away unless every requirement of the law has been complied with'.[16] Courts will not lightly hold that a contempt has been committed. As O'Connor J said in *P A Thomas & Co v Mould*:[17]

> 'where parties seek the power of the court to commit people to prison and deprive them of their liberty there has got to be quite clear certainty about it.'

Thus although persons are under a duty to comply strictly with the terms of an injunction, the courts will only punish a person for contempt upon adequate proof of the following points. First, it must be established that the terms of the injunction are clear and unambiguous; secondly, it must be shown that the defendant has had proper notice of such terms; and thirdly, there must be clear proof that the terms have been broken by the defendant. There is also a fourth issue, namely, the mens rea required in such cases. We will also refer, fifthly, to the question of who is responsible for the breach.

We shall now examine in detail each of these issues.

1   The terms of the injunction must be clear and unambiguous

No person will be held guilty of contempt for breaking an injunction unless the terms of the injunction are themselves clear and unambiguous. Luxmoore J said in *Iberian Trust Ltd v Founders Trust and Investment Co Ltd*,[18] 'If the court is to

---

12 [1973] ICR 1 at 10. See also in Canada, *Northwest Territories Public Service Association v Comr of the Northwest Territories* (1980) 97 DLR (3d) 202 at 233. For appeal see (107) DLR (3d) 458, and *Canadian Metal Co Ltd v Canadian Broadcasting Corpn (No 2)* (1975) 48 DLR (3d) 641 approved in this respect on appeal (1976) 65 DLR (3d) 231.

13 Per Chitty J in *A-G v Walthamstow UDG* (1895) 11 TLR 533 cited with approval in *Iberian Trust Ltd v Founders Trust and Investment Co Ltd* [1932] 2 KB 87.

14 Per Sir George Farwell in *Eastern Trust Co v McKenzie Mann & Co Ltd* [1915] AC 750, PC.

15 Per Sir John Donaldson in *Howitt Transport v Transport and General Workers Union* [1973] ICR 1 at 10.

16 Per Lord Denning MR in *McIlraith v Grady* [1968] 1 QB 468 at 477.

17 [1968] 2 QB 913, [1968] 1 All ER 963.

18 [1932] 2 KB 87 at 95. See also in Australia, *McNair Anderson Associates Pty Ltd v Hinch* [1985] VR 309, and in Canada, *Re Distillery Brewery, Winery, Soft Drinks and Allied Workers' Union 604 and British Columbia Distillery Co Ltd* (1975) 57 DLR (3d) 752 and *United Steelworkers of America Local 663 v Anaconda Co (Canada) Ltd* (1969) 67 WWR 744.

punish anyone for not carrying out its order the order must in unambiguous terms direct what is to be done.' In that case an order had been made which simply stated 'that the plaintiffs do have the return of the said shares within fourteen days'. The plaintiffs alleged that the defendant company had committed a contempt in not obeying the order, but the court rejected this contention. Luxmoore J refused to spell out of the order that the defendant company had been ordered to do something, since the terms of the order were too vague and in any case the order did not specify that the defendant company was to return the shares.

A similar point arose in a novel way in *P A Thomas & Co v Mould*.[19] The plaintiffs, a company specialising in the field of finance, brought an action claiming that during the course of their employment with the plaintiffs, the defendants had learnt the 'know-how' of four allegedly novel financial schemes which were the brain child of the plaintiffs. An interim injunction was granted in the terms asked for by the plaintiffs restraining the defendants from, inter alia:

> 'disclosing, divulging or making use of any confidential information acquired by them during the course of their employment by the plaintiffs or from any person who acquired such information in the course of his employment by the plaintiffs relating to (a) schemes providing for the sale of income; (b) schemes providing for splitting an endowment; (c) schemes concerned with death in service . . .'

In the course of preparing their case to meet the allegation that they were using confidential material, the defendants wrote to competitors in the field to discover whether the plaintiffs' schemes were in fact novel. The plaintiffs claimed that the defendants in making these enquiries had revealed confidential material and that they were therefore in breach of the interim injunction. The plaintiffs lost their action because the exact nature of the schemes had not been stated in the injunction, and the court was not prepared to infer that a breach had taken place. As O'Connor J said:[20]

> 'if the plaintiffs, seeking to protect their "know-how", are anxious to enforce any injunction which may be granted to them by seeking the help of the court to punish a breach of it, it seems to me to be quite essential that they should make it absolutely clear what it is they are seeking to protect.'

Where an order is ambiguous on its face it is submitted that that ambiguity cannot be resolved by examining the transcript of the proceedings.[1] On the other hand it may be possible to argue that an order is too wide given the background of the proceedings that preceded its making.[2]

Given the importance of certainty in an order, a material consideration in deciding whether an injunction should be granted in the first place is the difficulty of its enforcement and the courts may refuse to grant an injunction which is too widely drafted or which is too vague.[3]

---

19 [1968] 2 QB 913, [1968] 1 All ER 963.
20 [1968] 2 QB 913 at 922, [1968] 1 All ER 963 at 967. See also eg *Sega Enterprises Ltd v Richards* (1982) 127 Sol Jo 88 in which Sir Robert Megarry said that it was not right to hold a litigant in contempt for omitting to do what the order did not plainly require him to do.
1 Cf *Northwest Territories Public Service Association v Comr of the Northwest Territories* (1980) 107 DLR (3d) 458, where it was held (Morrow JA dissenting) that the court could not examine transcripts of proceedings to determine the scope of an undertaking.
2 See *MacMillan Bloedel (Alberni) Ltd v Swanson* (1972) 26 DLR (3d) 641.
3 See eg *Suhner & Co v Transradio Ltd* [1967] RPC 329 and *Technograph Printed Circuits Ltd v Chalwyn Ltd* [1967] RPC 339.

2   *The defendant must have proper notice of the terms of the injunction*

The defendant must be shown to have had proper notice of the terms, for it is an established principle that a 'person cannot be held guilty of contempt in infringing an order of the court of which he knows nothing'.[4] The rules regarding the proper means of bringing the terms of an injunction to the notice of the defendant are now, in the case of the High Court, embodied in RSC Ord 45, r 7 and by CCR 1981, Ord 29, r 1 in the case of county courts.[5] The general rule, as provided by Ord 45, r 7(2) is that no order can be enforced unless a copy of the order has been served personally on the person required to do or refrain from doing a specified act,[6] and in the case of an order requiring an act to be done within a specified time,[7] service must be effected before the expiration of the stated time.[8] Where the order is made against a body corporate, either to do or to abstain from doing a specified act, proceedings can be taken against an officer of that company, in addition to or instead of against the company itself, but, in that case the officer must be personally served with the order,[9] and in the case of an order requiring the company to do an act within a specified time, the copy must be served before expiration of the time limit.[10] Order 45, r 7(4)[11] provides that there must be indorsed on the copy of the order served, a notice, commonly referred to as a 'penal notice', warning the person so served that:

> 'disobedience to the order would be a contempt court punishable by imprisonment, or (in the case of an order requiring a body corporate to do or to abstain from doing an act) punishable by sequestration of [that body's] assets . . . and by imprisonment of any individual responsible.'

The object of requiring such indorsements is, in the words of Luxmoore J,[12] 'to call to the attention of the person ordered to do the act that the result of disobedience will be to subject him to penal consequences'.

Such indorsements are always required even where the defendant is a limited company[13] but although there are authoritative forms of indorsements[14] it has been held[15] that the actual form of the indorsement does not matter provided its effect substantially accords with the substance of the rule. In line with its general power to dispense with service (see below) the court has a discretion to dispense

---

4   Per Lyell J in *Husson v Husson* [1962] 3 All ER 1056, [1962] 1 WLR 1434.
5   Discussed further at p 643.
6   Ord 45, r 7(2)(a).
7   Failure to specify a time at all is fatal to an application to commit: *Temporal v Temporal* [1990] 2 FLR 98, CA.
8   Ord 45, r 7(2)(b) and see *Iberian Trust Ltd v Founders Trust and Investment Co Ltd* [1932] 2 KB 87; *Gordon v Gordon* [1946] P 99, [1946] 1 All ER 247. Note also *Beeston Shipping Ltd v Babanaft International SA* [1985] 1 All ER 923 CA (failure to serve judgment debtor with an amended order suitably indorsed detailing the new hearing date that he was required to attend, meant that his non-appearance could not be considered a contempt). See also *Kassebaum v Kassebaum* (1973) 5 SASR 411 (S Aust SC) and *Clifford v Middleton* [1974] VR 737 (Vict SC) cf *Warwick Corpn v Russell* [1964] 2 All ER 337, [1964] 1 WLR 613.
9   Ord 45, r 7(3)(a).
10   Ord 45, r 7(3)(b).
11   As amended by SI 1992/638.
12   In *Iberian Trust Ltd v Founders Trust and Investment Co Ltd* [1932] 2 KB 87 at 97.
13   *Benabo v W Jay & Partners Ltd* [1941] Ch 52, [1940] 4 All ER 196.
14   Such forms can be found in the *Supreme Court Practice* 45/7/6.
15   Per Luxmoore J in *Iberian Trust Ltd v Founders Trust and Investment Co Ltd* [1932] 2 KB 87 at 97.

with the failure to incorporate a penal notice in a prohibitory but not a mandatory order.[16]

The normal rule is that the copy of the order must be served personally on the person required to do or refrain from doing a specified act,[17] or in the case of a company a copy must be served on the company. In the case of a company, personal service can be effected by leaving the copy at the company's registered office,[18] but in other cases, the person entrusted with service should first satisfy himself that he has found the right person, and then hand to or leave with the person to be served the copy of the order and, if asked, show that person the original. If the person refuses to take the copy, he should tell him what it contains and leave it as nearly in his possession or control as he can.[19] Where an order has been made against parties jointly and severally liable (for example trustees) it has been held that, if one cannot be served, provided there has been the requisite service upon the other party, that other person can be committed.[20]

There are exceptions to the rule that there must be personal service of a copy of an order. Under Ord 45, r 7(6), where the order is prohibitory, it is provided that the order can be enforced:

'notwithstanding that service of a copy of the order has not been effected in accordance with this rule if the court is satisfied that, pending such service, the person against whom or against whose property it is sought to enforce the order has had notice thereof either:
(a)   by being present when the order was made, or
(b)   by being notified of the terms of the order, whether by telephone, telegram or otherwise.'

As Neill L J pointed out in *Sofroniou v Segetti*[1] before the major revision of the Rules of the Supreme Court in 1965, there was no requirement for a penal notice in the case of a negative or prohibitory injunction. Furthermore it was well established that some orders did not have to be served to be enforceable. In other words, r 7(6) preserves the previous practice in appropriate cases. Accordingly, the Court of Appeal rejected the contention based on the wording of r 7(4) that it is mandatory to serve a copy of an order backed with a penal notice even where that order is prohibitory. In the court's view, r 7(6) gives the court a discretion to enforce an order notwithstanding that service has not been effected in accordance with the general requirements laid down by r 7.

Order 45, r 7(6), it should be emphasised, applies only to an order requiring a person to abstain from doing an act. Further it does not dispense with the need to show that the defendant had notice of the order,[2] but merely that he need not be personally served with a correctly indorsed copy of it. As the rule itself says,

---

16   See *D v D (Access: Contempt: Committal)* [1991] 2 FLR 34, 40, sub nom *Dempster v Dempster* (1990) Independent, 9 November as cited by the *Supreme Court Practice* 45/7/6, per Dillon LJ, and *Moerman-Lenglet v Henshaw* (1992) Times, 23 November. See also *Sofroniou v Segetti* [1991] FCR 332, discussed below.

17   The copy must also be served personally upon an officer of the court before proceedings can be taken against him.

18   See Companies Act 1985, s 725. See also *Benabo v W Jay & Partners Ltd* [1941] Ch 52, [1940] 4 All ER 196.

19   See Ord 65, r 2 and for comments and cases see the *Supreme Court Practice* 65/2/1.

20   *Re Ellis, Hardcastle v Ellis* (1906) 54 WR 526.

 1   [1991] FCR 332 at 336.

 2   Indeed, such notice must be proved beyond all reasonable doubt, see *Churchman v Joint Shop Stewards' Committee of Workers of the Port of London* [1972] 3 All ER 603 at 606 per Lord Denning MR.

a person present in court at the time the order was granted will be deemed to have such notice,[3] or notice can be effected by telephone, fax or otherwise.[4] An example of notice being effected other than by telephone or telegraph is *Avery v Andrews,*[5] where an injunction had been granted against certain trustees of a certain society. At a meeting of the society, at which the defendants were present, a letter was read out advising the society to consent to the injunction. There was also a full account of the proceedings in a local newspaper. Shortly after the injunction had been made the trustees of the society retired and were replaced by new trustees against whom proceedings were brought in respect of an alleged breach. It was held that the new trustees had sufficient notice of the terms of the injunction both from the meeting and to a certain extent from the accompanying publicity and could therefore be punished for contempt in respect of the breach. In the past where notice was sent by telegram, etc it has been held[6] to be a desirable practice for it to be sent by the solicitor of the party who had obtained the order for then 'the person affected would have the responsibility of an officer of the court, for what he was doing'. Similar advice seems appropriate for sending notice by fax. Since it has been held[7] that a person charged with a breach who swears positively that he did not believe that an injunction had been granted, and who is not cross-examined on the point, will not be committed for contempt, the suggested practice is important since such a belief would be difficult to justify where the solicitor had served notice.[8]

Although as one author[9] has put it 'personal service is little more than a convenient way of establishing notice where the order is couched in negative or prohibitive terms', the procedure of serving notice should normally be observed.[10]

Order 45, r 7(7) reserves the court's power under Ord 65, r 4 to order substituted service[11] and also gives the court the power to dispense with service of a copy of any order, provided it thinks it just to do so. As McCowan LJ pointed out in *Sofroniou v Segetti*[12] unlike r 7(6) which operates retrospectively, r 7(7) is intended to operate prospectively. The courts will not lightly dispense with the need to serve a copy of the order under this provision, and, indeed, where the order is mandatory, personal notice is only likely to be dispensed with where it can be shown that the defendant, having notice of the terms of the order, was

---

3   See eg *Husson v Husson* [1962] 3 All ER 1056, [1962] 1 WLR 1434; *Pearce v Pearce* (1959) Times, 30 January; *Hearn v Tennant* (1808) 14 Ves (2nd Edn) 136; cf *Blome v Blome* (1976) Fam Law 215, (1976) 120 Sol Jo 315 rightly criticised by P H Pettit: (1977) 40 MLR 220.
4   In the past notice has been given by telegram, see eg *Re Bryant* (1876) 4 Ch 98 and *The Seraglio* (1885) 10 PD 120. See also *Re W (wards) (Publication of Information)* [1989] 1 FLR 246, sub nom *Cleveland County Council v W* (1988) Independent, 30 April in which it was held that newspapers and their editors, (but not indivdidual journalists) had sufficient notice of an injunction having learned about it from the Press Association to which they subscribed.
5   (1882) 51 LJ Ch 414.
6   Per James LJ in *Re Bishop, ex p Langley, ex p Smith* (1880) 13 Ch D 110 at 122.
7   In *Re Bishop ex p Langley, ex p Smith,* ibid, CA.
8   See also *The Seraglio* (1885) 10 PD 120.
9   Miller, *Contempt of Court* (2nd edn) p 423.
10 As the *Supreme Court Practice* at 45/7/1 says, the rule is most useful where negative orders are sought ex parte in circumstances of great urgency. It ought also to be remembered that an alleged offender has a defence if he can show that he had a bona fide and reasonable belief that no injunction had been granted: *Re Tuck Murch v Loosemore* [1906] 1 Ch 692.
11 Substituted service can be in the form of service by letter, advertisement, etc. For a more detailed assessment see the *Supreme Court Practice* 65/4/6–65/4/22 and the cases there cited. See also *Turner v Turner* (1978) 122 Sol Jo 696.
12 [1991] FCR 332 at 334.

deliberately evading service.[13] Merely to show that the defendant had notice, by for example being present in court at the time of the order, has been held not to be sufficient.[14]

3   The breach must be proved beyond all reasonable doubt

A person can only be held guilty of contempt for breaking the terms of an injunction if it can be proved that in fact a breach has been committed by the defendant. As Lawton J said in *W Watson & Sons Ltd v Garber*:[15]

> 'before the court would exercise its very special jurisdiction to punish for breach of an order, it was essential that proper proof of a breach be given.'

So far as English law is concerned it is established that the standard of proof is that applicable to criminal cases, so that the breach must be proved beyond all reasonable doubt.[16] In *Re Bramblevale Ltd* [17] the defendant, a managing director of a company which was being wound up, had been brought before Megarry J on a summons by the liquidator, for his alleged contempt in not complying with an order made by a Registrar to produce certain books belonging to the company. The defendant claimed that at the time of the order the books no longer existed, because as a result of a car accident a year earlier, the books had become soaked in petrol and inadvertently thrown away. Megarry J did not believe this story and committed the defendant indefinitely[18] for his contempt. The following month the defendant applied for his release. At this hearing Megarry J said in respect of the books:[19]

13 See *Re Tuck, Murch v Loosemore* [1906] 1 Ch 692 at 696 per Cozens Hardy LJ.
14 *Re Tuck; Murch v Loosemore*, ibid.
15 (1962) 106 So Jo 631.
16 A similar standpoint is taken in Canada see eg *Northwest Territories Public Service Association v Comr of the Northwest Territories* (1980) 107 DLR (3d) 458 at 479 and the cases there cited. See also *Crown Zellerbach Canada Ltd v Annand* (1972) 27 DLR (3d) 129; *Canadian Metal Co Ltd v Canadian Broadcasting Corpn (No 2)* (1975) 48 DLR (3d) 641 at 660; *Re Sheppard and Sheppard* (1976) 67 DLR (3d) 592 at 594 and *Re Regina and Monette* (1975) 64 DLR (3d) 470 at 473. In Australia, however, the position is much less certain. On the one hand cases such as *Foley v Herald Sun TV Pty Ltd* [1981] VR 315, *Clifford v Middleton* [1974] VR 737, *In the Marriage of Sahari* (1976) 11 ALR 679, *In the Marriage of Davis* (1976) 111 ALR 81, and, inferentially *AMIEU v Mugdinberri Station Pty Ltd* (1986) 66 ALR 577 (see the general statement at 585 'There is much to be said for the view that all contempts should be punished as if they are quasi-criminal in character'). Against this is *Jendell Australia Pty Ltd v Kesby* [1983] 1 NSWLR 127 in which McLelland J said, at 137 ' In my opinion the better view is that in the case of wholly civil contempt, the civil standard applies, but that "the degree of satisfaction for which the civil standard of proof calls may vary according to the gravity of the fact to be proved": *Reifek v McElroy* (1965) 112 CLR 517, at 521', which has been followed on numerous occasions, see eg *New South Wales Egg Corporation v Peek* (1987) 10 NSWLR 72, 81, and the cases there cited. With due respect this latter view seems questionable importing, as it seems, a third standard of proof following neither the standard civil nor criminal one. Interestingly attempts to introduce such a standard into English domestic family law have been decisively rejected; see *Re H and R (Child Sexual Abuse: Standard of Proof)* [1995] 1 FLR 643.
17 [1970] Ch 128, [1969] 3 All ER 1062.
18 NB sine die committals are no longer permissible under English law because of the Contempt of Court Act 1981, s 14, see p 626.
19 As reported in [1970] Ch 128 at 136.

'. . . there are only two possibilities . . . either he still has them, or else he no longer has them, whether by reason of loss, destruction, transfer to someone else or otherwise . . .'

In either event the defendant was still at fault since if he still had the books he ought to have handed them over, and if he had destroyed them he had been guilty of an offence under what was then the Companies Act 1948, s 328.[20] The learned judge concluded that if the defendant 'by his own voluntary act has put himself in difficulties, he has only himself to blame', and he therefore refused the application for release. An appeal was successfully made to the Court of Appeal. Lord Denning MR said:[1]

'A contempt of court is an offence of a criminal character. A man may be sent to prison for it. It must be satisfactorily proved. To use the time-honoured phrase, it must be proved beyond all reasonable doubt. It is not proved by showing that, when the man was asked about it, he told lies. There must be further evidence to incriminate him. Once some evidence is given, then his lies can be thrown into the scale against him. But there must be some other evidence.'

It was held that although the defendant may have lied about the car crash, that in itself did not prove that he had the books in his possession at the time of the order. There were in fact two equally likely possibilities—either the defendant at the time of the order had the books in his possession and had wrongfully refused to deliver them or he had got rid of them and could not deliver them. Lord Denning MR held that it was not possible to say which possibility was correct:

'The court cannot be satisfied beyond reasonable doubt that he still had the books . . . That would be conjecture rather than inference—surmise rather than proof. Where there are two equally consistent possibilities open to the court, it is not right to hold that the offence is proved beyond reasonable doubt.'

Re Bramblevale has since been followed by another Court of Appeal decision, *Knight v Clifton*[2] where Russell LJ said:

'Contempt of court, even of the type that consists in breach of an injunction or undertaking, is something that may carry penal consequences, even loss of liberty, and the evidence required to establish it must be appropriately cogent.'

The court therefore refused to interfere with a decision of a High Court judge that no contempt had been committed, since only part of the evidence was available before the Court of Appeal.

Notwithstanding this seemingly clear and undisputed[3] authority Hutchison J held in *West Oxfordshire District Council v Beratec Ltd*[4] that the appropriate standard of proof in civil contempt cases was the civil standard of the balance of probabilities. In doing so he relied on a statement by Lord Scarman in *R v Secretary of State for the Home Department, ex p Khawaja*,[5] a case concerning

---

20 See now s 208(1) of the Insolvency Act 1986.
1   [1970] Ch 128 at 137.
2   [1971] Ch 700 at 707, [1971] 2 All ER 378 at 381. See also *Churchman v Joint Shop Stewards' Committee of Workers of the Port of London* [1972] 3 All ER 603, [1972] 1 WLR 1094, CA. For other consequences of this standpoint see eg *Kent County Council v Batchelor* (1976) 75 LGR 151, discussed at p 654.
3   See *Dean v Dean* [1987] 1 FLR 517 at 522 where Stephen Brown LJ said 'Mr Munby's careful researches have shown that this principle has not been questioned in the substantial number of cases which have come before the courts since 1970'.
4   (1986) Times, 30 October.
5   [1984] AC 74, [1983] 1 All ER 765.

judicial review of a decision in an immigration case that there was no need 'to import into this branch of the civil law the formula used for the guidance of juries in criminal cases'. *Beratec Ltd*, however, was overruled by the Court of Appeal in *Dean v Dean*,[6], Dillon LJ commenting:[7]

> 'I have no doubt . . . that the procedure in contempt is of a criminal nature and that the case against the alleged contemnor must be proved to the criminal standard of proof. That was not a matter for decision in *Khawaja* ... the matter rests on long established practice, probably well before the *Bramblevale* case . . . and certainly repeated many times since in this court . . .'.

There can now be no doubt that the appropriate standard of proof is that of the criminal law.

4 What is the mens rea required?

As Lord Oliver said in *A-G v Times Newspapers Ltd*[8] liability for breaking a court order is strict:

> 'in the sense that all that requires to be proved is service of the order and the subsequent doing by the party bound of that which is prohibited.'

Accordingly, it is neither necessary to show that the defendant is intentionally contumacious nor that he intends to interfere with the administration of justice.[9] As Sachs LJ said in *Knight v Clifton*:[10]

> 'when an injunction prohibits an act, the prohibition is absolute and is not to be related to intent unless otherwise stated on the face of the order'

and in, what now must be regarded as the locus classicus, Warrington J said in *Stancomb v Trowbridge UDC*:[11]

> 'if a person or corporation is restrained by injunction from doing a particular act, that person or corporation commits a breach of the injunction, and is liable for process for contempt, if he or it in fact does the act, and it is no answer to say that the act was not contumacious in the sense that, in doing it, there was no direct intention to disobey the order.'

It was upon this basis that a contempt was held to have been established even though the acts were done 'reasonably and despite all due care and attention, in the belief based on legal advice, that they were not breaches'.[12] Similarly it is no

---

6 [1987] 1 FLR 517.
7 Ibid at 521.
8 [1992] 1 AC 191 at 217, [1991] 2 All ER 398 at 414–415, referred to by Lord Woolf in *M v Home Office* [1994] 1 AC 377 at 426, [1993] 3 All ER 537 at 568.
9 Cases to the contrary such as *Worthington v Ad-Lib Club Ltd* [1965] Ch 236, [1964] 3 All ER 674 are no longer good law and should be regarded as overruled by *Heatons Transport (St Helens) Ltd v Transport and General Workers' Union* [1973] AC 15 at 109, [1972] 3 All ER 101 at 117 per Lord Wilberforce.
10 [1971] Ch 700 at 721, [1971] 2 All ER 378 at 393.
11 [1910] 2 Ch 190 at 194 cited with approval by Lord Wilberforce in *Heatons Transport* [1973] AC 15 at 109 and [1972] 3 All ER 101 at 117 and by Lord Nolan in *Re Supply of Ready Mixed Concrete (No 2)* [1995] 1 AC 456, at 479–481, [1995] 1 All ER 135 at 152–157.
12 *Re Agreement of Mileage Conference Group of Tyre Manufacturers' Conference Ltd* [1966] 2 All ER 849 at 862 cited with approval in *C H Giles & Co Ltd v Morris* [1972] 1 All ER 960 at 970 per Megarry J and in *Re Rossminster Ltd and Tucker* (1980) Times, 23 May. See also *M v Home Office* [1994] 1 AC 377, [1993] 3 All ER 537 in which the Secretary of State for

defence for a company enjoined by a court order that it had expressly forbidden its employers from breaking its terms.[13]

Despite the foregoing statements it is equally established that casual or accidental and unintentional acts of disobedience will not be met by the full rigours of the law. In *Fairclough & Sons v Manchester Ship Canal Co (No 2)*,[14] for example, Lord Russell CJ said:

> 'We desire to make it clear that in such cases no casual or accidental and unintentional disobedience of an order would justify either commital or sequestration. Where the court is satisfied that the conduct was not intentional or reckless, but merely casual and accidental and committed under circumstances which negative any suggestion of contumacy, while it might visit the offending party with costs and might order an inquiry as to damages, it would not take the extreme course of ordering either of commitment or of sequestration.'

Although *Fairclough* and numerous cases[15] that followed it in this respect were decided in the context of the requirement under the old Rules of the Supreme Court[16] that a judgment or order made against a corporation could only be enforced if there had been 'wilful' disobedience, it is apparent that the practice has not changed even though the current rules[17] make no mention of 'wilful'. This is one result of *Heatons Transport (St Helens) Ltd v Transport and General Workers' Union*[18] which expressly followed the *Fairclough* line of cases. However, as Lord Wilberforce intimated[19] the omission of the word 'wilful' cannot be in favour of parties who disobey court orders, and it may be that as a result it will be easier to establish a prima facie case of contempt.

So far as disobedience to a positive order is concerned it has been held[20] that it is the duty of the defendants to find out the proper means of obeying the order and although it may be a defence to show that compliance with the order was impossible, the burden of proving such impossibility is upon the defendants. In *Lewis v Pontypridd, Caerphilly, and Newport Rly Co*[1] a railway company had been ordered to make a junction joining their line with the plaintiff's works. The

---

the Home Office was held liable in contempt in his official capacity even though he relied on legal advice and acted on a mistaken belief. See further p 573. In Australia see eg *McNair Anderson Associates Pty Ltd v Hinch* [1985] VR 309 and *Jendell Australia Pty Ltd v Kesby* [1983] I NSWLR 127 at 133. In Canada see *Canadian Metal Co Ltd v Canadian Broadcasting Corp (No 2)* (1975) 48 DLR (3d) 641 at 661 not overruled on this point at (1976) 65 DLR (3d) 231, *Re Sheppard and Sheppard* (1976) 67 DLR (3d) 592. See also *Re Gaglardi* (1961) 27 DLR (2d) 281. But cf *Morrow, Power v Newfoundland Telephone Co* (2 June 1994), Doc 83/91 (Nfld CA).

13 *Re The Supply of Ready Mixed Concrete (No 2)* [1995] 1 AC 456 at 479–81, [1985] 1 All ER 135 at 152–157, per Lord Nolan, and in Canada see eg *Baxter Travenol Laboratories of Canada Ltd v Cutter (Can) Ltd* (1987) 13 CIPR 41, [1987] 2 FC 557.

14 (1897) 41 Sol Jo 225 (the better report, see *Re Agreement of Mileage Conference etc* [1966] 2 All ER 849 at 861) [1897] WN 7.

15 For a list of such cases see *Heatons Transport* [1973] AC at 109, [1972] 3 All ER at 117.

16 Ord 42, r 31.

17 Ie Ord 45, r 5.

18 [1973] AC 15, [1972] 3 All ER 101. See also *United Kingdom Association of Professional Engineers and Newell v Amalgamated Union of Engineering Workers (TASS)* [1972] ICR 151 at 160 per Sir John Donaldson and *Marshall v Marshall* (1966) 110 Sol Jo 112.

19 Ibid at 109H and 117f; cf in Canada eg *R v Perry* (1982) 133 DLR (3d) 703.

20 *A-G v Walthamstow UDC* (1895) 11 TLR 533 per Chitty J.

1 (1895) 11 TLR 203. See also *R v Poplar Borough Council* [1922] 1 KB 95 in which (as Miller, *Contempt of Court* (2nd edn) at p 428 points out) disobedience for an order of mandamus requiring a rate to be levied was not excused by pleading that the borough was too poor to support it.

defendants argued that since they never had any funds to build the junction they could not have complied with the order and that therefore the breach could not be said to be 'wilful'. The court rejected this contention. The defendants had failed to discharge their burden of proving that compliance was impossible, because they had not shown that they could not have obeyed the judgment if they had used proper economy, which they were bound to do to comply with their obligation under the order.

5 Responsibility for breach

Insofar as an individual is enjoined by an order to do or refrain from doing a particular act the responsibility for obeying that order is clearly thrown on that individual.[2] More difficulty occurs where orders are made against a corporate body, a trade union, or a government department.

With regard to corporate bodies it seemed well established that liability was dependent upon the vicarious principle in that where an order had been made against the corporation, that body was liable for the deliberate acts of its servants, at any rate, where they were acting in the course of their employment. As Warrington J said in *Stancomb v Trowbridge Urban District Council:*[3]

> 'Such a body can only act by its agents or servants, and I think, if the act is in fact done, it is no answer to say that, done, as it must be, by an officer or servant of the council, the council is not liable for it, even though it may have been done by the servant through carelessness, neglect, or even in dereliction of his duty.'

It had also been held to be no defence for a company to show that its officers were unaware of the terms of the order, or that they failed to realise that the terms were being broken by their actions.[4]

Stancomb was subsequently cited with approval by the House of Lords in *Heaton's Transport (St Helens) Ltd v T&GWU*[5] in which it was held that the union was responsible for the acts of its agents, including shop stewards, within the scope of the authority.

Notwithstanding the foregoing authority, its ambit was called into question by the Court of Appeal in *The Supply of Ready Mixed Concrete.*[6] In that case several

2 But where an injunction is granted against a husband and wife and it is broken by one spouse and the other spouse is neither implicated nor to blame no liability will answer to the other: *Hope v Carnegie* (1868) LR 7 Eq 254. As Miller, *Contempt of Court* (2nd edn) at p 429 points out, RSC Ord 15 makes provision for representative proceedings which may include issuing injunctions binding both named individuals and other unidentified individuals who were members of an unincorporated association or of some other group acting in concert see *M Michaels (Furriers) Ltd v Askew* (1983) Times, 25 June. But for the limits of enforcing such others by contempt see *Harrington v North London Polytechnic* [1984] 3 All ER 666,CA.
3 [1910] 2 Ch 190 at 194.
4 *Re Garage Equipment Association's Agreement* (1964) LR 4 RP 491 at 505 and *Re Galvanized Tank Manufacturers Association's Agreement* [1965] 2 All ER 1003 at 1009, per Megaw P.
5 [1973] AC 15, [1972] 3 All ER 101. See also *Z Ltd v A-Z and AA-LL* [1982] QB 558 at 581, sub nom *A Ltd v A* [1982] 1 All ER 556 at 569, per Eveleigh L J and Miller, *Contempt of Court* (2nd edn) p 435. In Canada see eg *Baxter Travenol Laboratories Ltd v Cutter (Canada) Ltd (No 2)* (1985) 14 DLR (4th) 641 at 650 but cf, in the context of Ministerial liability, *Minister of Employment & Immigration v Bhatnager* (1990) 71 DLR (4th) 84 (Can Sup Ct), discussed further at p 573.
6 [1992] 1 QB 213, [1991] 4 All ER 150, commented upon by Robertson, 'Enforcement of the UK Restrictive Trade Practices Act: Judicial Limitations and Legislative Proposals' [1992] 2 ECLR 82.

companies had been brought before the Restrictive Trade Practices Court in 1979 and in consequence each was restrained by a court order from giving effect to the specific agreements uncovered by the Director General of Fair Trading's investigations and 'from giving effect to or enforcing or purporting to enforce (whether by itself or by its servants or agents or otherwise) any other agreements in contravention of s 35(1) of the [Restrictive Trade Practices] Act of 1976'. Despite this order it was subsequently found that employees of four of the companies enjoined had entered into a market sharing and price fixing cartel for ready mixed concrete. At first instance, three of the companies admitted their contempt and the fourth, Smiths, were held to have committed contempt. Smiths appealed. The Court of Appeal quashed the finding of contempt because since Smiths had forbidden its employees to enter into agreements which would contravene the 1979 injunction and had taken reasonable steps to enforce compliance it could not be said to be a party to the new agreement. In reaching that decision, Lord Donaldson MR distinguished *Heatons Transport*[7] on the ground that it was only dealing with whether the trade union had withdrawn or curtailed the authority of its shop stewards to instigate industrial action.

Perhaps not surprisingly, given this Court of Appeal decision, the other three companies obtained leave to appeal out of time[8] and subsequently the issue came before the House of Lords in *Re the Supply of Ready Mixed Concrete (No 2)*.[9] The House of Lords, however, overruled the earlier Court of Appeal decision and held that all the respondent companies had correctly been held to be in contempt. In Lord Templeman's view, since an employee who acts for the company within the scope of his employment is the company, by entering into the cartel in question the employees were committing their companies to that cartel and were thus causing a breach of the court order binding on the companies. Lord Nolan, whilst agreeing with that analysis (though confining it to the context of the Restrictive Trade Practices Act 1976) further considered the issue of what and whose mens rea was necessary for a finding of contempt against a company. In this respect he concluded:[10]

> 'Given that liability for contempt does not require any direct intention on the part of the employer to disobey the order, there is nothing to prevent an employing company from being found to have disobeyed an order "by" its servant as a result of a deliberate act by the servant on its behalf. In my judgment the decision in *Stancomb's* case is good law and should be followed in the present case.'

Assuming, as it is submitted it should be, that Lord Nolan's analysis is of general application, it now seems clear that corporate bodies will be considered to be in contempt if the terms of an injunction made against them are broken by a deliberate act of their agents or servants whilst acting within the course of their employment but regardless of whether the act in question was authorised or indeed expressly forbidden by the company. Their only defence is either that the acts in question were not deliberate but casual or accidental or unintentional[11] or

---

7 But note the criticisms by Robertson, op cit, at p 83.
8 [1994] ICR 57
9 [1995] 1 AC 456, [1995] 1 All ER 135, commented upon by Robertson, 'Corporate Liability for Contempt of Court under the Restrictive Trade Practices Act 1976' [1995] 3 ECLR 196.
10 Ibid at 481 and 156-157.
11 Ie the standard defence outlined by *Fairclough & Sons v Manchester Ship Canal Co (No 2)* (1897) 41 Sol Jo 225 and approved by *Heatons Transport (St Helens) Ltd v T&GWU* [1973] AC 15, [1972] 3 All ER 101, discussed at p 568.

that the agents or servants in question were not acting in the course of their employment.

So far as the individual directors are concerned, because RSC Ord 45, r 5(1)(b)(ii) and (iii) expressly permits enforcement measures to be taken against a director or officer of a company, it was thought at one time[12] that such persons could be personally liable for breach of an order made against the company even where they did not actively assist in procuring the breach. In *Director General of Fair Trading v Buckland*,[13] however, Anthony Lincoln J held that Ord 45, r 5 did not render an officer of a company liable in contempt by virtue of his office and his mere knowledge that the order sought to be enforced was made. In his view an officer is only liable to committal or sequestration where it can be shown that he was in contempt under the general law. But this view has since been considered by the Court of Appeal in *A-G for Tuvalu v Philatelic Distribution Corp Ltd*.[14] As Woolf LJ pointed out, Anthony Lincoln J's remarks were made in a case where there was no finding of culpable conduct against the director and it was not to be assumed that it is only where a director has actively participated in the breach of the order that Ord 45, r 5 can apply. In that case it was held that where a company was enjoined by a court not to do certain acts and a director of that company was aware of that order, he was under a duty to take reasonable steps to ensure that the order was obeyed and if he wilfully failed to take those steps and the order was breached he could be punished for contempt unless he reasonably believed that some other director or officer of the company was taking them.

In the light of these cases the current position seems to be that no action can be taken against a director or officer personally for breach of an order against a company, unless (a) the director knows of the order, and (b) he either actively assisted in the breach or wilfully[15] failed to take steps to ensure that the order was obeyed. It may be further added that in any event that it may be that where orders are made against a company contempt liability extends to directors only in so far as they act in their capacity as directors and not, for example, when they are acting as shareholders.[16] Of course orders may be made not only against the corporate body but against individuals as well. In such cases the individuals concerned are clearly bound to obey the order. On the other hand, however, those individuals should be brought before the court before any such order is made.[17]

---

12 See the second edition of this work at p 402 and Miller, *Contempt of Court* (2nd edn) at p 436.

13 [1990] 1 All ER 545.

14 [1990] 2 All ER 216.

15 Note the pertinent comment by Miller, [1990] All ER Annual Review at 55. 'The word "wilful" is hardly a precise one when used in this or any other context. Indeed, it used to appear in the old pre-1966 version of Ord 45, r 5(1) but was then abandoned [see the discussion at p 568— now, it seems to be reintroduced (by the courts) as the basis of a director's liability for a company's breach'.

16 See *Northern Counties Securities Ltd v Jackson and Steeple Ltd* [1974] 2 All ER 625, [1974] 1 WLR 1133. NB it may sometimes be possible to say that shareholders commit a contempt on the basis that they have aided and abetted or perhaps procured a breach of injunction, see below.

17 See eg *Marengo v Daily Sketch and Sunday Graphic Ltd* [1948] 1 All ER 406; cf in *Beecham Group Ltd v Bristol Laboratories Pty Ltd* (1967) 118 CLR 618, discussed by Miller, *Contempt of Court* (2nd edn) p 252.

In the past the extent of trade union liability for breach of court orders has proved a troublesome issue[18] but according to *Halsbury* [19] the current position seems to be:

'In deciding whether a trade union is liable for actions in contempt of a court order, the same rules as to authorisation or endorsement by a union apply as apply to the liability of the union for the tortious conduct in the original proceedings.'

This view is based on s 20(6) of the Trade Union and Labour Relations (Consolidation) Act 1992 which expressly provides that the provisions (s 20(2) to (4)) dealing with union authorisation or endorsement:

'apply in relation to proceedings for failure to comply with any injunction [restraining the union inter alia from breaking, inducing, interfering or threatening so to interfere with contracts] . . . as they apply in relation to the original proceedings.'

Section 20(2) and (3) provides:

'(2)   An act shall be taken to have been authorised or endorsed by a trade union if it was done, or was authorised or endorsed—
    (a)   by any person empowered by the rules to do, authorise or endorse acts of the kind in question, or
    (b)   by the principal executive committee or the president or general secretary, or
    (c)   by any other committee of the union or any other official of the union (whether employed by it or not),
(3)   For the purposes of paragraph (c) of subsection (2)—
    (a)   any group of persons constituted in accordance with the rules of the union is a committee of the union; and
    (b)   an act shall be taken to have been done, authorised or endorsed by an official if it was done, authorised or endorsed by, or by any member of, any group of persons of which he was at the material time a member, the purposes of which included organising or co-ordinating industrial action.'

By s 20(4) these provisions are expressly subject to s 21 which makes provision for the repudiation of certain acts:

'by the executive, president or general secretary as soon as reasonably practicable after coming to the knowledge of any of them.'

Strictly speaking these provisions only apply to the restraining of tortious acts by a trade union and although they provide sound criteria by which to judge liability it remains to be seen whether *Halsbury* [20] is right in saying that they will provide the criteria in *all* cases of contempt.

As we discussed earlier in this chapter it has now been established by *M v Home Office* [1] that a finding of contempt can be made against a government department or a minister of the Crown in his official capacity. Such liability must also be based on the principle of vicarious liability. In *M v Home Office* itself the

---

18   Formerly, what constituted effective compliance remained a matter of fact and argument, see eg *Richard Read (Transport) Ltd v NUM (South Wales Area)* [1985] IRLR 67, *Heaton's Transport (St Helens) Ltd v T&GWU* [1973] AC 15, [1972] 3 All ER 101 and *Express & Star Ltd v NGA (1982)* [1986] ICR 569.
19   47 *Halsbury's Laws* (4th edn) para 1514.
20   A similar view is taken in Bowers and Honeyball, *Textbook on Labour Law* (3rd end, Blackstones) p 394.
1   [1994] 1 AC 377, [1993] 3 All ER 537, discussed at p 557.

House of Lords distinguished the position of the Home Secretary in his official capacity from that in his personal capacity, holding that because he had not been personally at fault[2] the order was properly made against him only in his official capacity.[3] Implicit in this ruling is that a minister cannot be made personally liable on the basis of vicarious liability. Interestingly in *Ministry of Employment & Immigration v Bhatnager* [4] the Canadian Supreme Court expressly rejected the application of vicarious liability to a minister of the Crown. As Sopinka J (giving the judgment of the court) said:[5]

> 'Since a corporate entity cannot have a mind of its own, it was necessary to select some responsible official (the directing mind) whose mind was identified as that of the corporation. To now apply the theory of identification to natural persons would be to turn the principle on its head. It would be, in my view, a manifestly unjust application to an individual of simple vicarious liability under another name.'

B Aiding and abetting a breach of injunction or otherwise obstructing or frustrating a court order

Although prima facie court orders only bind parties to the action[6] it is nevertheless well established that third parties can be guilty of contempt if, knowing of the order, they either aid and abet the defendant in breaking it or otherwise do an act that obstructs or frustrates the object of the order. So far as English law is concerned[7] there are four key cases, namely *Lord Wellesley v Earl of Mornington*,[8] *Seaward v Paterson*,[9] *Z Ltd v AZ and AA-LL*[10] and *A-G v Times Newspapers Ltd.*[11]

---

2 Ie he was acting on advice which he was entitled to accept and under a mistaken view as to the law, see eg Lord Templeman [1994] 1 AC 377 at 396, [1993] 3 All ER 537 at 541.
3 See in particular Lord Woolf, ibid, at 427 and 568–569.
4 (1990) 47 DLR (4th) 84.
5 Ibid at 94.
6 Save in rare cases when the court has power to act in rem. See eg in wardship cases *X County Council v A* [1985] 1 All ER 53, but which was subsequently doubted by *R v Central Independent Television Plc* [1994] Fam 192 [1994] 3 All ER 641, CA.
7 In Australia see eg *Madeira Roggette Pty Ltd (No 2)* [1992] 1 QdR 394; *Sun Newspapers Pty Ltd v Brisbane TV (Ltd)* (1989) 92 ALR 535; *Re Inter Consultants Pty Ltd* [1986] 2 QdR 99; *Windsurfing International Inc v Sailboards Australia Pty Ltd* (1986) 69 ALR 534 and *Ellendale Pty Ltd v Graham Matthews Pty Ltd* (1986) 65 ALR 275. In Canada see eg *Northwest Territories Public Service Association v Commissioner of the Northwest Territories* (1980) 97 DLR (3d) 202 at 230–231 and on appeal see (1980) 107 DLR (3d) 458 at 482; *Catkey Construction Ltd v Moran* (1970) 8 DLR (3d) 413; *Re Tilco Plastics Ltd v Skurjat* (1966) 57 DLR (2d) 596; *Re Gaglardi* (1961) 27 DLR (2d) 281, 284–285 and *Tony Poje v A-G of British Columbia* [1953] 2 DLR 785 at 789–792. In New Zealand see *Malevez v Knox* [1977] 1 NZLR 463.
8 (1848) 11 Beav 181, 50 ER 786.
9 [1897] 1 Ch 545.
10 [1982] QB 558, sub nom *Z Ltd v A* [1982] 1 All ER 556.
11 [1992] 1 AC 191, [1991] 2 All ER 398. For other English cases see *Johnston v Moore* [1965] NI 128; *Elliot v Klinger* [1967] 3 All ER 141, [1967] 1 WLR 1165; *Acrow (Automation) Ltd v Rex Chainbelt Inc* [1971] 3 All ER 1175, [1971] 1 WLR 1676; *NUM v Taylor* (1985) Times, 20 November and, in the family law context, *Re K (minors) (Incitement to Breach Contact Order)* [1992] 2 FLR 108 and *Re S (Abduction: Sequestration)* [1995] 1 FLR 858.

1   *Lord Wellesley v Earl of Mornington*

The defendant Earl had been restrained from cutting timber on certain land. Subsequently, one Batley, who was the Earl's agent and manager, and who knew of the injunction, cut timber on the land concerned. An initial attempt to commit Batley for contempt for breaking the injunction failed because the injunction was solely against the Earl and did not extend to his servants and agents.[12] However, a second application for committal was brought against Batley for 'being part and privy to, and in aiding and abetting the breach of the injunction.' This action succeeded, although Lord Wellesley did not press for a committal order. Lord Langdale MR said 'if the matter had been pressed, I should have found it my duty to commit Mr Batley for his contempt in intermeddling with these matters.'

Although the motion of committal mentioned aiding and abetting, it has since been pointed out[13] that there is nothing in the report of the proceedings to suggest that the Earl was even aware of the agent's acts much less that he authorised them. Accordingly, while the case is 'clear authority for the propostion that an aider and abetter may be guilty of contempt, it also suggests that aiding and abetting or assisting was construed fairly widely to include acts done for the benefit of the person enjoined but in which that person did not personally participate.'[14]

2   *Seaward v Paterson*

An injunction had been granted restraining Paterson, his agents and servants, inter alia from:

> 'doing or suffering to be done anything which may interfere with the full and quiet enjoyment of the plaintiff . . . or his undertenants, of the premises adjoining or neighbouring to the first, second and third floors.'

In contravention of this injunction, Paterson allowed boxing matches to be held on his premises. The motion to commit was moved against both Paterson and others whom it was alleged had aided and abetted the breach. North J held that the court not only had jurisdiction to commit Paterson for the breach of the injunction but also to commit the other persons for aiding and abetting the breach. Murray, one of those committed for aiding and abetting the breach appealed, but the Court of Appeal upheld North J's decision, even though he was neither a party to the suit nor named in the injunction. Lindley LJ said:[15]

> 'There is no injunction against him—he is no more bound by the injunction granted against Paterson than any other member of the public. He is bound like other members of the public, not to interfere with, and not to obstruct, the course of justice; and the case, if any, made against him must be this—not that he has technically infringed the injunction, which was not granted against him in any sense of the word, but that he has been aiding and abetting others in setting the court at defiance, and deliberately treating the order of the court as unworthy of notice. If he has so conducted himself, it is perfectly idle to say that there is no jurisdiction to [punish] him for contempt as distinguished from the breach of the injunction, which has a technical meaning.'

12   See (1848) 11 Beav 181, 50 ER 785.
13   Per Lord Oliver in *A-G Times Newspapers Ltd* [1992] 1 AC 191 at 219, [1991] 2 All ER 398 at 416. See also Lord Ackner at 212 and 410 and Lord Jauncey at 228 and 424.
14   Per Lord Jauncey, ibid at 228 and 424.
15   [1897] 1 Ch 545 at 554.

The essence of the jurisdiction therefore is not to punish a technical infringement of a court order, but to punish the aiding and abetting of others in setting the court at defiance. As Eveleigh LJ said in *Z Ltd v A-Z and AA-LL*,[16] the third party:

'is liable for contempt of court by himself. It is true that his conduct may very often be seen as possessing a dual character of contempt of court by himself and aiding and abetting the contempt by another, but the conduct will always amount to contempt of court by himself.'

Although *Seaward v Paterson* specifically concerned a prohibitory injunction, the principle is of a more general application so that aiding and abetting the breach of any order of the court, including mandatory orders, or any undertaking[17] given to the court, will also amount to a contempt.

It is an essential element of the offence that the offender knows of the terms of the injunction but knowledge of the order does not depend upon the offending third party being served with notice of the order. In *Seaward v Paterson* [18] the court rejected Murray's argument that he had no notice of the injunction since he was not served with a copy of the order until after the boxing matches had been held, because it was satisfied that he did in fact know of the terms having been present during a great part of the trial and had been informed by Paterson of the result immediately afterwards. It was thus held to be irrelevant that notice of the order had been served only after the boxing matches. It would seem that no distinction should be drawn in this respect between prohibitory orders and mandatory orders. No such distinction was made in *Z Ltd v A-Z and AA-LL* [19] and it seems that in either case the fact of knowledge of the order is sufficient. Whether there are any limits on how that knowledge is gained remains to be established.

A second required element relates to the quality of the act. It seems evident from the cases that mere passivity is unlikely to attract contempt liability. In *Seaward v Paterson* two persons were held guilty of the contempt. One was 'master of the ceremonies' at the boxing matches and it was held that he was:[20]

'actively assisting in what took place and on his own shewing he has clearly been guilty of taking part in Paterson's disobedience to the injunction.'

Murray on the other hand claimed that he was a mere spectator and could not therefore be considered as an aider and abetter. The court rejected this contention because it was shown that far from being a mere spectator, Murray was, in fact acting as a promoter. The court did accept,[1] however, that being a mere spectator was not enough per se to prove that he was aiding and abetting the breach, and it can be reasonably concluded that before anyone will be held guilty of contempt for aiding and abetting a breach of injunction, it must be shown either that he actively assisted in the breach or, possibly, that he willingly acquiesced in the breach.

16   [1982] QB 558, at 578, sub nom *Z Ltd v A* [1982] 1 All ER 556 at 567.
17   See *Elliot v Klinger* [1967] 3 All ER 141, [1967] 1 WLR 1165 and *Thorne RDC v Bunting (No 2)* [1972] 3 All ER 1084. In New Zealand see *Malevez v Knox* [1977] 1 NZLR 463.
18   [1897] 1 Ch 545 at 550.
19   See [1982] QB 558 at 582–583, [1982] 1 All ER 556 at 570 where Eveleigh LJ thought that from the third party's point of view a Mareva injunction had elements of a mandatory order.
20   [1897] 1 Ch 545 at 549 per North J.
 1   Ibid at 557 per Smith LJ.

3   *Z Ltd v A-Z and AA-LL*

The application of the *Seaward v Paterson* principle to Mareva injunctions[2] was considered in *Z Ltd v A-Z and AA-LL*. According to the Supreme Court Act 1981, s 37(3), which gives statutory force to such orders, a Mareva injunction is:

> 'an interlocutory injunction restraining a party to any proceedings from removing from the jurisdiction of the High Court, or otherwise dealing with assets located within the jurisdiction.'

The efficacy of the order normally depends upon a bank[3] (who is not a party to the order) freezing the defendant's assets. The bank's duty to do this rests upon the *Seaward v Paterson* principle. In the simple case[4] a Mareva injunction is served on the defendant restraining him from disposing of his assets in his account at a named bank and the plaintiff will notify the bank of the injunction. If the defendant then, in breach of the injunction, draws a cheque in favour of a tradesman he clearly commits a contempt but so does the bank since under the *Seaward v Paterson* principle it is guilty of aiding and abetting the breach. In *Z Ltd,* however, the principle was held to be wider than simply aiding and abetting so that it could be a contempt for a bank knowing of the injunction to dispose of the defendant's assets, even though the defendant had not himself been served with the order and had therefore not himself committed any contempt to which the bank could be an accessory. The juristic basis of the contempt in these circumstances is the wrongful interference with the administration of justice by causing the order of the court to be thwarted.[5] Lord Denning MR thought[6] that like the arrest of a ship, a Mareva injunction operates in rem and attaches to the asset itself immediately the order is made. Disposal of the asset therefore obstructs the course of justice as prescribed by the court which granted the injunction.

The apparent width of this principle is tempered by a number of reservations laid down by the Court of Appeal. An important limitation relates to the mens rea requirement.[7] According to Eveleigh LJ[8] a bank can only be liable if it knows that what it is doing is inconsistent with the terms of the injunction.

4   *A-G v Times Newspapers Ltd* [9]

Although the three foregoing cases undoubtedly establish that aiding and abetting a breach of a court order is a contempt, as already intimated, they were

---

2 For a general account of these injunctions see the *Supreme Court Practice* 29/1/11E.
3 As Lord Denning MR pointed out, [1982] 2 QB 574 and [1982] 1 All ER at 563, Mareva injunctions can be directed to any person who holds assets of the defendant.
4 Per Lord Denning MR ibid at 572 and 561–2.
5 Per Lord Denning MR, ibid at 574 and 563, per Eveleigh LJ, ibid at 580 and 568.
6 Ibid at 572 and 562.
7 Other limitations include the legality of the bank to honour cheques supported by credit cards or cheque cards and payments under letters of credit. Concern was expressed particularly by Kerr LJ about the abuse of the Mareva procedure and for other limitations see eg *Galaxia Maritime SA v Mineralimportexport, The Eleftherios* [1982] 1 All ER 796, [1982] 1 WLR 539.
8 [1982] 2 QB 574 at 581 and [1982] 1 All ER at 569–70.
9 For further discussion of this case and the 'Spycatcher' litigation generally, see Ch 6 pp 211 ff. See also Miller, *1991 All ER Review* 65–66.

also suggestive of a wider principle, namely, that third parties can be guilty of contempt if they engage in conduct intending to interfere with the course of justice by causing a court order to be thwarted. The existence of this wider principle was confirmed by the House of Lords in *A-G Times Newspapers Ltd*. In that case interim injunctions had been granted against the *Observer* and *Guardian* newspapers restraining them from publishing material from the now infamous memoirs, *Spycatcher*, pending the determination of the breach of confidentiality action brought by the Government against the author, Peter Wright. Whilst these injunctions were still in force the *Sunday Times* published extracts from Wright's book. It was accepted that in doing this the *Sunday Times* was acting independently on its own behalf and could not therefore be regarded as 'aiding and abetting any breach of the order.' Importantly, it was conceded for the purposes of this final appeal that the publisher and editor intended to impede or prejudice the administration of justice, in this case by destroying the subject matter of the action between the Government and Wright. Accordingly, the sole issue before the House of Lords was whether in a case where the court grants A an injunction restraining B from doing certain acts it could be a contempt of court for a third person, with the intention of impeding or prejudicing the administration of justice by the court in the action between A and B, himself to do the acts which the injunction restrains B from doing. It was unanimously held that it could be and was on the facts of the case. As Lord Jauncey put it:[10]

> 'I am quite satisfied that . . . a person who knowingly acts in a way which will frustrate the operation of an injunction may be guilty of contempt even although he is neither named in the order nor has he assisted the person who is named to breach it. Indeed it would be extraordinary if orders of the court could be set at nought with impunity by third parties seeking to achieve that end.'

Although on the face of it *A-G v Times Newspapers Ltd* seems to set a wide precedent, Lord Jauncey, for example, could see 'no danger of the floodgates being opened' by it.[11] As he pointed out, not every order is capable of being frustrated by a third party stranger. He instanced the example of an injunction obtained by A against B trespassing on his land and pointed out that C's subsequent trespass on A's land in knowledge of that order, in no way impairs the effect of the order against B. In his Lordship's view:

> 'It can only be in a limited type of case that independent action by a third party will have the effect of interfering with the operation of an order to which he is not a party. Cases involving confidential information are obvious examples.'

His Lordship also adverted to the destruction of a valuable object or demolition of a listed building which is the subject of the restraining order but pointed out that it could only be in exceptional circumstances that a third party would be free to achieve that result without also incurring liabilities other than for contempt.

Time will tell whether Lord Jauncey was right to think that the decision has a limited application. In this regard it may be observed that his Lordship's own examples concerned the destruction of the subject matter of the litigation yet it is evident that they are not the only examples.[12] Lord Oliver instanced the example of C's obstructing a right of way the use of which is needed by A to

---

10 [1992] 1 AC 191 at 231, [1991] 2 All ER 398 at 426.
11 Ibid at 232 and 427.
12 Indeed as we point out at at p 217, it may not even be necessary to show that the conduct in question has destroyed the whole of the subject matter.

demolish a wall which A has undertaken to remove after proceedings have been commenced by B. In such a case, in Lord Oliver's view:[13]

'C has impeded the administration of justice by deliberately thwarting an undertaking given to the court and designed to secure the removal of the wall. In circumstances such as these, it would seem to me unarguable that C is not in contempt of court in exactly the same way as if he had obstructed an officer of the court and I cannot imagine any court accepting as a defence to a motion for committal the proposition that no contempt is committed because C was not a party to the action or undertaking.'

Even so all the examples postulated are extreme, comprising either the irremediable destruction of the subject matter of the litigation or conduct rendering further performance impossible. If it is subsequently held that the actus reas is confined to such extreme examples the occasions on which third parties can be guilty of such contempt will indeed be limited.

Of course another important limiting factor is the mens rea requirement. Since the point was conceded there was little discussion of this aspect by the House of Lords. However, it is evident that it must be shown that the third party must both know of the order (or undertaking) *and* intend to interfere with or impede the administration of justice. Although, as Lord Oliver said, such an intention may be inferred from the circumstances, it seems unlikely, outside the context of aiding and abetting[14] that the courts will infer such an intention save in the clearest circumstances. Again if this approach is adopted Lord Jauncey may well be right that the ruling in the Spycatcher case has limited application.

C Breach of an undertaking

An undertaking entered into, with or given to the court by a party or his counsel or solicitor has exactly the same force as an order made by the court, and accordingly breach thereof amounts to a contempt in the same way as a breach of an injunction. As Sir John Donaldson MR said:[15]

'Let it be stated in the clearest possible terms that an undertaking to the court is as solemn, binding and effective as an order of the court in the like terms . . .'

Once a party has given an undertaking to the court he is bound by its terms[16] and it has been held that the courts will not entertain an application to vary the

---

13 [1992] 1 AC 191 at 219 and [1991] 2 All ER 398 at 416.
14 It would seem relatively easy to infer an intention to interfere with the course of justice in cases where a third party, knowing of the court order, aids and abets a party to break it.
15 In *Hussain v Hussain* [1986] Fam 134 at 139, [1986] 1 All ER 961 at 963. See also *Gandolfo v Gandolfo* [1981] QB 359, [1980] 1 All ER 833; *Biba Ltd v Stratford Investments Ltd* [1973] 1 Ch 281, [1972] 3 All 1041; *Hallam v Hallam* (1961) Times, 29 September; *Milburn v Newton Colliery Ltd* (1908) 52 Sol Jo 317 and *Neath Canal Co v Ynisarwed Resolven Colliery Co* (1875) 10 Ch App 450, CA. Also accepted in Canada see eg *Northwest Territories Public Service Association v Comr of the Northwest Territories* (1980) 107 DLR (3d) 458 at 468 and in New Zealand in *Malevez v Knox* [1977] 1 NZLR 463. Also accepted but with some reservations in Australia see *Trade Practices Commission v C G Smith Pty Ltd* (1978) 30 ALR 368 at 375.
16 Technically even where the undertaking is recorded in an order of the court (as will now be the universal practice in England and Wales, see Fricker and Bean, *Enforcement of Injunctions and Undertakings* (1991, Jordans) para 2.10) it is the undertaking and not the order which requires the giver of the undertaking to act in accordance with its terms: per Sir John Donaldson MR in *Hussain v Hussain* [1986] Fam 134 at 140, [1986] 1 All ER 961 at 963.

terms of the undertaking. The proper procedure is to apply for a release and such an application should be supported by evidence showing why the litigant should be released from his undertaking.[17]

To establish a case of contempt for breach of an undertaking, as in the case of proving a breach of an injunction, it must be shown that the terms of the undertaking are themselves clear and unambiguous, that the defendant has had proper notice of the terms and the breach by the defendant is clearly established.

A person cannot be held guilty of contempt for breaking the terms of an undertaking unless the terms of the undertaking are themselves clear for as Jenkins J said:[18]

> 'a defendant cannot be committed for contempt on the ground that upon one of two possible constructions of an undertaking being given he has broken that undertaking. For the purpose of relief of this character I think the undertaking must be clear and the breach must be clear beyond all reasonable doubt.'

As the court observed in *O'Neill v Murray* [19] great care should be taken to ensure that undertakings are drafted in clear and precise terms so as to avoid long arguments about whether breaches have occurred. In determining the scope of the undertaking it has been held in a Canadian case[20] that the court should only look to the words of the formal order of the court and not examine the transcript of the proceedings.

No person will be held guilty of a breach of an undertaking unless he has had proper notice of its terms. So, for instance, an undertaking given in court on behalf of a person without his knowledge and which is not communicated to him will not be enforced by process of contempt.[1]

Where an undertaking has been given to the court on behalf of a company, then provided that the company is aware of its terms, it is under a duty to carry out the obligations pursuant to its undertaking, and will be guilty of contempt if it fails to do so. A company will be held to have committed contempt if the terms of its undertaking have been broken even if none of the individual officers of the company knew that the undertaking was being broken. In *Re Garage Equipment Associations' Agreement*, Megaw J said:[2]

> 'The court is prepared to accept that none of the officers of the company individually knew or realised that an undertaking given to the court was being broken or had been broken. But that does not in any way detract from the fact that the company—and this motion is only concerned with the company—was in contempt of court by these things being done when an undertaking had been given on behalf of the company and the company was aware of the existence of that undertaking.'

17 In *Cutler v Wandsworth Stadium Ltd* [1945] 1 All ER 103.
18 In *Redwing Ltd v Redwing Forest Products Ltd* (1947) 177 LT 387. See also in Australia, *Australian Consolidated Press Ltd v Morgan* (1965) 112 CLR 483; *Trade Practices Commission v C G Smith Pty Ltd* (1978) 30 ALR 368 and *Bryant v Keith* (1980) 33 ALR 437.
19 (1990) Times, 15 October, CA.
20 *Northwest Territories Public Service Association v Comr of the Northwest Territories* (1980) 107 DLR (3d) 458; cf *Chanel Ltd v F G M Cosmetics* (1981) 7 FSR 471, Ch D.
1 *Turner v Naval Military and Civil Service Co-operative Society of South Africa* (1907) Times, 21 January. However, if the alleged contemnor knows of the undertaking given on his behalf he will be liable for its breach: *Camden Borough Council v Alpenoak Ltd* (1985) NLJ Rep 1209. For the requisite procedure for the serving of notice of undertakings see the discussion at pp 619–620.
2 (1964) LR 4 RP 491 at 504; cf *Z Ltd v A-Z* [1982] QB 558, [1982] 1 All ER 556 discussed at p 576.

Indeed in the later decision of *Re Galvanized Tank Manufacturers' Association's Agreement*, Megaw P said:[3]

'We would, however, emphasize that a company which has given an undertaking to the court must be treated as having failed lamentably and inexcusably in its elementary duty if it fails to take adequate and continuing steps to ensure, through its responsible officers, that those officers themselves, and anyone to whom they may delegate the handling of matters which fall within the scope of the undertaking, do not forget or misunderstand or overlook the obligations imposed by such undertakings.'

A company can on occasion be liable for the undertaking given by the company it has taken over. In *Re British Concrete Pipe Association's Agreement*[4] it was held that because of the wording of the Iron and Steel Act 1969, s 8 and art 3 of the Steel Companies (Vesting) Order 1970, British Steel were bound by an undertaking given by a company which upon nationalisation had become a wholly owned subsidiary of the corporation. No such liability will accrue, however, if a new company formed in good faith takes over the assets of an old company that had given an undertaking.[5]

Company directors or other officers can also be personally liable for the company's breach of undertaking. In *Ronson Products Ltd v Ronson Furniture Ltd*[6] it was argued that although proceedings might be taken against a director, etc in respect of an order made against the company, as a matter of law, directors could never be proceeded against in respect of an undertaking given by the company. It was held by Stamp J that there was no such distinction and provided that it is satisfactorily established that the officers know of the terms of the undertaking and had procured its breach they will themselves be liable for proceeding in contempt. It has been further held in *Biba Ltd v Stratford Investments Ltd*[7] that because the Rules of the Supreme Court applying to injunctions should be construed as applying also to undertakings, a director could be liable under RSC Ord 45, r 5 for a company's breach of undertakings even if he had taken a purely passive role.

However, an officer of a company will only be held liable in contempt if it is proved that he has had proper notice of the terms of the undertaking. In this respect a distinction must be made between a positive and negative undertaking. *Ronson*'s case establishes the important point that where the undertaking is negative in character, the fact that the particular director or officer has not been served with an order containing the undertaking is not a bar to taking proceedings against such persons for its breach.[8] In such cases it must be proved beyond all reasonable doubt[9] that the particular person did know of the terms of the undertaking, but once it is so proved then the exact means of gaining that knowledge is not vital to the proceedings. Where the undertaking is of a

---

3 [1965] 2 All ER 1003 at 1009, (1965) LR 5 RP 315 at 350.
4 [1981] ICR 182 n, affd [1983] 1 All ER 203, [1983] ICR 215, CA.
5 *Bosch v Simms Manufacturing Co Ltd* (1909) 25 TLR 419. Query the position where a company takes over another company (that had given the undertaking) by acquiring all the shares? See also pp 569 ff.
6 [1966] Ch 603, [1966] 2 All ER 381.
7 [1973] 1 Ch 281, [1972] 3 All ER 1041.
8 Not following *Redwing Ltd v Redwing Forest Products Ltd* (1947) 177 LT 387.
9 See *United Telephone Co v Dale* (1884) 25 Ch D 778 cited with approval in *Ronson*'s case [1966] Ch 603 at 616; see also *Churchman*'s case [1972] 3 All ER 603, [1972] 1 WLR 1094.

positive nature, different considerations apply, for as Stamp J said in *Ronson*'s case:[10]

> 'If a man be ordered to do an act, so that his failure to do it may lead him to prison, justice requires that he know precisely what he has to do and by what time he has to do it.'

On this basis the conclusion must be that an:

> 'order ought not to be enforced against a director unless he has been served with it, so that he, like the company, knows precisely what is to be done and the period during which it has to be done.'

So far as the element of procuring a breach is concerned, penal proceedings are not likely to be taken against a director, etc unless he has played an active part in procuring the breach.[11] In practice, of course, since a company must of necessity act through its officers, there is almost bound to be some person who has actively procured the breach and provided he has the requisite knowledge, he will be liable in contempt. Indeed in a restrictive trade practices case, the Director General of Fair Trading was advised:[12]

> 'not to overlook the desirability of process being taken against responsible directors in cases in which their companies have been found guilty of contempt or have admitted having acted in contempt.'

It should be added that proceedings will only lie against an officer of the company if the company itself is liable. So in *A-G v Wheatley & Co Ltd* [13] the undertaking by the company did not specify the time within which a positive act had to be done, and there had been no order made against its directors to do it. As Stamp J commented in *Ronson*'s case:[14]

> 'It followed that the order could not be enforced against the company, which was not in contempt, and, because directors as such can only be proceeded against for a contempt if the company itself is in contempt, there could at that stage be no relief against the company's directors.'

It is important that liability of the company and its directors are separately considered. Accordingly, it was held wrong in principle to impose a fine jointly and severally on a company and one of its directors for breach of undertakings.[15]

As in the case of breaking the terms of an injunction, a breach of undertaking will amount to contempt even though such a breach is not wilful. In *Re Agreement of the Mileage Conference Group of the Tyre Manufacturers' Conference Ltd*,[16]

---

10 [1966] Ch 603 at 614, 615. No penal proceedings were taken against Mrs Ronson (at p 614). Stamp J said 'She claims to have played no active part in the affairs of the defendant company and apologises for any breach of undertaking. I accept that position and will make no order of a penal nature against her.'
11 In Canada see *Glazer v Union Contractors Ltd and Thornton* (1961) 26 DLR (2d) 349; *Canadian Metal Ltd v Canadian Broadcasting Corpn (No 2)* (1975) 48 DLR (3d) 641 at 660, appealed but not on this point (1976) 65 DLR (3d) 231.
12 Per Mocatta J in *Re British Concrete Pipe Association's Agreement* [1982] ICR 182 at 195 echoing the warning given in *Re Galvanized Tank Manufacturers' Association's Agreement* (1965) LR 5 RP 315 at 350.
13 (1903) 48 Sol Jo 116.
14 [1966] Ch 603 at 615.
15 *McMillan Graham Printers Ltd v RR (UK) Ltd* (1993) Times, 19 March, CA.
16 [1966] 2 All ER 849, [1966] 1 WLR 1137, not following *Worthington v Ad-Lib Club Ltd* [1965] Ch 236, [1964] 3 All ER 674. See also *West Oxfordshire District Council v Beratec Ltd* (1986) Times, 30 October; *Steiner Products Ltd v Willy Steiner* Ltd [1966] 2 All ER 387, [1966] 1 WLR 986 and the *Heaton's Transport* case [1973] AC 15.

for instance, certain tyre manufacturers had given an undertaking inter alia not to operate a certain scheme which the Restrictive Practices Court had declared contrary to the public interest. A new scheme was devised and operated which was held to be a breach of the undertaking. The companies argued, however, that since they had relied upon legal advice that the new scheme would not amount to a breach of their undertaking, they could not be said to have committed contempt because the breach had not been 'contumacious'. The court, held, however, that although reliance on legal advice might be a mitigating factor, if it was reasonable to rely on such advice, a contempt will nevertheless still have been committed. As Megaw P said:[17]

> 'We conclude . . . that the breaches of undertaking here were contempts of court, even though it were to be shown that they were things done, reasonably and despite all due care and attention, in the belief, based on legal advice, that they were not breaches.'

D   Disobeying an order for the payment of money into court

There are two types of judgment or order which direct a person to pay money, namely, that directing payment of money to another person and that directing payment of money into court. Disobedience to either type of order can amount to contempt but the importance of the distinction is that whereas the effect of an order directing a person to pay money to another person is to create a debt, an order to pay money into court does not necessarily imply the existence of a debt. In the former case the court's power to imprison persons who have disobeyed the court order is very limited and can only be exercised in the circumstances provided for by the Debtors Act 1869, s 4 and s 5.[18] In the latter case, however, where the order for payment into court is not in respect of any debt but merely for the security, for example, of a wife's costs, then the power of the court is not affected by the Debtors Act 1869, s 4, and the normal remedies of committal or sequestration are available. In *Bates v Bates* [19] the Court of Appeal held that their power to punish a husband who had defaulted in paying a sum of money into court, ordered for the security of his wife's costs in respect of her petition for judicial separation, was unaffected by the Debtors Act 1869. Lindley LJ said:[20]

> 'The question turns upon the words of the 4th section of the Debtors Act. It is said that the appellant is within the protection of the Act, because he has made default in payment of a sum of money. But what do the words "payment of money" in this section mean? In my opinion, they do not mean depositing a sum of money in court, to abide an order to be subsequently made.'

---

17 [1966] 2 All ER 849 at 863. For other cases concerning reliance upon legal advice see *Re National Federated Electrical Association's Agreement Ltd and National Federation of Retail Newsagents Booksellers and Stationers* (1961) LR 2 RP 447 and *Re Newspaper Proprietors' Association Agreement* [1961] 3 All ER 428. See also *Re Rossminster Ltd and Tucker* (1980) Times, 23 May.

18 See pp 647–651. In *Buckley v Crawford* [1893] 1 QB 105 it was held that an order to pay money to another person in pursuance of an undertaking had the same effect as an order made by the court directing a person to pay money, and that therefore the Debtors Act 1869, s 4, still applied.

19 (1888) 14 PD 17.

20 Ibid at 20.

On the other hand, where the order for the payment of money into court is in the nature of a debt, then the Debtors Act 1869 does apply. In *De Lossy v De Lossy*[1] it was held that an order directing a husband to pay permanent maintenance to his wife did amount to a debt. In *Farrant v Farrant*,[2] a husband had been ordered to pay school fees for three children, and it was held by Sachs J that:[3]

> 'in substance the husband's obligation was to pay a sum certain when it had been ascertained. The moment that sum had been ascertained his obligation was clearly to pay money, and any default on his part was in truth a "default in payment of a sum of money" within the meaning of section 4 [of the Debtors Act 1869]. Thus the court has in the present case no power to order a writ of attachment to issue.'

The essence of the distinction seems to be that the payment of money as security is not a debt within the meaning of the Debtors Act, because no definite and fixed obligation to pay a sum of money has thereby been created. As Chitty J said:[4]

> 'judgments or orders for payments into court are generally not final: the money paid in may be paid for security only for the safety of the fund, and the person ordered to pay in not infrequently is entitled to have some part of the money afterwards paid out to him.'

On the other hand once the sum has become fixed, a definite obligation to pay a sum of money is created and it is in essence therefore a debt.[5]

Where payment into court is held to fall outside the provisions of the Debtors Act 1869, the court can proceed to enforce payment by means of a committal or sequestration provided the time for payment is fixed,[6] and the same rules with regard to serving notice etc[7] will apply as are applicable, for instance, in respect of a breach of an injunction.

E Disobeying a judgment or order for the giving of possession of land or for the delivery of goods within a time specified

It is a contempt to disobey a judgment or order for the giving of possession of land, and such an order can be enforced by means of committal or sequestration.[8] However, enforcement by committal or sequestration is only possible where, pursuant to RSC Ord 45, r 5, the order giving possession specifies the time within which this act is to be done, and the defendant has refused or neglected to do it within that time. Commonly, orders for possession do not specify any time limit and accordingly the remedies of committal and sequestration will not be available and enforcement will depend upon the writ of possession.[9] Normally,

---

1 (1890) 15 PD 115.
2 [1957] P 188, [1957] 1 All ER 204.
3 Ibid at 191.
4 In *Re Greer, Napper v Fanshawe* [1895] 2 Ch 217 at 220. See also *Bates v Bates* (1889) 14 PD 17 at 19, per Cotton LJ, where emphasis was laid on the fact that the order related also to the giving of a bond.
5 As in *Farrant v Farrant* [1957] P 188, [1957] 1 All ER 204.
6 RSC Ord 45, r 1 (2)(b), (c), pursuant to Ord 45, r 5.
7 See Ord 45, r 7.
8 RSC Ord 45, r 3(1)(b), (c).
9 By Ord 45, r 3(1)(a). By r 3(2) leave of the court is required before a writ of possession will be issued, unless the order was given or made in a mortgage action to which Ord 88 applies. For the requirements of when leave will be given, see r 3(3).

this latter means will be a sufficient remedy, but in an extreme case where it is still thought necessary to enforce the order by committal or sequestration, an application to the court should be made under Ord 45, r 6[10] for an order fixing the time within which a defendant is required to give possession and it will also be necessary to comply with the rules relating to the service of notice.[11] Once this procedure has been adopted an application pursuant to Ord 45, r 5 for committal or sequestration can then be made.

A similar position obtains in the county court. Under the County Court Rules 1981, Ord 26, r 17 a judgment or order for the recovery of land is enforceable by warrant of possession and with leave of the court a warrant of restitution may be issued in aid of any warrant of possession.[12] Rule 17 does not prejudice the power to enforce a judgment by committal[13] though like the High Court any order for committal is dependent upon there being a fixed time limit in the original order.[14] In any event it has been held[15] that committal orders should only be sought where there is no alternative means of enforcing the judgment.

Sadly, the above procedure both in the county court and High Court can on occasion prove not only cumbersome but largely ineffective particularly in matrimonial cases where it is sought to evict a recalcitrant spouse from the matrimonial home so that it can be sold with vacant possession.[16] In one case[17] Ormrod LJ commented that the wife's attempts to obtain possession by seeking an order for possession followed by a writ of possession followed by a writ of restitution followed finally by an order for committal was ill-advised being a highly complex and old-fashioned property approach. Instead he advocated the following method for dealing with spouses who will not obey orders in divorce proceedings:

(1)   Obtain a personal order together with the proper penal notice against the spouse that he vacate the premises by a particular date and that he be restrained from returning thereafter. *However, at this stage no move should be made to commit the husband.*

(2)   Arrange for the contract of sale of the house to be made with vacant possession.

(3)   When the sale is imminent (ie when the contract is about to be signed), if the spouse is still in breach of the order, apply to the court to enforce the personal order. Ormrod LJ envisaged that in such cases the court would make an indefinite committal order pending the sale or until the spouse gives an undertaking not to interfere with the sale.

10   Discussed at pp 604–605.
11   Pursuant to RSC Ord 45, r 7, see pp 562 ff.
12   CCR 1981, Ord 26, r 17(4).
13   Ord 26, r 18.
14   Ord 29, r 1(1).
15   See *Danchevsky v Danchevsky* [1975] Fam 17 at 22B, 22G and 24E per Lord Denning MR and Buckley and Scarman LJJ, respectively.
16   Highlighted by *Danchevsky v Danchevsky* [1975] Fam 17, [1974] 3 All ER 934 and *Danchevsky v Danchevsky (No 2)* (1977) 128 NLJ 955, [1977] CA Transcript 416A and *Kavanagh v Kavanagh* [1978] CA Transcript 166 and *Kavanagh v Kavanagh (No 2)* [1978] CA Transcript 571 and at (1978) 128 NLJ 1007, both extensively discussed by Lowe, 'Evicting the Recalcitrant Spouse' [1979] Conv 337.
17   *Kavanagh v Kavanagh* [1978] CA Transcript 166. For a comment on this procedure see Lowe, op cit, at 341–343.

(4)   As soon as the husband is in prison sign the contract and let the purchaser into possession.

Ormrod LJ's suggested procedure was readily endorsed by Lord Denning MR. Both judges agreed that it was a practical and effective way of dealing with the problem. It enabled the court to use its contempt powers as a true aid to execution of the civil process (and not as a form of punishment) with the result that recalcitrant spouses would spend the shortest possible time in prison.

Unfortunately, the efficacy of this suggested procedure depended to some extent on the courts having the power to make sine die committals.[18] Under the Contempt of Court Act 1981, s 14, however, courts no longer have such a power.[19] The only alternative now it would seem is to make a committal order for a fixed term that is sufficiently long for the sale to be effected[20] but to add the condition that the spouse be released as soon as the sale has been completed if that is achieved earlier.[1]

It is contempt to disobey an order or judgment for the delivery of any goods, and where the order does not give the defendant the alternative of paying the assessed value of the goods, and provided a time is specified within which the act must be done,[2] the order may be enforced by committal or sequestration.[3] As in the case of an order for the giving of possession of land, in practice an order for delivery of goods does not normally specify any time limit. The normal remedy is by writ of specific delivery or by writ of delivery,[4] but in the event of a need to enforce the order by means of sequestration or committal, an application must be made for the fixing of a time limit within which the act may be done,[5] and again requisite notice must be served.[6]

F   Failure of a party to comply with an order for interrogatories, or for discovery, or production of documents

1   *Courts of law*

It is a contempt for a party not to comply with an order for the discovery or production of documents, or to disobey an order to answer interrogatories. In both cases, a person who fails to comply with such an order is liable to committal, and this liability does not detract from the court's power to dismiss the action or to strike out the defence and enter judgment accordingly, in consequence of the disobedience.[7]

---

18   Ie committals that have no fixed term.
19   See p 626.
20   The maximum term is two years, s 14 of the Contempt Court Act 1981.
 1   The order might have to be coupled with an undertaking from the other spouse to use every endeavour to effect a sale quickly and to inform the court of the progress of the sale.
 2   Pursuant to RSC Ord 45, r 5 or CCR 1981 Ord 29, r 1.
 3   RSC Ord 45, r 4(1)(b), (c). In the county court, however, there is only express power to make a committal order under CCR 1981, Ord 2. (which power to make such an order is expressly preserved by Ord 26, r 18). It was held in *Rose v Laskington Ltd* [1990] QB 562, [1989] 3 All ER 306 (discussed at p 643) that the remedy of sequestration is available in the county court.
 4   RSC Ord 45, r 4(1)(a), (2)(a). In the county court see CCR 1981, Ord 26.
 5   Ord 45, r 6.
 6   Ord 45, r 7.
 7   See Ord 24, r 16(2) (discovery, etc). It is also a contempt to disobey an Anton Piller order, for details of which see the *Supreme Court Practice* 29/2–3/16 and note the effect of the Supreme Court Act 1981, s 72. For contempt by abusing the process of discovery see pp 592 ff. See also Ord 26, r 6(2), committal for failure to answer interrogatories.

As in all cases of contempt, the court will not lightly make a committal order. As Kay J said in *Gay v Hancock*:[8] 'This Court should exercise very great care in putting into force its power of sending persons to prison.' Before a person can be found guilty of contempt for not producing documents pursuant to a court order, it must be proved beyond all reasonable doubt that the defendant, at the time that the order is made, has possession of the documents, so that he is able to produce them.[9]

Possession of the documents means both de facto and de jure possession. In *Eccles & Co v Louisville and Nashville Rly Co*,[10] a servant of a firm, who had been ordered to produce certain documents, argued that he had possession of the documents only in his capacity as a servant and that therefore it was for his master to produce the documents. The prosecution argued that once it was shown that the servant had de facto possession of the documents, the onus was on him to show that the master had refused to allow him to produce them. The Court of Appeal upheld the defence holding that, since the burden of making out the case was upon the prosecution it was for them to prove not only that the servant had de facto control but also that the master was willing for him to produce the documents. Where the documents are in possession of a company, an order should be made against the company, requiring it, by its proper officer, to produce the documents, but the order should not be made against an individual officer of the company since he will be able to argue that he had no authority to produce the documents.[11] Where an action is brought by one partner in the name of the partnership, but the other partner does not wish to be joined in the action, then provided that the partner is indemnified against any costs which might be incurred in the action, he is bound to comply with any order in respect of any document which he has in his possession.[12]

It must also be shown that the defendant has adequate notice of the court order and that he does in fact know of the terms of the order. RSC Ord 26, r 6(3) and Ord 24, r 16(3) respectively provide that service upon a party's solicitor of an order to answer interrogatories or for discovery or production of documents constitutes sufficient notice, but it is a defence if the party can show that he had no notice or knowledge of the order. It is also a contempt not to comply with certain orders peculiar to probate matters, as for example where an intermeddling executor fails upon a citation to prove a will,[13] or where a person disobeys a subpoena to bring in a will,[14] or fails to obey a citation to bring in a will[15] or disobeys an order to file an inventory.[16]

---

8   (1887) 56 LT 726. See also *Van Houten v Foodsafe Ltd* (1980) Times, 7 February.
9   *Re Bramblevale Ltd* [1970] Ch 128; cf *Re Rossminster Ltd and Tucker* (1980) Times, 23 May.
10 [1912] 1 KB 135, CA.
11 Per Lord Denning MR in *Penn-Texas Corpn v Murat Anstalt (No 2)* [1964] 2 All ER 594 at 598.
12 See *Seal and Edgelow v Kingston* [1908] 2 KB 579, CA.
13 *Re Lister's Goods* (1894) 70 LT 812, following *Mordaunt v Clarke and Clarke* (1868) LR 1 P & D 592, see also *Re Coates' Goods* (1898) 78 LT 820.
14 *Simmons v Dean* (1858) 27 LJP&M 103; *Parkinson v Thornton* (1867) 37 LJP&M 3.
15 *Evans v Evans* (1892) 67 LT 719.
16 *Marshman v Brookes* (1863) 32 LJPM & A 95; *Re Pergamon Press Ltd* [1971] Ch 388, [1970] 3 All ER 535.

2 Other statutory bodies

Under the Companies Act 1985, s 436, if any officer or agent of the company or other body corporate refuses to produce to inspectors (appointed by the Secretary of State) any document relating to the company or, as the case may be, the other body corporate which are in their custody or power, or to attend before the inspectors when required to do so, or to answer any question put by the inspectors in respect of the company's affairs, or otherwise not to give the inspectors all assistance in connection with the investigation which they are reasonably able to give the inspectors can certify that fact in writing to the court.[17] Thereupon, after inquiring into the case and after hearing any statement offered in defence, that court can punish the offender as if he had been guilty of contempt.[18]

It is a contempt (certifiable before the High Court) for officers and agents of a building society under investigation by the Building Societies Commission to refuse to produce to the inspectors (appointed by the Commission): (a) documents and materials relating to the society which are in their custody or possession; (b) to attend before the inspectors when required to do so; or (c) otherwise to give the inspectors all the assistance in connection with the investigation which they are reasonably able to give.[19] A similar position obtains to enforce co-operation with inspectors appointed to investigate the affairs of a Friendly Society.[20]

Under the Charities Act 1993, the Charity Commissioners are empowered inter alia to institute inquiries with regard to charities and in the course of such inquiries can require persons to furnish accounts or written statements in respect of any matter in question at the inquiry, or to attend at a specified time or place and give evidence or to produce documents which are in their control.[1] The Commissioners can also order any person having in his possession or control any books, records, deeds or papers relating to the charity, to furnish copies thereof to the Commissioners.[2] By s 88, disobedience to these orders or to an order made by the Commissioners requiring the transfer of property or payments to be made,[3] can on the application of the Commissioners to the High Court be dealt with as for disobedience to a High Court order, ie it can be treated as a contempt. Section 88 also provides that disobedience to an order of the Commissioners requiring a default under the Act to be made good, can also be taken before the High Court.[4]

There are a number of ways in which a person may be guilty of contempt of court under the Insolvency Act 1986. In the case of winding up a company the official receiver can apply to the court at any time for the public examination of any person who is or was an officer of that company[5] and the failure without

---

17 For the definition of which see s 744 of the 1985 Act.
18 A liquidator may also be subject to contempt proceedings if he fails to comply with a court order to send certain statements to the Registrar of Companies as required by the Insolvency Act 1985, s 192(1). In such proceedings, the court is not confined to the penalties provided by statute: *Re Grantham Wholesale Fruit, Vegetable and Potato Merchants Ltd* [1972] 1 WLR 559; *Re Diane (Stockport) Ltd* (1982) Times, 15, 16 July and 4 August.
19 Building Societies Act 1986, s 57(6).
20 Friendly Societies Act 1992, s 67(6).
 1 S 8(3).
 2 S 9(1).
 3 Pursuant to ss 18, 20.
 4 By s 42 charities are bound to submit annual statements of account and it is possible that such liability may be tested by a motion for contempt, cf *Re Gilchrist Educational Trust* [1895] 1 Ch 367.
 5 Insolvency Act 1986, s 133.

reasonable excuse of any such person to attend his public examination constitutes a contempt which may be punished accordingly.[6] Similarly, a bankrupt is under a duty to answer any questions put to him during any public examination of him by the court,[7] and it is a contempt to refuse to answer such questions.[8] It is well established that unlike civil cases generally[9] a bankrupt is not entitled to refuse to answer a question on the ground that an answer may incriminate him. As Lord Hanworth MR said *in Re Paget, ex p Official Receiver*:[10]

> 'the purpose of the Act [is to] secure a full and complete examination and disclosure of the facts relating to the bankruptcy in the interests of the public and not merely in the interests of those who are the creditors of the debtor.'

It has since been held that the '*Re Paget* principle' still applies under the Insolvency Act 1986.[11]

Where a bankruptcy order has been made, the bankrupt is under a duty to deliver to the official receiver possession of his estate and 'all books, papers and other records of which he has possession or control and which relate to his estate and affairs (including any which would be privileged from disclosure in any proceedings)'.[12] The bankrupt is also obliged to give the official receiver such inventory and such other information and to attend on the receiver at such times as is reasonable for the receivers to require.[13] Failure without reasonable excuse to comply with any of these obligations renders the bankrupt guilty of contempt and liable to punishment accordingly (in addition to any other punishment to which he may be subject).[14] Where a bankruptcy order has been made otherwise than on a debtor's petition, he must, on pain of contempt, submit a statement of his affairs to the official receiver within 21 days of the commencement of the bankruptcy.[15]

Not dissimilar provisions are made to enforce the bankrupt's obligations towards the trustee in bankruptcy.[16] An undischarged bankrupt or a discharged bankrupt whose estate is still being administered under Part V of the 1986 Act is obliged, on pain of contempt (and without prejudice to any other punishment to which he might be subject), to do all such things as he may be directed by the court for the purposes of his bankruptcy or, as the case may be, the administration of that estate.[17]

In any insolvency proceedings, orders of the court (including those made by the secondary court) may be enforced in the same manner as a judgment to the same effect.[18] The failure without reasonable excuse to co-operate with

---

6 Ibid s 134(1).
7 Insolvency Rules 1986, r 6.175.
8 Insolvency Act 1986, s 290(5).
9 See Civil Evidence Act 1968, s 14(1). For the position generally see Ch 2.
10 [1927] 2 Ch 85 at 88, following *Re Atherton* [1912] 2 KB 251.
11 See *Bishopsgate Investment Management Ltd v Maxwell* [1993] Ch 1, [1992] 2 All ER 856, CA.
12 S 291(1).
13 S 291(4).
14 S 291(6).
15 S 288.
16 Ie to deliver possession of property, books, papers of his (see s 312) and to give such information as to his affairs, to attend on the trustee at such times and to do all such other things as the trustee may reasonably require, see s 333.
17 S 363.
18 Insolvency Rules 1986, r 7.19. The relevant form is that provided by Sch 4 to the Rules, see r 12.7.

investigations into insider trading under s 17 of the Financial Services Act 1977, can be dealt with as a contempt.[19]

It can also be a contempt to refuse to comply with an order to produce documents etc made either by the Parliamentary Commissioner, the Local Commissioner (the Ombudsman and Local Ombudsmen respectively), the Legal Services Ombudsman, the Pensions Ombudsman and the Mental Health Commissioner.[20]

G Disobeying a prerogative writ or order of the court

It is a contempt to disobey prerogative writs or orders of the court, such as mandamus or habeas corpus.

The person to whom a writ of habeas corpus is directed is under a legal duty to produce the body of the person alleged to be unlawfully detained, before the court on the day specified, and to make a formal return to the writ. Failure to comply will render the party to whom the writ is directed, guilty of contempt.[1] Before a person can be held guilty of contempt for not complying with a writ of habeas corpus, the writ must have been served personally[2] upon the defendant, but if that is not possible, or if it is directed to a governor of a prison or public official, it must be served by leaving it with a servant or agent of the person to whom the writ is directed at the place where the person restrained is confined.[3] The original writ should be served but where the writ is directed to more than one person the original should be served upon the person first named in the writ and copies must be served upon the others,[4] and it has been held that failure to serve the original upon the principal renders service of the copies also invalid.[5]

An order of mandamus directs a person, corporation or inferior tribunal to do a particular act, and failure to comply with the order is a contempt.[6] Similarly, disobeying an order of prohibition (which operates to prohibit proceedings) or an order of certiorari (which operates to remove proceedings into the High Court) will also amount to contempt.[7] In each case a notice or summons must be served on all persons directly affected and where the order relates to any proceedings in or before a court, and the object is either to compel the court or an officer of the court to do any act, the notice or summons must be served on the clerk or registrar of the court and the other parties to the proceedings, and where any objection is to be made against the conduct of the judge, service must also be made upon the

---

19 Financial Services Act 1986, s 177(2).
20 See respectively the Parliamentary Commissioner Act 1967, s 9, the Local Government Act 1974, s 29(8), the Courts and Legal Services Act 1990, s 25, the Pension Schemes Act 1993, s 150(4) and the Mental Health Service Commissioners Act 1993, s 13. In each case the offence must be certified to the High Court.
1 See *Re Thompson, R v Woodward* (1889) 5 TLR 601.
2 RSC Ord 54, r 6(1).
3 Ord 54, r 6(2).
4 Ord 54, r 6(3).
5 *R v Rowe* (1894) 11 TLR 29; *R v Barnardo* (1889) 23 QBD 305. For the account of writs of habeas corpus generally, see 37 *Halsbury's Laws* (4th edn), paras 584ff and for the procedure, see RSC Ord 54.
6 *R v Poplar Borough Council (No 2)* [1922] 1 KB 95; *R v Worcester Corpn* (1903) 68 JP 130; *R v Leicester Union* [1899] 2 QB 632. In Australia see *Re The Municipal District of Lambton (No 2)* (1989) 20 NSWLR 378 and in Canada see *Re Axelrod and City of Toronto* (1985) 13 DLR (4th) 634.
7 *Mungean v Wheatley* (1851) 6 Exch 88.

judge.[8] The court has the power to adjourn proceedings in order that further persons may be served.[9] Where a writ or order is served upon a body corporate, etc it has been held[10] that the proper course in proceeding against an individual is to serve notice of committal upon the individual personally for:

> 'It is common justice that, where individuals are to be charged with contempt . . . they should have the opportunity of exculpating themselves.'[11]

Nevertheless such an irregularity may be waived, as for example by the individuals addressing the court.[12]

H   Disobeying other orders of the court

1   *Specific performance*

It is a contempt to disobey an order for specific performance.[13]

2   *Declarations*

As we said at the beginning of this chapter, not every order that the courts make is enforceable. As *Webster v Southwark London Borough Council*[14] established, since a declaratory order is not a coercive order a refusal to comply with it does not amount to contempt. If therefore a litigant or even the court[15] is in doubt as to whether a declaration will be observed they would be better advised to seek an injunction.

3   *Orders relating to family matters*

Court orders relating to family matters are no less binding than those relating to any other area of law. Indeed there are regrettably numerous instances of contempts comprising the breaking of orders restraining the use of violence or from otherwise molesting a spouse, cohabitant or child.[16] Similarly, the breaking of matrimonial orders relating to the possession of the matrimonial home or to

---

8   See the *Supreme Court Practice* 53/1–14/26.
9   See the *Supreme Court Practice* 53/1–14/26.
10   In *R v Poplar Borough Council (No 2)* [1922] 1 KB 95.
11   Per Lord Denman in *R v Ledgard* (1841) 1 QB 616 at 619, cited with approval in *R v Poplar Borough Council (No 2)* [1922] 1 KB 95. See also in Canada, *Re United Fisherman and Allied Workers' Union* (1968) 65 DLR (2d) 579 at 590.
12   See *R v Poplar Borough Council (No 2)*, where it was also held that the notice should normally contain details of the alleged contempt, but that this irregularity can also be waived. See also *R v Worcester Corpn* (1903) 68 JP 130.
13   *C H Giles & Co Ltd v Morris* [1972] 1 All ER 960, [1972] 1 WLR 307.
14   [1983] QB 698, [1983] 2 WLR 217, though note that in the special circumstances of that case leave to issue a writ of sequestration was held to have been rightly given. But see the discussion at p 606.
15   See Forbes J ibid at 708 and 224 respectively.
16   See eg *Szczepanksi v Szczepanksi* [1985] 1 FLR 468; *Juby v Miller* [1991] 1 FLR 133; *Jones v Jones* [1993] 2 FLR 377 and *Keeber v Keeber* [1995] 2 FLR 748.

the distribution of other family assets, is viewed as a serious contempt.[17] In principle there is no less a binding obligation to obey orders relating to children but this is subject to the important proviso that the order in question must be coercive or injunctive in form. Moreover, given that the sanctions of fining or imprisoning the offender are singularly inappropriate in most cases involving children, in this, perhaps more than any other area, resort to contempt should not be readily undertaken, and certainly only where other alternatives are thought to be ineffective.[18]

The requirement that the order be in injunctive form (ie stating explicitly precisely what it is that the person in question must do, or must refrain from doing) means that not all orders made under the Children Act 1989[19] and associated directions are enforceable. It is clear, for example, that the embargoes against changing the child's surname and removing him from the United Kingdom as provided for by s 13 of the Children Act 1989[1] and clearly stated on the face of a residence order[2] are not per se enforceable by committal orders.[3] If, therefore, sanctions for contempt are being sought it will be necessary to obtain a prohibited steps order under s 8 of the 1989 Act[4] clearly setting out what action must be refrained from and backed by a penal notice.

Before the Children Act 1989 there was authority for saying that it was a contempt to disobey what was then known as a custody order. As Simon P explained in *B (BPM) v B (MM)*:[5]

'order for custody vests the right of possession of a child in the person to whom custody is vouchsafed. An order for access derogates from that right only so far as the order for access operates. In so far, therefore, as a person with a right only to access retained the child in excess of the period of access, he or she is disobeying the order of the court.'

Under the Children Act 1989 custody orders have been replaced by residence orders. However, since such orders are said only to settle 'the arrangements to be made as to the person with whom a child is to live' they are clearly not injunctive in form and are not therefore enforceable in themselves in the county court or High Court.[6] To make such orders prima facie enforceable courts must attach

17 See eg *Danchevsky v Danchevsky* [1975] Fam 17 and *Kavanagh v Kavanagh (No 1)* [1978] CAT No 166 and *(No 2)* [1978] CAT No 571.
18 In particular note the power under s 34 of the Family Law Act 1986 for a court to make an order authorising an officer of the court or a constable to take charge of the child and deliver him to another person.
19 See generally White, Carr and Lowe, *The Children Act in Practice* (1995, Butterworths) paras 5.93ff and the authorities there cited. The 1989 Act extends to England and Wales and Northern Ireland. Similar problems of enforcement will be found by the Scottish Courts under the Children (Scotland) Act 1995 when it comes into force in relation to their powers under s 11.
1 See White, Carr and Lowe, op cit, at paras 5.23ff.
2 See Form C43.
3 See *Re P (minors) (Custody Order Penal Notice)* [1990] 1 WLR, 613, CA, discussed by Lowe, 'Enforcing orders relating to children' (1992) 4 Journal of Child Law 26.
4 Ie, an order prohibiting a person from taking a step which 'could be taken by a parent in meeting his parental responsibility for a child, and which is of a kind specified in the order' See generally White, Carr and Lowe, *The Children Act in Practice* (1995, Butterworths) paras 5.44ff.
5 [1969] P 103 at 117. See also *Gordon v Gordon* [1946] P 99, [1946] 1 All ER 247 and *Stark v Stark and Hitchins* [1910] P 190.
6 See White, Carr and Lowe, op cit, para 5.98. Note, however, that because of s 14 of the Children Act 1989 the position is different with regard to residence orders made by magistrates' courts, see p 645.

precise directions or conditions, for example that the child be returned to a specific place at a specific time, pursuant to their powers under s 11(7) of the 1989 Act.[7]

Although there was some authority for saying that disobeying an access order was a contempt,[8] the Court of Appeal ruled in *D v D (Access: Contempt: Committal)* [9] that if the order was declaratory in terms as for example, providing for access during the summer, dates to be arranged by the parties or simply for reasonable access, then it could not be enforced by committal. Under the Children Act 1989 access orders have been replaced by contact orders by which the person with whom the child lives or is to live is required:

> 'to allow the child to visit or stay with the person named in the order, or for that person and the child otherwise to have contact with each other.'

Although in their statutory form contact orders are injunctive in terms and are therefore prima facie enforceable it remains the case that orders that are declaratory in terms as, for example, providing for 'reasonable contact', cannot have a penal notice attached to it and cannot therefore be enforced by committal.[10] As the Children Act Advisory Committee said:[11]

> 'To be enforceable by committal, an order for contact . . . [has] . . . to specify when and probably where, the child [is] to be allowed contact as well as with whom.'

As is generally the case, orders relating to children are normally only enforceable against parties to the proceedings[12] but it can be a contempt for someone else knowingly to frustrate a court order by assisting or inciting and encouraging a party to break it.[13] In such cases not only is the interference regarded as a serious contempt but the normal reluctance to impose penalties because of the adverse effect that might have on the child will generally not be a relevant factor.

I   Abusing the process of discovery

1   *The general principle*

Discovery is the process whereby litigating parties are compelled in the course of preparing for the trial of a civil action to produce to one another for inspection and copying, all documents in their possession or control which contain information that may, either directly or indirectly, enable the other party either to advance his own cause or to damage the case of his adversary or which may fairly lead to a

---

7   S 11(7) is discussed in detail in White, Carr and Lowe, op cit, at paras 5.56ff.
8   See *Re K (a minor) (Access Orders: Breach)* [1977] 2 All ER 737, [1977] 1 WLR 533.
9   [1991] 2 FLR 34, CA.
10 The procedure for obtaining committals is set out by the Family Proceedings Rules 1991, r 4.21A.
11 Children Act Advisory Committee Annual Report 1992/93, p 44.
12 See White, Carr and Lowe, op cit, at para 5.99.
13 See *Re K (minors) (Incitement to Breach of Orders)* [1992] 2 FLR 108 (solicitor held guilty of contempt for advising a client mother to break an access order); *Re S (Abduction: Sequestration)* [1995] 1 FLR 858 (contempt for a friend to assist mother in abducting child). See also in Scotland where a Dundee firm of solicitors were reportedly fined £1,500 for advising a client to refuse access of her son to her former husband, reported at (1981) Times, 6 February.

chain of inquiry which may have either of these two consequences.[14] It is established[15] that the litigant and his legal adviser, on whom a list or affidavit of documents is served or to whom the documents are produced under the discovery process, impliedly undertakes not to use them for a collateral or ulterior purpose and that such improper use amounts to a contempt.[16] Precisely what amounts to a 'collateral or improper purpose' is unclear[17] but according to Lord Denning MR in *Riddick v Thames Board Mills* [18] 'documents disclosed on discovery are not to be made use of except for the purposes of the action in which they are disclosed'.

This general principle was reaffirmed by *Crest Homes Plc v Marks* [19] in which Lord Oliver said[20] that the implied undertaking 'applies not merely to the documents discovered themselves but also to information derived from those documents whether it be embodied in a copy or stored in the mind'. He also said the 'the implied undertaking is one which is given to the court ordering discovery and it is clear . . . that it can, in appropriate circumstances, be relieved or modified by the court'. In this latter regard Lord Oliver was of the opinion that such implied undertakings would only be released or modified in 'special circumstances' and not where it would occasion injustice to the person giving discovery.

---

14 Per Lord Diplock in *Home Office v Harman* [1983] 1 AC 280 at 299, [1982] 1 All ER 532 at 534. For the practice and procedure in discovery see RSC Ord 24 and the commentary thereto in the *Supreme Court Practice* at 24/1/3.
15 See eg *Alterskye v Scott* [1948] 1 All ER 469; *Distillers (Biochemicals) Ltd v Times Newspapers Ltd* [1975] QB 613, [1975] 1 All ER 41; *Home Office v Harman* [1983] 1 AC 280, [1982] 1 All ER 532 and *Seton's Judgments and Orders* (7th edn, 1912) Vol 1, p 76. A similar position obtains in Australia, see eg *Complete Technology Pty Ltd v Toshiba (Australia) Pty Ltd* (1994) 124 ALR 493; *Springfield Nominees Pty Ltd v Bridgelands Securities Ltd* (1992) 110 ALR 685; *Holpitt Pty Ltd* (1991) 103 ALR 648; *Ainsworth v Hanrahan* (1991) 25 NSWLR 155. In New Zealand, see eg *Green v Commissioner of Inland Revenue* [1991] 3 NZLR 8, 11 per Barker J, and *Brightwell v Accident Compensation Corporation* [1985] 1 NZLR 132 at 145 per Cooke J. In Canada, however, it seems that the courts are not prepared to accept that there is any rule of law that imposes an implied undertaking see eg *Goodman v Rossi* (1994) 120 DLR (4th) 557 (Ont Div Ct) (not following *Lac Minerals Ltd v New Cinch Uranuim Ltd* (1985) 17 DLR (4th) 745) and *Kyuquot Logging Ltd v BC Forest Products Ltd* (1986) 30 DLR (4th) 65 (BC CA). The position in the United States also seems to be that protection from disclosure must be based on an express court order rather that upon an implied undertaking of confidentiality, see eg *Re Halkin* (1979) 598 F 2nd 176; *Joy v North* (1982) 692) F 2nd 880 and *US v Davis* (1983) 702 F 2nd 418.
16 Contempt is not the only sanction. For example, any further action based upon the misused documents can be dismissed as an abuse of process, see eg *Riddick v Thames Board Mills* [1977] QB 881, [1977] 3 All ER 677.
17 The precise phrase seems to emanate from Jenkins J's judgment in *Alterskye v Scott* [1948] 1 All ER 469, which was derived from the statement in *Seton's Judgments and Orders* (7th edn, 1912) Vol 1, p 76 which referred to the 'vexatious or improper use' for a 'collateral object'. Jenkins J was not himself sure what the phrase meant for he said ([1948] 1 All ER at 470) 'The discussion before me makes it clear that there is room for considerable argument what a collateral or ulterior purpose is.'
18 [1977] QB 881 at 896. A good example of misuse occurred in *Association of Licensed Aircraft Engineers v British European Airways* [1973] 1 CR 601 where one union obtained, upon an order for discovery, the nominal roll of membership of another rival union. This information was then used to put pressure on some individuals to resign from the rival union. It was held that such a use was most improper and contrary to the implied undertaking. However, because the court was satisfied that there had been no deliberate misuse, no penalty was imposed.
19 [1987] AC 829, [1987] 2 All ER 1074, HL.
20 Ibid at 854 and 1074, agreeing with *Sybron Corporation v Barclays Bank Plc* [1985] Ch 299.

2   The Harman case

The point in issue in *Home Office v Harman* [1] was whether the implied undertaking continues to subsist even though the documents have been read out in open court. In the *Harman* case itself the defendant, who was then the legal officer of the National Council for Civil Liberties, had, in her capacity as a solicitor, obtained on discovery a considerable volume of documents belonging to the Home Office. After the hearing at which some 800 pages had been read out in open court, the defendant without referring to the Home Office, allowed a journalist to come to her office and there, under her surveillance, to inspect and make notes of the contents of the 800 pages. The journalist's object in doing this was, as the defendant knew, to write a feature article on the issues raised by the case. In fact the ensuing article was highly critical of the Home Office, ministers and civil servants.

It was held by a majority[2] in the House of Lords that the undertaking in these circumstances did continue to subsist and that therefore by showing the documents to the journalist, which conduct had nothing to do with the conduct of the case, the defendant had broken her undertaking and had committed a contempt. In reaching this decision the majority stressed the importance of the discovery process to the administration of justice and how necessary it is to safeguard the process from abuse. Perhaps the most convincing of the majority judgments is that of Lord Keith. He said:[3]

> 'The implied obligation not to make improper use of discovered documents is, however, independent of any obligation existing under the general law relating to confidentiality. It affords a particular protection accorded in the interests of the proper administration of justice. It is owed not to the owner of the documents but to the court, and the function of the court in seeing that the obligation is observed is directed to the maintenance of those interests, and not to the enforcement of the law relating to confidentiality. There is good reason to apprehend, that if the argument for the appellant were accepted, there would be substantially increased temptation to destroy or conceal the existence of relevant documents which would fall properly within the ambit of discovery.'

Despite this conclusion it was nevertheless accepted[4] that permitting journalists to see documents would not always be a contempt. In particular, the practice of assisting law reporters and press reporters concerned with day-to-day reporting (ie not feature writers) by showing them documents so that details can be checked was considered not to be a contempt, rather it should be regarded in the interests of fair and accurate reporting, as being for the immediate purpose of the litigation and not collateral or ulterior to it since it is in the interests of justice for a fair and accurate report of what is said in open court to be produced.

In a strong dissenting judgment Lord Scarman[5] said that the basis of the implied undertaking was to protect the confidentiality of the documents so that when that confidentiality was destroyed by the reading out of their contents in open court, the undertaking thereby ended. In his view the alleged anomaly in so concluding (ie that immunity depends upon the fortuitous circumstance that a

---

1   [1983] 1 AC 280, [1982] 1 All ER 532.
2   Ie Lords Diplock, Keith and Roskill.
3   [1983] 1 AC 580 at 308, [1982] 1 All ER 532 at 541.
4   Per Lord Diplock at 306 and 539 and Lord Roskill at 327 and 555.
5   With whom Lord Simon collaborated and agreed.

document is read out in open court) was less compelling than the anomalies that flow from the majority view, namely:[6]

'(1) once the document has been read in open court, a transcript of a shorthand note or mechanical recording of the proceedings setting out the contents of the document in question could be used by the litigant or his advisers, but not the document itself; (2) anyone may communicate the contents of and comment on the document once read in open court except the litigant and his advisers; (3) the use of the document itself even by a bona fide law reporter, would probably be at least a technical contempt of court (or, if not, involve a complex and artificial distinction).'

3   Subsequent developments

Perhaps not surprisingly the decision in *Harman* attracted widespread criticism.[7] As we ourselves commented in the second edition of this work,[8] while it is important to safeguard the process of discovery[9] and to prevent its abuse it is also important to preserve and promote open publicity to public legal proceedings. Even if it is accepted that the implied undertaking is not based upon the protection of the confidentiality of the documents[10] it seems an odd law that allows members of the public, including the media, to note or even record a verbatim account of proceedings yet at the same time penalise as contempt a litigant or his adviser for showing documents that have already been read out in open court. The majority view seemed to depend upon the cynical view that in most cases the de facto media coverage of proceedings will mean that disclosed documents that have been read out in open court will rarely come to the public notice. But that is surely a questionable way of justifying a finding of contempt. If it is felt that the disclosed documents should not be publicised, the safest and more principled method of securing privacy is to ensure that the documents are not read out in open court in the first place. This could be achieved, for example, by reading the documents silently or by hearing the relevant part of the case in camera or by an order preventing disclosure of the documents' contents.

Despite the outcry against the decision early attempts to amend the law were resisted.[11] However, following a ruling by the European Court of Human Rights that the application brought by Ms Harman against the United Kingdom under the Convention[12] was admissible,[13] the government reached a friendly settlement

---

6   Ibid at 318 and 548.
7   See in particular Eagles, 'Discovery of Material Obtained on Discovery' (1984) 47 MLR 284, and the editorials 'Contempt—The Harman Case' (1982) 132 NLJ 149, 'Proceedings in open court' (1992) 126 Sol Jo 105. For a trenchant criticism of the Court of Appeal and Divisional Courts' decisions see Lowe, 'Discovering Contempt' [1982] 1 Civil Justice Quarterly 10; cf (1982) 98 LQR 337–339.
8   At pp 421–422.
9   Fears that the courts might not be so ready to order discovery following the circumstances of the *Harman* case are supported by *Air Canada and Others v Secretary of State for Trade (No 2)* [1983] 1 All ER 910, [1983] 2 WLR 494 (*Harman* referred to in Court of Appeal but not in House of Lords).
10   Which contention, it is submitted, is of doubtful validity.
11   Repeated but unsuccessful attempts were made to include a provision in the Contempt of Court Bill and the Administration of Justice (1982) Bill.
12   For the relevance of the European Convention to the issue cf Lord Diplock [1983] 1 AC 280 at 299, [1982] 1 All ER 532 at 534 with Lord Scarman ibid at 316–17 and at 547.
13   *Harman v United Kingdom* [1985] 7 EHRR 146.

before the Commission undertaking to change the law.[14] As a result RSC Ord 24, r 14A now provides:

> 'Any undertaking, whether express or implied, not to use a document for any purposes other than those of the proceedings in which it is disclosed shall cease to apply to such document after it has been read to or by the court, or referred to, in open court, unless the court for special reasons has otherwise ordered on the application of a party or of the person to whom the document belongs.'

On the face of it r 14A not only reverses the *Harman* decision[15] but seems to provide that once a document has been read or referred to in open court the party is *completely* freed from all restrictions and might use the document for any purpose whatsoever. However, as Drake J pointed out in *Singh (Tejendra) v Christie* [16] such an interpretation would also mean that a disclosed document read out in open court (an attendance note in this case) could then be used against strangers to the action in which the document had been disclosed. Drake J was not prepared to hold that r 14A should be so interpreted and indeed seemed to hold that notwithstanding the new rule a person remained subject to his undertaking not to use a document obtained on discovery for any purposes other than those of the proceedings in which it was disclosed even where it had been read or referred to in open court. He seemed to suggest that all the rule did was to allow the party subject to the undertaking to make known the contents of any disclosed documents read or referred to in open court.

With respect to Drake J his approach seems unduly narrow and flies in the face of the actual wording of r 14A. The preferable interpretation, it is submitted, is that the rule has no application to non-parties and hence any obligation towards strangers to the action is not affected by open court disclosure.[17]

It is to be noted that r 14A only applies to documents referred to or read out in open court. It does not apply to documents read in camera nor in that regard should the rule be considered to have made a fundamental change in the approach which the court should adopt towards applications to release or discharge the implied undertaking. It remains for the applicant to make out a case for ordering the release.[18]

J   Breach of various obligations of solicitors[19]

As officers of the Supreme Court,[20] solicitors have always been subject to a special jurisdiction of the courts. As Lord Denning MR has said, the court:[1]

---

14   The text of the settlement is cited in *Bibby Bulk Carriers Ltd v Cansulex Ltd* [1989] QB 155 at 159, [1988] 2 All ER 820 at 824.
15   The new Rule, however, was held not to be retrospective in *Bibby Bulk Carriers Ltd v Cansulex Ltd*, ibid.
16   (1993) Times, 11 November.
17   Cf the *Supreme Court Practice* 24/14A/1 which states that r 14A represents a change in the onus of showing why there should not be a release from the implied undertaking where documents have been read or referred to in open court.
18   *Apple Corpn Ltd v Apple Computer Inc* [1992] 1 CMLR 969.
19   See generally *Cordery on Solicitors* (8th edn, 1988) pp 104ff and 44 *Halsbury's Laws* (4th edn) paras 252ff.
20   Solicitors Act 1974, s 50(1). The Supreme Court comprises the High Court, Court of Appeal and Crown Court.
1   *Silver and Drake v Baines* [1971] 1 QB 396 at 402, [1971] 1 All ER 473 at 475.

'has from time immemorial exercised a summary jurisdiction over solicitors. They are officers of the court and are answerable for anything that goes wrong in the execution of their office.'

The basis of this jurisdiction is to secure the honest conduct of court officers, for as Lord Esher MR said in *Re Grey*,[2] the principle:

'is that the court has a punitive and disciplinary jurisdiction over solicitors, as being officers of the court, which is exercised, not for the purpose of enforcing legal rights, but for the purpose of enforcing honourable conduct on the part of the court's own officers. That power of the court is quite distinct from any legal rights or remedies of the parties, and cannot, therefore, be affected by anything which affects the strict legal rights of the parties.'

As Balcombe LJ said in *Udall v Capri Lighting Ltd*:[3]

'Although the jurisdiction is compensatory and not punitive it still retains a disciplinary slant. It is only available where the conduct of the solicitor is inexcusable and such as to merit reproof . . .

If the misconduct of the solicitor leads to a person suffering loss, then the court has power to order the solicitor to make good the loss occasioned by his breach of duty . . .'

There seem to be two aspects of this special jurisdiction, namely, the contempt jurisdiction to discipline solicitors and an independent inherent jurisdiction which has been preserved by s 50(2) of the Solicitors Act 1974 and which can be exercised[4] so as to order a solicitor to pay the costs in cases where he has been guilty of neglect or misconduct and as a result of which costs have been needlessly incurred.[5] Formerly, the distinction between the two jurisdictions was important at least where the power was exercised by the Crown Court since there was no right of appeal against an order made under the inherent disciplinary jurisdiction. However, a right of appeal in such cases is now provided for by s 50(3) of the Solicitors Act 1974.[6]

Solicitors are not officers of inferior courts so there is no question of such courts exercising any *inherent* jurisdiction.[7] However, the county courts have a statutory right to enforce a solicitor's undertaking.[8]

---

2 [1892] 2 QB 440 at 443. See also *Myers v Elman* [1940] AC 282, 319, per Lord Wright and *Re Hilliard* (1845) 14 LJ QB 225. In Canada see *Northwest Territories Public Service Association v Comr of the Northwest Territories* (1980) 97 DLR (3d) 202 at 210, 212 and on appeal, see (1980) 107 DLR (3d) 458 at 467 and 477.
3 [1988] QB 907 at 917, [1987] 3 All ER at 269, relying on *R and T Thew Ltd v Reeves (No 2)* [1982] 2 QB 1283, and *Marsh v Joseph* [1897] 1 Ch 213.
4 By the Supreme Court, for definition of which, see n 20 above.
5 See eg *R v Smith (Martin)* [1975] QB 531, [1974] 1 All ER 651 and *Myers v Elman* [1940] AC 282 (query the limits of this jurisdiction?). See the discussion in *Weston v Central Criminal Court, Courts' Administrator* [1977] QB 32 and *R and T Thew Ltd v Reeves* [1982] 2 QB 1283, [1982] 3 All ER 1086. But see now *Gupta v Comer* [1991] 1 All ER 289, CA.
6 Added by the Supreme Court Act 1981, s 147.
7 Criticised by the Court of Appeal in *R v Smith (Martin)* [1975] QB 531, [1974] 1 All ER 651. See also the discussion in *Weston v CCC Administrator*, ibid.
8 Under the County Courts Act 1984, s 142.

1 Breach of undertakings

One consequence of this special jurisdiction is that the Crown Court, the High Court and Court of Appeal, and the county court[9] have the power summarily to enforce an undertaking given by a solicitor.[10] Provided the undertaking is given by a solicitor in his capacity as a solicitor, it can be enforced even though it has not been given to the court either directly or indirectly nor in connection with any legal proceedings.[11] An undertaking given directly to the court by a solicitor in his personal capacity will of course be enforceable in the same way as an undertaking given by any other person, but so far as the special jurisdiction is concerned the crucial requirement is that the solicitor must be acting in his capacity as a solicitor, for as Widgery LJ said in *Silver and Drake (a firm) v Baines*:[12]

> 'a remedy of this kind is intended primarily to discipline the officers of the court, to ensure the honesty of those officers. The court is thus concerned only with their activities as solicitors, and anything done by a solicitor in his private capacity is outside their jurisdiction.'

Although it is not always easy to determine whether or not a solicitor is acting in a professional capacity, where the undertaking is to pay money then, according to Lord Denning MR,[13] a solicitor will usually be acting professionally if he has the money 'in his hands on trust, or on an undertaking that he will apply it in a particular way'. So, in *Re A Solicitor*,[14] it was held that a solicitor who, in the course of acting for a client for the sale of land, gave an undertaking to a bank that he would pay over to the bank a proportion of the money, when received, was acting in his professional capacity. Again in *United Mining and Finance Corpn Ltd v Becher*[15] it was held that a solicitor was acting professionally when during the course of business, which he was conducting for clients with third parties, he gave an undertaking to hold a sum of money in his own hands pending the outcome of certain negotiations. On the other hand, in *Silver and Drake v Baines*[16] in which B, an admitted solicitor who conducted much of the defendant's firm's work, gave an undertaking, written on the defendant's professionally headed notepaper, to repay with interest by a specified date a certain sum of money advanced by the plaintiff who was a partner in another firm of solicitors, for the benefit of a client of the defendant's firm, was held by the Court of Appeal not to be an undertaking given in a professional capacity. As Lord Denning MR said:[17]

---

9   County Courts Act 1984, s 142 and County Court Rules 1981, Ord 29, r 2 by which the power to enforce undertakings by committal order is vested.

10   Though as Balcombe LJ pointed out in *Udall v Capri Lighting Ltd* [1988] QB 907 at 916, [1987] 3 All ER 262 at 268, solicitors' undertakings can also be enforced by (a) an action at law, if there is a cause of action, or (b) an application to the Law Society, under whose Professional Conduct Code a solicitor's failure to honour the terms of a professional undertaking amounts to prima facie guilt of professional misconduct.

11   See eg *United Mining and Finance Corpn Ltd v Becher* [1910] 2 KB 296 and see *Home Office v Harman* [1983] 1 AC 280, [1982] 1 All ER 532 discussed at p 594. In Canada see *R v Rowbotham (No 2)* (1977) 2 CR (3d) 222 at 233–234.

12   [1971] 1 QB 396 at 403, [1971] 1 All ER 473 at 476.

13   In *Silver and Drake v Baines*, ibid at 402 and 475.

14   [1966] 3 All ER 52, [1966] 1 WLR 1604.

15   [1910] 2 KB 296.

16   [1971] 1 QB 396, [1971] 1 All ER 473.

17   Ibid at 403 and 476.

'The solicitor here was not holding money in his hands at all. All that happened was that [B] received money and paid it over to a client . . . and promised to repay it to [the plaintiff]. It was an undertaking to repay money lent. That is all . . . The money may have been for the benefit of a client. But that does not matter. It was, in truth, nothing more nor less than an undertaking to repay money lent. That is not an undertaking in his capacity as a solicitor.'

Provided it is clear that the solicitor has undertaken an obligation in his professional capacity the use of the word 'undertaking' is not essential for the exercise of the summary jurisdiction.[18]

The position where a solicitor fails to honour a professionally given undertaking has been admirably summarised by Balcombe LJ in *Udall v Capri Lighting Ltd*,[19] namely:

'[1] Failure to implement a solicitor's undertaking is prima facie to be regarded as misconduct on his part, and this is so even though he has not been guilty of dishonourable conduct . . .

[2] Neither the fact that the undertaking was that a third party should do an act, nor the fact that the solicitor may have a defence to an action at law (eg the Statute of Frauds), precludes the court from exercising its supervisory jurisdiction . . . However, these are factors which the court may take into account in deciding whether or not to exercise its discretion and, if so, in what manner.

[3] The summary jurisdiction involves a discretion as to the relief to be granted . . . In the case of an undertaking, where there is no evidence that it is impossible to perform, the order will usually be to require the solicitor to do that which he had undertaken to do . . .

[4] Where it is inappropriate for the court to make an order requiring the solicitor to perform his undertaking, the court may . . . order the solicitor to compensate a person who has suffered loss in consequence of his failure to implement his undertaking.'

With regard to the first of Balcombe LJ's propositions cited above it is established that the undertaking is enforceable even if it was given gratuitously, or given to someone other than the solicitor's own client and even though the solicitor has ceased to act for his client. It has also been held that an undertaking can be enforced even though the solicitor's conduct involves no dishonourable conduct, for as Hamilton J explained in *United Mining and Finance Corporation Ltd v Becher*,[20] the jurisdiction may be invoked not only to secure honesty, in its moral sense, in court officers, but also to secure[1] 'the proper and professional observation of undertakings professionally given'. He added:

'The conduct which is required of solicitors is to this extent perhaps raised to a higher standard than the conduct required of ordinary men, in that it is subject to the special control which a court exercises over officers so that in certain cases they may be called upon summarily to perform their undertakings, even where the contention that they are not liable to perform them is entirely free from any taint of moral misconduct.'

On this basis an undertaking given by a solicitor can be enforced even though there is no personal fault at all on the part of the solicitor, as for example, where

18 *Hastingwood Property Ltd v Saunders Bearman Anselm (a firm)* [1990] 3 All ER 107.
19 [1988] QB 907 at 917–918, [1987] 3 All ER 262 at 269.
20 [1910] 2 KB 296.
1 Ibid at 305.

an employee is at fault.[2] An undertaking can also be enforced notwithstanding the client's fraud.[3]

With regard to the second of Balcombe LJ's propositions cited above, as *Udall* itself shows, while it may not necessarily be wise it is no answer to its enforcement that the undertaking given by the solicitor were that someone else would do an act (in *Udall*'s case that the defendant's directors would provide securities for its liabilities towards the plaintiff by creating secured charges in the plaintiff's favour on their personal properties). It is also well established that the supervisory jurisdiction can be exercised notwithstanding that the solicitor has a defence to any action at law, as for example under the Statute of Frauds[4] or the Limitation Act 1980.[5]

With regard to the third of Balcombe LJ's propositions it is well established that whether or not a particular undertaking will be enforced at all is a matter for the court's discretion[6] and will therefore depend upon the circumstances of each case. As Megaw LJ said:[7]

'There is and there has always been recognised a discretion in the court whether or not the circumstances of the case justify the exercise of this exceptional procedure.'

It has been emphasised, in the words of Lord Denning MR,[8] that the:

'solicitor is deprived of the advantages which ordinarily avail a defendant on trial. There are no pleadings; no discovery; and no oral evidence save by leave. The jurisdiction should, therefore, only be exercised in a clear case.'

This comment has subsequently been taken to mean that the court will only excercise its supervisory juisdiction where it has been clearly established that there has been a serious dereliction of professional duty by the solicitor.[9]

It is for the plaintiff to prove his case, 'beyond all reasonable doubt'.[10] If the court is not satisfied that a clear case has been made out for the exercise of its special powers, it will decline to enforce the undertaking. In *Thompson v Gordon*[11] the court declined to enforce an undertaking to make an arrangement with the defendant about the payment of a debt and costs, since it was said that the damages caused by non-performance could not be measured. In *Silver and Drake v Baines*,[12] one of the grounds for refusing to enforce the undertaking to pay money lent was that a clear case for the exercise of the jurisdiction had not been made out since the case involved disputed questions of fact, and it was pointed out that the summary mode of procedure was a highly inappropriate

2   Per Lord Denning MR in *Silver and Drake v Baines* [1971] 1 QB 396 at 402, [1971] 1 All ER 473 at 475 relying on *Myers v Elman* [1940] AC 282, [1939] 4 All ER 484, HL. See also *Re Woodfin and Wray* (1882) 51 LJ Ch 427; *Re Coolgardie Goldfields Ltd* [1900] 1 Ch 475.
3   See *Rooks Rider v Steel* [1993] 4 All ER 716.
4   See *Ex p Hughes* (1822) 5 B& Ald 482, and *In re Greaves* (1827) 1 Cr & J 374. Cf *Rooks Rider v Steel* [1993] 4 All ER 716.
5   *Bray v Stuart A West & Co* [1989] NLJR 753.
6   See *United Mining and Finance Corpn Ltd v Becher* [1910] 2 KB 296 and cases there cited.
7   In *Silver and Drake v Baines*, [1971] 1 QB 396 at 405 and [1971] 1 All ER 473 at 477–478.
8   In *Silver and Drake v Baines*, ibid at 402 and 475 respectively.
9   Per Sir John Donaldson MR in *John Fox v Bannister, King & Rigbeys* [1988] QB 925 at 931–932, [1987] 1 All ER 737 at 744.
10   Per Widgery LJ in *Silver and Drake v Baines* [1971] 1 QB 396 at 404 and [1971] 1 All ER 473 at 477.
11   (1846) 15 M & W 610.
12   [1971] 1 QB 396, [1971] 1 All ER 473.

method for resolving such issues. The courts have also refused to enforce an undertaking where it was given in ignorance of facts known to the other side,[13] or where it was given by mistake,[14] although an undertaking given by a solicitor in the mistaken belief that he had authority was not set aside.[15] Impossibility of performance has also been held to be a ground for not enforcing an undertaking[16] as has delay in seeking to enforce the undertaking.[17]

Examples of undertakings that have been held to be enforceable are: an undertaking to hold a client's lease to a bank's order and to pay over the proceeds of sale to the bank,[18] an undertaking to stamp a document,[19] an undertaking not to issue execution if payment of a judgment debt is expedited,[20] an undertaking in consideration of proceedings being adjourned to pay such sum of money as should be adjudged by magistrates to be due to the other side's clients,[1] an undertaking not to molest witnesses,[2] an undertaking to enter an appearance for a defendant in an action,[3] an undertaking given during the course of a business which the solicitor was conducting for clients with third parties that he would hold a sum of money pending the conclusion of certain negotiations,[4] and a statement made, in the course of legal proceedings, to a person who is not the solicitor's client that he is holding certain funds for the purpose of paying that person upon the happening of a certain event.[5]

As the fourth of Balcombe LJ's propositions cited above states, in cases where the court decides not to enforce the undertaking it may nevertheless decide to order the solicitor to compensate a person who has suffered loss. Furthermore, as *John Fox v Bannister, King & Rigbeys*[6] established, this power to order compensation is not limited to undertakings given in the course of proceedings.

Even though an undertaking may be one which the court is likely to enforce, it was held in *Re A Solicitor*[7] that the correct procedure is not to apply for a committal order immediately[8] upon an alleged breach of the undertaking, but first to obtain a mandatory order,[9] ordering the solicitor to perform his undertaking,

13 *Wade v Simeon* (1845) 13 M & W 647.
14 See *Mullins v Howell* (1879) 11 Ch D 763.
15 *The Gertrude* [1927] WN 265.
16 *Re A Solicitor* [1966] 3 All ER 52, [1966] 1 WLR 1604, but see *Udall v Capri Lighting Ltd* [1988] QB 907, [1987] 3 All ER 262 discussed further below.
17 See *Bray v Suart A West & Co Ltd* [1989] NLJR 753.
18 *Re A Solicitor* [1966] 3 All ER 52, [1966] 1 WLR 1604.
19 *Re Coolgardie Goldfield Ltd* [1900] 1 Ch 475.
20 *Re Commonwealth Land, Buildings, Estate and Auction Co Ltd, ex p Hollington* (1873) 43 LJ Ch 99.
 1 *Re C* (1908) 53 Sol Jo 119.
 2 *Lawford v Spicer* (1856) 27 LTOS 75.
 3 *Re Kerly, Son and Verden* [1901] 1 Ch 467, CA; see also *Practice Note* [1934] WN 228 where it was said that an undertaking to enter an appearance is implied where a respondent on a motion appears by counsel before appearance has been entered.
 4 *United Mining and Finance Corpn Ltd v Becher* [1910] 2 KB 296.
 5 *Re Solicitor, ex p Hales* [1907] 2 KB 539.
 6 [1988] QB 925, [1987] 1 All ER 737 and followed by *Udall v Capri Lighting Ltd* [1988] QB 907, [1987] 3 All ER 262.
 7 [1966] 3 All ER 52, per Pennycuick J approved in *Silver and Drake v Baines* [1971] 1 All ER 473 at 475, per Lord Denning MR.
 8 Though Pennycuick J did not say that the court had no jurisdiction to make such an order, see [1966] 3 All ER 52 at 56.
 9 Such applications are normally by motion but can be by simple application in an action where the conduct complained of occurred in the course of that action, and will not automatically or usually involve pleadings, discovery or oral evidence, per Sir John Donaldson MR in *John Fox v Bannister, King & Rigbeys* [1988] QB 925 at 931, [1987] 1 All ER 737 at 743–744.

and upon breach of that order to ask for a committal. In *Silver and Drake v Baines* Lord Denning MR suggested[10] that where the mandatory order is for the payment of money, as an alternative to committal, execution may be levied against the solicitor's property, ie by means of sequestration.

2   *Breach of other obligations*

The courts may also exercise their punitive and disciplinary jurisdiction over solicitors in respect of other acts amounting to misconduct in the performance of their duties as solicitors. In *Re Dudley*,[11] for instance, a solicitor paid the money he had received on behalf of his client into his own banking account and dealt with it for his own purposes. He later forwarded some of the money to his client but refused to pay the balance even after a court order had been made, ordering him to do so. It was held that the court could in the exercise of its punitive jurisdiction imprison the solicitor for his contempt in failing to comply with the court order, and since the order had been made against the offender in his capacity as a solicitor, it fell within one of the statutory exceptions[12] to the normal rule that persons cannot be imprisoned for debt.[13] As Bowen LJ said:[14]

> 'By the Debtors Act 1869, imprisonment for debt or default in the payment of money was with certain exceptions abolished. One of these exceptions relates to solicitors who make default, as officers of the Supreme Court, in payment of money, . . . When an order has been made for the payment of money by a solicitor it is not to be assumed against him that it has been made upon him as an officer of the court; but in the present case the proceedings shew that the order was made upon the solicitor in his capacity of officer of that court.'

Similarly, in *Re Freston*[15] it was held to be within the court's punitive jurisdiction to punish a solicitor who was ordered to deliver up certain documents, a certain sum of money and costs, but who only delivered some of the documents. Summary proceedings were then taken to enforce the order, and at this hearing the solicitor delivered the rest of the documents. The solicitor was ordered to pay the sum of money and costs within one week or be imprisoned for his contempt. The sum of money was paid but not the costs and he was therefore some time later arrested for his contempt, but since at the time of his arrest he was returning from court where he had been acting as an advocate, he claimed that he was entitled to privilege from arrest.[16] The Court of Appeal rejected this defence, holding that no such privilege existed when, as here, the courts punished an offender for misconduct. As Brett MR said:[17]

> 'The rights of those employing solicitors were not merely of a civil nature; . . . the courts dealt with defaulting solicitors on the ground that they had been guilty of breaches of duty and breaches of the law.'

10 Ibid at 402 and 475, respectively.
11 (1883) 12 QBD 44.
12 Ie under the Debtors Act 1869, s 4(4).
13 Debtors Act 1869, s 4 ; see generally p 650.
14 (1883) 12 QBD 44 at 49, CA
15 (1883) 11 QBD 545, CA. NB Solicitors may be punished in other ways and for this type of conduct they are likely to be struck off the roll. Solicitors can also be disciplined, inter alia, for failing to deliver accounts. See s 34(6) of the Solicitors Act 1974.
16 For privilege from arrest see p 661.
17 (1883) 11 QBD 545 at 554.

The punitive nature of the court's jurisdiction over solicitors was also stressed in *Re Grey*,[18] in which it was held that where a solicitor failed to pay over a sum of money received by him on behalf of his client in breach of his professional duty, the fact that an action had been brought and judgment given for the payment of the money did not automatically take away the disciplinary jurisdiction of the court summarily to enforce the payment. As Lord Esher MR said:[19]

> 'It appears to me that we can make the order asked for on the ground that the power of the court which is invoked is a punitive, disciplinary power to prevent breaches of their duty by its officers, quite distinct and separate from the client's legal right, and therefore unaffected by any alteration of such right.'

The Court of Appeal emphasised however that the court had a discretion whether or not to exercise its punitive jurisdiction and although Lord Esher MR was of the opinion[20] that such a jurisdiction could still be excercised even if a judgment had been recovered, in practice, except in exceptional circumstances it would not do so. In *Re Grey* itself, however, the judgment was ineffective since the solicitor was already in debt and had given a bill of sale on his goods, and it was held that the punitive jurisdiction should be exercised.

The Rules of the Supreme Court also provide instances where a solicitor can be committed for contempt. By RSC Ord 24, r 16(4), a solicitor on whom an order is served for the discovery of documents made against his client, is liable to committal if he fails without reasonable excuse to give notice of such an order to his client, and similarly by RSC Ord 26, r 6(4), for failing, without reasonable excuse to give notice to his client of an order for interrogatories, discovery or inspection.

By RSC Ord 75, r 9, a solicitor who fails to enter an appearance, or give bail or pay money into court in lieu of bail in an Admiralty action, in pursuance of a written undertaking to do so, is liable to committal. It has been held that an undertaking to give bail cannot be withdrawn by substituting the vessel for the bail, and parties do not waive their rights under the undertaking by arresting the vessel.[1] The courts have also refused to discharge an undertaking given by a solicitor even though the owners had subsequently repudiated their authority to do so.[2] It has been established that where ordered to do so, the defendants must complete their undertaking by putting in bail the value of the vessel at the date of the undertaking.[3]

III POWERS OF THE COURTS TO ENFORCE JUDGMENTS OR ORDERS OTHER THAN FOR THE PAYMENT OF A SUM OF MONEY

A High Court and Court of Appeal

The two major sanctions which the High Court and Court of Appeal can impose upon persons who have committed contempt by not obeying court orders or

---

18 [1892] 2 QB 440, CA.
19 Ibid at 444.
20 Ibid at 445.
1 *The Borre* [1921] P 390 per Sir Henry Duke P.
2 *The Gertrude* [1927] WN 265. See also *The Ring* [1931] P 58.
3 *The Borre* [1921] P 390.

judgments are sequestration and committal. These powers are provided for by RSC Ord 45, r 5, which states:

'(1) Where—

    (a)   a person required by a judgment or order to do an act within a time specified in the judgment or order refuses or neglects to do it within that time or, as the case may be, within that time as extended or abridged under Order 3, rule 5, or

    (b)   a person disobeys a judgment or order requiring him to abstain from doing an act,

then subject to the provisions of these rules, the judgment or order may be enforced by one or more of the following means, that is to say -

    (i)   with the leave of the court, a writ of sequestration against the property of that person;

    (ii)   where that person is a body corporate, with the leave of the court, a writ of sequestration against the property of any director or other officer of the body;

    (iii)   subject to the provisions of the Debtors Acts 1869 and 1878, an order of committal against that person or, where that person is a body corporate, against any such officer.'

By this rule the courts have identical powers to enforce both positive and negative orders[4] but the coercive methods of enforcing a positive order can only be exercised where that order specifically expresses the time within which the act must be done. Normally such positive orders will specify a time within which an act must be done, and indeed the courts are obliged to specify a time under Ord 42, r 2(1).[5] However, by Ord 42, r 2(2), no time limit need be specified in respect of an order or judgment requiring a person to pay money to some other person, or to give possession of any land or to deliver goods. In practice such orders will not normally specify any time limit and accordingly they cannot be enforced by sequestration or committal. However, where the original order does not specify a time limit (and this includes not only orders or judgments requiring persons to pay money to some other person, etc under Ord 42, r 2(2), but also other orders which either through inadvertence or omission have not complied with Ord 42, r 2(1)),[6] the courts are empowered to make a further order requiring the act to be done within a stated time.[7] This subsequent order can be enforced by sequestration

4   Formerly it was doubtful whether a negative order could be enforced by sequestration.

5   It has been held that an order to do an act 'forthwith' is a sufficient expression of time within the meaning of the rule. See *Thomas v Nokes* (1868) LR 6 Eq 521; *Favard v Favard* (1896) 75 LT 664, and *Halford v Hardy* (1899) 81 LT 721. The term 'forthwith' has been held to mean, for the purposes of what was then the Housing Act 1957, that the act is to be done as soon as it can reasonably be done, see *Hillingdon London Borough Council v Cutler* [1968] 1 QB 124, [1967] 2 All ER 361, CA. It is submitted that a similar interpretation would be applicable under this rule. See also the *Supreme Court Practice* 42/2/2.

6   Such an omission does not render the order ineffectual, but the court will make a supplemental order fixing the time, which in the Chancery Division is designated a 'four-day order'. The order, however, cannot be enforced (except in the case of an order directing a person to pay money to another or to give possession of land or to deliver goods) until a time has been fixed, see, eg *Re Wilde* [1910] WN 128, CA. A four-day order has, however, been held to be inapplicable to an order made under what is now the Inheritance (Provision for Family and Dependants) Act 1975: see *Re Jennery, Jennery v Jennery* [1967] Ch 280, [1967] 1 All ER 691, CA.

7   Ord 45, r 6(2). This rule is not applicable to prohibitory orders, see *Selous v Croydon Rural Sanitary Authority* (1885) 53 LT 209, nor is it applicable to an order made under the Inheritance (Provision for Family and Dependants) Act 1975, see *Re Jennery, Jennery v Jennery* [1967] Ch 280, [1967] 1 All ER 691, CA.

or committal, and accordingly where it is thought necessary so to enforce orders for giving possession of land[8] or for the delivery of goods, the procedure to adopt is to apply for this subsequent order. Such an application must be made by summons and the summons must be served upon the person required to do the act in question.[9] In cases where the order does express a time limit, the court has the power upon such terms as it thinks just, to extend or abridge that time[10] and an application for an extension may be granted even if it is made after the expiration of the original time limit.[11] The court also has the power to specify an entirely different time limit.[12]

A judgment or order requiring the delivery of goods cannot be enforced by committal if the person liable to execution has the alternative of paying the assessed value of the goods, but the court can, upon an application by the person entitled to enforce the judgment or order, make an order requiring that goods be delivered to the applicant within a specified time, and such an order can then be enforced by the committal.[13]

Order 45, r 5, makes it clear that the remedies of committal and sequestration are cumulative and not alternatives, thereby resolving any doubt that existed under the old rules.[14] The rule omits any reference to the remedy by way of attachment, which is in accordance with the general intention to abolish the remedy altogether,[15] though technically it may still be possible in appropriate cases to use the remedy.[16] In any case the provisions under this rule, while providing for the major sanctions, do not exhaustively define the court's powers. For example, the rule does not limit the court's powers to commit under the Debtors Act 1869, ss 4 and 5[17] nor does it prevent the courts from imposing lesser sanctions such as fines[18] or injunctions, nor does it affect the court's power to award costs.

We shall now examine, in more detail, the power of the courts.

8   See p 584 for the problems and procedure when seeking to evict a recalcitrant spouse from the matrimonial home.
9   Ord 45, r 6(3).
10   Ord 3, r 5(1), see also Ord 45, r 5(1)(a).
11   Ord 3, r 5(2).
12   Ord 45, r 6(1). Under Ord 45, r 6(3), an application must be made by a summons which must be served on the person required to do the act in question. Where such an amendment is made then references in Ord 45, r 5(1)(a) to a judgment or order, shall be construed as references to the order made under Ord 45, r 6, Ord 45, r 5(2).
13   Ord 45, r 5(3).
14   See *Phonographic Performance Ltd v Amusement Caterers (Peckham) Ltd* [1964] Ch 195 at 201 per Cross J doubting *Iberian Trust Ltd v Founders' Trust and Investment Co Ltd* [1932] 2 KB 87.
15   See the *Supreme Court Practice* 52/1/1. No mention of attachment is made in Ord 52.
16   For an account of the difference between committal and attachment, see *Annual Practice* (1966) p 1071. See also p 475.
17   See p 647.
18   See eg *Phonographic Performance Ltd v Amusement Caterers (Peckham) Ltd* [1964] Ch 195 [1963] All ER 493, discussed at p 636.

1   *Sequestration* [19]

(a)   The nature of the writ

Chitty J said in *Pratt v Inman* [20] 'Sequestration was and is a process of contempt', and as such the writ is normally only available as a means of enforcing a coercive order against someone who has committed a contempt by disobeying the order. In *Webster v Southwark London Borough Council*,[1] however, Forbes J held, in what he described as an exceptional and unique case, that leave to issue a writ of sequestration was properly given to force a local authority to comply with its legal duties under what is now the Representation of the People Act 1983, following a declaration (a non-coercive order[2]) made by the court as to the election candidate's legal rights. Although one might sympathise with Forbes J's desire to avoid the court standing by and confessing that it is powerless, his decision in this regard seems questionable especially in view of the Court of Appeal's subsequent decision in *IRC v Hoogstraten*[3] that sequestration only lies against a person actually in contempt. In that case it was held that a writ of sequestration had wrongly been issued since Hoogstraten had made good his breaches of a Mareva injunction and had apologised. Dillon LJ added:

> 'There can be no jurisdiction to commit a man to prison merely for fear that he will in the future dispose of his assets in breach of a Mareva injunction *and there can equally be no jurisdiction to sequestrate his assets for fear of future breaches . . .* '
> (emphasis added).

A writ of sequestration places property belonging to the contemnor temporarily into the hands of persons known as sequestrators who, in the case of land, manage the property and receive the rents and profits. Although it is a drastic remedy it is nevertheless primarily coercive. As Sir John Donaldson MR said in *Con-Mech Ltd v Amalgamated Union of Engineering Workers*:[4]

> 'A sequestration order is quite different from a fine. If someone is fined the money is lost to him for ever. If his assets are sequestered the money remains his but he cannot use it. The money stays in the sequestrator's possession until the court orders what shall be done with it. The man can come to the court at any time and ask for the money to be returned to him, but if he does so the court will require some explanation of his conduct.'

In the Australian case, *Australian Consolidated Press Ltd v Morgan*,[5] Windeyer J described the writ thus:

> 'When the property of a contemnor is actually sequestered and held under sequestration it is not confiscated. The contemnor is deprived of the enjoyment of

19   See generally 17 *Halsbury's Laws* (4th edn) paras 505 ff; Fricker and Bean, *Enforcement of Injunctions and Undertakings* (1991, Jordans) p 75ff; Jacob, 'Sequestration for Contempt of Court' (1986) Current Legal Problems 219 and O'Regan, 'Contempt of Court and the Enforcement of Labour Injunctions' (1991) 54 MLR 385 at 401–405. See also the account in the report of the Payne Committee on the Enforcement of Judgment Debts (1969, Cmnd 3909) para 900.
20   (1889) 43 Ch D 175 at 179. See also Romer LJ in *Re Pollard, ex p Pollard* [1903] 2 KB 41 at 47. In New Zealand see *Quality Pizzas Ltd v Canterbury Hotel Employees' Industrial Union* [1983] NZLR 612, 615, per Richardson J.
1   [1983] QB 698, 710, [1983] 2 WLR 217, 226.
2   See at p 590.
3   [1984] 3 All ER 25.
4   [1973] ICR 620 at 627.
5   (1965) 112 CLR 483 at 501, (1965) 39 ALJR 32 at 40. See also Romer LJ in *Re Pollard, ex p Pollard* [1903] 2 KB 41 at 47.

his rents and profits for the duration of the sequestration; but he does not forfeit his property in them. When whatever is considered necessary to clear the contempt has been done, the sequestration is discharged by the order of the court: and the sequestrators must then give up possession on having their costs and expenses. As it is put in *Bacon's Abridgment* under "Sequestration", "Then whoever hath been seized shall be accounted for and paid over to him (the party whose property was sequestered). However, the court have the whole under their power, and may do therein as they please and as shall be most agreeable to the justice and equity of the case." Sometimes it may be appropriate that the proceeds of the sequestration, or part thereof, should be applied to the discharge of an equitable obligation, as for example by a direction that equitable debts, the non-payment of which had led to the sequestration, be first paid out of the fund; or that the fund be applied so far as necessary in reparation of the damage caused by the contemnor's disobedience.'

Notwithstanding these foregoing comments the English courts have on occasion been prepared to order the sale of sequestered property to enable the innocent party to use the proceeds to finance proceedings abroad to recover a child wrongfully removed from England and Wales.[6]

(b)   Against whom sequestration lies

A writ of sequestration has been held to lie against a body corporate,[7] a peer,[8] a minor,[9] a married woman,[10] and against a person who after the order had been made, became of unsound mind.[11] On the other hand the writ does not lie to enforce a judgment against the Crown.[12] Whether a writ properly lies against third persons who are parties is not entirely clear. According to Gorrell Barnes J in *Craig v Craig* [13] it does not, but in *Re S (Abduction: Sequestration)* [14] Johnson J, upon being satisfied that the mother's friend, knowing of a court order that a child be returned to Israel, deliberately frustrated the order or aided and abetted the mother in avoiding compliance with it, granted the issue of a writ against the property of the friend. Although on the face of it this latter decision seems sensible it is open to the objection that as the contempt in question was criminal[15] rather than civil a writ of sequestration should not have been issued.[16]

---

6   See *Mir v Mir* [1992] Fam 79, [1992] 1 All ER 765, discussed at p 613.
7   Which, by reason of the Trade Union and Labour Relations (Consolidation) Act 1992, s 12(2), includes for these purposes trade unions.
8   See *Eyre v Countess of Shaftesbury* (1722) 2 P Wms 102 at 110 and *Shuttleworth v Earl of Lonsdale* (1788) 2 Cox Eq Cas 47.
9   *Anon* (1684) 2 Cas in Ch 163.
10   *Worrall v Worall and Jones* (1895) 11 TLR 573.
11   *Robinson v Galland* [1889] WN 108.
12   Ord 77, r 15(1), including for these puposes a government department or an officer of the Crown. Cf *M v Home Office* [1994] 1 AC 377 at 427, [1993] 3 All ER 537 at 568, per Lord Woolf.
13   [1896] P 171 at 174.
14   [1995] 1 FLR 858. *Craig v Craig* was not apparently cited to the court.
15   See p 657.
16   See *Pratt v Inman* (1889) 43 Ch D 175, 179, discussed further at p 661.

(c)   Procedure for an application for a writ of sequestration

No writ of sequestration can issue without leave of the court,[17] and an application for leave must be made to a judge by motion.[18] The motion is made in the Division in which the judgment or order was made and the grounds of the application must be stated in the motion, and supported by an affidavit. It must be shown on the motion that the requirements of the service of a correctly indorsed copy of the judgment or order have been complied with,[19] and the notice of the motion, stating the grounds of the application and accompanied by the affidavit in support, must be served personally on the person against whose property it is sought to issue the writ.[20] The court may, if it thinks it just to do so, dispense with service of the motion,[1] or it can order a substituted service.[2] The hearing of an application for leave to issue a writ of sequestration must be heard in open court, unless the case involves minors,[3] persons suffering from mental disorder within the meaning of the Mental Health Act 1983,[4] a secret process, discovery or invention, or unless it appears that it is in the interests of the administration of justice or for reasons of national security that the case should be heard in private. In these cases the court may hear the application in private.[5]

Since sequestration is a process of contempt a writ should only be allowed to issue where the court is satisfied beyond reasonable doubt that a contempt has been committed. The court's sole function when hearing an application for leave to issue the writ is to determine whether a contempt has been committed. It has no further jurisdiction to declare the rights of the parties inter se. In *Meters Ltd v Metropolitan Gas Meters Ltd*[6] the court, having found that no contempt had been committed, held that it had no further jurisdiction upon that application and therefore refused to give a declaration as to whether the patent in question had been infringed.

(d)   The form and effect of the writ

The writ itself is addressed to not less than four persons, called the sequestrators (of whom at least two must act) who are nominated by the person issuing the

---

17 Ord 45, r 5(1)(b)(i) and (ii).
18 Ord 46, r 5(1). Although there is no equivalent rule in Australia it has been held in *Trade Practices Commission v C G Smith Pty Ltd* (1978) 30 FLR 368 at 379 (per Bowen J) that for the purposes of the Federal Court of Australia applications should be made by substantive motion.
19 Thereby complying with Ord 45, r 7 unless, pursuant to Ord 45, r 7(7), notice has been dispensed with. See pp 564–565.
20 Ord 46, r 5(2).
 1 Ord 46, r 5(3). See eg *Hyde v Hyde* (1888) 13 PD 166.
 2 Pursuant to Ord 65, r 4, this power being expressly preserved by Ord 46, r 5(3).
 3 See eg *Re An Infant* [1965] 2 All ER 254, [1965] 1 WLR 754.
 4 See eg *White v Kirby* (1966) Times, 12 August.
 5 Ord 46, r 5(4) which provides that applications for sequestration may be heard in private in exactly the same circumstances as committals, pursuant to Ord 52, r 6. Query whether the circumstances in *Webster v Southwark London Borough Council* [1983] QB 698, [1982] 2 WLR 217 in which Forbes J sat in private fell within the 'interests of the administration of justice' exception? Cf *Salm Kyrburg v Posnanski* (1884) 13 QBD 218 and in Australia, *La Trobe University v Robinson and Pola* [1973] VR 682.
 6 (1907) 51 Sol Jo 499. Cf *Webster v Southwark London Borough Council* [1983] QB 698, [1982] 2 WLR 217 where leave to issue a writ was granted following a declaration.

writ,[7] and directs them to sequestrate the property of the contemnor. The sequestrators themselves need have no special qualification[8] other than that they must be capable of accounting for the moneys received by them, and they are not required to give security for what they may receive.[9] It was held by the Court of Appeal in *IRC v Hoogstraten*[10] that although a sequestrator is an officer of the court he nevertheless owes a duty of care to the owner of the sequestered property.

A writ of sequestration is effective from the date of its issue and not at its execution.[11] The writ binds both real[12] and personal property[13] as soon as it is issued, although the sequestrators cannot follow and seize property passing into the hands of other persons after the date of issue, if those persons are bona fide purchasers for value without notice of the writ.[14] The issue of the writ creates no charge on the land unless it is registered.[15] So far as choses in action are concerned, it has been held that the mere issue of the writ, and the service of it upon the party indebted to the judgment debtor is not enough to create a charge on the chose in action.[16]

It is now established[17] that once third parties know of the issue of the writ of sequestration they are under a duty not to take any action which they know would frustrate the object of the writ.[18] This means that they are obliged to comply with the sequestrator's demand either to reveal the property that they hold on behalf of the contemnor and/or to hand over to the sequestrators property belonging to the contemnor. In *Bucknell v Bucknell*[19] a writ of sequestration had been issued against a husband for non-payment of a maintenance order. The husband owned a house which he had mortgaged to a certain bank. The bank exercising its power of sale, sold the house, and there remained in its hands a substantial surplus. The sequestrators asked the bank to pay the money over to them, but the bank said that they would only do so following court order to that effect. Could the bank

---

7 The aggrieved party normally nominates the sequestrators because he is usually the prime mover in the sequestration but the court does have power to issue a writ itself and nominate the sequestrators, see below.
8 In *Webster v Southwark London Borough Council* [1983] QB 698, [1982] 2 WLR 217 one of the commissioners nominated as a sequestrator was the court tipstaff. This seems a good choice in terms of being able to enforce the writ.
9 *Rowley v Ridley* (1784) 2 Dick 622 at 630, where it was said 'the sequestrators are named by the plaintiff or the party who applies for the sequestration; the court hath no concern in the propriety of the nomination; and they do not give security for what they may receive'.
10 [1984] 3 All ER 25.
11 See *Burdett v Rockley* (1682) 1 Vern 58 and *Dixon v Rowe* (1876) 35 LT 548.
12 *Re Rush* (1870) LR 10 Eq 442.
13 *Dixon v Rowe* (1876) 35 LT 548 (annuity under a will).
14 *Coulston v Gardiner* (1681) 3 Swan 279n at 283n; *Vicars v Colclough* (1779) 5 Bro Parl Cas 31.
15 Land Charges Act 1972, s 6(4), it being void against a purchaser. For registration see ss 7, 8.
16 See eg *Re Hoare, ex p Nelson* (1880) 14 Ch D 41, CA; *Re Pollard, ex p Pollard* [1903] 2 KB 41.
17 See particularly the statement by Sir John Donaldson MR in *Eckman v Midland Bank Ltd* [1973] QB 519 at 528. Earlier cases to the contrary should now be regarded as wrong: eg *Guerrine v Guerrine* [1959] 2 All ER 594, [1959] 1 WLR 760; cf *Re Pollard, Pollard v Pollard* (1902) 18 TLR 717.
18 Ie the '*Seaward v Paterson* principle' applies (see pp 573 ff). According to Sir John Donaldson in *Eckman v Midland Bank Ltd* [1973] QB 519 at 528 even with knowledge of the writ, but in absense of express instructions from the sequestrators, banks can continue to honour cheques and stock-brokers can sell securities on the contemnor's authority unless in either case the transaction is exceptional and designed to obstruct or prevent the sequestration. To protect themselves, they can report the facts to the sequestrators.
19 [1969] 2 All ER 998, [1969] 1 WLR 1204.

properly refuse to pay without a court order to do so? Brandon J held that a court order was not necessary in every case, for as he said:[20]

> 'It is difficult to see why, if a writ entitles sequestrators to collect and get in choses in action, whether equitable as in *Claydon v Finch*[1] or legal as in the other cases cited,[2] and the contemnor's right to the chose in action is clear and undisputed, there should be any need for a further application to the court to do so .... To hold that a third party could properly, in all cases where sequestrators seek to collect a chose in action from him, insist on an application to the court for a specific order and recover his costs of such application, would have very disadvantageous consequences from a practical point of view.'

He pointed out, however, that an application to the court would be appropriate in circumstances where there is doubt as for instance as to whether the chose in action was liable to sequestration at all,[3] or, more commonly, where there is a dispute as to the contemnor's title to the chose.[4] Where there are no such doubts, Brandon J thought that a person insisting on an application would be held liable not only for his own costs but for those of the sequestrators as well.[5] Although there were no such doubts in *Bucknell* it was nevertheless held that it was not unreasonable for the bank to insist on an application since the same procedure had been adopted without comment in *Guerrine v Guerrine*,[6] which had involved the same bank and no order for costs was made.

Bucknell was followed in *Eckman v Midland Bank Ltd*[7] where it was held that the defendant's bank was wrong to insist on the sequestrators obtaining a specific order against them requiring them to make full disclosure of the contemnor union's assets held by them and to pay over money demanded by the sequestrators. Again no order for costs was made against the bank since the law was thought sufficiently unclear as to make the bank's action not unreasonable. However, Sir John Donaldson MR commented[8] that were such a situation to arise again 'the position will be quite different'.

Eckman was applied by the Court of Appeal in *Messenger Newspapers Group Ltd v National Graphical Association*[9] which established that the duty of third parties not knowingly to obstruct sequestrators in the performance of their duties applies regardless of whether that person holds property belonging to the contemnor. In that case it was held that auditors of a trade union against which a writ of sequestration had been issued was wrong to have refused the sequestrators' request to disclose information about the union's assets. In so holding the court also rejected the auditors' defence that the trade union had not consented to the

20 Ibid at 1005.
 1 (1873) LR 15 Eq 266.
 2 Eg *Wilson v Metcalfe* (1839) 1 Beav 263, and see other cases cited by Brandon J in *Bucknell* [1969] 2 All ER 998 at 1000–1005.
 3 See *Fenton v Lowther* (1787) 1 Cox Eq Cas 315, cited in *Bucknell*, supra, at 1005.
 4 *Craig v Craig* [1896] P 171 cited in *Bucknell*, supra, at 1005.
 5 Supra, at 1007.
 6 [1959] 2 All ER 594, [1959] 1 WLR 760.
 7 [1973] 1 QB 519, [1973] 1 All ER 609. See also *Con-Mech Ltd v Amalgamated Union of Engineering Workers* [1973] ICR 620 at 627 where Sir John Donaldson MR commented 'The AUEW [the contemnors] lent £100,000 to the council [Hebburn UDC] and the sequestrators acting under their authority from the court, required the council to repay this loan. The council had no choice but to comply.'
 8 Ibid at 529. Liability for costs may not be the full extent of liability since it seems that wrongful action by third parties will itself constitute a contempt.
 9 [1984] 1 All ER 293. See Gennard, 'Implications of the Messenger Group Dispute' (1984) 15 IRJ 7.

disclosure ruling that such consent had no relevance to their duty to give the requested information.

The present position, therefore, is that while the issue of the writ does not create a charge over choses in action, nevertheless in the absence of any dispute, third parties do not have a right to insist on an application being made to the court before handing the money to the sequestrators. If they do refuse to hand the money over, thereby forcing the sequestrators to apply to the court, then unless the refusal is reasonable, they will be liable for the costs of the application. Indeed an unreasonable refusal is itself a contempt.

A writ of sequestration does not give the person issuing the writ any charge over the property seized. As Romer LJ said in *Re Pollard, ex p Pollard:*[10]

> 'when the sequestration issues and the sequestrators seize under it property of the debtor, what result follows? I need scarcely point out that the seizure by the sequestrators does not convert the property seized into the property of the creditor. The next question is: Does the mere seizure by the sequestrators give the creditor a charge upon each part of the property of the debtor, which has been seized? The answer must be: Clearly it does not. It does nothing of the kind. In order that the creditor should obtain a special charge upon some specific part of the property seized under the writ, he must go further, and must obtain some order giving him a special right to or charge on a specific part of the property.'

It was held in *Re Pollard* that no charge had been created even though the moneys seized were paid into court. It has also been held that the issue of a writ, coupled with the receipt of the money of the debtor, does not in itself make the creditor a secured creditor within the meaning of what is now the Insolvency Act 1986. Accordingly, the trustee has priority over the person issuing the writ.[11]

If, however, the person seeking sequestration cannot prove in bankruptcy, as for example, where a spouse defaults on a judicially awarded maintenance order,[12] then it seems that provided the writ of sequestration precedes the bankruptcy[13] he will be fully protected.[14]

It has also been held that the title of the sequestrator prevails over that of a mortgagee, where the mortgage for value was made in order to avoid the effect of the writ, and with full knowledge on the part of the mortgagee of all the circumstances.[15]

(e) Property liable to sequestration

The issue of a writ of sequestration authorises the sequestrators to enter on the contemnor's property and take possession of all[16] his property which is liable to

---

10 [1903] 2 KB 41 at 47.
11 *Re Hastings, ex p Brown* (1892) 61 LJQB 654; *Re Browne, ex p Hughes* (1871) LR 12 Eq 137.
12 Cf an agreed non-judicial maintenance order or lump sum order. See Fletcher, *The Law of Insolvency* (1990, Sweet & Maxwell) pp 246–248.
13 See *Scharkie v Scharkie* (1971) 18 FLR 89 (NSW Sup Ct).
14 *Coles v Coles* [1957] P 68, [1956] 3 All ER 542.
15 *Ward v Booth* (1872) LR 14 Eq 195. See also *Re Rush* (1870) LR 10 Eq 442 where under the circumstances the title of the sequestrator was held to prevail over a volunteer.
16 Subject to the restriction that such tools, books, vehicles and other items of equipment as are necessary for the contemnor's personal use in employment, business or vocation and such clothing, bedding, furniture household equipment and provision as are necessary for the contemnor and his family are exempt: County Courts Act 1984, s 89(1) as substituted by the Courts and Legal Services Act 1990, s 15(2). So far as trade unions are concerned the property

be sequestered.[17] In practice, almost every type of property is liable to sequestration, the general underlying principle being that any property to which the contemnor has a clear and undisputed right and which is his exclusive property is liable to sequestration. It is established that estates in land, whether freehold[18] or leasehold[19] and the rents and profits of such real[20] or personal property, a rent charge,[1] and chattels whether choses in possession[2] or choses in action (including money or stocks) whether legal or equitable[3] are all liable to sequestration. It has also been held that pensions,[4] or a sum received in commutation of a pension[5] can be sequestered provided alienation is not restricted by statute. On the other hand, property of which the contemnor is merely a trustee[6] or a fund in court which is liable to solicitor's lien in another suit,[7] or choses in action which are not alienable by the contemnor such as a pension where alienation is prohibited by statute,[8] have all been held not to be subject to sequestration. It has been held that a salary of an equerry to a member of the Royal Family cannot be sequestered.[9]

Although sequestration can only be effective if the contemnor owns property it has nevertheless been established[10] that an applicant need not point to any particular property which can be sequestered; it is the burden of the contemnor to show that there is no property to sequester. As Lord Herschell said:[11]

> 'Prima facie, the person who has obtained an order of the court which has been treated with contempt has a right to the process of the court to secure that its orders shall not be so treated; and it seems to me to rest upon the debtor who alleges that the proceeding would be futile to shew to the court that it would be so.'

(f)   Application of the proceeds

Classically, the primary duty of the sequestrators, having taken possession of the contemnor's property, is to detain and hold the property in their hands until the contempt is cleared and the court makes a further order to the contrary.[12] In appropriate cases, however, the court can authorise the use of sequestered property to enable the innocent party to seek to remedy the breach for themselves.

    liable to sequestration is subject to the restrictions imposed under s 23 of The Trade Union and Labour Relations (Consolidation) Act 1992, see s 12(3) of the 1992 Act. Cf 47 *Halsbury's Laws* (4th edn reissue) para 1514 which suggests that there are no restrictions.
17   Ie to the amount ordered by the court.
18   See eg *Whitehead v Harrison* (1730) 1 Barn KB 431.
19   See eg *Wharam v Broughton* (1748) 1 Ves Sen 180.
20   See eg *Hyde v Greenhill* (1746) Dick 106.
 1   See eg *Wilson v Metcalfe* (1839) 1 Beav 263.
 2   See *Empringham v Short* (1844) 3 Hare 461 (farming stock, furniture, etc); *Dickinson v Smith* (1813) 4 Madd 177 (growing crops); *Dixon v Smith* (1818) 1 Swan 457 (growing crops).
 3   See *Bucknell v Bucknell* [1969] 2 All ER 998, [1969] 1 WLR 1204 and the cases there cited.
 4   See *Dent v Dent* (1867) LR 1 P & D 366 (retired naval officer); *Willcock v Terrell* (1878) 3 Ex D 323 (county court judge); *Sansom v Sansom* (1879) 4 PD 69 (civil servant).
 5   *Crowe v Price* (1889) 22 QBD 429.
 6   See 17 *Halsbury's Laws* (4th edn) para 511. But for the difficulties of applying this to trade unions see O'Regan: (1991) 54 MLR at 402–403.
 7   *Munt v Munt* (1862) 2 Sw & Tr 661.
 8   See *Birch v Birch* (1883) 8 PD 163 and *Lucas v Harris* (1886) 18 QBD 127.
 9   *Fenton v Lowther* (1787) 1 Cox Eq Cas 315.
10   *Hulbert and Crowe v Cathcart* [1896] AC 470, HL. See also *Capron v Capron* [1927] P 243 at 248.
11   In *Hulbert and Crowe v Lambert* ibid at 474.
12   See *Wharum v Broughton* (1748) 1 Ves Sen 180.

Before any property which has been sequestered can be sold an application for leave to do so must be made to the court.[13] At one time it was thought that leave could not be given authorising the sale of freehold land[14] but according to Scott Baker J in *Mir v Mir*[15] the underlying reason for this lack of power was the absence of any procedure whereby good title could be given to the purchaser rather than for any reason of principle. Since such a procedure is now provided for by s 39 of the Supreme Court Act 1981,[16] Scott Baker J considered that there were no longer any obstacles to ordering a sale even of freehold land and he accordingly made such an order in that case. The court has power to authorise the sale of leasehold[17] and any personal property. It also has power to enable the sequestrators to raise money against the security of the property or by letting it.[18]

So far as the actual application of the proceeds are concerned, the former practice was to distingush between sequestration to enforce payment of a sum of money and sequestration as punishment for some default other than in the payment of money. As Scarman J said in *Romilly v Romilly*:[19]

'In the former the court would, upon application, order the sequestrators, if they had the funds, to satisfy the demand whereas in the latter the property sequestered would only be held in medio until the contempt was purged.'

In *Richardson v Richardson*,[20] however, Scott Baker J did not think that he was bound to follow this old practice. As he said:[1]

'Sequestration is an ancient tool of the law used as a last resort for enforcing orders of the court. Ancient tools need, if possible, to be adapted for use in modern conditions. In my judgment, where otherwise the whole purpose of the sequestration would be defeated, the court is not constrained by ancient practice from using the seized assets in satisfaction of the order.'

In that case the judge authorised the sequestrators to let the contemnor's house and/or to raise money on it by way of a loan to fund the innocent spouse's costs in bringing proceedings in the Republic of Ireland to seek the children's return, following the latter's wrongful abduction to the Republic.

Although *Richardson* is a key decision there had been some evidence of flexibility before then. It had been held, for example, that where a writ of sequestration had issued against a person for disobeying an order directing him to transfer shares, the court nevertheless did have the jurisdiction to order payment out of the sequestered fund to be made to the plaintiff in respect of certain costs ordered against the defendant.[2] Similarly in *Romilly v Romilly*,[3] although sequestration had been issued against a husband for failing to

13   See *Desbrow v Crommie* (1729) 1 Barn KB 212.
14   See *Shaw v Wright* (1796) 3 Ves 22, 30 ER 872 and *Sutton v Stone* (1745) 1 Dick 107, 21 ER 209. But cf *Hipkin v Hipkin* [1962] 2 All ER 155 in which it was held that where the benefit of the contemnor's contract to sell freehold land was vested in the sequestrators the court could authorise the latter to convey the land under the contract.
15   [1992] Fam 79, 81, [1992] 1 All ER 765, 767–768.
16   Which emanated originally from the Supreme Court of Judicature Act 1884, before which there was no such power.
17   See *Ellard v Warren* (1681) 3 Rep Ch 87, 21 ER 737.
18   *Richardson v Richardson* [1989] Fam 95, [1989] 3 All ER 779, per Scott Baker J.
19   [1964] P 22 at 23–24.
20   [1989] Fam 95, [1989] 3 All ER 779.
 1   Ibid at 101 and 783 respectively.
 2   *Etherington v Big Blow Gold Mine Ltd* [1897] WN 21, thereby avoiding circuity of action.
 3   [1964] P 22. See also *Goad v Amalgamated Union of Engineering Workers (No 3)* [1973] ICR 108 at 112, per Sir John Donaldson.

comply with an order for the return to the jurisdiction of certain children, since the husband had committed a further contempt by not paying alimony pending suit, it was held that the court had the jurisdiction to order funds sequestered in respect of the one contempt to be used in respect of the other.

(g) Discharge of writ

A writ of sequestration will be discharged, upon an application to the court, once the contemnor has cleared his contempt.[4] Provided the contempt has been purged a formal apology is not a prerequisite for the ordering of a discharge. As Scott J said in *Richard Read Transport Ltd v NUM South Wales Area*[5] in the context of a trade union whose assets had been sequestrated to pay fines:

> 'The court's dignity did not depend upon or require an expressed public recantation, the sincerity of which, if offered, might in the circumstances be open to question.'

On the other hand it has been held[6] that the court should not make an order releasing and discharging a sequestrator until it has investigated, or made provision for the investigation of, any claims against a sequestrator of which the court has notice. It is not, however, bound to wait until the end of the normal period of limitation before making such an order.

There is no set form of order bringing sequestration to an end.[7] The terms of the order must depend upon the individual circumstances. Normally, however, the court will direct the sequestrators to withdraw from possession upon payment of their costs, expenses and proper allowances either out of the sequestered funds or by the contemnor.[8] The death of the contemnor does not discharge a writ of sequestration already issued against him, but instead continues in force against the contemnor's personal representatives,[9] unless it was issued for the purpose of enforcing a personal interlocutory order, as for example an order to answer interrogatories.[10]

---

4 *Goldsmith v Goldsmith* (1846) 5 Hare 123. The position of the trustee in bankruptcy when seeking a discharge will depend upon whether the person seeking sequestration can prove in bankruptcy and whether the issue of the writ preceded the bankruptcy, see p 611. See also RSC Ord 52, r 8(2), discussed at p 633.
5 [1985] 1RLR 67.
6 *ICR v Hoogstraten* [1984] 3 All ER 25, CA.
7 See Dillon LJ in *ICR v Hoogstraten*, ibid at 30–31.
8 Where the amounts sequestered are large, the expenses can be significant eg in a case involving SOGAT in which the union was fined £675,000 it was reported (see *Financial Times*, 27 December 1985) that the sequestrators' costs were £67,751. In addition legal fees were said to be as high as £800,000. In *Goad v AUEW (No 3)* [1973] ICR 108 at 110 it was mentioned that a £5,000 fine collected by sequestrators cost £995 while in *Goad (No 2)* they ordered the sequestrators to execute the costs both to collect a £50,000 fine and a further £5,000 'on account of the possible costs of collection' (ibid at 112) in connection with the fine. The application for costs by the sequestrators must be by motion in the name of the sequestrators and not their solicitor: *Crone v O'Dell* (1824) 2 Mol 355; see also *Re Shapland, ex p Hunt* (1874) 23 WR 40.
9 *Burdett v Rockley* (1682) I Vern 58; *Hyde v Greenhill* (1746) Dick 106 and *Pratt v Inman* (1889) 43 Ch D 175.
10 *Burdett v Rockley*, ibid and see *Pratt v Inman*, ibid at 179.

Leave to withdraw the writ is required once it has been issued. Furthermore the person who caused the writ to issue may be penalised in costs, if it was unreasonable to issue the writ in the first place.[11]

(h) When issued in practice

In theory sequestration can be issued in any case where a person or a company has disobeyed a judgment or order either to do or to abstain from doing a particular act.[12] In practice, however, sequestration is not often used in the High Court except to enforce financial orders in matrimonial cases,[13] or to enforce orders in the context of international child abduction,[14] or to enforce judgments or orders against a company or trade unions.

In the family law context sequestration is a particularly useful remedy where the contemnor is abroad but has assets in this country.[15] Indeed following the decisions in *Richardson* [16] and *Mir* [17] which, as we have seen,[18] establish that the proceeds from sequestered assets can be made available to allow the innocent spouse to institute proceedings abroad to seek recovery of a child wrongfully taken abroad, the remedy has become particularly potent.

So far as trade unions are concerned the issue of sequestration of their assets came into particular prominence during the life of the National Industrial Relations Court. Writs were issued either to enforce the payment of fines[19] or, on one occasion, to delay a decision as to what amount to fine the union.[20] It was in this context, namely, where there is public contumacy in ignoring a court order that it became established that the court has the power itself to issue a writ of sequestration, irrespective of the complainant's wishes.[1]

Where it is the practice to enforce a judgment or order by means of sequestration, it has been recognised that the remedy is a most drastic form of coercion[2] and the courts have generally been reluctant to allow the writ to issue except in the clearest cases. As Sir John Donaldson said in *Howitt Transport v Transport and*

---

11 *Showerings Ltd v Fern Vale Brewery Co Ltd* [1958] RPC 462.
13 Ord 45, r 5, see p 604.
13 See *Romilly v Romilly* [1964] P 22, [1963] 3 All ER 607; *Hipkin v Hipkin* [1962] 2 All ER 155, [1962] 1 WLR 491; *Capron v Capron* [1927] P 243; *Birch v Birch* (1883) 8 PD 163 and *Sansom v Sansom* (1879) 4 PD 69.
14 See eg *Re S (Abduction: Sequestration)* [1995] 1 FLR 858; *Mir v Mir* [1992] 1 All ER 765; *Richardson v Richardson* [1989] Fam 95, [1989] 3 All ER 779; *Charder v Charder* [1980] CLY 1837, *Romilly v Romilly* [1964] P 22, [1963] 3 All ER 607 and *Hyde v Hyde* (1888) 13 PD 166.
15 This is no less true, however, in the case of a company registered abroad where it has no officers or direction within the jurisdiction. See eg *Re Rose* (1989) 133 Sol Jo 1033.
16 [1989] Fam 95, [1989] 3 All ER 779.
17 [1992] Fam 79, [1992] 1 All ER 765.
18 At p 613.
19 See eg *Goad v AUEW (No 2)* [1973] ICR 42 and *(No 3)* [1973] ICR 108. In Australia see *AMIEU v Mudginberry Station Pty Ltd* (1986) 161 CLR 98 in which the Australian High Court rejected the contention that sequestration was not available as a means of executing an order imposing fines. See also Kidner, 'Sanctions for Contempt by a Trade Union' (1986) 6 Legal Studies 18, 27–30.
20 *Con-Mech (Engineers) Ltd v Amalgamated Union of Engineering Unions* [1973] ICR 620 at 627.
1 *Con-Mech (Engineers) Ltd v AUEW*, ibid at 626.
2 See eg the remarks of Edmund-Davies J in *Showerings Ltd v Fern Vale Brewery Co Ltd* [1958] RPC 462.

General Workers' Union[3] sequestration lies at the top end of the scale of severity in the means by which courts can enforce their orders. In the New Zealand case, *Quality Pizzas v Canterbury Hotel Employees' Industrial Union*[4] Richardson J commented:

> 'As a sanction sequestration is both drastic and blunt in its operation. It may also have devastating consequences on innocent third parties—as it would have had here on the employees of the company if the sequestration had continued in its simple custodial form—and that is obviously a powerful consideration militating against the making of an order . . .'

Under an old rule of the Supreme Court[5] it was expressly provided in the cases of disobedience by a corporation, that sequestration would only issue where the disobedience was 'wilful'. There were differing views as to what the word 'wilful' meant and indeed in one case it was held that no contempt at all was committed since the order had not been contumaciously disregarded.[6] This view has now been discredited, and it is clearly established that disobedience to a judgment or order will be a contempt per se.[7] However, it is submitted that even though the court may hold that a contempt has been committed, with regard to whether or not a writ of sequestration should issue, the better view is that although the present rule makes no mention of the word 'wilful', nevertheless it will not issue, where, in the words of Lord Russell CJ, the court:[8]

> 'is satisfied that the conduct was not intentional or reckless but merely casual and accidental and committed under circumstances which negative any suggestion of contumacy . . .'

Thus in *Steiner Products Ltd v Willy Steiner*[9] the court imposed a fine in lieu of sequestration, where the disobedience to the order was held not to be obstinate. A further alternative open to the court is to allow the issue of the writ but to direct that it should lie in the office for a specified period, thereby allowing the defendants further time to comply with the order.[10] The court also has the power to grant an injunction in lieu of sequestration.[11]

---

3 [1973] ICR 1 at 11.
4 [1983] NZLR 612 at 617–618.
5 Ie Ord 42, r 31.
6 See *Worthington v Ad-Lib Club Ltd* [1965] Ch 236, [1964] 3 All ER 674.
7 See *Steiner Products Ltd v Willy Steiner* [1966] 2 All ER 387, [1966] I WLR 986; *Re Agreement of the Mileage Conference Group of Tyre Manufacturers Conference Ltd* [1966] 2 All ER 849, [1966] 1 WLR 1137; *Knight v Clifton* [1971] Ch 700, [1971] 2 All ER 378.
8 In *Fairclough v Manchester Ship Canal Co* (1897) 41 Sol Jo 225. See also *Heatons Transport (St Helens) Ltd v Transport and General Workers' Union* [1973] AC 15 at 109, 110.
9 [1966] 2 All ER 387, [1966] 1 WLR 986. It is significant that a writ of sequestration was not issued in the *Mileage Conference* case [1966] 2 All ER 849, [1966] 1 WLR 1137.
10 See *A-G v Walthamstow UDC* (1895) 11 TLR 533; *Lee v Aylesbury UDC* (1902) 19 TLR 106 and *Stancomb v Trowbridge UDC* [1910] 2 Ch 190.
11 *Marsden & Sons Ltd v Old Silkstone Collieries Ltd* (1914) 13 LGR 342, cited in the *Supreme Court Practice*, 46/5/7.

2   Committal

(a)   General observations

Committal is a major remedy for civil contempt but, as has been said on numerous occasions,[12] because the liberty of the subject is in issue the proper procedures must be strictly observed. These procedures are designed to ensure, as Lord Donaldson MR said in *M v P (Contempt of Court: Committal Order), Butler v Butler*,[13] that:

> '(1) no alleged contemnor shall be in any doubt as to the charges which are made against him; (2) he shall be given a proper opportunity of showing cause why he should not be held in contempt of court; (3) if an order of committal is made, the accused (a) knows precisely in what respects he has been found to have offended and (b) is given a written record of those findings and of the sentence passed upon him.'

Although these objectives seem simple enough, as the voluminous case law, to which we shall refer, shows mistakes or misunderstandings have been legion. To some extent blame for these errors can be laid, at any rate, in the past, to poorly expressed rules and forms, and in this respect it seems unfortunate that there continue to be separate and not always consistent rules and forms governing High Court and county court procedure. However, during the 1990s procedure in the county court in particular has been considerably tightened (though the High Court forms are still in need of revision) so that now there can be little excuse, if there ever was, for not getting the procedure absolutely right.

While of course it is important from the contemnor's point of view that the procedure designed for his benefit is strictly observed it is equally important from the point of view of the party for whose benefit the original order was made. It is no protection for the innocent party, particularly a person who has been the victim of violence, that blatant contempts go unpunished because of defects in the committal process.[14]

(b)   Jurisdiction

So far as the High Court is concerned, RSC Ord 45, r 5 provides that a judgment or order either to do an act within a specified time or to abstain from doing an act may be enforced by committal.[15] A similar provision is made by CCR 1981, Ord 29, r 1(1) for enforcing orders in the county court.[16] This power of enforcement can either be used as an alternative or in addition to sequestration,[17] though in

---

12   See eg Lord Denning MR's comment in *McIlraith v Grady* [1968] 1 QB 468 at 477 that the fundamental principle is that 'no man's liberty is to be taken away unless every requirement of the law has been strictly complied with'. Cited subsequently in eg *Lee v Walker* [1985] QB 1191, [1985] 1 All ER 781; *Re C (a minor) (Contempt)* [1986] 1 FLR 578 and *B v B (Contempt: Committal)* [1991] 2 FLR 588.

13   [1993] Fam 167 at 174, [1992] 4 All ER 833 at 839. In Australia see *Doyle v Commonwealth of Australia* (1985) 60 ALR 567 (Aust HC).

14   In this respect it might be noted that the Court of Appeal seems more ready to remedy defects than in the past. See in particular *Duo v Osborne (Formerly Duo)* [1992] 3 All ER 121, CA discussed at p 538.

15   See Ord 45, r 5(1)(b)(iii).

16   See further p 643.

17   See the wording of Ord 45, r 5(1)(b). A similar position obtains in the county court by reason of the County Courts Act 1984, s 38 and *Rose v Laskington Ltd* [1990] 1 QB 562, [1984] 3 All ER 306, discussed at p 643.

practice, both remedies are only sought together where it is desired to enforce an order made against a company—sequestration might be used as against the company and committal against its officers.[18] The powers of committal do not detract from the powers under the Debtors Act 1869 which will be considered later.[19]

An order of committal does not lie against the Crown,[20] though the Crown is still nevertheless under a duty to comply with court orders[1] and it has been held that a person receiving payment from the Crown contrary to an order restraining him from doing so, is guilty of contempt even though no contempt proceedings could be taken against the Crown.[2] A company cannot be committed to prison for contempt:[3]

> 'for the simple reason that the officer of the Court would not be able to put his hand upon that which has no corporeal existence',[4]

but a committal order does lie against an officer of the company.[5] So far as enforcing an order or judgment against the company itself is concerned, the proper procedure is to apply for leave to issue a writ of sequestration against the company.[6]

Jurisdiction to commit a person for disobeying a judgment or order vests in the court whose judgment or order has been disobeyed,[7] and an application for committal should therefore be made to the appropriate court.[8] Where the application is made to a particular Division of the High Court, a single judge of that Division has jurisdiction to hear the application.[9] Thus, unlike its jurisdiction with respect to criminal contempts, the Divisional Court of the Queen's Bench Division has a limited jurisdiction to enforce judgments or orders, being restricted to enforcing its own orders such as writs of habeas corpus,[10] or orders of mandamus,[11] prohibition or certiorari.[12]

(c)   Procedure for applying for a committal order

The rules of procedure for obtaining an order of committal to enforce a judgment or order are governed by RSC Ord 52 in the High Court and CCR 1981 Ord 29

18   See eg *Phonographic Performance Ltd v Amusement Caterers (Peckham) Ltd* [1964] Ch 195, [1963] 3 All ER 493.
19   See pp 647 ff.
20   Ord 77, r 15. But cf *M v Home Office* [1994] 1 AC 377, [1993] 3 All ER 537 which held that findings of contempt can nevertheless be made against a Minister of the Crown or government department.
1   See *Eastern Trust Co v McKenzie Mann & Co Ltd* [1915] AC 750 at 759, per Sir George Farwell (Privy Council).
2   *Eastern Trust Co v McKenzie Mann & Co Ltd,* ibid.
3   *Re Hooley* (1899) 79 LT 706.
4   Per Darling J in *R v Hammond & Co Ltd* [1914] 2 KB 866 but that does not mean there can be no corporate liability for contempt (ie the company can be fined or have its property sequestered, see eg (in Canada) *R v United Fishermen and Allied Workers' Union* (1968) 65 DLR (2d) 579 at 595 (BCCA)).
5   Ord 45, r 5(1)(b)(iii).
6   Pursuant to Ord 45, r 5(1)(b)(ii) (High Court). There is no equivalent rule governing county court procedure for obtaining sequestration, see p 643.
7   Ord 52, r 1(3).
8   See *Ex p Heston and Isleworth Borough Council* (1964) 108 Sol Jo 920.
9   See Ord 52, r 1(3).
10   *R v Barnardo* (1889) 23 QBD 305.
11   *R v Poplar Borough Council (No 2)* [1922] 1 KB 95; *R v Worcester Corpn* (1903) 68 JP 130.
12   *Mungean v Wheatley* (1851) 6 Exch 88.

in the county court. So far as the High Court is concerned, where the Divisional Court has jurisdiction, the proper procedure is first to make an ex parte application for leave to apply for an order for committal.[13] If leave is granted, an application for committal should then be made by motion within 14 days of leave being granted[14] in the Divisional Court,[15] and notice of the motion, accompanied by a copy of the statement, and an affidavit in support of the application for leave must be served personally on the person sought to be committed.[16] The court can, however, order a substituted service[17] or dispense with the need to serve the notice of motion altogether if it thinks it just to do so.[18]

In other cases before the High Court the appropriate procedure is to apply for a committal by motion which must be supported by an affidavit.[19] In the Family Division, however, applications for committal are made by summons as provided for by r 7.2(1) of the Family Proceedings Rules 1991,[20] though in other respects the procedure is the same as in the other Divisions. Notice of the motion or summons stating the grounds of the application and accompanied by a copy of the affidavit must be served personally on the person sought to be committed,[1] but the court can order a substituted service[2] or dispense with the need to serve notice of the motion or summons altogether.[3] As *Lewis v Lewis* [4] makes clear with regard to county court procedure, substituted service applies at the time when the order is being made and dispensing at the time of enforcement. Accordingly, there is no power retrospectively to dispense with service after the breach.

Another distinction of relevance to the issue of notice is that between orders and undertakings. It was held in *Hussain v Hussain* [5] that although as binding and as effective as an order, an undertaking differs in that it is volunteered rather than imposed. Accordingly, the person giving the undertaking is presumed to know of it[6] so that proof of service is not therefore essential. Nevertheless Neill LJ said:[7]

13 Ord 52, r 2, discussed in more detail in Ch 12.
14 Otherwise leave will lapse; see Ord 52, r 3(2).
15 Ord 52, r 3(1).
16 Ord 52, r 3(3). Where the order is served on a group each person sought to be committed must be given notice, and therefore each individual name must be inserted in the motion and each member served with a copy of the notice accompanied by the affidavit, see *R v Poplar Borough Council (No 2)* [1922] 1 KB 95, but these irregularities can be waived, eg by joining the affidavits and addressing the court, see *R v Poplar Borough Council (No 2)*, ibid.
17 Under Ord 65, r 4; Ord 52, r 3(4).
18 Ord 52, r 3(4).
19 Ord 52, r 4(1). For a detailed discussion, see Ch 12.
20 A similar procedure is applicable to wardship. Statements to the contrary in *Re C (a minor) (Contempt)* [1986] 1 FLR 578 (and the commentary in the *Supreme Court Practice* at 52/4/1) must be regarded as having been superseded by FPR 1991, r 7.2(1). For the difference between applications by motion and those by summons, see p 495.
1 Ord 52, r 4(2). See *Manners v Brown* (1966) 110 Sol Jo 710 where it was held that ignorance of the defendant's christian name did not invalidate the service. For the procedure when seeking to enforce an injunction restraining domestic violence to which a power of arrest is attached see below. For the importance of stating the grounds of the application see below.
2 Ord 65, r 4; Ord 52, r 4(3).
3 Ord 52, r 4(3). Dispensing with service can be made either on an ex parte application, or at the hearing of the motion.
4 [1991] 3 All ER 251.
5 [1986] Fam 134, [1986] 1 All ER 961, CA, applying inter alia *D v A & Co* [1900] 1 Ch 484 and *Re Launder* (1908) 98 LT 554. See to similar effect in Australia. *Taylor v Whelan* [1962] VR 306 at 307 (Sup Ct of Victoria) and *Douglas v Douglas* (1976) 10 ALR 285 (Sup Ct of Queensland)).
6 Although as Sir John Donaldson MR pointed out, ibid at 140 and 964, ignorance of an undertaking given on behalf of the defendant 'may well, depending upon the circumstances, provide powerful mitigation.'
7 Ibid at 142 and 965.

'(1) The undertaking should be included as a recital or preamble in an order of the court; this should be done even where the substantive part of the order is merely "No Order". (2) The order incorporating the undertaking should be issued and served on the person who has given the undertaking. (3) The order should be endorsed with a suitably worded notice explaining the consequences of a breach of the undertaking.'

It should be noted that in the light of *Hussain* a new county court form, Form N117 has been issued which provides for the recording of the undertaking and contains a recital of the penal notice.[8] No equivalent changes have been made to High Court practice though as others have said,[9] it is clearly desirable that Neill LJ's advice should be followed. The courts will not often dispense with the need to serve notice of the motion, and indeed it has been held that mere knowledge on the part of the defendant of the plaintiff's intention to move to commit does not dispense with the need to effect personal service and, further, the defendant's appearance at the motion does not amount to waiver of this requirement.[10] Service of notice of the motion or summons has however been dispensed with where a husband remained with his children outside the jurisdiction contrary to a court order,[11] and where a husband's whereabouts were unknown.[12] Dispensing with the need to serve notice is also likely to be granted where the offender is deliberately evading service. The need to serve notice of the motion may also be dispensed with where the grounds upon which committal are sought are grave or where the need for relief is urgent, provided it is shown that the person sought to be committed has knowledge of the committal proceedings.[13]

Where there is more than one party to the proceedings and it is apparent to the plaintiff that there has been a breach of the court order, the better practice is to bring all the parties in default before the court.[14]

Committal for contempt is a serious matter and alleged contemnors must be afforded full knowledge of the allegations they have to face. The notice, which should be addressed to the alleged contemnor[15] and recite the relevant terms of the order or undertaking alleged to have been broken, should specify the precise breach of which complaint is made.[16] As Nicholls LJ said in *Harmsworth v Harmsworth*[17] the proper test for a notice initiating committal proceedings is whether it gives the alleged contemnor enough information to meet the charge. Such information must be contained in the notice itself, or if lengthy, in a schedule attached thereto. It is not sufficient to refer to a wholly different

8   See also CCR 1981, Ord 29, r 1A.
9   See Fricker and Bean, *Enforcement of Injunctions and Undertakings* (1991, Jordans) para 4.3. Note that in the Family Division, Practice Form D 787 should be issued and delivered to the person giving the undertaking.
10 See *Mander v Falcke* [1891] 3 Ch 488.
11 *O'Donovan v O'Donovan* [1955] 3 All ER 278; *Favard v Favard* (1896) 75 LT 664.
12 *Moran v Moran* (1959) Times, 25 September.
13 Per Scarman J in *Spooner v Spooner* (1962) 106 Sol Jo 1034. NB If the powers of dispensation are exercised that should be stated in the committal order: *Nguyen v Phung* [1984] FLR 773.
14 Per Whitford J in *Petrushkin Ltd v Stark's (London) Ltd* [1971] RPC 357 at 358.
15 See *Williams v Fawcett* [1986] QB 604, [1985] 1 All ER 787.
16 See eg *Chanel Ltd v FGM Cosmetics* (1981) FSR 471 where Whitford J held the committal notice bad even though he had 'very little doubt' that the defendants knew of the nature of the complaint that was being made against them.
17 [1987] 3 All ER 816 at 821. See also *Chiltern District Council v Keane* [1985] 2 All ER 118, CA and *Dorrell v Dorrell* [1985] FLR 1089, CA. For a similar statement of principle in Australia see eg *Clifford v Middleton* [1974] VR 737 (Sup Ct of Victoria) and in Canada see eg *Re Sheppard and Sheppard* (1976) 67 DLR (3d) 592 (Ont CA).

document[18] nor can any discussions be rectified by the contemnor's alleged admission.[19]

The notice must require the contemnor to attend the hearing, the time and place of which must be clearly set out.[20] When a hearing to commit is adjourned to a date to be notified, the new date must be notified to the contemnor by personal service.[1]

(d)   The relevance of a pending criminal prosecution arising out of the same incident as the contempt

A problem surprisingly only recently faced by the courts is how, if at all, to proceed with a contempt application where the defendant is being or could also be proceeded against for a criminal offence arising out of the same incident. Typically, the defendant will have committed serious breaches of an injunction or undertaking not to use violence against or otherwise interfere with a spouse or partner. The issues that this type of case raises are (1) can the defendant be punished both for the contempt and the crime? (2) if so, can or should the contempt proceedings be adjourned until after the criminal prosecution? (3) what sentence should be imposed for the contempt given the potential sentence for the crime? and (4) what is the effect of any finding in the contempt action in the subsequent criminal prosecution?

So far as the first question is concerned there seems little doubt that in principle an offender can be punished both for the contempt and the crime. As Stephen Brown LJ emphasised in *Szczepanski v Szczepanski*[2] the jurisdiction in contempt proceedings is 'quite separate from the criminal jurisdiction of any other court notwithstanding that it may arise out of the same set of factual circumstances'. The advantage of proceeding for contempt is that the punishment can be imposed quickly and could justifiably be used to secure compliance particularly in domestic violence cases.

Notwithstanding the availability of the contempt remedy it is generally accepted that the court has a discretion to adjourn those proceedings pending the outcome of the criminal proceedings. There is, however, less agreement on how that discretion should be exercised. In *Szczepanski* a husband broke an injunction restraining him from assaulting, molesting or interfering with his wife by committing a very serious assault on her (he struck her with a sledgehammer). He was brought before the judge for contempt. The judge, having been informed that criminal proceedings for the assault were pending, refused to adjourn and committed the husband for 12 months. In upholding this decision the Court of Appeal emphasised that it was important that the contempt proceedings should be dealt with switftly and decisively. The court could see no ground at all to accede to the application to adjourn the contempt proceedings until the pending criminal proceedings had been completed.

---

18   In *Harmsworth*, reference was made to the applicant's affidavit. See also *Lakin v Lakin* [1984] CAT No 488.
19   *Dorrell v Dorrell* [1985] FLR 1089, CA.
20   In the county court see CCR 1981, Form N 78.
 1   See eg *Chiltern District Council v Keane* [1985] 2 All ER 118, CA at 120, per Sir John Donaldson MR. See also *Phonographic Performance Ltd v Tsang* (1985) 82 LS Gaz 2331, CA.
 2   [1985] FLR 468 at 469.

In the subsequent decision *H v C (Contempt and Criminal Proceedings)*,[3] the Court of Appeal held that *Szczepanski* should not be interpreted as saying that the court had no discretion to adjourn the contempt proceedings. On the contrary the court always has a discretion not to go ahead with a set of proceedings if they might in fact prejudice the fairness of the trial of other proceedings. However, this discretion should only be exercised in Neill LJ's words, 'where there is a real risk of serious prejudice which may lead to injustice.'[4]

In *H v C* one factor that weighed with the court in remitting the case for reconsideration was that unlike *Szczepanski* the husband denied the allegations made against him, though whether a denial alone could always justify an adjournment remains to be seen.

On the face of it under English law the discretion to adjourn seems a narrow one[5] which is an interesting contrast to the position taken by the Family Court of Australia in *In the Marriage of Sahari*.[6] In that case a husband broke a non-molestation order inter alia by threatening his wife with an imitation pistol. Accepting that in such a case the court is called upon to exercise a discretion, it was observed that the exercise of that discretion could to some extent be assisted by the applicant's choice of remedy. If, for example, the applicant undertook not to bring a criminal action, that would be an important factor in deciding whether or not to invoke the contempt powers. Indeed it was suggested that where the offence is minor it might be more appropriate for a 'family' court to deal with the incident rather than a 'criminal' court. In such a case it was accepted that the Family Court had no power to grant immunity from criminal prosecution but it could, in an appropriate case, decline to proceed with the contempt hearing unless the applicant undertook not to prosecute the criminal offence.

Different considerations arise where the offence is more serious since a criminal prosecution might inevitably have to be brought regardless of the applicant's wishes. In such cases it might be preferable to allow the criminal prosecution to be heard first before deciding, what, if anything, should be done about the contempt. In summary, as the Full Court said:[7]

> 'Where the alleged facts constituting the contempt also constitute a crime the court has a careful and considered discretion to exercise. In some cases protection of the applicant will demand urgent action. In others the applicant's protection can be left to the processes of the criminal law. Where only the affront to the court's authority is involved and the same facts constitute a crime, the criminal processes should first be allowed to take their course. When they are concluded the court may then turn to the question whether the disobedience of its orders merits further punishment in the public interest.'

It is respectfully suggested that the position taken in *Sahari* provides a more reasoned basis for deciding whether or not to press ahead with a contempt

---

3 [1993] 1 FLR 787.
4 Ibid at 789, relying on *Jefferson Ltd v Bhetcha* [1979] 2 All ER 1108, CA.
5 See Posner, 'Civil Contempt and Criminal Trial' [1993] Fam Law 385 at 386, who concludes that it is hard to persuade judges to adjourn contempt cases. Note, for example, *Caprice v Boswell* [1986] Fam Law 52 where a judge was held wrong to have adjourned the contempt proceedings. In that case the husband had broken a non-molestation order assaulting the wife with an iron bar, threatening to kill her and smashing her property. See also *Keeber v Keeber* [1995] 2 FLR 748, CA.
6 (1976) 11 ALR 679 (Full Court).
7 Ibid at 696. In this case an ex parte committal for 28 days was set aside. The court took into consideration comments made (in relation to contempt in the face of the court) by the Phillimore Committee at para 34.

application than that so far provided by the English cases. In cases where the contempt application is heard first it is clear that the punishment should be for the contempt and not the offence. This was emphasised by the Court of Appeal in *Smith v Smith*.[8] As Neill LJ put it:[9]

> 'It seems to me that it is important to avoid the danger of double punishment in respect of the same incident or offence. Exercising its jurisdiction on contempt, the court should punish the contempt and not go on to punish in respect of any criminal offence which may be committed.'

Nevertheless those who break orders by committing an offence can expect severe punishment. As Lord Donaldson MR said in *Juby v Miller* [10] when upholding an eight-month sentence for a man's contempt comprising a serious assault on a former associate in breach of a non-molestation order:

> 'it cannot be too widely known that the court will regard as being in a wholly special category cases in which people commit criminal offences which constitute a breach of the court's orders. . . . [It] amounts to saying to the notional officer of the court standing by the victim, "You may think that you are going to protect this man or woman, but you are powerless to do so," and then assaulting the person concerned. That sort of conduct is wholly unacceptable and must be met with condign punishment.'

Case law is so far silent on how to punish the offence following punishment for the contempt.[11] It is, however, established that the accused cannot plead autrefois convict on the basis of any contempt finding.[12]

(e) The hearing of the application

An application for committal must normally be heard in open court unless the proceedings involve a child, a person suffering from a mental disability, a secret process or invention, or where it appears to the court that it is in the interests of justice that the hearing should take place in private, in which case the court may hear the application in private. If the application is heard in private[13] the court must state in open court the name of the person, the nature of the contempt and the length of the period for which he is being committed.[14] Notwithstanding this latter requirement it has been held[15] that applying RSC Ord 2, r 1 the failure to make the statement in open court should be treated as an irregularity rather than an omission nullifying the order. In order words in such circumstances the committal is initially valid but the court has a discretion to set it aside.

Unless leave is given, the only grounds which can be relied upon to support the application for committal at the hearing, are those set out in the statement or notice of motion.[16] It has been established, however, contrary to the general rule in civil proceedings, that the court itself can call evidence, and serve subpoenas

---

8   [1991] 2 FLR 55.
9   Ibid at 63. See also to similar effect Balcombe LJ at 64.
10   [1991] 1 FLR 133 at 135.
11   In theory it ought to have no effect if the punishment was solely for the contempt.
12   *R v Green (Bryan)* (1992) Times, 14 July, CA. This would resolve one of the concerns expressed in *In the Marriage of Sahari* (1976) 11 ALR 679 at 696.
13   Ord 52, r 6(1).
14   Ord 52, r 6(2).
15   *Re C (Contempt: Committal Order)* [1989] 1 FLR 288, CA.
16   See Ord 52, r 6(3).

upon its own motion to discover the truth, without the consent of either of the parties.[17]

It is a fundamental principle that the person sought to be committed must be given a proper opportunity to answer the charges put to him.[18] Accordingly, the defendant's legal representatives must be allowed adequate time to take proper instructions and to call such evidence as is considered necessary for the defence.[19] An unrepresented alleged contemnor should be invited to consider whether he wishes to be legally represented having been warned, preferably by the judge, of the possible penalty if the alleged contempt is proved.[20] The defendant must be given full opportunity to cross-examine any witness against him.[1] If he wishes to give oral evidence on his own behalf,[2] he is entitled to do so. However, in *Comet Products UK Ltd v Hawkex Plastics Ltd*[3] it was held that since civil contempt 'partakes of the nature of a criminal charge' the defendant is not a compellable witness in the contempt proceedings against him and therefore cannot be compelled to answer interrogatories or to give evidence himself to make him prove his guilt. If, however, a defendant voluntarily gives evidence then he cannot as of right decline to be cross-examined.[4] In *Comet Products UK Ltd*[5] it was held that where a defendant had sworn and filed an affidavit, which had been read as part of the defendant's case, the court had a discretion whether or not to allow cross-examination, but although such cross-examination would normally be allowed, it was refused in this case since it had little relevance to the issue of contempt.

In *Garvin v Domus Publishing Ltd*,[6] however, Walton J held that insofar as *Comet* purported to hold that defendants in civil contempt cases were not compellable witnesses it was obiter. He held that since civil contempt proceedings are not criminal proceedings then under the terms of s 14(1) of the Civil Evidence Act 1968[7] there was no privilege against self-incrimination. In *Bhimji v Chatwani (No 3)*,[8] however, Knox J refused to follow *Garvin*. In his view because a fine imposed by the court even for civil contempt was a 'penalty' for the purposes of s 14(1)(a) of the 1968 Act, that provision operated to confer the privilege against self incrimination.

It is submitted that this latter approach is to be preferred since it is in line with the general philosophy in cases of civil contempt that the safeguards devised by the criminal law should be applied wherever they are needed to protect the defendants who are at risk of criminal like penalties.

Notwithstanding the foregoing submission it is evident that not all rules of criminal procedure are applicable to proceedings for civil contempt. For example,

---

17 *Yianni v Yianni* [1966] 1 All ER 231. See also Ord 20, r 8.
18 See eg *Doyle v Commonwealth of Australia* (1985) 60 ALR 567 (Aust HC).
19 See *Duo v Osborne (Formerly Duo)* [1992] 3 All ER 121, CA.
20 *Shoreditch County Court Bailiffs v de Madeiros* (1988) Times, 24 February, CA.
 1 See *Aslam v Singh* [1987] 1 FLR 122, CA.
 2 Ord 52, r 6(4). Query whether there is an inherent power to order the attendance of the alleged contemnor? Cf *A-G for NSW v Hayden* (1994) 34 NSWLR 638 and *Registrar, Court of Appeal v Ritter* (1985) 34 NSWLR 641n, where the NSW, CA held that there is.
 3 [1971] 2 QB 67, [1971] 1 All ER 1141, CA. See especially Lord Denning MR at 73 and 1143–1144.
 4 See especially Megaw LJ, ibid at 1145, 1146. See also *Re B (a minor) (Contempt: Evidence)* (1995) Times, 15 November.
 5 Ibid. Cited with approval by Lord Oliver in *Crest Homes Plc v Marks* [1987] 1 AC 829 at 858. See also *A J Bekhor v Bilton & Co Ltd* [1981] 2 All ER 565 at 580.
 6 [1989] Ch 335, [1989] 2 All ER 344.
 7 Which statute, as Walton J pointed out, was not considered by the Court of Appeal in *Comet*.
 8 [1992] 4 All ER 912.

in *Barclays de Zoete Wedd Securities Ltd v Asil Nadir*[9] Knox J held that unlike criminal proceedings, when submitting that there is no case to answer, the defendant does not have an absolute right to withhold his evidence until after making that submission. It now[10] seems accepted that hearsay evidence is admissible. In *Savings and Investment Bank Ltd v Gasco Investments (Netherlands) BV (No 2)*[11] the Court of Appeal held first that proceedings for breach of an undertaking given in a civil action are themselves civil proceedings and as such fall within s 18(1)(a) of the Civil Evidence Act 1968 notwithstanding the punitive nature of the court order sought. Accordingly, hearsay evidence is admissible to the extent that the 1968 Act allows. Secondly, but more particularly, it held that where the purpose of the committal proceedings is to enforce an order ancillary to the main proceedings so as to further the proper conduct of the main action and the final resolution of the issues between the parties, they were properly classified as 'interlocutory proceedings' so that hearsay evidence contained in affidavits is admissible, pursuant to RSC Ord 41, r 5(2).

Just as the contemnor should have the fullest opportunity to present his defence so the court should only make a committal order after considering all the available evidence. In this regard the court has full powers to adjourn the hearing so as to be able to hear all the relevant witnesses.[12] This can be especially important in cases where the court is considering making an ex parte committal as the facts of *Boylan v Boylan*[13] well illustrate. In that case an injunction had been granted restraining the husband from visiting the former matrimonial home and attached to the order was a power of arrest. Subsequently, *at the wife's invitation* the husband went to the matrimonial home but whilst there the wife's lover (the cause of the initial problem) turned up but left after a short while. Meanwhile the wife had telephoned the police. The husband explained to the police that he had come for a reconciliation but he was nevertheless arrested. The wife told him not to worry as she would be in court the following morning. In fact she did not attend the hearing nor did she give counsel any instructions and the husband was committed to prison for 14 days. On appeal the committal was set aside, although the husband had served five days imprisonment. Ormrod LJ commented that there was no *necessity* to commit an offender to prison for breaking the order and that it:

> 'would seem as a matter of good practice, very doubtful whether a judge will feel justified in sending a husband to prison for breach of an injunction (unless it is absolutely gross) without at least finding what the wife's view is.'

9 (1992) Times, 25 March, full transcript on Lexis.
10 Cf *El Capistrano SA v ATO Marketing Ltd* [1989] 2 All ER 572, CA, where the affidavits in support of the original committal order were struck out for containing hearsay evidence in ignorance of the policy in *Gasco*. See eg the comments of Kerr LJ at 578.
11 [1988] Ch 422, [1988] 1 All ER 975, Note also *C v C (Contempt: Evidence)* [1993] 1 FLR 220, CA, in which hearsay evidence was admitted in a contempt case involving children on the basis of what was then the Children (Admissibility of Hearsay Evidence) Order 1991, art 2, see now the Children (Admissibility of Hearsay Evidence) Order 1993 (SI 1993/621), art 2.
12 See *Roberts v Roberts* [1991] 1 FLR 294, CA, where the county court judge relying on *Practice Direction (Contempt of Court: Committal)* [1991] 1 FLR 304 mistakenly thought he had no powers of adjournment. As the Court of Appeal pointed out that direction is concerned with the powers to remand.
13 (1980) 11 Fam Law 76.

Once the contempt has been proved no penalty should be imposed before the contemnor (whether legally represented or not) has been given full opportunity to address the court as to penalty and to apologise to it for the contempt.[14]

(f)   The powers of the court

At common law there was no limit to the period for which a contemnor could be committed nor was there any necessity to commit for a fixed term.[15] Indeed sine die committals were quite frequently made, the theory being that an open-ended committal provided a more powerful inducement to an offender to obey a court order than committal for a fixed term. Of course, once the contemnor intimated his willingness to comply with the court order, he would be released. The Phillimore Committee recommended[16] that the power to make sine die committals should cease. Their argument was that contemnors comprise 'those who obstinately refuse to obey in any circumstances, and those who can be persuaded to obey by the threat of committal or by, at most, a fairly short stay in prison'. In the Committee's view in both cases but especially in the former situation, there are advantages in fixed terms. As they said:

> 'Obstinate contemnors have to be released eventually, despite non-compliance.[17] A fixed term would save the appearance of a climb-down by the court and would obviate the need for an application for release and uncertainty as to the appropriate timing of it.'

The Phillimore Committee recommended[18] that for all cases of contempt the maximum sentence in the High Court should be for a fixed period for up to two years.

These proposals did not escape criticism.[19] In particular it was argued that the Committee underestimated the usefulness of sine die committals when directed to securing eventual compliance.[20] It was also pointed out[1] that while a fixed-term order might avoid in the immediate future an appearance of a climb-down in the event of the eventual release of an unrepentant contemnor, the problem of how to treat the repeated offender remained.

Despite these criticisms, the Phillimore Committee's recommendation was implemented by s 14(1) of the Contempt of Court Act 1981[2] so that now the maximum period of a committal is two years. Section 14(1), however, is without prejudice the court's power to order an earlier discharge[3] and this together with

---

14   *Javadi-Babreh v Javadi-Babreh* (1992) Independent, 16 November, CA; *Taylor v Persico* (1992) Times, 12 February, CA and *Shoreditch County Court v de Madeiros* (1988) Times, 24 February, CA.
15   See p 354 of the first edition of this work.
16   See para 172.
17   See eg *Re Davies* (1888) 21 QBD 236 (referred to at p 354 of the first edition of this work) and *Re Barrell Enterprises* [1971] 3 All ER 631, [1973] 1 WLR 19.
18   See paras 199-201 though it is not clear whether the Committee had civil contempts in mind in these paragraphs when fixing the maximum term.
19   See eg Miller, *Contempt of Court* (1st edn) p 18.
20   Ie as opposed to punishing past breache;s see Lord Denning MR in *Danchevsky v Danchevsky* [1975] Fam 17 at 21F-G.
1   See the second edition of this work at 442.
2   Sine die committals were not made in Scotland, but s 15(1) provides that committals should be for a fixed term..
3   See further pp 632-633.

the power to suspend (see below) the execution of a committal order for such period or on such terms or conditions as the court may specify, provide, as Miller points out,[4] an incentive for compliance. As we discuss in Chapter 12[5] it is established that s 14 operates to prevent a court from imposing a sentence of greater than two years imprisonment regardless of whether it relates to more than one application.[6] Subject to that proviso there is nothing to prevent a court from imposing consecutive committal orders where more than one contempt has been proved.[7]

The power to suspend a committal order, which is discretionary, derives from common law, and not s 22 of the Powers of Criminal Courts Act 1973 so that the statutory guidelines to that section do not apply.[8] This common law power is vested both in the High Court and county court. In the case of the former the procedure is prescribed by RSC Ord 52, r 7 and by r 7(2), the applicant for a committal order must, unless the court otherwise directs, serve on the person against whom the order was made, a notice informing him of the making and terms of the order of suspension.[9]

It is now established that the suspension of a committal must be for a specific time[10] and, it is submitted, it should not be made without specifying the terms and conditions. It seems doubtful that a suspended order can be made in circumstances where the breach has already been remedied.[11]

Both High Court and county courts have power to make an ex parte committal order[12] but as the Court of Appeal stressed in *Wright v Jess*,[13] such a course is a wholly exceptional one to take and can only be justified if no other means of upholding the authority of the court or protecting the applicant is available.[14] Although at a minimum the court has to be satisfied that the alleged contemnor has been served with or clearly knows of the order or undertaking and has clearly been warned of the consequences of the breach, as *Wright v Jess* shows, service of notice of the committal proceedings can be dispensed with.[15]

4   *Contempt of Court* (2nd edn) 31.
5   See p 524.
6   *Villiers v Villiers* [1994] 2 All ER 149, CA. See also *Re R (a minor) (Contempt: Sentence)* [1994] 2 All ER 144, CA.
7   See eg *Lee v Walker* [1985] QB 1191, [1985] 1 All ER 781, CA.
8   *Lee v Walker* [1985] 1 All ER 781, CA see also *B (BPM) v B(MM)* [1969] P 103 at 113; *Morris v Crown Office* [1970] 2 QB 114, [1970] 1 All ER 1079 and *Head v Head* [1982] 3 All ER 14 at 17. Note, however, that there is no power to *defer* a contempt sentence, see *Delaney v Delaney* (1995) Times, 2 November, CA.
9   So far as the county courts are concerned the rules are silent on this issue but such power is clearly assumed by Form 79.
10   *Pidduck v Molloy* [1992] 2 FLR 202, CA. By reason of s 14 of the Contempt of Court Act 1981, the maximum period in two years. See also *Loseby v Newman* [1995] 2 FLR 754, CA.
11   See *Bluffield v Curtis* [1988] 1 FLR 170, CA.
12   See RSC Ord 45, r 7(7), CCR 1981 Ord 29, r 1(7).
13   [1987] 2 All ER 1067. See also *Loseby v Newman* [1995] 2 FLR 754, CA; *Benesch v Newman* [1987] 1 FLR 262; *Lamb v Lamb* [1984] FLR 278. In Australia see eg *Doyle v Commonwealth of Australia* (1985) 60 ALR 567 (Aust HC) in which it was said that flagrancy of the breach does not per se justify an ex parte committal.
14   For example, in a case of domestic violence where a power of arrest has been attached to a non-molestation order the preferable course might well be to activate the power of arrest, cf *Benesch v Newman* [1987] 1 FLR 262.
15   Though in that case such a dispensation ought to be recorded in the committal order: *Wright v Jess* [1987] 2 All ER 1067.

Where an ex parte committal order is made the contemnor should be shown the order either upon arrest or shortly after he is in custody.[16] His attention should be expressly drawn to his right to apply to court for his earlier release.[17]

(g) Exercising the powers

The court has a wide discretion as to whether to punish a contempt by committal, and, if so, for how long. Nevertheless since a committal order represents the ultimate sanction that can be brought against an individual and given that it is being invoked in the aid of execution of civil process it should never be lightly resorted to.[18] It is certainly not obliged to punish every breach of an order or undertaking with a committal. As Sir John Donaldson said in *Howitt Transport Ltd v TGWU*,[19] non compliance with a court order can have a wide range of qualities comprising at the top end of the scale a flat defiance of the court's authority, and at the bottom end a genuine, whole-hearted use of the best endeavours to comply with the order, which nevertheless has been unsuccessful. It is only at the top end of the scale that committal orders should be made.

Committal orders should not be made where the contempt is merely accidental or technical. In *Stark v Stark and Hitchins*[20] following a divorce, a father had been given the custody of his daughter. Upon hearing that her father was to be remarried and she was to travel by train to London, the daughter wrote to her mother saying that she would leave the train at a certain station and stop there penniless, and she implored her mother to meet her. Not surprisingly the mother acceded to her daughter's request, but it was held by the Court of Appeal that although the mother thereby committed a technical contempt by breaking the terms of the custody order, she was not guilty of a contempt deserving of imprisonment. It was emphasised, however, that the decision was based upon the finding that the meeting had not been prearranged by the mother. As Cozens Hardy MR said:[1]

> 'Now we desire to state emphatically that the court ought not to hesitate to send to prison one of the parties to a divorce suit who deliberately defies the court and takes the law into her own hands.'

It is also established that where a committal order is suspended and the terms of the suspension are broken, the court still retains a discretion to do what is just

16 Cf CCR 1981 Ord 29, r 1(5) which allows 36 hours after service of the warrant.
17 See *Wright v Jess* [1987] 2 All ER 1067 and *Benesch v Newman* [1987] 1 FLR 262. Indeed as Fricker and Bean in *Enforcement of Injunctions and Undertakings* (1991, Jordans) at para 33.3, comment, on general principles an ex parte order is provisional and is made in the expectation that it will be reviewed. NB the practice in the Family Division is to include in the warrant a proviso that as soon as possible after his apprehension the contemnor shall be brought before the committing judge (or another if he is not available) to enable him to make representations.
18 See eg *Re Clements and Costa Rica Republic v Erlanger* (1877) 46 LJ Ch 375 at 385 per Jessel MR; *Seaward v Paterson* [1897] 1 Ch 545 at 553 per Lindley LJ; *Danchevsky v Danchevsky* [1975] Fam 17 at 22 per Lord Denning MR and *Ansah v Ansah* [1977] Fam 138 143 per Ormrod LJ. In Australia see *In the Marriage of Sahari* (1976) 11 ALR 679 at 686 and 702.
19 [1973] ICR 1 at 11.
20 [1910] P 190. See also the comments by Sir John Donaldson in *United Kingdom Association of Professional Engineers and Newell v Amalgamated Union of Engineering Workers (TASS)* [1972] ICR 151 at 160 and *Gay v Hancock* (1887) 56 LT 726 per Kay J.
1 Ibid at 192.
2 [1969] 2 Ch 50, [1969] 1 All ER 594.

in all the circumstances. In *Re W(B) (an infant)*[2] an injunction had been granted against the defendant restraining him from associating with a ward of court. The defendant broke the terms of the injunction and was committed for six months, but the order was suspended on condition that and so long as the injunction was complied with. The defendant broke the injunction again, but it was held that, even then, the six months' sentence did not automatically come into effect, for as Lord Denning MR said:[3]

'Imprisonment is not the inevitable consequence of a breach. The court has a discretion to do what is just in all the circumstances. It can reduce the length of the sentence or can impose a fine instead. It may indeed not punish at all. It all depends on how serious is the breach, how long has the man behaved himself, and so forth.'

On the facts of the case it was held that the appropriate penalty was a fine of £50 in lieu of imprisonment.

It has been argued that an application for the lifting of the suspension and implementation of committal should be made by way of an adapted notice of an application to commit and that the contemnor ought to be given precise details of the alleged further contempt.[4]

The understandable enjoinder not to impose committal orders too readily should not be misunderstood. Any deliberate breach is to be treated seriously. As we have said elsewhere,[5] there is certainly no concept of 'one free breach'[6] nor, in the case of domestic violence, is it a defence that the breach was oral rather than physical.[7] Blatant and aggravated contempts particularly when repeated by a person who has clearly been warned as to the possible consequences of defying an order, will quite properly attract an immediate custodial sentence as a mark both of the gravity of the contempt and the court's disapproval and to deter contemnors and others who might be tempted to breach such order.

So far as deciding the appropriate length of any committal regard should be had to Lord Donaldson MR's observations in *Lightfoot v Lightfoot*:[8]

'Sentences for contempt really fall into two different categories. There is the purely punitive sentence where the contemnor is being punished for breach of an order which has occurred but which was a once and for all breach. A common example, of course, is a non-molestation order where the respondent does molest the petitioner and that is an offence for which he has to be punished. In fixing the sentence there can well be an element of deterrence to deter him from doing it again and to deter others from doing it. That is one category.

There is a second category which I might describe as a coercive sentence where the contemnor has been ordered to do something and is refusing to do it. Of course, a sentence in that case also has a punitive element since he has to be punished for having failed to do so up to the moment of the court hearing, but, nevertheless, it also has a coercive element.'

---

3 Ibid at 56. See also *Banton v Banton* [1990] 2 FLR 465 where, in ignorance of *Re W (B)* the court at first instance activated a suspended sentence in the belief that this was the only option. The order was set aside on appeal. Note the admonishment of counsel by Ralph Gibson LJ at 468–469.
4 Fricker and Bean, *Enforcement of Injunctions and Undertakings* (1991, Jordans) at para 31.2, relying in part on *Lakin v Lakin* [1984] CAT 488.
5 At p 556.
6 See *Jordan v Jordan* [1993] 1 FLR 169 and *A v D (Contempt: Committal)* [1993] Fam Law 519.
7 See eg *Jones v Jones* [1993] 2 FLR 337, CA; *G v G (Contempt: Committal)* [1993] Fam Law 335; *Brewer v Brewer* [1989] 2 FLR 251 and *George v George* [1986] 2 FLR 347, CA.
8 [1989] 1 FLR 414 at 416–417.

In principle there would seem greater justification for making committals to secure future compliance, but that is not to deny the need to punish past contempts. In that regard there are no formal guidelines on sentencing for contempt, indeed in *Re H (a minor) (Injunction: Breach)*[9] Fox LJ thought that meaningful guidance would be impossible. Nevertheless certain factors do seem to carry some weight. Clearly one such factor must be the seriousness of the breach. For example, in the context of non-molestation orders violent breaches can expect to attract severe punishment. Another important factor is contrition. Where the contemnor shows no remorse he can expect to be punished more severely.[10] Another highly significant factor is repeated breaches (see further below). Mitigating factors include the contemnor's previous good character,[11] pressure that he might be under and the effect (where relevant) on children,[12] and genuine remorse.[13]

Where a committal is sought to secure future compliance with an order, particularly while the order is mandatory then it may be more appropriate to make an order provided, at any rate, there is no alternative means of securing compliance. With the abolition of sine die committals the courts are faced with the difficult problem of fixing the appropriate length. In *Lightfoot v Lightfoot*[14] Lord Donaldson MR suggested that it would be consistent with previous practice if, in the case of continuing and wilful breaches, the court considered imposing the full two year sentence. As he pointed out whilst there might be cases where such a sentence would be disproportionately severe, the contemnor has a remedy in his own hands by seeking his immediate release by ending his defiance, complying with the order and thereby purging his contempt. Such observations, however, do not appear to reflect current practice. Moreover the disadvantage of imposing the maximum sentence immediately is that the court has no further room for manoeuvre.

Of course in some cases committal orders will be deemed appropriate both because of past breaches *and* to secure future compliance. A particular headache for the courts is the continually obdurate contemnor. There is authority[15] for the view that where an offender repeatedly commits contempt then the courts may

---

9 [1986] 1 FLR 558 at 563. Nevertheless, the lack of guidance and the disparity of sentences has been criticised by *Butterworths' Family Law Service* at B [192.5].

10 See eg *Burton v Winters* [1993] 3 All ER 847, CA, discussed further below; *Brewer v Brewer,* [1989] 2 FLR 251, order might have been suspended in view of defendant's previous good character but was not, given his lack of contrition. See also *Re O (Contempt)* [1995] 2 FLR 767, CA in which the denial of contempt counted heavily against the contemnor.

11 See eg *Danchevsky v Danchevsky* [1975] Fam 17, and *Goff v Goff* [1989] 1 FLR 436, CA. See also *Leslie Knight Advertising and Associates v Deerhorn Brokers Ltd* (1968) 112 Sol Jo 759, CA. The defendants had been committed for three months but were released on appeal, having regard to their previous good character and also to their alleged failure to appreciate that they were committing contempt. Cf *Brown v Crowley (No 2)* [1964] 1 All ER 72, [1964] 1 WLR 147.

12 *Goff v Goff* [1989] 1 FLR 436, CA.

13 See *Re R (a minor) (Contempt: Sentence)* [1994] 2 All ER 144, credit given for acknowledgment of the breaches, apologies to the court and sparing the child the need to give evidence; sentence reduced from 18 to 12 months.

14 [1989] 1 FLR 414 at 417.

15 See *Yager v Musa* [1961] 2 QB 214, [1961] 2 All ER 561 per Devlin LJ. If this strategy is adopted care should be taken that a fresh order is made on each occasion lest a plea of auterefois convict is raised—see *Danchevsky v Danchevsky* [1977] CA Transcript No 416A and see Lowe, 'Evicting the Recalcitrant Spouse' [1979] Conv 337 at 339. It is fundamental that no-one can be sentenced to two committals for the same breach: *B v B (Contempt: Committal)* [1991] 2 FLR 588; *Lamb v Lamb* [1984] FLR 278.

impose increasingly longer sentences.[16] However, on another occasion the court has pointed out the ultimate futility of the strategy.[17] It has to be said that where a contemnor has proved obdurate despite imprisonment, subsequent committals may be little more than a gesture on the court's part to uphold its authority. At any rate a court should think hard before imposing a long sentence. Nevertheless it is commonly in the context of repeated breaches that the maximum term of two years has been imposed. In *Burton v Winters*,[18] for example, which concerned a neighbour dispute over the building of a garage, the maximum sentence was imposed following numerous breaches of an injunction not to interfere with her neighbour's property and following which the defendant remained defiantly unrepentant. As Lloyd LJ observed 'the defendant had been given every chance and afforded every indulgence but all to no avail.' He added:[19]

> 'There may come a time when it can be seen that prison is having no further coercive effect, but that time has not yet arrived. [At the time the contemnor had been in prison for two months.] No doubt the Official Solicitor will keep the case under review. In the meantime the punitive element in the sentence remains to be served.'

The maximum sentence was also imposed in *Mesham v Clarke*[20] following violent and repeated breaches of a non-molestation and exclusion order.

(h) The form and service of committal order

Based on the principle that the contemnor should know precisely in what respects he has been found to have been in breach it is a cardinal rule both in the High Court and county court that the order for committal should specify the exact nature of the contempt found proved and set out each particular head of contempt on the face of the order.[1] It is therefore insufficient merely to state that the contempt has been found proved,[2] nor does it cure the defect that though the order did not specify the matters found proved, the judge had previously set out in his judgment

---

16 That is not to say that there is or should be a standard tariff. See eg *Wilsher v Wilsher* [1989] 2 FLR 187 in which the Court of Appeal was at pains to point out that there was no standard tariff of 28 days for the first breach.
17 *Priest v Priest* [1980] CA Transcript No 570 per Ormrod LJ.
18 [1993] 3 All ER 847.
19 Ibid at 850.
20 [1989] 1 FLR 370, CA.
1 See *Chiltern District Council v Keane* [1985] 2 All ER 118, CA. See also *Langley v Langley* [1994] 1 FLR 383; *Smith v Smith (Contempt: Committal)* [1992] 2 FLR 40, CA; *Clarke v Clarke* [1990] 2 FLR 115, CA; *Re C (a minor) (Contempt)* [1986] 1 FLR 578, CA and *CBS (UK) v Manoli* (1985) NLJ rep 555, CA. *Chiltern* must be taken to have scotched the suggestion made by Eveleigh LJ in *Kavanagh v Kavanagh* [1978] CAT 571 that the same degree of particularity may not be required for an order made by a High Court judge as for an order by a county court judge—a suggestion which we criticised in the second edition of this work at p 445. Although failure to specify the date on which the contempt was committed may not always be fatal, see *Burrows v Iqbal* [1985] FLR 844, it should nevertheless be stated. See also *Javadi-Babreh v Javadi-Babreh* (1992) Independent, 16 November, CA in which it was held an order which contained contempts proved by the judge but which were not set out in the notice, was invalid.
2 *Chiltern District Council v Keane* [1985] 2 All ER 118, CA and which until this decision was apparently not uncommon practice in the High Court.

in chambers the matters he found proved.[3] The same requirements apply to suspended committal orders.[4]

Failure to comply with the requirement of particularity is a serious error which renders a committal order invalid.[5]

Not only must a committal order specify the full particulars of the contempt found proved but it must also be served on the contemnor personally[6] either at the time that the warrant is executed, or, in the case of the county court orders, if the judge has signed it, within 36 hours of its execution.[7] Again failure to comply with this requirement renders the order invalid. As Lord Donaldson MR said in *Clarke v Clarke*:[8]

> 'A failure to inform a citizen in writing and at the earliest practicable moment of precisely why he is being deprived of his liberty constitutes a fundamental breach of his rights.'

In *B v B (Contempt: Committal)*,[9] given that the requirements of personal service of a properly drafted order must strictly be obeyed, it was thought insufficient to leave the order at the police station. It was also pointed out in that case that a properly drafted order will also inform the prisoner of his right to apply for an earlier release and, as Purchas LJ said:[10]

> 'the purpose of the notice . . . is that [the prisoner] should know why he is in prison and what his position is, and that this information should be given to him in writing. It is difficult to think of a more important matter to draw to the attention of the incarcerated contemnor than the avenue open to him at all times to apply to the court to purge his contempt and obtain his release.'

(i)   Discharge

Where the term of imprisonment is fixed the gaoler is bound to discharge the prisoner at the expiration of that time,[11] but in any other case an application for discharge must be made by the prisoner or on his behalf.[12] Subject to the statutory provisions providing for earlier release,[13] it is not for the prison authorities to release the contemnor before he has completed his sentence.[14]

---

3   As in *Re M (minors)(Access: Contempt: Committal)* [1991] 1 FLR 355, CA. See also *Smith v Smith (Contempt: Committal)* [1992] 2 FLR 40, where an order was held defective because although it set out details of allegations admitted it failed to give any details of the contempts found proved.
4   See *Re M (minors)(Access: Contempt: Committal)* [1991] 1 FLR 355.
5   Cf *C v Hackney London Borough Council* [1995] 2 FCR 306, easier to remedy a defective committal order triggering a validly made suspended order. For the appellate court's powers to remedy defective committal orders generally see pp 538 ff.
6   See *M v P and Others (Contempt of Court: Committal Order); Butler v Butler* [1993] Fam 167, [1992] 4 All ER 833, CA; *B v B (Contempt: Committal)* [1991] 2 FLR 588, CA and *Clarke v Clarke* [1990] 2 FLR 115.
7   CCR 1991, Ord 29, r 1(5).
8   [1990] 2 FLR 115 at 119.
9   [1991] 2 FLR 588, CA. See also *Hegarty v O'Sullivan* (1985) 135 NLJ 577, CA.
10   Ibid at 598.
11   *Moone v Rose* (1869) IR 4 QB 486; *Re Edwards, Brooke v Edwards* (1882) 21 Ch D 230 (committal under the Debtors Act 1869, s 4).
12   There is no prescribed discharge application form but there is a suggested version in County Court Practice in the notes to CCR 1981, Ord 29, r 3.
13   In the case of terms of less than 12 months, after serving half the sentence and in the case of 12 months or more, after serving two-thirds of it: Criminal Justice Act 1991, ss 33 and 45.
14   *Parsons v Nasar* [1990] 2 FLR 103 at 104 per Parker LJ.

An application should, if possible, be made to the court which made the original committal order, and should be made by motion,[15] notice being served on the opposite party.[16] An application for discharge, which in the Chancery Division takes precedence over all other motions,[17] can be made in respect of any contempt and can be made at any time even if the period of imprisonment is fixed.[18] Where a person has been committed for failing to deliver anything and a writ of sequestration has also been issued, the sequestrators may, where that thing is in the offender's custody, take possession of it, as if it were the offender's property. The court may then discharge the offender giving such directions for dealing with the thing, as it thinks fit.[19]

Although an application for discharge can be made at any time, naturally the court will only order a discharge either where the offender has purged his contempt (as for example by complying with an order to produce documents) or where the court considers the offender to have been sufficiently punished[20] in which case a discharge will be ordered irrespective of the wishes of the party who sought committal.[1] The court, besides being empowered to refuse an application, can also stipulate that the offender be released at a fixed future date, though it should not state that no further application for discharge may be made for a fixed time.[2]

The order for discharge will usually direct that the contemnor pay the costs occasioned by the contempt, but in cases of civil contempt the discharge cannot be made conditional on such payment.[3]

(j)   The role of the Official Solicitor with regard to imprisoned contemnors[4]

Among the many and disparate functions of the Official Solicitor[5] is to keep the cases of contempt prisoners under review. His duties in this regard currently[6] derive from a Lord Chancellor's standing direction, dated 29 May 1963 which reads[7] as follows:

15   See *Practice Direction* [1952] WN 121. The Official Solicitor can apply by summons.
16   *Re Evans, Evans v Noton* [1893] 1 Ch 252.
17   *Ashton v Shorrock* (1880) 43 LT 530.
18   Ord 52, r 8(1). The power to grant an earlier discharge is expressly reserved by s 14(1) of the Contempt of Court Act 1981.
19   Ord 52, r 8(2).
20   Mere contrition may not be enough see eg *Taylor v Taylor* (1980) CA Transcript No 351 but cf *Enfield London Borough Council v Mahoney* [1983] 2 All ER 901, [1983] 1 WLR 749 where an obdurate contemnor was released (after being in prison for nearly a year) because further incarceration would have had no coercive effect upon him. See also *Re Barrell Enterprises* [1972] 3 All ER 631, CA and in Australia *Von Doussa v Owens (No 3)* (1983) 31 SASR 116.
 1   See *Re Davies* (1888) 21 QBD 236; *Brown v Crowley (No 2)* [1964] 1 All ER 72, [1964] 1 WLR 147 and *Re Barrell Enterprises* [1972] 3 All ER 631.
 2   *Yager v Musa* [1961] 2 QB 214, [1961] 2 All ER 561 and *Vaughan v Vaughan* [1973] 3 All ER 449; [1973] 1 WLR 1159.
 3   *Jackson v Mawby* (1875) 1 Ch D 86 and *Re Jarvis Ward v Jarvis* [1886] WN 118.
 4   For his role in bringing contempt proceedings on behalf of children see eg *Re H-S (minors) (Protection of Identity)* [1994] 3 All ER 390, [1994] 1 WLR 1141.
 5   For his duties generally see the Supreme Court Act 1981, s 90(3), (3A) and (3B), as amended by the Courts and Legal Services Act 1990, s 125(3), Sch 18, para 39. For a brief history of his office see Lowe and White, *Wards of Court* (2nd edn, 1986) 9-1-9-2 and *Clarke Hall & Morrison on Children*, 1 [1223]ff.
 6   Formerly this jurisdiction derived from the Court of Chancery Act 1860 but this was repealed by the Statute Law Revision Act 1963.
 7   It was first published in *Churchman v Joint Shop Stewards' Committee* [1972] 3 All ER 603 at 604, [1974] 1 WLR 1094 at 1095.

'I, the Right Honourable Reginald Edward, Baron Dilhorne, do hereby DIRECT that the Official Solicitor to the Supreme Court of Judicature do review all cases of persons committed to prisons for contempt of court, do take such action as he may deem necessary thereon and do report thereon quarterly on the 31st day of January, the 30th day of April, the 31st day of July and the 31st day of October in every year.'

The object of this direction is to require the Official Solicitor to bring to the court's notice any circumstances which might cause it to review a committal order. The procedure was designed, among other things, to prevent anyone being detained for a moment longer than was necessary, despite their own folly or obstinacy.

The Official Solicitor enjoys an independent status and carries out his duties as he personally sees fit. He can apply for a contemnor's release, irrespective of the prisoner's own wishes.[8] As Lord Denning MR has said:[9]

'He has authority to apply on behalf of any person in the land who is committed to prison [for contempt] and does not move the court on his own behalf.'

In the exercise of these powers he can institute an appeal[10] and take such proceedings even before the contemnor has actually been committed to prison. It seems that the power to decide exactly when to bring a contempt case to the court's notice rests solely in the discretion of the Official Solicitor. It seems clear that his powers extend to all types of contempt whether criminal or civil, though there is some doubt as to whether his duties extend to those imprisoned by magistrates as, for example, for the non-payment of council tax.[11]

To enable him to discharge his duty, courts (both civil and criminal) should send the Official Solicitor a copy of the committal order immediately a contemnor has been imprisoned for contempt where the sentence is in excess of 28 days.[12] The covering letter should state the date of the contemnor's arrest; whether or not the contemnor is legally represented and, if so, the name and address of his solicitor.

When such committals are notified, the Official Solicitor's office[13] will (1) scrutinise the papers to see if there are any obvious defects in the committal order (eg to make sure that there are no sine die committals and that the order states the contempt with particularity). (2) Ensure that the prisoner is advised as to the means by which he may seek to purge his contempt. (3) Request a medical report from the prison, if one is not received within 14 days of the committal. (4) If the

---

8 See *Churchman v Joint Shop Stewards' Committee*, ibid and *Midland Cold Storage Ltd v Turner* [1972] 3 All ER 773. On the question of costs when he is so acting see *Enfield London Borough Council v Mahoney* [1983] 1 WLR 749 at 756–757.

9 In *Churchman*'s case, ibid at 605.

10 As in *Churchman*'s case. For an explanation of the circumstances of this appeal see ibid at 609 per Lord Denning MR.

11 Apparently in the past the Official Solicitor has been known to refuse to intervene in a case involving non-payment of rates. Presumably there is no doubt as to his duties with respect to contemnors committed to prison under s 12 of the Contempt of Court Act 1981.

12 We are indebted to Mr H D S Venables, the former Official Solicitor, for showing us a copy of this direction. The period of 28 days is to be noted. The Phillimore Committee were concerned (at para 190) that cases in the county courts were not notified if the committal was for less than six weeks. NB prison governors also have a duty to notify inter alia the Official Solicitor of any prisoner committed to prison for contempt. For the treatment of contemnors in prison see Ch 12.

13 The procedure was outlined to us by Mr H D S Venables.

contemnor has his own solicitor, the position is monitored to ensure that the prisoner does not stay in prison unnecessarily but usually no positive action is taken. (5) If the prisoner wishes to purge his contempt an application is made but if he does not, the matter is kept under review, and an application may be made if (a) the contemnor changes his mind or (b) an application is considered appropriate because of the effluxion of time or (c) there is medical evidence that the contemnor's further detention is detrimental to his physical and mental health.

The Official Solicitor's role came into particular prominence during the life of the National Industrial Relations Court but his continued, if less spectacular role, provides a useful if somewhat unusual safeguard for contemnors. It had been expected[14] that his role in this regard would decline with the ending of sine die committals but in fact the abolition seems to have made little difference to the work load with the number of referrrals remaining at roughly the same level in both the 1980s and 1990s, as the following figures show:[15]

	References Made	References Disposed Of	References Pending At End Of Year
1980	253	270	256
1981	275	289	277
1991	180	227	172
1992	201	25	231
1993	352	464	119
1994	308	331	96

3   Fine

At one time it was thought[16] that the courts had no common law power to impose a fine in respect of a contempt committed by disobeying court orders.

The basis of this assumption seems to have rested upon a statement of Lord Selborne LC,[17] delivered during a House of Lords' debate on the Contempt of Court Bill in 1883. Speaking of contempts committed by disobeying a court order he said:[18]

'The object of punishing contempts of that class was partly penal and partly to compel obedience to the orders of the court. As cases of this class could not arise in courts purely criminal, but only in courts of civil jurisdiction, the power of punishment in those cases was by imprisonment only, and not by fine.'

Whatever the historical basis may have been for this statement, Lord Selborne's reasoning is not appropriate to modern courts, especially when it is remembered that courts of civil jurisdiction can impose a fine in respect of a criminal contempt committed, for example, by the publication of an article tending to prejudice the

14 See the Phillimore Committee's Report at paras 172 and 190.
15 Taken from the Judicial Statistics Table C10 for 1980 and 1981 and Table 8.2 for 1991–1994.
16 See Harnon, 'Civil and Criminal Contempts of Court' (1962) 25 MLR 179 at 181 and *Justice:* 'Contempt of Court' (1959), p 23.
17 See Fox, *The History of Contempt of Court* (1927) p 2
18 276 HL Official Report (3rd series) col 1709.

proceedings before such courts,[19] or by interrupting court proceedings.[20] A different, but perhaps more cogent reason for there being no power to fine for disobedience to a court order, was forcibly stated in the Australian High Court decision of *Australian Consolidated Press Ltd v Morgan*.[1] Windeyer J argued[2] that the processes by which the court enforces its orders are 'primarily coercive or remedial rather than punitive' and since a fine is essentially a penal sanction, it was entirely inappropriate as a means of enforcing judgments. He added:

> 'It is true that a fine may—depending upon its amount—be a less severe consequence of disobedience than attachment or committal in the case of an individual or sequestration in the case of a company. But that does not, to my mind, show that a power to fine is a legal or logical alternative to the other remedies.'

However, as Windeyer J himself recognised, there is a penal element involved in committing a person to prison for disobeying a court order:[3]

> 'I do not suggest that a person who contumaciously disobeys a decree may not in some cases be sentenced to remain in custody for a fixed term by way of expiation.'

It was this penal element in enforcing court orders which was stressed by Cross J in *Phonographic Performance Ltd v Amusement Caterers (Peckham) Ltd*.[4] He said:

> 'where there has been wilful disobedience to an order of the court and a measure of contumacy on the part of the defendants, then civil contempt, . . . "bears a two-fold character, implying as between the parties to the proceedings merely a right to exercise and a liability to submit to a form of civil execution, but as between the party in default and the state, a penal or disciplinary jurisdiction to be exercised by the court in the public interest." Civil contempt bears much the same character as criminal contempt.'

He concluded:[5]

> 'I cannot see the logic of saying that in a case of civil contempt the court has no alternative to sending the defendants to prison . . . I think the court must have power, in the case of a civil contempt, to impose the lesser penalty of a fine.'

On the facts of the case, however, Cross J felt that the contempt was not serious enough to warrant even the imposition of a fine, but, as the Australian High Court has observed,[6] there is now a strong stream of English and Australian authority to support the imposition of fines for disobedience to orders in circumstances where the disobedience is wilful.[7] There can be now little doubt that the courts

---

19   Ord 52, r 1(3) provides that in these cases the contempt can be tried by a single judge of the particular Division, in which the proceedings, alleged to be prejudiced, were being heard. See Ch 12.
20   As in *Morris v Crown Office* [1970] 2 QB 114, [1970] 1 All ER 1079.
1   (1965) 39 ALJR 32.
2   Ibid 38-40.
3   Ibid 39.
4   [1964] Ch 195 at 198–199, approving the statement in *Halsbury*.
5   Ibid 200.
6   *AMIEU v Mudginberry Station Pty Ltd* (1986) 161 CLR 98 at 109.
7   See *Re Garage Equipment Association's Agreement* (1964) LR 4 RP 491; *Re Galvanised Tank Manufacturer's Association's Agreement* [1965] 2 All ER 1003, [1965] 1 WLR 1074; *Steiner Products Ltd v Willy Steiner* [1966] 2 All ER 387, [1966] 1 WLR 986; *Re Agreement of Mileage Conference Group Tyre Manufacturers' Conference Ltd* [1966] 2 All ER 849 and *Re British Concrete Pipe Association's Agreement* [1982] ICR 182, note; [1981] ICR 421. *Heatons Transport (St Helens) Ltd v T&GWU* [1973] AC 15, [1972] 3 All ER 101; *Goad v AUEW (No 2)* [1973] ICR 42; *Goad v AUEW (No 3)* [1973] ICR 108 and *Con-Mech*

have the power to impose a fine for disobeying a court order. In *Steiner Products Ltd v Willy Steiner*[8] it was held that where the contempt in not observing an undertaking was not obstinate, the court might impose a fine in lieu of sequestration. In the Australian High Court decision, *AMIEU v Mudginberri Station Pty Ltd*[9] it was held that the court had power to impose a daily fine to secure compliance with an order. The court also lent support[10] to Miller's view[11] based on certain US cases[12] that the court has power to suspend a fine pending compliance with an order. Although there seem strong arguments to support this view it has to be noted that no such provision is made in RSC Ord 52, r 7(1), which deals with suspension of committal, Order 52, r 9, which deals with the power to fine, nor in s 16 of the Contempt of Court Act 1981, which deals with enforcement of fines.[13] It might be noted, however, that in *Con-Mech (Engineers) Ltd v Amalgamated Union of Engineering Workers (Engineering Section)*[14] the former National Industrial Relations Court ordered sequestration of the union's assets to the value of £100,000, but postponed a final decision on the amount of the fine which would become payable so as to give the union time for further reflection. This decision illustrates the flexibility of the court's powers in this regard.

As we said in Chapter 12 so far as the High Court and county court are concerned there are no statutory limits to the amount that a contemnor may be fined. It should be noted in particular that in the case of trade unions fines for contempt are not subject to the statutory limits on the award of damages in tort actions aginst them.[15]

In assessing the amount of the fine, it has been held that account must be made of the damage done to the public interest in addition to the seriousness of the contempt. As Megaw P said in *Re Agreement of Mileage Conference Group of Tyre Manufacturer's Conference Ltd*:[16]

> 'where the injunction or undertaking is given in litigation between the registrar [of Restrictive Trading Agreements], as representing the public interest, and an individual or a company, the court, in imposing a financial penalty, may take into account, in addition to other factors, the injury to the public interest which must be deemed to be involved in the breach.'

In this regard the length and area of defiance will be taken into account.

(Engineers) Ltd v AUEW [1973] ICR 620. Note also the comment by O'Regan, 'Contempt of Court and the Enforcement of Labour Injunctions' (1991) 54 MLR 385 at 400 that in 'eleven of the twelve contempt cases arising out of labour injunctions since 1974 ... fines were levied upon contemnors. It is therefore by far the most common initial sanction upon contemnors in labour injunctions'. For the position in Australia see *AMIEU v Mudginberri Station Pty Ltd* (1986) 161 CLR 98 and the cases there cited, ibid, at 109–110.

8 [1966] 2 All ER 387 at 390–391.
9 (1986) 161 CLR 98 at 113–115.
10 Ibid at 114. See also *Registrar of the Court of Appeal v Maniam (No 2)* (1992) 26 NSWLR 309 in which a fine was suspended on condition that the contemnor undertook community service; discussed further at p 641.
11 *Contempt of Court* (2nd edn) p 32.
12 *Doyle v London Guarantee Co* (1907) 204 US 599 and *US v United Mine Workers of America* (1947) 330 US 258.
13 As observed by Fricker and Bean, *Enforcement of Injunctions and Undertakings* (1991, Jordans) para 19.5.
14 [1973] ICR 620.
15 The restrictions under s 22 of the Trade Union and Labour Relations (Consolidation) Act 1992 do not apply, see s 12(2) and 47 *Halsbury's Laws* (4th edn, reissue) para 1514.
16 [1966] 2 All ER 849 at 862.

Another factor is the means of the contemnor since any fine has to bear some relation to the individual's, company's or trade union's assets. Accordingly, evidence ought ideally to be given of the contemnor's assets.[17] In this regard note might also be taken of whether the company named in the motion is a subsidiary company of a larger holding company or part of a large group of companies.[18]

Mitigating factors include contrition and, in the case of companies or trade unions, the existence of corporate compliance procedures.[19]

In cases involving large companies and trade unions where there is a considerable public interest in enforcing such judgments or orders, breaches of orders, undertakings, etc have been treated very seriously.[20] As Buckley J said in *In the Matter of Agreements Relating to the Supply of Ready Mixed Concrete*:[1]

'Fines should not be regarded as token gestures by the public or by those whose primary task is to maximise turnover and profit.'

In that case record fines totalling in excess of £6.5 million were imposed on a number of companies found to be operating restrictive trading agreements in blatant disregard of rulings by the Restrictive Practices Court. The highest individual fines in that case were in the case of Pioneer Mixconcrete, £2,225,000, and in the case of Tarmac, £1,500,000.

These fines, as the court was well aware, were considerably in excess of previous levels[2] and it may be that they in part reflect the peculiarity of the enforcement process under the Restrictive Trade Practices legislation, namely, that it relies solely upon the contempt power. Nevertheless not inconsiderable fines have been imposed upon trade unions ranging in recent times from a high of £525,000[3] to a low of £4,000.[4]

Of course the level of fines imposed upon individuals is much lower and in the case of labour injunction cases have ranged from £10,000[5] to £350, the latter being imposed on Mr Geraghty, secretary of the Fleet Street Press Bench of the EETPU for his much publicised contempt.[6]

---

17 See O'Regan, 'Contempt of Court and the Enforcement of Labour Injunctions' (1991) 54 MLR 385 at 405 relying on *News Group Newspapers v SOGAT '82*, (unreported, 10 February 1986).

18 Hinted at in *Re Galvanised Tank Manufacturers' Association's Agreements* (1965) LR 5 RP 315 at 349 and expressly adverted to by Buckley J in *In the Matter of Agreements relating to the Supply of Ready Mixed Concrete* (unreported, 4 August 1995).

19 Adverted to by Buckley in In *the Matter of Agreements Relating to the Supply of Ready Mixed Concrete*, ibid.

20 *Re British Concrete Pipe Associations Agreement* [1982] ICR 182n. Cf the level of fines imposed on trade unions, see below.

 1 Unreported, 4 August 1995. This case was the sequel to the House of Lords' ruling in *Re Supply of Ready Mixed Concrete (No 2)* [1995] 1 AC 456, [1995] 1 All ER 135, discussed at p 570.

 2 According to counsel in the *Ready Mixed Concrete* case the previous highest fine in real terms was that imposed in the *Galvanized Tank Manufacturers' Association Agreement* estimated to be about £250,000 when adjusted for inflation. A fine of £100,000 was imposed in *Re British Concrete Pipe Association's Agreement* [1982] 1 CR 182n. Cf the level of fines imposed on trade unions, see below.

 3 *Messenger Group Newspapers v NGA* [1984] 1 RLR 397. The total fines in that dispute amounted to £675,000.

 4 *Kent Free Press v NGA* [1987] 1 RLR 267. Other fines include £75,000 in *Con-Mech (Engineers) Ltd v AUEW* [1973] ICR 620, and in *News Group Newspapers Ltd v SOGAT '82* (unreported, 10 February 1986) where the union was first fined £50,000 and then £100,000 and sequestration.

 5 See *Mirror Group Newspapers v Harrison* (unreported, 7 November 1986) referred to by O'Regan, (1991) 54 MLR 385 at 400, n 92.

 6 *Express Newspapers plc v Mitchell* [1982] IRLR 465. See also in *Re Diane (Stockport) Ltd* (1982) Times, 4 August where a liquidator was fined £500.

Following recommendations of the Phillimore Committee,[7] s 16 of the Contempt of Court Act 1981 provides that payment of a fine for contempt of court imposed by a superior court other than the Crown Court, Court of Appeal (Criminal Division) or the House of Lords on appeal from that division[8] may be enforced upon the order of the court:

(a) in like manner as a judgment of the High Court for the payment of money;[9] or

(b) in like manner as a fine imposed by the Crown Court.[10]

Notwithstanding this power of enforcement it is common practice where fines remain unpaid by trade unions and companies for the courts to grant leave to issue a writ of sequestration to ensure payment.[11]

Perhaps curiously, given the penal element, it seems to be accepted that provided the fine is paid the source of the money is irrelevant. For example in *Con-Mech (Engineers) Ltd v AUEW*[12] the fines were paid by an anonymous donor, as was the fine imposed on Arthur Scargill during the miners strike in 1984.[13] It is to be noted, however, that trade unions are statutorily barred from assisting their members by paying their fines imposed for contempt.[14]

4   Other powers of the courts

A further power open to the courts is to take the more lenient course of granting an injunction to restrain either a threatened contempt or a repetition of the contempt. The court can grant an injunction in lieu of either sequestration[15] or committal.[16] It has been emphasised, however, that the power to grant an injunction does not lie at the instance of a litigant, but is a discretion vested in the court, acting upon its own initiative. In *Elliot v Klinger*[17] the court refused to grant an injunction against two companies which it was alleged had been aiding and abetting the breach of a previous injunction. As Stamp J said, the granting of an injunction is taken by the court:[18]

> 'on its own initiative and not at the instance of a plaintiff whose proper remedy, where an injunction has been disobeyed or where there has been aiding and

---

7 See para 188.
8 See s 16(4).
9 In which case s 16(2) operates so as to empower Her Majesty's Remembrancer to proceed to enforce payment of the sum 'as if it were due to him as a judgment debt'. According to O'Regan: (1991) 54 MLR 385 at 401, the fine levied against the TGWU in *Austin Rover v AUEW & Others* [1985] IRLR 162 was recovered in this way.
10 In which case s 16(3) operates so that ss 31 and 32 of the Powers of Criminal Courts Act 1973 apply 'as they apply to a fine imposed by the Crown Court'.
11 See O'Regan, (1991) 54 MLR 385 at 401.
12 [1973] ICR 620. In another case the British Printing and Communications Corporations having brought contempt proceedings against two unions, paid them the £75,000 that they had been fined, see Gennard, 'Implications of the Messenger Group Dispute' (1984) 15 IRJ 7,13.
13 See O'Regan, (1991) 54 MLR 385 at 421.
14 Under s 15(1) (a) of the Trade Union and Labour Relations (Consolidation) Act 1992.
15 *Marsden & Sons Ltd v Old Silkstone Collieries Ltd* (1914) 13 LGR 342 and see the *Supreme Court Practice* 46/5/7.
16 *Elliot v Klinger* [1967] 3 All ER 141, [1967] 1 WLR 1165.
17 Ibid.
18 Ibid at 144.

abetting by a third party of a breach of an injunction, is to move either to commit, or to apply, in the case of a company, for a writ of sequestration. It does not in the least follow that because the court may take the lenient course that the plaintiff is entitled to come to the court and ask the court to take that course without asking for committal.'[19]

It has been held that in a doubtful case, instead of proceeding for contempt, it is possible to apply for an order requiring the defendant to state whether he has in fact complied with his undertaking.[1]

As was emphasised by the Court of Appeal in *Knight v Clifton*,[2] the court has a complete discretion both with regard to whom and to what extent costs are to be paid. Costs can even be awarded against a successful defendant, but *Knight v Clifton* established that such an award should only be made in exceptional circumstances. So far as contempt proceedings are concerned such circumstances are not likely to arise for as Russell LJ said:[3]

'Motions to commit a man should not be launched except on solid grounds, and it would, I think, be unfortunate if plaintiffs were encouraged to think that where a defendant has acted rashly and foolishly, their threat to his liberty may, with luck, be made at his expense when they fail to establish a case of contempt.'

Where appropriate the court may make no order as to costs at all.[4] On the other hand the court may make a punitive order for costs by which the defendants pay costs as between solicitor and client, thereby affording the plaintiff an indemnity against the costs of his proceedings. This procedure has been adopted in a number of cases where an action was brought against a corporation to enforce an order, and where the court allowed the writ of sequestration to issue but directed that it should lie in the office thereby giving further time for compliance.[5] While stressing that this course of action was not a rule of the court, Warrington J said:[6]

'Dealing with the injunction alone, or rather with the contempt in not obeying it, I think, where the court does not actually direct the writ to issue, though it comes to the conclusion that the contempt has been committed, it is in a sense making a bargain with the defendants—that is to say, it is saving the defendants and the ratepayers from a very considerable pecuniary loss which would be incurred if the writ were actually issued, and it is saving them from that loss on the assumption that the court having expressed the opinion that their duty has not hitherto been performed, they will do their duty. In a case like that, where less is given to the

---

19 Cf the position where the applicant brings fresh proceedings for an injunction rather than seeking to enforce the original injunction. See *Acrow (Automation) Ltd v Rex Chainbelt Inc* [1971] 3 All ER 1175 at 1181 per Lord Denning MR.

1 *Kangol Industries v Alfred Bray & Sons Ltd* [1953] 1 All ER 444. It seems that such a course of action is also possible in respect of an injunction.

2 [1971] Ch 700, [1971] 2 All ER 378. In Australia see *McIntyre v Perkes* (1987) 15 NSWLR 417. In Canada (see *Canadian Metal Co Ltd v Canadian Broadcasting Corpn (No 2)* (1976) 59 DLR (3d) 430) it has been held wrong to deprive a man of costs where because a breach could not be proved with sufficient certainty he was not found to have committed a contempt.

3 [1971] Ch at 714, [1971] 2 All ER at 386–387.

4 As in *Bluffield v Curtis* [1988] 1 FLR 170, and *Bucknell v Bucknell* [1969] 2 All ER 998, [1969] 1 WLR 1204.

5 *A-G v Walthamstow UDC* (1895) 11 TLR 533; *Lee v Aylesbury UDC* (1902) 19 TLR 106 and *Stancomb v Trowbridge UDC* [1910] 2 Ch 190.

6 In *Stancomb v Trowbridge UDC*, ibid at 196. For the meaning of costs as between 'solicitor and client' see *Morgan v Carmarthen Corpn* [1957] Ch 455, [1957] 1 All ER 437, Ch D; revsd [1957] Ch 455, [1957] 2 All ER 232, CA.

plaintiff than he is found by the court to be entitled to, by way of concession to the defendants, I think it is only fair that the plaintiff should receive a complete indemnity so far as solicitor and client costs will give him one against the expenses of the proceedings.'

An award of costs on any basis may in itself amount to a substantial sanction and can be taken into account in determining what sum, if any, the contemnor should be fined.[7]

In Australia, the New South Wales Court of Appeal held it to be within their *inherent* powers to suspend the operation of a fine on condition that the contemnor undertook community service.[8] Whether courts in other jurisdictions will be disposed to follow this ruling remains to be seen[9] but, if they do, then as in the Australian case it would seem to be a minimum pre-requisite that the 'recipient' of the service consents.

Another 'remedy' was that imposed by Hollis J in *Re K (minors) (Incitement to Breach Contact Order),* [10] a case where the contempt of inciting a breach of order by a solicitor and his legal executive has not been found proved but where there was said to be a prima facie case against them, namely to report them to the Law Society.

Finally, mention may be made of *Midland Marts Ltd v Hobday*[11] in which Vinelott J held that where a breach of an undertaking necessarily involves a breach of contract between the plaintiff and the defendant the court may, on hearing the committal application by the plaintiff, order an inquiry into damages on the amount of compensation to be paid to him. In other words the plaintiff is not required to bring a separate action for damages. In *Midland Marts* itself the defendants were ordered to pay the plaintiffs' costs on a full indemnity basis and in addition £500 by way of liquidated damages. This case should be distinguished from *Chapman v Honig,* [12] which established that contempt does not *in itself* give rise to a claim for damages, in that here the damages claim was based on the breach of contract and not the contempt.

B   County courts

1   *Powers and means of enforcement*

The County Courts Act 1984, s 38 now provides:[13]

'(1)   Subject to what follows, in any proceedings in a county court the court may make any order which could be made by the High Court if the proceedings were in the High Court.

7   See eg *Sealink UK Ltd v National Union of Seamen* (1988) Independent, 12 February, per Michael Davies J.
8   *Registrar of the Court of Appeal v Maniam (No 2)* (1992) 26 NSWLR 309, see 318–319.
9   Under English law, the statutory power to make community service orders, provided for by s 14 of the Powers of Criminal Courts Act 1973 only applies 'where a person of over sixteen years of age is convicted of an offence punishable with imprisonment'. This provision is clearly inapplicable to civil contempts and probably to criminal contempts. Cf *R v Palmer* [1992] 3 All ER 289, CA in which was held that the similarly worded s 2(1) did not apply to contempt at all so that there is no power to make a probation order in such cases. See also p 526.
10   [1992] 2 FLR 108.
11   [1989] 3 All ER 246.
12   [1963] 2 QB 502, [1963] 2 All ER 513, discussed at pp 418 ff.
13   As substituted (as from 1 July 1991) by s 3 of the Courts and Legal Services Act 1990. This provision is now in a much simpler form than previously.

> (2)   Any order made by a county court may be—
>   (a)   absolute or conditional;
>   (b)   final or interlocutory.
> (3)   A county court shall not have power—
>   (a)   to order mandamus, certiorari or prohibition; or
>   (b)   to make any order of a prescribed kind.'

The importance of s 38 is that not only does it vest county courts with like powers as the High Court to grant such remedies as injunctions and to accept undertakings but it also vests them with like powers of enforcement. Accordingly, county courts are vested with wide contempt powers as was emphasised in *Jennison v Baker*.[14] After purchasing a leasehold, the defendant began terrorising her tenants with the object of driving them out. The tenants obtained interim injunctions restraining her inter alia from evicting or attempting to evict her tenants. These injunctions were, however, ignored and the policy of terror continued, and succeeded to the extent that all tenants eventually left. The defendant was imprisoned for her contempt in disobeying the terms of the injunction, and her subsequent application for release was refused.[15] The defendant then appealed to the Court of Appeal, arguing that the county court judge had no power to imprison her in the first place, since the injunction was no longer effective (as the tenants had no desire to return) and therefore could not be enforced. This argument was rejected. As Salmon LJ said, if that[16] 'is the correct view of the law, it follows that the law can be flouted and brought into disrepute with impunity.' The court emphasised that the power of the county court was to grant such remedy as could be given by the High Court and 'in as full and ample a manner'.[17] In this case, as Salmon LJ said:[18]

> 'Clearly a bare order not to evict would not have afforded the plaintiffs a "full and ample" remedy. The fact that the defendant was liable to be attached for its breach was an essential part of the remedy granted . . . It is the deterrent effect of an injunction plus the liability to imprisonment for its breach which is the remedy. It is the remedy as a whole which normally deters the defendant from evicting the plaintiffs.'

Under s 142, county courts can in the same circumstances as the High Court, enforce undertakings given by solicitors.[19]

Until March 1979 the enforcement process for contempt was by way of attachment[20] but the current process[1] is by way of committal which brings county court procedure into line with that of the High Court.[2]

---

14   [1972] 2 QB 52, [1972] 1 All ER 997; cf *Peart v Stewart* [1983] 2 AC 109, [1983] 1 All ER 859, HL discussed at p 644 but see now the County Courts (Penalties for Contempt) Act 1983 discussed at p 644.
15   Instead the court fixed a future date for her release, as it was empowered to do, see *Yager v Masa* [1961] 2 QB 214, [1961] 2 All ER 561 discussed above.
16   [1972] 2 QB 52 at 63.
17   It was conceded that the High Court did have power to commit in these circumstances. See also in Canada, *Re Pereira and Minister of Manpower and Immigration* (1979) 91 DLR (3d) 706 at 714.
18   Ibid at 63–64. See also *Ex p Martin* (1879) 4 QBD 212, affd at 491.
19   See pp 596 ff.
20   For details see p 360 of the first edition of this work.
1   County Court Rules 1981, Ord 29, discussed below.
2   See *County Court Practice* 1995 at 379ff.

Although neither the 1984 Act nor the 1981 Rules confer a specific power of sequestration it was held in *Rose v Laskington Ltd*[3] that county courts nevertheless do have such power. As Stuart-Smith LJ said:[4]

'if a sanction available in the High Court is a necessary or essential part of the relief, redress or remedy which the county court has jurisdiction to grant as regards the plaintiff's cause of action, then it is within the power of the [county] court under s 38 of the Act to impose that sanction.'

2 Procedure

The procedure for applying for and making committal orders is governed in general by the County Court Rules 1981, Ord 29. The procedure is similar to that applying in the High Court.[5] By Ord 29, r 1(2)(a) a copy of the order or judgment must be served personally on the person required to do[6] or abstain from doing the act in question. In the case of a body corporate, service upon the director or other officer of the body is required. Judgments or orders requiring a person to abstain from doing an act (ie prohibitory orders) can be enforced notwithstanding that there has been no personal service provided that the judge is satisfied that the alleged offender has had notice either by being present when the judgment or order was given or made or by being notified of the terms whether by telephone or otherwise.[7] In any event, the court has power both to order substituted service,[8] or to dispense with service altogether.[9]

All notices must be indorsed by a penal notice drawing attention to the consequences of disobedience of the order, ie that the offender can be imprisoned.[10] While absence of an indorsement will be fatal to the application[11] it has been held that the indorsement need not be in exactly the same terms as the wording of the rule provided it is to the same effect.[12]

If the order is disobeyed, then on application, the proper officer will issue a notice calling on the alleged offender to show cause why a committal order shall not be made against him.[13] The foregoing notice must identify the provisions of the injunction or undertaking which it is alleged have been disobeyed or broken and list the ways in which it is alleged that the injunction has been disobeyed or the undertaking has been broken.[14]

3 [1990] 1 QB 562, [1989] 3 All ER 306.
4 Ibid at 570 and 312 respectively. As was pointed out in that case unless county courts did have the power to make seqestration orders they would be powerless to impose sanctions on a company or corporation.
5 See pp 618 ff.
6 Before an order for committal can be applied for the order must specify a time by which the act must be done and the offender should have failed to have done so: Ord 29, r 1(1).
7 Ord 29, r 1(6).
8 Ord 29, r 1(7), referring to the power under Ord 7, r 8.
9 Ord 29, r 1(7).
10 See Form N 77.
11 *Hampden v Wallis* (1884) 26 Ch D 746 and *Iberian Trust Ltd v Founders Trust and Investment Co* [1932] 2 KB 87.
12 *Treherne v Dale* (1884) 27 ChD 66 and *Iberian Trust Ltd v Founders Trust and Investment Co*, ibid.
13 Ord 29, r 1(4): notice must be served personally unless substituted service has been ordered.
14 Ord 29, r 1(4A). Unless service has been dispensed with a copy of the affidavit should be served with the notice.

If a committal order is made then, unless the judge orders otherwise, a copy of it must be served on the contemnor either before or at the time of the execution of the warrant or, where the warrant has been signed by the judge, within 36 hours after the execution of the warrant.[15]

So far as the procedure to enforce an undertaking given by a solicitor is concerned, the procedure is governed by Order 29, r 2. If a judge is of the opinion that a solicitor has failed to carry out an undertaking, he may on his own motion direct the proper officer to issue a notice,[16] but where a party wishes to enforce an undertaking, he must make an application supported by an affidavit setting out the facts on which the application is based, and the proper officer will then issue the notice.[17] The notice and, where applicable, a copy of the affidavit, must be served personally on the solicitor.[18]

3   *Powers*

As we have seen, s 14(1) of the Contempt of Court Act 1981 stipulates that a committal order must be made for a fixed term. That section provides inter alia that a fixed term:

> 'shall not on any occasion exceed two years in the case of committal by a superior court, or one month in the case of committal by an inferior court.'

The question was raised in *Peart v Stewart*[19] as to whether this meant that county courts' powers to enforce their orders or judgments are limited to a committal for one month. The Court of Appeal[20] accepted that county courts are inferior courts within the meaning of the 1981 Act,[1] but nevertheless held that their powers are not so limited and that instead they have the same powers as the High Court and can therefore commit for a fixed period of up to two years. The reason for so holding was that there is nothing in s 14(1) which derogated from the power bestowed by s 38 of the County Courts Act 1984. The House of Lords reversed this decision holding that there was nothing in the 1981 Act to justify a distinction being made between county courts acting under s 38 and such courts acting for example under s 118 of the 1984 Act. Accordingly it was held that s 14(1) limited county courts' power of committal to one month.

The decision of the House of Lords seemed to leave county courts with inadequate powers and their decision was reversed by the County Courts (Penalties for Contempt) Act 1983. That Act provides that, for the purposes of s 14 of the 1981 Act, 'a county court shall be treated as a superior court and not as an inferior court'. Accordingly, county courts may commit for a fixed period not exceeding two years.

In deciding whether or not to make a committal order and, if so, for how long, the same considerations apply as those discussed in relation to the High Court.[2]

---

15 Ord 29, r 1(5).
16 Ord 29, r 2(2). See Form N 81.
17 Ord 29, r 2(3).
18 Ord 29, r 2(4). Enforcement is by committal see Ord 29, r 2(1) and Form N 82.
19 [1983] 2 AC 109, [1983] 1 All ER 859.
20 [1982] 2 All ER 369, [1982] 1 WLR 389.
 1 As is clear from the definition of 'superior court' in s 19 of the 1981 Act.
 2 See pp 628 ff.

If a committal order is deemed appropriate it is especially important that the breach for which the committal order is made is specified with particularity.[3] As Lord Denning MR said in *McIlraith v Grady*[4] the fundamental principle is that 'no man's liberty is to be taken away unless every requirement of the law has been strictly complied with'.

C Magistrates' courts

Magistrates' powers to punish offenders for disobeying their orders (other than for the payment of money) are provided for by the Magistrates' Courts Act 1980, s 63(3) which provides:[5]

> 'Where any person disobeys an order of a magistrates' court . . . to do anything other than the payment of money or to abstain from doing anything the court may—
> (a) order him to pay a sum not exceeding £50 for every day during which he is in default or a sum not exceeding £5,000; or
> (b) commit him to custody until he has remedied his default or for a period not exceeding 2 months
> but a person who is ordered to pay a sum for every day during which he is in default or who is committed to custody until he has remedied his default shall not by virtue of this section be ordered to pay more than [£5,000][6] or be committed for more than 2 months in all for doing or abstaining from doing the same thing contrary to the order (without prejudice to the operation of this section in relation to any subsequent default).'

By s 17 of the Contempt of Court Act 1981 the above powers may be exercised either of the court's own motion[7] or by order on complaint. Any fine imposed is to be treated as adjudged to be paid by a conviction.[8]

It is specifically provided by s 14 of the Children Act 1989 that where a residence order[9] is in force and 'any other person (including one in whose favour the order is also in force) is in breach of the arrangements settled by that order', the person named in the order, may, as soon as a copy of the residence order has been served on the other person, enforce the order under the Magistrates' Courts Act 1980, s 63(3), 'as if it were an order requiring the other person to produce the child to him'. Making express provision for the enforcement of residence orders is intended to obviate the argument that such orders are declaratory and therefore not enforceable.[10]

3 See Form N 79.
4 [1968] 1 QB 468 at 477. A number of cases have been impugned on this ground see eg *Wellington v Wellington* (1978) 122 Sol Jo 296; *Cinderby v Cinderby* (1978) 122 Sol Jo 436; *Pekesin v Pekesin* (1978) 8 Fam Law 244 and *Kavanagh v Kavanagh* (1978) CA Transcript 166. Not all defects will render a committal order bad, see *Palmer v Townsend* (1979) 123 Sol Jo 570, CA Transcript 422 of 1979.
5 As amended by the Criminal Justice Act 1991, s 17(3)(a), Sch 4, Pt I.
6 In fact this figure still reads as £1,000 but it is evident that it should be £5,000 to bring it into line with the maximum fine provided for in sub-s (3)(a).
7 In which case the Contempt of Court Act 1981, Sch 3 applies.
8 S 63(4). For the significance of this see p 649.
9 Ie orders made under s 8 of the Children Act 1989 settling the arrangements as to the person with whom the child is to live, see p 591.
10 See pp 591–592.

Section 63(3) enables magistrates to impose a fixed penalty for an infringement rather than a daily penalty as formerly.[11] This fixed penalty can either be a fine or a committal.[12] Nevertheless the current provision is still not happily worded and seems more apt for dealing with continuing breaches rather than punishing a past breach. However, as Wood J said in *P v W (Access Order: Breach)*[13] the word 'or' in both s 63(3)(a) and (b) makes it 'possible to argue that the first part of each phrase makes provision for continuing disobedience and the second half provides for punishment of a past contempt.' This latter point, however, was left open in *P v W* and has yet to be authoritatively resolved. It is, however, clear that further penalties can be imposed for the breaches of an order subsequent to a breach for which penalties have already been imposed under s 63(3).[14]

It should be emphasised that magistrates' powers to punish offenders for disobeying their orders other than for the payment of money are governed *solely* by s 63(3) and further, since it is a penal provision it must be construed strictly.[15] There is, for example, no power both to fine *and* commit an offender nor is there power to suspend any committal[16] (though there is power to grant a stay of execution pending an appeal).[17] It has been held[18] that committal to custody does not mean 'imprisonment' for the purposes of the 1980 Act so that a committal must take effect from the day on which it is ordered and therefore there is no power to make two committals the period of which are to run consecutively.

Where proceedings are pending in a higher court magistrates should not proceed to hear the default proceedings on a related matter.[19]

Unlike the higher courts there is no provision for adding a penal notice to a magistrates' courts' order.[20] Special provision is, however, made in relation to residence orders made under s 8 of the Children Act 1989, by r 24 of the Family Proceedings Courts (Children Act 1989) Rules 1991, namely, that a person (in whose favour a residence order has been made) wishing to enforce it must:

> 'file a written statement describing the alleged breach of the arrangements settled by the order, whereupon the justices' clerk shall fix a date, time and place for a hearing of the proceedings and give notice as soon as practicable, to the person whom it is alleged is in breach of the arrangements settled by that order, of the date fixed.'

---

11 Under the Domestic Proceedings and Magistrates' Courts Act 1978, s 78. The amendement implemented the recommendations of the Law Commission. See Law Com No 77: *Report on Matrimonial Proceedings in Magistrates' Courts* (1976) paras 5.48–5.52.

12 In this respect the provisions reverse *B (BPM) v B (MM)* [1969] P 103, [1969] 1 All ER 891.

13 [1984] Fam 32 at 40.

14 Ie it prevents the plea (which was successfully raised in certain county court proceedings in *Danchevsky v Danchevsky (No 2)* [1977] CA Transcript 416A, (1977) 128 NLJ 955) of autrefois convict being raised.

15 Per Simon P in *B (BPM) v B (MM)* [1969] P 103 at 113–114. According to Wood J in *P v W (Access Order: Breach)* [1984] Fam 32 at 38F–G, breaches must be 'wilful',

16 *B (BPM) v B (MM)*, above, ie what is now s 22 of the Powers of Criminal Courts Act 1973 does not apply.

17 *B (BPM) v B (MM)* following *Re S (an infant)* [1958] 1 All ER 783, [1958] 1 WLR 391.

18 *Head v Head* [1982] 3 All ER 14, [1982] 1 WLR 1186.

19 See *Thomason v Thomason* [1985] FLR 214.

20 The introduction of penal notices has, however, been recommended by the Children Act Advisory Committee in their Annual Report 1993/94 at p 53.

It seems sensible to assume that a similar procedure is applicable to the enforcement of other orders, under s 8 of the Children Act 1989[1] and possibly for any other order.[2]

Where a committal order is made magistrates should produce a note of the evidence that was put before them and on which they decided to make the order as they did and of their reasons for so doing.[3]

IV   POWERS OF THE COURTS TO ENFORCE THE PAYMENT OF A SUM OF MONEY

Although disobedience to a court order or judgment for payment of a sum of money amounts to contempt,[4] the remedy of committal has not generally been available to enforce such orders since the Debtors Act 1869. The general object of that Act was to prevent the imprisonment of persons for the non-payment of ordinary judgment debts,[5] ie judgments in respect of simple or civil debts 'contracted in the ordinary intercourse between man and man, where credit is given by one person to another'.[6]

This general rule is embodied in s 4 of the Debtors Act 1869, which states that subject to certain exceptions: 'no person shall, after the commencement of this Act, be arrested or imprisoned for making default in payment of a sum of money'.[7] Following the Report by the Committee on the Enforcement of Judgment Debts under the chairmanship of Mr Justice Payne[8] further restrictions on the courts' powers to commit a person to prison for non-payment of judgment debts were introduced by the Administration of Justice Act 1970. Nevertheless there still remain exceptional cases where debtors can be committed for not complying with a judgment or order for the payment of a sum of money,[9] and it is with the exceptions that we are now concerned. It is to be noted that the general rule under the Debtors Act 1869 only operates in respect of orders for the payment of a sum of money and it has been held to be inapplicable to orders to deliver bills or cheques or to deposit or to hand over bonds.[10] Secondly, orders for the payment of money into court, as we have seen, are not always classified as 'debts' and may therefore fall outside the scope of the Act.[11]

---

1   See White, Carr and Lowe, *The Children Act in Practice*, para 5.103.
2   In *P v W (Access Order: Breach)* [1984] Fam 32 it was said that a summons to enforce an order should give clear details of the breach, ie particulars of the date, time and place of the alleged breach so that a respondent is quite clear what is alleged against him.
3   Per Sheldon J in *Head v Head* [1982] 3 All ER 14 at 17.
4   See eg *Leavis v Leavis* [1921] P 299.
5   Per Cotton LJ in *Bates v Bates* (1888) 14 PD 17 at 19.
6   Per Lord Hatherly LC in *Middleton v Chichester* (1871) 6 Ch App 152 at 156.
7   See *Alexander v Alexander* (1962) Times, 14 September; *Farrant v Farrant* [1957] P 188, [1957] 1 All ER 204. The Debtors Act 1869 applies to debts owed to the Crown; see the Crown Proceedings Act 1947, s 26(2), cf *A-G v Randall* [1944] KB 709, [1944] 2 All ER 179.
8   1969, Cmnd 3909.
9   In such cases the remedy of sequestration is also available, see RSC Ord 45, r 1(1)(f).
10   See *Linwood v Andrews* (1887) 31 Sol Jo 410; *Digby v Turner* [1873] WN 65. The Act does not apply where an order is made directing that an act be done, or in the alternative that a sum of money be paid, see *Harvey v Hall* (1870) LR 11 Eq 31.
11   See eg *Bates v Bates* (1888) 14 PD 17, discussed, at p 582.

A   The courts' powers to imprison for the non-payment of an ordinary debt

Under the Debtors Act 1869, s 5 (as amended) the power to commit an offender for the non-payment of a debt is only exercisable:

(a) by the High Court[12] in respect of a High Court maintenance order; and

(b) by a county court in respect of—

   (i) a High Court or a county court maintenance order; or

   (ii) a judgment or order of any court for payment of income tax or any other tax recoverable under ss 65, 66 or 68 of the Taxes Management Act 1970 or national insurance contributions or state scheme pensions recoverable under Part 1 of the Social Security Contributions and Benefits Act 1992.

The power so vested is to commit the offender to prison for a fixed term not exceeding six weeks or until the payment of the sum due. The High Court or county court can suspend any order of committal on the terms that the debtor pays to the judgment creditor the amount due either at a specified time or by instalments.[13]

Before the power can be exercised at all it must be shown that the debtor has, or has had since the judgment was made, the means to pay the sum in default,[14] and has refused or neglected, or refuses or neglects to pay the same. Such 'means' must be proved to the satisfaction of the court[15] and in such manner as the court thinks just, and for the purposes of such proof the debtor and any witnesses may be summoned.[16]

The nature of the jurisdiction is essentially penal,[17] though it should nevertheless still be regarded as a mode for enforcing payment of the debt, in the sense that it is a means of coercing the debtor into paying the judgment debt.[18] Perhaps the best summary of the nature of the courts' powers pursuant to s 5 was expressed by Vaughan Williams LJ in *Re Edgcombe, ex p Edgcombe* [19] when he said that an order could only be made:

'when there is a contumacious debtor who has the means, or has had the means, to pay the debt, and his conduct is in the nature of a contempt. This imprisonment is for a fixed time not exceeding six weeks, and is a punishment for the contempt, and the suffering of that imprisonment in no way discharges the debt.'

Imprisonment under s 5 does not operate to discharge or satisfy the debt nor does it deprive any person of his right, if any, to take out execution against the lands, goods or chattels of the person imprisoned.[20]

---

12 The jurisdiction is confined to the Family Division. See Family Proceedings Rules 1991, rr 7.4–7.6.
13 FPR 1991, rr 7.4(10), 7.6(3) and County Court Rules 1981, Ord 28, r 7.
14 S 4, see *Buckley v Crawford* [1893] 1 QB 105.
15 In *Nesom v Metcalfe* [1921] 1 KB 400, McCardie J said the means 'should be of a reasonably direct character'; see also *Chard v Jervis* (1882) 9 QBD 178.
16 S 4. For the procedure upon an application under s 5 see in the High Court and divorce county court FPR 1991 rr 7.4–7.6, and in the county court see CCR 1981, Ord 28.
17 See *Mitchell v Simpson* (1890) 25 QBD 183, CA.
18 Per Smith MR in *Bailey v Plant* [1901] 1 KB 31 at 33.
19 [1902] 2 KB 403 at 410.
20 *Re Edgcombe, ex p Edgcombe*, ibid.

Although the right of appeal provided by s 13 of the Administration of Justice Act 1960 has no application to s 5 committals,[1] an appeal from a county court judgment might still lie under s 77 of the County Courts Act 1984, while the right to appeal from the High Court does not seem to be excluded by s 18 of the Supreme Court Act 1981.

Both the High Court and county court have the power when dealing with a s 5 application to make an attachment of earnings order instead.[2]

Under the Magistrates' Courts Act 1980, s 76 a magistrates' court has the power to issue a warrant to commit a person to prison for default in paying a sum adjudged to be paid by a conviction or order of that court.[3] Under s 92, however, in the case of civil debts the power is only exercisable in respect of default under:

'(a)   a magistrates' court maintenance order;
(b)   an order under section 23 of the Legal Aid Act 1988 (contribution by legally assisted person to the cost of his defence in a criminal case); or
(c)   an order for the payment of the taxes, contributions, premiums or liabilities specified in Schedule 4 to the Administration of Justice Act 1970.'

A magistrate may issue a warrant of committal pursuant to s 76, either where a warrant of distress had been issued but the property was insufficient to satisfy the sum together with the costs and charges of levying the sum,[4] or in lieu of a warrant of distress altogether.[5] By s 96 (1) of the Magistrates' Courts Act 1980, however, a magistrates' court cannot commit any person for non-payment of a civil debt:

'except by an order made on complaint, and on proof to the satisfaction of the court that that person has, or has had since the date on which the sum was adjudged to be paid, the means to pay the sum or any instalment of it on which he has defaulted, and refuses or neglects or, as the case may be, has refused or neglected to pay it.'

The maximum punishment for enforcing a civil debt under this section is imprisonment for six weeks.[6] Section 92 does not, however, affect their powers to issue a warrant of committal:

'in the case of default in paying a sum adjudged to be paid by a conviction, or treated (by any enactment relating to the collection or enforcement of fines, costs, compensation or forfeited recognisances) as so adjudged to be paid.'[7]

As Waite J emphasised in *R v Luton Magistrates' Court, ex p Sullivan*[8] the power of committal under s 76 is one of extreme severity to be exercised sparingly and only as a last resort. In his Lordship's view a spouse cannot be committed under s 76 unless (a) he is present in court; (b) his default amounts to a deliberate defiance or reckless disregard of the court order about which the court has conducted a full inquiry;[9] and (c) the justices are satisfied that all other

1 Administration of Justice Act 1960, s 13(5).
2 Attachments of Earnings Act 1971, s 3(4).
3 Note that for persons aged 18 or over but less than 21 the power is to fix a term of detention rather than imprisonment: s 96A.
4 S 76(2)(a).
5 S 76(2)(b).
6 See s 76(3) and Sch 4, para 3.
7 S 92(2).
8 [1992] 2 FLR 196.
9 In *Luton* itself the court had conducted no such inquiry with the result, as Waite J commented, ibid at 201 'A man who should never have lost his liberty was sent to prison by a bench which, with no knowledge of his poor health and present lack of means, treated him as a defiant or

methods of enforcing payment have been considered[10] and had either proved unsuccessful or were unlikely to do so.

B   The courts' power to imprison an offender pursuant to the Debtors Act 1869, s 4

The Debtors Act 1869, s 4, provides six exceptions to the rule that a person cannot be imprisoned for not paying a sum of money. They are:

'(1)   Default in payment of a penalty, or sum in the nature of a penalty, other than a penalty in respect of any contract.

(2)   Default in payment of any sum recoverable summarily before a justice or justices of the peace.

(3)   Default by a trustee or person acting in a fiduciary capacity and ordered to pay by a court of equity any sum in his possession or under his control.

(4)   Default by an attorney or solicitor in payment of costs when ordered to pay costs for misconduct as such, or in the payment of a sum of money when ordered to pay the same in his character of an officer of the court making the order.[11]

(5)   Default in payment for the benefit of creditors of any portion of salary or other income in respect of the payment of which any court having jurisdiction in bankruptcy is authorised to make an order.

(6)   Default in payment of sums in respect of the payment of which orders are in this Act authorised to be made.'

A further exception has since been added by the Crown Proceedings Act 1947, s 26(2),[12] namely, 'default in payment of inheritance tax'.

The general nature of the jurisdiction under s 4 differs in two important respects from that of s 5. First, although the jurisdiction under s 5 is penal, the better view is to regard those powers as not only being penal but also as being a means of coercing the debtor into paying the sums due. This view is supported by the fact that a debtor cannot be imprisoned under s 5 unless it is shown that he has had or has the means to pay the debt. On the other hand, the courts have tended to emphasise that their powers under s 4 are primarily[13] or even purely penal,[14] though it can be said that, incidentally, s 4 may have the effect of coercing payment. The essence of the jurisdiction is to punish a fraudulent or dishonest debtor, and in this sense the powers are 'vindictive and intended to be so'.[15] Lord

culpably negligent defaulter on the scantiest evidence after denying him the opportunity of professional advice, which he reasonably requested, and disregarding the alternatives which it was their statutory duty to consider'.

10   As Douglas points out at [1992] Fam Law 381, with the further mechanisms for enforcing maintenance orders introduced by the Maintenance Enforcement Act 1991, ie ordering payments by standing order and opening bank accounts, imprisonment for non-payment should become even rarer.

11   For the meaning of this exception see *Marris v Ingram* (1879) 13 Ch D 338 at 342 per Jessel MR, who also briefly reviews the nature of the other exceptions. See also *Middleton v Chichester* (1871) 6 Ch App 152 per Lord Hatherley LC.

12   As amended by the Finance Act 1972.

13   See, eg *Marris v Ingram* (1879) 13 Ch D 338 per Jessel MR; *Middleton v Chichester* (1871) Ch App 152; *Re Gent* (1888) 40 Ch D 190 and *Church's Trustee v Hibbard* [1902] 2 Ch 784 per Vaughan Williams LJ.

14   See *Church's Trustee v Hibbard*, ibid where Vaughan Williams LJ said 'these orders are not in the nature of remedies for the recovery of debts but are in the nature of punishment.'

15   Per Jessel MR, in *Marris v Ingram* (1879) 13 Ch D, 338 at 343.

Hatherley LC said in *Middleton v Chichester* [16] 'in every case there is something of the character of delinquency pointed out.' Secondly, whereas s 5 is concerned with the enforcement via the courts of simple debts owed by one person to another, s 4 is not concerned with simple debts at all but with debts incurred either through a monetary *penalty* imposed by or under the authorisation of the courts, or through the exercise of the office of trustee or solicitor. As Lord Hatherley said:[17]

> 'the exceptions are all of a character which indicates that the legislature wished merely to limit the term of imprisonment in regard to certain debts which were not simple debts, contracted in the ordinary intercourse between man and man, where credit is given by one person to another, but were debts the incurring of which was in some degree worthy of being visited with punishment.'

The difference in the penalties—imprisonment for a maximum period of six weeks under s 5 and one year in the case of s 4—is to be noted. Furthermore, there is no requirement under s 4 to inquire into the debtor's means, though the means may well be a material consideration in the exercise of the courts' discretionary powers under the Debtors Act 1878. In view of the penal nature of the jurisdiction under s 4, it has been held that an offender cannot be punished twice in respect of the same offence.[18] On the other hand, as in the case of s 5, punishment under these exceptions does not discharge the debt.[19]

There have been a number of reported cases, nearly all decided in the nineteenth century, which have determined the nature and scope of the exceptions under s 4. These cases were particularly concerned with the nature and scope of the third and fourth exceptions and indeed there has been a statutory amendment to both of these exceptions under the Debtors Act 1878, which gives the courts discretionary powers in relation to both of these provisions.[20] In practice, however, none of these exceptions seems to have been invoked in recent years (although they are still on the statute book) and for this reason it is not proposed to discuss their application.[1]

V   IS THERE A RULE THAT THE CONTEMNOR MAY NOT BE HEARD?

A   Historical background

A person who has committed a civil contempt by disobeying a court order may be subject to the so-called rule that a party in contempt cannot be heard or take proceedings in the same cause until he has purged his contempt. According to Denning LJ, in his classic exposition of the history and development of this rule, in *Hadkinson v Hadkinson*,[2] the origin of the rule lay not in common law but in canon law, which was adopted by the Chancery court and the Ecclesiastical

---

16   Ibid at 1567.
17   In *Middleton v Chichester* (1871) 6 Ch App 152 at 156.
18   *Church's Trustee v Hibbard* [1902] 2 Ch 784 at 791, per Vaughan Williams LJ.
19   S 4.
20   See Jessel MR, in *Marris v Ingram* (1879) 13 Ch D 338 at 343.
 1   For a detailed account of these exceptions see 9 *Halsbury's Laws* (4th edn) paras 79–80 and the *Supreme Court Practice* 45/1/24ff.
 2   [1952] P 285 at 295. See also *Chuck v Cremer* (1846) 1 Coop temp Cott 205.

courts. So far as the rule in Chancery was concerned, its origin lay in the ordinance of Lord Bacon in 1618 where it was laid down:

> 'they that are in contempt are not to be heard neither in that suit, nor in any other, except the court of special grace suspend the contempt.'

In these cases the rule only applied where a writ of attachment had issued, or where an order for committal had been made. However, as Denning LJ said:[3]

> 'The ordinance of Lord Bacon was . . . capable of working great injustice, and in the course of practice it came to be much restricted in its scope. It was confined to cases where a party in contempt, that is, a party against whom a writ of attachment had issued or an order for committal had been made, came forward voluntarily and asked for an indulgence in the self-same suit.'

So far as the Ecclesiastical courts were concerned, the rule was not tied to the issue of an attachment or committal and the rule applied was that:

> 'if a party was in contempt for disobeying an order, and his disobedience impeded the course of justice in the suit, the court might in its discretion refuse to allow him to take active proceedings in the suit until the impediment was removed.'[4]

B   The modern application

The leading modern authority on the rights of contemnors to be heard in the courts is *Hadkinson v Hadkinson*.[5] There a wife was given custody of the son of the marriage, subject to a direction that he should not be taken out of the jurisdiction. The wife broke the order by taking the child to Australia, and upon the husband's application a court order was made ordering the wife to bring the child back to England. The wife wished to appeal against the order, but the Court of Appeal refused to hear her application until she returned the child.

In reaching this decision, however, there was a difference of approach. On the one hand Romer LJ (with whom Somervell LJ agreed) considered there to be a general rule that a contemnor will not be heard until he has purged his contempt subject to certain specific exceptions.[6] Denning LJ on the other hand preferred a more flexible approach. He said:[7]

> 'I am of opinion that the fact that a party to a cause has disobeyed an order of the court is not of itself a bar to his being heard, but if his disobedience is such that, so long as it continues, it impedes the course of justice in the cause, by making it more difficult for the court to ascertain the truth or to enforce the orders which it may make, then the court may in its discretion refuse to hear him until the impediment is removed or good reason is shown why it should not be removed.'

In his view the case before him was:

> 'a good example of a case where the disobedience of the party impedes the course of justice. So long as this boy remains in Australia it is impossible for this court to enforce its orders in respect of him.'[8]

---

3 Ibid at 296.
4 Ibid at 297.
5 [1952] P 285.
6 Ibid at 288–291. The exceptions are outlined below at pp 653–654.
7 Ibid at 298.
8 This was in fact the first case since the setting up of the Divorce Court in 1857 in which the court refused to hear an appellant. See also *Leavis v Leavis* [1921] P 299 in which, having failed

Although subsequent cases can be found supporting Romer LJ's approach,[9] the growing weight of judicial opinion now favours Denning LJ's more flexible approach. Lord Bridge said in *X Ltd v Morgan-Grampian Ltd*:[10]

> 'I cannot help thinking that the more flexible treatment of the jurisdiction as one of discretion to be exercised in accordance with the principle stated by Denning LJ better accords with contemporary judicial attitudes to the importance of ensuring procedural justice than confining its exercise within the limits of a strict rule subject to defined exceptions.'

Lord Bridge also made the point, however, that in most cases the two different approches are likely to lead to the same conclusion. Indeed it remains unusual for a court not to hear a contemnor,[11] the modern application of the rule reflecting a general reluctance to refuse to hear a party. As Denning LJ said:[12]

> 'It is a strong thing for a court to refuse to hear a party to a cause and it is only to be justified by grave considerations of public policy.'

It is established, for instance, that the rule does not operate to bar applications made in *other* causes, even though these *other* proceedings may actually involve the same parties.[13] It is also been held that in any event the so-called rule does not prevent a contemnor from giving notice of a motion nor that the contemnor's action should be struck out rather than suspended. As Sir Robert Megarry V-C eloquently put it:[14]

> 'It was neither the law, nor ought it to be, that a person in contempt was an outlaw unable to take proceedings in the courts until he had purged his contempt and liable until then to have any proceedings that he brought struck out.'

According to Romer LJ's analysis in *Hadkinson v Hadkinson*[15] the rule is subject to the following exceptions namely where the contemnor is (1) applying

---

to comply with an order to give security for his wife's costs, the court refused to hear the husband's application to stay a petition for restitution of conjugal rights.

9   See eg *Astro Exito Navegacion SA v Southland Enterprise Co Ltd and Nan Jong Iron and Steel Co Ltd (The 'Messiniaki Tolmi')* [1981] 2 Lloyd's Rep 595, CA and *Maynard v Maynard* [1984] FLR 85, CA, and in Australia *Young v Jackman* (1986) 7 NSWLR 97 relying on *Short v Short* (1973) 7 SASR 1 and *Permewan Wright Consolidated Pty Ltd v AG (NSW), ex p Franklin's Stores Pty Ltd* (1978, unreported).

10   [1991] 1 AC 1 at 46, [1990] 2 All ER 1 at 11. See also *J (HD) v J (AM)* [1980] 1 All ER 156 at 161 (Sheldon J); *Clarke v Heathfield* [1985] 1 CR 203, CA and in Australia *Schumann v Schumann* (1964) 6 FLR 422 and *Woollahra Municipal Council v Shahini* (1990) 69 LGRA 435. A similarly flexible approach seems evident in Canada, see *Innovation and Development Partners/IDP Inc v The Queen* (1994) 114 DLR (4th) 326 and the cases there cited. For the relationship of the '*Hadkinson*' rule to the Canadian Charter see *Paul Magder Furs Ltd v Ontario (A-G)* (1991) 85 DLR (4th) 694 and the cases there cited.

11   See eg *Re A (a minor)(Appeal by Party in Contempt)* (1978) 1 FLR 140, CA; *Blome v Blome* (1976) 120 Sol Jo 315 where in questionable circumstances a husband had his leave to appeal struck out possibly because he 'was not taking seriously any order of the court'. For a criticism of this decision see Pettit, 'Injunctions Service and Committal' (1977) 40 MLR 220 at 222–223. In Australia see *Young v Jackman* (1986) 7 NSWLR 97.

12   In *Hadkinson v Hadkinson* [1952] P 285 at 298. See also at 295 where Denning LJ said 'I need hardly say that it is very rare for this court not to hear counsel for an appellant.'

13   *Bettinson v Bettinson* [1965] Ch 465, [1965] 1 All ER 102. In Canada see *Innovation and Development Partners/IDP Inc v The Queen* (1994) 114 DLR (4th) 326.

14   *Pyke v National Westminster Bank Ltd* (1977) Times, 9 December.

15   [1952] P 285 at 288–291 as explained by Lord Donaldson MR in *X Ltd v Morgan-Grampian Ltd* [1991] 1 AC 1 at 21, [1990] 1 All ER 616 at 627.

to purge his contempt, (2) appealing against the order which has not been obeyed,[16] (3) submitting that he is not or should not be treated as being in contempt,[17] (4) defending himself against subsequent applications, and (5) appealing against an order made against him, provided that the order was not made in the exercise of the court's discretion.

In short the rule prima facie has no application to subsequent attempts to clear the very contempt complained of. Nevertheless even with these so-called exceptions there remains a discretion not to hear the party, for example, on the ground that to put one party in a position of having to resist an appeal against an order made in his favour with which the other party has in any event no intention of complying is an abuse of the process of the court.[18]

There is some suggestion that the rule might be more readily applied where the welfare of minors is involved on the basis that where an order relates to a child the court is or should be adamant upon its due observance.[19] However, it is submitted that even in these cases the court retains a discretion whether to hear the case and the determining factor should be what is best in the interests of the child's welfare.[20]

VI   APPEALS

As in the case of criminal contempts the provisions relating to appeals in cases of civil contempt are governed by the Administration of Justice Act 1960, s 13.[1] This means that at the Court of Appeal level appeals are heard in the Civil Division. However, because civil contempts partake of a criminal nature appellate courts should hear the case as if it were a criminal offence and orders should be set aside if the evidence makes it unsafe to sustain the order.[2] It has also been held by the Court of Appeal in *Irtelli v Squatriti* [3] that since contemnors stand to lose

---

16   See also *Maynard v Maynard* [1984] FLR 85, application to discharge an ex parte order upon which the contempt was based, and *The Messiniaki Tolmi* [1981] 2 Lloyd's Rep 595. The rule may also be excluded when making application incidental to the appeal, see Nield J in the Australian case, *Price v Price (No 2)* (1961) 4 FLR 40 (NSW Sup Ct). This point was, however, left open on appeal at 4 FLR 43.

17   See *Gordon v Gordon* [1904] P 163, CA.

18   Per Brandon LJ in *The Messiniaki Tolmi* [1981] 2 Lloyd's Rep 595. However, it is incongruous to entertain the appeal to dismiss it and to give leave to appeal to the House of Lords but in the process to decline to hear counsel in support of the appeal, per Lord Bridge in *X Ltd v Morgan-Grampian Ltd* [1991] 1 AC 1 at 47, [1990] 2 All ER 1 at 12. In *Atlantic Capital Corporation v Johnson* (1994) Independent, 26 September, CA, it was said to be an exceptional case not to hear a contemnor in support of an appeal in respect of the order he is said to be in contempt.

19   Following *Corcoran v Corcoran* [1950] 1 All ER 495; *Hadkinson v Hadkinson* [1952] P 285; *Re A (a minor) (Appeal by Party in Contempt)* (1978) 1 FLR 140, and *The Messiniaki Tolmi* [1981] 2 Lloyd's Rep at 602, per Brandon LJ.

20   See *Re P (minors) (Wardship)(Access: Contempt)* [1991] 1 FLR 280, 288 per Russell LJ (decision to proceed taken on the basis of child's rather than the parties' interests). In Australia see *Short v Short* (1973) 22 FLR 320 and *Schumann v Schumann* (1964) 6 FLR 422. Cf *Clarke v Scargill* (1985) Times, 25 October, decision to proceed notwithstanding union's contempt taken in the interests of the union's members. This decision was upheld on appeal. See *Clarke v Heathfield* [1985] 1 CR 203, CA.

1   But note s 13(5) which excludes a right of appeal against an order made under the Debtors Act 1869, s 5 (discussed at p 648) and an order made under s 63(3) of the Magistrates' Courts Act 1980 (discussed at pp 645 ff). For discussion of the procedure and general powers of appellate courts see Ch 12.

2   *Kent County Council v Batchelor* (1976) 75 LGR 151.

3   [1993] QB 83, [1992] 3 All ER 294.

their liberty if the first instance judgment is upheld the court should act by analogy with the practice of the Court of Appeal (Criminal Division) to admit fresh evidence where justice requires it.[4]

VII THE DISTINCTION BETWEEN CIVIL AND CRIMINAL CONTEMPT

A The difficulty of classification

Notwithstanding attempts both to minimise the significance and, more recently, to suggest new classifications[5] contempts are traditionally classified as being either *civil* or *criminal*. However, a peculiar feature of contempt jurisprudence is the difficulty of satisfactorily classifying the different types of contempt. As *Justice* has said:[6]

> 'contempt being a growth of the common law, has no one authoritative definition or limitation . . . [and the] virtual absence of any precise definition has also made the task of classification one of considerable difficulty.'

Whilst not embarking upon the risky academic exercise[7] of attempting to give precise definitions of the two types of contempt it is proposed to highlight the difficulties of such a classification, to examine the current distinctions between the two types of contempt, and finally to explore possible new classifications.

In broad terms it is easy enough to distinguish criminal contempts from civil contempts. Criminal contempts are essentially offences of a public nature comprising publications or acts which interfere with the due course of justice as, for example, by tending to jeopardise the fair hearing of a trial or by tending to deter or frighten witnesses or by interrupting court proceedings or by tending to impair public confidence in the authority or integrity of the administration of justice. Civil contempts, on the other hand, are committed by disobeying court judgments or orders either to do or to abstain from doing particular acts, or by breaking the terms of an undertaking given to the court, on the faith of which a particular course of action or inaction is sanctioned, or by disobeying other court orders (for example not complying with an order for interrogatories, etc). Civil contempts are therefore essentially 'offences' of a private nature since they deprive a party of the benefit for which the order was made.[8] The essence of the

---

4 Ie the rule in *Ladd v Marshall* [1954] 1 WLR 1489 which is generally applicable to appeals in civil does not apply.
5 See in particular *A-G v Newspaper Publishing Plc* [1988] 1 Ch 333 at 362, [1987] 3 All ER 276 at 294, per Sir John Donaldson MR, discussed at pp 663–664.
6 *Contempt of Court* (1959) p 4. See also in Australia *Australian Building Construction Employees' and Builders' Labourers' Federation v David Syme & Co Ltd* (1982) 40 ALR 518 at 519 and *Australasian Meat Industry Employees' Union v Mudginberry Station Pty Ltd* (1986) 161 CLR 98, 106.
7 As Earl Loreburn said in *Scott v Scott* [1913] AC 417 at 445 such an exercise would require a 'treatise' and which in any case 'would be a treatise without authority, liable to the risk of error or misconception.'
8 In *Guildford Borough Council v Smith* (1993) Times, 18 May (full report on Lexis) Sedley J commented 'I am unable to accept that committal on the motion of an antagonist in civil proceedings is today in any admissible sense the private law right of which older dicta suggest it was. To all intents and purposes it is a form of private prosecution'. See also Cotton LJ in *O'Shea v O'Shea and Parnell* (1890) 15 PD 59 at 62. In Australia see the discussion by the Australian Law Reform Commission Report No 35: *Contempt* (1987) para 492. See also

courts' jurisdiction in respect of criminal contempts is penal, the aim being to protect the public interest in ensuring that the administration of justice is duly protected. On the other hand, the courts' jurisdiction in respect of civil contempts is primarily remedial, the basic object being to coerce the offender into obeying the court judgment or order, etc.[9] Reflecting this public/private dichotomy it is broadly true that the prime responsibility for prosecuting criminal contempts is that of the Attorney General or the court, but of the parties themselves in the case of civil contempt.[10]

While on the face of it, these distinctions between the two types of contempt are clear in practice it can be difficult to determine whether a particular act amounts to a criminal or civil contempt.[11] One of the reasons for this difficulty is that there is a punitive element even in cases of civil contempt, for it must be remembered that the law of contempt as a whole is concerned to uphold the due administration of justice, and it is obvious that disregard of a court order not only deprives the other party of the benefit of that order but also impairs the effective administration of justice. As Cross J said in *Phonographic Performance Ltd v Amusement Caterers (Peckham) Ltd*:[12]

> 'Where there has been wilful disobedience to an order of the court and a measure of contumacy on the part of the defendants, then civil contempt, what is called contempt in procedure, "bears a two-fold character, implying as between the parties to the proceedings merely a right to exercise and a liability to submit to a form of civil execution, but as between the party in default and the state, a penal or disciplinary jurisdiction to be exercised by the court in the public interest".'

In practice, therefore, the distinction between the two types of contempt has become blurred and there are certain border line types of contempt which defy easy classification. No case illustrates this point better than *Scott v Scott* which involved the publication of a copy of the official shorthand writer's notes of certain nullity proceedings, in contravention of an order directing that the case should be heard in camera. The case was heard before a full Court of Appeal[13] where by a majority of four to two it was held that since the order to hear the case in camera had been made in the public interest to protect the due course of justice, the publication amounted to a criminal contempt.[14] The House of Lords,[15]

AMIEU v Mudginberry Station Pty Ltd (1986) 161 CLR 98 at 108; *Adriatic Terrazo and Foundation Pty Ltd v Robinson* (1972) 4 SASR 294 at 295–296 per Wells J (S Aust SC). In Canada see the dissenting judgment of Husband JA in *R v Clement* (1980) 114 DLR (3d) 656 at 667–668. In Ireland see *Keegan v de Burra* (1973) IR 223 and *The State (Commins) v McRann* (1977) IR 78 at 89.

9   See Windeyer J in *Australian Consolidated Press Ltd v Morgan* (1965) 39 ALJR 32 at 38. See also *AMIEU v Mudginberri Station Pty Ltd* (1986) 161 CLR 98 at 108.

10   See eg Sopinka J in *United Nurses of Alberta v A-G for Alberta* (1992) 89 DLR (4th) 609 at 615. For a discussion of the Attorney General's role in contempt cases see at pp 480 ff and 500–501.

11   See the analysis in the context of labour disputes by O'Regan, 'Contempt of Court and the Enforcement of Labour Injunctions' (1991) 54 MLR 385.

12   [1964] Ch 195 at 198, cited with approval by Edmund-Davies LJ in *Jennison v Baker* [1972] 2 QB 52 at 69–70. See also *Re Barrell Enterprises* [1972] 3 All ER 631 at 639 per Russell LJ. Cf the position in Canada where public disobedience to court orders tends to be treated as criminal contempt. See eg *United Nurses of Alberta v A-G for Alberta* (1992) 89 DLR (4th) 609; *Tony Poje v A-G of British Columbia* [1953] 2 DLR 785; *Foothills Provincial General Hospital Board v Broard* (1975) 57 DLR (3d) 758 and *Re New Brunswick Electric Power Commission and Local Union No 1733* (1976) 73 DLR (3d) 94. See also *R v Clement* (1980) 114 DLR (3d) 656.

13   [1912] P 241.

14   See eg Farwell LJ, ibid at 291.

15   [1913] AC 417.

however, held that had a contempt been committed it would have been a civil contempt, since they treated the publication simply as being a breach of a court order.[16] How far *Scott v Scott* is authority for saying that publication of an account of proceedings heard in private will always amount to a civil contempt is a matter of debate (in *Scott v Scott* itself, for instance,[17] it was suggested that publications of proceedings concerning wards of court might well be treated on a different footing), and the issue remains unresolved despite the amendments under the Administration of Justice Act 1960, s 12.[18]

Another type of contempt which is difficult to classify is aiding and abetting a breach of injunction.[19] It can be argued that such an act amounts to a criminal contempt since the offence is not committed by a party to the action and the act clearly impedes the due course of justice.[20] On the other hand, it can equally well be argued that the act amounts to a civil contempt, the punishment of the offender being an indirect means of enforcing the court order for the benefit of the plaintiff.[1] Although support can be found for both views,[2] the weight of modern authority is that it is a criminal contempt.[3]

There are similar problems in classifying contempts committed by solicitors qua solicitors, for while there is authority to say that such contempts are civil[4] the courts have tended to emphasise the penal nature of their jurisdiction,[5] and a case could certainly be made out for saying such contempts are criminal.[6]

There is also no clear authority to say whether disobedience to a subpoena amounts to a criminal or civil contempt.[7]

It is suggested that some of the above difficulties of classification would disappear if it was accepted, as it is in Canada, that some acts, as for example, public disobedience of a court order[8] can convert what was prima facie a civil

16 See especially Lord Atkinson, ibid, at 456ff.
17 See Lord Atkinson, ibid at 462.
18 For a detailed discussion of this provision see Ch 8. In Australia the view has been taken that *Scott v Scott* turned purely on the wording of s 47 of the Supreme Court of Judicature Act 1873. See *La Trobe University v Robinson and Pola* [1973] VR 682 at 688 (Sup Ct of Victoria, Full Court); see also the decision at first instance [1972] VR 883 and 889.
19 For the discussion of which see pp 573 ff.
20 See Lindley LJ in *Seaward v Paterson* (1897) 1 Ch 545 at 553.
 1 See Salmon LJ in *Jennison v Baker* [1972] 2 QB, 52 at 64–65.
 2 Lord Atkinson in *Scott v Scott* [1913] AC 417 at 457, 459 emphatically stated that such an act amounted to a civil contempt, but Cross J, in *Phonographic Performance Ltd v Amusement Caterers (Peckham) Ltd* [1964] Ch 195 at 200, 201, assumed that the act amounted to a criminal contempt. It is also classified as criminal by Oswald, *Contempt* (3rd edn, 1910) p 106 and Fox, *Contempt of Court* (1927) pp 44, 45.
 3 See *A-G v Newspapers Publishing Plc* [1988] Ch 333, 342 (per Browne-Wilkinson V-C) and 377 (per Lloyd LJ) and *A-G v Times Newspapers Ltd* [1992] 1 AC 191, at 214 (per Lord Ackner) and 218 (per Lord Oliver) and Miller, *Contempt of Court* (2nd edn) p 430.
 4 See Lord Atkinson in *Scott v Scott* [1913] AC 417 at 459, 461, and *Seldon v Wilde* [1911] 1 KB 701, see especially Buckley LJ.
 5 See eg *Re Freston* (1883) 11 QBD 545 and *Re Gent, Gent-Davis v Harris* (1888) 40 Ch D 190.
 6 It is so classified in 9 *Halsbury's Laws* (4th edn) para 40.
 7 See *Re Evans, Evans v Noton* [1893] 1 Ch 252, CA where the question was left open. It is classified as criminal in the *Supreme Court Practice* 52/1/11. It was accepted as being criminal in the Australian case, *Registrar of the Court of Appeal v Manian* (1991) 25 NSWLR 459 at 467. Note also *DPP v Chidiac* (1991) 25 NSWLR 372 in which it was held that refusal to answer questions was a criminal contempt.
 8 Query whether some acts, eg wrongful interference with a ward of court contrary to an express court order could constitute both criminal and civil contempt. See Lowe and White, *Wards of Court* (2nd edn, 1986) at paras 8.27–8.28. See also *Scott v Scott* [1913] AC 417 in which a hybrid form of contempt was mooted.

into a criminal contempt. As Kelloch J said in *Tony Poje v A-G of British Columbia*:[9]

> 'there are many statements in the books that contempt proceedings for breach of an injunction are civil process, but it is obvious that conduct which is a violation of an injunction may, in addition to its civil aspect, possess all the features of criminal contempt of court. In case of a breach of purely civil nature, the requirements of the situation from the standpoint of enforcement of the rights of the opposite party constitute the criterion upon which the court acts. But a punitive sentence is called for where the act of violation has passed beyond the realm of the purely civil.'

As McLachlin J put it in *United Nurses of Alberta v A-G for Alberta:* [10]

> 'A person who simply breaches a court order is viewed as having committed a civil contempt. However, when the element of public defiance of the court's process in a way calculated to lessen societal respect for the courts is added to the breach it becomes criminal.'

B The relevance of classification

As far as English law is concerned it was formerly vital to distinguish criminal from civil contempts since a number of important consequences were dependent upon classification.[11] Even today, although the number of distinctions has declined some remain so that the issue of classification is by no means otiose.

Formerly, the most important distinction between criminal and civil contempts was the fact that there was no right of appeal in respect of criminal contempts, but this anomalous position was remedied by the Administration of Justice Act 1960, s 13, which as we have seen,[12] provides a right of appeal in *all* cases of contempt. Another important distinction was the fact that it was thought that the courts had no power to fine an offender in respect of a civil contempt, but it is now established[13] that the courts can and will fine an offender where it is appropriate to do so even in cases of civil contempt. Another distinction was that once an offender had been committed to prison for a fixed period in respect of a criminal contempt, the court had no power to discharge him before the expiration of the fixed period, whereas it had in respect of civil contempts.[14] This distinction has also disappeared, RSC Ord 52, r 8 (1) now providing that the court can discharge a prisoner committed to prison for *any* contempt, at any time. The Contempt of Court Act 1981, s 14 (1) has removed another distinction in that sine die committals can no longer be made in cases of civil contempt. In all cases of contempt committals must be for a fixed period.

---

9 [1953] 2 DLR 785 at 787.
10 (1992) 89 DLR (4th) 609, 636. See also *BCGEU v British Columbia (A-G)* (1989) 53 DLR (4th) 1 at 17.
11 For an excellent account of such distinctions see Harnon, (1962) 25 MLR 179. See also O'Regan, (1991) 54 MLR 385.
12 See Ch 12.
13 Per Cross J in *Phonographic Performance Ltd v Amusement Caterers (Peckham) Ltd* [1964] Ch 195, [1963] 3 All ER 493, see p 636.
14 *A-G v James* [1962] 2 QB 637, [1962] 1 All ER 255.

Another distinction which was thought to exist[15] was that since the jurisdiction in respect of civil contempts was primarily remedial, once the offender complied with a court order, he had a *right* to be released, whereas there was no such right in respect of criminal contempts. However, since it has been held[16] that eventual compliance with a court order does not necessarily preclude the court from punishing an offender for his original breach, if that breach was so contumacious as to deserve punishment, it is no longer possible to say that an offender has a *right* to be released upon compliance.

It was also thought that a civil contempt could be waived on the grounds that if the party for whose benefit an order is made is content that it should not be performed, the court generally had no interest to interfere,[17] whereas there is no right of waiver in cases of criminal contempt.[18] Although there was some authority to support this proposition,[19] the distinction was never firmly established.[20] Indeed in *Jennison v Baker* Salmon LJ said:[1]

'Rigby LJ, in *Seaward's case*[2] pointed out that the court might well send the defendant to prison even if the plaintiff having applied for attachment, relented and asked that the order in his favour should not be so enforced. The plaintiff cannot waive the order, but, as a rule, the court will pay attention to his wishes.'

The better view would seem to be that if a party does not seek to invoke the aid of the court to enforce a judgment, no contempt proceedings are likely to be brought, and to this extent the contempt can be waived, but once proceedings have been brought, then the party has no right to waive the contempt, and it is a matter for the court's discretion whether the offender should be punished.[3]

In some cases, however, for example where the disobedience is public, the court has the power to act upon its own motion so that no question of waiver can arise.[4]

Not only are the above distinctions no longer relevant or important, recent cases in emphasising the penal nature of the court's jurisdiction in respect of civil contempts have tended to merge the two types still further. It has been held, for

15 See Harnon, (1962) 25 MLR 179, 184–5. In *Corcoran v Corcoran* [1950] 1 All ER 495 it was argued, unsuccessfully, that a contemnor had a right to be released upon the waiver of the other party.
16 Per Cross J in *Phonographic Performance Ltd* [1964] Ch 195, [1963] 3 All ER 493 at 199 cited with approval in *Jennison v Baker* [1972] 2 QB 52 at 69–70 per Edmund-Davies LJ. See also in Canada *Re Pereira and Minister of Manpower and Immigration* (1979) 91 DLR (3d) 706.
17 See eg Lord Diplock in *A-G v Times Newspapers Ltd* [1974] AC 273 at 308A and *Home Office v Harman* [1983] 1 AC 280 at 307, [1982] 1 All ER 532 at 539–540; cf Lord Scarman at 319 and 549.
18 See *R v Newton* (1903) 19 TLR 627, where it was held that an attempt to settle in a case of criminal contempt itself amounted to contempt.
19 See the dictum of Lindley LJ in *Seaward v Paterson* [1897] 1 Ch 545 at 555, quoted by Harnon, (1962) 25 MLR 179 at 183. See also *Roberts v Albert Bridge Co* (1873) 8 Ch App 753.
20 See Harnon: (1962) 25 MLR 179, 182ff. See also O'Regan, (1991) 54 MLR at 387.
1 [1972] 2 QB 52 at 64.
2 [1897] 1 Ch 545 at 558ff.
3 It has been held that leave of the court is necessary before a writ of sequestration can be withdrawn. See *Showerings Ltd v Fern Vale Brewery Co Ltd* [1958] RPC 462. In *Mirror Group Newspapers v Harrison* (unreported 1986, referred to by O'Regan, (1991) 54 MLR at 387) the court refused permission for the plaintiff to withdraw contempt proceedings even though the dispute between the parties was settled. See also *Clarke v Chadburn* [1984] IRLR 350.
4 See the explanation by Sir John Donaldson in *Con-Mech Ltd v Amalgamated Union of Engineering Workers* [1973] ICR 620 at 625. See also *Churchman v Joint Shop Stewards' Committee* [1972] ICR 222, CA. A similar standpoint is taken in Canada, see eg *Foothills Provincial General Hospital Board v Board* (1976) 57 DLR (3d) 758.

instance, that the court can still punish an offender for past breaches of an injunction even though the terms of the injunction can no longer be effectively enforced. This shows that the jurisdiction even in respect of civil contempts can be *purely* penal.[5] It has also been established that since contempt of court as a whole is an offence of a criminal character, it is necessary even in cases of civil contempt to prove the offence beyond all reasonable doubt,[6] and similarly it has been held that a defendant in proceedings for civil contempt cannot be compelled to answer interrogatories or to give evidence against his will so as to incriminate himself.[7] It is also established that because proceedings for civil contempt are quasi criminal in character the defence of autrefois acquit and autrefois convict apply,[8] and that on appeal fresh evidence should be admitted according to the practice of the Criminal rather than the Civil Division of the Court of Appeal.[9] These decisions therefore suggest that in general, the same rules of evidence and procedure are applicable to both criminal and civil contempts. However, against this general proposition it has been held that unlike criminal contempt, hearsay evidence is admissible in cases of civil contempt.[10] It has also been held that the civil rather than the criminal procedure concerning the right to withhold evidence and submit there is no case to answer is applicable to civil contempts, namely, that the judge has a discretion to put the respondent to his election whether to adduce evidence before giving a ruling whether there is a case to answer.[11] It remains uncertain whether the same rules of discovery are applicable to civil and criminal contempts.[12]

Perhaps the most convincing explanation of the apparently differing positions just adverted to is that the basic rules of procedure and evidence remain those applicable to civil proceedings in respect of civil contempts save that where there is a justification for importing the protection devised by the criminal law for the benefit of the accused it will be imported.[13]

The distinctions that still exist are as follows:

(1)   The prerogative right of the Crown to grant pardons extends to criminal contempts but not civil contempts,[14] but the importance of this distinction is

---

5   *Jennison v Baker* [1972] 2 QB 52 and in Canada *Re Pereira* (1979) 91 DLR (3d) 706.
6   *Re Bramblevale Ltd* [1970] Ch 128, [1969] 3 All ER 1062, CA and see p 565.
7   See *Bhimji v Chatwani (No 3)* [1992] 4 All ER 912 (not following *Garvin v Domus Publishing Ltd* [1989] Ch 335, [1989] 2 All ER 344) and *Comet Products UK Ltd v Hawkex Plastics Ltd* [1971] 2 QB 67, [1971] 2 All ER 1141 and p 000. In Canada, see *Videotron Ltée v Industries Microlec Produits Electroniques Inc* (1993) 96 DLR (4th) 376 (Can SC)
8   See *Danchevsky v Danchevsky (No 2)* [1977] CA Transcript 416A, (1977) 128 NLJ 955; *Jelsen (Estates) Ltd v Harvey* [1984] 1 All ER 12, CA and *El Capistrano SA v Ato Marketing Ltd* [1989] 2 All ER 572, CA.
9   See *Irtelli v Squatriti* [1993] QB 83, [1992] 3 All ER 294, CA.
10 See *Savings and Investment Bank Ltd v Gasco Investments (Netherlands) BV (No 2)* [1988] Ch 422, [1988] 1 All ER 975, CA, and *C v C (Contempt: Evidence)* [1993] 1 FLR 220, CA, discussed at p 625.
11 *Barclays de Zoete Wedd Securities Ltd v Asil Nadir* (1992) Times, 25 March (full transcript on Lexis) per Knox J.
12 *In The Matter Relating to the Supply of Ready Mixed Concrete in the Restrictive Practices Court* (unreported, 4 August 1995) Buckley J apparently held that the duty of discovery should be nearer to that common to criminal proceedings than that in civil proceedings. See also *Crest Homes Plc v Marks* [1987] 1 AC 829 at 859 per Lord Oliver.
13 Per Knox J in *Barclays de Zoete Wedd Securities Ltd v Asil Nadir* (1992) Times, 25 March. See also the not dissimilar reasoning by the majority in the Canadian Supreme Court decision, *Videotron Ltée v Industries Microlec* (1993) 96 DLR (4th) 376, 395–401.
14 For a discussion of this prerogative see Ch 12.

minimal for in practice it was very rarely used and even in theory its importance has greatly diminished, since s 13 of the Administration of Justice Act 1960 now provides a right of appeal in cases of criminal contempt.

(2)   An officer executing process of arrest in respect of a criminal, but not a civil, contempt, may, after due notice, break open an outer door, perhaps may even execute the process on a Sunday.[15]

(3)   The writ of sequestration, though a process of contempt in its nature, is nevertheless a form of civil execution[16] and is therefore inapplicable to criminal contempts.

(4)   An order for the discharge of a person committed to prison can only be made conditional upon payment of costs in cases of criminal[17] and not civil contempt.[18]

(5)   Hearsay evidence is admissible in cases of civil contempt but not criminal contempt.[19]

(6)   Privilege from arrest may be relied upon in certain cases of civil contempt but not in cases of criminal contempt.[20] It is established that this privilege, which may be claimed by Members of Parliament, witnesses travelling to or from courts of justice, and solicitors and barristers attending court in discharge of their functions, can be raised where the committal is granted merely for the purpose of enforcing judgments in civil disputes, but not where the default is 'criminal in character' so that the application to commit 'is intended rather to punish than to compel'.[1] Whether or not such a privilege exists depends upon the facts of each case[2] and, moreover, it has been held that:[3]

> 'the privilege, if any, is not the privilege of the litigant, but the privilege of the court, and if it be the privilege of the court, nothing could be plainer than that it is open to the court itself to have the man arrested if it thinks proper to do so under a committal order, even though he be in that court.'

In practice the privilege is very rarely claimed and cannot be considered to be of vital significance.[4]

15 *Harvey v Harvey* (1884) 26 Ch D 644.
16 *Pratt v Inman* (1889) 43 Ch D 175 at 179. This can be of some importance in, eg wardship cases, see Lowe and White, *Wards of Court* (2nd edn, 1986) para 8–28.
17 See *Re M* (1876) 46 LJ Ch 24, CA but even in these cases where a contemnor is without means the court will, upon application, discharge him without directing him to pay costs. See *West Ham Corpn v Cunningham* (1906) Times, 12 October.
18 See, eg *Jackson v Mawby* (1875) 1 Ch D 86.
19 See *Savings and Investment Bank Ltd v Gasco Investments (Netherlands) BV (No 2)* [1988] Ch 422, [1988] 1 All ER 975, CA, discussed at p 625.
20 See the classic case of *Wellesley v Duke of Beaufort* (1831) 2 Russ & M 639. See also in Australia *La Trobe University v Robinson and Pola* [1972] VR 883 at 899 and in Canada *Re Ouellet* (1976) 72 DLR (3d) 95.
 1 See *Stourton v Stourton* [1963] P 302, [1963] 1 All ER 606 and the cases there cited.
 2 Per Scarman J in *Stourton v Stourton*, ibid at 310.
 3 *Re Hunt* [1959] 2 QB 69 at 77 per Romer LJ.
 4 It was successfully claimed in *Stourton v Stourton* [1963] P 302, [1963] 1 All ER 606.

(7)   Under s 1 of the Representation of the People Act 1981:

> 'A person found guilty of one or more offences . . . and sentenced or ordered to be
> imprisoned or detained . . . for more than one year, shall be disqualified for
> membership of the House of Commons while detained anywhere in the British
> Islands or the Republic of Ireland in pursuance of the sentence or order while
> unlawfully at large at a time when he would otherwise be so detained.'

This would appear to apply to criminal but not civil contempt since the Act
only applies to those found guilty of an offence.

(8)   Another key difference between civil and criminal contempt is the mens rea
requirement in connection with the breaking of court orders. Whereas parties
who deliberately do an act contrary to a court order are liable for civil contempt
regardless of intention, third parties can only be guilty of (criminal) contempt to
frustrate a court order if they both know of the order and intend to interfere or
impede the course of justice. This distinction can be important when considering
whether it is the Office, Ministry or department or its holder[5] or whether it is the
company or its individual members that are liable.[6] As Lord Oliver explained in
A-G v Times Newspapers Ltd:[7]

> 'One particular form of contempt by a party to proceedings is that constituted by
> an intentional act which is in breach of the order of a competent court. Where this
> occurs as a result of the act of a party who is bound by the order of others acting
> at his direction or on his instigation, it constitutes a civil contempt by him. The
> intention with which the act was done will, of course, be of the highest relevance
> in the determination of the penalty (if any) to be imposed by the court, but the
> liability here is a strict one in the sense that all that requires to be proved is service
> of the order and the subsequent doing by the party bound of that which is
> prohibited. When, however, the prohibited act is done not by the party bound
> himself, but by a third party, a stranger to the litigation, that person may also also
> be liable for contempt. There is, however, this essential distinction that his liability
> is for criminal contempt and arises not because the contemnor is himself affected
> by the prohibition contained in the order, but because his act constitutes a wilful
> interference with the administration of justice by the court in the proceedings in
> which the order was made. Here the liability is not strict in the sense referred to,
> for there has to be shown not only knowledge of the order but an intention to
> interfere with or impede the administration of justice—an intention which can, of
> course, be inferred from the circumstances.'

A further distinction, which might prove of relevance in a novel case, is that
criminal contempt is, for all its peculiarities, a crime, whereas a civil contempt
despite its criminal characteristics is not. In the former case it might be difficult
to argue for an extension of the law because of the general reluctance to extend
common law crime.[8] Such a consideration might not, however, be thought to

---

5   See eg the discussion in *M v Home Office* [1994] 1 AC 377 at 426–427, [1993] 3 All ER 537
     at 567–569, per Lord Woolf, discussed at pp 572–573.
6   See eg *Re Supply of Ready Mixed Concrete (No 2)* [1995] 1 AC 456, [1995] 1 All ER 135, HL,
     discussed at pp 569–571.
7   [1992] 1 AC 191, 217–218, [1991] 2 All ER 398, 415.
8   See eg the concerns expressed in the 'Spycatcher' litigation, particularly by Browne-
     Wilkinson V-C in *A-G v Newspaper Publishing Plc* [1988] Ch 333 at 346E–G but cf Lord
     Ackner in *A-G v Times Newspapers Ltd* [1992] 1 AC 191 at 215C–E that it was not a case of
     widening the law, but merely a new example of its application. See also in Canada, the
     concerns of Sopinka J (dissenting) in *United Nurses of Alberta v A-G for Alberta* (1992) 89
     DLR (4th) 609. Admittedly, however, this consideration has not prevented major developments,

apply to civil contempt.[9] It is also understood that the distinction between civil and criminal contempt can be important for tax purposes since companies' court expenses in the former case are thought to be tax deductible but not in the latter.

In other common law jurisdictions the distinction between criminal and civil contempt can be significant for other reasons. In Australia, for example, classification can be important in determining whether the issue is a state or federal matter[10] and it has been held[11] important in determining whether a superior court has supervisory jurisdiction in a case. In Canada, the classification issue may be important in relation to s 116 (1) of the Canadian Criminal Code in determining whether those who have disobeyed a court order must be proceeded against summarily as for contempt or whether they should be indicted[12] and in relation to the application of the Code of Civil Procedure and Canadian Charter of Rights and Freedoms.[13]

C   Should the distinction be retained?

From time to time judges have expressed dissatisfaction with the traditional distribution between civil and criminal contempt. In *Jennison v Baker,* [14] for instance, Salmon LJ said that he found it 'an unhelpful and almost meaningless classification' while in *A-G v Newspaper Publishing Plc* [15] Sir John Donaldson MR considered that the classification 'tends to mislead rather than assist'. Despite this, as we have seen, not only does the classification persist but there remain some not insignificant differences. It certainly cannot be said[16] that the issue of classification is of academic importance only. Moreover it may still be argued that the two types of contempt are essentially different in that criminal law is concerned to protect the *public* interest in the due administration of justice whereas civil contempt (at any rate where disobedience of court orders does not pass into the realm of public misconduct and therefore into the arena of criminal contempt) is concerned to protect the *private* interest in the enforcement of court orders. Even so two questions must be asked, namely, whether a better form of classification can be devised, and, if not,whether all the remaining distinctions between the two types of contempt are justified.

---

see eg *A-G v Butterworth* [1963] 1 QB 696, [1963] 3 All ER 326; cf in Australia, *Registrar of the Supreme Court v McPherson* [1980] 1 NSWLR 688 where the NSW CA were careful to say that they were not expanding the criminal law.

9   One wonders, eg whether the courts would have been quite so ready to find a contempt in *Home Office v Harman* [1983] 1 AC 280, [1982] 1 All ER 532 had the contempt involved been criminal rather than civil?

10   See eg *R v B* (1972) 20 FLR 368 (W Aust SC).

11   *Kassebaum v Kassebaum* (1973) 5 SASR 411 (S Aust SC).

12   See eg *Re Gerson, Re Nightingale* (1946) 87 CCC 143, [1946] SCR 538 affd, [1946] SCR 547 and *Re Regina and Monette* (1975) 64 DLR (3d) 470. In *R v Clement* (1980) 114 DLR (3d) 656 (Manitoba CA) where the majority held that distinction between criminal and civil contempt was irrelevant in interpreting s 116 (1) and that a charge on indictment does not lie but note the dissent by Husband JA. See now *United Nurses of Alberta v A-G for Alberta* (1992) 89 DLR (4th) 609 (Can SC).

13   See eg *Videotron Ltée v Industries Microlec Produits Electroniques Inc* (1993) 96 DLR (4th) 376 (Can Sup Ct) and *BCGEU v British Columbia (A-G)* (1989) 53 DLR (4th) 1 (Can SC).

14   [1972] 2 QB 52 at 61, [1972] 1 All ER 997 at 1001.

15   [1988] Ch 333 at 362, [1987] 3 All ER 276 at 294.

16   As we did in the first edition at pp 371 and 374.

With regard to the former issue, Sir John Donaldson MR suggested in *A-G v Newspaper Publishing Plc* [17] that of greater assistance would be the reclassification of contempt as:

> '(a) conduct which involves a breach, or assisting in the breach, of a court order and (b) any other conduct which involves an interference with the due administration of justice, either in a particular case or, more generally, as a continuing process.'

One undoubted advantage of such a reclassification is that it would obviate classifying disobedience of a court order as civil contempt, yet aiding and abetting as a breach as a criminal contempt. As Lloyd LJ said in *A-G v Newspapers Publishing Plc:* [18]

> 'it does not make sense that a stranger to the order, who aids and abets a breach should be criminally liable while the peson to whom the order is directed and who himself omits a breach, should only be liable for civil contempt. That is the sort of nonsense which does no credit to the law . . . '

However, what the suggested distinction leaves out of account is public disobedience of court orders which do deserve different treatment from other forms of disobedience and which are classified as criminal contempts in Canada. Morever, apart from solving the problem of aiding and abetting breaches, the suggested reclassification seems merely to substitute new synonyms for criminal and civil contempts. It does not address the problem of what, if any, distinctions should continue to attach to the different types of contempt.

So far as the current distinctions are concerned, the Phillimore Committee [19] could see no reason to maintain the rule conferring privilege from process for civil contempts and recommended its abolition. They also recommended that the rules as to waiver in civil contempt should be abolished and that the court should have power upon its own motion to act against a person who disobeys a court order and in appropriate cases to require a breach to be reported to it by the party in whose favour the order was made. They also recommended that the rules of execution should be the same for both types of contempt and that the power of pardon should be ended. Although these seem sensible proposals no legislative action has been taken, though, as have seen, some have since been adopted by the courts. [20]

---

17 [1988] Ch 333 at 362, [1987] 3 All ER 276 at 294.
18 Ibid at 377 and 306.
19 See paras 168–176. See also the Canadian Law Reform Commission Working Paper (1977) pp 24–29 and Final Report No 17 (1982) pp 23–24.
20 Ie those concerning waiver and the court having power to punish of its own motion breaches of a court order.

Contempt of Court Act 1981 (c 49) 27 July 1981

An Act to amend the law relating to contempt of court and related matters

BE IT ENACTED by the Queen's most Excellent Majesty, by and with the advice and consent of the Lords Spiritual and Temporal, and Commons, in this present Parliament assembled, and by the authority of the same, as follows:—

Strict liability

1 The strict liability rule

In this Act "the strict liability rule" means the rule of law whereby conduct may be treated as a contempt of court as tending to interfere with the course of justice in particular legal proceedings regardless of intent to do so.

2 Limitation of scope of strict liability

(1)   The strict liability rule applies only in relation to publications, and for this purpose "publication" includes any speech, writing, [programme included in a programme service] or other communication in whatever form, which is addressed to the public at large or any section of the public.

(2)   The strict liability rule applies only to a publication which creates a substantial risk that the course of justice in the proceedings in question will be seriously impeded or prejudiced.

(3)   The strict liability rule applies to a publication only if the proceedings in question are active within the meaning of this section at the time of the publication.

(4)   Schedule 1 applies for determining the times at which proceedings are to be treated as active within the meaning of this section.

[(5)   In this section "programme service" has the same meaning as in the Broadcasting Act 1990.]

Annotations

Sub-s (1): words in square brackets substituted by the Broadcasting Act 1990, s 203(1), Sch 20, para 31(1).

Sub-s (5): added by the Broadcasting Act 1990, s 203(1), Sch 20, para 31(1).

3   Defence of innocent publication or distribution

(1)   A person is not guilty of contempt of court under the strict liability rule as the publisher of any matter to which that rule applies if at the time of publication (having taken all reasonable care) he does not know and has no reason to suspect that relevant proceedings are active.

(2)   A person is not guilty of contempt of court under the strict liability rule as the distributor of a publication containing any such matter if at the time of distribution (having taken all reasonable care) he does not know that it contains such matter and has no reason to suspect that it is likely to do so.

(3)   The burden of proof of any fact tending to establish a defence afforded by this section to any person lies upon that person.

(4)   < ... >

Annotations

Sub-s (4): repeals the Administration of Justice Act 1960, s 11.

4   Contemporary reports of proceedings

(1)   Subject to this section a person is not guilty of contempt of court under the strict liability rule in respect of a fair and accurate report of legal proceedings held in public, published contemporaneously and in good faith.

(2)   In any such proceedings the court may, where it appears to be necessary for avoiding a substantial risk of prejudice to the administration of justice in those proceedings, or in any other proceedings pending or imminent, order that the publication of any report of the proceedings, or any part of the proceedings, be postponed for such period as the court thinks necessary for that purpose.

(3)   For the purposes of subsection (1) of this section and of section 3 of the Law of Libel Amendment Act 1888 (privilege) a report of proceedings shall be treated as published contemporaneously—

   (a)   in the case of a report of which publication is postponed pursuant to an order under subsection (2) of this section, if published as soon as practicable after that order expires;

   (b)   in the case of a report of *committal proceedings* [an application for dismissal under section 6 of the Magistrates' Courts Act 1980] of which publication is permitted by virtue only of *subsection (3) of section 8 of the Magistrates' Courts Act 1980* [subsection (5) or (7) of section 8A of that Act], if published as soon as practicable after publication is so permitted.

(4)   < ... >

Annotations

Sub-s (3): in para (b) words in italics prospectively repealed and subsequent words in square brackets prospectively substituted by the Criminal Justice and Public Order Act 1994, s 44, Sch 4, Part II, para 50, as from a day to be appointed.

Sub-s (4): repeals the Magistrates' Courts Act 1980, s 8(9).

5 Discussion of public affairs

A publication made as or as part of a discussion in good faith of public affairs or other matters of general public interest is not to be treated as a contempt of court under the strict liability rule if the risk of impediment or prejudice to particular legal proceedings is merely incidental to the discussion.

6 Savings

Nothing in the foregoing provisions of this Act—

    (a)   prejudices any defence available at common law to a charge of contempt of court under the strict liability rule;

    (b)   implies that any publication is punishable as contempt of court under that rule which would not be so punishable apart from those provisions;

    (c)   restricts liability for contempt of court in respect of conduct intended to impede or prejudice the administration of justice.

7 Consent required for institution of proceedings

Proceedings for a contempt of court under the strict liability rule (other than Scottish proceedings) shall not be instituted except by or with the consent of the Attorney General or on the motion of a court having jurisdiction to deal with it.

Annotations

This section does not extend to Scotland.

Other aspects of law and procedure

8 Confidentiality of jury's deliberations

(1)   Subject to subsection (2) below, it is a contempt of court to obtain, disclose or solicit any particulars of statements made, opinions expressed, arguments advanced or votes cast by members of a jury in the course of their deliberations in any legal proceedings.

(2)   This section does not apply to any disclosure of any particulars—

(a)   in the proceedings in question for the purpose of enabling the jury to arrive at their verdict, or in connection with the delivery of that verdict, or

(b)   in evidence in any subsequent proceedings for an offence alleged to have been committed in relation to the jury in the first mentioned proceedings,

or to the publication of any particulars so disclosed.

(3)   Proceedings for a contempt of court under this section (other than Scottish proceedings) shall not be instituted except by or with the consent of the Attorney General or on the motion of a court having jurisdiction to deal with it.

Annotations

Extent: sub-s (3) does not extend to Scotland.

9   Use of tape recorders

(1)   Subject to subsection (4) below, it is a contempt of court—

(a)   to use in court, or bring into court for use, any tape recorder or other instrument for recording sound, except with the leave of the court;

(b)   to publish a recording of legal proceedings made by means of any such instrument, or any recording derived directly or indirectly from it, by playing it in the hearing of the public or any section of the public, or to dispose of it or any recording so derived, with a view to such publication;

(c)   to use any such recording in contravention of any conditions of leave granted under paragraph (a).

(2)   Leave under paragraph (a) of subsection (1) may be granted or refused at the discretion of the court, and if granted may be granted subject to such conditions as the court thinks proper with respect to the use of any recording made pursuant to the leave; and where leave has been granted the court may at the like discretion withdraw or amend it either generally or in relation to any particular part of the proceedings.

(3)   Without prejudice to any other power to deal with an act of contempt under paragraph (a) of subsection (1), the court may order the instrument, or any recording made with it, or both, to be forfeited; and any object so forfeited shall (unless the court otherwise determines on application by a person appearing to be the owner) be sold or otherwise disposed of in such manner as the court may direct.

(4)   This section does not apply to the making or use of sound recordings for purposes of official transcripts of proceedings.

10 Sources of information

No court may require a person to disclose, nor is any person guilty of contempt of court for refusing to disclose, the source of information contained in a publication for which he is responsible, unless it be established to the satisfaction of the court that disclosure is necessary in the interests of justice or national security or for the prevention of disorder or crime.

11 Publication of matters exempted from disclosure in court

In any case where a court (having power to do so) allows a name or other matter to be withheld from the public in proceedings before the court, the court may give such directions prohibiting the publication of that name or matter in connection with the proceedings as appear to the court to be necessary for the purpose for which it was so withheld.

12 Offences of contempt of magistrates' courts

(1)   A magistrates' court has jurisdiction under this section to deal with any person who—

    (a)   wilfully insults the justice or justices, any witness before or officer of the court or any solicitor or counsel having business in the court, during his or their sitting or attendance in court or in going to or returning from the court; or

    (b)   wilfully interrupts the proceedings of the court or otherwise misbehaves in court.

(2)   In any such case the court may order any officer of the court, or any constable, to take the offender into custody and detain him until the rising of the court; and the court may, if it thinks fit, commit the offender to custody for a specified period not exceeding one month or impose on him a fine not exceeding [£2,500], or both.

[(2A) A fine imposed under subsection (2) above shall be deemed, for the purposes of any enactment, to be a sum adjudged to be paid by a conviction.]

(3)   < . . . >

(4)   A magistrates' court may at any time revoke an order of committal made under subsection (2) and, if the offender is in custody, order his discharge.

(5)   The following provisions of the Magistrates' Courts Act 1980 apply in relation to an order under this section as they apply in relation to a sentence on conviction or finding of guilty of an offence, namely: section 36 (restriction on fines in respect of young persons); sections 75 to 91 (enforcement); section 108 (appeal to Crown Court); section 136 (overnight detention in default of payment); and section 142(1) (power to rectify mistakes).

Annotations

Sub-s (2): sum in square brackets substituted by the Criminal Justice Act 1991, s 17(3), Sch 4, Part I.

Sub-s (2A): added by the Criminal Justice Act 1991, s 17(3), Sch 4, Part V, substituted by the Criminal Justice Act 1993, s 65(3), (4), Sch 3, para 6(4).

Sub-s (3): repealed by the Criminal Justice Act 1982, s 78, Sch 16.

Modification: reference in sub-s (2) to "any officer of the court" modified by the Criminal Justice Act 1991, s 100, Sch 11, para 29.

This section does not extend to Scotland.

Penalties for contempt and kindred offences

14   Proceedings in England and Wales

(1)   In any case where a court has power to commit a person to prison for contempt of court and (apart from this provision) no limitation applies to the period of committal, the committal shall (without prejudice to the power of the court to order his earlier discharge) be for a fixed term, and that term shall not on any occasion exceed two years in the case of committal by a superior court, or one month in the case of committal by an inferior court.

(2)   In any case where an inferior court has power to fine a person for contempt of court and (apart from this provision) no limit applies to the amount of the fine, the fine shall not on any occasion exceed [£2,500].

[(2A) A fine imposed under subsection (2) above shall be deemed, for the purposes of any enactment, to be a sum adjudged to be paid by a conviction.]

[(2A) In the exercise of jurisdiction to commit for contempt of court or any kindred offence the court shall not deal with the offender by making an order under section 17 of the Criminal Justice Act 1982 (an attendance centre order) if it appears to the court, after considering any available evidence, that he is under 17 years of age.]

(3)   < . . . >

(4)   Each of the superior courts shall have the like power to make a hospital order or guardianship order under [section 37 of the Mental Health Act 1983] [or an interim hospital order under [section 38 of that Act]] in the case of a person suffering from mental illness or [severe mental impairment] who could otherwise be committed to prison for contempt of court as the Crown Court has under that section in the case of a person convicted of an offence.

[(4A) Each of the superior courts shall have the like power to make an order under [section 35 of the said Act of 1983] (remand for report on accused's mental condition) where there is reason to suspect that a person who could be committed to prison for contempt of court is suffering from mental illness or severe mental impairment as the Crown Court has under that section in the case of an accused person within the meaning of that section.]

[(4A) For the purposes of the preceding provisions of this section a county court shall be treated as a superior court and not an inferior court.]

(5) The enactments specified in Part III of Schedule 2 shall have effect subject to the amendments set out in that Part, being amendments relating to the penalties and procedure in respect of certain offences of contempt in coroners' courts, county courts and magistrates' courts.

Annotations

Sub-s (2): sum in square brackets substituted by the Criminal Justice Act 1991, s 17(3), Sch 4, Part I; further prospectively substituted in relation to Northern Ireland by the Criminal Justice (Northern Ireland) Order 1994, SI 1994 No 2795, art 3(5), Sch 1, as from a day to be appointed.

Sub-s (2A): first sub-s (2A) added by the Criminal Justice Act 1991, s 17(3), Sch 4, Part V; substituted by the Criminal Justice Act 1993, s 65(3), (4), Sch 3, para 6(5); second sub-s (2A) added by the Criminal Justice Act 1982, s 77, Sch 14, para 60.

Sub-s (3): repealed by the Criminal Justice Act 1982, s 78, Sch 16.

Sub-s (4): first and final words in square brackets substituted by the Mental Health Act 1983, s 148, Sch 4, para 57; second words in square brackets added by the Mental Health (Amendment) Act 1982, s 65(1), Sch 3, para 59, words in square brackets therein substituted by the Mental Health Act 1983, s 148, Sch 4, para 57.

Sub-s (4A): first sub-s (4A) added by the Mental Health (Amendment) Act 1982, s 65(1), Sch 3, para 60, words in square brackets therein substituted by the Mental Health Act 1983, s 148, Sch 4, para 57; second sub-s (4A) added by the County Courts (Penalties for Contempt) Act 1983, s 1.

This section does not extend to Scotland.

15 Penalties for contempt of court in Scottish proceedings

(1) In Scottish proceedings, when a person is committed to prison for contempt of court the committal shall (without prejudice to the power of the court to order his earlier discharge) be for a fixed term.

(2) The maximum penalty which may be imposed by way of imprisonment or fine for contempt of court in Scottish proceedings shall be two years' imprisonment or a fine or both, except that—

(a) where the contempt is dealt with by the sheriff in the course of or in connection with proceedings other than criminal proceedings on indictment, such penalty shall not exceed three months' imprisonment or a fine of [level 4 on the standard scale] or both; and

(b) where the contempt is dealt with by the district court, such penalty shall not exceed sixty days' imprisonment or a fine of [level 4 on the standard scale] or both.

(3)   Section 207 (restriction on detention of young offenders) and sections 175 to 178 (persons suffering from mental disorder) of the Criminal Procedure (Scotland) Act 1975 shall apply in relation to persons found guilty of contempt of court in Scottish proceedings as they apply in relation to persons convicted of offences, except—

(a)   where subsection (2)(a) above applies, when sections 415 and 376 to 379 of the said Act shall so apply; and

(b)   where subsection (2)(b) above applies, when section 415 of the said Act and subsection (5) below shall apply.

(4)   Until the commencement of section 45 of the Criminal Justice (Scotland) Act 1980, in subsection (3) above for the references to sections 207 and section 415 of the Criminal Procedure (Scotland) Act 1975 there shall be substituted respectively references to section 207 and 208 and sections 415 and 416 of that Act.

(5)   Where a person is found guilty by a district court of contempt of court and it appears to the court that he may be suffering from mental disorder, it shall remit him to the sheriff in the manner provided by section 286 of the Criminal Procedure (Scotland) Act 1975 and the sheriff shall, on such remit being made, have the like power to make an order under section 376(1) of the said Act in respect of him as if he had been convicted by the sheriff of an offence, or in dealing with him may exercise the like powers as the court making the remit.

[(6)   For the purposes of section [22 of the Prisons (Scotland) Act 1989] (release on licence of prisoners serving determinate sentences) a penalty of a period of imprisonment imposed for contempt of court shall be treated as a sentence of imprisonment within the meaning of that Act.]

Annotations

Sub-s (2): fines converted to a level on the standard scale by the Criminal Justice Act 1982, s 56, Sch 7.

Sub-s (6): added with retrospective effect by the Criminal Justice (Scotland) Act 1987, s 70(1), Sch 1, words in square brackets substituted by the Prisons (Scotland) Act 1989, s 45, Sch 2, para 18; repealed with savings by the Prisoners and Criminal Proceedings (Scotland) Act 1993, s 47(3), Sch 7, Part I, for savings see Sch 6 thereof and SI 1993 No 2050, art 4.

This section extends to Scotland only.

16   Enforcement of fines imposed by certain superior courts

(1)   Payment of a fine for contempt of court imposed by a superior court, other than the Crown Court or one of the courts specified in subsection (4) below, may be enforced upon the order of the court—

(a)   in like manner as a judgment of the High Court for the payment of money; or

(b)   in like manner as a fine imposed by the Crown Court.

(2)   Where payment of a fine imposed by any court falls to be enforced as mentioned in paragraph (a) of subsection (1)—

(a)   the court shall, if the fine is not paid in full forthwith or within such time as the court may allow, certify to Her Majesty's Remembrancer the sum payable;

(b)   Her Majesty's Remembrancer shall thereupon proceed to enforce payment of that sum as if it were due to him as a judgment debt; < . . . >

(c)   < . . . >

(3)   Where payment of a fine imposed by any court falls to be enforced as mentioned in paragraph (b) of subsection (1), the provisions of sections 31 and 32 of the Powers of Criminal Courts Act 1973 shall apply as they apply to a fine imposed by the Crown Court.

(4)   Subsection (1) of this section does not apply to fines imposed by the criminal division of the Court of Appeal or by the House of Lords on appeal from that division.

(5)   The Fines Act 1833 shall not apply to a fine to which subsection (1) of this section applies.

(6)   < . . . >

Annotations

Sub-s (2): words omitted repealed by the Supreme Court Act 1981, s 152(4), Sch 7.

Sub-s (6): repeals the Employment Protection (Consolidation) Act 1978, Sch 11, para 23(1), and the Employment Act 1980, Sch 1, para 30.

This section does not extend to Scotland.

17   Disobedience to certain orders of magistrates' courts

(1)   The powers of a magistrates' court under subsection (3) of section 63 of the Magistrates' Courts Act 1980 (punishment by fine or committal for disobeying an order to do anything other than the payment of money or to abstain from doing anything) may be exercised either of the court's own motion or by order on complaint.

(2)   In relation to the exercise of those powers the provisions of the Magistrates' Court Act 1980 shall apply subject to the modifications set out in Schedule 3 to this Act.

Annotations

This section does not extend to Scotland.

Supplemental

18   Northern Ireland

(1)   In the application of this Act to Northern Ireland references to the Attorney General shall be construed as references to the Attorney General for Northern Ireland.

(2)   In their application to Northern Ireland, sections 12, 13, 14 and 16 of this Act shall have effect as set out in Schedule 4.

19   Interpretation

In this Act—

[< . . . >]

"court" includes any tribunal or body exercising the judicial power of the State, and "legal proceedings" shall be construed accordingly;

"publication" has the meaning assigned by subsection (1) of section 2, and "publish" (except in section 9) shall be construed accordingly;

"Scottish proceedings" means proceedings before any court, including the Courts-Martial Appeal Court, the Restrictive Practices Court and the Employment Appeal Tribunal, sitting in Scotland, and includes proceedings before the House of Lords in the exercise of any appellate jurisdiction over proceedings in such a court;

"the strict liability rule" has the meaning assigned by section 1;

"superior court" means the Court of Appeal, the High Court, the Crown Court, the Courts-Martial Appeal Court, the Restrictive Practices Court, the Employment Appeal Tribunal and any other court exercising in relation to its proceedings powers equivalent to those of the High Court, and includes the House of Lords in the exercise of its appellate jurisdiction.

Annotations

Definition "cable programme" added by the Cable and Broadcasting Act 1984, s 57(1), Sch 5, para 39(2), and repealed by the Broadcasting Act 1990, s 203(1), (3), Sch 20, para 31(2), Sch 21.

20   Tribunals of Inquiry

(1)   In relation to any tribunal to which the Tribunals of Inquiry (Evidence) Act 1921 applies, and the proceedings of such a tribunal, the provisions of this Act (except subsection (3) of section 9) apply as they apply in relation to courts and legal proceedings; and references to the course of justice or the administration of justice in legal proceedings shall be construed accordingly.

(2)   The proceedings of a tribunal established under the said Act shall be treated as active within the meaning of section 2 from the time when the tribunal is appointed until its report is presented to Parliament.

21   Short title, commencement and extent

(1)   This Act may be cited as the Contempt of Court Act 1981.

(2)   The provisions of this Act relating to legal aid in England and Wales shall come into force on such day as the Lord Chancellor may appoint by order made by statutory instrument; and the provisions of this Act relating to legal aid in Scotland and Northern Ireland shall come into force on such day or days as the Secretary of State may so appoint.

Different days may be appointed under this subsection in relation to different courts.

(3)   Subject to subsection (2), this Act shall come into force at the expiration of the period of one month beginning with the day on which it is passed.

(4)   Sections 7, 8(3), 12, 13(1) to (3), 14, 16, 17 and 18, Parts I and III of Schedule 2 and Schedules 3 and 4 of this Act do not extend to Scotland.

(5)   This Act, except sections 15 and 17 and Schedules 2 and 3, extends to Northern Ireland.

SCHEDULE 1

Times when Proceedings are Active for Purposes of Section 2

Section 2

Preliminary

1   In this Schedule "criminal proceedings" means proceedings against a person in respect of an offence, not being appellate proceedings or proceedings commenced by motion for committal or attachment in England and Wales or Northern Ireland; and "appellate proceedings" means proceedings on appeal from or for the review of the decision of a court in any proceedings.

2   Criminal, appellate and other proceedings are active within the meaning of section 2 at the times respectively prescribed by the following paragraphs of this Schedule; and in relation to proceedings in which more than one of the steps described in any of those paragraphs is taken, the reference in that paragraph is a reference to the first of those steps.

Criminal proceedings

3   Subject to the following provisions of this Schedule, criminal proceedings are active from the relevant initial step specified in paragraph 4 until concluded as described in paragraph 5.

4   The initial steps of criminal proceedings are:—

    (a)   arrest without warrant;

    (b)   the issue, or in Scotland the grant, of a warrant for arrest;

    (c)   the issue of a summons to appear, or in Scotland the grant of a warrant to cite;

    (d)   the service of an indictment or other document specifying the charge;

    (e)   except in Scotland, oral charge.

5   Criminal proceedings are concluded—

    (a)   by acquittal or, as the case may be, by sentence;

    (b)   by any other verdict, finding, order or decision which puts an end to the proceedings;

    (c)   by discontinuance or by operation of law.

6   The reference in paragraph 5(a) to sentence includes any order or decision consequent on conviction or finding of guilt which disposes of the case, either absolutely or subject to future events, and a deferment of sentence under section 1 of the Powers of Criminal Courts Act 1973, section 219 or 432 of the Criminal Procedure (Scotland) Act 1975 or Article 14 of the Treatment of Offenders (Northern Ireland) Order 1976.

7   Proceedings are discontinued within the meaning of paragraph 5(c)—

    (a)   in England and Wales or Northern Ireland, if the charge or summons is withdrawn or a *nolle prosequi* entered;

    [(aa)   in England and Wales if they are discontinued by virtue of section 23 of the Prosecution of Offences Act 1985;]

    (b)   in Scotland, if the proceedings are expressly abandoned by the prosecutor or are deserted *simpliciter;*

    (c)   in the case of proceedings in England and Wales or Northern Ireland commenced by arrest without warrant, if the person arrested is released, otherwise than on bail, without having been charged.

8   Criminal proceedings before a court-martial or standing civilian court are not concluded until the completion of any review of finding or sentence.

9   Criminal proceedings in England and Wales or Northern Ireland cease to be active if an order is made for the charge to lie on the file, but become active again if leave is later given for the proceedings to continue.

[9A   Where proceedings in England and Wales have been discontinued by virtue of section 23 of the Prosecution of Offences Act 1985, but notice is given by the accused under subsection (7) of that section to the effect that he wants the proceedings to continue, they become active again with the giving of that notice.]

10   Without prejudice to paragraph 5(b) above, criminal proceedings against a person cease to be active—

(a)   if the accused is found to be under a disability such as to render him unfit to be tried or unfit to plead or, in Scotland, is found to be insane in bar of trial; or

(b)   if a hospital order is made in his case under [section 51(5) of the Mental Health Act 1983] or [Article 57(5) of the Mental Health (Northern Ireland) Order 1986] or, in Scotland, where a transfer order ceases to have effect by virtue of [section 73(1) of the Mental Health (Scotland) Act 1984],

but become active again if they are later resumed.

11   Criminal proceedings against a person which become active on the issue or the grant of a warrant for his arrest cease to be active at the end of the period of twelve months beginning with the date of the warrant unless he has been arrested within that period, but become active again if he is subsequently arrested.

Other proceedings at first instance

12   Proceedings other than criminal proceedings and appellate proceedings are active from the time when arrangements for the hearing are made or, if no such arrangements are previously made, from the time the hearing begins, until the proceedings are disposed of or discontinued or withdrawn; and for the purposes of this paragraph any motion or application made in or for the purposes of any proceedings, and any pre-trial review in the county court, is to be treated as a distinct proceeding.

13   In England and Wales or Northern Ireland arrangements for the hearing of proceedings to which paragraph 12 applies are made within the meaning of that paragraph—

(a)   in the case of proceedings in the High Court for which provision is made by rules of court for setting down for trial, when the case is set down;

(b)   in the case of any proceedings, when a date for the trial or hearing is fixed.

14   In Scotland arrangements for the hearing of proceedings to which paragraph 12 applies are made within the meaning of that paragraph—

(a)   in the case of an ordinary action in the Court of Session or in the sheriff court, when the Record is closed;

(b)   in the case of a motion or application, when it is enrolled or made;

(c)   in any other case, when the date for a hearing is fixed or a hearing is allowed.

Appellate proceedings

15   Appellate proceedings are active from the time when they are commenced—

(a)   by application for leave to appeal or apply for review, or by notice of such an application;

(b)   by notice of appeal or of application for review;

(c)   by other originating process,

until disposed of or abandoned, discontinued or withdrawn.

16   Where, in appellate proceedings relating to criminal proceedings, the court—

(a)   remits the case to the court below; or

(b)   orders a new trial or a *venire de novo*, or in Scotland grants authority to bring a new prosecution,

any further or new proceedings which result shall be treated as active from the conclusion of the appellate proceedings.

Annotations

Para 7: sub-para (aa) added by the Prosecution of Offences Act 1985, s 31(5), Sch 1, Part I.

Para 9A: added by the Prosecution of Offences Act 1985, s 31(5), Sch 1, Part I.

Para 10: first words in square brackets substituted by the Mental Health Act 1983, s 148, Sch 4, para 57; second words in square brackets substituted by SI 1986 No 595, art 136(1), Sch 5, Part II; final words in square brackets substituted by the Mental Health (Scotland) Act 1984, s 127(1), Sch 3, para 48.

SCHEDULE 3
Application of Magistrates' Courts Act 1980 to Civil Contempt Proceedings under section 63(3)

Section 17

1   (1) Where the proceedings are taken of the court's own motion the provisions of the Act listed in this sub-paragraph shall apply as if a complaint had been made against the person against whom the proceedings are taken, and subject to the modifications specified in sub-paragraphs (2) and (3) below. The enactments so applied are:—

section 51 (issue of summons)

section 53(1) and (2) (procedure on hearing)

section 54 (adjournment)

section 55 (non-appearance of defendant)

section 97(1) (summons to witness)

section 101 (onus of proving exceptions etc.)

section 121(1) and (3)(a) (constitution and place of siting of court)

section 123(defect in process).

(2)   In section 55, in subsection (1) for the words "the complainant appears but the defendant does not" there shall be substituted the words "the defendant does not appear", and in subsection (2) the words "if the complaint has been substantiated on oath, and" shall be omitted.

(3)   In section 123, in subsections (1) and (2) the words "adduced on behalf of the prosecutor or complainant" shall be omitted.

2   Where the proceedings are taken by way of complaint for an order, section 127 of the Act (limitation of time) shall not apply to the complaint.

3   Where the proceedings are taken of the court's own motion or by way of complaint for an order, subsection (3) of section 55 shall apply as if the following words were added at the end of the sub-section:—

"or, having been arrested under section 18 of the Domestic Proceedings and Magistrates' Courts Act 1978 in connection with the matter of the complaint, is at large after being remanded under subsection (3)(b) or (5) of that section.".

Annotations

This Schedule does not extend to Scotland.

SCHEDULE 4

Sections 12, 13, 14 and 16 as Applied to Northern Ireland

Section 18

12   Offences of contempt of magistrates' courts

(1), (2)   < . . . >

13   Legal aid

(1)   In any case where—

(a)   a person is liable to be committed or fined—

(i)   by a magistrates' court under [Article 160 of the Magistrates' Courts (Northern Ireland) Order 1981];

(ii) by a county court under Article 55 of the County Courts (Northern Ireland) Order 1980; or

(iii) by any superior court for contempt in the face of that or any other court; and

(b)   it appears to the court that it is desirable in the interests of justice that he should have legal aid and that he has not sufficient means to enable him to obtain that aid;

the court may order that he shall be given legal aid for the purposes of the proceedings.

(2)   Unless the court orders that the legal aid to be given under this section shall consist of representation by counsel only or, in any court where solicitors have a right of audience, by a solicitor only, legal aid under this section shall consist of representation by a solicitor and counsel assigned by the court; and the court may assign for the purpose any counsel or solicitor who is within the precincts of the court at the time when the order is made.

(3)   If on a question of granting a person legal aid under this section there is a doubt whether his means are sufficient to enable him to obtain legal aid or whether it is desirable in the interests of justice that he should have legal aid, the doubt shall be resolved in favour of granting him legal aid.

(4)   Articles 32, 33, 36 and 40 of the Legal Aid, Advice and Assistance (Northern Ireland) Order 1981 shall apply in relation to legal aid under this section as they apply in relation to legal aid under Part III of that Order as if any legal aid under this section were given in pursuance of a certificate under Article 29 of that Order.

(5)   This section is without prejudice to any other enactment by virtue of which legal aid may be granted in or for purposes of civil or criminal proceedings.

14   Proceedings in Northern Ireland

(1)   In any case where a court has power to commit a person to prison for contempt of court and (apart from this provision) no limitation applies to the period of commital, the committal shall (without prejudice to the power of the court to order his earlier discharge) be for a fixed term, and that term shall not on any occasion exceed two years in the case of committal by a superior court, or one month in the case of committal by an inferior court.

(2)   In any case where an inferior court has power to fine a person for contempt of court and (apart from this provision) no limit applies to the amount of the fine, the fine shall not on any occasion exceed £500.

(3)   < . . . >

(4)   Each of the superior courts shall have the like power to make a hospital

order or guardianship order under [Article 44 of the Mental Health (Northern Ireland) Order 1986 or an interim hospital order under Article 45 of that Order] in the case of a person suffering from mental disorder who could otherwise be committed to prison for contempt of court as the Crown Court has under [that Article] in the case of a person convicted of an offence.

[(4A) Each of the superior courts shall have the like power to make an order under Article 42 of the said Order of 1986 where there is reason to suspect that a person who could be committed to prison for contempt of court is suffering from mental illness or severe mental impairment as the Crown Court has under that Article in the case of an accused person within the meaning of that Article.]

[(4A) For the purposes of the preceding provisions of this section a county court shall be treated as a superior court and not as an inferior court.]

(5)–(7)   < . . . >

16 Section 35 of the Criminal Justice Act (Northern Ireland) 1945 enforcement of fines imposed by superior courts shall apply to fines imposed for contempt of court by any superior court other than the Crown Court as it applies to fines imposed by the Crown Court.

Annotations

Section 12: sub-s (1) repealed by SI 1981 No 1675, art 170(3); sub-s (2) repeals SI 1980 No 704, Sch 1, para 26.

Section 13: words in square brackets substituted by SI 1981 No 1675, art 170(2), Sch 6, para 61.

Section 14: sub-s (3) amends the Children and Young Persons Act (Northern Ireland) 1968, s 72; in sub-s (4) words in square brackets substituted, and first sub-s (4A) added, by SI 1986 No 595, art 136(1), Sch 5, Part II; second sub-s (4A) added by the County Courts (Penalties for Contempt) Act 1983, ss 1, 2; sub-s (5) amends the Coroners Act (Northern Ireland) 1959, s 20; sub-s (6) repealed by SI 1981 No 1675, art 170(3), Sch 7; sub-s (7) amends SI 1980 No 397, art 55(2).

Index

Canada—*contd*
anonymity order in, 278
confession of accused, publication of, 142
criminal and civil contempt classification in,
663
editorial responsibility principle accepted in,
376
Law Reform Commission
jury deliberations, protection of, 373
sub judice period, 254, 255
merits of case, publication as to, 151-2
scandalising the court,
compatibility with Charter of Rights, 337-8
partiality allegations, 353-4
time for interference with criminal
proceedings, 249
Cartoon, 88, 340
Certiorari, order of
disobedience of, 589
Charity
inquiry into, 587
public benefit, and meaning of publication,
111-12
Child
abduction, and use of sequestered property,
607, 613-14, 615
application for order for committal in
proceedings concerning, 495
case concerning, reporting restrictions, 310-
16, 329-30. *See also* REPORTING COURT
PROCEEDINGS
adult court, in, discretion as to, 311-14
family proceedings, in, 314-16. *See also*
FAMILY PROCEEDINGS
order prohibiting publication on, under AJA
1960, 333
statutory prohibitions on private sitting,
330-1
identity protected, 310 *et seq*
leave of court, when required, 456-7
order relating to, enforcement of, 557, 590-2
residence order relating to. *See* RESIDENCE
ORDER
ward of court. *See* WARDSHIP
Child Support Appeal Tribunal, 490
Child witness
notice of transfer case, reporting restrictions,
309-10
Cinema proprietor, 397-8
Civil contempt, 3-4, 555 *et seq. See also*
COMMITTAL (CIVIL CONTEMPT)
aiding and abetting breach of injunction,
573-8
classification as civil contempt, problems
with, 657
interference with course of justice, link
with, 576-8
key cases, 574-8
Mareva injunction, 576
mere spectator not guilty, 575
notice on offending third party not required,
575
principal person need not participate, 574

Civil contempt—*contd*
appeals, 654-5
breach of injunction, 559-73
casual or accidental, 568
clear and unambiguous terms, need for,
560-1
corporate body, by, 569-71
director's personal liability, 571
establishing, 560
individual, by, 569
interim treated same as final, 560
nature of an injunction, and, 559-60
notice of terms, defendant must have had,
562-5
penal notice, and, 562
proof beyond reasonable doubt, need for,
565-7
responsibility for, who has, 569-73
service, need for, 563-5
strict liability, 567
trade union liability, 572
breach of undertaking, 578-82
clear and unambiguous terms, need for, 579
company, by, 579-80
director, or officer, personal liability, 580
effect of undertaking, 578
establishing, 579
notice of terms, need for, 579
strict liability, 581-2
classification of, 655-63
difficulty of, 655-8
need for, 658-63
whether to retain, 663-4
contemnor's right to be heard in a suit, 651-4
background, 651-2
present position, and court discretion, 652-4
delivery of goods, disobedience of order for,
585, 604-5
discovery, abuse of process. *See* DISCOVERY
discovery or document production, breach of
order for, 585-9
committal as remedy, 585-6
court, order made by, 585-6
statutory body, order made by, 587-9
distinction from criminal contempt, 655-64
blurring of, 656-7
common law jurisdictions outside England,
and, 663
procedural differences, 660-3
retention of distinction, whether need for,
663-4
enforcement powers,
non-money orders and judgments, 603-47
payment of sum of money, 647-51
See also COMMITTAL (CIVIL CONTEMPT),
JUDGMENT DEBT, SEQUESTRATION
fine, 635-9, 658
amount of, 637-8
arguments against imposition of, 635-6
mitigating factors, 638
Phillimore Committee recommendations,
639
power to impose, 636-7